THE CRIMINAL JURISDICTION
OF MAGISTRATES

THE CRIMINAL JURISDICTION OF MAGISTRATES

BY

BRIAN HARRIS, OBE, QC, LLB

ELEVENTH EDITION

BY

BRYAN GIBSON, BA

Barrister, Clerk to the Basingstoke justices,
co-editor of Justice of the Peace

BARRY ROSE, A DIVISION OF KLUWER LAW PUBLISHERS
1988

First edition 1969
Tenth edition 1986

©
KLUWER PUBLISHERS LTD
1988

ISBN 1 870080 51 3

The publishers are indebted for permission to reproduce in this book extracts from various Command Papers, Home Office Circulars, and other publications where the copyright vests in Her Majesty's Stationery Office, to the Controller and also to the Law Society's Gazette, the Justice of the Peace and the New Law Journal.

Typeset by Phoenix Photosetting, Chatham, Kent
Printed and bound in Great Britain by Dotesios Printers Ltd, Bradford on Avon, Wilts.

For Dawn

Introduction

This eleventh edition of *Criminal Jurisdiction of Magistrates* is different from the previous ten editions in several ways. Most significant, Brian Harris OBE, QC, LLB, former clerk to the Poole Justices – creator of the work – has relinquished control. His departure from the magistrates' courts arena at the end of 1985 to work in an unrelated field was as unexpected as it was sudden, and represents an incalculable loss to those courts. This seems to be an ideal place to record that his contribution to the summary criminal jurisdiction of this country – as *lawyer*, as *writer* and as a leading figure within the *Justices' Clerks' Society*, of which he was president in 1981-82 – has been second to none. In saying this, I am certain that there are numerous of his former professional colleagues and friends who will be delighted to see – albeit after a gap of some two years – that this, the best known of his many works, is to continue. There can, perhaps, be no greater tribute – and his presence will also continue to be felt in that he remains as consulting editor.

A mandate for change

Brian's own words when he entrusted *Criminal Jurisdiction* to me were to the effect that it was time '. . . a fresh mind was brought to bear'. The pace of new legislation and legal rulings was such that much had been added to the work over the years without the opportunity being taken to reconsider its overall structure, and it was indicated to me at the outset that perhaps some aspects might be improved upon, or profitably reduced, or even abandoned altogether. A degree of change was expected, then – and I only hope that I have not taken matters too far. There is almost a 'domino effect' once a step is taken towards any form of re-organization. Nonetheless, whilst *Criminal Jurisdiction* may have taken a new shape, I have also tried to remain true to the essential formula created by the very first edition in 1969 – and set out by Brian in the *Introduction* to what was then a work of only *345 pages* as follows:

'. . . Fundamentally, my approach has been to assemble together all the relevant Acts and Rules on any one topic, avoiding so far as possible undue repetition and cross-reference, so that each chapter aims at setting out completely the law concerning a separate aspect of the powers and procedures of magistrates' courts. However, as there is nothing so conducive to intellectual indigestion as a mass of undigested statutes, every chapter has been prefaced by an introduction stating in brief compass the outlines of its subject matter. . . . Within each chapter the statutes are set out in chronological order, the sections being followed by commentaries designed to assist the reader in understanding their statutory context as well as referring him to the relevant case law . . . (Sometimes), the greater part of the law is in the form of decided cases rather than statute, and in these circumstances the introduction has seemed the proper place to expound such general topics . . . rather than trying to force them artificially into any particular enactment'.

An overall context

Indeed, those with sufficiently long memories may find the present edition closer in its format to that very first one than many of those which came in between – apart, that is, from the vastly increased volume of material, over which no editor has any real control if a work is to remain authoritative. Apart from what I hope is a complete updating, the main change is that the entire contents have been placed – perhaps I should say replaced, to wit the first edition already referred to above – into an overall context. My aim has been to reduce the unruly nature of criminal procedure into some sort of logical progression – largely chronological – both as between the chapters themselves and within each. To achieve this, certain chapters have been retitled, or created from new material, or from material which was previously dispersed around the work, or moved from one place to another, and in one instance a chapter has been deleted altogether. The result is to bring more closely together associated parts of the law, and to make for ease of reference and cross-reference.

Within the chapters themselves, a system of numbering *based on paragraphs* has been introduced, each numbered paragraph being a self-contained exposition of some aspect of summary criminal procedure. Additionally, the title page to each chapter now contains not only the headings of the topics dealt with but also a note of the relevant paragraph numbers, an omission in previous editions which as a user of the work I found less than helpful. A secondary contribution has been the re-writing of much of the contents, particularly when there have been substantial developments in a particular area of law – but also to weld the newly shaped work together. Established readers may find amusement in trying to spot the joins!

A new structure
Criminal Jurisdiction of Magistrates now starts with a general introductory chapter *Magistrates' Courts – Constitution, Powers and Natural Justice.* I have long taken the view that a firm grasp of these topics is essential to an understanding of criminal procedure. They are fundamental matters, without which all else – what I prefer to regard as detail or 'gloss' – is hardly to be comprehended. I believe there is a good deal in this, as is suggested by the occasional glimpses which the Divisional Court and the House of Lords allow us into their thinking on 'the inherent jurisdiction of magistrates'. When magistrates purport to devise their own procedures in situations not covered, or not fully covered, by statutory or other legal authority, they do so by analogy with basic principle. Fairness, impartiality, equality of treatment and such important matters as the 'openness of proceedings' and 'acting judicially' are guaranteed not so much by the words in an Act of Parliament or legal rulings, but by the fundamental principles and modes of thought by which practitioners operate – and which underpin the application and interpretation of whatever legal rule happens to be in question. No-one who has mastered these basics need ever be at a loss for an acceptable procedure, nor concerned whether he or she has acted in a respectable fashion – and will find that, for the largest part, the statutory provisions fall more readily into place.

The substantive chapters follow as obvious a progression as I have been able to devise – although, in practice not all stages will apply to every case. However, users of this work can assume that generally they may work forward in the book in parallel with the proceedings. By way of example, Chapter 2 deals with *Commencing Criminal Proceedings*, whilst Chapter 3 now covers *Detention, Remand, Bail and Custody*, thereby bringing together all the possibilities by which liberty may be affected from the moment that a person is arrested until the time when, ultimately, he is sentenced by the court. Similarly, *Mode of Trial, Committal for Trial and Transfer to the Crown Court*, the last of which stems from the complex or serious fraud provisions of the Criminal Justice Act 1987 have now been brought together in Chapter 4.

One particular innovation is that Chapter 8, *Sentencing*, has been broken down into a series of 'sub-Chapters' 8a to 8e, which deal with the dispositions open to a court in as near to a progression of seriousness – (I almost used the forbidden word *tariff!*) – as that subject permits. In relation to *Custodial Sentences*, Chapter 8d, an amount of fresh case law has been added, with separate materials on sentencing *young offenders*, ie those below the age of 21, and to whom special statutory restrictions apply. There is also a completely new chapter on *Contempt of Court and Other Interferences*, bringing together the various strands which apply in this area of law. The intention is that practitioners can now find in one readily identifiable location material which by its very nature may be required at short notice.

In response to new statute law, a fresh Chapter 9 has been put together on *Costs and Witnesses' Allowances*, to take account of the Prosecution of Offences Act 1985 and the regulations and orders made thereunder, Chapter 9. The issue of warrants under the Police and Criminal Evidence Act 1984 and the Criminal Justice Act 1987, when fully in force, and which in real life preceeds what is generally thought of as 'criminal procedure', but which is not strictly part of it, has been moved to the end of the work – Chapter 12 – to be followed by what I hope are three worthwhile appendices – the *Codes of Practice* issued pursuant to the 1984 Act (Appendix I), the *Code for Crown Prosecutors*, pursuant to the Prosecution of Offenders Act 1985 (Appendix II) and the *Criminal Justice Bill/Act 1988* (Appendix III –mentioned further below).

In deciding how best to keep the ever increasing text within bounds, I resolved that the former chapter on *Road Traffic Offences* should be deleted. To my mind, that chapter – despite its central focus on disqualification and endorsement – seemed out of place in a general work on criminal procedure and not capable of effective treatment within these pages. I have retained a list of 'endorseable' offences and a brief *Note on 'Totting-up' under the Penalty Points System* within the *Table of Commonplace Offences*, now – for ease of reference – printed at the front of the work. Those who require a full treatment of traffic matters will find better texts than can be provided here – and more authoritative commentators.

Developments in the law

It would be impossible to catalogue all the many developments which have occurred since the tenth edition of *Criminal Jurisdiction* without taking up many pages. To the best of my ability, those changes are all to be found in the appropriate part of the text, and the more significant ones under their own paragraph headings.

But as the work goes to press, the Criminal Justice Bill is in the final stages of its passage through Parliament. Given that the Act will soon be law – but, on the best information available, understanding that most of it will not be brought in to force until 1989 – the following method has been adopted to cater for its effect. Firstly, the *Introductions* to the various chapters have been written so as to include *only* the law as it actually stood at the time of going to press – but *Notes*, mostly speaking in square brackets, have been entered at relevant points and in relation to the more significant changes brought about by the new provisions. Secondly, the provisions themselves have then been dealt with as follows: Appendix III reproduces all relevant parts of the new law in the form of the Criminal Justice *Act* 1988; and the sections on *Statutory Provisions* at the end of each chapter have been printed – in some cases in two completely separate versions – to include the alterations *in italics*. To complement those methods, a narrative guide to the main changes, *A Selection from the Criminal Justice Bill/Act 1988*, follows immediately after this introduction. In all cases, section numbers have been printed in brackets *as a reminder* that the changes are still in embryo, and that alterations to the numbering may occur before the Act reaches the Queen's Printers.

Acknowledgements

For someone whose preferences and inclinations are in the direction of the spontaneous weekly journalism of *Justice of the Peace*, the two years which it has taken to produce this edition represents an unusual experience – the commitment demanding both a degree of sustained effort, and that other capacity, possessed, I assume, more readily by some than others, of being able to 'go back' to matters after they have once been completed. In sustaining this effort, my thanks are due to numerous professional colleagues – both legal and journalistic – for their support, their assistance, the use of their knowledge, skills, articles, law reports, transcripts – and their own valuable time on occasion. I cannot overstate the willingness with which help was given, a constant source of reassurance that *Criminal Jurisdiction* must re-emerge.

Particularly, I would like to acknowledge the invaluable guidance given in the early stages by Barry Rose MBE, publisher of the first ten editions. He it was who telephoned me out of the blue towards the end of 1985 to say that Brian Harris had decided to call it a day and it was with him that I later discussed my original ideas (as well as partaking of the hospitality for which he is so famous!). Kluwer Law has since acquired his book publishing interests and I am grateful to Elizabeth Bramwell of Kluwer for her assistance and good humour over the past year or so.

I have to acknowledge the role played by Nick Stevens, clerk to the Bath and Vansdyke justices. It was his private tutorials which enabled me to write Chapter 9, *Costs and Witnesses' Allowances*, and without which I might still be wrestling with that subject. My thanks are also due to my personal assistant Nikki Kenny, both for her secretarial skills and for keeping people at bay so efficiently. The Basingstoke justices and staff, together with my colleagues at *Justice of the Peace*, all contributed to this work – by their support, and by withholding their demands from time to time.

Above all my thanks are due to Dawn, my wife, for her constant support and encouragement, and to Kara, Alex and Verity who might well be forgiven if they suggested that editing a text-book ought to be added to the grounds on which children may be removed into the care of the local authority!

My presumptive treatment of the Criminal Justice Act 1988 apart, I have tried to state the law as at *1 April, 1988*.

BRYAN GIBSON
The Court House
London Road
Basingstoke

Easter, 1988

A Selection from The Criminal Justice Bill/Act 1988

Key provisions contained in the Criminal Justice Bill/Act 1988 provide courts with more effective powers and procedures, assist them in dealing with victims of crime, widen the basis on which certain evidence is admissible, affect remands and bail, alter jurisdiction as between the Crown Court and magistrates' courts, and lay down new statutory stages and considerations in relation to the enforcement of fines. The following is an outline of changes which are likely to be of greatest interest to practitioners in the *magistrates' courts*. Full details can be found in Appendix III to this work and in the italic insertions to existing statutes under the heading *Statutory Provisions* at the end of each chapter. Throughout the work, the 'section/clause' numbers are printed in square brackets – as they stood in *April 1988* as the Criminal Justice Bill progressed through its final stages in Parliament – as *a reminder* to check the detail against the Act when published. At the time of writing, it seems unlikely that any of the relevant provisions will be activated until 1989, apart from those few which come into force when the Act receives the Royal Assent.

Re-classification of offences
Perhaps one of the most striking aspects of the Act is the reclassification of certain offences so as to make them triable summarily, as opposed to 'either way': see generally under the heading Mode of Trial in Chapter 4. This is achieved by [s.36] in relation to the offences of driving while disqualified under s.99 Road Traffic Act 1972 and taking a motor vehicle without authority under s.12 Theft Act 1968, with consequential reductions in the maximum penalties for these offences to a fine not exceeding level 5 on the standard scale and/or six months' imprisonment. Similarly, [s.37] increases five-fold, from £400 to £2,000, the threshold below which most offences of criminal damage will be triable only summarily. This amounts to a 10-fold increase since 1977, when summary criminal damage first appeared, considerably beyond inflation and thus representing a real shift in jurisdiction. A further, more subtle, shift is effected by [s.37(3)] under which jurisdiction in respect of 'a series' of offences of criminal damage is determined by the aggregate values involved. Both changes appear by way of an amendment to s.22 MCA 1980.

The law of assaults has suffered from piecemeal development for some two centuries and is now long overdue for reform. Yet another ad hoc adjustment is contained in [s.38] which provides that, 'Common assault and battery shall be summary offences . . .', subject again to the usual maximum penalties on summary conviction. But one welcome result of this is that it sweeps away the difficulties created by the decision of the Divisional Court in *R v Harrow Justices, ex p. Osaseri* (1985) 81 Cr App R 306 whereby mode of trial in relation to common assaults prosecuted 'by or on behalf of the party aggrieved' is presently a tortuous matter in terms of procedure.

As will be evident from national media coverage, the thorny question of the abolition of jury trial for theft and associated offences below a certain value has been avoided once again. It seems indefensible that special treatment is still being afforded to 'dishonesty' when most other aspects of criminal justice are having to bow to economic reality. The myth that jury trial somehow produces 'better justice' and to such extent that the country is prepared to sanction the expense involved where such matters do reach the Crown Court might usefully have been laid to rest in relation to petty theft as part of the present de-escalation.

Crown Court powers to deal with summary matters
In a much needed procedural change [ss.39-41] contain provisions which, *inter alia*, enable the Crown Court to dispose of summary offences – and thus in some instances to 'clear up' matters which have hitherto presented awkward problems in practice. It

becomes possible for certain summary offences to be included as additional counts when a more serious charge is to be tried on indictment [s.39]. These offences are limited to common assault, taking motor vehicles without consent, driving whilst disqualified and summary criminal damage – provided the offences are founded on the same facts or evidence as an indictable matter, or form part of a series with it. But under [s.39(4)] the Secretary of State is given power to specify further offences by way of statutory instrument, the only limitation being that such offences must be punishable with imprisonment or must involve mandatory or discretionary disqualification from driving.

Of wider import is [s.40], under which a magistrates' court which commits a person for trial on indictment for an offence which is triable either way may commit him 'to be dealt with' for any summary offence which is imprisonable, or disqualifiable, or which arises out of the same or connected circumstances as the triable either way matter. The chief effect of the remaining provisions of [s.40] is that if the defendant is convicted of an indictable offence, he may then *plead guilty* to the associated summary matters which the magistrates will have 'provisionally committed' to the Crown Court. He can then be sentenced by the Crown Court for those offences, but only *within the summary maxima*. If the defendant pleads *not guilty* to the summary matters, the jurisdiction of the Crown Court is ousted and the fact that the Crown Court has not dealt with the offences must be notified back to the clerk to the justices. In the absence of express provision (although rules will probably emerge), it appears that the clerk will then re-list the matters before the justices as outstanding. Finally [s.41] extends the powers of committal for sentence to include probationers convicted of subsequent offences, and summary offences committed during the term of a wholly or partially suspended sentence imposed by the Crown Court.

Police detention and committal in default

Among the changes affecting magistrates' powers, [s.48] repeals that presently contained in s.134 MCA 1980 (see 8d.71) to sentence a convicted defendant to be detained in a police cell for up to four days, seemingly on the basis that such sentences involve unsuitable accommodation for sentenced prisoners and that they result in the diversion of police effort from the more important prevention and detection of crime. A new table of 'increased periods of imprisonment for default' is substituted by [s.59] (see 8b.98) and [s.60] amends s.77 MCA 1980 and inserts new subsections (4A) and (5A) to (5F) in s.82 of that Act, and sets out the steps to be taken by a magistrates' court before it may issue a warrant committing a fine defaulter to custody at a hearing which the offender does not attend. Under the clause, the court is prohibited from issuing a warrant of commitment unless the clerk has served on the offender a notice in writing stating that the court intends to hold a hearing to consider whether to issue such a warrant and giving reasons why the court so intends.

The court need not inquire into the offender's means at such a hearing if it has previously inquired into them under the existing s.85(3)(*b*) and exercised the power to issue a 'suspended committal' under s.77(2). The notice to the defaulter must state the time and place appointed for the hearing 'not being less than 21 days after the issue of the notice' and must inform him that if he considers there are grounds why the warrant should not be issued, he may make representations to the court, either in person or in writing. The notice is deemed to have been served if sent by registered post or the recorded delivery service addressed to the defaulter at his last known address, even if returned as undelivered or not received by him for any other reason. Provided that the procedures are complied with '. . . the court may exercise its powers in relation to the issue of the warrant whether or not he makes respresentations'. Under a new s.77(3) to the 1980 Act, magistrates have power to postpone the issue of a warrant of commitment until a different time, or to vary the conditions of postponement.

An additional power for magistrates is the power to apply for an order controlling the assets of, or an order winding up, a company which is in default of payment of a fine imposed by a criminal court, provided a distress warrant has been issued and has failed to produce the sum outstanding – [s.61] which operates via an insertion to s.87 MCA 1980.

Two further items to be noted concerning fines and their enforcement are [s.64] which by amendments to ss.125 and 136 MCA 1980, permits 'civilian enforcement officers' to execute distress warrants and warrants for detention overnight at a police station, respectively; and [s.68] which makes fines imposed by coroners enforceable as if imposed by the magistrates' court for the area in which the coroner's court was held.

Compensation, forfeiture and confiscation

In line with the trend of giving priority to compensation, [ss.102–103] contain amendments to ss.35 and 37 Powers of Criminal Courts Act 1973, the effects of which are to require courts to give reasons, on passing sentence, for not making a compensation order in cases where they are empowered by s.35 to make such an order. A new s.35(3) will prohibit compensation due to an accident arising out of the presence of a motor vehicle on a road except damage treated as resulting from an offence under the Theft Act 1968, or in respect of injury, loss or damage as respects which the offender is uninsured (including loss of no claims bonuses – what is described as 'preferential rates').

In an extension of the court's powers, [s.105] provides that where a forfeiture order is made against the offender under s.43 of the 1973 Act in cases involving injury, loss or damage, the court may order that the proceeds arising from the sale of the property be paid *to the victim or victims*.

Courts will also wish to note that [ss.106–115] place the existing non-statutory Criminal Injuries Compensation Scheme on a statutory basis and lay down new entitlements to and conditions for such compensation. Those clauses also specify the basis of assessment for awards and the powers and obligations of the Board in the discharge of its functions.

The 1988 Act introduces the 'confiscation order' and an exhaustive code is contained in [ss.70 to 101], dealing with both the power to make confiscation orders [ss.'70–73] and their enforcement [ss.74–88] see Appendix III. Both the Crown Court and the magistrates' court are given the power, in addition to dealing with an offender in any other way, '. . . to make *an order requiring him to pay such sum under [s.70] as the court thinks fit*'. At present, magistrates' courts may *only* make such an order where the defendant is convicted of an offence listed in [Sch.4] to the 1988 Act – currently in relation to sex establishments, unclassified videos and unlicensed cinemas – whereas the Crown Court has much wider powers (a factor which may be relevant to *Mode of Trial, semble* – see Chapter 4). In either case, the court must be satisfied that the offender has benefitted from the offence and that the benefit is 'at least the minimum amount', currently £10,000.

The court can only make a confiscation order if the prosecutor has given written notice to the court '. . . to the effect that it appears to him that, were the court to consider that it ought to make such an order, it would be able to make an order requiring the offender to pay at least the minimum amount'. If the prosecutor does give such a notice, then the court must determine whether to make a confiscation order. The court must take into account information as to whether the victim is to pursue a civil remedy, and if it makes an order must do so *before* sentencing the offender and must then take account of the order if it imposes a financial penalty or, *inter alia*, it orders compensation. Subject to this, the confiscation order must be left out of account when sentencing.

Where the court makes both a compensation order and a confiscation order and it appears that the offender's means will not meet both orders, the court may order that the compensation order be met from the proceeds of confiscation: see, generally, [s.71]. Various special provision concerning statements relevant to the making of confiscation orders are contained in [s.72]. If the 'realisable property' ultimately proves to be inadequate, the High Court may issue a certificate to this effect under [s.82], when the offender may apply to the Crown Court or magistrates' court, depending on which court made the confiscation order for the amount to be recovered under the order to be reduced.

Young offenders

Several provisions affect the courts' powers to deal with young offenders, ie those below 21 years of age. Most notably, [s.121] introduces a 'generic' sentence of 'detention in a young offender institution' in place of the former sentence of youth custody and the detention centre order – and the phenomena of courts straining their reasoning to bring the length of sentence either over or under the 4 month barrier for youth custody thus disappears at the same time. Most references to detention centre in other statutory provisions are amended.

Additionally, [s.121] substitutes a new s.1(4) CJA 1982, under which there are enhanced and more precise restrictions on custodial sentences for all those below the age of 21. In particular, a court may not pass a sentence of detention in a young offender institution, *supra*, unless satisfied that the circumstances '. . . are such that if the offender were over 21 the court would pass a sentence of imprisonment'. *Qualification* (a new concept) for a custodial sentence is then made to depend, *inter alia*, on a '*history* of failure to respond to non-custodial measures', or the protection of the public from '*serious harm*', or – as previously – the seriousness of the offence (see the new s.1(4) and (4A) – 8d.74 *post*). A new s.2(4) of the 1982 Act adds the obligation for courts to give reasons for imposing custodial sentences on young offenders to explaining '. . . to the offender in open court and in *ordinary language* why it is passing the custodial sentence on him'.

The 1988 Act also contains a number of provisions directed exclusively towards juvenile offenders, full treatment of which is outside the scope of this work – but it should be noted that there are limits on the length of detention below the age of 17 (the new s.1B CJA 1982); and a substituted s.12 CYPA 1969 to strengthen supervision orders made in criminal proceedings, in particular power (highly contentious) to include a 'school attendance requirement', and a duty on the court to announce the fact if it is using supervision requirements – 'stipulated activities' – as an *alternative to custody* (new s.12 D, *ibid*). Finally, and although at the time of writing the question of detention by the Crown Court in respect of 'grave crimes' under s.53 CYPA 1933 remains a topic of much debate, it must be noted that [s.124] – (whatever its eventual form) – alters the basis upon which such orders can be made under *s.53(2)* of the 1933 Act, and hence the powers of the juvenile court to decline jurisdiction.

Of the lesser changes, [s.125] requires a court, except in two specified instances, to order that a fine imposed on a juvenile for failing to comply with the requirements of a supervision order or a community service order be paid by his or her parent or guardian except where he cannot be found, or where '. . . it would be unreasonable . . . having regard to the circumstances of the case'. This is achieved by an amendment to s.55 CYPA 1933 and has the effect of bringing such fines into line with those imposed on conviction.

Remands and bail

What must be one of the most wasteful practices ever invented is the weekly production from prison of those remand prisoners who, although not convicted, have no particular wish to be produced, or to apply for bail. To an extent, s.128 (3A) MCA 1980 – which allows remand decisions to be taken in the defendant's absence subject to a number of pre-conditions – was an attempt to solve this problem (as is s.131 of the 1980 Act, which permits a remand in custody before conviction for up to 28 days where the defendant is already serving a *prison sentence*). A welcome provision, therefore, is [s.147], which introduces a new s.128A into the 1980 Act, and which confronts the issue in more direct fashion. Subject to regulations being made and in relation to whatever class of proceedings and areas of the country the Secretary of State may determine, courts will be able to remand in custody for *up to 28 days*, the prerequisites are a previous remand for the same offence, the presence of the defendant, an opportunity to make representations and the setting of a date on which the court expects 'the next stage in the proceedings' other than a purely remand hearing to take place. The accused is not prevented from applying for bail during the period of the remand, and the court, in applying its mind to considerations under the Bail Act 1976, is required to have regard to the total length of time which an accused would spend in custody if it were to exercise the power.

Another pertinent measure is [s.129], which, by an amendment to the Bail Act, empowers courts to require a defendant who as a condition of bail is required to reside in a bail hostel or probation hostel to enable a report to be made on his suitability to receive a disposal which would involve a condition of hostel residence to comply with the rules of the hostel: see the new s.3(6ZA) Bail Act 1976.

(At the time of writing, the Government is tabling two amendments affecting the Bail Act: firstly, to require a court to give reasons *for granting bail* in relation to charges of murder, attempted murder, manslaughter, rape and attempted rape where the prosecution objects to bail – a thing which, however viewed, and however justified in certain well publicised cases, comes dangerously close to removing the 'presumption of bail'; and secondly, to emphasize the need for the court to consider whether or not bail should be granted *each time an accused is brought before it*, notwithstanding that it is not required to hear arguments upon which it has previously based its decision – cf: *R v Nottingham Justices, ex p. Davies* (1980) 71 Cr App R 178 (3.27, *post*). Unfortunately, it is too late to include details of any resultant amendments in the text).

Other changes

Of the remaining changes, the following seem to merit special mention:

In [s.148] it is provided that when the Crown Court hears an appeal against sentence imposed by a magistrates' court where 'no separate penalty' was imposed by the magistrates for another offence dealt with on the same occasion, then the Crown Court may impose a penalty for that other offence.

A much publicised provision is [s.150], which alters ss.4 and 6 Sexual Offences (Amendment) Act 1976. The two-fold effect is that the anonymity guaranteed to complainants in rape cases is extended back to the time of the allegation; whilst s.6 – which normally prevented the disclosure of the name of any person who had been accused of an offence of rape until conviction – is repealed *in toto*.

Restitution orders under s.28 Theft Act 1968 are made to apply to the Crown by [s.155].

Evidence

Parts [II and III] of the 1988 Act contain a variety of changes concerning the law of evidence. All of these provisions are reproduced in full in Appendix III and where appropriate under the heading *Statutory Provisions* in Chapter 6, *Evidential Matters*.

The provisions deal with 'documentary evidence': [s.22], which makes a 'first-hand hearsay' documentary statement admissible in criminal proceedings where the witness cannot be called for one of the reasons set out, the statement was made to some person charged with investigating offences and charging offenders and the witness 'does not give oral evidence through fear or because he is kept out of the way'; [s.23], which widens the scope for the admission of 'business documents' and other similar records (the present provision for this in s.68 PACE Act 1984 also being repealed by [Sch.15]: see 6.68); and [ss.24 to 27], which deal with associated matters. Of particular note is the *'exclusionary'* discretion contained in [s.24], under which the court may direct that the statement shall not be admitted, if '. . . of the opinion that in the interests of justice a statement which is admissible by virtue of sections 22 or 23 . . . nevertheless ought not to be admitted'. Where such a document has been *prepared for the purposes of criminal proceedings or criminal investigation*, the discretion is *'inclusionary'* and the statement cannot be put in evidence without the leave of the court, which leave cannot be given unless the 'interests of justice' demand this.

The remaining provisions contain several new departures. Completely novel is [s.28] which empowers a justice to issue a 'letter of request' to a court or authority outside the United Kingdom asking for assistance in obtaining evidence. The idea of taking 'evidence on commission' for use in criminal proceedings was a suggestion contained in the Report of the Fraud Trials Commission (the 'Roskill Report) and whilst [s.28] obviously complements the *serious or complex fraud* provisions of the Criminal Justice Act 1987 (see Chapter 4), it is wider in its effect and applies in relation to *all* criminal proceedings.

An adjustment to the law is contained in [s.29], which *inter alia* makes an 'expert report' admissible whether or not the person making it attends to give oral evidence – but subject to the *leave* of the court where the expert *does not attend* to give evidence. The provision applies to experts generally, and a report, once admitted, '. . . shall be evidence of any fact or opinion of which the person making it could have given oral evidence'.

Modern techniques

Much has been made by the media concerning the use of modern techniques, modern technology and modern methods (or lack of their use) in criminal trials and, again, Lord Roskill was quite critical in this regard. Thus [s.30] provides for *Crown Court* rules to be made to allow evidence of a *complicated* or *technical nature* to be furnished 'in any form' – eg by means of charts and visual aids – and for 'glossaries' to be provided to juries. In analogous vein, and perhaps the most innovative provision of the entire 1988 Act, [s.31] enables evidence from a witness outside the United Kingdom to given *in the Crown Court* in a trial on indictment by means of a 'live video link', and for evidence from child witnesses under the age of 14 (less than the impression given in many public pronouncements, perhaps) in respect of certain specified violent and sexual offences to be given in the same way. Corresponding to that provision, [s.32] sustitutes a new s.103 MCA 1980 (see 4.58), widening the categories of offences in respect of which children need not appear before magistrates' in committal proceedings unless the defence requires otherwise. It is, perhaps, a pity that this provision, which has received much public attention – though without any great care as to detail – only applies to childen below 14. Similarly, there seems to be no good reason why 'video links' should be confined to the Crown Court.

Finally, [s.33] abolishes the corroboration requirement which presently attaches to the *unsworn* evidence of a child under s.38 CYPA 1933. This is an encouraging development, the underlying rationale being that courts should be concerned more with the *weight* to be attached to evidence than with its *admissibility* – a development which could point the way for the future in relation to a much wider range of potential evidence.

Contents

Table of Abbreviations

The following commonplace abbreviations are used in this work:

CYPA 1933, 1963, 1969	Children and Young Persons Act 1933, 1963, 1969
CJA 1925, 1948, 1961, 1967, 1977, 1982, 1987	Criminal Justice Act 1925, etc
CLA 1967, 1977	Criminal Law Act 1967, 1977
LAA 1974, 1982	Legal Aid Act 1974, 1982
MCA 1980	Magistrates' Courts Act 1980
MHA 1983	Mental Health Act 1973
OAPA 1961	Offences Against the Person Act 1861
PACE Act 1984	Police and Criminal Evidence Act 1984
PCCA 1973	Powers of Criminal Courts Act 1973
POA 1985	Prosecution of Offenders Act 1985
RTA 1972, 1974, 1976	Road Traffic Act 1972, 1974, 1976
RTRA 1984	Road Traffic Regulations Act 1984
MC Rules 1981	Magistrates' Courts Rules 1981
HOC	Home Office Circular
LCD(C)	Lord Chancellor's Department Circular

TABLE OF CASES

TABLE OF STATUTES

The bold references indicate where sections (or part thereof) are set out in full

STATUTORY TABLE OF RULES AND REGULATIONS

Table of Commonplace Offences

PART I **General** – List of Commonplace Offences, Including Maximum Punishments and Mode of Trial arranged in alphabetical order of statute.

PART II **Road Traffic** – List of Offences Attracting Disqualification or Penalty Points, together with a note on 'Totting-up' at 13.49.

The 'Standard Scale of Fines is as follows:
Level 1   £50
Level 2   £100
Level 3   £400
Level 4   £1,000
Level 5   £2,000
[Section 37 CJA 1982 – As at 1 April 1988]
References to the 'prescribed sum' are to that set pursuant to s.32 MCA 1980, currently £2,000.

PART I – GENERAL

Section	Offence	Mode of Trial	Maximum Punishment

BAIL ACT 1976

6.	Failure to surrender to bail.	If committed for sentence or dealt with as for a contempt in the Crown Court.	12 months and/or a fine.
		Summarily.	3 months and/or a fine not exceeding **Level 5**.

Special Conditions: Unique procedural provisions apply to this offence: see Practice Direction (Bail: Failure to surrender to Custody) [1986] *The Times*, 20 December and Chapter 3.

BRITISH TRANSPORT COMMISSION ACT 1949

55.	Trespass on the railway.	Summarily.	Fine not exceeding **Level 3**.

CONTEMPT OF COURT ACT 1981

12.	Contempt of magistrates' courts.	Summarily.	One month and/or a fine not exceeding £1,000; and/or the contemnor maybe taken into custody and detained until the rising of the court: s.12(2). Committal orders maybe revoked: s.12(4).

Section	Offence	Mode of Trial	Maximum Punishment

CRIMINAL ATTEMPTS ACT 1981

9.	Interfering with vehicles.	Summarily.	3 months and/or a fine not exceeding **Level 4**.

CRIMINAL DAMAGE ACT 1971

1.(1)	Destroying or damaging property.	On indictment.	10 years/life where arson (s.4(1)).
		Summarily.	6 months or a fine not exceeding the prescribed sum, or both.
		Where triable only summarily.	3 months and/or **Level 4**.

---

1 Special Considerations:
  (i)   Triable *only on indictment*, if defendant also charged before court with offence under s.17(1) or (2) Firearms Act 1968: see para 3, Part II, Sch.6, *ibid*.
  (ii) Triable *only summarily* where value of damage below £400 (£2,000 under CJA 1988); or where value 'unclear' and defendant accepts offer of summary trial – except where a 'series of offences'; or arson: see s.22 MCA 1980, 4.49.
  (iii) *Triable either way* in all other circumstances – including 'arson'. But contrast aggravated offence in s.1(2), *post*.
  (iv) Criminal Damage by fire must be charged as 'arson': s.1(3) Criminal Damage Act 1971.

1.(2)	Destroying or damaging property with intent to endanger life etc.	Indictable only.	Life (s.4(3)).
2.	Threats to destroy or damage property.	On indictment. Summarily.	10 years. 6 months and/or a fine not exceeding the prescribed sum.
3.	Possessing anything with an *intent to destroy or damage*.	On indictment.	10 years.
		Summarily.	6 months and/or a fine not exceeding the prescribed sum.

CRIMINAL JUSTICE ACT 1967

91.	Drunk and disorderly.	Summarily.	Fine not exceeding **Level 3**.

For 'Simple Drunk', see Licensing Act 1872, *post*.

CRIMINAL LAW ACT 1967

5.(2)	Causing wasteful employment of police.	Summarily.	6 months and/or a fine not exceeding **Level 4**.

DOG LICENCES ACT 1959

12.	Keeping a dog without a licence.	Summarily.	Fine not exceeding **Level 1**.
13.	Failing to produce dog licence.	Summarily.	Fine not exceeding **Level 1**.

FIREARMS ACT 1968
(Extracts from SCHEDULE 6)
PROSECUTION AND PUNISHMENT OF OFFENCES
[*As amended by s.28, Sch.6, 6 CJA 1972, s.28(2), Sch.12 CLA 1977, Sch.7 MCA 1980, ss.38 and 46 CJA 1982*].

Section	Offence	Mode of Trial	Maximum Punishment

PART I

Section	Offence	Mode of Trial	Maximum Punishment
1.(1)	Possessing etc firearm or ammunition without firearm certificate.	Summary.	6 months and/or a fine of the statutory maximum.
		On indictment.	(i) where the offence is committed in an aggravated form within the meaning of s.4(4) of this Act, 5 years, or a fine, or both. (ii) in any other case, 3 years and/or a fine.
1.(2)	Non-compliance with condition of firearm certificate.	Summary.	6 months and/or a fine not exceeding **Level 5**.
2.(1)	Possessing etc shot gun without shot gun certificate.	Summary.	6 months and/or a fine not exceeding **Level 5**.
2.(2)	Non-compliance with conditions of shot gun certificate.	Summary.	6 months and/or a fine not exceeding **Level 5**.
3.(1)	Trading in firearms without being registered as firearms dealer.	Summary.	6 months and/or a fine not exceeding the statutory maximum.
		On indictment.	3 years and/or a fine.
3.(2)	Repairing, testing etc firearm for person without a certificate.	Summary.	6 months and/or a fine not exceeding the statutory maximum, or both.
		On indictment.	3 years and/or a fine.
4.(1)	Shortening a shot gun; conversion of firearms.	Summary.	6 months and/or a fine not exceeding the statutory maximum.
		On indictment.	5 years and/or a fine, or both.
5.(1)	Possessing or distributing prohibited weapons or ammunition.	Summary.	6 months and/or a fine not exceeding the statutory maximum, or both.
		On indictment.	5 years and/or a fine.
7.(2)	Making false statement in order to obtain police permit.	Summary.	6 months and/or a fine not exceeding **Level 5**.
16.	Possession of firearm with intent to endanger life or injure property.	Indictable only.	Life imprisonment or a fine, or both.
17.(1)	Use of firearms to resist arrest.	Indictable only.	Life imprisonment and/or a fine, or both.
17.(2)	Possessing firearm while commiting an offence specified in Sch.1.	Indictable only.	14 years and/or a fine, or both.

Special provisions: In relation to charges under either s.17(1) or (2), where a person is also charged 'before the court' with any offence 'listed' in Sch.1 MCA 1980 (see 4.61), the court must proceed as if the 'listed' offence is also triable only on indictment unless and until it determines not to commit the firearms offence for trial, or proceedings in respect of that offence are discontinued: see further paras 3 to 5 Part II, Sch.I, Firearms Act 1968.

Section	Offence	Mode of Trial	Maximum Punishment
18.(1)	Carrying firearm or imitation firearm with intent to commit indictable offence or to resist arrest.	Indictable only.	14 years and/or a fine.
19.	Carrying loaded firearm in public place.	Summary.	6 months and/or a fine not exceeding the statutory maximum.
		On indictment (*but not if the firearm is an air weapon*).	5 years and/or a fine.

Section	Offence	Mode of Trial	Maximum Punishment
20.(1)	Trespassing with firearm in a building.	Summary.	6 months and/or a fine not exceeding the statutory maximum.
		On indictment (*but not if the firearm is an air weapon*).	5 years and/or a fine.
20.(2)	Treaspassing with firearm on land.	Summary.	3 months and/or a fine not exceeding **Level 4** on the standard scale, or both.
21.(4)	Contravention of provisions denying firearms to ex-prisoners and the like.	Summary.	6 months and/or a fine not exceeding the statutory maximum.
		On indictment.	3 years and/or a fine.
21.(5)	Supplying firearms to person denied them under s.21.	Summary.	6 months and/or a fine not exceeding the statutory maximum.
		On indictment.	3 years and/or a fine.
22.(1)	Person under 18 acquiring firearm.	Summary.	6 months and/or a fine not exceeding **Level 5**.
22.(2)	Person under 14 having firearm in his possession without lawful authority.	Summary.	6 months and/or a fine not exceeding **Level 5**.
22.(3)	Person under 15 having with him a shot gun without adult supervision.	Summary.	Fine not exceeding **Level 3**.

Forfeiture and disposal of *any* firearm or ammunition found in the offender's possession may be ordered: see para 8 Part II, Sch.6 Firearms Act 1968.

Section	Offence	Mode of Trial	Maximum Punishment
22.(4)	Person under 14 having with him an air weapon or ammunition therefor.	Summary.	Fine not exceeding **Level 3**.
22.(5)	Person under 17 having with him an air weapon in a public place.	Summary.	Fine not exceeding **Level 3**.
23.(1)	Person under 14 making improper use of air weapon when under supervision; person supervising him permitting such use.	Summary.	Fine not exceeding **Level 3**.

In relation to s.22(4), (5) and s.23(1), forfeiture and disposal of the air weapon in respect of which the offence was committed and *any* firearm or ammunition found in the offender's possession may be ordered: see paras 7 and 8, Part II, Sch.6, Firearms Act 1968.

Section	Offence	Mode of Trial	Maximum Punishment
24.(1)	Selling or letting on hire a firearm to person under 17.	Summary.	6 months and/or a fine not exceeding **Level 5**.
24.(2)	Supplying firearm or ammunition (being of a kind to which s.1 of this Act applies) to person under 14.	Summary.	6 months and/or a fine not exceeding **Level 5**.
24.(3)	Making gift of shot gun to person under 15.	Summary.	Fine not exceeding **Level 3**.

In relation to s.24(3), forfeiture of the shot gun or ammunition in respect of which the offence was committed may be ordered: see para 9, Part II, Sch.6, Firearms Act 1968.

Section	Offence	Mode of Trial	Maximum Punishment
24.(4)	Supplying air weapon to person under 14.	Summary.	Fine not exceeding **Level 3**.

Section	Offence	Mode of Trial	Maximum Punishment

> In relation to s.24(4), the power to order forfeiture is as set out in relation to ss.22(4), (5) and s.23(1), *supra*.

Section	Offence	Mode of Trial	Maximum Punishment
25.	Supplying firearm to person drunk or insane.	Summary.	3 months and/or a fine not exceeding **Level 3**.
26.(5)	Making false statement in order to procure grant or renewal of a firearm or shot gun certificate.	Summary.	6 months and/or a fine not exceeding **Level 5**.
29.(3)	Making false statement in order to procure variation of a firearm certificate.	Summary.	6 months and/or a fine not exceeding **Level 5**.
30.(4)	Failing to surrender certificate on revocation.	Summary.	Fine not exceeding **Level 3**.
47.(2)	Failure to hand over firearm or ammunition on demand by constable.	Summary.	3 months and/or a fine not exceeding **Level 4**.
48.(3)	Failure to comply with requirement of a constable that a person shall declare his name and address.	Summary.	Fine not exceeding **Level 3**.
49.(3)	Failure to give constable facilities for examination of firearms in transit, or to produce papers.	Summary.	3 months and/or, for each firearm or parcel of ammunition in respect of which the offence is committed, a fine not exceeding **Level 3**.

> In relation to s.49(3), forfeiture of the firearm or ammunition may be ordered provided that the offender is the owner: see para 2, Part II, Sch.6, Firearms Act 1968.

Section	Offence	Mode of Trial	Maximum Punishment
52.(2)	Failure to surrender firearm or shot gun certificate cancelled by court on conviction.	Summary.	Fine not exceeding **Level 3**.

FOOD ACT 1984

Section	Offence	Mode of Trial	Maximum Punishment
	Any offence under the Act except those listed below (s.92).	On indictment. Summarily.	2 years and/or a fine. Fine not exceeding the statutory maximum.
5.(3)	Disclosure of information etc.	On indictment. Summarily.	2 years and/or a fine. 3 months and/or a fine not exceeding the statutory maximum.
18.(4)	Failing to give notice of change of use.	Summarily.	Fine not exceeding **Level 4**.
27.(1)	Failing to display name and address.	Summarily.	Fine not exceeding **Level 1**.
28.(1)	Failing to give notice of disease.	Summarily.	Fine not exceeding **Level 1**.
28.(3)	Using etc ice cream in contravention of notice.	Summarily.	Fine not exceeding **Level 5**.
31.(1)	Using etc food in contravention of notice.	Summarily.	Fine not exceeding **Level 5**.
53.(4)	Demanding or accepting a greater charge.	Summarily.	Fine not exceeding **Level 2**.
56.(1)	Selling or exposing for sale.	Summarily.	Fine not exceeding **Level 2**.
58.	Refusing to weigh or measure	Summarily.	Fine not exceeding **Level 2**.

Section	Offence	Mode of Trial	Maximum Punishment
65.	Contravention of s.64 (food hawkers)	Summarily.	Fine not exceeding **Level 3**.
87.(5)	Disclosure of information	Summarily.	3 months and/or a fine not exceeding **Level 3**.
91.(1)	Wilful obstruction.	Summarily.	Fine not exceeding **Level 5**.
91.(3)	Failure to give information or assistance.	Summarily.	Fine not exceeding **Level 5**.

FORGERY AND COUNTERFEITING ACT 1981

Section	Offence	Mode of Trial	Maximum Punishment
1.	Forgery.	On indictment.	10 years (s.6).
2.	Copying a false instrument.		
3.	Using a false instrument.		
4.	Using a copy of a false instrument.	Summarily.	3 months imprisonment and/or a fine not exceeding the statutory maximum (s.6).
5.(1)	Having custody or control of a false instrument with intent.		
5.(2)	Having custody or control of a false instrument without lawful authority or excuse.	On indictment.	Two years (s.6).
5.(3)	Offences related to machines etc, adapted etc, for making a false instrument.	On indictment. Summarily.	10 years. Six months and/or a fine not exceeding the statutory maximum.
5.(4)	Making or controlling such machine etc.	On indictment.	Two years.
14.(1)	Making counterfeit notes or coins with intent to pass as genuine.	On indictment. Summarily.	10 years and/or a fine (s.22). Six months and/or a fine not exceeding the statutory maximum (s.22).
14.(2)	Making counterfeit notes or coin without lawful authority or excuse.	On indictment. Summarily.	2 years and/or a fine. Six months and/or a fine not exceeding the statutory maximum.
15.(1)	Passing or delivering as genuine counterfeits.	On indictment. Summarily.	10 years and/or a fine. Six months and/or a fine not exceeding the statutory maximum.
15.(2)	Delivering counterfeits without lawful authority or excuse.	On indictment. Summarily.	Two years and/or a fine. Six months and/or a fine not exceeding the statutory maximum.
16.(1)	Having custody or control of counterfeit with intent.	On indictment. Summarily.	10 years and/or a fine. Six months and/or a fine not exceeding the statutory maximum.
16.(2)	Having custody or control of counterfeit without lawful authority or excuse.	On indictment. Summarily.	Two years and/or a fine. Six months and/or a fine not exceeding the statutory maximum.
17.(1)	Making etc things for purpose of counterfeiting.	On indictment. Summarily.	10 years and/or a fine. Six months and/or a fine not exceeding the statutory maximum.
17.(2)	Making etc anything specially designed or adapted for counterfeiting.	On indictment. Summarily.	Two years and/or a fine. Six months and/or a fine not exceeding the statutory maximum.

Section	Offence	Mode of Trial	Maximum Punishment
17.(3)	Making etc any implement capable of making a resemblance.	On indictment. Summarily.	Two years and/or a fine. Six months and/or a fine not exceeding the statutory maximum.
18.	Reproducing British currency notes.	On indictment. Summarily.	Fine. Fine not exceeding the statutory maximum.
19.	Making etc, imitation British coins.	On indictment. Summarily.	Fine. Fine not exceeding the statutory maximum.

HIGHWAYS ACT 1835

72.	Riding or driving on footpath.	Summarily.	Fine not exceeding **Level 2**.

HIGHWAYS ACT 1980

137.	Wilful obstruction.	Summarily.	Fine not exceeding **Level 2**.
148.(1)	Depositing things on the highway.	Summarily.	Fine not exceeding **Level 3**.
155.	Straying animals.	Summarily.	Fine not exceeding **Level 3**.
161.(2)	Discharging firearms or firework.	Summarily.	Fine not exceeding **Level 3**.

INDECENCY WITH CHILDREN ACT 1960

1.	Indecent conduct towards children.	On indictment. Summarily.	Two years. Six months or a fine not exceeding the statutory maximum.

LICENSING ACT 1872

12.	Found drunk.	Summarily.	A fine not exceeding **Level 1** on the standard scale.

For 'drunk and disorderly' see CJA 1967, *ante*.

LICENSING ACT 1964

168.	Children in bars.	Summarily.	Fine not exceeding **Level 1**.
169.(1)	Serving liquor to minors.	Summarily.	Fine not exceeding **Level 2***.
169.(2)	Minors, etc buying liquor.	Summarily.	Fine not exceeding **Level 3** (s.169(9)).
169.(3)	Buying liquor for minors.	Summarily.	Fine not exceeding **Level 3**.
169.(5)	Delivering liquor to minors for consumption off the premises.	Summarily.	Fine not exceeding **Level 2***.
170.	Employing minor in bar.	Summarily.	Fine not exceeding **Level 1** (s.169(9)).
172.	Permitting drunkenness in licensed premises.	Summarily.	Fine not exceeding **Level 2** (s.172(4)).

Special provisions: *s.169(8), applies which gives power to forfeit a licence on a person's second or subsequent conviction if the offence was committed by him as the holder of a justices' licence. Any conviction which took place more than five years previously must be disregarded: s.194(2).

LITTER ACT 1983

1.	Depositing litter.	Summarily.	Fine not exceeding **Level 2**.

MISUSE OF DRUGS ACT 1971 (Sch.4 as amended)

			Class A drug	Class B Drug	Class C drug	General
4.(2)	Production, or being concerned in the production, of a controlled drug.	Summary.	6 months and/or the statutory maximum.	6 months and/or the statutory maximum.	3 months and/or £500.	
		On indictment.	Life and/or a fine.	14 years and/or a fine.	5 years and/or a fine.	
4.(3)	Supplying or offering to supply a controlled drug or being concerned in the doing of either activity by another.	Summary.	6 months and/or the statutory maximum.	6 months and/or the statutory maximum.	3 months and/or £500.	
		On indictment.	Life and/or a fine.	14 years and/or a fine.	5 years and/or a fine.	
5.(2)	Having possession of a controlled drug.	Summary.	6 months and/or the statutory maximum.	3 months and/or £500.	3 months and/or £200.	
5.(3)	Having possession of a controlled drug with intent to supply it to another.	On indictment.	7 years and/or a fine.	5 years and/or a fine.	2 years and/or a fine.	
		Summary.	6 months and/or the statutory maximum.	6 months and/or the statutory maximum.	3 months and/or £500.	
6.(2)	Cultivation of cannabis plant.	Summary.	—	—	—	6 months and/or the statutory maximum.
		On indictment.	—	—	—	14 years and/or a fine.
8.	Being the occupier, or concerned in the management, of premises and permitting or suffering certain activities to take place there.	Summary.	—	—	—	6 months and/or the statutory maximum.
		On indictment.	14 years and/or a fine.	14 years and/or a fine.	5 years and/or a fine.	
9.	Offences relating to opium.	Summary.	—	—	—	6 months and/or **Level 5**.
		On indictment.	—	—	—	14 years and/or a fine.
9.A	Prohibition of supply etc of articles for administering or preparing controlled drugs.	Summary.	—	—	—	6 months and/or the statutory maximum.

	Offence		Class A drug	Class B Drug	Class C drug	General
11.(2)	Contravention of directions relating to safe custody of controlled drugs.	Summary.	—	—	—	—
		On indictment.	—	—	—	2 years and/or a fine.
12.(6)	Contravention of direction prohibiting practitioner etc. from possessing, supplying etc. controlled drugs.	Summary.	6 months and/or the statutory maximum.	6 months and/or the statutory maximum.	3 months and/or £500.	—
		On indictment.	14 years and/or a fine.	14 years and/or a fine.	5 years and/or a fine.	—
13.(3)	Contravention of direction prohibiting practitioner etc. from prescribing, supplying etc. controlled drugs.	Summary.	6 months and/or the statutory maximum.	6 months and/or the statutory maximum.	3 months and/or £500.	—
		On indictment.	14 years and/or a fine.	14 years and/or a fine.	5 years and/or a fine.	—
17.(3)	Failure to comply with notice requiring information relating to prescribing, supply etc. of drugs.	Summary.	—	—	—	Level 3.
		On indictment.	—	—	—	6 months and/or the statutory maximum.
17.(4)	Giving false information in purported compliance with notice requiring information relating to prescribing, supply etc. of drugs.	Summary.	—	—	—	—
		On indictment.	—	—	—	2 years and/or a fine.
18.(1)	Contravention of regulations (other than regulations relating to addicts).	Summary.	—	—	—	6 months and/or the statutory maximum.
		On indictment.	—	—	—	2 years and/or a fine.
18.(2)	Contravention of terms of licence or other authority (other than licence issued under regulations relating to addicts).	Summary.	—	—	—	6 months and/or the statutory maximum.
		On indictment.	—	—	—	2 years and/or a fine.

18.(3)	Giving false information in purported compliance with obligation to give information imposed under or by virtue of regulations.	Summary.	—	—	6 months and/or the statutory maximum.
		On indictment.	—	—	2 years and/or a fine.
18.(4)	Giving false information, or producing document etc. containing false statement etc., for purposes of obtaining issue or renewal of a licence or other authority.	Summary.	—	—	6 months and/or the statutory maximum.
		On indictment.	—	—	2 years and/or a fine.
20.	Assisting in or inducing commission outside United Kingdom of an offence punishable under a corresponding law.	Summary.	—	—	6 months and/or the statutory maximum.
		On indictment.	—	—	14 years and/or a fine.
23.(4)	Obstructing exercise of powers of search etc. or concealing books, drugs, etc.	Summary.	—	—	6 months and/or the statutory maximum.
		On indictment.	—	—	2 years and/or a fine.

Section	Offence	Mode of Trial	Maximum Punishment

NATIONAL ASSISTANCE ACT 1948

52.	False statements.	Summarily.	3 months and/or a fine not exceeding **Level 3**.

OFFENCES AGAINST THE PERSON ACT 1861

16.	Threats to kill.	On indictment. Summarily.	10 years. 6 months and/or the statutory maximum.
18.	Wounding *with intent to do grievous bodily harm.*	Indictable only.	Life.
20.	Inflicting bodily injury with or without a weapon.	On indictment. Summarily – but see below.	5 years. 6 months and/or the statutory maximum.
27.	Exposing child.	On indictment. Summarily.	5 years. 6 months and/or the statutory maximum, or both.
38.	Assaults with intent to resist apprehension.	On indictment. Summarily – but see below.	2 years. 6 months and/or the statutory maximum, or both.
43.	Aggravated assault on women and children.	Summarily.	6 months and/or a fine not exceeding **Level 4**.
47.	Assault occasioning actual bodily harm.	On indictment. Summarily.	5 years. 6 months and/or statutory maximum.
47.	Common assault.	On indictment. Summarily.	1 year. 6 months and/or the statutory maximum.

Special provision concerning all offences which are otherwise triable either way under OAPA 1861, above:
triable only on indictment if the defendant is also charged before the court with an offence under s.17(1) or (2) Firearms Act 1968: see para 3, Part II, Sch.6.

A complaint for common assault contrary to s.47, *supra* made *by or on behalf of the aggrieved* is triable *summarily* at the discretion of the justices pursuant to s.42 OAPA 1861. If they decide to try it summarily the accused has no right to elect trial by jury. The justices also have a discretion to decline summary trial under s.46, *ibid*, when the offence becomes indictable: see *R v Harrow Justices ex p. Osaseri* [1985] 3 WLR 819 and *R v Blythe Valley Magistrates' Court ex p. Dobson* (1987) *The Times*, 7 November (neither the court nor the accused can choose for the matter to be treated as an either way offence under the standard mode of trial provisions of the MCA 1980); and see generally in 4.02 *et seq.*. But note that *common assault* becomes triable *summarily only* under the CJA 1988: [s.37].

57.	Bigamy.	On indictment. Summarily.	2 years. 6 months and/or the statutory maximum.
60.	Concealing the birth of a child.	On indictment. Summarily.	2 years. 6 months and/or the statutory maximum.

POLICE ACT 1964

51.(1)	Assault on constable.	Summarily.	6 months and/or a fine not exceeding **Level 5**.
51.(3)	Resisting or obstructing a constable.	Summarily.	1 month and/or a fine not exceeding **Level 3**.

Section	Offence	Mode of Trial	Maximum Punishment

PREVENTION OF CRIME ACT 1953

1.	Carrying offensive weapons.	On indictment. Summarily.	2 years and/or a fine. 3 months and/or the statutory maximum. Power to order forfeiture or disposal of any weapon in respect of which the offence was committed (s.1(2)).

PUBLIC ORDER ACT 1986

1.	Riot.	Indictable only.	10 years and/or a fine.
2.	Violent Disorder.	On indictment. Summarily.	5 years and/or a fine. 6 months and/or a fine not exceeding the statutory maximum.
3.	Affray.	On indictment. Summarily.	3 years and/or a fine. 6 months and/or a fine not exceeding the statutory maximum.
4.	Threatening abusive or insulting words or behaviour or display etc. *Fear or provocation of violence.*	Summarily.	6 months and/or a fine not exceeding **Level 5**.
5.	Threatening abusive or insulting words or behaviour or display etc. *Harassment, alarm or distress.*	Summarily.	Fine not exceeding **Level 3**.
18.	Threatening, abusive or insulting words or behaviour, or display. *Intended or likely to stir up racial hatred.*	On indictment. Summarily.	2 years and/or a fine. 6 months and/or a fine not exceeding the statutory maximum.
19.	Publishing material intended or likely to stir up racial hatred.		
20.	Presenting or directing a public performance at a play intended or likely to stir up racial hatred.	The consent of the Attorney-General is required to proceedings relating to offences under ss.18 to 23.	
21.	Distributing etc recordings intended or likely to stir up racial hatred.		
22.	Broadcasting etc programme intended or likely to stir up racial hatred.		
23.	Possession of racially inflammatory material.		

> Special provisions: s.25 Public Order Act 1986 requires the court to order forfeiture of written material or recordings produced to the court in relation to ss.18, 19, 21 and 23.

38.	Contaminating etc goods with intent to cause public alarm or economic loss (s.38(2)). Threats etc to contaminate etc (s.38(2)).	On indictment. Summarily.	10 years and/or a fine. 6 months and/or a fine not exceeding the statutory maximum.
	Possession with a view to contaminating etc goods etc (s.38(3)).		

Section	Offence	Mode of Trial	Maximum Punishment

PUBLIC PASSENGER VEHICLES ACT 1981

Section	Offence	Mode of Trial	Maximum Punishment
24.	Breach of regulations concerning drivers, inspectors and conductors.	Summarily.	Fine not exceeding **Level 2**.
25.	Breach of regulations concerning passengers.	Summarily.	Fine not exceeding **Level 3**.

REGULATION OF RAILWAYS ACT 1889

Section	Offence	Mode of Trial	Maximum Punishment
5.(3)	Avoiding payment of fare with intent.	Summarily.	3 months and/or a fine not exceeding **Level 3**.

ROAD TRAFFIC ACT 1972
See PART II, *post.*

ROAD TRAFFIC REGULATION ACT 1984
See PART II, *post.*

SEXUAL OFFENCES ACT 1956 – Schedule 2, PART I

Section	Offence	Mode of Trial	Maximum Punishment
1.	Rape (and attempts to commit this offence).	Indicatable only. Indictable only.	Life. Life.
5.	Intercourse with a girl under 13. (and attempts to commit this offence).	Indictable only. Indictable only.	Life. 7 years.
12.	Buggery.	Indictable only.	If with a boy under the age of 16 or with a woman or an animal, life; otherwise the relevant punishment prescribed by s.3 Sexual Offences Act 1967.
	(and attempts to commit this offence).	Indictable only.	If with a boy under the age of 16 or with a woman or an animal, 10 years.
17.	Abduction of a woman by force or for the sake of her property.	Indictable only.	14 years.
25.	Permitting girl under 13 to use premises for intercourse.	Indictable only.	Life.

SEXUAL OFFENCES ACT 1956 – Sch. 2, PART II

Section	Offence	Mode of Trial	Maximum Punishment
2.	Procurement of woman by threats (and attempts to commit this offence).	Indictable only. Indictable only.	2 years. 2 years.
3.	Procurement of woman by false pretences.	Indictable only.	2 years.
4.	Administering drugs to facilitate intercourse.	Indictable only.	2 years.
6.	Intercourse with a girl under 16	On indictment: a prosecution may not be commenced more than 12 months after the offence charged. Summarily.	2 years. 6 months and/or a fine not exceeding the statutory maximum.
	(and attempts to commit this offence).	[As above.]	[As above.]
7.	Intercourse with defective (and attempts to commit this offence).	Indictable only. Indictable only.	2 years. 2 years.

Section	Offence	Mode of Trial	Maximum Punishment
9.	Procurement of defective (and attempts to commit this offence).	Indictable only. Indictable only.	2 years. 2 years.
10.	Incest by man.	Indictable only; a prosecution may not be commenced except by or with the consent of the Director of Public Prosecutions.	If with a girl under 13, and so charged in the indictment, life; otherwise 7 years.
	(and attempts to commit this offence).	Indictable only; a prosecution may not be commenced except by or with the consent of the Director of Public Prosecutions.	If with a girl under 13 who is stated to have been so in the indictment, 7 years; otherwise 2 years.
11.	Incest by a woman	Indictable only; a prosecution may not be commenced except by or with the consent of the Director of Public Prosecutions.	7 years.
	(and attempts to commit this offence).	Indictable only: a prosecution may not be commenced except by or with the consent of the Director of Public Prosecutions.	2 years.
13.	Indecency between men.	On indictment. Summarily.	If by a man of or over the age of 21 with a man under that age, 5 years; otherwise 2 years. 6 months and/or a fine not exceeding the statutory maximum.
	(and attempts to procure the commission by a man of an act of gross indecency with another man).	On indictment. Summarily.	If the attempt is by a man of or over the age of 21 to procure a man under that age to commit an act of gross indecency with another man, 5 years; otherwise 2 years. 6 months and/or a fine not exceeding the statutory maximum.
14.	Indecent assault on a woman.	On indictment. Summarily (ie by virtue of s.17(1) 1980).	10 years. 6 months and/or a fine not exceeding the prescribed sum under s.32(1) MCA 1980.
15.	Indecent assault on a man.	On indictment. Summarily (ie by virtue of s.17(1) 1980).	10 years. 6 months and/or a fine not exceeding the prescribed sum.
16.	Assault with intent to commit buggery.	Indictable only.	10 years.
19.	Abduction of girl under 18 from parent or guardian.	Indictable only.	2 years.
20.	Abduction of girl under 16 from parent or guardian.	Indictable only.	2 years.
21.	Abduction of defective from parent or guardian.	Indictable only.	2 years.
22.	Causing prostitution of a woman (and attempts to commit this offence).	Indictable only. Indictable only.	2 years. 2 years.
23.	Prostitution of girl under 21 (and attempts to commit this offence).	Indictable only. Indictable only.	2 years. 2 years.
24.	Detention of woman in brothel.	Indictable only.	2 years.
26.	Permitting girl under 16 to use premises for intercourse.	On indictment. Summarily.	2 years. 6 months and/or a fine not exceeding the statutory maximum.

Section	Offence	Mode of Trial	Maximum Punishment
27.	Permitting defective to use premises for intercourse.	Indictable only.	2 years.
28.	Causing or encouraging prostitution etc of girl under 16.	Indictable only.	2 years.
29.	Causing or encouraging prostitution of defective.	Indictable only.	2 years.
30.	Living on earnings of prostitution.	On indictment. Summarily.	7 years. 6 months and/or a fine not exceeding the statutory maximum.
31.	Controlling a prostitute.	On indictment. Summarily.	7 years. 6 months and/or a fine not exceeding the statutory maximum.
32.	Solicitation by a man.	On indictment. Summarily.	2 years. 6 months and/or a fine not exceeding the statutory maximum.
33.	Keeping a brothel.	Summarily.	For an offence committed after a previous conviction, 6 months, and/or a fine not exceeding **Level 4**; otherwise 3 months and/or a fine not exceeding **Level 3**.
34.	Letting premises for use as brothel.	Summarily.	For an offence committed after a previous conviction, 6 months and/or a fine not exceeding **Level 4**; otherwise, 3 months and/or a fine not exceeding **Level 3**.
35.	Tenant permitting premises to be used as brothel.	Summarily.	For an offence committed after a previous conviction, 6 months and/or a fine not exceeding **Level 4**; otherwise, 3 months and/or a fine not exceeding **Level 3**.
36.	Tenant permitting premises to be used for prostitution.	Summarily.	For an offence committed after a previous conviction, 6 months and/or a fine not exceeding **Level 4**; otherwise, 3 months and/or a fine not exceeding **Level 3**.

SEXUAL OFFENCES ACT 1985

1.	Kerb crawling.	Summarily.	Fine not exceeding **Level 3**.
2.	Persistent soliciting of women for the purpose of prostitution.	Summarily.	Fine not exceeding **Level 3**.

SOCIAL SECURITY ACT 1975

146.	Failing to pay contribution.	Summarily.	Fine not exceeding **Level 3**.

> *Note:* Unpaid contributions must be ordered under s.150: *R v Melksham Justices, ex p. Williams* (1983) 147 JP 283.

STREET OFFENCES ACT 1959

1.(2)	Loitering or soliciting.	Summarily.	Fine not exceeding **Level 2** or, for an offence committed after a previous conviction, a fine not exceeding **Level 3**.

SUPPLEMENTARY BENEFITS ACT 1976

21.	False statements.	Summarily.	3 months and/or a fine not exceeding **Level 5**.

Section	Offence	Mode of Trial	Maximum Punishment
25.	Failure to maintain.	Summarily.	3 months and/or a fine not exceeding **Level 4.**

TELECOMMUNICATIONS ACT 1984

42.	Fraudulent use of telecommunications.	On indictment. Summarily.	2 years and/or a fine, or both. 6 months and/or a fine not exceeding the statutory maximum.

THEFT ACT 1968

Special provisions: All triable either way offences under the Theft Act 1968 are subject to para 3, Part II, Sch.6, Firearms Act 1968 so that if the defendant is also charged before the court with an offence under s.17(1) or (2) Firearms Act 1968, then the Theft Act offence also becomes indictable only.

Section	Offence	Mode of Trial	Maximum Punishment
7.	Theft. [For theft of vehicle, see Part II of this Table].	On indictment. Summarily.	10 years. 6 months and/or a fine not exceeding the prescribed sum.
8.	Robbbery or assault with intent to rob.	Indictable only.	Life.
9.	Burglary. Burglary except burglary comprising the commission of or an intention to commit an offence which is triable only on indictment and burglary in a dwelling if any person in the dwelling was subjected to violence or the threat of violence: Sch.1 MCA 1980.	On indictment. Summarily.	14 years. 6 months or the prescribed sum, or both.
10.	Aggravated burglary.	Indictable only.	Life.
11.	Removal of articles from place open to the public.	On indictment. Summarily.	10 years. 6 months and/or a fine not exceeding the prescribed sum.
12.(1)	Taking motor vehicle or other conveyance without authority. [See also Part II of this Table].	On indictment. Summarily.	3 years. 6 months and/or a fine not exceeding the prescribed sum.
12.(5)	Taking, etc pedal cycle.	Summarily.	Fine not exceeding **Level 3.**
13.	Abstracting electricity.	On indictment. Summarily.	5 years. 6 months and/or a fine not exceeding the prescribed sum.
15.	Obtaining property by deception.	On indictment. Summarily.	10 years. 6 months and/or a fine not exceeding the prescribed sum.
16.	Obtaining pecuniary advantage by deception.	On indictment. Summarily.	5 years. 6 months and/or a fine not exceeding the prescribed sum.
17.	False accounting.	On indictment. Summarily.	7 years. 6 months and/or a fine not exceeding the prescribed sum.
19.	False statements by company directors etc.	On indictment. Summarily.	7 years. 6 months and/or a fine not exceeding the prescribed sum, or both.
20.(1)	Suppression of documents.	On indictment. Summarily.	7 years. 6 months and/or a fine not exceeding the prescribed sum, or both.

Section	Offence	Mode of Trial	Maximum Punishment
20.(2)	Procuring the execution of a valuable security.	On indictment. Summarily.	7 years. 6 months and/or a fine not exceeding the prescribed sum, or both.
21.	Blackmail.	Indictable only.	14 years.
22.	Handling stolen goods.	On indictment. Summarily.	14 years. 6 months and/or a fine not exceeding the prescribed sum.
23.	Advertising reward for goods stolen or lost.	Summarily.	Fine not exceeding **Level 3**.
25.	Going equipped for stealing.	On indictment. Summarily.	3 years. 6 months and/or a fine not exceeding the prescribed sum.

[For going equipped for theft of vehicle, see Part II of this Table].

Section	Offence	Mode of Trial	Maximum Punishment
Sch.1, para. 2.(1)	Taking or destroying fish.	Summarily.	3 months and/or a fine not exceeding **Level 3**.
Sch.1, para. 2.(2)	Taking or destroying fish by angling in the daytime.	Summarily.	Fine not exceeding **Level 1**.

THEFT ACT 1978

Section	Offence	Mode of Trial	Maximum Punishment
1.	Obtaining services by deception.	On indictment. Summarily.	5 years. 6 months and/or a fine not exceeding the prescribed sum.
2.	Evasion of liability by deception.	On indictment. Summarily.	5 years. 6 months and/or a fine not exceeding the prescribed sum.
3.	Making off without payment.	On indictment. Summarily.	2 years. 6 months and/or a fine not exceeding the prescribed sum.

TRADE DESCRIPTIONS ACT 1968

Section	Offence	Mode of Trial	Maximum Punishment
28.	All offences except s.29(1).	On indictment. Summarily.	2 years and/or a fine, or both. Fine not exceeding the statutory maximum.
29.(1)	Obstruction of authorised officers. Summarily.	Fine not exceeding **Level 3**.	

TRANSPORT ACT 1968

Section	Offence	Mode of Trial	Maximum Punishment
96.(11)	Breaches of domestic drivers' code	Summarily.	Fine not exceeding **Level 4**.
96.(11A).	Breach of Community rules.	Summarily.	Fine not exceeding **Level 4**.
98.(4)	Written records of driving hours – breach of regulations.	Summarily.	Fine not exceeding **Level 4**.
99.(5)	False entries on written records.	On indictment. Summarily.	2 years. Fine not exceeding the statutory maximum.

VAGRANCY ACT 1824

Section	Offence	Mode of Trial	Maximum Punishment
3.	Idle and disorderly person (various offences).	Summarily.	1 month and/or a fine not exceeding **Level 3**. (s.34(3) MCA 1980).
4.	Rogues and vagabonds (various offences).	Summarily.	3 months or a fine not exceeding **Level 3** (s.34 MCA 1980).
5.	Incorrigible rogues.	On indictment.	1 year.

Section	Offence	Mode of Trial	Maximum Punishment

VEHICLES (EXCISE) ACT 1971

Section	Offence	Mode of Trial	Maximum Punishment
8.	Using and keeping vehicles without a licence.	Summarily.	Not exceeding **Level 3** or an amount equal to five times the amount of duty chargeable in respect of the vehicle. The court must order payment of an amount of 'back duty' calculated in accordance with s.8(2)–(4): s.9(1). There are corresponding provisions governing written pleas under s.34 Vehicles (Excise) Act 1971.
12.(4)	Failure to exhibit licence.	Summarily.	Fine not exceeding **Level 1**.
16.(7)	Misuse of trade plates.	Summarily.	Not exceeding **Level 3** or an amount equal to five times the amount of the duty chargeable in respect of the vehicle or vehicles.
18.	Higher rate of duty chargeable.	Summarily.	Not exceeding **Level 3** or an amount equal to five times the amount of the duty chargeable in respect of the vehicle or vehicles.
22.	Failure to fix and obscuration of marks and signs.	Summarily.	Fine not exceeding **Level 3**.
26.(1)	Fraudulent alteration or use.	On indictment. Summarily.	2 years. Fine not exceeding the statutory maximum.
26.(2)	False or misleading details.	On indictment. Summarily.	2 years. Fine not exceeding the statutory maximum.

WIRELESS TELEGRAPHY ACT 1949

Section	Offence	Mode of Trial	Maximum Punishment
1.	Unlicensed use or installation.	Summarily.	Fine not exceeding **Level 3** (s.14).

PART II – ROAD TRAFFIC

Note on 'Totting-up' under the Penalty Points System

Offenders must be disqualified for a minimum period of *6 months* – except where there are 'mitigating circumstances' – on reaching *12 points*. The key provisions concerning the way in which the total number of points is calculated, the prohibition on putting forward the same 'mitigating circumstances' twice and the effect of a previous 'totting-up' on the minimum period of disqualification are contained in s.19(2) to (5) Transport Act 1981 (to be construed as if contained in Part III Road Traffic Act 1972), as follows:

Disqualification for repeated offences

19. (1) . . .

(2) Where a person is convicted of an offence involving obligatory or discretionary disqualification and the penalty points to be taken into account under subs. (3) number 12 or more, the court shall order him to be disqualified for not less than the minimum period in subs. (4) unless the court is satisfied, having regard to all the circumstances not excluded by subs. (6), that there are grounds for mitigating the normal consequences of the conviction and thinks fit to order him to be disqualified for a shorter period or not to order him to be disqualified.

(3) The penalty points to be taken into account on the occasion of a person's conviction are–
(a) any that on that occasion will be ordered to be endorsed on any licence held by him or would be so ordered if he were not then ordered to be disqualified; and
(b) any that were on a previous occasion ordered to be so endorsed, unless the offender has since that occasion and before the conviction been disqualified, whether under subs. (2) or under s.93 of the 1972 Act;
but if any of the offences was commited more than three years before another the penalty points in respect of that offence shall not be added to those in respect of the other.

(4) The minimum perod referred to in subs. (2) is–
(a) six months if no previous disqualification imposed on the offender is to be taken into account; and
(b) one year if one, and two years if more than one, such disqualification is to be taken into account;
and a previous disqualification imposed on an offender is to be taken into account if it was imposed within the three years immediately preceding the commission of the latest offence in respect of which penalty points are taken into account under subs. (3).

(5) Where an offender is convicted on the same occasion of more than one offence involving obligatory or discretionary disqualification–
(a) not more than one disqualification shall be imposed on him under subs. (2); and
(b) in determining the period of the disqualification the court shall take into account all the offences; and
(c) for the purposes of any appeal any disqualification imposed under subs. (2) shall be treated as an order made on the conviction of each of the offences.

(6) No account is to be taken under subs. (2) of–
(a) any circumstances that are alleged to make the offence or any of the offences not a serious one;
(b) hardship, other than exceptional hardship; or
(c) any circumstances which, within the three years immediately preceding the conviction have been taken into account under that subsection in ordering the offender to be disqualified for a shorter period or not ordering him to be disqualified.'

References in the third columns of the table are to DVLC endorsement codes. Note that where the offence consists of:

Aiding and/or Abetting and/or Counselling and/or Procuring
Offences are coded with zero changed to '2', eg UT10 becomes UT12.

Causing or Permitting
Offences are coded with zero changed to '4', eg PL10 becomes PL14.

Inciting
Offences are codes with zero changed to '6', eg DD30 becomes DD36.

Section	Offence	Code	Maximum punishment	Penalty Points

ROAD TRAFFIC ACT 1972

Section	Offence	Code	Maximum punishment	Penalty Points
2	Reckless driving	DD30	£2,000 [the 'prescribed sum'] and/or 6 months	10

> *Note:* The offence is *triable either way* and attracts a mandatory 12 month disqualification (except for 'special reasons' when 4 penalty points are imposed) if committed within 3 years of a previous conviction for either reckless driving or causing death by reckless driving (ie under s.1 RTA 1972–DD70). The maximum punishment on indictment is 2 years imprisonment and/or a fine.

Section	Offence	Code	Maximum punishment	Penalty Points
3	Careless driving/	CD10	£1,000 [level 4]	2–5
	Inconsiderate driving	CD20	£1,000 [level 4]	2–5
5 (1)	*Driving* or *attempting to drive* whilst unfit through *drink* or *drugs*	DR20	£2,000 [level 5] and/or 6 months	4

> *Note:* The offence attracts a mandatory 12 months disqualification except for 'special reasons' when 4 penalty points imposed.

Section	Offence	Code	Maximum punishment	Penalty Points
5 (2)	*In charge* when unfit through *drink* or *drugs*	DR50	£1,000 [level 4] and/or 3 months	10
6 (1) (a)	*Driving* or *attempting* to drive – 'excess alcohol'	DR10	£2,000 [level 5] and/or 6 months	4

> *Note:* The offence attracts a mandatory 12 month disqualification except for 'special reasons' when 4 penalty points imposed.

Section	Offence	Code	Maximum punishment	Penalty Points
6 (1) (b)	In charge – 'excess alcohol'	DR40	£1,000 [level 4] and/or 3 months.	10
7 (4)	Failing to provide a specimen for *breath test*	DR70	£400 [level 3]	4
8 (7)	Failing to provide specimen *for analysis*, (Intoximeter, blood or urine sample). Driving or attempting to drive	DR30	£2,000 [level 5] and/or 6 months	(4)

> *Note:* The offence attracts a mandatory 12 months disqualification except for 'special reasons' when 4 penalty points imposed.

Section	Offence	Code	Maximum punishment	Penalty Points
	In all other circumstances	DR60	£1,000 [level 4] and/or 3 months	10
14	Racing and speed trials on the highway	MS50	£1,000 [level 4]	(4)

> *Note:* The offence attracts a mandatory 12 months disqualification except for 'special reasons' when 4 penalty points imposed.

Section	Offence	Code	Maximum punishment	Penalty Points
22	Failing to comply with:			
	Traffic lights	TS10		
	White lines	TS20		
	Stop sign	TS30		
	Directions of constable or warden	TS40	£400 [level 3]	3
	Other traffic signs	TS50		
	Undefined	TS70		

> *Note:* For TS60, 'School Crossing patrol', – see s.28 RTRA 1984, *infra.*

Section	Offence	Code	Maximum punishment	Penalty Points
24	Dangerous parking	MS10	£400 [level 3]	3
25 (4)	Failing to stop after an accident	AC10	£2,000 [level 5]	5–9
	Failing to report	AC20	£2,000 [level 5]	4–9

Section	Offence	Code	Maximum punishment	Penalty Points
40 (5)	Defective brakes	CU10	£1,000 [level 4]	3
	Causing or likely to cause danger – by reason of *condition*, etc	CU20	£1,000 [level 4]	3
	Defective tyre	CU30	£1,000 [level 4]	3
	Defective steering	CU40	£1,000 [level 4]	3
	Causing or likely to cause danger – by reason of *load* etc	CU50	£1,000 [level 4]	3
	Undefined failure	CU60	£1,000 [level 4]	3

Note: The maximum fine for 'construction and use' offences is £2,000 [level 5] in the case of a *goods vehicle*.

Section	Offence	Code	Maximum punishment	Penalty Points
84 (1)	No driving licence	LC10	£400 [level 3]	2 (no endorsement where failure to renew *full* licence or 'permitting')
88 (6)	Provisional licence offences:			
	No 'L' plates	PL10		
	Not under supervision	PL20		
	Unqualified passenger	PL30	£400 [level 3]	2
	Towing	PL40		
	Undefined offence	PL50		
91 (1)	Driving with uncorrected eyesight	MS70	£400 [level 3]	2
91 (2)	Refusing to submit to eye test	MS80	£400 [level 3]	2
99 (b)	Driving whilst disqualified: Under a court order	BA10	£2,000 [the 'prescribed sum'] and/or six months	6
	Under age	BA20	£2,000 [the 'prescribed sum'] and/or 6 months	2

Note: The offence is triable either way. The maximum punishment on indictment is 12 months imprisonment and/or a fine.

Section	Offence	Code	Maximum punishment	Penalty Points
143	No insurance	IN10	£1,000 [level 4]	4–8

ROAD TRAFFIC REGULATIONS ACT 1984

Section	Offence	Code	Maximum punishment	Penalty Points
17 (4)	Contravention of traffic regulations on special roads (motorways for 'speeding', see SP50, *infra*).	MW10	£1,000 [level 4]	3
23 (5)	Pedestrian crossing offences:			
	Moving vehicle	PC20		
	Stationary vehicle	PC30	£400 [level 3]	3
	Undefined	PC10		
28 (3)	Disobeying school crossing patrols	TS60	£400 [level 3]	3
81	Exceeding *statutory speed limit*	SP30	£400 [level 3]	3
89	Exceeding *goods vehicle* speed limit	SP10	£400 [level 3]	3
	Exceeding speed limit *for type of vehicle* (except passenger vehicles, SP40, *infra*)	SP20	£400 [level 3]	3
	Exceeding *passenger vehicle* speed limit	SP40	£400 [level 3]	3
	Exceeding *motorway* limit (for other 'motorway offences', see MW10, *supra*)	SP50	£1,000 [level 4]	3

Section	Offence	Code	Maximum punishment	Penalty Points

THEFT ACT 1968

1	Theft (or attempt under Criminal Atempts Act 1981) of vehicle	UT20	£2,000 [the prescribed sum'] and/or 6 months	8

> *Note:* The offence is triable either way. The maximum punishment on indictment is 10 years imprisonment and/or a fine – see, generally, Part I of this table.

12	Taking (or attempting to take under Criminal Attempts Act 1981) vehicle without consent being carried in or on such a vehicle	UT40	£2,000 [the 'prescribed sum'] and/or 6 months	8

> *Note:* The offence is triable either way. The maximum punishment on indictment is 3 years imprisonment and/or a fine.

25	Going equipped for theft or taking of vehicle	UT30	£2,000 [the 'prescribed sum'] and/or 6 months	8

> *Note:* The offence is triable either way. The maximum punishment on indictment is 3 years and/or a fine.

CHAPTER 1

Magistrates' Courts – Constitution, Powers and Natural Justice

Magistrates' Courts – Constitution, Powers and Natural Justice

1.00   INTRODUCTION

In everyday conversation, the term 'magistrates' court' signifies the *place*, usually some designated building, where magistrates – or 'justices of the peace', as they are equally correctly described – habitually sit to dispense local justice. From a different perspective, a slightly more sophisticated observer might use the same words to describe the *event* which occurs when 'a bench of magistrates' sits in the formal surroundings of a courtroom to adjudicate on matters brought or placed before *the court*. Legally speaking, however, the term has a more precise meaning. This legal meaning certainly encompasses the notion of 'a bench sitting in court', but goes much further. Essentially it connotes *any* discharge of duty or exercise of power by *any* justice of the peace. By definition, a magistrates' court is '. . . any justice or justices of the peace acting under any enactment or by virtue of his or their commission or under the common law': s.148 MCA 1980; Sch 2 Interpretation Act 1978. It follows that, eg a single justice of the peace dealing with an 'emergency' application in his own home is as much a 'magistrates' court' as a bench of three sitting formally in court to try criminal charges; and – since it is probably true to say that the search for all the common law powers of justices remains to be exhausted – the absolute meaning of the term 'magistrates court' is yet to be discovered.

The *place* where magistrates are accustomed to sit is only relevant to the definition of the term 'magistrates' court' indirectly, to the extent that certain of their (more common) powers can only be exercised in either a duly appointed *petty sessional court house* or in an *occasional court house, post*.

It is often said that magistrates' courts are 'creatures of statute', having been created, in their modern form, by Act of Parliament, and the vast bulk of their powers, jurisdiction and procedures being regulated thereby. But whilst many summary procedures are laid down by statute (principally, now, the Magistrates' Courts Act 1980 and Magistrates' Courts Rules 1981 (SI No 552)), and some of these procedures in considerable detail, it is also certain that courts have inherent power to regulate their own proceedings where statutory provision is lacking, or where the provisions do not sufficiently cover the situation, provided always that the higher courts have not already ruled on the matter: see the views of Lord Roskill in *Chief Constable of Norfolk v Clayton* [1983] 2 AC 473, [1983] 1 All ER 984; *sub nom R v Hunstanton Justices, ex p. Clayton*; also, eg *Att-Gen v Leveller Magazine Ltd* [1979] AC 440; *R v Denbigh Justices, ex p. Williams and Evans* [1974] QB 759. It is inescapable that this should be so in the day-to-day affairs of magistrates' courts, and in the sometimes unforeseeable procedural situations which arise. In the exercise of magistrates' inherent jurisdiction, the guiding principles are *'fairness'* and *'natural justice'* (see *Clayton's* case, *supra*) and, it is suggested, analogy and comparison with existing rules. An important aspect of this inherent jurisdiction is that, for example, although barristers and solicitors have *rights* of audience, the court may, as a matter of discretion, hear *whom it sees fit*: see *O'Toole v Scott* [1965] 2 All ER 240; and under *Summary Trial* see Chapter 6, *post*.

In certain instances, practice and procedure is governed by none of these sources, but by *Practice Directions* issued by the Lord Chief Justice. Generally speaking, such directions tend to be issued in response to some frequently occurring difficulty which is not readily – or is not being adequately – addressed via the regular appeal processes, eg *The Role of the Clerk in Court* [1981] 2 All ER 831. In 1986 this method was extended to the clarification of a High Court ruling on the procedure to be followed in cases of 'failure to surrender to court bail': see *Schiavo v Anderton* [1986] 3 WLR 177 and *Practice Direction (Bail: Failure to Surrender to Custody)* [1987] 1 WLR 79; 3.40, *post*

CONSTITUTION OF THE COURT (INCLUDING POWERS OF A SINGLE JUSTICE)   1.01

Statute dictates whether one, or more than one, justice is required to discharge a particular function. The effect of s.148 MCA 1980 is that a magistrates' court may comprise a single justice unless some other statutory provision requires otherwise. Additionally, s.121 MCA 1980 lays down a number of rules in relation to common types of proceeding. Thus, eg a magistrates' court may not try an information summarily, or hear a complaint, or hold a means enquiry except when composed of *at least two justices*, unless (in relation to 'informations' and 'complaints' only) the trial or hearing is one which by virtue of any enactment may take place before *a single justice*: s.121(1), (2). The maximum number of justices is *seven*: r.3 Justices of the Peace (Size and Chairmanship of Bench Rules) 1986 (SI No 923). Another provision of s.121 states that where a single justice acts (ie under some other express provision) his powers are limited to a maximum of 14 days imprisonment or a fine or other financial order of £1: s.121(5). A common situation not caught by s.122 in which a single justice is regularly encountered in practice is at 'remand hearings', to deal with bail issues: see 3.19, *post*; particularly at 'special' or 'occasional' courts held outside normal sitting times.

Both 'mode of trial' and 'committal for trial' may occur before a single justice: see s.18(5) and s.4(1) MCA 1980, respectively; and generally for those subjects at 4.00, *post*. A bind-over on complaint under s.115 requires two justices as a result of s.121(1); but not a bind-over pursuant to the Justices of the Peace Act 1361, at the instigation of the court, semble: see *Veater v Glennon* [1981] 2 All ER 304. A limited range of the more straightforward 'lesser' functions of a single justice may be discharged by the justices' clerk, eg the issue of a summons, adjournments, 'extensions of bail' where there is no alteration in the terms or conditions, and the granting of further time to pay a fine etc: Justices' Clerks Rules 1970 (SI No 231); but such duties remain 'judicial' ones, and cannot be delegated further: *R v Gateshead Justices, ex p. Tesco Stores Ltd* [1981] QB 470, [1981] 1 All ER 1027; and see under *The Justices' Clerk, post*.

Except where the contrary is expressed or implied, anything required to be done by justices may be done by one on behalf of the others present: s.150(2).

Stipendiary magistrates are empowered to adjudicate alone under special provisions outlined at 1.09 *post*.

The justices comprising a court must be present throughout the proceedings: s.121(6); and see *R v Guerin* (1888) 53 JP 468 (magistrate 'disqualified' when he left bench for a while); and *R v Manchester Justices, ex p. Burke* (1961) 125 JP 387 ('disqualified' where entered court late); except that a differently constituted bench may sentence following an adjournment after conviction, provided that full inquiry is made into the facts and circumstances: s.121(7)—including where sentence has been deferred for up to six months: *Cf R v Jacobs* (1976) 62 Cr App R 116.

1.02   **COURT HOUSES**

Subject to any statutory provision, a magistrates' court may sit where it will. However, a magistrates' court may only try a 'summary offence', hold a means inquiry or impose imprisonment when sitting in a *petty sessional court house* or an *occasional court house*, and the summary trial of an indictable offence may only take place in the former: s.121(3) MCA 1980. Licensed premises may not be used as either type of court house: s.190 Licensing Act 1964.

A 'petty sessional court house' is a court house or place at which justices are accustomed to assemble for holding special or petty sessions or for the time being appointed as a substitute for such a court house or place (including where justices are accustomed to assemble for either special or petty sessions at more than one court house or place in a petty sessional division, any such court house or place) and a court house or place at which a stipendiary magistrate is authorised by law to discharge any act authorised to be done by more than one justice of the peace: s.150(1) MCA 1980.

The justices acting for a petty sessions area may appoint as an occasional court house any place that is not a petty sessional court house for each petty sessions area, and an occasional court house may be outside the area for which it is appointed: s.147.

1.03   **TIMES OF SITTINGS**

There are no statutory limits upon the times when magistrates' courts may sit. In practice, they arrange their sittings at fixed hours which are published locally, but these do not prevent them sitting at any other time, or on any other day, or (subject to s.121 MCA 1980, *supra*) at any other place to discharge their duties. They are empowered to sit, if they think fit, on any day of the year, including Christmas Day, Good Friday and Sunday: see s.153 MCA 1980 – although these days are usually excepted in statutory provisions which affect the days on which courts might otherwise be required to be held.

1.04   **OPEN COURT (INCLUDING EXCEPTIONS)**

It is one of the proud claims of English law that the courts are open to the public, and that justice is administered publicly. Even the privacy of the retiring room falls to be considered here. Lord Hailsham LC, in a speech made at the Magistrates' Association's 1986 annual meeting, commended the practice of 'open clerking' ie the giving of advice in the court-room in the hearing of the parties, and the *Practice Direction on the Role of the Clerk in Court* [1981] 2 All ER 831, which provides at para 3 that 'If no request for advice has been made by the justices, the justices' clerk shall discharge his responsibility in open court'. The rule that justices may not remain anonymous to *bona fide* inquirers, *infra*, may be viewed as having as much to do with 'openness' in the administration of justice as with the rule against bias: see *R v Felixstowe Justices, ex p. Leigh* [1987] 2 WLR 380; and *The Rule against Anonymity, post* 1.21.

More generally, the principle of 'open court' defines who may enter the courtroom, and the extent of magistrates' jurisdiction to regulate their own proceedings by excluding the public, sections of the public, or individuals. Whenever magistrates are required to sit in a petty sessional or occasional court house they must sit in open court: s.121 MCA 1980. This and similar provisions are merely declaratory of the common law. 'Every court of justice is open to every subject of the King', *per* Lord Halsbury in *Scott v Scott* [1913] AC 1417. But, per Viscount Haldane LC in the same case

'while the broad principle is that the courts in this country must, as between parties administer justice in public, this principle is subject to apparent exceptions (*which however*) are themselves the outcome of a yet more fundamental principle that the chief object of courts of justice must be to secure that justice is done . . . As the paramount object must always be to do justice, the general rule as to publicity . . . must accordingly yield. But the burden lies on those seeking to displace its application . . . The question is by no means one which . . . can be dealt with by the judge as resting in his mere discretion as to what is expedient. The latter must treat it as one of principle, and as turning not on convenience but on necessity.'

Or as Lord Diplock said in *Att-Gen v Leveller Magazine Ltd* [1979] AC 440 at 449:

'As a general rule the English system of administering justice does require that it be done in public: *Scott v Scott* [1913] AC 417. If the way that courts behave cannot be hidden from the public ear and eye this provides a safeguard against judicial arbitrariness or idiosyncrasy and maintains the public confidence in the administration of justice. The application of this principle of open justice has two aspects: as respects proceedings in the court itself it requires that they should be held in open court to which the press and public are admitted and that, in criminal cases at any rate, all evidence communicated to the court is communicated publicly. As respects the publication to a wider public of fair and accurate reports of proceedings that have taken place in court the principle requires that nothing should be done to discourage this. However, since the purpose of the general rule is to serve the ends of justice it may be necessary to depart from it where the nature or circumstances of the particular proceeding are such that the application of the general rule in its entirety would frustrate or render impracticable the administration of justice or would damage some other public interest for whose protection Parliament has made some statutory derogation from the rule. Apart from statutory exceptions, however, where a court in the exercise of its inherent power to control the conduct of proceedings before it departs in any way from the general rule, the departure is justified to the extent and to no more than the extent that the court reasonably believes it to be necessary in order to serve the ends of justice.'

Thus, where magistrates have power to sit in private it is an acceptable alternative in a proper case to allow a witness to conceal his identity by a pseudonym. Where this is done a warning should be given as to the intended effects of this ruling: *Att-Gen v Leveller Magazine Ltd and Others* [1979] AC 440 ('Colonel X'). Recently, it has been stated that the occasions when justices should sit in private are 'rare' and only when justice cannot be achieved by sitting in open court; see *R. v Malvern Justices, ex p. Evans; R. v Evesham Justices, ex p. McDonagh* (1987) *The Times*, 1 August, although they may sit *in camera* in order to make their decision whether to hold the hearing itself *in camera*, otherwise the point of doing the latter might be lost: *R v Tower Bridge Justices, ex p. Osborne* (1987) *The Times*, 4 December.

Justices have power in a proper case to hear mitigation *although the decision to hear in camera* should itself be announced in open court: *R v Ealing Justices, ex p. Weafer* (1982) 74 Cr App R 206. Mitigation can also be submitted in a sealed form although the prosecution are entitled to see it, *per* Donaldson LJ, *ibid*. The hearing of mitigation *in camera* should be a very exceptional step and should be avoided if there is any alternative, for example by the advocate drawing the court's attention to relevant passages in written documents: *R v Reigate Justices, ex p. Argus Newspapers Ltd and Another* (1983) 5 Cr App R (S) 181.

'The actual presence of the public is never, of course, necessary', *per* Lord Blanesburgh in *McPherson v McPherson* [1935] All ER Rep 105 at p 109 (a divorce case). The injunction to the judge or magistrate is for him to do his best to enable the public to come in and see what was happening, having proper commonsense regard to the facilities available and the necessity for keeping order, security and the like. Although it is difficult to imagine a case which could be said to be held publicly if the press had been actively excluded, the fact that the press is present is not conclusive the other way because one must not overlook the open factor of an open and public proceeding: one to which members of the public could come if they had sufficient interest in the proceedings to make it worth their while to do so. If, having regard to all the prevailing circumstances, the judge or magistrate on the spot had shown himself conscious of his duty and reached a reasonable conclusion the Divisional Court would not substitute their own views as to whether the facilities were sufficient or not: *R v Denbigh Justices, ex p. Williams and Evans* [1974] QB 759 (exclusion of demonstrators justified).

'It is one of the essential qualities of a court of justice that its proceedings should be public, and that all persons who may be desirous of hearing what is going on, if there be room in the place for that purpose – provided they do not interrupt the proceedings and provided there is no specific reason why they should be removed – have a right to be present for the purpose of hearing what is going on': *Daubney v Cooper* (1829) 10 B & C 236. 'The court may be closed or cleared if such a precaution is necessary for the administration of justice. Tumult or disorder or the just apprehension of it, would certainly justify the exclusion of all from whom such interruption is expected, and if such discrimination is impossible, the exclusion of the public in general', *per* Lord Loreborn in *Scott v Scott* [1911–13] All ER Rep 1 at p. 13.

1.05   Contempt and restrictions on publication

The term 'open court' must be understood in the light of the quite separate powers of justices to act to prevent disorders or other interferences with the administration of justice. Also the court may order that publication of any legal proceedings held in public or any part of those proceedings be *postponed* but only where it appears necessary for avoiding a substantial risk of prejudice to the administration of justice in those or other proceedings: s.4(2) Contempt of Court Act 1981; and see further at **7.00**, *post*.

1.06   Statutory exceptions

Examining justices must sit in open court except when any enactment contains an express provision to the contrary and except where it appears to them as respects the whole or any part of committal proceedings that the ends of justice would not be served by their sitting in open court: s.4(2) MCA 1980. The court may on the application of the prosecutor order that all or any portion of the public may be excluded during any part of the hearing of proceedings under the Official Secrets Act on the grounds that the publication of evidence would be prejudicial to public safety: s.8(4) Official Secrets Act 1920.

The public, but not the press, may be excluded during the evidence of a juvenile witness in proceedings in relation to an offence against or any conduct contrary to decency or morality: s.37 CYPA 1933. Children other than babes in arms may not in general be allowed in court except as witnesses: s.36 CYPA 1933.

THE RETIRING ROOM   1.07

The privacy of the retiring room is sanctioned by custom and long usage, and a considerable body of law has built up concerning the circumstances and the matters upon which the justices may properly receive advice from their clerk in private whilst during the disposal of a case: see under *The Clerk to the Justices, post.* Discussions which take place in the retiring room remain private, except in so far as it is appropriate to disclose them in open court by way of explanation of a decision, or to allow further representations – or where statute requires reasons to be given: see eg Bail Act 1976 (grounds and reasons); s.1(4) Criminal Justice Act 1982 (reasons for breaching restrictions on custodial sentences for young offenders). It is suggested that, as a matter of practice, in the interests of the open administration of justice and to allow representations by the parties, magistrates should always indicate publicly anything from their private discussions which is material to the decision they are about to make.

Notwithstanding the terms of para 3 of the *Practice Direction on the Role of the Clerk in Court, ante,* it is clear that the court clerk may enter the retiring room to prevent the justices falling into error. Indeed, this has been elevated by the High Court into a duty: *R v Uxbridge Justices, ex p. Smith* (1985) 149 JP 620; and see under *The Court Clerk,* 1.24 *post. Natural Justice,* 1.10 *post,* requires that the court clerk should not enter the retiring room when this is not within his proper functions, since this may give the impression that he is interferring in matters which are the exclusive province of the justices. Justices should not receive a record of previous convictions in the retiring room even though they have already come to a decision to convict: *Hastings v Ostle* (1930) 94 JP 209; *Hill v Tothill* [1936] W N 126. A witness even as to character only may not be interviewed by justices in their retiring room: *R v Bodmin Justices, ex p. McEwan* [1947] KB 321; nor may a social worker be, even after a conviction: *R v Aberdare Justices, ex p. Jones* [1973] Crim LR 45. But *certiorari* will not issue simply because anyone, even the informant, enters the justices' retiring room, although the conviction will be quashed where it appears he did so specifically to make a point: *R v Stratford Upon Avon Justices, ex p. Edmunds* [1973] Crim LR 241. It is the practice, in many courts, to deal with ex parte applications in the privacy of the retiring room, outside the times normally set aside for the disposal of cases.

All decisions of a magistrates court are 'unanimous', and dissenting views are not announced or permitted.

1.08   **JUSTICES OF THE PEACE**

The term 'magistrate' in relation to a county or London commission area of the City of London means a justice of the peace for the county, London commission area or the City as the case may be other than a justice whose name is for the time being entered in the supplemental list; and in relation to a part of a county or of a London commission area, means a person who is a magistrate for that county or area and ordinarily acts in and for that part of it: s.70 Justices of the Peace Act 1979.

A justice of the peace holds his office by virtue of the *commission of the peace*. There is a commission of the peace for each commission area addressed generally and not by name to all such persons as may from time to time hold office as justices of the peace for the area: s.5 Justices of the Peace Act 1979. Each county, London commission area and the City of London is a commission area: s.1.

Although a justice is appointed to a commission area he is assigned by the Lord Chancellor administratively to a *petty sessions area* as defined in s.4(1) and (2) Justices of the Peace Act 1979. A justice of the peace for any commission area may act as a justice for that area in any adjoining commission area: s.66(1); and see the special provisions in relation to Surrey and Kent contained in s.66(2). In relation to remand hearings, it has been held that the fact that justices are appointed to a county commission area enables 'cross-court' remands *within the county*: see *R v Avon Magistrates' Courts Committee, ex p. Bath Law Society* (1987) 151 JP 825 and generally at 3.15 *et al, post*.

A justice of the peace must reside in or within 15 miles of his commission area, but no act of his is invalidated by reason only of his being disqualified thereby: s.7. Once a justice becomes 70 his name is normally entered in the supplemental list: s.8. His powers thereafter are limited to those specified in s.10(2), but other acts are not disqualified: s.10(4).

1.09 **Stipendiary magistrates**

Stipendiary magistrates and *acting stipendiary magistrates* must be barristers or solicitors of not less than seven years' standing. The former are appointed by the Queen on the recommendation of the Lord Chancellor; whilst the latter may be 'authorised' to act for periods of up to 3 months at a time by the Lord Chancellor himself. Both have the same jurisdiction, powers and duties. The provisions relating to appointment, removal, jurisdiction and place of sitting vary according to whether the person is appointed to be a *metropolitan stipendiary*, or a stipendiary *outside the inner London area and the City of London*: see ss.31 to 35 Justices of the Peace Act 1979 and ss.13 to 16, respectively (apart from s.16, not reproduced herein). The Lord Chancellor must 'designate' one of the metropolitan stipendiaries to be the chief metropolitan stipendiary magistrate: s.31(3).

A stipendiary magistrate is *ex officio* a justice of the peace for his area, and metropolitan stipendiaries are also justices of the peace for each of the London Commission areas *and* for Essex, Hertfordshire, Kent and Surrey. A stipendiary magistrate sitting at a place appointed for that purpose has power to do any act and to exercise alone any jurisdiction which can be done or exercised by two justices under any law other than any law made after 2 August, 1858 which expressly provides to the contrary: s.16(3), as applied to metropolitan stipendiaries by s.33(4).

NATURAL JUSTICE 1.10

The two rules of natural justice are usually stated by way of the latin maxims *audi alteram partem* and *nemo judex in causa sua* or 'hear both sides' and 'no-one can be a judge in his own cause', respectively. As to the first of these rules, the pages of this work contain numerous examples of situations in which proceedings before magistrates have been successfully challenged because the magistrates failed to hear or allow representations on some point, or where they acted precipitately without regard to the views of the parties, or failed to allow adequate time for a party to prepare his case. A number of such cases can be found under *Adjournment*, 5.06 *post*, and also under *Judicial Review*, 11.06 *post*. It will perhaps, suffice for present purposes to emphasise that the principle operates equally in favour of the prosecutor: see, in more recent times, eg *R v Clerkenwell Magistrates Court, ex p. Director of Public Prosecutions* (1987) *The Times*, 20 May; and *R v Lewes Magistrates' Court, ex p. Oldfield* (1987) *The Times*, 6 May. The second rule, also known as the 'rule against bias' lies at the heart of criminal procedure and is treated in the next section.

Procedurally speaking, the requirements of natural justice, in the more modern cases, have been said to be satisfied if a court 'acts fairly'; and this is also the basis upon which a court must proceed when it devises its own procedures in the absence of statutory provision: see *Chief Constable of Norfolk v Clayton*; *sub nom R v Hunstanton Justices, ex p. Clayton* [1983] 2 AC 473 per Lord Roskill. A sound sense of natural justice and of fair procedures is essential to all aspects of summary justice, and fundamental to everything contained in this work.

Bias and disqualification 1.11

Justices may be disqualified from acting as such in court by failing to conform to residence qualifications: s.7 Justices of the Peace Act 1979; sitting in proceedings in which they are interested as members of local authorities: s.64 or when on the supplemental list: s.10(1). But such disqualifications do not *in themselves* invalidate their acts: s.10(4). Solicitor justices are restricted from practising before their own bench by s.38 Solicitors Act 1974 and there are many other statutory restrictions upon justices sitting to hear cases with which they have a connection.

The Lord Chancellor's Department has offered advice to magistrates in cases (a) where the solicitor prosecuting or defending is the magistrates' personal and/or business adviser; and (b) where the firm prosecuting or defending is one in which a justice's son is a partner or salaried assistant in another office: see August 1982 issue of *The Magistrate*, at p.121.

Pecuniary interest 1.12

The common law distinguishes, somewhat cynically perhaps, between *pecuniary* and *non-pecuniary interest*. Any direct pecuniary interest, however small, in the subject of inquiry disqualifies a person from acting as a judge in the matter. *per* Blackburn J, in *R v R*; *R v Justices of Blandford* (1866) 30 JP 293 (a civil case – *a fortiori* it is suggested in a criminal one). If a justice 'has a pecuniary interest or an interest capable of being measured pecuniarily the law raises a conclusive presumption of bias', *per* Vaughan Williams LJ in *R v Sutherland JJ* (1901) 65 JP 594, 598.

(But see *R v Burton ex p. Young* (1897) 61 JP 727. A shareholder in the victim company should not adjudicate: *R v Hammond* (1863) 27 JP 793.

The fact that a magistrate is a ratepayer does not disqualify him from ordering costs against a party: *Sierzant v Anderton* (1982) 4 Cr App R(S) 275: exemptions or disqualifications of this type only apply where there is an interest in the subject matter of the proceedings and have no application to ancillary matters such as costs or sentence, *per* Ormrod LJ, *ibid*.

1.13   Non-pecuniary interest

Where the alleged bias is *not of a pecuniary nature* the test is, 'would a reasonable and fair-minded person sitting in court and knowing all the relevant facts have a reasonable suspicion that a fair trial for the accused was not possible?' *per* Ackner LJ in *R v Liverpool City Justices, ex p. Topping* [1983] 1 All ER 490 and see *per* Lord Goddard CJ in *R v Caernarvon Licensing Justices, ex p. Bensen* (1948) 113 JP 23; and *per* Lord Widgery CJ in *R v McLean, ex p. Aiken and Others* (1975) 139 JP 261 at p.266.

Justices who are interested in a criminal proceeding should not act therein: *R v Glamorganshire Justices* (1857) 21 JP 773. The reason is that 'It is highly desirable that justice should be administered by persons who cannot be suspected of improper motives', *per* Mellor J, in *R v Allan* (1864) 4 B & S 915 at p.926. The most flagrant example of this rule is where a magistrate adjudicates in a matter to which he is substantially a party, since no man may be a judge in his own cause: *R v Hoseason* (1811) 14 East 605. It is bias for a magistrate to declare his preference for police evidence: *R v Bingham Justices, ex p. Jowitt* (1974) *The Times*, 3 July.

A conviction was quashed when a presiding magistrate was a member of the *education committee* whose schools were said to have been short weighted by a firm of contractors *R v Altrincham Justices, ex p. Pennington and Another* [1975] QB 549 in which Bridge J, said that, if one visualised almost any kind of association between a magistrate and a private victim of an offence, it would be obvious that it ought to disqualify. If the plain outcome of an association between a magistrate and a private commercial undertaking which was the victim of the offence to be tried was that he should not sit without disclosing his position, the same outcome should result from a comparable association between a magistrate and a non-commercial undertaking, such as an education authority, which was the victim. In the same case, Lord Widgery CJ observed *obiter* that the situation of a magistrate member of a *police authority* is wholly different: the police authority are concerned with the administration of the force; they are not concerned with the rights and wrongs of the individual prosecution. They are not given such an interest merely because the prosecutor is a police officer.

An acquittal was quashed where the husband of one of the justices had formerly been a member of the defendant local authority: *R v Smethwick Justices, ex p. Hands* (1980) *The Times*, 4 December.

1.14   Bias and the justices' clerk or prosecutor

The same principles would appear to apply to the clerk of the court: *R v Camborne Justices, ex p. Pearce* [1955] 1 QB 41. In *R v Uxbridge Justices, ex p. Burbridge* (1972) *The Times*, 20 June it was held that an alleged remark of a clerk out of court which might have disclosed bias could not affect all the magistrates on a particular bench when the clerk did not sit in the proceedings.

In *R v Dunstable Justices, ex p. Cox* [1986] NLJ 310, a conviction was
quashed where, according to Watkins LJ, the accused was faced with the
'alarming prospect' of being prosecuted by a solicitor who had earlier
advised him on his defence. It was 'absolutely vital for the appearance of
fairness' that this should not occur.

Waiver of objection   1.15

Objection on ground of interest can be waived: *R v Cheltenham Commissioners* (1841) 10 LJMC 99; and cannot be made afterwards unless the
objector shows that both he and his advocate were unaware of the
interest: *R v Justices of Richmond* (1860) 24 JP 422; *R v Justices of Kent*
1880) 44 JP 298 (a licensing case). There can be no waiver in ignorance of
the interest: *R v Cumberland Justices, ex p. Midland Rail Co* (1880) 52 JP
402. But an advocate is under no duty to put 'fishing' questions to justices
when he suspects interest: *R v Barnsley Licensing Justices, ex p. Barnsley
& District LVA* [1960] 2 QB 167.

Avoidance of bias   1.16

The proper course for any magistrate with a multiplicity of outside
interests before embarking on a judicial task on the day when he or she
was sitting, is to look at the list of cases to see whether there is something
which involves an organisation with which he or she has an interest. If in
the list there is a case involving an organisation in which the magistrate is
actively employed, then the magistrate ought either to disqualify himself
or herself, or at all events bring the matter to the parties' attention before
the case is opened to see if there is any objection – which is really doing
the same thing, *per* Lord Widgery CJ, in *R v Altrincham Justices, ex p.
Pennington* [1975] QB 549.
Magistrates who are interested should not even appear to form part of a
court or place themselves in a position where they could exert any
influence: *R v Byles & Others, ex p. Hollidge* (1912) 77 JP 40 (see also *R v
Suffolk JJ* (1852) 16 JP 296 – a rating appeal in which justices were
recommended to absent themselves from the court – it may be the better
view that justices should leave the bench but be visible in the court, at
least during any period when the justices are in the retiring room, unless
the disqualified justice has left the premises entirely). If an interested
justice remains upon the bench that is sufficient to invalidate the proceedings, *per* Kay LJ, in *R v Budden & Others, Kent Justices* (1896) 60 JP 166
notes passed from interested magistrate). The Lord Chancellor in a
letter dated 12 January 1967 has condemned the practice of '*sitting back*'
and expressed the view that magistrates who do not sit as a member of a
court should remove themselves completely from its vicinity. (This rule is
difficult to apply if the justice is to adjudicate on matters later in the list,
when the 'visibility' approach suggested above can dispel any suggestion
of behind the scenes involvement.)

Knowledge of the parties   1.17

As to a justice's personal knowledge of the parties before him, it was said
in a civil case that it would be a preposterous thing if a suggestion were
made that there was bias or possibility of bias because of the mere fact
that some sort of acquaintance exists between a justice and parties, or
even the fact that they have discussed business matters entirely unconnected with the case. 'The whole essence of the local administration of justice
and the great value of the functions of justices are that they do administer

justice amongst people with whom they are acquainted and of whose lives and family history they know something', *per* Sir Boyd Merriman P in *Cottle v Cottle* [1939] 2 All ER 535 at p.539 (decision quashed where there was sufficient evidence upon which the litigant husband might reasonably have formed the impression that the justice, who was a friend of the wife's mother, could not give the case an unbiased hearing). It is desirable in criminal proceedings that an accused should come before a magistrate who does not have an intimate knowledge of his record or background, but that desirability cannot be elevated into a proposition of law: *R v Metropolitan Stipendiary Magistrate, ex p. Gallagher and Another* (1972) 136 JPN 80. Thus, there is no rule of law that a magistrate is disqualified from hearing a case by reason of his having been concerned with the same defendant in other proceedings: *R v McLean, ex p. Aikens and Others* (1975) 139 JP 261.

In *R v Liverpool City Justices, ex p. Topping* [1983] 1 All ER 490 disapproval was expressed of the practice of placing before justices court lists prepared by computer which contained, not only the present charge, but details of all other charges, related or unrelated, which were outstanding and of all convictions. The decision was later tempered in *R v Weston-Super-Mare Justices, ex p. Shaw* [1987] 2 WLR 305; applying same *Ex p. Stone* (1984) unreported where it was stated that whether there is any 'real or ostensible bias' is a matter for the justices themselves, whilst a clerk may use his 'good sense' in producing the court list.

If a justice becomes aware of previous convictions during a hearing, it is his duty to disclose this fact, even if the trial has to start again before a fresh bench: *R v Birmingham Justices, ex p. Robinson* (1985) 150 JP 1; similarly where convictions have been revealed to a magistrate in a legal aid application: *R v Blythe Valley Juvenile Court, ex p. S* (1987) 151 JP 805.

1.18 Knowledge of the circumstances

Although magistrates may without hearing evidence take cognizance of any matter covered by the doctrine of *judicial notice*, they may not otherwise act on their own local knowledge. Thus, it is proper on the one hand for magistrates to make use of their *general local knowledge* in deciding whether a car park known to all three members of the bench was a public place or not (*Clift v Long* [1961] Crim LR 121); similarly, justices in dealing with local geography in the sense that they are dealing with matters which are *notorious locally and which are within their own local knowledge*, are entitled to supplement the evidence (as to road user) by their knowledge that the journey in question inevitably involved passage over public roads, *per* Lord Widgery CJ in *Borthwick v Vickers* [1973] RTR 390; but on the other hand, the *private knowledge* of one member of the bench as to the use to which a car park was put on a particular occasion cannot be a substitute for evidence: *Williams v Boyle* [1963] Crim LR 204.

Magistrates may *not* act on their *own expert evidence* by taking a tyre gauge with them into the retiring room for the purpose of measurement: *R v Tiverton Justices, ex p. Smith* [1980] RTR 280.

1.19 Specialised knowledge

It is *not improper* for a justice with specialised knowledge, such as a doctor, to draw on that knowledge in interpreting the evidence. However, he should not go on, as it were, *to give evidence to himself* in contradiction of that heard in court. In the retiring room, a justice with such knowledge ought to wait until asked to make a contribution on his speciality. *Wetherall v Harrison* [1976] QB 773; see also *Kent v Stamps* [1982] RTR 273 (knowledge of road). Neither should justices try to become 'amateurs in Science' where expert evidence is needed: *Dawson v Lunn* [1986] RTR 234.

Magistrates' conduct on the bench   1.20

If a responsible observer seriously believes a justice to have been asleep on the bench the justice should withdraw from the case even if the belief is unfounded: *R v Weston-Super-Mare Justices, ex p. Taylor* [1981] Crim LR 179.

The rule against anonymity   1.21

Until 1987, it seems to have been correct that magistrates were under no duty to disclose their names to anyone: *cf Newton v Saunders* (1972) 31 October, mentioned at 137 JPN 432; and, as a matter of practice, names were commonly withheld, ostensibly on such grounds as security, other misuse of the information or 'collective responsibility'. But it is now clear that magistrates' names cannot be withheld as a matter of course and that *bona fide* inquirers such as the parties (who may need to know the names in order to assess whether a particular magistrate should be asked to stand down on the ground of 'bias', *supra*) and the press (at least at the time of the events) are entitled to know who it is that is adjudicating: *R v Felixstowe Justices, ex p. Leigh* [1987] 2 WLR 380. According to the declaration granted by the Divisional Court in that case, there is a public interest in the open administration of justice, and the practice of withholding names, whether at the behest of the court or the justices' clerk, is '. . . inimical to the proper administration of justice, and an unwarranted and unlawful obstruction of the right to know who sits in judgment': per Watkins LJ. It was, however, recognised that there is a discretion to withhold names where there appears to be some 'mischievous purpose', and, additionally, it must be noted that, whilst a declaration was granted in this case, *mandamus* to compel the Felixstowe Justices to divulge names to the chief reporter of the *Observer* newspaper (who had not been present in court at the original hearing, but requested the names some three weeks later in connection with an article which he was writing) was refused on the ground that he did not have sufficient *locus standi*. The report also suggests that any decision to withhold names can only be taken *judicially*, so that whilst a justices' clerk might well act to refuse disclosure until the hearing, any final decision should be taken by the court itself.

The following principles can be *suggested* as flowing from the *Felixstowe* case:
(a) Routine non-disclosure is unwarranted and unlawful;
(b) Certain persons should normally be accommodated, as follows:
    (i) the parties
    (ii) their legal representatives
    (iii) the press present in court, and possibly where they seek the information close to the events
    (iv) there is no general right of individual members of the public to the information (at least no such right was suggested)

(v) there must be a discretion to give names in other circumstances to *bona fide* inquirers, *semble*; eg another lawyer might have legitimate reasons to ask for the names of justices who have heard certain matters, researchers etc

(vi) a 'reasonable belief' (*Ex p. Leigh*) that a request is 'mischievous' justifies refusal

(vii) a lapse of time between the proceedings and the request may justify refusal. Here, the more remote the applicant, or the less 'essential or material' (*Ex p. Leigh*) the information to him, the stronger the ground for refusal, *semble*

(viii) the ultimate decisions in individual cases should be taken by *the court* under its inherent discretion to control its own proceedings, at least where such a reference is practicable

(ix) subject to (i) to (viii) *supra*, the justices' clerk must have a discretion to deal with day to day inquiries as he sees fit, including asking for credentials and written confirmation if necessary.

1.22   LIABILITY OF JUSTICES

The action on the case for tort against justices for acting *within their jurisdiction* maliciously and without reasonable and probable cause no longer lies. However, they are liable for acts *outside their jurisdiction* even though they act without malice: see *Re McC (a minor)* [1985] AC 528 (justices liable for committing a young offender to training school without regard to the rules concerning legal representation).

,No action may be brought in respect of the acts of a justice in excess of his jurisdiction until the conviction, order, etc, has been quashed by the High Court: s.45 Justices of the Peace Act 1979 (not reproduced herein). Damages for anything done by a justice *in the execution of his office* as such a justice are limited to a nominal amount: s.52 (not reproduced). It has been held that justices may act within their office even when they have no jurisdiction to make the order made: see *R v Waltham Forest Justices, ex p. Solanke* [1985] 3 All ER 727, confirmed in *same* [1986] 2 All ER 981; but contrast *R v Manchester City Justices, ex p. Davies* (1987) *The Times*, 25 November (distress/committal for non-payment of rates), where the justices were held liable in damages at large on the basis of an 'insufficient' committal procedure.

A justice or a justice's clerk may be indemnified for damages etc out of local funds if he acted *reasonably and in good faith*: s.53 (not reproduced). The Lord Chancellor may reimburse costs awarded against a justice or a justices' clerk in proceedings for a prerogative order: s.54(2) (not reproduced).

1.23   THE CLERK TO THE JUSTICES

The functions of the clerk to the justices ie the person or persons appointed to this post under s.25 Justices of the Peace Act 1979 (not printed herein), are only partially defined by statute. They *include* the giving to the justices to whom he is clerk or any of them, at the request of the justices or justice, advice about law, practice or procedure on questions arising in connection with the discharge of their or his functions, including questions arising when the clerk is not personally attending on the justices or justice. In particular the clerk may, at any time when he thinks he should do so, bring to the attention of the justices or justice any point of law, practice or procedure that is or may be involved in any question so arising: s.28(3). This provision does not define – or in any respect limit – the powers and duties of the justices' clerk or the matter on which justices may obtain assistance from him: s.28(4).

Certain things authorised to be done by, to or before a single justice may be done by, to or before a justices' clerk: Justices' Clerks Rules 1970 (SI No 231, as amended). In acting under those Rules, any enactment or rule of law regulating the exercise of any jurisdiction or powers of justices or relating to the exercise of such jurisdiction or powers applies to the clerk as if he were one of the justices: s.28(2) Justices of the Peace Act 1979.

The justices' clerk's responsibilities under the Rules are non-delegable: see *R v Gateshead Justices, ex p. Tesco Stores Ltd* [1981] QB 470 (contrast his power to grant legal aid, which is: see 10.02, *post*). But when performing such duties the justices' clerk has a full judicial function. Thus he may, eg query delay in laying an information upon which he is requested to issue a summons: *R v Clerk to the Medway Justices, ex p. DHSS* (1986) 150 JP 401 (even though the 'preferable course' for both justices and justices' clerks may be to leave such issues until the hearing).

Where outside Inner London someone acts as a substitute for the clerk to the justices he is treated as acting as deputy to the clerk and must make a return to the latter: s.30. Except in Inner London there is no statutory post of deputy to the clerk to the justices although such appointments are commonly made.

For a discussion of the legal position and status of the 'deputy clerk to the justices', see the article at (1988) JPN 486 and 151 by J A Davis and C Boulter, respectively.

Court clerks 1.24

From the earliest days, justices of the peace have sat in court with a clerk. For a long time this was usually the person holding the office of clerk to the justices, but with the growth in work of the modern magistrates' courts increasingly this role has come to be discharged by assistants, whilst the clerk to the justices is becoming, increasingly, an administrator, or 'manager' – though still subject to the many duties cast on him by statute, including those of a personal nature towards his own bench: *supra* and the *Practice Directions* below. Although, remarkably, there is no requirement that justices must have the assistance of a clerk when sitting in court, no person may be employed as a clerk in court unless he is (a) qualified (any age limits apart) to be appointed a justices' clerk by virtue of s.27 Justices of the Peace Act 1979 or (b) he is qualified by virtue of r.4 of the Justices' Clerks (Qualifications of Assistants) Rules (SI No 570, as amended, not reproduced herein): s.30 Justices of the Peace Act 1979. A person who is not so qualified may be employed as a clerk in court if he holds a valid training certificate granted by a magistrates' courts' committee: r.5. The Secretary of State may grant authority for any such person as may be specified by him to be employed as a clerk in court for such period not exceeding six months as may be specified if he is satisfied that the person is in the circumstances a suitable person to be so employed and that no other arrangement can reasonably be made for the hearing of proceedings before the court: r.6.

Any staff provided for a justices' clerk work under his direction: s.27(6).

The role of the clerk in court is governed by the following *Practice Direction-Role of the Clerk in Court* [1981] 2 All ER 831 issued by the Lord Chief Justice on 2 July 1981.

1 A justices' clerk is responsible to the justices for the performance of any of the functions set out below by any member of his staff acting as court clerk and may be called in to advise the justices even when he is not personally sitting with the justices as clerk to the court.

2 It shall be the responsibility of the justices' clerk to advise the justices as follows:
   (a) on questions of law or of mixed law and fact;
   (b) as to matters of practice and procedure.

3 If it appears to him necessary to do so, or he is so requested by the justices, the justices' clerk has the responsibility to:
   (a) refresh the justices' memory as to any matter of evidence and to draw attention to any issues involved in the matters before the court;
   (b) advise the justices generally on the range of penalties which the law allows them to impose and on any guidance relevant to the choice of penalty provided by the law, the decisions of the superior courts or other authorities.

   If no request for advice has been made by the justices, the justices' clerk shall discharge his responsibility in court in the presence of the parties.

4 The way in which the justices' clerk should perform his functions should be stated as follows:
   (a) The justices are entitled to the advice of their clerk when they retire in order that the clerk may fulfil his responsibility outlined above.
   (b) Some justices may prefer to take their own notes of evidence. There is, however, no obligation upon them to do so. Whether they do so or not, there is nothing to prevent them from enlisting the aid of their clerk and his notes if they are in any doubt as to the evidence which has been given.
   (c) If the justices wish to consult their clerk solely about the evidence or his notes of it, this should ordinarily, and certainly in simple cases, be done in open court. The object is to avoid any suspicion that the clerk has been involved in deciding issues of fact.

5, 6 (*Domestic Proceedings*).

Paragraph 3 of the *Practice Direction* is not referable to the clerk's obligation to advise justices on the law but goes to refreshing the justices' memory. So long as there is no suspicion that the clerk is involved in deciding issues of fact he is entitled to give advice on a point of law to justices who have retired and who have not requested advice: *R v Uxbridge Justices, ex p. Gina Smith* (1985) 149 JP 620. According to this case it is wrong for a court clerk to sit 'mute and immobile' so as to allow the justices to fall into error.

A failure to comply strictly with the *Practice Direction* which caused 'no material injustice, just a question of appearances', nevertheless resulted in a conviction being quashed in *R v Warley Justices, ex p. SJ Nash* [1982]

QBD (clerk failed to return to court before magistrates on an issue of fact). But *cf R v Southampton Justices, ex p. Atherton* [1974] Crim LR 108, where a different view was taken.

It is normal for the clerk to conduct the ordinary arrangements inside the court and in doing so he *does not usurp* the judicial function of the bench, *per* Lord Parker CJ in *R v Consett Justices, ex p. Postal Bingo* [1967] 1 All ER 605 (not improper for a clerk to retire with his justices for substantially the whole two and a half hours of their retirement and to call his shorthand writer in with him where questions of fact and law were closely interwoven). Lord Parker CJ, stating that 'there is hardly a decision which falls to be made which is not mixed law and fact.'

Since the magistrates and not their clerks are in theory responsible for all decisions, including decisions of law, there is no division corresponding to that between judge and jury in the Crown Court. The magistrates may for example have to read a document themselves before deciding whether it is admissible before them. However, in *R v Weston-super-Mare Justices, ex p. Townsend* (1968) 132 JP 526, Lord Parker CJ dealing with problems that arise under the Criminal Evidence Act 1898 said that where an unrepresented defendant attacks prosecution witnesses the prosecutor should ask for an adjournment and in the justices' absence enlist the help of their clerk in warning the defendant of the risk he runs.

The extent to which the clerk in court should assist the parties was considered in *Simms v Moore* [1970] 2 QB 327 where Lord Parker CJ laid down the following points.

(1) In general, neither the court nor the justice's clerk should take an active part in the proceedings except to clear up ambiguities in the evidence. (2) So far as examining witnesses is concerned, this should never be done if the party concerned is legally represented: see *Hobby v Hobby* [1954] 2 All ER 395 where Sachs J said:

"Both parties were represented at the trial by solicitors. Accordingly neither of them was in need of assistance as to how to present the case to the court. Both parties were entitled within the limits of relevancy and reasonableness, so to conduct their cases as seemed best to their legal representatives in court. In those circumstances a justices' clerk is no more entitled to step into the arena and conduct a litigant's case for him than is a justice himself. Indeed, it is important in the interests of justice that the clerk should not give even the appearance of seeking himself to conduct the case of either party or to limit the way in which the case is conducted."

Nor in my opinion should this be done where a party, although unrepresented, is competent to and desires to examine the witnesses himself. (3) Where however, the unrepresented party, whoever he may be, is not competent through a lack of knowledge of court procedure or rules of evidence or otherwise, to examine the witnesses properly, the court can at its discretion permit the clerk to do so. (4) When this is permitted, there is no reason why the clerk should not do so by reference to a proof of evidence or statement handed in to him, provided always that an opportunity is given to the other side to see it or to have a copy. (5) Where notes of evidence have to be or are taken, care should be taken not to use the proof or statement as the basis of the notes: see *Hobby v Hobby*, already referred to. The best course is for it to be arranged that someone else, possible a member of the court itself, should take the note. (6) Generally, the discretion in the court should be so exercised that examination of witnesses by the clerk should only be permitted when there are reasonable grounds for thinking that thereby the interests of justice would be best promoted, care being taken to see that nothing is done which conflicts with the rules of natural justice or the principle that justice must manifestly be seen to be done.'

Notes of evidence 1.25

There is no statutory or common law duty on the clerk of a magistrates' court to keep any notes of evidence in a criminal case, nor is there any *Practice Direction* to that effect, as there is in domestic proceedings. Nonetheless, it seems essential that a clerk makes a sufficient note of the evidence for him to properly perform his duties. In *Lancashire County Council v Clarke* (1984) 148 JPN 656, Watkins LJ stated that '. . . It is incumbent on a clerk to keep notes in prosecutions so that they may be referred to either during the hearing of the case itself or at some later time when, for example, the justices are asked to state a case'. The remark echoes a similar comment by the same judge in *R v Fareham Justices, ex p. Long* [1976] Crim LR 269. But the non co-ercive nature of the position has been re-affirmed on a number of occasions: see eg *R v Clerk to the Highbury Corner Justices, ex p. Hussein* [1986] 1 WLR 1266.

Similarly, special provision apart, there is no duty on the clerk to provide the parties with a copy of any note of evidence which does exist although justices' clerks have been urged to 'view sympathetically requests for notes from the solicitor of a defendant who is appealing a conviction, provided proper reasons are given for the request: *Ex p Hussein, supra*. Where a legal aid order is made in respect of an appeal to the Crown Court, the justices' clerk must supply – on the application of the solicitor assigned – copies of any notes of evidence which were taken see r.16 Legal Aid in Criminal Proceedings (General) Regulations 1968 SI No 1231 as amended; but the argument that this ought, *as a matter of law*, to place a privately instructed solicitor and client in the same position has been rejected by the Divisional Court: see *Ex p. Hussein, supra*; and *cf Hill v Wilson, infra*.

A justices' clerk is in no privileged position so far as resisting a subpoena to produce his notes of evidence at a higher court is concerned *Hill v Wilson* (1984) 149 JP 252 – and *Practice Note* [1956] 1 QB 451 recommended that justices' clerks furnish the appellate court with notes in such circumstances. But a subpoena will not issue where the evidence would be inadmissible: *R v Barking Justices, ex p. Goodspeed* (1983) 148 JPN 33; and no power exists in the High Court to direct the justices' clerk to furnish notes of evidence to the Crown Court for the purposes of an appeal to that court: *Ex p. Hill, supra, Ex p. Hussein, supra*.

Under r.17(1) M C Rules 1981, the justices' clerk is required to forward to the Crown Court a copy of any notes of evidence taken in the magistrates' court (with other documents) on *committal for sentence*; or on *committal for a hospital order with an order restricting discharge*: r.18 The justices' clerk must also send such notes to the other magistrates court when an offender is *remitted for sentence*: r.19(1).

Statutory Provisions

1.26   **SOLICITORS ACT 1974**

Solicitor who is justice of the peace not to act in certain proceedings

38. (1) Subject to the provisions of this section, it shall not be lawful for any solicitor who is one of the justices of the peace for any area, or for any partner of his, to act in connection with proceedings before any of those justices as solicitor or agent for the solicitor for any person concerned in those proceedings.

(2) Where the area for which a solicitor is a justice of the peace is divided into petty sessional divisions, his being a justice for the area shall not subject him or any partner of his to any disqualification under this section in relation to

proceedings before justices acting for a petty sessional division for which he does not ordinarily act.

(3) Where a solicitor is a justice of the peace for any area, that shall not subject him or any partner of his to any disqualification under this section if his name is entered in the supplemental list kept under s.80 of the Justices of the Peace Act 1979.

(4) Where a solicitor is, as being Lord Mayor or alderman, a justice of the peace for the City of London, that shall not subject him or any partner of his to any disqualification under this section, if he is in accordance with the proviso to s.39(1) of the Justices of the Peace Act 1979 excluded from the exercise of his functions as a justice for the City.
[*as amended by Sch. 2 Justices of the Peace Act 1979*].

COMMENTARY
As a matter of conduct, the Law Society consider that the prohibition against acting imposed by this section upon a solicitor who becomes a JP and his partner should apply to any assistant solicitor employed by the firm in question: see August 1982 issue of *The Magistrate* at p.122.

JUSTICES OF THE PEACE ACT 1979

General form of commissions of the peace   **1.27**
   5. (1) The commission of the peace for any commission area shall be a commission under the Great Seal addressed generally, and not by name, to all such persons as may from time to time hold office as justices of the peace for the commission area.

COMMENTARY
The present commission of the peace reads as follows:

ELIZABETH THE SECOND by the Grace of God of the United Kingdom of Great Britain and Northern Ireland and of Our other Realms and Territories Queen Head of the Commonwealth Defender of the Faith To all such persons as may from time to time hold office as justices of the peace for Our County of . . . .

GREETING Know ye that you are and each of you is by these Presents assigned to keep Our peace in Our said county and to keep and cause to be kept in all points in Our said County the rules of law and enactments from time to time obtaining for the good of Our peace and for the preservation of the same and for the quiet rule and government of Our people And to deal according to law with all persons that offend against any of those rules of law or enactments And also to cause to come before you and to deal according to law with all persons against whom anything is alleged giving just cause under any rule of law or enactment for the time being in force why they should find security to keep the peace or be of good behaviour towards Us and Our people. And to exercise all such other jurisdiction and powers as by any rule of Law or enactment may from time to time belong to justices of the peace And therefore We command you and each of you that you diligently apply yourselves in Our said county to the keeping of Our peace and of the rules of law and enactments aforesaid and to other matters hereinbefore mentioned doing therein what to justice appertains according to law
   In Witness whereof We have cause these Our Letters to be made Patent
   WITNESS Ourself at Westminster the   day of   in the year of Our Reign.

[*The Crown Office (Commissions of the Peace) Order 1973, SI No 2099*]

Residence qualification   **1.28**
   7. (1) Subject to the provisions of this section, a person shall not be appointed as a justice of the peace for a commission area in accordance with s.6

of this Act, nor acts as a justice of the peace by virtue of any such appointment, unless he resides in or within fifteen miles of that area.

(2) If the Lord Chancellor is of the opinion that it is in the public interest for a person to act as a justice of the peace for a particular area though not qualified to do so under subs (1) above, he may direct that, so long as any conditions specified in the direction are satisfied, that subsection shall not apply in relation to that person's appointment as a justice of the peace for the area so specified.

(3) Where a person appointed as a justice of the peace for a commission area in accordance with s.6 of this Act is not qualified under the preceding provisions of this section to act by virtue of the appointment, he shall be removed from office as a justice of the peace in accordance with s.6 of this Act if the Lord Chancellor is of opinion that the appointment ought not to continue having regard to the probable duration and other circumstances of the want of qualification.

(4) No act or appointment shall be invalidated by reason only of the disqualification or want of qualification under this section of the person acting or appointed.

COMMENTARY

s.7(1): Commission area, defined in s.1 of the Act (not reproduced).

15 miles, measured in a straight line on a horizontal plane: s.8 Interpretation Act 1978.

s.7(2): Lord Chancellor, in the counties of Greater Manchester, Merseyside and Lancashire this refers to the Chancellor of the Duchy of Lancaster: s.68(1).

1.29 **Place of sitting and powers of stipendiary magistrates**
16. (1) Subject to subs (5) below, nothing in the Magistrates' Courts Act 1980 requiring a magistrates' court to be composed of two or more justices, or to sit in a petty sessional court-house, or limiting the powers of a magistrates' court composed of a single justice, or when sitting elsewhere than in a petty sessional court-house, shall apply to any stipendiary magistrate sitting in a place appointed for that purpose.

(2) A stipendiary magistrate appointed under s.13 of this Act in any commission area shall sit at such court houses in the area, on such days and at such times as may be determined by, or in accordance with, directions given by the Lord Chancellor from time to time.

(3) Subject to subs (5) below, a stipendiary magistrate so appointed, sitting at a place appointed for the purpose, shall have power to do any act, and to exercise alone any jurisdiction, which can be done or exercised by two justices under any law, other than any law made after 2 August 1958 which contains an express provision to the contrary; and all the provisions of any Act which are auxilliary to the jurisdiction exercisable by two justices of the peace shall apply also to the jurisdiction of such a stipendiary magistrate.

(4) Subsection (3) above shall apply to cases where the act or jurisdiction in question is expressly required to be done or exercised by justices sitting or acting in petty sessions as it applies to other cases; and any enactment authorizing or requiring persons to be summoned or to appear at petty sessions shall in the like cases authorize or require persons to be summoned or to appear before such a stipendiary magistrate at the place appointed for his sitting.

(5) (*Domestic proceedings*)
[*as amended by Sch. 7 MCA 1980*]

COMMENTARY

See under *Stipendiary Magistrate* in the introduction.

Chairman and deputy chairman of justices   **1.30**
    17. (1) In any petty sessions area there shall be a chairman and one or more
deputy chairmen of the justices chosen from amongst themselves by the
magistrates for the area by secret ballot.

    (2) Subject to subs (3) below, if the chairman or a deputy chairman of the
justices for a petty sessions area is present at a meeting of those justices, he
shall preside unless he requests another justice to preside in accordance with
rules made under the next following section.

    (3) Subsection (2) above shall not confer to the chairman and deputy
chairman of the justices as such any right to preside in a juvenile or domestic
court or at meetings of a committee or other body of justices having its own
chairman, or at meetings when any stipendiary magistrate is engaged as such in
administering justice.

COMMENTARY
s.17(1): Secret ballot, ie in accordance with the Justices of the Peace (Size and Chairmanship
of Bench) Rules 1986 (SI 923), *post.*

s.17(2); Meeting, ie any sitting of the court. Before exercising the discretion to ask another
justice to preside, the elected chairman or deputy chairman must satisfy himself as to the
suitability of that justice for this purpose': r.9, *ibid.*

General powers and duties of justices' clerks   **1.31**
    28. (1) *(Rules).*

    (2) Any enactment (including any enactment contained in this Act) or any
rule of law regulating the exercise of any jurisdiction or powers of justices of
the peace, or relating to things done in the exercise or purported exercise of
any such jurisdiction or powers, shall apply in relation to the exercise or
purported exercise thereof by virtue of subs (1) above by the clerk to any
justices as if he were one of those justices.

    (3) It is hereby declared that the functions of a justices' clerk include the
giving to the justices to whom he is clerk or any of them, at the request of the
justices or justice, of advice about law, practice, or procedure on questions
arising in connection with the discharge of their or his functions, including
questions arising when the clerk is not personally attending on the justices or
justice, and that the clerk may, at any time when he thinks he should do so,
bring to the attention of the justices or justice any point of law, practice or
procedure that is or may be involved in any question so arising.
    In this subsection the reference to the functions of justices or a justice is a
reference to any of their or his functions as justices or a justice of the peace,
other than functions as a judge of the Crown Court.

    (4) The enactment of subs (3) above shall not be taken as defining or in any
respect limiting the powers and duties belonging to a justices' clerk or the
matters on which justices may obtain assistance from their clerk.
[*as amended by Sch.7 MCA 1980*]

COMMENTARY
s.28(3): Justices' clerk, menas a clerk to the justices for a petty sessions area: s 70.

Questions of law, including questions of mixed law and fact. Compare the *Practice Direction*
[1981] 2 All ER 831 and *R v Consett Justices, ex p. Postal Bingo* [1967] 1 All ER 605.

Person acting as substitute clerk to justices   **1.31a**
    30. (1) The provisions of this section shall have effect where, in any petty
sessions area outside the inner London area, a person who is not the justices'
clerk or one of the justices' clerks appointed in that petty sessions area by the
magistrates' courts committee acts as clerk to the justices for that petty
sessions area.

(2) Subject to any rules made under s.144 of the Magistrates' Courts Act 1980 and to subs (3) below, the person so acting shall be treated as having acted as deputy to the justices' clerk appointed by the magistrates' courts committee in that petty sessions area, and shall make a return to the justices' clerk so appointed of all matters done before the justices and of all matters that the clerk to the justices is required to register or record.

(3) In relation to a petty sessions area in which there are two or more justices' clerks appointed by the magistrates' courts committee, any reference in subs (2) above to the justices' clerk so appointed shall be construed as a reference to such one of them as may be designated for the purpose by the committee.

[*as amended by Sch.7 MCA 1980*]

COMMENTARY

s.30(1): Petty sessions area, defined in s.4.

Justices' clerk means a clerk to the justices for a petty sessions area: s.70.

1.32 **Disqualification in certain cases of justices who are members of local authorities**

64. (1) A justice of the peace who is a member of a local authority shall not act as a member of the Crown Court or of a magistrates' court in any proceedings brought by or against, or by way of appeal from a decision of, the authority or any committee or officer of the authority.

(2) For the purposes of subs (1) above–
(a) any reference to a committee of a local authority includes a joint committee joint board, joint authority or other combined body of which that authority is a member or on which it is represented; and
(b) any reference to an officer of a local authority refers to a person employed or appointed by the authority, or by a committee of the authority, in the capacity in which he is employed or appointed to act.

(3) A justice of the peace who is a member of the Common Council of the City of London shall not act as a member of the Crown Court or of a magistrates' court in any proceedings brought by or against, or by way of appeal from a decision of, the Corporation of the City or the Common Council or any committee or officer of the Corporation or Common Council; and subs (2) above shall apply for the purposes of this subsection, with the substitution for references to a local authority, of references to the Corporation or the Common Council.

(4) Nothing in this section shall prevent a justice from acting in any proceedings by reason only of their being brought by a police officer.

(5) No act shall be invalidated by reason only of the disqualification under this section of the person acting.

(6) In this section 'local authority' means a local authority within the meaning of the Local Government Act 1972 or the Local Government (Scotland) Act 1973, the Inner London Education Authority and a joint authority established by Part IV of the Local Government Act 1985.

[*as amended by Schs.14 and 17 Local Government Act 1985*]

COMMENTARY

s.64(1) Local authority means a county council, a district council, a London borough council or a parish or community council: s.270 Local Government Act 1972. A 'residuary body' established under Part VII Local Government Act 1985 is *treated as* a local authority for the purposes of s.64: see Sch.13, para 13 of the 1985 Act. A justices' clerk is not disqualified: see *R v Camborne Justices, ex p. Pearce* [1955] 1 QB 41.

s.64(3): Magistrates' court defined in s.5 and Sch.1 Interpretation Act 1978.

Acts done by justices outside their area   **1.33**
66. (1) A justice of the peace for any commission area may act as a justice
for that area in any commission area which adjoins the commission area for
which he is a justice.

(2) Justices for the county of Surrey or the county of Kent may hold special
or petty sessions for any division of their county at any place in Greater
London; and for all purposes relating to sessions so held the place at which
they are held shall be deemed to be within the county and the division for
which the justices holding them are justices.

COMMENTARY
s.66(1): Commission area defined in s.1 (not reproduced).

MAGISTRATES' COURTS ACT 1980

Orders other than for payment of money   **1.34**
63. (1) Where under any Act passed after 31 December 1879 a magistrates'
court has power to require the doing of anything other than the payment of
money, or to prohibit the doing of anything, any order of the court for the
purpose of exercising that power may contain such provisions for the manner
in which anything is to be done, for the time within which anything to be done,
or during which anything is not to be done, and generally for giving effect to
the order, as the court thinks fit.

(2) The court may by order made on complaint suspend or rescind any such
order as aforesaid.

(3) Where any person disobeys an order of a magistrates' court made under
an Act passed after 31 December 1879 to do anything other than the payment
of money or to abstain from doing anything the court may–
  (a) order him to pay a sum not exceeding £50 for every day during which he
      is in default or a sum not exceeding £2,000; or
  (b) commit him to custody until he has remedied his default or for a period
      not exceeding two months;
but a person who is ordered to pay a sum for every day during which he is in
default or who is committed to custody until he has remedied his default shall
not by virtue of this section be ordered to pay more than £1,000 or be
committed for more than two months in all for doing or abstaining from doing
the same thing contrary to the order (without prejudice to the operation of this
section in relation to any subsequent default).

(4) Any sum ordered to be paid under subs (3) above shall for the purposes
of this Act be treated as adjudged to be paid by a conviction of a magistrates'
court.

(5) The preceding provisions of this section shall not apply to any order for
the enforcement of which provision is made by any other enactment.
[*as amended by SI 1984 No 447*]

COMMENTARY
The power under this section may be exercised either of the court's own motion or by order
on complaint: s.17(1) Contempt of Court Act 1981: see **7.23,** *post.*
  There is no power to make consecutive commitments to prison under this section: *Head v
Head* [1982] 3 All ER 14. Instead of being committed to prison a person *under 21 but not less
than 17* may be detained under s.9 CJA 1982.

Constitution and place of sitting of court   **1.35**
121. (1) A magistrates' court shall not try an information summarily or
hear a complaint except when composed of at least two justices unless the trial

or hearing is one that by virtue of any enactment may take place before a single justice.

(2) A magistrates' court shall not hold an inquiry into the means of an offender for the purposes of s.82 above [*or determine under that section at a hearing at which the offender is not present whether to issue a warrant of commitment*] except when composed of at least two justices.

(3) A magistrates' court shall not–
(a) try summarily an information for an indictable offence or hear a complaint except when sitting in a petty-sessional court-house;
(b) try an information for a summary offence or hold an inquiry into the means of an offender for the purposes of s.82 above, or impose imprisonment, except when sitting in a petty-sessional court-house or an occasional court-house.

(4) Subject to the provisions of any enactment to the contrary, where a magistrates' court is required by this section to sit in a petty-sessional or occasional court-house, it shall sit in open court.

(5) A magistrate's court composed of a single justice, or sitting in an occasional court-house, shall not impose imprisonment for a period exceeding 14 days or order a person to pay more than £1.

(6) Subject to the provisions of subs (7) below, the justices composing the court before which any proceedings take place shall be present during the whole of the proceedings; but, if during the course of the proceedings any justice absents himself, he shall cease to act further therein and, if the remaining justices are enough to satisfy the requirements of the preceding provisions of this section, the proceedings may continue before a court composed of those justices.

(7) Where a trial of an information is adjourned after the accused has been convicted and before he is sentenced or otherwise dealt with, the court which sentences or deals with him need not be composed of the same justices as that which convicted him, but, where among the justices composing the court which sentences or deals with an offender there are any who were not sitting when he was convicted, the court which sentences or deals with the offender shall before doing so make such inquiry into the facts and circumstances of the case as will enable the justices who were not sitting when the offender was convicted to be fully acquainted with those facts and circumstances.

(8) Domestic proceedings.
[*the words in italics in subs (2) will be added by [s.60] CJA 1988 from a date to be appointed*]

COMMENTARY

s.121(1): At least two justices. The number of justices sitting to deal with a case as a magistrates' court shall not be greater than seven r.2(2) Justices of the Peace (Size and Chairmanship of Bench) Rules 1964, *infra*. It is the Lord Chancellor's opinion that only in special circumstances should more than five justices constitute a court: circular letter of 30 November 1950. There should preferably be an odd number of justices, *per* Lord Goddard CJ in *Barnsley v Marsh* (1947) 111 JP 363. Today, the normally accepted number is three.

By virtue of any enactment, eg ss.3 and 4 Vagrancy Act 1982; s.12 Licensing Act 1872. For a full list see vol 29 *Halsbury's Laws* 4th edn at para 244. *But note the restriction of subs (5).*

s.121(3): Indictable/summary offence defined in Sch.1 Interpretation Act 1978.

Petty sessional court-house defined in s.150 Magistrates' Courts Act 1980. Licensed premises may not be used as a petty sessional court-house: s.190 Licensing Act 1964.

Occasional court-house ie appointed under s.147, *infra*.

s.121(4): Any provision to the contrary, see eg s.8(4) Official Secrets Act 1920; s.4(2) MCA 1980 (examining justices); s.37 CYPA 1933 (evidence of juveniles in certain cases); and s.47(2), not reproduced herein (juvenile courts).

Open court, see under this title in the introduction.

s.121(6): Present during the whole of the proceedings. Thus if even one justice joins the others the hearing must be begun afresh. A conviction has been quashed where a justice who had not heard the case joined the bench and appeared to (though did not actually) participate in the adjudication: *R v Walton, ex p. Dutton* (1911) 75 JP 558; similarly *R v Guerin* (1888) 53 JP 468 (justice left bench temporarily); and *R v Manchester Justices, ex p. Burke* (1961) 125 JP 387 (justice arrived late). But see s.121(7) for the position on adjournment after conviction.

Fees **1.36**
137. (1) Subject to the provisions of this section, the court fees set out in Part I of Sch 6 to this Act, and no others, shall be chargeable by clerks of magistrates' courts; and any enactment providing for the payment of any fees for the payment of which provision is made in the said Part I shall have effect accordingly.

(2) No fee shall be chargeable by a clerk of a magistrates' court in respect of any matter specified in Part II of the said Schedule.

(3) – (6) . . .

Clerks of justices **1.37**
141. (1) Any reference in this Act to a clerk of any magistrates' court shall be construed as a reference to the clerk to the justices for the petty sessions area for which the court is acting, or was acting at the relevant time.

(2) Where there is more than one clerk to the justices for any petty sessions area, anything that this Act requires or authorises to be done by or to the clerk to the justices shall or may be done by or to any of the clerks or by or to such of the clerks as the magistrates' courts committee having power over the appointment of clerks to justices for that area generally or in any particular case may direct.

(3) Subsections (1) and (2) above shall apply to the justices' clerks for the inner London area as if the reference in subs (2) to the magistrates' courts committee were a reference to the committee of magistrates.

COMMENTARY
s.141(1): Petty sessions area. Defined in s.150(1) (not reproduced herein).

Occasional court-house **1.38**
147. (1) The justices acting for a petty sessions area may appoint as an occasional court-house any place that is not a petty-sessional court-house.

(2) A place appointed as an occasional court-house after 31 May 1953 shall not be used as such unless public notice has been given that it has been appointed.

(3) There may be more than one occasional court-house for each petty sessions area; and an occasional court-house may be outside the petty sessions area for which it is appointed, and if so shall be deemed to be in that area for the purpose of the jurisdiction of the justices acting for that area.

COMMENTARY
s.147(1): Occasional court-house, for the powers of justices sitting in occasional court-houses see s.121, *supra.*
Petty sessional court-house, see the note to s.121, *supra.*
s.147(2): Public notice, no method of giving notice is prescribed. *Chislett* suggests a notice by the clerk in newspapers circulating in the district. The earlier law required that notice be given 'in such manner as the justices think expedient'.

'Magistrates' court' **1.38a**
148. (1) In this Act the expression 'magistrates' court' means any justice or

justices of the peace acting under any enactment or by virtue of his or their commission or under the common law.

(2) Except where the contrary is expressed, anything authorized or required by this Act to be done by, to or before the magistrates' court by, to or before which any other thing was done, or is to be done by, to or before any magistrates' court acting for the same petty sessions area as that court.

COMMENTARY

s.148(1): Magistrates' court As to where and in what numbers justices sit to form a magistrates' court see s.121, *supra*. The term includes examining justices: *Atkinson v United States Government* [1971] AC 197.

1.39 **Interpretation**
150. (2) Except where the contrary is expressed or implied, anything required or authorised by this Act to be done by justices may, where two or more justices are present, be done by one of them on behalf of the others. [*as amended by s.12 Local Government Act 1985*]

1.39a **Magistrates' court may sit on Sundays and public holidays**
153. It is hereby declared that a magistrates' court may sit on any day of the year, and in particular (if the court thinks fit) on Christmas Day, Good Friday or any Sunday.

COMMENTARY

This declaratory provision is in *permissive* and not mandatory terms.

SCHEDULE 6
(Section 137)

1.40 **Fees**
PART II: MATTERS IN RESPECT OF WHICH NO FEES ARE CHARGEABLE
2. Any criminal matter, but this paragraph shall not prevent the charging of a fee for supplying, for use in connection with a matter which is not a criminal matter, a copy of a document prepared for use in connection with a criminal matter.

1.41 ## JUSTICES' CLERKS RULES 1970
(SI 1970 No 231, as amended by SI 1971 No 809, SI 1975 No 30, SI 1976 No 1767, SI 1978 No 754, SI 1983 No 527)

3. The things specified in the schedule to these rules, being things authorised to be done by, to or before a single justice of the peace for a petty sessions area, may be done by, to or before the justices' clerk for that area.

SCHEDULE

1. The laying of an information or the making of a complaint, other than an information or complaint substantiated on oath.

2. The issue of any summons, including a witness summons.

3. . . .

4. (1) The further adjournment of criminal proceedings with the consent of the prosecutor and the accused if, but only if,

(a) the accused, not having been remanded on the previous adjournment, is not remanded on the further adjournment; or

(b) the accused, having been remanded on bail on the previous adjournment is remanded on bail on the like terms and conditions.

(2) The remand of the accused on bail at the time of further adjourning the proceedings in pursuance of subpara (1)(b) above.

5. . . .

6. The allowing of further time for payment of a sum enforceable by a magistrates' court.

6A. The varying of the number of instalments payable, the amount of any instalment payable and the date on which any instalment becomes payable where a magistrates' court has ordered that a sum adjudged to be paid by a conviction shall be paid by instalments.

7. The making of a transfer of fine order, that is to say, an order making payment by a person of a sum adjudged to be paid by a conviction enforceable in the petty sessions area in which he is residing.

8. The making of an order before an inquiry into the means of a person under s.84 of the Magistrates' Courts Act 1980 that that person shall furnish to the court a statement of his means in accordance with s.84(1).

9. *(Repealed).*

10. The giving of consent for another magistrates' court to deal with an offender for an earlier offence in respect of which, after the offender had attained the age of 17 years, the court had made a probation order or an order for conditional discharge, where the justices' clerk is the clerk of the court which made the order or, in the case of a probation order, of that court or of the supervising court.

11. The amending, in accordance with para 2(1) of Sch 1 to the Powers of Criminal Courts Act 1973, of a probation order made after the probationer had attained the age of 17 years by substituting for the petty sessions area named in the order the area in which the probationer proposes to reside or is residing.

12. The signing of a certificate given to the Crown Court under s.16(4) of the Powers of Criminal Courts Act 1973 as to non-compliance with a community service order.

13, 14, 15. . . .

16. The acceptance under subs (3) of s.14 of the Magistrates' Courts Act 1980 (which relates to process for minor offences) of service of such statutory declaration as is mentioned in subs (1) of that section.

17. The fixing under s.86(3) of the Magistrates' Courts Act 1980 of a later day in substitution for a day previously fixed for the appearance of an offender to enable an inquiry into his means to be made under s.82 of that Act or to enable a hearing required by subs (5) of s.82 to be held.

COMMENTARY

See s.28(2) Justices of the Peace Act 1979.

MAGISTRATES' COURTS RULES 1981

(SI 1981 No 552, as amended by SI 1983 No 523, SI 1984 No 1552, SI 1985 Nos 1695, 1944 and SI 1986 No 1332).

1.42   Register of convictions, etc

66. (1) The clerk of every magistrates' court shall keep a register in which there shall be entered–
(a) a minute or memorandum of every adjudication of the court;
(b) a minute or memorandum of every other proceeding or thing required by these rules or any other enactment to be so entered.

(2) The register shall be in the prescribed form, and entries in the register shall include, where relevant, such particulars as are provided for in the said form.

(3) Particulars of any entry relating to a decision about bail or the reasons for any such decision or the particulars of any certificate granted under s.5(6A) of the Bail Act 1976 may be made in a book separate from that in which the entry recording the decision itself is made, but any such separate book shall be regarded as forming part of the register.

(3A) Where, by virtue of subs (3A) of s.128 of the Act of 1980, an accused gives his consent to the hearing and determination in his absence of any application for his remand on an adjournment of the case under ss.5, 10(1) or 18(4) of that Act, the court shall cause the consent of the accused, and the date on which it was notified to the court, to be entered in the register.

(3B) Where any consent mentioned in para (3A) is withdrawn, the court shall cause the withdrawal of the consent and the date on which it was notified to the court to be entered in the register.

(4) On the summary trial of an information the accused's plea shall be entered in the register.

(5) Where a court tries any person summarily in any case in which he may be tried summarily only with his consent, the court shall cause his consent to be entered in the register and, if the consent is signified by a person representing him in his absence, the court shall cause that fact also to be entered in the register.

(6) Where a person is charged before a magistrates' court with an offence triable either way the court shall cause the entry in the register to show whether he was present when the proceedings for determining the mode of trial were conducted and, if they were conducted in his absence, whether they were so conducted by virtue of s.18(3) of the Act of 1980 (disorderly conduct on his part) or by virtue of s.23(1) of that Act (consent signified by person representing him).

(7) In any case to which s.22 of the Act of 1980 (certain offences triable either way to be tried summarily if value involved is small) applied, the court shall cause its decision as to the value involved, or, as the case may be, the fact that it is unable to reach such a decision to be entered in the register.

(8) Where a court has power under s.53(3) of the Act of 1980 to make an order with the consent of the defendant without hearing evidence, the court shall cause any consent of the defendant to the making of the order to be entered in the register.

(9) The entry in the column of the register headed 'Nature of Offence' shall show clearly, in case of conviction or dismissal, what is the offence of which the accused is convicted or, as the case may be, what is the offence charged in the information that is dismissed.

(10) An entry of conviction in the register shall state the date of the offence.

(11) The entries shall be signed by one of the justices, or the justice, before whom the proceedings to which they relate took place, or by the clerk who was present when those proceedings took place or, in the case of an entry required by paras (3A) and (3B), where the consent or withdrawal of consent was not

given or made (as the case may be) when the accused was present before the court, by the clerk or justice who received the notification.

Provided that, where the proceedings took place before a justice or justices sitting elsewhere than in a petty sessional court-house, the justice or, as the case may be, one of the justices may instead of signing an entry in the register, send to the clerk whose duty it is to keep the register a signed return of the proceedings containing the particulars required to be entered in the register, and the clerk shall enter the return in the register.

(12) Every register shall be open to inspection during reasonable hours by any justice of the peace, or any person authorised in that behalf by a justice of the peace or the Secretary of State.

COMMENTARY
Para 1: Clerk of . . . magistrates' court, see s.141 MCA 1980.

Para 12 A request to justices' clerks to afford the police access to the register for statistical purposes was made by the Secretary of State: see HO Circular, 9 February 1893 57 JP Jo 105.

Proof of proceedings   **1.43**
    68.   The register of a magistrates' court, or any document purporting to be an extract from the register and to be certified by the clerk as a true extract, shall be admissible in any legal proceedings as evidence of the proceedings of the court entered in the register.

COMMENTARY
Extract, see form 154.

Signature of forms prescribed by rules made under the Act of 1980   **1.43a**
    109. (1) Subject to para (2), where any form prescribed by Rules made or having effect as if made under s.144 of the Act of 1980 contains provision for signature by a justice of the peace only, the form shall have effect as if it contained provision in the alternative for signature by the clerk of a magistrates' court.

(2) This rule shall not apply to any form of warrant, other than a warrant of commitment or of distress, or to any form prescribed in the Magistrates' Court (Forms) Rules 1981.

COMMENTARY
In addition to the provisions of this rule the clerk of a magistrates' court may sign any document in the Schedule to the Magistrates' Courts (Forms) Rules 1981 which admits of his signature.

The clerk of a magistrates' court, that is, the clerk to the justices: see s.141(1) MCA 1980.

Magistrates' Courts (Forms) Rules 1981 SI No 553, as amended (not reproduced herein).

JUSTICES OF THE PEACE (SIZE AND CHAIRMANSHIP OF BENCH) RULES 1986
(SI No 923, as amended by 1987 SI No 1137)

Size of bench   **1.44**
    3. The number of justices sitting to deal with a case as a magistrates' court, other than such a court sitting as a juvenile court or hearing domestic proceedings within the meaning of s.65 of the Magistrates' Courts Act 1980(a), shall not be greater than seven.

Election of chairman and deputy chairman   **1.44a**
    4. (1) Subject to para (3) below, the justices for each petty sessions area

shall, in accordance with the following provisions of these Rules, elect from among their number a chairman and one or more deputy chairmen, and the justices for the City of London shall so elect from among their number one or more deputy chairmen, at a meeting (hereinafter referred to as an 'election meeting') to be held in the month of October every year of which at least seven days' notice shall be given to each justice for the petty sessions area.

(2) etc, (Rules governing election)

1.45   **Period of office and eligibility for re-election**
6. (1) A chairman elected under these Rules shall hold office for one year from 1 January next after the date of his election and, shall, subject to paragraph (2) below, be eligible for re-election.

(2) A person who has held office as chairman shall not be eligible for re-election as chairman at an election meeting if on 1 January next after the election meeting he will have held such office for five consecutive years and less than three years will have elapsed from when he last held office unless–
    (a) at the time when the election meeting is held he holds office as chairman, and
    (b) the justices entitled to vote at the election meeting decide, in accordance with para (3) below, that the restriction on eligibility imposed by this paragraph shall not apply in relation to the election to be held at that meeting.

(4) . . . (7)

Vacancy in office
7. If the office of chairman or deputy chairman becomes or is about to become vacant for any reason, the justices shall, as soon as practicable, proceed to elect, in the manner provided for under these Rules, another chairman or deputy chairman, as the case may be, who shall hold office for the remainder of the term of the appointment of the justice whom he replaces.

Absence of chairman or deputy chairman
8. In the absence of a chairman or deputy chairman elected under these Rules, nothing in Rule 4, 5, 6 or 7 shall prevent the appointment by justices present of one of their number to preside at a court sitting to deal with any case.

Requests to a justice to preside
9. Before a chairman or deputy chairman of the justices for a petty sessions area who is present at a meeting of those justices requests another justice to preside under the provisions of s.17(2) of the Justices of the Peace Act 1979, he shall satisfy himself as to the suitability of that justice for this purpose.

CHAPTER 2

Commencing Criminal Proceedings

Commencing Criminal Proceedings

2.00   **THE RIGHT TO PROSECUTE**

Subject to any statutory restrictions, any private individual or public authority may seek to initiate and to conduct the prosecution of another person for an offence: *Gouriet v Union of Post Office Workers* [1977] 3 All ER 70. This right is preserved by s.6(1) Prosecution of Offences Act 1985, except where the Director of Public Prosecutions or the Director of the Serious Fraud Office is under a duty to take over the conduct of criminal proceedings: s.6(1); or where the former takes over proceedings under his wide discretionary powers: s.6(2). So far as the police are concerned, the Director of Public Prosecutions is under a duty to take over the conduct of all criminal proceedings instituted by or on behalf of a police force, other than 'specified proceedings', ie as presently defined, in effect 'paperwork' cases under s.12 MCA 1980 (s.3(2) Prosecution of Offences Act 1985, 2.64, *post* – which sets out a range of other situations in which the duty exists; and see 2.89 for a list of 'specified proceedings'; 5.30 under the title Written Pleas of Guilty for 'paperwork courts'). In addition to this, r.3 Prosecution of Offences Regulations 1978 (SI No 1357, as amended) provides that it is the duty of the Director of Public Prosecutions to 'institute, undertake or carry on criminal proceedings in any case which appears to him to be of importance or difficulty or which for any other reason requires his intervention'. It may be that the eventual effect of the still relatively young Crown Prosecution Service, via which the Director's functions are discharged locally will be that the traditional right to bring a 'private prosecution' may recede in significance, save for the initial instigating of the proceedings – particularly since a prosecution may not only be taken over, but may also be 'discontinued' by the Crown Prosecutor under the provisions of s.23 at 2.82, *post*, regardless of the private prosecutor's wishes in the matter.

2.01   **The Crown Prosecution Service**

The structure of the Crown Prosecution Service is that it is headed by the Director of Public Prosecutions under the superintendence of the Attorney-General, through whom the service is answerable to Parliament. The service is divided into areas which, outside the Metropolitan Police District, are based on police areas or combinations thereof, each being headed and managed by a Chief Crown Prosecutor. In practice, there is substantial delegation of responsibility within areas for both management and criminal justice decisions to local Branch Crown Prosecutors. Within the context of court proceedings, whichever Crown Prosecutor is present may have to make decisions which will affect the outcome of cases. Subject to the directions of the Director, any Crown Prosecutor may exercise any of the Director's powers relating to the institution or conduct of proceedings: see s.1(6) Prosecution of Offences Act 1985. Under s.4, barristers and solicitors designated as Crown Prosecutors have the rights of audience of practising solicitors.

The principle function of the service is to conduct all criminal proceedings instituted (ie following information or charge: see s.15(2)) *on behalf of a police force*. Thereafter, the service – and not the chief constable – assumes total responsibility for the case including, where appropriate, the making of representations in bail applications. It is for the Crown Prosecutor to conduct an independent review of the evidence and to make his own decision as to what proceedings it is appropriate to pursue. The Crown Prosecutor must also conduct binding over proceedings on behalf of a police force, proceedings concerning the forfeiture of obscene articles, and bring any appeals. But the *general duty does not extend* to taking over 'specified proceedings', ie those listed in the Prosecution of Offences Act 1985 (Specified Proceedings) Order 1985, SI No 2010, see 2.89, *post*, essentially matters of a routine nature where no real advocacy is involved and an independent legal review is unnecessary. The Crown Prosecutor also has a *discretion* to take over criminal proceedings in all circumstances where he is *not under a duty* to do so: s.6(2).

The Director is empowered, by s.5, to appoint solicitors who are not Crown Prosecutors, or who are barristers employed by another public authority, to undertake prosecutions, ie what are generally termed 'agents'. Such prosecutors must exercise the powers of a Crown Prosecutor 'subject to any directions given to him by a Crown Prosecutor': s.5(2).

The 'public interest' 2.02

Under s.10 POA 1985, the Director of Public Prosecutions is required to issue a Code for Crown Prosecutors giving guidance on general principle. The present Code for Crown Prosecutors is reproduced at Appendix II, *post*. A significant feature of the Code is the requirement for Crown Prosecutors to have regard to the 'public interest' when making decisions concerning the bringing, conduct or continuance of proceedings. This implies that issues other than those of pure justice may be legitimate considerations, a fact borne out by certain other aspects of the Code. It might be suggested that the Code – and particularly the 'public interest' requirement – illustrates the true potential which the Crown Prosecution Service possesses to alter the nature of criminal business coming before the courts.

Discontinuance 2.03

The 1985 Act introduced the concept of the formal *discontinuance* of proceedings. Under s.23, the Crown Prosecutor may drop all or any charges against a defendant in a case for which he is responsible without first consulting the court, provided that in indictable cases the defendant has not yet been committed for trial, and in summary cases (or either way cases which are being tried summarily) that the court has not yet begun to hear the evidence: see s.23(2). Where a case is discontinued, *the defendant has a right to insist* that it be heard before a court.

The procedure is by way of notice to the court under s.23(3) anc counter-notice by the accused under s.23(7). Notwithstanding that the leave of the court is not required in order to discontinue, the Crown Prosecutor's notice to the court must contain the reasons for his wishing to discontinue the proceedings: s.23(5). The effect of a counter-notice i to leave matters as if the initial notice had not been given, except that any remand conditions lapse: s.23(7). The clerk to the court is required to inform the director of any counter-notice: s.23(8).

The Crown Prosecutor's notice to the accused must inform him that a notice of discontinuance has been issued under s.23(3), *supra*, and of his right to issue a counter-notice, but there is no requirement for the accused to be given a copy of the notice or the reasons for its issue: see s.23(6); but the accused must be told that he may issue a counter-notice: *ibid*. Special provisions apply where the proceedings are discontinued before they reach court at all, when the court need not be informed and there is no provision for the accused to serve a counter-notice: see s.23(4).

Discontinuance does not prevent fresh proceedings being brought for the same offence: s.23(9). Contrast, generally, *Withdrawal of proceedings* under that title in the introduction to Chapter 5.

2.04 Other prosecuting authorities

Crown Prosecutors, each of whom, provided he is employed in the Crown Prosecution Service (ie as opposed to being an 'agent' – who may only operate subject to any directions given by a Crown Prosecutor, *post*) 'may give consents or take steps required by an enactment from the Director'.

Where the police do prosecute, then they are in no different position to any other private citizen. The primary responsibility for police prosecutions probably resides with each chief constable; see the report of the Royal Commission on Criminal Procedure, Vol II at paras 136, 137; and *Hawkins v Bepey* [1980] 1 WLR 419.

The provisions of the POA 1985 in relation to Crown Prosecutors apart, there is no statutory definition of the term 'prosecutor'. In general he is the person named as informant. Where an officer of a local authority purports (wrongly) to act on its behalf, he is regarded personally as the prosecutor: *Cole v Coulton* (1860) 24 JP 596; *R v Bushell* (1888) 52 JP 136 *Giebler v Manning* (1906) 70 JP 181; *Lake v Smith* (1911) 76 JP 71 *Duchesne v Finch* (1912) 76 JP 377; *Snodgrass v Topping* (1952) 166 JP 322; *Lund v Thompson* [1958] 3 WLR 594.

Where a prosecution may only be brought with *consent or authority* it is the duty of the person issuing the summons to see that that consent is available. There is a *presumption* that this has been done unless objection is taken, when the prosecution must prove the necessary consent or authority. If the defence wish to challenge this, they should object before the prosecution case is closed, otherwise it will be presumed to be good and properly authorised: *Price v Humphries* (1958) 122 JP 423; *Frost v Frank Hoyles Transport Ltd* (1983) 11 May (unreported).

The Attorney-General's *fiat* (or consent) is required before proceedings are instituted or continued for certain offences; and the DPP must be notified in relation to certain offences. By various statutes, some offence may not be prosecuted save by or on behalf of certain officials. The Solicitor General may exercise any of the functions of the Attorney General if the latter is absent or incapacitated or if he is specifically authorised to do so: s.1 Law Officers Act 1944.

Where a private citizen abuses his right to initiate proceedings by habitually bringing vexatious matters, s.42 Supreme Court Act 1981 (as amended by s.24 POA 1985) enables the Attorney-General to seek an order of the High Court declaring that person to be a 'vexatious litigant'. If granted, this means that that individual may not then institute criminal proceedings without leave of the High Court.

ADVANCE DISCLOSURE 2.05

Where someone is accused of an *either way offence* the prosecutor must furnish him with *advance information* of the case against him as soon as practicable after receiving a request from the accused or his representative. The request must be made *before* the mode of trial decision or, in the case of a juvenile, before plea: r.4(1) Magistrates' Courts (Advance Information) Rules 1985, made under s.144 MCA 1980, as extended by s.48 CLA 1977.

The information may consist, at the prosecutor's discretion, of a copy of every statement which contains information as to the facts and matters of which the prosecutor proposes to adduce evidence or a summary of those matters: r.4. In order to inform the accused of his rights the prosecutor must provide him with a written notice as soon as practicable after charge or summons: r.3); and the court must satisfy itself before the mode of trial decision (or plea in the case of a juvenile), that he is aware of the prosecutor's duty in this respect: r.6. Disclosure may only be withheld for possible *intimidation* or other *interference* with the course of justice: r.5. If the court is satisfied that a request to a prosecutor has not been complied with, it must adjourn the proceedings unless satisfied that the conduct of the case for the accused will not be substantially prejudiced: r.7.

Dismissal for failure to provide advance disclosure does not prevent proceedings being re-commenced at a later date, in the absence of abuse of process: *R v Willesden Justices, ex p. Clemmings* (1987) *The Times*, 21 October.

BRINGING THE ACCUSED TO COURT 2.06

A person may be caused to appear before a magistrates' court in one of two ways: he may be arrested (*with* or *without* warrant) or he may appear in answer to a summons. The *laying of an information* is a pre-requisite to the issue of a summons or warrant. In the case of a person arrested otherwise than on warrant, the information is usually regarded as being laid when it is read out before a justice at the first appearance in court. In other instances it is the time when the information is received at the clerk's office for the purpose of issuing process upon it: *post*.

Powers of arrest without warrant are dealt with at Chapter 12.

Although it has been held to amount to the commencement of proceedings for a limited purpose (see *R v Brentwood Justices, ex p. Jones* [1979] RTR 155), a charge at a police station does not constitute the laying of an information and does not, it is suggested, represent the commencement of time for jurisdictional purposes: (see the report of the Royal Commission on Criminal Procedure, Vol II, para 182; and *Rees v Barlow* [1974] Crim LR 713).

2.07   **THE INFORMATION**

An information is simply 'the statement by which the magistrate is informed of the offence', *per* Huddleston B in *R v Hughes* (1879) 43 JP 556. The information need not be in writing or on oath, r.4(2) MC Rules 1981, except when a warrant is sought: s.1(3) MCA 1980.

The information is sufficient if it describes the offence in ordinary language, avoiding as far as possible the use of technical terms and without necessarily stating all the elements of the offence, and if it contains such particulars as may be necessary for giving reasonable information of the nature of the charge: r.100(1). It must contain a reference to the section or provision under which the offence is created: r.100(2), but it is not necessary to negative any exception, proviso, excuse or qualification: r.4(3). A court may not try an information charging more than one offence: r.12(1) (see under *'Duplicity'* at 5.11, *post*). But there is nothing to prevent a number of informations being set out on one piece of paper: r.12(2).

The practice of laying alternative informations when there is doubt was commended in *R v Newcastle Justices, ex p. Bryce* [1976] 1 WLR 517.

Defective informations may sometimes be cured by s.123 MCA: see 5.00 *post*.

2.08 **Laying the Information**

An information may be laid by the prosecutor in person or by his counsel or solicitor or other person authorised in that behalf: r.4(1) MCA Rules. It may be laid before a justice of the peace; s.1 MCA 1980 or before a clerk to the justices: Justices' Clerks Rules 1970 (SI No 231, as amended); and is *laid* for the purposes of s.127 MCA 1980 when it is received at the office of the clerk to the justices for the relevant area. It is *not necessary for the information to be personally received* by a justice of the peace or by the clerk to the justices. It is enough that it is received by any member of the staff of the clerk to the justices, expressly or impliedly authorised to receive it, for onward transmission to a justice of the peace or the clerk to the justices: *R v Manchester Stipendiary Magistrate, ex p. Hill* [1983] AC 328, HL. The House found it unnecessary to decide whether similar reasoning applies to an information laid orally, but expressed the view that in the ordinary course such oral information will in practice and should as a matter of prudence be addressed by the informant or his authorised agent to a justice of the peace or the clerk to the justices in person.

The 'precautionary' laying of an information before the prosecutor has decided to prosecute may be an *abuse* of the process of the court: *R v Brentford Justices, ex p. Wong* [1981] 1 All ER 884; *R v Fairford Justices, ex p. Brewster* (1975) 139 JP 574, except where there are administrative difficulties in getting the case together; see also *R v South Western Magistrates' Court, ex p. Beaton* [1980] RTR 35; and *'Oppression and Abuse of Process'* at 5.16, *post*. The justice or justice's clerk has a discretion to query delay and to refuse to issue a summons on this ground even though the delay is within the statutory time bar for summary proceedings: *R v Clerk to the Medway Justices, ex p. DHSS* (1986) 150 JP 401 (12 months under the provision in question in that case, normally 6 months under s. 127(1) MCA 1980 – although it was stated that it is 'preferable' to leave such issues until the hearing); and see further at 2.10 *Summonses* and 2.23 *Limitation of time, post*.

Juveniles   2.09

Anyone who decides to lay an information against someone he has reason
to believe to be a juvenile is under a duty to notify the appropriate local
authority: s.5(8) CYPA 1969. In the case of a juvenile of 13 years or
older, a probation officer must also be notified: s.34(2). Whenever a
juvenile is charged with an offence, his parents or guardians must be
required to attend court unless this is unreasonable: s.34(1) CYPA 1933.
A summons or warrant may issue in the same manner as if the information had been laid against them, and a summons to the juvenile may
include a summons to the parent or guardian: r.26 Magistrates' Courts
(Children and Young Persons) Rules 1970 (SI No 1792 as amended).
Where a juvenile is in *police detention* all practicable steps must be taken
to notify a person responsible for his welfare: s.34(2)–(11) CYPA 1933.

SUMMONSES   2.10

Unlike the *laying* of an information, the *issue* of a summons 'is the result
of a judicial act', *per* Lord Goddard CJ in *R v Wilson, ex p. Battersea BC*
[1947] 2 All ER 569; *R v Manchester Stipendiary Magistrate, ex p. Hill*
[1983] AC 328.

The circumstances in which a summons may be issued are set out in
s.1(2) MCA 1980. They should be distinguished from the *jurisdiction to
try offences* which is continued in ss.2, 3.

A summons may be issued by a justice of the peace s.1 MCA 1980, or
by a justices' clerk: Justices' Clerks Rules 1970 (SI No 231). This duty
cannot be delegated by the clerk to any of his assistants: *R v Gateshead
Justices, ex p. Tesco Stores* [1981] QB 470; *R v Manchester Stipendiary
Magistrate, ex p. Hill, supra.* When the clerk acts, he acts as a justice, *per*
Donaldson LJ in *R v Worthing Justices, ex p. Norvell* [1981] 1 WLR 413.
He may thus *refuse* as well as *grant.*

If a justice authorises the issue of a summons *without having applied his
mind to the information* then he is guilty of dereliction of duty, *per* Lord
Widgery CJ in *R v Brentford Justices, ex p. Catlin* [1975] QB 455.

'In the exercise of his discretion whether or not to accede to an application for the issue of a
summons a justice must at the very least ascertain:
(i) whether the allegation is of an offence known to the law and if so whether the essential
   ingredients of the offence are *prima facie* present;
(ii) that the offence alleged is not out of time;
(iii) that the court has jurisdiction;
(iv) whether the informant has the necessary authority to prosecute.
'In addition to these specific matters it is clear that he may and indeed should consider
whether the allegation is vexatious. Since the matter is properly within the magistrate's
discretion it would be inappropriate to attempt to lay down an exhaustive catalogue of
matters to which consideration should be given. Plainly he should consider the whole of the
relevant circumstances. The magistrate must be able to satisfy himself that it is a proper case
in which to issue a summons. There can be no question, however, of conducting a preliminary hearing. Until a summons has been issued there is no allegation to meet: no charge
has been made. A proposed defendant has no *locus standi* and no right at this stage to be
heard. Whilst it is conceivable that a magistrate might seek information from him in
exceptional circumstances it must be entirely within the discretion of the magistrate whether
to do so'

per Lord Widgery CJ in *R v West London Justices, ex p. Klahn* [1979] 1
WLR 933; see also *R v Gateshead Justices, ex p. Tesco Stores* [1981] 2
WLR 419.

Examples of magistrates *wrongly refusing* to issue process are: *R v*

Adamson [1875] 1 QBD 201 (distaste for views expressed at public meetings); *R v Byrde and Pontypool Gas Co, ex p. Williams* (1980) 65 JP 210 (having previously dismissed a summons based on similar facts, justices declined process without exercising judicial discretion); *R v Bennett and Bond, ex p. Bennett* (1908) 72 JP 362 (first summons having been dismissed in the absence of the prosecutor who had knowledge of the hearing, the magistrates declined a second, commenting that the prosecutor had a civil remedy); and *R v Beacontree Justices, ex p. Mercer* [1970] Crim LR 103 (practice always to refuse applications of a particular nature).

Refusals to grant process were *upheld* in the following cases: *Ex p. Lewis* (1888) 52 JP 773 (where the High Court had earlier decided that the facts did not disclose an offence); *Utting v Berney* (1888) 52 JP 806 (two informations laid against two different people for the same offence, informant refusing to select either); and *R v Clerk to the Medway Justices, ex p. DHSS* (1986) 150 JP 401 (delay). An order of *mandamus* will not be issued unless it can be shown that in declining to grant process a magistrate's decision was governed by extraneous or irregular matters: *R v Metropolitan Magistrate, ex p. Bennion* (1971) 135 JPN 491.

In *R v Mead, ex p. National Insurance Commissioners* (1916) 80 JP 332, it was held that a magistrate could not decline to issue process against an employer simply because his servants were not being prosecuted. Ridley J stated *obiter*:

'It is quite true that in considering the matter brought before him the magistrate may decline to issue a summons because he thinks that there will not be evidence by which the offence could be proved if it were brought before a jury.'

It may be doubted whether it is proper for justices to decide, as a matter of discretion, to entertain a second application for a summons on exactly the same material as has been considered by other justices of the same bench, *per* Donaldson LJ in *R v Worthing Justices, ex p. Norvell* [1981] 1 WLR 413. Although it may sometimes be useful to give reasons for the refusal of a summons there is no obligation to do so and it is not usually done, *per* Donaldson LJ, *ibid*. The charge to be preferred is in the discretion of the prosecution, not the justices: *R v Nuneaton Justices, ex p. Parker* (1954) 118 JP 524 (magistrate refused summons for careless driving where he felt dangerous driving more appropriate), and see the remarks of Lord Roskill in *R v Seymour* [1983] 3 WLR 349 at p.359. But in *R v Old Street Magistrate, ex p. Simons* (1976) 140 JPN 25, a magistrate's decision to refuse a summons for criminal damage after he had granted one for common assault arising out of the same incident was upheld where he considered that this could satisfactorily dispose of the case.

2.11   Not essential to jurisdiction

A summons, as distinct from an information, is not essential to jurisdiction. In *R v Hughes* (1879) 43 JP 556, Hawkins J in a considered judgment in the Court for Crown Cases Reserved approved also by Coleridge LCJ said:

'There is a marked distinction between the jurisdiction to take cognizance of an offence and the jurisdiction to issue a particular process to compel the accused to answer it. The former may exist, the latter may be wanting . . . process is not essential to the jurisdiction of the justices to hear and adjudicate.'

See also *R v Shaw* (1865) 29 JP 339; *R v Tabrum and Quayle, ex p. Dash* (1907) 71 JP 325; *Gray v Customs Commissioners* (1884) 48 JP 343. The effect of this is that an *oral information* may be laid against a person present in court and the trial begun immediately. This is of course subject to the principles of 'natural justice', and if the accused seeks an adjournment it would seem that he is entitled to it, whereupon a summons should issue.

Contents of a summons 2.12

A summons must state shortly the matter of the information and the time and place at which the defendant is required to appear: r.4(2) MC Rules 1981. The summons is sufficient if it describes the specific offence in *ordinary language avoiding so far as possible the use of technical terms and without necessarily stating all the elements of the offence, and gives such particulars as may be necessary for giving reasonable information of the nature of the charge*: r.100(1). If a statutory offence it must refer to the section of the Act etc: r.100(2). A single summons may contain a number of informations: r.4(3). It must be signed by the justice issuing it, or be authenticated by the clerk: r.4(1). If issued by the clerk it must be signed by him.

Sufficiency of a summons 2.13

Certain defects in a summons may be cured by s.123 MCA 1980: see under 'Defective process' at Chapter 5.

If a sumons does not give sufficient particulars, the proper course for the defendant is to apply for an adjournment and if the justices are satisfied that he has been misled in any way they should always be willing to grant such an application: *Neal v Devenish* (1894) 58 JP 246. If the prosecution reject an adjournment to enable them to supply sufficient particulars the information may be dismissed: *Robertson v Rosenburg* (1951) 115 JP 128. Application for particulars may be made at any time after the charge is preferred, but the accused is not in general entitled *to see* the information before committal for trial: *R v Aylesbury Justices, ex p. Wisbey* (1965) 129 JP 287. In *Hickmott v Curd* (1971) 135 JP 519 a conviction was upheld on particulars different from those stated in the charge where the alternative particulars had been 'sufficiently ventilated' in argument. It is suggested that this decision is one which should be regarded very much as being dependent on its particular facts. The question whether sufficient particulars have been supplied may now also fall to be assessed in the light of any 'advance information' provided under the Magistrates' Courts (Advance Information) Rules 1985 (SI No 601): 2.88 *post*.

Service 2.14

A distinction must be made between the methods by which a summons may be served and the means by which service of a summons may be proved.

A summons may be served:

(a) by delivering it to the person to whom it is directed;
(b) by leaving it for him with some person at his last known or usual place of abode or at an address given by him for that purpose; or
(c) by sending it by post in a letter addressed to him at such place of abode or address: r.99(1), (8) MC Rules 1981.

However, in the case of an *indictable offence* service by method (b) or (c) must not be treated as established unless it is proved *that the summons came to the defendant's knowledge* and for that purpose any letter or other communication purporting to be written by him or on his behalf in such terms as reasonably to justify the inference that the summons came to his knowledge is admissible as evidence of that fact: r.99(2). There is no need for proof that the summons came to the defendant's knowledge in the case of a summary offence, but where service is by post it must be by recorded delivery or registered letter: *ibid* r.99(2), proviso.

A witness summons and certain other summonses may not be served by methods (b) or (c): r.99(6).

A summons to a corporation may be served by delivery to, or sending it by post to, the registered office: r.99(3).

The fact that a summons has been properly served may be proved by evidence on oath or in any other admissible form, but the most usual way is a certificate under r.67 MC Rules 1981; when the provisions concerning proof of service are then satisfied 'unless the contrary is proved': see r.67(2) and *Hawkins v Crown Prosecution Service* (1987) *The Times*, 24 August.

2.15   VOIDING PROCEEDINGS UNKNOWN TO ACCUSED

When a summons has been issued and a magistrates' court has begun to try the information the accused may make a *statutory declaration* that he did not know of the proceedings or summons until a date after the court had begun to try the information. If this declaration is served on the clerk to the justices within 21 days of the date mentioned in the declaration the summons and all subsequent proceedings are void: s.14(1) Magistrates Courts Act 1980. The date for service may be *extended* if the court, or the justices' clerk (Justices' Clerks Rules 1970) is satisfied that it was not reasonable to expect the accused to serve the statement within time: s.14(3). When a statutory declaration is made a fresh summons may issue on the original information, but the information cannot be tried by the same justices: s.14(1), (4).

2.16   WARRANTS

The vast majority of summary offenders are proceeded against by way of summons, but a warrant for the arrest of the accused is usually issued in a serious case or when the accused is unlikely to attend as a result of a summons: *O'Brien v Brabner* (1885) 49 JPN 227; *Dumbell v Roberts* [1944] 1 All ER 326. In the case of an adult the power to issue a warrant *in the first instance* is confined to

  (i) indictable offences;
 (ii) offences punishable with imprisonment; and
(iii) cases where the defendant's address is not sufficiently established for a summons to be served on him: s.1(4) MCA 1980.

The *jurisdiction* in which a warrant may be issued is set out in s.1(2), (5) MCA 1980. This should be distinguished from the *jurisdiction to try offences* which is contained in ss.2, 3. Where the offence is *indictable* a warrant may issue *at any time* notwithstanding that a summons has previously been issued: s.1(6).

Contents of a warrant 2.17

A warrant of arrest must require the persons to whom it is directed to arrest the person against whom the warrant is issued: r.96(1) MC Rules 1981. It must name or otherwise describe the person to be arrested and must contain a statement of the offence charged: r.96(2). The warrant is sufficient if it describes the offence charged in *ordinary language* avoiding so far as possible the use of technical terms and without necessarily stating all the elements of the offence, and gives such particulars as may be necessary for giving reasonable information of the nature of the charge: r.100(1). It must refer to the section of the Act: r.100(2). The warrant must be signed by the justice or, in certain cases, his clerk: r.95. The warrant may be endorsed for bail: s.117 MCA 1980; except in a case of treason: s.47. Certain defects in a warrant may be cured by s.123 MCA 1980: see Chapter 5, *post*.

Execution of a warrant 2.18

A warrant may be executed *anywhere in England and Wales* by any person to whom it is directed or by any constable acting within his police area: s.125(2) MCA 1980. It *remains in force* until executed or withdrawn: s.125(1); notwithstanding the death of the issuing justice: s.124. When a warrant is *lost or destroyed* a duplicate may be issued after proper inquiry: *R v Leigh Justices, ex p. Kara* (1981) 72 Cr App R 327.

PROCESS OUTSIDE ENGLAND AND WALES 2.19

A *warrant* issued in England or Wales for the arrest of a person charged with an offence may be executed in Scotland or Northern Ireland and *vice versa* without endorsement: s.38 CLA 1977. No endorsement is required.

A warrant issued in England and Wales for the arrest of a person in any part of the United Kingdom including the Channel Islands and the Isle of Man may be executed after endorsement in those places (and *vice versa*) under ss.12–14 Indictable Offences Act 1848. Effectively, because of the simpler machinery of s.38 Criminal Law Act 1977, the 1848 Act is used now only in respect of the Channel Islands and the Isle of Man, and for civil process. That Act has been extended to a wider range of warrants of arrest and to warrants of commitment by s.126 MCA 1980.

A *summons* requiring a person charged with an offence to appear before a court in England or Wales may be served on him in Scotland or Northern Ireland: s.39(1) CLA 1977. Methods of service and proof of service are dealt with in rr.67, 99 MC Rules 1981. A summons issued for appearance in a court in Northern Ireland may similarly be served in England or Wales: s.39(2) Criminal Law Act 1977. Service is prescribed for in the Magistrates' Courts (Amendment) Rules (Northern Ireland) 1980; not reproduced herein.

Citation of a person charged with a crime or offence to appear before a Scottish court may be effected in England or Wales or Northern Ireland in like manner as it may be in Scotland: s.39(3) CLA 1977.

The endorsement and execution in England or Wales of warrants granted in the Republic of Ireland is dealt with in a separate code laid down in the Backing of Warrants (Republic of Ireland) Act 1965, and rules made thereunder. There are no reciprocal arrangements between the two countries for the execution of summonses.

The ordinary process of a magistrates' court in criminal cases (ie summonses and warrants) cannot be executed outside the United

Kingdom and the Republic of Ireland except under the Extradition Acts 1870 and 1873, or the Fugitive Offenders Act 1967 (which are not dealt with in this work).

2.20   JURISDICTION

Jurisdiction is both *territorial* and *temporal*.

Territorial jurisdiction

Indictable offences may, in general, be dealt with by magistrates either as examining justices or on summary trial, wherever committed in England and Wales: ss.2(3), (4) and 155(6) MCA 1980. Various statutes extending the powers of English courts over specific offences committed abroad are outside the scope of this work, but certain general principles apply to the general run of offences and where the act in question affects events within the jurisdiction. Where acts are committed outside this country, the rules of international comity do not call for more than that each sovereign state should refrain from punishing persons for their conduct within the territory of another sovereign state where that conduct has had no harmful consequences within the territory of the state which imposes the punishment, *per* Lord Diplock in *Treacy v Director of Public Prosecutions* [1971] 2 WLR 112 (defendant could be tried for blackmail where he posted in England a letter received by someone in Germany). But a person in the UK does not assist an offence abroad which is not, in fact, committed: see *R v Panayi and Karte* (1987) *The Times*, 24 July. An attempt to obtain property by deception is committed within the jurisdiction where letters posted in Northern Ireland were received in England: *R v Baxter* (1971) 135 JP 345; *R v Wall* [1974] 2 All ER 245 (knowingly concerned in fraudulent evasion of import restriction); *R v Markus* (1975) 139 JP 19 (fraudulent inducement to invest).

In *DPP v Stonehouse* [1977] 2 All ER 909, Lord Edmund Davies approved the proposition that 'If a person, being outside England, initiates an offence, part of the essential elements of which take effect in England, he is amenable to English jurisdiction'. That case concerned an attempted deception to obtain insurance monies where acts committed abroad had resulted in the intended payment of those monies in England.

'Where a crime is committed in England a secondary party (accessory or abettor) can be punished even though he was not within British territorial jurisdiction at the time when the crime was committed or when he gave his assistance, *at least if he is a citizen of the United Kingdom*'

Professor Glanville Williams, quoted with approval in *R v Robert Millar (Contractors) Ltd* [1970] 2 QB 54. (Scottish company convicted of counselling and procuring death by dangerous driving – now obsolete – in England when tyre of vehicle driven by their employee was defective.)

The jurisdiction of English courts in *indictable* cases extends over British ships on the high seas or waters where great ships go, as far as the tide ebbs and flows: *R v Anderson* [1861–73] All ER Rep 999. This jurisdiction is extended by s.686 Merchant Shipping Act 1894 over aliens committing offences on board British ships and British subjects committing offences on board any foreign ship to which they do not belong. See *R v Kelly* [1981] 2 All ER 1098. Justices are given jurisdiction over ships lying off the coast by s.685. For jurisdiction in territorial waters see s.2

Territorial Waters Jurisdiction Act 1878 (not reproduced herein) and *R v Kent Justices, ex p. Lye and Others* [1967] 2 WLR 765.

For jurisdiction over criminal acts committed in aircraft see the Civil Aviation Act 1982 (not reproduced herein).

Local jurisdiction 2.21

Summary offences may be tried only by the justices of the county within which they are alleged to have been committed: s.2(1) Magistrates' Courts Act 1980; except when process is issued under s.2(1)(b) in order to allow a person accused of an offence committed elsewhere to be charged *jointly with or in the same place as* a person for whose alleged offence the justices already have jurisdiction: s.2(2). Similarly, when a defendant is already being tried for an offence before magistrates they have jurisdiction to try him for any summary offence wherever allegedly committed: s. 2(6). Special rules apply to offences committed on boundaries, on journeys or begun in one jurisdiction and completed in another s.3. For the purposes of the Magistrates' Courts Act 1980, the Isles of Scilly form part of the County of Cornwall: s.149.

Jurisdiction of the London courts 2.22

Greater London is divided into five London commission areas by s.2 Justices of the Peace Act 1979. Each commission area is 'deemed to be a county for all purposes of the law relating to commissions of the peace, justices of the peace, magistrates' courts, the *custos rotulorum*, justices' clerks and matters connected with any of these matters': s.2(3). Thus, magistrates for any London commission area may try any summary offence arising within the area in accordance with s.2(1) MCA 1980. A justice in any London commission area may act as a justice for his area in any other commission area or county adjoining his own area by virtue of s.33.

The Inner London area is in turn divided into a number of petty sessional divisions by virtue of s.36 Justices of the Peace Act 1979 and Orders made thereunder.

Before the coming into operation of the Administration of Justice Act 1964 there were two separate and, geographically at least, coextensive systems of petty sessional courts in the metropolitan area – the courts of the metropolitan stipendiary magistrates and those of the lay justices for the county of London. The effect of that Act was substantially, to merge these two jurisdictions. The present position is as follows:

The Metropolitan Stipendiary Magistrates
— exercise the jurisdiction conferred on them by statute except that the inner London area replaces the metropolitan police courts area: Justices of the Peace Act 1979, s.33(2).
— have the jurisdiction conferred on any two justices of the peace sitting together by any enactment, their commission or by the common law (s.33(1), (3)).
— are by virtue of their office justices of the peace for each of the London commission areas and for the counties of Essex, Hertfordshire, Kent and Surrey (s.31(4)); notwithstanding that they may be assigned by the Lord Chancellor to a particular petty sessional division (s.32(1)).

Lay Justices
— share the jurisdiction conferred on all justices of the peace, by any enactment, by their commission and by the common law *ibid.* s.33(1)).
— When sitting with at least one other, are given the jurisdiction conferred on metropolitan stipendiary magistrates as such by any enactment except
  (a) the Extradition Acts 1870–1935
  (b) the Fugitive Offenders Act 1967
  (c) s.26 of the Pilotage Act 1983 (to be repealed by s.32 Pilotage Act 1987 from a day to be appointed)
  (d) s.25 of the Children and Young Persons Act 1933

2.23 Limitation of time

Nullum tempus occurrit regi (time never runs against the Crown) is the rule with regard to any indictable offence when tried on indictment and this rule is applied to the summary trial of an offence triable either way by s.127(2), (3) MCA 1980. But where any enactment imposes a limitation on the time for taking proceedings on indictment for that offence no summary proceedings may be taken after the latest time for taking proceedings on indictment: s.127(4).

Subject only to the exception concerning *indictable offences*, a magistrates' court may not try an information unless *the information is laid within six months* from the time when the offence was committed: s.127(1). But it is always necessary to consult the statute concerned (usually that creating the offence) to establish whether any special limitation period applies. The limit is not breached by failure *to serve* the summons: *R v Clerkenwell Magistrates' Court ex p. Ewing; Ewing v Clark* (1987) *The Times*, 3 June.

The purpose of the six months' limitation is to ensure that summary offences are charged and tried as soon as reasonably possible after their alleged commission so that the recollection of witnesses may still be reasonably clear and so that there shall be no unnecessary delay in the disposal of summary offences, *per* May J in *R v Newcastle-upon-Tyne Justices, ex p. Bryce (Contractors) Ltd* [1976] 1 WLR 517; see also *R v Brentford Justices, ex p. Wong* [1981] 1 All ER 884. Thus, undue delay between the laying of an information and the issue of process may amount to 'Oppression and Abuse of Process': see under that heading at Chapter 5. *Delay* in laying an information may justify the refusal of process, or the court in refusing to proceed with the case, notwithstanding that the information is laid within the limitation period: *R v Clerk to the Medway Justices ex p. DHSS* (1986) 150 JP 401 (refusal of summons justified where information laid on the final day of a twelve months' limitation period).

The laying of a subsequent information out of time was held not to bar the re-issue of a warrant on an earlier information laid within time: *R v Leigh Justices, ex p. Kara* (1981) 72 Cr App R 327. The Act lays down no period within which a summons must issue upon the information but it cannot be delayed indefinitely to the prejudice of the defendant: *R v Fairford Justices, ex p. Brewster* (1975) 139 JP 574.

For calculating the period of limitation, the day on which the offence was committed is to be excluded and the day the information was laid included: *Radcliffe v Bartholomew* (1892) 56 JP 262; *Stewart v Chapman* (1951) 115 JP 473; *Marren v Dawson, Bentley and Co Ltd* [1961] 2 All ER 270.

The relevant date is that of the information and not that of the hearing: *Beardsley v Giddings* (1904) 68 JP 222; *Abraham v Jutson* [1963] 1 WLR 658, *Morris v Duncan* (1899) 62 JP 823. Where a *doubt* is raised as to whether an information was laid in time, the defendant is entitled to be acquitted: *Lloyd v Young* [1963] Crim LR 703. When the evidence fails to show that the offence was committed within the time, it is immaterial that the evidence available to the prosecution at the time of instituting the proceedings did: *R v Lewis* (1979) 143 JP 588.

In some cases where enactments set their own time limits, limitation is dependent upon the date on which information came to the prosecutor's knowledge. But where an information was laid within time but not accompanied by the necessary certificate as to knowledge it was held that the magistrate had been wrong to decline jurisdiction: *R v Clerkenwell Magistrates' Court, ex p. Director of Public Prosecutions* (1984) 79 Cr App R 141.

Where a statute permits a justice to grant a certificate allowing the prosecutor to lay an information out of time, it is imperative that either the clerk or one of his assistants should be called upon to give advice, *per* Watkins LJ in *R v Harvey, ex p. Select Livestock Producers Ltd* (1985) 149 JP 389.

Aiders and abettors are subject to the same time limit as principal offenders: *Gould and Co v Houghton* (1921) 85 JP 93; *Homolka v Osmond* [1939] 1 All ER 154.

The same, but no other, justice may issue a second summons out of time, 'or a series of summonses, if necessary', where the information is laid in time and the first summons not served: *R v Pickford* (1861) 25 JP 549 (a bastardy case); and see *Ex p. Fielding* (1861) 25 JP 759.

Continuing offences   2.24

With continuing offences, time runs not from first discovery but from each day on which the offence was committed: *Barrett v Barrow-in-Furness Corporation* (1887) 51 JP 803; *Rowley v Everton (TA) and Sons, Ltd* (1940) 104 JP 461; *R v Chertsey Justices, ex p. Franks* [1961] 2 WLR 442. A continuing offence is one which is committed afresh each day, not a single transaction, albeit taking place over a length of time: *Anderton v Cooper* (1980) 72 Cr App R 232 ('keeping' and 'managing' a brothel over various dates not bad for duplicity).

'It is not an essential characteristic of a criminal offence that any prohibited act or omission, in order to constitute a single offence, should take place once and for all on a single day. It may take place, whether continuously or intermittently, over a period of time.'

per Lord Roskill in *Chiltern District Council v Hodgetts* [1983] 1 All ER 1057 at 1060 (contravention of an enforcement notice under s.89 Town and Country Planning Act 1971) in which the House of Lords distinguished a '*do*' notice from a '*desist*' notice:

'The initial offence created by subs (1) in the case of non-compliance with a 'do notice' is complete once and for all when the period of compliance with the notice expires; but it is plainly contemplated that the further offence of non-compliance with a 'do notice' created by subs (4), though it too is a single offence, may take place over a period of time, since the penalty for it is made dependent on the number of days on which it takes place. Similarly, as respects non-compliance with a 'desist notice', it is . . . clear that the initial offence (as well as the further offence), though it too may take place over a period, whether continuously or intermittently (eg holding a Sunday market), is a single offence and not a series of separate offences committed each day that the non-compliance prior to the first conviction for non-compliance continues.'

The illegal erection of a partition wall is not a 'continuing offence'; *Marshall v Smith* (1873) 29 JP 36; and neither is letting at an excessive rent: *R v Wimbledon Justices, ex p. Derwent* [1953] 1 All ER 390; nor 'depositing and leaving' litter contrary to the Litter Act 1958: *Vaughan v Biggs* [1960] 1 WLR 622. There is a Scottish decision to the effect that acts required by statute to be performed *'forthwith'* are not continuing offences and time runs from the date the act falls to be performed; *A and C McLennon (Blairgowrie) Ltd v Macmillan* 1964 SLT 2. It is not a continuing offence for a non-partial to remain unlawfully in this country contrary to the s.24(1)(b)(i) Immigration Act 1971: *Singh (Gurdev) v The Queen* [1974] 1 All ER 26. The offence of knowingly remaining in the UK beyond time in s.24(1)(b) can only be committed on the day following the expiry of the limited leave: *Grant v Borg* [1982] 2 All ER 257.

2.25   TIME LIMITS

Section 22 POA 1985 *post*, gives wide powers to the Secretary of State to make regulations with respect to the *preliminary stages* of criminal proceedings, laying down the maximum time allowed to the prosecution to complete a particular step – what are called *general time limits*. The section also confers power to specify the maximum period for which an accused may be held in custody in relation to an offence whilst awaiting completion of a particular preliminary stage – *'custody time limits'*. It is expressly stated in s.22(2) that regulations may '. . . be made so as to apply in specified areas' (s.22(2)(a)) and that they may '. . . make different provision with respect to proceedings in different areas' (s.22(2)(b)). Following the field trials in the counties of Avon, Kent, Somerset, the West Midlands and some further areas, the Secretary of State has made the Prosecution of Offences (Custody Time Limit) Regulations 1987 (SI No 299) see 3.120, *post*) applying certain pre-trial custody limits to places within the areas already mentioned by name above '. . . but not elsewhere' (see r.3(1)). The 1987 Regulations have been extended to further areas of the country by the Prosecution of Offences (Custody Time Limits) Regulations 1988 SI No 164. At the time of going to press, no 'general time limits' have been made.

2.26   SPECIAL SITUATIONS

The Crown and diplomatic immunity

The court may be deprived of jurisdiction in cases involving a head of state.

'The doctrine of regal immunity really rests upon the fact that no British tribunal has a jurisdiction under which the Sovereign can be tried. That this is so is shown by the rules . . . under which the servants of the Crown cannot plead superior orders as an excuse for any offence which they may have committed':

Russell on Crime 12th ed at p.96. The principle that statutes do not bind the Crown except by clear expression to the contrary is not derogated from by the many Acts of Parliament protecting the Crown or saving Crown rights: *Hornsey Urban District Council v Hennell* [1900–3] All ER 392; *Cooper v Hawkins* (1904) 68 JP 25. An example of a statute being applied to persons and property in the service of the Crown is the s.188 Road Traffic Act 1972.

A diplomatic agent as defined in art.1 of Sch.1 to the Diplomatic

Privileges Act 1964 enjoys immunity from the criminal jurisdiction of this country, (*ibid*, art.31), but such immunity may be waived by his State (*ibid*, art.32). For the corresponding provisions concerning consular officers and employees see the Consular Relations Act 1968, and for representatives of Commonwealth countries the Diplomatic and Other Privileges Act 1971. Proceedings brought against anyone entitled to diplomatic immunity are without jurisdiction and null and void until there is a valid waiver, but immunity is a procedural bar which can be lost by change of circumstances: *R v Madan* [1961] 2 WLR 231; as explained in *Empson v Smith* [1965] 2 All ER 881.

Accomplices   2.27

Since s.1 Criminal Law Act 1967, (which abolished all distinctions between felonies and misdemeanours and provided that on all matters in which a distinction had previously been made the law and practice should be that applicable to felony), the only categories of accomplice have been principals in the first degree and principals in the second degree (or aiders and abettors). A person may no longer be charged as an accessory after the fact, although s.4 of the Act of 1967 makes it an offence to assist persons who have committed an arrestable offence.

By s.8 of the Accessories and Abettors Act 1861, every person who aids, abets, counsels or procures the commission of a misdemeanour (and thus, now, any offence) is liable to be tried, indicted and punished as a principal. By s.44(1) MCA 1980, a person who aids, abets, counsels or procures the commission by another of a summary offence is guilty of the like offence and may be tried (whether or not charged as a principal) either by a court having jurisdiction to try the other person or by a court having jurisdiction to try him.

'Two things must be proved before an accused can be held guilty of aiding and abetting the commission of the offence: first, he must have full knowledge of the facts which constitute the offence . . . Secondly, there must be some form of voluntary assistance in the commission of the offence. Sometimes the word used is "encouragement". . .'

per Parker LCJ in *Tuck v Robson* [1970] 1 WLR 741, in which was approved the dictum of Devlin J in *National Coal Board v Gamble* [1958] 3 WLR 434, where he said:

It would be wrong to conclude . . . that proof of encouragement is necessary to every form of aiding and abetting . . . Presence on the scene of the crime without encouragement or assistance is no aid to the criminal; the supply of essential material is . . . If voluntary presence is *prima facie* evidence of encouragement and therefore aiding and abetting, it appears to me to be *a fortiori* that the intentional supply of an essential article must be *prima facie* evidence of aiding and abetting.'

And see *Cassady v Reg Morris (Transport) Ltd* [1975] Crim LR 398. Mere presence at the scene of a crime is not enough. In *R v Coney* (1882) 8 QBD at 557, Hawkins J said:

'In my opinion, to constitute an aider and abettor some active steps must be taken by word, or action, with the intent to instigate the principal, or principals. Encouragement does not of necessity amount to aiding and abetting, it may be intentional or unintentional, a man may unwittingly encourage another in fact by his presence, be misinterpreted words, or gestures, or by his silence, or non-interference, or he may encourage intentionally by expressions, gestures, or actions intended to signify approval. In the latter case he aids and abets, in the former he does not. It is no criminal offence to stand by, a mere passive spectator of a crime, even of a murder. Non-interference to prevent a crime is not itself a crime. But the fact that a person was voluntarily and purposely present witnessing the commission of a crime, and offered no opposition to it, though he might reasonably be expected to prevent and had the power to do so, or at least to express his dissent, might under some circumstances, afford cogent evidence upon which a jury would be justified in finding that he wilfully encouraged and so aided and abetted. But it would be purely a question for the jury whether he did so or not.'

And see *R v Clarkson* (1971) 135 JP 533.

In the case of *D Stanton and Sons Ltd v Webber* (1972) 136 JPN 68, it was said that to convict a person as an aider or abettor it must be proved that he knew the material and relevant facts which constituted a substantive offence either by actual knowledge or from knowledge deemed to be had from the fact that he deliberately shut his eyes to the obvious.

It is still necessary to distinguish between principals in the first and second degree (even if not charged as such) in the case of offences of strict liability, owing to the fact that *mens rea* will in general attach to the latter but not to the former. See, for example: *John Henshall (Quarries) Ltd v Harvey* [1965] 2 WLR 758.

Aiders and abettors are liable to the same time limit as principal offenders: *Gould and Co Ltd v Houghton* (1921) 85 JP 93; *Homolka v Osmond* [1939] 1 All ER 154.

In misdemeanours (and now, by virtue of s.1 Criminal Law Act 1967, all offences) the acquittal or conviction of the principal in the second degree is a matter of evidence so that, for example, notwithstanding that the principal offender has been acquitted for lack of admissible evidence, the offence can be proved to have taken place by evidence which, as against the aider and abettor, is admissible and cogent: *per* Judge Chapman in *R v Humphreys and Turner* [1965] 3 All ER 689; affirmed by the Court of Appeal in *R v Cogan; R v Leak* [1975] 3 WLR 316. But an accomplice cannot be convicted when the principal offender has not committed the offence: *R v Davis* [1977] Crim. LR 542.

2.28   Husbands and wives

A husband and wife cannot conspire together to commit a crime: s.2(2)(a) CLA 1977. Nor can there be any publication of a criminal libel between them: *R v Lord Mayor of London* [1886] 16 QBD 772. A husband may not be convicted of rape upon his wife: 1 Hale 629; except after a separation order: *R v Clarke* [1949] 2 All ER 448; a decree *nisi: R v O'Brien (Edward)* (1974) 138 JP 798; or an undertaking not to molest: *R v Steele* (1977) 65 Cr App R 22.

Except in treason or murder it is a defence for a wife to prove that the offence was committed in the presence of and under the coercion of her husband: s.47 CJA 1925.

The common law rule that husbands and wives could not steal from one another, at least when living together, modified by the Larceny Act 1916, has been reversed altogether by the s.30 Theft Act 1968. The consent of the Director of Public Prosecutions is necessary to certain prosecutions made possible by this section.

2.29   Incitement

It is an offence at common law to incite the commission of any offence. It matters not whether the offence is committed or not but, if committed, the inciter will become guilty of the substantive offence.

Any offence consisting in the incitement to commit a summary offence is triable only summarily: s.45(1) MCA 1980.

Attempts to commit offences   2.30

If, with intent to commit an indictable offence, a person does an act which is more than merely preparatory to the commission of the offence, he is guilty of attempting to commit the offence: s.1(1) Criminal Attempts Act 1981. By virtue of *ibid*, s.1(4), attempts to commit conspiracy, aiding and abetting, counselling, procuring or suborning the commission of an offence and offences under ss.4(1) and 5(1) CLA 1967 are excluded. A person may be guilty of attempting to commit an offence even though the facts are such that the commission of the offence is impossible: s.1(2), *ibid*, He is also regarded as having had an intent to commit an offence where, apart from the act, his intention would not be regarded as having amounted to an intent to commit an offence, so long as, if the facts of the case had been as he believed them to be, his intention would have been so regarded: *ibid*, s.1(3). These subsections are applied to offences of attempt under other enactments by *ibid*, s.3.

Certain penal and procedural provisions governing the substantive offences are applied to attempts by virtue of *ibid*, s.2.

If the offence attempted is triable only on indictment the attempt is also so triable: *ibid*, s.4(1). If the offence attempted is triable either way the accused is liable on summary conviction to any penalty to which he would have been liable on summary conviction of that offence: *ibid*, s.4(1). Where the court may proceed to summary trial of an information charging a person with an offence and in information charging him with an attempt to commit it the court may, without his consent, try the informations together. *ibid*, s.4(2). Only those provisions of the 1981 Act relating to criminal *procedure* are reproduced herein.

Statutory Provisions

INDICTABLE OFFENCES ACT 1848

English warrants may be backed in Ireland and vice versa   2.31

12. That if any person against whom a warrant shall be issued in any county, riding, division, liberty, city, borough, or place in England or Wales, by any justice of the peace, or by any Judge of Her Majesty's court of Queen's Bench, or the Crown Court, for any indictable offence against the laws of that part of the United Kingdom, shall escape, go into, reside, or be, or be supposed or suspected to be, in any county or place in that part of the United Kingdom called Ireland, or if any person against whom a warrant shall be issued in any county or place in Ireland, by any justice of the peace, or by any Judge of Her Majesty's Court of Queen's Bench there, or the Crown Court for any crime or offence against the laws of that part of the United Kingdom, shall escape, go into, reside, or be, or be supposed or suspected to be, in any county, riding, division, liberty, city, borough, or place in that part of the United Kingdom called England or Wales, it shall and may be lawful for any justice of the peace in and for the county or place into which such person shall escape or go, or where he shall reside or be, or be supposed or suspected to be, to make an endorsement on the warrant, signed with his name, authorizing the execution of the warrant within the jurisdiction of the justice making the endorsement, or to the like effect, and which warrant so endorsed shall be sufficient authority to the person or persons bringing such warrant, and to all persons to whom such warrant was originally directed, and also to all constables or other peace officers of the county or place where such warrant shall be endorsed, to execute the said warrant in the county or place where the justice so endorsing it shall have jurisdiction, by apprehending the person against whom such warrant shall have been granted, and to convey him before the justice or justices who granted the same, or before some other justice or justices of the peace in and for the same county or place, and which the said justice or justices before whom he shall be so brought shall thereupon proceed in such manner as if the said person had been apprehended in the said last-mentioned county or place. [*as amended by Sch.5 MCA 1952, Sch.8 Courts Act 1971*]

COMMENTARY

Sections 12–14 of the 1848 Act have been applied to (a) warrants of arrest issued under s.1 MCA 1980 for offences other than those referred to in this section; (b) warrants of arrest issued under *ibid*, s.13; and (c) warrants of commitment issued under s.126 *ibid*. But the 1848 Act is effectively superseded so far as concerns a warrant of arrest of a person charged with an offence by s.38 CLA 1977. By s.32 of the 1848 Act the town of Berwick upon Tweed is deemed to be in England.

Indictable offence, defined in Sch.1 Interpretation Act 1978.

Ireland, to be construed as referring to Northern Ireland only: s.9 Backing of Warrants (Republic of Ireland) Act 1965.

2.32   **Backing English warrants in the Isles of Man, Guernsey, Jersey, Alderney, or Sark, and vice versa**
    13. That if any person against whom a warrant shall be issued in any county, riding, division, liberty, city, borough, or place in England or Wales, by any justice of the peace, or by any Judge of Her Majesty's Court of Queen's Bench, or the Crown Court, for any indictable offence, shall escape, go into, reside, or be, or supposed to be, or suspected to be, in any of the Isles of Man, Guernsey, Jersey, Alderney, or Sark, it shall be lawful for any officer within the district into which such accused person shall escape or go, or where he shall reside or be, or be supposed or suspected to be, who shall have jurisdiction to issue any warrant or process in the nature of a warrant for the apprehension of offenders within such district, to endorse such warrant in the manner hereinbefore mentioned, or to the like effect; or if any person against whom any warrant, or process in the nature of a warrant, shall be issued in any of the Isles aforesaid, shall escape, go into, reside, or be, or be supposed or suspected to be, in any county, riding, division, liberty, city, borough, or place in England or Wales, it shall be lawful for any justice of the peace in and for the county or place into which such person shall escape or go, or where he shall reside or be, or be supposed or suspected to be, to endorse such warrant or process in manner hereinbefore mentioned, and every such warrant or process, so endorsed, shall be a sufficient authority to the person or persons bringing the same, and to all persons to whom the same respectively was originally directed, and also to all constables and peace officers in the county, district, or jurisdiction within which such warrant or process shall be so endorsed, to execute the same within the county, district, or place where the justice or officer endorsing the same has jurisdiction, and to convey such offender, when apprehended, into the county or district wherein the justice or person who issued such warrant or process shall have jurisdiction and carry him before such justice or person, or before some other justice or person within the same county or district who shall have jurisdiction to commit such offender to prison for trial, and such justice or person may thereupon proceed in such and the same manner as if the said offender had been apprehended within his jurisdiction.
[*as amended by Sch.8 Courts Act 1971*].

COMMENTARY

This section has ben extended by s.126 MCA 1980; see commentary to s.12 1848 Act, *supra*. It is still necessary to use this provision because s.38 CLA 1977, does not apply to territories named herein.

Channel Islands, for the endorsement of warrants in the Channel Islands, see s.18 Criminal Justice Administration Act 1851.

English or Irish warrants may be backed in Scotland 2.33
14. That if any person against whom a warrant shall be issued by any justice of
the peace for any county or place within England or Wales or Ireland, or by any
Judge of Her Majesty's Court of Queen's Bench or the Crown Court in England
or Ireland for any crime or offence against the laws of those parts respectively of
the United Kingdom of Great Britain and Ireland, shall escape, go into, reside,
or be, or be supposed or suspected to be, in any place in Scotland it shall be lawful
for the sheriff or steward depute or substitute, or any justice of the peace of the
county or place where such person or persons shall go into, reside, or be, or be
supposed or suspected to be, to endorse the said warrant in manner hereinbefore mentioned, or to the like effect, which warrant so endorsed shall be a
sufficient authority to the person or persons bringing such warrant, and to all
persons to whom such warrant was originally directed, and also to all sheriffs'
officers, stewards' officers, constables, and other peace officers of the county or
place where such warrant shall be so endorsed, to execute the same within the
county or place where it shall have been so endorsed, by apprehending the
person against whom such warrant shall have been granted, and to convey him
into the county or place in England, Wales or Ireland where the justice or
justices who first issued the said warrant shall have jurisdiction in that behalf,
and to carry him before such justice or justices, or before any other justice or
justices of the peace of and for the same county or place, to be there dealt with
according to law, and which said justice or justices are hereby authorised and
required thereupon to proceed in such and the same manner as if the said
offender had been apprehended within his or their jurisdiction.
[*as amended by Sch.8 Courts Act 1971*]

COMMENTARY
See Commentary to s.12 1848 Act, *supra.*

Ireland, to be construed as referring to Northern Ireland only: s.9 Backing of Warrants
(Republic of Ireland) Act 1965.

Scottish warrants may be backed in England or Ireland 2.34
15. That if any person against whom a warrant shall be issued by the Lord
Justice General, Lord Chief Justice Clerk, or any of the Lords Commissioners of
Justiciary, or by any sheriff or steward depute or substitute, or justice of the
peace, of Scotland, for any crime or offence against the laws of that part of the
United Kingdom, shall escape, go into, reside, or be, or shall be supposed or
suspected to be, in any county or place in England or in Ireland, it shall be lawful
for any justice of the peace in and for the county or place into which such person
shall escape or go, or where he shall reside or be, or shall be supposed or
suspected to be, to endorse the said warrant in manner hereinbefore mentioned,
and which said warrant so endorsed shall be a sufficient authority to the person
or persons bringing the same, and to all persons to whom the same was originally
directed, and also to all constables and other peace officers of the county or place
where the justice so endorsing such warrant shall have jurisdiction, to execute
the said warrant in the county or place where it is so endorsed, by apprehending
the person against whom such warrant shall have been granted, and to convey
him into the county or place in Scotland next adjoining England, and carry him
before the sheriff or steward depute or substitute or one of the justices of the
peace, of such county or place, and which said sheriff, steward, depute or
substitute, or justice of the peace, is hereby authorised and required thereupon
to proceed in such and the same manner according to the rules and practice of the
law of Scotland, as if the said offender had been apprehended within such county
or place in Scotland last aforesaid.

COMMENTARY
See Commentary to s.12 1848 Act, *supra.* By s.32, the town of Berwick upon Tweed is deemed
to be in England.

Ireland, to be construed as referring to Northern Ireland only. s.9 Backing of Warrants
(Republic of Ireland) Act 1965.

2.35 # CRIMINAL JUSTICE ACT 1925

Abolition of presumption of coercion of married women by husband
47. Any presumption of law that an offence committed by a wife in the presence of her husband is committed under the coercion of the husband is hereby abolished, but on a charge against a wife for any offence other than treason or murder it shall be a good defence to prove that the offence was committed in the presence of, and under the coercion of, the husband.

COMMENTARY
See *Husbands and Wives* at 2.28.

2.36 # CHILDREN AND YOUNG PERSONS ACT 1933

Attendance at court of parents of child or young person brought before court
34. (1) Where a child or young person is charged with any offence or is for any other reason brought before a court, any person who is a parent or guardian of his may be required to attend at the court before which the case is heard or determined during all stages of the proceedings, and any such person shall be so required at any stage where the court thinks it desirable, unless the court is satisfied that it would be unreasonable to require his attendance.

(2) Where a child or young person is in police detention, such steps as are practicable shall be taken to ascertain the identity of a person responsible for his welfare.

(3) If it is practicable to ascertain the identity of a person responsible for the welfare of the child or young person, that person shall be informed, unless it is not practicable to do so–
(a) that the child or young person has been arrested;
(b) why he has been arrested; and
(c) where he is being detained.

(4) Where information falls to be given under sub(3) above, it shall be given as soon as it is practicable to do so.

(5) For the purposes of this section the persons who may be responsible for the welfare of a child or young person are–
(a) his parent or guardian; or
(b) any other person who has for the time being assumed responsibility for his welfare.

(6) If it is practicable to give a person responsible for the welfare of the child or young person the information required by subs (3) above, that person shall be given it as soon as it is practicable to do so.

(7) If it appears that at the time of his arrest a supervision order, as defined in s.11 of the Children and Young Persons Act 1969, is in force in respect of him, the person responsible for his supervision shall also be informed as described in subs (3) above as soon as it is reasonably practicable to do so.

(8) The reference to a parent or guardian in subs (5) above is–
(a) in the case of a child or young person in the care of a local authority, a reference to that authority; and
(b) in the case of a child or young person in the care of a voluntary organisation in which parental rights and duties with respect to him are vested by virtue of a resolution under s.64(1) of the Child Care Act 1980, a reference to that organisation.

(9) The rights conferred on a child or young person by subs (2) to (8) above are in addition to his rights under s.56 of the Police and Criminal Evidence Act 1984.

(10) The reference in subs (2) above to a child or young person who is in police detention includes a reference to a child or young person who has been detained under the terrorism provisions and in subs (3) above 'arrest' includes such detention.

(11) In subs (10) above 'the terrorism provisions' has the meaning assigned to it by s.65 of the Police and Criminal Evidence Act 1984.
[as substituted by s.25 CYPA 1963, as amended by Schs 5 and 6, s.57 PACE Act 1984].

COMMENTARY

'Where a child or young person is charged with an offence, or is for any other reason brought before a court, a summons or warrant may be issued by a court to enforce the attendance of a parent or guardian under s.34 CYPA 1933, in the same manner as if an information were laid upon which a summons or warrant could be issued against a defendant under the r,26 MCA 1980, and a summons to the child or young person may include a summons to the parent or guardian to enforce his attendance for the said purpose': r.26 Magistrates' Courts (Children & Young Persons) Rules 1970.

Child, means a person *under the age of 14 years*: s.107(1) CYPA 1933.

Young person, means a person who has *attained the age of 14 years and is under the age of 17 years*: s.107(1) CYPA 1933.

Parent, this term is not defined. It is *suggested* that it is restricted to natural and adoptive parents, whether having legal custody or not and does not apply to step-parents or others having custody. As to adoptive parents, see Sch.1, para 3 Children Act 1975. For children in care, see s.34(8).

Guardian, in relation to a child or young person, 'guardian' includes any person who, in the opinion of the court having cognizance of any case in relation to the child or young person or in which the child or young person is concerned, has for the time being the charge of or control over the child or young person: s.107(1) CYPA 1933. For children in care, see s.34(8).

BACKING OF WARRANTS (REPUBLIC OF IRELAND) ACT 1965

2.37

Endorsement of warrants issued in Republic of Ireland
1.(1) Where–
(a) a warrant has been issued by a judicial authority in the Republic of Ireland (in this Act referred to as the Republic) for the arrest of a person accused or convicted of an offence against the laws of the Republic, being an indictable offence or an offence punishable on summary conviction with imprisonment for six months; and
(b) an application for the endorsement of the warrant is made to a justice of the peace in the United Kingdom by a constable who produces the warrant and states on oath that he has reason to believe the person named or described therein to be within the area for which the justice acts;
then, subject to the provisions of this section, the justice shall endorse the warrant in the prescribed form for execution within the part of the United Kingdom comprising the are a for which he acts.

(2) A warrant for the arrest of a person accused of an offence which under the laws of the Republic is not an indictable offence but is punishable on summary conviction with imprisonment for six months shall not be endorsed under this section unless–
(a) he has failed to appear in answer to a summons issued by or on behalf of a court in the Republic requiring his presence before the court for the trial of the offence and, not less than 14 days before the date named in the summons for his appearance, the summons was served on him personally in the Republic or a notice of the issue of the summons, together with a copy of the summons, was served on him personally in the United Kingdom; or

(b) having entered into a recognizance for his appearance before a court in the Republic for the trial of the offence, he has failed to appear in pursuance of the recognizance; or

(c) having appeared before a court in the Republic for the trial of the offence, he has subsequently failed to appear on any date to which the proceedings were adjourned.

(3) A warrant for the arrest of a person convicted of any offence against the laws of the Republic shall not be endorsed under this section unless the purpose of the arrest is to enable him–

(a) to be brought before a court in the Republic for sentence in respect of the conviction; or

(b) to be taken to a place where he is to undergo imprisonment under such a sentence, not being imprisonment in default of the payment of a fine or other sum.

(4) The endorsement of a warrant under this section by a justice of the peace in any part of the United Kingdom shall be treated for the purposes of any enactment or rule of law relating to warrants of arrest as if it were for the arrest of a person charged with an offence committed in that part.

COMMENTARY

This Act was introduced following the case of *R v Metropolitan Police Commissioner, ex p. Hammond* [1965] AC 810, which disclosed defects in the pre-existing law. It is complemented by Part III Extradition Act 1965, an Act of the Republic of Ireland, as to which see HOC 178/1965; and see generally HOC 240/1965.

The task of the justices is to look first at the warrant and any certificate or affidavit in support of it and to decide whether it comes within s.1(1). If the matter is raised that it is a case within s.1(3), the justices ought to look at the matter and examine it in some detail and with such evidence as may be placed before them, *per* Michael Davies J in *Re Lawlor* (1978) 66 Cr App R 75, at p.79. It is not essential to separate proof of the fact of the prisoner's conviction: it is enough that the warrant is a warrant for the arrest of a person who has been convicted of an offence against the laws of the Republic of Ireland: *R v Governor of Risley Remand Centre, ex p. Marks* [1984] Crim LR 238.

A judicial authority Means a court, judge or justice of a court or peace commissioner: s.10, *infra*.

Republic of Ireland Defined in s.1 Ireland Act, 1949, s.1 Eire (Confirmation of Agreements) Act 1938.

Indictable offence Defined in s.10(1), *infra*.

United Kingdom, ie England and Wales, Scotland or Northern Ireland: s.10(2). It also extends to Jersey and Guernsey: s.12.

Shall endorse Once the matters mentioned in (1) are proved, the magistrate is obliged to endorse the warrant: *Re Arkins* (1966) 130 JP 427.

The prescribed form, see form No 1 Magistrates' Courts (Backing of Warrants) Rules 1965 (SI No 1906).

s.1(2): for evidence by affidavit, see s.7 and r.5, *infra*.

Not less than 14 days before the date, this means at least *14 clear days* exclusive of the day of service and exclusive of the return date: *R v Turner* (1910) 74 JP 81; *Re Hector Whaling Ltd.* [1935] All ER Rep. 302; *Thompson v Stimpson* [1960] 3 All ER 500.

Imprisonment, includes any form of detention: s.10, *infra*.

2.38   **Proceedings before magistrates' court**

2.(1) So soon as is practicable after a person is arrested under a warrant endorsed in accordance with s.1 of this Act, he shall be brought before a magistrates' court and the court shall, subject to the following provisions of this section, order him to be delivered at some convenient point of departure from the United Kingdom into the custody of a member of the police force (Garda Siochana) of the Republic, and remand him until so delivered.

(2) An order shall not be made under subs (1) of this section if it appears to the

court that the offence specified in the warrant does not correspond with any offence under the law of the part of the United Kingdom in which the court acts which is an indictable offence or is punishable on summary conviction with imprisonment for six months; nor shall such an order be made if it is shown to the satisfaction of the court–

(a) that the offence specified in the warrant is an offence of a political character, or an offence under military law which is not also an offence under the general criminal law, or an offence under an enactment relating to taxes, duties or exchange control; or

(b) that there are substantial grounds for believing that the person named or described in the warrant will, if taken to the Republic, be prosecuted or detained for another offence, being an offence of a political character or an offence under military law which is not also an offence under the general criminal law; or

(c) that the warrant is for the arrest of a person accused of an offence committed in Northern Ireland which constitutes an extra-territorial offence under the law of the Republic of Ireland as defined in s.3 of the Criminal Jurisdiction Act 1975; or

(d) that the person named or described in the warrant has been acquitted or convicted in a trial in Northern Ireland for an extra-territorial offence as defined in s.1 of the said Act of 1975 in respect of which the warrant is issued.

(3) In any case where the court does not make an order under subs (1) of this section, the court shall order the person named or described in the warrant to be discharged.

(4) The provisions of the schedule to this Act shall apply in relation to proceedings under this section.
[*as amended by the Sch.3 Criminal Jurisdiction Act, 1975*].

COMMENTARY

s.2(1): A magistrates' court, for composition and powers see schedule, *infra*.

Remand, see s.5 and r.3, *infra*.

Correspond with any offence These words refer to the ingredients of the offence, whether it be murder, grievous bodily harm, child neglect or whatever it may be, and in no sense dealing with the classification of the offence according to whether it is indictable or both summary and indictable or summary only, *per* Lord Parker CJ in *Re Arkins* (1966) 130 JP 427. As to proof of the laws of the Republic, see s.7(b), *infra*.

United Kingdom, see note to s.1, *supra*.

Indictable offence, defined in s.10, *infra*.

s.2(2): In relation to any warrant issued in the Republic of Ireland which specified an offence to which s.1 Suppression of Terrorism Act 1978 applies, being a warrant to which para (c) of subs (3) of that section applies, this section has effect as if at the end of s.2(2) there were added the following words:
'or (e) that there are substantial grounds for believing–
(i) that the warrant was in fact issued in order to secure the return of the person named or described in it to the Republic for the purpose of prosecuting or punishing him on account of his race, religion, nationality or political opinions; or
(ii) that he would, if returned there, be prejudiced at his trial or punished, detained or restricted in his personal liberty by reason of his race, religion, nationality or political opinions.'
Suppression of Terrorism Act 1978.

Offence of a political character The fact that the defendant will be tried by a court set up under the (Irish) Offences Against the State Act 1939 is no acknowledgement that the offence is a political one: *R v Governor of Winson Green Prison, Birmingham, ex p. Littlejohn* [1975] 3 All ER 208. Unless this issue is raised before the justice, it is not a matter upon which fresh or additional evidence is admissible in an application for *habeas corpus: Re Nobbs* [1978] 1 WLR 1302.

In relation to extradition, it has been held that (1) burglaries by members of the Church of Scientology which had not taken place in order to challenge the political control or government of the United States of America but simply to further the interests of the Church and its members were not offences of a political character, (ii) when the offence had not been shown to be of a political character, our courts would not entertain allegations of bad faith on the part of the requesting country: *R v Budlong and Kember* (1980) NLJ 90.

Genocide is not an offence of a political character: s.2(2) Genocide Act 1969.

For the purposes of this Act:

(a) no offence to which this section applies shall be regarded as an offence of a political character; and

(b) no proceedings in respect of an offence to which this section applies shall be regarded as a criminal matter of a political character or as criminal proceedings of a political character.

[s.1(2) Suppression of Terrorism Act 1978].

s.2(2)(b): Another offence This must be an offence already committed or alleged to have been already committed: *Keane v Governor of Brixton Prison* [1972] AC 204.

2.39   **Statement of case by court**

2A.(1) *If the court refuses to make an order in relation to a person under s.2 above, the chief officer of police for the area of the force to which the constable making the application under s.1 above belongs or, if the application is made in Northern Ireland, the chief constable of the Royal Ulster Constabulary may question the proceeding on the ground that it is wrong in law by applying to the court to state a case for the opinion of the High Court on the question of law involved.*

(2) *Where the court refuses to state a case, the High Court may, on the application of the chief officer or chief constable, make an order requiring the court to state a case.*

(3) *The High Court shall have power–*

(a) *to remit the case to the magistrates' court to decide it according to the opinion of the High Court on the question of law; or*

(b) *to dismiss the appeal.*

(4) *In any case where it dismisses the appeal, it shall discharge the person named or described in the warrant.*

(5) *Where an appeal is brought under this section, the court may make an order providing for the detention of the person to whom it relates, or directing that he shall not be released except on bail, which may be granted by the court as under s.4 of the Administration of Justice Act 1960 or para 3 of Sch.1 to the Judicature (Northern Ireland) Act 1978 so long as the appeal is pending.*

(6) *In relation to a decision of a court on an appeal under this section, s.1 of the Administration of Justice Act 1960 or s.41 of the Judicature (Northern Ireland) Act 1978 (right of appeal to House of Lords) shall have effect as if so much of subs (2) as restricts the grant of leave to appeal were omitted.*

(7) *In the application to Scotland of this section–*

(a) *for the references to the chief officer of police or the chief constable of the Royal Ulster Constabulary there shall be substituted references to the procurator fiscal;*

(b) *for the references to the High Court there shall be substituted references to the High Court of Justiciary; and*

(c) *subs (5) and (6) above shall be omitted, but, in relation to an appeal under this section in Scotland, the court may make an order providing for the detention of the person to whom it relates, or may grant bail; and section 446(2) of the Criminal Procedure (Scotland) Act 1975 shall apply for the purpose of such an appeal as it applies for the purpose of an appeal such as is mentioned in section 444 of that Act.*

[*As added by Sch.1, Pt II Criminal Justice Act 1988 from a day to be appointed*].

2.40   **Review of orders of magistrates' courts**

3. (1) Where an order is made by a magistrates' court under s.2(1) of this Act in respect of any person–

(a) he shall not be delivered up under the order until the expiration of the period of 15 days beginning with the date on which the order is made, unless he gives notice in the prescribed manner that he consents to his earlier removal;

(b) if within that period an application is made by him or on his behalf for a writ of habeas corpus *ad subjiciendum* or, in the case of an order made in Scotland, an application for review is made by him under subs (2) of this section, he shall not be so delivered up while proceedings on the application are pending;

and the magistrates' court shall inform him that he will not be delivered up under the order during that said period of 15 days unless he gives notice as aforesaid, and that he has the right to apply for a writ of habeas corpus *ad subjiciendum* or, as the case may be, to make an application for review under subs (2) of this section.

(2) . . .

(3) For the purposes of this section proceedings on an application for a writ of habeas corpus *ad subjiciendum* shall be treated as pending until any appeal in those proceedings is disposed of; and an appeal shall be treated as disposed of at the expiration of the time within which the appeal may be brought or, where leave to appeal is required, within which the application for leave may be made, if not brought or made within that time.

COMMENTARY

Notice in the prescribed manner, to be signed in the presence of a justice or justices' clerk: 2(1) Magistrates Courts (Backing of Warrants) Rules 1965 (SI No 1906).

Provisional warrants

2.41

4. (1) A justice of the peace in the United Kingdom, on the application of a constable who states on oath–

(a) that he has reason to believe that a warrant has been issued by a judicial authority in the Republic for the arrest of a person accused or convicted of an indictable offence against the laws of the Republic, but that the warrant is not yet in his possession; and

(b) that he has received a request made on grounds of urgency by a member of the police force of the Republic holding the rank of inspector or above for the issue in the United Kingdom of a warrant for the arrest of that person; and

(c) that he has reason to believe that person to be within the area for which the justice acts;

may issue a warrant in the prescribed form (in this section referred to as a provisional warrant) for the arrest of that person.

Provided that where the warrant issued in the Republic was for the arrest of a convicted person, a provisional warrant shall not be issued unless the applicant states on oath that he has reason to believe the requirements of s.1(3) of this Act to be satisfied.

(2) A provisional warrant issued in any part of the United Kingdom shall be treated for the purposes of any enactment or rule of law relating to warrants of arrest as if it were a warrant for the arrest of a person charged with an offence committed in that part, but the warrant shall not be authority for the making of an arrest more than five days after the date of issue.

(3) So soon as is practicable after a person is arrested under a provisional warrant he shall be brought before a magistrates' court, and–

(a) if there is produced to the court the warrant issued in respect of him in the Republic, endorsed in accordance with s.1 of this Act, the court shall proceed as if he had been arrested under that warrant;

(b) in any other case the court may remand him for not more than three days.

(4) Where at any time there is produced to a constable having custody of a person remanded under this section the warrant issued in respect of that person in

the Republic, endorsed in accordance with s.1 of this Act, the period of th
remand shall determine, and he shall thereafter be treated as if arrested at tha
time under that warrant.

(5) If the period of a remand under this section is not determined under sub
(4) thereof the person remanded shall be discharged at the end of the period

COMMENTARY

s.4(1): A judicial authority, defined in s.10, *infra*.

Indictable offence, defined in s.10, *infra*.

The prescribed form, see form 3 Magistrates' Courts (Backing of Warrants) Rules 1965 (S
No 1906).

s.4(3): Remand, see s.5 and r.3, *infra*.

.42 **Remand**

5. (1) Where under s.2(1) or s.4(3) of this Act a magistrates' court ha
power to remand a person, the court may–

   (a) remand him in custody, that is to say, commit him for the period of th
remand to prison or, in the case of a remand under s.4(3) of this Act, t
the custody of a constable; or

   (b) remand him on bail in accordance with the Bail Act 1976, that is to sa
direct him to surrender himself into the custody of the officer in charg
of a specified police station at the time to be appointed by that offic
and notified in writing to the person so remanded;

and where his release on bail is conditional on his providing one or more surety
sureties and, in accordance with s.8(3) of that Act, the court fixes the amount
which the surety is to be bound with a view to his entering into his recognizan
subsequently in accordance with subs (4) and (5) or (6) of that section the court sha
in the meantime commit him to the custody of a constable.

(2) The time to be appointed for the purpose of subs (1) above by the offic
and notified to the person so remanded shall not be more than 24 hours befo
the time at which it appears to the officer in charge of the police station that t
period of remand is likely to end.

(3) During the period between the surrender of a person as aforesaid a
the end of the period of remand he shall be treated as if committed to t
custody of a constable, but where it appears to the officer to whom
surrenders that the end of the period of remand will be unexpectedly delaye
the officer shall grant him bail in accordance with the Bail Act 1976 subject t
duty to surrender himself into the custody of the officer in charge of the stati
specified under subs (1) above at the time appointed by that officer and notifi
in writing to him; and subs (2) above shall apply to the appointment of a tir
for the purposes of this subsection as it applies to the appointment of a time f
the purposes of subs (1) above.

(4) If a person fails to surrender as aforesaid, the court by which he w
remanded may issue a warrant in the prescribed form for his arrest; and on
arrest under the warrant subs (3) of this section shall apply as if he h
surrendered to the officer in charge of the police station specified under su
(1) above, but that officer shall not grant him bail as provided by that subs
tion unless he is satisfied that it is proper to do so.

A warrant issued under this subsection in any part of the United Kingd
shall be treated for the purposes of any enactment or rule of law relating
warrants of arrest as if it were a warrant for the arrest of a person charged w
an offence committed in that part.

(5) . . .

[*as amended by Schs.2 and 3 Bail Act 1976*].

COMMENTARY

Commit him . . . to prison Persons *under the age of 21* shall be committed to the institution to which they would be committed if charged with an offence: s.34 CJA 1967, *infra*; as to which institution, see s.27 CJA 1948.

Warrant in the prescribed form, see Form 9. As to where the warrant should be sent, see r.4.

Discharge of persons not taken to Republic   2.43
6. (1) If the person in respect of whom an order has been made by a magistrates' court under s.2(1) of this Act is not delivered up under the order within one month after it was made, a superior court exercising jurisdiction in the part of the United Kingdom within which it was made, upon application by or on behalf of that person, may, unless reasonable cause is shown for the delay, order him to be discharged.

In this subsection 'superior court' means the High Court, the High Court of Justiciary in Scotland or the High Court of Northern Ireland.

(2) If, in the case of a person in respect of whom an order has been made under s.2(1) of this Act, it appears to a justice of the peace acting for the same area as that of the court by which the order was made, or in Scotland to the sheriff, that for any reason the police force of the Republic no longer require the delivery of that person into their custody he shall order him to be discharged.

COMMENTARY

Within one month, ie one calendar month: Sch.1 Interpretation Act 1978. The first day is to be excluded, and the last included: *Goldsmiths' Co v West Metropolitan Rail Co* [1900–03] All ER Rep 667; *Stewart v Chapman* [1951] 2 All ER 613.

Evidence as to matters originating in Republic   2.44
7. For the purposes of this Act–
(a) a document purporting to be a warrant issued by a judicial authority in the Republic or a copy of a summons issued by or on behalf of a court in the Republic, if verified in the prescribed manner, may be taken to be such a warrant or, as the case may be, a copy of such a summons, and the warrant or summons shall be taken to have been duly issued;
(b) evidence with respect to the laws of the Republic may be given by affidavit or other written statement on oath, but a certificate purporting to be issued by or on behalf of the judicial authority in the Republic by whom a warrant was issued, or another judicial authority acting for the same area, and certifying that the offence specified in the warrant can be dealt with under the laws of the Republic in the manner described in the certificate shall be sufficient evidence of matters so certified;
(c) a desposition purporting to have been made in the Republic, or affidavit or written statement purporting to have been sworn therein, may be admitted if verified in the prescribed manner.

COMMENTARY

For the verification of warrants, summonses and depositions under s.7, see r.5, *infra*.

7(b): Evidence, the only evidence required is a statement to the effect that the offence specified in the warrant is an indictable offence under Republic of Ireland law, all other words are surplus and do not affect the validity of the warrant. Surplus words are *only significant* if they alter the nature of the certificate: *Re Hawkins (Francis)* (1987) *The Times*, 1 February.

Interpretation   2.45
10. (1) In this Act–
'imprisonment' includes any form of detention;
'indictable offence' does not include an offence which is triable on indictment only at the instance or with the consent of the accused;
'judicial authority' means a court, judge or justice of a court, or peace commissioner;

'prescribed' means prescribed in accordance with s.8 of this Act;
'the Republic' means the Republic of Ireland.

(2) Subject to s.12(1) of this Act, references in this Act to a part of the
United Kingdom are references to England and Wales, to Scotland, or to
Northern Ireland.

(3) . . .

(4) Any reference in this Act to any other enactment is a reference thereto
as amended, and includes a reference thereto as extended or applied, by or
under any other enactment.

COMMENTARY

s.10(1): Indictable offence This definition would not include an offence triable either way
As such it is *inconsistent* with the definition of this term in Sch.1 Interpretation Act 1978
which can thus have no application to this statute.

2.46   **Application to Channel Islands and Isle of Man**
         12. (1) Subject to the provisions of this section, this Act shall extend to the
         Channel Islands and the Isle of Man (in this section collectively referred to as
         the Islands) and shall have effect as if each of them were a part of the United
         Kingdom.

         (2), (3) (*Orders in Council*).

COMMENTARY

SI 1965 No 1874 (Guernsey), 1875 (Isle of Man), 1876 (Jersey) apply this Act to those areas.

2.47   **SCHEDULE**

Supplementary provisions as to proceedings under s.2
Proceedings in England or Wales
1. Paragraphs 2 to 4 of this Schedule shall apply to proceedings in England
or Wales under s.2 of this Act.

2. The court shall consist of at least two justices and shall sit in open court in
a petty-sessional court-house or an occasional court-house: provided that
s.16(1) of the Justices of the Peace Act 1979 (which exempts stipendiary
magistrates from certain restrictions imposed by the Magistrates' Courts Act
1980) shall apply as if the foregoing provisions of this paragraph were contained in the Magistrates' Courts Act 1980.

3. Subject to para 2 of this Schedule, the court shall have the like powers
including power to adjourn the case and meanwhile to remand the person
arrested under the warrant either in custody or on bail, and the proceedings
shall be conducted as nearly as may be in the like manner, as if the court were
acting as examining justices inquiring into an indictable offence alleged to have
been committed by that person.

4. Without prejudice to the generality of para 3 of this Schedule, s.1 of the
Costs in Criminal Cases Act 1973 (award of costs by examining justices out of
central funds) and s.2 of the Poor Prisoners Defence Act, 1930 (legal aid
before examining justices) shall apply in relation to the proceedings as if the
person arrested under the warrant were charged with an indictable offence or
the prosecution of the constable on whose application the warrant was
endorsed and, where the court discharges that person, as if it had determined
not to commit for trial.

5–10. . . .
[*as amended by s.71 Justices of the Peace Act 1979; s.21(1), Sch.1 Costs in
Criminal Cases Act 1973; s.154, Sch.7 MCA 1980.*]

COMMENTARY

Para 3: The caution required by the MC Rules 1981, is inapt to proceedings under this Act; nor is there any need for any inquiry into whether there is strong or probable presumption of guilt: *Re Arkins* [1966] 3 All ER 651. The words 'in like manner' refer to the manner in which proceedings are to be conducted and not to issues to be tried. The schedule does not provide for any inquiry by the magistrate into the merits of the charges: *Keane v Governor of Brixton Prison* [1971] 2 WLR 1243. It is *suggested* that this phrase does not import the restrictions on publication contained in s.8 MCA 1980.

Para 4: s.2 Poor Prisoners Defence Act 1930, now s.28 LAA 1974.

CRIMINAL JUSTICE ACT 1967   2.48

Committal of persons under 21 accused of extradition crimes, etc.

34. Any person under the age of 21 who apart from this section would be committed to prison under s.10 of the Extradition Act, 1870 (committal of a person alleged to have committed an extradition crime) or s.5(1)(a) of the Backing of Warrants (Republic of Ireland) Act 1965 (remand in custody of a person for whose arrest a warrant has or is alleged to have been issued in the Republic of Ireland) shall be committed to an institution to which he could be committed if he were charged with an offence before the court which commits him, and any reference in those provisions to prison shall be construed accordingly.

COMMENTARY

Under the age of 21 For the determination of age, see s.150(4) MCA 1980.

An institution For the appropriate institutions, see s.27 CJA 1948.

THEFT ACT 1968

Prosecution of husband or wife   2.49

30. (1) This Act shall apply in relation to the parties to a marriage, and to the property belonging to the wife or husband whether or not by reason of an interest derived from the marriage, as it would apply if they were not married and any such interest subsisted independently of the marriage.

(2) Subject to subs (4) below, a person shall have the same right to bring proceedings against that person's wife or husband for any offence (whether under this Act or otherwise) as if they were married, and a person bringing any such proceedings shall be competent to give evidence for the prosecution at every stage of the proceedings.

(3) *(Repealed)*.

(4) Proceedings shall not be instituted against a person for any offence of stealing or doing unlawful damage to property which at the time of the offence belongs to that person's wife or husband, or for any attempt, incitement or conspiracy to commit such an offence, unless the proceedings are instituted by or with the consent of the Director of Public Prosecutions.

Provided that–

(a) this subsection shall not apply to proceedings against a person for an offence–
  (i) if that person is charged with committing the offence jointly with the wife or husband; or
  (ii) if by virtue of any judicial decree or order (wherever made) that person and the wife or husband are at the time of the offence under no obligation to cohabit;

(b) *(Repealed)*.

(5) Notwithstanding s.6 of the Prosecution of Offences Act 1979 subs (4) of this section shall apply–
   (a) to an arrest (if without warrant) made by the wife or husband, and
   (b) to a warrant of arrest issued on an information laid by the wife or husband.
[*as amended by Sch.5 Criminal Jurisdiction Act 1975, Sch.1 POA 1979, Sch.7 PACE Act 1984*].

COMMENTARY
See under *Husbands and Wives* 2.28.

CHILDREN AND YOUNG PERSONS ACT 1969

2.50   **Restrictions on criminal proceedings for offences by young persons**
   5. (1)–(7) (*Not yet in force*).

(8) It shall be the duty of a person who decides to lay an information in respect of an offence in a case where he has reason to believe that the alleged offender is a young person to give notice of the decision to the appropriate local authority unless he is himself that authority.

(9) In this section–

'the appropriate local authority', in relation to a young person, means the local authority for the area in which it appears to the informant in question that the young person resides or, if the young person appears to the informant not to reside in the area of a local authority, the local authority in whose area it is alleged that the relevant offence or one of the relevant offences was committed. . .

COMMENTARY
Young person, includes a child who has attained the age of 10 years: SI 1970 No 1882.

Resides, means 'habitually resides': s.70.

2.51   **Transitional modifications of Part I for persons of specified ages**
   34. (1) . . .

(2) In the case of a person who has not attained the age of 17 but has attained such lower age as the Secretary of State may by order specify, no proceedings under s.1 of this Act or for an offence shall be begun in any court unless the person proposing to begin the proceedings has, in addition to any notice falling to be given by him to a local authority in pursuance of s.2(3) or 5(8) of this Act, given notice of the proceedings to a probation officer for the area for which the court acts: and accordingly in the case of such a person the reference in s.1(1) of this Act to the said s.2(3) shall be construed as including a reference to this subsection.
[*as amended by Sch.12 CLA 1977, Sch.16 CJA 1982*].

COMMENTARY
Such lower age, the *age of 13* has been specified in SI 1970 No 1882, as amended by SI 1973 No 485, SI 1974 No 1083, SI 1977 No 240, SI 1979 No 125 and SI 1981 No 81.

CRIMINAL LAW ACT 1977

2.52   **Execution throughout United Kingdom of warrants of arrest**
   38. (1) A warrant issued in Scotland or Northern Ireland for the arrest of a person charged with an offence may be executed in England or Wales by any constable acting within his police area; and subs (3) of s.125 of the Magistrates' Courts Act 1980 (execution without possession of the warrant) shall apply to the execution in England or Wales of any such warrant.

(2) A warrant issued in England, Wales or Northern Ireland for the arrest of a person charged with an offence may be executed in Scotland by any constable

appointed for a police area in the like manner as any such warrant issued in Scotland.

(3) A warrant issued in England, Wales or Scotland for the arrest of a person charged with an offence may be executed in Northern Ireland by any member of the Royal Ulster Constabulary or the Royal Ulster Constabulary Reserve; and para (4) and (5) of Art 158 of the Magistrates' Courts (Northern Ireland) Order 1981 (execution without possession of the warrant and execution on Sunday) shall apply to the execution in Northern Ireland of any such warrant.

(4) A warrant may be executed by virtue of this section whether or not it has been endorsed under ss.12, 14 or 15 of the Indictable Offences Act 1848 or under ss.27, 28 and 29 of the Petty Sessions (Ireland) Act 1851.

(5) Nothing in this section affects the execution in Scotland or Northern Ireland of a warrant to which s.123 of the Bankruptcy Act 1914 applies.
[*as amended by Sch.7 MCA 1980, Magistrates' Courts (Northern Ireland) Order 1981*].

COMMENTARY
The effects of this section are described in HOC 44/1980.

s.38(2): **Charged with an offence.** These words distinguish between civil and criminal cases. A warrant for the arrest of a convicted person for the purpose of passing sentence is a warrant for the arrest of a person 'charged with an offence': *cf Evans v Macklen* [1976] Crim LR 120.

Service of Summonses and citation throughout United Kingdom   2.53
39. (1) A summons requiring a person charged with an offence to appear before a court in England and Wales may, in such manner as may be prescribed by rules of court, be served on him in Scotland or Northern Ireland.

(2) A summons requiring a person charged with an offence to appear before a court in Northern Ireland may, in such manner as may be prescribed by rules of court, be served on him in England, Wales or Scotland.

(3) Citation of a person charged with a crime or offence to appear before a court in Scotland may be effected in any other part of the United Kingdom in like manner as it may be done in Scotland, and for this purpose the persons authorised to effect such citation shall include (a) in England and Wales and Northern Ireland, constables and prison officers serving in those parts of the United Kingdom (b) persons authorised by a chief officer of police in England or Wales to serve summonses there.
[*as amended by Sch.7 Criminal Justice (Scotland) Act 1980*].

COMMENTARY
The effects of this section are described in HOC 44/1980 and 105/1980. The latter contains details of the procedure which has been agreed with the Northern Ireland court service for personal service of a non-police summons in Northern Ireland.

MAGISTRATES' COURTS ACT 1980   2.54

Issue of summons to accused or warrant for his arrest
1. (1) Upon an information being laid before a justice of the peace for an area to which this section applies that any person has, or is suspected of having committed an offence, the justice may, in any of the events mentioned in subs (2) below, but subject to subs (3) to (5) below–
    (a) issue a summons directed to that person requiring him to appear before a magistrates' court for the area to answer to the information, or
    (b) issue a warrant to arrest that person and bring him before a magistrates' court for the area or such magistrates' court as is provided in subs (5) below.

(2) A justice of the peace for an area to which this section applies may issue a summons or warrant under this section–

(a) if the offence was committed or is suspected to have been committed within the area, or

(b) if it appears to the justice necessary or expedient, with a view to the better administration of justice, that the person charged should be tried jointly with, or in the same place as, some other person who is charged with an offence, and who is in custody, or is being or is to be proceeded against, within the area, or

(c) if the person charged resides or is, or is believed to reside or be, within the area, or

(d) if under any enactment a magistrates' court for the area has jurisdiction to try the offence, or

(e) if the offence was committed outside England and Wales and, where it is an offence exclusively punishable on summary conviction, if a magistrates' court for the area would have jurisdiction to try the offence if the offender were before it.

(3) No warrant shall be issued under this section unless the information is in writing and substantiated on oath.

(4) No warrant shall be issued under this section for the arrest of any person who has attained the age of 17 unless–

(a) the offence to which the warrant relates is an indictable offence or is punishable with imprisonment, or

(b) the person's address is not sufficiently established for a summons to be served on him.

(5) Where the offence charged is not an indictable offence–

(a) no summons shall be issued by virtue only of para (c) of subs (2) above, and

(b) any warrant issued by virtue only of that paragraph shall require the person charged to be brought before a magistrate's court having jurisdiction to try the offence.

(6) Where the offence charged is an indictable offence, a warrant under this section may be issued at any time notwithstanding that a summons has previously been issued.

(7) A justice of the peace may issue a summons or warrant under this section upon an information being laid before him notwithstanding any enactment requiring the information to be laid before two or more justices.

(8) The areas to which this section applies are any county, any London commission area and the City of London.

COMMENTARY

s.1(1): Information, see under *The Information* 2.07.

Laid before a justice. Informations, other than those substantiated on oath, may be laid before a clerk to justices who may issue any summons thereon: Justices' Clerks Rules 1970, (SI No 231). In exercising this power the clerk is acting as a justice and may refuse as well as grant: *R v Worthing Justices, ex p. Norvell* [1981] 1 WLR 413. As to what constitutes the *Laying of an Information*, see under that title at 2.08.

A summons was held to be invalid where it was considered by two justices and signed by a third who had not considered the complaint: *Dixon v Wells* (1890) LR 25 QB 249. When a summons is granted by a justice it may be signed by him or authenticated by a justices' clerk: r.98(1) MC Rules 1981. It is the duty of the clerk to see that any necessary formalities are in order, *per* Dibben J in *Price v Humphries* [1958] 3 WLR 304.

Any person includes a body corporate and incorporate Sch.1 Interpretation Act 1978.

Offence, an Act prohibited on pain of an excise penalty is not an offence *Brown v Allweather Mechanical Grouting Co Ltd* [1953] 2 WLR 402, but see now s.156(2) Customs and Excise Management Act 1979. Non-compliance with an abatement notice under the Public Health Act 1936 constitutes an offence: *Northern Ireland Trailers Ltd v County Borough of Preston* [1972] 1 All ER 260.

Issue a summons, see *Summonses* 2.10.

Issue a warrant, see *Warrants* 2.16.

s.1(2): If it appears to the justice necessary or expedient, ie to the justice issuing the warrant, not the justice hearing the case: *Turf Publishers Ltd v Davies* [1927] WN 190.

s.1(2)(b): A receiver may thus be charged along with the thief: *R v Blandford; R v Freestone* [1955] 1 WLR 331.

s.1(2)(c): Resides 'A person resides where he lives, where he has his bed and where he dwells.' It includes the place where one works provided the work is not merely temporary: *Stoke-on-Trent Borough Council v Cheshire County Council* (1915) 79 JP 452; *South Shields Corporation v Liverpool Corporation* (1943) 107 JP 77. '"To reside" is a somewhat elegant expression for what used to be called "to live",' *per* Cockburn CJ in *R v St. Leonards* (1865) 29 JP 728. It is essentially a question of fact, *per* Lord Buckmaster in *IRC v Lysaght* [1928] All ER Rep 575, at p.582. To constitute *constructive residence* there must be both an intention to return and a place to return to: *R v Guardians of Glossop Union* (1886) 30 JP 215 (a pauper case). It may include residence in an institution: *Worcestershire County Council v Warwickshire County Council* (1934) 98 JP 347.

The House of Lords, in a taxation case, has expressed the view that a man may have two homes, one abroad and one in the United Kingdom, but if he is a wanderer spending most of his time in hotels then it is a question of *fact and of degree* which must be determined on the circumstances of the case: *Leven v IRC* [1928] All ER Rep 746; and see *Langford Property Co Ltd v Athamassoglou* [1948] 2 All ER 722.

Is, or is believed to . . . be. A person does not 'happen to be' at a place to which he comes in response to a summons: *Johnson v Colam* (1875) 40 JP 135. In *R v Hitchin Justices, ex p. Hilton* (1975) 139 JP 252, similar words in the Transport Act 1968 were held to relate to the point at which the proceedings were commenced.

s.(2)(e), see HOC 162/1971.

s.1(3): Substantiated on oath. Not necessarily by the original informant.

s.1(4): Indictable offence, means an offence which, if committed by an adult, is triable on indictment, whether it is exclusively so triable or triable either way: s.5, Sch.1 Interpretation Act 1978.

s.1(7): it is *suggested* that the effect of this subsection, when read with s.11 MCA 1980, is to allow a court to issue a warrant under s.1 for an indictable offence prior to the return date of a summons already granted, and not, impliedly, to preclude the grant of a warrant for a non-indictable offence after the return date of a summons previously issued.

Jurisdiction to deal with charges   2.55

2. (1) A magistrates' court for a county, a London commission area or the City of London shall have jurisdiction to try all summary offences committed within the county, the London commission area or the City (as the case may be).

(2) Where a person charged with a summary offence appears or is brought before a magistrates' court in answer to a summons issued under para (b) of s.1(2) above, or under a warrant issued under that paragraph, the court shall have jurisdiction to try the offence.

(3) A magistrates' court for a county, a London commission area or the City of London shall have jurisdiction as examining justices over any offence committed by a person who appears or is brought before the court, whether or not the offence was committed within the county, the London commission area or the City (as the case may be).

(4) Subject to ss.18 to 22 below and any other enactment (wherever contained) relating to the mode of trial of offences triable either way, a magistrates' court shall have jurisdiction to try summarily an offence triable either way in any case in which under subs (3) above it would have jurisdiction as examining justices.

(5) A magistrates' court shall, in the exercise of its powers under s.24 below, have jurisdiction to try summarily an indictable offence in any case in which under subs (3) above it would have jurisdiction as examining justices.

(6) A magistrates' court for any area by which a person is tried for an offence

shall have jurisdiction to try him for any summary offence for which he could be tried by a magistrates' court for any other area.

(7) Nothing in this section shall affect any jurisdiction over offences conferred on a magistrates' court by any enactment not contained in this Act.

COMMENTARY

It is a principle engrained in our law that jurisdiction cannot be conferred by consent, *per* Davey LJ in *Farquharson v Morgan* (1894) 58 JP 495 (a civil case).

s.2(1): Summary offence. This means an offence which, if committed by an adult, is triable only summarily: s.5, Sch.1 Interpretation Act 1978.

Committed within the county. Jurisdiction is not, therefore, confined to the petty sessional division: *R v Beacontree JJ* [1914–15] All ER 1180. The Isles of Scilly form part of the county of Cornwall: s.149, *infra*.

s.2(3): for the extent of the court's indictable jurisdiction see *Territorial Jurisdiction* 2.20.

s.2(4): An offence triable either way, means an offence which, if committed by an adult, is triable either on indictment or summarily: s.5, Sch.1 Interpretation Act 1978.

s.2(5): Indictable offence, means an offence which, if committed by an adult, is triable on indictment, whether it is exclusively so triable or triable either way: s.5, Sch.1 Interpretation Act 1978.

2.56   **Offences committed on boundaries, etc**
     3. (1) Where an offence has been committed on the boundary between two or more areas to which this section applies, or within 500 yards of such a boundary, or in any harbour, river, arm of the sea or other water lying between two or more such areas, the offence may be treated for the purposes of the preceding provisions of this Act as having been committed in any of those areas.

(2) An offence begun in one area to which this section applies and completed in another may be treated for the purposes of the preceding provisions of this Act as having been wholly committed in either.

(3) Where an offence has been committed on any person, or on or in respect of any property, in or on a vehicle or vessel engaged on any journey or voyage through two or more areas to which this section applies, the offence may be treated for the purposes of the preceding provisions of this Act as having been committed in any of those areas; and where the side or any part of a road or any water along which the vehicle or vessel passed in the course of the journey or voyage forms the boundary between two or more areas to which this section applies, the offence may be treated for the purposes of the preceding provisions of this Act as having been committed in any of those areas.

(4) The areas to which this section applies are any county, any London commission area and the City of London.

COMMENTARY

s.3(1): Five hundred yards, ie measured in a straight line on a horizontal plane: s.8 Interpretation Act 1978, *Stokes v Grissell* (1854) 18 JP 378.

s.13(2): Begun in one county Normally an offence takes place where it is completed: *Athersmith v Dewry* (1858) 22 JP 735. But, by the operation of this section, a letter seeking to obtain money by false pretences, posted in one jurisdiction and delivered in another, may be the subject of a prosecution in either: *R v Leech* (1856) 20 JP 278. The offence of exacting an excessive cab fare, however, is committed where the fare is exacted, although the journey may have begun in another jurisdiction: *Ely v Godfrey* (1922) 86 JP 82. The offence of forwarding cattle into a prohibited area is committed only in the latter area: *Midland Rail Co v Freeman* (1884) 48 JP 660.

s.13(3): In or on a vehicle Not the mere unlawful use of the vehicle: *Wardhaugh (AF) Ltd v Mace* (1952) 116 JP 360.

2.57   **Proceedings invalid where accused did not know of them**
     14. (1) Where a summons has been issued under s.1 above and a magistrates'

court has begun to try the information to which the summons relates, then if–
  (a) the accused, at any time during or after the trial, makes a statutory declaration that he did not know of the summons or the proceedings until a date specified in the declaration, being a date after the court has begun to try information; and
  (b) within 21 days of that date the declaration is served on the clerk to the justices,
without prejudice to the validity of the information, the summons and all subsequent proceedings shall be void.

(2) For the purposes of subs (1) above a statutory declaration shall be deemed to be duly served on the clerk to the justices if it is delivered to him, or left at his office, or is sent in a registered letter or the recorded delivery service addressed to him at his office.

(3) If on the application of the accused it appears to a magistrates' court (which for this purpose may be composed of a single justice) that it was not reasonable to expect the accused to serve such a statutory declaration as is mentioned in subs (1) above within the period allowed by that subsection, the court may accept service of such a declaration by the accused after that period has expired; and a statutory declaration accepted under this subsection shall be deemed to have been served as required by that subsection.

(4) Where any proceedings have become void by virtue of subs.(1) above, the information shall not be tried again by any of the same justices.

COMMENTARY

s.14(1): Statutory declaration This means a declaration made by virtue of the Statutory Declarations Act 1835: Sch.1 Interpretation Act 1978. This procedure is to be used, where applicable, in preference to *certiorari*, which will not normally be granted in such a case: *R v Brighton Justices, ex p. Robinson* [1973] 1 WLR 69.

Within 21 days, the date specified is to be excluded and the 21st day included: *Goldsmiths Co. v Metropolitan Rail Co.* (1904) 68 JP 41; *Steward v Chapman* (1951) 115 JP 473. *Note* that time runs from the date mentioned in the declaration, not the date of conviction; see also s.14(3).

Served on the clerk, who must note it in the register and inform the prosecutor or in the case of a private prosecutor the chief officer of police: r.20 MC Rules 1981.

Without prejudice, this allows a second summons to be issued on the original information without the necessity for a further information which might be out of time; and *cf R v Clerkenwell Magistrates' Court ex p. Ewing; Ewing v Clark* (1987), *The Times*, 3 June.

s.14(3), a justices' clerk may perform this function of a single justice: (Justices' Clerks Rules 1970, SI No 231).

Aiders and abettors   2.58

44. (1) A person who aids, abets, counsels or procures the commission by another person of a summary offence shall be guilty of the like offence and may be tried (whether or not he is charged as a principal) either by a court having jurisdiction to try that other person or by a court having by virtue of his own offence jurisdiction to try him.

(2) Any offence consisting in aiding, abetting, counselling or procuring the commission of an offence triable either way (other than an offence listed in Sch.1 of this Act) shall by virtue of this subsection be triable either way.

COMMENTARY

See generally *Accomplices* 2.27.

Aids, abets, counsels or procures These words may properly be used conjunctively ('aids abets, counsels *and* procures') 'to charge a person who is alleged to have participated in an offence otherwise than as a principal in the first degree': *Ex p. Smith* (1858) 22 JP 45; *Ferguson v Weaving* [1951] 1 All ER 412. The words '*aid and abet*' refer to principals in the second degree. The words '*counsel and procure*' refer to accessories before the fact as they were formerly called. The word '*procure*' means to produce by endeavour, thus there may be a procuring of a crime by another even though there is no sort of conspiracy or even discussion between the two: *Attorney General's Reference (No 1 of 1975)* [1975] QB 773 (laced drink).

A summary offence, defined in Sch.1 Interpretation Act 1978 as meaning an offence which, if committed by an adult, is triable only summarily.

Guilty of the like offence and subject to the same penalties. This section, like s.8 Accessories and Abettors Act 1861, is declaratory of the common law at which there was no distinction between the principal and accessory in misdemeanour. Thus the fact that a defendant was an accomplice other than a principal in the first degree does not prevent him from being convicted as such: *Stacey v Whitehurst* (1865) 29 JP 136: *Du Cros v Lambourne* [1907] 1 KB 40. S.1 CLA 1967 assimilated the law of felony to that of misdemeanour and the same rules now apply to all offences.

s.44(2): Offence triable either way, defined in Sch.1 Interpretation Act 1978 as an offence which, if committed by an adult, is triable either on indictment or summarily.

2.59   **Incitement**
            45. (1) Any offence consisting in the incitement to commit a summary offence shall be triable only summarily.

            (2) Subsection (1) above is without prejudice to any other enactment by virtue of which any offence is triable only summarily.

            (3) On conviction of an offence consisting in the incitement to commit such a summary offence a person shall be liable to the same penalties as he would be liable to on conviction of the last-mentioned offence.

2.60   **Service of summons out of time after failure to prove service by post**
            47. Where any enactment requires, expressly or by implication, that a summons in respect of an offence shall be issued or served within a specified period after the commission of the offence, and service of the summons may under the rules be effected by post, then, if under the rules service of the summons is not treated as proved, but it is shown that a letter containing the summons was posted at such time as to enable it to be delivered in the ordinary course of post within that period, a second summons may be issued on the same information; and the enactment shall have effect, in relation to that summons, as if the specified period were a period running from the return of the original summons.

            COMMENTARY
            Any enactment, for example, s.179 RTA 1972.

2.61   **Construction of references to complaint in enactments dealing with offences**
            50. In any enactment conferring power on a magistrates' court to deal with an offence, or to issue a summons or warrant against a person suspected of an offence, on the complaint of any person, for references to a complaint there shall be substituted references to an information.

            COMMENTARY
            This provision standardised nomenclature so as to confine the term 'complaint' to civil and the term 'information' to criminal proceedings. It does not affect the substantive law by converting a ground for civil complaint into an offence: *R v Nottingham Justices, ex p. Brown* [1960] 3 All ER 625 (dangerous dog); see also *Northern Ireland Trailers Ltd v County Borough of Preston* [1972] 1 All ER 260.

2.62   **False statements in declaration proving service, etc**
            107. If, in any solemn declaration, certificate or other writing made or given for the purpose of its being used in pursuance of the rules as evidence of the service of any document or the handwriting or seal of any person, a person makes a statement that he knows to be false in a material particular, or recklessly makes any statement that is false in a material particular, he shall be liable on summary conviction to imprisonment for a term not exceeding six months or a fine not exceeding level 3 on the standard scale or both.
            [*as amended by ss.38, 46 CJA 1982*].

Warrant endorsed for bail **2.63**

117. (1) A justice of the peace on issuing a warrant for the arrest of any person may grant him bail endorsing the warrant for bail, that is to say, by endorsing the warrant with a direction in accordance with subs (2) below.

(2) A direction for bail endorsed on a warrant under subs (1) above shall–
(a) in the case of bail in criminal proceedings, state that the person arrested is to be released on bail subject to a duty to appear before such magistrates' court and at such time as may be specified in the endorsement.
(b) in the case of bail otherwise than in criminal proceedings, state that the person arrested is to be released on bail on his entering into such a recognizance (with or without sureties) conditioned for his appearance before a magistrates' court as may be specified in the endorsement;
and the endorsement shall fix the amounts in which sureties and, in the case falling within para (b) above, that person is or are to be bound.

(3) Where a warrant has been endorsed for bail under subs (1) above–
(a) where the person arrested is to be released on bail on his entering into a recognizance without sureties, it shall not be necessary to take him to a police station, but if he is so taken, he shall be released from custody on his entering into the recognizance; and
(b) where he is to be released on his entering into a recognizance with sureties, he shall be taken to a police station on his arrest, and the custody officer there shall (subject to his approving any surety tendered in compliance with the endorsement) release him from custody as directed in the endorsement.
[*as amended by s.47 PACE Act 1984.*]

COMMENTARY

The general right to bail (s.4 Bail Act 1976) does not aply to endorsement of warrants.

s.117(1): A warrant for the arrest of any person Thus if a warrant is merely for the arrest of 'persons hunting, resorting and playing' in premises it is not a warrant for the arrest of a named person to which this section applies: *Coughtry v Porter* (1950) 114 JP 129 (which dealt with a warrant under the Gaming Act 1845, now replaced by s.51 Betting, Gaming and Lotteries Act 1963); see also r.96 MC Rules 1981.

Endorsing A separate document to the warrant is not endorsement: *R v Metropolitan Police Commissioner, ex p. Melia* [1958] 1 WLR 1065.

s.117(2): Released on bail For the conditions of bail, see s.3 Bail Act 1976.

Process valid notwithstanding death, etc of justice **2.64**

124. A warrant or summons issued by a justice of the peace shall not cease to have effect by reason of his death or his ceasing to be a justice.

Warrants **2.65**

125. (1) A warrant of arrest issued by a justice of the peace shall remain in force until it is executed or withdrawn.

(2) A warrant of arrest, warrant of commitment, warrant of distress or search warrant issued by a justice of the peace may be executed anywhere in England and Wales by any person to whom it is directed or by any constable acting within his police area.

A warrant of arrest, warrant of commitment or warrant of distress which is issued by a justice of the peace for the enforcement of a fine may also be executed by a person who–
(a) is employed by an authority of a prescribed class;
(b) is authorised in the prescribed manner to execute such warrants; and
(c) is acting within the area for which the authority that employs him performs its functions.
This subsection does not apply to a warrant of commitment or a warrant of distress issued under Part VI of the General Rate Act 1967.

(3) A warrant to which this subsection applies may be executed by a constabl notwithstanding that it is not in his possession at the time; but the warrant shall, o the demand of the person arrested, be shown to him as soon as practicable.

(4) The warrants to which subs (3) above applies are–
(a) a warrant to arrest a person in connection with an offence;
    (b) without prejudice to paragraph (a) above, a warrant under s.186(3) o the Army Act 1955, s.186(3) of the Air Force Act 1955, s.105(3) of th Naval Discipline Act 1957 or Sch.5 to the Reserve Forces Act 198 (desertion etc.);
(c) a warrant under–
    (i) s.102 or 104 of the General Rate Act 1967 (insufficiency of distress)
    (ii) s.18(4) of the Domestic Proceedings and Magistrates' Courts Ac 1978 (protection of parties to marriage and children of family) and
    (iii) ss.55, 76, 93 or 97 above.

[*as amended by s.33 PACE Act 1984. The words in italics in subs (2) will be added by [s.64] CJA 1988 from a date to be appointed*].

COMMENTARY

s.125(2): Constable, ie a police officer of any rank.

The paragraph in italics will be inserted by s.59 Criminal Justice Act 1988 when that sectio comes into force.

Police area, defined in s.62 and Sch.8 Police Act 1964.

2.66   **Execution of certain warrants outside England and Wales**
126. Sections 12 to 14 of the Indictable Offences Act 1848 (which relate among other things, to the execution in Scotland, Northern Ireland, the Isle o Man and the Channel Islands of warrants of arrest for the offences referred to in those sections) shall, so far as applicable, apply to–
(a) warrants of arrest under s.1 above for offences other than those referred to in the said ss.12 to 14;
(b) warrants of arrest issued under s.13 above;
(c) warrants of arrest issued under s.97 above other than warrants issued in bastardy proceedings to arrest a witness; and
(d) warrants of commitment issued under this Act.

2.67   **Limitation of time**
127. (1) Except as otherwise expressly provided by any enactment and subject to subs (2) below, a magistrates' court shall not try an information or hear a complaint unless the information was laid, or the complaint made, within six months from the time when the offence was committed or the matter of complaint arose.

(2) Nothing in–
(a) subs (1) above; or
(b) subject to subs (4) below, any other enactment (however framed or worded) which, as regards any offence to which it applies, would but for this section impose a time-limit on the power of a magistrates' court to try an information summarily or impose a limitation on the time for taking summary proceedings,
shall apply in relation to any indictable offence.

(3) Without prejudice to the generality of para (b) of subs (2) above, that paragraph includes enactments which impose a time-limit that applies only in certain circumstances (for example, where the proceedings are not instituted by or with the consent of the Director of Public Prosecutions or some other specified authority).

(4) Where, as regards any indictable offence, there is imposed by any enactment (however framed or worded, and whether falling within subs (2)(b)

above or not) a limitation on the time for taking proceedings on indictment for that offence no summary proceedings for that offence shall be taken after the latest time for taking proceedings on indictment.

COMMENTARY

See generally *Limitation of Time* 2.23.

While this section may bar an information laid against a third party outside the time limit under a statutory third party procedure it does not prevent the original defendant from invoking that procedure: *R v Bicester Justices, ex p. Unigate Ltd* [1975] 1 WLR 207.

s.127(1): Try an information This does not apply to the preferment of a charge under para 4 Part IV of Sch.4 to RTA 1972: *R v Coventry Justices, ex p. Sayers* [1979] RTR 22.

Six months, ie calendar months: Sch.1 Interpretation Act 1978.

The information was laid, see *Laying the Information* 2.08.

s.127(2): Indictable offence, see the note to s.2(5), *supra.*

Isles of Scilly	**2.68**

149. For the purposes of this Act the Isles of Scilly form part of the county of Cornwall.

[The next paragraph is 2.70]

CRIMINAL ATTEMPTS ACT 1981

Application of procedural and other provisions to offences under s.1   **2.70**
2. (1) Any provision to which this section applies shall have effect with respect to the offence attempted.

(2) This section applies to provisions of any of the following descriptions made by or under any enactment (whenever passed)–
  (a) provisions whereby proceedings may not be instituted or carried on other-wise than by, or on behalf or with the consent of, any person (including any provisions which also make other exceptions to the prohibition);
  (b) provisions conferring power too institute proceedings;
  (c) provisions as to the venue of proceedings;
  (d) provisions whereby proceedings may not be instituted after the expi-ration of a time limit;
  (e) provisions conferring a power of arrest or search;
  (f) provisions conferring a power of seizure and detention of property;
  (g) provisions whereby a person may not be convicted or committed for trial on the uncorroborated evidence of one witness (including any provision requiring the evidence of not less than two credible witnesses);
  (h) provisions conferring a power of forfeiture, including any power to deal with anything liable to be forfeited;
  (i) provisions whereby, if an offence committed by a body corporate is proved to have been committed with the consent or connivance of another person, that person also is guilty of the offence.

COMMENTARY

Offences under s.1 ie attempts to commit offences, the procedural provisions of s.2 have *not been applied* to other offences of attempt created specially by other statutes, and now governed by s.3 of the Act in that, for *substantive law* purposes, they are assimilated with attempts under s.1.

Trial and penalties   **2.71**
4. (1) A person guilty by virtue of s.1 above of attempting to commit an offence shall–
  (a) if the offence attempted is murder or any other offence the sentence for which is fixed by law, be liable on conviction on indictment to imprison-ment for life; and

(b) if the offence attempted is indictable but does not fall within para (a) above, be liable on conviction on indictment to any penalty to which he would have been liable on conviction on indictment of that offence; and

(c) if the offence attempted is triable either way, be liable on summary conviction to any penalty to which he would have been liable on summary conviction of that offence.

(2) In any case in which a court may proceed to summary trial of an information charging a person with an offence and an information charging him with an offence under s.1 above of attempting to commit it or an attempt under a special statutory provision, the court may, without his consent, try the informations together.

(3) Where, in proceedings against a person for an offence under s.1 above, there is evidence sufficient in law to support a finding that he did an act falling within subs (1) of that section the question whether or not his act fell within that subsection is a question of fact.

(4) Where, in proceedings against a person for an attempt under a special statutory provision, there is evidence sufficient in law to support a finding that he did an act falling within subs (3) of s.3 above, the question whether or not his act fell within that subsection is a question of fact.

(5) Subsection (1) above shall have effect–

(a) subject to s.37 of Sch.2 to the Sexual Offences Act 1956 (mode of trial of and penalties for attempts to commit certain offences under that Act); and

(b) notwithstanding anything–

(i) in s.32(1) (no limit to fine on conviction on indictment) of the Criminal Law Act 1977; or

(ii) in s.31(1) and (2) (maximum of six months' imprisonment on summary conviction unless express provision made to the contrary) of the Magistrates' Courts Act 1980.

COMMENTARY

s.4(1): An attempt to commit an offence triable either way is by virtue of this subsection triable and punishable in the same way as the substantive offence and itself an offence triable either way.

s.4(3): an act falling within subs 1, ie an act which is 'more than merely preparatory', s.4(3) making clear that this is a question of fact.

s.4(4): an act falling within subs 3 of s.3, ie an act which is 'more than merely preparatory', s.4(4) making clear that this is a question of fact.

PROSECUTION OF OFFENCES ACT 1985

PART I

2.72   **Constitution and functions of Service**

1. (1) There shall be a prosecuting service for England and Wales (to be known as the 'Crown Prosecution Service') consisting of–

(a) the Director of Public Prosecutions, who shall be head of the Service;

(b) the Chief Crown Prosecutors, designated under subs (4) below, each of whom shall be the member of the Service responsible to the Director for supervising the operation of the Service in his area; and

(c) the other staff appointed by the Director under this section.

(2) The Director shall appoint such staff for the Service as, with the approval of the Treasury as to numbers, remuneration and other terms and conditions of service, he considers necessary for the discharge of his functions.

(3) The Director may designate any member of the Service who is a barrister or solicitor for the purposes of this subsection, and any person so designated shall be known as a Crown Prosecutor.

(4) The Director shall divide England and Wales into areas and, for each of those areas, designate a Crown Prosecutor for the purposes of this subsection and any person so designated shall be known as a Chief Crown Prosecutor.

(5) The Director may, from time to time, vary the division of England and Wales made for the purposes of subs (4) above.

(6) Without prejudice to any functions which may have been assigned to him in his capacity as a member of the Service, every Crown Prosecutor shall have all the powers of the Director as to the institution and conduct of proceedings but shall exercise those powers under the direction of the Director.

(7) Where any enactment (whenever passed)–
(a) prevents any step from being taken without the consent of the Director or without his consent or the consent of another; or
(b) requires any step to be taken by or in relation to the Director;
any consent given by or, as the case may be, step taken by or in relation to, a Crown Prosecutor shall be treated, for the purposes of that enactment, as given by or, as the case may be, taken by or in relation to the Director.

The Director of Public Prosecutions   **2.73**
2. (1) The Director of Public Prosecutions shall be appointed by the Attorney General.

(2) The Director must be a barrister or solicitor of not less than ten years' standing.

(3) There shall be paid to the Director such remuneration as the Attorney General may, with the approval of the Treasury, determine.

Functions of the Director   **2.74**
3. (1) The Director shall discharge his functions under this or any other enactment under the superintendence of the Attorney General.

(2) It shall be the duty of the Director, subject to any provisions contained in the Criminal Justice Act 1987–
(a) to take over the conduct of all criminal proceedings, other than specified proceedings, instituted on behalf of a police force (whether by a member of that force or by any other person);
(b) to institute and have the conduct of criminal proceedings in any case where it appears to him that–
  (i) the importance or difficulty of the case makes it appropriate that proceedings should be instituted by him; or
  (ii) it is otherwise appropriate for proceedings to be instituted by him;
(c) to take over the conduct of all binding over proceedings instituted on behalf of a police force (whether by a member of that force or by any other person);
(d) to take over the conduct of all proceedings begun by summons issued under s.3 of the Obscene publications Act 1959 (forfeiture of obscene articles);
(e) to give, to such extent as he considers appropriate, advice to police forces on all matters relating to criminal offences;
(f) to appear for the prosecution, when directed by the court to do so, on any appeal under–
  (i) s.1 of the Administration of Justice Act 1960 (appeal from the High Court in criminal cases);
  (ii) Part I or Part II of the Criminal Appeal Act 1968 (appeals from the Crown Court to the criminal division of the Court of Appeal and thence to the House of Lords); or
  (iii) s.108 of the Magistrates' Courts Act 1980 (right of appeal to Crown Court) as it applies, by virtue of subs (5) of s.12 of the Contempt of Court Act 1981, to orders made under s.12 (contempt of magistrates' courts); and

(g) to discharge such other functions as may from time to time be assigned t
him by the Attorney General in pursuance of this paragraph.

(3) In this section–
'the court' means–
(a) in the case of an appeal to or from the criminal division of the Court o
Appeal, that division;
(b) in the case of an appeal from a Divisional Court of the Queen's Benc
Division, the Divisional Court; and
(c) in the case of an appeal against an order of a magistrates' court, the Crow
Court;
'police force' means any police force maintained by a police authority under th Police Act 1964 and any other body of constables for the time being specified b order made by the Secretary of State for the purposes of this section; and
'specified proceedings' means proceedings which fall within any category for th time being specified by order made by the Attorney General for the purposes o this section.

(4) The power to make orders under subs (3) above shall be exercisable b statutory instrument subject to annulment in pursuance of a resolution of eith House of Parliament.
[*as amended by Sch.2 Criminal Justice Act 1987*].

COMMENTARY

s.3(2)(a): Specified proceedings see the Prosecution of Offenders (Specified Proceeding Order 1985 (SI No 2010), *post*.

2.75 **Crown Prosecutors**

4. (1) Crown Prosecutors shall have, in any court, the rights of audien enjoyed by solicitors holding practising certificates and shall have suc additional rights of audience in the Crown Court as may be given by virtue o subs (3) below.

(2) The reference in subs (1) above to rights of audience enjoyed in any court b solicitors includes a reference to rights enjoyed in the Crown Court by virtue of ar direction given by the Lord Chancellor under s.83 of the Supreme Court Act 198

(3) *Crown Court – power to prescribe additional rights of audience.*

(4), (5) *Practising certificates.*

(6) . . .

2.76 **Conduct of prosecutions on behalf of the service**

5. (1) The Director may at any time appoint a person who is not a Crow Prosecutor but who is–
(a) a solicitor; or
(b) a barrister who is a member of the staff of a public authority;
to institute or take over the conduct of such criminal proceedings as the Direct may assign him.

(2) Any person conducting proceedings assigned to him under this sectic shall have all the powers of a Crown Prosecutor but shall exercise those powe subject to any instructions given to him by a Crown Prosecutor.

2.77 **Prosecutions instituted and conducted otherwise than by the Service**

6. (1) Subject to subs (2) below, nothing in this Part shall preclude a person from instituting any criminal proceedings or conducting any crimin proceedings to which the Director's duty to take over the conduct of procee ings does not apply.

(2) Where criminal proceedings are instituted in circumstances in which th Director is not under a duty to take over their conduct, he may nevertheless d so at any stage.

Delivery of recognizances etc to Director 2.78

7. (1) Where the Director or any Crown Prosecutor gives notice to any justice of the peace that he has instituted, or is conducting, any criminal proceedings, the justice shall–

(a) at the prescribed time and in the prescribed manner; or

(b) in a particular case, at that time and in the manner directed by the Attorney General;

send him every recognizance, information, certificate, deposition, document and thing connected with those proceedings which the justice is required by law to deliver to the appropriate officer of the Crown Court.

(2) *Regulations.*

(3) The Director or, as the case may be, Crown Prosecutor shall–

(a) subject to the regulations, cause anything which is sent to him under subs (1) above to be delivered to the appropriate officer of the Crown Court; and

(b) be under the same obligation (on the same payment) to deliver to an applicant copies of anything so sent as that officer.

(4) It shall be the duty of every justices' clerk to send to the Director, in accordance with the regulations, a copy of the information and of any depositions and other documents relating to any case in which–

(a) a prosecution for an offence the magistrates' court to which he is clerk is withdrawn or is not proceeded with within a reasonable time;

(b) the Director does not have the conduct of the proceedings; and

(c) there is some ground for suspecting that there is no satisfactory reason for the withdrawal or failure to proceed.

Guidelines for Crown Prosecutors 2.79

10. (1) The Director shall issue a Code for Crown Prosecutors giving guidance on general principles to be applied by them–

(a) in determining, in any case–

(i) whether proceedings for an offence should be instituted or, whether proceedings have been instituted, whether they should be discontinued; or

(ii) what charges should be preferred; and

(b) in considering, in any case, representations to be made by them to any magistrates' court about the mode of trial suitable for that case.

(2) The Director may from time to time make alterations in the Code.

(3) The provisions of the Code shall be set out in the Director's report under s.9 of this Act for the year in which the Code is issued; and any alteration in the Code shall be set out in his report under that section for the year in which the alteration is made.

COMMENTARY

10(1): Code for Crown Prosecutors, see Appendix II, *post.*

Interpretation of Part I 2.80

15. (1) In this Part–

'binding over proceedings' means any proceedings instituted (whether by way of complaint under s 115 of the Magistrates' Courts Act 1980 or otherwise) with a view to obtaining from a magistrates' court an order requiring a person to enter into a recognizance to keep the peace or to be of good behaviour;

'Director' means the Director of Public Prosecutions;

'police force' has the same meaning as in section 3 of this Act;

'prosecution functions' means functions which by virtue of this Part becomes functions of the Director;

'public authority' has the same meaning as in section 17 of this Act;

'Service' means the Crown Prosecution Service; and

'solicitor' means a solicitor of the Supreme Court.

(2) For the purposes of this Part, proceedings in relation to an offence ar instituted–
  (a) where a justice of the peace issues a summons under s.1 of the Magistrate Courts Act 1980, when the information for the offence is laid before him
  (b) where a justice of the peace issues a warrant for the arrest of any perso under that section, when the information for the offence is laid before him
  (c) where a person is charged with the offence after being taken into custod without a warrant, when he is informed of the particulars of the charge
  (d) where a bill of indictment is preferred under s.2 of the Administration c Justice (Miscellaneous Provisions) Act 1933 in a case falling within par (b) of subs (2) of that section, when the bill of indictment is preferre before the court;
and where the application of this subsection would result in there being mor than one time for the institution of the proceedings, they shall be taken to hav been instituted at the earliest of those times.

(3) For the purposes of this Part, references to the conduct of any procee ings include references to the proceedings being discontinued and to the takin of any steps (including the bringing of appeals and making of representations i respect of applications for bail) which may be taken in relation to them.

(4) For the purposes of ss.3(2)(b), 5, 6 and 7(1) of this Act, binding ove proceedings shall be taken to be criminal proceedings.

(5) For the purposes of s.5 of this Act, proceedings begun by summons issue under s.3 of the Obscene Publications Act 1959 (forfeiture of obscene article shall be taken to be criminal proceedings.

(6) The functions which become functions of the Director by virtue of th Part shall be treated as transferred functions for the purposes of s.95 of th Employment Protection (Consolidation) Act 1978 (effect of certain provisior where functions are transferred to the Crown) but shall not be so treated for th purposes of para 1(2) of Sch.3 to the Pensions (Increase) Act 1971 (meaning c 'last employing authority').

(7) The person who, immediately before the commencement of s.2 of th Act, holds the office of Director shall be treated on the commencement of tha section as holding that office in pursuance of an appointment made by th Attorney General.

PART III
MISCELLANEOUS

2.81   **Power of Secretary of State to set time limits in relation to preliminary stage of criminal proceedings**
  22. (1) The Secretary of State may be regulations make provision, wit respect to any specified preliminary stage of proceedings for an offence, as to th maximum period–
  (a) to be allowed to the prosecution to complete that stage;
  (b) during which the accused may, while awaiting completion of that stage, be
    (i) in the custody of a magistrates' court; or
    (ii) in the custody of the Crown Court;
  in relation to that offence.

(2) The regulations may, in particular–
  (a) be made so as to apply only in relation to proceedings instituted specified areas;
  (b) make different provision with respect to proceedings instituted different areas;
  (c) make such provision with respect to the procedure to be followed criminal proceedings as the Secretary of State considers appropriate consequence of any other provision of the regulations;

(d) provide for the Magistrates' Courts Act 1980 and the Bail Act 1976 to apply in relation to cases to which custody or overall time limits apply subject to such modifications 'as may be specified (being modifications which the Secretary of State considers necessary in consequence of any provision made by the regulations); and

(e) make such transitional provision in relation to proceedings instituted before the commencement of any provision of the regulations as the Secretary of State considers appropriate.

(3) The appropriate court may, at any time before the expiry of a time limit imposed by the regulations, extend, or further extend, that limit if it is satisfied–

(a) that there is good and sufficient cause for doing so; and

(b) that the prosecution has acted with all due expedition.

(4) Where, in relation to any proceedings for an offence, an overall time limit has expired before the completion of the stage of the proceedings to which the limit applies, the accused shall be treated, for all purposes, as having been acquitted of that offence.

(5) Where–

(a) a person escapes from the custody of a magistrates' court or the Crown Court before the expiry of a custody time limit which applies in his case; or

(b) a person who has been released on bail in consequence of the expiry of a custody time limit–

  (i) fails to surrender himself into the custody of the court at the appointed time; or

  (ii) is arrested by a constable on a ground mentioned in s.7(3)(b) of the Bail Act 1976 (breach, or likely breach, of conditions of bail);

the regulations shall, so far as they provide for any custody time limit in relation to the preliminary stage in question, be disregarded.

(6) Where–

(a) a person escapes from the custody of a magistrates' court or the Crown Court; or

(b) a person who has been released on bail fails to surrender himself into the custody of the court at the appointed time;

the overall time limit which applies in his case in relation to the stage which the proceedings have reached at the time of the escape or, as the case may be, at the appointed time shall, so far as the offence in question is concerned, cease to have effect.

(7) Where a magistrates' court decides to extend, or further extend, a custody or overall time limit, the accused may appeal against the decision to the Crown Court.

(8) Where a magistrates' court refuses to extend, or further extend, a custody or overall time limit the prosecution may appeal against the refusal to the Crown Court.

(9) An appeal under subs (8) above may not be commenced after the expiry of the limit in question; but where such an appeal is commenced before the expiry of the limit the limit shall be deemed not to have expired before the determination or abandonment of the appeal.

(10) Where a person is convicted of an offence to any proceedings, the exercise, in relation to any preliminary stage of those proceedings, of the power conferred by subs (3) above shall not be called into question in any appeal against that conviction.

(11) In this section–

'appropriate court' means–

(a) where the accused has been committed for trial or indicted for the offence, the Crown Court; and

(b) in any other case, the magistrates' court specified in the summons or warrant in question or, where the accused has already appeared or been brought before a magistrates' court, a magistrates' court for the same area; 'custody of the Crown Court' includes custody to which a person is committed in pursuance of–

(a) s.6 of the Magistrates' Courts Act 1980 (magistrates' court committing accused for trial); or

(b) s.43A of that Act (magistrates' court dealing with a person brought before it following his arrest in pursuance of a warrant issued by the Crown Court);

'custody of a magistrates' court' means custody to which a person is committed in pursuance of s.128 of the Magistrates' Courts Act 1980 (remand);

'custody time limit' means a time limit imposed by regulations made under subs (1)(b) above or, where any such limit has been extended by a court under subs (3) above, the limit as so extended;

'preliminary stage', in relation to any proceedings, does not include any stage of the proceedings after the accused has been arraigned in the Crown Court or, in the case of a summary trial, the magistrates' court has begun to hear evidence for the prosecution at the trial;

'overall time limit' means a time limit imposed by regulations made under subs (1)(a) above or, where any such limit has been extended by a court under subs (3) above, the limit as so extended; and

'specified' means specified in the regulations.

(12) For the purposes of the application of any custody time limit in relation to a person who is in the custody of a magistrates' court or the Crown Court–

(a) all periods during which he is in the custody of a magistrates' court in respect of the same offence shall be aggregated and treated as a single continuous period; and

(b) all periods during which he is in the custody of the Crown Court in respect of the same offence shall be aggregated and treated similarly.

COMMENTARY

s.22(1): Preliminary stage, partially defined in s.22(11).

Be . . . in the custody, see the Prosecution of Offences (Custody Time Limits) Regulations 1987 (SI No 299), which apply to certain limited areas of the country and which are reproduced at 3.00, *ante*.

2.82   **Discontinuance of proceedings in magistrates' courts**

23. (1) Where the Director of Public Prosecutions has conduct of proceedings for an offence, this section applies in relation to the preliminary stages of those proceedings.

(2) In this section, 'preliminary stage' in relation to proceedings for an offence does not include–

(a) in the case of a summary offence, any stage of the proceedings after the court has begun to hear evidence for the prosecution at the trial;

(b) in the case of an indictable offence, any stage of the proceedings after–

(i) the accused has been committed for trial; or

(ii) the court has begun to hear evidence for the prosecution at a summary trial of the offence.

(3) Where, at any time during the preliminary stages of the proceedings, the Director gives notice under this section to the clerk of the court that he does not want the proceedings to continue, they shall be discontinued with effect from the giving of that notice but may be revived by notice given by the accused under subs (7) below.

(4) Where, in the case of a person charged with an offence after being taken into custody without a warrant, the Director gives him notice, at a time when no magistrates' court has been informed of the charge, that the proceedings against him are discontinued, they shall be discontinued with effect from the giving of that notice.

(5) The Director shall, in any notice given under subs (3) above, give reasons for not wanting the proceedings to continue.

(6) On giving any notice under subs (3) above the Director shall inform the accused of the notice and of the accused's right to require the proceedings to be continued; but the Director shall not be obliged to give the accused any indication of his reasons for not wanting the proceedings to continue.

(7) Where the Director has given notice under subs (3) above, the accused shall, if he wants the proceedings to continue, give notice to that effect to the clerk of the court within the prescribed period; and where notice is so given the proceedings shall continue as if no notice had been given by the Director under subs (3) above.

(8) Where the clerk of the court has been so notified by the accused he shall inform the Director.

(9) The discontinuance of any proceedings by virtue of this section shall not prevent the institition of fresh proceedings in respect of the same offence.

(10) In this section 'prescribed' means prescribed by rules made under s.144 of the Magistrates' Courts Act 1980.

COMMENTARY

s.2(1): Preliminary stages, as partially defined in s.2(2) and see s.2(4) for discontinuance before the matter reaches court.

s.2(9): Note that 'discontinuance' does not prevent fresh proceedings for the same offence.

s.2(10): Prescribed . . . by rules see the Magistrates' Courts (Discontinuance of Proceedings) Rules 1986 (SI No 367), *post.*

Consents to prosecutions etc   **2.83**
25. (1) This section apples to any enactment which prohibits the institution or carrying on of proceedings for any offence except–
   (a) with the consent (however expressed) of a Law Officer of the Crown or the Director; or
   (b) where the proceedings are instituted or carried on by or on behalf of a Law Officer of the Crown or the Director;
and so applies whether or not there are other exceptions to the prohibition (and in particular whether or not the consent is an alternative to the consent of any other authority or person).

(2) An enactment to which this section applies–
   (a) shall not prevent the arrest without warrant, or the issue or execution of a warrant for the arrest, of a person for any offence, or the remand in custody or on bail of a person charged with any offence; and
   (b) shall be subject to any enactment concerning the apprehension or detention of children or young persons.

(3) In this section 'enactment' includes any provision having effect under or by virtue of any Act; and this section applies to enactments whenever passed or made.

Consents to be admissible in evidence   **2.84**
26. Any document purporting to be the consent of a Law Officer of the Crown, the Director or a Crown Prosecutor for, or to–
   (a) the institution of any criminal proceedings; or
   (b) the institution of criminal proceedings in any particular form;
and to be signed by a Law Officer of the Crown, the Director or, as the case may be, a Crown Prosecutor shall be admissible as prima facie evidence without further proof.

2.85　　　　　　**MAGISTRATES' COURTS (BACKING OF WARRANTS) RULES 1965**

(SI No 1965 No 1906)

1. (1) *(Forms)*.

(2) Where a requirement is imposed by the Act for the use of a prescribed form, and an appropriate form is contained in the schedule to these rules, that form or a form to the like effect shall be used.

2. (1) A notice given under s.3(1)(a) of the Act (consent to surrender earlier than is otherwise permitted) shall be signed in the presence of a justice of the peace of a justices' clerk.

(2) Any such notice given by a person in custody shall be delivered to the governor of the prison in whose custody he is.

(3) If a person on bail gives such notice, he shall deliver it to, or send it by post in a registered letter or by recorded delivery service addressed to, the police officer in charge of the police station specified in his recognizance.

(4) Any such notice shall be attached to the warrant ordering the surrender of that person.

3. The person taking the recognizance of a person remanded on bail under s.2(1) or s.4(3) of the Act shall furnish a copy of the recognizance to the police officer in charge of the police station specified in the recognizance.

(2) The clerk of a magistrates' court which ordered a person to be surrendered and remanded him on bail shall deliver to, or send by post in a registered letter or by recorded delivery service addressed to, the police officer in charge of the police station specified in the recognizance the warrant ordering the person to be surrendered.

4. (1) The clerk of the magistrates' court which ordered a person to be surrendered shall deliver to, or send by post in a registered letter or by recorded delivery service addressed to–

(a) if he is remanded in custody under s.5(1)(a) of the Act, the prison governor to whose custody he is committed.

(b) if he is remanded on bail under s.5(1) of the Act, the police officer in charge of the police station specified in the recognizance,

(c) if he is committed to the custody of a constable pending the taking from him a recognizance under s.5(1) of the Act, the police officer in charge of the police station specified in the warrant of commitment,

the warrant of arrest issued by a judicial authority in the Republic and endorsed in accordance with s.1 of the Act.

(2) The governor or police officer to whom the said warrant of arrest is delivered or sent shall arrange for it to be given to the member of the police force of the Republic into whose custody the person is delivered when the person is so delivered.

5. (1) A document purporting to be a warrant issued by a judicial authority in the Republic shall, for the purposes of s.7(a) of the Act, be verified by a certificate purporting to be signed by a judicial authority, a clerk of a court or a member of the police force of the Republic and certifying that the document is a warrant and is issued by a Judge or justice of a court or a peace commissioner.

(2) A document purporting to be a copy of a summons issued by a judicial authority in the Republic shall, for the purposes of the said s.7(a), be verified by a certificate purporting to be signed by a judicial authority, a clerk of a court or a member of the police force of the Republic and certifying that the document is a true copy of such a summons.

(3) A deposition purporting to have been made in the Republic, or affidavit or written statement purporting to have been sworn therein, shall, for the purposes

of s.7(c) of the Act, be verified by a certificate purporting to be signed by the person before whom it was sworn and certifying that it was so sworn.

6. (1) In these Rules–
'the Act' means the Backing of Warrants (Republic of Ireland) Act 1965; a reference to a person ordered to be surrendered means a reference to a person ordered by a magistrates' court to be delivered into the custody of a member of the police force of the Republic under s.2(1) of the Act; and cognate expressions shall be construed accordingly,
'the Republic' means the Republic of Ireland.

(2) The Interpretation Act, 1978, shall apply to the interpretation of these rules as it applies to the interpretation of an Act of Parliament.

MAGISTRATES' COURTS RULES 1981   2.86
(SI 1981 No 552 as amended by SI 1982 No 245, 1983 No 523, 1984 No 1552, 1985 Nos 1695 and 1944, 1986 No 1332.)

Information and complaint
4. (1) An information may be laid or complaint made by the prosecutor or complainant in person or by his counsel or solicitor or other person authorised in that behalf.

(2) Subject to any provision of the Act of 1980 and any other enactment, an information or complaint need not be in writing or on oath.

(3) It shall not be necessary in an information or complaint to specify or negative an exception, exemption, proviso, excuse or qualification, whether or not it accompanies the description of the offence or matter of complaint contained in the enactment creating the offence or on which the complaint is founded.

COMMENTARY
For the laying of the information, see s.1 MCA 1980. For the contents of the information, see 100 MC Rules 1981, and Form 1.

Para (1): The prosecutor, see *The Right to Prosecute* 2.00.

Other person authorised, eg authorised officers of local authorities and Ministries. The informant is the person named in the information, not the one who usually lays the information: Glanville Williams [1956] Crim LR 169.

Para (2): Any provision of the Act, see s.1(3) MCA 1980.

Para (3): See s.101 of the Act for the substantive law. The words '*proviso*', '*exception*' have no technical meaning, and the word 'unless' is equally covered by this provision: *Roche v Willis* (1934) 98 JP 227.

Duty of the clerk receiving statutory declaration under s.14(1) of Act of 1980
20. Where the clerk of a magistrates' court receives a statutory declaration which complies with s.14(1) of the Act of 1980, he shall–
(a) note the receipt of the declaration in the register against the entry in respect to the trial of the information to which the declaration relates; and
(b) inform the prosecutor and, if the prosecutor is not a constable, the chief officer of police of the receipt of the declaration.

Proof of service, handwriting, etc.
67. (1) The service on any person of a summons, process, notice or document required or authorised to be served in any proceedings before a magistrates' court, and the handwriting or seal of a justice of the peace or other person on any warrant, summons, notice process or documents issued or made in any such proceedings, may be proved in any legal proceedings by a document purporting to be a solemn declaration in the prescribed form made before a justice of the peace, commissioner for oaths, clerk of a magistrates' court or registrar of a county court or a sheriff or sheriff clerk (in Scotland) or a clerk of petty sessions (in Northern Ireland).

(2) The service of any process or other documents required or authorised be served, the proper addressing, pre-paying and posting or registration f the purposes of service of a letter containing such a document, and the plac date and time of posting or registration of any such letter, may be proved in a proceedings before a magistrates' court by a document purporting to be certificate signed by the person by whom the service was effected or the lett posted or registered.

(3) References in para (2) to the service of any process shall, in the application to a witness summons, be construed as including references to t payment or tender to the witness of his costs and expenses.

COMMENTARY

False statements in documents made under this rule are punishable in accordance with s. MCA 1980.

Para (1): Seal of a justice, this means court stamps which are used as seals: *R v W verhampton Deputy Recorder, ex p. Director of Public Prosecutions* [1951] 1 All ER 62

Prescribed form, see Forms 136 and 139.

Para (2): Certificate, see Forms 140 and 141. Rule 67(2) is satisfied '. . . unless the contra is proved': *Hawkins v Crown Prosecution Service* (1987) *The Times*, 24 August (analys report re blood/alcohol concentration).

Warrant to be signed

95. Except where a signature by the clerk of a magistrates' court is perm ted by rule 109 or by the Magistrates. Courts (Forms) Rules 1981, eve warrant order under the Act of 1980 shall be signed by the justice issuing i

Warrant of arrest

96. (1) A warrant issued by a justice of the peace for the arrest of any pers shall require the persons to whom it is directed, that is to say, the constables of t police area in which the warrant is issued, or the authorised persons for the poli area specified in the warrant, or any persons named in that behalf in the warrant, arrest the person against whom the warrant is issued.

(2) The warrant shall name or otherwise describe the person for who arrest it is issued, and shall contain a statement of the offence charged in t information or, as the case may be, the ground on which the warrant is issue

COMMENTARY

Para (1): Police area, defined in s.62 and Sch.8 Police Act 1964 (not reproduced herein)

The authorised persons, this is a reference to the persons employed by a local authority that area or by the chief officer of police or the police authority for that area who a authorised by the chief officer of police to execute warrants: r.2(4).

Para (2): Name or otherwise describe, a constable is liable to an action for false impriso ment if he arrests a person not properly named in the warrant even though that is the pers against whom it was desired the warrant should issue: *Hoye v Bush* [1835–42] All ER R 286. A conviction for wounding in the course of resisting arrest upon a warrant which mer stated the defendant's surname and the name of his father was quashed where the father h four sons living at the same address: *R v Hood* (1830) 1 MCC 281.

It is not improper to issue a warrant on description, but justices should be careful that t description is specific (and substantiated by the information) and not capable of applicati to a substantial proportion of the population, eg 'dark-haired male, aged about 30'.

Statement of the offences, see r.100, *infra*.

2.87   **Form of summons**

98. (1) A summons shall be signed by the justice issuing it or state his nan and be authenticated by the signature of the clerk of a magistrates' court.

(2) A summons requiring a person to appear before a magistrates' court answer to an information or complaint shall state shortly the matter of t

information or complaint and shall state the time and place at which the defendant is required by the summons to appear.

(3) A single summons may be issued against a person in respect of several informations or complaints; but the summons shall state the matter of each information or complaint separately and shall have effect as several summonses, each issued in respect of one information or complaint.

OMMENTARY

ra (1): A summons may also be issued (and thus signed in his own right) by the clerk to stices: Justices' Clerks Rules 1970 (SI No 231).

summons, see Form 2.

gned, a signature may be affixed to a rubber stamp facsimile not only by the justice himself t also by another person expressly authorised to do so or, if he is subject to the directions and ntrol of the justices, if he is acting in accordance with an established practise in the justices' fice. In no case may a document be signed in blank: *R v Brentford Justices, ex p. Catlin* 975) 139 JP 516.

ate shortly, see r.100, *infra*.

Service of summons, etc.

99. (1) Service of a summons issued by a justice of the peace on a person other than a corporation may be effected–
  (a) by delivering it to the person to whom it is directed; or
  (b) by leaving it for him with some person at his last known or usual place of abode; or
  (c) by sending it by post in a letter addressed to him at his last known or usual place of abode.

(2) If the person summoned fails to appear, service of a summons in manner authorised by sub-para (b) or (c) of para (1) shall not be treated as proved unless it is proved that the summons came to his knowledge; and for that purpose any letter or other communication purporting to be written by him or on his behalf in such terms as reasonably to justify the inference that the summons came to his knowledge shall be admissible as evidence of that fact; provided that this paragraph shall not apply to any summons in respect of a summary offence served in the manner authorised by–
  (a) the said sub-para (b); or
  (b) the said sub-para (c) in a registered letter or by recorded delivery service.

(3) Service for the purposes of the Act of 1980 of a summons issued by a justice of the peace on a corporation may be effected by delivering it at, or sending it by post to, the registered office to the corporation, if that office is in the United Kingdom or, if there is no registered office in the United Kingdom, any place in the United Kingdom where the corporation trades or conducts its business.

(4) Paragraph (3) shall have effect in relation to a document (other than a summons) issued by a justice of the peace as it has effect in relation to a summons so issued, but with the substitution of references to England and Wales for the references to the United Kingdom.

(5) Any summons or other document served in a manner authorised by the preceding provisions of this rule shall, for the purposes of any enactment other than the Act of 1980 or these rules requiring a summons or other document to be served in any particular manner, be deemed to have been as effectively served as if it had been served in that manner, and nothing in this rule shall render invalid the service of a summons or other document in that manner.

(6) Sub-paragraph (c) of para (1) shall not authorise the service by post of–
  (a) a summons requiring the attendance of any person to give evidence or produce a document or thing; or
  (b) a summons issued under any enactment relating to the liability of members of the naval, military or air forces of the Crown for the maintenance of their wives and children, whether legitimate or illegitimate.

(7) . . .

(8) Where this rule or any other of the rules provides that a summons or other document may be sent by post to a person's last known or usual place of abode that rule shall have effect as if it provided also for the summons or other document to be sent in the manner specified in the rule to an address given by that person for that purpose.

(9) This rule shall not apply to a judgment summons.

COMMENTARY

The effects of this rule are summarised under *Service of the Summons* 2.14. So far as summons for a summary offence is concerned, ordinary post may be used in the first instance but if the accused fails to acknowledge in the manner referred to in para (2) the hearing of summary offence may be adjourned for service by registered letter or recorded delivery, i which case the lack of acknowledgment at the adjourned date will not be a bar to trial in the absence of the accused. The trial of an indictable offence cannot proceed in the absence of the accused without either proof of service, normally personal service (sub-para (a) of para (1) or acknowledgment or other proof of service in accordance with para (2).

Para (1): Leaving it for him, this may including posting: *Stylo Shoes Ltd v Price Tailors Lt* [1959] 3 All ER 901. If a summons is served by leaving it with another person such perso should be told who it is for and made to understand the nature of the summons, *per* Quain J, i *R v Smith* (1875) 39 JP 313.

Last known or usual place of abode, does not include a shop where the defendant does nc reside: *R v Lilley, ex p. Taylor* (1910) 75 JP 95; not a lock-up shop: *R v Rhodes, ex p. McVitti* (1915) 79 JP 527. 'Place of abode' includes the last place of abode if the defendant no longe has one: *R. v Evans and Yale* (1850) 1 LM & P 357; 19 LJMC 151. But where the defendant ha obtained a fixed place of abode abroad, his last address in England is not his 'last known plac of abode': *R v Farmer* (1892) 56 JP 341. Note para (8) however.

Sending it by post, where an Act passed on or after January, 1890, authorises or requires an document to be served by post, whether the expression 'serve' or the expression 'give' o 'send' or any other expression is used, then, unless the contrary intention appears, the servic shall be deemed to be effected by properly addressing, prepaying and posting a lette containing the document, and, unless the contrary is proved, to have been effected at the tim at which the letter would be delivered in the ordinary course of post: s.7 Interpretation Ac 1978. For proof of such service see para (2).

Proviso to para (2), note as a corollary the provisions of s.14 MCA 1980 (proceedings may b made invalid when accused did not know of them).

Summary offence, defined in Sch.1 Interpretation Act 1978.

Principal office, ie the place where the company's business is managed and controlled as whole: *Garton v GWR Co* (1858) EB & E 837; *Palmer v Caledonian Rail Co.* [1892] 1 QB 82? When a summons is improperly served on an assistant at a shop occupied by a limited compan and the company answers the summons simply to point out the irregularity this is not a appearance sufficient to effect a waiver of the irregularity: *Pearks, Gunston, Tee and Co Richardson* (1902) 66 JP 119.

Statement of offence

100. (1) Every information, summons, warrant or other document laid, issue or made for the purposes of, or in connection with, any proceedings before magistrates' court for an offence shall be sufficient if it described the specific offenc with which the accused is charged, or of which he is convicted, in ordinary languag avoiding as far as possible the use of technical terms and without necessarily statin all the elements of the offence, and gives such particulars as may be necessary fo giving reasonable information of the nature of the charge.

(2) If the offence charged is one created by or under any Act, the description c the offence shall contain a reference to the section of the Act, or, as the case may be the rule, order, regulation, byelaw or other instrument creating the offence.

COMMENTARY

Defects in an information, summons or warrant may be cured by s.123 MCA 1980.

Technical terms, in *Lomas v Peek* [1947] 2 All ER 574, the court held that the word 'knowingly and wilfully' were technical terms, omission of which was permissible in an information. This rule was not considered in the later case of *Waring v Wheatley* (1951) 115 JP 630, which came to the contrary conclusion on special facts.

Such particulars as may be necessary for giving reasonable information of the nature of the charge, in *Stephenson v Johnson* [1954] 1 WLR 375, a conviction for failing to pay a minimum wage was quashed when the information failed to quote the statutory order involved, the nature of the worker's employment, the amounts paid and alleged to be due, etc. Other examples of insufficient information are given in *Herniman v Smith* [1938] 1 All ER 1, at p.7; *Atterton v Brown* (1945) 109 JP 25; *Cording v Halse* [1954] 3 WLR 625.

When the date of offence is not known it is sufficient to allege commission between specified dates: *R v Simpson* (1715) 10 Mod Rep 248; *Onley v Gee* (1861) 25 JP 342. The place of offence may be omitted if unknown and immaterial, as in an indictable offence: *R v Wallwork* (1958) 122 JP 299.

Para (2): 'When the elements of an old common law offence are plainly covered by the words of a modern statute, it is preferable that the indictment should be framed, to use the old expression, *contra formam statuti*', *per* Veale J in *R v Pollock and Divers* [1966] 2 WLR 1145.

A failure to comply with this rule may be cured under s.123 MCA 1980, see note *supra*, provided that the accused has not been misled: *Thornley v Clegg* [1982] Crim LR 523; [1982] RTR 405 (information recited the precise words of the statute and quoted the regulations but not the statute). The rule is statutory only.

MAGISTRATES' COURTS (ADVANCE INFORMATION) RULES 1985

2.88

(SI 1985 No 601)

1. (*Citation, etc*).

2. These Rules apply in respect of proceedings against any person ('the accused') for an offence triable either way other than proceedings where the accused was charged or an information was laid before the coming into operation of these Rules.

3. As soon as practicable after a person has been charged with an offence in proceedings in respect of which these Rules apply or a summons has been served on a person in connexion with such an offence, the prosecutor shall provide him with a notice in writing explaining the effect of Rule 4 below and setting out the address at which a request under that Rule may be made.

4. (1) If, in any proceedings in respect of which these Rules apply, either before the magistrates' court considers whether the offence appears to be more suitable for summary trial or trial on indictment or, where the accused has not attained the age of 17 years when he appears or is brought before a magistrates' court, before he is asked whether he pleads guilty or not guilty, the accused or a person representing the accused requests the prosecutor to furnish him with advance information, the prosecutor shall, subject to Rule 5 below, furnish him as soon as practicable with either–

(a) a copy of those parts of every written statement which contain information as to the facts and matters of which the prosecutor proposes to adduce evidence in the proceedings, or

(b) a summary of the facts and matters of which the prosecutor proposes to adduce evidence in the proceedings.

(2) In paragraph (1) above, 'written statement' means a statement made by a person on whose evidence the prosecutor proposes to rely in the proceedings and, where such a person has made more then one written statement one of which contains information as to all the facts and matters in relation to which the prosecutor proposes to rely on the evidence of that person, only that statement is a written statement for purposes of para (1) above.

(3) Where in any part of a written statement or in a summary furnished under para (1) above reference is made to a document on which the prosecutor proposes to rely, the prosecutor shall, subject to Rule 5 below, when furnishing the part of

the written statement or the summary, also furnish either a copy of the document or such information as may be necessary to enable the person making the request under para (1) above to inspect the document or a copy thereof.

5. (1) If the prosecutor is of the opinion that the disclosure of any particular fact or matter in compliance with the requirements imposed by Rule 4 above might lead to any person on whose evidence he proposes to rely in the proceedings being intimidated, to an attempt to intimidate him being made or otherwise to the course of justice being interfered with, he shall not be obliged to comply with those requirements in relation to that fact or matter.

(2) Where, in accordance with para (1) above, the prosecutor considers that he is not obliged to comply with the requirements imposed by Rule 4 in relation to any particular fact or matter, he shall give notice in writing to the person who made the request under that Rule to the effect that certain advance information is being withheld by virtue of that paragraph.

6. (1) Subject to para (2) below, where an accused appears or is brought before a magistrates' court in proceedings in respect of which these Rules apply, the court shall, before it considers whether the offence appears to be more suitable for summary trial or trial on indictment, satisfy itself that the accused is aware of the requirements which may be imposed on the prosecutor under Rule 4 above.

(2) Where the accused has not attained the age of 17 when he appears or is brought before a magistrates' court in proceedings in respect of which these Rules apply, the court shall, before the accused is asked whether he pleads guilty or not guilty, satisfy itself that the accused is aware of the requirements which may be imposed on the prosecutor under Rule 4 above.

7. (1) If, in any proceedings in respect of which these Rules apply, the court is satisfied that, a request under Rule 4 of these Rules having been made to the prosecutor by or on behalf of the accused, a requirement imposed on the prosecutor by that Rule has not been complied with, the court shall adjourn the proceedings pending compliance with the requirement unless the court is satisfied that the conduct of the case for the accused will not be substantially prejudiced by non-compliance with the requirement.

(2) Where, in the circumstances set out in para (1) above, the court decides not to adjourn the proceedings, a record of that decision and of the reasons why the court was satisfied that the conduct of the case for the accused would not be substantially prejudiced by non-compliance with the requirement shall be entered in the register kept under Rule 66 of the Magistrates' Courts Rules 1981.

COMMENTARY
See generally, HOC 26/1985 reproduced at 149 JP 286, 203.

An offence triable either way, this phrase is defined in Sch.1 Interpretation Act 1978, as meaning an offence which, if committed by an adult, is triable either on indictment or summarily. However, this term is to be construed without regard to the effect, if any, of s.22 MCA 1980 (criminal damage below £400 etc or below £2,000 when s.35 CJA 1988 comes into force) on the mode of trial in a particular case. It follows that the defendant enjoys the right to advance disclosure in all offences of criminal damage, even those where the damage involved does not exceed the relevant sum.

2.89
PROSECUTION OF OFFENCES ACT 1985 (SPECIFIED PROCEEDINGS) ORDER 1985
(SI No 2010)

1. (*Citation etc*)

2. (1) Subject to paras (2) and (3) below, proceedings for the offences mentioned in the Schedule to this Order are hereby specified for the purposes of s.3 of the Prosecution of Offences Act 1985 (which, amongst other things, places a duty on the Director of Public Prosecutions to take over the conduct of all criminal proceedings, other than specified proceedings, instituted on behalf of a police force).

(2) Where a summons has been issued in respect of an offence mentioned in the Schedule to this Order, proceedings for that offence cease to be specified when the summons is served on the accused unless the documents described in paras (a) and (b) of s.12(1) of the Magistrates' Courts Act 1980 (pleading guilty by post etc) are served upon the accused with the summons.

(3) Proceedings for an offence cease to be specified if at any time a magistrates' court begins to receive evidence in those proceedings; and for the purpose of this paragraph nothing read out before the court under section 12(4) of the Magistrates' Courts Act 1980 shall be regarded as evidence.

SCHEDULE

Offences Proceedings for which are specified by Article 2(1)
1. Fixed penalty offences within the meaning of s.27(5) of the Transport Act 1982.

2. The offence under s.8(1) of the Vehicles (Excise) Act 1971.

3. The offences under ss.18, 20, 21, 30(1) and (2), 33(2), 33AA(3), 44(1), 161(4) and (5), 162(1), 164(1) and 168(3) of the Road Traffic Act 1972.

4. All offences under the Road Traffic Regulation Act 1984 other than those under ss.35(5), 43(5) and (12), 47(3), 52(1), 108(3), 115(1) and (2), 116(1) and 129(3) and paragraph 6(3) of Sch.12 or those mentioned para 1 above.

5. The offences arising by contravention of Regulations 3(9) (involving a pedal cycle) and 4(27), (28) and (30) of the Royal and other Parks and Gardens Regulations 1977.

COMMENTARY
The Order specifies proceedings for the offences set out in the Schedule for the purposes of s.3 if those proceedings are commenced by the prosecution so as to give the accused the opportunity of pleading guilty by post under s.12 MCA 1980. But they cease to be specified if at any time the court begins to receive evidence in those proceedings. The effect is that the duty of the Director of Public Prosecutions to take over the conduct of all criminal proceedings instituted on behalf of a police force does not include a duty to take over the conduct of proceedings specified in the order.

MAGISTRATES' COURTS (DISCONTINUANCE OF PROCEEDINGS) RULES 1986

2.90

1. (*Citation etc*).

2. In these Rules 'section 23' means s.23 of the Prosecution of Offences Act 1985.

3. The period within which an accused person may give notice under subs (7) of s.23 that he wants proceedings against him to continue is 35 days from the date when the proceedings were discontinued under that section.

4. Notice under subs (3), (4) or (7) of s.23 shall be given in writing and shall contain sufficient particulars to identify the particular offence to which it relates; and, without prejudice to any other lawful method of giving notice, may be given by post in a registered letter or by the recorded delivery service, in which case it shall be treated as having been given on the date on which it is received for dispatch by the Post Office.

5. On giving notice under subs (3) or (4) of s.23 the Director of Public Prosecutions shall inform any person who is detaining the accused person for the offence in relation to which the notice is given that he has given such notice and of the effect of the notice.

6. On being given notice under subs (3) of s.23 in relation to an offence for which the accused person has been granted bail by a court, the clerk of a magistrates' court shall inform–
  (a) any sureties of the accused, and
  (b) any persons responsible for securing the accused's compliance with any conditions of bail
that he has been given such notice and of effect of the notice.

COMMENTARY

Under s.23(3) Prosecution of Offences Act 1985 *ante*, where the Director has the conduct of proceedings for an offence he may, *at any time during the preliminary stages* (as defined in subs (2)) of those proceedings, by notice to the clerk of the court effect their discontinuance. The proceedings may, however, under s.23(7) be revived by notice given by the accused to the clerk of the court within 35 days: see r.3.

The Director may, under s.23(4), in a case where a person has been charged with an offence after being taken into custody without a warrant but no magistrates' court has yet been informed of the charge, effect a discontinuance by giving notice of discontinuance to the accused. Rule 4 provides that notice must be given in writing, with sufficient particulars to identify the offence concerned, and deals with the giving of notice by registered post or the recorded delivery service, which is permissible, but *inter alia* 'without prejudice to any other lawful method' – ie provided in writing.

Rules 5 and 6 impose obligations to inform certain persons that a notice of discontinuance has been given and of the effect of the notice. Under r.5 the Director is to inform any person who is detaining the accused for an offence to which the notice relates. Where the accused is on bail granted by any court, the clerk of the court who receives notice under s.23(3) is to inform any sureties of the accused and any persons responsible for securing his compliance with bail conditions.

CHAPTER 3

Detention, Remand, Bail and Custody

[NB For the definition of 'serious arrestable offence', see Chapter 12, Investigation and Arrest.]

Detention, Remand, Bail and Custody

INTRODUCTION 3.00

The law concerning the liberty or otherwise of those suspected or, ultimately, charged with criminal offences is contained in the Police and Criminal Evidence Act 1984 and the Bail Act 1976. Respectively, the PACE Act 1984 deals with police powers to arrest and detain suspects, and with magistrates' powers to extend the maximum lawful period of police detention beyond 36 hours, the Bail Act 1976 with the position once a person has been charged with a criminal offence and brought before the court. Both provisions contain considerable safeguards as respects the liberty of the individual, the underlying presumption being in favour of release unless stringent statutory requirements are complied with. Not all cases will necessarily involve 'police detention', which only follows from arrest and which in any event may be of short duration before the suspect is charged. In practice, only a small proportion of the more serious cases run the full 36 hours and are such as to require extension beyond that period by a court. At worst, however, an accused might have to run the full gauntlet of the PACE Act and Bail Act provisions which are thus discussed and set out in that chronological order in this chapter.

POLICE DETENTION

Procedure on arrest 3.01

Where a person is arrested otherwise than by being informed that he is under arrest the arrest is not lawful unless he is informed that he is arrested as soon as practicable after arrest; s.28(1) PACE Act 1984. Nor is an arrest lawful unless the arrested person is informed of the ground for the arrest at the time or as soon as practicable after the arrest: s.28(2).

The duty to inform does not apply where it is not reasonably practicable for the arrested person to be informed by reason of his having escaped from arrest before the information could be given: s.28(5). Where a person is arrested or taken into custody by a constable *otherwise than at a police station* he must be taken to a police station as soon as reasonably practicable: s.30(1). Certain statutory powers of arrest are exempted by s.30(12).

The police station must be a *designated police station* (as to which see s.35) if it appears that it may be necesary to keep the accused in police detention *for more than 6 hours* unless the constable will be unable to take him to a designated police station without injury and he lacks the necessary assistance: s.30(2), (3), (5).

Delay in taking the arrested person to a police station is authorised by s.30(10) in the case of investigations which it is reasonable to carry out immediately. A person arrested otherwise than at a police station must be released if the constable is satisfied that there are no grounds for keeping him under arrest: s.30(7).

Where a person attends voluntarily at a police station or other place where a constable is present for the purpose of assisting with investigations or accompanies a constable there without having been arrested he is entiled to leave at will unless placed under arrest and if a decision is taken to prevent him from leaving at will he must be informed at once that he is under arrest: s.29.

If it appears to a constable that an arrested person who is at a police station would, if released, be liable to arrest for another offence he must be arrested for that other offence: s.31.

See also Code C of the Codes of Practice at Appendix I, *post*, under which a person brought to a police station under arrest or who is arrested at the police station should be informed by the custody officer of the following rights and of the fact that they need not be exercised immediately:

   (i) the *Right to have someone informed* of his arrest under s.56 (see 3.12).

   (ii) the right to consult a solicitor – *Access to legal advice* under s.58 (see 3.13); and

   (iii) the right to consult the Codes of Practice.

3.02 Search for arrested person

A person arrested otherwise than at a police station may be searched by a constable:

  — if the cosntable has reasonable grounds for believing that he may present a danger to himself or others:

  — for anything which he might use to escape or which might be evidence relating to an offence: s.32(1), (2)(a).

But only if the constable has reasonable grounds for believing that the person searched may have concealed on him anything for which a search is permitted: s.32(5). A constable may not require a person to remove any of his clothing in public other than an outer coat, jacket or gloves: s.32(4).

A constable may enter and search any premises in which the arrest took place or in which the arrested person was before he was arrested for evidence relating to the offence: s.32(2)(b); but only if the constable has reasonable grounds for believing that there is evidence for which a search is permitted on the premises: s.32(6).

Custody officers and their duties   3.03

Certain police stations must be designated by the chief officer of police to be used for detaining arrested persons: s.35. One or more *custody officers* must be appointed for each designated police station: s.36(1). He must be of at least the rank of sergeant: s.36(3); but a non-involved officer of any rank may perform the functions of a custody officer if a custody officer is not readily available: s.36(4), (5).

It is the duty of the custody officer to ensure that all persons in police detention are treated in accordance with the Act and the Code of Practice: s.39(1); except where custody is transferred to another officer: s.39(2), (3). He is also responsible for the keeping of the custody record.

Where an arrested person is taken to a police station which *is not a designated police station* the function of the custody officer must be performed by an officer not involved in the investigation or, if no such officer is available, the officer who took him to the station or any other officer: s.35(7).

If *at any time* a custody officer becomes aware that the grounds of detention have ceased to apply and is not aware of any other grounds on which continued detention could be justified he *must order the immediate release from custody of a person in police detention*: s.34(2); unless the person was unlawfully at large when arrested: s.34(4). A person so released must be released *without bail* unless it appears that there is a need for further investigation or that proceedings may be taken against him: s.34(5).

Where a person is arrested for an offence or returns to a police station to answer to bail the custody officer must as soon as practicable determine whether he has sufficient evidence to charge that person with the offence for which he was arrested and may detain him for such period as is necessary to enable him to do so: s.37(1), (10). If he does not have sufficient evidence, the arrested person must be released with or without bail unless the custody officer has reasonable grounds for believing that his detention is necessary to secure or preserve evidence or to obtain evidence by questioning him: s.37(2); when he may authorise continued detention: s.37(3). If the custody officer determines that he *has sufficient evidence to charge the arrested person he must be charged or released without charge* with or without bail: s.37(7). Following a charge, the custody officer *must order the release* either with or without bail of anyone arrested without warrant, except where, in summary, his identity is suspect, it is feared he would commit violence or damage, or would abscond or interfere with the administration of justice, or with the investigation, or in the case of a juvenile, that he should be detained in his own interests: s.38(1), when he may authorise the keeping of that person in detention.

Review of police detention   3.04

Periodic review of persons in police detention *must* be carried out by the *review officer* who is, in the case of a person arrested and charged, the custody officer, and in the case of a person arrested but not charged, a non-involved inspector: s.40(1). The first review must take place not later than 6 *hours* after detention is first authorised, the second review not later than 9 *hours* after the first, and subsequent reviews at intervals of not more than 9 *hours*: s.40(1). All times are to be treated as 'approximate' only: s.45(2); and a review may be postponed in certain circumstances when it must be carried out as soon as practicable thereafter: s.40(4), (5).

The criteria for review are the same as on arrest and charge: s.40(8); see *Custody officers and their duties, supra.*

The detained person or, if asleep, his solicitor must be given the opportunity to make *oral or written representations* except where the detained person's condition or behaviour makes him unfit to do so: s.40(12)–(14).

3.05 Limits of detention without charge

A person must not be kept in police detention for more than 24 hours without being charged: s.41(1); this limit may be extended up to 36 hours by a senior police officer but only in the case of a *serious arrestable offence*: see 3.06. Detention beyond 36 hours may be authorised by a magistrates' court: see 3.07.

The time from which the period of detention is calculated (the relevant time) is the time at which the arrested person arrives at the first police station to which he is taken: s.41(2)(d); or, in the case of a person who attends voluntarily at the police station or who accompanied a constable there without having been arrested, the time of his arrest: s.41(2)(c). Special rules apply to a person arrested in one police area whose arrest is sought in another: s.41(2)(a), (5); and to a person arrested outside England or Wales: s.41(2)(b). All times are 'approximate': s.45(2).

3.06 Police authorisation of continued detention

A person who has not been charged at the expiry of *24 hours* after the relevant time *must be released* from police detention: s.41(7); unless his continued detention is authorised or permitted in accordance with ss.42 or 43: s.41(8). A person so released may not be re-arrested without warrant unless new evidence justifying a further arrest has come to light since his release; s.41(9).

A police officer of the rank of *superintendent or above* who is responsible for the police station may authorise the keeping of a person in police detention for a period of up to *36 hours* after the relevant time if he has *reasonable grounds for believing* that:

(a) detention without charge is necessary to *secure or preserve evidence or to obtain evidence by questioning* him;
(b) the offence is *a serious arrestable offence*; and
(c) the investigation is being conducted *diligently* and *expeditiously*: s.42(1).

Such authorisation can only be given *within 24 hours* of the relevant time and not until after the second review of his detention: s.42(2).

The arrested person or his solicitor must be given opportunity to make representations *before any period of detention is authorised*: s.42(6). The representations may be made *orally or in writing*: s.42(7), but the officer may refuse to hear oral representations from the arrested person if he considers that he is unfit to make them by reason of his condition or behaviour: s.42(8).

When detention for a person of less than 36 hours is authorised a further period expiring not more than 36 hours after the relevant time may be authorised, provided the conditions are still satisfied: s.42(2).

3.07 WARRANTS FOR FURTHER DETENTION

A magistrates' court may issue a warrant of further detention authorising the keeping of a person in police detention: s.43(1). In this context, the term 'magistrates' court' means a court consisting of *two or more justices of the peace sitting otherwise than in open court:* s.45(1). Application must be made by a constable *on oath* and supported by *an information*. The information must contain the matters specified in s.43(14). The court must be *satisfied* that there are reasonable grounds for believing that further detention is justified: s.43(1). Further detention is only justifiable by the same criteria as govern the exercise of the superintendent's discretion: s.43(4); see the previous section.

Application for a warrant of further detention may only be made:

(a) *before* the expiry of *36 hours* from the relevant time; or

(b) where it is not practicable for the magistrates' court to sit at the expiry of 36 hours after the relevant time but the court will sit during the 6 hours following the end of that period, before the expiry of those 6 hours: s.43(5).

This six hour period of lee-way is not limited to the situation where the 36 hour period expires and no court is sitting at all; justices also have a discretion during the course of a sitting whether to hear such an application straight away or to wait, provided they do so for no longer than six hours: *R v Slough Justices, ex p. Stirling* (1987) 151 JP 603.

The Code of Practice recognises the impracticability of a court being held outside the hours of 9 am and 10 pm: see Code V. Appendix I, *post.*

Where application is made *after the expiry of 36 hours* and it appears that it would have been reasonable for the police to have made it before the expiry of that period, the court *must dismiss* the application: s.43(7). The requirement to dismiss where it would have been reasonable to apply within 36 hours is mandatory: *ex p. Stirling, supra.* Where the court is not satisfied that further detention is justified it *must refuse* the application *or adjourn the hearing for up to 36 hours from the relevant time*: s.43(8).

An application may not be heard unless the person in police detention has been furnished with a copy of the information and he has been brought before the court for the hearing: s.43(2). He is *entitled* to legal representation and if he is not so represented and wishes to be the case must be adjourned: s.43(3). The person remains detained during any adjournment: s.43(9).

A warrant of further detention must state the *time* when it was issued (ie hours and minutes): s.43(10). The period authorised must be such period as the court thinks fit having regard to the evidence before it, but no longer than 36 hours: s.43(11), (12). Here it will be relevant how long the criteria for detention are likely to subsist, whether eg the court should, in effect, set a time limit for questioning. Further applications can then be made, if need be, for the warrant to be extended: *post.*

If the application is refused the arrested person must be charged forthwith or released with or without bail: s.43(15). However he need not be released before the expiry of 24 hours after the relevant time, or before the expiry of any longer period for which his continued detention has been authorised by a superintendent: s.43(16). Following refusal to issue a warrant, no further application may be made unless supported by evidence which has come to light since refusal: s.43(17).

A warrant of further detention may be *extended* by a magistrates' court on application by a constable supported by an information: s.44(1). The extension may be for such period as the court thinks fit but *not longer than 36 hours nor ending later than 96 hours* after the relevant time: s.44(2), (3). Where the extension is for a period ending before the 96 hours, the warrant may be further extended – but not beyond that time: s.44(4).

All times are 'approximate' only: s.45(2).

3.08
 PROCEDURE AFTER CHARGE

A person who after being charged with an offence is kept in police detention or detained by a local authority must be brought before a magistrates' court: s.46(1). If he is brought before a magistrates' court for the petty sessions area in which the police station is situated he must be brought before the court as *soon as practicable and in any event not later than the first sitting after he is charged* with the offence: s.46(2). If no magistrates' court is due to sit on the day he is charged or the next day the custody officer must inform the clerk to the justices: s.46(3).

The bringing of an accused before a magistrates' court for a different area is dealt with in s.46(5). In both cases the clerk who is informed *must arrange* for a magistrates' court to sit not later than the day after the relevant day: s.46(6). Christmas Day, Good Friday and Sundays are exempted: s.46(8). The 'relevant day' is as defined in s.46(7).

3.09 **SEARCH AND RIGHTS OF DETAINED PERSONS**

A custody officer must ascertain and record everything which an arrested person has with him: s.54(1). The officer has discretion to seize and retain any such thing or cause it to be seized or retained: s.54(2). Clothing and personal effects may only be seized if the custody officer:
(a) *believes* that the arrested person may use them –
    (i) to cause physical injury;
    (ii) to damage property;
    (iii) to interfere with evidence; or
    (iv) to assist him to escape; or if he
(b) has *reasonable grounds for believing* that they may be evidence relating to an offence: s.54(4).

3.10 **Search**

An officer of the rank of *superintendent or above* may authorise the search of a person who has been arrested and is in police detention if he has reasonable grounds for believing:
(a) that he may have concealed on him anything which –
    (i) he could use to cause physical injury; and
    (ii) he might so use while in police detention or in the custody of a court; or
(b) that such a person –
    (i) may have a Class A drug concealed on him; and
    (ii) was in possession of it with the appropriate criminal intent before his arrest: s.55(1).

3.11 **Intimate search**

An *intimate search* may not be authorised without reasonable grounds for believing that the object of the search cannot be found without such a search: s.55(2). Authority may be given *orally or in writing*, but if given orally must be confirmed in writing as soon as practicable: s.55(3). An intimate search is a search which consists of the physical examination of a person's bodily orifices: s.118(1). An intimate search which is only a drug offence search must be by way of examination by a suitably qualified person: s.55(4). Other intimate searches must be by a suitably qualified person unless an officer of at least the rank of superintendent considers that it is not practicable: s.55(6); when it must be carried out by a constable: s.55(7). A constable may *not* carry out an intimate search of a person of the opposite sex: s.55(8). An intimate search may only be carried out at a *police station*, a *hospital*, a registered medical practitioner's *surgery* or *some other place used for medical purposes*: s.55(9). A purely drug offence intimate search may not be carried out at a police station: s.55(10).

The custody officer may seize and retain anything found on an intimate search or cause it to be seized and retained in the same circumstances as on a search of a detained person: s.55(12); see *supra*.

Right to have someone informed   3.12

A person arrested and held in custody in a police station or other premises is *entitled if he so requests* to have a friend or relative or other person known to him or who is likely to take an interest in his welfare told as soon as is practicable, that he has been arrested and is being detained: s.56(1). An officer of at least the rank of superintendent may authorise delay in the case of a person in police detention for a *serious arrestable offence* where he has reasonable grounds for believing that this will lead to interference with or harm to evidence concerned with a serious arrestable offence or interference with or harm to other persons, will lead to the alerting of other suspects not yet arrested or will hinder the recovery of property: s.56(5). Delay may not exceed 36 hours from the relevant time: s.56(3); and see Code C, Codes of Practice at Appendix I, *post*.

Special provisions apply to terrorism offences: s.56(11).

Note: the amendments to s.56 which will be effected by [s.97] CJA 1988 when in force: see 3.93.

Access to legal advice   3.13

A person arrested and held in custody in a police station or other premises is entitled if he so requests to consult a solicitor privately at any time: s.58(1); and such request shall be recorded in the custody record. Consultation must be permitted as soon as is practicable except to the extent that delay is permitted, but in any case within *36 hours* from the relevant time: s.58(4). An officer of at least the rank of superintendent may authorise delay in the case of a *serious arrestable offence:* s.58(6). The officer must have reasonable grounds for believing that any of the grounds for delaying notification of a friend applies: s.58(8). Delay may only be authorised in accordance with the Code of Practice (see Code C, Appendix I, *post*). While the right is to consult privately, an *assistant chief constable or commander* may authorise consultation to take place only in the sight and hearing of a qualified officer of the uniformed branch: s.58(15), (16), (17).

Special provisions apply to terrorism offences: s.58(13), (14).

IDENTIFICATION, PHOTOGRAPHS AND   3.14
FINGERPRINTS

The conduct of an *identity parade* and other methods of identification – and photography – is dealt with in the *Code of Practice for the Identification of Persons by Police Officers*: see Code D, Appendix I, *post*. *Evidence of identification* is also dealt with by way of an extended extract from *R v Turnbull* [1977] QB 224, reproduced in Chapter 6.

A person's *fingerprints* may be taken by the police:
   (i) with his consent: s.61(1); which, if he is at a police station, must be *in writing*;

(ii) without consent in the case of a person detained at a police station on the authority of an officer of at least the rank of *superintenden* who has reasonable grounds for suspecting the subject's involve ment in a criminal offence and for believing that his fingerprint will tend to confirm or disprove it: s.61(3)(a), (4);

(iii) without consent in the case of a person detained in a police station who has been *charged* with a recordable offence (ie an offence defined in regulations), or informed that he will be reported fo such an offence: s.61(3)(b); or

(iv) without consent in the case of a person *convicted* of a recordable offence: s.61(6).

Where a person has been convicted of a recordable offence, has no been in police detention for it and has not had his fingerprints taken an constable may within a month after the date of conviction require him t attend at a police station in order that his fingerprints may be taken: s.27 Fingerprints include palm prints: s.65. *Reasonable force* may be used i necessary to take fingerprints where there is authority for doing s without consent: s.117. Fingerprints must be destroyed in accordance with s.64.

3.15   # ADJOURNMENTS AND REMANDS

When the hearing of criminal proceedings is adjourned the defendan may (and in some circumstances must) be remanded, that is, he must b granted bail or committed to custody. Bail may also be granted or refuse by the court on a committal for trial or sentence, on appeal and in a number of other circumstances. The law concerning remands is dealt wit mainly in the Magistrates' Courts Act 1980 and the principles upon whic bail may be granted or refused in the Bail Act 1976.

While a magistrates' court always had power at common law to adjourn the hearing of an information, that power is now regulated by statute an depends, as does the power to remand the defendant, upon the stage o the procedings as follows:

— *Mode of trial proceedings* (for an offence triable either way): The powe of adjournment is contained in s.18 MCA 1980 which also *permits* an adult t be *remanded* whenever he is present and *requires* him to be remanded i certain circumstances. There is no obligation to remand where these proceed ings are conducted by a legal representative in accordance with s.25, or whe the court changes over to act as examining justices.

— *Committal proceedings:* The power of *adjournment* is contained i s.10 MCA 1980, which *permits the accused to be remanded* in any case an *requires* an adult to be remanded on an offence triable either way i certain circumstances.

A remand is an order of a court disposing of the person of someone appearing before it during the period of an adjournment. A remand ma be either on bail or in custody: s.128 MCA 1980. Remands in summar proceedings will usually be for the accused to appear before the sam magistrates' court as that remanding him – but there is power to reman to a court nearer to the prison where the accused is to be held: s.130 MCA 1980; and there is a general power to 'cross-remand' between courts in th same commission area: see *R v Avon Magistrates' Court Committee, ex p. Bath Law Society* (1987) 151 JP 805. In that case, the Divisional Cour chose to express 'no opinion' on whether 'cross-remanding' on any wide basis is lawful.

The maximum periods of remand are as follows:

— *before conviction*
in custody — eight clear days
on bail — eight clear days unless both sides consent to a longer period: s.128(6) MCA 1980.

n either case the eight-day period may be exceeded in the case of an offence *triable either way* where necessary to obtain a properly constiuted court.

— *after conviction or for medical reports*
in custody — three weeks
on bail — four weeks: ss.10 and 128(6) MCA 1980.

There is power to remand further: s.128(3); which may be exercised in he absence of the defendant: s.129.

When the accused is already serving a custodial sentence there is power n certain circumstances to remand in custody for *up to 28 days*: s.131 MCA 1980.

Note: the new s.128A MCA 1980 inserted by [s.147] CJA 1988 which, vhen in force, will enable, subject to any regulations, custodial remands or up to 28 days by consent where the defendant is present and has previously been remanded in custody for the same offence, see 3.62a.

Remand in absence   3.16

A magistrates' court may remand an accused in his absence where:
   (i) he is aged 17 or over;
   (ii) he has already been remanded in custody;
   (iii) he has given his consent to this course (and was 17 when he did so);
   (iv) that consent has not been withdrawn;
   (v) not more than two immediately preceding remands have been in his absence under this provision: s.128(3A) MCA 1980.

This provision must be explained on all relevant remands in custody vhere the accused is 17 or over and legally represented: s.128(1A); and nis consent must then be sought: s.128(1C). Where on an adjourned nearing the court is not satisfied that these conditions are or were met it nust adjourn the case for the shortest period possible to allow the accused to be produced (*ibid.* s.128(3C), (3D), (3E)).

Young adult offenders and juveniles   3.17

The places to which a person aged 17–20 years may be remanded *in custody* are dealt with in s.27 CJA 1948. A juvenile (ie under 17) not granted bail is remanded to the care of the local authority in accordance vith s.23 CYPA 1933; except that in certain narrowly defined circumstances a boy aged 15 or over may be remanded to prison: s.23(2) and the Certificates of Unruly Character (Conditions) Order 1977 (SI No 1037), *post*.

First appearance apart, the court can only issue a certificate where it is satisfied of certain prescribed matters on the basis of a written report from he local authority. Provided there is such a report, it is open to the court o reject the local authority view as to whether the young offender can be safely accommodated in a community home: see *R v Leicester Juvenile Court, ex p. Capenhurst* (1984) 80 Cr App R 320; but where the local authority 'fails' or 'declines' to submit the necessary report the court is powerless: *R v Dudley Magistrates' Court, ex p. G* (1988) *The Times*, 13 February.

3.18 Local remands

Where the court has power to remand a person in custody it may instead commit him to detention at a police station if the remand does not exceed *three clear days*: s.128(7) MCA 1980. The maximum period in the case of a juvenile is 24 hours: s.23(5) CYPA 1969. A person may not be kept in such detention unless this is needed for the purposes of inquiries into other offences: s.128(8) MCA 1980.

Note: that [s.144] CJA 1988, when in force, introduces remands of up to 192 hours to customs detention.

3.19   BAIL

The remand of an adult defendant otherwise than in custody *must* be on bail.

3.20 General right to bail

Anyone accused of an offence who appears or is brought before a magistrates' court in the course of or in connection with proceedings for the offence or who applies to a court for bail in connection with an offence *must be granted bail* unless his case falls within one of the *exceptions* in Sch.1 Bail Act 1976, when the court has a *discretion* to grant or refuse bail: s.4(1); except in a case of treason when bail may not be granted: s.4(7).

By s.4(2) the *general right to bail does not apply after 'conviction'* (a term widely defined in s.2(1)), *unless* the adjournment is *for the purpose of enabling inquiries* to be made to assist the court in dealing with him for the offence: s.4(4); or for proceedings under ss.6 or 16 PCCA 1973 (breach of requirement of probation and community service respectively): s.4(3). Thus while the general right to bail applies on a committal to the Crown Court for trial it does not apply on:

  (i) an appeal to the Crown Court or High Court;
 (ii) a committal to the Crown Court *for sentence*; or
(iii) a committal *to be dealt with* for breach of a suspended sentence; or to
(iv) warrants for the appearance of a defendant, nor, it is suggested, to warrants for fine defaulters.

3.21 Exceptions

Where the *general right to bail* applies a defendant may be refused bail only in the following circumstances:

— *in relation to all offences:*
  (i) if he has been arrested under s.7 Bail Act 1976 for absconding or breaching bail conditions in the present proceedings: para 6, Part I and para 5, Part II of Sch.1;
 (ii) for his own protection or, if a juvenile, for his welfare: para 3, Part I; and para 3: Part II, Sch.1;
(iii) if he is in custody in pursuance of a sentence of a court or under the Services Acts: para 4, Part I; and para 4, Part II, Sch.1;

— *in the case of non-imprisonable offences only:*
(iv) if he has previously failed to answer bail *and* the court believes that, if released, he would fail to surrender to custody: para 2, Part II, Sch.1;

— *in the case of imprisonable offences only:*
  if the court is satisfied there are 'substantial grounds' for
  believing that he would if released on bail

fail to surrender to custody: para 2(a), Part I, Sch.1;
  (vi) commit an offence while on bail: para 2(b), Part I, Sch.1;
  (vii) interfere with witnesses or otherwise obstruct the course of
     justice; para 2(c), Part I, Sch.1.

if the court is 'satisfied' that:
  (viii) it has not been practicable since the proceedings were instituted to
     obtain sufficient information to take the bail decision: para 5, Part I;
  (ix) he has been convicted and it is impracticable to complete any
     necessary inquiries or report on bail: para 7, Part I, Sch.1.

Of these objections by far the most important in practice are (v), (vi)
and (vii). It is suggested that the requirement that there should be
'substantial grounds' connotes something more than a mere possibility
and something less than proof beyond reasonable doubt. Indeed, it would
not appear to connote any particular degree of 'proof'. Much of the
information put before a court in a remand application is necessarily
incapable of proof in an evidential sense.

'Substantial likelihood of absconding' 3.22

Statistically, very few persons granted bail fail to attend and where there
is reason to fear absconding the problem can often be dealt with by
sureties and 'conditions' of bail. Courts are justified in taking greater risks
with those charged with less serious offences. Thus, it has been said that
the court must weigh the gravity of the offence and all the other facts of
the case against the likelihood of the accused absconding: *R v Phillips*
(1947) 32 Cr App R 47.

'Substantial likelihood of offending' 3.23

In *R v Phillips* (1947) 32 Cr App R 47, Atkinson J in the Court of Appeal
said that housebreaking particularly is a crime which will very probably
be repeated if a prisoner is released on bail, especially in the case of a man
who has a record of housebreaking. It is an offence which can be committed with a considerable measure of safety. Referring to a defendant
who had committed nine offences while on bail, he said: 'To turn such a
man loose on society until he has received his punishment for an offence
which is not in dispute is, in the view of the court, a very inadvisable step
to take. The court wish justices who release on bail young housebreakers
such as this to know that in 19 cases out of 20 it is a very wrong step to
take.' This applies, *a fortiori* in the case of offenders with bad records: *R v
Gentry; R. v Wharton* [1955] Crim LR 565; *R v Pegg* [1955] Crim LR 308.
The Home Office working party on bail agreed with this view and
commented that there were indications that there is a significantly greater
risk of offences being committed on bail by persons charged with *robbery*
or *burglary* than those charged with other offences: para 67 of the report.
At the other extreme, they added, if a person is charged with a comparatively minor offence a greater risk of similar offences being committed if
bail is granted *can reasonably be accepted*: para 68.

'Substantial likelihood of interference with witnesses' 3.24

The Home Office working party on bail commented: 'The possibility of
the defendant interfering with witnesses arises less frequently and will

usually be relevant only when the alleged offence is comparatively serious and there is some other indication, such as a past record of violence or threatening behaviour by the defendant. When there is a substantial ground for fearing such interference, this seems to us to be a very strong reason for refusing bail: para 69.

3.25 Factors to be considered

In taking a bail decision in the case of an *imprisonable offence* the court may consider the following factors as well as any others which may be relevant: para 9, Part I of Sch.1 Bail Act 1976.

The nature and seriousness of the offence or default: The Home Office working party on bail commented:

'. . . the more serious the offence charged, the stronger the temptation to abscond is likely to be, since a defendant who is liable, if convicted, to receive a long sentence of imprisonment has more inventive to abscond than one facing a less serious charge. Moreover, the more serious the offence, the smaller is the risk that can justifiably be taken either of the defendant's absconding or of his committing offences similar to that with which he is charged . . . At the other extreme, the comparative triviality of the offence may of itself indicate that a remand in custody is not justified, whatever the other considerations.

'57. While the seriousness of the class of offence is an important factor, it is not necessarily conclusive. The nature of the particular offence may also be relevant. The circumstances of a dometic murder, for example, may of themselves preclude any likelihood of repetition and there may be virtually no risk of the defendant's absconding. Similarly, the case of certain types of fraud, the possibility of repetition may not be a factor, although a remand in custody may, of course, be justifiable on other grounds.'

'Default' is defined in para 4, Part III, Sch.1.

The following observations were made by Dunn LJ, in the Court of Appeal in respect of committal proceedings on a charge of murder:

It is unnecessary to say that it is in the interests of the accused himself that he should be examined by a prison doctor whenever there is a charge of murder so that the various relevant matters affecting his state of mind at the time of the offence may be considered by the doctor, and in particular the possibility of a defence of diminished responsibility. This situation is not expressly provided for in the 1976 Act, which gives a right to bail, subject to the exceptions set out in Part I of Sch.I. Nothing that we say is intended to derogate from the terms of the 1976 Act so far as those exceptions are concerned. However, in para 9 of Part I of Sch. I, it is provided that in taking the decision required by para 2 of Part I of the Schedule (that is to say the decision whether or not to grant bail) the court shall have regard to four specified considerations as well as to any others which appear to be relevant. It appears to this court that the consideration in a charge of murder that in his own interests an accused should be examined by a prison doctor is a proper consideration for the magistrates to take into account. They should consider, before granting bail whether it would not be desirable to remand the accused in custody at any rate for a period long enough for the necessary reports to be prepared. Once that is done, the accused will then of course be in a position to apply for bail to the Crown Court.' *R v Vernege* [1982] 1 All ER 403.

See also s.3(6A), (6B) Bail Act 1976, which provides that where bail is granted in a murder case a condition must normally be imposed requiring the accused to undergo examination into his 'mental condition'.

The probable method of dealing with the defendant: The Home Office working party on bail commented:

'60. The court should also have regard to the likely sentence if the defendant is convicted, since his perception of the likely consequences of a conviction may be expected to have a considerable influence on his reaction to bail. The defendant will have much less incentive to abscond if the likely penalty is a fine or probation than if a custodial sentence is in prospect. If a person is remanded in custody and subsequently receives a sentence of imprisonment, the time spent on remand counts towards the sentence by virtue of s.67 of the Criminal Justice Act 1967. If however, he does not receive a sentence of imprisonment, he cannot of course gain 'credit' for his period in custody. Although it is wrong to assume that where a custodial remand is followed by a non-custodial sentence bail should have been granted initially, it is clearly desirable that, where an eventual custodial sentence is unlikely, bail should be granted unless there are strong grounds for a remand in custody. We would suggest that in a borderline case the court might give the defendant the benefit of the doubt, if a non-custodial sentence seems the likeliest outcome.

'61. This is not to say that a person who is likely to receive a custodial sentence if convicted should necessarily be refused bail. It has been suggested that, where a defendant is likely to receive a custodial sentence, it is doing him no kindness to give him a preliminary period of liberty. We do not think that this is a conclusive argument; much depends on whether the likely sentence of imprisonment will be short or long, since there is a danger, if the sentence is likely to be short, that the period on remand may exceed it. It seems to us, therefore, that the likely sentence if the defendant is convicted should be considered more in relation to the danger of his absconding than as a factor in its own right.'

Defendant's character and anecedents: The working party commented:

'59. The court should next consider the defendant's antecedents. These are a valuable guide, but need to be interpreted with some care. If the defendant has abused the grant of bail in the past or is already on bail in respect of another charge these facts should count strongly against him. In other cases, however, the defendant's previous convictions may not provide a reliable guide to his likely reaction to the grant of bail, unless, for example, they disclose a large number of serious offences. A long string of petty offences does not automatically justify a remand in custody. Clearly a man who, although convicted on a number of occasions in the past, has always answered his bail, is likely to be a good bail risk.'

Antecedents include previous convictions. They should be submitted to the court in writing and not *viva voce: R v Dyson* (1943) 107 JP 178. 'Antecedents' is as wide a term as can be conceived, *per* Lord Goddard CJ in *R v Vallet* [1951] 1 All ER 231 (where it was held in another context to extend to offences taken into consideration). A justice who has been informed of a defendant's previous convictions must not take part in trying the issue of his guilt: s.42(1) MCA 1980.

Defendant's associations and community ties: The working party commented:

'The extent to which the defendant has a stable background and settled employment – what are generally called his "community ties" – is likely to be of considerable influence in determining whether he is a good bail risk.

'65. One aspect of the defendant's community ties is the type of accommodation in which he lives. The fact that a defendant has no fixed abode is often advanced as a good reason for opposing bail. We accept that this is a material consideration, but we think it important that courts should ascertain precisely what is meant when a person is said to have no fixed abode. Does it mean that he is sleeping rough or that he is staying with friends or in a hostel or merely that he is living in a furnished flat to which he has only moved very recently?'

Probation 'bail hostels' are increasingly seeking to cater for this category of offender in particular.

Defendant's record as respects previous grants of bail: self-explanatory.

The strength of the evidence (before conviction only): The working party commented:

'58. Where the nature of the prosecution evidence of the alleged offence is known, this should be considered in conjunction with the seriousness and nature of the offence. If the case against the defendant appears to the court to be weak, this should be an additional ground for considering the grant of bail. In many cases the evidence will not be available at the time the court is considering the bail application, particularly if it is the defendant's first appearance in court. Where, however, the court is considering the question of bail on committal for trial, it may at that stage have a good idea of the strength of the evidence.'

Thus, even on committal for trial 'without consideration of the evidence' (see 4.10), justices may quite properly consider the contents of written statements, *semble*.

3.26 Procedure

No procedure is laid down. The usual practice is that after it has been decided whether to adjourn the case, the prosecution is asked whether it is aware of any reasons why bail should not be granted. The defendant is then given the opportunity to put forward considerations in favour of bail which he wished the court to take account of and to comment on any points made by the prosecution. Evidence is *not essential* on either side. In any event the strict rules of evidence do not apply: *Re Moles* [1981] Crim LR 170.

Unlike a trial, a decision about bail is not a contest between two parties with the court neutrally holding the ring. The court is under a *duty* to consider the question of bail and it may grant bail against the objection of the prosecutor as much as it may refuse bail in the absence of such objection. The extent to which evidence affecting proof of guilt or innocence might properly be called at a remand hearing would seem to be one of degree in the circumstances of a particular case. There is no rule that such evidence cannot be placed before the court, and, indeed, the purpose of an investigating officer giving 'formal evidence', or 'evidence of arrest' as it is sometimes called, a fairly common occurrence in the more serious cases, may often be to connect the accused sufficiently with the offence, as much as to claim that he may eg fail to surrender. Since the Bail Act itself actually requires that the court shall 'have regard' *inter alia* to the strength of the evidence, any case against allowing matters relevant to guilt to be put forward seems unarguable. What cannot be allowed, it seems, is a rehearsal of the trial, but this is not to say that the accused cannot, eg say that 'The evidence against me is weak because of a, b and c . . .' In pursuance of this duty the court may seek the views not only of the prosecutor and defendant, but also of anyone else who it believes can offer useful assistance.

The court may properly direct a probation officer to make inquiries, eg about the defendant's background and the possibility of 'bail hostel', or other accommodation. In the case of a bail decision taken after conviction, the facts of the case and the circumstances of the defendant will usually be within the court's knowledge and the role of the parties may accordingly be much less.

The doctrine of *functus officio* has to be applied with 'common sense' in relation to bail decisions: *R v Governor of Ashford Remand Centre, ex p. Harris* [1984] Crim LR 618 (magistrate rescinded bail after defendant made a disparaging remark to a police officer on leaving the dock).

3.27 Subsequent applications

Once a bench is satisfied that one of the statutory exceptions exists, it is a finding of the court analogous to *res judicata*. Thereafter a subsequent bench can only investigate whether that situation has changed: *R v Nottingham Justices, ex p. Davies* [1981] QB 38. The question is not, 'Has there been a change?' It is, 'Are there any new considerations which were not before the court when the accused was last remanded in custody?' Lapse of time may amount to fresh circumstances, particularly, but by no means only, because of *delay* on the part of the prosecution. It is suggested that for a decision to have this binding effect it must be one taken after the accused has had the opportunity to mount a fully prepared application for bail. The first appearance, which may take place soon after arrest and without legal representation, is seldom such an occasion. The later court is bound to investigate any alleged change of circumstances: *Re Moles* [1981] Crim LR 170.

A refusal on the part of justices to look behind the fresh grounds to grounds which had been put forward before was held to be wrong in *R v Barking Justices, ex p. Shankshaft* (1983) 147 JP 399. In many cases there will be a *material change in circumstances at the committal for trial stage* justifying a review of the bail decision, eg the strength of the prosecution case may be better known or it may be possible to re-evaluate the seriousness of the offence or the time likely to elapse before the case comes to trial, but the fact that the committal stage has been reached is not *ipso facto* a 'material change': *R v Slough Justices, ex p. Duncan and Embling* (1982) 75 Cr App R 384.

Where a magistrates' court has heard 'full argument' and issued a certificate to that effect – whether following a change of circumstances or otherwise – application lies to the Crown Court: see *Applications to the Crown Court for bail*, 3.36.

Conditional Bail   3.28
The defendant's own recognizance may not be taken in criminal proceedings: Bail Act 1976. But he may be required to:
(a) provide *sureties*;
(b) comply with *requirements* imposed by the court; and
(c) give *security*.

Sureties   3.29
A bailed person may be required to provide sureties: s.3(4) Bail Act 1976. In considering the suitability of a surety regard may be had among other things to his
— financial resources
— character and any previous convictions
— proximity to the bailed person: s.8(2).

As s.8 makes clear, these are not the only matters which may be considered. It is essential that the person being put forward should be interested in looking after and, if necessary, using powers he has to prevent the accused from escaping: *Petersdorff on Bail* quoted with approval by North J in *Consolidated Exploration and Finance Co v Musgrave* (1900) 64 JP 89. But a court may not refuse a surety for his political opinions or otherwise inquire into his private interest or character: *R v Badger* (1843) 7 JP 128. 'Excessive' bail is forbidden by the Bill of Rights 1688. A solicitor ought not to stand bail for his client: *R v Scott Jervis* (1876) *The Times*, 20 November. As well as being an illegal contract (*R v Porter* (1910) 74 JP 159) it is an offence to agree to indemnify a surety in criminal proceedings: s.9(1) Bail Act 1976.

Forfeiture of recognizances   3.30
The court may declare a recognizance forfeited: s.120(1) MCA 1980. No procedure is laid down but since the section confers a *discretion* on the justices whether to forfeit *in whole or in part or not at all* (s.120(3)), it seems essential that the surety should have an opportunity to show cause why the recognizances should not be 'estreated'. A notice of hearing would appear to be sufficient for this purpose provided there is proof of service.

The principles to be applied to questions of forfeiture were summarised by McCullough J in *R v Uxbridge Justices, ex p. Heward Mills* [1983] 1 WLR 56:

1. When a defendant for whose attendance a person has stood surety fails to appear, the full recognizance should be forfeited, unless it appears fair and just that a lesser sum should be forfeited or none at all.
2. The burden of satisfying the court that the full sum should not be forfeited rests on the surety and is a heavy one. It is for him to lay before the court the evidence of want of culpability and of means on which he relies.
3. Where a surety is unrepresented the court should assist him by explaining these principles in ordinary language, and giving him the opportunity to call evidence and advance argument in relation to them.

See also *R v Southampton Justices, ex p. Green* [1976] QB 11; *R v Southampton Justices, ex p. Corker* (1976) *The Times*, 11 February; *R v Horseferry Road Magistrate' Court, ex p. Pearson* [1976] 1 WLR 511; *R v Waltham Forest Justices, ex p. Parfrey* (1980) 2 Cr App R (S) 208; *R v Tottenham Magistrates' Court, ex p. Ricardi* (1978) 66 Cr App R 150); and *R v York Crown Court ex p. Coleman* (1987) *The Times*, 12 May, where a judge erred in ordering the estreatment of the whole of the recognizances of two sureties in circumstances where the accused attended court on the day of his trial but absconded during the luncheon adjournment.

Means other than the surety's own must be disregarded: *R v Southampton Justices, ex p. Green* [1976] QB 11; but the system of sureties would be defeated if the amount to be forfeited was limited to the defendant's means: *R v Southampton Justices, ex p. Corker* (1976) *The Times*, 11 February. The justices are under no obligation to inquire as to the ability of the surety to pay: *R v Waltham Forest Justices, ex p. Parfrey* (1980) 2 Cr App R (S) 208. However, an order of forfeiture was quashed where justices declined to hear evidence of means: *R v Uxbridge Justices, ex p. Heward-Mills* [1983] 1 WLR 56.

It is the duty of the surety to stay in touch with the bailed person to see that he will appear in court. The court in considering the culpability of the surety will look to what he did to see that the accused surrendered and what he did to alert the police if there was any known risk of absconding. It is the duty of the surety to keep himself informed of the bail conditions and he can help himself by entering into the recognizance only from one remand to another rather than on continuous bail: *R v Wells St. Magistrates' Court, ex p. Albanese* [1981] 3 All ER 769. While the fact that a surety has reported to the police under s.7(3) Bail Act 1976 does not relieve the surety of his obligations it is a factor which the court may take into account when considering forfeiture: *R v Ipswich Crown Court, ex p. Reddington* [1981] Crim LR 618.

There is no right of appeal to the Crown Court against an order to forfeit a recognizance: *R v Durham JJ, ex p. Laurent* (1945) 109 JP 21. But *certiorari* will lie where an error in law is disclosed in the affidavits: *R v Southampton Justices, ex p. Green, supra*.

3.31 Requirements of bail

A person bailed by the court may be *required* to comply with requirements (commonly referred to as '*conditions*') necessary to ensure that:
— he *surrenders* to custody

— he does *not commit an offence* while on bail

— he does *not interfere with witnesses* or otherwise *obstruct the course of justice*

— he *makes himself available for* the purpose of *inquiries or a report*: s.3(6) Bail Act 1976.

(This provision is duplicated for imprisonable offences by para 8 of Part I, Sch.1).

There is no statutory power to add requirements for any other purpose. Whilst the first three grounds are similar to the main exceptions to the right to bail, justices are here not obliged to have substantial grounds. It is, eg enough if they perceive a real and not a fanciful risk of an offence being committed, *per* Lord Lane CJ in *R v Mansfield Justices, ex p. Sharkey* [1985] QB 613 (bail conditions imposed in the miners' strike).

There is no power to place a bailed person under the supervision of a probation officer but it is part of the duties of a probation officer to advise, assist and befriend any person who is for the time being remanded on bail and is willing to be assisted: r.34 Probation Rules 1984 (SI No 647).

A *parent or guardian* who stands as *surety* may additionally be required to *secure* that the child or young person complies with any such requirement except where the child or young person will become 17 before he is required to surrender and not in respect of a sum greater than £50: s.3 Bail Act 1976.

HOC 206/1977 asks justices 'to ensure that the defendant is able to comply with any conditions they intend to impose under s.3(6) and that any such conditions are enforceable. Difficulty has been encountered where, for example, a court has required *residence* at a particular address without first checking that accommodation was available there; a court has delegated the approval of a place of residence to the police or probation service; a court has required the defendant not to enter any licensed premises for the period of bail; a court has imposed a *reporting condition* without specifying the police station or has named a station without checking that it is continuously manned. Courts are requested to be especially selective in requiring regular reporting to a police station since this can be burdensome for the police and also raise identification problems. A condition of bail sometimes imposed by courts is that the defendant *surrender his passport* prior to release. Since this is simply a device to prevent the defendant from absconding abroad it should be accompanied by a post-release condition stipulating that the defendant shall not leave Great Britain during the period of bail. When a passport condition is imposed but the defendant is committed to custody pending its surrender or the finding of sureties, it would be of assistance to prison governors and help to avoid unnecessary delay in releasing the defendant if any information available to the court about the whereabouts of the passport (eg that it is already in the hands of airport police or Customs and Excise authorities) could be noted on the committal warrant.'

A condition that the accused should *not drive* is lawful, but courts ought to consider whether it might have unexpected and possibly unjust results eg in effect, a period of disqualification in excess of a mandatory one later imposed, and which cannot then be mitigated or reduced on account of the earlier bail conditions: *R v Kwame* (1975) 60 Cr App R 65.

It is not an offence to break conditions of bail, this simply results in possible withholding of bail if the accused is arrested and brought before the court: see *Exceptions* at 3.21, *ante*.

3.32 Security

A bailed person may be required to give security *where he is unlikely to remain in Great Britain*: s.3(5) Bail Act 1976. In the case of an imprisonable offence security may only be called for for the reasons set out in para 8, Part I, Sch.1 (see *Sureties* at 3.29 *supra*).

The term 'security' is not defined. HOC 206/1977 comments that 'it may take the form of *cash, travellers' cheques or any other article of value*. In exercising their discretion in a particular case, courts or the police should have regard to the ease with which the security could be held and converted into pounds sterling in the event of forfeiture. For example it would be unwise to accept as security any perishable articles or any article which would create problems of storage or valuation.' The court may direct how the requirement to give security is to be complied with: r.8 MC Rules 1981. For further advice see HOC 11/1978.

Security may be forfeited in whole or part upon a failure to surrender: s.5(4)(8) 1976. The order does not take effect until 21 days after it is made: 5(8A), and the court may in this period revoke or vary it if the defendant shows good reason for failing to surrender. The court may also *remit* or *reduce* the amount of the forfeiture after the order has taken effect: s.5(8B). HOC 206/1977 comments that it is expected that an application for variation or remission will normally be made within the 21 day period, but there may be occasions when this is not possible, and therefore would be unreasonable for a period which is fixed for administrative convenience to fetter rights of the individual.

3.33 Variation of bail terms

A court may *vary the conditions* of any bail it has granted or *impose conditions* where there were none before on application by or on behalf of the bailed person or by the prosecutor or a constable: s.3(8) Bail Act 1976.

3.34 INFORMATION FOR THE DEFENDANT

Whenever bail is *granted* in criminal proceedings or *withheld* from anyone enjoying the general right to bail a record of the decision must be made in prescribed manner and a copy given on request to the defendant: s.5(1) Bail Act 1976. A court dealing with anyone enjoying the general right to bail and imposing conditions, or varying them, or witholding bail *must* give its *resons* for the purpose of enabling him to consider making an application to another court: s.5(3). The reason must be noted in the court register and a copy given to the defendant: s.5(4).

When a magistrates' court withholds bail to anyone who is not legally represented it must tell him of his right to apply to the High Court and, where appropriate, the Crown Court: s.5(6).

3.35 APPLICATION TO THE HIGH COURT FOR BAIL

Where in criminal proceedings a magistrates' court *withholds bail or imposes conditions* in granting bail, the High Court may grant bail or vary the conditions: s.22(1) CJA 1967.

3.36 APPLICATION TO THE CROWN COURT FOR BAIL – INCLUDING 'FULL ARGUMENT CERTIFICATES'

The Crown Court may grant bail, *inter alia*, to anyone:
— (i) who has been committed in custody for appearance before that court;

— (ii) who is in custody pursuant to a sentence of a magistrates' court
and who has appealed to the Crown Court; or
— (iii) who has been remanded in custody by a magistrates' court and
who has a *full argument certificate*: s.81(1), (1J) Supreme Court
Act 1981. Such a certificate must be granted by a magistrates'
court upon hearing full argument on a bail application for the
first time and on hearing argument after a change in circumstances or on new considerations: s.5(6A) Bail Act 1976.

ENFORCEMENT

Duty to surrender   3.37

A person granted bail is under a *duty to surrender to custody*: s.3(1) Bail
Act 1976; failure to comply constitutes an offence under s.6(1) or (2). A
person surrenders to custody when he complies with the procedures of
the court where he is due to appear and reports to the appropriate person
eg the court usher. Surrendering to a judicial officer is not necessary:
Director of Public Prosecutions v Richards (1988) *The Times*, 25 February. Courts should thus make it clear to defendants what their obligations are in this regard: *ibid*.

NB It is no offence to break 'conditions' of bail, this simply resulting in
possible witholding of bail if the accused is then arrested and brought
before the court. A remand on bail is a direction to appear before the
court:
— at the end of the period of remand, or
— at every time and place to which the hearing may be adjourned:
s.128(1), (4), MCA 1980.
See *Exceptions* at 3.21 ante.

Arrest of a bailed person without warrant   3.38

A *constable* may arrest *without warrant* a bailed person where he has
*reasonable grounds for believing that he will abscond or is likely to break
or has broken any bail condition* or where he is notified in writing by a
surety that the bailed person is unlikely to surrender and the surety wishes
to be relieved of his obligations: s.7(3) Bail Act 1976. As soon as practicable (and in any event within 24 hours) a person so arrested must be
brought before a justice for the petty sessions area *in which he was
arrested* unless he was arrested within 24 hours of the time appointed for
surrender: s.7(4); when he must be brought before the court at which he
was to have surrendered to custody. The justice must give him bail on the
same conditions unless satisfied that he is not likely to surrender or has
broken a bail condition, when the defendant may be remanded on *bail or
in custody*: s.7(5).

At common law the surety of a bailed person had a power to detain. Thus, 'if
it comes to (the knowledge of sureties) that (the bailed person) is about to
abscond they should at once inform the police of the fact,' *per* Lord
Alverstone CJ in *R v Porter* (1910) 74 JP 159. 'Hence, they may seize his
person at any time (as on a Sunday) or at any place to carry him to a justice to
find new sureties, or be committed in their discharge, and in surrendering the
principal they may command the co-operation of the sheriff and any of his
officers': *Petersdorff on Bail* cited in *Consolidated Exploration and Finance
Co v Musgrave* (1900) 64 JP 89. It is suggested that this power of the surety has
not been superseded by the Act of 1976, although a *constable* would normally
be wise to rely on the procedure provided in s.7(3).

3.39 Arrest on warrant

If a person released on bail in criminal proceedings *fails to surrender*, a warrant may be issued for his arrest: s.7(1) Bail Act 1976. There is a similar power when a defendant who has surrendered *absents himself without leave* from the court: s.7(2). **NB** The power to issue a warrant does not extend to 'breach of conditions' of bail where the only remedy is 'arrest' under s.7(3), or possibly 'detention' at common law: 3.07, *ante*.

3.40 Absconding from bail – 'Failure to surrender'

It is an *offence* for a bailed person to *fail without reasonable cause to surrender to custody*: s.6(1) Bail Act 1976. Similarly, it is an offence, having had reasonable cause to fail to surrender, to fail to surrender as soon as reasonably practicable thereafter: s.6(2). The burden of proof of reasonable cause lies on the bailed person: s.6(3). Both offences are punishable either on summary conviction or as a criminal contempt of court: s.6(5). On summary conviction the offender is liable to imprisonment for up to three months or a fine not exceeding level 5 (£2,000) on the standard scale or both: s.6(7).

The offence of 'failure to surrender to bail' is not subject to the normal procedural rule whereby proceedings are commenced by the laying of an information, is not (despite certain indicators) an offence 'triable either way' and is an offence in respect of which proceedings can only be commenced 'by the court's own motion'. Following rulings to this effect by Watkins LJ in *Schiavo v Anderton* [1986] 3 WLR 177, Lord Lane CJ took the unusual step of issuing the *Practice Direction (Bail: Failure to Surrender to Custody)* [1987] 1 WLR 79 in order to 'clarify the effect' of that ruling, principally to indicate that although 'acting of its own motion' it was 'more appropriate' that the initiation of proceedings should follow from an express invitation by the prosecutor, who would then '. . . naturally conduct the proceedings'. The *Practice Direction* also clarifies that the rule against commencing proceedings by way of an information applies only to '*court bail*' (as in *Schiavo v Anderton*) and not to '*police bail*' where proceedings should be initiated by the normal methods of charge or information. The key points from *Schiavo v Anderton* are as follows:

— (a) The magistrates' court and the Crown Court each required separately a power to punish for the offence of absconding.
— (b) The offence was not subject to the general rule that trial be commenced by an information.
— (c) The only proper way to proceed was by the initiation of the simple procedure for trial by the court's own motion and not by formal charge.
— (d) The offence was not triable on indictment or either way.
— (e) The offence was only triable in the court at which proceedings were to be heard in respect of which bail had been granted.
— (f) The Bail Act offence should be tried immediately following the disposal of a substantive offence in respect of which bail had been granted.

Without further qualification, that ruling leaves open the question who should conduct the proceedings. In the earlier case of *R v Gateshead Justices, ex p. Usher* [1981] Crim LR 491, Ormerod LJ described as 'a legal pantomime' the idea that the clerk should prosecute and give evidence in such cases and Donaldson J said that it is *wrong* for a clerk to prosecute. This problem, *inter alia*, the *Practice Direction* resolves as follows:

1. This *Practice Direction* is issued with a view to clarifying any misunderstandings as to the effect of the decision in *Schiavo v Anderton* [1986] 3 WLR 177 in which, *inter alia*, the Divisional Court of the Queen's Bench Division provided guidance on the procedure to be adopted in magistrates' courts when dealing with allegations of failure to surrender to custody contrary to s.6 of the Bail Act 1976.

2. *Bail granted by a magistrates' court*

Where a person has been granted bail by a court and subsequently fails to surrender to custody as contemplated by s.6(1) or 6(2) of the Bail Act 1976, on arrest that person should be brought before the court at which the proceedings in respect of which bail was granted are to be heard. It is neither necessary nor desirable to lay an information in order to commence proceedings for the failure to surrender. Having regard to the nature of the offence which is tantamount to the defiance of a court order, it is more appropriate that the court itself should initiate the proceedings by its own motion, following an express invitation by the prosecutor. The court will only be invited so to move if, having considered all the circumstances, the prosecutor considers proceedings are appropriate. Where a court complies with such an invitation, the prosecutor will naturally conduct the proceedings and, where the matter is contested, call the evidence. Any trial should normally take place immediately following the disposal of the proceedings in respect of which bail was granted.

3. *Bail granted by a police officer*

Where a person has been bailed from a police station subject to a duty to appear before a magistrates' court or to attend a police station on an appointed date and/or time, a failure so to appear or attend cannot be said to be tantamount to the defiance of a court order. There does not exist the same compelling justification for the court to act by its own motion. Where bail has been granted by a police officer, any proceedings for a failure to surrender to custody, whether at a court or a police station, should accordingly be initiated by charging the accused or by the laying of an information.

Practice Direction [1987] 1 WLR 79.

In *Laidlaw v Atkinson* (1986) *The Times*, 2 August, where a defendant failed to appear through mistake (ie due to some confusion concerning both him, his solicitors and the bail notice which led him to think that he was due to appear the following week) '. . . The error was his responsibility and it could not be said that it amounted to reasonable cause. But contrast *France v Dewsbury Magistrates' Court* (1987) *The Times*, 7 December in which a decision by justices not to initiate proceedings of their own motion – 'the court agreed not to proceed' – where the defendant failed to appear because the solicitor 'got the days mixed up', passed without comment from the Divisional Court. This latter ruling establishes that it is not open to justices to proceed of their own motion on a later occasion in respect of an earlier failure to surrender which has been consciously 'overlooked'. See also *Ex p. Usher, supra* (7 minutes late, no offence on the facts).

Breach of bail conditions is not an offence: 3.31.

A person in custody in pursuance of a Crown Court warrant with a view to his appearance before that court must be brought before either the Crown Court or a magistrates' court: s.81 Supreme Court Act 1981. Where such a person is brought before magistrates he must be dealt with in accordance with s.43 MCA 1980.

3.41 **LEGAL AID**

An application for legal aid *must* be granted, subject to means, when a defendant is brought before the court *in pursuance of a remand in custody* on an occasion *when he may be again remanded or committed in custody* and is not (but wishes to be) legally represented, not having been legally represented on the first occasion: s.29(1) (CC) LAA 1974. This requirement does *not* apply after conviction s.29(1A). Such a legal order may be confined to so much of the proceedings as relates to the grant of bail: s.29(1A). Legal aid confined to bail applications does not extend to the services of counsel: s.30(2).

Legal aid must similarly be granted, subject to means, when it is applied for by a person who is to be sentenced or dealt with for an offence by a magistrates' court or the Crown Court and is to be kept in custody for inquiries or report: s.29(1)(d) LAA 1974.

3.42 **TIME LIMITS (PRESCRIBED AREAS ONLY)**

Section 22 POA 1985 empowers the Secretary of State to prescribe time limits with respect to the preliminary stages of criminal proceedings, laying down the maximum time allowed to the prosecution to complete a particular step. Following field trials in the counties of Avon, Kent, Somerset, the West Midlands and some further areas, the Secretary of State has made the Prosecution of Offences (Custody Time Limit) Regulations 1987 (SI No 299), and the Prosecution of Offences (Custody Time Limits) (Amendment) Regulations 1988 (SI No 164) applying pre-trial custody limits to certain areas. The Custody Time Limit regulations impose a limit on the length of time for which a person may be held in custody *awaiting trial*. This limit varies according to whether the matter is before the Crown Court, the magistrates' court (and which magistrates' court – see below), and upon whether a 'mode of trial' decision has been made by magistrates in favour of summary trial.

Custody limits in the magistrates' court: The regulations apply only where the accused is in custody and facing proceedings for an *indictable offence* or an *offence triable either way* (see r.4 for detail). No limits apply to offences which are summary only (an anomaly, in that, in theory at least, a 'summary' remand prisoner might be held for longer than someone charged with a much more serious offence, or one in respect of which summary trial has been deemed more suitable). In most areas there is a custody limit of *70 days* between first appearance and summary trial or committal. By 'committal' is meant '. . . the time when the court decides whether or not to commit the accused to the Crown Court for trial': see r.4(2). By a process of deduction, this particular time measure applies only where the committal is a 'paper committal' under s.6(2) MCA 1980, since where the court proceeds to inquire into the information as examining justices pursuant to s.6(1) of the 1980 Act the relevant time is when the court '. . . begins to hear evidence for the prosecution': see r.4(5). The custody limit in the West Midlands is higher, at *84 days* – and it has been intimated that this will be reduced when circumstances permit.

Where the justices decide on summary trial, there is a tighter limit of *56 days* between first appearance and summary trial, but this limit only applies if the decision to proceed takes place within the 56 days, so that where it is not practicable to make such a decision within 56 days the regular limits of 70 or 84 days will apply.

First appearance before magistrates: Under r.2(2), the reference to a person's 'first appearance' is defined as meaning '. . . the time when first he appears or is brought before the court on an information charging him with that offence', whilst r.2(4) makes it clear that the maximum period set by the regulations does not include the day on which custody commenced. Rule 2(5) excludes weekends and public and bank holidays from being expiry days.

Custody limits in the Crown Court: In the specified Crown Court centres, the custody limit is *112 days* from committal to arraignment (defined as 'the time when he is asked to plead: r.5(7)). The time limits apply where cases have been instituted in the specified areas, wherever they may later be transferred. The Crown Court limits apply both to cases committed for trial and to cases begun in the Crown Court by voluntary bill of indictment under s.2(2). Administration of Justice Act 1933, the single standard limit being 112 days between committal or preferring the bill and arraignment.

When a time limit expires: In effect a custody limit places a responsibility on the prosecutor to ensure that cases are dealt with within the time limits, or risk the accused being released on bail. If a custody limit does expire, this result is automatic – so that the court, deprived of its custody powers when the relevant time – has run, must release on bail – unless it allows further time and extends the custody limit under s.22(3) POA 1985, which provides that '. . . the appropriate court may, at anytime before the expiry of a time limit imposed by the regulations, extend, or further extend, that limit if satisfied – (a) that there is good and sufficient cause for doing so; and (b) that the prosecution has acted with all due expedition'. There is thus no question of treating the accused as acquitted (as there will be in relation to overall time limits, if and when introduced: see s.22(4)). For the relevant procedure see r.7.

Bail: Where bail is (ie, has to be) granted, this may be unconditional or conditional according to normal principles. Since a remand in custody will no longer be an option, there may be a temptation to strengthen conditions of bail to compensate for this. Clearly, however, a condition of bail which is so restrictive as to contradict the very fact of bail would seem to be both inappropriate and improper. Rule 8 contains a number of modifications to the Bail Act 1976. These are reproduced by way of the regulations, *post*, since to amend or modify the Bail Act provisions might cause confusion for areas to which the regulations have not yet been applied.

Statutory Provisions

CRIMINAL JUSTICE ACT 1948

Remand of persons aged 17 to 20

3.43

27. (1) Where a court remands a person charged with or convicted of an offence or commits him for trial or sentence and he is not less than 17 but under 21 years old and is not released on bail, then, if the court has been notified by the Secretary of State that a remand centre is available for the reception from the court of persons of his class or description, it shall commit him to a remand centre and, if it has not been so notified, it shall commit him to prison.

(2) Where a person is committed to a remand centre in pursuance of this section, the centre shall be specified in the warrant and he shall be detained

there for the period for which he is remanded or until he is delivered thence in due course of law.

(3) In this section 'court' includes a justice; and nothing in this section affects the provisions of s.128(7) of the Magistrates' Courts Act, 1980 (which provides for remands to the custody of a constable).

[*as substituted by Sch.5 CYPA 1969, as amended by Sch.7 MCA 1980*].

COMMENTARY

For determination of age, see s.80(3) CJA 1948. For the disposal of juveniles remanded or committed for trial or sentence see s.23 CYPA 1969, *infra*.

s.27(1): Remand centre, defined in s.43 Prison Act 1952, as substituted by s.11 CJA 1982 (see s.80 of the 1948 Act).

CHILDREN AND YOUNG PERSONS ACT 1969

3.44   **Remand to care of local authorities etc**

23. (1) Where a court–

(a) remands or commits for trial a child charged with homicide or remands a child convicted of homicide; or

(b) remands a young person charged with or convicted of one or more offences or commits him for trial or sentence,

and he is not released on bail, then, subject to the following provisions of this section, the court shall commit him to the care of a local authority in whose area it appears to the court that he resides or that the offence or one of the offences was committed.

(2) If the court aforesaid certifies that a young person is of so unruly a character that he cannot safely be committed to the care of a local authority under the preceding subsection, then if the court has been notified by the Secretary of State that a remand centre is available for the reception from the court of persons of his class or description, it shall commit him to a remand centre and, if it has not been so notified, it shall commit him to a prison.

(3) If, on the application of the local authority to whose care a young person is committed by a warrant under subs (1) of this section, the court by which he was so committed or any magistrates' court having jurisdiction in the place where he is for the time being certifies as mentioned in subs (2) of this section, the provisions of the said subs (2) relating to committal shall apply in relation to him and he shall cease to be committed in pursuance of the said subs (1).

(4) The preceding provisions of this section shall have effect subject to the provisions of s.37 of the Magistrates' Courts Act 1980 (which relates to committal to the Crown Court with a view to a youth custody sentence).

(5) In this section 'court' and 'magistrates' court' include a justice; and notwithstanding anything in the preceding provisions of this section, s.128(7) of the said Act of 1980 (which provides for remands to the custody of a constable for periods not exceeding three clear days) shall have effect in relation to a child or young person as if for the reference to three clear days there were substituted a reference to 24 hours.

[*as amended by Sch.8 Courts Act 1971, Sch.7 MCA 1980, Sch.14 CJA 1982*].

COMMENTARY

s.23(1): A court, see s.23(5).

A child, means a person under the age of 14: s.70(1) of the Act.

A young person, includes in s.23(1) a child who has attained the age of 10 years: CYPA 1969 (Transitional Modifications of Part 1) Order 1979 (SI No 125). For the determination of age, see s.99 CYPA 1933.

The care of a local authority, except when the contrary intentions appears a child in the care of a local authority under a warrant under s.23(1) of this season is treated in accordance with

Part II of the Child Care Act 1980: s.17. Note, particularly, s.18(3) which states that: 'If it appears to the local authority that it is necessary, for the purpose of protecting members of the public, to exercise their powers in relation to a particular child in their care in a manner which may not be consistent with their duty . . . the authority may, notwithstanding that duty, act in that manner.' For other powers and duties of the authority, see s.24 CYPA 1969.

Resides, means 'habitually resides': s.70(1) of the Act.

s.23(2): So unruly a character, when a young person is committed to a remand centre or a prison under s.23(2), the court shall include in the order of committal a certificate that the young person is of so unruly a character that he cannot safely be committed to the care of a local authority: r.27 MC (CYP) Rules 1970.

Certifies, the court may not make a certificate under this subsection unless one or more of the conditions in the Certificates of Unruly Character (Conditions) Order 1977, as amended, *post*, is satisfied. First appearance apart, the court or justice must be satisfied of the prescribed matters on the basis of a written report from the local authority. Provided there is such a report it is open to the court to reject the local authority view as to whether the young offender can be safely accommodated in a community home: see *R v Leicester City Juvenile Court, ex p. Capenhurst* (1985) 80 Cr App R 320; but where the local authority 'fails' or 'declines' to submit the necessary report the court is powerless: *R v Dudley Magistrates' Court, ex p. G* (1988) *The Times*, 13 February.

Young person, means a person who has attained the age of 14 and is under the age of 17: s.70(1) of the Act. The references in s.23(2) and (3) to a young person do not include a female person under the age of 17: CYPA 1969 (Transitional Modifications of Part I) Order 1979 (SI 1979 No 125). They also exclude references to a male person who has not attained the age of 15 years: CYPA 1969 (Transitional Modifications of PartI) Order 1981 (SI 1981, No 81).

s.23(3): Certifies, see note to s.23(2).

Young person, see note to s.23(2).

Recognizance on release of arrested child or young person **3.45**
29. A child or young person arrested in pursuance of a warrant shall not be released unless *he or* his parent or guardian (with or without sureties) enters into a recognizance for such amount as the custody officer at the police station where he is detained considers will secure his attendance at the hearing of the charge; and the recognizance entered into in pursuance of this section may, if the custody officer thinks fit, be conditioned for the attendance of the parent or guardian at the hearing in addition to the child or young person.
[*as substituted by Sch.6 PACE 1984. The words 'he or' shall be repealed when [Sch.15] CJA 1988 comes into force*].

BAIL ACT 1976

Meaning of 'bail in criminal proceedings'; **3.46**
1. (1) In this Act 'bail in criminal proceedings' means–
(a) bail grantable in or in connection with proceedings for an offence to a person who is accused or convicted of the offence, or
(b) bail grantable in connection with an offence to a person who is under arrest for the offence or for whose arrest for the offence a warrant (endorsed for bail) is being issued.

(2) In this Act 'bail' means bail grantable under the law (including common law) for the time being in force.

(3) Except as provided by s.13(3) of this Act, this section does not apply to bail in or in connection with proceedings outside England and Wales.

(4) This section does not apply to bail granted before the coming into force of this Act.

(5) This section applies–
(a) whether the offence was committed in England or Wales or elsewhere, and

(b) whether it is an offence under the law of England and Wales, or of any other country or territory.

(6) Bail in criminal proceedings shall be granted (and in particular shall be granted unconditionally or conditionally) in accordance with this Act.

COMMENTARY

s.1(1): Bail, defined in s.1(2).

An offence, includes an alleged offence: s.2(2), *infra.* Seemingly, this does not include a breach of the peace which does not itself constitute an offence.

Convicted, partially defined in s.2(1), *infra.*

3.47   **Other definitions**
2. (1) In this Act, unless the context otherwise requires, 'conviction' includes–
(a) a finding of guilt,
(b) a finding that a person is not guilty by reason of insanity,
(c) a finding under s.30(1) of the Magistrates' Courts Act 1980 (remand for medical examination) that the person in question did the act or made the omission charged, and
(d) a conviction of an offence for which an order is made placing the offender on probation or discharging him absolutely or conditionally, and 'convicted' shall be construed accordingly.

(2) In this Act, unless the context otherwise requires–
'bail hostel' and 'probation hostel' have the same meanings as in the Powers of Criminal Courts Act 1973.
'child' means a person under the age of 14,
'court' includes a Judge of a court, or a justice of the peace and, in the case of a specified court, includes a Judge or (as the case may be) justice having powers to act in connection with proceedings before that court.
'Courts-Martial Appeal rules' means rules made under s.49 of the Courts-Martial (Appeals) Act, 1968,
'Crown Court rules' means rules made under s.15 of the Courts Act, 1971,
'magistrates' courts rules' means rules made under s.15 of the Justices of the Peace Act, 1949,
'offence' includes an alleged offence,
'proceedings against a fugitive offender' means proceedings under s.9 of the Extradition Act, 1870, s.7 of the Fugitive Offenders Act, 1967 or s.2(1) or s.4(3) of the Backing of Warrants (Republic of Ireland) Act, 1965.
'Supreme Court rules' means rules made under s.99 of the Supreme Court of Judicature (Consolidation) Act, 1925.
'surrender to custody' means, in relation to a person released on bail, surrendering himself into the custody of the court or of the constable (according to the requirements of the grant of bail) at the time and place for the time being appointed for him to do so,
'vary', in relation to bail, means imposing further conditions after bail is granted, or varying or rescinding conditions,
'young person' means a person who has attained the age of 14 and is under the age of 17.

(3) Where an enactment (whenever passed) which relates to bail in criminal proceedings refers to the person bailed appearing before a court it is to be construed unless the context otherwise requires as referring to his surrendering himself into the custody of the court.

(4) Any reference in this Act to any other enactment is a reference thereto as amended, and includes a reference thereto as extended or applied, by or under any other enactment, including this Act.
[as amended by Sch.12 CLA 1977, Sch.7 MCA 1980. The words in italics in subs (2) will be added when [Sch.14] CJA 1988 comes into force].

COMMENTARY

s.2(2): Surrendering to custody, thus, a defendant answers to his bail when he reports his presence at the place and time appointed. If there is any gap between that moment and his appearance in court he is, for that period, not on bail but in the custody of the court. If he absents himself from the court without leave during that period a warrant for his arrest may be issued: s.7(2). Unless there is some good reason. HOC 206/1977 suggested that defendants surrendering to the custody of the court should not be held in the secure area pending the beginning of their case since it is undesirable that a person who has been at liberty prior to the hearing should be locked up upon his arrival at the court.

General provisions

3.48

3. (1) A person granted bail in criminal proceedings shall be under a duty to surrender to custody, and that duty is enforceable in accordance with s.6 of this Act.

(2) No recognizance for his surrender to custody shall be taken from him.

(3) Except as provided by this section–
(a) no security for his surrender to custody shall be taken from him,
(b) he shall not be required to provide a surety or sureties for his surrender to custody, and
(c) no other requirement shall be imposed on him as a condition of bail.

(4) He may be required, before release on bail, to provide a surety or sureties to secure his surrender to custody.

(5) If it appears that he is unlikely to remain in Great Britain until the time appointed for him to surrender to custody, he may be required, before release on bail, to give security for his surrender to custody.
The security may be given by him or on his behalf.

(6) He may be required (but only by a court) to comply, before release on bail or later, with such requirements as appear to the court to be necessary to secure that–
(a) he surrenders to custody,
(b) he does not commit an offence while on bail,
(c) he does not interfere with witnesses or otherwise obstruct the course of justice whether in relation to himself or any other person,
(d) he makes himself available for the purpose of enabling inquiries or a report to be made to assist the court in dealing with him for the offence.

(6A) In the case of a person accused of murder the court granting bail shall, unless it considers that satisfactory reports on his mental condition have already been obtained, impose as conditions of bail–
(a) a requirement that the accused shall undergo examination by two medical practitioners for the purpose of enabling such reports to be prepared; and
(b) a requirement that he shall for that purpose attend such an institution or place as the court directs and comply with any other directions which may be given to him for that purpose by either of those practitioners.

(6B) Of the medical practitioners referred to in subs (6A) above at least one shall be a practitioner approved for the purposes of s.12 of the Mental Health Act 1983.

(6ZA) Where he is required under subsection (6) above to reside in a bail hostel (or probation hostel, he may also be required to comply with the rules of the hostel).

(7) If a parent or guardian of a child or young person consents to be surety for the child or young person for the purposes of this subsection, the parent or guardian may be required to secure that the child or young person complies with any requirement imposed on him by virtue of subs (6) or (6A) above, but–

(a) no requirement shall be imposed on the parent or the guardian of a young person by virtue of this subsection where it appears that the young person will attain the age of seventeen before the time to be appointed for him to surrender to custody; and

(b) the parent or guardian shall not be required to secure compliance with any requirement to which his consent does not extend and shall not, in respect of those requirements to which his consent does extend, be bound in a sum greater than £50.

(8) Where a court has granted bail in criminal proceedings that court, or, where that court has committed a person on bail to the Crown Court for trial or to be sentenced or otherwise dealt with, that court or the Crown Court may on application (a) by or on behalf of the person to whom bail was granted, or (b) by the prosecutor or a constable, vary the conditions of bail or impose conditions in respect of bail which has been granted unconditionally.

(9) This section is subject to subs (2) of s.30 of the Magistrates' Courts Act 1980 (conditions of bail on remand for medical examination).

[*as amended by Sch.12 CLA 1977, Sch.7 MCA 1980, s.34 Mental Health (Amendment) Act 1982, Sch.4 Mental Health Act 1983.*]

COMMENTARY

s.3(1): Surrender to custody, defined in s.2(2), *supra.*

s.3(2): this rules out the defendant's own recognizances.

s.3(3): Security, except as provided for in s.3(5) this rules out cash bail.

Surety, the effect of para. (b) and s.3(4) is to rule out sureties for any purpose other than securing the surrender to custody of the bailed person. But note s.3(7).

s.3(4)–(7): No condition may be imposed under these subsections in the case of an imprisonable offence save for the purpose of preventing any of the events in para 2 of Part I of Sch.I, *infra* or, in the case of a condition under s.3(6)(d), where it is necessary to enable inquiries or a report concerning the defendant's physical or mental condition: para 8(1), *ibid.* This would not seemingly permit a remand to assess suitability for a bail hostel. (See 142 JPN 287).

s.3(4): Surety, see 3.29 and s.8, *infra.* In the event of non-appearance the recognizance of a surety may be estreated in accordance with s.120 MCA 1980. For the persons who may take the recognizance, see r.86.

s.3(5): Security, see 3.29.

Great Britain, ie England, Scotland and Wales: Union with Scotland Act 1706; s.3 Wales and Berwick Act 1746. Great Britain is specified rather than the United Kingdom because there is power to arrest and return an absconder who has gone to Scotland: see HOC 706/1977.

s.3(6): see under *Requirements of bail,* 3.31. A requirement under this subsection amounts to a 'condition' of bail, breach of which would justify the bailed person's arrest under s.7, *infra.* When the requirement has to be complied with before release the court may give directions as to the manner in which and the person(s) before whom they are to be complied with: r.85 MC Rules 1981.

A court, defined in s.2(2), *supra.*

s.3(6A): see also the comments of Dunn LJ, in *R v Vernege* [1928] 1 All ER 403 under *Factors to be Considered,* 3.25.

s.3(6ZA), will be added by [s.129] CJA 1988 from a date to be appointed.

s.3(7): this places a limit on the extent to which a parent or guardian may be requried to stand surety for his child (in this case anyone who will be under 17 at the adjourned date) in respect of any *requirements* under s.3(6). It does not limit the amount of the parent's or guardian's recognizance for the *appearance of his child.*

Parent/guardian, not defined.

Child/young person, defined in s.2(2), *supra.*

Conditions of bail, these include, not merely the special requirements under s.3(6), but the number and value of any sureties. Note also the restrictions in para 8 of Part I of Sch.I, *infra.*

s.3(8): Vary, defined in s.2(2). There is no duty of the court to notify a surety of variation of bail conditions, but the court might wish to warn the surety of this fact. Where the court thinks that a variation might affect a surety's willingness to continue, it might decline to continue bail unless the surety agrees, knowingly, to continue: *R v Wells St Magistrates' Court, ex p. Albanese* [1981] 3 All ER 769.

General right of bail to accused persons and others   3.49
4. (1) A person to whom this section applies shall be granted bail except as provided in Sch.1 to this Act.

(2) This section applies to a person who is accused of an offence when–
(a) he appears or is brought before a magistrates' court or the Crown Court in the course of or in connection with proceedings for the offence, or
(b) he applies to a court for bail in connection with the proceedings.
This subsection does not apply as respects proceedings on or after a person's conviction of the offence or proceedings against a fugitive offender for the offence.

(3) This section also applies to a person who, having been convicted of an offence, appears or is brought before a magistrates' court to be dealt with under s.6 or s.16 of the Powers of Criminal Courts Act, 1973 (breach of requirement of probation or community service order).

(4) This section also applies to a person who has been convicted of an offence and whose case is adjourned by the court for the purpose of enabling inquiries or a report to be made to assist the court in dealing with him for the offence.

(5) Schedule 1 to this Act also has effect as respects conditions of bail for a person to whom this section applies.

(6) In Sch.1 to this Act 'the defendant' means a person to whom this section applies and any reference to a defendant whose case is adjourned for inquiries or a report is a reference to a person to whom this section applies by virtue of subs (4) above.

(7) This section is subject to s.41 of the Magistrates' Courts Act 1980 (restriction of bail by magistrates' court in cases of treason).
[*as amended by Sch.7 MCA 1980*].

COMMENTARY
s.4(2): One effect of the concluding sentence of s.4(2) is that Sch.1 does not apply *after conviction* except in the cases referred to in s.3(3) and (4).

Offence, see the note to s.1, *supra.*

Proceedings against a fugitive offender, defined in s.2(1), *supra.*

s.4(4): this refers to an adjournment under s.10 MCA 1980.

Supplementary provisions about decisions on bail   3.50
5. (1) Subject to subs (2) below, where–
(a) a court or constable grants bail in criminal proceedings, or
(b) a court withholds bail in criminal proceedings from a person to whom s.4 of this Act applies, or
(c) a court, officer of a court or constable appoints a time or place or a court or officer of a court appoints a different time or place for a person granted bail in criminal proceedings to surrender to custody, or
(d) a court varies any conditions of bail or imposes conditions in respect of bail in criminal proceedings,
that court, officer or constable shall make a record of the decision in the prescribed manner and containing the prescribed particulars and, if requested to do so by the person in relation to whom the decision was taken, shall cause him to be given a copy of the record of the decision as soon as practicable after the record is made.

(2) Where bail in criminal proceedings is granted by endorsing a warrant of arrest for bail the constable who releases on bail the person arrested shall make the record required by subs (1) above instead of the judge or justice who issued the warrant.

(3) Where a magistrates' court or the Crown Court–
(a) withholds bail in criminal proceedings, or
(b) imposes conditions in granting bail in criminal proceedings, or
(c) varies any condition of bail or imposes conditions in respect of bail in criminal proceedings,
and does so in relation to a person to whom s.4 of this Act applies, then the court shall, with a view to enabling him to consider making an application in the matter to another court, give reasons for withholding bail or for imposing or varying the conditions.

(4) A court which is by virtue of subs (3) above required to give reasons for its decision shall include a note of those reasons in the record of its decision and shall (except in a case where, by virtue of subs (5) below, this need not be done) give a copy of that note to the person in relation to whom the decision was taken.

(5) . . .

(6) Where a magistrates' court withholds bail in criminal proceedings from a person who is not represented by counsel or a solicitor, the court shall–
(a) if it is committing him for trial to the Crown Court, or if it issues a certificate under subs (6A) below, inform him that he may apply to the High Court or to the Crown Court to be granted bail;
(b) in any other case, inform him that he may apply to the High Court for that purpose.

(6A) Where in criminal proceedings–
(a) a magistrates' court remands a person in custody under any of the following provisions of the Magistrates' Court Act 1980–
   (i) s.5 (adjournment of inquiry into offence);
   (ii) s.10 (adjournment of trial);
   (iii) s.18 (initial procedure on information against adult for offence triable either way); or
   (iv) s.30 (remand for medical examination),
after hearing full argument on an application for bail from him; and
(b) either–
   (i) it has not previously heard such argument on an application for bail from him in those proceedings; or
   (ii) it has previously heard full argument from him on such an application but it is satisfied that there has been a change in his circumstances or that new considerations have been placed before it,
it shall be the duty of the court to issue a certificate in the prescribed form that they heard full argument on his application for bail before they refused the application.

(6B) Where the court issues a certificate under subs(6A) above in a case to which para (b)(ii) of that subsection applies, it shall state in the certificate the nature of the change of circumstances or the new considerations which caused it to hear a further fully argued bail application.

(6C) Where a court issues a certificate under subs (6A) above it shall cause the person to whom it refuses bail to be given a copy of the certificate.

(7) Where a person has given security in pursuance of s.3(5) above and a court is satisfied that he failed to surrender to custody then, unless it appears that he had reasonable cause for his failure, the court may order the forfeiture of the security.

(8) If a court orders the forfeiture of a security under subs (7) above, the

court may declare that the forfeiture extends to such amount less than the full value of the security as it thinks fit to order.

(8A) An order under subs (7) above shall, unless previously revoked, take effect at the end of 21 days beginning with the day on which it is made.

(8B) A court which has ordered the forfeiture of a security under subs (7) above may, if satisfied on an application made by or on behalf of the person who gave it that he did after all have reasonable cause for his failure to surrender to custody, by order remit the forfeiture or declare that it extends to such amount less than the full value of the security as it thinks fit to order.

(8C) An application under subs (8B) above may be made before or after the order for forfeiture has taken effect, but shall not be entertained unless the court is satisfied that the prosecution was given reasonable notice of the applicant's intention to make it.

(9) A security which has been ordered to be forfeited by a court under subs (7) above shall, to the extent of the forfeiture–
  (a) if it consists of money, be accounted for and paid in the same manner as a fine imposed by that court would be;
  (b) if it does not consist of money, be enforced by such magistrates' court as may be specified in the order.

(9A) Where an order is made under subs (8B) above after the order for forfeiture of the security in question has taken effect, any money which would have fallen to be repaid or paid over to the person who gave the security if the order under subs (8B) had been made before the order for forfeiture took effect shall be repaid or paid over to him.

(10) *(Rules)*.

[*as amended by Sch.12 CLA 1977, s.60 CJA 1982*].

COMMENTARY

Records required by this section must be made by way of an entry in the register: r.90 MC Rules 1981.

.5(1): A court, defined in s.2(2), *supra*.

Bail in criminal proceedings, defined in s.1(1), *supra*.

The prescribed manner/particulars, see forms 149–152.

.5(2): Give reasons, advice as to the form the reasons should take is contained in HOC 1/1978.

.5(3): Varies, defined in s.2(2), *supra*.

Conditions of bail, seemingly under s.4(4)–(7).

.5(4): The record of its decision, the record must be made by ways of an entry in the court register: r.90 MC Rules 1981.

A note of those reasons, incorporated in forms 149–153.

.5(6): the right to apply to the Crown Court is contained in s.81 Supreme Court Act 1981, and to the High Court in s.22 CJA 1967.

.5(6A): the purpose of the certificate is to facilitate an application to the Crown Court for bail under s.81 Supreme Court Act 1981. The reference to *changed circumstances and new considerations* seems to import the principles laid down by the Divisional Court in the *Nottingham Justices* case: see under *Subsequent Applications*, 3.27.

.5(7): Forfeiture, note s.5(8)–(9A).

Offence of absconding by person released on bail   **3.51**
  6. (1) If a person who has been released on bail in criminal proceedings fails without reasonable cause to surrender to custody he shall be guilty of an offence.

(2) If a person who–

(a) has been released on bail in criminal proceedings, and

(b) having reasonable cause therefor, has failed to surrender to custody

fails to surrender to custody at the appointed place as soon after the appointe time as is reasonably practicable he shall be guilty of an offence.

(3) It shall be for the accused to prove that he had reasonable cause for h failure to surrender to custody.

(4) A failure to give to a person granted bail in criminal proceedings a cop of the record of the decision shall not constitute a reasonable cause for the person's failure to surrender to custody.

(5) An offence under subs (1) or (2) above shall be punishable either c summary conviction or as if it were a criminal contempt of court.

(6) Where a magistrates' court convicts a person of an offence under sub (1) or (2) above the court may, if it thinks–

(a) that the circumstances of the offence are such that greater punishmer should be inflicted for that offence than the court has power to inflict, c

(b) in a case where it commits that person for trial to the Crown Court fc another offence, that it would be appropriate for him to be dealt with fc the offence under subs (1) or (2) above by the court before which he tried for the other offence,

commit him in custody or on bail to the Crown Court for sentence.

(7) A person who is convicted summarily of an offence under subs (1) or (2) above and is not committed to the Crown Court for sentence shall be liable t imprisonment for a term not exceeding three months or to a fine not exceedir level 5 on the standard scale or to both and a person who is so committed fc sentence or is dealt with as for such a contempt shall be liable to imprisonmer for a term not exceeding 12 months or to a fine or to both.

(8) In any proceedings for an offence under subs (1) or (2) above a docu ment purporting to be a copy of the part of the prescribed record which relat to the time and place appointed for the person specified in the record t surrender to custody and to be duly certified to be a true copy of that part of th record shall be evidence of the time and place appointed for that person surrender to custody.

(9) For the purposes of subs (8) above–

(a) 'the prescribed record' means the record of the decision of the cour officer or constable made in pursuance of s.5(1) of this Act;

(b) the copy of the prescribed record is duly certified if it is certified by th appropriate officer of the court or, as the case may be, by the constab who took the decision or a constable designated for the purpose by th officer in charge of the police station from which the person to whom th record relates was released;

(c) 'the appropriate officer' of the court is–

(i) in the case of a magistrates' court, the justices' clerk or such oth officer as may be authorized by him to act for the purpose;

(ii) in the case of the Crown Court, such officer as may be designate for the purpose in accordance with arrangements made by th Lord Chancellor;

(iii) in the case of the High Court, such officer as may be designated fc the purpose in accordance with arrangements made by the Lor Chancellor;

(iv) in the case of the Court of Appeal, the registrar of criminal appea or such other officer as may be authorized by him to act for th purpose;

(v) in the case of the Courts-Martial Appeal Court, the registrar c such other officer as may be authorized by him to act for the purpos

[*as amended by ss.38, 46 CJA 1982*].

COMMENTARY

This section makes it an offence for a bailed person to fail without reasonable cause to surrender to custody at the time appointed (s.6(1)) or if he had a reasonable cause for such failure, as soon as reasonably practicable thereafter (s.6(2)). It would seem that s.6(3) applies to proceedings under both s.6(1) and (2).

For the procedure in respect of the offence of 'failure to surrender to bail', see the case of *Schiavo v Anderton* [1986] 3 WLR 177, and the *Practice Direction (Bail: Failure to Surrender to Custody)* [1987] 1 WLR 79, discussed under *Absconding from bail*, 3.40.

Although this offence may be dealt with *ab initio* at the Crown Court, it would, by virtue of subs (5), not be triable on indictment. It is not therefore an offence triable either way within the meaning of Sch.1 Interpretation Act 1978.

A magistrates' court has power in certain circumstances to commit an offender to the Crown Court to be dealt with: subs (6).

6(1), in *R v Gateshead Justices, ex p. Usher* [1981] Crim LR 491, it was held that no offence had been committed where the accused arrived 7 minutes late, but his decision may be confined to special facts since there can be no proposition of law that there is any fixed margin of time which affords defence; and cf *France v Dewsbury Magistrates* (1987) *The Times* 7 December (3 days late where solicitor 'got the days mixed up' – justices agreed not to proceed); but see *Laidlaw v Atkinson* (1986) *The Times*, 2 August where failure to appear through mistake was held to be the defendants' own responsibility.

Bail in criminal proceedings, defined in s.1(1), *supra*.

Without reasonable cause, see s.6(3) and (4).

Surrender to custody, defined in s.2(2), *supra*. A person surrenders to custody when he complies with the procedures of the court where he is due to appear and reports to the appropriate person, eg the court usher. Surrendering to a judicial officer is not required: *DPP v Richards* (1988) *The Times*, 25 February.

6(4): Copy of the record, presumably that referred to in s.5(4), *supra*. The legislature appear to have taken the view that it was unnecessary to provide that a failure on the part of the court to perform its duty under s.5(3) constitutes reasonable cause within the meaning of s.6(1).

6(5): the purpose of the provision is to create swift and simple alternative remedies, either by way of proceedings for a summary offence or by way of committal for what is to be treated as a criminal contempt of court, without the necessity for more elaborate proceedings of a kind which sometimes are necessary when questions of criminal contempt of court arise. It is designed to give a court other than a magistrates' court, that is the Crown Court, power to deal with an offender as if he had committed a criminal contempt of court, leaving the Crown Court to deal with him in whatever way as the Crown Court could do if he were guilty of criminal contempt of court. In some cases it may not be appropriate to deal with the offender summarily this way, eg where there is a dispute whether or not particular facts amounted to absconding; the judge might then direct that summary proceedings should be begun before a magistrates' court, or he might think he could deal with the matter adequately himself: *R v Harbax Singh* (1979) 143 JP 214.

An offence, sufficient to activate a suspended sentence: *R v Tyson* (1979) 68 Cr App R 314.

6(6): The power to commit to the Crown Court for sentence otherwise than on a committal for trial is confined to 'the circumstances of the offence'. The past record of the defendant, including any previous failures to surrender to bail, would not appear to justify such a committal. HOC 206/1977 comments: 'The mode of trial procedure is designed to give maximum flexibility, to take account of both the seriousness of the offence and the stage in the proceedings at which it occurs; on occasions it will be better to deal with a relatively minor infringement immediately after the person is rearrested; on other occasions it will be appropriate for sentence to be passed for the absconding offence at the same time as the main offence finally disposed of.'

There is nothing to prevent a defendant convicted summarily of an offence under this section being committed to the Crown Court to be dealt with (s.56 CJA 1967).

6(7): Convicted, partially defined in s.2(1).

Liability to arrest for absconding or breaking conditions of bail   3.52

7. (1) If a person who has been released on bail in criminal proceedings and is under a duty to surrender into the custody of a court fails to surrender to custody at the time appointed for him to do so the court may issue a warrant for his arrest.

(2) If a person who has been released on bail in criminal proceedings absents

himself from the court at any time after he has surrendered into the custody of th court and before the court is ready to begin or to resume the hearing of th proceedings, the court may issue a warrant for his arrest; but no warrant shall b issued under this subsection where that person is absent in accordance with leav given to him by or on behalf of the court.

(3) A person who has been released on bail in criminal proceedings and i under a duty to surrender into the custody of a court may be arrested withou warrant by a constable–

(a) if the constable has reasonable grounds for believing that that person is n likely to surrender to custody;

(b) if the constable has reasonable grounds for believing that that person i likely to break any of the conditions of his bail or has reasonable ground for suspecting that that person has broken any of those conditions; or

(c) in a case where that person was released on bail with one or more surety o sureties, if a surety notifies a constable in writing that that person is unlikel to surrender to custody and that for that reason the surety wishes to b relieved of his obligations as a surety.

(4) A person arrested in pursuance of subs (3) above–

(a) shall, except where he was arrested within 24 hours of the time appointe for him to surrender to custody, he brought as soon as practicable and i any event within 24 hours after his arrest before a justice of the peace fo the petty sessions area in which he was arrested; and

(b) in the said excepted case shall be brought before the court at which he wa to have surrendered to custody.

In reckoning for the purposes of this subsection any period of 24 hours, n account shall be taken of Christmas Day, Good Friday or any Sunday.

(5) A justice of the peace before whom a person is brought under subs (4 above may, subject to subs (6) below, if of the opinion that that person–

(a) is not likely to surrender to custody, or

(b) has broken or is likely to break any condition of his bail,

remand him in custody or commit him to custody, as the case may require, o alternatively, grant him bail subject to the same or to different conditions, but i not of that opinion shall grant him bail subject to the same conditions (if any) a were originally imposed.

(6) Where the person so brought before the justices is a child or young perso and the justice does not grant him bail, subs (5) above shall have effect subject t the provisions of s.23 of the Children and Young Persons Act 1969 (remands t the care of local authorities).

[*as amended by Sch.12 CLA 1977*].

COMMENTARY

s.7(1): Bail in criminal proceedings, defined in s.1(1), *supra*.

Surrender to custody, defined in s.2(2), *supra*.

Warrant, no information is necessary.

s.7(2): by absenting himself in this manner the accused is not committing an offence under s.6

s.7(3): Constable, all members of a police force are, in law, constables.

Reasonable grounds for believing, by analogy, these words should be read as 'has reasonabl grounds for believing and believes' cf *R v Banks* (1916) 80 JP 432; *R v Harrison* [1938] 3 All E 134.

The conditions of his bail, in this context the phrase appears to relate solely to requirement imposed under s.3(6), *supra*.

s.7(3)(c): Relieved of his obligations, but not, it is suggested, of the liability to have hi recognizance estreated: see 143 JPN 585 and *R v Ipswich Crown Court, ex p. Reddington* [1981 Crim LR 618, noted under s.20 MCA 1980.

s.7(4)(a): the justice must cause a copy of the bail record to be sent to the clerk of the court: r.9 MC Rules 1981.

s.7(5): note that the power to remand only arises if the justice forms either opinion (a) or (b), or both. It does not require these matters to be proved and, while it is open to the parties to call evidence, it is suggested that the justice can in a proper case form an opinion on the basis solely of representations made to him.

Commit him to custody, defined in s.150(1) MCA 1980. For the place to which persons aged 17–20 years of age should be committed, see s.27 CJA 1948. For the treatment of juveniles, see s.7(6). Committals to custody must be by warrant: r.94 MC Rules 1981.

s.7 Subsection (6): a suggested procedure and specimen letter for the use of courts are contained in HOC 11/1978.

Child or young person, defined in s.2(2), *supra*.

Bail with sureties   3.53

8. (1) This section applies where a person is granted bail in criminal proceedings on condition that he provides one or more surety or sureties for the purpose of securing that he surrenders to custody.

(2) In considering the suitability for that purpose of a proposed surety, regard may be had (amongst other things) to–
  (a) the surety's financial resources;
  (b) his character and any previous convictions of his; and
  (c) his proximity (whether in point of kinship, place of residence or otherwise) to the person for whom he is to be surety.

(3) Where a court grants a person bail in criminal proceedings on such a condition but is unable to release him because no surety or no suitable surety is available, the court shall fix the amount in which the surety is to be bound and subs (4) and (5) below, or in a case where the proposed surety resides in Scotland subs (6) below, shall apply for the purpose of enabling the recognizance of the surety to be entered into subsequently.

(4) Where this subsection applies the recognizance of the surety may be entered into before such of the following persons or descriptions of persons as the court may by order specify or if it makes no such order, before any of the following persons, that is to say–
  (a) where the decision is taken by a magistrates' court, before a justice of the peace, a justices' clerk or a police officer who either is of the rank of inspector or above or is in charge of a police station or, if magistrates' courts rules so provide, by a person of such other description is specified in the rules;
  (b) where the decision is taken by the Crown Court, before any of the persons specified in para (a) above or, if Crown Court rules so provide, by a person of such other description as is specified in the rules;
  (c) where the decision is taken by the High Court or the Court of Appeal, before any of the persons specified in para (a) above or, if Supreme Court rules so provide, by a person of such other description as is specified in the rules;
  (d) where the decision is taken by the Courts-Martial Appeal Court, before any of the persons specified in para (a) above or, if Courts-Martial Appeal rules so provide, by a person of such other description as is specified in the rules;
and Supreme Court rules, Crown Court rules, Courts-Martial Appeal rules or magistrates' courts rules may also prescribe the manner in which a recognizance which is to be entered into before such a person is to be entered into and the persons by whom and the manner in which the recognizance may be enforced.

(5) Where a surety seeks to enter into his recognizance before any person in accordance with subs (4) above but that person declines to take his recognizance because he is not satisfied of the surety's suitability, the surety may apply to–
  (a) the court which fixed the amount of the recognizance in which the surety was to be bound, or
  (b) a magistrates' court for the petty sessions area in which he resides,

for that court to take his recognizance and that court shall, if satisfied of his suitability, take his recognizance.

(6) Where this subsection applies, the court, if satisfied of the suitability of the proposed surety, may direct that arrangements be made for the recognizance of the surety to be entered into in Scotland before any constable, within the meaning of the Police (Scotland) Act 1967, having charge at any police office or station in like manner as the recognizance would be entered into in England or Wales.

(7) Where, in pursuance of subss (4) or (6) above, a recognizance is entered into otherwise than before the court that fixed the amount of the recognizance, the same consequences shall follow as if it had been entered into before that court.

COMMENTARY

s.8(2): Among other things, for other factors which may be considered see *Sureties*, 3.29.

s.8(3): Fix the amount, the court will supply a certificate of the amount and conditions of the recognizance or a statement of the requirement: r.86(2) MC Rules 1981.

s.8(4): The effect is that in the absence of any special direction a recognizance may be taken before anyone in categories (a)–(d), but the court may reserve this function to any one or more of those categories. Presumably a court can also reserve this function to itself.

Magistrates' Courts Rules, see rr.86–88, *infra.*

s.8(6), HOC 11/1978 suggests the arrangements referred to.

3.54   **Offence of agreeing to indemnify sureties in criminal proceedings**
      9. (1) If a person agrees with another to indemnify that other against any liability which that other may incur as a surety to secure the surrender to custody of a person accused or convicted of or under arrest for an offence, he and that other person shall be guilty of an offence.

(2) An offence under subs (1) above is committed whether the agreement is made before or after the person to be indemnified becomes a surety and whether or not he becomes a surety and whether the agreement contemplates compensation in money or in money's worth.

(3) Where a magistrates' court convicts a person of an offence under subs (1) above the court may, if it thinks–
(a) that the circumstances of the offence are such that greater punishment should be inflicted for that offence than the court has power to inflict, or
(b) in a case where it commits that person for trial to the Crown Court for another offence, that it would be appropriate for him to be dealt with for the offence under subs (1) above by the court before which he is tried for the other offence,
commit him to custody or on bail to the Crown Court for sentence.

(4) A person guilty of an offence under subs (1) above shall be liable–
(a) on summary conviction, to imprisonment for a term not exceeding three months or to a fine not exceeding £1,000 or to both; or
(b) on conviction on indictment or if sentenced by the Crown Court on committal for sentence under subs (3) above, to imprisonment for a term not exceeding 12 months or to a fine or to both.

(5) No proceedings for an offence under subs (1) above shall be instituted except by or with the consent of the Director of Public Prosecutions.
[*as amended by s.32(2) MCA 1980*].

SCHEDULE 1

3.55   **Persons entitled to Bail: Supplementary Provisions**

PART 1:

DEFENDANTS ACCUSED OR CONVICTED OF IMPRISONABLE OFFENCES
Defendants to whom Part 1 applies
      1. Where the offence or one of the offences of which the defendant is

accused or convicted in the proceedings is punishable with imprisonment the following provisions of this Part of this schedule apply.

Exceptions to right to bail

2. The defendant need not be granted bail if the court is satisfied that there are substantial grounds for believing that the defendant, if released on bail (whether subject to conditions or not) would–

(a) fail to surrender to custody, or

(b) commit an offence while on bail, or

(c) interfere with witnesses or otherwise obstruct the course of justice, whether in relation to himself or any other person.

3. The defendant need not be granted bail if the court is satisfied that the defendant should be kept in custody for his own protection or, if he is a child or young person, for his own welfare.

4. The defendant need not be granted bail if he is in custody in pursuance of the sentence of a court or of any authority acting under any of the Services Acts.

5. The defendant need not be granted bail where the court is satisfied that it has not been practicable to obtain sufficient information for the purpose of taking the decisions required by this Part of this schedule for want of time since the institution of the proceedings against him.

6. The defendant need not be granted bail if, having been released on bail in or in connection with the proceedings for the offence, he has been arrested in pursuance of s.7 of this Act.

Exception applicable only to defendant whose case is adjourned for inquiries or a report

7. Where his case is adjourned for inquiries or a report, the defendant need not be granted bail if it appears to the court that it would be impracticable to complete the inquiries or make the report without keeping the defendant in custody.

Restrictions of conditions of bail

8. (1) Subject to sub-para (3) below, where the defendant is granted bail, no conditions shall be imposed under subss (4) to (7) of s.3 of this Act unless it appears to the court that it is necessary to do so for the purposes of preventing the occurrence of any of the events mentioned in para 2 of this Part of this schedule or, in the case of a condition under subs (6)(d) of that section, that it is necessary to impose it to enable inquiries or a report to be made into the defendant's physical or mental condition, *or, where the condition is that the defendant reside in a bail hostel or probation hostel, that it is necessary to impose it to assess his suitability for being dealt with for the offence in a way which would involve a period of residence in a probation hostel.*

(2) Sub-paragraph (1) above also applies on any application to the court to vary the conditions of bail or to impose conditions in respect of bail which has been granted unconditionally.

(3) The restriction imposed by sub-para (1) above shall not operate to override the direction in s.30(2) of the Magistrates' Courts Act 1980 to a magistrates' court to impose conditions of bail under s.3(6)(d) of this Act of the description specified in the said s.30(2) in the circumstances so specified.

Decisions under para 2

9. In taking the decisions required by para 2 of this Part of this schedule, the court shall have regard to such of the following considerations as appear to it to be relevant, that is to say–

(a) the nature and seriousness of the offence or default (and the probable method of dealing with the defendant for it),

(b) the character, antecedents, associations and community ties of the defendant,

(c) the defendant's record as respects the fulfilment of his obligations under previous grants of bail in criminal proceedings,

(d) except in the case of a defendant whose case is adjourned for inquiries or a report, the strength of the evidence of his having committed the offence or having defaulted,

as well as to any others which appear to be relevant.

9A. *(1) If–*

(a) the defendant is charged with an offence to which this paragraph applies; and

(b) representations are made as to any of the matters mentioned in paragraph 2 of this Part of this Schedule; and

(c) the court decides to grant him bail,

the court shall state the reasons for its decision and shall cause those reasons to be included in the record of the proceedings.

(2) The offences to which this paragraph applies are–

(a) murder;

(b) manslaughter;

(c) rape;

(d) attempted murder; and

(e) attempted rape.

[*as amended by Sch.7 MCA 1980*].

COMMENTARY

In this schedule the term 'defendant' means a person to whom s.4 applies (s.4(6)), ie someone who enjoys the general right to bail.

Para 1: Punishable with imprisonment, see para 1 of Part III, *infra.*

Para 2 in taking a decision under this paragraph the court may have regard to the considerations referred to in para 9. See generally under *Exceptions* to the general right to bail at 3.21 *et seq.*

Para 3: Kept in custody, includes in the case of a juvenile being kept or being in the care of a local authority under an s.23 warrant: para 3 of Part III, *infra.*

His welfare The court must in a proper case take steps for removing a juvenile from undesirable surroundings: s.44 CYPA 1933.

Para 4: Court, see para 4 of Part III, *infra.*

Services Acts, see para 4 of Part III, *infra.*

Para 5: Sufficient information, HOC 155/1975 recommended a standardised procedure for the collection of this information. The Home Office working party on bail commented that the length of remands of this nature should be kept to the minimum necessary to enable the inquiries to be completed. A week's remand should not be ordered as a matter of course (para 72). They recommended for this purpose greater use of remands in police custody under s.128(7) MCA 1980.

Para 6: failure to surrender to custody in proceedings for earlier offences are evidence to support a refusal to bail under para 2 (a).

Para 7: unlike para 5 (which deals with inquiries concerning the bail application) this paragraph appears to relate to inquiries after conviction under s.10 MCA 1980.

Para 8: this duplicates s.3(6) of the Act: see *R v Mansfield Justices, ex p. Sharkey* [1984] 3 WLR 1328 at 1337. The words in italics will be added by [s.129] CJA 1988 from a date to be appointed.

Para 9: see *Factors to be Considered*, 3.25.

Para 9A will be added by [s.145] CJA 1988 from a date to be appointed.

PART II:

DEFENDANTS ACCUSED OR CONVICTED OF NON-IMPRISONABLE OFFENCES

Defendants to whom Part II applies

1. Where the offence or every offence of which the defendant is accused or convicted in the proceedings is one which is not punishable with imprisonment the following provisions of this Part of this schedule apply.

Exceptions to right to bail

2. The defendant need not be granted bail if–
   (a) it appears to the court that, having been previously granted bail in criminal proceedings, he has failed to surrender to custody in accordance with his obligations under the grant of bail; and
   (b) the court believes, in view of that failure, that the defendant, if released on bail (whether subject to conditions or not) would fail to surrender to custody.

3. The defendant need not be granted bail if the court is satisfied that the defendant should be kept in custody for his own protection or, if he is a child or young person, for his own welfare.

4. The defendant need not be granted bail if he is in custody in pursuance of the sentence of a court or of any authority acting under any of the Services Act.

5. The defendant need not be granted bail if, having been released on bail or in connection with the proceedings for the offence, he has been arrested in pursuance of s.7 of this Act.

COMMENTARY

In this schedule the term 'defendant' means a person to whom s.4 of the Act applies by virtue of s.4(4): s.4(6), ie a person who enjoys the general right to bail.

Para 1: Punishable with imprisonment, see note to para 1 of Part I.

Para 2: Note that both (a) and (b) must be satisfied before bail may be refused, but condition (a) is not restricted to absonsions in proceedings for the present offence.

Bail in criminal proceedings: defined in s.1(1), *supra.*

Para 3: In custody in the case of a juvenile, see para 3 of Part III, *infra.*

Para 4: The sentence of a court, this does not seemingly extend to a remand in custody for another offence, nor to a commitment to prison in default of payment of a fine etc: cf s.150(1) MCA 1980.

The Services Acts, defined in para 4 of Part III, *infra.*

PART IIA
DECISIONS WHERE BAIL REFUSED ON PREVIOUS HEARING

If the court decides not to grant the defendant bail, it is the court's duty to consider, at each subsequent hearing while the defendant is a person to whom section 4 above applies and remains in custody, whether he ought to be granted bail, but the court need not hear arguments as to fact or law which it has heard previously.
[as added by [s.146] CJA 1988 from a date to be appointed].

PART III:
INTERPRETATION

1. For the purposes of this schedule the question whether an offence is one which is punishable with imprisonment shall be determined without regard to any enactment prohibiting or restricting the imprisonment of young offenders or first offenders.

2. References in this schedule to previous grants of bail in criminal proceedings include references to bail granted before the coming into force of this Act.

3. References in this schedule to a defendant's being kept in custody or being in custody include (where the defendant is a child or young person) references to his being kept or being in the care of a local authority in pursuance of a warrant of commitment under s.23(1) of the Children and Young Persons Act 1969.

4. In this schedule–
'court' in the expression 'sentence of a court', includes a services court as defined in s.12(1) of the Visiting Forces Act 1952 and 'sentence' in that

expression, shall be construed in accordance with that definition;
'default', in relation to the defendant, means the default for which he is to be
dealt with under s.6 or s.16 of the Powers of Criminal Courts Act 1973;
'the Services Acts' means the Army Act 1955, the Air Force Act 1955 and the
Naval Discipline Act 1957.

MAGISTRATES' COURTS ACT 1980

3.56   **Restriction on grant of bail in treason**
    41. A person charged with treason shall not be granted bail except by order
of a judge of the High Court or the Secretary of State.

COMMENTARY
By order of a judge of the High Court, such an order cannot be altered by magistrates:
s.119(3) MCA 1980.

3.57   **Restriction on justices sitting after dealing with bail**
    42. (1) A justice of the peace shall not take part in trying the issue of an
accused's guilt on the summary trial of an information if in the course of the
same proceedings the justice has been informed, for the purpose of determining whether the accused shall be granted bail, that he has one or more previous
convictions.

(2) For the purposes of this section any committal proceedings from which
the proceedings on the summary trial arose shall be treated as part of the trial.

COMMENTARY
This is a mandatory provision, breach of which would give rise to an order of prohibition *per*
Lord Widgery CJ in *R v McLean, ex p. Aikens and Others* (1975) 139 JP 261.

Trying the issue of an accused's guilt on the summary trial of an information, thus, this
section does not operate to prevent a justice from dealing with subsequent remands, from
sentencing a convicted offender, nor from acting as an examining justice.

In the course of the same proceedings, not in earlier proceedings for offences on other days:
R v Sandwich Justices, ex p. Berry (1982) 74 Cr App R 132.

s.42(2): this deals with the situation where the court had begun as examining justices and
then reverted to summary trial under s.25 MCA 1980.

Committal proceedings, defined in s.150(1).

3.58   **Bail on arrest**
    43. (1) Where a person has been granted bail under the Police and
Criminal Evidence Act 1984 subject to a duty to appear before a magistrates'
court the court before which he is to appear may appoint a later time as the
time at which he is to appear and may enlarge the recognizances of any sureties
for him at that time.

(2) The recognizance of any surety for any person granted bail subject to a
duty to attend at a police station may be enforced as if it were conditioned for
his appearance before a magistrates' court for the petty sessions area in which
the police station named in the recognizance is situated.
[as substituted by s.47 Police and Criminal Evidence Act 1984].

3.59   **Functions of magistrates' court where a person in custody is brought before it
with a view to his appearance before the Crown Court**
    43A. (1) Where a person in custody in pursuance of a warrant issued by the
Crown Court with a view to his appearance before the Crown Court is brought
before a magistrates' court in pursuance of s.81(5) of the Supeme Court Act
1981–
        (a) the magistrates' court shall commit him in custody or release him on bail
            until he can be brought or appear before the Crown Court at the time
            and place appointed by the Crown Court;

(b) if the warrant is endorsed for bail, but the person in custody is unable to satisfy the conditions endorsed, the magistrates' court may vary those conditions, if satisfied that it is proper to do so.

(2) A magistrates' court shall have jurisdiction under subs (1) whether or not the offence was committed, or the arrest was made, within the court's area. [*as inserted by Sch.5 Supreme Court Act 1981*].

COMMENTARY
For the duties of the clerk to the justices see r.89 MC Rules 1981.

Postponement of taking recognizance   **3.60**
119. (1) Where a magistrates' court has power to take any recognizance, the court may, instead of taking it, fix the amount in which the principal and his sureties, if any, are to be bound, and thereafter the recognizance may be taken by any such person as may be prescribed.

(2) Where, in pursuance of this section, a recognizance is entered into otherwise than before the court that fixed the amount of it, the same consequences shall follow as if it had been entered into before that court; and references in this or any other Act to the court before which a recognizance was entered shall be construed accordingly.

(3) Nothing in this section shall enable a magistrates' court to alter the amount of a recognizance fixed by the High Court or the Crown Court.
[*as amended by Sch.14 CJA 1982*].

COMMENTARY
s.119(1): Such person as may be prescribed, r.86(1) MC Rules 1981.

Forfeiture of recognizance   **3.61**
120. (1) Where a recognizance to keep the peace or to be of good behaviour has been entered into before a magistrates' court or any recognizance is conditioned for the appearance of a person before a magistrates' court or for his doing any other thing connected with a proceeding before a magistrates' court, and the recognizance appears to the court to be forfeited, the court may, subject to subs (2) below, declare the recognizance to be forfeited and adjudge the persons bound thereby, whether as principal or sureties, or any of them, to pay the sum in which they are respectively bound.

(2) Where a recognizance is conditioned to keep the peace or to be of good behaviour, the court shall not declare it forfeited except by order made on complaint.

(3) The court which declares the recognizance to be forfeited may, instead of adjudging any person to pay the whole sum in which he is bound, adjudge him to pay part only of the sum or remit the sum.

(4) Payment of any sum adjudged to be paid under this section, including any costs awarded against the defendant, may be enforced, and any such sum be applied, as if it were a fine and as if the adjudication were a summary conviction of an offence not punishable with imprisonment and so much of s.85(1) above as empowers a court to remit fines shall not apply to the sum but so much thereof as relates to remission after a term of imprisonment has been imposed shall so apply; but at any time before the issue of a warrant of commitment to enforce payment of the sum, or before the sale of goods under a warrant of distress to satisfy the sum, the court may remit the whole or any part of the sum either absolutely or on such conditions as the court thinks just.

(5) A recognizance such as is mentioned in this section shall not be enforced otherwise than in accordance with this section, and accordingly shall not be transmitted to the Crown Court nor shall its forfeiture be certified to that Court.

COMMENTARY

s.120(1): Any recognizance . . . conditioned for the appearance of a person before a magistrates' court: ie under s.43 MCA 1980 and s.29 CYPA 1969 (bail by police) or ss.128, 129 MCA 1980, s.3(4) Bail Act 1976, s.81 (1H) Supreme Court Act 1981 (bail by the court).

Forfeited, see *Forfeiture of recognizances*, 3.30.

s.120(4): Enforced as if it were a fine, notice must be given to the defendant if he is absent or time to pay is allowed: r.46 MC Rules 1981.

An order of discharge in bankruptcy does not release the debt on the recognizance: s.28(1)(a) Bankruptcy Act 1914.

Remit, recognizances estreated by the Crown Court may not be remitted by magistrates except with the permission of that court: s.47(8) CJA 1967. Any order of remission must be entered in the register or separate record: r.65 MC Rules 1981.

3.62   **Remand in custody or on bail**

128. (1) Where a magistrates' court has power to remand any person, then, subject to s.4 of the Bail Act 1976 and to any other enactment modifying that power, the court may–

(a) remand him in custody, that is to say, commit him to custody to be brought before the court subject to subs (3A) below at the end of the period of remand or at such earlier time as the court may require; or

(b) where it is inquiring into or trying an offence alleged to have been committed by that person or has convicted him of an offence, remand him on bail in accordance with the Bail Act 1976, that is to say, by directing him to appear as provided in subs (4) below; or

(c) except in a case falling within para (b) above, remand him on bail by taking from him a recognizance (with or without sureties) conditioned as provided in this subsection;

and may, in a case falling within para (c) above, instead of taking recognizances in accordance with that paragraph, fix the amount of the recognizances with a view to their being taken subsequently in accordance with s.119 above.

(1A) Where–

(a) on adjourning a case under ss.5, 10(1) or 18(4) above the court proposes to remand or further remand a person in custody; and

(b) he is before the court; and

(c) he has attained the age of 17; and

(d) he is legally represented in that court,

it shall be the duty of the court–

(i) to explain the effect of subss (3A) and (3B) below to him in ordinary language; and

(ii) to inform him in ordinary language that, notwithstanding the procedure for a remand without his being brought before a court, he would be brought before a court for the hearing and determination of at least every fourth application for his remand, and of every application for his remand heard at a time when it appeared to the court that he had no solicitor acting for him in the case.

(1B) For the purposes of subs (1A) above a person is to be treated as legally represented in court if, but only if, he has the assistance of counsel or a solicitor to represent him in the proceedings in that court.

(1C) After explaining to an accused as provided by subs (1A) above the court shall ask him whether he consents to the hearing and determination of such applications in his absence.

(2) Where the court fixes the amount of a recognizance under subs (1) above or s.8(3) of the Bail Act 1976 with a view to its being taken subsequently the court shall in the meantime commit the person so remanded to custody in accordance with para (a) of the said subs (1).

(3) Where a person is brought before the court after remand, the court may further remand him.

(3A) Subject to subs (3B) below, where a person has been remanded in custody, *and the remand was not a remand under s.128A below for a period exceeding 8 clear days,* the court may further remand him *(otherwise than in the exercise of the power conferred by that section)* on an adjournment under s.5, 10(1) or 18(4) above without his being brought before it if it is satisfied–
   (a) that he gave his consent, either in response to a question under subs (1C) above or otherwise, to the hearing and determination in his absence of any application for his remand on an adjournment of the case under any of those provisions; and
   (b) that he has not by virtue of this subsection been remanded without being brought before the court on more than two such applications immediately preceding the application which the court is hearing; and
   (c) that he had attained the age of seventeen years when he gave his consent to the hearing and determination of such applications in his absence; and
   (d) that he has not withdrawn his consent to their being so heard and determined.

(3B) The court may not exercise the power conferred by subs (3A) above if it appears to the court on an application for a further remand being made to it, that the person to whom the application relates has no solicitor acting for him in the case (whether present in court or not).

(3C) Where–
   (a) a person has been remanded in custody on an adjournment of a case under ss.5, 10(1) or 18(4) above; and
   (b) an application is subsequently made for his further remand on such an adjournment; and
   (c) he is not brought before the court which hears and determines the application; and
   (d) that court is not satisfied as mentioned in subs (3A) above,
the court shall adjourn the case and remand him in custody for the period for which it stands adjourned.

(3D) An adjournment under subs (3C) above shall be for the shortest period that appears to the court to make it possible for the accused to be brought before it.

(3E) Where–
   (a) on an adjournment of a case under ss.5, 10(1) or 18(4) above a person has been remanded in custody without being brought before the court; and
   (b) it subsequently appears–
      (i) to the court which remanded in custody; or
      (ii) to an alternate magistrates' court to which he is remanded under s.130 below,
that he ought not to have been remanded in custody in his absence, the court shall require him to be brought before it at the earliest time that appears to the court to be possible.

(4) Where a person is remanded on bail under subs (1) above the court may, where it remands him on bail in accordance with the Bail Act 1976 direct him to appear or, in any other case, direct that his recognizance be conditioned for his appearance–
   (a) before that court at the end of the period of remand; or
   (b) at every time and place to which during the course of proceedings the hearing may be from time to time adjourned;
and, where it remands him on bail conditionally on his providing a surety during an inquiry into an offence alleged to have been committed by him, may direct that the recognizance of the surety be conditioned to secure that the person so bailed appears–

(c) at every time and place to which during the course of the proceedings the hearing may be from time to time adjourned and also before the Crown Court in the event of the person so bailed being committed for trial there.

(5) Where a person is directed to appear or a recognizance is conditioned for a person's appearance in accordance with para (b) or (c) of subs (4) above the fixing at any time of the time for him next to appear shall be deemed to be a remand; but nothing in this subsection or subs (4) above shall deprive the court of power at any subsequent hearing to remand him afresh.

(6) Subject to the provisions of *ss.128A and* 129 below, a magistrates' court shall not remand a person for a period exceeding eight clear days, except that—
   (a) if the court remands him on bail, it may remand him for a longer period if he and the other party consent;
   (b) where the court adjourns a trial under ss.10(3) or 30 above, the court may remand him for the period of the adjournment;
   (c) where a person is charged with an offence triable either way, then, if it falls to the court to try the case summarily but the court is not at the time so constituted, and sitting in such a place, as will enable it to proceed with the trial, the court may remand him until the next occasion or which it will be practicable for the court to be so constituted, and to sit in such a place, as aforesaid, notwithstanding that the remand is for a period exceeding eight clear days.

(7) A magistrates' court having power to remand a person in custody may, if the remand is for a period not exceeding three clear days, commit him to detention at a police station.

(8) Where a person is committed to detention at a police station under subs (7) above—
   (a) he shall not be kept in such detention unless there is a need for him to be so detained for the purposes of inquiries into other offences;
   (b) if kept in such detention, he shall be brought back before the magistrates' court which committed him as soon as that need ceases;
   (c) he shall be treated as a person in police detention to whom the duties under s.39 of the Police and Criminal Evidence Act 1984 (responsibilities in relation to persons detained) relate;
   (d) his detention shall be subject to periodic review at the times set out in s.40 of that Act (review of police detention).
   [*as amended by Sch.9 CJA 1982, s.48 Police and Criminal Evidence Act 1984. The words in italics in subs (3A) and (6) will be added by [Sch.14] CJA 1988 from a date to be appointed*].

COMMENTARY

s.128(1): Power to remand any person, eg during committal proceedings (s.5(1) of the Act) summary trial (s.10(3)) and for medical reports (s.30(1)).

In custody, it is not necessary for sworn 'evidence of arrest' to be given before remanding in custody: *R v Guest, ex p. Metropolitan Police Commissioner* [1961] 3 All ER 1118.
   The committal must be by warrant: r.94 MC Rules 1981. For the contents of the warrant see r.97. For the place to which persons aged 17–20 years of age should be remanded in custody see s.27 CJA 1948. For the remand of juveniles otherwise than on bail see s.23 CYPA 1969.

Such earlier time, this allows a defendant to be brought back earlier than the remand date if the court so orders. HOC 107/1971 recommends that this power should be used where reports after conviction are available earlier than the remand date; see also HOC 116/1972.

s.128(1)(b): Where a magistrates' court remands a person on bail pursuant to this section, but thereafter another magistrates' court, in connection with the criminal charges, remands him in custody, neither the Secretary of State nor the governor of the prison in which he is held are under an unconditional duty to produce him at court in accordance with the terms of the remand on duly notified dates. The duty of the Home Secretary or the governor acting under powers delegated to him, is merely to consider, in accordance with the terms of s.29 CJA 1961, whether he is satisfied that it is desirable in the interests of justice that such a person should be so produced and, if he is so satisfied, then not unreasonably refuse to produce him: *Walsh v Governor of Brixton Prison* (1985) 80 Cr App R 186.

A recognizance, a recognizance may not be required of the defendant himself in criminal proceedings: s.3(3) Bail Act 1976.

s.128(3): Further remand, there is power to remand further in the absence of the defendant udner s.129, *infra*. The justices' clerk may order such remands on bail: Justices' Clerks Rules 1970. When a transfer direction has been made by the Secretary of State, the managers of the hospital must be notified in writing of any further remand: r.26 MC Rules 1981.

s.128(3A): where the court is satisfied under this subsection, the power to further remand is adapted in accordance with s.130(4A), *infra*.

s.128(4): Appear . . . before that court, to be construed as referring to surrendering himself into the custody of the court: s.2(3) Bail Act 1976.

Every time and place, such a remand is sometimes described as *continuous bail* and avoids the need for sureties attending at each remand.

s.128(5): Remand afresh, thus a court is empowered to fix different terms of remand at an adjourned hearing despite the fact that the defendant is on 'continuous bail.'

s.128(6): this subsection does *not apply* to further remands arising from *illness* or *accident*: s.129, *infra*. When the accused is committed to custody in default of sureties the warrant must direct production at the end of eight clear days or sooner unless the sureties enter into their recognizances: r.23 MC Rules 1981. For the power to remand in custody up to 28 days where the accused is serving a custodial sentence, see s.131, *infra*.

Eight clear days, ie disregarding the day of remand and the day of the adjourned hearing.

Exception (b): both these sections are subject to their own time limits.

Exception (c): this proviso is appropriate where a single magistrate sits to deal with the mode of trial procedure.

Offence triable either way, defined in Sch.1 Interpretation Act 1978.

s.128(7): a warrant is required by r.94 MC Rules 1981, see form 5.

Three clear days, ie disregarding the day of remand and the day of the adjourned hearing. This subsection has effect in relation to a *juvenile* as if for the reference to three clear days there were substituted a reference to *twenty-four hours*: s.23(5) CYPA 1969.

Remands in custody for more than eight days   **3.62a**
128A (1) The Secretary of State may by order made by statutory instrument provide that this section shall have effect–
(a) in an area specified in the order; or
(b) in proceedings of a description so specified,
in relation to any accused person ('the accused') who has attained the age of 17.

(2) A magistrates' court may remand the accused in custody for a period exceeding 8 clear days if–
(a) it has previously remanded him in custody for the same offence; and
(b) he is before the court,
but only if, after affording the parties an opportunity to make representations, it has set a date on which it expects that it will be possible for the next stage in the proceedings, other than a hearing relating to a further remand in custody or on bail, to take place, and only–
(i) for a period ending not later than that date; or
(ii) for a period of 28 clear days,
whichever is the less.

(3) Nothing in this section affects the right of the accused to apply for bail during the period of the remand.

(4) A statutory instrument containing an order under this section shall not

be made unless a draft of the instrument has been laid before Parliament and been approved by a resolution of each House.
[as added by [s.147] CJA 1988 from a date to be appointed].

3.63   **Further remand**
        129. (1) If a magistrates' court is satisfied that any person who has been remanded is unable by reason of illness or accident to appear or be brought before the court at the expiration of the period for which he was remanded, the court may, in his absence, remand him for a further time; and s.128(6) above shall not apply.

(2) Notwithstanding anything in s.128(1) above, the power of a court under subs (1) above to remand a person on bail for a further time–
   (a) where he was granted bail in criminal proceedings, includes power to enlarge the recognizance of any surety for him to a later time;
   (b) where he was granted bail otherwise than in criminal proceedings, may be exercised by enlarging his recognizance and those of any sureties for him to a later time.

(3) Where a person remanded on bail is bound to appear before a magistrates' court at any time and the court has no power to remand him under subs (1) above, the court may in his absence–
   (a) where he was granted bail in criminal proceedings, appoint a later time as the time at which he is to appear and enlarge the recognizances of any sureties for him to that time;
   (b) where he was granted bail otherwise than in criminal proceedings, enlarge his recognizance and those of any sureties for him to a later time;
and the appointment of the time or the enlargement of his recognizance shall be deemed to be a further remand.

(4) Where a magistrates' court commits a person for trial on bail and the recognizance of any surety for him has been conditioned in accordance with para (a) of subs (4) of s.128 above the court may, in the absence of the surety enlarge his recognizance so that he is bound to secure that the person so committed for trial appears also before the Crown Court.

COMMENTARY
This is an unnecessarily confusing section. s.129(1) gives power to remand for a further time persons unable to appear through *illness* or *accident*. s.129(2) gives the court the option in such circumstances to enlarge the recognizance of any surety, while s.129(3) gives a general power to appoint a later date for the appearance of the accused and to enlarge the recognizances of his sureties where the non-appearance is due to circumstances *other than illness or accident*. s.129(1) is not subject to the general prohibition (and exceptions) against remands for more than eight clear days contained in s.128(6) and applies to remands on bail and in custody; s.129(2) and (3) to remands on bail only.

s.129(1): A magistrates' court, the clerk to justices may order the further adjournment of criminal proceedings with the consent of the prosecutor and the accused if, but only if . . . (b) the accused, having been remanded on bail on the previous adjournment, is remanded on bail on the like terms and conditions. When the clerk adjourns proceedings under this rule he may also remand the accused on bail in pursuance of (b) above: Justices' Clerks Rules 1970. Remands under this rule may be ordered by the clerk in the absence of the defendant under s.129(2) or (3). The clerk may not fix bail in the first instance, strangely enough, even when the defendant has been bailed by police to attend court.

Accident, the first definitions in the *Concise Oxford Dictionary* are: 'Event without apparent cause, unexpected, unforeseen course of events.' It has been held in Northern Ireland that an industrial dispute cannot constitute an 'accident' for the purpose of similarly phrased legislation: 143 JPN 29.

Remand . . . for a further time, see form 10. Notice msut be given to the accused and his sureties under r.91 MC Rules 1981.

s.129(4): Enlarging his recognizance, notice must be given to the surety: r.84 MC Rules 1981.

Transfer of remand hearings **3.64**

130. (1) A magistrates' court adjourning a case under ss.5, 10(1) or 18(4) above, and remanding the accused in custody may, if he has attained the age of 17, order that he be brought up for any subsequent remands before an alternate magistrates' court nearer to the prison where he is to be confined while on remand.

(2) The order shall require the accused to be brought before the alternate court at the end of the period of remand or at such earlier time as the alternate court may require.

(3) While the order is in force, the alternate court shall, to the exclusion of the court which made the order, have all the powers in relation to further remand (whether in custody or on bail) and the grant of legal aid which that court would have had but for the order.

(4) The alternate court may, on remanding the accused in custody, require him to be brought before the court which made the order at the end of the period of remand or at such earlier time as that court may require; and, if the alternate court does so, or the accused is released on bail, the order under subs (1) above shall cease to be in force.

(4A) Where a magistrates' court is satisfied as mentioned in s.128(3A) above–
(a) subs (1) above shall have effect as if for the words 'he be brought up for any subsequent remands before' there were substituted the words 'applications for any subsequent remands be made to';
(b) subs (2) above shall have effect as if for the words 'the accused to be brought before' there were substituted the words 'an application for a further remand to be made to'; and
(c) subs (4) above shall have effect as if for the words 'him to be brought before' there were substituted the words 'an application for a further remand to be made to'.

(5) Schedule 5 to this Act shall have effect to supplement this section.
[*as amended by Sch.9 CJA 1982*].

COMMENTARY

This section must be read in conjunction with Sch.5, *infra*.

The Home Office advise that the cases in which transfer under this provision seem likely to provide positive advantages are those where bail is not likely to be granted, when several remands in custody are likely to be necessary before trial or committal, and transport to and from the prison:
(1) is likely to involve a significant security risk; in the main, these are likely to involve prisoners who are provisionally in category A (a category A prisoner is one whose escape would be highly dangerous to the public, the police or the security of the state); or
(2) when the journey between the original magistrates' court and the prison or remand centre is particularly lengthy or in some other way inconvenient. (When, however, the original magistrates' court is on or close to the route of a daily prison van to a Crown Court centre, this consideration is less likely to apply: HOC dated 10 July 1978.

The consent of the accused is not necessary. For the documents to be sent to the alternate court see r.25 MC Rules 1981.

For the general power to remand from one court to another (cross-remanding) within the same commission area, see *R v Avon Magistrates' Courts Committee ex p. Bath Law Society* (1987) *The Times*, 28 July.

Remand of accused already in custody **3.65**

131. (1) When a magistrates' court remands an accused person in custody and he is already detained under a custodial sentence, the period for which he is remanded may be up to 28 clear days.

(2) But the court shall inquire as to the expected date of his release from that detention; and if it appears that it will be before 28 clear days have

expired, he shall not be remanded in custody for more than eight clear days
(if longer) a period ending with that date.

(3) *(Repealed)*.
[*as amended by Schs.9, 16 CJA 1982*].

COMMENTARY

The practice of remanding a sentenced prisoner on 'notional bail' in order to avoid the ne
to have him produced to court every eight days for further remand in custody was criticis
by the Chief Inspector of the Prison Service in his report of March, 1977, on the escape
William Thomas Hughes on the grounds that not only does it involve a legal fiction bu
may also mislead people into thinking that the court has a real intention of granting bail
the end of the custodial sentence. This provision avoids the need to use notional bail in th
circusmtances.

s.131(1): A custodial sentence, not a mere remand.

28 clear days, ie disregarding the day of the remand and the day of the adjourned heariι

SCHEDULE 5

3.66　　　TRANSFER OF REMAND HEARINGS

1. A court which, on adjourning a case, makes an order under s.130(1)
this Act is not required at that time to fix the time and place at which the case
to be resumed but shall do so as soon as practicable after the order ceases to
in force.

2. Where an order under subs (1) of s.130 of this Act is made in the course
proceedings which, for the purpose of s.8 of this Act, are committal procee
ings, proceedings relating to the accused before the alternate court are a
committal proceedings for these purposes.

3. A court making an order under subs (1) of s.130 of this Act or remandi
the accused under subs (4) shall at once notify the terms of the order or rema
to the court before which the accused is to be brought for the hearing on a
application for a subsequent remand or, as the case may be, before which a
such application is to be made without his being brought before it.

4. A person to whom an order under s.130(1) of this Act applies shall,
released on bail, be bailed to appear before the court which made the orde

5. Section 130 of this Act and this schedule have effect notwithstandi
anything in ss.5, 10 or 18(4) of this Act.
[*as amended by Sch.9 CJA 1982*].

COMMENTARY

The memorandam accompanying HOC 39/1978 comments on the paragraphs of t
schedule as follows:
 '1. When a magistrates' court adjourns a case and makes an order under s.130 it will ha
 to specify a date on which the accused is to be brought up before the alternate co
 (subject to the alternate court specifying an earlier date). The first court is n
 however, required, when making the order, to fix the date and time on which the ca
 will be resumed before it – indeed it would seldom know at that stage when the ca
 would be ready to proceed. Instead, it is required to fix a date for resumption as so
 as possible after the order ceases to be in force (which occurs either when the accus
 is remanded back to the alternate court or when the accused is released on bail).
 '2. The effect of para 2 of (Sch.5) is that when an order under s.130 is made in the cou
 of proceedings for such an offence, the provisions of s.8 of the Act will apply equa
 to proceedings before the alternate court. Thus if an order lifting those restrictions l
 been made by the original court that order will continue to have effect during
 proceedings before the alternate court; similarly if no such order has been made wh
 the case is transferred, the reporting restrictions will continue in force at the altern
 court unless the accused applies to the alternate court to have them lifted.
 '3. When remand hearings are transferred to or from the alternate court, under s.130
 and (4) respectively, the court making the transfer must notify the court before whi
 the defendant will next appear.

4. When a person is *released* on bail the transfer order ceases to have effect by virtue of s.130(4). The order granting bail must therefore require him to surrender to the custody of the court which made the transfer order and not the alternate court. Where the alternate court *grants* bail for surrender to the original court but commits the defendant to custody until he complies with pre-release conditions, he is to be produced to the alternate court after eight days if he has been unable to comply with those conditions and is consequently still in custody. He returns to the jurisdiction of the original court only after his release on bail (or on transfer back by the alternate court).

5. This paragraph contains a saving for s.130 from specified enactments which require that a person who is remanded on an adjournment must be brought back before the same court at the end of the period of remand.'

SUPREME COURT ACT 1981

Bail 3.67

81. (1) The Crown Court may grant bail to any person–

(a) who has been committed for appearance before the Crown Court or in relation to whose case a notice of transfer has been given under s.4 CJA 1987.

(b) who is in custody, pursuant to a sentence imposed by a magistrates' court, and who has appealed to the Crown Court against his conviction or sentence; or

(c) who is in the custody of the Crown Court pending the disposal of his case by that court; or

(d) who, after the decision of his case by the Crown Court, has applied to that court for the statement of a case for the High Court on that decision; or

(e) who has applied to the High Court for an order of certiorari to remove proceedings in the Crown Court in this case into the High Court, or has applied to the High Court for leave to make such an application;

(f) to whom the Crown Court has granted a certificate under ss.1(2) or 11(1A) of the Criminal Appeal Act 1968 or under subs (1B) below; or

(g) who has been remanded in custody by a magistrates' court on adjourning a case under–

    (i) s.5 (adjournment of inquiry into offence);

    (ii) s.10 (adjournment of trial);

    (iii) s.18 (initial procedure on information against adult for offence triable either way);

    (iv) s.30 (remand for medical examination) of the

Magistrates' Courts Act 1980; and the time during which a person is released on bail under any provision of this subsection shall not count as part of any term of imprisonment or detention under his sentence.

(1A)–(1G) . . .

(1H) Where the Crown Court grants a person bail under subs (1)(g) it may direct him to appear at a time and place which the magistrates' court could have directed and the recognizance of any surety shall be conditioned accordingly.

(1J) The Crown Court may only grant bail to a person under subs (1)(g) if the magistrates' court which remanded him in custody has certified under s.5(6A) of the Bail Act 1976 that it heard full argument on his application for bail before it refused the application.

(2) (*Rules*).

(3) Any reference in any enactment to a recognizance shall include, unless the context otherwise requires, a reference to any other decription of security given instead of a recognizance, whether in pursuance of subs (2)(a) or otherwise.

(4) The Crown Court, on issuing a warrant for the arrest of any person, may endorse the warrant for bail, and in any such case–

(a) the person arrested under the warrant shall, unless the Crown Cou otherwise directs, be taken to a police station; and

(b) the officer in charge of the station shall release him for custody if he, ar any sureties required by the endorsement and approved by the office enter into recognizance of such amount as may be fixed by th endorsement.

Provided that in the case of bail in criminal proceedings (within the meani of the Bail Act 1976) the person arrested shall not be required to enter into recognizance.

(5) A person in custody in pursuance of a warrant issued by the Crow Court with a view to his appearance before that court shall be broug forthwith before either the Crown Court or a magistrates' court.

(6) A magistrates' court shall have jurisdiction, and a justice of the pea may act, under or in pursuance of rules under subs (2) whether or not th offence was committed, or the arrest was made, within the court's area, or th area for which he was appointed.

[*as amended by ss.29, 60 CJA 1982, Sch.2 CJA 1987*].

COMMENTARY

The procedure for an application under this section is dealt with in the *Practice Directi* (1983) 77 Cr App R 69.

s.81(4): A person arrested in pursuance of this subsection and brought before a magistrate court must be dealt with in accordance with s.43A MCA 1980.

POLICE AND CRIMINAL EVIDENCE ACT 1984

3.68   **Fingerprinting of certain offenders**
27. (1) If a person–
(a) has been convicted of a recordable offence;
(b) has not at any time been in police detention for the offence; and
(c) has not had his fingerprints taken–
    (i) in the course of the investigation of the offence by the police; or
    (ii) since the conviction,
any constable may at any time not later than one month after the date of th conviction require him to attend a police station in order that his fingerprin may be taken.

(2) A requirement under subs (1) above–
(a) shall give the person a period of at least 7 days within which he must s attend; and
(b) may direct him to so attend at a specified time of day or betwee specified times of day.

(3) Any constable may arrest without warrant a person who has failed t comply with a requirement under subs (1) above.

(4), (5) (*Regulations*).

COMMENTARY

A recordable offence, defined in s.118(1), *post.*

Constable, includes a police officer of any rank.

One month, means a calendar month: Sch.1 Interpretation Act 1978.

Police detention, defined in s.118(2).

3.69   **Information to be given on arrest**
28. (1) Subject to subs (5) below, where a person is arrested, otherwis than by being informed that he is under arrest, the arrest is not lawful unle the person arrested is informed that he is under arrest as soon as is practicab after his arrest.

(2) Where a person is arrested by a constable, subs (1) above applies regardless of whether the fact of the arrest is obvious.

(3) Subject to subs (5) below, no arrest is lawful unless the person arrested is informed of the ground for the arrest at the time of, or as soon as is practicable after, the arrest.

(4) Where a person is arrested by a constable, subs (3) above applies regardless of whether the ground for the arrest is obvious.

(5) Nothing in this section is to be taken to require a person to be informed–
(a) that he is under arrest; or
(b) of the ground for the arrest,
if it was not reasonably practicable for him to be so informed by reason of his having escaped from arrest before the information could be given.

Voluntary attendance at police station etc 3.70
29. Where for the purpose of assisting with an investigation a person attends voluntarily at a police station or at any other place where a constable is present or accompanies a constable to a police station or any such other place without having been arrested–
(a) he shall be entitled to leave at will unless he is placed under arrest;
(b) he shall be informed at once that he is under arrest if a decision is taken by a constable to prevent him from leaving at will.

Arrest elsewhere than at police station 3.71
30. (1) Subject to the following provisions of this section, where a person–
(a) is arrested by a constable for an offence; or
(b) is taken into custody by a constable after being arrested for an offence by a person other than a constable,
at any place other than a police station, he shall be taken to a police station by a constable as soon as practicable after the arrest.

(2) Subject to subs (3) and (5) below, the police station to which an arrested person is taken under subs (1) above shall be a designated police station.

(3) A constable to whom this subsection applies may take an arrested person to any police station unless it appears to the constable that it may be necessary to keep the arrested person in police detention for more than six hours.

(4) Subsection (3) above applies–
(a) to a constable who is working in a locality covered by a police station which is not a designated police station; and
(b) to a constable belonging to a body of constables maintained by an authority other than a police authority.

(5) Any constable may take an arrested person to any police station if–
(a) either of the following conditions is satisfied–
  (i) the constable has arrested him without the assistance of any other constable and no other constable is available to assist him;
  (ii) the constable has taken him into custody from a person other than a constable without the assistance of any other constable and no other constable is available to assist him; and
(b) it appears to the constable that he will be unable to take the arrested person to a designated police station without the arrested person injuring himself, the constable or some other person.

(6) If the first police station to which an arrested person is taken after his arrest is not a designated police station, he shall be taken to a designated police station not more than six hours after his arrival at the first police station unless he is released previously.

(7) A person arrested by a constable at a place other than a police station shall be released if a constable is satisfied, before the person arrested reaches a police station, that there are no grounds for keeping him under arrest.

(8) A constable who releases a person under subs (7) above shall record the fact that he has done so.

(9) The constable shall make the record as soon as is practicable after the release.

(10) Nothing in subs (1) above shall prevent a constable delaying taking a person who has been arrested to a police station if the presence of that person elsewhere is necessary in order to carry out such investigations as it is reasonable to carry out immediately.

(11) Where there is delay in taking a person who has been arrested to a police station after his arrest, the reasons for the delay shall be recorded when he first arrives at a police station.

(12) Nothing in subs (1) above shall be taken to affect–
(a) paragraphs 16(3) or 18(1) of Sch.2 to the Immigration Act 1971;
(b) section 34(1) of the Criminal Justice Act 1972; or
(c) paragraph 5 of Sch.3 to the Prevention of Terrorism (Temporary Provisions) Act 1984 or any provision contained in an order under s.13 of that Act which authorises the detention of persons on board a ship or aircraft.

(13) Nothing in subs (10) above shall be taken to affect para 18(3) of Sch.2 to the Immigration Act 1971.

COMMENTARY

Designated police station, defined in s.35(4), *post*: s.118(1).

Police detention, defined in s.118(2).

Six hours, the 'approximating' provision of s.45(2) has not been applied to this section.

Designated police station, defined in s.35(4): s.118(1).

3.72   **Arrest for further offence**
31. Where–
(a) a person–
(i) has been arrested for an offence; and
(ii) is at a police station in consequence of that arrest; and
(b) it appears to a constable that, if he were released from that arrest, he would be liable to arrest for some other offence,
he shall be arrested for that other offence.

3.73   **Search upon arrest**
32. (1) A constable may search an arrested person, in any case where the person to be searched has been arrested at a place other than a police station, if the constable has reasonable grounds for believing that the arrested person may present a danger to himself or others.

(2) Subject to subs (3) to (5) below, a constable shall also have power in any such case–
(a) to search the arrested person for anything–
(i) which he might use to assist him to escape from lawful custody; or
(ii) which might be evidence relating to an offence; and
(b) to enter and search any premises in which he was when arrested or immediately before he was arrested for evidence relating to the offence for which he has been arrested.

(3) The power to search conferred by subs (2) above is only a power to

search to the extent that is reasonably required for the purpose of discovering any such thing or any such evidence.

(4) The powers conferred by this section to search a person are not to be construed as authorising a constable to require a person to remove any of his clothing in public other than an outer coat, jacket or gloves.

(5) A constable may not search a person in the exercise of the power conferred by subs (2)(a) above unless he has reasonable grounds for believing that the person to be searched may have concealed on him anything for which a search is permitted under that paragraph.

(6) A constable may not search premises in the exercise of the power conferred by subs 2(b) unless he has reasonable grounds for believing that there is evidence for which a search is permitted under that paragraph on the premises.

(7) In so far as the power of search conferred by subs(2)(b) above relates to premises consisting of two or more separate dwellings, it is limited to a power to search–
(a) any dwelling in which the arrest took place or in which the person arrested was immediately before his arrest; and
(b) any parts of the premises which the occupier of any such dwelling uses in common with the occupiers of any other dwellings comprised in the premises.

(8) A constable searching a person in the exercise of the power conferred by subs.(1) above may seize and retain anything he finds, if he has reasonable grounds for believing that the person searched might use it to cause physical injury to himself or to any other person.

(9) A constable searching a person in the exercise of the power conferred by subs.(2)(a) above may seize and retain anything he finds, other than an item subject to legal privilege, if he has reasonable grounds for believing–
(a) that he might use it to assist him to escape from lawful custody; or
(b) that it is evidence of an offence or has been obtained in consequence of the commission of an offence.

(10) Nothing in this section shall be taken to affect the power conferred by para 6 of Sch.3 to the Prevention of Terrorism (Temporary Provisions) Act 1984.

COMMENTARY

Constable, includes a police officer of any rank.

Premises, defined in s.23, *ante*: s.118(1).

Item subject to legal privilege, defined in s.10: s.118(1).

Limitations on police detention   3.74
34. (1) A person arrested for an offence shall not be kept in police detention except in accordance with the provisions of this Part of this Act.

(2) Subject to subs (3) below, if at any time a custody officer–
(a) becomes aware, in relation to any person in police detention, that the grounds for the detention of that person have ceased to apply; and
(b) is not aware of any other grounds on which the continued detention of that person could be justified under the provisions of this Part of this Act,
it shall be the duty of the custody officer, subject to subs (4) below, to order his immediate release from custody.

(3) No person in police detention shall be released except on the authority of a custody officer at the police station where his detention was authorised or, if it was authorised at more than one station, a custody officer at the station where it was last authorised.

(4) A person who appears to the custody officer to have been unlawfully a large when he was arrested is not to be released under subs (2) above.

(5) A person whose release is ordered under subs (2) above shall be released without bail unless it appears to the custody officer–
(a) that there is need for further investigation of any matter in connection with which he was detained at any time during the period of his detention; or
(b) that proceedings may be taken against him in respect of any such matter,
and, if it so appears, he shall be released on bail.

(6) For the purposes of this Part of this Act a person arrested under s.7(5) of the Road Traffic Act 1972 is arrested for an offence.

COMMENTARY

Child, sections 34–51 do not apply to a child arrested without warrant otherwise than for homicide, to whom s.28(4)(5) CYPA 1969 applies: s.52.

Police detention, defined in s.118(2); and see s.34(1).

Custody officer, see s.36.

3.75   **Designated police stations**
35. (1) The chief officer of police for each police area shall designate the police stations in his area which, subject to s.30(3) and (5) above, are to be the stations in that area to be used for the purpose of detaining arrested persons.

(2) A chief officer's duty under subs (1) above is to designate police stations appearing to him to provide enough accommodation for that purpose.

(3) Without prejudice to s.12 of the Interpretation Act 1978 (continuity of duties) a chief officer–
(a) may designate a station which was not previously designated; and
(b) may direct that a designation of a station previously made shall cease to operate.

(4) In this Act 'designated police station' means a police station for the time being designated under this section.

3.76   **Custody officers at police stations**
36. (1) One or more custody officers shall be appointed for each designated police station.

(2) A custody officer for a designated police station shall be appointed–
(a) by the chief officer of police for the area in which the designated police station is situated; or
(b) by such other police officer as the chief officer of police for that area may direct.

(3) No officer may be appointed a custody officer unless he is of at least the rank of sergeant.

(4) An officer of any rank may perform the function of a custody officer at a designated police station if a custody officer is not readily available to perform them.

(5) Subject to the following provisions of this section and to s.39(2) below, none of the functions of a custody officer in relation to a person shall be performed by an officer who at the time when the function falls to be performed is involved in the investigation of an offence for which that person is in police detention at that time.

(6) Nothing in subs (5) above is to be taken to prevent a custody officer–
(a) performing any function assigned to custody officers–

(i) by this Act; or

(ii) by a code of practice issued under this Act;

(b) carrying out the duty imposed on custody officers by s.39 below;

(c) doing anything in connection with the identification of a suspect; or

(d) doing anything under s.8 of the Road Traffic Act 1972.

(7) Where an arrested person is taken to a police station which is not a designated police station, the functions in relation to him which at a designated police station would be the functions of a custody officer shall be performed–

(a) by an officer who is not involved in the investigation of an offence for which he is in police detention, if such an officer is readily available; and

(b) if no such officer is readily available, by the officer who took him to the station or any other officer.

(8) References to a custody officer in the following provisions of this Act include references to an officer other than a custody officer who is performing the functions of a custody officer by virtue of subs (4) or (7) above.

(9) Where by virtue of subs (7) above an officer of a force maintained by a police authority who took an arrested person to a police station is to perform the functions of a custody officer in relation to him, the officer shall inform an officer who–

(a) is attached to a designated police station; and

(b) is of at least the rank of inspector,

that he is to do so.

(10) The duty imposed by subs (9) above shall be performed as soon as it is practicable to perform it.

COMMENTARY

Child, see note to s.34.

Designated police station, see s.35(4).

Custody officer, see s.36.

Police detention, defined in s.118(2), *post*; and see s.34(1).

Duties of custody officer before charge   **3.77**

37. (1) Where–

(a) a person is arrested for an offence–

(i) without a warrant; or

(ii) under a warrant not endorsed for bail, or

(b) a person returns to a police station to answer to bail,

the custody officer at each police station where he is detained after his arrest shall determine whether he has before him sufficient evidence to charge that person with the offence for which he was arrested and may detain him at the police station for such period as is necessary to enable him to do so.

(2) If the custody officer determines that he does not have such evidence before him, the person arrested shall be released either on bail or without bail, unless the custody officer has reasonable grounds for believing that his detention without being charged is necessary to secure or preserve evidence relating to an offence for which he is under arrest or to obtain such evidence by questioning him.

(3) If the custody officer has reasonable grounds for so believing, he may authorise the person arrested to be kept in police detention.

(4) Where a custody officer authorises a person who has not been charged to be kept in police detention, he shall, as soon as is practicable, make a written record of the grounds for the detention.

(5) Subject to subs (6) below, the written record shall be made in the

presence of the person arrested who shall at that time be informed by th custody officer of the grounds for his detention.

(6) Subsection (5) above shall not apply where the person arrested is, at th time when the written record is made–

(a) incapable of understanding what is said to him;
(b) violent or unlikely to become violent; or
(c) in urgent need of medical attention.

(7) Subject to s.41(7) below, if the custody officer determines that he ha before him sufficient evidence to charge the person arrested with the offenc for which he was arrested, the person arrested–

(a) shall be charged; or
(b) shall be released without charge, either on bail or without bail.

(8) Where–

(a) a person is released under subs (7(b) above; and
(b) at the time of his release a decision whether he should be prosecuted fo the offence for which he was arrested has not been taken,

it shall be the duty of the custody officer so to inform him.

(9) If the person arrested is not in a fit state to be dealt with under subs (7 above, he may be kept in police detention until he is.

(10) The duty imposed on the custody officer under subs (1) above shall b carried out by him as soon as practicable after the person arrested arrives at th police station or, in the case of a person arrested at the police station, as soo as practicable after the arrest.

(11)–(14) (*Not yet in force*).

(15) In this Part of this Act–

'arrested juvenile' means a person arrested with or without a warrant wh appears to be under the age of 17 and is not excluded from this Part of this Ac by s.52 below;

'endorsed for bail' means endorsed with a direction for bail in accordanc with s.117(2) of the Magistrates' Courts Act 1980.

COMMENTARY

Custody officer, see s.36, *ante.*

Arrested juvenile, defined in s.37(15).

Endorsed for bail, defined in s.37(15).

3.78   **Duties of custody officer after charge**

38. (1) Where a person arrested for an offence otherwise than under warrant endorsed for bail is charged with an offence, the custody officer shal order his release from police detention, either on bail or without bail, unles

(a) if the person arrested is not an arrested juvenile–
  (i) his name or address cannot be ascertained or the custody office has reasonable grounds for doubting whether a name or addres furnished by him as his name or address is his real name or address
  (ii) the custody officer has reasonable grounds for believing that th detention of the person arrested is necessary for his own protectio or to prevent him from causing physical injury to any other perso or from causing loss of or damage to property; or
  (iii) the custody officer has reasonable grounds for believing that th person arrested will fail to appear in court to answer to bail or tha his detention is necessary to prevent him from interfering with th administration of justice or with the investigation of offences or o a particular offence;
(b) if he is an arrested juvenile–

(i) any of the requirements of para (a) above is satisfied; or

(ii) the custody officer has reasonable grounds for believing that he ought to be detained in his own interests.

(2) If the release of a person arrested is not required by subs (1) above, the custody officer may authorise him to be kept in police detention.

(3) Where a custody officer authorises a person who has been charged to be kept in police detention, he shall, as soon as practicable, make a written record of the grounds for the detention.

(4) Subject to subs (5) below, the written record shall be made in the presence of the person charged who shall at that time be informed by the custody officer of the grounds for his detention.

(5) Subs (4) above shall not apply where the person charged is, at the time when the written record is made–

(a) incapable of understanding what is said to him;

(b) violent or likely to become violent; or

(c) in urgent need of medical attention.

(6) Where a custody officer authorises an arrested juvenile to be kept in police detention under subs (1) above, the custody officer shall, unless he certifies that it is impracticable to do so, make arrangements for the arrested juvenile to be taken into the care of a local authority and detained by the authority; and it shall be lawful to detain him in pursuance of the arrangements.

(7) A certificate made under subs (6) above in respect of an arrested juvenile shall be produced to the court before which he is first brought thereafter.

(8) In this Part of this Act 'local authority' has the same meaning as in the Children and Young Persons Act 1969.

COMMENTARY

Child, see note to s.34, *ante.*

Endorsed for bail, defined in s.37(15).

Custody officer, see s.36.

Arrested juvenile, defined in s.37(15); see Note 17A of the Code of Practice for the Detention, Treatment and Questioning etc: Appendix I, *post.*

Police detention, defined in s.118(2); and see s.34(1).

Local authority, defined in s.38(8).

Responsibilities in relation to persons detained   **3.79**

39. (1) Subject to subs (2) and (4) below, it shall be the duty of the custody officer at a police station to ensure–

(a) that all persons in police detention at that station are treated in accordance with this Act and any code of practice issued under it and relating to the treatment of persons in police detention; and

(b) that all matters relating to such persons which are required by this Act or by such codes of practice to be recorded are recorded in the custody records relating to such persons.

(2) If the custody officer, in accordance with any code of practice issued under this Act, transfer or permits the transfer of a person in police detention–

(a) to the custody of a police officer investigating an offence for which that person is in police detention; or

(b) to the custody of an officer who has charge of that person outside the police station,

the custody officer shall cease in relation to that person to be subject to the duty imposed on him by subs (1)(a) above; and it shall be the duty of the office to whom the transfer is made to ensure that he is treated in accordance with the provisions of this Act and of any such codes of practice as are mentioned in subs (1) above.

(3) If the person detained is subsequently returned to the custody of the custody officer, it shall be the duty of the officer investigating the offence to report to the custody officer as to the manner in which this section and the codes of practice have been complied with while that person was in his custody

(4) If an arrested juvenile is transferred to the care of a local authority in pursuance of arrangements made under s.38(6) above, the custody officer shall cease in relation to that person to be subject to the duty imposed on him by subs (1) above.

(5) It shall be the duty of a local authority to make available to an arrested juvenile who is in the authority's care in pursuance of such arrangements such advice and assistance as may be appropriate in the circumstances.

(6) Where–
(a) an officer of higher rank than the custody officer gives directions relating to a person in police detention; and
(b) the directions are at variance–
  (i) with any decision made or action taken by the custody officer in the performance of a duty imposed on him under this Part of this Act; or
  (ii) with any decision or action which would but for the directions have been made or taken by him in the performance of such a duty,
the custody officer shall refer the matter at once to an officer of the rank of superintendent or above who is responsible for the police station for which the custody officer is acting as custody officer.

COMMENTARY

Child, see note to s.34, *ante.*

Custody officer, see s.36.

Persons in police detention, defined in s.118(2); and see s.34(1).

Arrested juvenile, defined in s.37(15).

Local authority, defined in s.38(8).

3.80   **Review of police detention**
40. (1) Reviews of the detention of each person in police detention in connection with the investigation of an offence shall be carried out periodically in accordance with the following provisions of this section–
(a) in the case of a person who has been arrested and charged, by the custody officer; and
(b) in the case of a person who has been arrested but not charged, by an officer of at least the rank of inspector who has not been directly involved in the investigation.

(2) The officer to whom it falls to carry out a review is referred to in this section as a 'review officer'.

(3) Subject to subs (4) below–
(a) the first review shall be not later than six hours after the detention was first authorised;
(b) the second review shall be not later than nine hours after the first;
(c) subsequent reviews shall be at intervals of not more than nine hours.

(4) A review may be postponed–
(a) if, having regard to all the circumstances prevailing at the latest time for it specified in subs (3) above, it is not practicable to carry out the review at that time;

(b) without prejudice to the generality of para (a) above–
  (i) if at that time the person in detention is being questioned by a police officer and the review officer is satisfied that an interruption of the questioning for the purpose of carrying out the review would prejudice the investigation in connection with which he is being questioned; or
  (ii) if at that time no review officer is readily available.

(5) If a review is postponed under subs (4) above it shall be carried out as soon as practicable after the latest time specified for it in subs (3) above.

(6) If a review is carried out after postponement under subs (4) above, the fact that it was so carried out shall not affect any requirement of this section as to the time at which any subsequent review is to be carried out.

(7) The review officer shall record the reasons for any postponement of a review in the custody record.

(8) Subject to subs (9) below, where the person whose detention is under review has not been charged before the time of the review, s.37(1) to (6) above shall have effect in relation to him, but with the substitution–
  (a) of references to the person whose detention is under review for references to the person arrested; and
  (b) of references to the review officer for references to the custody officer.

(9) Where a person has been kept in police detention by virtue of s.37(9) above, s.37(1) to (6) shall not have effect in relation to him but it shall be the duty of the review officer to determine whether he is yet in a fit state.

(10) Where the person whose detention is under review has been charged before the time of the review, s.38(1) to (6) above shall have effect in relation to him, but with the substitution of references to the person whose detention is under review for references to the person arrested.

(11) Where–
  (a) an officer of higher rank than the review officer gives directions relating to a person in police detention; and
  (b) the directions are at variance–
    (i) with any decision made or action taken by the review officer in the performance of a duty imposed on him under this Part of this Act; or
    (ii) with any decision or action which would but for the directions have been made or taken by him in the performance of such a duty,
the review officer shall refer the matter at once to an officer of the rank of superintendent or above who is responsible for the police station for which the review officer is acting as review officer in connection with the detention.

(12) Before determining whether to authorise a person's continued detention the review officer shall give–
  (a) that person (unless he is asleep); or
  (b) any solicitor representing him who is available at the time of the review,
an opportunity to make representations to him about the detention.

(13) Subject to subs (14) below, the person whose detention is under review or his solicitor may make representations under subs (12) above either orally or in writing.

(14) The review officer may refuse to hear oral representations from the person whose detention is under review if he considers that he is unfit to make such representations by reason of his condition or behaviour.

COMMENTARY

For review *by telephone* see Note 16B of the Code of Practice for the Detention, Treatment and Questioning etc: Appendix I, *post*.

Child, see note to s.34.

Person in police detention, defined in s.118(2); and see s.34(1).

Custody officer, see s.36.

Six/Nine hours, to be treated as *approximate only*: s.45(2).

The review officer, see s.40(2).

3.81   **Limits on period of detention without charge**
    41. (1) Subject to the following provisions of this section and to ss.42 and 43 below, a person shall not be kept in police detention for more than 24 hours without being charged.

(2) The time from which the period of detention of a person is to be calculated (in this Act referred to as 'the relevant time')–
    (a) in the case of a person to whom this paragraph applies, shall be–
        (i) the time at which that person arrives at the relevant police station; or
        (ii) the time 24 hours after the time of that person's arrest, whichever is the earlier;
    (b) in the case of person arrested outside England and Wales, shall be–
        (i) the time at which that person arrives at the first police station to which he is taken in the police area in England or Wales in which the offence for which he was arrested is being investigated; or
        (ii) the time 24 hours after the time of that person's entry into England and Wales,
    whichever is the earlier;
    (c) in the case of a person who–
        (i) attends voluntarily at a police station; or
        (ii) accompanies a constable to a police station without having been arrested,
    and is arrested at the police station, the time of his arrest;
    (d) in any other case, except where subs (5) below applies, shall be the time at which the person arrested arrives at the first police station to which he is taken after his arrest.

(3) Subsection (2)(a) above applies to a person if–
    (a) his arrest is sought in one police area in England and Wales;
    (b) he is arrested in another police area; and
    (c) he is not questioned in the area in which he is arrested in order to obtain evidence in relation to an offence for which he is arrested;
and in sub-para (i) of that paragraph 'the relevant police station' means the first police station to which he is taken in the police area in which his arrest was sought.

(4) Subsection (2) above shall have effect in relation to a person arrested under s.31 above as if every reference in it to his arrest or his being arrested were a reference to his arrest or his being arrested for the offence for which he was originally arrested.

(5) If
    (a) a person is in police detention in a police area in England and Wales ('the first area'); and
    (b) his arrest for an offence is sought in some other police area in England and Wales ('the second area'); and
    (c) he is taken to the second area for the purposes of investigating that offence, without being questioned in the first area in order to obtain evidence in relation to it,
    the relevant time shall be–
        (i) the time 24 hours after he leaves the place where he is detained in the first area; or

(ii) the time at which he arrives at the first police station to which he is taken in the second area,

whichever is the earlier.

(6) When a person who is in police detention is removed to hospital because he is in need of medical treatment, any time during which he is being questioned in hospital or on the way there or back by a police officer for the purpose of obtaining evidence relating to an offence shall be included in any period which falls to be calculated for the purposes of this Part of this Act, but any other time while he is in hospital or on his way there or back shall not be so included.

(7) Subject to subs (8) below, a person who at the expiry of 24 hours after the relevant time is in police detention and has not been charged shall be released at that time either on bail or without bail.

(8) Subsection (7) above does not apply to a person whose detention for more than 24 hours after the relevant time has been authorised or is otherwise permitted in accordance with ss.42 or 43 below.

(9) A person released under subs (7) above shall not be re-arrested without a warrant for the offence for which he was previously arrested unless new evidence justifying a further arrest has come to light since his release.

COMMENTARY

Child, see note to s.34, *ante.*

24 hours, to be treated as *approximate only*: s.45(2).

The relevant police station, defined in s.41(3).

Person in police detention, defined in s.118(2); see s.34(1).

Authorisation of continued detention   **3.82**
  42. (1) Where a police officer of the rank of superintendent or above who is responsible for the police station at which a person is detained has reasonable grounds for believing that–
  (a) the detention of that person without charge is necessary to secure or preserve evidence relating to an offence for which he is under arrest or to obtain such evidence by questioning him;
  (b) an offence for which he is under arrest is a serious arrestable offence; and
  (c) the investigation is being conducted diligently and expeditiously,
he may authorise the keeping of that person in police detention for a period expiring at or before 36 hours after the relevant time.

(2) Where an officer such as is mentioned in subs (1) above has authorised the keeping of a person in police detention for a period expiring less than 36 hours after the relevant time, such an officer may authorise the keeping of that person in police detention for a further period expiring not more than 36 hours after that time if the conditions specified in subs (1) above are still satisfied when he gives the authorisation.

(3) If it is proposed to transfer a person in police detention to another police area, the officer determining whether or not to authorise keeping him in detention under subs (1) above shall have regard to the distance and the time the journey would take.

(4) No authorisation under subs (1) above shall be given in respect of any person–
  (a) more than 24 hours after the relevant time; or
  (b) before the second review of his detention under s.40 above has been carried out.

(5) Where an officer authorises the keeping of a person in police detention under subs (1) above, it shall be his duty–
(a) to inform that person of the grounds for his continued detention; and
(b) to record the grounds in that person's custody record.

(6) Before determining whether to authorise the keeping of a person in detention under subs (1) or (2) above, an officer shall give–
(a) that person; or
(b) any solicitor representing him who is available at the time when it falls to the officer to determine whether to give the authorisation,
an oppportunity to make representations to him about the detention.

(7) Subject to subs (8) below, the person in detention or his solicitor may make representations under subs (6) above either orally or in writing.

(8) The officer to whom it falls to determine whether to give the authorisation may refuse to hear oral representations from the person in detention if he considers that he is unfit to make such representations by reason of his condition or behaviour.

(9) Where–
(a) an officer authorises the keeping of a person in detention under subs (1) above; and
(b) at the time of the authorisation he has not yet exercised a right conferred on him by ss.56 or 58 below,
the officer–
(i) shall inform him of that right;
(ii) shall decide whether he should be permitted to exercise it;
(iii) shall record the decision in his custody record; and
(iv) if the decision is to refuse to permit the exercise of the right, shall also record the grounds for the decision in that record.

(10) Where an officer has authorised the keeping of a person who has not been charged in detention under subs (1) or (2) above, he shall be released from detention, either on bail or without bail, not later than 36 hours after the revelant time, unless–
(a) he has been charged with an offence; or
(b) his continued detention is authorised or otherwise permitted in accordance with s.43 below.

(11) A person released under subs (10) above shall not be re-arrested without a warrant for the offence for which he was previously arrested unless new evidence justifying a further arrest has come to light since his release.

COMMENTARY

Child, see note to s.34, *ante.*

Serious arrestable offence, defined in s.116, *post.*

36 hours, to be treated as *approximate only*: s.45(2).

The relevant time, defined in s.41(2).

Person in police detention, defined in s.118(2); and see s.34(1).

3.83   **Warrants of further detention**
43. (1) Where, on an application on oath made by a constable and supported by an information, a magistrates' court is satisfied that there are reasonable grounds for believing that the further detention of the person to whom the application relates is justified, it may issue a warrant of further detention authorising the keeping of that person in police detention.

(2) A court may not hear an application for a warrant of further detention unless the person to whom the application relates–
(a) has been furnished with a copy of the information; and
(b) has been brought before the court for the hearing.

(3) The person to whom the application relates shall be entitled to be legally represented at the hearing and, if he is not so represented but wishes to be so represented–

(a) the court shall adjourn the hearing to enable him to obtain representation; and

(b) he may be kept in police detention during the adjournment.

(4) A person's further detention is only justified for the purposes of this section or s.44 below if–

(a) his detention without charge is necessary to secure or preserve evidence relating to an offence for which he is under arrest or to obtain such evidence by questioning him;

(b) an offence for which he is under arrest is a serious arrestable offence; and

(c) the investigation is being conducted diligently and expeditiously.

(5) Subject to subs (7) below, an application for a warrant of further detention may be made–

(a) at any time before the expiry of 36 hours after the relevant time; or

(b) in a case where–

(i) it is not practicable for the magistrates' court to which the application will be made to sit at the expiry of 36 hours after the relevant time; but

(ii) the court will sit during the 6 hours following the end of that period, at any time before the expiry of the said 6 hours.

(6) In a case to which subs (5)(b) above applies–

(a) the person to whom the application relates may be kept in police detention until the application is heard; and

(b) the custody officer shall make a note in that person's custody record–

(i) of the fact that he was kept in police detention for more than 36 hours after the relevant time; and

(ii) of the reason why he was so kept.

(7) If–

(a) an application for a warrant of further detention is made after the expiry of 36 hours after the relevant time; and

(b) it appears to the magistrates' court that it would have been reasonable for the police to make it before the expiry of that period,

the court shall dismiss the application.

(8) Where on an application such as is mentioned in subs (1) above a magistrates' court is not satisfied that there are reasonable grounds for believing that the further detention of the person to whom the application relates is justified, it shall be its duty–

(a) to refuse the application; or

(b) to adjourn the hearing of it until a time not later than 36 hours after the relevant time.

(9) The person to whom the application relates may be kept in police detention during the adjournment.

(10) A warrant of further detention shall–

(a) state the time at which it is issued;

(b) authorise the keeping in police detention of the person to whom it relates for the period stated in it.

(11) Subject to subs (12) below, the period stated in a warrant of further detention shall be such period as the magistrates' court think fit, having regard to the evidence before it.

(12) The period shall not be longer than 36 hours.

(13) If it is proposed to transfer a person in police detention to a police area

other than that in which he is detained, when the application for a warrant of further detention is made, the court hearing the application shall have regard to the distance and the time the journey would take.

(14) Any information submitted in support of an application under this section shall state–
  (a) the nature of the offence for which the person to whom the application relates has been arrested;
  (b) the general nature of the evidence on which that person was arrested;
  (c) what inquiries relating to the offence have been made by the police and what further inquiries are proposed by them;
  (d) the reasons for believing the continued detention of that person to be necessary for the purposes of such further inquiries.

(15) Where an application under this section is refused, the person to whom the application relates shall forthwith be charged or, subject to subs (16) below, released, either on bail or without bail.

(16) A person need not be released under subs (15) above–
  (a) before the expiry of 24 hours after the relevant time; or
  (b) before the expiry of any longer period for which his continued detention is or has been authorised under s.42 above.

(17) Where an application under this section is refused, no further application shall be made under this section in respect of the person to whom the refusal relates, unless supported by evidence which has come to light since the refusal.

(18) Where a warrant of further detention is issued, the person to whom it relates shall be released from police detention, either on bail or without bail, upon or before the expiry of the warrant unless he is charged.

(19) A person released under subs (18) above shall not be re-arrested without a warrant for the offence for which he was previously arrested unless new evidence justifying a further arrest has come to light since his release.

COMMENTARY

Child, note to s.34, *ante.*

A magistrates' court, defined in s.45(1), *post.*

Serious arrestable offence, defined in s.116.

36/6/24 hours, to be treated as *approximate only*: s.45(2).

Police detention, defined in s.118(2); and see s.34(1).

The relevant time, defined in s.41(2).

(1): Information, see s.43(14).

(5): application should be made between 10 am and 9 pm and, if possible, during normal court hours: see Code A, Codes of Practice, Appendix I, *post.*

s.43(7): The requirement to dismiss where it would have been reasonable to apply within 36 hours is *mandatory: Ex p. Stirling, supra.* The six hour period of lee-way is not limited to the situation where the 36 hour period expires and no court is sitting at all; justices also have a discretion during the course of sittings whether to hear such an application straight away or to wait, provided that they do so for no longer than 6 hours: *R v Slough Justices, ex p. Stirling* (1987) 151 JP 603.

3.84   **Extension of warrants of further detention**
      44. (1) On an application on oath made by a constable and supported by an information a magistrates' court may extend a warrant of further detention issued under s.43 above if it is satisfied that there are reasonable grounds for believing that the further detention of the person to whom the application relates is justified.

(2) Subject to subs (3) below, the period for which a warrant of further

detention may be extended shall be such a period as the court thinks fit, having regard to the evidence before it.

(3) The period shall not–
(a) be longer than 36 hours; or
(b) end later than 96 hours after the relevant time.

(4) Where a warrant of further detention has been extended during subs (1) above, or further extended under this subsection, for a period ending before 96 hours after the relevant time, on an application such as is mentioned in that subsection a magistrates' court may further extend the warrant if it is satisfied as there mentioned; and subss (2) and (3) above apply to such further extensions as they apply to extensions under subs (1) above.

(5) A warrant of further detention shall, if extended or further extended under this section, be endorsed with a note of the period of that extension.

(6) Subs (2), (3) and (14) of s.43 above shall apply to an application made under this section as they apply to an application made under that section.

(7) Where an application under this section is refused, the person to whom the application relates shall forthwith be charged or, subject to subs (8) below, released, either on bail or without bail.

(8) A person need not be released under subs (7) above before the expiry of any period for which a warrant of further detention issued in relation to him has been extended or further extended on an earlier application made under this section.

COMMENTARY

Child: see note to s.34, *ante.*

Magistrates' court, defined in s.45(1), *post.*

36/39 hours, to be treated as *approximate only*: s.45(2).

Detention before charge – supplementary　　　　　　　　　　**3.85**
45. (1) In s.43 and 44 of this Act 'magistrates' court' means a court consisting of two or more justices of the peace sitting otherwise than in open court.

(2) Any reference in this Part of this Act to a period of time or a time of day is to be treated as approximate only.

Detention after charge　　　　　　　　　　　　　　　　　　**3.86**
46. (1) Where a person–
(a) is charged with an offence; and
(b) after being charged–
　　(i) is kept in police detention; or
　　(ii) is detained by a local authority in pursuance of arrangements made under s.38(6) above,
he shall be brought before a magistrates' court in accordance with the provisions of this section.

(2) If he is to be brought before a magistrates' court for the petty sessions area in which the police station at which he was charged is situated, he shall be brought before such a court as soon as is practicable and in any event not later than the first sitting after he is charged with the offence.

(3) If no magistrates' court for that area is due to sit either on the day on which he is charged or on the next day, the custody officer for the police station at which he was charged shall inform the clerk to the justices for the area that there is a person in the area to whom subs (2) above applies.

(4) If the person charged is to be brought before a magistrates' court for a petty sessions area other than that in which the police station at which he was

charged is situated, he shall be removed to that area as soon as is practicable and brought before such a court as soon as is practicable after his arrival in the area and in any event not later than the first sitting of a magistrates' court for that area after his arrival in the area.

(5) If no magistrates' court for that area is due to sit either on the day on which he arrives in the area or on the next day–
(a) he shall be taken to a police station in the area; and
(b) the custody officer at that station shall inform the clerk to the justices for the area that there is a person in the area to whom subs (4) applies.

(6) Subject to subs (8) below, where a clerk to the justices for a petty sessions area has been informed–
(a) under subs (3) above that there is a person in the area to whom subs (2) above applies; or
(b) under subs (5) above that there is a person in the area to whom subs (4) above applies,
the clerk shall arrange for a magistrates' court to sit not later than the day next following the relevant day.

(7) In this section 'the relevant day'–
(a) in relation to a person who is to be brought before a magistrates' court for the petty sessions area in which the police station at which he was charged is situated, means the day on which he was charged; and
(b) in relation to a person who is to be brought before a magistrates' court for any other petty sessions area, means the day on which he arrives in the area.

(8) Where the day next following the relevant day is Christmas Day, Good Friday or a Sunday, the duty of the clerk under subs (6) above is a duty to arrange for a magistrates' court to sit not later than the first day after the relevant day which is not one of those days.

(9) Nothing in this section requires a person who is in hospital to be brought before a court if he is not well enough.

COMMENTARY

Child, see note to s.34, *ante* and s.56, *post.*

Local authority, defined in s.38(8).

The relevant day, defined in s.46(7).

3.87   **Bail after arrest**
47. (1) Subject to subs (2) below, a release on bail of a person under this Part of this Act shall be released on bail granted in accordance with the Bail Act 1976.

(2) Nothing in the Bail Act 1976 shall prevent the re-arrest without warrant of a person released on bail subject to a duty to attend at a police station if new evidence justifying a further arrest has come to light since his release.

(3) Subject to subs (4) below, in this Part of this Act references to 'bail' are references to bail subject to a duty–
(a) to appear before a magistrates' court at such time and such place; or
(b) to attend at such police station at such time,
as the custody officer may appoint.

(4) Where a custody officer has granted bail to a person subject to a duty to appear at a police station, the custody officer may give notice in writing to that person that his attendance at the police station is not required.

(5) Where a person arrested for an offence who was released on bail subject to a duty to attend at a police station so attends, he may be detained without charge in connection with that offence only if the custody officer at the police

station has reasonable grounds for believing that his detention is necessary–
    (a) to secure or preserve evidence relating to the offence; or
    (b) to obtain such evidence by questioning him.

(6) Where a person is detained under subs (5) above, any time during which he was in police detention prior to be granted bail shall be included as part of any period which falls to be calculated under this Part of this Act.

(7) Where a person who was released on bail subject to a duty to attend at a police station is re-arrested, the provisions of this Part of this Act shall apply to him as they apply to a person arrested for the first time.

(8) (*Amendment*).

COMMENTARY
Child, see note to s.34, *ante* and s.52, *post.*

The custody officer, see s.36.

Person . . . in police detention, defined in s.118(2).

Savings   **3.88**
    51. Nothing in this Part of this Act shall affect–
    (a) the powers conferred on immigration officers by s.4 of and Sch.2 to the Immigration Act 1971 (administrative provisions as to control on entry etc);
    (b) the powers conferred by or by virtue of ss.12 or 13 of the Prevention of Terrorism (Temporary Provisions) Act 1984 (powers of arrest and detention and control of entry and procedure for removal);
    (c) any duty of a police officer under–
        (i) sections 129, 190 or 202 of the Army Act 1955 (duties of governors of prisons and others to receive prisoners, deserters, absentees and persons under escort);
       (ii) sections 129, 190 or 202 of the Air Force Act 1955 (duties of governors of prisons and others to receive prisoners, deserters, absentees and persons under escort);
      (iii) section 107 of the Naval Discipline Act 1957 (duties of governors of civil prisons etc); or
      (iv) paragraph 5 of Sch.5 to the Reserve Forces Act 1980 (duties of governors of civil prisons); or
    (d) any right of a person in police detention to apply for a writ of habeas corpus or other prerogative remedy.

Children   **3.89**
    52. This Part of this Act does not apply to a child (as for the time being defined for the purposes of the Children and Young Persons Act 1969) who is arrested without a warrant otherwise than for homicide and to whom s.28(4) and (5) of that Act accordingly apply.

COMMENTARY
This Part of this Act, see ss.46–52.

Children and Young Persons Act 1969, defines a child as a person under the age of 14: s.70(1) CYPA 1969.

Abolition of certain powers of constables to search persons   **3.90**
    53. (1) Subject to subs (2) below, there shall cease to have effect any Act (including a local Act) passed before this Act is so far as it authorises–
    (a) any search by a constable of a person in police detention at a police station; or

(b) an intimate search of a person by a constable;
and any rule of common law which authorises a search such as is mentioned in para (a) or (b) above is abolished.

(2) Nothing in subs (1)(a) above shall affect para 6(2) of Sch.2 to the Prevention of Terrorism (Temporary Provisions) Act 1984.

COMMENTARY

A person in police detention, defined in s.118(2), *post.*

Intimate search, defined in s.118(1).

3.91   **Searches of detained persons**
54. (1) The custody officer at a police station shall ascertain and record or cause to be recorded everything which a person has with him when he is–
(a) brought to the station after being arrested elsewhere or after being committed to custody by an order or sentence of a court; or
(b) arrested at the station after–
(i) having attended voluntarily there; or
(ii) having accompanied a constable there without having been arrested.
(b) arrested at the station or detained there under s.47(5) above.

(2) In the case of an arrested person the record shall be made as part of his custody record.

(3) Subject to subs (4) below, a custody officer may seize and retain any such thing or cause any such thing to be seized and retained.

(4) Clothes and personal effects may only be seized if the custody officer–
(a) believes that the persons from whom they are seized may use them–
(i) to cause physical injury to himself or any other person;
(ii) to damage property;
(iii) to interfere with evidence; or
(iv) to assist him to escape; or
(b) has reasonable grounds for believing that they may be evidence relating to an offence.

(5) Where anything is seized, the person from whom it is seized shall be told the reason for the seizure unless he is–
(a) violent or likely to become violent; or
(b) incapable of understanding what is said to him.

(6) Subject to subs (7) below, a person may be searched if the custody officer considers it necessary to enable him to carry out his duty under subs (1) above and to the extent that the custody officer considers necessary for that purpose.

(6A) A person who is in custody at a police station or is in police detention otherwise than at a police station may at anytime be searched in order to ascertain whether he has with him anything which he could use for any of the purposes specified in subsection (4)(a) above.

(6B) Subject to subsection (6C) below, a constable may seize and retain, or cause to be seized and retained, anything found on such a search.

(6C) A constable may only seize clothes and personal effects in the circumstances specified in subsection (4) above.

(7) An intimate search may not be conducted under this section.

(8) A search under this section shall be carried out by a constable.

(9) The constable carrying out a search shall be of the same sex as the person searched.
[Subs (1)(b) will be replaced by the words in italics and subs (6A)–(6C) will be inserted by [s.140] CJA 1988 from a date to be appointed].

COMMENTARY

See para 4.1 and Annex A Code of Practice for Detention, Treatment and Questioning etc: Appendix I, *post.*

Custody officer, see s.36, *ante.*

Intimate search, defined in s.118(1), *post.*

Intimate search 3.92

55. (1) Subject to the following provisions of this section, if an officer of at least the rank of superintendent has reasonable grounds for believing–

    (a) that a person who has been arrested and is in police detention may have concealed on him anything which–

        (i) he could use to cause physical injury to himself or others; and

        (ii) He might so use while he is in police detention or in the custody of a court; or

    (b) that such a person–

        (i) may have a Class A drug concealed on him; and

        (ii) was in possession of it with the appropriate criminal intent before his arrest,

he may authorise such a search of that person.

(2) An officer may not authorise an intimate search of a person for anything unless he has reasonable grounds for believing that it cannot be found without his being intimately searched.

(3) An officer may give an authorisation under subs (1) above orally or in writing but, if he gives it orally, he shall confirm it in writing as soon as is practicable.

(4) An intimate search which is only a drug offence search shall be by way of examination by a suitably qualified person.

(5) Except as provided by subs (4) above, an intimate search shall be by way of examination by a suitably qualified person unless an officer of at least the rank of superintendent considers that this is not practicable.

(6) An intimate search which is not carried out as mentioned in subs (5) above shall be carried out by a constable.

(7) A constable may not carry out an intimate search of a person of the opposite sex.

(8) No intimate search may be carried out except–

    (a) at a police station;

    (b) at a hospital;

    (c) at a registered medical practitioner's surgery; or

    (d) at some other place used for medical purposes.

(9) An intimate search which is only a drug offence search may not be carried out at a police station.

(10) If an intimate search of a person is carried out, the custody record relating to him shall state–

    (a) which parts of his body were searched; and

    (b) why they were searched.

(11) The information required to be recorded by subs (10) above shall be recorded as soon as practicable after the completion of the search.

(12) The custody officer at a police station may seize and retain anything which is found on an intimate search of a person, or cause any such thing to be seized and retained–

    (a) if he believes that the person from whom it is seized may use it–

        (i) to cause physical injury to himself or any other person;

        (ii) to damage property;

        (iii) to interfere with evidence; or

    (iv) to assist him to escape; or
  (b) if he has reasonable grounds for believing that it may be evidence relating to an offence.

    (13) Where anything is seized under this section, the person from whom it is seized shall be told the reason for the seizure unless he is–
    (a) violent or likely to become violent; or
    (b) incapable of understanding what is said to him.

    (14)–(16) (*Annual reports*).

    (17) In this section–
'the appropriate criminal intent' means an intent to commit an offence under–
    (a) section 5(3) of the Misuse of Durgs Act 1971 (possession of controlled drug with intent to supply to another); or
  (b) section 68(2) of the Customs and Excise Management Act 1979 (exportation etc with intent to evade a prohibition or restriction);
'Class A drug' has the meaning assigned to it by s.2(1)(b) of the Misuse of Drugs Act 1971;
'drug offence search' means an intimate search for a Class A drug which an officer has authorised by virtue of subs (1)(b) above; and
'suitably qualified person' means–
    (a) a registered medical practitioner; or
    (b) a registered nurse.

Note
Subs (1) will be amended by [Sch.14] CJA 1988 from a date to be appointed as follows:
    (1) Subject to the following provisions of this section, if an officer of at least the rank of superintendent has reasonable grounds for believing–
    (a) that a person who has been arrested and is in police detention may have concealed on him anything which–
      (i) he could use to cause physical injury to himself or others; and
      (ii) he might so use while he is in police detention or in the custody of a court; or
    (b) that such a person–
      (i) may have a Class A drug concealed on him; and
      (ii) was in possession of it with the appropriate criminal intent before his arrest,
he may authorise an intimate search.

COMMENTARY

See para 4.1 and Annex A Code of Practice for Detention, Treatment and Questioning etc: Appendix I, *post*.

Police detention, defined in s.118(2), *post*.

Class A drug, defined in s.55(17).

Appropriate criminal intent, defined in s.55(17).

Intimate search, defined in s.118(1).

Suitably qualified person, defined in s.55(17).

Drug offence search, defined in s.55(17).

Custody officer, see s.36.

s.55(1): The seemingly undefined phrase 'such a search' suggests an ill considered Parliamentary amendment. It is suggested that s.55(1) can only be read sensibly as being confined (as the side note indicates) to intimate searches.

3.93   **Right to have someone informed when arrested**
    56. (1) Where a person has been arrested and is being held in custody in a police station or other premises, he shall be entitled, if he so requests, to have

one friend or relative or other person who is known to him or who is likely to take an interest in his welfare told, as soon as is practicable except to the extent that delay is permitted by this section, that he has been arrested and is being detained there.

(2) Delay is only permitted–
(a) in the case of a person who is in police detention for a serious arrestable offence; and
(b) if an officer of at least the rank of superintendent authorises it.

(3) In any case the person in custody must be permitted to exercise the right conferred by subs (1) above within 36 hours from the relevant time, as defined in s.41(2) above.

(4) An officer may give an authorisation under subs (2) above orally or in writing but, if he gives it orally, he shall confirm it in writing as soon as is practicable.

(5) Subject to subs (5A) below an officer may only authorise delay where he has reasonable grounds for believing that telling the named person of the arrest–
(a) will lead to interference with or harm to evidence connected with a serious arrestable offence or interference with or physical injury to other persons; or
(b) will lead to the altering of other persons suspected of having committed such an offence but not yet arrested for it; or
(c) will hinder the recovery of any property obtained as a result of such an offence.

(5A) An officer may also authorise delay where the serious arrestable offence is a drug trafficking offence *or an offence to which Part VI of the Criminal Justice Act 1988 applies (offences in respect of which confiscation orders under that Part may be made)* and the officer has reasonable grounds for believing–
(a) that the detained person has benefited from drug trafficking, and
(b) that the recovery of the value of that person's proceeds of drug trafficking will be hindered by telling the named person of the arrest.

(6) If a delay is authorised–
(a) the detained person shall be told the reason for it; and
(b) the reason shall be noted on his custody record.

(7) The duties imposed by subs (6) above shall be performed as soon as is practicable.

(8) The rights conferred by this section on a person detained at a police station or other premises are exercisable whenever he is transferred from one place to another; and this section applies to each subsequent occasion on which they are exercisable as it applies to the first such occasion.

(9) There may be no further delay in permitting the exercise of the right conferred by subs (1) above once the reason for authorising delay ceases to subsist.

(10) In the foregoing provisions of this section references to a person who has been arrested include references to a person who has been detained under the terrorism provisions and 'arrest' includes detention under those provisions.

(11) (*Terrorism provisions*).
[*as amended by s.32 Drug Trafficking Offences Act 1986*].
Note: the words in italics in subs (5A) will be added by [s.97] CJA 1988 from a date to be appointed and [s.97] will substitute the following paragraphs for (a) and (b) in subs (5A):
(a) where the offence is a drug trafficking offence, that the detained person

> *has benefited from drug trafficking and that the recovery of the value of that person's proceeds of drug trafficking will be hindered by telling the named person of the arrest; and*
>
> (b) *where the offence is one to which Part VI of the Criminal Justice Act 1988 applies, that the detained person has benefited from the offence and that the recovery of the value of the property obtained by that person from or in connection with the offence or of the pecuniary advantage derived by him from or in connection with it will be hindered by telling the named person of the arrest.*

COMMENTARY

Serious arrestable offence, defined in s.116, *post.*

36 hours, the 'approximating' provision in. s.45(2) has not been applied to this section.

The terrorism provisions/Terrorism, defined in s.65.

3.94   **Access to legal advice**

58. (1) A person arrested and held in custody in a police station or other premises shall be entitled, if he so requests, to consult a solicitor privately at any time.

(2) Subject to subs (3) below, a request under subsection (1) above and time at which it was made shall be recorded in the custody record.

(3) Such a request need not be recorded in the custody record of a person who makes it at a time while he is at a court after being charged with an offence.

(4) If a person makes such a request, he must be permitted to consult a solicitor as soon as is practicable except to the extent that delay is permitted by this section.

(5) In any case he must be permitted to consult a solicitor within 36 hours from the relevant time, as defined in s.41(2) above.

(6) Delay in compliance with a request is only permitted–
(a) in the case of a person who is in police detention for a serious arrestable offence; and
(b) if an officer of at least the rank of superintendent authorises it.

(7) An officer may give an authorisation under subs (6) above orally or in writing but, if he gives it orally, he shall confirm it in writing as soon as is practicable.

(8) Subject to subs (8A) below an officer may only authorise delay where he has reasonable grounds for believing that the exercise of the right conferred by subs (1) above at the time when the person detained desires to exercise it–
(a) will lead to interference with or harm to evidence connected with a serious arrestable offence or interference with or physical injury to other persons; or
(b) will lead to the altering of other persons suspected of having committed such an offence but not yet arrested for it; or
(c) will hinder the recovery of any property obtained as a result of such an offence.

(8A) An officer may also authorise delay where the serious arrestable offence is a drug trafficking offence *or an offence to which Part VI of the Criminal Justice Act 1988 applies* and the officer has reasonable grounds for believing–

(a) that the detained person has benefited from drug trafficking, and

(b) that recovery of the value of that person's proceeds of drug trafficking will be hindered by the exercise of the right conferred by subsection (1) above.

(9) If delay is authorised–
(a) the detained person shall be told the reason for it; and
(b) the reason shall be noted on his custody record.

(10) The duties imposed by subs (9) above shall be performed as soon as is practicable.

(11) There may be no further delay in permitting the exercise of the right conferred by subs (1) above once the reason for authorising delay ceases to subsist.

(12) The reference in subs (1) above to a person arrested includes a reference to a person who has been detained under the terrorism provisions.

(13) (*Terrorism provisions*).

(14) If an officer of appropriate rank has reasonable grounds for believing that, unless he gives a direction under subs (15) below, the exercise by a person arrested or detained under the terrorism provisions of the right conferred by subs (1) above will have any of the consequences specified in subs (8) above (as it has effect by virtue of subs (13) above), he may give a direction under that subsection.

(15) A direction under this subsection is a direction that a person desiring to exercise the right conferred by subs (1) above may only consult a solicitor in the sight and hearing of a qualified officer of the uniformed branch of the force of which the officer giving the direction is a member.

(16) An officer is qualified for the purpose of subs (15) above if–
(a) he is of at least the rank of inspector; and
(b) in the opinion of the officer giving the direction he has no connection with the case.

(17) An officer is of appropriate rank to give a direction under subs (15) above if he is of at least the rank of Commander or Assistant Chief Constable.

(18) A direction under subs (15) above shall cease to have effect once the reason for giving it ceases to subsist.
[*as amended by s.32 Drug Trafficking Offences Act 1986*].

Note: the words in italics in subs (8A) will be added by [s.97] CJA 1988 from a date to be appointed and [s.97] will substitute the following paragraphs for (a) and (b) in subs (8A):
(a) *where the offence is a drug trafficking offence, that the detained person has benefited from drug trafficking and that the recovery of the value of that person's proceeds of drug trafficking will be hindered by the exercise of the right conferred by subsection (1) above; and*
(b) *where the offence is one to which Part VI of the Criminal Justice Act 1988 applies, that the detained person has benefited from the offence and that the recovery of the value of the property obtained by that person from or in connection with the offence or of the pecuniary advantage derived by him from or in connection with it will be hindered by the exercise of the right conferred by subsection (1) above.*

COMMENTARY

36 hours, the 'approximating' provision in s.45(2) has not been applied to this section.

Serious arrestable offence, defined in s.116

Terrorism provisions, defined in s.65.

Officer of appropriate rank, see s.58(17).

Qualified officer, see s.58(17).

3.95   **Fingerprinting**

61. (1) Except as provided by this section no person's fingerprints may be taken without the appropriate consent.

(2) Consent to the taking of a person's fingerprints must be in writing if it is given at a time when he is at a police station.

(3) The fingerprints of a person detained at a police station may be taken with the appropriate consent–
- (a) if an officer of at least the rank of superintendent authorises them to be taken; or
- (b) if–
  - (i) he has been charged with a recordable offence or informed that he will be reported for such an offence; and
  - (ii) he has not had his fingerprints taken in the course of the investigation of the offence by the police.

(4) An officer may only give an authorisation under subs (3)(a) above if he has reasonable grounds–
- (a) for suspecting the involvement of the person whose fingerprints are to be taken in a criminal offence; and
- (b) for believing that his fingerprints will tend to confirm or disprove his involvement.

(5) An officer may give an authorisation under subs (3)(a) above orally or in writing but, if he gives it orally, he shall confirm it in writing as soon as is practicable.

(6) Any person's fingerprints may be taken without the appropriate consent if he has been convicted of a recordable offence.

(7) In a case where by virtue of subs (3) or (6) above a person's fingerprints are taken without the appropriate consent–
- (a) he shall be told the reason before his fingeprints are taken; and
- (b) the reason shall be recorded as soon as is practicable after the fingerprints are taken.

(8) If he is detained at a police station when the fingerprints are taken, the reason for taking them shall be recorded on his custody record.

(9) Nothing in this section–
- (a) affects any power conferred by para 18(2) of Sch.2 to the Immigration Act 1971; or
- (b) applies to a person arrested or detained under the terrorism provisions.

COMMENTARY

Fingerprints, include palm prints: s.65.

The appropriate consent, defined in s.65.

Recordable offence, defined in s.118(1).

The terrorism provisions, defined in s.65.

3.96   **Intimate samples**

62. (1) An intimate sample may be taken from a person in police detention only–
- (a) if a police officer of at least the rank of superintendent authorises it to be taken; and
- (b) if the appropriate consent is given.

(2) An officer may only give an authorisation if he has reasonable grounds–
- (a) for suspecting the involvement of the person from whom the sample is to be taken in a serious arrestable offence; and
- (b) for believing that the sample will tend to confirm or disprove his involvement.

(3) An officer may give an authorisation under subs (1) above orally or in writing but, if he gives it orally, he shall confirm it in writing as soon as is practicable.

(4) The appropriate consent must be given in writing.

(5) Where–
(a) an authorisation has been given; and
(b) it is proposed that an intimate sample shall be taken in pursuance of the authorisation,
an officer shall inform the person from whom the sample is to be taken–
(i) of the giving of the authorisation; and
(ii) of the grounds for giving it.

(6) The duty imposed by subs (5)(ii) above includes a duty to state the nature of the offence in which it is suspected that the person from whom the sample is to be taken has been involved.

(7) If an intimate sample is taken from a person–
(a) the authorisation by virtue of which it was taken;
(b) the grounds for giving the authorisation; and
(c) the fact that the appropriate consent was given,
shall be recorded as soon as is practicable after the sample is taken.

(8) If an intimate sample is taken from a person detained at a police station, the matters required to be recorded by subs (7) above shall be recorded in his custody record.

(9) An intimate sample, other than a sample of urine or saliva, may only be taken from a person by a registered medical practitioner.

(10) Where the appropriate consent to the taking of an intimate sample from a person was refused without good cause, in any proceedings against that person for an offence–
(a) the court, in determining–
(i) whether to commit that person for trial; or
(ii) whether there is a case to answer; and
(b) the court or jury, in determining whether that person is guilty of the offence charge,
may draw such inferences from the refusal as appear proper; and the refusal may, on the basis of such inferences, be treated as, or as capable of amounting to, corroboration of any evidence against the person in relation to which the refusal is material.

(11) Nothing in this section affects ss.5 to 12 of the Road Traffic Act 1972.

COMMENTARY
Intimate sample, defined in s.65.

The appropriate consent, defined in s.65.

Other samples   3.97
63. (1) Except as provided by this section, a non-intimate sample may not be taken from a person without the appropriate consent.

(2) Consent to the taking of a non-intimate sample must be given in writing.

(3) A non-intimate sample may be taken from a person without the appropriate consent if–

(a) he is in police detention or is being held in custody by the police on the authority of a court; and
(b) an officer of at least the rank of superintendent authorises it to be taken without the appropriate consent.

(4) An officer may only give an authorisation under subs (3) above if he has reasonable grounds–

(a) for suspecting the involvement of the person from whom the sample is to be taken in a serious arrestable offence; and

(b) for believing that the sample will tend to confirm or disprove his involvement.

(5) An officer may give an authorisation under subs (3) above orally or in writing but, if he gives it orally, he shall confirm it in writing as soon as is practicable.

(6) Where–

(a) an authorisation has been given; and

(b) it is proposed that a non-intimate sample shall be taken in pursuance of the authorisation,

an officer shall inform the person from whom the sample is to be taken–

(i) of the giving of the authorisation; and

(ii) of the grounds for giving it.

(7) The duty imposed by subs (6)(ii) above includes a duty to state the nature of the offence in which it is suspected that the person from whom the sample is to be taken has been involved.

(8) If a non-intimate sample is taken from a person by virtue of subs (3) above–

(a) the authorisation by virtue of which it was taken; and

(b) the grounds for giving the authorisation,

shall be recorded as soon as is practicable after the sample is taken.

(9) If a non-intimate sample is taken from a person detained at a police station, the matters required to be recorded by subs (8) above shall be recorded in his custody record.

COMMENTARY

Non-intimate sample, defined in s.65.

Person . . . in police detention, defined in s.118(2).

The appropriate consent, defined in s.65.

Serious arrestable offence, defined in s.116.

3.98   **Destruction of fingerprints and samples**

64. (1) If–

(a) fingerprints or samples are taken from a person in connection with the investigation of an offence; and

(b) he is cleared of that offence,

they must be destroyed as soon as is practicable after the conclusion of the proceedings.

(2) If–

(a) fingerprints or samples are taken from a person in connection with such an investigation; and

(b) it is decided that he shall not be prosecuted for the offence and he has not admitted it and been dealt with by way of being cautioned by a constable,

they must be destroyed as soon as is practicable after that decision is taken.

(3) If–

(a) fingerprints or samples are taken from a person in connection with the investigation of an offence; and

(b) that person is not suspected of having committed the offence,

they must be destroyed as soon as is practicable after that decision is taken.

(4) Proceedings which are discontinued are to be treated as concluded for the purposes of this section.

(5) If fingerprints are destroyed, any copies of them shall also be destroyed.

(5) If fingerprints are destroyed–
(a) any copies of the fingerprints shall also be destroyed; and
(b) any chief officer of police controlling access to computer data relating to the fingerprints shall make access to the data impossible, as soon as it is practicable to do so.

(6) A person who asks to be allowed to witness the destruction of his fingerprints or copies of them shall have a right to witness it.

(6A) If–
(a) subsection (5)(b) above falls to be complied with; and
(b) the person to whose fingerprints the data relate asks for a certificte that it has been complied with,
such a certificate shall be issued to him by the responsible chief officer of police or a person authorised by him or on his behalf for the purposes of this section.
(6B) In this section–
'chief officer of police' means the chief officer of police for an area mentioned in Schedule 8 to the Police Act 1964; and
'the responsible chief officer of police' means the chief officer of police in whose area the computer data were put on to the computer.

(7) Nothing in this section–
(a) affects any power conferred by para 18(2) of Sch.2 to the Immigration Act 1971; or
(b) applies to a person arrested or detained under the terrorism provisions.
[Subs (5) will be substituted by the subsection in italics and subs (6A) and (6B) will be added by [s.141] CJA 1988 from a date to be appointed].

COMMENTARY

Fingerprints. Include, palm prints: s.65.

The terrorism provisions, defined in s.65.

Part V – supplementary   **3.99**
  65. In this Part of this Act–
'appropriate consent' means–
(a) in relation to a person who has attained the age of 17 years, the consent of that person;
(b) in relation to a person who has not attained that age but has attained the age of 14 years, the consent of that person and his parent or guardian; and
(c) in relation to a person who has not attained the age of 14 years, the consent of his parent or guardian;
'drug trafficking' and 'drug trafficking offences' have the same meaning as in the Drug Trafficking Offences Act 1986;
'fingerprints' includes palm prints;
'intimate sample' means a sample of blood, semen or any other tissue fluid, urine, saliva or pubic hair, or a swab taken from a person's body orifice;
'non-intimate' sample means–
(a) a sample of hair other than pubic hair;
(b) a sample taken from a nail or from under a nail;
(c) a swab taken from any part of a person's body other than a body orifice;
(d) a footprint or a similar impression of any part of a person's body other than a part of his hand;
'the terrorism provisions' means–
(a) section 12(1) of the Prevention of Terrorism (Temporary Provisions) Act 1984; and
(b) any provision conferring a power of arrest or detention and contained in an order under s.13 of that Act; and
'terrorism' has the meaning assigned to it by s.14(1) of that Act and references

in this Part to any person's proceeds of drug trafficking are to be construed in accordance with the Drug Trafficking Offences Act 1986.
[*as amended by s.32 Drug Trafficking Offences Act 1986*].

COMMENTARY
Parent or guardian, defined in s.118(1), *post.*

3.100   **Codes of practice**
66. The Secretary of State shall issue codes of practice in connection with–
(a) the exercise by police officers of statutory powers–
    (i) to search a person without first arresting him; or
    (ii) to search a vehicle without making an arrest;
(b) the detention, treatment, questioning and identification of persons by police officers;
(c) searches of premises by police officers; and
(d) the seizure of property found by police officers on persons or premises.

COMMENTARY
Codes of practice, these are reproduced in Appendix I, *post.*

3.101   **Codes of practice – supplementary**
67. (1)–(7) (*Procedure*).

(8) A police officer shall be liable to disciplinary proceedings for a failure to comply with any provision of such a code, unles such proceedings are precluded by s.104 below.

(9) Persons other than police officers who are charged with the duty of investigating offences or charging offenders shall in the discharge of that duty have regard to any relevant provision of such a code.

(10) A failure on the part–
(a) of a police officer to comply with any provision of such a code; or
(b) of any person other than a police officer who is charged with the duty of investigating offences or charging offenders to have regard to any relevant provision of such a code in the discharge of that duty,
shall not of itself render him liable to any criminal or civil proceedings.

(11) In all criminal and civil proceedings any such code shall be admissible in evidence; and if any provision of such a code appears to the court or tribunal conducting the proceedings to be relevant to any question arising in the proceedings it shall be taken into account in determining that question.

(12) In this section 'criminal proceedings' includes–
(a) proceedings in the United Kingdom or elsewhere before a court-martial constituted under the Army Act 1955, the Air Force Act 1955 or the Naval Discipline Act 1957 or a disciplinary court constituted under s.50 of the said Act of 1957;
(b) proceedings before the Courts-Martial Appeal Court; and
(c) proceedings before a Standing Civilian Court.

COMMENTARY
Criminal proceedings, s.67(12).

Codes of practice, these are reproduced in Appendix I, *post.*

3.102   **Meaning of 'serious arrestable offence'**
116. (1) This section has effect for determining whether an offence is a serious arrestable offence for the purposes of this Act.

(2) The following arrestable offences are always serious–
(a) an offence (whether at common law or under any enactment) specified in Part I of Sch.5 to this Act; and

(aa) any of the offences mentioned in paras (a) to (d) of the definition of 'drug trafficking offence' in s.38(1) of the Drug Trafficking Offences Act 1986; and

(b) an offence under an enactment specified in Part II of that schedule.

(3) Subject to subs (4) and (5) below, any other arrestable offence is serious only if its commission–
(a) has led to any of the consequence specified in subs (6) below; or
(b) is intended or is likely to lead to any of those consequences.

(4) An arrestable offence which consists of making a threat is serious if carrying out the threat would be likely to lead to any of the consequences specified in subs (6) below.

(5) An offence under ss.1, 9 or 10 of the Prevention of Terrorism (Temporary Provisions) Act 1984 is always a serious arrestable offence for the purposes of s.56 or 58 above, and an attempt or conspiracy to commit any such offence is also always a serious arrestable offence for those purposes.

(6) The consequences mentioned in subs (3) and (4) above are
(a) serious harm to the security of the State or to public order;
(b) serious interference with the administration of justice or with the investigation of offences or of a particular offence;
(c) the death of any person;
(d) serious injury to any person;
(e) substantial financial gain to any person; and
(f) serious financial loss to any person.

(7) Loss is serious for the purposes of this section if, having regard to all the circumstances, it is serious for the person who suffers it.

(8) In this section 'injury' includes any disease and any impairment of a person's physical or mental condition.

[*as amended by s.36 Drug Trafficking Offences Act 1986*].

Power of constable to use reasonable force **3.103**
117. Where any provision of this Act–
(a) confers a power on a constable; and
(b) does not provide that the power may only be exercised with the consent of some person, other than a police officer,
the officer may use reasonable force, if necessary, in the exercise of the power.

General interpretation **3.104**
118. (1) In this Act–
'arrestable offence' has the meaning assigned to it by s.24 above;
'designated police station' has the meaning assigned to it by s.35 above;
'document' has the same meaning as in Part I of the Civil Evidence Act 1968;
'intimate search' means a search which consists of the physical examination of a person's body orifices;
'item subject to legal privilege' has the meaning assigned to it by s.10 above;
'parent or guardian' means–
(a) in the case of a child or young person in the care of a local authority, that authority; and
(b) in the case of a child or young person in the care of a voluntary organisation in which parental rights and duties with respect to him are vested by virtue of a resolution under s.64(1) of the Child Care Act 1980, that organisation;
'premises' has the meaning assigned to it by s.23 above;
'recordable offence' means any offence to which regulations under s.27 above apply;
'vessel' includes any ship, boat, raft or other apparatus constructed or adapted for floating on water.

(2) A person is in police detention of the purposes of this Act if–
(a) he has been taken to a police station after being arrested for an offence; or
(b) he is arrested at a police sation after attending voluntarily at the station or accompanying a constable to it,

and is detained there or is detained elsewhere in the charge of a constable, except that a person who is at a court after being charged is not in police detention for those purposes.

SCHEDULE 5

3.105   **Serious Arrestable Offences**
Part I
OFFENCES MENTIONED IN SECTION 116(2)(A)
1. Treason.
2. Murder.
3. Manslaughter.
4. Rape.
5. Kidnapping.
6. Incest with a girl under the age of 13.
7. Buggery with–
(a) a boy under the age of 16; or
(b) a person who has not consented.
8. Indecent assault which constitutes an act of gross indecency.

Part II
OFFENCES MENTIONED IN SECTION 116(2)(B)
Explosive Substances Act 1883
1. Section 2 (causing explosion likely to endanger life or property).

Sexual Offences Act 1956
2. Section 5 (intercourse with a girl under the age of 13).

Firearms Act 1968
3. Section 16 (possession of firearms with intent to injure).
(4) Section 17(1) (use of firearms and imitation firearms to resist arrest).
5. Section 18 (carrying firearms with criminal intent).

Road Traffic Act 1972
6. Section 1 (causing death by reckless driving);

Taking of Hostages Act 1982
7. Section 1 (hostage-taking).

Aviation Security Act 1982
8. Section 1 (hi-jacking).

3.106   # CERTIFICATES OF UNRULY CHARACTER (CONDITIONS) ORDER 1977
SI 1977 No 1037

2. (1) In this Order–
'appropriate local authority' means the local authority in whose area the court is sitting or the young person resides;
'court' includes a justice; and
'local authority' means the council of a county (other than a metropolitan county) a metropolitan district or a London borough, or the Common Council of the City of London;
'young person' means a person who has attained the age of 14 and is under the age of 17.

(2) The Interpretation Act [1978] shall apply to the Interpretation of this Order as it applies to the interpretation of an Act of Parliament.

3. The court shall not certify under s.22(5) or s.23(2) or (3) of the Children and Young Persons Act 1969 (committals to remand centres or prisons) that a young person is of so unruly a character that he cannot safely be committed to the care of a local authority unless one or more of the following conditions is satisfied in relation to him–

- (a) the young person is charged with an offence punishable in the case of an adult with imprisonment for 14 years or more, and–
  - (i) the court is remanding him for the first time in the proceedings and is satisfied that there has not been time to obtain a written report from the appropriate local authority on the availability of suitable accommodation for him in a community home, or
  - (ii) the court is satisfied on the basis of such a report that no suitable accommodation is available for him in a community home where he could be accommodated without substantial risk to himself or others;
- (b) the young person is charged with an offence of violence or has been found guilty on a previous occasion of an offence of violence, and–
  - (i) the court is remanding him for the first time in the proceedings and is satisfied that there has not been time to obtain a written report from the appropriate local authority on the availability of suitable accommodation for him in a community home, or
  - (ii) the court is satisfied on the basis of such a report that no suitable accommodation is available for him in a community home where he could be accommodated without substantial risk to himself or others;
- (c) the young person has persistently absconded from a community home or, while accommodated in a community home, has seriously disrupted the running of the home, and the court is satisfied on the basis of a written report from the appropriate local authority that accommodation cannot be found for him in a suitable community home where he could be accommodated without risk of his absconding or seriously disrupting the running of the home.

COMMENTARY

'The Secretary of State suggests that where the court is satisfied that a young person before it cannot properly be released on bail, and where it has reason to think that it might not be appropraite to commit him to the care of the local authority under s.23(1) CYPA 1969, the court will wish to make such inquiries as it thinks relevant concerning the previous history of the young person in respect of the matters mentioned in the prescribed conditions; ie, whether he has any previous findings of guilt for offences of violence, or a history of absconding from local authority care or of particularly disruptive behaviour while in such care. The court may also consider it a matter of good practice to state the grounds on which it is proposed to issue the certificate and give the young person and his parents (if present) or legal adviser an opportunity to address the court': HOC 19/1977.

Para 3, the effect of this paragraph is not to deprive the court of its power, but to regulate its exercise by imposing conditions which have to be fulfilled: *R v Leicester City Juvenile Court, ex p. Capenhurst* (1984) 80 Cr App R 320. Thus, where a written report from the local authority indicated that accommodation was available for the accused in a remand unit of a community home but that he did not satisfy the social services committee's criteria for admission to secure accommodation or for an unruly certificate, it was held that it was for the juvenile court to satisfy itself on the availablity of secure accommodation. But the court is powerless to issue an unruly certificate where the local authority declines or fails altogether to submit a written report: *R v Dudley Magistrates' Court, ex p. G* (1988) *The Times*, 13 February.

MAGISTRATES' COURTS RULES 1981
SI 1981 No 552 (as amended by SI 1984 No 1552)

Remand on bail for more than eight days where sureties have not entered into recognizances   **3.107**

23. Where the court, with a view to a person's being remanded on bail under para (a) of s.128(6) of the Act of 1980 for a period exceeding eight days, has fixed the amount of the recognizances to be taken for that purpose but commits that person to custody because the recognizances of the sureties have not yet been taken, the warrant of commitment shall direct the governor or keeper of the prison or place to which he is committed to bring him before the court at the end of eight clear days or at such earlier time as may be specified in the warrant unless in the meantime the sureties have entered into their recognizances.

3.108   **Transfer of remand hearings**
           25. (1) Where a magistrates' court, under s.130(1) of the Act of 1980, orders that an accused who has been remanded in custody be brought up for any subsequent remands before an alternate magistrates' court, the clerk of the first-mentioned court shall, as soon as practicable after the making of the order and in any case within two days thereafter (not counting Sundays, Good Friday, Christmas Day or bank holidays), send to the clerk of the alternate court–
           (a) a statement indicating the offence or offences charged;
           (b) a copy of the record made by the first-mentioned court in pursuance of s.5 of the Bail Act 1976 relating to the withholding of bail in respect of the accused when he was last remanded in custody;
           (c) a copy of any legal aid order previously made in the same case;
           (d) a copy of any legal aid application;
           (e) a copy of any contribution order previously made in the case under s.7 of the Legal Aid Act 1982;
           (f) if the first-mentioned court has made an order under s.8(2) of the Act of 1980 (removal of restrictions on reports of committal proceedings), a statement to that effect;
           (g) a statement whether or not the accused has a solicitor acting for him in the case and has consented to the hearing and determination in his absence of any application for his remand on an adjournment of the case under ss.5, 10(1) and 18(4) of the Act of 1980 together with a statement indicating whether or not that consent has been withdrawn;

           (h) a statement indicating the occasions, if any, on which the accused has been remanded under s.128(3A) of the Act of 1980 without being brought before the first-mentioned court.

           (1A) Where the first-mentioned court is satisfied as mentioned in s.128(3A) of the Act of 1980, para (1) shall have effect as if for the words 'an accused who has been remanded in custody be brought up for any subsequent remands before' there were substituted the words 'applications for any subsequent remands of the accused be made to'.

           (2) The clerk of an alternate magistrates' court before which an accused who has been remanded in custody is brought up for any subsequent remands in pursuance of an order made as aforesaid shall, as soon as practicable after the order ceases to be in force and in any case within two days thereafter (not counting Sundays, Good Friday, Christmas Day or bank holidays), send to the clerk of the magistrates' court which made the order–
           (a) the documents referred to in sub-para (c), (d) and (e) of para (1);
           (b) a copy of the record made by the alternate court in pursuance of s.5 of the Bail Act 1976 relating to the grant or withholding of bail in respect of the accused when he was last remanded in custody or on bail;
           (c) a copy of any legal aid order made by the alternate court;
           (d) a copy of any legal aid application made to the alternate court;
           (e) any statement of means submitted to the alternate court; and
           (ee) a copy of any contribution order made in the case by the alternate court under s.7 of the Legal Aid Act 1982;
           (f) if the first-mentioned court has made an order under s.8(2) of the Act of 1980 (removal of restrictions on reports of committal proceedings), a statement to that effect;

(g) a statement indicating whether or not the accused has a solicitor acting for him in the case and has consented to the hearing and determination in his absence of any application for his remand on an adjournment of the case under ss.5, 10(1) and 18(4) of the Act of 1980 together with a statement indicating whether or not that consent has been withdrawn;

(h) a statement indicating the occasions, if any, on which the accused has been remanded by the alternate court under s.12(3)A) of the Act of 1980 without being brought before that court.

(2A) Where the alternate court is satisfied as mentioned in s.128(3A) of the Act of 1980 para (2) shall have effect as if for the words 'an accused who has been remanded in custody is brought up for any subsequent remands' there shall be substituted the words 'applications for the further remand of the accused are to be made'.

Notice of further remand in certain cases   **3.109**
26. Where a transfer direction has been given by the Secretary of State under s.73 of the Mental Health Act 1959 in respect of a person remanded in custody by a magistrates' court and the direction has not ceased to have effect, the clerk of the court shall give notice in writing to the managers of the hospital where he is detained of any further remand under s.128 of the Act of 1980.

Notice of enlargement of recognizances   **3.110**
84. (1) If a magistrates' court before which any person is bound by a recognizance to appear enlarges the recognizance to a later time under s.129 of the Act in his absence, it shall give him and his sureties, if any, notice thereof.

(2) If a magistrates' court, under s.129(4) of the Act of 1980, enlarges the recognizance of a surety for a person committed for trial on bail, it shall give the surety notice thereof.

Directions as to security, etc   **3.111**
85. Where a magistrates' court, under s.3(5) or (6) of the Bail Act 1976, imposes any requirement to be complied with before a person's release on bail, the court may give directions as to the manner in which and the person or persons before whom the requirement may be complied with.

Requirements to be complied with before release   **3.112**
86. (1) Where a magistrates' court has fixed the amount in which a person (including any surety) is to be bound by a recognizance, the recognizance may be entered into–

(a) in the case of surety in connection with bail in criminal proceedings where the accused is in a prison or other place of detention, before the governor or keeper of the prison or place as well as before the persons mentioned in s.8(4)(a) of the Bail Act 1976;

(b) in any other case, before a justice of the peace, a justices' clerk, a police officer who either is of the rank of inspector or above or is in charge of a police station or, if the person to be bound is in prison or other place of detention, before the governor or keeper of the prison or place.

(2) The clerk of a magistrates' court which has fixed the amount in which a person (including any surety) is to be bound by a recognizance or, under s.3(5), (6) or (6A) of the Bail Act 1976, imposed any requirement to be complied with before a person's release on bail or any condition of bail shall issue a certificate in the prescribed form showing the amount and conditions, if any, of the recognizance, or as the case may be, containing a statement of the requirement or condition of bail; and a person authorised to take the recognisance or do anything in relation to the compliance with such requirement or condition of bail shall not be required to take or do it without production of the certificate as aforesaid.

(3) If any person proposed as a surety for a person committed to custody by a magistrates' court produces to the governor or keeper of the prison or other place of detention in which the person so committed is detained a certificate in the prescribed form to the effect that he is acceptable as a surety, signed by any of the justices composing the court or the clerk of the court and signed in the margin by the person proposed as surety, the governor or keeper shall take the recognisance of the person so proposed.

(4) Where the recognisance of any person committed to custody by a magistrates' court of any surety of such a person is taken by any person other than the court which committed the first-mentioned person to custody, the person taking the recognisance shall send it to the clerk of that court.

Provided that, in the case of a surety, if the person committed has been committed to the Crown Court for trial or under any of the enactments mentioned in r.17(1), the person taking the recognisance shall send it to the appropriate officer of the Crown Court.

3.113   **Notice to governor of prison, etc where release from custody is ordered**
87. Where a magistrates' court has, with a view to the release on bail of a person in custody, fixed the amount in which he or any surety of such a person shall be bound or, under s.3(5) or (6) or 6A of the Bail Act 1976, imposed any requirements to be complied with before his release or any condition of bail–
     (a) the clerk of the court shall give notice thereof to the governor or keeper of the prison or place where that person is detained by sending him such a certificate as is mentioned in r.86(2);
     (b) any person authorised to take the recognisance of a surety or do anything in relation to the compliance with such requirement shall, on taking or doing it, send notice thereof by post to the said governor or keeper in the prscribed form and, in the case of a recognisance of a surety, shall give a copy of the notice to the surety.

COMMENTARY

(b) Notice . . . in the prescribed form, see forms 129 and 130. The Home Office requests that the prison governor should also be notified by telephone in cases where it is impracticable for the surety's copy to be presented at the prison the same day: HOC 104/1972.

3.114   **Release when recognizances have been taken or requirements complied with**
88. Where a magistrates' court has, with a view to the release on bail of a person in custody, fixed the amount in which he or any surety of such a person shall be bound or, under s.3(5) or (6) of the Bail Act 1976, imposed any requirement to be complied with before his release and given notice thereof in accordance with these rules to the governor or keeper of the prison or place where that person is detained, the governor or keeper shall, when satisfied that the recognizances of all sureties required have been taken and that all such requirements have been complied with–
     (a) in the case of bail in criminal proceedings, unless he is in custody for some other cause, release him;
     (b) in the case of bail otherwise than in criminal procedings, take the recognizances of that person if that has not already been done and, unless he is in custody for some other cause, release him.

3.115   **Procedure under [s.43A of the Magistrates' Courts Act 1980]**
89. Where under [s.43A of the Magistrates' Courts Act 1980] a magistrates' court commits to custody or releases on bail a person who has been arrested in pursuance of a warrant issued by the Crown Court, or the officer in charge of a police station releases such a person on bail under s.13(6) of that Act, the clerk of the magistrates' court or the officer, as the case may be, shall forthwith notify the appropriate officer of the Crown Court of the action which has been taken and, if that person has been released, shall transmit to the appropriate officer of the Crown Court as soon as practicable–

(a) in the case of bail in criminal proceedings, a copy of the record made in pursuance of s.5 of the Bail Act 1976 relating to such bail;
(b) in the case of bail otherwise than in criminal proceedings, the recognizances of that person.

Bail records to be entered in register   **3.116**
90. Any record required by s.5 of the Bail Act 1976 to be made by a magistrates' court (together with any note of reasons required by subs (4) of that section to be included) and the particulars set out in any certificate granted under subs(6A) of that section shall be made by way of an entry in the register and shall contain the particulars set out in the appropriate form prescribed for the purpose.

Notice of change of time for appearance   **3.117**
91. Where–
(a) a person has been granted bail under s.43(1) of the Act of 1980 and the magistrates' court before which he is to appear appoints, under s.43(2), a later time as the time at which he is to appear; or
(b) a magistrates' court further remands a person on bail under s.129 of that Act in his absence,
it shall give him and his sureties, if any, notice thereof.

Notification of bail decision after arrest while on bail   **3.118**
92. Where a person who has been released on bail and is under a duty to surender into the custody of a court is brought under s.7(4)(a) of the Bail Act 1976 before a justice of the peace, the justice shall cause a copy of the record made in pursuance of s.5 of that Act relating to his decision under s.7(5) of that Act in respect of that person to be sent–
(a) in the case of a magistrates' court, the clerk thereof; or
(b) in the case of any other court, to the appropriate officer thereof.
    Provided that this rule shall not apply where the court is a magistrates' court for the same petty sessions area as that for which the justice acts.

Variation of arrangements for bail on committal to Crown Court   **3.119**
93. Where a magistrates' court has committed a person on bail to the Crown Court for trial or under any of the enactments mentioned in r.17(1) and subsequently varies any conditions of the bail or imposes any conditions in respect of the bail, the clerk of the court shall send to the appropriate officer of the Crown Court a copy of the record made in pursuance of s.5 of the Bail Act 1976 relating to such variations or impositions of conditions.

PROSECUTION OF OFFENCES (CUSTODY TIME LIMITS) REGULATIONS 1987
(SI 1987 No 299)

Application   **3.120**
3. (1) Subject to paragraph (3) below these Regulations shall apply in relation to proceedings instituted in any of the areas mentioned in paragraph (2) below, but shall not apply in relation to proceedings instituted elsewhere.

(2) The areas referred to in paragraph (1) above are the following counties, namely–
Avon
Kent
Somerset
West Midlands
Cheshire
Clwyd
Cornwall

Devon
Dorset
Dyfed
Gloucestershire
Greater Manchester
Gwent
Gwynedd
Hampshire
Isle of Wight
Mid Glamorgan
Powys
South Glamorgan
West Glamorgan
Wiltshire.

(3) (Transitional provision).

Custody time limits in magistrates' courts

4. (1) In proceedings in relation to which these Regulations apply, the maximum period during which a person accused of an indictable offence other than treason may be in the custody of a magistrates' court in relation to that offence while awaiting completion of any preliminary stage of the proceedings specified in the following provisions of this Regulation shall be as stated in those provisions.

(2) Except as provided in paragraph (3) below, in the case of an offence triable either way the maximum period of custody between the accused's first appearance and the commencement of summary trial or, as the case may be, the time when the court decides whether or not to commit the accused to the Crown Court for trial shall be–

(a) in the case of proceedings instituted in the county of West Midlands, 84 days; and

(b) in the case of proceedings instituted elsewhere, 70 days.

(3) In the case of an offence triable either way if, before the expiry of 56 days following the day of the accused's first appearance, the court decides to proceed to summary trial in pursuance of sections 19 to 24 of the 1980 Act the maximum period of custody between the accused' first appearance and the commencement of the summary trial shall be 56 days.

(4) In the case of an offence triable on indictment exclusively the maximum period of custody between the accused's first appearance and the time when the court decides whether or not to commit the accused to the Crown Court for trial, shall be–

(a) in the case of proceedings instituted in the county of West Midlands, 84 days; and

(b) in the case of proceedings instituted elsewhere, 70 days.

(5) Where a court proceeds to inquire into an information as examining justices in pursuance of section 6(1) of the 1980 Act, the foregoing provisions of this Regulation shall have effect as if any reference therein to the time when the court decides whether or not to commit the accused to the Crown Court for trial was a reference to the time when it begins to hear evidence for the prosecution at the inquiry.

5. (Crown Court).

Application for extension of custody time limit

7. (1) An application to a court for the extension or further extension of a custody time limit under section 22(3) of the 1985 Act may be made orally or in writing.

(2) Subject to paragraphs (3) and (4) below the prosecution shall–
(a) (Crown Court) . . .

(b) not less than 2 days before making such an application in a magistrates' court,

give notice in writing to the accused or his representative . . . stating that it intends to make such an application.

(3) It shall not be necessary for the prosecution to comply with paragraph (2) above if the accused or his representative has informed the prosecution that he does not require such notice.

(4) If the court is satisfied that it is not practicable in all the circumstances for the prosecution to comply with paragraph (2) above, the court may direct that the prosecution need not comply with that paragraph or that the minimum period of notice required by that paragraph to be given shall be such lesser minimum period as the court may specify.

Application of Bail Act 1976
8. (1) The Bail Act 1976 shall apply in relation to cases to which a custody time limit applies subject to the modifications specified in paragraph (2) below, being modifications necessary in consequence of the foregoing provisions of these Regulations.

(2) That Act shall apply as if–
(a) in section 3 (general provisions) at the end there were inserted the following subsection–
'(10) Where a custody time limit has expired this section shall have effect as if–
  (a) subsections (4) and (5) (sureties and security for his surrender to custody) were omitted:
  (b) in subsection (6) (conditions of bail) for the words "before release on bail or later" there were substituted the words "after release on bail"';
(b) in section 4 (general right to bail of accused persons and others) at the end there were inserted the following subsection–
'(8) Where a custody time limit has expired this section shall have effect as if, in subsection (1), the words "except as provided in Schedule 1 to this Act" were omitted.';
(c) in section 7 (liability to arrest for absconding or breaking conditions of bail) at the end there were inserted the following subsection–
'(7) Where a custody time limit has expired this section shall have effect as if, in subsection (3), paragraphs (a) and (c) were omitted.'.

[*as amended by the Prosecution of Offences (Custody Time Limits) (Amendment) Regulations 1988 (SI No 164]*.

COMMENTARY

These Regulations make provision as to the maximum period during which a person accused of any indictable offence except treason (including an offence triable either way) in the specified counties may be kept in custody while awaiting trial or committal for trial.

Regulation 4 is concerned with custody time limits in relation to proceedings in magistrates' courts. The limit between the first appearance of the accused in court and the commencement of summary trial or, as the case may be, committal for trial is 70 days, except where the proceedings are commenced in the West Midlands in which case the limit is 84 days. If a decision to proceed to summary trial is taken within 56 days following the accused's first appearance, the limit up to the commencement of the trial is reduced to 56 days in all cases.

Regulations 5 and 6 are concerned with custody time limits in relation to proceedings in the Crown Court sitting at specified centres (not reproduced herein). The limit between committal (or the preferment of a voluntary bill of indictment) and arraignment is 112 days.

Regulation 7 deals with the procedure for applying to the Crown Court or a magistrates' court for an extention of a custody time limit. In particular, the prosecution is normally required to give the accused 5 days notice before applying to the Crown Court and 2 days before applying to a magistrates' court.

Regulation 8 makes consequential modifications in the application of the Bail Act 1976 in cases where a custody time limit applies.

CHAPTER 4

Mode of Trial, Committal for Trial and Transfer to the Crown Court

Note: For '*Trials within Trials*' as that subject applies in relation to the admissibility of confessions or admissions in committal proceedings, see under that heading in the introduction to Chapter 6, Evidence and for '*Editing Statements*', under that heading in the same chapter.

Mode of trial, committal for trial, and transfer to the Crown Court

INTRODUCTION   4.00

There are two methods of trial under English law, trial on indictment and summary trial: the former takes place in the Crown Court before a judge and jury, the latter in the magistrates' court. For the purpose of ascertaining how they are to be tried, offences are divided into the three following types:

> indictable only;
> summary only; and
> triable either way

So far as adults are concerned, the function of magistrates in relation to 'indictable only' offences is solely to hold a preliminary inquiry, or 'committal proceedings' to establish whether or not there is a case to go before a jury, any eventual trial taking place before the Crown Court. Offences which are 'summary only' proceed straight to trial in the magistrates' court: they cannot be tried by the Crown Court, no matter how interconnected they may be with more serious matters (but note the effect of [s.40] CJA 1988 when in force: see App III, *post*. This will enable the trial of certain connected summary offences in the Crown Court. Note also [s.41] which will permit the committal of summary offences 'to be dealt with' – enabling the accused to plead guilty only to summary matters in the Crown Court following committal for trial for an either way offence).

Offences which are 'triable either way' may be tried either in the Crown Court or the magistrates' court. This will depend on decisions made by the magistrates' court and, where applicable, the accused under the 'mode of trial' procedures set out in ss.19 to 23 MCA 1980. The procedures have two distinct stages. First, the justices must consider which of the two courts is the *more suitable* court for trial, and before taking this decision must afford first the prosecutor, then the accused, an *opportunity to make representations* – and have regard to four prescribed matters:

— the *nature* of the case;

— whether the circumstances make the offence one of a *serious character*;

— whether their powers of *punishment* would be adequate; and

— *any other circumstances* affecting suitability for trial in either court [s.19(2) MCA 1980; these criteria are considered in the commentary at 4.46 *post*].

If the decision is in favour of summary trial, there is a second stage to mode of trial. Under s.20 MCA 1980, the justices' conclusion must be explained to the accused *in ordinary language*, as must the fact that he may consent to summary trial and that if he does so, and if convicted, he may still be committed to the Crown Court for sentence if the justices' powers appear inadequate because of his *character and antecedents* – or that, alternatively, he may if he wishes be tried by a jury.

A decision by either the court or the accused in favour of trial in the Crown Court leads to 'committal proceedings' when – as will always be the case with 'indictable only' offences – the court sits as 'examining justices'. Both mode of trial and committal proceedings can, in fact, take place before a single justice although this is relatively unusual with lay benches.

Committals for trial take one of two forms:

— *'conventional'* or *'old style'* committals under s.6(1) MCA 1980, when the justices listen to the evidence (either 'live' witnesses whose evidence is taken down in the form of depositions, or written statements which are 'read aloud' pursuant to s.102 MCA 1980, or a mix of both) and consider whether it is sufficient to go before a jury – whether there is a *prima facie* case; or

— *'paper'* or *'section six-two'* committals 'without consideration of the evidence' in accordance with s.6(2) MCA 1980. The evidence is confined to written statements under s.102 – which are simply served on the court and the other party and *not read out* in the proceedings. In effect, committal is by agreement of the accused, who must have a solicitor 'acting for him in the proceedings' (though not necessarily present in court). The justices are obliged to commit for trial if the formalities are in order and the statutory procedures complied with. The fact that the committal is 'without consideration of the evidence' does not preclude the court from considering matters disclosed in the written statements for ancillary purposes such as bail, legal aid, and determining the appropriate type of witness orders to be made. Similarly, although legal aid may be disallowed for appearances by solicitors in 'paperwork committals' (see HOC 71/1986), associated matters may demand legal representation in their own right.

There are *four* special cases in relation to mode of trial, where the correct procedures do not follow automatically from the status, or apparent status, of the offence. First, with the offence of 'criminal damage', mode of trial depends upon the value of the damage – ie whether or not it exceeds the 'relevant sum', currently £400. *Above* this figure, the offence is triable either way; *on and below it*, the justices must proceed 'as if the matter were triable only summarily'. Where value is 'unclear', the justices may, with the accused's consent, proceed as if the offence is a purely summary one. In all instances, however, these provisions are ousted and the offence remains triable either way if the offence charged is '. . . part of a *series* of two or more offences of the same or a similar character' with which the accused is charged 'on the same occasion'. All these matters are contained in s.22 and Sch.2 MCA 1980. Note that [s.38] CJA 1988, when in force, increases the relevant sum to £2,000 and imports 'aggregate' value for a series of offences, see App III, *post*.

The second special case is that highlighted by the ruling in *R v Harrow Justices, ex p. Osaseri* [1986] QB 589, in relation to the offence of 'common assault' contrary to s.47 OAPA 1861. Where such an allegation is prosecuted '*by or on behalf of the party aggrieved*' it attracts the 'procedural' provisions of s.42 OAPA 1861 and what would otherwise be an either way offence may, under s.42 and at the discretion of the justices, be treated as one which is triable summarily only. Alternatively, justices may decline jurisdiction under s.46 of the 1861 Act, when the matter must be committed to the Crown Court for trial. When ss.42 and 46 apply they oust the mode of trial provisions of the MCA 1980 completely: *R v Blyth Valley Magistrates' Court, ex p. Dobson* (1987) 152 JP 142. It should be noted that under [s.39] CJA 1988, when in force, all common assaults become triable summarily only, see App III, *post*.

Thirdly, certain law officers may insist that an either way matter be tried on indictment, when a magistrates' court must give way: see s.19(4) MCA 1980; and fourthly, summary jurisdiction may be ousted by a 'claim of title' to do the act complained of, a claim rarely made before magistrates in practice, but discussed at 4.09, *post*.

Under new procedures introduced by the Criminal Justice Act 1987, cases of '*serious and complex fraud*' by-pass the committal for trial procedures and '*transfer*' direct to the Crown Court for trial where the Director of the Serious Fraud Office gives '*notice of transfer*' to the magistrates' court. The functions of the justices then cease, save for ancillary matters such as bail and legal aid. An overview of the new provisions (the only surviving aspect of the pre-1987 election Criminal Justice Bill), together with those provisions of the 1987 Act which are of direct application to magistrates' courts have been incorporated into this introduction: see 4.63. The provisions are based on recommendations contained in the Report of the Fraud Trials Committee (The Roskill Committee) and could point the way to a more straightforward and expeditious procedure in a wider range of cases in the future. At the time of going to press, a commencement order relating to the transfer provisions (ss.4–6) of the 1987 Act is still awaited. Sections 1–3 and 12–18 are in force (s.15 for certain purposes only).

CLASSIFICATION OF OFFENCES   4.01

For the purposes of statutory provisions, there are three categories of offence defined by s.5 and Sch. 1 Interpretation Act 1978 as follows:
— *an indictable offence* means an offence which, if committed by an adult, is triable on indictment, whether it is exclusively so triable or triable either way;
— *a summary offence* means an offence which, if committed by an adult, is triable only summarily; and
— *an offence triable either way* means an offence which, if committed by an adult, is triable either on indictment or summarily.

These references to the way or ways in which an offence is triable must be construed without reference to the effect of s.22 MCA 1980 (criminal damage) on the mode of trial in a particular case.

[Note that [s.40] CJA 1988, when in force, will enable the Crown Court to try or deal with [s.41], certain summary offences: App III, *post*.

Offences *triable either* way consist of:
 (i) the offences listed in Sch.1 MCA 1980: s.17(1) MCA 1980; and
(ii) offences which are triable either summarily or on indictment by virtue of any (other) statutory provision: s.17(2) – usually the statute creating the offence.

Under Pt II of Sch.6 Firearms Act 1968, certain offences listed in Sch.1

MCA 1980 become triable only on indictment if the accused is also charged before the court with an offence under s.17(1) or (2) of that Act (use of firearm to resist arrest – widely defined via s.17(2)): 4.44, *post*.

It should be noted that [ss.37–38] CJA 1988, when in force, alter the status of certain offences: App III, *post*.

The maximum penalty on summary conviction of an offence listed in Sch. 1 is 6 months imprisonment and/or a fine on level 5, unless the penalty on indictment is less: s.32(1) MCA 1980. For all other either way offences, the maximum fine is level 5 or any larger sum prescribed by statute: s.32(2), (7). The maximum imprisonment is 6 months unless the statute in question sets a shorter term: s.31(1), (2). The six months' limitation period fixed by s.127 MCA 1980 does not apply to either way offences: s.127(2). Failure to follow the correct procedure for an 'either way' offence will result in the proceedings being quashed: see *R v Tottenham Justices, ex p. Arthur's Transport Services* [1981] Crim LR 180; and *R v Cardiff City Magistrates' Court, ex p. Cardiff City Council* (1987) *The Times* 24 February (failure to identify a 'non-scheduled' offence as 'either way').

4.02   **MODE OF TRIAL**

When a person who has attained 17 years of age appears in relation to an either way matter, the court must cause the charge to be written down and read to him: s.19(2) MCA 1980. First the prosecution and then the accused must be given an opportunity to make representation as to the mode of trial: s.19(2). The court must then make *an initial decision as to which mode of trial is more suitable*, having regard to the criteria listed in s.19(3) – and set out at 4.01, *supra*. Guidance on the application of the criteria is contained in the commentary to s.19(3) at 4.46, *post*.

If the court decides that trial on indictment is more appropriate, it will proceed with the inquiry without more ado: s.21. If it decides that summary trial is more appropriate, the accused must be so informed and 'cautioned' as to his rights: s.20(2). If he then consents to summary trial, the matter proceeds accordingly; if he does not, the court will begin to inquire into the information as examining justices: s.20(2). Where a third party is involved in committal proceedings, eg under the food and drugs legislation, the third party must be allowed to make representations at the initial mode of trial stage. If either the principal defendant or the third party elects trial by jury, then both should face committal proceedings: *R v Uxbridge Justices, ex p. Co-operative Retail Services Ltd* (1985) 150 JPN 154.

If the prosecution is carried on by a law officer or the Director of Public Prosecutions and he applies for trial on indictment, neither the court nor the accused has any discretion in the matter: s.19(4).

The restrictions on the reporting of committal proceedings (see 4.22) apply to the mode of trial proceedings: *ibid*, s.8(8). Mode of trial may be determined by a single 'justice': s.18(5).

4.03   Offences of criminal damage

Special rules apply to the mode of trial of certain offences of criminal damage, *except arson*. The offence's relevant provisions are contained in s.22 and Sch.2 MCA 1980. Note that these are affected by [s.38] CJA 1988, when in force, see App III, *post*.

Before evidence is called, (s.18(2)) the court must first consider, *having regard to any representations made by the prosecutor or accused*, whether the value (as defined in s.22(10) and Sch.2) involved exceeds the relevant sum: s.22(1), currently £400 [£2,000]. Where the accused is charged jointly with a juvenile, the latter may also make representations: s.22(9).

If the value involved is *on or below* the relevant sum, the offence is tried summarily. The maximum penalty in such cases is 3 months imprisonment or a fine up to £1,000; there is no power to commit to the Crown Court for greater sentence: s.33. If the value involved *exceeds* the relevant sum the ordinary mode of trial procedure for either way offences applies.

If it is *not clear* whether the value *does or does not exceed* the relevant sum, a special procedure takes place before representations are heard: s.22(4). The purpose of this procedure appears to be to induce the offender to accept summary trial by offering him a reduced maximum penalty should he be convicted. The accused is cautioned as to his right to trial by jury but informed that if he consents to summary trial his liability to punishment will be limited to a lower maximum penalty of 3 months or £1,000, with no possibility of being committed to the Crown Court for greater sentence: s.33. If the accused consents to summary trial the proceedings continue accordingly. If he does not, the normal mode of trial procedure is followed: s.22(6). There is no right of appeal to the Crown Court against the magistrates' decision as to value: s.22(8); which is determined in accordance with Sch.2.

This procedure does not apply when the offence charged is *one of two or more offences charged on the same occasion* appearing to constitute or form part of a *series of offences* of like character, or where the offence consists in the incitement to commit two or more offences listed in Sch.2: s.22(7). But note that where other charges in the series are eg withdrawn or no evidence is offered, a single surviving charge which is below the £400 [£2,000] limit cannot be committed for trial, and the court must proceed to summary trial: *R v Braden* (1987) *The Times*, 14 October.

By definition, all offences of criminal damage remain indictable offences, no matter that they may be triable only summarily: Sch.1 Interpretation Act 1978. Costs may therefore be ordered from central funds in accordance with the Prosecution of Offences Act 1985.

Presence of the accused   4.04

Selection of mode of trial must take place before any evidence is called and *in the presence of the accused* (s.18(2) Magistrates' Courts Act 1980), except

(i) when this is *impracticable* by reason of his disorderly conduct before the court (s.18(3)); or

(ii) when the accused is represented by counsel or a solicitor who in his absence signifies the accused's consent for the proceedings for determining the mode of trial to take place in his absence and the court is satisfied there is good reason for so proceeding (s.23(1)).

In both these cases, the proceedings may take place in the absence of the accused. The caution need not be put and the legal representative, if any, may signify his consent to summary trial. If there is no legal representative and the accused is himself absent (ie a disorderly conduct case – see 4.15) or if the legal representative does not consent to summary trial, or if – in accordance with s.21 – the court considers trial on indictment more appropriate, the magistrates will proceed to inquire into the information as examining justices and may adjourn the hearing without remanding the accused s.23(5).

If the court is not satisfied that there is good reason for proceeding in the absence of the accused or if for any reason the court decides to proceed as examining justices, process may issue to compel the personal attendance of the accused: s.26.

4.05 Corporations

A representative may, on behalf of a corporation, consent to the corporation being tried summarily: Sch.3, para 1(2) Magistrates' Courts Act 1980. Any requirement that anything shall be done in the presence of the accused or said to him applies to a representative if he appears: Sch.3, para 3.

4.06 'Switching'

The fact that a court has commenced to act as examining justices does not necessarily fix the procedure irrevocably. Except in the case of the special criminal damage procedure where the accused has opted for summary trial under s.22(6) Magistrates' Courts Act 1980, the court may change from summary trial to inquiry at any time before the conclusion of the evidence for the prosecution: s.25(2). But where a defendant has elected summary trial and pleaded not guilty, the justices have no jurisdiction to commit him for trial under s.25(2) without first having *begun to hear evidence* in the summary trial: See *R v St Helens Justices ex p. Critchley* (1987) 152 JP 102; and where a plea of guilty is *unequivocal* justices cannot direct a plea of not guilty for the purposes of switching to committal proceedings under s.25(2): see *R v Telford Justices, ex p. Darlington* (1987) *The Times*, 23 November.

To change from an inquiry to summary trial the court must first explain its decision to the accused and obtain his consent, informing him, if this has not already been done, of its power to commit him to the Crown Court for sentence: s.25(3). If the prosecution is being carried on by a law officer or the Director of Public Prosecutions his consent is essential to a conversion to summary trial: s.25(3). Evidence given during the inquiry is deemed to have been given in and for the purposes of the summary trial: s.28. However, the witnesses must be recalled for cross-examination unless not required by the accused or the prosecutor, r.21 MC Rules 1981.

4.07 Adjournment and remands

Procedurally, the trial of an offence triable either way is divided into three possible stages. The first, which is common to all, is the mode of trial procedure. This commences as soon as the accused appears or is brought before a magistrates' court: s.18(1) MCA 1980. From that time until the decision as to mode of trial is taken the power to adjourn is contained in s.18(4). On such an adjournment the accused *may* be remanded whenever he is present and *must* be remanded if:
(a) on the occasion on which he first appeared or was brought before the court he was in custody or, having been released on bail, surrendered to the custody of the court; *or*
(b) if he has been remanded at any time in the course of the proceedings, s.18(4).

4.08 Juveniles

A juvenile charged with an indictable offence *other than homicide* must be tried summarily unless:
(i) he is aged 14–16 and charged with certain grave offences and the court feels that if found guilty it ought to be possible for him to be detained for the longer periods available in such cases: see s.53 CYPA 1933 and *R v*

Fairhurst [1986] 1 WLR 1374 – and note s.53(2) as amended by [s.124] CJA 1988, when in force, see 4.30a and App III; *or*

(ii) he is charged jointly with an adult and the court considers it necessary in the interests of justice to commit both for trial: s.24(1) MCA 1980.

In the latter case the juvenile may also be committed for trial for any other indictable offence with which he is charged (whether jointly or not) arising out of the same or connected circumstances: s.24(2).

If a juvenile is tried summarily for an indictable offence the maximum fine may not exceed £400 if a young person: s.24(3); or £100 if a child: s.24(3).

The *right* to trial by jury for an indictable offence arises at the age of 17. There is a special situation where an accused person attains that age during the course of the proceedings. In *R v Islington North Juvenile Court, ex p. Daley* [1983] AC 347, it was held that the date at which to determine whether an accused person has attained an age which entitles him to elect to be tried by a jury for an offence triable either way is *the date of his appearance before the magistrates' court on the occasion when the court makes its decision as to the mode of trial*. *Daley's* case concerned a 16-year-old charged with an either way offence who, after pleading not guilty before a juvenile court, had subsequently attained the age of 17. At an adjourned hearing he claimed trial by jury. The decision in *Daley* has been followed in *R v Vale of Glamorgan Juvenile Justices, ex p. Beattie* (1985) 149 JP 120, where the accused wished to be tried in the juvenile court. *Daley* was distinguished in *R v Lewes Juvenile Court, ex p. Turner* (1984) 149 JP 186. In that case the court made the mode of trial decision when it adjourned the hearing of a charge of theft against a 16-year-old for the purpose of summary trial and it was held that when the trial was about to begin some six months later when he was 17 it was too late to elect trial by jury. McNeil J. advised that, 'Where a person under the age of 17 pleads not guilty before a juvenile court, and the circumstances set out in s.24 of the Magistrates' Courts Act 1980 do not apply, but when the juvenile court is not there and then able to take the evidence in the trial which is to follow, the register of the court should be marked "remanded for summary trial".'

Where there is a mix of adults and juveniles and a juvenile becomes separated for any reason, committal proceedings may take place on different days, provided the defendants were together for mode of trial to be determined: *R v Doncaster Crown Court, ex p. Crown Prosecution Service* (1987) 151 JP 167 (juvenile arrested again on day of committal proceedings – and thus 'unavailable' – committed on day following).

Ouster of jurisdiction

4.09

There are certain circumstances in which justices have no jurisdiction in matters involving a *bona fide* claim of title: *R v Speed* (1700) 1 Ld Raym 583. In cases such as this the magistrates must commit for trial: *R v Holsworthy and Another, ex p. Edwards* [1952] 1 All ER 411. At common law, the main effect of the rule was in respect of prosecutions for malicious damage. However, s.7(2) Criminal Damage Act 1971 specifically excludes the rule from prosecutions under that Act or any other offences of destroying or damaging property. A rule of ouster in relation to charges of assault or battery still obtains by virtue of s.46 OAPA 1861. The elements of the rule at common law are that:

(i) it is confined to claims of title *to real* property: *Eagling v Wheatley* [1977] Crim LR 165.

(ii) It is confined to claims to *private* title. Thus magistrates can properly hear informations in which are raised disputes over public highways: *R*

v Critchlow (1878) 26 WR 681; *White v Fox* (1880) 44 JP 618 (bu
compare *Edwards v Cook* (1894) 58 JP 398). Nor are they excluded by
mere contractual claim to enter land: *Lucan v Barrett* (1915) 79 JP 463

(iii) There must be a *bona fide* claim to title and not a mere pretence o
assertion. Assertions may be disregarded where on either the defen
dant's own showing or other manifest grounds it is apparent the claim i
baseless: *R v Sandford* (1874) 39 JP 118. The justices must decide
whether the claim is *bona fide: Legg v Pardoe* (1860) 25 JP 39; *Birnie*
Marshall (1876) 41 JP 22 (a borderline case where ouster was upheld)
Hudson v Macrea (1863) 33 LJMC 65; *Croyden RDC v Cowley an*
Another (1909) 73 JP 205; *Burton v Hudson* (1909) 73 JP 401. But if, in
order to decide whether a legal claim exists, it is necessary to determine
some disputed question of fact, the jurisdiction of magistrates is ousted
per Ridley J in *Arnold v Morgan* (1911) 75 JP 105.

(iv) The claim must be part of the defendant's case: *Cornwell v Sanders*
(1862) 27 JP 148.

It is important to distinguish the principles by which the jurisdiction o
magistrates is ousted from a claim of right which may be pleaded as a
defence to certain offences. Such claims are matters of substantive law and
are thus not dealt with in this work.

There are other cases where a statute may give jurisdiction to decide
questions of title: *Duplex Settled Investment Trust Ltd v Worthing Borough*
Council [1952] 1 All ER 545, *London, Brighton and South Coast Railway*
Fairbrother (1900) 16 TLR 167.

4.10   **COMMITTAL PROCEEDINGS**

A person may be tried on indictment by a bill of indictment preferred:
   (i) by the direction or with the consent of the Court of Appeal or a judge o
       the High Court;
  (ii) pursuant to an order made under s.9 of the Perjury Act 1911; or
 (iii) upon committal for trial following a preliminary inquiry.
[Administration of Justice (Miscellaneous Provisions) Act 1933, s.2(2)]

Additionally a case may now be 'transferred' to the Crown Court for tria
where it is one of 'serious or complex fraud': see under *Transfer to the Crown*
Court, post.

Of these, by far the most usual procedure is committal by examining
justices.

There are two types of committals, namely 'paper' or 'six-two' committals
'without consideration of the evidence' under s.6(2) MCA 1980; and 'con
ventional' or 'old style' committals under s.6(1) MCA 1980.

A single justice may discharge the functions of an examining justice
s.4(1) MCA 1980.

4.11 **'Paper' committals**

A person can be committed to the Crown Court for trial by justices without
consideration of the evidence where:
   (i) all the evidence consists of written statements under s.102 MCA 1980;
  (ii) the accused has a solicitor *acting for him in the proceedings*; and
 (iii) no submission is made that the evidence is insufficient: s.6(2) MCA
       1980.

The procedure for 'paper' committals is set out in r.6 MC Rules 1981. I
the conditions set out above do not obtain, proceedings take the conven
tional form: r.6(3).

'Conventional' or 'old style' committals

4.12

In 'conventional' committal proceedings, the examining justice must consider the evidence and if there is sufficient evidence to put the accused on trial for any indictable offence the accused must be committed for trial. If not, he must be discharged: s.6(1) MCA 1980.

The procedure for such a committal is set out in r.7 MCR Rules 1981.

The function of committal proceedings is to ensure that no one stands his trial unless a *prima facie* case has been made out, not a rehearsal for the defence to try out their cross-examination on the prosecution witnesses with a view to using the results to their advantage in the Crown Court. It is thus not incumbent upon the prosecution to call even a very important witness if they deem this unnecessary or undesirable: *R v Epping and Harlow Justices, ex p. Massaro* [1973] 1 QB 433 (girl victim of sex assault). In the course of his judgment in *R v Colchester Stipendiary Magistrate, ex p. Beck* [1979] QB 674, Kilner Brown J said 'There is regrettably a tendency in committals under both (subs.(1) and (2) of s.6 of this Act) for quantities of irrelevant or inadmissible, or it may be highly prejudicial, material to be collected by prosecuting authorities and served without any attempt to remove such material before consideration by the court. It may place an intolerable burden on committing magistrates, and it certainly does on trial judges in cases of committals under (subs.(2)). Speaking for myself, I would hope that more careful selection would be made in appropriate cases. It would be preferable if there is a concentration on the essential evidence to be tendered at committal stages. Any lacunae can always be corrected by a notice of additional evidence.

In *R v Grays Justices, ex p. Tetley* (1980) 70 Cr App R 11, Eveleigh LJ said: 'To ask a court to call witnesses for any other purpose than to ask them to consider whether the evidence is sufficient to commit for trial would be an improper use of that section. The section is not intended to allow the accused to explore the evidence as a rehearsal for trial. It is to consider the situation when the magistrates may have properly argued before them the sufficiency of the evidence and for no other purpose' (prosecutor went back on undertaking to call witness).

In *R v Carden* (1879) 44 JP 122 Cockburn CJ said, at p.137: 'The duty of the magistrate [in committal proceedings] is simply upon hearing the evidence for the prosecution, and evidence if it is to be adduced, on the part of the defence, to consider and decide whether there is a presumption of guilt . . It is no part of his duty or his province to try the case.'

What constitutes a *prima facie* case is usually described in the following terms: 'There must be such evidence that, if uncontradicted at the trial, a reasonably minded jury could convict upon it,' *per* Swift J in *R v Brixton Prison Governor, ex p. Bidwell* [1937] 1 KB 305; approved by the House of Lords in *Schtraks v Government of Israel* [1964] AC 556 (and see also *Armah v Government of Ghana* [1967] Crim LR 240), all cases turning upon extradition or the like proceedings in which the court held that the test is the same as in committal proceedings. When a defendant gives evidence in committal proceedings in support of a defence it is open to the justices to refuse to commit if, on the whole of the evidence, they are satisfied no reasonable jury would convict: *Re Roberts* [1967] 1 WLR 474.

Oppression and abuse of process

4.13

The power of magistrates to stop a prosecution because of oppression or abuse of process of the court (see under this title at 5.00, *post*) applies to committal proceedings as much as trial. In *R v Horsham Justices, ex p.*

Reeves (1982) 75 Cr App R 236, prohibition was granted to prevent examining justices from hearing fresh charges against the applicant (albeit simplified and shortened charges) when he had been discharged on similar charges after a three-day hearing. In *R v Derby Justices ex p. Brooks* (1984) 80 Cr App R 164, application for judicial review of committal proceedings was refused where the delay had not prejudiced the defendant who was admitting his guilt. A refusal by examining justices to discharge defendants in committal proceedings was upheld in *R v Guildhall Justices, and Director of Public Prosecutions, ex p. Carson Selman and Others* (1984) 148 JP 392. Justices have the right to invite the prosecution to tell them about the state of the case, but that right should be exercised only in exceptional circumstances, for example where the delay is truly excessive, *per* Watkins LJ *ibid*, at p.399.

4.14   Evidence

Evidence at 'conventional' committal proceedings may be in the form either of 'live witnesses', whose depositions are taken down in writing or of written statements under s.102 MCA 1980, or both. Admissions may also be made under s.10 CJA 1967. But a committal cannot rest on s.10 admissions alone where the prosecution itself offers 'no evidence': *R v Horseferry Road Magistrates' Court, ex p. O'Regan* (1986) 150 JP 535.

Despite the fact that it is improper to take a deposition by means of leading questions, this will not invalidate a committal: *R v Walker* (1950) 114 JP 578; and in general a committal for trial is not invalidated simply because inadmissible evidence was admitted by the examining justices: *R v Norfolk Quarter Sessions, ex p. Brunson* (1953) 117 JP 100; *R v Ipswich Justices, ex p. Edwards* (1979) 143 JP 699; *R v Oxford Justices, ex p. Berry* [1987] 1 All ER 1244. A prerogative order will issue only when a magistrate has refused to exercise discretion and not when the matter complained of is the exercise of that discretion: *R v Wells Street Stipendiary Magistrate, ex p. Seillon and Others* (1980) 69 Cr App R 78 (refusal to allow questions of witness). In committal proceedings magistrates have no discretion to admit or reject legally admissible evidence on the ground that its prejudicial effect outweighs its probative value: *R v Horsham Justices, ex p. Bukhari* (1981) 74 Cr App R 291 (dock identification); *R v Highbury Corner Magistrates' Court, ex p. Boyce and Others* (1984) 79 Cr App R 132. In all other respects, it is suggested, the normal rules of evidence apply in committal proceedings, including the holding of '*Trials within trials*' to determine the admissibility of confessions and admissions: see under that title at 6.26, *post*.

The evidence of a child in committal proceedings for a sexual offence must be dealt with in accordance with s.103 MCA 1980 and received by way of written statement unless one of the exceptions to this in s.103(2) applies, eg where the defence objects to this course.

[But note the new s.103 substituted by [s.32] CJA 1988, when in force, reproduced at 4.58, which, inter alia, extends the requirements to offences involving 'assault or injury or a threat of injury to a person'.]

4.15   Presence of the accused

Evidence in committal proceedings must be given in the presence of the accused unless (a) the court considers this impracticable by reason of his disorderly conduct or (b) he cannot be present for health reasons, but is represented by counsel or solicitor and has consented to that course: s.4(3), (4) MCA 1980. This does not prevent the magistrate from reading the papers in advance of the hearing: *R v Colchester Magistrate, ex p. Beck and Others* [1979] QB 674.

Open court 4.16

Examining justices must sit in open court except when statute allows otherwise or when it appears to them as respects the whole or part of the proceedings that the ends of justice would not be served by sitting in open court: s.4(2) MCA 1980.

Multiple charges and defendants 4.17

Two charges (even against different defendants) can be properly committed jointly for trial wherever two offences can be properly tried jointly on indictment: *R v Camberwell Green Justices, ex p. Christie* [1978] QB 602. See also under *Joinder of Offences and Defendants* at 5.10.

Adjournment of inquiry 4.18

Examining justices may adjourn their inquiry at any time and on doing so must remand the accused to a fixed date: s.5 MCA 1980. Examining justices have a *judicial discretion* to allow the prosecutor an adjournment: *R v West London Metropolitan Stipendiary Magistrate, ex p. Karminski* [1983] Crim LR 40.

Place of trial 4.19

The examining justices must specify the location of the Crown Court at which the accused will be tried in accordance with the criteria in the s.7 MCA 1980. This discretion is also governed by directions given by the Lord Chief Justice: see 4.77, *post* and HOC 3/1988.

Bail or custody 4.20

A committal for trial must be either in custody or on bail; s.6(3) MCA 1980; although magistrates may review their decision to commit in custody at a later date: s.6(4). The defendant enjoys the general right to bail: s.4 Bail Act 1976. Magistrates may not grant bail to a person charged with treason: s.41 MCA 1980; s.4(7) Bail Act 1976. Once a person has been committed in custody by a magistrates' court, the Crown Court may admit him to bail: s.81 Supreme Court Act 1981.

Corporations 4.21

A corporation may be committed for trial by an order in writing empowering the prosecutor to prefer a bill of indictment: Sch.3, para 1 MCA 1980. The requirement that evidence must be given in the presence of the defendant applies if the corporation appears by a representative but not otherwise: Sch.3, para 3.

Reporting restrictions 4.22

The press are allowed to report only certain prescribed formalities unless the court makes an order removing the restrictions. Such an order may be made only on the application of a defendant, and if an application is made the court must so order, it has no discretion in the matter: s.8 MCA 1980. As a corollary, even in cases where the press restrictions are lifted, the clerk must, subject to the Sexual Offences (Amendment) Act 1976 display particulars of the proceedings in or near the court house: s.6(5) MCA 1980. That notice may not identify any juvenile concerned unless by direction of the justices for the purposes of avoiding injustice to him: s.6(6).

For the purposes of this provision committal proceedings are deemed to include any proceedings in the magistrates' court before the court proceeds to inquire into the information as examining justices: s.8(8) MCA 1980.

In any legal proceedings held in public the court may, where it appears to be necessary for avoiding a substantial risk of prejudice to the administration of justice in those proceedings, or in any other proceedings pending or imminent, order that the publication of any report of the proceedings, or any part of the proceedings be postponed for such period as the court thinks necessary for that purpose: Contempt of Court Act 1981, s.4(2) reproduced at 7.17.

4.23   Rape

Restrictions on the identification of the complainant and defendant in committal proceedings for a rape offence are contained in the Sexual Offences (Amendment) Act 1976, which defines the term 'rape offence' in s.7.

On the application of the defendant, a magistrates' court may at any time before the commencement of the trial remove the restrictions upon his identification: s.6(2). Otherwise, the only person who can remove the restrictions is a judge of the Crown Court.

[But note the amendments made by [s.150] CJA 1988, when in force. See 4.36].

4.24   The alibi warning

On a trial on indictment the defendant may not without the leave of the court adduce evidence in support of an *alibi* unless within seven days from the end of the proceedings before the examining justices he gives notice of particulars of the alibi: s.11(1), (8) CJA 1967. During committal proceedings the court is obliged to warn the defendant of this fact unless, having regard to the nature of the offence, it appears to the court unnecessary to do so: rr.6(4), 7(9) MC Rules 1981.

4.24a   Expert evidence

As soon as practicable *after* committal for trial, each party is required to disclose to the other any expert evidence which it is prepared to adduce at the trial: see Crown Court (Advance Notice of Expert Evidence) Rules 1987 (SI No. 716), explained in HOC 35/1987. The purpose of the rules is to resolve, as far as possible, technical arguments about scientific findings outside the court room. There are no comparable rules relating to summary proceedings, or to 's.6(1) Committals' themselves.

4.25   Witness orders

Witnesses at committal proceedings, even those whose evidence is in the form of written statements, must be made the subject of an order to attend the trial, which may be 'full witness orders' or 'conditional witness orders', ie conditional upon their later being given notice to attend at the Crown Court and give evidence: s.1 Criminal Procedure (Attendance of Witnesses) Act 1965.

4.26   Exhibits

'Once an article has become an exhibit, the court has a responsibility in relation to it. That responsibility is to preserve and retain it, or to arrange for its preservation and retention, for the purpose of justice. The usual course is for the court to entrust the exhibits to the police or to the Director of Public Prosecutions subject to the same responsibility. That responsibility is: (1) to take all proper care to preserve the exhibits safe from loss or damage, (2) to co-operate with the defence in order to allow them reasonable access to the exhibits for the purpose of inspection and examination, and (3) to produce the exhibits at the trial. Where a court entrusts exhibits to the police or the prosecutor, it can impose such restrictions as it considers proper in all the circumstances. In the case of a private prosecutor it would be more likely to impose such restrictions than in the case of a public prosecutor and indeed might well decide to retain the exhibits itself or to deliver them into the custody of the police. But if the court imposes no restrictions, it is for the recipient of the exhibits to deal with them in whatever way appears best for the purposes of justice. If the recipient has doubts as to where his duty lies, he can apply to the court for directions, but he is under no obligation so to do. Equally, the accused can apply to the court for directions if he thinks it appropriate.'

per Sir John Donaldson MR in *R v Lambeth Metropolitan Stipendiary Magistrate, ex p. McComb* [1983] 2 WLR 259; and see r.11(1), (2) MC Rules 1981.

Autrefois convict and *autrefois acquit*

4.27

The discharge of a defendant in committal proceedings is *not an acquittal* and does not bar the bringing of further proceedings in respect of the same offence, but the High Court has a discretion to see that the use of repeated committal proceedings is not allowed to become vexatious or an abuse of the court: *R v Manchester City Magistrates' Court, ex p. Snelson* [1977] 1 WLR 911.

A defendant wrongly committed for trial in respect of offences triable only summarily cannot claim *autrefois acquit*. The committal is a nullity and the justices may proceed to convict the defendant summarily: *Bannister v Clarke* (1920) 85 JP 12.

Despite *dicta* in *R v West* (1962) 126 JP 352, it would appear that the doctrines of *autrefois acquit* and *convict* can debar examining justices from committing for trial where there has been a previous trial: *cf. Re Roberts* [1967] 1 WLR 474.

TRANSFER TO THE CROWN COURT

4.28

Among the innovative provisions of the CJA 1987 – and in direct response to the recommendations contained in the Report of the Fraud Trials Committee (The Roskill Report) – are provisions which allow for the *transfer* of cases to the Crown Court for trial without either committal proceedings or a voluntary bill of indictment. Section 4 provides that where a person has been charged with an indictable offence and in the opinion of the designated authority, *infra*, evidence would be sufficient for the person charged to be committed for trial, and that it reveals '. . . a case of fraud of such seriousness and complexity that it is appropriate that the management of the case should without delay be taken to the Crown Court' – then, provided that the magistrates have not started to inquire into the offence as examining justices, a *notice of transfer* may be given to the court certifying the prosecutor's opinion. If this happens, then, in the terms of s.4 . . . the functions of the magistrates' court *shall cease* in relation to the case. The only exceptions are in relation to bail and legal aid: see s.5(3); and witness orders: s.5(9).

In addition to the Director of the Serious Fraud Office, the authorities designated for the above purpose are the Director of Public Prosecutions, the Commissioners of Inland Revenue, the Commissioners of Customs and Excise and the Secretary of State: s.4(2), in all instances the power extending to officers acting on the authorities' behalf: s.4(1).

Under s.4(3), the decision to give a notice of transfer . . . shall not be subject to appeal or liable to be questioned in any court, an unusually all embracing provision which, taken at face value, would exclude all forms of judicial review.

4.29 Procedure

A notice of transfer must specify the proposed place of trial and in selecting the venue the designated authority is required to have regard to the considerations contained in s.7 MCA 1980 – ie those matters which, ordinarily, the magistrates are obliged to have regard to: convenience, expediting the trial, and any *directions* by the Lord Chief Justice under s.4(5) Courts Act 1971 see 4.77, *post*. The notice must specify the charge or charges to which it relates and include or be accompanied by such matters as may later be prescribed by regulations: ss.5(1) and (2).

By s.6(9), the Attorney-General is placed under a *duty* to make regulations requiring the person charged and the Crown Court to be given a copy of the notice of transfer, together with a statement of the evidence on which any charge to which the notice of transfer relates is based. The Attorney General *may* also make further regulations in relation to notices of transfer, including . . . provision as to the duties of a designated authority in relation to such notices.

Where the magistrates have already remanded a person in custody to which the notice of transfer relates, then, as already indicated, s.5(3) gives that court power – subject to s.4 Bail Act 1976 and s.22 Prosecution of Offenders Act 1985 – to either order that '. . . he shall be safely kept in custody until delivered in due course of law, or to release the person on bail with a direction that he appear before the Crown Court for trial. Where bail is *conditional on sureties* being taken, the magistrates *must* order custody in the meantime.'

With the written consent of the accused and provided that the court is satisfied that when this consent was given the accused knew that the notice of transfer had been issued, the court may deal with custody matters in the absence of the accused – provided the case would otherwise have been covered by the analogous provisions of s.128(3A) MCA 1980: s.5(4) and (5). The duty to surrender to bail before examining justices evaporates once a notice of transfer is served and is replaced automatically by a duty to surrender to the custody of the Crown Court when called upon to do so: the effect of s.5(6) and (7) summarised. The notice of transfer can, by way of exception to the general rule, require the accused to surrender to bail before the justices – presumably, eg a procedure to be used where there is to be an attempt to have bail revoked, or a variation of conditions of bail is requested.

By way of a fiction, the justices continue to be regarded as examining magistrates for the purposes of the Criminal Procedure (Attendance of Witnesses) Act 1965, *post*, so that they can still make witness orders in respect of anyone whose written statement is tendered in evidence for the purposes of the notice of transfer (ie, in accordance with regulations to be made under s.5(9)). The 'witness' is treated as if he had been examined by the court, and the justices are deemed to be examining magistrates for this limited purpose.

A provision contained in Sch.2 (not reproduced herein) amends s.11(8) CJA 1967 under which the period for giving an *alibi warning* in committal proceedings is seven days from the end of the proceedings before the examining justices. A similar period from the time of the 'notice of transfer' applies where that notice has been given under s.4 of the 1987 Act: see Sch.2, para 2. Magistrates are empowered to grant legal aid for the trial: Sch.2, para 7.

The effect of the procedure is to produce what will hopefully prove to be an expeditious and effective means of processing complex cases to the

Crown Court (as envisaged by Roskill) – and it might well prove that such procedures will not necessarily be confined to fraud cases for the future. The overall effect is not unlike that of a 'paper committal' under s.6(2) MCA 1980 but without the involvement of the magistrates, or the justices' clerk and his administration, except in peripheral matters. In place of the 'preliminary inquiry', and where the accused wishes to object, his challenge will go before a Judge of the Crown Court via another new form of procedure, the application to dismiss.

Application to the Crown Court to dismiss 4.30
The final limb of the new 'transfer' procedure is the right of the accused to apply to the Crown Court for the charge to be dismissed. Under s.6, where notice of transfer has been given, the person charged may at any time *before his arraignment* apply orally or in writing to the Crown Court for the charge to be dismissed on the ground that '. . . the evidence which has been disclosed would not be sufficient for a jury properly to convict him'. This test – a truncated version, it seems, of the *prima facie* case test in committal proceedings – substitutes for the fact that the latter type of proceedings have been by-passed by the transfer of the case direct to the Crown Court. In fact, by s.6(7), a discharge under this section has the same effect as a refusal by examining magistrates to commit, subject to the qualification that no further proceedings may be brought on the charge – except by way of a voluntary bill of indictment.

The remaining provisions of s.6 contain various aspects of the procedure on application to a Judge. There are also controls over the emerging case, and powers concerning 'disclosure'. These Crown Court procedures are not further dealt with in this work, but are set out, principally, in ss.7 to 11 CJA 1987.

Statutory Provisions

CHILDREN AND YOUNG PERSONS ACT 1933 4.30a
Punishment of certain grave crimes

53. (1) A person convicted of an offence who appears to the court to have been under the age of eighteen years at the time the offence was committed shall not, if he is convicted of murder, be sentenced to imprisonment for life, nor shall sentence of death be pronounced on or recorded against any such person; but in lieu thereof the court shall (notwithstanding anything in this or any other Act) sentence him to be detained during Her Majesty's pleasure, and if so sentenced he shall be liable to be detained in such place and under such conditions as the Secretary of State may direct.

(2) Where a child or young person is convicted on indictment of any offence punishable in the case of an adult with imprisonment for fourteen years or more, not being an offence the sentence for which is fixed by law and the court is of opinion that none of the other methods in which the case may legally be dealt with is suitable, the court may sentence the offender to be detained for such period [not exceeding the maximum term of imprisonment with which the offence is punishable in the case of an adult] as may be specified in the sentence; and where such a sentence has been passed the child or young person shall, during that period, be liable to be detained in such place and on such conditions as the Secretary of State may direct.

COMMENTARY
See also *R v Fairhust* [1986] 1 WLR 1374.

Subsection (2) will be amended by [s.124] CJA 1988, when in force, to read as follows:
(2) Where–
   (a) a young person is convicted on indictment of any offence punishable in the case of an
       adult with imprisonment for fourteen years or more, not being an offence the
       sentence for which is fixed by law; or
   (b) a child is convicted of manslaughter, and the court is of opinion that none of the other
       methods in which the case may legally be dealt with is suitable, the court may
       sentence the offender to be detained for such period [not exceeding the maximum
       term of imprisonment with which the offence is punishable in the case of an adult] as
       may be specified in the sentence; and where such a sentence has been passed the child
       or young person shall, during that period, be liable to be detained in such place and
       on such conditions as the Secretary of State may direct.

4.31   **CRIMINAL PROCEDURE (ATTENDANCE OF**
                        WITNESSES) ACT 1965

Order by examining justices for attendance of witness at court of trial
   1. (1) A magistrates' court acting as examining justices shall in respect of
each witness examined by the court, other than the accused and any witness of
his merely to his character, make an order (in this Act referred to as a witness
order) requiring him to attend and give evidence before the Crown Court.

   (2) Where it appears to the court, after taking into account any representation made by the accused or the prosecutor, that the attendance at the trial of
any witness is unnecessary on the ground that his evidence is unlikely to be
required or is unlikely to be disputed, then—
   (a) any witness order to be made by the court in his case shall be a
       conditional order requiring him to attend the trial if notice in that behalf
       is given to him and not otherwise; and
   (b) if a witness order other than a conditional order has previously been
       made by the court in his case, the court shall direct that that order be
       treated as a conditional order.

   (3) A magistrates' court on committing any person for trial shall inform him
of his right to require the attendance at the trial of any witness in respect of
whom a conditional witness order, or an order treated as a conditional witness
order, has been made, and of the steps he must take for the purpose of
enforcing the attendance.
   [*As amended by Sch.8 Courts Act 1971, Statute Law (Repeals) Act 1974*].

COMMENTARY
If a witness fails to appear at the Crown Court in response to a witness order that Court has
power to issue a warrant under s.14 of the Act. The Home Office expressed the view that no
attempt should be made to effect service upon a witness outside the UK, but that the
prosecutor or defendant should be asked to make suitable arrangements for his attendance
[HOC 118/1970].

s.1(1): A witness order see generally, r.8 MC Rules 1981, and Form 17. Disobedience to a
witness order is punishable as a contempt: s.3 of the 1965

Examining justices, note that for the purposes of this section magistrates are deemed to be
examining justices in cases of serious and complex fraud where a notice of transfer has been
given: s.5(a) CJA 1987, when in force.

s.1(2): Evidence . . . unlikely to be disputed eg a medical man whose evidence is unchall-
enged and really only formal, as is often the case in cases of carnal knowledge, or of
wounding, where there is no dispute as to the nature and extent of the injuries: *Practice Note*
[1952] WN 245.

A conditional order A conditional order must be served on a witness who has been examined as soon as practicable after committal for trial except where made at the conclusion of his examination when it must be served on him immediately after the deposition is signed: r.8 MC Rules 1981. For the admissibility of the deposition of such a witness at the trial see s.13(3) CJA 1925 and s.7 CJA 1967 (not reproduced herein). Inability to warn a conditional witness does not necessarily prevent his deposition being read at the trial: *R v Dadlani Meyrow* [1974] Crim LR 627. Unless there are reasons for not doing so, exhibits produced by a witness subject to a conditional witness order must be retained by the court: r.11(1) MC Rules 1981.

s.1(3) Presumably, the steps consist of informing the appropriate officer of the Crown Court.

CRIMINAL JUSTICE ACT 1967

Signature of depositions   **4.32**
    7. An examining justice who signs a certificate authenticating one or more depositions or statements tendered under s.102 of the Magistrates' Courts Act 1980 shall be treated for the purposes of s.13(3)(c) of the Criminal Justice Act 1925 (requirement that depositions read at the trial must have been signed by an examining justice) as signing that deposition or statement or each of those depositions and statements).
    [*as amended by Sch.7 MCA 1980*].

COMMENTARY
Expressions used in this section have the same meaning as in the MCA 1980; s.36(2) CJA.

A certificate see Form 11.

Section 13(3)(c) of the Criminal Justice Act 1925 (not reproduced herein) provides that the depositions and statements shall be admissible in a trial on indictment provided, *inter alia*, that they are signed by the justices.

Notice of alibi   **4.33**
    11. (1) On a trial on indictment the defendant shall not without the leave of the court adduce evidence in support of an alibi unless, before the end of the prescribed period, he gives notice of particulars of the alibi.

    (2) Without prejudice to the foregoing subsection, on any such trial the defendant shall not without the leave of the court call any other person to give such evidence unless—
    (a) the notice under that subsection includes the name and address of the witness or, if the name or address is not known to the defendant at the time he gives the notice, any information in his possession which might be of material assistance in finding the witness:
    (b) if the name or the address is not included in that notice, the court is satisfied that the defendant, before giving the notice, took and thereafter continued to take all reasonable steps to secure that the name or address would be ascertained;
    (c) if the name or the address is not included in that notice, but the defendant subsequently discovers the name or address or receives other information which might be of material assistance in finding the witness, he forthwith gives notice of the name, address or other information, as the case may be; and
    (d) if the defendant is notified by or on behalf of the prosecutor that the witness has not been traced by the name or at the address given, he forthwith gives notice of any such information which is then in his possession or, on subsequently receiving any such information, forthwith gives notice of it.

(3) The court shall not refuse leave under this section if it appears to the court that the defendant was not informed in accordance with rules under s.144 of the Magistrates' Courts Act 1980 (rules of procedure for magistrates' courts) of the requirements of this section.

(4) Any evidence tendered to disprove an alibi may, subject to any directions by the court as to the time it is to be given, be given before or after evidence is given in support of the alibi.

(5) Any notice purporting to be given under this section on behalf of the defendant by his solicitor shall, unless the contrary is proved, be deemed to be given with the authority of the defendant.

(6) A notice under subs. (1) of this section shall either be given in court during, or at the end of, the proceedings before the examining justices or be given in writing to the solicitor for the prosecutor, and a notice under para (c) or (d) of subs (2) of this section shall be given in writing to that solicitor.

(7) A notice required by this section to be given to the solicitor for the prosecutor may be given by delivering it to him, or by leaving it at his office, or by sending it in a registered letter or by the recorded delivery service addressed to him at his office.

(8) In this section—
'evidence in support of an alibi' means evidence tending to show that by reason of the presence of the defendant at a particular place or in a particular area at a particular time he was not, or was unlikely to have been, at the place where the offence is alleged to have been committed at the time of its alleged commission.
'the prescribed period' means the period of seven days from the end of the proceedings before the examining justices or, where a notice of transfer has been given under s.4 of the Criminal Justice Act 1987, of the giving of that notice.

(9) In computing the said period a Sunday, Christmas Day, Good Fiday, a day which is a bank holiday under the Bank Holidays Act 1871, in England and Wales or a day appointed for public thanksgiving or mourning shall be disregarded.
[*as amended by Sch.7 MCA 1980; Sch.2 CJA 1987*].

COMMENTARY

For the proposals on which this provision was based, see the Ninth Report of the Criminal Law Revision Committee, Cmnd. 3145. The provisions of this section do not apply to summary trials wherein 'sprung alibis' may be readily met by an adjournment. Expressions used in this section have the same meaning as in MCA 1980: s.36(2) CJA 1967.

s.11(1) includes evidence which the defendant himself may give; s.11(2) deals with evidence given by persons other than the accused: *R v Jackson and Robertson* [1973] Crim LR 356. In order to enable clerks of assize (now Crown Court) to make more reliable estimates of the length of criminal trials, the prosecution are requested, so soon as any notice of alibi is given to them under s.11 to send a copy thereof to the court of trial. *Practice Note* [1969] 1 All ER 1042.

s.11(1): Evidence in support of an alibi see s.11(8). This applied only to evidence relative to the whereabouts of the accused at the time when the crime is alleged to have been committed: evidence relative to another occasion is not subject to the restrictions however significant to the issues of the case: *R v Lewis* [1969] 1 All ER 79. Any question as to the place or date at or on which the offence was committed must be resolved on the material then available to the accused, namely, the committal charges and the depositions: *ibid*.
'This phrase envisages an offence which necessarily involves the accused being at a particular place at a particular time. Thus s.11 is inapplicable to an offence of a continuing nature such as living on the earnings of prostitution alleged to have been committed 'in the city of Cardiff': *R v Hassan* [1970] 1 QB 423. The defence of alibi is inapplicable to a person charged with driving while disqualified who admits that he was in the car but denies that he was the driver: *R v Westlake* [1970] Crim LR 652.

Before the end of the prescribed period See s.11(8), (9).

s.11(3): Informed in accordance with rules MC Rules 1981, and Form 23, rr.6(4), and 7(9), (13).
s.11.(7): A notice may be given This implies that these are not the only methods of notice.

s.11(8): Evidence in support of an alibi Includes evidence by the accused himself: *R v Jackson and Robertson* [1973] Crim LR 356.

FIREARMS ACT 1968

Schedule 6   4.33a

PART II

SUPPLEMENTARY PROVISIONS AS TO TRIAL AND PUNISHMENT OF OFFENCES

1. (*Scotland.*)

2. In the case of an offence against ss.6(3) or 49(3) or this Act, the court before which the offender is convicted may, if the offender is the owner of the firearms or ammunition, make such order as to the forefeiture of the firearms or ammunition as the court thinks fit.

3. (1) Where in England or Wales a person who has attained the age of 17 is charged before a magistrates' court with an offence triable either way listed in Sch.1 to the Magistrates' Court Act 1980 ('the listed offence') and is also charged before that court with an offence under s.17(1) or (2) of this Act, the following provisions of this paragraph shall apply.

(2) Subject to the following sub-paragraph the court shall proceed as if the listed offence were triable only on indictment and ss.18 to 23 of the said Act of 1980 (procedure for determining mode of trial of offences triable either way) shall not apply in relation to that offence.

(3) If the court determines not to commit the accused for trial in respect of the offence under s.17(1) of (2), or if proceedings before the court for that offence are otherwise discontinued, the preceding sub-paragraph shall cease to apply as from the time when this occurs and–
   (a) If at that time the court has not yet begun to inquire into the listed offence as examining justices, the court shall, in the case of the listed offence, proceed in the ordinary way in accordance with the said ss.18 to 23; but
   (b) if at that time the court has begun so to inquire into the listed offence, those sections shall continue not to apply and the court shall proceed with its inquiry into that offence as examining justices, but shall have power in accordance with s.25(3) and (4) of the said Act of 1980 to change to summary trial with the accused's consent.

4. Where a person commits an offence under s.17(1) of this Act in respect of the lawful arrest or detention of himself for any other offence committed by him, he shall be liable to the penalty provided by Part I of this schedule in addition to any penalty to which he may be sentenced for the other offence.

5. If on the trial of a person for an offence under s.,17(1) of this Act the jury are not satisfied that he is guilty of that offence but are satisfied that he is guilty of an offence under s.17(2), the jury may find him guilty of the offence under s.17(2) and he shall then be punishable accordingly.

6. The punishment to which a person is liable for an offence under s.17(2) of this Act shall be in addition to any punishment to which he may be liable for the offence first referred to in s.17(2).

7. The court by which a person is convicted of an offence under s.22(4) or (5), 23(1) or 24(4) of this Act may make such order as it thinks fit as to the forfeiture or disposal of the air weapon or ammunition in respect of which the offence was committed.

8. The court by which a person is convicted of an offence under s.22(3), (4) or (5), 23(1) or 24(4) may make such order as it thinks fit as to the forfeiture or disposal of any firearm or ammunition found in his possession.

9. The court by which a person is convicted of an offence under s.24(3) of this Act may make such order as it thinks fit as to the forfeiture or disposal of the shot gun or ammunition in respect of which the offence was committed. [*as amended by Sch.12 CLA 1977 Sch.7 MCA 1980*].

COMMENTARY

Paragraph 3. Sch.1, as amended by the Criminal Damage Act 1971, the Criminal Attempts Act 1981 and the Child Abduction Act 1984, lists the following offences to which s.17(2) of the Act (use of firearm to resist arrest) apply:

1. Offences under s.1 of the Criminal Damage Act 1971.

2. Offences under any of the following provisions of the Offences against the Person Act 1861;–

ss. 20 to 22 (inflicting bodily injury; garrotting; criminal use of stupefying drugs);

s. 30 (laying explosives to buildings etc.);

s. 32 (endangering railway passengers by tampering with track);

s.38 (assault with intent to commit felony or resist arrest);

s. 47 (criminal assaults);

s. 56 (child-stealing and abduction).

2A. Offences under Pt I of the Child Abduction Act 1984 (abduction of children).

3. Repealed.

4. Theft, burglary, blackmail and any offence under s.12(1) (taking of motor vehicle or other conveyance without owner's consent) of the Theft Act 1968.

5. Offences under s.51(1) of the Police Act 1964, or s.41 of the Police (Scotland) Act 1967 (assaulting constable in execution of his duty).

6. Offences under any of the following provisions of the Sexual Offences Act, 1956;–

s. 1 (rape);

ss. 17, 18 and 20 (abduction of women).

7. (*Repealed*): Theft Act 1968.

8. Aiding or abetting the commission of any offence specified in paras. 1 to 6 of this schedule.

9. Attempting to commit and offence so specified.

This Schedule operates on s.17(2) so as to shift the burden to the accused to prove that when committing a listed offence he had the firearm for a 'lawful object', failing which he is deemed to have had the firearm for a purpose prohibited by s.17(1). The Schedule should not be confused with the basis upon which an offence which is otherwise triable either way becomes indictable only. Schedule 1 Firearms Act 1968 is a part of substantive criminal law. Paragraph 3 of Pt II of Sch.6 of the 1968 Act alters the status of certain offences – which may coincide with some only of those in the above list – by reference to Sch.1 MCA 1980.

SEXUAL OFFENCES (AMENDMENT) ACT 1976

4.34   **Restrictions on evidence at trials for rape etc.**

2.(1) If at a trial any person is for the time being charged with a rape offence to which he pleads not guilty, then, except with the leave of the judge, no evidence and no question in cross-examination shall be adduced or asked at the trial, by or on behalf of any defendant at the trial, about any sexual experience of a complainant with a person other than that defendant.

(2) The judge shall not give leave in pursuance of the preceding subsection for any evidence or question except on an application made to him in the absence of the jury by or on behalf of a defendant; and on such an application the judge shall give leave if and only if he is satisfied that it would be unfair to that defendant to refuse to allow the evidence to be adduced or the question to be asked.

(3) In subs. (3) of this section 'complainant' means a woman upon whom, in a charge of a rape offence to which the trial in question relates, it is alleged that rape was committed, attempted or proposed.

(4) Nothing in this section authorises evidence to be adduced or a question to be asked which cannot be adduced or asked apart from this section.

COMMENTARY

s.2(1): A rape offence, defined in s.7, *infra*.

The leave of the judge, in *R v Lawrence* [1977] Crim LR 492 May J said:
'. . . before a judge is satisfied or may be said to be satisfied that to refuse to allow a particular question or a series of questions in cross-examination would be unfair to a defendant he must take the view that it is more likely than not that the particular question or line of cross-examination, if allowed, might reasonably lead the jury, properly directed in the summing-up, to take a different view of the complainant's evidence from that which they might take if the question or series of questions was or were not allowed.'

This statement was approved by the Court of Appeal in *R v Mills* (1979) 68 Cr App R 327 and *R v Viola* [1982] 3 All ER 73.

Complainant, defined in s.2(3).

Other than that defendant, thus a defendant is restricted in respect of evidence of sexual experience with a co-defendant. The defendant may be of good character and able to put his character in issue by attacking the character of a prosecution witness even though the co-defendant is of bad character and therefore does not wish to do so. This may be a ground for an application to lift the restriction.

s.2(2): Unfair to that defendant, unfairness to another defendant or even prejudice to another defendant are not material.

Application of s.2 to committal proceedings, courts-martial and summary trials   4.35

    3. (1) Where a magistrates' court inquires into a rape offence as examining justices, then, except with the consent of the court, evidence shall not be adduced and a question shall not be asked at the inquiry which, if the inquiry were a trial at which a person is charged as mentioned in subs (1) of the preceding section and each of the accused at the inquiry were charged at the trial with the offences of which he is accused at the inquiry, could not be adduced or asked without leave in pursuance of that section.

    (2) On an application for consent in pursuance of the preceding subsection for any evidence or question the court shall–
    (a) refuse the consent unless the court is satisfied that leave in respect of the evidence or question would be likely to be given at a relevant time; and
    (b) give the consent if the court is so satisfied.

    (3) (*Courts-martial and juvenile court*).

COMMENTARY

s.3(1): A magistrates' court, includes a single justice: s.4(1) MCA 1980.

A rape offence, defined in s.7, *infra*.

s.3(2), the criteria are the same as in s.2.

An application for consent, i.e. by the defendant. The prosecutor does not need consent.

Anonymity of complainants in rape etc. cases   4.36

    4. (1) Subject to subs (7)(a) of this section, after a person is accused of a rape offence no matter likely to lead members of the public to identify a woman as the complainant in relation to that accusation shall either be published in England and Wales in a written publication available to the public or be broadcast or included in a cable programme in England and Wales except as authorised by a direction given in pursuance of this section.

    (2)–(5) . . .

    (6) For the purposes of this section a person is accused of a rape offence if –
    (a) an information is laid alleging that he has committed a rape offence; or
    (b) he appears before a court charged with a rape offence; or
    (c) a court before which he is appearing commits him for trial on a new charge alleging a rape offence; or

 (d) a bill of indictment charging him with a rape offence is preferred before a court to which he may lawfully be indicted for the offence,

and references in this section and s.7(5) of this Act to an accusation alleging a rape offence shall be construed accordingly; and in this section–

'a broadcast' means a broadcast by wireless telegraphy of sound or visual images intended for general reception, and cognate expressions shall be construed accordingly;

'cable programme' means a programme included in a cable programme service;

'complainant', in relation to a person accused of a rape offence or an accusation alleging a rape offence, means the woman against whom the offence is alleged to have been committed; and

'written publication' includes a film, a sound track and any other record in permanent form but does not include an indictment or other document prepared for use in particular legal proceedings.

 (7) Nothing in this section–

 (a) prohibits the publication, broadcasting or inclusion in a cable programme, in consequence of an accusation alleging a rape offence, of matter consisting only of a report of legal proceedings other than proceedings at, or intended to lead to, or on an appeal arising out of, a trial at which the accused is charged with that offence; or

 (b) affects any prohibition or restriction imposed by virtue of any other enactment upon a publication, broadcast or inclusion in a cable programme;

  and a direction in pursuance of this section does not effect the operation of subs (1) of this section at any time before the direction is given.

[as amended by Sch.5 Cable and Broadcasting Act 1984 and note the substitution effected by [s.150] CJA 1988, when in force, reproduced below].

 (1) Except as authorised by a direction given in pursuance of this section–

 (a) after an allegation that a woman has been the victim of a rape offence has been made by the woman or by any other person neither the woman's name nor her address nor a still or moving picture of her shall during her lifetime–

  (i) be published in England and Wales in a written publication available to the public; or

  (ii) be broadcast or included in a cable programme in England and Wales,

if that is likely to lead members of the public to identify her as an alleged victim of such an offence; and

 (b) after a person is accused of a rape offence no matter likely to lead members of the public to identify a woman as the complainant in relation to that accusation shall during her lifetime–

  (i) be published in England and Wales in a written publication available to the public; or

  (ii) be broadcast or included in a cable programme in England and Wales,

but nothing in this subsection prohibits the publication or broadcasting or inclusion in a cable programme of matter consisting only of a report of criminal proceedings other than proceedings at, or intended to lead to, or on an appeal arising out of, a trial at which the accused is charged with the offence.

 (1A) In subsection (1) above 'picture' includes a likeness however produced.

 (5A) Where a person is charged with an offence under subsection (5) of this section in respect of the publication or broadcast of any matter or the inclusion of any matter in a cable programme, it shall be a defence, subject to subsection (5B) below, to prove that the publication, broadcast or cable programme in which the matter appeared was one in respect of which the woman had given written consent to the appearance of matter of that description.

 (5B) Written consent is not a defence if it is proved that any person interfered unreasonably with the woman's peace or comfort with intent to obtain the consent.

ᶜOMMENTARY

ʰhe following guidance was given to clerks to justices in an annex to HO Circ 194/1976:
ᶦt may be considered appropriate if, at the commencement of committal proceedings in
ᵉspect of a rape offence, the Chairman or the Clerk reminds all persons present that,
₀otwithstanding that the court may make an order under [s.6(5) MCA 1980] removing the
ᵉstrictions on reports of committal proceedings:
(i) it is a criminal offence to publish or broadcast at any time in the future any report of the
      proceedings or indeed any matter which is likely to identify the complainant except as
      authorised by a direction of the Crown Court; and
ii) no such report or matter may be published, except as authorised by the court, which is
      likely to lead members of the public to identify the defendant in those proceedings
      unless and until the defendant is convicted of the offence by the Crown Court.
Ðhe duty imposed upon the clerk to the justices by [s.6(5) MCA 1980] in respect of giving
₀otice of the result of committal proceedings no longer applies in respect of rape offences, so
ₐr as the inclusion in such notice of the defendant's name, address and age. The notice
ʰould not contain any particulars which identify or are likely to identify the complainant.
ₐlthough there will be no breach of anonymity under the Act if names are used in court,
ₑevertheless clerks to the justices may consider it expedient to advise justices and advocates
₀ refrain from addressing the complainant and the defendant by name whenever possible.
ᶜlerks are also advised that in notices posted in the courthouse giving details of the cases to
ₑe heard in various courtrooms, the name of the defendant should not – as is the usual
ₚractice – be included where a rape offence is charged. Therefore the notice should indicate
ₙ which courtroom such a case is being heard by some other names, for example:
ᶜase 1 – Committal Proceedings
    (officer in charge of case on behalf of Police – Det/Sgt Smith)
Ⱳith regard to the citing of such cases, it is recommended that the current practice used in
ᵉspect of cases involving juveniles should be followed with the addition of the symbol "[R]"
ₙdicating that it is a rape case.'

.4(1): A rape offence, defined in s.7, *infra.*

ᶜomplainant/written publication/broadcast/cable programme, defined in s.4(6).

ₐ direction given in pursuance of this section, i.e. by a judge of the Crown Court under s.4(2)
ₒr (3), or by the Court of Appeal under s.4(4).

Anonymity of defendants in rape etc. cases   **4.37**
   6. (1) After a person is accused of a rape offence no matter likely to lead
members of the public to identify him as the person against whom the accusation is made shall either be published in England and Wales in a written
publication available to the public or be broadcast or included in a cable
programme in England and Wales except–
    (a) as authorised by a direction given in pursuance of this section or by s.
        4(7)(a) of this Act as applied by subs (6) of this section; or
    (b) after he has been convicted of the offence at a trial before the Crown
        Court.

   (2) If person accused of a rape offence applies to a magistrates' court,
before the commencement of his trial for that offence, for a direction in
pursuance of this subsection, the court shall direct that the preceding subsection shall not apply to him in consequence of the accusation; and if at a trial
before the Crown Court at which a person is charged with a rape offence in
respect of which he has not obtained such a direction–
    (a) the judge is satisfied that the effect of the preceding subsection is to
        impose a substantial and unreasonable restriction on the reporting of
        proceedings at the trial and that it is in the public interest to remove the
        restriction of that person; or
    (b) that person applies to the judge for a direction in pursuance of this
        subsection;
the judge shall direct that the preceding subsection shall not apply to that
person in consequence of the accusation alleging that offence.

   (3) *(Crown Court).*

   (4) *(Services Acts).*

(5) (Juvenile Court).

(6) Subsections (5) to (7) of s.4 of this Act shall have effect for the purpose of this section as if for references to that section there were substitute references to this section; and–

(a) in relation to a person charged as mentioned in subs (4) of this section s.4(6) of this Act, as applied by this subsection, shall have effect as if fc paras. (a) to (d) there were substituted the words 'he is charged with rape offence in pursuance of any provision of the Naval Discipline A 1957, the Army Act 1955 or the Air Force Act 1955;

(b) in s.5(2) of this Act the reference to the purposes of s.4(2) of this A shall be construed as including a reference to the purposes of subs (and (3) of this section; and

(c) in relation to a person charged by virtue of this subsection with such a offence as is mentioned in subs (5) of s.5 of this Act, that subsection sha have effect as if for the reference to s.4(1) of this Act there wer substituted a reference to subs (1) of this section.

[*as amended by Sch.5 Cable and Broadcasting Act 1984. To be repealed b [Sch.15] CJA 1988 when in force*].

COMMENTARY

s.6(2): A rape offence, defined in s.7, *infra.*

A magistrates' court, includes a single justice: s.4(1) MCA 1980.

4.38   **Citation, interpretation, commencement and extent**
         7. (2) In this Act–
'a rape offence' means any of the following, namely rape, attempted rape aiding, abetting, counselling and procuring rape or attempted rape, an incitement to rape; and
references to sexual intercourse shall be construed in accordance with s.44 c the Sexual Offences Act 1956 so far as it relates to natural intercourse (unde which such intercourse is deemed complete on proof of penetration only); and s.46 of that Act (which relates to the meaning of 'man' and 'woman' in tha Act) shall have effect as if the reference to that Act included a reference to thi Act.

COMMENTARY

Section 44 of the Sexual Offences Act 1956, reads: 'Where on the trial of an offence under thi Act it is necessary to prove sexual intercourse (whether natural or unnatural) it shall not b necessary to prove the completion of the intercourse by the emission of seed, but th intercourse shall be deemed complete upon proof of penetration only.'

Section 46 of that Act reads: 'The use in any provision of this Act of the word 'man' withou the addition of the word 'boy', or *vice versa*, shall not prevent the provision applying to an person to whom it would have applied if both words had been used, and similarly with th words 'woman' and 'girl'.

MAGISTRATES' COURTS ACT 1980

4.39   **General nature of committal proceedings**
         4. (1) The functions of examining justices may be discharged by a singl justice.

(2) Examining justices shall sit in open court except where any enactmen contains an express provision to the contrary and except where it appears t them as respects the whole or any part of committal proceedings that the end of justice would not be served by their sitting in open court.

(3) Subject to subs (4) below and s.102 below, evidence given befor examining justices shall be given in the presence of the accused, and th defence shall be at liberty to put questions to any witness at the inquiry.

(4) Examining justices may allow evidence to be given before them in the absence of the accused if–

    (a) they consider that by reason of his disorderly conduct before them it is not practicable for the evidence to be given in his presence, or

    (b) he cannot be present for reasons of health but is represented by counsel or a solicitor and has consented to the evidence being given in his absence.

COMMENTARY

4(2): Express provision to the contrary, see s.37 CYPA 1933, s.105 MCA 1980, and s.8(4) Official Secrets Act 1920.

4(3): see under *Evidence* at 4.14 and *Presence of the Accused* at 4.04.

Evidence given before examining justices, since written statements put in under s.102 MCA 1980 are evidence, this section applies equally to committals under s.6, *infra*.

The defence shall be at liberty, there is no corresponding provision in the Act or Rules in respect of the prosecution, but they are in practice always accorded the privilege of cross-examination of any witnesses called by the defendant.

Adjournment of inquiry 4.40

5. (1) A magistrates' court may, before beginning to inquire into an offence as examining justices, or at any time during the inquiry, adjourn the hearing, and if it does so shall remand the accused.

(2) The court shall when adjourning fix the time and place at which the hearing is to be resumed; and the time fixed shall be that at which the accused is required to appear or be brought before the court in pursuance of the remand or would be required to be brought before the court but for s.128(3A) below. [*as amended by Sch.9 CJA 1982*].

COMMENTARY

5(1): May . . . adjourn, the justices' clerk has power further to adjourn criminal proceedings in certain circumstances with the consent of the prosecutor and the accused: Justices' Clerks Rules 1970 (SI No 231).

Shall remand the accused, see Form 5. The remand must be on bail or in custody: s.128 MCA 1980. The general right to bail applies: see Bail Act 1976.

5(2): Fix the time, it is not therefore possible to adjourn a preliminary inquiry without fixing a date.

Discharge or committal for trial 4.41

6. (1) Subject to the provisions of this and any other Act relating to the summary trial of indictable offences, if a magistrates' court inquiring into an offence as examining justices is of opinion, on consideration of the evidence [and of any statement of the accused], that there is sufficient evidence to put the accused on trial by jury for any indictable offence, the court shall commit him for trial; and, if it is not of that opinion, it shall, if he is in custody for no other cause than the offence under inquiry, discharge him.

(2) A magistrates' court inquiring into an offence as examining justices may, if satisfied that all the evidence before the court (whether for the prosecution or the defence) consists of written statements tendered to the court under s.102 below, with or without exhibits, commit the accused for trial for the offence without consideration of the contents of those statements, unless–

    (a) the accused or one of the accused has no solicitor acting for him in the case (whether present in court or not);

    (b) counsel or a solicitor for the accused or one of the accused, as the case may be, has requested the court to consider a submission that the statements disclose insufficient evidence to put that accused on trial by jury for the offence;

and subs (1) above shall not apply to a committal for trial under th
subsection.

(3) Subject to s. 4 of the Bail Act 1976 and s.41 below, the court ma
commit a person for trial–
  (a) in custody, that is to say, by committing him to custody there to be safe
      kept until delivered in due course of law, or
  (b) on bail in accordance with the Bail Act 1976, that is to say, by directin
      him to appear before the Crown Court for trial;
and where his release on bail is conditional on his providing one or more suret
or sureties and, in accordance with s.8(3) of the Bail Act 1976, the court fix
the amount in which the surety is to be bound with a view to his entering in
his recognizance subsequently in accordance with subs (4) and (5) or (6) of th
section the court shall in the meantime commit the accused to custody
accordance with paragraph (a) of this subsection.

(4) Where the court has committed a person to custody in accordance wit
para (a) of subs (3) above, then, if that person is in custody for no other caus
the court may, at any time before his first appearance before the Crown Cour
grant him bail in accordance with the Bail Act 1976 subject to a duty to appe
before the Crown Court for trial.

(5) Where a magistrates' court acting as examining justices commits an
person for trial or determines to discharge him, the clerk of the court shall, o
the day on which the committal proceedings are concluded or the next day
cause to be displayed in a part of the court house to which the public hav
access a notice–
  (a) in either case giving that person's name, address, and age (if known)
  (b) in a case where the court so commits him, stating the charge or charge
      on which he is committed and the court to which he is committed;
  (c) in a case where the court determines to discharge him, describing th
offence charged and stating that it has so determined;
      but this subsection shall have effect subject to ss.4 and 6 of the Sexu
      Offences (Amendment) Act 1976 (anonymity of complainant an
      accused in rape etc cases).

(6) A notice displayed in pursuance of subs (5) above shall not contain th
name or address of any person under the age of 17 unless the justices i
question have stated that in their opinion he would be mentioned in the notic
apart from the preceding provisions of this subsection and should be men
tioned in it for the purpose of avoiding injustice to him.
[*as amended by s.61 CJA 1982*].

COMMENTARY

This section provides for two types of committals: (a) *on consideration of the evidence* (c
conventional committal proceedings) under s.6(1); and (b) *without consideration of th
evidence* (or 'paper' committals) under s.6(2).

The court's permission is not needed for the prosecutor to offer no evidence on a charge
committal proceedings: *R v Canterbury and St Augustine's Justices, ex p. Klisiak* [1982] Q
398.

Legal aid may be granted in the proceedings: s.28 LAA 1974. For the power to awar
costs, see Chapter 9.

The provisions of s.42 MCA 1980 (restriction of justices sitting after dealing with bail) d
not apply to committals for trial, nor is there apparently any objection in principle t
magistrates who are aware of previous convictions acting as examining justices. If th
committal proceedings are discontinued and the matter dealt with summarily, then by s.4
such a magistrate is debarred from trying the issue of guilt: *R v Brixton Prison Governor, e
p. Thompson* (1970) 134 JPN 371 (an extradition case).

'It shall be the duty of the clerk to the examining justices before whom a person is charged wit
murder, manslaughter or infanticide to inform the coroner who is responsible for holding a
inquest upon the body of the making of the charge, and of the committal for trial or discharge, a
the case may be, of the person charged': s.20(5) Coroners (Amendment) Act 1926. This sectio
has been applied to the offence of causing death by reckless driving by s.1(2) RTA 1972, and t
aiding, abetting, counselling or procuring suicide by Sch.1 Suicide Act 1961.

s.6(1), the effect of s.6(1) is that if the justices are of opinion that there is sufficient evidence to put the accused on trial for any indictable offence (ie the offence the subject of the inquiry or any other offence which, if committed by an adult is triable on indictment, whether it is exclusively so triable or not) they *must* commit him for trial on such offence. The procedure in ss.18–22 of the Act for the summary trial of an indictable offence is not available: *R v Cambridge Justices, ex p. Fraser* [1985] 1 WLR 1391. The words 'subject to the provisions of this and any other Act relating to the summary trial of indictable offences . . .' refer at the very least to the powers conferred by s.25, *per* Webster J., *ibid.*

For the procedure to be followed in a committal under this subsection, see r.7 MC Rules 1981 Courts Rules 1981, *infra.*

Indictable offence, defined in Sch.1 Interpretation Act 1978, as an offence which, if committed by an adult, is triable on indictment, whether it is exclusively so triable or not.

Examining justices, this term is defined in s.49 CJA 1925 as 'the justices before whom a charge is made against any person for an indictable offence, and references to examining justices include a reference to a single examining justice.'

Of opinion, justices evenly divided may adjourn for re-hearing before a differently constituted bench: *R v Hertfordshire Justices, ex p. Larsen* (1926) 89 JP 205; in which it was also said to be desirable that the bench should preferably consist of an odd number of justices.

The evidence, see under this title in the introduction.

Statement of the accused, it would appear that the words in square brackets have been repealed by s.72 CJA 1982.

Sufficient evidence, see the introduction under *Conventional committals*

For any indictable offence, not merely the offences charged by the prosecutor, but any disclosed in the evidence. If the defendant is committed in respect of a different offence from that charged it must be read to him: r.7(12) MC Rules 1981. Other and additional counts may be subsequently added to the indictment under the proviso to s.2(2) Administration of Justice (Miscellaneous Provisions) Act 1933.

Commit him for trial, the committing magistrate must specify the *place* of trial in accordance with s.75 Supreme Court Act 1981; and see the *directions* of the Lord Chief Justice, at 4.77, *post.*

The court shall . . . discharge him, for the power to award costs, see Chapter 9.

s.6(2), for the procedure in a committal under this subsection see r.6 MCA 1981, *infra.*

A magistrates' court . . . may, this terminology would appear to give the court an *overriding discretion* to refuse to deal with the procedings under the procedure laid down in this section.

All the evidence before the court, this is merely a reference to the statements and not to the nature or admissibility of their contents: *R v Brooker* (1977) 65 Cr App R 181. It is suggested that the wording of this subsection precludes the use of a written statement by a child taken in accordance with s.27 CYPA 1963.

Commit . . . for trial, see the corresponding note to s.6(1), *supra.*

For the offence, i.e. unlike committal proceedings under s.6(1), *supra,* a committal under this subsection may *only* be in respect of *the charge or charges preferred by the prosecutor.* Other and additional counts may be added to the indictment later under the proviso to s.2(2) Administration of Justice (Miscellaneous Provisions) Act 1933: *R v James William* [1972] Crim LR 436. But the indictment will be quashed where the defendant is committed for trial in respect of an offence which has been repealed: *R v Lamb (Thomas)* (1969) 133 JP 89.

A solicitor, the fact that the solicitor has no practising certificate is irrelevant to the validity of the committal: *R v Scott (John)* (1978) 68 Cr App R 164.

s.6(3): In custody, see Form 18. Juveniles not granted bail are committed to the care of the local authority: s.23 CYPA 1969. Unless certified as unruly: s.23(2). For the committal to custody of persons aged 17–20 see s.27 CJA 1948. The reasons for refusing bail are set out in the Bail Act 1976. Bail may be granted by the High Court (s.22 CJA 1967) and the Crown Court (s.81 Supreme Court Act 1981) and the defendant, if unrepresented, must be informed that he may apply thereto: s.5(6) Bail Act 1976.

On bail, except in treason: s.41 MCA 1980. The conditions and other incidents of bail are governed by the Bail Act 1976. The general right to bail applies: s.4, *ibid.* If bail is offered on unacceptable terms, the High Court has power to admit to bail: s.22 CJA 1967. Notice must be sent to the prison governor, etc.: r.9 MC Rules 1981.

s.6(5): Cause to be displayed, no minimum period of display is prescribed. HOC 209/1967 recommends 'at least (*sic*) two to three days' and adds: 'If it is not practicable to post up the notice in the building in which the court sits, it should be posted as near as possible to the entrance of the building.' The reference to s.6 Sexual Offences (Amendment) Act 1976 will be deleted when that section is repealed by CJA 1988.

4.42   Place of trial on indictment
   7. (1) A magistrates' court committing a person for trial shall specify the place at which he is to be tried, and in selecting that place shall have regard to–
   (a) the convenience of the defence, the prosecution and the witnesses,
   (b) the expediting of the trial, and
   (c) any direction given by or on behalf of the Lord Chief Justice with the concurrence of the Lord Chancellor under s.4(5) of the Courts Act 1971.

COMMENTARY
The *directions* of the Lord Chief Justice are reproduced at 4.77, *post.*

4.43   Restrictions on reports of committal proceedings
   8. (1) Except as provided by subs (2), (3) and (8) below, it shall not be lawful to publish in Great Britain a written report, or to broadcast or include in a cable programme in Great Britain a report, of any committal proceedings in England and Wales containing any matter other than that permitted by subs (4) below.

   (2) Subject to subs 2(A) below a magistrates' court shall, on application for the purpose made with reference to any committal proceedings by the accused or one of the accused, as the case may be, order that subs (1) above shall not apply to reports of those proceedings.

   (2A) Where in the case of two or more accused one of them objects to the making of an order under subs (2) above, the court shall make the order if, and only if, it is satisfied, after hearing the representations of the accused, that it is in the interests of justice to do so.

   (2B) An order under subs (2) above shall not apply to reports of proceedings under subs (2A) above, but any decision of the court to make or not to make such an order may be contained in reports published, broadcast or included in a cable programme before the time authorised by subs (3) below.

   (3) It shall not be unlawful under this section to publish, broadcast or include in a cable programme a report of committal proceedings containing any matter other than that permitted by subs (4) below–
   (a) where the magistrates' court determines not to commit the accused, or determines to commit none of the accused, for trial after it so determines;
   (b) where the court commits the accused or any of the accused for trial, after the conclusion of his trial or, as the case may be, the trial of the last to be tried;
and where at any time during the inquiry the court proceeds to try summarily the case of one or more of the accused under s.25(3) or (7) below, while committing the other accused or one or more of the other accused for trial, it shall not be unlawful under this section to publish, broadcast or include in a cable programme as part of a report of the summary trial, after the court determines to proceed as aforesaid, a report of so much of the committal proceedings containing any such matter as takes place before the determination.

   (4) The following matters may be contained in a report of committal proceedings published, broadcast or included in a cable programme, without an order under subs (2) before the time authorised by subs (3) above, that is to say–

(a) the identity of the court and the names of the examining justices;

(b) the names, addresses and occupations of the parties and witnesses and the ages of the accused and witnesses;

(c) the offence or offences, or a summary of them, with which the accused is or are charged;

(d) the names of counsel and solicitors engaged in the proceedings;

(e) any decision of the court to commit the accused or any of the accused for trial, and any decision of the court on the disposal of the case of any accused not committed;

(f) where the court commits the accused or any of the accused for trial, the charge or charges, or a summary of them, on which he is committed and the court to which he is committed;

(g) where the committal proceedings are adjourned, the date and place to which they are adjourned;

(h) any arrangements as to bail or committal or adjournment;

(i) whether legal aid was granted to the accused or any of the accused.

(5) If a report is published, broadcast or included in a cable programme in contravention of this section, the following persons, that is to say–

(a) in the case of a publication of a written report as part of a newspaper or periodical, any proprietor, editor or publisher of the newspaper or periodical;

(b) in the case of a publication of a written report otherwise than as part of a newspaper or periodical, the person who publishes it;

(c) in the case of a broadcast of a report, any body corporate which transmits or provides the programme in which the report is broadcast and any person having functions in relation to the programme corresponding to those of the editor of a newspaper or periodical;

(d) in the case of an inclusion of a report in a cable programme, any body corporate which sends or provides the programme and any person having functions in relation to the programme corresponding to those of an editor of a newspaper.

shall be liable on summary conviction to a fine not exceeding level 5 on the standard scale.

(6) Proceedings for an offence under this section shall not, in England and Wales, be instituted otherwise than by or with the consent of the Attorney-General.

(7) Subsection (1) above shall be in addition to, and not in derogation from, the provisions of any other enactment with respect to the publication of reports and proceedings of magistrates' and other courts.

(8) For the purposes of this section committal proceedings shall, in relation to an information charging an indictable offence, be deemed to include any proceedings in the magistrates' court before the court proceeds to inquire into the information as examining justices; but where a magistrates' court which has begun to try an information summarily discontinues the summary trial in pursuance of s.25(2) or (6) below and proceeds to inquire into the information as examining justices, that circumstance shall not make it unlawful under this section for a report of any proceedings on the information which was published or broadcast before the court determined to proceed as aforesaid to have been so published, broadcast or included in a cable programme.

(9) (*Repealed*).

(10) In this section–

'broadcast' means broadcast by wireless telegraphy sounds or visual images intended for general reception;

'cable programme' means a programme included in a cable programme service;

'publish', in relation to a report, means publish the report, either by itself or as part of a newspaper or periodical, for distribution to the public.

[*as amended by s.1 Criminal Justice (Amendment) Act 1981, s.4(4) Contempt of Court Act 1981, ss.38, 46 CJA 1982, Sch.5 Cable and Broadcasting Act 1984*].

COMMENTARY

The court is required to give the defendant, whether represented or not, an explanation of the effects of this section: r.5(1) MC Rules 1981. The existence of this section does not prevent the court from making an order under s.4(2) Contempt of Court Act 1981: *R v Horsham Justices, ex p. Farquharson and Another* [1982] 2 All ER 269.

s.8(1): Great Britain. i.e. England, Scotland and Wales: Union with Scotland Act 1706; s.1 Wales and Berwick Act 1746.

A written report, writing includes typing, printing, lithography, photography and other modes of representing or reproducing words in a visible form: Interpretation Act 1978.

Committal proceedings, defined in s.150(1) as meaning proceedings before a magistrates court acting as examining justices.

s.8(2), once a court has made an order under this subsection, the fact must be stated at an adjourned hearing on a later date, r5(3) MC Rules 1981. The order must be recorded in the register. Jurisdiction to make the order is not confined to magistrates sitting as examining justices, but may be made at an earlier stage of the proceedings. When an order is made the particular committal proceedings to which it relates must be ascertained in the light of the circumstances prevailing at the time when the order was made: *R v Bow Street Magistrate, ex. p. Kray* [1969] 1 QB 473; *R v Blackpool Justices, ex p. Beaverbrook Newspapers Ltd* [1972] 1 W LR 95. An order under s.8(2) applied to a variety of charges being heard together is not extinguished by reason of the fact that the charges are later dealt with separately: *R v Bow Street Magistrate, ex p. Kray, supra.* There is, seemingly, no power to reimpose the restrictions once they have been removed, see *R v Blackpool JJ, supra.*

s.8(2A): The interests of justice, it is the interests of justice as affecting the defendant that the court must consider, *per* Shaw LJ in *R v Horsham Justices, ex p. Farquharson* [1982] 2 All ER 269 (application by newspaper reporter and union). *Dictum* approved in *R v Leeds Justices, ex p. Sykes* [1983] 1 All ER 460. The phrase 'the interests of justice' incorporates as a *paramount consideration* that the defendant should have a fair trial. Only if a powerful case is made out should justices lift reporting restrictions if one of the defendants objects: *R v Leeds Justices, supra.* (Magistrates wrong to lift restrictions in order to give publicity to defendant's grievance against the police where a co-defendant feared publicity would prejudice a fair trial.)

s.8(4)(h): Arrangements as to bail, that is to say, the terms and conditions and not the evidence or submissions.

s.8(6): The consent of the Attorney-General, see s.26 Prosecution of Offences Act 1985. A document purporting to be the consent of a Law Officer of the Crown and to be signed by him . . . shall be admissible as *prima facie* evidence without further proof. For the Solicitor General's powers to discharge his functions see Law Officers Act 1944 (not reproduced herein).

s.8(7): Any other enactment, see, eg, the Judicial Proceedings (Regulation of Reports) Act 1926 (in relation to indecent details), s.39 CYPA 1933 (identifications of juveniles) and the Sexual Offences (Amendment) Act 1976, s.6, *supra.*

s.8(8), this means that the restrictions of this section apply from the first moment the defendant is brought before the court. Compare the remarks of Lord Widgery CJ, in *R v Bow Street Magistrate, ex p. Kray* [1969] 1 QB 473.

Indictable offence, defined in Sch.1 Interpretation Act 1978.

4.44   Certain offences triable either way

17. (1) The offences listed in Sch.1 to this Act shall be triable either way

(2) Subsection (1) above is without prejudice to any other enactment by virtue of which any offence is triable either way.

COMMENTARY

Note: (i) the effect of para 3 of Pt II, Sch.6 Firearms Act 1968 on offences contained in Sch.1 MCA 1980, see 4.33a *ante*;

(ii) [ss.36–48] CJA 1988 which reduce the status of certain either way offences: Appendix II, *post*.
s.17(1): Offence triable either way, defined in Sch.1 Interpretation Act 1978 (see Commentary to s.18, *infra*).

Initial procedure on information against adult for offence triable either way.   4.45

18. (1) Sections 19 to 23 below shall have effect where a person who has attained the age of 17 appears or is brought before a magistrates' court on an information charging him with an offence triable either way.

(2) Without prejudice to s.11(1) above, everything that the court is required to do under ss.19 to 22 below must be done before any evidence is called and, subject to subs (3) below and s.23 below, with the accused present in court.

(3) The court may proceed in the absence of the accused in accordance with such of the provision sof ss.19 to 22 as are applicable in the circumstances if the court considers that by reason of his disorderly conduct before the court it is not practicable for the proceedings to be conducted in his presence; and subss (3) to (5) of s.23 below, so far as applicable, shall have effect in relation to proceedings conducted in the absence of the accused by virtue of this subsection (references in those subsections to the person representing the accused being for this purpose read as references to the person, if any, representing him).

(4) A magistrates' court proceeding under ss.19 to 23 below may adjourn the proceedings at any time, and on doing so on any occasion when the accused is present may remand the accused, and shall remand him if–
  (a) on the occasion on which he first appeared, or was brought, before the court to answer the information he was in custody or, having been released on bail, surrendered to the custody of the court; or
  (b) he has been remanded at any time in the course of proceedings on the information;
and where the court remands the accused, the time fixed for the resumption of the proceedings shall be that at which he is required to appear or be brought before the court in pursuance of the remand or would be required to be brought before the court but for s.128(3A) below.

(5) The functions of a magistrates' court under ss.19 to 23 below may be discharged by a single justice, but the foregoing provision shall not be taken to authorise the summary trial of an information by a magistrates' court composed of less than two justices.
[*as amended by Sch.9 CJA 1982*]

COMMENTARY

This section and ss.19 to 23 *infra*, do not apply where the defendant is charged with an offence under s.17(1) or (2) Firearms Act 1968 (using firearm to resist arrest and possessing firearms while committing certain offences) and is also charged with a Sch.1 offence. For the procedure in such cases see Sch.6, Part II Firearms Act 1968.
  Whilst a large number of the more common 'either way' offences are listed in Sch.1 MCA 1980, *post*, a considerable number, particularly of a regulatory nature, are given this status by the enactment creating the offence. Failure to follow the procedure in ss.19–24 will result in any ensuing conviction being quashed: *R v Tottenham Justices, ex p. Arthur's Transport Services* [1981] Crim LR 180; *R v Cardiff City Magistrates' Court, ex p. Cardiff City Council* (1987), *The Times* 24 February (summary proceedings a nullity where correct procedure not followed in respect of a 'non-scheduled' offence).

s.18(1): Attained the age of 17, for the determination of age, see s.150(4) MCA 1980. For the stage at which a juvenile loses the right to jury trial, see under *Juveniles* in the introduction.

s.18(1): Offence triable either way, this phrase is defined in Sch.1 Interpretation Act 1978, as meaning an offence which, if committed by an adult, is triable either on indictment or summarily.

s.18(2): Before any evidence is called, this would appear to relate to evidence in the trial and not to statements made on oath during a bail application.

s.18: The accused present in court, the effect of this is that the decision as to mode of trial may not be taken without the defendant being personally present in court unless he is legally represented and the conditions of s.23 are satisfied (This subsection is drafted so as to exclude the general right of an accused contained in s.122 to appear by a legal representative). The subsection does not affect s.11 MCA 1980 which prescribes what may take place if the defendant does not appear, but in that case appearance by a legal representative under s.122 is sufficient unless, for any other purpose, the accused's appearance in person is required, eg to surrender to bail.

s.18(3): This allows the court to exclude the defendant personally in the circumstances referred to and as such is an exception to the common law right of a defendant to be present at his trial. This subsection ceases to operate after evidence has been called: s.18(2), *supra.* The comparable provisions in s.4(4) apply only when committal proceedings begin. Note the powers of a legal representative under s.23, *infra,* as applied by this subsection.

s.18(4): The remand will be in accordance with s.128 MCA 1980. The general right to bail applies: s.4 Bail Act 1970. The period of the remand must be co-terminous with the adjournment. The powers of adjournment contained in ss.5 and 10 MCA 1980 are not available at this stage of the proceedings. There is no overriding necessity for evidence of arrest before a remand in custody: *R v Guest, ex p. Metropolitan Police Commissioner* [1961] 3 All ER 1118.

4.46   **Court to begin by considering which mode of trial appears more suitable**
    19. (1) The court shall consider whether having regard to the matters mentioned in subs (3) below and any representations made by the prosecutor or the accused, the offence appears to the court more suitable for summary trial or for trial on indictment.

    (2) Before so considering, the court–
    (a) shall cause the charge to be written down, if this has not already been done, and read to the accused; and
    (b) shall afford first the prosecutor and then the accused an opportunity to make representations as to which mode of trial would be more suitable.

    (3) The matters to which the court is to have regard under subs. (1) above are the nature of the case; whether the circumstances make the offence one of serious character; whether the punishment which a magistrates' court would have power to inflict for it would be adequate; and any other circumstances which appear to the court to make it more suitable for the offence to be tried in one way rather than the other.

    (4) If the prosecution is being carried on by the Attorney General, the Solicitor General or the Director of Public Prosecutions and he applies for the offence to be tried on indictment, the preceding provisions of this section and ss.20 and 21 below shall not apply, and the court shall proceed to inquire into the information as examining justices.

    (5) The power of the Director of Public Prosecutions under subs (4) above to apply for an offence to be tried on indictment shall not be exercised except with the consent of the Attorney General.
    [*as amended by Sch.1 Prosecution of Offences Act 1985*].

COMMENTARY
This section applies in the circumstances set out in s.18(1), *supra.* Its requirements must be completed *before* any evidence is called and, subject to s.23 *infra,* with the accused present in court: s.18(2). By analogy with the position under s.24(1), *post,* it seems that the initial mode of trial decision may be reviewed at any point before the accused makes his election and arguably until a plea is entered – *but only* where a change of circusmtances has occurred or if there are new or additional factors: *cf. R v Newham Juvenile Court, ex p. F (a minor),* [1986] 3 All ER 17. But the bringing of further indictable offences will not suffice, *semble: R v Southend Justices, ex p. Wood* (1986) *The Times,* 8 March; and once there has been both election and plea the court is restricted to the 'switching' provisions of s.25(2), *post*: see *R v*

St Helens Justices, ex p. Critchley (1987) *The Times*, 22 October; or s.25(3) if the court has begun as examining justices.

.19(1): Representations, the court is not bound by these (unless s.19(4) applies) but must consider them, if made. The court may not at this stage investigate whether the accused has any previous convictions: *R v Colchester Justices, ex p. North Essex Building Co Ltd* [1977] 3 All ER 567 (limited company which could not be committed for sentence). It is a matter of *fundamental importance* that this provision should be complied with and *the clerk should make a record of the fact that the accused was asked for representations and of his response: R v Horseferry Road Magistrates' Court, ex p. Constable* [1981] Crim LR 504 (form of words used by the clerk satisfactory but preferable to follow the statutory wording). It is suggested that the fact that the accused wishes other offences to be taken into consideration is not a matter which should be relied upon by the court in taking its decision under this section because this is a matter which can justify a committal to the Crown Court for sentence. See the articles at 145 JPN 647 and 735; and see *R v Derby and South Derbyshire Magistrates, ex p. McCarthy and McGovern* (1981) mentioned therein.

s.19(2): Cause the charge to be written down, the charge sheet or summons will usually suffice.

.19(3): it was wrong for the prosecutor to prefer a charge of wounding contrary to s.18 Offences Against the Person Act 1861 solely in order to obtain trial on indictment after the magistrates had accepted summary trial of a charge under s.20: *R v Brooks* [1985] Crim LR 385.

The nature of the case eg the trial of a councillor in a small borough: *Afford v Pettit* (1949) 33 JP 433.

Offence . . . of serious character, justices must exercise their discretion judicially. Grave offences, such as a stabbing which barely falls short of murder, were not intened to be tried summarily; although the Divisional Court will not in such a case interfere by means of *certiorari*. In *R v Middlesex Quarter Sessions, ex p. Director of Public Prosecutions* [1950] 2 KB 589, Lord Goddard CJ said: 'Serious cases ought to be dealt with by the superior courts,' and in *R v Norfolk Justices, ex p. Director of Public Prosecutions* [1950] 2 KB 558, 'When a case is of a serious character – and surely a case of a man committing 13 bankruptcy offences is one of a serious character – that case ought to go for trial. It is not merely a matter of what the sentence may be . . . serious cases ought to be dealt with by a superior court.' In *R v Everest* (1968) 53 Cr App R 20, Lord Parker CJ said: 'Serious offences must be dealt with on indictment, which would enable appropriate sentences to be given.' And see also *R v Coe* [1968] 1 WLR 1950 and *R v Pitson* (1972) 56 Cr App R 391: 'Large scale thieving and receiving should be dealt with by the Crown Court. While trivial burglaries may be tried by magistrates, cases of breaking and entering, particularly at night, should not, *per* Lord Lane CJ in *R v Hardman* (1982) *The Times*, 10 November. But see generally the comments concerning the adequacy of justices' powers to sentence for certain levels of offence which a few years ago might have attracted sentences within the power of the Crown Court, under the titles *Sentencing Powers* and *Custodial Sentences for particular offences* at Chapter 8d.

Punishment, appears to include the award of compensation: *R v McLean, ex p. Metropolitan Commissioner of Police* [1975] Crim LR 289.

.19(4): see the commentary to s.18(6), *supra*.

Procedure where summary trial appears more suitable   4.47

20.(1) If, where the court has considered as required by s.19(1) above, it appears to the court that the offence is more suitable for summary trial, the following provisions of this section shall apply (unless excluded by s.23 below).

(2) The court shall explain to the accused in ordinary language–
  (a) that it appears to the court more suitable for him to be tried summarily for the offence, and that he can either consent to be so tried or, if he wishes, be tried by a jury; and
  (b) that if he is tried summarily and is convicted by the court, he may be committed for sentence to the Crown Court under s.38 below if the convicting court, on obtaining information about his character and antecedents, is of opinion that they are such that greater punishment should be inflicted than the convicting court has power to inflict for the offence.

(3) After explaining to the accused as provided by subs (2) above the court

shall ask him whether he consents to be tried summarily or wishes to be tried by a jury, and–

(a) if he consents to be tried summarily, shall proceed to the summary trial of the information;

(b) if he does not so consent, shall proceed to inquire into the information as examining justices.

COMMENTARY

This section applies in the circumstances set out in s.18(1), *supra*. It does not apply where the presence of the accused has been dispensed with under s.18(3), or when the accused's representative has signalled his consent under s.23, *infra*. The requirements must be complied with *before* any evidence is called and, subject to s.23, *infra*, with the accused present in court: s.18(2). When a person is tried summarily under this section 'the court shall cause his consent to be entered in a register and if the consent was signified by a person representing him in his absence' that fact too: r.66(5) MC Rules 1981.

s.20(2): Explain to the accused, it is essential that the accused understands the nature and significance of the choice that is open to him: see *R v Birmingham Justices, ex p. Hodgson* [1985] QB 1131; *R v Highbury Corner Magistrates' Court ex p. Weekes* [1985] QB 1147; *R v Slough Magistrates' Court, ex p. Thomas* (1986) (reported at 150 JPN 545) noted in the commentary to s.20(3), *infra*. Failure to give the caution would seemingly render a committal for sentence invalid: cf *R v Kent Justices, ex p. Machin* [1952] 2 QB 355; *R v Newcastle under Lyme Justices, ex p. Whitehouse* [1952] 2 All ER 531. Where the omission of the caution is discovered and the proceedings withdrawn a fresh information may seemingly be laid: *Davis v Morton* (1913) 77 JP 223.

Tried by a jury, this phrase can be misleading since the procedure of this section applies as much to defendants intending to plead 'guilty' as to those intending to plead 'not guilty': *R v Birmingham Justices, ex p. Hodgson* [1985] QB 1131.

Character and antecedents, this term has been considered judicially in relation to its use in s.38 MCA 1980: see Chapter 8e.

s.20(3): If he consents, although the caution must be put to the defendant in person it was held under the pre-existing provisions that a consent to summary trial by counsel or solicitor in the presence and the hearing of the defendant is sufficient if not contradicted at the time: *R v Latham, ex p. Roberts* (1943) 41 LGR 99; and see *R v Salisbury and Amesbury Justices, ex p. Greatbatch* (1954) 118 JP 392. A legal representative may act in the absence of the accused in the circumstances set out in s.23, *infra*. A representative may consent to summary trial on behalf of a corporation: para 2 of Sch.3. Where a representative does not appear the corporation's consent to summary trial is not required: para 3.

Withdrawal of consent, consent may be withdrawn at any time before evidence is given: *R v Craske, ex p. Metropolitan Police Commissioner* [1957] 2 QB 591 confirmed by the Court of Criminal Appeal in *R v Ibrahim* (1958) 42 Cr App R 38, and re-affirmed in *R v Southampton City Justices, ex p. Robins* (1981) 144 JP 288. Justices have a discretion whether or not to permit withdrawal of consent which will depend on how they see the broad justice of the whole situation: *R v Southampton Justices, ex p. Briggs* (1972) 136 JP 237.

Recently the courts have adopted a more generous attitude towards applications to withdraw consent to summary trial:

'Justices faced with an application [to change an election] may take the view that the case is more suitable for summary trial, but I do not see this as a factor which should tell against the application. If the defendant demonstrates that his original choice was exercised when he did not properly understand the nature and significance of the choice which he was making, then it is as if he had never made that choice, and I repeat that regardless of the justices' view about which was the more suitable court to deal with the case. On the other hand if the justices hearing such an application take the view that the case is now one more suitable for trial on indictment, or even if it is now less clearly more suitable for summary trial, for example because further evidence is not to be relied upon by the Crown, this would be a factor which underlined the justice of allowing the defendant to re-elect.'

per McCullough J in *R v Birmingham Justices, ex p. Hodgson* [1985] QB 1131 (applicants elected summary trial and pleaded guilty when they were unrepresented, pleas not accepted by the court and the applicants, now represented, sought unsuccessfully to vacate the election for summary trial on the ground that they had thought they had no defence to the charge and that their election for summary trial was purely for the purpose of being sentenced: *held* the broad justice of the situation demanded that they be allowed to re-elect.) *Hodgson's* case was followed in *R v West London Metropolitan Stipendiary*

Magistrate, ex p. Keane (1985) *The Times*, 9 March. In *R v Highbury Corner Magistrates' Court, ex p. Weekes* [1985] QB 1147, it was held that a magistrate had erred in not allowing a change of election on the part of a 17-year-old who had not understood the choice which he had been asked to make. The magistrate had misdirected himself in failing to appreciate the very limited use to which his own view as to the more suitable mode of trial could be put. In this case McCullough J declined to lay down as a principle that an unrepresented defendant of any age should, in relation to 'serious' charges, never be put to his election when he first appears before justices. It is not every *claim* that the original election was made without full understanding which will succeed, even where that claim is fully supported by the lawyer in the case: see *R v Slough Magistrates' Court, ex p. Thomas* (1986) (reported at 150 JPN 545) intelligent, responsible and educated professional golfer).

Consent may not be withdrawn after evidence has been given: *R v Bennett ex p. R* [1960] 1 All ER 335. However, the court has the power to abandon summary trial at this stage and convert to committal proceedings under s.25(2), *infra*. The court's refusal to allow consent to be withdrawn cannot be attacked by an application for prerogative orders unless it was wrongly exercised, that is to say, exercised on a wrong principle or exercised having regard to factors which ought to have been ignored or exercised without reference to factors which ought to have been included, or indeed not exercised at all: *R v Lambeth Metropolitan Stipendiary Magistrate, ex p. Wright* [1974] Crim LR 444.

The summary trial, any subsequent adjournment must be in accordance with s.10, not s.18(4). The court may subsequently discontinue the summary trial and proceed as examining justices in accordance with s.25(2), *supra*.

Examining justices, any subsequent adjournment must be in accordance with s.5, not s.18(4). The court may with the defendant's consent subsequently change over to summary trial in accordance with s.25(3), *infra*; see note to s.2, *supra*.

Procedure where trial on indictment appears more suitable 4.48

21. If, where the court has considered as required by s.19(1) above, it appears to the court that the offence is more suitable for trial on indictment, the court shall tell the accused that the court has decided that it is more suitable for him to be tried for the offence by a jury, and shall proceed to inquire into the information as examining justices.

COMMENTARY

The requirements of this section must be complied with before any evidence is called, and subject to s.23, *infra*, with the accused present in court: s.18(2). This section does not apply when the accused has been excluded under s.18(3), *supra*, when the accused's legal representative has signified his consent under s.23, *infra*.

Examining justice. See note to s.20.

Certain offences triable either way to be tried summarily if value involved is small 4.49

22. (1) If the offence charged by the information is one of those mentioned in the first column of Sch.2 to the Act (in this section referred to as 'scheduled offences') then, subject to subs 17 below, the court shall, before proceeding in accordance with s.19 above consider whether, having regard to any representations made by the prosecutor or the accused, the value involved (as defined in subs (10) below) appears to the court to exceed the relevant sum.

For the purpose of this section the relevant sum is £400 [£2,000].

(2) If, where subs (1) above applies, it appears to the court clear that, for the offence charged, the value involved does not exceed the relevant sum, the court shall proceed as if the offence were triable only summarily, and ss.19 to 21 above shall not apply.

(3) If, where subs (1) above applies, it appears to the court clear that, for the offence charged, the value involved exceeds the relevant sum, the court shall thereupon proceed in accordance with s.19 above in the ordinary way without further regard to the provisions of this section.

(4) If, where subs (1) above applies, it appears to the court for any reason not clear whether, for the offence charged, the value involved does or does not exceed the relevant sum, the provisions of subs. (5) and (6) below shall apply.

(5) The court shall cause the charge to be written down, if this has not already been done, and read to the accused, and shall explain to him in ordinary language–
   (a) that he can, if he wishes to be tried summarily for the offence and that if he consents to be so tried, he will definitely be tried in that way; and
   (b) that if he is tried summarily and is convicted by the court, his liability to imprisonment or a fine will be limited as provided in s.33 below.

(6) After explaining to the accused as provided by subs (5) above the court shall ask him whether he consents to be tried summarily and–
   (a) if he so consents, shall proceed in accordance with subs (2) above as if that subsection applied;
   (b) if he does not so consent, shall proceed in accordance with subs (3) above as if that subsection applied.

(7) Subsection (1) above shall not apply where the offence charged–
   (a) is one of two or more offences with which the accused is charged on the same occasion and which appear to the court to constitute or form part of a series of two or more offences of the same or a similar character; or
   (b) consists in the incitement to commit two or more scheduled offences.

(8) Where a person is convicted by a magistrates' court of a scheduled offence, it shall not be open to him to appeal to the Crown Court against the conviction on the ground that the convicting court's decision as to the value involved was mistaken.

(9) If, where subs (1) above applies, the offence charged is one with which the accused is charged jointly with a person who has not attained the age of 17 the reference in that subsection to any representations made by the accused shall be read as including any representations made by the person under 17.

(10) In this section 'the value involved', in relation to any scheduled offence, means the value indicated in the second column of Sch.2 to this Act measured as indicated in the third column of that schedule; and in that schedule 'the material time' means the time of the alleged offence.

(11) Where–
   (a) the accused is charged on the same occasion with two or more scheduled offences and it appears to the court that they constitute or form part of a series of two or more offences of the same or a similar character; or
   (b) the offence charged consists in incitement to commit two or more scheduled offences,
this section shall have effect as if any reference in it to the value involved were a reference to the aggregate of the values involved.
[as amended by SI 1984 No. 447 and subs (11) added by [s.37] CJA 1988].

COMMENTARY

This section applies to most offences of criminal damage except arson (see Sch.2), except in the circumstances referred to in s.22(7). It contemplates three contingencies:
   (i) when it appears *clear* to the court that the value involved (as defined in s.22(10) and Sch.2) is *the relevant sum or less*, in which case the court proceeds to summary trial in accordance with s.22(2);
   (ii) when it appears *clear* to the court that the value involved *exceeds the relevant sum*, in which case the court proceeds according to the provisions of ss.19–21, which govern the selection of method of trial of offences triable either way; and
   (iii) when it is *not clear* whether the value involved does or does not exceed the relevant sum, in which case the special procedure of s.22(5) and (6) is applied by s.22(4). If the accused does not consent to summary trial thereunder, the procedure under s.19 is followed in accordance with s.22(3). Under this he has a second opportunity to consent to summary trial but will suffer disadvantages if he does consent; in particular, he will be subject on conviction to a greater maximum penalty, he can be committed to the Crown Court for sentence and the magistrates can revert to trial on indictment in accordance with s.24.
The relevant sum is defined in s.22(1), by virtue of which the procedure of this section takes

place *before representations* are heard from prosecutor and defendant *under s.19, supra.* Its requirements must be complied with before any evidence is called and, subject to s.23, *infra*, with the accused present in court: s.18(2). The court's decision as to value must be recorded in the register: r.66(7) MC Rules 1981.

NB The relevant sum will be increased to £2,000 when [s.37] CJA 1988 comes into force but will not apply to offences charged in respect of acts done before the section comes into force.

s.22(1): Representations Representations under this section are confined to *value only.* The court is not bound by these but must consider them, if made. Unlike the 'single procedure' neither side has any specific right to speak first. A juvenile jointly charged with an adult is entitled to make representations: s.22(9).

While the court may in its discretion hear evidence on the value involved it need not do so. Representations imply something less than evidence. The nearest analogy is a speech in mitigation: *R v Canterbury and St. Augustine's Justices, ex p. Klisiak* (1981) 145 JP 344.

s.22(2), the maximum penalty for an offence tried summarily is provided in s.33, *infra*, ie currently £1,000 or 3 months' imprisonment, or both.

s.22(4), this is a procedural device which seeks to avoid argument about the value of the property involved by giving the accused the right to select the mode of trial wherever there is doubt in the matter. In such cases, s.33 encourages the accused to opt for summary trial by limiting the maximum penalties thereon, by removing the power of the court to commit an offender to the Crown Court for greater sentence and by taking away the power of the court to change to committal proceedings.

s.22(5), see the notes to ss.18 and 20, *supra.* s.22(5) and (6) do not apply where the accused has been excluded from the court under s.18(3), *supra*, or where his legal representative signals consent in accordance with s.23. There is *no power* to commit for sentence under s.38 of the Act.

Fine, includes any pecuniary penalty: s.150(1) MCA 1980.

Definitely, the power in s.25, *infra*, to change from summary trial to committal proceedings does not apply to summary trial under s.22(2).

s.22(6), see note to s.22(5).

s.22(7), the object of this subsection is to allow the defendant to be tried on indictment when, although the criminal damage charge is a very minor one, there are other charges which may make a minor matter more serious, *per* Lord Lane CJ in *R v Tottenham Justices, ex p. Tibble* (1981) 73 Cr App R 55. This subsection will be repealed when [Sch.15] CJA 1988 comes into force.

A series of offences, to form part of a series the offences must be separated in time: *R v Hatfield Justices, ex p. Castle* [1981] 1 WLR 217; *R v Canterbury and St. Augustine's Justices, ex p. Klisiak, supra.* In *R v St Helens Justices, ex p. McClorie* [1983] 1 WLR 1332 (two criminal damage offences were held to be a series). In such a case the value of the damage is immaterial. But note that where other charges are eg withdrawn or no evidence is offered, a single surviving charge which is below the £400 limit cannot be committed for trial, and the court must proceed to summary trial: *R v Braden* (1987) *The Times*, 14 October.

The same or similar character An offence of common assault is not of similar character to an offence of criminal damage. Generally speaking, similar offences will be other offences under s.1 of Criminal Damage Act 1971: *R v Tottenham Justices, ex p. Tibble, supra*, disapproving *R v Leicester Justices, ex p. Lord* [1980] Crim LR 581. In *Re Prescott* (1980) 70 Cr App R 244, it was held that an offence of obstructing a police officer was not of the same or similar character as an offence of criminal damage to the officer's trousers. In *R v Hatfield Justices, ex p. Castle, supra*, it was held that threatening behaviour and obstruction were not similar to criminal damage. To be of similar character the other offence must be triable either way: *R v Hatfield Justices, ex p. Castle, supra: R v Considine* [1980] Crim LR 179. Where no evidence is offered in circumstances where the series ceases to exist, then the offence becomes triable summarily only, see *R v Braden, supra.*

Incitement to commit a schedule offence, is itself a scheduled offence: Sch.1, para 35.

s.22(8), this would not rule out an appeal to the High Court by way of case stated, eg, if the court came to a decision as to value for which there were no possible grounds. Nor would it prevent an appeal to the Crown Court against the making of a compensation order in a particular amount.

4.50   **Power of court, with consent of legally represented accused, to proceed in his absence**

23. (1) Where–

(a) the accused is represented by counsel or a solicitor who in his absence signifies to the court the accused's consent to the proceedings for determining how he is to be tried for the offence being conducted in his absence; and

(b) the court is satisfied that there is good reason for proceeding in the absence of the accused

the following provisions of this section shall apply.

(2) Subject to the following provisions of this section, the court may proceed in the absence of the accused in accordance with such of the provisions of ss.19 to 22 above, as are applicable in the circumstances.

(3) If, in a case where subs (1) of s.22 above applies, it appears to the court as mentioned in subs (4) of that section, subss (5) and (6) of that section shall not apply and the court–

(a) if the accused's consent to be tried summarily has been or is signified by the person representing him, shall proceed in accordance with subs (2) of that section as if that subsection applied; or

(b) if that consent has not been and is not so signified, shall proceed in accordance with subs (3) of that section as if that subsection applied.

(4) If, where the court has considered as required by s.19(1) above, it appears to the court that the offence is more suitable for summary trial then–

(a) if the accused's consent to be tried summarily has been or is signified by the person representing him, s.20 above shall not apply, and the court shall proceed to the summary trial of the information; or

(b) if that consent has not been and is not so signified, s.20 above shall not apply and the court shall proceed to inquire into the information as examining justices and may adjourn the hearing without remanding the accused.

(5) If, where the court has considered as required by s.19(1) above, it appears to the court that the offence is more suitable for trial on indictment, s.21 above shall not apply, and the court shall proceed to inquire into the information as examining justices and may adjourn the hearing without remanding the accused.

COMMENTARY

This section allows the accused's legal representative to signify his consent to the mode of trial proceedings being conducted in his absence. However, the court must also be satisfied that there is good reason for so proceeding. It is an exception to the general rule in s.18(2) that the accused must be personally present during the selection of the mode of trial. The court register must show whether the accused was present: r.66(6) MC Rules 1981.

This section does not relieve the accused, if he has been bailed to attend court, from his duty to surrender. This section has effect for the purposes set out in s.18(1), *supra*.

s.23(1)(a), when the court is not satisfied there is good reason for proceeding in the absence of the accused it may issue a summons or warrant under s.25, *infra*.

s.23(4)(a): Section 20, ie the caution must not be put.

s.23(4)(b), (5), when the hearing is adjourned without the accused being remanded, a summons or warrant may issue under s.25, *infra*.

4.51   **Summary trial of information against child or young person for indictable offence.**

24. (1) Where a person under the age of 17 appears or is brought before a magistrates' court on an information charging him with an indictable offence other than homicide, he shall be tried summarily unless–

(a) he has attained the age of 14 and the offence is such as is mentioned in subs (2) of s.53 of the Children and Young Persons Act 1933 (under which young persons convicted on indictment of certain grave crimes may be sentenced to be detained for long periods) and the court considers that if he is found guilty of the offence it ought to be possible to sentence him in pursuance of that subsection; or

(b) he is charged jointly with a person who has attained the age of 17 and the court considers it necessary in the interests of justice to commit them both for trial;

and accordingly in a case falling within para (a) or (b) of this subsection the court shall commit the accused for trial if either it is of the opinion that there is sufficient evidence to put him on trial or it has power under s.6(2) above so to commit him without consideration of the evidence.

(2) Where, in a case falling within subs (1)(b) above, a magistrates' court commits a person under the age of 17 for trial for an offence with which he is charged jointly with a person who has attained that age, the court may also commit him for trial for any other indictable offence with which he is charged at the same time (whether jointly with the person who has attained that age or not) if that other offence arises out of circumstances which are the same as or connected with those giving rise to the first-mentioned offence.

(3) If on trying a person summarily in pursuance of subs (1) above the court finds him guilty, it may impose a fine of an amount not exceeding £400 or may exercise the same powers as it could have exercised if he had been found guilty of an offence for which, but for s.1(1) of the Criminal Justice Act 1982, it could have sentenced him to imprisonment for a term not exceeding–

(a) the maximum term of imprisonment for the offence on conviction on indictment; or

(b) six months.

whichever is the less.

(4) In relation to a person under the age of 14 subs (3) above shall have effect as if for the words '£400' there were substituted the words '£100'; but this subsection shall cease to have effect on the coming into force of s.4 of the Children and Young Persons Act 1969 (which prohibits criminal proceedings against children).

[*as amended by Sch.14 Criminal Justice Act 1982, SI 1984 No 447*].

COMMENTARY

There are now no circumstances in which juveniles have a right to claim trial by jury but they must be so tried in the circumstances specified in s.24(1).

Justices are not obliged in taking a decision under this section to consider the evidence: they are merely required to hear representations and to determine in an interlocutory and preliminary fashion whether there should be a summary trial or whether there should be a committal for trial: *R v South Hackney Juvenile Court, ex p. RB (a minor) and CB (a minor)* (1983) 77 Cr App R 294. While no mention may be made in arriving at this decision of the defendant's bad character there is no harm in the defendant drawing to the attention of the court his good character: *R v South Hackney Juvenile Court, ex p. RB (a minor) and CB (a minor), supra.* Once the court has considered all factors placed before the court that are relevant to the exercise of its discretion and has ordered summary trial, there is no power to review the decision on the same material. Such a review is, however, permissible at any stage up to the beginning of summary trial if a change of circumstances has occurred or there are new or additional factors: *R v Newham Juvenile Court, ex p. F (a minor)* [1986] 3 All ER 17 (court purported to review determination by earlier bench): see also *R v Hammersmith Juvenile Court, ex p. O (a minor)* [1987] Crim LR 369. For the stage at which a juvenile acquires the adult's right to elect trial by jury for an indictable offence see under *Juveniles* at 4.08.

For the restrictions on evidence concerned with the sexual experience of a complainant in a rape offence see s.2 Sexual Offences (Amendment) Act 1976 and for their application to the trial of a juvenile under this section *ibid*, s.3(3).

The age of 17, for the determination of age, see s.150(4) MCA 1980.

A magistrates' court, not necessarily a juvenile court: see s.46 CYPA 1933 and s.18 CYPA 1963.

Indictable offence, see *Classification of Offences* in the introduction.

Homicide Homicide would appear to include the offence of causing death by reckless driving.

s.53(2) CYPA 1933 reads:
'Where a child or young person is convicted on indictment of (any offence punishable in the case of an adult with imprisonment for 14 years or more, not being an offence the sentence for which is fixed by law) and the court is of opinion that none of the other methods in which the case may legally be dealt with is suitable, the court may sentence the offender to be detained for such period (not exceeding the maximum term of imprisonment with which the offence is punishable in the case of an adult) as may be specified in the sentence; and where such sentence has been passed the child or young person shall, during that period . . . be liable to be detained in such place and on such conditions as the Secretary of State may direct.'

Charged jointly In *R v Newham Justices, ex p. Knight* [1976] Crim LR 323, the court accepted that a mother and child involved in the same incident but separately charged with theft could be regarded as having been jointly charged. To comply with s.24(1)(6), it is necessary that *both* adult and juvenile defendants appear before the court *at the same time*, but once any decision to commit both for trial has been made it is not essential that the committal proceedings in respect of each be held on the same occasion: *R v Doncaster Crown Court, ex p. Crown Prosecution Service* (1987) 151 JP 167.

Sufficient evidence, this relates to a committal under s.6(1), *supra*.

s.24(3), the powers of the adult court in dealing with a juvenile are restricted in accordance with s.7(8) CYPA 1969.

4.52   **Power to change from summary trial to committal proceedings and vice versa**
25. (1) Subsections (2) to (4) below shall have effect where a person who has attained the age of 17 appears or is brought before a magistrates' court on an information charging him with an offence triable either way.

(2) Where the court has (otherwise than in pursuance of s.22(2) above) begun to try the information summarily, the court may, at any time before the conclusion of the evidence for the prosecution, discontinue the summary trial and proceed to inquire into the information as examining justices and, on doing so, may adjourn the hearing without remanding the accused.

(3) Where the court has begun to inquire into the information as examining justices, then, if at any time during the inquiry it appears to the court, having regard to any representations made in the presence of the accused by the prosecutor, or made by the accused, and to the nature of the case, that the offence is after all more suitable for summary trial, the court may, after doing as provided in subs (4) below, ask the accused whether he consents to be tried summarily and, if he so consents, may proceed subject to subs (3A) below, to try the information summarily; but if the prosecution is being carried on by the Attorney General, the Solicitor General or the Director of Public Prosecutions, the court shall not act under this subsection without his consent.

(3A) Where the prosecution is being carried on by the Attorney General or the Solicitor General, the court shall not exercise the power conferred by subsection (3) above without his consent and, where the prosecution is being carried on by the Director of Public Prosecutions, shall not exercise that power if the Attorney General directs that it should not be exercised.

(4) Before asking the accused under subs (3) above whether he consents to be tried summarily, the court shall in ordinary language–
  (a) explain to him that it appears to the court more suitable for him to be tried summarily for the offence, but that this can only be done if he consents to be so tried; and
  (b) unless it has already done so, explain to him, as provided in s.20(2)(b) above, about the court's power to commit to the Crown Court for sentence.

(5) Where a person under the age of 17 appears or is brought before a

magistrates' court on an information charging him with an indictable offence other than homicide, and the court–

(a) has begun to try the information summarily on the footing that the case does not fall within para (a) or (b) of s.24(1) above and must therefore be tried summarily, as required by the said s.24(1); or

(b) has begun to inquire into the case as examining justices on the footing that the case does so fall,

subs (6) or (7) below, as the case may be, shall have effect.

(6) If, in a case falling within subs (5)(a) above, it appears to the court at any time before the conclusions of the evidence for the prosecution that the case is after all one which under the said s.24(1) ought not to be tried summarily, the court may discontinue the summary trial and proceed to inquire into the information as examining justices and, on doing so, may adjourn the hearing without remanding the accused.

(7) If, in a case falling within subs (5)(b) above, it appears to the court at any time during the inquiry that the case is after all one which under the said s.24(1) ought to be tried summarily, the court may proceed to try the information summarily.

[*as amended by Sch.1 Prosecution of Offences Act 1985*].

COMMENTARY

s.25(1): Attained the age of 17, for the determination of age, see s.150(4) MCA 1980.

s.25(2): The conclusion of the evidence for the prosecution Where a defendant has elected summary trial and pleaded not guilty, the justices have *no jurisdiction* to commit him for trial under s.25(2) without first having *begun* to hear evidence in the summary trial: see *R v St Helens Justices, ex p. Critchley* (1987) 152 JP 102; and where a plea of guilty is *unequivocal* justices cannot direct a plea of not guilty for the purposes of switching to committal proceedings under s.25(2): see *R v Telford Justices, ex p. Darlington* (1987) *The Times*, 23 November. Once a magistrates' court has either convicted or acquitted a defendant accused of an indictable offence, it has no power to change to committal proceedings: *R v Dudley Justices, ex p. Gillard* [1985] 3 WLR 936 (applicant consented to summary trial and pleaded guilty. His co-defendant elected to be tried at the Crown Court and after a remand in custody the magistrates decided to discontinue summary trial and commit both defendants for trial.)

The restrictions on press publicity do not apply to reports of a summary trial published or broadcast before a decision to change over to inquiry: s.8(8), *supra*. Where a bench of two justices failed to agree and the case had been put back for re-hearing it could not be said that the prosecution case had been concluded: *R v Coventry City Justices, ex p. Wilson* [1981] Crim LR 787.

Examining justice, see note to s.6, *supra*.

s.25(3), the procedure in s.25(3) only applies where a defendant appears or is brought before the court on an information charging him with an offence triable either way: *R v Cambridge Justices, ex p. Fraser* [1985] 1 WLR 1391. Witnesses who have already given evidence must be recalled for cross-examination: r.21 MC Rules 1981.

Representations, except in the cases mentioned later in this subsection the court is not bound by the representations but must consider them, if made. There would seem to be nothing to preclude the court from taking the initiative to effect a change-over to an inquiry so long as it gives the parties opportunity to make representations. Justices are entitled to refuse an application to change to summary trial where the election for trial on indictment was made in order to obtain the prosecution statements: *R v Warrington Justices, ex p. McDonagh* [1981] Crim LR 629.

The nature of the case, compare note to s.19.

If he consents, see note to s.20.

Try the information summarily, as to the receipt of evidence given in the inquiry see s.28.

s.25(7), see note to s.25(3), *supra*.

Power to issue summons to accused in certain circumstances **4.53**
26. (1) Where–
(a) in the circumstances mentioned in s.23(1)(a) above the court is not

satisfied that there is good reason for proceeding in the absence of the accused; or

(b) subss (4)(b) or (5) of s.23 or subss (2) or (6) of s.25 above applies, and the court adjourns the hearing in pursuance of that subsection without remanding the accused,

the justice or any of the justices of which the court is composed may issue a summons directed to the accused requiring his presence before the court.

(2) If the accused is not present at the time and place appointed–

(a) in a case within subs (1)(a) above, for the proceedings under s.19(1) above, as the case may be; or

(b) in a case within subs (1)(b) above, for the resumption of the hearing, the court may issue a warrant for his arrest.

COMMENTARY

s.26(1): Issue a summons, there is no power to issue a warrant at this stage.

s.26(2): Issue a warrant no further information is called for nor need the information be substantiated on oath.

4.54   Effect of dismissal of information for offence triable either way
27. Where on the summary trial of an information for an offence triable either way the court dismisses the information, the dismissal shall have the same effect as an acquittal on indictment.

COMMENTARY

Thus the defendant can plead *autrefois acquit* if subsequently indicted on the same offence: *Wemyss v Hopkins* (1875) 39 JP 549.

An offence triable either way, see *Classification of Offences* at 4.01.

4.55   Using in summary trial evidence given in committal proceedings
28. Where under ss.25(3) or (7) above a magistrates' court, having begun to inquire into an information as examining justices, proceeds to try the information summarily, then, subject to ss.102(9) and 103(3) below, any evidence already given before the court shall be deemed to have been given in and for the purposes of the summary trial.

COMMENTARY

Witnesses must be recalled for cross-examination unless not required by the accused or the prosecutor, r.21 MC Rules 1981. This section does not apply to written statements before examining justices under s.102, s.102(9).

Any evidence This section does not apply to written statements of child witnesses in sexual cases tendered under s.103, s.102(3).

4.56   Penalties on summary conviction for offences triable either way
32. (1) On summary conviction of any of the offences triable either way listed in Sch.1 to this Act a person shall be liable to imprisonment for a term not exceeding six months or to a fine not exceeding the prescribed sum or both, except that–

(a) a magistrates' court shall not have power to impose imprisonment for an offence so listed if the Crown Court would not have that power in the case of an adult convicted of it on indictment;

(b) on summary conviction of an offence consisting in the incitement to commit an offence triable either way a person shall not be liable to any greater penalty than he would be liable to on summary conviction of the last-mentioned offence.

(2) For any offence triable either way which is not listed in Sch.1 to this Act, being an offence under a relevant enactment, the maximum fine which may be imposed on summary conviction shall by virtue of this subsection be the

prescribed sum unless the offence is one for which by virtue of an enactment other than this subsection a larger fine may be imposed on summary conviction.

(3) Where, by virtue of any relevant enactment, a person summarily convicted of an offence triable either way would, apart from this section, be liable to a maximum fine of one amount in the case of a first conviction and of a different amount in the case of a second or subsequent conviction, subs (2) above shall apply irrespective of whether the conviction is a first, second or subsequent one.

(4) Subsection (2) above shall not affect so much of any enactment as (in whatever words) makes a person liable on summary conviction to a fine not exceeding a specified amount for each day on which a continuing offence is continued after conviction or the occurrence of any other specified event.

(5) Subsection (2) above shall not apply on summary conviction of any of the following offences–
(a) offences under s.5(2) of the Misuse of Drugs Act 1971 (having possession of a controlled drug) where the controlled drug in relation to which the offence was committed was a Class B or Class C drug;
(b) offences under the following provisions of that Act, where the controlled drug in relation to which the offence was committed was a Class C drug, namely–
  (i) section 4(2) (production, or being concerned in the production, of a controlled drug);
  (ii) section 4(3) (supplying or offering a controlled drug or being concerned in the doing of either activity by another);
  (iii) section 5(3) (having possession of a controlled drug with intent to supply it to another);
  (iv) section 8 (being the occupier, or concerned in the management, of premises and permitting of suffering certain activities to take place there);
  (v) section 12(6) (contravention of direction prohibiting practitioner etc. from possessing, supplying etc. controlled drugs).

(6) Where, as regards any offence triable either way, there is under any enactment (however framed or worded) a power by subordinate instrument to restrict the amount of the fine which on summary conviction can be imposed in respect of that offence–
(a) subsection (2) above shall not affect that power or override any restriction imposed in the exercise of that power; and
(b) the amount to which that fine may be restricted in the exercise of that power shall be any amount less than the maximum fine which could be imposed on summary conviction in respect of the offence apart from any restriction so imposed.

(7) Where there is under any relevant enactment (however framed or worded) a power by subordinate instrument to impose penal provisions, being a power which allows the creation of offences triable either way–
(a) the maximum fine which may in the exercise of that power be authorised on summary conviction in respect of an offence triable either way shall by virtue of this subsection be the prescribed sum unless some larger maximum fine can be authorised on summary conviction in respect of such an offence by virtue of an enactment other than this subsection; and
(b) subsection (2) above shall not override any restriction imposed in the exercise of that power on the amount of the fine which on summary conviction can be imposed in respect of an offence triable either way created in the exercise of the power.

(8) In subs (5) above 'controlled drug', 'Class B drug' and 'Class C drug' have the same meaning as in the Misuse of Drugs Act 1971.

(9) In this section–
'fine' includes a pecuniary penalty but does not include a pecuniary forfeiture or pecuniary compensation;
'the prescribed sum' means £2,000 or such sum as if for the time being substituted in this definition by an order in force under s.143(1) below;
'relevant enactment' means an enactment contained in the Criminal Law Act 1977 or in any Act passed before, or in the same Session as, that Act.
[*as amended by the Criminal Attempts Act 1981, Sch., SI 1984 No. 447*].

COMMENTARY
See generally HOC 39/1978.

s.32 (1): A fine, see s.32(9).

The prescribed sum, see s.32(9).

s.32 (2): This does not affect (a) continuing penalties (see s.32(4)); (b) limitation by subordinate instrument (see s.32(6) and (7)), or (c) the maximum term of imprisonment available which continues to be that prescribed in the relevant enactment, but not exceeding six months (s.31).

A relevant enactment, see s.32(9).

4.57   **Maximum penalties on summary conviction in pursuance of section 22**
33. (1) Where in pursuance of subs (2) of s.22 above a magistrates' court proceeds to the summary trial of an information, then, if the accused is summarily convicted of the offence–
(a) the court shall not have power to impose on him in respect of that offence imprisonment for more than three months or a fine greater than £1,000; and
(b) section 38 below shall not apply as regards that offence.
(2) In subs (1) above 'fine' includes a pecuniary penalty but does not include a pecuniary forfeiture or pecuniary compensation.
[*as amended by SI 1984 No 447*].

COMMENTARY
s.33(1), note that the terms of para (a) do not prescribe the maximum penalty available in a trial under s.22(2); they are merely limitations on the penalty allowed in s.32. The effect of the two sections read together therefore is that the maximum penalty in a s.22(2) case is imprisonment for a term not exceeding three months or a fine of £1,000 or both.
    This section does not appear to preclude a committal to the Crown Court to be dealt with under the distinctly separate provisions of s.56 CJA 1967, where the offender is already being committed for sentence in respect of another offence: see generally Chapter 8E *post.*

NB
For s.102 MCA 1980 see Chapter 6, Evidence.

4.58   **Evidence of children in committal proceedings for sexual offences**
103. (1) In any proceedings before a magistrates' court inquiring into a sexual offence as examining justices–
(a) a child shall not be called as a witness for the prosecution; but
(b) any statement made in writing by or taken in writing from the child shall be admissible in evidence of any matter of which his oral testimony would be admissible,
except in a case where the application of this subsection is excluded under subs (2) below.

(2) Subsection (1) above shall not apply–
(a) where at or before the time when such a statement is tendered in evidence the defence objects to the application of that subsection; or
(b) where the prosecution requires the attendance of the child for the purpose of establishing the identity of any person; or
(c) where the court is satisfied that it has not been possible to obtain from the child a statement that may be given in evidence under this section; or

(d) where the inquiry into the offence takes place after the court has discontinued to try it summarily and the child has given evidence in the summary trial.

(3) Section 28 above shall not apply to any statement admitted in pursuance of subs (1) above.

(4) In this section 'child' has the same meaning as in the Children and Young Persons Act 1933 and 'sexual offence' means any offence under the Sexual Offences Act 1956 or the Indency with Children Act 1960 or s.1(1)(a) of the Protection of Children Act 1978, or any attempt to commit such an offence.

COMMENTARY

s.103 is replaced by a new section (see below) when [s.32] CJA 1988 comes into force.

s.103(1), before a statement is received in evidence under this subsection its effect must be explained to an unrepresented defendant in ordinary language and, if he does not object to its operation, he must be informed that he may ask questions about the circumstances in which the statement was made or taken: r.7(4) MC Rules 1981.

Child, see s.103(4) and note thereto.

Sexual offence, see s.103(4).

Shall not be called as a witness, this does not seemingly preclude the use of written statements under s.102, *supra*, but note the comments thereto under the heading *Liable to Prosecution*.

In writing, includes typing, printing, lithography, photography and other modes of representing or reproducing words in a visible form: Interpretation Act 1978, Sch.1. The statement must be made an exhibit: r.7(5) MC Rules 1981.

Subs (4): Child, defined in s.107 CYPA 1933, as 'a person under the age of 14 years'.

Evidence of persons under 14 in committal proceedings for assault, sexual offences etc.

103. *(1) In any proceedings before a magistrates' court inquiring into an offence to which this section applies as examining justices–*

(a) a child shall not be called as a witness for the prosecution; but

(b) any statement made by or taken from a child shall be admissible in evidence of any matter of which his oral testimony would be admissible,

except in a case where the application of this subsection is excluded under subsection (3) below.

(2) This section applies–

(a) to an offence which involves an assault, or injury or a threat of injury to, a person;

(b) to an offence under section 1 of the Children and Young Persons Act 1933 (cruelty to persons under 16);

(c) to an offence under the Sexual Offences Act 1956, the Indecency with Children Act 1960, the Sexual Offences Act 1967, section 54 of the Criminal Law Act 1977 or the Protection of Children Act 1978; and

(d) to an offence which consists of attempting or conspiring to commit, or of aiding, abetting, counselling, procuring or inciting the commission of, an offence falling within paragraph (a), (b) or (c) above.

(3) The application of subsection (1) above is excluded–

(a) where at or before the time when the statement is tendered in evidence the defence objects to its admission; or

(b) where the prosecution requires the attendance of the child for the purpose of establishing the identity of any person; or

(c) where the court is satisfied that it has not been possible to obtain from the child a statement that may be given in evidence under this section; or

(d) where the inquiry into the offence takes place after the court has discontinued to try it summarily and the child has given evidence in the summary trial.

(4) Section 28 above shall not apply to any statement admitted in pursuance of subsection (1) above.

(5) In this section 'child' means a person under the age of 14.

COMMENTARY

As substituted by [s.32] CJA 1988.

4.59   **Deposition of person dangerously ill**
105. (1) Where a person appears to a justice of the peace to be able and willing to give material information relating to an indictable offence, and–
  (a) the justice is satisfied, on a representation made by a duly qualified medical practitioner, that the person able and willing to make the statement is dangerously ill and unlikely to recover, and
  (b) it is not practicable for examining justices to take the evidence of the sick person in accordance with the provisions of this Act and the rules, the justice may take in writing the deposition of the sick person on oath.

(2) A deposition taken under this section may be given in evidence before examining justices inquiring into an information against the offender or in repect of the offence to which the deposition relates, but subject to the same conditions as apply, under s.6 of the Criminal Law Amendment Act 1867, to its being given in evidence upon the trial of the offender or offence.

COMMENTARY

s.105(1): A justice of the peace, not necessarily one of the examining justices.

Indictable offence, see *Classification of Offences* at 4.01.

Duly qualified medical practitioner, ie a person fully registered under the Medical Act 1956, s.52 *ibid.*

The justice may take It was held under the previously existing provisions that a magistrate was bound to attend a witness who is dangerously ill: *R v Bros, ex p. Hardy* (1910) 74 JP 483. Reasonable notice must be given to the other side of the intention to take the deposition and full opportunity of cross-examining allowed. The procedure for taking the deposition is set out in r.33(1),(2) MC Rules 1981. The depositions must be sent to the examining justice or the court of trial: r.33(3).

In writing, includes typing, printing, lithography, photography and other modes of representing or reproducing words in a visible form: Sch.1 Interpretation Act 1978.

s.105(2): Section 6 of the Criminal Law Amendment Act 1867, this permits the deposition to be read at the trial if the person who made it is dead or there is no reasonable probability that such person will ever be able to travel or give evidence, provided certain conditions are satisfied.

4.60   **False written statements tendered in evidence**
106. (1) If any person in a written statement tendered in evidence in criminal proceedings by virtue of s.102 above wilfully makes a statement material in those proceedings which he knows to be false or does not believe to be true, he shall be liable on conviction on indictment to imprisonment for a term not exceeding two years or a fine or both.

(2) The Perjury Act 1911 shall have effect as if this section were contained in that Act.

COMMENTARY

s.106(2), an effect is that an offence under s.106(1) is triable either way: Sch.1, para 14, *infra.*

4.61   **SCHEDULE 1**

Offences triable either way by virtue of section 17
  1. Offences at common law of public nuisance.

2. Offences under s.8 of the Disorderly Houses Act 1751 (appearing to be keeper of bawdy house etc.).

3. Offences consisting in contravention of s.13 of the Statutory Declarations Act 1835 (administration by a person of an oath etc. touching matters in which he has no jurisdiction).

4. Offences under s.36 of the Malicious Damage Act 1861 (obstructing engines or carriages on railways).

5. Offences under the following provisions of the Offences Against the Person Act 1861–
   (a) section 16 (threats to kill);
   (b) section 20 (inflicting bodily injury, with or without a weapon);
   (c) section 26 (not providing apprentices or servants with food etc.);
   (d) section 27 (abandoning or exposing child);
   (e) section 34 (doing or omitting to do anything so as to endanger railway passengers);
   (f) section 36 (assaulting a clergyman at a place of worship etc.);
   (g) section 38 (assault with intent to resist apprehension);
   (h) section 47 (assault occasioning bodily harm – *common assault*);
   (i) section 57 (bigamy);
   (j) section 60 (concealing birth of a child).

6. Offences under s.20 of the Telegraph Act 1868 (disclosing or intercepting messages).

7. Offences under s.13 of the Debtors Act 1868 (transactions intended to defraud creditors).

8. Offences under s.5 of the Public Stores Act 1875 (obliteration of marks with intent to conceal).

9. Offences under s.12 of the Corn Returns Act 1882 (false returns).

10. Offences under s.22 of the Electric Lighting Act 1882 (injuring works with intent to cut off electricity supply).

11. Offences under s.3 of the Submarine Telegraph Act 1885 (damaging submarine cables).

12. Offences under s.13 of the Stamp Duties Management Act 1891 (offences in relation to dies and stamps).

13. Offences under s.8(2) of the Cremation Act 1902 (making false representations etc. with a view to procuring the burning of any human remains).

14. All offences under the Perjury Act 1911 except offences under–
   (a) section 1 (perjury in judicial proceedings);
   (b) section 3 (false statements etc. with reference to marriage);
   (c) section 4 (false statements etc. as to births or deaths).

15. (*Repealed*).

16. Offences under s.17 of the Deeds of Arrangement Act 1914 (trustee making preferential payments).

17. Offences under s.3(4) of the Checkweighing in Various Industries Act 1919 (false statements).

18. Offences under s.8(2) of the Census Act 1920 (disclosing census information).

19. Offences under s.36 of the Criminal Justice Act 1925 (forgery of passports etc.).

20. Offences under s.11 of the Agricultural Credits Act 1928 (frauds by farmers).

21. (*Repealed*).

22. Offences under the following provisions of the Post Office Act 1953–
    (a) section 53 (unlawfully taking away or opening mail bag);
    (b) section 55 (fraudulent retention of mail bag or postal packet);
    (c) section 57 (stealing, embezzlement, destruction etc. by officer of Post Office of postal packet);
    (d) section 58 (opening or delaying of postal packets by officers of the Post Office).

23. Offences under the following provisions of the Sexual Offences Act 1956–
    (a) section 6 (unlawful sexual intercourse with a girl under 16);
    (b) section 13 (indecency between men);
    (c) section 26 (permitting a girl under 16 to use premises for sexual intercourse).

24. Offences under s.3(1) of the Shipping Contracts and Commercial Documents Act 1964 (offences), so far as it relates to the contravention of any directions given under that Act before March 20, 1980.

25. (*Repealed*).

26. The following offences under the Criminal Law Act 1967–
    (a) offences under s.4(1) (assisting offenders); and
    (b) offences under s.5(1) (concealing arrestable offences and giving false information),
    where the offence to which they relate is triable either way.

27. Offences under s.4(1) of the Sexual Offences Act 1967 (procuring others to commit homosexual acts).

28. All indictable offences under the Theft Act 1968 except–
    (a) robbery, aggravated burglary, blackmail and assault with intent to rob;
    (b) burglary comprising the commission of, or an intention to commit, an offence which is triable only on indictment;
    (c) burglary in a dwelling if any person in the dwelling was subjected to violence or the threat of violence.

29. Offences under the following provisions of the Criminal Damage Act 1971–
    section 1(1) (destroying or damaging property);
    section 1(1) and (3) (arson);
    section 2 (threats to destroy or damage property);
    section 3 (possessing anything with intent to destroy or damage property).

30. Offences in relation to stamps issued for the purpose of national insurance under the provisions of any enactments as applied to those stamps.

31. (*Repealed*).

32. Committing an indecent assault upon a person whether male or female.

33. Aiding, abetting, counselling or procuring the commission of any offence listed in the preceding paragraphs of this schedule except para 26.

34. (*Repealed*).

35. Any offence consisting in the incitement to commit an offence triable either way except an offence mentioned in para 33.
    [*as amended by Sch. Criminal Attempts Act 1981, Sch. Forgery and Counterfeiting Act 1981, Sch.1 Housing (Consequential Provisions Act 1985, s.32(2) Wages Act 1986 and the words in italics in para 5(h) will be repealed when [Sch.15] CJA 1988 comes into force*].

COMMENTARY

This schedule is *not a complete list* of all offences triable either way: see the commentary to s.18, *supra*. In *R v Cardiff City Magistrates' Court, ex p. Cardiff City Council* (1987) *The Times*, 24 February, summary proceedings were quashed as a nullity where the 'either way' procedure was not followed in respect of a 'non-scheduled' either way offence under s.89 Town and Country Planning Act 1971; see also *R v Tottenham Justices, ex p. Arthur's Transport Services* [1981] Crim LR 180. Note also the effect of para 3, Pt II of Sch.6 to the Firearms Act 1968 on offences contained in Sch.1 MCA 1980, see 4.33a, *ante*.

Para 5(h): s.47 of the Offences Against the Person Act 1861, *R v Harrow Justices, ex p. Osaseri* [1986] QB 589, appears to decide:
1. Section 47 Offences Against the Person Act 1861 creates a statutory offence of assault occasioning actual bodily harm which, by virtue of s.17 and Sch.1 MCA 1980, is triable either way.
2. Section 47 also creates an entirely independent offence of 'common assault', which is also triable either way.
3. A complaint for 'common assault' (only) made *by or on behalf of the person aggrieved, is triable summarily at the discretion of the justices* under s.42. *If the justices do so decide* to try the matter summarily, then *the accused has no right to elect trial by jury.*
4. The justices have a general discretion to refuse jurisdiction and therefore to commit for trial under s.46, this in addition to the specific ouster cases mentioned under that section. The offence then becomes triable on indictment only.
5. *If there remains an offence of common assault at common law* it is triable only on indictment.
Note that under [s.38] CJA 1988, when in force, all offences of common assault become triable summarily only.

Para 33: Aiding, abetting, any offence consisting in aiding, abetting, counselling or procuring the commission of an offence triable either way *not* listed in this schedule is triable either way: s.44(2).

Para 35: Incitement, the offender is not liable to any greater penalty than if convicted summarily of the completed act: s.32(1)(b).

SCHEDULE 2   4.62

Offences for which the value involved is relevant to the mode of trial (Section 22)

Offence	*Value involved*	*How measured*
1. Offences under s.1 of the Criminal Damage Act 1971 (destroying or damaging property) excluding any offence committed by destroying or damaging property by fire.	As regards property alleged to have been destroyed, its value.	What the property would probably have cost to buy in the open market at the material time,
	As regards property alleged to have been damaged, the value of the alleged damage.	(a) If immediately after the material time the damage was capable of repair– (i) what would probably then have been the market price for the repair of the damage, or (ii) what the property alleged to have been damaged would probably have cost to buy in the open market at the material time, whichever is the less;

Offence	Value involved	How measured
		or
		(b) If immediately after the material time the damage was beyond repair, what the said property would probably have cost to buy in the open market at the material time.
2. The following offences, namely– (a) aiding, abetting, counselling or procuring the commission of any offence mentioned in para 1 above; (b) attempting to commit any offence so mentioned; and (c) inciting another to commit any offence so mentioned.	The value indicated in para 1 above for the offence alleged to have been aided, abetted, counselled or procured, or attempted or incited.	As for the corresponding entry in para 1 above.

CRIMINAL JUSTICE ACT 1987

4.63   **Notices of transfer and designated authorities**
    4. (1) If–
    (a) a person has been charged with an indictable offence; and
    (b) in the opinion of an authority designated by subsection (2) below or of one of such an authority's officers acting on the authority's behalf the evidence of the offence charged–
        (i) would be sufficient for the person charged to be committed for trial; and
        (ii) reveals a case of fraud of such seriousness and complexity that it is appropriate that the management of the case should without delay be taken over by the Crown Court; and
    (c) before the magistrates' court in whose jurisdiction the offence has been charged begins to inquire into the case as examining justices the authority or one of the authority's officers acting on the authority's behalf gives the court a notice (in this Act referred to as a 'notice of transfer') certifying that opinion,
the functions of the magistrates' court shall cease in relation to the case, except as provided by section 5(3) and (8) below and by section 28(7A) of the Legal Aid Act 1974.

    (2) The authorities mentioned in subsection (1) above (in this Act referred to as 'designated authorities') are–
    (a) the Director of Public Prosecutions;
    (b) the Director of the Serious Fraud Office;
    (c) the Commissioners of Inland Revenue;
    (d) the Commissioners of Customs and Excise; and
    (e) the Secretary of State.

    (3) A designated authority's decision to give notice of transfer shall not be subject to appeal or liable to be questioned in any court.

4.64   **Notices of transfer – procedure**
    5. (1) A notice of transfer shall specify the proposed place of trial and in selecting that place the designated authority shall have regard to the con-

siderations to which section 7 of the Magistrates' Courts Act 1980 requires a magistrates' court committing a person for trial to have regard when selecting the place at which he is to be tried.

(2) A notice of transfer shall specify the charge or charges to which it relates and include or be accompanied by such additional matter as regulations under subsection (9) below may require.

(3) If a magistrates' court has remanded a person to whom a notice of transfer relates in custody, it shall have power, subject to section 4 of the Bail Act 1976 and regulations under section 22 of the Prosecution of Offences Act 1985–

(a) to order that he shall be safely kept in custody until delivered in due course of law; or

(b) to release him on bail in accordance with the Bail Act 1976, that is to say, by directing him to appear before the Crown Court for trial;

and where his release on bail is conditional on his providing one or more surety or sureties and, in accordance with section 8(3) of the Bail Act 1976, the court fixes the amount in which the surety is to be bound with a view to his entering into his recognizance subsequently in accordance with subsections (4) and (5) or (6) of that section, the court shall in the meantime make an order such as is mentioned in paragraph (a) of this subsection.

(4) If the conditions specified in subsection (5) below are satisfied, a court may exercise the powers conferred by subsection (3) above without the person charged being brought before it in any case in which by virtue of section 128(3A) of the Magistrates' Courts Act 1980 it would have power further to remand him on an adjournment such as is mentioned in that subsection.

(5) The conditions mentioned in subsection (4) above are–

(a) that the person charged has given his written consent to the powers conferred by subsection (3) above being exercised without his being brought before the court; and

(b) that the court is satisfied that, when he gave his consent, he knew that the notice of transfer had been issued.

(6) Where notice of transfer is given after the person charged has been remanded on bail to appear before examining justices on an appointed day, the requirement that he shall so appear shall cease on the giving of the notice, unless the notice states that it is to continue.

(7) Where the requirement that a person charged shall appear before examining justices ceases by virtue of subsection (6) above, it shall be his duty to appear before the Crown Court at the place specified by the notice of transfer as the proposed place of trial or at any place substituted for it by a direction under section 76 of the Supreme Court Act 1981.

(8) For the purposes of the Criminal Procedure (Attendance of Witnesses) Act 1965–

(a) any magistrates' court for the petty sessions area for which the court from which a case was transferred sits shall be treated as examining magistrates; and

(b) a person whose written statement is tendered in evidence for the purposes of the notice of transfer shall be treated as a person who has been examined by the court.

(9) The Attorney General–

(a) shall by regulations make provisions requiring the giving of a copy of a notice of transfer, together with a statement of the evidence on which any charge to which it relates is based–

(i) to the person charged; and

(ii) to the Crown Court sitting at the proposed place of trial;

and

(b) may by regulations make such further provision in relation to notices of transfer, including provision as to the duties of a designated authority in relation to such notices, as appears to him to be appropriate.

(10) The power to make regulations conferred by subsection (9) above shall be exercisable by statutory instrument subject to annulment in pursuance of a resolution of either House of Parliament.

(11) Any such regulations may make different provision with respect to different cases or classes of case.

4.65   *Note:*

Relevant parts of sections 1 to 3 which concern, *inter alia*, the duties and investigative powers of the Director of Serious Fraud and the issue of warrants by justices in response to applications by the Director and members of his office are reproduced in Chapter 12, and see generally Warrants under the Criminal Justice Act 1987 in that chapter.

Sections 6 to 11 of the Act deal with procedures in the Crown Court including applications to a judge to dismiss (s.6); preparatory hearings (ss.7–9); and reporting restrictions (s.11); as noted in the introduction, but not reproduced herein.

SCHEDULE 1

4.66   **Procedure**

4. (1) Where any enactment (whenever passed) prohibits the taking of any step–
 (a) except by the Director of Public Prosecutions or except by him or another; or
 (b) without the consent of the Director of Public Prosecutions or without his consent or the consent of another,
it shall not prohibit the taking of any such step by the Director of the Serious Fraud Office.

(2) Northern Ireland.

5. (1) Where the Director has the conduct of any criminal proceedings in England and Wales, the Director of Public Prosecutions shall not in relation to those proceedings be subject to any duty by virtue of section 3(2) of the Prosecution of Offences Act 1985.

(2) Northern Ireland.

6. (1) Where the Director or any member of the Serious Fraud Office designated for the purposes of section 1(4) above ('designated official') gives notice to any justice of the peace that he has instituted, or is conducting, any criminal proceedings in England and Wales, the justice shall–
 (a) at the prescribed time and in the prescribed manner; or
 (b) in a particular case, at the time and in the manner directed by the Attorney General;
send him every recognizance, information, certificate, deposition, document and thing connected with those proceedings which the justice is required by law to deliver to the appropriate officer of the Crown Court.

(2) Northern Ireland.

(3), (4) *Regulations.*

7–9 *Regulations.*

MAGISTRATES' COURTS RULES 1981
SI 1981 No 552, as amended.

4.67   **Restrictions on reports of committal proceedings**

5. (1) Except in a case where evidence is, with the consent of the accused, to be given in his absence under s.4(4)(b) of the Act of 1980 (absence caused by ill health), a magistrates' court acting as examining justices shall before admitting in evidence any written statement or taking depositions of witnesses in accordance with r.7 explain to the accused the restrictions on reports of committal proceedings imposed by s.8 of the Act of 1980 and inform him of his right to apply to the court for an order removing those restrictions.

(2) Where a magistrates' court has made an order under s.8(2) of the Act of 1980 removing restrictions on the reports of committal proceedings, such order shall be entered in the register.

(3) Where the court adjourns any such proceedings to another day, the court shall, at the beginning of any adjourned hearing, state that the order has been made.

COMMENTARY

Para (1): Explain to the accused.
'It is not intended that this should be done at hearings which are only remand proceedings and at which the prosecution does not present the evidence against the accused; at these hearings the accused may not be represented; it might be unfair to expect him to make this decision without proper advice at so early a stage; and the case may, in the event, be tried summarily. It is therefore suggested that the information should be given to the accused at the beginning of the committal proceedings proper, ie before depositions are taken or written statements tendered in evidence. It should be borne in mind that the accused may apply to the court for an order at any time during the proceedings (in which event the order will be applied retrospectively), but the court may think it advisable, in appropriate cases, to remind the accused that if his application is deferred until a later stage in the proceedings there is likely to be less opportunity for the evidence to be reported.

Where no reporter is present in court when the restrictions are lifted the Home Office suggest that the court should consider adjourning the case for a short period to enable the press to attend':
[HOC 109/1968].

Committal for trial without consideration of evidence   **4.68**
 6. (1) This rule applies to committal proceedings where the accused has a solicitor acting for him in the case (whether present in court or not) and where the court has been informed that all the evidence for the prosecution is in the form of written statements copies of which have been given to the accused.

(2) A magistrates' court inquiring into an offence in committal proceedings to which this rule applies shall cause the charge to be written down, if this has not already been done, and read to the accused and shall then ascertain whether he wishes to–
    (a) object to any of the prosecution statements being tendered in evidence;
    (b) give evidence himself or call witnesses; or
    (c) submit that the prosecution statements disclose insufficient evidence to put him on trial by jury for the offence with which he is charged.

(3) If the court is satisfied that the accused or, as the case may be, each of the accused does not wish to take any of the steps mentioned in sub-paras. (a), (b) and (c) of para (2) and determines, after receiving any written statements tendered by the prosecution and the defence under s.102 of the Act of 1980, to commit the accused for trial without consideration of the evidence, the court shall proceed in accordance with para (4) and in any other case shall proceed in accordance with r.7.

(4) The court shall then say to the accused–

'You will be committed for trial but I must warn you that at that trial you may not be permitted to give evidence of an alibi or to call witnesses in support of an alibi unless you have earlier given particulars of the alibi and of the witnesses. You or your solicitor may give those particulars now to this court or at any time in the next seven days to the solicitor for the prosecution.', or words to that effect.

Provided that the court shall not be required to give this warning in any case where it appears to the court that, having regard to the nature of the offence with which the accused is charged, it is unnecessary to do so.

(5) Where the court has given to the accused the warning required by para (4) the clerk of the court shall give to him written notice of the provisions of s.11 of the Criminal Justice Act 1967, about giving notice of particulars of alibi to the solicitor for the prosecution and the solicitor's name and address shall be stated in the notice.

COMMENTARY

This rule applies to committal proceedings under s.6(2) MCA 1980.

The effect of this and the preceding rule is that a committal by consent proceeds as follows:

(i) The court explains the restrictions on reports of committal proceedings and informs the defendant of his right to apply for an order removing them.
(ii) The prosecution informs the court that all their evidence is in the form of written statements, copies of which have been given to all defendants.
(iii) The court verifies that the defendant has a solicitor acting for him (whether present or not).
(iv) The clerk reads the charge.
(v) The court asks the defendant if he:
    (a) objects to any of the written statements being put in;
    (b) wishes to give evidence or call witnesses; or
    (c) is making a submission of no case.

Provided that none of these questions is answered in the affirmative, the defendant is given the alibi warning: otherwise the proceedings revert to the conventional form under r.7, *infra*: *R v Pontypool JJ, ex p. McCann* [1969] Crim LR 148.

The magistrate may delegate to his clerk his duty to inform the defendant of his rights at a committal: *R v Horseferry Road Justices, ex p. Farooki* (1982) *The Times*, 29 October.

Proviso to para (4), the discretion resides in the court, not the parties.

Para (5): written notice of the provisions of s.11. See Form 24.

4.69   **Taking depositions of witnesses and statement of accused**

7. (1) This rule does not apply to committal proceedings where under s.6(2) of the Act of 1980 a magistrates' court commits a person for trial without consideration of the evidence.

(2) A magistrates' court inquiring into an offence as examining justices shall cause the evidence of each witness, including the evidence of the accused, but not including any witness of his merely to his character, to be put into writing; and as soon as may be after the examination of such a witness shall cause his deposition to be read to him in the presence and hearing of the accused, and shall require the witness to sign the deposition:

Provided that where the evidence has been given in the absence of the accused under s.4(4) of the Act of 1980 this shall be recorded on the deposition of the witness and the deposition need not be read in the presence and hearing of the accused.

(3) The depositions shall be authenticated by a certificate signed by one of the examining justices.

(4) Where the accused is not represented by counsel or a solicitor, before a statement made in writing by or taken in writing from a child is received in evidence under subs (1) of s.103 of the Act of 1980 the court shall cause the effect of that subsection to be explained to the accused in ordinary language and, if the defence does not object to the applications of that subsection, shall inform him that he may ask questions about the circumstances in which the statement was made or taken.

(5) Any such statement as aforesaid which is received in evidence shall be made an exhibit.

(6) After the evidence for the prosecution (including any statements tendered under s.102 of the Act of 1980, has been given and after hearing any submission, if any is made, the court shall, unless it then decides not to commit for trial, cause the charge to be written down, if this has not already been done, and, if the accused is not represented by counsel or a solicitor, shall read the charge to him and explain it in ordinary language.

*[(7) The courts shall then ask the accused whether he wishes to say anything in answer to the charge and, if he is not represented by counsel or a solicitor, shall before asking the question say to him–

'You will have an opportunity to give evidence on oath before us and to call witnesses. But first I am going to ask you whether you wish to say anything in answer to the charge. You need not say anything unless you wish to do so. Anything you say will be taken down and may be used in evidence at your trial. You should take no notice of any promise or threat which any person may have made to persuade you to say anything',

or words to that effect.]

*[(8) Whatever the accused says in answer to the charge shall be put into writing, read over to him and signed by one of the examining justices and also, if the accused wishes, by him.]

(9) The court shall then say to the accused–

'I must warn you that if this court should commit you for trial you may not be permitted at that trial to give evidence of an alibi or to call witnesses in support of an alibi unless you have earlier given particulars of the alibi and of the witnesses. You may give those particulars now to this court or to the solicitor for the prosecution not later than seven days from the end of these committal proceedings.',

or words to that effect and, if it appears to the court that the accused may not understand the meaning of the term 'alibi', the court shall explain it to him:

Provided that the court shall not be required to give this warning in any case where it appears to the court that, having regard to the nature of the offence with which the accused is charged, it is unnecessary to do so.

(10) After complying with the requirements of this rule relating to the statement of the accused, and whether or not he has made a statement in answer to the charge, the court shall give him an opportunity to give evidence himself and to call witnesses.

(11) Where the accused is represented by counsel or a solicitor, his counsel or solicitor shall be heard on his behalf, either before or after the evidence for the defence is taken, at his discretion, and may, if the accused gives evidence himself and calls witnesses, be heard on his behalf with the leave of the court both before and after the evidence is taken:

Provided that, where the court gives leave to counsel or the solicitor for the accused to be heard after, as well as before, the evidence is taken, counsel or the solicitor for the prosecution shall be entitled to be heard immediately before counsel or the solicitor for the accused is heard for the second time.

(12) Where the court determines to commit the accused for trial in respect of a charge which differs from that which was read to him in accordance with the provisions of para (6), the court shall cause the new charge to be read to him.

(13) Where the court has given to the accused the warning required by para (9) the clerk of the court shall give to him written notice of the provisions of s.11 of the Criminal Justice Act 1967 about giving notice of particulars of alibi to the solicitor for the prosecution and the solicitor's name and address shall be stated in the notice.

*It would appear that both these paragraphs have been repealed by the Criminal Justice Act 1982, s.72.

COMMENTARY

Para (2): Cause the evidence . . . to be put in writing Statements voluntarily interposed by the defendant should, if material, be taken down: *R v Walker* (1846) 2 Car & Kir 223; *R v Watson* (1851) 3 Car & Kir 111.

It is improper for depositions taken in respect of one defendant to be read over and confirmed in the inquiry respecting another co-defendant subsequently joined: *R v Phillips, R v Quayle* (1938) 102 JP 467. In *Ex p. Bottomley* (1909) 73 JP 246, it was held that where in a preliminary inquiry a magistrate was unable to conclude a case the witnesses who had already given evidence might affirm their earlier depositions before a different justice if the depositions were read over to them and they were given the opportunity to correct inaccuracies and make additions. The defendant must be allowed to cross-examine even if he did so on the earlier occasion. *Bottomley's* case was partially distinguished in *R v Phillips, supra,* and the force of this decision must now be doubted. *Prejudicial evidence* should go 'unvarnished' into the depositions, any editing may be done at the trial: *R v Weaver* [1967] 2 WLR 1244.

Read to him in the presence and hearing of the accused Where the depositions were not taken in the presence of the justice or defendant, the fact that they were subsequently read over in their presence does not cure the defect: *R v Christopher, Smith and Thornton* (1850) 14 JP 83; and this applies equally to the practice of giving the heads of evidence before the magistrate and detailed depositions before the clerk: *R v Watts* (1863) 27 JP 821. In *R v Bates* (1860) 2 F & F 317, the practice of taking abbreviated notes before the justice which were copied out in full, read before the justice and defendant and signed was not condemned. But in *R v Gee, R v Bibby, R v Dunscombe* (1936) 100 JP 227 (in which *R v Bates, supra,* was not referred to) the practice of checking in court a proof of evidence which had been taken otherwise than in the presence of the defendant was disapproved, and this is certainly the safer view: see also *R v Wharmby, Lindley and Lindley* (1946) 31 Cr App R 174.

Require the witness to sign the deposition, this is merely directory and not a condition of admissibility at the trial on indictment, *per* Wills J in *R v Holloway* (1901) 65 JP 712.

Para (3): A certificate, see Form 16. The Court of Criminal Appeal refused to set aside convictions on the ground that depositions taken on three separate days were not signed as to one of those days: *R v Edgar, etc.* (1958) 42 Cr App R 192.

Para 6: this paragraph is wholly procedural. An examining magistrate has a discretion after the prosecution have closed their case to adjourn the hearing to allow the prosecution to call a witness to clarify his written statement: *R v West London Justices, ex p. Kaminski* [1983] Crim LR 40.

Para (7), (8): see footnote in the text.

Para (9): The meaning of the term 'alibi', see s.11(8) CJA 1967.

Para (10): Opportunity to give evidence himself and to call witnesses, justices should not discourage witnesses for the defence from giving evidence at this stage, *per* Channell J in *R v Nicholson* (1909) 73 JP 347. The defendant is not precluded from giving evidence simply because his submission of no case has been overruled: *R v Horseferry Rd. Magistrates' Court, ex p. Adams* (1978) 142 JP 127.

Para (13): Written notice, see Form 24.

4.70   **Order for attendance of witness at court of trial**

8. (1) A witness order under s.1 of the Criminal Procedure (Attendance of Witnesses) Act 1965 shall be in the prescribed form and shall be served on the witnesses as soon as practicable after the accused has been committed for trial:

Provided that where, at the conclusion of the examination of a witness, the court determines that the witness order shall be a conditional order, the order shall be served on him immediately after the deposition has been signed.

(2) Where a court has directed under subs (2)(b) of the said s.1 that a witness order shall be treated as a conditional order, it shall give notice to the witness in the prescribed form.

(3) If a witness order has been made as aforesaid and the court determines not to commit the accused for trial, it shall give notice to the witness that he is no longer required to attend.

(4) A notice given under this rule shall be in writing and signed by one of the justices composing the court or the clerk of the court.

(5) A witness order under the said s.1 and a notice given under this rule shall be served by delivering it to the witness or by leaving it for him with some person at his last known or usual place of abode or by sending it by post in a letter addressed to him at his last known or usual place of abode.

COMMENTARY
Para (1): Witness order, see Form 22.

Para (2): see Form 23.

Notice to governor of prison of committal on bail   **4.71**
9. (1) Where the accused is committed for trial on bail, the clerk of the court shall give notice thereof in writing to the governor of the prison to which persons of the sex of the person committed are committed by that court if committed in custody for trial and also, if the person committed is under 21, to the governor of the remand centre to which he would have been committed if the court had refused him bail.

(2) Where a corporation is committed for trial, the clerk of the court shall give notice thereof to the governor of the prison to which would be committed a man committed by that court in custody for trial.

COMMENTARY
Para (1): Notice, see Form 19.

Para (2): Notice, see Form 20.

Notices on committal of person subject to transfer direction   **4.72**
10. Where a transfer direction has been given by the Secretary of State under s.47 of the Mental Health Act 1983 in respect of a person remanded in custody by a magistrates' court, and before the direction ceases to have effect, that person is committed for trial, the clerk of the court shall give notice in the prescribed form–
    (a) to the governor of the prison to which persons of the sex of that person are committed by that court if committed in custody for trial; and
    (b) to the managers of the hospital where he is detained.

COMMENTARY
Notice, see Form 21.

Documents and exhibits to be retained and sent to court of trial   **4.73**
11. (1) A magistrates' court that commits a person for trial shall, unless there are reasons for not doing so, retain any documents and articles produced by a witness who is subject to a conditional witness order or in whose case the court has directed that a witness order be treated as a conditional order.

(2) As soon as practicable after the committal of any person for trial, and in any case within four days from the date of his committal (not counting Sundays, Good Friday, Christmas Day or Bank Holidays), the clerk of the magistrates' court that committed him shall, subject to the provisions of s.5 of the Prosecution of Offences Act 1979 (which relates to the sending of documents and things to the Director of Public Prosecutions), send to the appropriate officer of the Crown Court–
    (a) the information, if it is in writing;
    (b) the depositions and written statements tendered in evidence, together with a certificate authenticating the depositions and statements, and any admission of facts made for the purposes of the committal proceedings under s.10 of the Criminal Justice Act 1967 and not withdrawn;
    (c) all statements made by the accused before the magistrates' court;
    (d) a list of the names, addresses and occupations of the witnesses in respect of whom witness orders have been made;

(e) a copy of the record made in pursuance of s.5 of the Bail Act 1976 relating to the grant or withholding of bail in respect of the accused on the occasion of the committal;

(f) any recognizance entered into by any person as surety for the accused together with a statement of any enlargement thereof under s.129(4) of the Act of 1980;

(g) a list of the documents and articles produced in evidence before the justices or treated as so produced;

(h) such of the documents and articles referred to in the last preceding subparagraph as have been retained by the justices;

(i) a certificate showing whether the accused was informed at the committal proceedings of the requirements of s.11 of the Criminal Justice Act 1967 (notice of alibi) and a record of any particulars given by him to the magistrates' court under that section;

(j) if the committal was under s.6(2) of the Act of 1980 (committal for trial without consideration of the evidence), a statement to that effect;

(k) if the magistrates' court has made an order under s.8(2) of the Act of 1980 (removal of restrictions on reports of committal proceedings), a statement to that effect;

(l) the certificate of the examining justices as to costs of prosecution (Form B in the Schedule to the Costs in Criminal Cases Regulations 1908);

(m) if any person under the age of 17 is concerned in the committal proceedings, a statement whether the magistrates' court has given a direction under s.39 of the Children and Young Persons Act 1933 (prohibition of publication of certain matter in newspapers);

(n) a copy of any legal aid order previously made in the case;

(o) a copy of any contribution order previously made in the case under s.7 of the Legal Aid Act 1982;

(p) a copy of any legal aid application previously made in the case which has been refused;

(q) any statement of means already submitted.

(3) The clerk shall retain a copy of any list sent in pursuance of para (2)(d).

(4) The period of four days specified in para (2) may be extended in relation to any committal for so long as the appropriate officer of the Crown Court directs, having regard to the length of any document mentioned in that paragraph or any other relevant circumstances.

COMMENTARY

The Home Office also asks justices' clerks to notify the liaison probation officer at the Crown Court of the matters specified in HOC 28/71, para 36.

Para (1): Reasons for not doing so, eg that the exhibit is perishable.

Para (2): (b) A certificate authenticating the depositions and statements, see Form 16.
(c) Statements made by the accused, see Form 17.
(d) A list of the names, addresses and occupations of witnesses, this must be drawn up with care: Practice Note [1961] 1 All ER 875 (relating to the former document).
(g) A list of documents and articles, see Form 25.
(h) No means of identification is prescribed, but a signed label is commonly used: *cf* r.70(4). As to what should be done with the exhibits see under *Exhibits* at 4.26.
(i) Certificate of committal, An erroneous certificate under r.11(2)(i) does not invalidate a lawful committal: *R v Hall* [1981] 1 WLR 1510.

4.74   **Duty to recall witnesses who have given evidence before examining justices**
     21. Where under s.25(3) of the Act of 1980 a magistrates' court, having begun to inquire into an information as examining justices, proceeds to try the information summarily, then, unless the accused pleads guilty, the court shall recall for cross-examination any witnesses who have already given evidence, except any not required by the accused or the prosecutor to be recalled for that purpose.

Preservation of depositions where offence triable either way is dealt with summarily   **4.75**
22. The clerk of the magistrates' court by which any person charged with an offence triable either way has been tried summarily shall preserve for a period of three years such depositions as have been taken.

Deposition of person dangerously ill   **4.76**
33. (1) Where a justice of the peace takes the deposition of a person under s.105 of the Act of 1980 and the deposition relates to an offence with which a person has been charged, the justices shall give the person, whether prosecutor or accused, against whom it is proposed to use it reasonable notice of the intention to take the deposition, and shall give that person or his counsel or solicitor full opportunity of cross-examining the deponent.

(2) The justice shall sign the deposition and add to it a statement of his reason for taking it, the day when, and the place where it was taken and the names of any persons present when it was taken.

(3) The justice shall send the deposition, with the statement, to the clerk to the justices for the petty sessions area for which the justice acts and the clerk shall–
(a) if the deposition relates to an offence for which a person has been committed for trial, send the deposition and statement to the appropriate officer of the Crown Court;
(b) if the deposition relates to proceedings which are pending before a magistrates' court acting for another area, send the deposition and statement to the clerk of that court.

COMMENTARY
Para (1): Give . . . reasonable notice, the notice should be in writing: *R v Harris* (1918) 82 JP 196 (in which it was held that one hour's notice was not reasonable).

Full opportunity of cross-examining, includes cross-examination following questions put by the magistrate: *R v Prestridge* (1881) 72 LTN 93.

Para (2): Persons present, it was ruled in *R v May* (1891) *The Times*, 7 December, that omission of the name of the prisoner's husband did not render the deposition inadmissible.

Practice Direction (Crime: Crown Court Classification and Allocation)   4.77
Lord Lane, Lord Chief Justice, with the concurrence of the Lord Chancellor and pursuant to sections 75(1) and (2) of the Supreme Court Act 1981 directed on 2 November that with immediate effect the following directions were to supersede *Practice Direction (Crime: Crown Court Business* [1971] 1 WLR 1535 as amended.

Classification
1. For the purposes of trial in the crown court, offences are to be classified as follows:
Class 1: (1) any offences for which a person may be sentenced to death; (2) misprision of treason and treason felony; (3) murder; (4) genocide; (5) an offence under section 1 of the Official Secrets Act 1911; (6) incitement, attempt or conspiracy to commit any of the above offences.
Class 2: (1) manslaughter; (2) infanticide; (3) child destruction; (4) abortion (section 58 of the Offences against the Person Act 1861); (5) rape; (6) sexual intercourse with a girl under 13; (7) incest with a girl under 13; (8) sedition; (9) an offence under section 1 of the Geneva Conventions Act 1957; (10) mutiny; (11) piracy; (12) incitement, attempt or conspiracy to commit any of the above offences.
Class 3: all offences triable only on indictment other than those in Classes 1, 2 and 4.
Class 4: (1) wounding or causing grievous bodily harm with intent (section 18

of the Offences against the Person Act 1861); (2) robbery or assault with intent to rob (section 8 of the Theft Act 1968); (3) incitement or attempt to commit any of the above offences; (4) conspiracy at common law, or conspiracy to commit any offence other than those included in Classes 1 and 2; (5) all offences which are triable either way.

Committals for trial

2. A magistrates' court on committing a person for trial under section 6 of the Magistrates' Courts Act 1980 shall, if the offence or any part of the offences is included in Classes 1 to 3, specify the most convenient location of the crown court where a High Court judge regularly sits and, if the offence is in Class 4, shall specify the most convenient location of the crown court.

3. In selecting the most convenient location of the crown court, the justices shall have regard to the considerations referred to in section 7 of the Magistrates' Courts Act 1980 and to the location or locations of the crown court designated by a presiding judge as the location to which cases should normally be committed from their petty sessions area.

4. Where on one occasion a person is committed in respect of a number of offences, all the committals shall be to the same location of the crown court and that location shall be the one where a High Court judge regularly sits if such a location is appropriate for any of the offences.

Committals for sentence or to be dealt with

5. Where a probation order, order for conditional discharge or a community service order has been made, or suspended sentence passed and the offender is committed to be dealt with for the original offence or in respect of the suspended sentence, he shall be committed in accordance with the paragraphs below.

6. If the order was made or the sentence was passed by the crown court, he shall be committed to the location of the crown court where the order was made or suspended sentence was passed, unless it is inconvenient or impracticable to do so.

7. If he is not so committed and the order was made by a High Court judge he shall be committed to the most convenient location of the crown court where a High Court judge regularly sits.

8. In all other cases where a person is committed for sentence or to be dealt with he shall be committed to the most convenient location of the crown court.

9. In selecting the most convenient location of the crown court the justices shall have regard to the location or locations of the crown court designated by a presiding judge as the locations to which cases should normally be committed from their petty sessions area.

Appeals and proceedings under the crown court's original civil jurisdiction

10. The hearing of an appeal or of proceedings under the civil jurisidiction of the crown court shall take place at the location of the crown court designated by a presiding judge as the appropriate location for such proceedings originating in the areas concerned.

Application for removal of a driving disqualification

11. Application should be made to the location of the crown court where the order of disqualification was made.

Transfer of proceedings between locations of the crown court

12. Without prejudice to the provisions of section 76 of the Supreme Court Act 1981 (committal for trial: alteration of place of trial) directions may be given for the transfer from one location of the crown court to another of: (i) appeals; (ii) proceedings on committal for sentence, or to be dealt with; (iii) proceedings under the original civil jurisidiction of the crown court where that appears desirable for expediting the hearing, or for the convenience of the parties.

13. Such directions may be given in a particular case by an officer of the crown court, or generally, in relation to a class or classes of case, by the presiding judge or a judge acting on his behalf.
14. If dissatisfied with such directions given by an officer of the crown court, any party to the proceedings may apply to a judge of the crown court who may hear the application in chambers.

Directions for allocation of business within crown court
General
1. Cases in Class 1 are to be tried by a High Court judge. A case of murder, or incitement, attempt or conspiracy to commit murder may be released, by or on the authority of a presiding judge, for trial by a circuit judge approved for the purpose by the Lord Chief Justice.
2. Cases in Class 2 are to be tried by a High Court judge unless a particular case is released by or on the authority of a presiding judge for trial by a circuit judge. A case of rape, or of a serious sexual offence against a child of any Class may be released by a presiding judge for trial only by a circuit judge approved for the purpose by the Lord Chief Justice.
3. Cases in Class 3 may be tried by a High Court judge or, in accordance with general or particular directions given by a presiding judge, by a circuit judge or a recorder.
4. Cases in Class 4 may be tried by a High Court judge, a recorder or an assistant recorder. A case in Class 4 shall not be listed for trial by High Court judge except with the consent of that judge or of a presiding judge.
5. Appeals from decisions of magistrates and committals to the crown court for sentence shall be heard by: (i) a resident or designated judge, or (ii) a circuit judge, nominated by the resident or designated judge, who regularly sits at the crown court centre, or (iii) an experienced recorder specifically approved by the presiding judges for the purpose, or (iv) where no circuit judge or recorder satisfying the requirements above is available and it is not practicable to obtain the approval of the presiding judges, by a circuit judge or recorder selected by the resident or designated judge to hear a specific case or cases.
6. Applications or matters arising before trial (including those relating to bail) should be listed where possible before the judge by whom the case is expected to be tried. Where a case is to be tried by a High Court judge who is not available, the application or matter should be listed before any other High Court judge then sitting at the crown court centre at which the matter has arisen; before a presiding judge; before the resident or designated judge for the centre; or, with the consent of the presiding judge, before a circuit judge nominated for the purpose.
   In other cases, if the circuit judge, recorder or assistant recorder who is expected to try the case is not available, the matter shall be referred to the resident or designated judge or, if he is not available, to any judge or recorder then sitting at the centre.
7. Matters to be dealt with (eg in which a probation order has been made or suspended sentence passed) should, where possible, be listed before the judge who originally dealt with the matter or, if not, before a judge of the same or higher status.

Allocation of proceedings to a court comprising lay justices
8. In addition to the classes of case specified in section 74 of the Supreme Court Act 1981 (appeals and proceedings on committals for sentence) any other proceedings apart from cases listed for pleas of not guilty which in accordance with those directions are listed for hearing by a circuit judge or recorder are suitable for allocation to a court comprising justices of the peace.

Transfer of cases between circuits
9. An application that a case be transferred from one circuit to another should not be granted unless the judge is satisfied that: (i) the approval of the

presiding judges and circuit administrator for each circuit has been obtained, or (ii) the case may be transferred under general arrangements approved by the presiding judges and circuit administrators.

10. When a resident or designated judge is absent from his centre, the presiding judges may authorise another judge who sits regularly at the same centre to exercise his responsibility.

Presiding judge's directions

11. For the just, speedy and economical disposal of the business of a circuit, presiding judges shall with the approval of the senior presiding judge issue directions as to the need where appropriate to reserve a case for trial by a High Court judge and as to the allocation of work between circuit judges, recorders and assistant recorders and where necessary the devolved responsibility of resident or designated judges for such allocation.

In such directions specific provision should be made for cases in the following categories: (a) cases where death or serious risk to life, or the infliction of grave injury are involved, including motoring cases of this category arising from reckless driving and/or excess alcohol; (b) cases where loaded firearms are alleged to have been used; (c) cases of arson or criminal damage with intent to endanger life; (d) cases of defrauding government departments or local authorities or other public bodies of amounts in excess of £25,000; (e) offences under the Forgery and Counterfeiting Act 1981 where the amount of money or the value of goods exceeds £10,000; (f) offences involving violence to a police officer which result in the officer being unfit for duty for more than 28 days; (g) any offence involving loss to any person or body of a sum in excess of £100,000; (h) cases where there is a risk of substantial political or racial feeling being excited by the offence or the trial; (i) cases which have given rise to widespread public concern; (j) cases of robbery or assault with intent to rob where gross violence was used, or serious injury was caused, or where the accused was armed with a dangerous weapon for the purpose of the robbery, or where the theft was intended to be from a bank, building society or a post office; (k) cases involving the manufacture or distribution of substantial quantities of drugs; (l) cases the trial of which is likely to last more than 10 days; (m) cases involving the trial of more than five defendants; (n) cases in which the accused holds a senior public office, or is a member of a profession or other person carrying a special duty or responsibility to the public, including a police officer when acting as such; (o) cases where a difficult issue of law is likely to be involved, or a prosecution for the offence is rare or novel.

12. With the approval of the senior presiding judge, general directions may be given by the presiding judges of the South Eastern Circuit concerning the distribution and allocation of business of all Classes at the Central Criminal Court.

4 November 1987

CHAPTER 5

Summary Trial (including written pleas of guilty)

Summary Trial

5.00 INTRODUCTION

Subject to the statutory provisions, 'magistrates have always had an inherent power to regulate the procedure in their courts in the interests of justice and a fair and expeditious trial', *per* Lord Parker CJ, in *Simms v Moore* (1970) 134 JP 573; and see *Chief Constable of Norfolk v Clayton sub nom R v Hunstanton Justices ex p. Clayton* [1983] 2 AC 473.

5.01 LEGAL REPRESENTATION

Either party may be represented by counsel or solicitor. s.122(1) MCA 1980. A party so represented is *deemed not to be absent* except for any enactment or any condition of a recognizance expressly requiring his presence: s.122(2), (3).

5.02 Representation otherwise than by a lawyer

The Privy Council have decided (in relation to an appeal from New South Wales) that the enactment which was replaced by the MCA 1952 'did not deprive magistrates of their pre-existing *discretionary power* to allow a person, not being the informant or his counsel or attorney, to conduct the case for the informant,' *per* Lord Pearson in *O'Toole v Scott* [1965] 2 All ER 240 at p. 246. Furthermore, there is no limitation on the magistrates' discretion: 'it can be exercised on general grounds common to many cases or on special grounds arising in a particular case . . . It should be regarded as proper for a magistrate to exercise the discretion in order to secure or promote convenience or expedition and efficiency in the administration of justice.' These comments apply to prosecutors before magistrates' courts in this country: *R v Uxbridge Justices, ex p. Smith* [1977] RTR 93. That case dealt with a particular instance where in an emergency it was sought to allow someone other than the named prosecutor to read out in his absence the statement of facts (a requirement itself superseded by s.12(4) MCA 1980 – 5.48, *post*). The court stressed the need for each case to be considered on its merits.

5.03 'McKenzie friends'

Legal representation is to be distinguished from assistance in presenting the case by a person who *does not act as an advocate* – or 'silent assistance' as it is sometimes termed. 'Any person, whether he be a professional man or not, may attend as a friend of either party, may take notes, may quietly make suggestions, and give advice; but no-one can demand to take part in the proceedings as an advocate contrary to the regulations of the court as settled by the discretion of the justices,' *per* Lord Tenterden CJ in *Collier v Hicks* (1831) 2 B & Ad 663, LJOSMC 138; approved by the Court of Appeal in *McKenzie v McKenzie* [1970] 3 All ER 1034.

DUTIES OF THE PROSECUTOR 5.04

In the words of the *Code of Conduct for the Bar of England and Wales:*

It is not the duty of the prosecuting counsel to obtain a conviction by all means at his command but rather to lay before the jury fairly and impartially the whole of the facts which comprise the case for the prosecution and to see that the jury are properly instructed in the law applicable to those facts.

It follows that there are certain duties laid upon the prosecutor which are not imposed on the defence. According to the Law Society *Guide to the Professional Conduct of Solicitors:*

12.13 (1) The prosecutor should state all relevant facts and should limit his expressions of opinion to those fairly required to present his case. He should reveal any mitigating circumstances; he should inform the court of its sentencing powers if invited to do so and whenever it appears to be under a misapprehension about those powers.

12.13 (2) If a prosecutor obtains evidence which he does not intend to use but which may assist the defence, he must supply particulars of witnesses to the defence, but is not obliged to supply copies of the statements made by those witnesses. He must reveal to the defence factual evidence of which he has knowledge and which is inconsistent with that which he, as prosecutor, has presented or proposes to present to the court.

12.13 (3) The prosecutor must reveal all relevant cases and statutory provisions known to him whether it be for or against his case. This is so whether or not he has been called upon to argue the point in question. (See above Principle 12.01).

Lay justices should have explained to them in difficult cases exactly what sort of knowledge the prosecution desires to be found, *per* Devlin J, in *Taylor's Central Garages (Exeter) Ltd v Roper* (1951) 115 JP 445 at p. 449.

When the police have taken a statement from a witness but decide not to call him they are under a duty to make that person available as a witness for the defence: *R v Bryant and Dickson* (1946) 31 Cr App R 146; *R v Leyland Justices, ex p. Hawthorn* [1979] 1 All ER 209. However they are not obliged to supply the defence with a copy of the statement they took: *R v Bryant and Dickson, supra*; but contrast the Magistrates' Courts (Advance Information) Rules 1985 (SI No 601) (Chapter 2, *ante*) under which prosecutors have certain duties in respect of matters on which they propose to rely.

When a witness whom the prosecution call or tender gives evidence in the witness box on the material issue and the prosecution have in their possession an earlier statement from that witness which is materially inconsistent with such evidence the prosecution should at any rate inform the defence of that fact: *Archbold*, 42nd edn at para 443a. When a prosecution witness is of known bad character the prosecution must inform the defence of this fact: *R v Colliston and Warhurst* (1955) 39 Cr App R 100; *R v Matthews* (1975) 60 Cr App R 292.

The prosecution is under a duty to supply the defence with the previous *convictions of the accused* in accordance with the *Practice Direction* [1966] 2 All ER 929, which deals with trial on indictment.

5.05   TRIAL IN ABSENCE

An accused has, in general, a right to be present at his trial. This right is
subject to the discretion of the court to proceed in his absence if it is
voluntarily waived, eg (i) where the accused *abuses his right* to be present
for the purpose of obstructing the proceedings of the court by unseemly,
indecent or outrageous behaviour; or (ii) where he *ceases to claim his
right* to be present by deliberately jumping bail. This is a discretion which
(in serious cases at least) should be exercised with great reluctance and
with a view rather to the due administration of justice than to the comfort
or convenience of anyone: *R v Jones (REW), (No 2)* [1972] 2 All ER 731.
In an appropriate case the court has a discretion to continue a trial in the
absence of the accused through *illness*, but it is a discretion which should
be sparingly exercised and never if the accused's defence could be prejudiced by his absence: *R v Howson* (1982) 74 Cr App R 172.

Subject to these considerations the court may proceed with the trial of
an information in the absence of the accused: s.11(1) MCA 1980; but
where a summons was issued the information may not be tried unless (a)
it is proved that the summons was served a reasonable time before the
trial or (b) the accused has appeared on a previous occasion: s.11(2).

Where neither prosecutor nor accused appear, the court may dismiss
the information or, if evidence was received on a previous occasion,
proceed in their absence: s.16. A *warrant* may issue for the arrest of the
accused if the information has been substantiated on oath: s.13(1);
subject to the restrictions in s.13(2), (5).

5.06   ADJOURNMENT

Magistrates have always had power at common law to adjourn their
proceedings and s.10 MCA 1980 now provides that a trial may be
adjourned both before and after the court has begun to try the information. The clerk to the justices may order the further adjournment of
criminal proceedings with the consent of the prosecutor and the accused
if, but only if (a) the accused, not having been remanded on the previous
adjournment is not remanded in this further adjournment, or (b) the
accused having been remanded on bail on the previous adjournment is
remanded on bail on the like terms and conditions: Justices' Clerks Rules
1970 (SI No 231). For restrictions on the period of certain adjournments
see Chapters 3, *ante*.

All the justices composing the court must be present during the whole
proceedings, but if any justice absents himself he must cease to act further
therein and if the remaining justices are enough to satisfy the s.121 MCA
1980 the proceedings may continue before them: s.121(6). If at an
adjourned hearing the court comprises *different* magistrates the trial must
be recommenced: *Re Guerin* (1888) 53 JP 468; *R v Walton, ex p. Dutton*
(1911) 75 JP 558. Evidence already given must be repeated and not read
over: *Fulker v Fulker* (1937) 101 JP 8.

The accused has no claim to an adjournment as a matter of right for the
purpose of obtaining legal assistance: *R v Lipscombe, ex p. Biggins* (1882)
26 JP 244; nor will the High Court interfere where justices have refused
an adjournment after being satisfied that the defendant had sufficient
time to instruct a solicitor: *R v Cambridgeshire Justices* (1880) 44 JP 168.
It is a breach of natural justice if a party, especially a defendant in a
criminal case, is not given a reasonable opportunity to present his case.
This is not confined to addressing the court, but entails a reasonable

opportunity to prepare the case before presentation: *R v Thames Magistrates' Court ex p. Polemis* [1974] 1 WLR 1371. The question magistrates should ask themselves is: if we proceed now, can the inquiry be conducted with due regard to natural justice? Magistrates' refusal to allow a further adjournment to an accused who had already received one and who had been notified that the case would go ahead was upheld in *R v Macclesfield Justices, ex p. Jones* [1983] RTR 143. It was otherwise in *R v Afan Justices, ex p. Chaplin* [1983] RTR 168 where the justices had overlooked a sentencing formality.

Magistrates' refusal to allow an adjournment to the prosecutor was upheld in *Taylor v Baird and Watters* (1983) *The Times* 3 May (owing to a confusion the prosecutor's case had been in disarray). However, where the prosecution were refused an adjournment to enable them to call their principal witness the justices erred in proceeding directly to acquittal without offering the prosecution opportunity to call the rest of their evidence: *Re Harrington* (1984) 148 JP 211.

In *R v Lewes Justices ex p. Oldfield* (1987) *The Times*, 6 May it was stated that justices had erred in dismissing 42 summonses when the prosecution and defence had been informed in advance that the date was a 'holding date', on which a date for trial would be fixed (although judicial review was refused as a matter of discretion); and see *R v Clerkenwell Magistrates' Court, ex p. Director of Public Prosecutions* (1987) *The Times*, 20 May where it was held that the prosecutor had been treated unfairly by the magistrate's insistence that he proceed on the first appearance when the defendant changed his election to summary trial at the invitation of the court.

When a case is dismissed because an adjournment is refused to the prosecutor he may challenge it by application for *judicial review*; not by preferring further process before the magistrates, *per* Donaldson LJ in *R v Swansea Justices, ex p. Purvis* (1981) 145 JP 252. Where a prosecutor declines to accept a medical certificate tendered in support of the defendant's absence he should notify the defendant's solicitors so as to give them an opportunity of calling the doctor to give evidence: *R v King's Lynne Justices, ex p. Whitelam* (1982) *The Times*, 23 June. A hearing should not be adjourned for long periods for the purposes of civil litigation: *R v Evans* (1890) 54 JP 47. The High Court will interfere in the case of an unduly long adjournment which is in effect a refusal of jurisdiction, *per* Alverstone J, in *R v Southampton JJ, ex p. Lebern* (1907) 71 JP 332.

It is a question for the discretion of the magistrates under s.10(1) MCA 1980 whether it is unfair to continue a part-heard case after a lengthy adjournment: *R v Ali* (1987) *The Times*, 6 July where, on the facts, the Divisional Court refused to interfere following a five months' adjournment.

As to the impropriety of making an adjournment conditional upon payment of costs see the Irish case of *R (Roche) v County Clare Justices* (1912) 46 ILT 80.

PRELIMINARY POINTS   5.07

It is permissible for the accused to address the court *before* the prosecutor to raise a preliminary point. Preliminary points are of three types:

(1) those which go to *jurisdiction* and which cannot be waived, eg where the information is not laid in time, or where necessary

consent to jurisdiction is lacking. If these matters are not raised by the defence, they should be raised by the court:

(2) those which may be *cured* by amendment under s.123 MCA 1980, but if not amended or waived should result in an acquittal, eg lack of a summons, insufficient (or insufficiently correct) particularity of the information, or duplicity; and

(3) those which are so *trivial* as not even to require amendment, eg minor misdescriptions of property, persons or venue. The test is whether the defendant has been misled, or injustice might otherwise occur.

Preliminary points should be taken *as early as possible*, preferably before any evidence is given: *R v Brown* (1857) 21 JP 357; *R v Salop Justices* (1859) 2 El & El 386; but may be raised at any time before the decision is pronounced. A solicitor should *as a matter of courtesy* inform the other party that he intends to take a preliminary point: *Re Mundy, ex p. Shead* (1885) 15 QBD 338.

If there is objection:

'the magistrates may or may not at that stage be in a position to decide whether the act complained of was or was not done (*in circumstances which render it outside their jurisdiction*). It is however always within the jurisdiction of magistrates to inquire whether they have jurisdiction to try the case before them, and in circumstances such as these the magistrates ought to continue the hearing despite the objection until they have reached the stage in which the facts are sufficiently clear for them to reach a conclusion on this point. If at that point they decide that (*they have jurisdiction*), they will complete the hearing and the matter can be tested if necessary by way of appeal. If, on the other hand, the magistrates conclude that (*they have not*), and that the proceedings before them cannot continue, they will discontinue the proceedings accordingly and leave the disappointed prosecutor to move for *mandamus* if so advised.'

R v Bracknell Justices, ex p. Griffiths (1975) 139 JP 368. Justices should be extremely careful before agreeing to treat submissions as preliminary points: *Williams v Mohamed* [1977] RTR 12. Where justices decline jurisdiction on a preliminary point, the proper remedy is *mandamus*: *Davies v May* (1937) 101 JP 250. A case dismissed on a preliminary objection is *not decided on its merits: R v Middlesex Justices* (1877) 41 JP 629 and so will not rank as a previous acquittal: see *Autrefois convict and autrefois acquit*, 5.13.

Where confession evidence is sought to be excluded, the justices may hold a *trial within a* trial, for that limited purpose: see 6.28, *post*. Chapter 6.

5.08 Objections and 'waiver'

Informalities may be waived if before the close of the prosecution case an accused with knowledge of the defect makes no objection: *Grimble & Co. v Preston* (1914) 78 JP 72; *R v Banks* (1972) 136 JP 306. An appearance to answer the charge without objection cures the want of information or summons: *Eggington v Pearl* (1875) 40 JP 56; *Gray v Customs Commissioners* (1886) 48 JP 343; *R v Garrett Pegge, ex p. Brown* (1911) 75 JP 169. In the words of Blackburn J in *R v Shaw* (1865) 29 JP 339 (quoted with approval in *R v Hughes* (1879) 43 JP 556):

'When a man appears before justices and a charge is then made against him, if he has not been summoned, he has a good ground for asking for an adjournment; if he waives that and answers the charge, a conviction would be perfectly good against him . . .'

An appearance simply in order to point out an irregularity of service is not a waiver: *Pearks, Gunston & Tee Ltd v Richardson* (1902) 56 JP 119. There is no waiver where the accused is ignorant of the objection or his right to raise it: *R v Essex Justices, ex p. Perkins* (1927) 91 JP 94. Objection to certain formalities, once waived, may not be renewed: *Turner v Postmaster General* (1864) 34 LJMC 10; but only where jurisdiction is otherwise satisfied.

Defective process   5.09

No objection may be allowed to any information, summons or warrant for any defect in it in substance or form or for any variance between it and the evidence at the hearing: s.123(1) MCA 1980. If it appears that any variance between a summons or warrant and the evidence adduced by the prosecutor at the hearing has *misled* the defendant the court must on his application adjourn the hearing: s.123(2). In *Wright v Nicholson* [1970] 1 WLR 142 Lord Parker CJ said:

'It of course has always been held that (subs (1)) cannot be read literally as meaning: there can be no attack on an information however fundamental the defect. It depends in every case whether, for instance, the variance between it and the evidence is such as to require an amendment: a misdescription of premises might not even require an amendment. (If), unless the information is amended there might be grave injustice to the accused, an amendment is called for. Once an amendment is called for and granted, then (s.123(2)) operates, which requires the court on the application of the defendant to adjourn', (conviction quashed where failure to amend date of offence).

In *Hutchison (Cinemas) Ltd v Tyson* [1970] Crim LR 350 Lord Parker CJ said:

'It seems to me that one might find an information which was so defective, so fundamentally bad, that it could not be cured at all and the only proper course would be for the justices to dismiss the information. At the other end of the scale there may be informations which are deficient in some minor particular, a misdescription of premises or data, where there could be no prejudice and where no amendment or further particulars are required at all. In between there are informations, which are perfectly good as informations, albeit deficient, and can be cured, not merely by a formal amendment, but by the delivery of particulars to supplement their contents'.

(Informations cured by delivery of particulars of statutory conditions said to be contravened by unlawful gaming); see also *Lee v Coles* (1972) 136 JPN 226. If the court is minded to rely on this section the defendant must be made aware of this, *per* Lord Widgery CJ in *Morriss v Lawrence* [1977] RTR 205.

Justices are entitled to amend under s.123 MCA 1980 after conviction and at any time before they are *functi officio: Allen v Wiseman* [1975] RTR 217; but not afterwards: *Cole v Wolkind* [1981] Crim LR 252.

Joinder of offences and defendants   5.10

The rule on joinder was described as follows by Lord Roskill in *Chief Constable of Norfolk v Clayton* [1983] 2 AC 473:

'The practice in magistrates' courts should be analogous to the practice prescribed in *Assim's* case in relation to trials on indictment. Where a defendant is charged on several informations and the facts are connected, for example motoring offences or several charges of shoplifting, I can see no reason why those informations should not, if the justices think fit, be heard together. Similarly, if two or more defendants are charged on separate informations but the facts are connected, I can see no reason why they should not, if the justices think fit, be heard together. In the present cases there were separate informations against the husband and the wife and a joint information against them both. I can see no rational objection to all those informations being heard and determined together. Of course, when this question arises, as from time to time it will arise, justices will be well advised to inquire both of the prosecution and of the defence whether either side has any objection to all the informations being heard together. If consent is forthcoming on both sides there is no problem. If such consent is not forthcoming, the justices should then consider the rival submissions and, under any necessary advice from their clerk, rule as they think right in the overall interests of justice. If the defendant is absent or not represented, the justices, of course, should seek the views of the prosecution and again if necessary the advice of their clerk and then rule as they think fit in the overall interests of justice. Absence of consent, either express where the defendant is present or represented and objects or necessarily brought about by his absence or the absence of representation, should no longer in practice be regarded as a complete and automatic bar to hearing more than one information at the same time or informations against more than one defendant charged on separate informations at the same time when in the justices' view the facts are sufficiently closely connected to justify this course and there is no risk of injustice to the defendants by its adoption. Accordingly, the justices should always ask themselves whether it would be fair and just to the defendant or defendants to allow a joint trial. Only if the answer is clearly in the affirmative should they order a joint trial in the absence of consent by or on behalf of the defendant. To give magistrates' courts this discretion and to change the practice and procedure which has seemingly prevailed in recent years is not to invite magistrates' courts to embark on long and complicated summary trials with many charges being heard and many offenders being tried all at the same time. As Sachs J said in *Assim's* case, it is impossible to lay down general rules applicable to every case which may arise, but if justices ask themselves, before finally ruling, the single question, what is the fairest thing to do in all the circumstances in the interests of everyone concerned, they are unlikely to err in their conclusion, for the aim of the judicial process is to secure a fair trial and rules of practice and procedure are designed to that end and not otherwise.'

In *Clayton's* case it was decided that there was no reason why separate information against a husband and wife, and a joint information against them both should not be heard together. In *R v Assim* [1966] 2 QB 249, referred to in *Clayton's* case by Lord Roskill, Sachs J said:

'As a general rule it is, of course, no more proper to have tried by the same jury several offenders on charges of committing individual offences that have nothing to do with each other, than it is to try before the same jury offences committed by the same person that have nothing to do with each other. Where, however, the matters which constitute the individual offences of the several offenders are on the available evidence so related, whether in time or by other factors, that the interests of justice are best served by their being tried together, then they can properly be the subject of counts in one indictment and can, subject always to the discretion of the court, be tried together. Such a rule, of course, includes cases where there is evidence that several offenders acted in concert but is not limited to such cases. Again, while the court has in mind the classes of case that have been particularly the subject of discussion before it, such as incidents which, irrespective of there appearing in a joint charge in the indictment, are contemporaneous (as where there has been something in the nature of an affray), or successive (as in protection racket cases), or linked in a similar manner as where two persons individually in the course of the same trial commit perjury as regards the same or a closely connected fact, the court does not intend the operation of the rule to be restricted so as to apply only to such cases as have been discussed before it.'

5.10a   The rule on indictment is that accused who are *jointly charged* may apply to be tried separately, but in the majority of cases it is in the public interest for persons jointly charged to be tried together: *R v Hoggins and Others* [1967] 1 WLR 1223. There is no rule of law that separate trials should be ordered where the defence of one accused consists of an attack on the other: *R v Marion Grondkowski and Henryck Malinowski* (1946) 110 JP 19; and it is a matter of discretion whether justices should refuse to try a second or subsequent case, but they should do so where there would be real problems in approaching the second case in a proper and impartial manner: *R v Sandwick Justices ex p. Berry* [1982] Crim LR 121.

When two accused are charged with a *joint offence* it is open to the prosecution to secure a conviction of both on the ground that they acted *ointly* or, no matter how either pleaded, of *either* or *both* on the ground of **n** *independent* commission of the offence: *Director of Public Prosecutions v Merriman* [1973] AC 584. Where two or more persons are **harged** *on separate informations*, but the facts are connected, the justices **nay**, if they think fit, hear the information together, when the same **rinciples** will apply: see *Clayton's* case, *supra*. Principals and aiders and **bettors** may be treated as *jointly charged*, it is suggested.

When two accused charged with a *joint offence* are tried together and **ne** gives evidence against the other he is liable to be cross-examined by he other's counsel: *R v Hadwen* (1902) 66 JP 456; and this applies equally **o** the summary trial of co-accused: *Rigby v Woodward* (1957) 121 JP 120. **The** rule is not dependent upon the one accused implicating his co-**accused**: *R v Hilton* (1971) 135 JP 590.

The defendant's consent is unnecessary to the joint trial of an informa-**ion** charging an offence and an information charging an attempt to **ommit** that offence: s.4(2) Criminal Attempts Act 1981.

Justices do not have power even with consent to permit the simultane-**us** trial of *cross-summonses; R v Epsom Justices, ex p. Gibbons* [1983] 3 **ll** ER 523; and an *information* should not be tried at the same time as a **ivil complaint:** *R v Dunmow Justices, ex p. Anderson* [1964] 1 WLR 1039 **(**dangerous dog); where it was suggested that the criminal proceedings **hould** be heard *first*, and the parties invited to accept the evidence *given* herein in the subsequent civil proceedings.

As with multiple offences, justices faced with multiple defendants **hould** inquire of the prosecution and the defence whether either has any **bjection** to all matters being heard together and if consent is not forth-**oming** then the court should rule as it thinks fit in the overall interests of **ustice:** *Clayton's* case, *supra*; and see *R v Liverpool Juvenile Court, ex p.* **3** (1986) *The Times*, 13 May. It does not affect this position that the **rosecutor** is the instigator of the application for separate trials, but the **ourt** should be slow to exerise its discretion in favour of a joint trial in **ircumstances** where all parties want separate trials: *R v Highbury Corner* **Magistrates'** *Court, ex p. McGinley* (1986) 150 JP 257.

In relation to remand hearings, the practice of putting into the dock **ogether** defendants who are not jointly charged and have been arrested **n** different occasions has been criticised on the ground that it gives the **ppearance** of 'group justice': *R v Mansfield Justices, ex p. Sharkey* [1985] **B** 613. It is permissible to hold 'joint committal proceedings', even **vithout** the consent of the accused, if the charges could properly be the **ubject** matter of counts in the same indictment: *R v Camberwell Green* **tipendiary** *Magistrate, ex p. Christie* [1978] QB 602.

A number of statutory provisions create special rules which apply to **oint charges** against adults and juveniles. The charge must be heard in the **adult'** magistrates' court, as opposed to the juvenile court: the effect of **.46(1)** CYPA 1933; but if the adult pleads guilty on summary trial and he juvenile pleads not guilty, then the magistrates' court may remit the **uvenile** to the juvenile court *before any evidence is called*. Similarly, **vhere** the magistrates' court proceeds to inquire into the information as **xamining** justices in the case of the adult and the juvenile pleads not **uilty:** s.29(2) MCA 1980. Usually, a juvenile is tried summarily unless he **s** charged jointly with an adult and the court considers it necessary – *in the* **nterests** *of justice* – to commit both defendants for trial: s.24 MCA 1980. **Vhere** this occurs, the juvenile may also be committed for trial to the **Crown** Court in respect of any other indictable offence with which he is

charged at the same time, provided that this offence arises out of circum
stances which are *the same as or connected with* those giving rise to th
joint offence: *ibid*.

A charge against a juvenile may also be heard by a magistrates' court
an adult is charged at the same time and either is charged with aiding ar
abetting etc the other: s.46 CYPA 1933, s.18 CYPA 1963; or where th
offences arise out of the same or connected circumstances: s.18 CYP.
1963. A magistrates' court which does find a juvenile guilty of an offenc
must remit the case to the juvenile court for sentence unless it is satisfie
that this course is undesirable: s.56 CYPA 1933; a provision which mu
be read in conjunction with s.7(8) CYPA 1969, which – without prejudic
to s.56 – *requires* the magistrates' court to remit except where the case ca
properly be dealt with by means of an absolute or conditional discharge,
fine or a parental bind-over, together with any ancillary orders, eg com
pensation.

5.11   Duplicity

The court may not proceed to the trial of an information that charge
more than one offence: r.12(1) MC Rules 1981, but this does not preve
several *separate informations* being set out in *one document*; and if wor
are common to a number of informations the use of a preamble contai
ing these words followed by ensuing paragraphs clearly detailing th
separate offences is not contrary to this rule: *Shah v Swallow* [1984]
WLR 908.

The rule arises in practice in three main circumstances: (i) where it
difficult to know from the wording of the statute whether Parliame
intended to create one or more offences; (ii) in relation to continuir
offences; and (iii) where a number of similar acts are charged as one.

So far as (i) is concerned, the two sets of behaviour may in a proper cas
be charged conjunctively where they comprise a single act or incident: *R*
Clow (1963) 127 JP 371 (driving at a speed and in a manner dangerous
the public); *Vernon v Paddon* [1973] 1 WLR 663 (words and behaviou
conducive to a breach of the peace). The Public Order Act 1986 express
provides that certain offences under that Act may be charged in a simil
fashion.

Concerning (ii), earlier cases have used the term '*continuing offence*'
two senses. A statute which creates a series of separate offences is caug
by this rule but one which charges one transaction, albeit taking plac
over a length of time, is not: *Anderton v Cooper* (1980) 72 Cr App R 2
(managing a brothel).

Concerning (iii) the test is whether the various acts can properly an
fairly be described, having regard to all the circumstances of the case,
forming part of one activity: *Heaton v Costello* (1984) 148 JP 688. Thus
R. v Ballysingh (1953) 37 Cr App R 28, it was held that where, in a case
shoplifting, the evidence showed that a number of articles had been take
from different parts of a large store the proper course was to make eac
taking the subject of a separate count. In *Jemmison v Priddle* [1972] 1 Q
489, Lord Widgery CJ, after referring to that case, said:

'Thus, if the accused is alleged to have gone to one department and picked up a handful
tomatoes, or whatever it might be, it is perfectly legitimate to charge that as a single offenc
whereas if the accused spends a substantial time going round the floors picking up a separa
article here and another article there those individual articles ought to be charge
separately.'

n *R v Jones & Others* (1974) 59 Cr App R 120, at p.122, the Court of
Appeal applied the approach of Lord Parker in *Ware v Fox* [1967] 1 WLR
79, by asking the question 'Does the single count charge more than one
ctivity even though that activity may involve more than one act?'
unlawful assembly). In *Horrix v Malam* [1984] RTR 112, the rule was
eld to allow an information for careless driving which alleged driving on
ifferent roads over a period of some 35 minutes. In *R v Bristol Crown
Court, ex p. Willets* (1985) 149 JP 416 it was applied to save an information
lleging that the defendant had a number of obscene articles in his
ossession for gain.

Curing duplicity 5.12

The prosecutor should be invited *before the trial begins* to decide on which
ffence he *elects* to proceed, and the remaining offence should be struck
ut. If the prosecutor refuses to elect, the information should be dis-
issed: *Edwards v Jones* [1947] KB 659. There is no power to amend the
nformation to cure duplicity once the trial has begun: *Hargreaves v
Alderson* [1962] 3 All ER 1019. If the summons is not amended, either
orthwith or after an adjournment, and the justices proceed to conviction
n a bad information it will be quashed: *Hunter v Coombs* [1962] 1 WLR
73. Where a question of duplicity was *not taken before the magistrates*
nd their conviction was a good one if certain dates were to be regarded as
urplusage, the Divisional Court declined to interfere: *Blakey Transport
Ltd v Baggott* [1973] Crim LR 776.

Autrefois convict and *autrefois acquit* 5.13

When a magistrates' court dismisses an information for an offence triable
ither way the effect is the same as acquittal on indictment: s.27 MCA
980. This corresponds to the special pleas in bar of *autrefois acquit* and
utrefois convict*, by pleading which on indictment the accused asserts
hat the charge has already been the subject of a prior acquittal or
onviction of a court of competent jurisdiction. Most of the cases concern
rial on indictment and for this reason these terms are commonly used in
elation to summary trial to which, strictly speaking, they are not applic-
ble. Thus, in *Wemyss v Hopkins* (1875) 39 JP 549, Blackburn J, said of a
revious conviction by justices:

The defence does not arise on a plea of *autrefois convict* but on the well established rule at
ommon law, that where a person has been convicted and punished for an offence by a court
f competent jurisdiction *transit in rem judicatem*, that is, the conviction shall be a bar to all
rther proceedings for the same offence, and he shall not be punished again for the same
atter; otherwise there might be two different punishments for the same offence.'

ee also the remarks of counsel in *Welton v Taneborne* (1908) 72 JP 419,
nd of Lord Goddard CJ, in *Flatman v Light* (1946) 110 JP 273. The whole
ubject of *autrefois acquit* and *convict* was reviewed by the House of
Lords in *Connelly v Director of Public Prosecutions* [1964] AC 1254, in
which Lord Morris quoted with approval the following dictum of Law-
ence J:

'or a plea of *autrefois acquit* to be maintainable, the offence of which the accused has been
cquitted and that with which he is charged must be the same in the sense that each must
ave the same essential ingredients. The factors which constitute the one must be sufficient
o justify a conviction for the other': (*R v Kupferberg* (1918) 3 Cr App R 166).

n *Connelly's* case the House held that an acquittal of murder in the course of armed robbery did not preclude a subsequent indictment fo robbery where the accused had relied on a defence of alibi at the earlie trial. Commenting on *Connelly*, Lord Parker CJ, said in *United State Government v Atkinson* [1969] 2 All ER 1151:

'The question is not a question of whether the actual facts examined on the trial of each of the offences are the same, but whether the facts necessary to support a conviction for eac offence are the same.'

(NB certain other aspects of *Connelly* were disapproved by the Lords i *Atkinson v United States Government* [1969] 3 All ER 1317.)

It is wrong to convict of two offences *arising out of the same act* if one o them is a lesser form of the other: *R v Haddock* [1976] Crim LR 37 (damaging property with intent to endanger life and damaging property)

It is an essential ingredient of the plea that the defendant should hav been *in peril* at the earlier proceedings. An acquittal *on the merits* simpl means that the accused must have been *in jeopardy* of conviction. I does not necessarily imply that there was a hearing and balancing c evidence but merely that the acquittal was *not on some technical o jurisdictional point*; *British Railways Board v Warwick* [1980] Crim L 590; *R v Swansea Justices, ex p. Purvis* (1981) 145 JPN 252 (case dis missed where prosecution witness not available). Thus the doctrine doe not apply to a summons which was dismissed for irregularities in th prosecution: *Foster v Hull* (1869) 33 JP 629; or for failing to giv advance disclosure: *R v Willesden Justices, ex p. Clemmings* (1987) *Th Times*, 21 October; or in respect of a conviction based on unswor evidence: *R v Marsham JJ, ex p. Pethick Lawrence* (1912) 76 JP 284; o following a committal for trial of an offence triable only summarily *Bannister v Clarke* (1920) 85 JP 12; or which could have been quashe for reciting the wrong date: *R v West* [1962] 2 All ER 624. The doctrin does not apply to a summons which has been withdrawn: *Brooks Bagshaw* (1904) JP 514; *Davies v Morton* (1913) 77 JP 223; unless th withdrawal was on the merits of the case: *Pickavance v Pickavanc* [1901] P 60 (cited in *Davies v Morton, supra*). There was no question o *double jeopardy* where the prosecution preferred a revised informatio and the magistrates dismissed the original information which it wa intended to supersede: *Broadbent v High* (1984) 148 JP 115. In *R Bedford and Sharnbrook Justices, ex p. Ward* [1974] Crim LR 109 *prohibition* was refused to prevent the prosecution of a person agains whom no evidence had been offered when he had previously answered charge against someone of the same name. The doctrine *does not appl to convictions reversed through errors of law*: *R v Drury* (1849) 18 LJMC 189; but a conviction quashed on appeal becomes an acquittal. A con viction requires for this purpose both a finding of guilty and a fina disposal of the case: *R v Gordon* [1983] Crim LR 735.

The court must be a court of *competent jurisdiction*: *R v Bitton* (1833) C & P 92; *R v Flower* (1956) 40 Cr App R 189. But a conviction for summary offence will act equally as a bar to subsequent proceedings fo what is, effectively, the same offence, even though under a differen statute: *Wemyss v Hopkins, supra*; see also s.27 MCA 1980. The fact tha the earlier conviction was not recorded in the court register does nc prevent application of the doctrine of *autrefois convict*: *R v Mancheste Justices, ex p. Lever* [1937] 3 All ER 4; *Iremonger v Vissenga and Anothe* [1976] Crim LR 524. The *burden of proof* lies upon the accused and mus be discharged on the balance of probabilities: *R v Coughlin (Martin)* (1976) 63 Cr App R 33.

The formal pleas obtain, but the doctrine of *issue estoppel* is no part of the criminal law: *Director of Public Prosecutions v Humphrys* [1976] 2 WLR 857.

Nemo debet and road traffic cases   5.14

The rule against *double punishment* (*nemo debet bis puniri*) frequently arises in relation to traffic offences where the defendant is charged both with a substantive offence of bad driving, such as reckless or careless driving, and with an offence of strict liability arising out of the same facts, such as excess speed or failure to conform to traffic lights. The prohibition against double punishment is now contained in statutory form in s.18 Interpretation Act 1978, as follows:

'Where an act or omission constitutes an offence under two or more Acts or both under an Act and at common law, whether any such Act was passed before or after the commencement of this Act, the offender shall unless the contrary intention appears, be liable to be prosecuted and punished under either or any of those Acts or at common law but shall not be liable to be punished twice for the same offence.'

The proper course to follow in cases where there has been a plea of guilty to the more serious offence has been laid down by Lord Parker CJ, in *R v Burnham Justices, ex p. Ansorge* [1959] 1 WLR 597, as follows:

'Before the magistrates can decide whether to convict or not on the second information they must inquire into the matter to see what are the facts. If, having inquired into the matter, they find that the facts are the very facts which have given rise to the conviction on the first information their proper course would be to *proceed no further*.' (author's italics).

This course was first laid down in respect of summary proceedings in *Welton v Taneborne* (1908) 72 JP 419, where the Divisional Court held that a conviction for dangerous driving was a bar to a conviction for exceeding the speed limit. The magistrate in this case said that 'in deciding the first information I took into consideration, besides other circumstances, the question of speed which I considered to be an element of danger'. The Court by a majority held that the magistrate after convicting on the first information was right in refusing to hear the second. Lawrence J, in the course of his judgment pointed out that this was not an inflexible rule:

'You might have a case [of dangerous driving] in which you might have a man convicted of driving to the danger of the public without there being any evidence of excessive speed. Then a policeman might come and say he was driving at over 20 miles an hour (the speed limit in 1908), and then the magistrate could convict [of speeding].'

In *R v Burnham Justices, supra.* the Divisional Court quashed a conviction for causing a motor car to wait in a restricted area when the defendant had already been convicted *on the same facts* and on the same occasion of having caused a motor car to wait on a road so as to cause unnecessary obstruction. The *proper course* in these circumstances, it is suggested, is to adjourn the less serious information *sine die* and to convict only on the more serious offence.

Where charges of both *careless* and *reckless driving* are preferred in respect of the same incident and the prosecutor indicates his willingness to accept a plea to the lesser charge this is subject to the agreement of the bench (a rule which would appear to hold good notwithstanding the wide and varied powers of the Crown Prosecutor). If after inquiring into the facts as presented by the prosecutor, they appear to warrant the more serious charge, the magistrates can properly refuse to accept the plea to the lesser offence: *R v Bedwellty Justices, ex p. Munday* [1970] Crim LR 601.

It was held in *Pilgram v Dean* [1974] 1 WLR 601 that magistrates could convict a motorist of both using a vehicle without a current excise licence and of failing to display such a licence. A request by the defendant that two charges should be tried together may preclude him from objecting to a dual conviction on the same evidence: *Williams v Hallam* (1943) 112 LJKB 353.

5.15   Military and civil convictions

A special application of the rule against double punishment is contained in s.133 Army Act 1955:

'Where a person subject to military law (a) has been tried for an offence by a court martial or has had an offence committed by him taken into consideration by a court martial in sentencing him, or (b) has been charged with an offence under this Act and has had the charge dealt with summarily by his commanding officer or the appropriate superior authority, a civil court shall be debarred from trying him subsequently for an offence substantially the same as that offence; but except as aforesaid nothing in this Act shall be construed as restricting the jurisdiction of any civil court to try a person subject to this Act for an offence.'

There is a provision in s.133 Air Force Act 1955, in identical terms but with the submission of 'air force law' for 'military law'; and in similar terms in s.129 Naval Discipline Act 1957. See also ss.3 and 4 Visiting Forces Act 1952 (not reproduced herein).

5.16   Oppression and abuse of process (including *Delay* and *Manipulation*)

A line of cases now establishes that magistrates' courts share with the higher courts a power to control 'oppression' and 'abuse of the process': see eg *R v Brentford Justices, ex p. Wong* [1981] 1 All ER 884; *R v West London Stipendiary Magistrate, ex p. Anderson* (1984) 148 JP 683 and *R v Derby Magistrates' Court, ex p. Brooks* (1984) 80 Cr App R 164. This power to stop a prosecution should *only be used in 'very exceptional circumstances'*, per Viscount Dilhorne in *Director of Public Prosecutions v Humphrys, supra* and in magistrates' courts its use is 'very strictly confined', per Lord Lane CJ in *R v Oxford City Justices, ex p. Smith* [1982] RTR 201 at p.206. The law was summarised as follows by Sir Roger Ormrod in *R v Derby Magistrates' Court, ex p. Brooks* (1984) 80 Cr App R 164:

'The power to stop a prosecution arises only when it is an abuse of the process of the court. It may be an abuse of process if either (a) the prosecution have manipulated or misused the process of the court so as to deprive the defendant of a protection provided by the law or to take unfair advantage of a technicality, or (b) on the balance of probability the defendant has been, or will be, prejudiced in the preparation or conduct of his defence by delay on the part of the prosecution which is unjustifiable: for example, not due to the complexity of the inquiry and preparation of the prosecution case, or to the action of the defendant or his co-accused, or to genuine difficulty in effecting service. We doubt whether the other epithets which are sometimes used in relation to delay, such as "unconscionable", "inordinate" or "oppressive" do more than add an emotive tone to an already sufficiently difficult problem. The ultimate objective of this discretionary power is to ensure that there should be a fair trial according to law, which involve fairness both to the defendant and the prosecution, for, as Lord Diplock said in *R v Sang* (1979) 69 Cr App R 282 at p.290. ". . . the fairness of a trial . . . is not all one-sided; it requires that those who are undoubtedly guilty should be convicted as well as that those about whose guilt there is any reasonable doubt should be acquitted". It is, as Lord Diplock also said in that case, "no part of a judge's function to exercise disciplinary powers over the police or prosecution as respects the way in which evidence to be used at the trial is obtained by them". Or, we would add, in regard to the preparation of the case, unless this has prejudiced the defendant in the way we have indicated. If the delay is not shown to have prejudiced the defendant in this way, lengthy inquiries into the reasons for the delay should not be necessary.'

(Judicial review was refused because the applicant had always admitted his guilt and would, inevitably, plead guilty at his trial: he had not therefore been prejudiced by the delay.)

Delay

Delay is the most common ground of objection. As Robert Goff LJ said in *R v West London Stipendiary Magistrate, ex p. Anderson* (1984) 148 JP 683 at 687:

'One particular type of case in which the power may be exercised occurs where delay has elapsed between the laying of an information within the six-month-period prescribed in s.127 of the Magistrates' Courts Act 1980, and the service of the summons on the defendant. The cases show that if delay of this kind has occurred in such circumstances, and has continued for such a time that it may be described as unconscionable, then the continuance of the prosecution may be regarded as an abuse of the process of the court and the magistrates may exercise their jurisdiction to decline to allow the prosecution to proceed further. A characteristic case for the exercise of the jurisdiction occurs where a substantial delay of this kind has been caused either by a deliberate act of the prosecution [for example, some "improper" or "mala fides" use of the procedure of the court – see *Graham* p.235, *per* May LJ, or by inefficiency on the part of the prosecution [see *Smith*], or even something having "gone wrong" with the system (see *Outrim*); and where the defendant has not himself caused or contributed to the delay. In such a case, if the defendant is shown to have suffered prejudice as a result of the delay, or even if such prejudice is to be inferred from the fact of the delay [see *Smith*], the magistrates may exercise the jurisdiction; indeed, the longer the delay, the more ready may the magistrates be to draw the inference of prejudice. In contrast where the sole, or even substantial, cause of the delay is the conduct of the defendant, then it is difficult to see how the continuance of the prosecution could be held to be an abuse of the process. There may however be cases where substantial delay has occurred, and this delay can be attributed in part to, for example, inefficiency on the part of the prosecution, and in part to the conduct of the defendant. In such circumstances the magistrates must consider, taking into account the conduct of the defendant, to what extent the delay which has occurred is attributable to the inefficiency of the prosecution; and if they consider that there has been substantial delay resulting from the inefficiency of the prosecution and that the defendant has been or must have been prejudiced by such delay, so that the continuance of the prosecution can be regarded as an abuse of the process of the court, they may exercise their jurisdiction to decline to allow the prosecution to proceed.'

In *R v Grays Justices, ex p. Graham* [1982] 3 WLR 596, it was held that delay of itself if sufficiently long can be an abuse of process but the delay in that case (four months between committal proceedings and two years since date of offence) was not sufficient. In *R v Oxford City Justices, ex p. Smith* [1982] RTR 201 magistrates were prevented from proceeding with the trial of the applicant on a charge of driving with excess alcohol where, owing to the fact that because the police were unobservant or inefficient or both, it took over two years after the commission of the alleged offence before a summons was served on him notwithstanding that the information was laid in time. The facts and outcome of *R v Watford Justices, ex p. Outrim* [1983] RTR 26 were broadly similar. A justice or justices' clerk may be justified in refusing to issue process on the grounds of delay, even though the information has been laid within the statutory time limit for summary proceedings: see *R v Clerk to the Medway Justices, ex p. DHSS* (1986) 150 JP 401.

In the absence of abuse of process, there is nothing to prevent proceedings being re-commenced after they have been dismissed for failing to give advance disclosure: *R v Willesden Justices, ex p. Clemmings* (1987) *The Times*, 21 October.

5.16a   *'Manipulation' or 'misuse' of procedure*

The other category of case identified by the court in *R v Derby Magistrates' Court, ex p. Brooks* (1984) 80 Cr App R 164, is where the prosecutor can be said to have manipulated or misused the rules of procedure. Thus, in *R v Brentford Justices, ex p. Wong* [1981] 1 All ER 884 the police laid an information two days before the expiry of the time limit but did not seek issue of the summons until over four months later: prohibition issued because the police *had deliberately attempted to gain time by the use of the 'precautionary' information*; and see *R v Clerk to the Medway Justices, supra*. In *Doyle v Leroux* [1981] RTR 438 the applicant, who was charged with driving with excess alcohol, had destroyed his specimen after being (wrongly) informed by the police that he would not be prosecuted. His appeal from conviction at the Crown Court was dismissed on the basis that this could not be described as an abuse of process and the applicant had not been prejudiced because he had already enjoyed sufficient time to get the specimen analysed. In *R v Newcastle upon Tyne Justices, ex p. Hindle* [1984] 1 All ER 770: *sub nom Thynn v Hindle* [1984] RTR 231 *prohibition* issued on the ground, *inter alia*, that, although the prosecution had acted in good faith by laying a charge which was ambiguous in the sense that it could be read as referring to one or other of two inconsistent offences, and by failing to give the necessary particulars when asked to do so, they had preserved an opportunity to advance their case on the basis of either of the two offences.

5.17   **WITHDRAWAL AND DISCONTINUANCE**

Process may with the leave of the court be withdrawn: *R v Broad* (1970) 68 Cr App R 281. The power to permit withdrawal is shared by a magistrates' court: *R v Phipps, ex p. Alton* [1964] 2 QB 420; *R v Redbridge Justices, ex p. Sainty* [1981] RTR 12; and see *Pickavance v Pickavance* [1901] P 60. However, the justices' consent is not necessary to a withdrawal of charges in committal proceedings: *R v Canterbury and St. Augustine's Justices, ex p. Klisiak* [1982] QB 398; and if the prosecutor offers 'no evidence' and prefers a lesser charge which is triable only summarily, this is not necessarily an abuse of the process of the court; *ibid*. Where the charges are of criminal damage, then withdrawl of one or more charges may prevent there being a 'series of offences' (see under that title in Chapter 2) so that a remaining charge becomes triable only summarily: *R v Braden* (1987) *The Times*, 14 October.

An information, as distinct from a summons, once laid, may not be withdrawn: *R v Leigh Justices, ex p. Kara* [1981] Crim LR 628. But when a prosecutor abandons the charge on which the defendant appears before the court, and proposes to proceed on a new charge, then a new information must be prepared: *Ex p. Klisiak, supra*. If the defendant so wishes, an adjournment should be granted: *ibid*. Where the defendant elects to continue with a case which the prosecutor wishes to withdraw, he cannot later change his mind and object: *Eggington v Pearl* (1875) 40 JP 56; *Conn v Turnbull* (1925) 89 JP Jo 300; and see *Peek v De Rutzen* (1882) 46 JP 313.

Since the creation of the Crown Prosecution Service, there is no longer the more general duty on the clerk to the justices to notify the Director of Public Prosecutions in a range of cases when charges are withdrawn or not proceeded with. But pursuant to the provisions of s.7(4) POA 1985 it *is* the duty of the clerk to send to the Director a copy of any information and other documents relating to a case in which:

(a) a prosecution is withdrawn or is not proceeded with within a reasonable time
(b) *the Director does not have the conduct of the proceedings*; and
(c) there is some ground for suspecting that there is no satisfactory reason for the withdrawal or failure to proceed.

According to *R v Preswick* [1978] Crim LR 377, where there has been an adjudication, whether or not a trial on the merits, the decision is binding and the matter cannot be prosecuted again. In contrast, it seems that – where there has been a withdrawal – there is no bar to subsequent proceedings on the same information, and that a withdrawal cannot thus amount to a 'dismissal on the merits' for the purposes of *autrefois acquit* (5.13, see *Davis v Morton* [1913] 2 KB 479; *Owens v Minoprio* [1942] 1 KB 193; *R (McDonnell) v Tyronne Justices* [1912] 2 IR 44; and *cf* now *R v Willesden Justices, ex p. Clemmings* (1987) *The Times*, 21 October, where even a dismissal for 'want of prosecution' was no bar to subsequent proceedings on the same information, and the defendant's contention that this amounted to an abuse of the processes of the court was rejected on the facts. Withdrawal should be distinguished from the unfettered *right* of the Crown Prosecutor *to discontinue* proceedings at a preliminary stage (including those which he has taken over from a private prosecutor): see Chapter 2, which is subject to the right of the accused to have the case continued with. The accused's insistence that proceedings *continue* will not, however, prevent either withdrawal by the prosecutor with the leave of the court where required, *supra*, or, even where the justices do not grant leave, the prosecutor offering 'no evidence', thereby obliging the justices to dismiss the charge.

For the power to award costs when an information is not proceeded with see s.16 Prosecution of Offences Act 1985, see Chapter 9.

PUTTING THE CHARGE   5.18

If the accused appears the court must state to him *the substance* of the information and ask him whether he pleads guilty or not guilty: s.9, MCA 1980. The court is under a duty not to accept a plea of guilty which is not 'equivocal' (a relatively common occurrence in practice, notably with unrepresented defendants, and *written pleas* of guilty under s.12 MCA 1980, *post* which are accompanied by 'exculpatory' mitigation – as to which see the discretion to 'abandon' the written plea procedure provided by s.12(2)(6), *post*). By contrast, the court has a discretion to permit an unambiguous plea of guilty to be changed to one of not guilty.

The entering of a plea of not guilty does *not* mark the commencement of the trial but simply establishes the need for one: *Quazi v Director of Public Prosecutions* [1988] *The Times*, 9 March (an immigration case in which jurisdiction turned on whether a certificate was signed before trial).

5.19 'Equivocal' pleas

A plea of guilty accompanied by words denying an essential element of the offence is really a plea of not guilty: *R v Golathon* (1915) 79 JP 270; *R v Durham Quarter Sessions, ex p. Virgo* [1952] 2 QB 1. This applies equally to statements made in mitigation: *R v Ingleson* [1915] 1 KB 512; to statements made to the police and read in court by the prosecutor: *R v Tottenham Justices, ex p. Rubens* [1970] 1 WLR 800 and to reported statements of the accused in a social inquiry report: *Maurice Leahy v Rawlinson* [1978] Crim LR 106. A plea is equivocal if, after a represented accused pleads guilty, his counsel interrupts and states that his client does not precisely understand the proceedings: *R v Halliwell* [1980] Crim LR 49; as is a plea of guilty to 'one twenty-eighth' of the value of a charge of theft: *R v South Sefton Justices ex p. Rabaca* (1986) *The Times*, 20 February.

Note, however, that where the plea is unequivocal, the court is bound to accept it, even though the precise basis of fact may be in dispute. If, subsequently, justices are confronted with a conflict of facts which are *extraneous to the offence* itself, the justices must then proceed to hear evidence on the disputed facts: *R v Telford Justices, ex p. Darlington* (1987) *The Times*, 25 November.

5.20 Change of plea

The accused can apply at any time before final adjudication to change his plea of guilty and it is for the court then to decide whether justice requires that this should be permitted. There is no difference in this respect in the practice of the superior and inferior courts and the doctrine of *functus officio* has no application to the acceptance of a plea: *S (an infant) v Manchester City Recorder* (1970) 134 JP 3. The court refused to upset an advocate's application to change a plea of guilty to one of not guilty in *R v Ali Tasamulug* [1971] Crim LR 441. Magistrates should only allow a change of plea where justified by the interests of justice and not by expediency: *R v Uxbridge Jutices, ex p. Smith* [1977] RTR 93. In *R v South Thameside Magistrates' Court, ex p. Rowland* [1983] 3 All ER 689 magistrates' refusal to allow a change of plea was upheld where they took the view that a likely reason for the application was fear of a custodial sentence. The court's power to allow an unequivocal plea of guilty to be changed at a later stage of the proceedings to one of not guilty should only be exercised in clear cases and very sparingly, *per* O'Connor J in *P Foster (Haulage) Ltd v Roberts* (1978) 142 JP 447 (solicitor mistakenly thought offence was absolute).

Magistrates cannot entertain an application to change a plea *after sentence: R v Campbell, ex p. Hoy* (1953) 117 JP 189; *R v McNally* [1954] 2 All ER 372; nor should they do so after a committal to the Crown Court for sentence: *R v Mutford & Lothingland Justices, ex p. Harber* [1971] 2 QB 291, except where the committal was invalid: *R v Norfolk Justices, ex p. Director of Public Prosecutions* [1950] 2 KB 558. Although the circumstances in which it would be proper to admit it are rare, the fact that a plea of guilty was entered (though subsequently withdrawn) may have some degree of probative value according to the circumstances of the case: *R v Rimmer* (1972) 136 JP 242.

5.21 Standing mute and 'fitness to plead'

In a trial *on indictment* a jury is empanelled to determine the issue of 'fitness to plead' s.4 Criminal Procedure (Insanity) Act 1964, but there is no analogous procedure which can be applied to magistrates' courts: *R v Metropolitan Stipendiary Magistrate, ex p. Aniifowoski* (1985) *The Times*, 5 August. Sometimes the prosecution, on hearing of the defendant's state of mind, will discontinue the proceedings and call in the mental welfare officer. If they do not, it is suggested that the preferred course is for magistrates to commit the defendant for trial in the case of an indictable offence and to enter a plea of not guilty in the case of a summary offence. Alternatively, the magistrates can proceed to hear the case and rely upon the provisions of the Mental Health Act 1983, *post*.

PROCEDURE ON A PLEA OF 'NOT GUILTY'   5.22

The order of proceedings following a plea of Not Guilty is mainly (but not entirely) set out in r.13 MC Rules 1981. Following any *preliminary points* which may be raised (see under that heading) the prosecutor may first 'open his case' in what is technically described as the 'opening speech', and then proceed to call his witnesses as well as producing any written statements or admissions in accordance with ss.9, 10, CJA 1967. At the close of his case, the court should consider whether a *prima facie* case has been made out and for this purpose hear any submission of *no case to answer*.

In a criminal trial the court has power to call a witness which neither prosecution nor defence wish to call. This is a power which is exercised only rarely and for compelling reasons: *R v Roberts* (1985) 80 Cr App R 89.

Case for the prosecution   5.23
It is a fundamental rule of English criminal law that it is the duty of the prosecution to prove every element of the offence alleged and that the offence has been committed by the person who is accused of it. To this general rule that the onus is on the prosecution, there are a limited number of exceptions discussed in Chapter 6, *Evidence*. But even in those rare instances where the onus *is* on the accused, the prosecutor must present the basic case and the evidence to the court. In practice, regular prosecutors tend to adopt as neutral a stance as their duty to present the case permits – 'laying the facts before the justices' as it is sometimes put, rather than pressing hard for a particular outcome. The prosecution case must be established by *evidence* in the form of oral testimony, written statements, documents and exhibits (as to all of which see Chapter 6).

No case to answer   5.24
In *R v Galbraith* (1981) Lord Lane CJ said in relation to trial by jury:

'(1) If there is no evidence that the crime alleged has been committed by the defendant, there is no difficulty. The judge will of course stop the case.
 (2) The difficulty arises where there is some evidence but it is of a tenuous character, for example because of inherent weakness or vagueness or because it is inconsistent with other evidence. (a) Where the judge comes to the conclusion that the prosecution evidence, taken at its highest, is such that a jury properly directed could not properly convict upon it, it is his duty, upon a submission being made, to stop the case. (b) Where however the prosecution evidence is such that its strength or weakness depends on the view to be taken of a witness's reliability, or other matters which are generally speaking within the province of the jury and where on one possible view of the facts there *is* evidence upon which a jury could properly come to the conclusion that the defendant is guilty, then the judge should allow the matter to be tried by the jury.'

This direction is supplemented in magistrates' courts by the *Practice Note* [1962] 1 All ER 448; which, it was said in *Stonely v Coleman* [1974] Crim LR 25, should always be brought to the attention of the presiding justice. That *Note* reads:

'A submission that there is no answer may properly be made and upheld:
  (a) when there has been no evidence to prove an essential element in the alleged offence;
  (b) when the evidence adduced by the prosecution has been so discredited as a result of
      cross-examination or is so manifestly unreliable that no reasonable tribunal could
      safely convict on it.
Apart from these two situations a tribunal should not in general be called on to reach a decision as to conviction or acquittal until the whole of the evidence which either side wishes to tender has been placed before it. If, however, a submission is made that there is no case to answer the decision should depend, not so much on whether the adjudicating tribunal (if compelled to do so) would at that stage convict or acquit, but on whether the evidence is such that a reasonable tribunal might convict. If a reasonable tribunal might convict on the evidence so far laid before it, there is a case to answer'.

Even if the defence makes no submission at the close of the prosecution case, it will, in appropriate cases, be the *duty of the court* to take the initiative itself: *R v Burdett* [1820] 4 B & Ald 95. It has been held in relation to civil proceedings that justices have a power at common law rather than under the rules to stop a case at the conclusion of the complainant's case, either of their own motion or on the complainant's submission: *Mayes v Mayes* [1971] 1 WLR 679. But, in contrast, it is not wrong for the court, of its own motion, to adjourn to allow the *prosecution* to obtain further *important* evidence: *R v Central Criminal Court, ex p. Garnier* (1987) *The Times*, 16 March; except possibly where evidence is a 'mere formality' or where a matter has arisen *ex improviso*: cf. *R v Pilcher* (1974) 60 Cr App R 1; *Royal v Prescott-Clarke* [1966] 1 WLR 788.

A submission of 'no case' is a submission *of law*. The prosecutor is thus entitled to reply to it and the clerk to advise upon it. It has been held that there is a case to answer when the only evidence of identification is the fact that the defendant who appears in answer to the summons bears the same name as appeared on a driving licence produced by the offender to a traffic warden: *Cooke v McCann* [1973] Crim LR 522; or even when counsel appears in answer to a summons and there is evidence that the driver gave the same name as the defendant: *Creed v Scott* [1976] Crim LR 381; see also *Stickings v George* [1980] RTR 237 (identity of driver).

In civil proceedings upon a submission of no case the court may have a discretion to insist that the defendant elects either to rely upon his submission or call evidence, but not both. But so far as criminal prosecutions are concerned, 'there is no question of putting a man to his election in a magistrates' court', *per* Lord Parker CJ, in *Jones v Metcalfe* (1967) 131 JP 494. But it is important that justices should ascertain whether what is submitted is *part of the final speech of the defence advocate or whether he makes the submission while reserving his right to call evidence thereafter*. The proper practice should be to ask a defendant: 'Are you making a final speech or are you making a submission and reserving the right to call evidence hereafter?', *per* Lord Parker CJ in *R v Gravesend Justices, ex p. Sheldon* [1968] 1 WLR 1699; see also *R v Birkenhead Justices, ex p. Fisher* [1962] 1 WLR 1410; *R v Essex Justices, ex p. Final; Same v Same* [1962] 3 All ER 924.

Where through a misunderstanding, justices, having retired to consider a submission of no case, return and announce a conviction, and the error is subsequently pointed out to them, they may on the authority of *S (an infant) v Manchester City Recorder* (1970) 134 JP 3, direct a re-hearing of the case by a differently constituted bench: *R v Midhurst Justices, ex p. Thompson* [1974] QB 137. The court may dismiss a case after rejecting a submission, even where no evidence is given for defence: *Lyons Maid Ltd v John Hardy Burrows* (1974) 138 JPN 701; *De Filipo v De Filipo* (1963) 108 SJ 56 (a civil case).

Case for the accused   5.25
Following the close of the prosecution case the accused may give evidence and call witnesses in accordance with r.13 MC Rules 1981.

He is not entitled to make a statement without being sworn, but an *unrepresented* accused may *address* the court otherwise than on oath on any matter on which, if he were represented, his advocate could do so: s.72(1),(2) CJA 1982.

The accused *must* be called before any other witness to the facts of the case *unless* the court in its discretion otherwise directs: s.79 PACE Act 1984.

Evidence in rebuttal   5.26
At the conclusion of the evidence for the defence the prosecutor may call evidence to *rebut* that evidence: r.13(3) MC Rules 1981. Such evidence must be confined to matters arising unexpectedly: *R v Whelan* (1881) 14 Cox CC 595; 8 LR Ir 314. That is to say, 'matters arising *ex improviso* which no human ingenuity can foresee': *R v Harris* (1927) 91 JP 152. If the prosecution could *reasonably have foreseen* that a particular piece of evidence was necessary to prove their case they must call it as part of their case and not wait until the defendant has given evidence: *R v Scott* [1984] Crim LR 235 (a 'shoplifting' offence, to which class of case this rule was said to be particularly important); see also *R v Levy & Tait* [1966] Crim LR 454.

Re-opening otherwise than in rebuttal   5.27
There are circumstances where the prosecution may make application to *re-open* their case otherwise than in rebuttal of the defence evidence. Justices should always allow a case to be re-opened where the matter is one 'of technicality such as the proof of a statutory rule or order', *per* Devlin J, in *Price v Humphries* [1958] 2 QB 353; see also *Palastanga v Solman* [1962] Crim LR 334. 'In all ordinary circumstances and in the absence of any conduct on the part of the prosecution which might properly be described as misconduct or election not to call other evidence and in the absence of any grave potential prejudice to the accused, there is only one way in which the discretion (ie to grant an adjournment) can properly be exercised', *per* Winn LJ in *Royal v Prescott Clarke* [1966] 1 WLR 788 (proof of notices and regulations allowed after submission of no case to answer).

But this applies only to highly technical or formal evidence. Where the prosecution omit to give any evidence *on a matter of substance*, such as the identity of the driver in a charge of careless driving, the justices have a *discretion* in the matter which they need not automatically exercise in favour of the prosecutor: *Middleton v Rowlett* [1954] 1 WLR 831, *Jones v Carter* [1956] Crim LR 275. In *Saunders v Johns* [1965] Crim LR 49, the Divisional Court held that, while evidence of identity could be called by the prosecutor or the court following the close of the prosecution case and even after a submission of no case, it could not be called after the defence had closed their case. In *Piggott v Simms* [1972] Crim LR 595, the failure of the prosecution to put in the analyst's certificate in a drunken driving case was treated as a matter of substance rather than a procedural error; and see *Matthews v Morris* [1981] Crim LR 495.

The power to re-open is *not* confined to evidence of formal nature. Justices have power to allow a case to be re-opened and to adjourn to enable any necessary proof to be obtained. This extends to any evidence omitted owing to accident or mistake or lack of foresight: *Duffin v Markham* (1981) 82 JP 281 (magistrates' dismissal on a submission of no case reversed where prosecutor failed to prove order). Similarly, when after two defence witnesses had been called, two of six other witnesses in court discovered their own capacity to contribute something to the trial the judge's decision to allow the prosecutor to re-open his case was upheld: *R v Doran* (1972) 56 Cr App R 429. As a general rule and in the absence of some special circumstances, it would certainly be wholly wrong for justices to purport to exercise a discretion to allow evidence to be called *once they had retired*: *Webb v Leadbetter* [1966] 1 WLR 245; followed in *Phelan v Back* [1972] 1 WLR 273; *French's Dairies (Sevenoaks) Ltd v Davis* [1973] Crim LR 630. This applies even where the irregularity takes place at the request of the defence: *R v Nixon* (1968) 132 JP 309: *R v Corless* (1972) 56 Cr App R 341 (evidence by formal admission wrongly admitted after jury had retired). No question about re-opening arises where what is in issue is whether the proceedings were properly authorised and the prosecution have been allowed to close their case without objection; assuming awareness by the defendant (*semble*) such an objection should have been made by the defence before the prosecution close their case: *Price v Humphries* [1958] 2 QB 353.

5.28 Majority decision

The decision of justices is that of the *majority* and the chairman has *no casting vote*. It has been said that if, on a division of opinion, one justice withdraws there is no objection to the ensuing majority verdict: *Ex p. Evans* (1894) 58 JP 260 (licensing); but this was disapproved in *Barnsley v Marsh,* [1947] KB 672, and the better course for justices equally divided is to adjourn the case for hearing before a fresh bench: *Bagg v Colquhoun* (1904) 68 JP 205; *Barnsley v Marsh, supra*. If they do not adjourn, the information should be dismissed: *R v Ashplant* (1888) 52 JP 474. A further summons cannot be preferred after a dismissal in these circumstances: *Kinnis v Graves* (1898) 67 LJQB 583. Where there is an uneven number of justices they must not '*fail to adjudicate*', and *mandamus* has issued to compel them to hear a case and come to a decision; also *prohibition* to prevent them remitting to another bench: *R v Bridgend Justices, ex p. Randall* [1975] Crim LR 297. A decision by a bench of *three* magistrates to remit the case for a re-hearing to a fresh bench on the basis that they were unable to come to a conclusion was quashed in *R v Bromley Justices, ex p. Haymills (Contractors) Ltd* (1984) 148 JP 363.

5.29 Ordering a re-trial

When the accused is convicted following a plea of not guilty or after the hearing has proceeded in his absence the same court or, if the court consisted of three or more justices, a court consisting of or including a majority of that court, may *within 28 days* beginning with the day of conviction order a re-trial before a different bench: s.142(2) MCA 1980.

In no other case can a finding of guilt once pronounced in open court be changed because the magistrates are *functi officio*: cf *R v Manchester Justices, ex p. Lever* (1937) 101 JP 407; *R v Essex Justices, ex p. Final* [1963] 2 QB 816; but it is an open question whether justices have an inherent power to treat proceedings as a complete nullity where they have acted without jurisdiction: cf those cases where a declaration of nullity has been granted, and query whether this remedy does any more than state what the position has always been: see *Appeals*, Chapter 11.

WRITTEN PLEAS OF GUILTY   5.30

Under the special 'paperwork' procedures provided for in s.12 MCA 1980, a plea of guilty may be received *in writing*, and in the absence of the accused. Cases dealt with under this procedure are commonly referred to as 'paperwork cases' or 'MCA cases', the latter after the Magistrates' Courts Act 1957 which originally introduced the procedure.

In outline, the procedure, which is *confined to summary offences punishable by not more than three months' imprisonment* (see s.12(1)), requires service on the accused – along with the summons – of a *statement of facts* and an explanatory note. If the clerk receives a written plea of guilty purporting to come from the accused or his solicitor and a statement that the accused does not wish to be present, then both the statement of facts, the plea, and anything which the accused has written in mitigation or concerning his financial position is read to the court. Under an amended s.12(4), the duty of reading out both the prosecutor's and the accused's documents is cast on *the clerk of the court.*

The written plea of guilty must relate to each offence alleged: *R v Burnham Justices, ex p. Ansorge* [1959] 3 All ER 505; but receipt may be at any time before the hearing, even where there has been an adjournment: *R v Norham and Islandshire Justices, ex p. Sunter Bros Ltd* [1961] 1 All ER 455. Where the offence is endorseable, the defendant must also give details of his or her date of birth and sex: s.104 Road Traffic Act 1972.

The court may of its own volition discontinue the procedure under s.12 in favour of regular proceedings, but whilst it is in operation no information may be given to the court by or on behalf of the prosecutor other than that contained in the documents already referred to, except following an adjournment after conviction together with due notice. The written plea of guilty may be withdrawn by the accused at any time before sentence.

The procedure under s.12 is *strict* and deviation from it – such, eg as a failure to *read out* the defendant's mitigation, or to read it out in full – will render the proceedings a nullity: see, eg *R v Oldham Justices, ex p. Morissey* [1959] 1 WLR 58; *R v Epping and Ongar Justices, ex p. Shippam* (1986) 150 JP 425. There is no power to rectify such an omission under s.142 MCA 1980: *ibid*; but the 'consent procedure' for judicial review is available: see *Practice Direction (Crown Office List: Criminal Proceedings)* [1983] 2 All ER 1020.

Under a recent and at first sight rather peculiar provision, the court may – provided that the accused consents – proceed under the written plea procedure where he is actually present '. . . as if he were absent': see s.12(9). The purpose of this provision would appear to be to overcome the need either for a prosecutor or an adjournment if the court abandons the written plea procedure. But a problem will still arise, eg if the accused wishes to go beyond the strict code of procedure, eg by adding his own oral comments.

A corporation may give notice via a director or secretary and the court may act upon such purported notification: Sch.3, para 1, MCA 1980. The procedure is *not* available in the juvenile court: see s.12(1).

Many cases proceed under s.12 – the option to do so being that of the prosecutor at the outset – becoming 'specified proceedings' within the meaning of the POA 1985 (Specified Proceedings) Order 1985 (SI No 2010) when the summons is served, so that they will not, eg be prosecuted by the Crown Prosecution Service – see, generally, Chapter 2. They cease to be 'specified proceedings' if the court begins to receive 'evidence', for which purpose the receipt of information under s.12(4) does not count.

Notwithstanding the bar on extraneous information, previous convictions may be cited in accordance with the provisions of s.104 MCA 1980, following conviction and provided that the notice requirement in s.104 has been complied with.

5.31   **TRIAL OF JUVENILES**

A charge against a juvenile *must* be heard in the juvenile court, except that magistrates in the adult court *may* deal with a juvenile charged with aiding and abetting an adult or *vice versa*, and where the offence arose out of circumstances which are the same as or connected with those giving rise to an offence with which an adult is at the same time charged; and *must* hear an information against a juvenile *jointly charged* with an adult s.46(1) CYPA 1933 and s.18 CYPA 1963. There is, additionally, a saving in the former provision whereby a defendant who is *discovered to be a juvenile only in the course of proceedings* in the adult court *may nevertheless be dealt with thereby*. The restrictions on the jurisdiction of the adult court do not prevent it from hearing remand applications: s.46(2) CYPA 1933. Notwithstanding these provisions, when a juvenile is jointly charged with an adult or a corporation and the latter pleads guilty and is committed for trial or is discharged and the juvenile pleads not guilty the juvenile *may* be remitted to the juvenile court for trial before evidence is called: s.29, MCA 1980.

A juvenile unwittingly dealt with in the adult court on a written plea of guilty under s.12 MCA 1980 is *deemed* to have attained the age of 17: s.46(1A) CYPA 1983.

A juvenile appearing in court must be *prevented from associating with adults who have been charged* and, if a girl, must be under the care of a woman: s.31 CYPA 1933. The terms *'conviction'* and *'sentence'* are replaced for juveniles by the clumsy euphemisms *'finding of guilt'* and *'order made upon a finding of guilt'*: s.59 CYPA 1933. A special form of oath (ie the 'promise') is prescribed for juveniles by s.28 CYPA 1963. At every stage of the proceedings the court must have regard (among other things) *to the welfare of a juvenile* and must take steps in a proper case to remove him from undesirable surroundings: s.44 CYPA 1933.

The rule that the names of juveniles involved in proceedings in the juvenile court may not be reported in the press: s.49, does not apply to the adult court except in cases involving the variation of supervision orders; s.10 CYPA 1969. But in any proceedings the court *may* make an order preventing the press from identifying any juvenile concerned in any way therein: s.39 CYPA 1933. Furthermore, the public, *but not the press*, may be excluded by direction of the court when a juvenile gives evidence in

roceedings in relation to an offence against or conduct contrary to, ecency or morality: *ibid*, s.37.
'ote The position of juveniles in the adult court is set out in the chart at .63.

'resumption of incapacity 5.32

is *conclusively presumed* that no child *under the age of 10* can be guilty f any offence: s.50 CYPA 1933. At common law a child *under 14* was resumed not to know right from wrong and thus to be *doli incapax*, a resumption which, in the case of those of (now) 10 years and over may e rebutted by strong proof of mischievous disposition: *malitia supplet etatem: R v Gorrie* (1918) 83 JP 136. The rule was considered in *JM (a iinor) v Runeckles* (1984) 79 Cr App R 255 where Robert Goff LJ said at .260:

. . the prosecution has to prove that the child knew that what he or she was doing was riously wrong. The point is that it is not enough that the child realised that what he or she as doing was naughty or mischievous. It must go beyond childish things of that kind. That, 5 I understand it, is the real point underlying the presumption that a child under the age of 4 has not yet reached the age of discretion, because children under that age may think what iey are doing is nothing more than mischievous. It would not be right for a child under that 3e to be convicted of a crime, even if they had committed the relevant *actus reus* and had ie relevant *mens rea* specified in the statute, unless they appreciated that what they were oing was seriously wrong and so went beyond childish activity of that kind.'

.nd where Mann J said at p.259:

think it is unnecessary to show that the child appreciated that his or her action was morally rong. It is sufficient that the child appreciated the action was seriously wrong. A court has look for something beyond mere naughtiness or childish mischief.'

'he younger the child, the stronger the evidence required: *B v R* (1958) 23 JP 61. But it is dangerous to deduce capacity from the demeanour of ie accused in court. While this may be evidence it is evidence to which *ery little weight* should be given: *Ex p. N* [1959] Crim LR 523. Evidence f background should be heard to decide whether a child has been rought up with a knowledge of right or wrong: *R v Padwick* [1959] Crim .R 439. The prosecution can call any relevant evidence, including pre-ious convictions, to rebut the presumption: *R v B* [1979] 3 All ER 360. If ie prosecution fail to call evidence to rebut the presumption of inca-acity the information *must* be dismissed upon the close of the pros-cution case: *JBH and JH (Minors) v O'Connell* [1981] Crim LR 632. 'here is an irrebuttable presumption *against sexual capacity* in the case of child *under 14 years* in respect of certain sexual and unnatural offences ich as rape: *R v Phillips* (1839) 8 C & P 736; *R v Waite* [1892] 2 QB 600. 'ut a child *is* capable of aiding and abetting such an offence.

REFERENCE TO THE EUROPEAN COURT 5.33

Jnder the EEC Treaty (the Treaty of Rome), art 177:

'he Court of Justice shall have jurisdiction to give preliminary rulings concerning: (a) the terpretation of this Treaty; (b) the validity and interpretation of acts of the institutions of ie Community; (c) the interpretation of the statutes of bodies established by an act of the ouncil, where those statutes so provide.
Where such a question is raised before any court or tribunal of a member state, that court r tribunal may, if it considers that a decision on the question is necessary to enable it to give idgment, request the Court of Justice to give ruling thereon.
Whereon any such question is raised in a case pending before a court or tribunal of a

member state, against whose decisions there is no judicial remedy under national law, th
court or tribunal shall bring the matter before the Court of Justice.

In *An Bord Bainne Co-Operative Ltd (Irish Dairy Board) v Mil*
Marketing Board (No 2) (1985) *The Times*, 26 May it was held that:

1. An English court could only refer a question to the European court if the English cou
considered that a decision on the question was necessary to enable it to give judgmen
see art. 177 of the Treaty and *HP Bulmer Ltd v J Bollinger SA* [1974] Ch 401.
2. The word 'necessary' should not be construed too narrowly. Thus in *Polydor Ltd*
Harlequin Record Shops Ltd [1980] 2 CMLR 413 Lord Justice Ormrod said (at p.428
'I would not, for my part, be inhibited by any nice questions of necessity, and woul
regard the word 'necessary' as meaning 'reasonably necessary' in ordinary English an
not "unavoidable".'
See also *R v Plymouth Justices, ex p. Rogers* [1982] 863.
On the other hand the word 'necessary' was clearly much stronger than 'desirable' ∈
'convenient': see Lord Denning, Master of the Rolls, in the *Bollinger* case at p.423.
3. The power conferred on a court of first instance to refer questions under art 177 wa
wholly discretionary. Furthermore, it was for the English court to decide at what stage i
the proceedings it was appropriate to refer questions to the European court: see *Iris*
Creamery Milk v Ireland [1981–3] EC 735, 747.
4. As a general rule a reference should not be made until the facts had been found by th
English court and therefore a reference should not be made at an interlocutory stage: se
Lord Denning in the *Bollinger* case at p. 423 and Lord Justice Templeman in *Polydor*
p. 426. See also *Bethell v Sabena* [1983] 3 CMLR 1, 5 *per* Parker J.
There might be cases, however, where it would be appropriate to refer questions to th
European court at any early stage in the proceedings in the national court: see, fc
example, *Customs and Excise Commissioners v Aps Samex* [1983] 1 All ER 1042.

A magistrates' court is a 'court or tribunal' falling within the secon
paragraph of the article which has a discretion to refer a question if
considers it 'necessary' to enable it to give judgment. The position of th
magistrates' court to be contrasted with that of a court against whos
decision there is no judicial remedy who must refer such a matter to th
European Court: *R v Plymouth Justices, ex p. Rogers, supra*, wher
Donaldson LJ said:

'The test is not more stringent in a magistrates' court but in the ordinary case it would l
highly undesirable for the justices to decide to refer until all the evidence had been calle
and until they could be satisfied that there was no question of the respondent being acquitte
on the facts (but in this case the justices were correct in not so waiting). In the ordinary wa
justices should exercise considerable caution before referring even after they hear all th
evidence. If they come to a wrong decision on Community law, a higher court can make th
reference and frequently the higher court would be the more suitable forum to do so. Th
higher court is as a rule in a better position to assess whether any reference is desirable. C
references the form of the question referred is of importance and the higher court w
normally be in a better position to assess the appropriateness of the question and to assist
formulating it clearly. Leaving it to the higher court will often also avoid delay.'

Statutory Provisions

5.34   **CHILDREN AND YOUNG PERSONS ACT 1933**

Separation of children and young persons from adults in police stations, court
etc.
    31. Arrangements shall be made for preventing a child or young perso
while detained in a police station, or while being conveyed to or from ar
criminal court, or while waiting before or after attendance in any crimin

court, from associating with an adult (not being a relative) who is charged with any offence other than an offence with which the child or young person is jointly charged, and for ensuring that a girl (being a child or young person) shall while so detained, being conveyed, or waiting, be under the care of a woman.

COMMENTARY

Waiting, 'It is desirable that a child witness should be able to wait in privacy and comfort – if possible in a separate room – and should have a trusted adult close at hand at all times, especially when giving evidence': HOC No 208/1964.

Prohibition against children being present in court during the trial of other persons

5.35

36. No child (other than an infant in arms) shall be permitted to be present in court during the trial of any other person charged with an offence, or during any proceedings preliminary thereto, except during such time as his presence is required as a witness or otherwise for the purposes of justice; and any child present in court when under this section he is not to be permitted to be so shall be ordered to be removed:

Provided that this section shall not apply to messengers, clerks, and other persons required to attend at any court for purposes connected with their employment.

Power to clear court while child or young person is giving evidence in certain cases

5.36

37. (1) Where, in any proceedings in relation to an offence against, or any conduct contrary to, decency or morality, a person who, in the opinion of the court, is a child or young person is called as a witness, the court may direct that all or any persons, not being members or officers of the court or parties to the case, their counsel or solicitors, or persons otherwise directly concerned with the case, be excluded from the court during the taking of the evidence of that witness:

Provided that nothing in this section shall authorise the exclusion of *bona fide* representatives of a newspaper or news agency.

(2) The powers conferred on a court by this section shall be in addition and without prejudice to any other powers of the court to hear proceedings in camera.

COMMENTARY

The object of this section is more likely to be attained if the court is closed before the witness enters: HOC 208/1964. The Home Office also recommends that justices' attention should be drawn to their powers under this section in certain cases: see Commentary on s.39, *infra*.

s.37(1): Provided that, without a direction under s.39, *infra*, the press are not prevented from publishing what is said simply by virtue of the fact that an order is made under this section.

s.37(2): Any other powers, eg s.4(2) MCA 1980 (committal proceedings) and s.8(4) Official Secrets Act 1920 (proceedings under the Official Secrets Acts).

Power to prohibit publication of certain matter in newspaper

5.37

39. (1) In relation to any proceedings in any court, the court may direct that–
  (a) no newspaper report of the proceedings shall reveal the name, address, or school, or include any particulars calculated to lead to the identification, of any child or young person concerned in the proceedings, either as being the person by or against or in respect of whom the proceedings are taken, or as being a witness therein;
  (b) no picture shall be published in any newspaper as being or including a picture of any child or young person so concerned in the proceedings as aforesaid:

except in so far (if at all) as may be permitted by the direction of the court

(2) Any person who publishes any matter in contravention of any such direction shall on summary conviction be liable in respect of each offence to fine not exceeding level 5 on the standard scale.

[*As amended by s.57 CYPA 1963, s.31, Sch.6 CLA 1977 ss.39, 46, Sch.3 CJA 1982, Sch.5 Cable and Broadcasting Act 1984.*]

COMMENTARY

This section, with the necessary modification, applies in relation to sound and television broadcasts as it applies in relation to newspapers: s.57(4) CYPA 1963.

'In Home Office Circular No. 18/1956 the Secretary of State suggested that, in all cases to which s.39 applied, the clerk to the justices should remind the court of its powers under this section and, in a case committed for trial, include with the depositions a statement that the examining justices, having had their attention drawn to those powers, did or did not exercise them. Section 39, as extended by s.57(1) of the 1963 Act, will apply in any proceeding against or in respect of a person under 17, or in which such a person is a witness. The Secretary of State thinks that it would be sufficient to draw the court's attention especially to its powers under that section only in cases where:
  (a) one of the defendants before an ordinary magistrates' court is under the age of 17, or
  (b) the proceedings arise (in the current phrase) "out of an offence against or conduct contrary to decency or morality."
'In the second class of case the justices' attention might also be drawn to their power under s.37 of the Act of 1933 to exclude the public while a witness under 17 gives evidence. If in a case of the kinds mentioned at (a) and (b) above (or in any other case in which the justices have given a direction under s.37 or s.39) the defendant is committed to a superior court for trial or for sentence, it would be helpful if the statement suggested in the Home Office Circ. 18/1956 could be included with the depositions or other documents sent to the clerk of that court.' HOC 17/1964.

Rule 11(2)(m) MC Rules 1981 requires the justices' clerk to send to the court of trial statement whether the court has given a direction under s.39 in every case where a person under 17 is concerned in the committal proceedings (whether as defendant or witness).

5.38   **General considerations**
      44. (1) Every court in dealing with a child or young person who is brought before it, either as an offender or otherwise, shall have regard to the welfare of the child or young person and shall in a proper case take steps for removing him from undesirable surroundings, and for securing that proper provision is made for his education and training.
      [*As amended by Sch.6 CYPA 1969.*]

5.39   **Assignment of certain matters to juvenile courts**
      46. (1) Subject as hereinafter provided, no charge against a child or young person, and no application whereof the hearing is by rules made under this section assigned to juvenile courts, shall be heard by a court of summary jurisdiction which is not a juvenile court:
      Provided that:
      (a) a charge made jointly against a child or young person and a person who has attained the age of 17 years shall be heard by a court of summary jurisdiction other than a juvenile court; and
      (b) where a child or young person is charged with an offence, the charge may be heard by a court of summary jurisdiction which is not a juvenile court if a person who has attained the age of 17 years is charged at the same time with aiding, abetting, causing, procuring, allowing or permitting that offence; and
      (c) where, in the course of any proceedings before any court of summary jurisdiction other than a juvenile court, it appears that the person to whom the proceedings relate is a child or young person, nothing in this subsection shall be construed as preventing the court, if it thinks fit so to do, from proceeding with the hearing and determination of those proceedings.

(1A) If a notification that the accused desires to plead guilty without appearing before the court is received by the clerk of a court in pursuance of section 12 of the Magistrates' Courts Act 1980 and the court has no reason to believe that the accused is a child or young person, then, if he is a child or young person he shall be deemed to have attained the age of 17 for the purposes of subs.(1) of this section in its application to the proceedings in question.

(2) No direction, whether contained in this or any other Act, that a charge shall be brought before a juvenile court shall be construed as restricting the powers of any justice or justices to entertain an application for bail or for a remand, and to hear such evidence as may be necessary for that purpose.

[*As amended by Sch.9 Education Act 1944, Sch.7 Justices of the Peace Act 1949, Sch.5 CYPA 1969 and Sch.7 MCA 1980.*]

COMMENTARY

The powers of an adult court to hear cases involving juveniles were extended largely by s.18 CYPA 1963, *infra*. For the *power* to remit a juvenile for trial to a juvenile court in certain circumstances see s.29 MCA 1980, *infra*. For the *duty* to remit to the juvenile court after a finding of guilt see s.56 of the 1933 Act and s.7(8) CYPA 1969, Chapter 8.

s.46(1): Charge, it is suggested that this does not extend to a complaint for a bind-over under s.115 MCA 1980, or even to a juvenile arrested for a breach of the peace without such a complaint or any charge being preferred.

Rules made under this section, none has been made.

Proviso (a), but see s.29 MCA 1980, *infra*. (Power to remit to juvenile court for trial).

Charge made jointly, see the note to s.6 CYPA 1969, infra.

Attained the age of 17 years, for the determination of age, see s.99; also s.46(1A), *supra*.

Shall be heard/may be heard, the difference in wording clearly implies that the court has a discretion in para (b), but not in para (a).

Aiding, abetting, see s.44 MCA 1980.

Age of criminal responsibility   5.40
50. It shall be conclusively presumed that no child under the age of 10 years can be guilty of any offence.
[*As amended by s.16(1) CYPA 1963.*]

COMMENTARY

The provisions of s.4 CYPA 1969 (which would prevent prosecutions for offences committed by children) have not been brought into effect. For the *Presumption of Incapacity* in the case of children see under that title in the introduction.

Note
For s.56 CYPA 1933 (power of court to remit juvenile offenders to juvenile courts on finding of guilt) see Chapter 8.

Miscellaneous provisions as to summary proceedings against juvenile offenders   5.41
59. (1) The words 'conviction' and 'sentence' shall cease to be used in relation to children and young persons dealt with summarily and any reference to any enactment whether passed before or after the commencement of this Act to a person convicted, a conviction or a sentence shall, in the case of a child or young person, be construed, as including a reference to a person found guilty of an offence, a finding of guilt or an order made upon such finding, as the case may be.
[*As amended by Sch.9 CJA 1948, Costs in Criminal Cases Act 1952, s.8(1).*]

COMMENTARY

The effect of this section is purely terminological; thus a finding of guilt remains a previous conviction for the purpose of attracting higher penalties, for the penalty points provisions under the Transport Act 1981, and for all other purposes. But see s.16 CYPA 1963, *infra*, as to the citation of findings of guilt which occurred when the offender was under the age of 14.

5.42   **Presumption and determination of age**
    99. (1) Where a person, whether charged with an offence or not, is brought before any court otherwise than for the purpose of giving evidence, and it appears to the court that he is a child or young person, the court shall make due enquiry as to the age of that person, and for that purpose shall take such evidence as may be forthcoming at the hearing of the case, but an order or judgment of the court shall not be invalidated by any subsequent proof that the age presumed or declared by the court to be the age of the person so brought before it shall, for the purposes of the Act, be deemed to be the true age of that person, and where it appears to the court that the person so brought before it has attained the age of 17 years, that person shall for the purposes of this Act be deemed not to be a child or young person.

(2) Where in any charge or indictment for any offence under this Act or any of the offences mentioned in the First Schedule to this Act, except as provided in that Schedule, it is alleged that the person by or in respect of whom the offence was committed was a child or young person or was under or had attained any specified age, and he appears to the court to have been at the date of the commission of the alleged offence a child or young person, or to have been under or to have attained the specific age, as the case may be, he shall for the purpose of this Act be presumed at that date to have been a child or young person or to have been under or to have attained that age, as the case may be, unless the contrary is proved.

(3) Where, in any charge or indictment for any offence under this Act or any of the offences mentioned in the First Schedule to this Act, it is alleged that the person in respect of whom the offence was committed was a child or was a young person, it shall not be a defence to prove that the person alleged to have been a child was a young person or the person alleged to have been a young person was a child in any case where the acts constituting the alleged offence would equally have been an offence if committed in respect of a young person or child respectively.

(4) Where a person is charged with an offence under this Act in respect of a person apparently under a specified age it shall be a defence to prove that the person was actually of or over that age.
    [*As amended by Sch.3 Sexual Offences Act 1956.*]

COMMENTARY
s.99(1): This Act, includes the 1969 Act s.70(3) CYPA 1969.

5.43   **FIRST SCHEDULE**

Offences against children and young persons, with respect to which special provisions of this Act apply
The murder or manslaughter of a child or young person.

Infanticide.

Any offence under ss.27, 56, of the Offences against the Persons Act 1861, and any offences against a child or young person under ss.5, 42, 43, of that Act.

Any offence under ss.1, 3, 4, 11 or 23, of this Act.

Any offence against a child or young person under any of the following sections of the Sexual Offences Act 1956, that is to say, ss.2 to 7, 10 to 16, 19, 20, 22 to 26, and 28 and any attempt to commit against a child or young person an offence under ss.2, 5, 6, 7, 10, 11, 12, 22 or 23 of that Act. Provided that for the purposes of s.99(2) of this Act this entry shall apply so far only as it relates

to offences under ss.10, 11, 12, 14, 15, 16, 20 and 28 of the Sexual Offences Act 1956, and attempts to commit offences under ss.10, 11 and 12 of that Act.
Any other offence involving bodily injury to a child or young person.
[*As amended by Sch.3 Sexual Offences Act 1956.*]

CHILDREN AND YOUNG PERSONS ACT 1963   5.44

Offences committed by children
16. (2) In any proceedings for an offence committed or alleged to have been committed by a person of or over the age of 21, any offence of which he was found guilty while under the age of 14 shall be disregarded for the purposes of any evidence relating to his previous convictions; and he shall not be asked, and if asked shall not be required to answer, any question relating to such an offence, notwithstanding that the question would otherwise be admissible under s.1 of the Criminal Evidence Act 1898.

COMMENTARY
This Act is to be construed as one with the CYPA 1933; s.65(3) 1963.

The age of 21, for the determination of age, see s.150(4) MCA 1980, and s.99 CYPA 1933, *supra.*

Disregarded for the purposes of any evidence relating to his previous convictions, but not for the purposes of informing the court as to antecedents: *Practice Direction* [1966] 2 All ER 929.

Section 1 of the Criminal Evidence Act 1898, proviso (f) thereof lists the cases in which a witness may be questioned as to previous offences.

MAGISTRATES' COURT ACT 1980   5.45

Procedure on trial
9. (1) On the summary trial of an information, the court shall, if the accused appears, state to him the substance of the information and ask him whether he pleads guilty or not guilty.

(2) The court, after hearing the evidence and the parties, shall convict the accused or dismiss the information.

(3) If the accused pleads guilty, the court may convict him without hearing evidence.

COMMENTARY
s.9(1): An information See under this title in the introduction to Chapter 2. For the trial of two or more informations at the same time see under *Joinder of Offences and Defendants* at 5.10.

State . . . the substance of the information, loquacity rather than justice served by reading out the formal wording of the information in full and this applies *a fortiori* to the young and inarticulate.

Ask him, the question must be asked personally of the accused whether he pleads guilty or not and a plea of guilty by a solicitor without the question being so put will be quashed: *R v Wakefield Justices, ex p. Butterworth* [1970] 1 All ER 1181. So long as the charges are put to the accused personally there is nothing wrong in his solicitor pleading guilty even if such a plea was not justified by his instructions, provided the accused did not show dissatisfaction with the plea: *ibid*; and see *R v Gowerton Justices, ex p. Davies* [1974] Crim LR 253.
    Despite the wording of this provision it has long been universal practice in magistrates' courts to accept a plea of guilty from a solicitor or counsel representing under s.122 MCA 1980 an accused who is not personally present.

Pleads guilty, the plea must be entered in the register: r.66(4) MC Rules 1981.
    For the conduct of a trial following a plea of guilty, see the note *Ascertaining the Facts on a Plea of Guilty*, Chapter 8. For *Ambiguous Pleas* and *Change of Plea* see under those headings in Chapter 8.

Or not guilty, the plea must be entered in the register: r.66(4) MC Rules 1981.

s.9(2): Hearing the evidence and the parties, as to the order of speeches on a plea of not guilty, see r.13 MC Rules 1981, and s.79 PACE Act 1984, *post.*

Convict the accused or dismiss the information, the terms 'conviction' and 'sentence' may not be used in relation to juveniles for whom the terms 'finding of guilt' or an 'order upon a finding of guilt' have been prescribed by s.59(1) CYPA 1933.

There is no power in a magistrates' court to substitute a conviction for a lesser offence. *Martin v Brickhill* (1864) 28 JP 359. In *Lawrence v Same* [1968] 2 QB 93, Lord Parker CJ said that if the justices consider that the accused was guilty of some lesser offence, they can always acquit him of the offence charged and direct that a summons be served forthwith on the accused for the offence of which they consider him to be guilty. That charge can then be heard.

It has always been accepted (in relation to a charge of stealing a number of articles) that it is unnecessary that the prosecution should prove that all the articles mentioned in the information have been stolen. But the register should note a conviction in respect only of the property found to be stolen and not the other items: *Machent v Quinn* (1970) 134 JP 501.

For the powers of the court to re-open a case after a finding of guilt see the note *Ordering a Re-trial,* 5.29.

For the form of conviction, see r.16 MC Rules 1981. For an order of dismissal, see Form 37.

5.46   **Adjournment of trial**

10. (1) A magistrates' court may at any time, whether before or after beginning to try an information, adjourn the trial, and may do so, notwithstanding anything in this Act, when composed of a single justice.

(2) The court may when adjourning either fix the time and place at which the trial is to be resumed, or, unless it remands the accused, leave the time and place to be determined later by the court; but the trial shall not be resumed at that time and place unless the court is satisfied that the parties have had adequate notice thereof.

(3) A magistrates' court may, for the purpose of enabling inquiries to be made or of determining the most suitable method of dealing with the case, exercise its power to adjourn after convicting the accused and before sentencing him or otherwise dealing with him; but, if it does so, the adjournment shall not be for more than four weeks at a time unless the court remands the accused in custody and, where it so remands him, the adjournment shall not be for more than three weeks at a time.

(4) On adjourning the trial of an information the court may remand the accused and, where the accused has attained the age of 17, shall do so if the offence is triable either way and–

   (a) on the occasion on which the accused first appeared, or was brought, before the court to answer the information he was in custody or, having been released on bail, surrendered to the custody of the court; or

   (b) the accused has been remanded at any time in the course of proceedings on the information;

and, where the court remands the accused, the time fixed for the resumption of the trial shall be that at which he is required to appear or be brought before the court in pursuance of the remand or would be required to be brought before the court but for s.128(3A) below.

[*As amended by Sch.9 CJA 1982*].

COMMENTARY

For guidance on the exercise of discretion in granting and refusing *Adjournment* at 5.06. Note that the powers of adjournment and remand contained in this section apply only to the trial of an information. They do not apply to committal proceedings or to proceedings for determining the mode of trial (as to which ss.5, 18 MCA 1980).

s.10(1): May . . . adjourn the trial, this subsection is restricted to an adjournment before a verdict is returned, *per* Lord Widgery CJ in *R v Talgarth Justices, ex p. Bithell* [1973] 1 WLR 1327.

s.10(2): Unless it remands the accused, an adjournment where the defendant is remanded ay not, therefore, be without a date. Certain cases *must* be remanded in accordance with 10(4). A remand in custody of an adult may be to an alternate magistrates' court nearer to e prison: s.130 of Act, *infra*; but there is strictly speaking, no general authority for 'cross urt remands', either in custody or on bail – though the latter is widely practised. An ccused already detained under a custodial sentence may be remanded for up to 28 clear ays: s.131.

dequate notice The clerk must give written notice of the time and place at which the trial is be resumed and this may be served in accordance with paras (1) and (3) of r.99 MC Rules 81, proof of which may be given under para (2) of r.99. A trial which is resumed without rvice of such a notice is a nullity: *R v Seisdon Justices, ex p. Dougan* [1983] 1 All ER 6.
When the adjournment follows a decision not to proceed under s.12 the notice must give e reason for the adjournment: s.12(6), *post*.
When a court proposes to disqualify an absent offender and adjourns the trial in accord-ce with this section and s.11(4) the notice of resumption must include notice of the reason r the adjournment, *ibid*.
Notice is required to advance the date of hearing even when the accused has indicated his tention not to attend on the original date: *R v Haverfordwest Justices, ex p. George* (1964) 8 SJ 199.

10(3): This sub-section is directory not mandatory and an excessively long adjournment es not necessarily deprive the court of jurisdiction: *R v Manchester City Justices, ex p. liley and Another* (1977) 16 February. As to the composition of the bench after conviction e s.121(7) of the Act.
Justices adjourning under this subsection should adjourn 'the whole question of sentenc-g' and should not, for example, impose a fine and adjourn to consider disqualification: *R v algarth Justices, ex p. Bithell, supra*. (This decision was apparently overlooked in the case Dyson v Ellison* [1975] 1 All ER 276).
The periods of limitation in this subsection have no application to a deferment of sentence der s.1 PCCA 1973, *supra*.
Any remand must be on bail or in custody: s.128(1) MCA 1980. The general right to bail plies: s.4 Bail Act 1976.
For the effects of an adjournment under this subsection see *Adjournment for Inquiries* 06 and see generally Chapter 8.

10(4) A remand for the purposes of s.10(4) may be for the period of the adjournment: 128(6).

fence triable either way Defined in Sch.1 Interpretation Act 1978.

Non-appearance of accused: general provisions

5.47

11. (1) Subject to the provisions of this Act, where at the time and place appointed for the trial or adjourned trial of an information the prosecutor appears but the accused does not, the court may proceed in his absence.

(2) Where a summons has been issued, the court shall not begin to try the information in the absence of the accused unless either it is proved to the satisfaction of the court, on oath or in such other manner as may be prescribed, that the summons was served on the accused within what appears to the court to be a reasonable time before the trial or adjourned trial or the accused has appeared on a previous occasion to answer the information

(3), (4).

Note
For s.11(3), (4) (prohibition on imprisonment or detention in absence, and restriction on disqualification in absence, respectively) see Chapter 8.

OMMENTARY

1(1): Appears,** appearance may be by counsel or solicitor: s.122 MCA 1980.

oceed in his absence,** this course should only be taken where the court has strong grounds r believing that the defendant is wilfully disobeying the summons, *per* Cockburn J in *R v nith* (1875) 39 JP 613; and, obviously, at the accused's request in trivial cases. For the right the accused to be present at his trial and the qualifications thereto see *Trial in the Absence the Accused* 5.05. The Divisional Court refused *certiorari* when the defending solicitor uld not establish that he had been misled into thinking that the case would be adjourned to ater date: *R v Pembroke Justices, ex p. Perrins* (1961) 26 October.

For proof of the service of a summons see r.99 MC Rules 1981, Chapter 2. When a accused is found guilty after the court has proceeded in his absence under s.11(1), the sam bench of justices or (if there were three or more) a court consisting of or comprising majority thereof may direct a retrial before a differently constituted bench where th appears to be in the interest of justice: s.142.

s.11(2): s.1(6) MCA 1980, provides that a warrant may be issued under that section respect of an indictable offence even where a summons has already issued. There is r express provision prohibiting a warrant being issued in respect of a summary offence und that section where a summons has been issued earlier.

Such other manner as may be prescribed, ie, under r.67 MC Rules 1981.

A reasonable time before the trial 'In considering the reasonableness of the time the justic are the proper judges', *per* Erle J in *Ex p. Williams* (1851) 15 JP 757 (a 19th century ca which upheld the reasonableness of a summons to appear the following day). But tl justices' decision may be upset if they were not in full possession of the facts: *Ex p. Smi* (1875) 39 JP 613; *R v Anwyl & Others, Merionethshire Justices, ex p. Cookson* (1909) 73 J 485. The problem is less likely to occur in modern times, although, when it does, a adjournment of 14 days is generally considered to be a fair minimum period f adjournment.

5.48 **Non-appearance of accused: plea of guilty**

12. (1) Subject to subs (7) below, this section shall apply where a summot has been issued requiring a person to appear before a magistrates' court, oth than a juvenile court, to answer to an information for a summary offence, n being an offence for which the accused is liable to be sentenced to l imprisoned for a term exceeding three months, and the clerk of the court notified by or on behalf of the prosecutor that the following documents ha been served upon the accused with the summons, that is to say–

(a) a notice containing such statement of the effect of this section as may l prescribed; and

(b) a concise statement in the prescribed form of such facts relating to tl charge as will be placed before the court by or on behalf of the pro ecutor if the accused pleads guilty without appearing before the cour

(2) Subject to subss (3) to (5) below, when the clerk of the court receives notification in writing purporting to be given by the accused or by a solicit acting on his behalf that the accused desires to plead guilty without appeari before the court, the clerk of the court shall inform the prosecutor of tl receipt of the notification and if at the time and place appointed for the trial adjourned trial of the information the accused does not appear and it is prov to the satisfaction of the court, on oath or in such other manner as may l prescribed, that the notice and statement of facts referred to in subs (1) abo have been served upon the accused with the summons, then–

(a) subject to s.11(3) and (4) above, the court may proceed to hear a dispose of the case in the absence of the accused, whether or not tl prosecutor is also absent, in like manner as if both parties had appear and the accused had pleaded guilty; or

(b) if the court decides not to proceed as aforesaid, the court shall adjou or further adjourn the trial for the purpose of dealing with the inform tion as if the notification aforesaid had not been given.

(3) If at any time before the hearing the clerk of the court receives a intimation in writing purporting to be given by or on behalf of the accused th he wishes to withdraw the notification aforesaid, the clerk of the court sh inform the prosecutor thereof and the court shall deal with the information if this section had not been passed.

(4) Before accepting the plea of guilty and convicting the accused in l absence under subs (2) above, the court shall cause the notification a statement of facts aforesaid, including any submission received with the noti cation which the accused wishes to be brought to the attention of the court wi a view to mitigation of sentence, to be read out before the court by the clerk the court.

(5) If the court proceeds under subs (2) above to hear and dispose of the case in the absence of the accused, the court shall not permit any statement to be made by or on behalf of the prosecutor with respect to any facts relating to the offence charged other than the statement of facts aforesaid except on a resumption of the trial after an adjournment under s.10(3) above.

(6) In relation to an adjournment by reason of the requirements of para (b) of subs (2) above or to an adjournment on the occasion of the accused's conviction in his absence under that subsection, the notice required by s.10(2) above shall include notice of the reason for the adjournment.

(7), (8) . . .

(9) Where the clerk of the court has received such a notification as is mentioned in subs (2) above but the accused nevertheless appears before the court at the time and place appointed for the trial or adjourned trial the court may, if the accused consents, proceed under this section as if he were absent. [*As amended by Sch.1 POA 1985.*]

COMMENTARY

Juveniles, since, following conviction, a juvenile must often be remitted to the juvenile court (see s.56 CYPA 1933 Act and s.7(8) CYPA 1969 Act) it will seldom be appropriate to use the procedure of this Act with regard to juveniles even in the rare cases when they may must appear in the adult court (s.46(1) CYPA 1933 and s.18 CYPA 1963). But note s.46(1A) CYPA 1933: 'If a notification that the accused desires to plead guilty without appearing before the court is received by the clerk of a court in pursuance of s.12 MCA 1980, and the court has no reason to believe that the accused is a child or young person, then, if he is a child or young person he shall be deemed to have attained the age of 17, for the purposes of subs (1) of this section in its application to the proceedings in question.'

12(1): Summary offence, defined in Sch.1 Interpretation Act 1978, Sch.1 as meaning an offence which, if committed by an adult, is triable only summarily.

statement in the prescribed form see Form 30. A copy must be sent to the clerk r.73 MC Rules 1981.

12(2): The clerk of the court receives Once the procedure of this Act is invoked 'an accused has the right up to the very last moment to enter a plea of guilty on the conditions laid down', and not merely at the return date of the summons, *per* Lord Parker CJ in *R v Norham & Islandshire Justices, ex p. Sunter Bros Ltd* [1961] 1 WLR 364.

notification in writing No form of notice is prescribed, but a form of notice is suggested in 51/1957. If the accused ignores this and writes his own letter pleading guilty it is equally effective. In the case of a corporation, notification of a plea or intimation of withdrawal may be given by a director or the secretary: Sch.3, para 4(1).

desires to plead guilty, One set of forms may properly be used for two or more offences, but conviction will be quashed unless it is clear that the accused intended to plead guilty to all the offences: *R v Burnham Justices, ex p. Ansorge* [1959] 1 WLR 1041.

proved . . . in the prescribed manner, see r.67 MC Rules 1981.

served upon the accused, certain methods of service are prescribed in r.99(5) MC Rules 1981.

decides not to proceed as aforesaid, *certiorari* issued where magistrates so adjourned but subsequently reverted to the procedure under this section because of a misapprehension: *R v Liverpool City Justices, ex p. Wallace* (1973) 12 December (unreported). Where the court declines to use the procedure of this section the statement of facts is inadmissible in evidence cross examination of a witness of fact who had taken no part in its preparation and cannot be put to him as an inconsistent statement: *Roger v Sullivan* [1978] RTR 181.

12(4): Accepting the plea of guilty, see under *Equivocal pleas* and *Changes of plea*, 5.19 and 5.20 respectively.

read out before the court, failure to observe this provision deprives the court of jurisdiction: *v Oldham Justices, ex p. Morrissey* [1959] 1 WLR 58. The onus of proving failure to read out rests on the defendant: *R v Davies* [1958] 3 All ER 559; but the provision is strict: see *v Epping and Ongar Justices ex p. Shippam* (1986) 150 JP 425 (failure to read out the whole of solicitor's letters); but this is no bar to further proceedings on the same information: *ibid.*

By the clerk These words were added by the Prosecution of Offences Act 1985 an effectively relieved the prosecutor of any need to attend the proceedings, other than i relation to ancillary matters, eg applications for costs.

s.12(5), thus the court may not even inquire of the prosecutor whether the facts of no-driving-licence offence make it an endorsable matter or not: *R v Liskerett Justices, ex p Child* [1972] RTR 141.

A court may not make an order of disqualification without first giving the accuse opportunity to attend: s.11(4), *supra*.

s.12(6): Notice of the reason for the adjournment, if there has been any adjournment for particular reason of which the defendant was notified, the court may not deal with him in an other way without adjourning again and giving further notice: *R v Mason* [1965] 2 All E 308.

5.49   Non-appearance of the accused: issue of warrant

13. (1) Subject to the provisions of this section, where the court, instead c proceeding in the absence of the accused, adjourns or further adjourns th trial, the court may, if the information has been substantiated on oath, issue warrant for his arrest.

(2) Where a summons has been issued, the court shall not issue a warran under this section unless it is proved to the satisfaction of the court, on oath o in such other manner as may be prescribed, that the summons was served o the accused within what appears to the court to be a reasonable time before th trial or adjourned trial or the accused has appeared on a previous occasion t answer the information.

(3) A warrant for the arrest of any person who has attained the age of 1 shall not be issued under this section unless–
   (a) the offence to which the warrant relates is punishable with imprison ment; or
   (b) the court, having convicted the accused, proposes to impose a dis qualification on him.

(4) This section shall not apply to an adjournment by reason of the require ments of para (b) of s.12 above or to an adjournment on the occasion of th accused's conviction in his absence under that subsection.

(5) Where the court adjourns the trial–
   (a) after having, either on that or on a previous occasion, received an evidence or convicted the accused without hearing evidence on hi pleading guilty under s.9(3) above; or
   (b) after having on a previous occasion convicted the accused withou hearing evidence on his pleading guilty under s.12(2) above,
the court shall not issue a warrant under this section unless it thinks i undesirable, by reason of the gravity of the offence, to continue the trial in th absence of the accused.

COMMENTARY

s.13(1): Adjourns the trial s.13(4) makes it clear that a trial for the purposes of this sectio begins before evidence is heard. As to the composition of the bench at an adjourned tria see s.121(6). Written notice of the time and place of the adjourned hearing must be given t the accused, if absent: r.15 MC Rules 1981; see Form 32.

Issue a warrant, see Chapter 2, *Warrants, Contents of a Warrant*, and *Execution of Warrant*.

s.13(2): section 1(6) provides that a warrant may be issued under that section in respect of a indictable offence even where a summons has already issued. There is no express provisio prohibiting a warrant being issued in respect of a summary offence under that section whe a summons has been issued earlier.

Such other manner as may be prescribed, ie under r.67 MC Rules 1981.

A reasonable time before the trial, 'In considering the reasonableness of the time the justice are the proper judges', *per* Erle J, in *Ex p. Williams* (1851) 15 JP 757 (a 19th century cas which upheld the reasonableness of a summons to appear the following day). But the justices' decision may be upset if they were not in full possession of the facts: *ex p. Smith* (1875) 39 JP 613; *R v Anwyl, Merionethshire Justices, ex p. Cookson* (1909) 73 JP 485; and see the commentary to s.11(2), *supra*. 14 days would generally be considered 'reasonable'.

s.13(3): Punishable with imprisonment Partially defined in s.150(6).

Non-appearance of prosecutor

15. (1) Where at the time and place appointed for the trial or adjourned trial of an information the accused appears or is brought before the court and the prosecutor does not appear, the court may dismiss the information or, if evidence has been received on a previous occasion, proceed in the absence of the prosecutor.

(2) Where, instead of dismissing the information or proceeding in the absence of the prosecutor, the court adjourns the trial, it shall not remand the accused in custody unless he has been brought from custody or cannot be remanded on bail by reason of his failure to find sureties.

5.50

COMMENTARY

s.15(1): The prosecutor does not appear, appearance may be by counsel or solicitor: s.122 MCA 1980.

Dismiss the information For a discussion of the effects of such a dismissal on future proceedings see under the title *Autrefois Convict* and *Autrefois Acquit*, 5.13.

Non-appearance of both parties

16. Subject to s.11(3) and (4) and to s.12 above, where at the time and place appointed for the trial or adjourned trial of an information neither the prosecutor nor the accused appears, the court may dismiss the information or, if evidence has been received on a previous occasion, proceed in their absence.

5.51

COMMENTARY

Appears Appearance may be by counsel or solicitor: s.122 MCA 1980.

Dismiss the information see note to s.15, *supra*.

Proceed in their absence Witnesses cannot be called by absent parties, but they can be called by the court. The only other proceedings which can be undertaken in the absence of both parties are adjournments and for the court to announce its adjudication following an adjourned hearing.

Power of magistrates' court to remit a person under 17 for trial to a juvenile court in certain circumstances

29. (1) Where–
(a) a person under the age of 17 ('the juvenile') appears or is brought before a magistrates' court on an information jointly charging him and one or more other persons with an offence; and
(b) that other person, or any of those other persons, has attained that age, subs (2) below shall have effect notwithstanding proviso (a) in s.46(1) of the Children and Young Persons Act 1933 (which would otherwise require the charge against the juvenile to be heard by a magistrates' court other than a juvenile court).

In the following provisions of this section 'the older accused' means such one or more of the accused as have attained the age of 17.

(2) If–
(a) the court proceeds to the summary trial of the information in the case of both or all of the accused, and the older accused or each of the older accused pleads guilty; or
(b) the court–
(i) in the case of the older accused or each of the older accused, proceeds to inquire into the information as examining justices and either commits him for trial or discharges him; and

5.52

(ii) in the case of the juvenile, proceeds to the summary trial of the information,

then, if in either situation the juvenile pleads not guilty, the court may before any evidence is called in his case remit him for trial to a juvenile court acting for the same place as the remitting court or for the place where he habitually resides.

(3) A person remitted to a juvenile court under subs (2) above shall be brought before and tried by a juvenile court accordingly.

(4) Where a person is so remitted to a juvenile court–
(a) he shall have no right of appeal against the order of remission; and
(b) the remitting court may give such directions as appear to be necessary with respect to his custody or for his release on bail until he can be brought before the juvenile court.

(5) The preceding provisions of this section shall apply in relation to a corporation as if it were an individual who has attained the age of 17.

COMMENTARY

This section gives an adult court power to remit a juvenile where (a) he had been jointly charged with an adult or a corporation, (b) the adult or corporation pleads guilty or is committed for trial or is discharged, and (c) the juvenile pleads not guilty. Without these provisions, the charge against the juvenile would have to be heard in the adult court in accordance with the s.46(1)(a) CYPA 1933.

s.29(1): Age, for the determination of age, see s.99 CYPA 1933.

5.53   Corporations
46. The provision of Sch.3 to this Act shall have effect where a corporation is charged with an offence before a magistrates' court.

5.54   Appearance by counsel or solicitor
122. (1) A party to any proceedings before a magistrates' court may be represented by counsel or solicitor.

(2) Subject to subs (3) below, an absent party so represented shall be deemed not to be absent.

(3) Appearance of a party by counsel or solicitor shall not satisfy any provision of any enactment or any condition of a recognizance expressly requiring his presence.

COMMENTARY

The effects of this section are summarised under *Legal Representation*, 5.01. When can magistrates issue a warrant under s.13 of this Act to compel personal appearance of an accused who appears by his legal representative only? The issue of such a warrant was held successfully to found an action for trespass in *Bessell v Wilson* (1853) 17 JP 567, but this case appears to have concerned fine enforcement proceeding now dealt with by statute. *Certiorari* issued to quash a similar warrant against an accused who appeared by solicitor in answer to a speeding charge, the court having considered the pre-existing legislation which was framed in similar but not identical terms to s.13: *R v Montgomery, ex p. Long* (1910) 74 JP 110. Nevertheless the judgment of Alverstone LCJ, was hedged about by the following qualifications:

'Where there is a proper appearance and where the justices must hear and determine, and where there is an admission by the defendant of what the prosecution desire to prove, and the defendant has not been shown to be contumacious, no warrant ought to be issued by the justices'. The position may be different after conviction.

s.122(1): Represented by counsel or solicitor 'Acting properly upon his client's instructions must, it is suggested, be added by inference.'

s.122(3): Any provision of any enactment, eg see s.4(4) (committal proceedings) and s.18(2) (mode of trial proceedings). When a representative of a corporation appears 'any requirement of this Act that anything shall be done in the presence of the accused, or shall be read or said to the accused, shall be construed as a requirement that that thing shall be done in the presence of the representative or read or said to the representative': para 3(1) of Sch.3 MCA 1980.

Defect in process
5.55

123. (1) No objection shall be allowed to any information or complaint, or to any summons or warrant to procure the presence of the defendant, for any defect in it in substance or in form, or for any variance between it and the evidence adduced on behalf of the prosecutor or complainant at the hearing of the information or complaint.

(2) If it appears to a magistrates' court that any variance between a summons or warrant and the evidence adduced on behalf of the prosecutor or complainant is such that the defendant has been misled by the variance, the court shall, on the application of the defendant, adjourn the hearing.

COMMENTARY

The effects of this section are described under *Defective Process*, 5.09. A dismissal after a refusal to allow amendment of a summons *on the grounds of evidence* is sufficient to found a plea of *autrefois acquit: Halstead v Clark* (1944) 108 JP 70.

The identity of the defendant, the section has been held to apply where the defendant's proper name was wrongly spelt, the court adding that such a defect does not even require amendment: *Dring v Mann* (1948) 112 JP 270. The section does not contemplate a different defendant: *City of Oxford Tramway Co v Sankey* (1890) 54 JP 564; but when summonses intended for a man were mistakenly addressed to his wife and he wrote to the court for an adjournment of 'the summonses against me', the convictions were upheld: *R v Norkett, ex p. Geach* (1915) 139 LT Jo 316; and see also *R v — (1825) R & R* 489 (defendant refused name). Amendment of the defendant's surname was allowed under this section where it was not disputed that he was the accused: *Allen v Wiseman* [1975] RTR 217. However, a conviction was quashed where the prosecution had at first prosecuted the wrong company, albeit one in the same group; and the magistrates had allowed the information to be amended: *Marco (Croydon) Ltd v Metropolitan Police* [1983] Crim LR 395.

Different offence, this section does not allow a defendant to be convicted of an offence different from that with which he is charged: *Martin v Pridgeon* (1859) 23 JP 630; *R v Brickill* (1864) 28 JP 359 (but see the doubts cast on the reasoning of these cases in *Lawrence v Same* [1968] 2 QB 93; *Loadman v Cragg* (1862) 26 JP 743. 'The section does not operate to prevent an objection being effective where the error alleged is fundamental, such as, for instance, where one offence is charged in the information and a different offence is found in the conviction recorded by the justices', per Humphreys J in *Atterton v Browne* [1945] KB 122. But in *R v Newcastle-upon-Tyne Justices, ex p. Bryce (Contractors) Ltd* [1976] 2 All ER 611, amendment of an information was allowed so as to allege a different offence even after the expiry of six months from its commission. *Prohibition* was refused to prevent justices from hearing informations which had been amended after the six months' period of limitation so as to alter the description of the tyres concerned in offences of using tyres with insufficient tread: *R v Sandwell Justices, ex p. West Midlands Passenger Transport Executive* [1979] RTR 17. An amendment to an information should not have been allowed which changed it from a (confusing) allegation of abandoning a dog to one of failing to feed a dog: *Simpson v Roberts* (1984) *The Times,* 21 December (in which it was said that an information which was good enough to enable a defendant to identify the misdoing alleged against him could be amended so long as it continued to allege the same mischief).

Repealed statute, 'It seems to me to be quite plain that if a person is charged before justices under a repealed statute, they have a choice which they can exercise. They can say, in effect, to the defendant: "If you do not object to an amendment, this summons can be amended forthwith". and if there is no objection than can be done. They can say: "We will adjourn this case so that this summons may be amended" and put the prosecution on whatever terms they please as the result of the adjournment. Or they can dismiss the summons leaving it to the prosecution to charge the offence under the correct statute in a fresh summons', per Byrne J in *Meek v Powell* [1952] 1 KB 164; quoted with approval in *Hunter v Coombs* [1962] 1 WLR 573; *R v Crook* (1977) 65 Cr App R 66. Where the information is not amended, a conviction on a repealed statute cannot stand: *Stowers v Darnell* [1973] RTR 459.

s.123(1): Any defect . . . in substance or in form, superfluous words may be deleted: *Rogerson v Stephens* [1950] 2 All ER 144; *Roberts v Griffiths* [1978] RTR 362. However, no amendment is required to delete purely superfluous words when the defendant has not been misled: *Roberts v Griffiths* [1978] RTR 362. An information which referred to the Act but not the section was held to be curable under this section: *R v Doncaster Justices, ex p. Doncaster Corpn* (1962) 106 SJ 879.

A justice's failure to sign the copy of a summons served on the defendant is not fatal when the original was in fact signed: *R v Hay Halkett, ex p. Rush* (1929) 93 JP 209 (the Court expressly refrained from deciding whether an unsigned original could be saved by this provision). Omission from the summons of the date on which the information was laid is a defect curable by this section where there is no reason for thinking that it had any relevance to the case: *R v Godstone Justices, ex p. Secretary of State for the Environment* [1974] Crim LR 110.

This sub-section has no application when the summons is void *ab initio: Garman v Plaice* [1969] 1 WLR 19, (language of the information disclosed no offence). By virtue of r.12 MC Rules 1981, an information bad for duplicity may not be amended under this section after the trial has begun: *Hargreaves v Alderson* [1964] 2 QB 159.

A failure to refer in the information to the Act and section can be cured under this provision where the accused is not misled: *Thornley v Clegg* [1982] RTR 405 (see r.100(2) MC Rules 1981).

s.123(2): Variance, this provision has been applied to variance between the date charged and the evidence: *Exeter Corporation v Heaman* (1877) 42 JP 503; *Wright v Nicholson* [1970] 1 WLR 142; *Wright v Eldred* (1971) 135 JPN 491; the place of the offence: *Fowler v St Mary Abbott's Vestry* (1872) 36 JP 69; *Lee v Coles* (1972) 136 JPN 226; *Moulder v Judd* [1974] Crim LR 111; *Darnell v Holiday* [1973] RTR 276; *Taylor v Grey* [1973] RTR 281; and as to ownership of property maliciously damaged: *Ralph v Howell* (1875) 40 JP 119; *Pike v Morrison* [1981] Crim LR 492. Magistrates erred in refusing to allow an information to be amended so as to correct the name of the street in which the offence was committed: *Cotterill v Johal* [1982] Crim LR 523. No amendment is needed to the information where the variance between it and the fact is slight: *Creek v Peck and Jones* (1983) 147 JP 537 (two young men were found to have formed the intention to steal a bicycle later in the day and in a different street from that charged).

5.56   **SCHEDULE 3**

Corporations (section 46)

1. (1) A magistrates' court may commit a corporation for trial by an order in writing empowering the prosecutor to prefer a bill of indictment in respect of the offence named in the order.

(2) An order under this paragraph shall not prohibit the inclusion in the bill of indictment of counts that under s.2 of the Administration of Justice (Miscellaneous Provisions) Act 1933 may be included in the bill in substitution for, or in addition to, counts charging the offence named in the order.

2. A representative may on behalf of a corporation–
(a) make a statement before examining justices in answer to the charge;
(b) consent to the corporation being tried summarily;
(c) enter a plea of guilty or not guilty on the trial by a magistrates' court of an information.

3. (1) Where a representative appears, any requirement of this Act that anything shall be done in the presence of the accused, or shall be read or said to the accused, shall be construed as a requirement that that thing shall be done in the presence of the representative or read or said to the representative.

(2) Where a representative does not appear, any such requirement, and any requirement that the consent of the accused shall be obtained for summary trial, shall not apply.

4. (1) Notification or intimation for the purposes of subs (2) and (3) of s.12 above may be given on behalf of a corporation by a director or the secretary of the corporation; and those subsections shall apply in relation to a notification or intimation purporting to be so given as they apply to a notification or intimation purporting to be given by an individual accused.

(2) In this paragraph 'director', in relation to a corporation which is estab-

lished by or under any enactment for the purpose of carrying on under national ownership any industry or part of an industry or undertaking and whose affairs are managed by the members thereof, means a member of that corporation.

5. The provisions of this Act relating to committal to the Crown Court for sentence shall not apply to a corporation.

6. Subject to the preceding provisions of this schedule, the provisions of this Act relating to the inquiry into, and trial of, indictable offences shall apply to a corporation as they apply to an adult.

7. Where a corporation and an individual who has attained the age of 17 are jointly charged before a magistrates' court with an offence triable either way, the court shall not try either of the accused summarily unless each of them consents to be so tried.

8. Subsection (6) of s.33 of the Criminal Justice Act 1925 shall apply to a representaive for the purposes of this Schedule as it applies to a representative for the purposes of that section.

COMMENTARY

Para 1(1): An order in writing, see Form 14. Notice must be given to the prison governor, r.9(2) MC Rules 1981.

Para (2): A representative, see para 8.

Para 3: Anything shall be done in the presence of the accused, for a list of such things see notes to s.122.

Para 6: Indictable offences, defined in Sch.1 Interpretation Act 1978.

An adult, ie a person aged *17 years and over.*

An offence triable either way, defined in Sch.1 Interpretation Act 1978.

Para 8: Section 33(6) of the Criminal Justice Act 1925, this section, as amended, defines a 'representative' as 'a person duly appointed by the corporation to represent it for the purpose of doing any act or thing which the representative of a corporation is by this section authorised to do, but a person so appointed shall not, by virtue only of being so appointed, be qualified to act on behalf of the corporation before any court for any other purpose. A representative for the purposes of this section need not be appointed under the seal of the corporation, and a statement in writing purporting to be signed by a managing director of the corporation, or by any person (by whatever name called) having, or being one of the persons having, the management of the affairs of the corporation, to the effect that the person named in the statement has been appointed as the representative of the corporation for the purposes of this section shall be admissible without further proof as *prima facie* evidence that that person has been so appointed.'

CRIMINAL JUSTICE ACT 1982   5.57

Abolition of right of accused to make unsworn statement

72. (1) Subject to subs (2) and (3) below, in any criminal proceedings the accused shall not be entitled to make a statement without being sworn, and accordingly, if he gives evidence, he shall do so on oath and be liable to cross-examination; but this section shall not affect the right of the accused if not represented by counsel or a solicitor, to address the court or jury otherwise than on oath on any matter on which, if he were so represented, counsel or a solicitor could address the court or jury on his behalf.

(2) Nothing in subs (1) above shall prevent the accused making a statement without being sworn–
  (a) if it is one which he is required by law to make personally; or
  (b) if he makes it by way of mitigation before the court passes sentence upon him.

(3) Nothing in this section applies–
  (a) to a trial; or

(b) to proceedings before a magistrates' court acting as examining justices which began before the commencement of this section.

5.58   ## POLICE AND CRIMINAL EVIDENCE ACT 1984

Time for taking accused's evidence
79. If at the trial of any person for an offence–
(a) the defence intends to call two or more witnesses to the facts of the case; and
(b) those witnesses include the accused,
the accused shall be called before the other witness or witnesses unless the court in its discretion otherwise directs.

MAGISTRATES COURTS' RULES 1981
SI 1981 No 552, as amended by SI 1983 No 523

5.59   **Information to be for one offence only**
12. (1) Subject to any Act passed after 2 October, 1848, a magistrates' court shall not proceed to the trial of an information that charges more than one offence.

(2) Nothing in this rule shall prohibit two or more informations being set out in one document.

COMMENTARY
Para (1): see under *Duplicity*, 5.11.

Para (2): thus, two or more informations may be laid in writing *on the same sheet*, provided they are set out separately.

5.60   **Order of evidence and speeches: information**
13. (1) On the summary trial of an information, where the accused does not plead guilty, the prosecutor shall call the evidence for the prosecution, and before doing so may address the court.

(2) At the conclusion of the evidence for the prosecution, the accused may address the court, whether or not he afterwards calls evidence.

(3) At the conclusion of the evidence, if any, for the defence, the prosecutor may call evidence to rebut that evidence.

(4) At the conclusion of the evidence for the defence and the evidence, if any, in rebuttal, the accused may address the court if he has not already done so.

(5) Either party may, with the leave of the court, address the court a second time, but where the court grants leave to one party it shall not refuse leave to the other.

(6) Where both parties address the court twice the prosecutor shall address the court for the second time before the accused does so.

COMMENTARY
Paragraphs (2) and (4) have been amended in accordance with s.72 CJA 1982, *supra*. The provisions of this rule deal only with the order of proceedings, and are merely *directory* rather than *mandatory*, per Lord Parker CJ, in *Simms v Moore* (1970) 134 JP 573. Thus where the prosecutor was also a witness it was open to the justices to take the view that the examination of prosecution witnesses should be taken out of his hands.
     This rule does not provide a comprehensive code of procedure on summary trial. For *No Case To Answer* see 5.24.

Para (3): Evidence . . . for the defence, by s.1(g) Criminal Evidence Act 1898, 'Every person called as a witness in pursuance of this Act (that is, the defendant and his spouse) shall, unless otherwise ordered by the court, give his evidence from the witness box or other place from which the other witnesses give their evidence.' The accused is not to be deprived of this right without good reason: *R v Symonds* (1924) Cr App R 100.

Evidence to rebut, see 5.26.

Para (4): The accused may address the court, this includes an unrepresented person who has a right to make a speech as well as give evidence: *R v Great Marlborough St. Magistrates' Court, ex p. Fraser* [1974] Crim LR 47; *R v Middlesex Crown Court, ex p. Riddle* [1976] Crim LR 731 (a case on indictment). But in *R v Knightsbridge Crown Court, ex p. Martin* [1976] Crim LR 463, the High Court refused to intervene where the Crown Court failed to give an opportunity to an unrepresented appellant to address them, distinguishing *Fraser's* case on the basis that the accused was positively denied the right to make a further speech [NB The appellant in this case was a solicitor and a justices' clerk who might have been expected to make the point at the time]. Where the justices omit to give the accused opportunity to address them and announce a conviction they cannot thereafter rectify the fault but should order a re-trial: *R v Marylebone Justices, ex p. Yasmin Farras* [1981] Crim LR 182.

Para (5), the peremptory nature of this rule is different from the procedure on indictment: *cf. R v Bryant* (1978) 142 JP 460.

Adjournment of trial of information 5.61

15. (1) Where in the absence of the accused a magistrates' court adjourns the trial of an information, the clerk of the court shall give to the accused notice in writing of the time and place at which the trial is to be resumed.

(2) Service of the notice required to be given by para (1) may be effected in any manner in which service of a summons may be effected under para (1) or (3) or r.99 and para (2) of that rule shall apply to the proof of service of the notice as it applies to the proof of service of a summons in respect of the offence charged in the information.

COMMENTARY

Para (1): The absence of the accused, an accused who is legally represented in court is *deemed* not to be absent: s.122(2) MCA 1980.

Clerk to have copies of documents sent to defendant under s.12(1) of the Act of 5.62 1980

73. Where the prosecutor notifies the clerk of the court that the documents mentioned in paras (a) and (b) of s.12(1) of the Act of 1980 have been served upon the accused, the prosecutor shall send to the clerk a copy of the document mentioned in para (b).

5.63

JUVENILES IN THE ADULT COURT

J appears with A in the Adult Court because either–

(i) J is jointly charged with A (s.46 CYPA 1933)
(ii) A is charged with aiding, abetting, causing, procuring, allowing J's offence (s.46 CYPA 1933)
(iii) J is charged with aiding, abetting, etc. A's offence (s.18 CYPA 1963)
(iv) J is charged with an offence arising out of circumstances which are the same as or connected with A's offence (s.18 CYPA 1963)

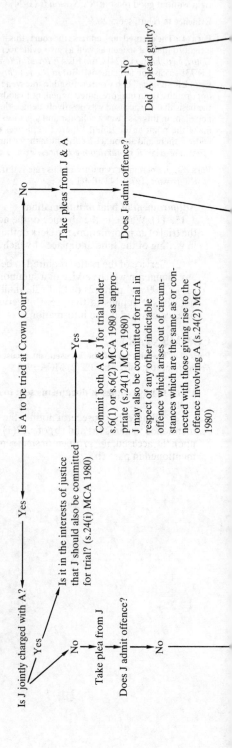

Is J jointly charged with A?

Yes → Is A to be tried at Crown Court → Yes → Is it in the interests of justice that J should also be committed for trial? (s.24(i) MCA 1980)

→ Yes → Commit both A & J for trial under s.6(1) or s.6(2) MCA 1980 as appropriate (s.24(1) MCA 1980) J may also be committed for trial in respect of any other indictable offence which arises out of circumstances which are the same as or connected with those giving rise to the offence involving A (s.24(2) MCA 1980)

No → Take pleas from J & A → Does J admit offence?

No

Take plea from J

Does J admit offence?

No

Did A plead guilty?

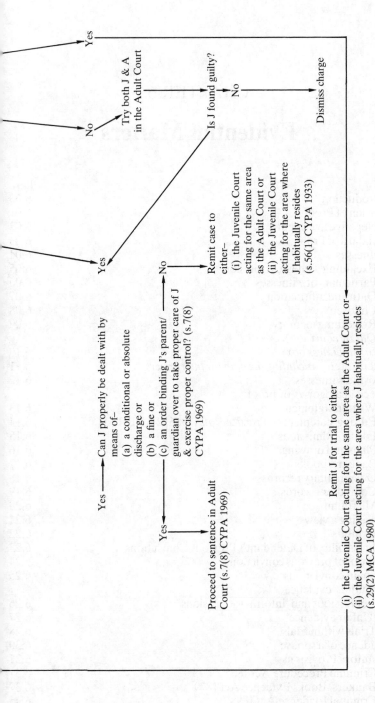

Yes

No

Try both J & A
in the Adult Court

Is J found guilty?

No

Dismiss charge

Yes

Can J properly be dealt with by
means of–
(a) a conditional or absolute
discharge or
(b) a fine or
(c) an order binding J's parent/
guardian over to take proper care of J
& exercise proper control? (s.7(8)
CYPA 1969)

No

Remit case to
either–
   (i) the Juvenile Court
acting for the same area
as the Adult Court or
   (ii) the Juvenile Court
acting for the area where
J habitually resides
(s.56(1) CYPA 1933)

Yes

Proceed to sentence in Adult
Court (s.7(8) CYPA 1969)

Remit J for trial to either
   (i) the Juvenile Court acting for the same area as the Adult Court or
   (ii) the Juvenile Court acting for the area where J habitually resides
(s.29(2) MCA 1980)

Devised by Steve Wilton, Leeds Magistrates' Court, and reproduced by permission of the *New Law Journal.*

CHAPTER 6
Evidential Matters

Note: For the tape recording of police interviews, see the Draft Code issued pursuant to the Police and Criminal Evidence Act 1984, reproduced at Appendix I and *R v Rampling* (1987) *The Times*, 29 August, noted thereunder concerning the use of tape recordings *in the Crown Court*.

Evidential Matters

INTRODUCTION   6.00

It is impossible to treat all relevant aspects of the law of evidence within a general work. Accordingly, the approach of this chapter is to provide a selection of frequently recurring aspects of this area of the law, together with those statutory provisions and judicial authorities which are of especial relevance to proceedings before magistrates. In certain instances – eg the emerging law concerning 'trials within trials' to determine the admissibility or otherwise of certain evidence – it is debatable whether the matter is primarily one of evidence, or one of procedure. The approach adopted has been to treat such matters as evidential ones within this chapter, and to insert appropriate references in Chapters 4 and 5 under the titles *Committal for Trial* and *Summary Trial*, respectively.

Note that Pts II and III CJA 1988, when in force, introduce new provisions concerning *documentary evidence* and deal with a number of specific aspects of the law of evidence as it affects summary criminal procedure. The new provisions are set out in full in Appendix III, *post*.

BURDEN OF PROOF   6.01

The term 'burden of proof' is often used imprecisely to mean one of two things. On the one hand, there is the *evidential* burden, the onus of *adducing* evidence to raise specific issues or facts. This burden may devolve on either prosecutor or defendant and may shift from one to another during the trial. On the other, there is the *legal* or *persuasive* burden of proof – the context in which the term is used in this work – which (subject to what is said below) is always borne by the prosecution in an English criminal trial: *R v Schama* (1914) 79 JP 184; *Woolmington v Director of Public Prosecutions* [1935] AC 462. In the words of Sankey LC in the latter case, 'Throughout the web of the English criminal law one golden thread is always to be seen, that is the duty of the prosecution to prove the prisoner's guilt, subject to . . . the defence of insanity and subject also to any statutory exceptions . . . No attempt to whittle it down will be entertained.'

In some statutes an evidential burden may be placed on the accused once the prosecution has established certain facts, eg where the accused wishes to raise lawful authority or reasonable excuse for the possession of an offensive weapon contrary to s.1 Prevention of Crimes Act 1953.

6.02   **Negative averments**

When an accused relies for his defence on any *exception, exemption, proviso, excuse* or *qualification* the *burden of proving* it lies on him: s.101 MCA 1980; which sets out the common law rule in statutory form. Section 101 does *not* depend on the defendant having *peculiar knowledge* enabling him to prove the positive of any negative averment. It shifts the *legal* or *persuasive*, but not the *evidential*, burden of proof to the defendant: *R v Edwards* (1974) 138 JP 621. For a general review of the common law position see *R v Oliver* (1943) 108 JP 30 and see *R v Hunt (Richard)* [1986] 3 WLR 1115, in which the House of Lords, although upholding the rule in *R v Edwards*, suggested a change of emphasis under which, *semble*, the more serious the offence the more likely it is that '. . . any ambiguity in the burden of proof, should be resolved in favour of the defendant. In the final analysis, each case has to turn on the construction of the particular legislation to determine whether the defence was an exception within the meaning of s.101 . . .': per Lord Griffiths and NB the *Standard of Proof* in such cases, *infra*.

It has been held that the burden of proof that a defendant held a driving licence lies upon him: *John v Humphreys* (1955) 119 JP 39; *Tynan v Jones* [1975] RTR 465. Similarly, with unauthorised possession of game: *R v Turner* (1816) 5 M & S 511, supplying drugs without a licence: *R v Oliver, supra*, possessing drugs without a prescription: *R v Ewens* [1966] 2 All ER 470; using a motor vehicle without insurance: *Leathley v Drummond* [1972] RTR 293; or without a test certificate: *Davey v Towle* [1973] RTR 328, offering taxi service without a licence: *R v Edwards, supra*; but not as to the proportion of morphine in a sample: *R v Hunt, supra*.

It is not necessary in an information to specify or negative an exemption, etc.: r.4(3) MC Rules 1981.

6.03   **STANDARD OF PROOF**

The prosecution must prove their case '*beyond reasonable doubt.*' It is often said that this term is designed to exclude the 'fanciful' or 'remote' or, as Sir James Stephen would have had it, 'improbable' doubt. Despite doubts which had been cast on the value of the 'reasonable doubt' test its use was confirmed by Lord Goddard CJ in *R v Hepworth; R v Fearnley* [1955] 2 QB 600 who said: 'One would be on safe ground if one said in a criminal case to a jury: "You must be satisfied beyond reasonable doubt" and one could also say "You, the jury, must be completely satisfied" or, better still, "You must feel sure of the prisoner's guilt".' It is best not to put any gloss on these terms: *R v Yap Chuan Ching* (1976) 63 Cr App R 7. In directing a jury it is generally sufficient and safe to say that they must be satisfied beyond reasonable doubt so that they feel sure of the defendant's guilt: *Ferguson v The Queen* [1979] 1 All ER 877.

When the burden of proof is on the defendant in respect of any issue it is well established that the test is not the same as that on the prosecutor, but is akin to that in civil cases, namely the *balance of probabilities*: *Sodeman v R* [1936] 2 All ER 1138; *R v Carr Briant* (1943) 29 Cr App R 76; *Islington London Borough v Panico* [1973] 3 All ER 485. When the civil burden applies this means that 'the balance must be tipped by the efendant, but no more [is] necessary': per O'Connor LJ in *R v waysland* (1987) *The Times*, 15 April.

WITNESSES 6.04

is the task of the party calling a witness to ensure his attendance at ourt. However, if a justice of the peace is satisfied that a person in ngland or Wales is likely to be able to give *material evidence* or to roduce any document or thing likely to be *material evidence* and that that erson will *not voluntarily attend* as a witness or produce the document or uing the justice must issue a witness summons: s.97(1) MCA 1980. The astices' clerk has a similar power and duty under the Justices' Clerks ules 1980 (SI No 231). A warrant may be issued for this purpose by a astice only if he is satisfied by evidence on oath of these matters and that is probable that a summons would not produce attendance of the itness: s.97(2) MCA 1980. Witnesses, whether appearing on process ider this section or not, may be compelled to give evidence, etc; s.97(4).

It is incumbent on the person applying for a summons or warrant to atisfy the justices (or justices' clerk, where applicable) with 'some mater-l to show that the potential witness is likely to give material evidence', id inquiry should be made into the nature of the evidence the witness in give and whether it is material: *R v Peterborough Magistrates' Court,* *p. Willis* (1987) 151 JP 785.

Note. For the position where the prosecution fails to reveal to the efence that a witness has made inconsistent statements, or that evidence known to be unreliable, see under *Judicial Review* at Chapter 11.

Witnesses may be witnesses as to *fact* or witnesses as to *opinion*, but the tter kind of evidence is restricted to 'experts' giving evidence within eir particular field of expertise and where the matter is 'outside the xperience of the court': see eg *R v Turner* [1975] 1 All ER 70; *DPP v rdan* [1977] AC 699. *Note* that under [s.29] CJA 1988, when in force id subject to the provisions thereto, an expert report will be admissible criminal proceedings, 'whether or not the person making it attends to ve evidence': see Appendix III, *post.*

xcluding witnesses from court 6.05

is *time honoured practice*, but not a rule of law, that persons who are to called as witnesses (with the exception of professional men giving idence in that capacity) should be ordered out of court before they are lled: *Southey v Nash* (1837) 7 C & P 632; *R v Bexley Justices, ex p. King* 980] RTR 49. Exclusion is thus purely within the discretion of the court. ut if witnesses remain in court, even in disobedience of the court's der, the court has no right to refuse to hear their evidence: *Moore v The egistrar of Lambeth County Court* [1969] 1 All ER 782 (a civil case); obbett v Hudson* (1852) 17 JP 39 although the weight which a court ight give to such evidence would, presumably, be reduced to the extent at it might have been influenced by what may have been heard in court the witness before giving his own evidence.

articulars of witnesses 6.06

ie normal rule is that a witness giving evidence must state publicly his me and address*. However, this rule may be departed from when there e overwhelming reasons as for example in the case of a victim of ackmail: see per Lord Widgery CJ in *R v Socialist Worker, ex p.*

Attorney General [1975] 1 All ER 142 at p.144. There is special provisic
concerning victims of rape: see Sexual Offences (Amendment) Act 197(
post. Where the court may sit in camera it is an acceptable alternative in
proper case to allow a witness to conceal his identity by a pseudonyn
Attorney General v Leveller Magazine Limited and Others (1979) (Col(
nel 'X'). When a court allows a name or other matter to be withheld fro
the public it may give such *directions prohibiting its publication* in co
nection with the proceedings as appear necessary for the purpose f(
which it was withheld: s.11 Contempt of Court Act 1981, see Chapter

6.07   Oath and Affirmation

Evidence given before a magistrates' court must be given on oath: s.(
MCA 1980. The accused is not entitled to make a statement without bei
sworn: s.72 CJA 1982; see 5.25 *ante*. The general form of Christian oath
administered to a witness without question unless he voluntarily object
s.1(1)(2) Oaths Act 1978. An oath may be administered to anyone not
Christian or a Jew in any lawful manner: s.1(3). Anyone who *objects
being sworn must be permitted to make a solemn affirmation* instead
taking the oath: s.5(1). The affirmation may also be used when it is n
reasonably practical without inconvenience or delay to administer tl
oath in the proper manner: *ibid*. s.5(2). The form of affirmation
prescribed in s.6.

Every person called as a witness in pursuance of the Criminal Eviden(
Act 1898 must, unless otherwise ordered by the court, give his eviden(
from the witness box or other place from which the other witnesses gi'
their evidence: s.1(g) of the 1898 Act.

6.08   Children

A child of tender years may give *unsworn* evidence when he does n
understand the nature of the oath if possessed of sufficient intelligence
justify the reception of the evidence and if he understands the duty
speaking the truth: s.38 CYPA 1933. For the problems which can ari
with regard to corroboration in respect of such unsworn evidence see tl
commentary to s.38 at 6.49 and [s.33] CJA 1988 which, when in force, w
abolish the corroboration requirement: Appendix III, *post*. For the e'
dence of a child witness in committal proceedings see the introduction
Chapter 4 and the new s.103 MCA 1980 which will be substituted by [s.3
CJA 1988 when in force: Appendix III, *post*.

Note that s.39 CYPA 1933 enables the court to direct, *inter alia*, th
particulars calculated to lead to the identification of a child or you
person concerned in the proceedings – eg as a witness – shall not
published, see s.37.

6.09   Refreshing memory
Out of court

A witness may not generally give evidence by referring the court tc
'previous *consistent* statement' made out of court – an application of t
rule against 'self-corroboration' (although this rule must be understood
the light of the special provisions relating to 'tendered evidence' and t
right of a party to call a witness whose evidence has been tendered: s
s.9(4) CJA 1967, closely analogous, it is the practice of the courts not
allow a witness to *refresh his memory* in the witness box by reference tc
note or statement. But there is an exception to this where it is establish
that it was made contemporaneously with or as soon as possible after t

vent. But witnesses for the prosecution are normally (though not in all ircumstances) entitled, if they so request, to copies of any statement taken om them by police officers. Witnesses for the defence are normally llowed to have copies of their statements and to refresh their memories om them at *any time up to the moment they go into the witness box*. While it ould be wrong for a number of witnesses to be handed statements in ircumstances which allowed one to compare with another what each had aid, there can be no general rule that witnesses may not before trial see the tatement they made at some period reasonably close to the time of the vent which is the object of the trial, *per* Sachs LJ in *R v Richardson* [1971] 2 All ER 773; *Warley v Bentley* [1976] Crim LR 31. But there is *no rule that itnesses must be allowed to see their statements*, nor need the prosecution aform the defence that a witness has seen his statement: *R v Westwell* 1976] Crim LR 441 (but *cf R v Webb* [1975] Crim LR 159).

n the witness box 6.10

witness should not be shown his statement once he is in the witness box: *v Graham* [1973] Crim LR 628. However, a witness may refresh his lemory by reference to any writing made or verified by himself concern- lg and *contemporaneously* with the facts to which he testifies: *Archbold*, 0th ed at para 515; approved in *Attorney General's Reference No 3 of 979* (1979) 69 Cr App R 411 (a police officer may refer to a full note of uestions and answers where drawn up accurately from brief notes made t the time): see also *R v Cheng* (1976) 63 Cr App R 2 (fuller transcription f notes made at the time; and *R v Britton* [1987] 1 WLR 579). The ocument must have been written either at the time of the transaction or) shortly afterwards that the facts were fresh in the witness's memory: *hipson on Evidence*, 11th ed at p.1528, approved in *R v Richardson* 1971] 2 All ER 773 at p.777, where it was said that that definition does rovide *a measure of elasticity* and should not be taken to confine itnesses to an over-short period. In *R v Fotheringham* [1975] Crim LR 10, a witness was allowed to look at a statement made 27 days after the vent. The most common application of the principle in practice is in :lation to *'police officers' notebooks'* the added rationale being that the olice can hardly be expected to recall the detail of every incident with ccuracy. But the rule remains that police officers – like other witnesses – re only permitted to give evidence from *recall*, albeit aided and :freshed by the note: *R v Benjamin* (1913) 8 Cr App R 146. In *R v ekhon* (1987) 85 Cr App R 19, it was stated by Woolf LJ that there is no ifference in principle between 'notes' and a 'police log' (ie a document ompiled by one officer and summarising his own observations *and* those f other officers). The Court of Appeal identified eight considerations in :lation to both categories of *aide memoire*, as follows:

1 Both may be referred to by witnesses to refresh memory (provided, on indictment, that the basis for this is established without putting the record before the jury).
2 Such documents must be available for inspection by the other party, who may cross-examine, if relevant. In most cases this will not require the document to be exhibited.
3 Where the cross-examination suggests that a witness has made up his evidence (usually, although not necessarily, involving an allegation of 'concoction') the record might be admissible to show consistency, because made contemporaneously with the events.

4 Where inconsistent with present testimony, the record may b
admitted as evidence of that inconsistency.

5 It is also appropriate for the record (in practice, copies of the record
to go before a jury where it would otherwise be difficult for them t
follow the cross-examination of a witness who has refreshed hi
memory.

6 Subject to the following exception (see 8 below), the record o
statement will not become evidence of the truth of its contents, an
cannot corroborate the evidence of the witness refreshing hi
memory from it. Rather, it is 'a tool' to assist in the evaluation of th
truth of the evidence given by the witness from the witness box
Whether appropriate to treat the document as an exhibit is of n
practical importance.

7 There might be cases where it is convenient to use the record as a
aide memoire to the witnesses' evidence, where that evidence is lon
and involved. But care should be exercised in adopting this cours
where the evidence and record are bitterly contested.

8 Although the document is not normally evidence of the truth of it
contents, in cases where, because of its nature, it provides materia
by which its authenticity can be judged, then in respect of tha
material and for the limited purpose of assessing its authenticity it i
capable of being evidence in the case.

[Summarised].

The defence is entitled to see documents from which memory has bee
refreshed, subject to two well established rules: a witness can be cross
examined upon the material from which he has refreshed his memor
without the notebook being made evidence in the case; whereas if he i
cross-examined beyond those limits into other matters, the cross
examiner takes the risk of the material being made evidence in the cas
and the document being exhibited and therefore available for use by th
fact finding tribunal: *Owen v Edwards* (1983) 147 JP 245; *R v Benjamir
supra; R v Sekhon, supra.*

It suffices if the note was made by someone else so long as the witnes
adopted it contemporaneously as his own: *Groves v Redbart* [1975] Crir
LR 158 (another officer's notebook which the witness had checked an
signed at the time); *R v Kelsey* (1982) 74 Cr App R 213 (witness allowed t
refresh memory from note he had dictated to a policeman who then rea
it back to him without showing it). 'What must be shown is that witness /
has verified in the sense of satisfying himself whilst the matters are fresh i
his mind (1) that a record has been made, and (2) that it is accurate. If /
makes a 'contemporaneous' note himself, or if A reads and adopts at th
time a 'contemporaneous' note made by B, A may refresh his memor
from it without need of another witness. In a case such as the present
second witness will be required': *ibid*; and see now *R v Sekhon, supr*
('police logs').

6.11 Interpreters – including the oath for interpreters

'When a foreigner is on trial on an indictment for a criminal office, and he is ignorant of th
English language and is undefended, the evidence given at the trial must be translated f
him. If he states that he understands part of the evidence and does not wish that pa
translated it need not be translated unless the judge in his discretion thinks otherwise
because the object of the translation is already achieved. For example, if an agreement i
writing signed by the accused is put in evidence by the Crown, it might well be that th
accused knew the contents and did not wish a translation. He is not thereby admitting an
part of the case against him, but merely that he understands that part of the evidence. If h

does not understand the English language he cannot waive compliance with the rule that the evidence must be translated; he cannot dispense with it by express or implied consent, and it matters not that no application is made by him for the assistance of an interpreter. It is for the court to see that the necessary means are adopted to convey the evidence to his intelligence, notwithstanding that, either through ignorance or timidity or disregard of his own interests, he makes no application to the court,'

per Lord Reading CJ in *R v Lee Kun* (1916) 80 JP 166. Analogous principles apply in summary proceedings and to deaf defendants: see eg *R v Kingston-upon-Thames Magistrates' Court, ex p. Davey* (1985) 149 JP 744.

A conviction was quashed where the interpreter was a waiter at the same restaurant as waiters who were witnesses for the prosecution: *R v Mitchell* [1970] Crim LR 153. A police officer's evidence of what a witness said out of court as translated to him by an interpreter is hearsay and inadmissible: *R v Attard* (1958) 43 Cr App R 90.

The customary form of oath for interpreters is: 'I swear by Almighty God that I will well and faithfully interpret and true explanation make of all such matters and things as shall be required of me according to the best of my skill and understanding', (cf Welsh Courts (Oath and Interpreters) Rules 1943.

Although it is for the court to assign an interpreter, chief officers of police are prepared to continue arrangements for the obtaining of interpreters where this is desired: HOC 86/1973.

In any legal proceeding in Wales or Monmouthshire the *Welsh language* may be spoken by any party, witness or other person who desires to use it; and any necessary provision for interpretation shall be made accordingly: s.1(1) Welsh Language Act 1967.

For costs payable to interpreters see Chapter 9.

The Home Office will meet expenditure on a sign language interpreter employed to assist a defendant who is deaf and dumb where the provisions of s.17 of the Act of 1973 otherwise apply: HOC 3/1979.

'Hostile witnesses'   6.12

Whilst any statement *inconsistent* with a witness's present testimony may be put to that witness in *cross-examination*, this is not permitted in *examination in chief*, except with the leave of the court – what is sometimes called the rule against impeaching a party's own witness. The circumstances of the previous inconsistent statement must then he put to the witness and he must be asked whether he has made such a statement: ss.3, 4 Criminal Procedure Act 1865. Whilst the precise basis of law seems to defeat even the most authoritative of commentators (see eg *Cross on Evidence*), the phrase 'hostile witness' which is often used in such circumstances is, it seems, strictly reserved for more serious situations, ie where the witness is not simply failing to tell or avoiding the truth, but is actually showing bias towards the party calling him. In such circumstances, the party calling the witness may seek leave to cross-examine him, the effect of this being to 'nullify' his present testimony rather than to give the court a choice between the witness's own competing statements: *Greenough v Eccles* (1859) 7 WR 341, and see *Ewer v Ambrose* (1825) 3 B & C 746. In summary proceedings, the justices may hear about and, if it is in writing, look at the previous statement in order to determine whether the witness is 'hostile' and for the purpose of giving leave. If they reject such a suggestion they must then dismiss the previous statement from their minds.

In relation to summary proceedings, there is no statutory provision or other legal authority for there to be a '*trial within a trial*' (*cf Confessions and 'informal admissions*' at 6.26, *post*) and since the situation of the 'hostile witness' is one which by its very nature tends to arise *impromptu* it may not be possible to consider dealing with this 'as a separate issue'. Also, in practice (and particularly, since the introduction of the Crown Prosecution Service) it may be unlikely that a case would proceed where the outcome turns entirely on whether a particular witness might or might not stick to his original statement – in circumstances where this is doubted by the prosecutor in advance.

SPECIAL CATEGORIES OF PROOF

6.13 Written statements

Provided certain conditions are satisfied, a written statement is admissible as evidence to the like extent and effect as oral evidence in summary proceedings. 9 CJA 1967; and committal proceedings. 102 MCA 1980. The form of the statement is the same in both types of proceedings, so that any statement taken from a witness under these provisions may be used in either. The conditions are that:

(a) the statement purports to be *signed* by the person who made it;
(b) it contains a prescribed declaration as to its truth: s.9(2) CJA 1967; s.102(2) MCA 1980;
(c) if made by a person under 21 it must give his age;
(d) if made by a person who cannot read it must be read to him before signature and must contain a declaration that this has been done: s.9(3) CJA 1967; s.102(3) MCA 1980.

The *procedure* for dealing wth the statement differs according to the type of proceedings.

In *committal proceedings* it is required by s.102(2) MCA 1980 that:

(i) before it is tendered in evidence a copy of the statement must be given to each of the other parties along with a copy of any exhibit or details of how to inspect it; and
(ii) none of the other parties objects before the statement is tendered.

In summary trial it is required by s.9(2) CJA 1967 that:

(i) before the hearing a copy of the statement must be given to each of the other parties along with a copy of any exhibit or details of how to inspect it (this may be waived by agreement of the parties).
(ii) none of the other parties or their solicitor serves notice of objection within 7 days of service, (this condition may be waived by agreement of the parties).

In addition, a copy of the statement and any exhibit must be given to the justices' clerk as soon as practicable after it is given to or served on the parties: r.70(2) MC Rules 1981. The court may *of its own motion* or *on the application of a party* require the maker of any statement to attend and given evidence: s.9(4) CJA 1967; s.102(4) MCA 1980. Additionally, in the case of *summary trial* the party tendering the statement may call the person who made it: s.9(4) CJA 1967.

Except in the case of a s.6(2) 'paper' committal the statement must be *read aloud* unless the court directs otherwise, when an *oral account* must be given of so much of the statement as is not read aloud: s.9(6) CJA 1967; s.102(5) MCA 1980. The name and address of the person who made the statement must be read aloud unless the court otherwise directs: r.70(6) MC Rules 1981.

Editing statements – *Practice Note* [1986] 2 All ER 511   6.14

The method of dealing with inadmissible material in written statements is laid down in r.70(5) MC Rules 1981. Written statements may be edited in accordance with *Practice Note* [1986] 2 All ER 511. The Note sets out various requirements and makes it clear that editing should in all circumstances be done by a Crown Prosecutor, or if the prosecution is not being conducted by the CPS, by a legal representative. It should *not be undertaken* by a police officer. The guidance applies to cases where the prosecution proposes to tender written statements under either s.102 MCA 1980, or s.9 CJA 1967, and Lord Lane instanced two situations in which editing might be necessary. First, where a witness has made more than one statement whose contents should conveniently be reduced into a single comprehensive statement; secondly, where a statement contains 'inadmissible, prejudicial or irrelevant material'. A *composite* statement, containing the result of the editing of two or more statements must be prepared in accordance with the appropriate provisions of the 1967 and 1980 Acts, and must then be *signed* by the witness.

The *Practice Note* deals at length with the proper procedure for editing single statements. This may occur in one of two ways. It may either be achieved by marking copies of the statement in a way which indicates the passages on which the prosecution will not rely, or by obtaining a fresh statement, signed by the witness, omitting the offending material. The former method is generally to be preferred to the latter, but there are *four instances when it may be more appropriate to prepare a new statement*:

1 When a police (or other investigating) officer's statement contains details of interviews with more suspects than are eventually charged, a fresh statement should omit all details of interview with those not charged except . . . for the bald fact that a certain named person was interviewed at a particular time, date and place.

2 When a suspect is interviewed about more offences than are eventually made the subject of committal charges, a fresh statement should omit all questions and answers about the uncharged offences unless, either they might appropriately be taken into consideration or evidence about them is admissible as evidence of system. The omitted questions and answers might however be replaced by a phrase such as, 'After referring to some other matters, I then said . . .' so as to make it clear that part of the interview has been omitted.

3 A fresh statement should normally be prepared and signed if the only part of the original on which the prosecution are relying is only a small proportion of the whole, although it remains desirable to use the alternative method if there is reason to believe that the defence

might themselves wish to rely, in mitigation or for any other purpose, on at least some of those parts which the prosecution do not propose to adduce.

4 When the passages contain material which the prosecution is entitled to withhold from disclosure from the defence.

The *Practice Note* specifically refers to the use of s.9 CJA in summary proceedings and states that in that situation there will be greater need to have a fresh statement prepared to exclude inadmissible or prejudicial material, rather than using the striking out or bracketing method. None of the principles in the *Note* applies in respect of committal proceedings to *exhibited documents*, nor to *oral statements of a defendant which are recorded in the witness statements of interviewing police officers*, except as in 2 above.

There is a further requirement in that whenever a fresh statement is taken from a witness, a copy of the earlier unedited statements(s) will be given to the defence, save in exceptional circumstances. This accords with the Attorney General's guidelines.

The *Note* recognises that in most cases where editing is necessary, the method used will be by marking the statement by indicating passages on which the prosecutor does not intend to rely. The *original* signed statement to be tendered to the court is *not to be marked in any way*. The method of marking on the copy statement is by lightly striking out the passage to be edited so that what appears beneath can still be read, or by bracketing, or by a combination of both. It must *not be done by producing a photocopy* which deletes the material obliterated. It is suggested that where this striking out/bracketing method is used, the following phrase should appear at the foot of the frontispiece or index to any bundle of copy statements to be tendered: 'The prosecution does not propose to adduce evidence of those passages of the attached copy statements which have been struck out and/or bracketed (nor will it seek to do so at the trial unless a Notice Of Further Evidence is served).'

6.15 Formal admissions

Any fact of which oral evidence may be given may be *admitted* by or on behalf of the prosecutor or defendant and the admission is, as against that party, conclusive evidence of the fact admitted: Criminal Justice Act 1967, s.10(1). An admission may be made *before or at* the proceedings: s.10(2). If made otherwise than in court it must be written down and purported to be signed by the person making it, and if made on behalf of a corporation it must purport to be signed by one of a number of prescribed representatives: s.10(2). Only *counsel* or a *solicitor* may make an admission *on behalf* of an individual. If made before the trial by an individual it must be *approved by counsel or solicitor*: s.10(2). If made in court it must be written down and signed by the maker: r.71 MC Rules 1981.

An admission may with the leave of the court be withdrawn: Criminal Justice Act 1967, s.10(4). It was held in *R v Horseferry Road Magistrates' Court ex p. O'Regan* (1986) 150 JP 535, that where 'no evidence is offered' by the prosecutor in committal proceedings, the committal cannot proceed on the basis of residual s.10 admissions alone.

6.16 Plans and drawings

Plans and drawings may be proved by certificate in accordance with the s.41 CJA 1948.

Banker's books 6.17

A banker or bank officer is not *compellable* to produce any bank book in proceedings to which the bank is not a party except by order of a judge: s.6 Banker's Books Evidence Act 1879. Once criminal proceedings are *begun* against any person a magistrates' court may make an order under s.7 that either the prosecutor or the defendant shall be at liberty *to inspect* and *take copies* of any entries in a banker's book.

The purpose of the provision is that, to save bankers from the inconvenience of having their books and their staff in courts for the purposes of supplying evidence, it shall be possible for the police officers concerned to obtain an order from the court, and by virtue of that order to be at liberty to inspect the accounts and take notes from them in the bank. Then when the trial comes on the bank will be undisturbed in its business, *per* Lord Widgery CJ in *R v Marlborough Street Magistrates' Court Metropolitan Stipendiary Magistrate, ex p. Simpson* (1980) 70 Cr App R 291.

'In criminal proceedings, justices should warn themselves of the importance of the step which they are taking in making an order under s.7: should always recognise the care with which the jurisdiction should be exercised; should take into account amongst other things whether there is other evidence in the possession of the prosecution to support the charge; or whether the application under s.7 is a fishing expedition in the hope of finding some material on which the charge can be hung. If justices approach these applications with a due sense of responsibility and a recognition of the importance of that which they are being asked to do, if they are always alive to the requirement of not making the order extend beyond the true purposes of the charge before them, and if in consequence they limit the period of the disclosure of the bank account to a period which is strictly relevant to the charge before them; and if finally they recognise the importance of considering whether there is other evidence in the possession of the prosecution before they provide the bank account as perhaps the only evidence, I feel if they observe those precautions and pay heed to those warnings, they will in fact produce a situation in which the section is used properly, wisely, and in support of the interests of justice, and will not allow it to be used as an instrument of oppression which on its face it might very well be . . . it would be perfectly proper when justices are faced with a difficult case in which they are genuinely disturbed whether they should use this jurisdiction or not, for them to decline to make the order and to say that they decline because they feel that it is an application more appropriate to the High Court.'

per Lord Widgery CJ in *Williams and Others v Summerfield* (1972) 136 JP 616; *R v Marlborough Street Magistrates' Court Metropolitan Stipendiary Magistrate, ex p. Simpson, supra.*

It is the duty of magistrates to take great care, when deciding whether or not to issue an order under this section, to ensure that the person whose bank account is to be inspected is not oppressed and, with a view to seeing that that is not the case, they must limit the period of time in respect of which disclosure is made. They must also be very wary that the prosecution are not using the section for ulterior purposes; that is to say for purposes other than inquiring into the matters with which the person concerned is charged. Nevertheless, the fact that a defendant intends to plead guilty does not mean that the prosecution should cease their efforts to collect sufficient evidence or that magistrates should refuse an order, *per* Donaldson LJ in *Owen v Sambrook* [1981] Crim LR 329.

The power to make an order under s.7 is a power which must be exercised with caution and must not be allowed to be used for the purpose of fishing in order to find out whether there is a case. The power may be used only where there is evidence for the prosecution of the commission of an offence and for the purpose of adding to the evidence upon that offence: *R v Nottingham Justices, ex p. Lynn* (1984) 79 Cr App R 238.

6.18 Documentary records

As an exception to the rule against hearsay s.68 PACE Act 1984 allows a statement in a document to be admissible in any criminal proceedings as evidence of any fact stated therein of which direct oral evidence would be admissible if certain conditions are satisfied. These are the *primary condition* in s.68(1) and any of the *secondary conditions* in s.68(2). The primary condition is that the document is or forms part of a record compiled by a person acting under a duty from information supplied by a person who had or may be reasonably supposed to have had, personal knowledge of the matters dealt with in that information. The secondary conditions are that:

(a) the person who supplied the information is *dead* or *unfit to attend* as a witness; is *outside the United Kingdom* and it is not reasonably practicable to secure his attendance; or cannot be *reasonably expected to have any recollection* of the matters;

(b) all *reasonable steps* have been taken to identify *the person who supplied the information* but he cannot be identified; or

(c) his identity being known, *he cannot be found* despite all reasonable steps.

Section 68 is supplemented by Parts I and III of Sch.3. In particular:

(i) secondhand hearsay (and third and fourth without number) is admissible but only if each person in the chain was under a duty: para 1;

(ii) the statement may be proved by the production of the original document or an authenticated copy (or a copy of the material part): para 13.

(iii) a witness's proof of evidence may fall within the section but cannot be admitted without the leave of the court which may not be given unless it is of the opinion that the statement ought to be admitted in the interests of justice having regard to the factors set out in para 2 of Sch.3.

Note that new and additional provisions affecting the admissibility of *documentary evidence* are contained in [ss.22-27] and [Sch.2] CJA 1988, see Appendix III, *post*.

Note also that [Sch.15] CJA 1988 repeals, when in force, s.68 PACE Act 1984 and that situation will then be subsumed within the more general provisions of [s.23] CJA 1988.

6.19 Computer records

A computer record may or may not comprise hearsay evidence, but by virtue of s.69(1) PACE Act 1984 such a record is *not admissible* in criminal proceedings *unless* it is shown that:

(i) there are no reasonable grounds for believing that the statement is inaccurate because of improper use of the computer;

(ii) at all material times the computer was operating properly or, if not, that the fault did not affect the production of the document or the accuracy of its contents; and

(iii) that any rules of court are complied with.

These matters may be *proved by a certificate* 'to the best of the knowledge and belief' of the signatory *unless the court requires oral evidence*: Sch.3, paras 8, 9. The record may be proved by the production of the original document or an authenticated copy (or a copy of the material part): Sch.3, para 13.

Note that computer records *per se* are not affected by the CJA 1988, the provisions of which are expressly stated to be, 'subject to section 69 of the Police and Criminal Evidence Act 1984' – see [s.22(1)(c)] and [s.23(1)(c)] of the 1988 Act: Appendix III, *post*.

Microfilm 6.20

An enlargement of an authenticated microfilm copy of a document (or the material part of it) is admissible in criminal proceedings to prove the contents of the document, whether or not the document still exists: s.71 PACE Act 1984.

Taking a view 6.21

There is nothing improper in magistrates viewing an immovable exhibit outside the court or inspecting the scene of a crime. A view is a part of the evidence and evidence must be given in the presence of both parties, a point which was reiterated in *Parry v Boyle* [1986] Crim LR 551 in which a reminder was issued to justices that whilst they have a discretion to view the scene of a crime they should only do so after informing both parties of their intention so to do. The parties or their representatives should be invited to be present, since they may wish to comment on whether any feature has changed, or on what the justices have seen. The only exception is when a judge goes by himself to see some public place, such as the site of a road accident, *per* Denning LJ in *Goold v Evans & Co* (1951) 2 TLR 1189 (a civil case). This applies to a magistrates' court: see for example *Houghton v Schofield* [1973] RTR 239.

There would be no objection to a witness who has already given evidence attending and taking part in a view so long as he is recalled to be cross-examined, if desired: *Karamat v R* (1957) 120 JP 136.

It is improper to conduct a view after a jury (and thus, seemingly, the magistrates) have retired: *R v Lawrence* (1968) 132 JP 173, but this was waived where the view took place *at the express wish* of the defence: *R v Nixon* (1968) 132 JP 309. In *Parry v Boyle, supra*, it was stated that the view should take place before the evidence is concluded or at its conclusion. If a view should happen to take place after the addresses, then the parties must be given the opportunity to comment on any feature which they themselves have observed.

Exhibits 6.22

Exhibits are looked at by the court but are not shown to the public who have no claim to see them. This includes the showing of films the subject of prosecution, *per* Lawton LJ in *R v Waterfield* (1975) 60 Cr App R 296, a judgment which also contains advice on the circumstances in which the public or press should be allowed to see such films.

ADMISSIBILITY OF DEFENDANT'S PREVIOUS CONVICTIONS 6.23

The defendant, if he gives evidence, may not be asked or required to answer any questions *tending to show* that he has committed or been convicted of or been charged with any other offence except in the three circumstances set out in the s.1(f) Criminal Evidence Act 1898, commonly referred to as 'provisos'. They are:

(i) where such evidence is admissible to show that he is guilty of the offence. This is sometimes known as the *similar facts rule*;

(ii) where the accused 'puts his character in issue' by asking questions of the prosecution witness with a view to establishing his own good character or has himself given evidence of such character or the nature and conduct of the defence is such as to involve imputations as to the character of the prosecutor or his witness;

(iii) where the accused gives evidence against any other person charged in the same proceedings.

Each 'proviso' is further treated in the commentary to s.1(f), *post*.

6.24 Proving previous convictions

Where proof of the commission of an offence – whether by the accused or another person – *is relevant* to any issue in criminal proceedings the fact that a person has been convicted of the offence is admissible: s.74(1) PACE Act 1984.

The effect of proof of conviction depends upon whom it refers to. If it is anyone other than the accused he must be taken to have committed the offence unless the contrary is proved: s.74(2). The same effect follows with regard to the accused but only in so far as proof of the commission of the offence *is relevant to any matter in issue for a reason other than a tendency to show in the accused a disposition to commit the kind of offence with which he is charged*: s.74(3). It has been said that s.74 should be 'sparingly used', particularly where there is any danger of a contravention of s.78, *infra*: *R v Robertson*; *R v Golder* [1987] 3 WLR 327, (per Lord Lane CJ) where evidence is admitted, it is important to remember the effect and limitations: *ibid*.

Once the conviction is admissible the contents of any charge sheet and related documents is also admissible: s.75.

In relation to a person over 21 years any *finding of guilt* while under the age of 14 must be disregarded: s.16(2) CYPA 1963.

Previous convictions may be *proved* under any of the following provisions:

— s.39 CJA 1948 (proof of previous convictions by finger-print):
— s.104 MCA 1980; r.72 MC Rules 1981 (proof of previous convictions);
— r.68 MC Rules 1981 (proof of proceedings);
— s.11(4A) RTA 1972 (endorsement of licences);
— s.182 RTA 1972 (records of the Secretary of State);
— s.73 PACE Act 1984 (proof of convictions and acquittals).

A previous conviction in any part of the United Kingdom may be proved against a prisoner in any other part of the United Kingdom under the Prevention of Crimes Act 1871.

6.25 Spent convictions

The *Practice Note* [1975] 2 All ER 172, reads:

1. The effect of s.4(1) of the Rehabilitation of Offenders Act 1974 is that a person who has become a rehabilitated person for the purpose of the Act in respect of a conviction (known

as a 'spent' conviction) shall be treated for all purposes in law as a person who has not committed or been charged with or prosecuted for or convicted of or sentenced for the offence or offences which were the subject of that conviction.

2. Section 4(1) of the 1974 Act does not apply however to evidence given in criminal proceedings (s.7(2)(a)). Convictions are often disclosed in such criminal proceedings. When the Bill was before the House of Commons on 28 June 1974 the hope was expressed that the Lord Chief Justice would issue a practice direction for the guidance of the Crown Court with a view to reducing disclosure of spent convictions to a minimum and securing uniformity of approach.

3. During the trial of a criminal charge reference to previous convictions (and therefore to spent convictions) can arise in a number of ways. The most common is when the character of the accused or a witness is sought to be attacked by reference to his criminal record, but there are, of course, cases where previous convictions are relevant and admissible as, for instance, to prove system.

4. It is not possible to give general directions which will govern all these different situations, but it is recommended that both court and counsel should give effect to the general intention of Parliament by never referring to a spent conviction when such reference can be reasonably avoided. If unnecessary references to spent convictions are eliminated much will have been achieved.

5. After a verdict of guilty the court must be provided with a statement of the defendant's record for the purposes of sentence. The record supplied should contain all previous convictions, but those which are spent should, so far as practicable, be marked as such.

6. No one should refer in open court to a spent conviction without the authority of the judge, which authority should not be given unless the interests of justice so require.

7. When passing sentence the judge should make no reference to a spent conviction unless it is necessary to do so for the purpose of explaining the sentence to be passed.

A breach of para 6 of this Note cannot be a ground for upsetting a conviction which would otherwise be perfectly proper: *R v Smallman* [1982] Crim LR 175 (prosecution cross-examined defence witness as to previous conviction).

EXCLUDING EVIDENCE

Confessions and 'informal admissions' 6.26

A *confession* by the accused may be given in evidence against him in so far as it is relevant to any matter in issue and is not excluded by the court: s.76(1) PACE Act 1984. A confession includes *any statement* wholly or partly adverse to the person who made it, whether made to a person in authority or not and whether made in words or otherwise: s.82(1). This provision has the effect of dispensing with the former distinction in treatment as between 'confessions' and 'informal' or 'adverse admissions', *semble*. Confessions may be excluded under either s.76(2) or under s.78 (discretion to exclude 'unfair evidence') and for the purposes of reaching a decision on this the justices must (s.76(2)) or may (s.78) hold a *Trial within a trial*, see 6.27 and 6.28.

A confession obtained by *oppression* or in circumstances which make it unreliable is inadmissible: s.76(2). 'Oppression' is defined in s.76(8). The court may of *its own motion* require the prosecution to *prove beyond reasonable doubt* that a confession was not so obtained; s.76(3); and if it is represented to the court that the confession was or may have been so obtained *must* do so: s.76(2). the word 'oppression' is to be given its ordinary dictionary meaning, ie 'exercise of authority or power in a burdensome, harsh or wrongful manner; unjust or cruel treatment of subjects, inferiors, etc; the imposition of unreasonable or unjust burdens', and connotes *impropriety* on the part of the investigator: see *R v Fulling* [1987] 2 WLR 923. But 'unreliability' (see s.76(2)(b)) does not require impropriety: *ibid*.

The fact that facts were discovered as a result of an inadmissible confession is not admissible unless given in evidence by the accused or his witness: s.76(5).

There is special need for caution in the case of a *mentally handicapped person* where his confession was not made in the presence of an independent person: s.77.

6.27 'Unfair evidence'

The court has a discretion in criminal proceedings to exclude evidence if it appears having regard to all the circumstances in which the evidence was obtained that its admission would have such an *adverse effect on the fairness of the proceedings* that the court ought not to admit it: s.78(1) PACE Act 1984. This provision does not prejudice any power of the court to exclude evidence: s.82(3). Confessions may be excluded under s.76(2) or s.78 see *Trials within trials*, 6.28.

6.28 Trials within trials

Despite the former uncertainty, it is now established that justices can hold a 'trial within a trial' to determine the admissibility of a confession where this has been challenged under s.76 PACE Act 1984: *R v Liverpool Juvenile Court, ex p. R* [1987] 2 All ER 668. Indeed, according to *Ex p. R* they *must* do so. In that case, Russell LJ laid down the following rules of procedure based on submissions which the Divisional Court found to be 'totally valid':

1 The effect of s.76(2) is that in summary proceedings justices must now hold a trial within a trial if it is represented to them *by the defence* that a confession was, or might have been, obtained by either of the improper processes set out in s.76(2) (ie 'oppression', or in circumstances which might render the confession 'unreliable').

2 In such a trial within a trial the defendant may give evidence confined to the question of admissibility, and the justices will not *then* be concerned with the truth or otherwise of the confession.

3 Therefore, the defendant is entitled to a ruling on the admissibility of a confession *before* or *at the end of the prosecution case*.

4 There remains a discretion in the defendant as to the stage at which he chooses to attack the alleged confession . . . a trial within a trial will only take place before the close of the prosecution case if it is represented to the court that the confession was or might have been improperly obtained. If no such representation is made, the defendant is at liberty to raise the admissibility or weight of the confession at any subsequent stage of the trial . . . 'Representation' is not the same as, nor does it include, cross-examination, and the court is therefore not obliged to embark on a trial within a trial merely because of a suggestion in cross-examination that the alleged confession was obtained improperly.

5 It should never be necessary to call the prosecution evidence relating to the obtaining of the confession twice.

[Italics added]

6.29 So far as other situations are concerned, the following rules are discernable in what has been a much litigated area since the PACE Act provisions came into force:

(a) The power and duty to hold a 'trial within a trial' extends confessions sought to be excluded under s.78 PACE Act 1984: *Carlisle v DPP* (1987) 152 JPN 227; but not to other varieties of 'unfair evidence': ibid. Under s.78, there is a discretion – as opposed to a duty (cf. s.76(2) – to hold a trial within a trial in relation to confession evidence: *ibid*. This apart, the discretion to hold trials within trials does not extend to any other questions of admissibility. It should be noted that whereas s.76(2) creates a *mandatory* exclusion once 'oppression' or 'unreliability' are established, s.78 gives only a *discretion* to exclude 'unfair evidence'. During a trial within a trial, a defendant cannot be asked about the *truth of* a confession: *R v Wong Kam-ming* [1980] AC 247.

(b) The stage at which the matter is dealt with will depend on the point at which the defence seeks to raise the issue, or at which the court raises the issue of its own motion: *Ex p. R, supra*. In the absence of specific statutory provision it will be for the court to devise its own procedure, in the nature of a *voir dire*:

(c) Section 76 ('oppression' and 'unreliability') and s.78 are *not mutually exclusive*, so that a confession or admission can be excluded under either section: see *R v Mason (Carl)* (1987) *The Times* 23 May where it was held that s.78 applies to confessions even though they are specifically referred to by s.76 (police 'conned defendant' into admitting involvement by falsely stating that his finger-prints had been found at the scene of crime – conviction quashed because 'unfairness' not considered).

(d) The provisions of the 1984 Act *do not reduce* a court's discretion to exclude 'unfair evidence' as that discretion existed at common law: *Matto v Wolverhampton Crown Court* (1987) *The Times* 27 May.

(e) Notwithstanding that there are instances where a 'trial within a trial' is not possible in the magistrates' court, justices have a *discretion* to decide a particular matter 'as a separate issue', and at such point in the proceedings as is deemed appropriate, *semble: SJF (an Infant) v Chief Constable of Kent* [1982] Crim LR 682; *ADC v Chief Constable of Greater Manchester* (1983) (unreported, but see 151 JPN 274); *Vel v Chief Constable of North Wales* [1987] Crim LR 496 (discretion to treat as a 'preliminary point', a case since superceded by, or re-interpreted in, *Carlisle v DPP, supra*).

(f) The holding of a trial within a trial is confined to the summary trial of an information: *Ex p. R, supra*; although this conclusion of Russell LJ may have been based on too wide a reading of *R v Oxford City Justices, ex p. Berry* [1987] 1 All ER 1244, in which the justices were criticised – but a committal was not quashed – where they had 'failed to enter upon the inquiry required by s.76(2)'. That refusal was based on there being sufficient other evidence to support the committal. It is clear from *Ex p. Berry* that '. . . judicial review will lie where justices have failed to enter upon the inquiry required by s.76(2)': per May LJ, albeit it was refused as a matter of discretion in that case. If a trial within a trial is inappropriate, then the 'separate issue' approach at '(e)' above must apply, *semble*.

(g) Sections 76 and 78 are *both* applicable to committal proceedings, *semble* – notwithstanding that the magistrates' court is concerned at that point only with whether there is a *prima facie* case: the effect of *R v Oxford City Justices, supra* applied in the light of *R v Mason (Carl), supra.*

6.30　　　　　　　　**EVIDENCE OF A SPOUSE**

A distinction must be drawn between the 'competence' of a spouse to give evidence, and 'compellability'.

The *spouse* of the accused is in general a *competent witness* for the prosecution, the defence and any co-defendant: s.80(1) PACE Act 1984.

The spouse of the accused is always a *compellable* witness *for the accused*: s.80(2) but she is only *compellable* for the *prosecution* where the offence:
  (i) involves an assault or an injury or threat of injury to herself or a person under 16;
 (ii) is a sexual offence on a person under 16;
(iii) consists of attempting, conspiring or aiding, abetting, counselling or procuring such an offence: s.80(3).

Where husband and wife are *jointly charged* neither is *competent* for the prosecution or *compellable* for the co-accused spouse unless he or she is no longer liable to be convicted: s.80(4). These rules do not apply to persons who are no longer married: s.80(5).

The prosecution may not comment on a failure by a spouse of the accused to give evidence: s.80(8).

Up to the point where she goes into the witness box, the wife has a choice: she may refuse to give evidence or waive her right of refusal. The waiver is effective only if made with full knowledge of her right to refuse. If she waives her right of refusal, she becomes an ordinary witness. She is by analogy in the same position as a witness who waives privilege which would entitle him to refuse to answer questions on a certain topic. If the nature of her evidence justifies it, an application may be made to treat her as a hostile witness, *per* Peter Pain J in *R v Pitt* [1982] 3 All ER 63.

Statutory Provisions

CRIMINAL PROCEDURE ACT 1865

6.31　　**How far witness may be discredited by the party producing**
　　　　3. A party producing a witness shall not be allowed to impeach his credit by general evidence of bad character; but he may, in case the witness shall in the opinion of the judge prove adverse, contradict him by other evidence, or by leave of the judge, prove that he has made at other times a statement inconsistent with his present testimony; but before such last-mentioned proof can be given the circumstances of the supposed statement, sufficient to designate the particular occasion, must be mentioned to the witness, and he must be asked whether or not he has made such a statement.

COMMENTARY
This provision has not removed the common law right of the court to allow at its discretion cross-examination of a hostile witness: *R v Thompson* (1977) 64 Cr App R 96; and see generally under the title 'Hostile witnesses'.

As to proof of contradictory statements of adverse witness   6.32
4. If a witness, upon cross-examination as to a former statement made by him relative to the subject matter of the indictment or proceeding, and inconsistent with his present testimony, does not distinctly admit that he has made such statement, proof may be given that he did in fact make it; but before such proof can be given the circumstances of the supposed statement, sufficient to designate the particular occasion, must be mentioned to the witness, and he must be asked whether or not he has made such statement.

Cross-examinations as to previous statements in writing   6.33
5. A witness may be cross-examined as to previous statements made by him in writing, or reduced into writing, relative to the subject matter of the indictment or proceeding, without such writing being shown to him; but if it is intended to contradict such witness by the writing, his attention must, before such contradictory proof can be given, be called to those parts of the writing which are to be used for the purpose of so contradicting him. Providing always, that it shall be competent for the judge, at any time during the trial, to require the production of the writing for his inspection, and he may thereupon make such use of it for the purposes of the trial as he may think fit.

Proof of conviction of witness for felony or misdemeanour may be given   6.34
6. A witness may be questioned as to whether he has been convicted for any felony or misdemeanour, and upon being so questioned, if he either denies or does not admit the fact, or refuses to answer, it shall be lawful for the cross-examining party to prove such conviction.
[*as amended by Sch.7 Police and Criminal Evidence Act 1984*].

Proof of instrument to validity of which whereof attestation is not necessary   6.35
7. It shall not be necessary to prove by the attesting witness any instrument to the validity of which attestation is not requisite, and such instrument may be proved as if there had been no attesting witness thereto.

Comparison of disputed writing with writing proved to be genuine   6.36
8. Comparison of a disputed writing with any writing proved to the satisfaction of the judge to be genuine shall be permitted to be made by witnesses; and such writings, and the evidence of witnesses respecting the same, may be permitted to the court and jury as evidence of the genuineness or otherwise of the writing in dispute.

COMMENTARY
Proof beyond reasonable doubt is required under this section in criminal proceedings: *R v Ewing* (1983) *The Times*, 15 March.

BANKERS' BOOKS EVIDENCE ACT 1879

Mode of proof of entries in bankers' books   6.37
3. Subject to the provisions of this Act, a copy of any entry in a banker's book shall in all legal proceedings be received as prima facie evidence of such entry, and of the matters, transactions, and accounts therein recorded.

Proof that book is a banker's book   6.38
4. A copy of an entry in a banker's book shall not be received in evidence under this Act unless it be first proved that the book was at the time of the making of the entry one of the ordinary books of the bank, and that the entry was made in the usual and ordinary course of business, and that the book is in the custody or control of the bank.
Such proof may be given by a partner or officer of the bank, and may be given orally or by an affidavit sworn before any commissioner or person authorised to take affidavits.

6.39   Verification of copy
5. A copy of an entry in a banker's book shall not be received under this Act unless it be further proved that the copy has been examined with the original entry and is correct.

Such proof shall be given by some person who has examined the copy with the original entry, and may be given either orally or by an affidavit sworn before any commissioner or person authorised to take affidavits.

6.40   Case in which banker, etc, not compellable to produce book, etc
6. A banker or officer of a bank shall not, in any legal proceeding to which the bank is not a party, be compellable to produce any banker's book the contents of which can be proved under this Act, or to appear as a witness to prove the matters, transactions, and accounts therein recorded, unless by order of a judge made for special cause.

COMMENTARY
Banker, bank defined in s.9, *infra.*

Proved under this Act see ss.4 and 5, *supra.*

6.41   Court or judge may order inspection, etc
7. On the application of any party to a legal proceeding a court or judge may order that such party be at liberty to inspect and take copies of any entries in a banker's book for any of the purposes of such proceedings. An order under this section, may be made either with or without summoning the bank or any other party, and shall be served on the bank three clear days before the same is to be obeyed, unless the court or judge otherwise directs.

COMMENTARY
For the principles on which the court should act see the introduction. The power under this section extends to banks in Scotland and Northern Ireland: *Kissam v Link* (1896) 1 QB 574. For the Isle of Man see *R v Grossman* (1981) 73 Cr App R 302.

The court (including the justices) has power to order the costs of any application against the bank: s.8, *infra.*

Legal proceeding defined in s.10, *infra.*

A court or judge may The terms 'court' and 'judge' are defined in s.10, *infra.*

Order Disclosure need not be limited to the periods charged: *Owen v Sambrook* [1981] Crim LR 329. The order should be limited in time: *Williams and Others v Summerfield* (1972) 136 JP 616; *R v Marlborough St. Magistrates' Court Metropolitan Stipendiary Magistrate, ex p. Simpson* (1980) 70 Cr App R 291.

A banker's book defined in s.9, *infra.* This is not confined to the books of the defendant, but extends to third parties: *Waterhouse v Wilson Baker* [1924] All ER 777 (a civil case); *R v Andover Justices, ex p. Rhodes* [1980] Crim LR 644 (husband of accused).

Summoning the bank or any other person It is in the court's discretion whether to issue a summons or to make the order *ex parte*, although *ex parte* orders are more common. A summons would appear to be indicated when the books are those of someone other than the accused: *Cf R v Grossman* (1981) 73 Cr App R 302.

Three clear days ie excluding the day of service and the day on which the order is to be obeyed.

6.42   Costs
8. The costs of any application to a court or judge under or for the purposes of this Act, and the costs of anything done or to be done under an order of a court or judge made under or for the purposes of this Act shall be in the discretion of the court or judge, who may order the same or any part thereof to be paid to any party by the bank where the same have been occasioned by any default or delay on the part of the bank. Any such order against a bank may be enforced as if the bank was a party to the proceeding.

Interpretation of 'bank', 'banker' and 'banker's books'   **6.43**
9. (1) In this Act the expressions 'bank' and 'banker' mean–
(a) a recognised bank, licensed institution or municipal bank, within the meaning of the Banking Act 1979;
(b) a trustee savings bank within the meaning of the Trustee Savings Banks Act 1981;
(c) the National Savings Bank; and
(d) the Post Office, in the exercise of its powers to provide banking services.

(2) Expressions in this Act relating to 'bankers' books' include ledgers, day books, cash books, account books and other records used in the ordinary business of the bank, whether those records are in written form or are kept on microfilm, magnetic tape or any other form of mechanical or electronic data retrieval mechanism.
[*as substituted by Sch.6 Banking Act 1979, as amended by Sch.6 Trustee Savings Bank Act 1981*].

COMMENTARY
Letters contained in a bank correspondence file are not banker's books: *R v Dadson* (1983) 147 JP 509.

Interpretation of 'legal proceedings', 'court', 'judge'   **6.44**
10. In this Act–
The expression 'legal proceeding' means any civil or criminal proceeding or inquiry in which evidence is or may be given, and includes an arbitration and an application to, or an inquiry or other proceeding before, the Solicitors Disciplinary Tribunal or any body exercising functions in relation to solicitors in Scotland or Northern Ireland corresponding to the functions of that Tribunal;
The expression 'the court' means the court, judge, arbitrator, persons or person before whom a legal proceeding is held or taken;
The expression 'a judge' means with respect to England a judge of the High Court . . .
[*as amended by s.86 Solicitors Act 1974*].

COMMENTARY
Persons or person includes a magistrates' court: *R v Kinghorn* (1908) 72 JP 478.

CRIMINAL EVIDENCE ACT 1898

Competency of witnesses in criminal cases   **6.45**
1. Every person charged with an offence shall be a competent witness for the defence at every stage of the proceedings, whether the person so charged is charged solely or jointly with any other person. Provided as follows–
(a) A person so charged shall not be called as a witness in pursuance of this Act except upon his own application:
(b) The failure of any person charged with an offence to give evidence shall not be made the subject of any comment by the prosecution:
(c), (d) (*Repealed*).
(e) A person charged and being a witness in pursuance of this Act may be asked any question in cross-examination notwithstanding that it would tend to criminate him as to the offence charged:
(f) A person charged and called as a witness in pursuance of this Act shall not be asked, and if asked shall not be required to answer, any question tending to show that he has committed or been convicted of or been charged with any offence other than that wherewith he is then charged, or is of bad character, unless–
    (i) the proof that he has committed or been convicted of such other offence is admissible evidence to show that he is guilty of the offence wherewith he is then charged; or

(ii) he has personally or by his advocate asked questions of the witnesses for the prosecution with a view to establish his own good character, or has given evidence of his good character, or the nature or conduct of the defence is such as to involve imputations on the character of the prosecutor or the witnesses for the prosecution; or

(iii) he has given evidence against any other person charged in the same proceedings:

(g) Every person called as a witness in pursuance of this Act shall, unless otherwise ordered by the court, give his evidence from the witness box or other place from which the other witnesses give their evidence.

[as amended by s.1 Criminal Evidence Act 1979, Sch.16 CJA 1982 s.80(9), Sch.7 PACE Act 1984].

COMMENTARY

Wife or husband see the introduction.

Witness for the defence including the defence of a co-defendant. But the person charged is not a compellable witness: see proviso (a).

Proviso (a): once a co-defendant is acquitted he becomes a compellable witness: *R v Conti* (1974) 85 Cr App R 387.

Proviso (e): the phrase 'tend to criminate him as to the offence charged' means 'tend to connect him with the commission of the offence charged' rather than 'tend to convince or persuade the jury that he is guilty,' *per* Lord Reid and Viscount Simonds in *Jones v Director of Public Prosecutions* [1962] AC 635.

Any question When the accused gives evidence on behalf of another accused he may be cross-examined to show that he is guilty of the offence charged: *R v Rowland* (1910) 74 JP 144.

Proviso (f): 'the substantive part of proviso (f) is negative in form and as such is universal and is absolute unless the exceptions come into play. Then come the three exceptions, but it does not follow that when the absolute prohibition is superseded by a permission, the permission is as absolute as the prohibition. When it is sought to justify a question it must not only be brought within the terms of the permission, but also must be capable of justification according to the general rules of evidence and in particular must satisfy the test of relevance. Exception (i) deals with evidence falling within the rule that where issues of intention or design are involved in the charge or defence, the prisoner may be asked questions relevant to these matters, even though he has himself raised no question of his good character. Exceptions (ii) and (iii) come into play when the prisoner by himself or his witnesses has put his character in issue, or has attacked the character of others. Dealing with exceptions (i) and (ii), it is clear that the test of relevance is wider in (ii) than in (i). In the latter, proof that the prisoner has committed or been convicted of some other offence can only be admitted if it goes to show that he was guilty of the offence charged. In the former (exception (ii)) the questions permissible must be relevant to the issue of his own good character and if not so relevant cannot be admissible', *per* Lord Sankey LC in *Maxwell v Director of Public Prosecutions* (1934) 98 JP 387.

Ignoring exception (i), the rules governing cross-examination of the accused where summarised by Viscount Simonds in *Stirling v Director of Public Prosecutions* (1945) 109 JP 1 as follows:

(1) The accused in the witness box may not be asked any question 'tending to show that he had committed or been convicted of or been charged with any offence other than that wherewith he is then charged, or is of bad character, unless' one or other of the three conditions set out in s.1(f) of the Act of 1898 is fulfilled.

(2) He may however be cross-examined as to any of the evidence he has given in chief, including statements as to his good record, with a view to testing his veracity or accuracy, or to showing that he is not to be believed on his oath.

(3) An accused who 'puts his character in issue' must be regarded as putting the whole of his past record in issue. He cannot assert his good character in certain respects without exposing himself to inquiry as to the rest of his record so far as this tends to disprove a claim for good character.

(4) An accused is not to be regarded as depriving himself of the protection of the section, because the proper conduct of his defence necessitates the making of injurious reflections on the prosecutor or his witnesses: *R v Turner* [1944] 1 All ER 599.

(5) It is no disproof of good character that a man has been suspected, or accused, of a previous crime. Such questions as 'Were you suspected?' or 'Were you accused?' are inadmissible because they are irrelevant to the issue of character, and can only be asked if the accused has sworn expressly to the contrary (see r.2, *supra*).

(6) The fact that a question put to the accused is irrelevant is in itself no reason for quashing his conviction, though it should have been disallowed by the judge. If the question is not only irrelevant but is unfair to the accused as being likely to distract the jury from considering the real issues, and so lead to 'a miscarriage of justice' (Criminal Appeal Act, 1907, s.4(1)). it should be disallowed, and, if not disallowed, is a ground on which an appeal against conviction may be based.

And see *R v Nelson* (1979) 68 Cr App R 12 (cross examination should not have been allowed when defence put it to police officer that conversation recorded in his notebook never took place).

'It is necessary that an unrepresented defendant should be warned of the risk he runs if he persists in attacking prosecution witnesses. The proper practice should be for those representing the prosecution, who alone know whether the defendant has got previous convictions, to ask for an adjournment and, when the justices have retired, to enlist the help, which I am sure would only too readily be given, of the justices' clerk in order that they may both explain, as simply as possible, to the unrepresented defendant the risk which he runs if he continues in that course of conduct', *per* Lord Parker CJ in *R v Weston-Super-Mare Justices, ex p. Townsend* (1968) 132 JP 526. Where justices hear inadmissible evidence they should not dismiss the case but should adjourn it for a re-hearing before a different bench: *Elkington v Kelsey* [1948] 2 KB 256. Where the defendant has *forfeited his shield* he may be cross-examined about subsequent as well as previous convictions: *R v Coltress* (1979) 68 Cr App R 193.

Proviso (f)(i): sometimes known as the similar facts rule. The present test was described as follows: is the evidence capable of tending to persuade a jury of the accused's guilt on some ground other than his bad character and disposition to commit the sort of crime with which he is charged? In the case of an alleged homosexual offence, just as in the case of an alleged burglary, evidence which proves merely that the accused has committed crimes in the past and is therefore disposed to commit the crime charged is clearly inadmissible. It has, however, never been doubted that if the crime charged is committed in an uniquely or strikingly similar manner to other crimes committed by the accused the manner in which the other crimes were committed may be evidence upon which a jury could reasonably conclude that the accused was guilty of the crime charged. The similarity would have to be so unique or striking that commonsense makes it inexplicable on the basis of coincidence, *per* Lord Salmon in *Boardman v Director of Public Prosecutions* (1975) 139 JP 52. In *R v Rance and Herron* (1976) 62 Cr App R 118 at p.121, Lord Widgery CJ was forced to say that 'one must be careful not to attach too much importance to Lord Salmon's vivid phrase "uniquely or strikingly similar".' The gist of what is being said both by Lord Cross (at p.185) and by Lord Salmon, is that evidence is admissible as similar fact evidence if, but only if, it goes beyond showing a tendency to commit crimes of this kind and is positively probative in regard to the crime now charged; see also *R v Scarrott* [1978] QB 1016.

In *R v Seaman* (1978) 67 Cr App R 234, the appellant had gone into a supermarket carrying a shopping bag, ordered a packet of bacon which the assistant had given him and placed it in a wire basket. He then bought some bottles of beer and slipped the bacon into the same bag. He left the supermarket without paying for the bacon and was stopped outside. At his trial for the theft of the bacon evidence was given of two previous occasions. On the first the store detective had seen the appellant buying bacon and put in it a wire basket which was later seen to be empty. However, as he had been lost sight of for a minute or so, no action had been taken against him. On the second occasion, the appellant, noticing that he was being watched, had returned the bacon on the shelf. Although it was said to be a borderline case, the evidence of the prior acts was held to have been properly admitted.

Evidence may be admitted of facts subsequent to the offence: *R v Armstrong* (1922) 86 JP 209; see also *R v Barrington* (1980) 72 Cr App R 280, and *Thompson v R* (1917) 81 JP 266.

Charged means 'charged before a court': *Stirland v Director of Public Prosecutions* (1945) 109 JP 1. This prohibits questions in regard to a charge of which the accused was acquitted: *R v Cokar* (1960) 124 JP 313. The mere fact that a man has been charged with an offence is no proof that he committed the offence and is irrelevant unless asked as a step in cross-examination leading to a question of whether the witness was convicted, or in order to elicit some evidence of statements made or evidence given by the prisoner on the trial of a charge which failed which tends to throw doubt on evidence which he is

6.46

giving or in order to show anger on the part of the accused against the person attacked for having brought a charge against the accused which proved to be unfounded, *per* Viscount Sankey LC in *Maxwell v Director of Public Prosecutions* (1934) 98 JP 387.

Proviso (f)(ii): the following guidelines have been set out for the exercise of discretion in favour of defendants:

'First, it should be used if there is nothing more than a denial, however emphatic or offensively made, of an act or even a short series of acts amounting to one incident or in what was said to have been a short interview. Examples are provided by the kind of evidence given in pickpocket cases and where the defendant is alleged to have said: "Who grassed on me this time?" The position would be different however if there were a denial of evidence of a long period of detailed observation extending over hours and just as in this case and in *R v Tanner*, where there were denials of long conversations. Second, cross-examination should only be allowed if the judge is sure that there is no possibility of mistake, misunderstanding or confusion and that the jury will inevitably have to decide whether the prosecution witnesses have fabricated evidence. Defendants sometimes make wild allegations when giving evidence. Allowance should be made for the strain of being in the witness box and the exaggerated use of language which sometimes results from such strain or lack of education or mental instability. Particular care should be used when a defendant is led into making allegations during cross-examination. The defendant who, during cross-examination, is driven to explaining away the evidence by saying it has been made up or planted on him usually convicts himself without having his previous convictions brought out. Finally, there is no need for the prosecution to rely on s.1(f)(ii) if the evidence against a defendant is overwhelming.

per Lawton LJ in *R v Britzman and Hall* (1983) 76 Cr App R 134.

Cross-examination of the accused is permissible under this exception, notwithstanding that the imputations are a necessary part of the accused's defence, but the court has a discretion to refuse to permit cross-examination: *Selvey v Director of Public Prosecutions* (1968) 52 Cr App R 443. A statement that amounts to no more than a denial of the charge expressed in emphatic language should not be regarded as coming within this section: *Selvey v Director of Public Prosecutions, supra*. It is wrong in principle to allow cross-examination as to character and previous convictions where the convictions are minor and took place long before: *R v Nye* (1982) 75 Cr App R 247 (spent convictions).

Proviso (f)(iii): Evidence against, the following guidelines were laid down for deciding whether evidence by an accused was 'evidence against' his co-accused: (1) If it is established that a person jointly charged has given evidence against the co-defendant that defendant has a right to cross-examine the other as to previous convictions and the trial judge has no discretion to refuse an application. (2) Such evidence may be given either in chief or during cross-examination. (3) It has to be objectively decided whether the evidence either supports the prosecution case in a material respect or undermines the defence of the co-accused. A hostile intent is irrelevant. (4) If consideration has to be given to the undermining of the other's defence care must be taken to see that the evidence clearly undermines the defence. Inconvenience to or inconsistency with the other's defence is not of itself sufficient. (5) Mere denial of participation in a joint venture is not of itself sufficient to rank as evidence against the co-defendant. For the proviso to apply, such denial must lead to the conclusion that if the witness did not participate then it must have been the other who did. (6) Where the one defendant asserts or in due course would assert one view of the joint venture which is directly contradicted by the other such contradiction may be evidence against the co-defendant: *R v Varley* [1982] 2 All ER 519.

6.47   Evidence of person charged
2. Where the only witness to the facts of the case called by the defence is the person charged, he shall be called as a witness immediately after the close of the evidence of prosecution.

6.48   Right of reply
3. The fact that the person charged has been called as a witness shall not of itself confer on the prosecution the right of reply.

CHILDREN AND YOUNG PERSONS ACT 1933

Evidence of child of tender years   **6.49**

38. (1) Where, in any proceedings against any person for any offence, any child of tender years called as a witness does not in the opinion of the court understand the nature of the oath, his evidence may be received, though not given upon oath, if, in the opinion of the court, he is possessed of sufficient intelligence to justify the reception of the evidence, and understands the duty of speaking the truth; and his evidence, though not given on oath, but otherwise taken and reduced into writing in accordance with the provisions of s.17 of the Indictable Offences Act 1848, or this Part of this Act, shall be deemed to be a deposition within the meaning of that section and that Part respectively:

Provided that where evidence admitted by virtue of this section is given on behalf of the prosecution the accused shall not be liable to be convicted of the offence unless the evidence is corroborated by some other material evidence in support thereof implicating him.

(2) If any child whose evidence is received as aforesaid wilfully gives false evidence in such circumstances that he would, if the evidence had been given on oath, have been guilty of perjury, he shall be liable on summary conviction to be dealt with as if he had been summarily convicted of an indictable offence punishable in the case of an adult with imprisonment.

COMMENTARY

s.38(1): This was always a rule of the common law: *R v Southern* [1930] All ER Rep 16. There may be cases in which witnesses should be called on the child's capacity to take the oath: *R v Reynolds* (1950) 114 JP 115. For an example of the examination of a child on this point see *R v Dent* (1907) 71 JP 511; and see *R v Lyons* (1921) 15 Cr App R 144. The Court of Appeal has tended to play down the importance of an awareness of the divine sanction. The important consideration, it was said in *R v Hayes* (1977) 64 Cr App R 194, at p.196, is whether the child has a sufficient appreciation of the solemnity of the occasion and the added responsibility to tell the truth which is involved in taking an oath over and above the duty to tell the truth which is an ordinary duty of normal social conduct. There are two aspects when considering whether a child should properly be sworn: first that the child has sufficient appreciation of the particular nature of the case and, secondly, a realisation that taking the oath involves more than the ordinary duty of telling the truth in ordinary day to day life: *R v Campbell* (1982) *The Times*, 10 December. Where a court admits the unsworn evidence of a child without first satisfying itself of the factors set out in subs (1) the conviction will not necessarily be quashed: *R v Surgenor* (1940) 104 JP 213. The assessment should be made in *open court*.

The evidence of a child before examining justices in sexual cases *must* in general be tendered in writing under the s.27 CYPA 1963, *infra*. The public, but *not the press*, may be excluded during the evidence of a juvenile witness in proceedings in relation to an offence against or any conduct contrary to, decency or morality: s.37 CYPA 1933.

Of tender years, 'whether a child is of tender years is a matter for the good sense of the court': *R v Campbell* [1956] 2 QB 432. What 'tender years' means differs according to the child. In general for a proffered witness under the age of 14 the precautions are necessary: *R v Khan* [1981] Crim LR 330. In *R v Hayes* (1977) 64 Cr App R 82 it was said that the borderline dividing children who are not normally considered old enough to take the oath properly falls between the ages of eight and 10. It is undesirable in any circumstances to call a child of five years old: *R v Wallwork* (1958) 42 Cr App R 153.

On oath includes an affirmation: Sch.1 Interpretation Act 1978.

Section 17 of the Indictable Offences Act 1848, now r.7 MC Rules 1981.

Corroborated

(a) The unsworn evidence of a child must be corroborated by sworn evidence if then the only evidence implicating the accused is that of unsworn children the judge must stop the case.

(b) It makes no difference whether the child's evidence relates to an assault on himself or herself or to any other charge, for example, when an unsworn child says that he saw the accused person steal an article.

(c) The sworn evidence of a child need not as a matter of law be corroborated, but a jury should be warned, not that they must find corroboration, but that there is a risk in acting on the uncorroborated evidence of young boys or girls, though they may do so if convinced that the witness is telling the truth.

(d) Such warning should also be given when a young boy or girl is called to corroborate the evidence either of another child whether sworn or unsworn or of an adult.

(e) As the statute which permits a child of tender years to give unsworn evidence expressly provides for such evidence being given in any proceeding against any person for any offence, the unsworn evidence of a child can be given to corroborate the evidence of another person given on oath, but in such a case a particularly careful warning should be given, *per* Lord Goddard CJ in *R v Campbell*, [1956] 2 QB 432, approved by the House of Lords in *Director of Public Prosecutions v Hester* [1973] AC 296, in which it was further decided that the evidence of an unsworn child (admitted pursuant to s.38(1)) could amount to corroboration of evidence given on oath by another child (the complainant) provided that the unsworn evidence was corroborated as required by the proviso: 'What was principally contemplated by the proviso was the situation where a child of tender years had been assaulted and the child's unsworn evidence was received. Corroboration of "that" evidence was then essential before a conviction could result.'

There is *no rule of law* that the sworn evidence of a child which requires corroboration cannot corroborate the sworn evidence of another child which requires corroboration: *Director of Public Prosecutions v Kilbourne* (1973) 57 Cr App R 381.

Note that [s.33] CJA 1988, when in force, will abolish the corroboration requirement and the proviso to s.38(1): see Appendix III, *post*.

CRIMINAL JUSTICE ACT 1948

6.50   **Proof of previous convictions by fingerprints**

39. (1) A previous conviction may be proved against any person in any criminal proceedings by the production of such evidence of the conviction as is mentioned in this section, and by showing that his fingerprints and those of the person convicted are the fingerprints of the same person.

(2) A certificate purporting to be signed by or on behalf of the Commissioner of Police of the Metropolis, containing particulars relating to a conviction extracted fro the criminal records kept by him, and certifying that the copies of the fingerprints exhibited to the certificate are copies of the fingerprints appearing from the said records to have been taken under or by virtue of any enactment in that behalf in force in part of the United Kingdom (including an enactment of the Parliament of Northern Ireland), from the person convicted on the occasion of the conviction, shall be evidence of the conviction and evidence that the copies of the fingerprints exhibited to the certificate are copies of the fingerprints of the person convicted.

(3) A certificate purporting to be signed by or on behalf of the governor of a prison or remand centre in which any person has been detained in connection with any criminal proceedings, certifying that the fingerprints exhibited thereto were taken from him while he was so detained, shall be evidence in those proceedings that the fingerprints exhibited to the certificate are the fingerprints of that person.

(4) A certificate purporting to be signed by or on behalf of the Commissioner of Police of the Metropolis, and certifying that the fingerprints, copies of which are certified as aforesaid by or on behalf of the Commissioner to be copies of the fingerprints of a person previously convicted and the fingerprints certified by or on behalf of the governor aforesaid, or otherwise shown, to be the fingerprints of the person against whom the previous conviction is sought to be proved are the fingerprints of the same person shall be evidence of the matter so certified.

(5) The method of proving a previous conviction authorised by this section shall be in addition to any other method of proving the conviction.

[*as amended by Sch.4 Criminal Justice Act 1961*].

COMMENTARY

Previous conviction to be construed as including a reference to a previous conviction by a court in any part of Great Britain: s.8(2) CJA 1948.

ingerprints to be construed as including a reference to palm prints: s.33 CJA 1967.
Any other method see *Proof of previous convictions* at 6.24.

Evidence by certificate 6.51
41. (1) In any criminal proceedings, a certificate purporting to be signed by a constable, or by a person having the prescribed qualifications, and certifying that a plan or drawing exhibited thereto is a plan or drawing made by him of the place or object specified in the certificate, and that the plan or drawing is correctly drawn to a scale so specified, shall be evidence of the relative position of the things shown on the plan or drawing.

(2), (3) (*Repealed*).

(4) Nothing in this section shall be deemed to make a certificate admissible as evidence in proceedings for any offence–
- (a) unless a copy thereof has, not less than seven days before the hearing or trial, been served in the prescribed manner on the person charged with the offence; or
- (b) if that person, not later than three days before the hearing or trial or within such further time as the court may in special circumstances allow, serves notice in the prescribed form and manner of the prosecutor requiring the attendance at the trial of the person who signed the certificate.

(6) In this section the expression 'prescribed' means prescribed by rules made by the Secretary of State.
[*as amended by Sch.18 RTA 1960 and Sch.3 Theft Act 1968*].

COMMENTARY
Constable, ie a police officer of any rank.

The prescribed qualifications, the Evidence by Certificate Rules 1961 (SI No 248) prescribe:
a) registration as an architect under the Architects (Registration) Acts 1931 to 1938; or
b) membership of any of the following bodies, that is to say, the Royal Institution of Chartered Surveyors, the Institution of Civil Engineers, the Institution of Municipal Engineers and the Land Agents Society.

Not less than seven days before, ie seven clear or intervening days: *R v Turner* (1910) 74 JP 1; *Re Hector Whaling Ltd* [1935] All ER Rep 302; *Thompson v Stimpson* [1960] 3 All ER 00.

The prescribed manner, the Evidence by Certificate Rules 1961 (SI No 248) prescribe:
a) where the person to be served is a corporation, by addressing it to the corporation and leaving it at, or sending it by registered post or by recorded delivery service to, the registered office of the corporation or, if there is no such office, its principal office or place at which it conducts its business;
b) in any other case, by delivering it personally to the person to be served or by addressing it to him and leaving it at, or sending it by registered post or by the recorded delivery service to, his last or usual place of abode or place of business.'

CHILDREN AND YOUNG PERSONS ACT 1963

Form of oath for use in juvenile courts and by children and young persons in other courts 6.52
28. (1) Subject to subs (2) of this section. In relation to any oath administered to and taken by any person before a juvenile court or administered to and taken by any child or young person before any other court, s.1 of the Oaths Act 1978, shall have effect as if the words 'I promise before Almighty God' were set out in it instead of the words 'I swear by Almighty God that'.

(2) Where in any oath otherwise duly administered and taken either of the forms mentioned in this section is used instead of the other, the oath shall nevertheless be deemed to have been duly administered and taken.
[*as amended by s.2 Oaths Act 1978*].

COMMENTARY

This section must be construed as one with the CYPA 1933: s.65(3) CYPA 1963.

WELSH LANGUAGE ACT 1967

6.53   **Use of Welsh in legal proceedings**

1. (1) In any legal proceedings in Wales or Monmouthshire the Welsh language may be spoken by any party, witness or other person who desires to use it, subject in the case of proceedings in a court other than a magistrates court to such prior notice as may be required by rules of court; and any necessary provision for interpretation shall be made accordingly.

COMMENTARY

The Lord Chancellor has powers under s.2 Welsh Courts Act 1942 to prescribe translation in the Welsh language of any form of oath or affirmation and has done so in the Welsh Courts (Oaths and Interpreters) Rules 1943, SR & O No 683, as amended by SI 1959 No 157.

CRIMINAL JUSTICE ACT 1967

6.54   **Proof by written statement**

9. (1) In any criminal proceedings, other than committal proceedings, a written statement by any person shall, if such of the conditions mentioned in the next following subsection as are applicable are satisfied, be admissible as evidence to the like extent as oral evidence to the like effect by that person.

(2) The said conditions are–

(a) the statement purports to be signed by the person who made it;

(b) the statement contains a declaration by that person to the effect that it is true to the best of his knowledge and belief and that he made the statement knowing that, if it were tendered in evidence, he would be liable to prosecution if he wilfully stated in it anything which he knew to be false or did not believe to be true;

(c) before the hearing at which the statement is tendered in evidence, a copy of the statement is served, by or on behalf of the party proposing to tender it, on each of the other parties to the proceedings; and

(d) none of the other parties or their solicitors, within seven days from the service of the copy of the statement, serves a notice on the party so proposing objecting to the statement being tendered in evidence under this section:

Provided that the conditions mentioned in paras (c) and (d) of this subsection shall not apply if the parties agree before or during the hearing that the statement shall be so tendered.

(3) The following provisions shall also have effect in relation to any written statement tendered in evidence under this section, that is to say–

(a) if the statement is made by a person under the age of 21, it shall give his age;

(b) if it is made by a person who cannot read it, it shall be read to him before he signs it and shall be accompanied by a declaration by the person who so read the statement to the effect that it was so read; and

(c) if it refers to any other document as an exhibit, the copy served on any other party to the proceedings under para (c) of the last foregoing subsection shall be accompanied by a copy of that document or by such information as may be necessary in order to enable the party on whom it is served to inspect that document or a copy thereof.

(4) Notwithstanding that a written statement made by any person may be admissible as evidence by virtue of this section–

(a) the party by whom or on whose behalf a copy of the statement was served may call that person to give evidence; and

(b) the court may, of its own motion or on the application of any party to the proceedings, require that person to attend before the court and give evidence.

(5) . . .

(6) So much of any statement as is admitted in evidence by virtue of this section shall, unless the court otherwise directs, be read aloud at the hearing and where the court so directs an account shall be given orally of so much of any statement as is not read aloud.

(7) Any document or object referred to as an exhibit and identified in a written statement tendered in evidence under this section shall be treated as if it had been produced as an exhibit and identified in court by the maker of the statement.

(8) A document required by this section to be served on any person may be served–
(a) by delivering it to him or to his solicitor; or
(b) by addressing it to him and leaving it at his usual or last known place of abode or place of business or by addressing it to his solicitor and leaving at his office; or
(c) by sending it in a registered letter or by the recorded delivery service addressed to him at his usual or last place of abode or place of business or addressed to his solicitor at his office; or
(d) in the case of a body corporate, by delivering it to the secretary or clerk of the body at its registered office or sending it in a registered letter or by the recorded delivery service addressed to the secretary or clerk of that body at that office.

COMMENTARY

See under *Written Statements* at 6.13. So far as admissibility of the statements is concerned, a distinction is apparently to be drawn between the 'conditions' referred to in subs (2) and the 'provisions' referred to in subs (3). Any failure to comply with the former renders the statement wholly inadmissible under this section. (It may of course be admissible for other purposes.) Breach of the 'provisions' on the other hand would, *it is suggested*, give the court a discretion to exclude the statement. For the background to this section see the 9th Report of the Criminal Law Revision Committee (Cmnd 3145).

Expressions used in this section have the same meaning as in the MCA 1980: s.36(2) CJA 1967.

This section, except subss (2), (6) and (3A), applies to written statements made in the Isle of Man: Isle of Man Act 1979, s.5(3), (9); and to written statements made in Scotland and Northern Ireland as well as to written statements made in England and Wales: s.46 CJA 1972.

.9(1): Committal proceedings means proceedings before a magistrates' court acting as examining justices: s.36(1) of the Act.

A written statement For the editing of statements see the *Practice Note* [1986] 2 All ER 511, noted under *Editing statements* at 6.14. For the use of a written statement for the purpose of *Refreshing memory; Out of Court* and *In the witness box* see those titles at 6.08 and 6.09. It is desirable for the prosecution to call witnesses in person who are central to their case and not use s.9 statements, *per* Stephen Brown J, in *Lister v Quaife* [1983] 2 All ER 29.

Admissible as evidence to the like extent as oral evidence thus a written statement under this section which identifies the accused by name only has the same effect as if evidence had been given orally from the witness box to the like effect, and in the absence of any suggestion that the person named is not the accused, is sufficient to constitute a case to answer: *Ellis v Jones* (1973) 137 JP 581.

.9(2)(b): Contains a declaration Unlike the statement itself, this declaration need not be signed and may be at the beginning of (preferably) the end of the statement: *Chapman v Ingleton* (1973) 57 Cr App R 476.

A copy of the statement is served . . . on each of the other parties together with a notice of the accused's right to object. A copy of the statement must as soon as practicable be given to the clerk: r.7(2) MC Rules 1981. For the method of service see s.9(8) of this Act. No minimum period is prescribed: it is left to the party seeking to tender the statement to serve it within seven days in accordance with s.9(2)(d) of this Act. For proof of service see r.67. Service may be waived by agreement: see the proviso to s.9(2).

Within seven days from: this term implies that the first day is to be excluded and the last included: *Goldsmiths' Co v West Metropolitan Rail Co* (1904) 68 JP 41; *Stewart v Chapman* (1951) 115 JP 473.

Under the age of 21, for the determination of age see s.150(4) MCA 1980.

Exhibit, for the identification of exhibits see r.70(4) MC Rules 1981.

s.9(4) The provisions of this subsection do not override the general rule that once justices have retired to consider the evidence further evidence should be admitted only in the most exceptional cases: *French's Dairies (Sevenoaks) Ltd v Davis* [1973] Crim LR 630; and see the note to (4) MCA 1980.

s.9(6) The statement must be read aloud or, with the consent of the court, summarised by the party tendering it: r.70(7) Magistrates' Courts Rules 1981. The name and address of the witness must, unless the court directs otherwise, be read out: r.70(6), *ibid*.

6.55   **Proof by formal admission**
   10. (1) Subject to the provisions of this section, any fact of which oral evidence may be given in any criminal proceedings may be admitted for the purpose of those proceedings by or on behalf of the prosecutor or defendant and the admission by any party of any such fact under this section shall as against that party be conclusive evidence in those proceedings of the fact admitted.

   (2) An admission under this section–
   (a) may be made before or at the proceedings;
   (b) if made otherwise than in court, shall be in writing,
   (c) if made in writing by an individual, shall purport to be signed by the person making it and, if so made by a body corporate, shall purport to be signed by a director or manager, or the secretary or clerk, or some other similar officer of the body corporate;
   (d) if made on behalf of a defendant who is an individual, shall be made by his counsel or solicitor;
   (e) if made at any stage before the trial by a defendant who is an individual must be approved by his counsel or solicitor (whether at the time it was made or subsequently) before or at the proceedings in question.

   An admission under this section for the purpose of proceedings relating to any matter shall be treated as an admission for the purpose of any subsequent criminal proceedings relating to that matter (including any appeal or retrial).

   (4) An admission under this section may with the leave of the court be withdrawn in the proceedings for the purpose of which it is made or any subsequent criminal proceedings relating to the same matter.

COMMENTARY

Expressions used in this section have the same meaning as in the MCA 1980: s.36(2) CJA 1967. Admissions made orally in court must be written down and signed: r.71 MC Rules 1981.

Any fact of which oral evidence may be given in a trial on indictment it was held that the practice of admitting the contents of the prosecutor's opening speech should be adopted rarely and with extreme caution because of the difficulties of jurors distinguishing facts, law and comment: *R v Lewis* (1971) 55 Cr App R 386. It is not possible for a layman to admit what only an expert can know: *R v Lang and Evans* [1977] Crim LR 286 (whether substance was cannabis). There is not a sufficient case to be committed for trial where the prosecutor offers no evidence and the only remaining evidence is a 's.10 admission': *R v Horseferry Road Magistrates' Court, ex p. O'Regan* (1986) 150 JP 535; and *quaere* therefor whether the same principle must apply at the *no case to answer* stage in relation to summary trial.

In writing includes typing, printing, lithography, photography, and other modes of representing or reproducing words in a visible form: Sch.1 Interpretation Act 1978. This document should be retained as it must be sent to the Crown Court in the event of an appeal r.74(6) MC Rules 1981.

Director in relation to a body corporate which is established by or under any enactment for the purpose of carrying on under national ownership any industry or part of an industry or undertaking and whose affairs are managed by the members thereof means a member of that body: s.36(1) CJA 1967.

Made/approved by his counsel or solicitor This does not imply that an unrepresented defendant may not make an admission, merely that admissions by represented defendants must be made or approved by their legal representatives – see para 28 of the 9th Report of the Criminal Law Revision Committee (Cmnd 3145).

s.10(4): Withdrawn 'If necessary the court, in allowing a withdrawal, might adjourn the hearing for a witness to prove the fact admitted': para 29, 9th Report of the Criminal Law Revision Committee (Cmnd 3145). For a discussion of the effects of a withdrawn admission see para 3, *ibid*.

Taking and use of fingerprints and palm prints 6.56

33. In s.39 of the Criminal Justice Act 1948 (proof of previous convictions by fingerprints) any reference to fingerprints shall be construed as including a reference to palm prints.
[*as amended by Sch.1 MCA 1980*].

CRIMINAL JUSTICE ACT 1972

Admissibility of written statements made outside England and Wales 6.57

46. (1) Section 12 of the Magistrates' Courts Act 1980 and s.9 of the Criminal Justice Act 1967 (which respectively allow written statements to be used as evidence in committal proceedings and in other criminal proceedings) and s.16 of the said Act of 1980 and s.89 of the said Act of 1967 (which punishes the making of false statements which are tendered in evidence under the said ss.12 or 9, as the case may be) shall apply to written statements made in Scotland or Northern Ireland as well as to written statements made in England and Wales.

(2) The said s.12 shall apply also to written statements made outside the United Kingdom, but, in relation to such statements, that section shall have effect with the omission of subss.(2)(b), (3A) and (7).
[*as amended by Sch.7 MCA 1980*].

OATHS ACT 1978

Manner of administration of oaths 6.58

1. (1) Any oath may be administered and taken in England, Wales or Northern Ireland in the following form and manner–
The person taking the oath shall hold the New Testament, or, in the case of a Jew, the Old Testament, in his uplifted hand, and shall say or repeat after the officer administering oath the words 'I swear by Almighty God that . . .', followed by the words of the oath prescribed by law.

(2) The officer shall (unless the person about to take the oath voluntarily objects thereto, or is physically incapable of so taking the oath) administer the oath in the form and manner aforesaid without question.

(3) In the case of a person who is neither a Christian nor a Jew, the oath shall be administered in any lawful manner.

(4) In this section 'officer' means any person duly authorised to administer oaths.

COMMENTARY

Subs (1): His uplifted hand, the requirements that the Bible shall be held in the uplifted hand is directive only so that a failure to comply does not invalidate the witness's testimony: *R v Chapman* [1980] Crim. LR 42. Contrary to popular belief, there is *no absolute requirement* that only the *right* hand should be used.

'**I swear by Almighty God**', for the words to be substituted in the case of children and young persons see s.28 CYPA 1963, *supra*.

s.38(2): Voluntarily objects, this places the onus upon the witness to object. A person objecting is entitled to affirm under s.5(1), *infra*, or he may be sworn in any lawful manner: s.5(3).

6.59   Swearing with uplifted hand
3. If any person to whom an oath is administered desires to swear with uplifted hand, in the form and manner in which an oath is usually administered in Scotland, he shall be permitted so to do, and the oath shall be administered to him in such form and manner without further question.

6.60   Validity of oaths
4. (1) In any case in which an oath may lawfully be and has been administered to any person, if it has been administered in a form and manner other than that prescribed by law, he is bound by it if it has been administered in such form and with such ceremonies as he may have declared to be binding.

(2) Where an oath has been administered and taken, the fact that the person to whom it was administered had, at the time of taking it, no religious belief, shall not for any purpose affect the validity of the oath.

COMMENTARY
For a list of oaths binding upon persons of different religions see *A Handbook of Cautions, Oaths and Recognizances Etc.* by Shannon. For doubts as to the validity of commonly used Hindu, Sikh and Muhammedan oaths see 136 JPN 831.

6.61   Making of solemn affirmations
5. (1) Any person who objects to being sworn shall be permitted to make his solemn affirmation instead of taking an oath.

(2) Subsection (1) above shall apply in relation to a person to whom it is not reasonably practicable without inconvenience or delay to administer an oath in the manner appropriate to his religious belief as it applies in relation to a person objecting to be sworn.

(3) A person who may be permitted under subs (2) above to make his solemn affirmation may also be required to do so.

(4) A solemn affirmation shall be of the same force and effect as an oath.

COMMENTARY
The form of the affirmation is prescribed in s.6, *infra*.

6.62   Form of affirmation
6. (1) Subject to subs (2) below, every affirmation shall be as follows:
'I,   do solemnly, sincerely and truly declare and affirm,
                    and then proceed with the words of the oath prescribed by law omitting any words of imprecation or calling to witness.

(2) 'Every affirmation in writing shall commence:
'I,   of   , do solemnly and sincerely affirm,
                    and the form in lieu of jurat shall be 'Affirmed
at   this   day of 19   , Before
me   '.

MAGISTRATES' COURTS ACT 1980

6.63   Summons to witness and warrant for his arrest
97. (1) Where a justice of the peace for any county, any London commission area or the City of London is satisfied that any person in England and Wales is likely to be able to give material evidence, or produce any document

or thing likely to be material evidence, at an inquiry into an indictable offence by a magistrates' court for that county, that London commission area or the City (as the case may be) or at the summary trial of an information or hearing of a complaint by such a court and that that person will not voluntarily attend as a witness or will not voluntarily produce the document or thing, the justice shall issue a summons directed to that person requiring him to attend before the court at the time and place appointed in the summons to give evidence or to produce the document or thing.

(2) If a justice of the peace is satisfied by evidence on oath of the matters mentioned in subs (1) above, and also that it is probable that a summons under that subsection would not procure the attendance of the person in question, the justice may instead of issuing a summons issue a warrant to arrest that person and bring him before such a court as aforesaid at a time and place specified in the warrant; but a warrant shall not be issued under this subsection where the attendance is required for the hearing of a complaint.

(3) On the failure of any person to attend before a magistrates' court in answer to a summons under this section, if–
(a) the court is satisfied by evidence on oath that he is likely to be able to give material evidence or produce any document or thing likely to be material evidence in the proceedings; and
(b) it is proved on oath, or in such other manner as may be prescribed, that he has been duly served with the summons, and that a reasonable sum has been paid or tendered to him for costs and expenses; and
(c) it appears to the court that there is no just excuse for the failure, the court may issue a warrant to arrest him and to bring him before the court at a time and place specified in the warrant.

(4) If any person attending or brought before a magistrates' court refuses without just excuse to be sworn or give evidence, or to produce any document or thing, the court may commit him to custody until the expiration of such period not exceeding one month as may be specified in the warrant or until he sooner gives evidence or produces the document or thing or impose on him a fine not exceeding £1,000 or both.
[*as amended by Sch.2 Contempt of Court 1981*].

COMMENTARY

Application for process may be made either personally or by the applicant's counsel or solicitor and may in the case of a summons be in writing to the clerk: r.17(1) MC Rules 1981. The clerk himself may issue a witness summons: Justices' Clerks Rules 1970 (SI No 231). 'No process for compelling the production of any document kept by the registrar shall issue from any court except with the leave of that court; and any such process if issued shall bear on it a statement that it is issued with leave of the court': s.710(1) CA 1985.

Process may issue under this section against a juvenile notwithstanding that someone of that age may not be imprisoned for disobedience to the order: *R v Greenwich JJ, ex p. Carter* [1973] Crim LR 444.

Discovery, the machinery of this section is intended merely to get the document into court. It does not allow the party to inspect it before it is produced. Each document has to be considered individually by the magistrate granting the summons: *R v Greenwich Juvenile Court, ex p. Greenwich London Borough Council* (1977)*The Times*, 11 May. This section does not give a general power of discovery in magistrates' courts *R v Sheffield Magistrates' Court ex p. Wrigley (Note)* [1985] RTR 78 (summons to produce tape recording quashed where the purpose was to examine it out of court).

Crown privilege, the issue of process under this section is normally made *ex p.* However an application to produce material subject to Crown privilege should be heard *inter partes* and the justices' decision should be based on the same reasoning as the Crown Court in such cases as *R v Hennessy* (1979) 68 Cr App R 419; *R v Guildhall Justices and Carson Selman, ex p. Director of Public Prosecutions* (1984) 148 JP 386 (tape recordings).

London commission area has the same meaning as in the Justices of the Peace Act 1979: s.150(1) MCA 1980.

6.64   Give material evidence, the issuing justice must be satisfied and thus should inquire into the nature of the potential witness's evidence and consider whether it *is* material: *R v Peterborough Magistrates' Court, ex p. Willis* (1987) 151 JP 785. It is within the inherent jurisdiction of the Divisional Court to set aside a witness summons where there has been an abuse of the process of the court or if it is clear in fact that the witness cannot give relevant evidence. An application could also be made to the magistrates' court for this purpose, *per* Lord Parker CJ in *R v Lewes Justices, ex p. Gaming Board of Great Britain* (1971) 135 JP 442 (Crown privilege invoked); and see *R v Howe JJ, ex p. Donne* (1967) 131 JP 460. There is no right to demand production of documents which are inadmissible as evidence: *R v Cheltenham JJ, ex p. Secretary of State for Trade* (1977) 141 JP 175 (copies of transcripts of evidence which could only be used in cross-examination). In *R v Barking Justices, ex p. Goodspeed* [1985] RTR 70, justices were held rightly to have refused a witness summons to compel the production of a justices' clerk's notes where the evidence (of an inconsistent statement) went merely to the credit of the witness and not to a fact in issue.

Document, a cinematograph film was held to be a document for the purposes of a county court summons *duces tecum: Senior v Holdsworth* [1975] 2 All ER 1009 (ITN film). For the application of this principle to the Lion Intoximeter, see *R v Skegness Magistrates' Court ex p. Cardy* [1985] RTR 49; *R v Coventry Magistrates' Court, ex p. Perks* [1985] RTR 76.

Indictable offence, defined in Sch.1 Interpretation Act 1978.

Issue a summons, see Form 136. A witness summons may not be served by post: see r.99 MC Rules 1981. Note that the summons cannot later be enforced by warrant unless *conduct money* is tendered under s.97(3)(b). No subpoena *ad testificandum* or *duces tecum* shall issue in respect of any proceedings for the purpose of which a witness summons may be issued under this section: s.8 Criminal Procedure (Attendance of Witnesses) Act 165. For an example of a case in which such a subpoena may still be appropriate, see 123 JCL 16.

Issue a warrant, see Forms 137, 138. For the signature, contents and execution of a warrant see rr.95, 96 MC Rules 1981. The warrant may be backed for bail: s.117. Since bail on a warrant issued under this section is *not bail in criminal proceedings* within the meaning of Bail Act 1976, the provisions of that Act do not apply. A warrant remains in force until it is executed or withdrawn: s.125 MCA 1980; notwithstanding the death of the issuing justice: s.124.

A person brought before the court on a '*forthwith*' warrant may not, seemingly, be remanded by the court: [1955] Crim LR 561.

s.97(3): Such other manner as may be prescribed, see r.67 MC Rules 1981.

s.97(4): Any person attending, the power to commit is not confined to persons attending in answer to a witness summons or warrant: *R v Flavell* (1884) 49 JP 406.

Without just excuse, where he had reasonable grounds for believing that he would be criminated by his answers: *Ex p. Reynolds* (1882) 46 JP 533.

Produce any document or thing, the fact that a document is deposited by two persons on condition that it is not to be given up except with permission of both is no ground for refusing to produce it: *R v Daye* (1908) 72 JP 269.

Commit him to custody, means *commit to prison* or, where any enactment authorises or requires committal to some other place of detention instead of to prison, to that other place: s.150(1). In the case of young offenders, this means *detention* under s.9 Criminal Justice Act 1982 see Chapter 8d. Note the restraint in *ibid*, s.1(5) which in turn attracts *ibid*, ss.2(1), (5) and 7. The need for legal representation of the contemnor was stressed by Watkins LJ in *R v K* (1984) 148 JP 410 at 415. Where a witness *refuses to testify* his sentence should be postponed until the end of the trial. This will allow him to change his mind and will assist the court in determining what might have been the weight of his evidence: *R v Phillips* (1983) 78 Cr App R 88.

6.65   Evidence on oath
98. Subject to the provisions of any enactment or rule of law authorising the reception of unsworn evidence, evidence given before a magistrates' court shall be given on oath.

COMMENTARY

Any enactment eg s.38 CYPA 1933 (evidence of child of tender years), s.9 CJA 1967 and MCA 1980.

A magistrates' court means any justice of the peace acting under any enactment or by the virtue of his or their commission or under common law: s.148(1) of the Act.

On oath Includes affirmations and declaration: Sch.1 Interpretations Act 1978.

Onus of proving exceptions, etc   6.66

101. Where the defendant to an information or complaint relies for his defence on any exception, exemption, proviso, excuse or qualification, whether or not it accompanies the description of the offence or matter of complaint in the enactment creating the offence or on which the complaint is founded, the burden of proving the exception, exemption, proviso, excuse or qualification shall be on him; and notwithstanding that the information or complaint contains an allegation negativing the exception, exemption, proviso, excuse or qualification.

COMMENTARY

See under *Negative Averments* at 6.02.

Written statements before examining justices   6.67

102. In committal proceedings a written statement by any person shall, if the conditions mentioned in subs (2) below are satisfied, be admissible as evidence to the like extent as oral evidence to the like effect by that person.

(2) The said conditions are–
(a) the statement purports to be signed by the person who made it;
(b) the statement contains a declaration by that person to the effect that it is true to the best of his knowledge and belief and that he made the statement knowing that, if it were tendered in evidence, he would be liable to prosecution if he wilfully stated in it anything which he knew to be false or did not believe to be true;
(c) before the statement is tendered in evidence, a copy of the statement is given, by or on behalf of the party proposing to tender it, to each of the parties to the proceedings; and
(d) none of the other parties, before the statement is tendered in evidence at the committal proceedings, objects to the statement being so tendered under this section.

(3) The following provisions shall also have effect in relation to any written statement tendered in evidence under this section, that is to say–
(a) if the statement is made by a person under 21 years old, it shall give his age;
(b) if it is made by a person who cannot read it, it shall be read to him before he signs it and shall be accompanied by a declaration by the person who so read the statement to the effect that it was so read; and
(c) if it refers to any other document as an exhibit, the copy given to any other party to the proceedings under subs (2)(c) above shall be accompanied by a copy of that document or by such information as may be necessary in order to enable the party to whom it is given to inspect that document or a copy thereof.

(4) Notwithstanding that a written statement made by any person may be admissible in committal proceedings by virtue of this section, the court before which the proceedings are held may, of its own motion or on the application of any party to the proceedings, require that person to attend before the court and give evidence.

(5) So much of any statement as is admitted in evidence by virtue of this section shall, unless the court commits the accused for trial by virtue of s.6(2) above or the court otherwise directs, be read aloud at the hearing, and where

the court so directs an account shall be given orally of so much of any statement as is not read aloud.

(6) Any document or object referred to as an exhibit and identified in a written statement tendered in evidence under this section shall be treated as if it had been produced as an exhibit and identified in court by the maker of the statement.

(7) Subsection (3) of s.13 of the Criminal Justice Act 1925 (reading of deposition as evidence at the trial) shall apply to any written statement tendered in evidence in committal proceedings under this section as it applies to a deposition taken in such proceedings, but in its application to any such statement that subsection shall have effect as if para (b) thereof were omitted.

(8) In s.2(2) of the Administration of Justice (Miscellaneous Provisions) Act 1933 (procedure for preferring bills of indictment) the reference in proviso (i) to facts disclosed in any deposition taken before a justice in the presence of the accused shall be construed as including a reference to facts disclosed in any such written statement as aforesaid *and s.37(2) of the Criminal Justice Act 1988 (power to join in indictment count for common assault etc) shall be given a corresponding construction.*

(9) Section 28 above shall not apply to any such statement as aforesaid.

(10) A person whose written statement is tendered in evidence in committal proceedings under this section shall be treated for the purposes of s.1 of the Criminal Procedure (Attendance of Witnesses) Act 1965 (witness orders) as a witness who has been examined by the court.

COMMENTARY
See under *Written Statement* at 6.13.

s.102(1): Committal proceedings means proceedings before a magistrates' court acting as examining justices: s.150(1).

A written statement in the prescribed form: r.70(1) MC Rules 1981, see Form 13. For the editing of written statements see the *Practice Note* [1986] 2 All ER 511 noted under *Editing Statements* at 6.14.

Admissible as evidence to the like extent as oral evidence for the method of excluding inadmissible evidence see.

s.102(2): Liable to prosecution this would be under s.16 MCA 1980. HOC 29/1967 expressed the view that since a child under the age of eleven is not liable to prosecution his evidence cannot be put in by way of a statement under this section.
Written statements made in Scotland or Northern Ireland are included in this provision: s.46(1) CJA 1972. Written statements made outside the United Kingdom are also admissible with the omissions of s.102(2)(b), (3A) and (7): s.46(2) CJA 1972.

A copy of the statement is given not 'served' as in statements under the s.9 CJA 1967. No minimum period of time is prescribed, but the other party has a right to object to the statement being put in. A copy must also be given to the clerk.

The other parties to the proceedings It is sufficient if the statement is given to the party's solicitor, *per* Veale J in *R v Bott* (1968) 132 JP 199.

Objects Where the accused objects without having given notice of objection, the court must, if necessary, adjourn to enable the witness to be called: r.70(3) MC Rules 1981.

s.102(3): Under 21 years old for the determination of age, see s.150(4).

s.102(4): it is *suggested* that the statement may first be put in as evidence under this section (not as an exhibit) and the witness then sworn for cross examination.

s.102(5): the effect of this subsection and r.70(6) MC Rules 1981 is that the statement must be *read aloud* or, with the consent of the court, *summarised by the party tendering it*, except where it is put in in proceedings under s.6(2) of the Act, where only the names and addresses of the witnesses should be read out, but even these particulars may be omitted by direction of the court.

s.102(6): the statement must be *read aloud* or, with the consent of the court, *summarised by* *the party tendering it*: r.70(7) MC Rules 1981. The name and address of the witness must, unless the court directs otherwise, be read out: r.70(6).

s.102(8): the words in italics will be added by Sch.12 para 50 CJA 1988 from a date to be appointed.

POLICE AND CRIMINAL EVIDENCE ACT 1984

Evidence from documentary records   **6.68**

68. (1) Subject to s.69 below, a statement in a document shall be admissible in any proceedings as evidence of any fact stated therein of which direct oral evidence would be admissible if–

(a) the document is or forms part of a record compiled by a person acting under a duty from information supplied by a person (whether acting under a duty or not) who had, or may reasonably be supposed to have had, personal knowledge of the matters dealt with in that information; and

(b) any condition relating to the person who supplied the information which is specified in subs (2) below is satisfied.

(2) The conditions mentioned in subs (1)(b) above are–

(a) that the person who supplied the information–

   (i) is dead or by reason of his bodily or mental condition unfit to attend as a witness;

  (ii) is outside the United Kingdom and it is not reasonably practicable to secure his attendance; or

 (iii) cannot reasonably be expected (having regard to the time which has elapsed since he supplied or acquired the information and to all the circumstances) to have any recollection of the matters dealt with in that information;

(b) that all reasonable steps have been taken to identify the person who supplied the information but that he cannot be identified; and

(c) that, the identity of the person who supplied the information being known, all reasonable steps have been taken to find him, but that he cannot be found.

(3) Nothing in this section shall prejudice the admissibility of any evidence that would be admissible apart from this section.

COMMENTARY

NB this section will be repealed by [Sch.15] CJA 1988 from a date to be appointed and the situation will then be subsumed within the more general provisions of [s.23] of the 1988 Act, see Appendix III, *post.*

This provision replaced that contained in the Criminal Evidence Act 1965, as a result of the recommendations of the Royal Commission on Criminal Procedure. It is supplemented by Parts I and III of Sch.3: s.70, *post.*

Copy/Statement have the same meaning as in Part I Civil Evidence Act 1968: s.72 *post.*

Proceedings defined in s.72 *post.*

Record 'Although it is not an exhaustive definition of the word, 'record' in this context means a history of events in some form which is not evanescent. How long the record is likely to be kept is immaterial: it may be something which will not survive the end of the transaction in question; it may be something which is indeed more lasting than bronze, but the degree of permanence does not seem to us to make or mar the fulfilment of the definition of the word 'record'. The record in each individual case will last as long as commercial necessity may demand.' *per* Geoffrey Lane LJ in *R v Jones* (1978) 142 JP 453 (bills of lading and cargo manifests held to be records). Records made outside the jurisdiction are admissible under *ibid*, s.1(1). In *R v Tirado* (1974) 59 Cr App R 80, it was doubted whether a file of correspondence maintained simply as a file of correspondence and added to from time to time as letters came in is or could be a record. 'The language of s.1 seems on its face to contemplate the making or keeping of a record. That means the keeping of a book or file or card index into which information is deliberately put in order that it may be available to others another day. A cash book, a ledger, a stockbook: all these may be records because they contain information deliberately entered in order that the information may be preserved', *per* Lord Widgery CJ, *ibid*.

A person acting under a duty see para 6 of Sch.3, *post*.

6.69 **Evidence from computer records**
　　69. (1) In any proceedings, a statement in a document produced by a computer shall not be admissible as evidence of any fact stated therein unless it is shown–
　　(a) that there are no reasonable grounds for believing that the statement is inaccurate because of improper use of the computer;
　　(b) that at all material times the computer was operating properly, or if not, that any respect in which it was not operating properly or was out of operation was not such as to affect the production of the document or the accuracy of its contents; and
　　(c) that any relevant conditions specified in rules of court under subs (2) below are satisfied.

　　(2) (*Rules of court*).

COMMENTARY
Copy/Statement have the same meaning as in Part I Civil Evidence Act 1968: s.72, *post*.

Proceedings defined in s.72, *post*.

Computer this term is not defined. It is *suggested* that the following definition from the Concise Oxford Dictionary is the most apposite: 'Automatic electronic apparatus for making calculations or controlling operations that are expressible in numerical or logical terms'.
　　Note that computer records *per se* are not affected by the CJA 1988, the provisions of which are expressly stated to be 'subject to section 69 of the Police and Criminal Evidence Act 1984': see [s.22(1)(c)] and [s.23(1)(c)] of the 1988 Act, Appendix III, *post*.

6.70 **Provisions supplementary to sections 68 and 69**
　　70. (1) Part I of Sch.3 to this Act shall have effect for the purpose of supplementing s.68 above.

　　(2) Part II of that schedule shall have effect for the purpose of supplementing s.69 above.

　　(3) Part III of that schedule shall have effect for the purpose of supplementing both sections.

6.71 **Microfilm copies**
　　71. In any proceedings the contents of a document may (whether or not the document is still in existence) be proved by the production of an enlargement of a microfilm copy of that document or of the material part of it, authenticated in such manner as the court may approve.

COMMENTARY
Copy defined in s.72, *post*.

6.72 **Part VII – Supplementary**
　　72. (1) In this Part of this Act–
'copy' and 'statement' have the same meaning as in Part I of the Civil Evidence Act 1968; and
'proceedings' means criminal proceedings, including–
　　(a) proceedings in the United Kingdom or elsewhere before a court-martial constituted under the Army Act 1955 or the Air Force Act 1955;
　　(b) proceedings in the United Kingdom or elsewhere before the Courts-Martial Appeal Court–
　　　　(i) on an appeal from a court-martial so constituted or from a court-martial constituted under the Naval Discipline Act 1957; or

(ii) on a reference under s.34 of the Courts-Martial (Appeals) Act 1968; and

(c) proceedings before a Standing Civilian Court.

(2) Nothing in this Part of this Act shall prejudice any power of a court to exclude evidence (whether by preventing questions from being put or otherwise) at its discretion.

Proof of convictions and acquittals   **6.73**
73. (1) Where in any proceedings the fact that a person has in the United Kingdom been convicted or acquitted of an offence otherwise than by a Service court is admissible in evidence, it may be proved by producing a certificate of conviction or, as the case may be, of acquittal relating to that offence, and proving that the person named in the certificate as having been convicted or acquitted of the offence is the person whose conviction or acquittal of the offence is to be proved.

(2) For the purposes of this section a certificate of conviction or of acquittal–
(a) shall, as regards a conviction or acquittal on indictment, consist of a certificate, signed by the clerk of the court where the conviction or acquittal took place, giving the substance and effect (omitting the formal parts) of the indictment and of the conviction or acquittal; and
(b) shall, as regards a conviction or acquittal on a summary trial, consist of a copy of the conviction or of the dismissal of the information, signed by the clerk of the court where the conviction or acquittal took place or by the clerk of the court, if any, to which a memorandum of the conviction or acquittal was sent;
and a document purporting to be a duly signed certificate of conviction or acquittal under this section shall be taken to be such a certificate unless the contrary is proved.

(3) References in this section to the clerk of a court include references to his deputy and to any other person having the custody of the court record.

(4) The method of proving a conviction or acquittal authorised by this section shall be in addition to and not to the exclusion of any other authorised manner of proving a conviction or acquittal.

COMMENTARY
Proceedings defined in s.82, *post.*

A service court defined in s.82, *post.*

Document has the same meaning as in Part I Civil Evidence Act 1968: s.118(1).

s.73(4): Any other authorised method see under *Previous Convictions* in the introduction.

Conviction as evidence of commission of offence   **6.74**
74. (1) In any proceedings the fact that a person other than the accused has been convicted of an offence by or before any court in the United Kingdom or by a Service court outside the United Kingdom shall be admissible in evidence for the purpose of proving, where to do so is relevant to any issue in those proceedings, that that person committed that offence, whether or not any other evidence of his having committed that offence is given.

(2) In any proceedings in which by virtue of this section a person other than the accused is proved to have been convicted of an offence by or before any court in the United Kingdom or by a Service court outside the United Kingdom, he shall be taken to have committed that offence unless the contrary is proved.

(3) In any proceedings where evidence is admissible of the fact that the accused has committed an offence, in so far as that evidence is relevant to any

matter in issue in the proceedings for a reason other than a tendency to show in the accused a disposition to commit the kind of offence with which he is charged, if the accused is proved to have been convicted of the offence–
  (a) by or before any court in the United Kingdom; or
  (b) by a Service court outside the United Kingdom,
he shall be taken to have committed that offence unless the contrary is proved.

  (4) Nothing in this section shall prejudice–
  (a) the admissibility in evidence of any conviction which would be admissible apart from this section; or
  (b) the operation of any enactment whereby a conviction or a finding of fact in any proceedings is for the purposes of any other proceedings made conclusive evidence of any fact.

COMMENTARY
Proceedings defined in s.82, *post*.

Service court defined in s.82, *post*.

s.74(3). It is *suggested* that this somewhat densely constructed provision is designed to refer to the similar facts rule, ie the rule in s.1(f)(i) Criminal Evidence Act 1898 whereby evidence of similar facts is admissible if it is positively probative of the crime of which the accused is charged, but not if it tends merely to show a tendency in the accused to commit crimes of that character.

6.75   **Provisions supplementary to section 74**
      75. (1) Where evidence that a person has been convicted of an offence is admissible by virtue of s.74 above, then without prejudice to the reception of any other admissible evidence for the purpose of identifying the facts on which the conviction is based–
  (a) the contents of any document which is admissible as evidence of the conviction; and
  (b) the contents of the information, complaint, indictment or charge-sheet on which the person in question was convicted,
shall be admissible in evidence for that purpose.

  (2) Where in any proceedings the contents of any document are admissible in evidence by virtue of subs (1) above, a copy of that document, or of the material part of it, purporting to be certified or otherwise authenticated by or on behalf of the court or authority having custody of that document shall be admissible in evidence and shall be taken to be a true copy of that document or part unless the contrary is shown.

  (3) Nothing in any of the following–
  (a) section 13 of the Powers of Criminal Courts Act 1973 (under which a conviction leading to probation or discharge is to be disregarded except as mentioned in that section);
  (b) section 392 of the Criminal Procedure (Scotland) Act 1975 (which makes similar provision in respect of convictions on indictment in Scotland); and
  (c) section 8 of the Probation Act (Northern Ireland) 1950 (which corresponds to s.13 of the Powers of Criminal Courts Act 1973) or any legislation which is in force in Northern Ireland for the time being and corresponds to that section,
shall affect the operation of s.74 above; and for the purposes of that section any order made by a court of summary jurisdiction in Scotland under s.182 and s.183 of the said Act of 1975 shall be treated as a conviction.

  (4) Nothing in s.74 above shall be construed as rendering admissible in any proceedings evidence of any conviction other than a subsisting one.

COMMENTARY
Document has the same meaning as in Part I Civil Evidence Act 1968: s.118(1).

Proceedings defined in s.82, *post.*

Confessions   **6.76**

76. (1) In any proceedings a confession made by an accused person may be given in evidence against him in so far as it is relevant to any matter in issue in the proceedings and is not excluded by the court in pursuance of this section.

(2) If, in any proceedings where the prosecution proposes to give in evidence a confession made by an accused person, it is represented to the court that the confession was or may have been obtained–
    (a) by oppression of the person who made it; or
    (b) in consequence of anything said or done which was likely, in the circumstances existing at the time, to render unreliable any confession which might be made by him in consequence thereof,
the court shall not allow the confession to be given in evidence against him except in so far as the prosecution proves to the court beyond reasonable doubt that the confession (notwithstanding that it may be true) was not obtained as aforesaid.

(3) In any proceedings where the prosecution proposes to give in evidence a confession made by an accused person, the court may of its own motion require the prosecution, as a condition of allowing it to do so, to prove that the confession was not obtained as mentioned in subs (2) above.

(4) The fact that a confessoin is wholly or partly excluded in pursuance of this section shall not affect the admissibility in evidence–
    (a) of any facts discovered as a result of the confession; or
    (b) where the confession is relevant as showing that the accused speaks, writes or expresses himself in a particular way, of so much of the confession as is necessary to show that he does so.

(5) Evidence that a fact to which this subsection applies was discovered as a result of a statement made by an accused person shall not be admissible unless evidence of how it was discovered is given by him or on his behalf.

(6) Subsection (5) above applies–
    (a) to any fact discovered as a result of a confession which is wholly excluded in pursuance of this section; and
    (b) to any fact discovered as a result of a confession which is partly so excluded, if the fact is discovered as a result of the excluded part of the confession.

(7) Nothing in Part VIII of this Act shall prejudice the admissibility of a confession made by an accused person.

(8) In this section 'oppression' includes torture, inhuman or degrading treatment, and the use or threat of violence (whether or not amounting to torture).

COMMENTARY
Proceedings, defined in s.82, *post.*

Confession, partially defined in s.82(1), *post.*

Oppression, partially defined in s.76(8); must be given its '. . . ordinary dictionary meaning . . . [ie] . . . the exercise of authority or power in a burdensome, harsh or wrongful manner; unjust or cruel treatment of subjects, inferiors, etc; the imposition of unreasonable or unjust burdens . . . there is not a word in our language which expresses more detestable wickedness than oppression . . . it is hard to envisage any circumstances in which oppression would not entail some impropriety on the part of the interrogator', per Lord Lane CJ in *R v Fulling* [1987] 2 WLR 923.

s.76(2): Represented in court, it would seem that representations may be made by the defendant or his counsel or solicitor without evidence being called, although evidence may also amount to a representation. Justices must hold a '*Trial within a trial*' to determine the admissibility of a confession in summary proceedings: see *R v Liverpool Juvenile Court, ex p. R* [1987] 2 All ER 668 and the extended commentary under that heading at 6.28.

NB the fine distinctions which have been drawn between determining admissibility under ss.76 and 78, and between summary trial and committal proceedings.

6.77   **Confessions by mentally handicapped person**
    77. (1) Without prejudice to the general duty of the court at a trial on indictment to direct the jury on any matter on which it appears to the court appropriate to do so, where at such a trial–
       (a) the case against the accused depends wholly or substantially on a confession by him; and
       (b) the court is satisfied–
          (i) that he is mentally handicapped; and
          (ii) that the confession was not made in the presence of an independent person,
    the court shall warn the jury that there is special need for caution before convicting the accused in reliance on the confession, and shall explain that the need arises because of the circumstances mentioned in paras (a) and (b) above.

    (2) In any case where at the summary trial of a person for an offence it appears to the court that a warning under subs (1) above would be required if the trial were on indictment, the court shall treat the case as one in which there is a special need for caution before convicting the accused on his confession.

    (3) In this section–
'independent person' does not include a police officer or a person employed for, or engaged on, police purposes;
'mentally handicapped', in relation to a person, means that he is in a state of arrested or incomplete development of mind which includes significant impairment of intelligence and social functioning; and
'police purposes' has the meaning assigned to it by s.64 of the Police Act 1964.

COMMENTARY
Confession, partially defined in s.82, *post.*

Mentally handicapped, defined in s.77(3).

An independent person, partially defined in s.77(3).

The Police Act 1964, s.64(1) provides that:

'In this Act the expression "police purposes", in relation to a police area, includes the purposes of special constables appointed for that area, of police cadets undergoing training with a view to becoming members of the police force maintained for that area and of civilians employed for the purposes of that force or of any such special constables or cadets'.

6.78   **Exclusion of unfair evidence**
    78. (1) In any proceedings the court may refuse to allow evidence on which the prosecution proposes to rely to be given if it appears to the court that, having regard to all the circumstances, including the circumstances in which the evidence was obtained, the admission of the evidence would have such an adverse effect on the fairnes of the proceedings that the court ought not to admit it.

    (2) Nothing in this section shall prejudice any rule of law requiring a court to exclude evidence.

COMMENTARY
The provision does not derive from the report of the Philips Commission but was added to the Bill during its passage through Parliament. Without judicial interpretation it is difficult to be sure of the scope of subs (1) or its interrelationship with the exclusionary rules of the common law preserved by subs (2). It should be noted however that the 'unfairness' at which the provision is aimed is unfairness in the proceedings and not unfairness to the accused during the investigation, except of course to the extent that the circumstances in which the evidence was obtained may have made the proceedings unfair. Justices have a *discretion* to exclude evidence under this section, although presumably this will be *compulsive* if prejudice really is likely to occur. For the *discretion* to hold a *trial within a trial* where it is sought

o exclude confession evidence under s.78 (as opposed to s.76(2) – where there is a duty to old such a proceeding), see *Carlisle v DPP* (1987) 152 JPN 227 and under that heading at .28.

NB the fine distinctions which have been drawn between determining admissibility under s.76 and 78, and between summary trial and committal proceedings.

Proceedings defined in s.82, *post.*

s.78(2): notably, the rule that the court may exclude evidence the probative value of which is outweighed by its prejudicial effect, see *R v Sang* [1979] 2 All ER 1222, HL.

Competence and compellability of accused's spouse   6.79

80. (1) In any proceedings the wife or husband of the accused shall be competent to give evidence–
   (a) subject to subs (4) below, for the prosecution; and
   (b) on behalf of the accused or any person jointly charged with the accused.

(2) In any proceedings the wife or husband of the accused shall, subject to subs (4) below, be compellable to give evidence on behalf of the accused.

(3) In any proceedings the wife or husband of the accused shall, subject to subs (4) below, be compellable to give evidence for the prosecution or on behalf of any person jointly charged with the accused if and only if–
   (a) the offence charged involves an assault on, or injury or a threat of injury to, the wife or husband of the accused or a person who was at the material time under the age of sixteen; or
   (b) the offence charged is a sexual offence alleged to have been committed in respect of a person who was at the material time under that age; or
   (c) the offence charged consists of attempting or conspiring to commit, or of aiding, abetting, counselling, procuring or inciting the commission of, an offence falling within paras (a) or (b) above.

(4) Where a husband and wife are jointly charged with an offence neither spouse shall at the trial be competent or compellable by virtue of subs (1)(a), (2) or (3) above to give evidence in respect of that offence unless that spouse is not, or is no longer, liable to be convicted of that offence at the trial as a result of pleading guilty or for any other reason.

(5) In any proceedings a person who has been but is no longer married to the accused shall be competent and compellable to give evidence as if that person and the accused had never been married.

(6) Where in any proceedings the age of any person at any time is material for the purposes of subs (3) above, his age at the material time shall for the purposes of that provision be deemed to be or to have been that which appears to the court to be or to have been his age at that time.

(7) In subs (3)(b) above 'sexual offence' means an offence under the Sexual Offences Act 1956, the Indecency with Children Act 1960, the Sexual Offences Act 1967, s.54 of the Criminal Law Act 1977 or the Protection of Children Act 1978.

(8) The failure of the wife or husband of the accused to give evidence shall not be made the subject of any comment by the prosecution.

(9) (*Amendment*).

COMMENTARY
Proceedings defined in s.82, *post.*
A sexual offence see s.80(7).

Part VIII – interpretation   6.80

82. (1) In this Part of this Act–
'confession', includes any statement wholly or partly adverse to the person

who made it, whether made to a person in authority or not and whether made in words or otherwise;
'court-martial' means a court-martial constituted under the Army Act 1955 the Air Force Act 1955 or the Naval Discipline Act 1957 or a disciplinary cour constituted under s.50 of the said Act of 1957;
'proceedings' means criminal proceedings, including–
  (a) proceedings in the United Kingdom or elsewhere before a court-martia constituted under the Army Act 1955 or the Air Force Act 1955;
  (b) proceedings in the United Kingdom or elsewhere before the Courts Martial Appeal Court–
    (i) on an appeal from a court-martial so constituted or from a court martial constituted under the Naval Discipline Act 1957; or
    (ii) on a reference under s.34 of the Courts-Martial (Appeals) Ac 1968; and
  (c) proceedings before a Standing Civilian Court; and
'Service court' means a court-martial or a Standing Civilian Court.

(2) In this Part of this Act references to conviction before a Service Cour are references–
  (a) as regards a court-martial constituted under the Army Act 1955 or the Air Force Act 1955, to a finding of guilty which is, or falls to be treatec as, a finding of the court duly confirmed;
  (b) as regards–
    (i) a court-matrial; or
    (ii) a disciplinary court,
    constituted under the Naval Discipline Act 1957, to a finding of guilty which is, or falls to be treated as, the finding of the court;
and 'convicted' shall be construed accordingly.

(3) Nothing in this Part of this Act shall prejudice any power of a court tc exclude evidence (whether by preventing questions from being put or other wise) at its discretion.

6.81   # SCHEDULE 3

Provisions Supplementary to Sections 68 and 69

PART I: PROVISIONS SUPPLEMENTARY TO SECTION 68
1. Section 68(1) above applies whether the information contained in the document was supplied directly or indirectly but, if it was supplied indirectly only if each person through whom it was supplied was acting under a duty; anc applies also where the person compiling the record is himself the person by whom the information is supplied.

2. Where–
  (a) a document setting out the evidence which a person could be expected to give as a witness has been prepared for the purpose of any pending o contemplated proceedings; and
  (b) it falls within subs (1) of s.68 above,
a statement contained in it shall not be given in evidence by virtue of tha section without the leave of the court, and the court shall not give leave unless it is of the opinion that the statement ought to be admitted in the interests of justice, having regard–
    (i) to the circumstances in which leave is sought and in particular to the contents of the statement; and
    (ii) to any likelihood that the accused will be prejudiced by its admission in the absence of the person who supplied the information on which it is based.

3. Where in any proceedings a statement based on information supplied by any person is given in evidence by virtue of s.68 above–

(a) any evidence which, if that person had been called as a witness, would have been admissible as relevant to his credibility as a witness shall be admissible for that purpose in those proceedings;
(b) evidence may, with the leave of the court, be given of any matter which, if that person had been called as a witness, could have been put to him in cross-examination as relevant to his credibility as a witness but of which evidence could not have been adduced by the cross-examining party; and
(c) evidence tending to prove that that person, whether before or after supplying the information, made a statement (whether oral or not) which is inconsistent with it shall be admissible for the purpose of showing that he has contradicted himself.

4. A statement which is admissible by virtue of s.68 above shall not be capable of corroborating evidence given by the person who supplied the information on which the statement is based.

5. In deciding for the purposes of s.68(2)(a)(i) above whether a person is unfit to attend as a witness the court may act on a certificate purporting to be signed by a registered medical practitioner.

6. Any reference in s.68 above or this Part of this Schedule to a person acting under a duty includes a reference to a person acting in the course of any trade, business, profession or other occupation in which he is engaged or employed or for the purposes of any paid or unpaid office held by him.

7. In estimating the weight, if any, to be attached to a statement admissible in evidence by virtue of s.68 above regard shall be had to all the circumstances from which any inference can reasonably be drawn as to the accuracy or otherwise of the statement and, in particular–
(a) to the question whether or not the person who supplied the information from which the record containing the statement was compiled did so contemporaneously with the occurrence or existence of the facts dealt with in that information; and
(b) to the question whether or not that person, or any other person concerned was compiling or keeping the record containing the statement, had any incentive to conceal or misrepresent the facts.

PART II: PROVISIONS SUPPLEMENTARY TO SECTION 69
8. In any proceedings where it is desired to give a statement in evidence in accordance with s.69 above, a certificate–
(a) identifying the document containing the statement and describing the manner in which it was produced;
(b) giving such particulars of any device involved in the production of that document as may be appropriate for the purpose of showing that the document was produced by a computer;
(c) dealing with any of the matters mentioned in subs (1) of s.69 above; and
(d) purporting to be signed by a person occupying a responsible position in relation to the operation of the computer,
shall be evidence of anything stated in it, and for the purposes of this paragraph it shall be sufficient for a matter to be stated to the best of the knowledge and belief of the person stating it.

9. Notwithstanding para 8 above, a court may require oral evidence to be given of anything of which evidence could be given by a certificate under that paragraph.

10. Any person who in a certificate tendered under para 8 above in a magistrates' court, the Crown Court or the Court of Appeal makes a statement which he knows to be false or does not believe to be true shall be guilty of an offence and liable–
(a) on conviction on indictment to imprisonment for a term not exceeding two years or to a fine or to both;

(b) on summary conviction to imprisonment for a term not exceeding six months or to a fine not exceeding the statutory maximum (as defined in s.74 of the Criminal Justice Act 1982) or to both.

11. In estimating the weight, if any, to be attached to a statement regard shall be had to all the circumstances from which any inference can reasonably be drawn as to the accuracy or otherwise of the statement and, in particular–
(a) to the question whether or not the information which the information contained in the statement reproduces or is derived from was supplied to the relevant computer, or recorded for the purpose of being supplied to it, contemporaneously with the occurrence or existence of the facts dealt with in that information; and
(b) to the question whether or not any person concerned with the supply of information to that computer, or with the operation of that computer or any equipment by means of which the document containing the statement was produced by it, had any incentive to conceal or misrepresent the facts.

12. For the purposes of para 11 above information shall be taken to be supplied to a computer whether it is supplied directly or (with or without human intervention) by means of any appropriate equipment.

PART III: PROVISIONS SUPPLEMENTARY TO SECTIONS 68 AND 69
13. Where in any proceedings a statement contained in a document is admissible in evidence by virtue of s.68 above or in accordance with s.69 above it may be proved–
(a) by the production of that document; or
(b) (whether or not that document is still in existence) by the production of a copy of that document, or of the material part of it,
authenticated in such manner as the court may approve.

14. for the purpose of deciding whether or not a statement is so admissible the court may draw any reasonable inference–
(a) from the circumstances in which the statement was made or otherwise came into being; or
(b) from any other circumstances, including the form and contents of the document in which the statement is contained.

15. Provision may be made by rules of court for supplementing the provisions of sections 68 or 69 above or this schedule.

COMMENTARY
Paragraphs 1 to 7 and 13 of Sch.3 will be repealed when [Sch.15] CJA 1988 comes into force.

PROSECUTION OF OFFENCES ACT 1985

6.82   **Other awards**
19. (1), (2) . . .

(3) The Lord Chancellor may by regulations make provision for the payment out of central funds, in such circumstances and in relation to such criminal proceedings as may be specified, of such sums as appear to the court to be reasonably necessary–
(a) to compensate any witness in the proceedings for the expense, trouble or loss of time properly incurred in or incidental to his attendance;
(b) to cover the proper expenses of an interpreter who is required because of the accused's lack of English;
(c) to compensate a duly qualified medical practitioner who–
(i) makes a report otherwise than in writing for the purpose of s.30 of the Magistrates' Courts Act 1980 (remand for medical examination); or

(ii) makes a written report to a court in pursuance of a request to which s.32(2) of the Criminal Justice Act 1967 (report by medical practitioner on medical condition of offender) applies;

for the expenses properly incurred in or incidental to his reporting to the court.

MAGISTRATES' COURTS RULES 1981 6.83

(SI 1981 No 552 as amended by SI 1983 No 523 and SI 1984 No 1552)

Written statements in committal proceedings or summary trial

70. (1) Written statements to be tendered in evidence under s.12 of the Act of 1980 or s.9 of the Criminal Justice Act 1967 shall be in the prescribed form.

(2) When a copy of such a statement is given to or served on any party to the proceedings a copy of the statement and of any exhibit which accompanied it shall be given to the clerk of the magistrates' court as soon as practicable thereafter, and where a copy of any such statement is given or served by or on behalf of the prosecutor, the accused shall be given notice by or on behalf of the prosecutor of his right to object to the statement being tendered in evidence.

(3) Where before a magistrates' court enquiring into an offence as examining justices the accused objects to a written statement being tendered in evidence and he has been given a copy of the statement but has not given notice of his intention to object to the statement being tendered in evidence, the court shall if necessary, adjourn to enable the witness to be called.

(4) Where a written statement to be tendered in evidence under the said s.12 or 9 refers to any document or object as an exhibit, that document or object shall wherever possible be identified by means of a label or other mark of identification signed by the maker of the statement, and before a magistrates' court treats any document or object referred to as an exhibit in such a written statement as an exhibit produced and identified in court by the maker of the statement, the court shall be satisfied that the document or object is sufficiently described in the statement for it to be identified.

(5) If it appears to a magistrates' court that any part of a written statement is inadmissible there shall be written against that part–

(a) in the case of a written statement tendered in evidence under the said s.102 the words 'Treated as inadmissible' together with the signature and name of the examining justice or, where there is more than one examining justice, the signature and name of one of the examining justices by whom the statement is so treated;

(b) in the case of a written statement tendered in evidence under the said s.9 the words 'Ruled inadmissible, together with the signature and name of the justice or, where there is more than one justice, the signature and name of one of the justices who ruled the statement to be inadmissible.

(6) Where a written statement is tendered in evidence under the said s.12 or 9 before a magistrates' court the name and address of the maker of the statement shall be read aloud unless the court otherwise directs.

(7) Where under subs (5) of the said s.12 or subs (6) of the said s.9 in any proceedings before a magistrates' court any part of a written statement has to be read aloud, or an account has to be given orally of so much of any written statement as is not read aloud, the statements shall be read or the account given by or on behalf of the party which has tendered the statement in evidence.

(8) Written statements tendered in evidence under the said s.12 before a magistrates' court acting as examining justices shall be authenticated by a certificate signed by one of the examining justices.

(9) A written statement tendered in evidence under the said ss.12 or 9 before a magistrates' court and not sent to the Crown Court under r.11, 17 or 18, shall be preserved for a period of three years by the clerk of the magistrates' court.

Proof of proceedings
78. The register of a magistrates' court, or any document purporting to be an extract from the register and to be certified by the clerk as a true extract, shall be admissible in any legal proceedings as evidence of the proceedings of the court entered in the register.

COMMENTARY
Para 1: The prescribed form See Form 13.

Para 5: *cf* also *Practice Note* on the editing of written statements [1986] 2 All ER 511, summarised at 6.14 *ante*. under the title *Editing statements*.

Para (8): Written statements Failure of one of the examining justices to sign the certificate does not invalidate a committal: *R v Carey* [1983] Crim LR 111.

Proof by formal admission
71. Where under s.10 of the Criminal Justice Act 1967 a fact is admitted orally in court by or on behalf of the prosecutor or defendant for the purposes of the summary trial of an offence or proceedings before a magistrates' court acting as examining justices the court shall cause the admission to be written down and signed by or on behalf of the party making the admission.

Proof of previous convictions
72. Service on any person of a notice of intention to cite previous convictions under s.14 of the Act of 1980 or s.182(2A)(c) of the Road Traffic Act 1972 may be effected by delivering it to him or by sending it by post in a registered letter or by recorded delivery service addressed to him at his last known or usual place of abode.

COMMENTARY
Extract see Form 154.

Application for summons to witness or warrant for his arrest
107. (1) An application for the issue of a summons or warrant under s.97 of the Act of 1980 may be made by the applicant in person or by his counsel or solicitor.

(2) An application for an issue of such a summons may be made by delivering or sending the application in writing to the clerk of the magistrates' court.

6.84   **IDENTIFICATION**

Extended extract from *R v Turnbull* (1976) 63 Cr App R 132, in which Lord Widgery CJ laid down the following guidelines:

Evidence of visual identification in criminal cases '. . . can bring about miscarriages of justice and has done so in a few cases in recent years. The number of such cases, although small compared with the number in which evidence of visual identification is known to be satisfactory, necessitates steps being taken by the courts, including this court, to reduce that number as far as is possible. In our judgment the danger of miscarriage of justice occurring can be much reduced if trial judges sum up to juries in the way indicated in this judgment.

'First, whenever the case against an accused depends wholly or substantially on the correctness of one or more identifications of the accused which the defence alleges to be mistaken, the judge should warn the jury of the special need for caution before convicting the accused in reliance on the correctness of the identification or identifications. In addition, he should instruct them as to the reason for the need for such a warning and should make some reference to the possibility that a mistaken witness can be a convincing one and that a number of such witnesses can all be mistaken. Provided this is done in clear terms the judge need not use any particular form of words. Secondly, the judge should direct the jury to examine closely the circumstances in which the identification by each witness came to be made. How long did the witness have the accused under observation? At what distance? In what light? Was the observation impeded in any way, as for example by passing traffic or a press of people? Had the witness ever seen the accused before? How often? If only occasionally, had he any special reason for remembering the accused? How long elapsed between the original observation and the subsequent identification to the police? Was there any material discrepancy between the description of the accused given to the police by the witness when first seen by them and his actual appearance? If in any case, whether it is being dealt with summarily or on indictment, the prosecution have reason to believe that there is such a material discrepancy they should supply the accused or his legal advisors with particulars of the description the police were first given. In all cases if the accused asks to be given particulars of such descriptions, the prosecution should supply them. Finally, he should remind the jury of any specific weakness which had appeared in the identification evidence. Recognition may be more reliable than identification of a stranger, but, even when the witness is purporting to recognise someone whom he knows, the jury should be reminded that mistakes in recognition of close relatives and friends are sometimes made.

'All these matters go to the quality of the identification evidence. If the quality is good and remains good at the close of the accused's case, the danger of a mistaken identification is lessened; but the poorer the quality, the greater the danger. In our judgment, when the quality is good, as for example when the identification is made after a long period of observation, or in satisfactory conditions by a relative, a neighbour, a close friend, a workmate and the like, the jury can safely be left to assess the value of the identifying evidence even though there is no other evidence to support it; provided always, however, that an adequate warning has been given about the special need for caution. Were the courts to adjudge otherwise, affronts to justice would frequently occur. A few examples, taken over the whole spectrum of criminal activity, will illustrate what the effects on the maintenance of law and order would be if any law were enacted that no person could be convicted on evidence of visual identification alone.

'Here are the examples. A had been kidnapped and held to ransom over many days. His captor stayed with him all the time. At last he was released but he did not know the identity of his kidnapper nor where he had been kept. Months later the police arrested X for robbery and as a result of what they had been told by an informer they suspected him of the kidnapping. They had no other evidence. They arranged for A to attend an identity parade. He picked out X without hesitation. At X's trial, is the trial judge to rule at the end of the prosecution's case that X must be acquitted?

'This is another example. Over a period of a week two police officers, B and C, kept observations in turn on a house which was suspected of being a distribution centre for drugs. A suspected supplier, Y, visited it from time to time. On the last day of the observation B saw Y enter the house. He at once signalled to other waiting police officers, who had a search warrant to enter. They did so; but by the time they got in, Y had escaped by a back window. Six months later C saw Y in the street and arrested him. Y at once alleged that C had mistaken him for someone else. At an identity parade he was picked out by B. Would it really be right and in the interests of justice for a judge to direct Y's acquittal at the end of the prosecution's case?

'A rule such as the one under consideration would gravely impeded the police in their work and would make the conviction of street offenders such as pickpockets, car thieves and the disorderly very difficult. But it would not only be the police who might be aggrieved by such a rule. Take the case of a factory worker, D, who during the course of his work went to the locker room to get something from his jacket which he had forgotten. As he went in he saw workmate, Z, whom he had known for years and who worked near him in the same shop, standing by D's open locker with his hand inside. He hailed the thief by name. Z turned round and faced D; he dropped D's wallet on the floor and ran out of the locker room by another door. D reported what he had seen to the chargehand. When the chargehand went to find Z, he saw him walking towards his machine. Z alleged that D had been mistaken. A directed acquittal might well be greatly resented not only by D but by many others in the same shop.

'When, in the judgment of the trial judge, the quality of the identifying evidence is poor, as for example when it depends solely on a fleeting glance or on a longer observation made in difficult conditions, the situation is very different. The judge should then withdraw the case from the jury and direct an acquittal unless there is other evidence which goes to support the correctness of the identification. This may be corroboration in the sense lawyers use the word; but it need not be so if its effect is to make the jury sure that there had been no mistaken identification. For example, X sees the accused snatch a woman's handbag; he gets only a fleeting glance of the thief's face as he runs off but he does see him entering a nearby house. Later he picks out the accused in an identity parade. If there was no more evidence than this, the poor quality of the identification would require the judge to withdraw the case from the jury; but this would not be so if there was evidence that the house into which the accused was alleged by X to have run was his father's. Another example of supporting evidence not amounting to corroboration in a technical sense is to be found in *R v Long* (1973) 57 Cr App R 871. The accused, who was charged with robbery, had been identified by three witnesses in different places on different occasions, but each had only a momentary opportunity for observation. Immediately after the robbery the accused had left his home and could not be found by the police. When later he was seen by them he claimed to know who had done the robbery and offered to help to find the robbers. At his trial he put forward an alibi which the jury rejected. It was an odd coincidence that the witnesses should have identified a man who had behaved in this way. In our judgment odd coincidence can, if unexplained, be supporting evidence.

'The trial judge should identify to the jury the evidence which he adjudges is capable of supporting the evidence of identification. If there is any evidence or circumstance which the jury might think was supporting when it did not have this quality, the judge should say so. A jury, for example, might think that support for identification evidence could be found in the fact that the accused had not given evidence before them. An accused's absence from the witness box cannot provide evidence of anything and the judge should tell the jury so. But he would be entitled to tell them that when assessing the quality of the identification evidence they could take into consideration the fact that it was uncontradicted by any evidence coming from the accused himself.

'Care should be taken by the judge when directing the jury about the support for an identification which may be derived from the fact that they have rejected an alibi. False alibis may be put forward for many reasons: an accused, for example, who has only his own truthful evidence to reply on may stupidly fabricate an alibi and get lying witnesses to support it out of fear that his own evidence will not be enough. Further, alibi witnesses can make genuine mistakes about dates and occasions like any other witnesses can. It is only when the jury are satisfied that the sole reason for the fabrication was to deceive them and there is no other explanation for its being put forward, that fabrication can provide any support for identification evidence. The jury should be reminded that proving the accused has told lies about where he was at the material time does not by itself prove that he was where the identifying witness says he was.

'In setting out these guidelines for trial judges, which involve only changes of practice, not law, we have tried to follow the recommendations set out in the report which Lord Devlin's committee made to the Secretary of State for the Home Department in April 1976. We have not followed that report in using the phrase 'exceptional circumstances' to describe situations in which the risk of mistaken identification is reduced. In our judgment, the use of such a phrase is likely to result in the build-up of case law as to what circumstances can properly be described as exceptional and what cannot. Case law of this kind is likely to be a fetter on the administration of justice when so much depends on the quality of the evidence in each case. Quality is what matters in the end. In many cases the exceptional circumstances to which the report refers will provide evidence of good quality, but they may not; the converse is also true.

'A failure to follow these guidelines is likely to result in a conviction being quashed and will do so if in the judgment of this court on all the evidence the verdict is either unsatisfactory or unsafe.'

This advice should be followed with great care by justices: *McShane v Northumbria Chief Constable* (1981) 72 Cr App R 28; but it does not make any new principles of law. (Court could convict when constable saw back of man's head in good light for a quarter of an hour). The judgment in *Turnbull* should not be applied inflexibly: *R v Keane* (1977) 65 Cr App R 247. *Turnbull* is intended to deal with 'the ghastly risk run in fleeting encounters', not the suggestion that a constable may be confused as to whether the man who knocked him down was the man standing beside him when he got up: *R v Oakwell* (1978) 142 JP 259.

Lord Lane CJ gave this direction in *R v Weeder* (1980) 71 Cr App R 288:

'When the quality of the identifying evidence is poor the judge should withdraw the case from the jury and direct an acquittal unless there is other evidence which goes to support the correctness of the identification. The identification evidence can be poor, even though it is given by a number of witnesses. They may all have had only the opportunity of a fleeting glance or a longer observation made in difficult conditions, eg the occupants of a bus who observed the incident at night as they drove past. Where the quality of the identification evidence is such that the jury can be safely left to assess its value, even though there is no other evidence to support it, then the trial judge is fully entitled, if so minded, to direct the jury that an identification by one witness can constitute support for the identification by another *provided* that he warns them in clear terms that even a number of honest witnesses can all be mistaken.'

The importance of this direction in all identification cases was stressed in: *R v Breslin* (1985) 80 Cr App R 236 CA.

CHAPTER 7

Contempt of Court and other Interferences

Contempt of Court and other Interferences

7.00   **INTRODUCTION**

The very nature of contempt and other interferences with court proceed
ings means that it is impossible to anticipate every possible situation an
every variety of conduct which might adversely affect proceedings. Th
law provides a range of powers which courts can use to deal with suc
matters and of which those contained in the Contempt of Court Act 198
are by far the most significant – particularly since the Act enables th
court to penalise, *inter alia*, a person who '*misbehaves in court*', condu
which could hardly be more widely defined. It should be noted, howeve
that the common law offence of contempt can still be committed i
relation to a magistrates' court just as it can in relation to the highe
courts. This position is expressly preserved by s.6(c) of the 1981 Ac
which provides that nothing in the Act '. . . restricts liability for contem
of court in respect of conduct intended to impede or prejudice th

dministration of justice'. In February 1988, eg, The *Sun* newspaper was
ined a substantial sum in respect of the common law offence committed
ia several publications, each of which fell outside the scope of the
tatutory contempt provisions affecting this situation: *Attorney-General v
News Group Newspapers Ltd* (1988) *The Times*, 20 February. In the
Divisional Court, Watkins LJ remarked that:
. . . The common law was not a worn-out jurisprudence rendered incap-
ble of further development by the ever increasing incursion of parliamentary legislation. It was a lively body of law capable of adaptation and
expansion to meet fresh needs calling for the exertion and discipline of
he law'.

Other general powers which may be called upon by magistrates in those
unusual situations which fall outside the scope of the statutory contempt
provisions are the power to bind-over persons, and the inherent jurisdic-
ion of the court to control its own proceedings. Under the latter, eg
persons may be required to leave the courtroom or the number of
pectators allowed to enter 'open court' can be controlled where either
ourse is necessary in the interests of the administration of justice. In
elation to certain kinds of conduct – where this amounts to a substantive
riminal offence in its own right – the general criminal law applies, as eg
where an assault occurs in court, or a person attempts to escape from
awful custody. Over and above such general powers both the Contempt
f Court Act 1981 and other specific legislation create prohibitions and
ffences concerning the publication of reports or details of proceedings.
These provisions are directed towards securing a fair trial, and/or the
protection of certain categories of individuals involved in criminal pro-
eedings and are set out under *Restrictions on Publication*, 7.07 *et seq*.

CONTEMPT

i) Statutory provisions 7.01

Under s.12 Contempt of Court Act 1981 it is an offence for anyone:
  wilfully to insult a justice or justices, any witness before or officer of the
  court or any solicitor or counsel having business in the court during his
  or her sitting or attendance or in going to or returning from court:
  s.12(1)(a); or–
  wilfully to interrupt the proceedings of the court or otherwise mis-
  behave in court; s.12(1)(b).
The court may *if it thinks fit*:
  (a) order any officer of the court or any constable to take the offender
      into custody and detain him until the rising of the court; and
  (b) commit him for a specified period not exceeding one month and/or
      impose a fine not exceeding £1,000 [s.12(2)].
The order may be revoked at any time, eg in the event of an apology to the
ourt which has not been forthcoming earlier, and the court may order
he discharge of an offender who is in custody: s.12(4).

There is always a danger that action taken by the court over contempt
may come into conflict with the normal principles of *Natural Justice*,
particularly, where misbehaviour or a contempt is committed in the face
f the court, the rule that no man should be a judge in his own cause: see
.05. It is suggested that wherever possible there should at least be a
period for 'cooling off', possibly by way of an adjournment, and that the
ontemnor should always be given an opportunity to apologise. There
may be circumstances in which the case should be put back to be dealt

with before a fresh bench, although there remains an insoluble dilemma in terms of natural justice if the original justices or clerk then have to give evidence before their colleagues. Recognising the need to preserve so far as possible the rights of the contemnor from a 'Draconian' law, the Court of Appeal stated in *R v Moran* (1985) 81 Cr App R 51 the following principles should be borne in mind:

1. *The decision to imprison* a man for contempt *should never be taken at once*, but there should always be time for reflection as to what is the best course to take.

2. The judge should consider whether that *time for reflection* should extend overnight.

3. If it is possible for the contemnor to have legal advice, he should be given an opportunity of having it. However, the court did not accept that justice required a contemnor to have a *right* to legal advice. Situations arise in court sometimes where a judge has to act quickly and to pass such a sentence as he thinks proper at once. Giving an offender the opportunity to apologise is one of the most important aspects of the summary procedure which in many ways is Draconian.

As to the desirability of an opportunity for legal representation as mentioned in *Moran, supra*, it has also been held that the restriction on imposing imprisonment on persons who are not legally represented as contained in s.21(1) PCCA 1973 is inapplicable: *R v Newbury Justices, ex p. Du Pont* (1984) 78 Cr App R 225.

The same can presumably be said of the similar restriction in relation to *young offenders* contained in s.3 Criminal Justice Act 1982. Young offenders may – provided that they have attained the age of 17 – be ordered *to be detained* for contempt in accordance with the provisions of s.9 of the 1982 Act. Whatever the legal position, justices are encouraged to consider asking a lawyer to speak to alleged contemnors who have been taken into custody: *Ex p. Du Pont, supra*. Legal aid may be granted in accordance with s.13 CJA 1982 once a commencement order is made in respect of that section.

Both the offence of contempt and the procedure in relation to it would appear to be *sui generis*, and without there being the benefit of an information or in most instances any process whatsoever. It is thus essential that the court keeps a proper record of the facts and of the basis of any order by the justices in case there should be further proceedings, eg with a view to revocation; or an appeal: see *R v Goult* (1982) 76 Cr App R 140, and note that *inter alia* s.108 MCA 1980 (appeal to the Crown Court) is applied to offences under s.12: s.12(6).

Although this should go without saying, it is important to note that the defendant's contempt must not be allowed to deprive him of a fair trial on the substantive matter with which he stands charged: cf, eg *Logicrose Ltd v Southend United Football Club Ltd* (1988) *The Times*, 5 March (a civil case). Neither should it be allowed to increase his sentence for that offence: *R v Powell* (1985) 11 July, unreported (defendant swore at judge from dock as sentence being imposed; the judge erred in increasing the sentence rather than dealing with the defendant for contempt).

7.02   (ii) Common law

As indicated in the *Introduction*, 7.00, contempt of court continues to be punishable at common law notwithstanding the Contempt of Court Act 1981: see s.6(c) and *Attorney-General v News Group Newspapers Ltd* (1988) *The Times*, 20 February. The example from that case of publications which avoid statutory restrictions concerning reports of proceedings apart, the common law might be used where eg an alleged contemnor insults a person present or travelling to court other than one who falls within the categories mentioned in s.12(1)(a), *supra*; and where this could not be dealt with as an interruption under s.12(1)(b). Such 'misbehaviour' *outside court* is not caught by s.12; although it might be suitable material for a *Bind-over, post*; or, depending on the facts, a *criminal offence* in its own right, *post*.

Common law contempt, even of a magistrates' court is punishable only by the High Court: cf *R v Parke* [1903] 2 KB 432; *R v Davies* [1906] 1 KB 32.

Binding Over 7.03

Prior to the Contempt of Court Act 1981, the only order magistrates could make with respect to disorderly behaviour in court was a bind-over see generally 8a.07, *post*. Where this course is adopted, there is no need for a complaint and the court may act of its own motion under the Justices of the Peace Act 1361. This may still have a place where the 1981 Act is inappropriate or to prevent future misbehaviour. It was said in Hawk PC c 61, p.327 that surety for good behaviour could be required for *disrespectful or unmannerly expressions in the face of the court or words out of court disparaging the magistrate in his office, and of obstructing officers of the court in the execution of their duty*. Where the behaviour consists of defaming a particular justice he should not comprise the court which orders the bind-over: *R v Lee* (1701) 12 Mod 514. In the case of other behaviour *in court* there is no objection to a magistrate who has witnessed it ordering the bind-over: *R v Butt* (1957) 41 Cr App R 82, unless the behaviour is disputed, when it should be tried by a different bench.

This need for a warning does not apply where the court binds over applicants seeking cross summonses who engage in verbal argument in the face of the court which there is fear will lead to a breach of the peace: *R v North London Metropolitan Magistrate, ex p. Haywood* [1973] 3 All ER 50.

The courts' powers in respect of a *refusal to be bound over* exceed those for contempt of court under s.12, ie for those over 21 years of age, the sanction is up to six months' imprisonment or until the person concerned complies, as opposed to one month for contempt. Those aged 17–20 may be ordered to be detained for refusal to be bound over in accordance with s.9 CJA 1982: *Howley v Oxford* (1985) 81 Cr App R 246. But juveniles cannot be detained or imprisoned for such a refusal: *Veater v Glennon* [1981] 1 WLR 567, and see generally at 8a.05. Any warant should make clear the basis of the committal, and not confuse refusal to be bound over with contempt: *Dean's Case* (1599) Cro Eliz 689.

Inherent Powers – Closing the Court 7.04

A magistrates' court has inherent powers to control its own proceedings, which extend to clearing the court of spectators, or limiting the number of spectators who may be present in court where this is genuinely necessary in the interests of justice and the proper administration thereof. It is suggested that the power to exclude persons from the court – which is further discussed at *Open Court (Including Exceptions)*, 1.04 – should be exercised with caution and not merely on some vague notion that potential problems might occur in fact.

Experience suggests that expected trouble often does not materialise once the court is in session, and it is important that the principle of open justice is preserved whenever possible. *A fortiori* when consideration is being given to excluding the body of the public from court on grounds, eg of 'security': see generally 1.04, particularly *R v Denbigh Justices, ex p. Williams and Evans* [1974] QB 759 (Welsh language demonstrators); *R v Malvern Justices, ex p. Evans*; *R v Evesham Justices, ex p. Donagh* (1987) *The Times*, 1 August; and *R v Governor of Lewes Prison, ex p. Doyle* [1917] 2 KB 254. But note *R v Tower Bridge Justices, ex p. Osborne* (1987) *The Times*, 4 December in which it was held that justices may sit *in camera* in order to determine whether to sit in camera.

The legal basis for the removal of a person from court would appear to be firstly the inherent power to order this, then with actual physical removal – into detention if necessary – taking place pursuant to s.12 Contempt of Court Act 1981.

7.05   The General Criminal Law

Substantive criminal offences committed in court may be charged as such, in the same way as if committed elsewhere. In the case of serious offences, the powers contained in the Contempt of Court Act 1981 may be wholly inadequate. Apart from offences such as assaults, escaping from lawful custody and carrying weapons it should be noted that various offences under the Public Order Act 1986 may be applicable to circumstances occurring in and around court houses, depending on the seriousness of the events in question. Where it does become necessary to charge a person with a substantive criminal offence committed in court, it is recommended that the matter should be adjourned for hearing before a fresh bench and that in appropriate cases consideration should be given whether the matter should be transferred to another petty sessional division altogether, and in some instances whether summary jurisdiction should be declined in favour of greater 'suitability' for trial in the Crown Court. There is no reason why a summons should not be issued and served *instanter*: see *R v Butt* (1957) 41 Cr App R 82.

7.06   RESTRICTIONS ON PUBLICATION

A number of statutory provisions concern the publication of matters arising in court proceedings:

7.07   The Contempt of Court Act 1981

Section 11 Contempt of Court Act 1981 proves that where a court, having power to do so, allows a name or other matter to be withheld from the public in proceedings before the court, the court may give such directions prohibiting publication in connection with the proceedings as appear to be necessary for the purpose for which it is so withheld. Any such order must be committed to writing, stating its precise scope, the time when it ceases to have effect, if appropriate, and the specific purpose in making the order. In addition, the press should be given notice in some form that the order has been made. The onus then rests with the press to ensure that no breach of the order occurs, and enquiry should be made by the press in cases of doubt: see *Practice Direction* [1982] 1 WLR 1475. There is *no authority* to give a direction *where the name is* allowed to be *mentioned in open court*: *R v Arundel Justices, ex p. Westminster Press Ltd* [1986] 1 WLR 676. It is suggested that, whenever possible, an indication of the reason for the withholding of the name is announced in open court.

The court has power under s.4 of the 1981 Act to order that the publication of any report of the proceedings or part of the proceedings to be *postponed* for such period as it thinks necessary where, '. . . it appears to be *necessary for avoiding a substantial risk of prejudice to the administration of justice* in those proceedings, or in any other proceedings pending or imminent': s.4(2) Contempt of Court Act 1981. The subsection applies to committal proceedings, notwithstanding that there is also a specific provision relating to those proceedings contained in s.8 MCA, *post*: *R v Horsham Justices, ex p. Farquharson* [1982] QB 762. The order should be no wider than is necessary '. . . for the prevention of prejudice to the administration of justice': *ibid.*

Failure to observe the terms of the order is a contempt of court, and one which is subject to the strict liability rule, even where the report was fair, accurate, published contemporaneously and in good faith: see ss.1 to 4 Contempt of Court Act 1981 (the relevant parts of which are not reproduced in this work).

Children   7.08

Under s.39 CYPA 1933, the court has power to direct – *in relation to any proceedings in any court* – that no newspaper, sound or television reports shall publish any particulars *calculated* to lead to the identification of the child or young person concerned in the proceedings: s.39(1). The probition may be applied whether the child is the defendant, or a witness: *ibid.* Publication is a summary offence punishable by a fine not exceeding level 5, currently £2,000. For the avoidance of doubt the restriction should be re-announced after any adjournment.

There is a wider all embracing and absolute restriction in relation to such publication regarding the *juvenile court* – *unless* either the court or the Secretary of State dispenses with this restriction '. . . for the purpose of avoiding injustice to a child or young person': s.49 CYPA 1963. Again, the maximum penalty on summary conviction, is a fine on level 5: s.49(2). Discharge of a supervision order in respect of a person of 17 years of age attracts a modified extension of this rule, but in which the restriction lapses unless announced: see s.10 CYPA 1969.

Rape   7.09

Section 4 Sexual Offences (Amendment) Act 1976 contains provisions which are designed to protect the anonymity of complainants in rape cases. Publication or broadcasting of offending material is an offence punishable on summary conviction with a fine up to level 5, currently £2,000: s.4(5). A similar restriction and a similar penalty is provided in respect of the anonymity of *defendants* in rape cases: see s.6(1), (6). The restriction applies from the time '. . . after the accused is charged' (s.6(1)) until lifted under one of the provisions of s.6, or until conviction. The accused may himself apply to the magistrates for this restriction to be so lifted: see s.6(2). *Note*, however, the amendments to s.4 of the 1976 effected by [s.150] CJA 1988, when in force. The same provision repeals s.6: see Appendix III, *post* and the *statutory provisions* at 4.36, 4.37.

Sexual Offences   7.10

Whilst the headnotes to both ss.4 and 6 Sexual Offences (Amendment) Act 1976 concern '. . . rape etc cases', the restrictions are closely confined to rape and secondary forms of participation in that offence: see s.7(2) of the 1976 Act. Any protection in relation to eg a child who has been indecently assaulted, is by a direction under s.39 CYPA 1933, *supra*, and not under the 1976 Act.

7.11 Committals for trial

Section 8 MCA 1980 contains restrictions on the reporting of committal proceedings unless the accused applies for these to be lifted: see Chapter 4.

7.12 TAPE RECORDING

The tape recording of proceedings *without the leave of the court* – and the mere bringing of tape recorders into court without leave – is prohibited under s.9 Contempt of Court Act 1981, which also forbids the publication of such recordings and gives the court power to forfeit the instrument. The practice governing the official use of tape recorders is contained in *Practice Direction* [1982] 1 WLR 1475, which is noted under the Commentary to s.9, 7.19.

The penalty for breach of the terms of s.9 is one month's imprisonment or a fine: s.14.

7.13 PHOTOGRAPHY

Photography in court – and sketching there with a view to publication – are prohibited under s.41 CJA 1925. The prohibition extends to 'the building' and to the 'precincts' of the court, and to the photographing or sketching of '. . . . any judge juror or witness' entering or leaving either part of the premises. It also extends to any subsequent publication. As to the meaning of 'precincts': see the Commentary to s.41(2), 7.15.

The section creates a summary offence punishable by a fine on level 3 (currently £400).

7.14 DISOBEDIENCE OF COURT ORDERS – CIVIL CONTEMPTS

Section 63(3) MCA 1980 provides that where any person disobeys an order of a magistrates' court to do anything other than the payment of money, or to abstain from doing anything, the court may order him to pay a sum not exceeding £50 for every day during which he is in default or a sum not exceeding £2,000, or to commit him to custody until he has remedied his default or for a period not exceeding 2 months.

Statutory Provisions

CRIMINAL JUSTICE ACT 1925

7.15 **Prohibition on taking photographs, etc in court**
   41. (1) No person shall–
   (a) take or attempt to take in any court any photograph, or with a view to
    publication make or attempt to make in any court any portrait or sketch,
    of any person, being a judge of the court or a juror or a witness in or a
    party to any proceedings before the court whether civil or criminal; or

(b) publish any photograph, portrait or sketch taken or made in contravention of the foregoing provisions of this section or any reproduc-
tion thereof;

and if any person acts in contravention of this section he shall, on summary
conviction, be liable in respect of each offence to a fine not exceeding level 3 on
the standard scale.

(2) For the purposes of this section–

(a) the expression 'court' means any court of justice, including the court of a
coroner;

(b) the expression 'judge' includes registrar, magistrate, justice and
coroner,

(c) a photograph, portrait or sketch shall be deemed to be a photograph,
portrait or sketch taken or made in court if it is taken or made in the
court-room or in the building or in the precincts of the building in which
the court is held, or if it is a photograph, portrait or sketch taken or
made of the person while he is entering or leaving the court-room or any
such building or precincts as aforesaid.

[*as amended by Sch.11 Courts Act 1971, ss.38, 46 CJA 1982*].

COMMENTARY

s.41(2): Precincts, the first meaning given in the *Shorter Oxford Dictionary* is 'the space
enclosed by the walls or other boundaries of a particular place or building, or by an
imaginary line drawn about it, *esp* the ground immediately surrounding a religious house or
place of worship'.

MAGISTRATES' COURTS ACT 1980

Orders other than for payment of money   7.16

63. (1) Where under any Act passed after 31 December 1879 a magistrates'
court has power to require the doing of anything other than the payment of
money, or to prohibit the doing of anything, any order of the court for the
purpose of exercising that power may contain such provisions for the manner
in which anything is to be done, for the time within which anything is to be
done, or during which anything is not to be done, and generally for giving
effect to the order, as the court thinks fit.

(2) The court may by order made on complain suspend or rescind any such
order as aforesaid.

(3) Where any person disobeys an order of a magistrates' court made under
an Act passed after 31 December 1879 to do anything other than the payment
of money or to abstain from doing anything the court may–

(a) order him to pay a sum not exceeding £50 for every day during which he
is in default or a sum not exceeding £2,000; or

(b) commit him to custody until he has remedied his default or for a period
not exceeding *two months*;

but a person who is ordered to pay a sum for every day during which he is in
default or who is committed to custody until he has remedied his default shall
not by virtue of this section be ordered to pay more than £1,000 or be
committed for more than two months in all for doing or abstaining from doing
the same thing contrary to the order (without prejudice to the operation of this
section in relation to any subsequent default).

CONTEMPT OF COURT ACT 1981

Contemporary reports of proceedings   7.17

4. (1) . . .

(2) In any such proceedings the court may, where it appears to be necessary
for avoiding a substantial risk of prejudice to the administration of justice in

those proceedings, or in any other proceedings pending or imminent, order that the publication of any report of the proceedings, or any part of the proceedings, be postponed for such a period as the court thinks necessary for that purpose.

(3), (4) . . .

COMMENTARY

Despite the existence of a separate (but different) power to restrict the reporting of committal proceedings this section may also be used for that purpose: _R v Horsham Justices, ex p. Farquharson_ [1982] 2 All ER 269.

Any such proceedings, ie legal proceedings held in public.

The court, includes any tribunal or body exercising the judicial power of the State and 'legal proceedings' must be construed accordingly: s.19 of the Act.

Substantial risk of prejudice, the only relevant risk to be considered is the risk to the proceedings being heard at the relevant time which, in the case of committal proceedings, is the committal proceedings. The proceedings at the Crown Court may be considered as 'proceedings pending or imminent': _R v Horsham Justices, ex p. Farquharson_ [1982] 2 All ER 269.

Order, disobedience to such an order is punishable either on complaint or on the court's own motion under s.63(3) MCA 1980.

Under s.4(2) Contempt of Court Act 1981, a court may, where it appears necessary for avoiding a substantial risk of prejudice to the administration of justice in the proceedings before it or in any other pending or imminent, order that publication of any report of the proceedings or part thereof be postponed for such period as the court thinks necessary for that purpose. Section 11 of the Act provides that a court may prohibit the publication of any name or other matter in connection with the proceedings before it which (having power to do so) it has allowed to be withheld from the public.

It is necessary to keep a permanent record of such orders for later reference. For this purpose all orders made under s.4(2) must be formulated in precise terms, having regard to the decision of _R v Horsham Justices, ex p. Farquharson_ [1982] 2 All ER 269, and orders under both sections must be committed in writing either by the judge personally or by the clerk of the court under the judge's directions. An order must state (a) its precise scope, (b) the time at which it shall cease to have effect, if appropriate, and (c) the specific purpose of making the order. Courts will normally give notice to the press in some form that an order has been made under either section of the Act and court staff should be prepared to answer any inquiry about a specific case, but it is, and will remain, the responsibility of those reporting cases, and their editors, to ensure that no breach of any order occurs and the onus rests with them to make inquiry in any case of doubt. _Practice Direction_ [1982] 1 WLR 1475.

Publication, this term is defined in s.2(1) as including any speech, writing, broadcast or other communication in whatever form, which is addressed to the public at large or any section of the public: _ibid_, s.19.

7.18   **Savings**

6. Nothing in the foregoing provisions of this Act–
   (a) . . .
   (b) . . .
   (c) restricts liability for contempt of court in respect of conduct intended to impede or prejudice the administration of justice.

COMMENTARY

This provision preserves the common law offence of contempt of court, _inter alia_, in relation to magistrates' courts.

7.19   **Use of tape recorders**

9. (1) Subject to the subs (4) below, it is contempt of court–
   (a) to use in court, or bring into court for use, any tape recorder or other instrument for recording sound, except with the leave of the court;
   (b) to publish a recording of legal proceedings made by means of any such instrument, or any recording derived directly or indirectly from it, by

playing it in the hearing of the public or any section of the public, or to dispose of it or any recording so derived, with a view to such publication;

(c) to use any such recording in contravention of any condition of leave granted under para (a).

(2) Leave under para (a) of subs (1) may be granted or refused at the discretion of the court, and if granted may be granted subject to such conditions as the court thinks proper with respect to the use of any recording made pursuant to the leave; and where leave has been granted the court may at the like discretion withdraw or amend it either generally or in relation to any particular part of the proceedings.

(3) Without prejudice to any other power to deal with an act of contempt under para (1) of subs (1), the court may order the instrument, or any recording made with it, or both, to be forfeited; and any object so forfeited shall (unless the court otherwise determines on application by a person appearing to be the owner) be sold or otherwise disposed of in such manner as the court may direct.

(4) This section does not apply to the making or use of sound recordings for purposes of official transcripts of proceedings.

COMMENTARY

The following *Practice Direction* [1981] 3 All ER 848 has been issued in the Supreme Court but its principles would seem to be of equal application in the magistrates' courts:

1. Section 9 of the Contempt of Court Act 1981 contains provisions governing the unofficial use of tape recorders in court. Among other things it provides that it is a contempt of court to use in court, or bring into court for use, any tape recorder or other instrument for recording sound, except with the leave of the court; and it is also a contempt of court to publish a recording of legal proceedings or to use any such recording in contravention of any conditions which the court may have attached to the grant of permission to use the machine in court. These provisions do not apply to the making or use of sound recordings for purposes of official transcripts of proceedings, on which the Act imposes no restriction whatever.

2. The discretion given to the court to grant, withhold or withdraw leave to use tape recorders or to impose conditions as to the use of the recording is unlimited, but the following factors may be relevant to its exercise: (a) the existence of any reasonable need on the part of the applicant for leave, whether a litigant or a person connected with the press or broadcasting, for the recording to be made; (b) in a criminal case, or a civil case in which a direction has been given excluding one or more witnesses from the court, the risk that the recording could be used for the purpose of briefing witnesses out of court; (c) any possibility that the use of a recorder would disturb the proceedings or distract or worry any witnesses or other participants.

3. Consideration should always be given whether conditions as to the use of a recording made pursuant to leave should be imposed. The identity and role of the applicant for leave and the nature of the subject matter of the proceedings may be relevant to this.

4. The particular restriction imposed by s.9(1)(b) of the 1981 Act applies in every case, but may not be present to the mind of every applicant to whom leave is given. It may, therefore, be desirable on occasion for this provision to be drawn to the attention of those to whom leave is given.

5. The transcript of a permitted recording is intended for the use of the person given leave to make it and is not intended to be used as, or to compete with, the official transcript mentioned in s.9(4) of the 1981 Act.

Sources of information   7.20

10. No court may require a person to disclose, nor is any person guilty of contempt of court for refusing to disclose, the source of information contained in a publication for which he is responsible, unless it be established to the satisfaction of the court that disclosure is necessary in the interests of justice or national security or for the prevention of disorder or crime.

COMMENTARY

'**In the interests of justice**', these words are given the meaning 'in the technical sense of the administration of justice in the course of legal proceedings': per Lord Diplock in *Secretary of*

State for Defence v Guardian Newspapers Ltd [1985] AC 339; and see *Maxwell v Pressdram Ltd* (1986) *The Times*, 12 November. For a journalist to be required to disclose his source of information, the court must be satisfied that disclosure is *necessary* in this technical sense: *ibid*. But a journalist may be required to disclose his sources where necessary for the *detection* of crime, as well as its prevention as envisaged by s.10: *Re Inquiry under the Company Securities (Insider Dealing) Act 1985* (1987) *The Times*, 7 May.

7.21   **Publication of matters exempted from disclosure in court**

    11. In any case where a court (having power to do so) allows a name or other matter to be withheld from the public in proceedings before the court, the court may give such directions prohibiting the publication of that name or matter in connection with the proceedings as appear to the court to be necessary for the purpose for which it was so withheld.

COMMENTARY

See the *Practice Direction* [1982] 1 WLR 1475 noted under s.4, *supra*. Breach of directions is a contempt of court which may be punished by the High Court or by the magistrates' court under s.63(3) MCA 1980 and in accordance with s.17 Contempt of Court Act 1981.

Allows a name to be withheld, thus, where the name is allowed to be mentioned in open court there is no authority to give a direction under this section: *R v Arundel Justices, ex p. Westminster Press Ltd* [1986] 1 WLR 676.

7.22   **Offences of contempt of magistrates' courts**

    12. (1) A magistrates' court has jurisdiction under this section to deal with any person who–

    (a) wilfully insults the justice or justices, any witness before or officer of the court or any solicitor or counsel having business in the court, during his or their sitting or attendance in court or in going to or returning from the court; or

    (b) wilfully interrupts the proceedings of the court or otherwise misbehaves in court.

    (2) In any such case the court may order any officer of the court, or any constable, to take the offender into custody and detain him until the rising of the court; and the court may, if it thinks fit, commit the offender to custody for a specified period not exceeding one month or impose on him a fine not exceeding £1,000, or both.

    (3) *(Repealed)*.

    (4) A magistrates' court may at any time revoke an order of committal made under subs (2) and, if the offender is in custody, order his discharge.

    (5) The following provisions of the Magistrates' Courts Act 1980 apply in relation to an order under this section as they apply in relation to a sentence on conviction or finding of guilty of an offence, namely: s.36 (restriction on fines in respect of young persons); ss.75 to 91 (enforcement); s.108 (appeal to Crown Court); s.136 (overnight detention in default of payment); and s.142(1) (power to rectify mistakes).

    [as amended by Sch.16 CJA 1982, SI 1984 No. 447].

COMMENTARY

See generally under *Contempt*; 7.01.

    Legal aid is available where anyone is liable to be fined under this section: s.28 (11A) LAA 1974.

s.12(1): It has been held under the corresponding County Court legislation that abuse of a judge in a newspaper did not take place 'in court': *R v Lefray* (1873) 37 JP 566.

Wilfully, despite conflicting decisions in other fields it is suggested that this term imports *mens rea* of all the elements of the offence.

Officer of the court, it is suggested that this includes the clerk to the justices and his staff and any probation officer attached to the court.

In the court It is suggested that this term is confined to the court room and its adjacent offices rather than the whole building in which the court room is situated.

Interrupts, it is not an interruption to threaten a witness outside the court room: *R v Havant Justices, ex p. Palmer* (1985) 149 JP 609.

Misbehaves, it is suggested that this is not confined to interruptions. Note that misbehaviour (unlike an interruption) must take place in court.

s.12(2): In *Balogh v Crown Court at St Albans* [1974] 3 All ER 283, Lord Denning MR said that the power to commit summarily for contempt should be exercised by the judge of his own motion 'only when it is urgent and imperative to act immediately – so as to maintain the authority of the court – to prevent disorder – to enable witnesses to be free from fear . . . and the like.'

Commit the offender to custody, the restrictions on the use of prison sentences contained in ss.20, 20A and 21 Powers of Criminal Courts Act 1973 do not apply, nor may the sentence be suspended in whole or in part. Young offenders may be committed to be detained under s.9 CJA 1982. For the place of detention see s.12(10), *ibid.* Note ss.1(5), 2(1), (5), (7).

A probation order may not be made for an offence at the same time as commitment to custody for a contempt: *R v Socratous* [1984] Crim LR 301.

Where there was a very serious contempt in the face of the court which prevented the court from carrying on its business it was held that natural justice did not require the magistrates to afford the contemnors opportunity of seeking legal representation, although this is desirable, wherever practicable, even if only by inviting counsel or solicitors present in court to have a word with the person taken into custody: *R v Newbury Justices, ex p. Du Pont* (1984) 148 JP 248.

It would seem that the order and warrant of commitment should specify the particular matter of contempt: cf. *McIlraith v Grady* [1967] 3 All ER 625.

s.12(5), in *R v Havant Justices, ex p. Palmer* (1985) 149 JP 609 the view was expressed *obiter* that the jurisdiction of the Crown Court is limited to the hearing of an appeal against the penalty and does not extend to hearing an appeal against a finding of contempt.

Proceedings in England and Wales   7.22a
14. (1), (2) . . .

(2A) In the exercise of jurisdiction to commit for contempt of court or any kindred offence the court shall not deal with the offender by making an order under s.17 of the Criminal Justice Act 1982 (an attendance centre order) if it appears to the court after considering any available evidence, that he is under 17 years of age.

(3) (*Repealed*).

(4), (4A), (5) . . .
[*as amended by Schs.14, 16 CJA 1982*].

Disobedience to certain orders of magistrates' courts   7.23
17. (1) The powers of a magistrates' court under subs (3) of s.63 of the Magistrates' Courts Act 1980 (punishment by fine or committal for disobeying an order to do anything other than the payment of money or to abstain from doing anything) may be exercised either of the court's own motion or by order on complaint.

(2) In relation to the exercise of those powers the provisions of the Magistrates' Court Act 1980 shall apply subject to the modifications set out in Sch.3 to this Act.

COMMENTARY
The court's own motion, if the court acts of its own motion, natural justice demands that, except where it is impracticable, the person to be punished is first given notice of the court's intention and the opportunity to make representations to the court . . .

SCHEDULE 3

7.24 **Application of Magistrates' Courts Act 1980 to Civil Contempt Proceedings under Section 63(3)**

1. (1) Where the proceedings are taken of the court's own motion the provisions of the Act listed in this sub-paragraph shall apply as if a complaint had been made against the person against whom the proceedings are taken, and subject to the modifications specified in sub-para (2) and (3) below. The enactments so applied are–

    s.51 (issue of summons)
    s.53(1) and (2) (procedure on hearing)
    s.54 (adjournment)
    s.55 (non-appearance of defendant)
    s.97(1) (summons to witness)
    s.101 (onus of proving exceptions etc.)
    s.121(1) and (3)(a) (constitution and place of sitting of court)
    s.123 (defect in process).

(2) In s.55, in subs (1) for the words 'the complainant appears but the defendant does not' there shall be substituted the words 'the defendant does not appear', and in subs (2) the words 'if the complaint has been substantiated on oath, and' shall be omitted.

(3) In s.123 in subs (1) and (2) the words 'adduced on behalf of the prosecutor or complainant' shall be omitted.

2. Where the proceedings are taken by way of complaint for an order, s.127 of the Act (limitation of time) shall not apply to the complaint.

CHAPTER 8

Sentencing Powers – General Introduction

Sentencing Powers – General Introduction   8.00

The purpose of Chapters 8a to 8e is to produce an analysis of the range of
sentences available, culminating in the ultimate sanction of a custodial

order. As far as practicable, matters with similar or comparable backgrounds have been grouped together as follows:

Binding Over   8a

Fines, Compensation and Property Orders   8b
Including: Fines
            Compensation
            Restitution
            Deprivation of property
            Transfer of fine
            Enforcement

Non-custodial Orders   8c
Including: Absolute and conditional discharges
            Probation
            Community service
            Medical treatment
            Attendance centre orders
            and Deportation

Custodial Orders   8d
Including: Imprisonment
            Suspended sentences of imprisonment
            Young offenders – youth custody and detention centres*
            Factors affecting sentence
            Sentences for particular offences

Committal for sentence   8e

In accordance with the general scheme of this work, sentencing in *Road
Traffic* cases is not dealt with beyond the details contained in the *Table of
Commonplace Offences, ante*, the outline structure of the *Penalty Points*
system contained therein and the references to *Reckless driving* under the
title *Sentences for particular offences* in Chapter 8d.

Note that sentences of youth custody and detention centre orders are
both replaced by 'a sentence of detention in a young offender institution',
by means of a new s.1(3A) CJA 1982, inserted by [s.121] CJA 1988, when
in force: see Appendix III and the insertions under statutory provisions in
Chapter 8d. For confiscation orders see [s.70-88] of the 1988 Act:
Appendix III.

    Once an accused person has been convicted the court must proceed to
sentence him, or to make some order *in lieu of sentence*. First, however, it
may *adjourn* the case to enable it to determine the most suitable method
of dealing with the offender, eg with the benefit of a social inquiry report
from a probation officer – or, in a proper case, the court might *defer*
sentence for up to six months under the provisions of s.1 PCCA 1973,
post. In general, the court may take such steps as it desires – or, in certain
cases, is required to take – to inform itself of the circumstances of the
case, of the offender, and of the availability or suitability of particular
'sentencing' options. Deferment apart, adjournments after conviction
are limited to four weeks at a time where the offender is remanded on
bail, three weeks at a time in custody.

    In certain situations, the conventional view is that the court may exercise
powers or duties of *remission* to another court, *infra*. Where the offence is

riable either way, the magistrates may commit the offender to the Crown Court for sentence where, by reason of his *'character and antecedents'*, they consider that a more severe penalty should be imposed than is within their own maximum powers – in summary, 6 months' imprisonment, or 12 months' in aggregate where there are two or more such offences: see Chapter 8e.

These situations apart, the magistrates are under a duty to proceed to impose a sentence or an order in lieu of sentence in respect of *each offence* of which the offender stands convicted. (Whilst there is no authority in relation to magistrates' courts for the use of devices such as 'no separate penalty' and 'no separate adjudication', neither is there anything to prohibit this and it is *suggested* that such formulae may serve a useful purpose in relation to minor offences, on occasion – and this view would appear to be corroborated by [s.148] (CJA 1988: see Appendix III.) A list of possible dispositions is set out below. With the exception of bind-overs, compensation orders and, in certain circumstances, orders for the payment of costs, the court cannot make an order from the list of *ancillary orders* without also *sentencing* the offender, or making *an order in lieu of sentence*. What sentences or orders are available in a particular case will depend on the offence in question and on any statutory rules concerning eligibility for particular sentences and orders, notably in relation to the age of the offender. All of the dispositions are subject to special provisions and procedures, and in some cases, eg imprisonment, youth custody, detention centre, to close restrictions on their use. All relevant aspects of the law concerning each disposition are discussed under the appropriate title in Chapters 8a to 8d.

Powers available to the Court

8.01

	For powers, procedures and any special restrictions see
Sentences:	Chapters
Imprisonment, including a suspended and partly suspended sentence (21 years and over)	8d
Youth custody sentence (15–20)*	8d
Detention centre order (14–20, males only)*	8d
Hospital order	8c
Guardianship order	8c
Attendance centre order (14–20)	8c
Order of detention in cells of police station or court (21)	8d
Community service order (16 years and over)	8c
Fine	8b
Compensation order	8b
Bind-over – statutory	8
Bind-over of a parent (ie specifically provided for by the statute creating the offence)	8a
Charge and control order (in respect of a youngster already in care)	8d

Orders in lieu of sentence:

Probation order (17 and over)	8c
Absolute or conditional discharge	8c

Orders ancillary to sentence:

Costs	9
Disqualification	⎰ Table of
Endorsement of driving licence	⎱ commonplace offences
Compensation	8b
Restitution or 'forfeiture'	8b
Deprivation of property	8a
Confiscation order	Appendix III
Bind-over	8a
Recommendation for deportation	8c

Note (i) Deferment of sentence is not a sentence or order in lieu of sentence, but a type of adjournment to which special rules and principles apply: see 8.20, *post*.

(ii) It is wrong to impose over a period of time a number of sentences or orders upon an offender each of which could give rise to punishment in default because of the commission there after of a relatively minor offence could result in the imposition of sentences which in aggregate would be disproportionate to the offence: *R v Docker* (1979) Cr App R (S) 151.

(iii) Youth custody and detention centre are replaced by 'deletion in a young offender institution' by [s.121] CJA 1988, when in force.

8.02   This work is concerned with two separate and distinct aspects of sentencing. First, the *existence of the power* to impose sentences or make other orders. Based almost entirely on statute, the various powers are set out in Chapters 8a to 8b; second, with the problem 'Which sentence to order?' To the extent that it is possible to deal with this second aspect within the confines of a general work, advice is set out at a number of points in the text, including under the titles *Custodial Sentences and Particular Offences, Imprisonment*, and *Restrictions on Custodial Sentences for Young Offenders*, at Chapter 8d *post*. It is, in fact, at the point where courts must decide whether or not to impose custody that much parliamentary and judicial activity has occurred in recent years and it is impossible to comprehend the provisions fully without an understanding of the changes which have taken place.

Notwithstanding a rising prison population, recent years have seen an increased 'tolerance' of certain kinds of criminal behaviour – thus the level of sentence for some non-violent offences, as discernible from the reports of appeal cases, show a noticeable downward trend, eg in relation to 'breach of trust', 'social security frauds' and 'taking motor vehicles without consent'. At the same time, the removal of imprisonment for persons under the age of 21 by s.1(1) CJA 1982, together with the still relatively new statutory restrictions on youth custody and detention centre orders contained in s.1(4) of the 1982 Act – and the proliferation of 'alternatives to custody' – has precipitated much re-thinking. These changes have not yet worked themselves out, so that it is essential for sentencers and their advisors always to consider the latest reported cases. A selection of the more important decisions since 1982 is set out under *Restrictions on custodial sentences for Young Offenders*, Chapter 8d, *post*.

8.03   Some dispositions are, in fact, more often than not thought of as '*alternatives to custody*', principally, in relation to adults (in the present context

1 and over) and young offenders (17 to 20 inclusive), community service, Chapter 8c, *post*, see eg *R v Stewart* [1987] *The Times*, 27 March where community service was equated with imprisonment probation orders with presenting and participating requirements, 8c, *post*, and probation day centre orders, 8c, *post*. Here, the use of these options be considered n the context of local practice, as much as within the statutory framework.

Under s.1(4) of the 1982 Act, and in relation to 'young offenders', a court, before using custody, must be '. . . of the opinion that no other method of dealing with him is appropriate because it appears to the court that he is *unable or unwilling* to respond to non-custodial penalties or because a custodial sentence is necessary for the *protection of the public* or because the offence was *so serious* that a non-custodial sentence cannot be justified'.

There is no appellate sentencing tribunal to promulgate guidelines in elation to sentences imposed by magistrates, but rulings by the Court of Appeal in relation to sentences in the Crown Court indicate – notably in elation to the the most common '*so serious*' exception – that fewer and fewer offences are intrinsically so serious that they automatically exclude a non-custodial penalty. Offence 'labels', it has been said, are less important than the individual circumstances of the offence: see *R v Bradbourn* 1985) 7 Cr App R (S) 180 (breach of trust involving small amount not '*so serious*' that custody appropriate). It is increasingly the case that the Court of Appeal has settled in favour of 'alternatives', see Chapter 8d, *post*. But it seems important to recognise that what happens to young offenders cannot be without its effect on thinking in relation to the sentencing of older offenders also. Where the Court of Appeal has refused to sanction the use of 'alternatives' is in relation to certain offences of violence, particularly serious violence, unprovoked attacks, attacks with weapons, and attacks on the old or young – see *Restrictions on custodial sentences for young offenders* and *sentencing for particular offences* Chapter 8d, *post*.

n relation to commonplace summary offences, most, if not all, benches **8.04** employ 'sentencing guidelines', and in some instances guidelines have been produced which deal with the more common triable either way offences also. 'Guidelines' do not constitute 'policy', and each offence falls to be dealt with on its own individual merits. This aspect – which applies across the whole range of sentencing and offending – can make it difficult to draw general conclusions from individual appeal rulings. Nonetheless, broad trends can usually be discerned and an attempt has been made to identify such trends in the sections already referred to, *supra*.

The justices' clerk is not only competent to advise on sentencing matters, but under a duty to do so within the terms of the *Practice Direction on the role of the clerk in court* [1981] 2 All ER 1121, as follows: . . . advise the justices generally on the range of penalties which the law allows them to impose and on any guidance relevant to the choice of penalty provided by the law, the decisions of superior courts or other authorities'. Among such 'other authorities', it seems, must be included the views of the Home Office concerning the purpose for which particular sentences are provided, as set out in *The Sentence of the Court – A Handbook for Courts on the Treatment of Offenders*, 4th edn, 1986 HMSO).

8.05   Procedure on a plea of guilty or conviction

Following a *plea of guilty* it is the duty of the prosecutor (a) to outline dispassionately but fully the facts of the case, laying before the court any statements made by the accused; (b) to inform the court of his previous convictions, if any; and (c) to inform the court of his antecedent history including his work record and family circumstances. As to conviction following a plea of *not guilty*, the position is as at (b) and (c) only. The prosecutor may also correct any erroneous statements of law concerning sentence and he should be prepared, if required, to address the court on the maximum sentence permitted by law in a particular case. Finally, he may indicate any claims for compensation, restitution and the like.

In contrast to the position in foreign jurisdictions, the convention in this country – indirectly sanctioned by a number of rulings – is that the prosecutor is not concerned with and does not address the court on the appropriate level of sentence, or seek a particular sentence from the court. In relation to the still relatively new Crown Prosecution system (see Chapter 2, *ante*), however, it might be questioned how far the present absolute rule is consistent with the Crown Prosecutor's earlier duties and powers concerning the commencement and conduct of proceedings, in particular the 'public interest' criterion contained in the *Code for Crown Prosecutors*, as to which, see Appendix II, *post*. The present position of the prosecutor in relation to sentence is set out in the *Code of Conduct for the Bar of England and Wales* as follows: '. . . prosecuting counsel should not attempt by advocacy to influence the court in regard to sentence. If, however, an accused person is unrepresented, it is proper for prosecuting counsel to inform the court of any mitigating circumstances as to which he is instructed.' And see the comments of Lord Scarman in *R v Atkinson (Leslie)* (1977) 67 Cr App R 201.

8.06   Ascertaining the facts on a plea of guilty

'Often it may be desirable to hear some evidence on oath, but this is not necessary in the many cases which are very trivial and the facts can be stated informally. Of course, if the accused person says that the facts have not been stated correctly, the justices would be well advised to have the informant sworn so that he can be cross-examined.' *per* Lord Goddard CJ in *R v Recorder of Grimsby, ex p. Purser* (1951) 115 JP 637, and see *R v Milligan* (1982) 4 Cr App R (S) 2 and see *Ex p. Darlington, infra.*

Where on a plea of guilty there is *serious conflict* between the prosecutor's version of the facts and the defendant's it can be resolved as follows: by directing a plea of not guilty and having the issue tried, or by allowing the parties to call evidence on the issue and by hearing submissions from each side. If submissions only are heard and there is still conflict the version of the defendant must so far as possible be accepted: *R v Newton* (1978) 77 Cr App R 13. Whether an issue should be tried in this way is for the court to decide and does not depend on the consent of the parties: *R v Williams* (1984) 148 JP 375. The court need not hear evidence if there is no substantial divergence or conflict of evidence which would materially affect the likely sentence: *R v Hall* (1984) 6 Cr App R (S) 321. Matters of mitigation such as a change of heart do not fall within the *Newton* principle: *R v Odey* (1984) 6 Cr App R (S) 318; and note that where the plea is *unequivocal*, the court is bound to accept it, even though the precise basis of fact may be in dispute. If, subsequently, justices are confronted with a conflict of facts which are *extraneous to the offence* itself the justices must then proceed to hear evidence on the disputed facts: *R v Telford Justices, ex p. Darlington* (1987) *The Times*, 23 November.

It has been stated that where evidence is called the normal criminal burden of proof applies: *R v Ahmed* (1984) 6 Cr App R (S) 391.

Previous convictions and antecedents 8.07

Previous convictions are convictions which *antedate the offence in question*. Convictions after that date and prior to the court hearing should be referred to in the antecedents (see the *Practice Direction* at [1966] 2 All ER 929 which concerns trial on indictment, and *R v Van Pelz* [1943]). *Findings of guilt* while under the age of 14 must be disregarded for the purposes of previous convictions of persons over 21: s.16 CYPA 1963; but they may be referred to as antecedent history: *Practice Direction* (1966) 130 JP 387. The relevance of previous convictions is that they reduce the scope of mitigation: see, eg *R v Webster* (1985) 7 Cr App R (S) 359; and generally under title *Previous Convictions* at Chapter 8d, *post*.

Where an alleged previous conviction which is in dispute is *trivial* or *irrelevant*, the court should state that it will ignore it: *per* Lord Goddard CJ, in *R v Butterwasser* [1948] KB 4; (see *R v Campbell* (1911) 75 JP 216).

A previous conviction should never be mentioned to magistrates in circumstances which prevent its being challenged by the defendant: *Hastings v Ostle* (1930) 94 JP 209. Details of antecedents need not be based strictly on the laws of evidence: *R v Elley* (1921) 85 JP 144; but the officer should not be allowed or invited to make allegations which are incapable of proof and which he has reason to think will be denied by the defendant: *R v Van Pelz* [1943] KB 157; *R v Robinson* (1969) 53 Cr App R 314; *R v Bibby* [1972] Crim LR 513; *R v Sargeant* (1974) 60 Cr App R 74; *R v Wilkins* (1978) 66 Cr App R 49.

The Law Society's *Guide to the Professional Conduct of Solicitors* advises:

Unlike the advocate for the prosecution, a solicitor who appears for the defendant is under no duty of disclosure to the prosecution or the court, save that he is bound to reveal all relevant cases and statutory provisions. Moreover, save in exceptional and specific circumstances, the client's privilege precludes him from making a disclosure of privileged material without the client's consent. Consequently, he must not, without instructions, disclose facts known to him regarding his client's character or antecedents nor must he correct any information which may be given to the court by the prosecution if the correction would be to his client's detriment. However, the defence advocate should not act in such a way that, in the context of the language used by him, his failure to disclose amounts to a positive deception of the court.

Previous convictions may be proved by any of the methods set out at Chapter 6.00, *ante*.

Spent Convictions 8.08

The Secretary of State considers that magistrates' courts will wish to follow, so far as possible, a practice which reflects the *Practice Direction* [1975] 2 All ER 172: see under *Spent Convictions*. Broadly speaking this means that no oral reference should be made to spent convictions unless they have influenced the court in determining sentence: see also HOC 98/1975.

Offences taken into consideration – 'tic's' 8.09

As a matter of practice, the court may *take into consideration* certain other offences committed by the accused of which he has *not been convicted*: *R v Syres* (1908) 73 JP 13; *Director of Public Prosecutions v Anderson* [1978] AC 964; a power shared by magistrates: *R v Marquis* (1951) 35 Cr App R 33. But an offence should *not be taken into consideration*.

— (i) if the offence is triable only by a higher court: *R v Warn* (1938) 102 JP 46; *R v Simons* (1953) 117 JP 422;
— (ii) unless the offence was committed within the territorial jurisdiction, ie not in a foreign country: *R v Warn, supra; R v Davies* (1912) 28 LTR 431;
— (iii) if the offence is *not of the same class* as that of which the defendant stands convicted: *R v Davies, supra;*
— (iv) if disqualification or endorsement may be ordered thereupon under the Road Traffic Act 1972: *R v Collins* [1947] KB 560; *R v Simons, supra*. This objection does not apply where the principal offence is also disqualifiable: *R v Jones* [1970] 3 All ER 815;
— (v) in respect of breaches of probation or of conditions of discharge: *R v Webb* [1953] 2 QB 390.

The court has a *discretion* whether to take other offences into consideration, but where they are similar to those on which the defendant has just been convicted it is *'practically the duty'* of the court to do so: *R v Smith* (1921) 85 JP 224. As to the procedure which should be followed, Lord Goddard CJ, in *R v Marquis, supra* said:

It is not enough for the court to be told that the prisoner has signed a form on which the other offences are mentioned. The prisoner should be told what those other offences are, and himself asked whether he admits them and desires them to be taken into consideration. It is not necessary in every case to put the details of each offence, but he may be asked: 'Have you received and signed this list of cases showing the other offences which are outstanding against you?' If he says 'Yes', he should then be asked: 'Do you admit those offences and wish them to be taken into consideration?' Then he can say 'Yes' or 'No' as the case may be, or he can say: 'Yes, I admit some, and I do not admit others.'

When 'sample' charges are preferred the ordinary procedure for taking other offences into consideration should be followed: *Director of Public Prosecutions v Anderson* [1978] AC 964. It is essential that there is no suggestion of pressure being put on the offender: *R v Nelson* [1967] 1 All ER 358. (Recorder criticized for explaining that if prisoner did not wish offences taken into consideration prosecution would be entitled to have them tried).

It is for the accused himself and not his counsel or solicitor to admit the other offences and ask for them to be considered: *R v Davis* (1943) 107 JP 75; but the court refused to upset sentence where the accused had heard his counsel speak and had himself signed the form.

Offences taken into consideration *do not rank as convictions* and are probably not sufficient upon which to found a plea of *autrefois convict*; although 'normally no proceedings follow on them'; *R v Nicholson* [1947] 1 All ER 535; *R v Neal* [1949] 2 KB 590.

Note that the maximum sentence allowed by law is unaffected, no matter how many offences are taken into consideration; but compensation may be ordered in respect of t.i.c's: s.35 PCCA 1973.

Adjournment for inquiries 8.10

There is express power in s.10(3) MCA 1980 to adjourn for limited periods after conviction for the purpose of enabling inquiries to be made or for determining the most suitable method of dealing with the case. Adjournments may be repeated and there is no overall statutory period within which sentence must follow upon conviction. But the power must be exercised judicially, and the practice of postponing sentence and remanding in custody is disapproved of unless there is some legitimate purpose: *R v Easterling* (1946) 175 LT 520.

Simply asking for a social inquiry report *does not commit the court* to a non-custodial sentence, unless the request is accompanied by something of a promise, express or implied, that a favourable report will lead to that result: *R v Moss and others* (1984) 5 Cr App R (S) 209; *R v Hatherall* [1977] Crim LR 755. However, when a court adjourns a case after conviction for the purpose of obtaining a probation report in order to ascertain the offender's *suitability for community service* and the report shows the offender to be suitable for such an order, the court ought to make it because otherwise a feeling of injustice would be aroused: *R v Gillam* [1981] Crim LR 55; see also *R v Ward* (1982) 4 Cr App R (S) 103 (report on suitability for bail hostel followed by borstal sentence); and *R v Moss and others* [1983] Crim LR 751. It is otherwise where no expectation of a non-custodial sentence has been raised: *R v Horton and Alexander* (1985) 7 Cr App R (S) 299; and see again *R v Moss* and the other cases quoted, *supra*.

Part sentencing improper 8.11

It is improper to fine a convicted offender and adjourn the case for consideration of the rest of the sentence: *R v Talgarth JJ, ex p. Bithell* [1973] 1 WLR 1327.

SOCIAL INQUIRY REPORTS 8.12

When a report is essential

A social inquiry report *must* be obtained:

(i) before a court can be satisfied that there is no *appropriate method* other than imprisonment to deal with an offender *aged 21 or over* who has *not previously received* such a sentence: s.20A(1) PCCA 1973

(ii) before a court can be satisfied that there is no *appropriate method* other than youth custody or detention centre to deal with an offender aged *under 21*: ss.1(4), 2(2) CJA 1982

(iii) before making a community service order: s.14(2) PCCA 1973.

Obtaining the report

A probation officer is *under a duty* to inquire in accordance with any directions of the court into the circumstances or home surroundings of any person with a view to assisting the court in determining *the most suitable method of dealing with his case*: sch.3, para 8(1) PCCA 1973.

Solicitors representing an accused person *should not make a request for a report direct to the probation service*. Any such request must be made through the court: *R v Adams* [1970] Crim LR 693.

In the case of a juvenile, a local authority notified that criminal proceedings are being brought is, unless it considers it unnecessary, *under a duty* to make investigations and produce certain reports to the court: s.9(1) CYPA 1969; in addition, the court may request investigations and reports, when the local authority is obliged to respond: s.9(2).

8.13   Presentation of the report

A copy of any probation officer's report must be given by the court to the offender or his legal representative or, if under 17 and unrepresented, to his parent or guardian: s.46 PCCA 1973.

The Home Office has given the following advice:

'27. The Secretary of State shares the view of the Morison Committee that the probation officer's report should be provided to the defendant or his adviser by the court itself, and that it is not the probation officer's responsibility to do so. The court will wish to bear in mind the desirability of allowing the defence to see a copy of the report in sufficient time to digest its contents and to clarify or challenge any points of doubt. A copy of a prison report is, under s.37 of the Criminal Justice Act 1961, similarly required to be provided by the court. It will not normally be necessary to supply a copy of a social inquiry report to the prosecution, though there may be cases where the court thinks it right to do so – eg if it considers that the prosecution can assist in clearing up any conflict between the report and the police antecedents. If a copy of the report is given to the prosecution arrangements should be made for it to be returned to the court . . . when the prosecution has given such assistance as may be required.

'28. The Secretary of State's view, with which the Lord Chief Justice agrees, is that, as a general rule, it is undesirable that reports by probation officers should be read aloud in open court: it is likely to be only in exceptional circumstances that the court will wish to depart from normal practice in this respect. (This view is supported by judicial remarks made in the Court of Appeal in the unreported case of *R v Albert Edwin Smith* (1967), on the ground that a report usually contains many things which, for the prisoner's sake, are better not emphasized). If it is known that a report may be read aloud, the frankness of the defendant in talking to the probation officer, and of the latter in preparing his report, may be impaired.

'29. The Streatfeild Committee expressed the view that ordinarily the prison reporting officer need not be in court to present his report; and both the Streatfeild and Morison Committees recognized that it was impracticable for the reporting probation officer to attend court in every case. The reporting officer will, however, attend if the accused is already under supervision, or if requested to do so by either the court or the defence; . . .

'30. The Streatfeild and Morison Committee further expressed the view, with which the Secretary of State agrees, that, when a probation officer gives evidence, he should not appear as a witness for the defence or prosecution, but should be called by the court (para 367 of the Streatfeild report and para 44 of the Morison report).'
(Extracts from HOC 28/1971.)

8.14   The contents of a Social Inquiry Report

Guidance on the contents of social inquiry reports is given in HOC 17/1983.

As to *recommendations* in probation reports:

The Secretary of State and Lord Widgery CJ, shared the view that a probation officer can go further in commenting on an offender's 'treatment needs'. They suggested that if an experienced probation officer feels able to make a specific recommendation in favour of (or against) any particular form of decision being reached he should state it clearly in his report. Further, when offering advice in a report on the suitability of an offender for probation, probation officers should be encouraged to suggest the terms of an order, taking into account their assessment of the offender's needs, his likely response to supervision and any other relevant factors:

HOC 195/1974. Further guidance on recommendations in probation reports is contained in HOC 18/1983.

8.15   MEDICAL AND MENTAL REPORTS

Reports on the *physical* and *mental condition* of an accused person may be called for:

(a) where the court is satisfied that the accused *did the act or made the omission charged* in the case of an offence punishable with imprisonment: s.30 MCA 1980;
(b) after a *finding of guilt* in the case of any offence: s.10(3) MCA 1980; see *Boaks v Reece* (1956) 121 JP 51; and
(c) where the offence is punishable by imprisonment, by way of a remand to hospital (*infra*).

For provisions concerning medical evidence see the s.54 Mental Health Act 1983 (Chapter 8c, *post*).

The costs of a doctor giving oral evidence may be ordered from central funds: s.19 POA 1985 and r.25 Costs in Criminal Cases (General) Regulations 1986 (SI No 1335), and similar provision is made for written reports in s.32(2) CJA 1967: see *Costs*, Chapter 9.

REMAND TO HOSPITAL   8.16

The DHSS Memorandum on the Mental Health Act 1983 states:

Section 35 empowers the courts to order the remand to hospital of an accused person for the preparation of a report on his mental condition. This provides an alternative to remanding the accused person in custody for a medical report, in circumstances where it would not be practicable to obtain the report if he were remanded on bail (for instance because he might decide to break a condition of bail that he should reside at a hospital, and the hospital would then be unable to prevent him for discharging himself).

A magistrates' court may *remand to hospital* for a report on his mental condition (i) anyone convicted of an offence punishable on summary conviction with imprisonment and (ii) anyone charged with such an offence (a) if satisfied that he *did the act or made the omission charged*; or (b) *he has consented* to this course: s.35(1) Mental Health Act 1983. The *pre-conditions* are that the court should be satisfied *on the written or oral evidence of a medical practitioner* that the accused is suffering from mental illness, psychopathic discorder, severe mental impairment or mental impairment and that it is of the opinion that it would be impracticable to obtain the report on bail: s.35(3).

The court must also be satisfied on the written or oral evidence of the medical practitioner who would make the report or someone representing the managers of the hospital that *arrangements have been made for his admission* within the seven days beginning from the remand: s.38(4). Further remand may be ordered if justified by the doctor's report: s.35(5); and this may take place in the absence of the accused if he is represented by counsel or solicitor who is given an opportunity of being heard: s.35(6). The remand may not be for more than *28 days* at a time and *12 weeks in all*: s.35(7).

The accused is entitled to obtain at his own expense *an independent report* and to apply to the court for his remand to be terminated: s.35(8). Directions for conveyance to and detention in a place of safety may be given by the court: s.35(4). The duties of the constable and hospital managers are set out in s.35(9). For absconscion see s.35(10).

SENTENCING CO-ACCUSED   8.17

Special problems arise when two or more accused with different backgrounds and criminal records and, perhaps, ages, are convicted of the same offence. Normally a court will strive to apply uniform sentences on co-defendants unless there are grounds for discriminating between them: *R v Richards* (1955) 39 Cr App R 191; *R v Gardiner, R v Ryall* [1962] Crim LR 853. 'But when two persons are convicted together of a crime or series of crimes in which they have been acting in concert, it may be right, and very often is right, to discriminate between the two and to be lenient to the one and not the other . . . The argument that a severe sentence on one prisoner must be unjust because his fellow prisoner, who was convicted of the same crime, received a light sentence or not at all, has neither validity nor force. The differentiation in treatment is justified if the court, in considering the public interest, has regard to the difference in characters and antecedents of the two convicted men and discriminates between them because of those differences', *per* Hilbery J in *R v Ball* (1951) 35 Cr App R 164; and see *R v Coe* [1969] 1 All ER 65.

The fact that one of the defendants is a *woman* is not of itself sufficient to warrant discriminating in her favour, unless she was a young woman operating under the influence of a man: *R v Williams* (1953) 37 Cr App R 71; *R v Okuya and Nwaobi* [1984] Crim LR 766.

Complete legal consistency is impossible and it may not be wrong for a young man to go to a detention centre when older men were treated more leniently: *R v Midgley* [1975] Crim LR 469. But see the new s.1(4) CJA 1982, substituted by [s.121] CJA 1988, when in force. Section 1(4)(a) and (b)(i) will prevent a custodial sentence in respect of a person below 21 years of age unless '. . . if the offender were aged 21 or over the court would pass a sentence of imprisonment': see Appendix III. What must be avoided is such disparity between sentences as would leave a reasonable man with a burning sense of grievance: *R v Dickinson* [1977] Crim LR 303. When *deterrent sentences* are passed, individual circumstances may be irrelevant: *R v Goldsmith & Oakley* [1964] Crim LR 729; *R v Colley, Mills & Greenland* (1967) *The Times*, 20 March. It is undesirable, if it can be avoided, that members of a gang should be dealt with at different times and by different judges: *R v Pitson* (1972) 56 Cr App R 391; *R v Stroud* (1977) 65 Cr App R 150; *R v Weekes and Others* (1982) 74 Cr App R 161.

When one of a number of co-accused is *convicted before the others sentence should be postponed until the trial is concluded, except in the rare case where it is necessary to sentence one accused in order to allow him to be called against his co-accused without any suspicion that his evidence will be coloured by considerations of sentence: R v Payne* (1950) 34 Cr App R 43. The object of sentencing in advance a co-accused who is going to give evidence for the prosecution is that there should be no suggestion that he is under any *inducement* which will result in his getting a lesser sentence than otherwise: *R v Stone* [1970] 1 WLR 1112. This practice is not obligatory: *R v Potter* (1977) 15 September. There may be exceptions: *R v Woods* (1977) 25 October. There is no corresponding rule where it is proposed to call one accused as a witness for another: *R v Coffey* [1977] Crim LR 45. Where one accused is sentenced before his co-accused the later court should be fully informed of the sentence passed at the first trial: *R v Pleasance* [1974] Crim LR 20.

8.18   **PRESENCE OF THE OFFENDER**

A sentence of *imprisonment, an order that a suspended sentence shall take effect*, and a sentence of detention in a *detention centre*, may *not be passed or made in the absence of the accused*, and anyone convicted of an endorsable traffic offence may not be *disqualified* in his absence without notice and an opportunity of attending: s.11(3), (4) MCA 1980.

MITIGATION 8.18a

After any reports have been read, the accused must be given an opportunity to address the court *in mitigation*. Failure to allow this is a breach of the rules of natural justice: *R v Billericay Justices, ex p. Rumsey* [1978] Crim LR 305. The right of the offender to address the court in mitigation otherwise than on oath is preserved by s.72(2) CJA 1982. In appropriate circumstances there is no reason why the accused should not give *evidence in mitigation*: *R v Cross* [1975] Crim LR 591. Certain aspects of mitigation, as for example special reasons for not disqualifying in a traffic case, require that the defendant discharge a burden of proof. Therefore such reasons should be advanced on oath: *Jones v English* [1951] 2 All ER 853.

The form of oath (the *voire dire*) for statements made after conviction is as follows:

'You shall true answer make to all such questions as the court shall demand of you.'

The court can then demand any information it thinks fit, *per* Lord Goddard CJ, in *R v Butterwasser* [1948] KB 4. When the accused gives *evidence on oath after conviction* he is subject to cross-examination by the prosecutor, who may, if necessary, call rebutting evidence. Where statements are made in *mitigation not on oath* which the prosecutor wishes to *challenge* it is suggested that he has the same duty as he bears throughout the trial to intervene and point out any inaccuracy of facts so as to give the accused an opportunity to substantiate what he says by sworn testimony. For the position where the defendant pleads guilty but there is a 'conflict of facts', see *R v Telford Justices, ex p. Darlington* (1987) *The Times*, 23 November, noted at 5.20. *Before* the court is addressed in mitigation it should receive and read any social inquiry reports which are available: *R v Kirkham* [1968] Crim LR 210.

See also the relevance of *Previous convictions* in relation to mitigation at 8.07, *supra*, and Chapter 8d, *post*.

REMISSION 8.19

Remission to another court for sentence

When an *adult* convicted by a magistrates' court of an offence *punishable by imprisonment or a motoring offence for which he may be disqualified* is also convicted of such an offence at another magistrates' court he may be remitted to the latter court for sentence either on bail or in custody: s.39 MCA 1980. The remitting court may at the same time make an order of *restitution*: s.39(4). The other court may deal with the offender in any way he could have been dealt with by the convicting court including the remission of the offender to the convicting or any other magistrates' court.

Remission of juveniles

After a *finding of guilt* an adult court (which has reached this stage under one of the exceptions to the trial of a juvenile in the juvenile court) must remit a juvenile offender to a juvenile court to be dealt with *unless* satisfied this would be *undesirable*: s.56 CYPA 1933; *and* that the case can properly be dealt with by means of a *fine, absolute or conditional discharge or the binding-over of a parent* with or without any ancillary orders: s.7(8) CYPA 1969.

8.20   **DEFERMENT**

Deferment of sentence should be distinguished from *disposal of* the case, deferment being a form of adjournment to which special rules and principles apply.

A court may *defer* passing sentence on a convicted offender for a single period of *up to six months* for the purpose of enabling the court to have regard in determining sentence to his conduct after conviction (including, where appropriate, the making by him of reparation for his offence) or to any change of circumstances: s.1(1) PCCA 1973. This can only be done with the offender's *consent* and if the court is satisfied, having regard to the nature of the offence and the character and circumstances of the offender, that it would be *in the interests of justice* to do so: s.1(3). Following deferment the offender may be dealt with in any way in which the court which deferred sentence could have dealt with him, including the power to commit him to the Crown Court for sentence, if available: s.1(8) PCCA 1973.

If a person the subject of a deferred sentence is convicted in Great Britain of any offence prior to the adjourned date the court which deferred sentence: s.1(4) PCCA 1973; or the convicting court, if different: s.1(4A); may proceed to sentence for the original offence except that a magistrates' court may not pass sentence where the Crown Court deferred: s.1(4A). When a person is convicted of a further offence during the operational period of a suspended sentence and the passing of sentence for the further offence is deferred no action should be taken on the suspended sentence during the period of deferment. Furthermore, where the suspended sentence was imposed by the Crown Court and the subsequent conviction is before a magistrates' court the better course is to commit the offender to the Crown Court: *R v Salmon* (1973) 57 Cr App R 953. The use of the power to defer sentence is governed by the following '*guideline judgment*' of the Court of Appeal in *R v George* (1984) 6 Cr App R (S) 211:

The purpose of deferment is . . . to enable the court to take into account the defendant's conduct after conviction or any change in circumstances and then only if it is in the interests of justice to exercise the power. It will, one imagines, seldom be in the interests of justice to stipulate that the conduct required is reparation by the defendant. The power is not to be used as an easy way out for a court which is unable to make up its mind about the correct sentence [see *Burgess* (July 18, 1974 unreported)]. Experience has shown that great care should be exercised by the court when using this power . . . The consent of the defendant must of course be obtained to the making of the order. The court should make it clear to the defendant what the particular purposes are which the court has in mind under s.1(1) of the Act and what conduct is expected of him during deferment. The failure to do so, or more often the failure on the part of the defendant or his representatives to appreciate what those purposes are or that conduct is, has been a fruitful source of appeals to this Court. It is essential that the deferring court should make a careful note of the purposes for which the sentence is being deferred and what steps, if any, it expects the defendant to take during the period of deferment. Ideally, the defendant himself should be given notice in writing of what he is expected to do or refrain from doing, so that there can be no doubt in his mind what is expected of him. Thus the task of the court which comes to deal with the offender at the expiration of the period of deferment is as follows:

First the purpose of the deferment and any requirement imposed by the deferring court must be ascertained. Secondly the court must determine if the defendant has substantially conformed or attempted to conform with the proper expectations of the deferring court, whether with regard to finding a job or as the case may be. If he has, then the defendant may legitimately expect that an immediate custodial sentence will not be imposed.* If he has not, then the court should be careful to state with precision in what respects he has failed.

If the court does not set out its reasons in this way, there is a danger, particularly where the sentencing court is differently constituted from the deferring court, that it may appear that the former is disregarding the deferment and is saying in effect that the sentence should never have been deferred and that the defendant should have been sentenced to immediate imprisonment by the latter [see *Glossop* (1981) 3 Cr App R (S) 347]. In many cases a short probation order may be preferable to a deferment of sentence. Such an order enables the defendant's behaviour to be monitored by the probation officer, it ensures that formal notice of the requirements of the court are given to the defendant. On the other hand a deferment of sentence will be more appropriate where the conduct required of the defendant is not sufficiently specific to be made the subject of a condition imposed as part of a probation order without creating uncertainty in the mind of the probation officer and the defendant as to whether there has been a breach of the order; for example, where the defendant is making a real effort to find work, or where the sentencer wishes to see whether a change in the defendant's attitude and circumstances, which appears to be a possibility at the time of deferment, does in fact come about. Again, deferment may be the appropriate course where the steps to be taken by the defendant could not of their nature be the subject of a condition, for example where he is to make reparation, or at least demonstrate a real intention and capacity to do so.

These are only examples. It is unnecessary and undesirable to attempt an exhaustive definition of the circumstances in which the procedure should be employed. It is sufficient to say that it should not be adopted without careful consideration of whether the sentencer's intentions could not best be achieved by other means, and that if deferment is decided upon, care must be taken to avoid the risk of misunderstanding and a sense of injustice when the defendant returns before the court.'

[*These remarks do not amount to an absolute rule of law: *R v Head* (1976) 63 Cr App R 157. Thus, it would not necessarily be wrong for the court subsequently to impose a suspended sentence for a prior offence which was inadvertently not disclosed at the time of deferment. *R v Harling* (1977) 65 Cr App R 320.]

The provision does not give a general discretion to defer sentence: *R v McQuaide* (1975) 60 Cr App R 239. Deferment cannot be used to require an offender to keep in touch with a probation officer or pay fines: *R v Dwyer* (1975) 60 Cr App R 39; nor may it be subject to any condition or undertaking: *R v Skelton* [1983] Crim LR 686, CA (undertaking to reside in hospital). **8.21**

If the purpose of the court is to enable a social inquiry report to be produced this should be achieved by way of adjournment, not deferment: *R v Gilby* (1975) 61 Cr App R 112; *R v George* (1984) 79 Cr App R 26. All aspects of sentencing must be deferred: *R v Dwyer, supra; including disqualification: R v Fairhead* [1975] 2 All ER 737. An exception is the power to order restitution under s.28 Theft Act 1968.

It is *normally desirable* for the offender to be sentenced by the bench which deferred passing sentence, but this is *not essential*: s.121 MCA 1980. To guard against this possibility it is advisable for the clerk to make a note of the court's reasons for deferment: *R v Jacobs* (1976) 62 Cr App R 116.

Despite the terms of the statute a failure to sentence the offender on the due date is not fatal, whether it arises from administrative difficulties: *R v Ingle* [1974] 3 All ER 811; or error: *R v Anderson* (1983) 5 Cr App R(S) 338.

POWER TO RE-OPEN CASES – 'RECTIFICATION' **8.22**

Within 28 days beginning with the day on which a sentence or order was imposed or made a magistrates' court may *vary or rescind* that sentence or order and this power extends to the alteration of invalid sentences or orders: s.142(1) MCA 1980. The power is exercisable only by the court which passed sentence or, if three or more justices sat originally, by a court consisting of or including a majority of that court: s.142(4). Unless there is a direction to the contrary, the revised sentence, etc., takes effect from the beginning of the day when it was originally imposed.

This provision also extends to the re-opening of *convictions*, but only where the accused was *found guilty*: see s.142(2). It thus has no application to a conviction following a plea of guilty, in particular under s.12 MCA 1980 (*Written Pleas of Guilty*, Chapter 5, *ante*): see *R v Epping and Ongar JJ ex p. C Shippam* (1986) 150 JP 425; although failure to observe the s.12 procedure will render the proceedings a *nullity*: see *Appeals* at Chapter 11, *post*, and the comments contained therein concerning whether magistrates may simply treat the proceedings as such.

Statutory Provisions

CHILDREN AND YOUNG PERSONS ACT 1933

8.23   *Note:*
Certain aspects of this Act relevant to summary proceedings in general are set out at Chapter 5, *ante*, as follows:
s.31 separation of children and young persons from adults in police stations, courts, etc;
s.36 prohibition on children being present in court during the trial of other persons;
s.37 power to clear court while child or young person is giving evidence in certain cases;
s.39 power to prohibit publication of certain matter in newspapers;
s.44 general considerations;
s.46 assignment of certain matters to juvenile courts.

8.24   **Power of other courts to remit juvenile offenders to juvenile courts**
56. (1) Any court by or before which a child or young person is found guilty of an offence other than homicide, may, and, if it is not a juvenile court, shall, unless satisfied that it would be undesirable to do so, remit the case to a juvenile court acting for the place where the offender was committed for trial, or, if he was not committed for trail, to a juvenile court acting either for the same place as the remitting court or for the place where the offender habitually resides; and, where any such case is so remitted, the offender shall be brought before a juvenile court accordingly, and that court may deal with him in any way in which it might have dealt with him if he had been tried and found guilty by that court.

(2) Where any case is so remitted the offender shall have the same right of appeal against any order of the court to which the case is remitted as if he had been found guilty by that court, but shall have no right of appeal against the order of remission.

(3) A court by which an order remitting a case to a juvenile court is made under this section may give such directions as appear necessary with respect to the custody of the offender or for his release on bail until he can be brought before the juvenile court, and shall cause to be transmitted to the clerk of the juvenile court a certificate setting out the nature of the offence and stating that the offender has been found guilty thereof, and that the case has been remitted for the purpose of being dealt with under this section.
[*as amended by Sch.3 CYPA 1963, Sch.5 CYPA 1969, Sch.11 Courts Act 1971*].

COMMENTARY

The power to remit under this section only arises *after* and not before a finding of guilty.

Undesirable to do so The court has no discretion but to remit unless it proposes to make one or more of the orders contained in s.7(8) CYPA 1969, *infra*.

Remit For the form of order, see Form 51 Magistrates' Courts (Children & Young Persons) Rules 1970 (SI No 1792, as amended). There is no right of appeal against an order of remission.

The custody of the offender The Home Office booklet on Part 1 of the CYPA 1969 states:

'Courts may wish to use the remand procedure for this purpose. If there is no release on bail, remand would be in accordance with s.23 of the 1969 Act, if the person was under 17, or with s.27 of the Criminal Justice Act 1948, if he had reached the age of 17 since the proceedings were begun.'

Note:
Section 59 CYPA 1933 (miscellaneous provisions as to summary proceedings against juvenile offenders;
    Section 99 (presumption and determination of age); and
    Schedule 1 to this Act
    are set out at Chapter 5, *ante*.

Section 16 CYPA 1963 (offences committed by children –
    evidence of *previous convictions*)
    is set out at Chapter 5, *ante*.

CHILDREN AND YOUNG PERSONS ACT 1969

Alterations in treatment of young offenders, etc   **8.25**
    7. (7) Subject to subs (7A) of this section and to the enactments requiring cases to be remitted to juvenile courts and to s.53(1) of the Act of 1933 (which provides for detention for certain grave crimes), where a child is found guilty of homicide or a young person is found guilty of any offence by or before any court, that court or the court to which his case is remitted shall have power–
    (a), (b) (*Refer to juvenile court*), or
    (c) with the consent of his parent or guardian, to order the parent or guardian to enter into a recognizance to take proper care of him and exercise proper control over him,
and, if it makes such an order as is mentioned in this subsection while another such order made by any court is in force in respect of the child or young person, shall also have power to discharge the earlier order; and subs (13) of s.2 of this Act shall apply to an order under para (c) of this subsection as it applies to such an order as is mentioned in that subsection.

    (7A) . . .

    (8) Without prejudice to the power to remit any case to a juvenile court which is conferred on a magistrates' court other than a juvenile court by s.56(1) of the Act of 1933, in a case where such a magistrates' court finds a person guilty of an offence and either he is a young person or was a young person when the proceedings in question were begun, it shall be the duty of the court to exercise that power unless the court is of the opinion that the case is one which can properly be dealt with by means of–
    (a) an order discharging him absolutely or conditionally, or
    (b) an order for the payment of a fine; or
    (c) an order requiring his parent or guardian to enter into a recognizance to take proper care of him and exercise proper control over him,
with or without any other order that the court has power to make when absolutely or conditionally discharging an offender.
[*as amended by Sch.5 CJA 1972, Sch.6 PCCA 1973, s.23, Ssch.16 CJA 1982*].

COMMENTARY

s.7(7): The enactments requiring cases to be remitted see s.56 CYPA 1933, and s.7(8), *supra*.

Young person The definition in s.70 CYPA 1969 has been extended to include in this section a child who has attained the age of 10 years: CYPA 1969 (Transitional Modifications of Part 1) Order 1970, SI 1970 No 1882.

Enter into a recognizance This power is in addition to the common law powers of magistrates. *Note* that it may only be made by consent of the parent or guardian and is subject to the limitations of s.2(13) CYPA 1969.

Section 2(13) of this Act reads as follows:

'Such an order as is mentioned in subs (3)(a) of the preceding section shall not require the parent or guardian in question to enter into a recognizance for an amount exceeding £50 or for a period exceeding three years or, where the relevant infant will attain the age of 18 in a period shorter than three years, for a period exceeding that shorter period, and s.120 of the MCA 1980 (which relates to the forfeiture of recognizances) shall apply to a recognizance to keep the peace.'

s.7(8): Thus an adult court *may not make* a supervision or detention centre order in respect of a juvenile offender, or commit him to the Crown Court for sentence.

Was a young person when the proceedings were begun Thus an adult court must remit even an adult to a juvenile court if he was a juvenile when the proceedings began, unless it proposes to make one or more of the specified orders; see also the note *Young Person, supra*. It has been held that proceedings are begun on the date the accused is served with the summons: *R v Billericay Justices, ex p. Johnson* (1979) 143 JP 697.

A recognizance to take proper care *see s.7(7).*

8.26   **Investigations by local authorities**
         9. (1) Where a local authority or a local education authority bring proceedings under s.1 of this Act or proceedings for an offence alleged to have been committed by a young person or are notified that any such proceedings are being brought, it shall be the duty of the authority, unless they are of the opinion that it is unnecessary to do so, to make such investigation and provide the court before which the proceedings are heard with such information relating to the home surroundings, school record, health and character of the person in respect of whom the proceedings are brought as appear to the authority likely to assist the court.

         (2) If the court mentioned in subs (1) of this section requests the authority aforesaid to make investigation and provide information or to make further investigations and provide further information relating to the matters aforesaid, it shall be the duty of the authority to comply with the request.

COMMENTARY

s.9(1): Proceedings under s.1 of this Act ie care proceedings.

Young person The definition in s.70 CYPA 1969 has been extended to include a child who has attained the age of 10 years: CYPA 1969 (Transitional Modifications of Part 1) Order 1970, SI 1970 No 1882. Where local arrangements allow of reports by the probation service of young persons to the age of 13, the duty of the local authority under this section is removed by s.34(3) (SI 1970 No 1882 refers).

Notified The prosecutor is under a duty to notify the local authority when he decides to lay an information against a juvenile s.5(8) CYPA 1969.

POWERS OF CRIMINAL COURTS ACT 1973

8.27   **Deferment of Sentence**
         1. (1) Subject to the provisions of this section, the Crown Court or a magistrates' court may defer passing sentence on an offender for the purpose of enabling the court or any other court to which it falls to deal with him to have regard, in dealing with him, to his conduct after conviction (including, where

appropriate, the making by him of reparation for his offence) or to any change in his circumstances.

(2) Any deferment under this section shall be until such date as may be specified by the court, not being more than six months after the date on which the deferment is announced by the court; and subject to subs (8A) below where the passing of sentence has been deferred under this section it shall not be further deferred thereunder.

(3) The power conferred by this section shall be exercisable only if the offender consents and the court is satisfied, having regard to the nature of the offence and the character and circumstances of the offender, that it would be in the interests of justice to exercise the power.

(4) A court which under this section has deferred passing sentence on an offender may deal with him before the expiration of the period of deferment if during that period he is convicted in Great Britain of any offence.

(4A) If an offender on whom a court has under this section deferred passing sentence in respect of one or more offences is during the period of deferment convicted in England and Wales of any offence ('the subsequent offence'), then, without prejudice to subs (4) above, the court which (whether during that period or not) passes sentence on him for the subsequent offence may also, if this has not already been done, deal with him for the first-mentioned offence or offences:

Provided that–

(a) the power conferred by this subsection shall not be exercised by a magistrates' court if the court which deferred passing sentence was the Crown Court; and

(b) the Crown Court, in exercising that power in a case in which the court which deferred passing sentence was a magistrates' court, shall not pass any sentence which could not have been passed by a magistrates' court in exercising it.

(5) Where a court which under this section has deferred passing sentence on an offender proposes to deal with him, whether on the date originally specified by the court or by virtue of subs (4) above before that date, or where the offender does not appear on the date so specified, the court may issue a summons requiring him to appear before the court, or may issue a warrant for his arrest.

(6) It is hereby declared that in deferring the passing of a sentence under this section a magistrates' court is to be regarded as exercising the power of adjourning the trial which is conferred by s.10(12) of the Magistrates' Courts Act 1980, and that accordingly ss.11(1) and 13(1), (2) and (5) of that Act (non-appearance of the accused) apply (without prejudice to subs (5) above) if the offender does not appear on the date specified in pursuance of subs (2) above.

(6A) Notwithstanding any enactment, a court which under this section defers passing sentence on an offender shall not on the same occasion remand him.

(7) . . .

(8) The power of a court under this section to deal with an offender in a case where the passing of sentence has been deferred thereunder–

(a) includes power to deal with him in any way in which the court which deferred passing sentence could have dealt with him; and

(b) without prejudice to the generality of the foregoing, in the case of a magistrates' court, includes the power conferred by ss.37 or 38 of the Magistrates' Courts Act 1980 to commit him to the Crown Court for sentence.

(8A) Where, in a case where the passing of sentence on an offender in respect of one or more offences has been deferred under this section, a magistrates' court deals with him by committing him to the Crown Court under ss.37 or 38 of the Act of 1980, the power of the Crown Court to deal with him includes the same power to defer passing sentence on him as if he had just been convicted of the offence or offences on indictment before the court.
[*as amended by Sch.12 CLA 1977, Sch.7 MCA 1980, s.63 CJA 1982*].

COMMENTARY
See generally the introduction, under *Deferment* 8.20.

s.1(2): the prohibition of further deferment beyond the six months period is confined to deferments 'under this section'. It would not seem to exclude, eg a remand under ss.10 or 30 MCA 1980, if, at this last date, it became clear that such a remand was desirable. *Cf R v Ingle* [1974] 3 All ER 811; *R v James Anderson* (1983) 5 Cr App R (S) 338.

s.1(3): Consents Consent should be obtained from the accused personally: *R v Gilby* [1975] 1 WLR 924; but where counsel appeared and requested deferment lack of a personal consent was not held to be fatal: *R v Fairhead* [1975] 2 All ER 737.

s.1(4): Any offence whether committed before or after the date of conviction of the present offence. The clerk of the convicting court must notify the clerk of the court which has deferred sentence: r.27 MC Rules 1981.

Great Britain ie England, Scotland and Wales: Union with Scotland Act 1706; s.3 Wales & Berwick Act 1746. Excluding the Channel Isles and the Isle of Man.

s.1(4A): see the note to s.1(4).

s.1(6A). Thus, a deferment is an adjournment s.1(6) *on which the defendant cannot be bailed or remanded in custody*.

s.1(8): This reverses the decision in *R v Gilby* [1975] 1 WLR 924.

8.28   **Reports of Probation Officers**
46. (1) Subject to subs (2) below, where a report by a probation officer is made to any court (other than a juvenile court) with a view to assisting the court in determining the most suitable method of dealing with any person in respect of an offence, a copy of the report shall be given by the court to the offender or his counsel or solicitor.

(2) If the offender is under 17 years of age and is not represented by counsel or a solicitor, a copy of the report need not be given to him but shall be given to his parent or guardian if present in court.

COMMENTARY
Failure to comply with the provisions of this section is probably not in itself a ground for upsetting the order of the court: *Re Philpot* (1960) 124 JP 124. See generally the heading *Presentation of Social Inquiry Reports* Chapter 8c.

s.46(2), a juvenile offender must be remitted to a juvenile court for sentence *unless* the court is satisfied this would be undesirable: Children & Young Persons Act 1933, s.56 *and* the court is of the opinion the case can properly be dealt with in one or more of a number of specified ways: s.7(8) CYPA 1969.

Parent or guardian, for their attendance at court see s.34 CYPA 1933.

MAGISTRATES COURTS ACT 1980

Note Section 10 of this Act (Adjournment of trial), which deals with adjournments and remands both *before* and *after* conviction is set out in full in Chapter 5, *ante*; see, in particular, s.10(3) and the commentary thereon.

8.29   **Non-appearance of accused: general provisions**
11. (1), (2)

(3) A magistrates' court shall not in a person's absence sentence him to imprisonment or detention in a detention centre or make an order under s.23

of the Powers of Criminal Courts Act 1973 that a suspended sentence passed on him shall take effect.

(4) A magistrates' court shall not in a person's absence impose any disqualification on him, except on resumption of the hearing after an adjournment under s.10(3) above; and where a trial is adjourned in pursuance of this subsection the notice required by s.10(2) above shall include notice of the reason for the adjournment.

COMMENTARY

s.11(3): A person's absence By s.122 of the Act, an accused represented by counsel or solicitor is *deemed not to be absent*.

s.11(4): Notice of the reason for the adjournment If notice was given in respect of one course of action, the court may not take any other course without first adjourning and giving further notice: *R v Mason* [1965] 2 All ER 308.

Note Section 11(1), (2), which concerns trial in absence, is set out in Chapter 5, *ante*.

See also s.12 which *inter alia*, contains one specific circumstance (written plea of guilty) in which the court may 'hear and *dispose*' of a case in the offender's absence (see particularly s.12(2) – which is inoperative where s.11(3), (4), *supra*, apply); and ss.13, 15 and 16 which concern non-appearance of the 'accused', 'prosecutor' and 'both parties' respectively, and which may affect the position after conviction. The net effect is that it is possible (if sometimes undesirable in practice, perhaps) for magistrates to sentence in absence, provided the case is not caught by s.11(3), (4), *supra*, whilst, on the other hand, the accused cannot be compelled to attend, except in those circumstances where there is power to issue a warrant: see s.13. All the provisions are set out in full in Chapter 5, *ante*.

Remand for medical examination   **8.30**

30. (1) If, on the trial by a magistrates' court of an offence punishable on summary conviction with imprisonment, the court is satisfied that the accused did the act or made the omission charged but is of opinion that an inquiry ought to be made into his physical or mental condition before the method of dealing with him is determined, the court shall adjourn the case to enable a medical examination and report to be made and shall remand him; but the adjournment shall not be for more than three weeks at a time where the court remands him in custody nor for more than four weeks at a time where it remands him on bail.

(2) Where on an adjournment under subs (1) above the accused is remanded on bail, the court shall impose conditions under para (d) of s.3(6) of the Bail Act 1976 and the requirements imposed as conditions under that paragraph shall be or shall include requirements that the accused–

(a) undergo medical examination by a duly qualified medical practitioner or, where the inquiry is into his mental condition and the court so directs, two such practitioners; and

(b) for that purpose attend such an institution or place, or on such practitioner, as the court directs and, where the inquiry is into his mental condition, comply with any other directions which may be given to him for that purpose by any person specified by the court or by a person of any class so specified.

(3) (Repealed).

[*as amended by Ssch.2 Prosecution of Offences Act 1985*].

COMMENTARY

When the examination is completed some time before the remand date the prison will inform the clerk of the court to enable the hearing to be advanced where practicable in accordance with s.128(1)(a) MCA 1980, or the accused released on bail if the court considers this appropriate: HOC 28/1971. Most reports by prison officers and medical officers can be prepared within 14 days: HOC 116/1972.

s.30(1): Offence punishable on summary conviction with imprisonment there is power to remand for medical reports under s.10(3) of the Act in the case of offences not so punishable: *Boaks v Reece* (1957) 121 JP 51.

Shall remand him either in custody or on bail: s.128 MCA 1980. If on bail note s.30(2). The general right to bail applies: s.4 Bail Act 1976, but para 7 of Sch.1, *ibid*, allows bail to be refused in the case of an imprisonable offence if it appears *impracticable* to make the report otherwise. HOC 206/1977 suggests the use of outpatient facilities (HOC 155/1975 refers), and, in the case of reports on suitability for detention centre training, the police surgeon (HOC 179/1972 refers).

The institution or place of remand must be given a statement of the reasons for the remand and any information before the court about his physical or mental condition: Magistrates' Courts Rules 1981, r.24.

s.30(2): Para (d) of s.3(6) ie a condition that the offender makes himself available for the purpose of enabling inquiries to be made to assist the court in dealing with him for the offence.

Duly qualified medical practitioner ie a fully registered person, namely a person registered under ss.7 or 8 Medical Act 1956.

Costs, these may now be ordered under s.19 Prosecution of Offences Act 1985 and r.25 Costs in Criminal Cases (General) Regulations 1986 (SI 1986 No 1335) (oral reports); and s.32(2) CJA 1967 (written reports).

8.31   **Mitigation of penalties, etc.**

34. (1) Where under any enactment whether passed before or after the commencement of this Act a magistrates' court has power to sentence an offender to imprisonment for a period specified by the enactment, then, except where an Act passed after 31 December, 1879 expressly provides to the contrary, the court may sentence him to imprisonment for less than that period or, as the case may be, to a fine of less than that amount.

(2) Where under any such enactment an offender sentenced on summary conviction to imprisonment or a fine is required to enter into a recognizance with or without sureties to keep the peace or observe any other condition, the court convicting him may dispense with or modify the requirement.

(3) Where under any such enactment a magistrates' court has power to sentence an offender to imprisonment or other detention but not to a fine, then, except where an Act passed after 31 December, 1879 expressly so provides to the contrary, the court may, instead of sentencing him to imprisonment or other detention, impose a fine which–
  (a) for an offence triable either way, shall not exceed the prescribed sum within the meaning of s.32 above; and
  (b) for a summary offence, shall–
    (i) not exceed £400, and
    (ii) not be of such an amount as would subject the offender, in default of payment of the fine, to a longer term of imprisonment or detention than the term to which he is liable on conviction of the offence.
[*as amended by SI 1984 No 447*]

COMMENTARY

s.34(1) This power does not extend to the reduction of any minimum penalty prescribed by statute: *Osborn v Wood Bros* (1897) 61 JP 118; see, eg s.78(3) Reserve Forces Act 1980.

31 December, 1879 the date when the Summary Jurisdiction Act 1879 came into force.

A Fine Arrears of national insurance, although 'recoverable as a penalty', are neither a 'penalty' nor 'pecuniary compensation' so as to make them a fine under s.126(1) *Leach v Litchfield* [1960] 1 WLR 1392.

s.34(3): An offence triable either way/a summary offence defined in sch.1 Interpretation Act 1978.

Cases where magistrates' court may remit offender to another such court for sentence **8.32**

39. (1) Where a person who has attained the age of 17 ('the offender') has been convicted by a magistrates' court ('the convicting court') of an offence to which this section applies ('the instant offence') and–

(a) it appears to the convicting court that some other magistrates' court ('the other court') has convicted him of another such offence in respect of which the other court has neither passed sentence on him nor committed him to the Crown Court for sentence nor dealt with him in any other way; and

(b) the other court consents to his being remitted under this section to the other court,

the convicting court may remit him to the other court to be dealt with in respect of the instant offence by the other court instead of by the convicting court.

(2) The offender, if remitted under this section, shall have no right of appeal against the order of remission.

(3) Where the convicting court remits the offender to the other court under this section, it shall adjourn the trial of the information charging him with the instant offence, and–

(a) section 128 below and all other enactments (whenever passed) relating to remand or the granting of bail in criminal proceedings shall have effect in relation to the convicting court's power or duty to remand the offender on that adjournment as if any reference to the court to or before which the person remanded is to be brought or appear after remand where a reference to the court to which he is being remitted; and

(b) subject to subs (4) below, the other court may deal with the case in any way in which it would have power to deal with it (including where applicable, the remission of the offender under this section to another magistrates' court in respect of the instant offence) if all proceedings relating to that offence which took place before the convicting court had taken place before the other court.

(4) Nothing in this section shall preclude the convicting court from making any order which it has power to make under s.28 of the Theft Act 1968 (orders for restitution) by virtue of the offender's conviction of the instant offence.

(5) Where the convicting court has remitted the offender under this section to the other court, the other court may remit him back to the convicting court; and the provisions of subs (3) above (so far as applicable) shall apply with the necessary modifications in relation to any remission under this subsection.

(6) This section applies to–

(a) any offence punishable with imprisonment; and

(b) any offence in respect of which the convicting court has a power or duty to order the offender to be disqualified under s.93 of the Road Traffic Act 1972 (disqualification for certain motoring offences);

and in this section 'conviction' includes a finding under s.30(1) above that the person in question did the act or made the omission charged, and 'convicted' shall be construed accordingly.

COMMENTARY

Note that both the instant offence and the offence at the other court must fall within the categories of s.39(6). For the documents to be transmitted to the other court, see r.19(1) MC Rules 1981.

s.39(1): Attained the age of 17 for the determination of age, see s.99 CYPA 1933.

Convicted includes a finding under s.30(1) of the Act: s.39(6).

Dealt with him in any other way it is suggested that this does not prevent remission where the other court has *deferred sentence* on the offender.

s.39(3): Remand The general right to bail (s.4 Bail Act 1976) only applies *if the case is also adjourned for inquiries or a report.*

s.39(5): for the documents to be sent to the other court, see r.30(2) MC Rules 1981.

8.33   Proof of previous convictions

104. Where a person is convicted of a summary offence by a magistrates' court, other than a juvenile court, and–

(a) it is proved to the satisfaction of the court, on oath or in such other manner as may be prescribed, that not less than seven days previously a notice was served on the accused in the prescribed form and manner specifying any alleged previous conviction of the accused of a summary offence proposed to be brought to the notice of the court in the event of his conviction of the offence charged; and

(b) the accused is not present in person before the court,

the court may take account of any such previous conviction so specified as if the accused had appeared and admitted it.

COMMENTARY

This section is confined to the proof of previous convictions of summary offences after conviction of a summary offence.

Summary offence defined in sch.1 Interpretation Act 1978 as meaning an offence which, if committed by an adult, is triable only summarily.

Proved . . . in the prescribed manner see r.67 MC Rules 1981.

Not less than seven days previously ie seven clear days or intervening days: *R v Turner* (1910) 74 JP 81; *Re Hector Whaling Ltd* [1935] All ER Rep 302; *Thompson v Stimpson* [1960] 3 All ER 500.

Notice . . . in the prescribed form see Form 29.

Previous conviction, although in the ordinary procedure a court is permitted to hear *subsequent* convictions as *antecedents*, there is no means of adducing them under this section. For the contrary opinion, see 125 JPN 404.

8.34   Power of magistrates' court to re-open cases to rectify mistakes etc

142. (1) Subject to subs (4) below, a magistrates' court may vary or rescind a sentence or other order imposed or made by it when dealing with an offender, and it is hereby declared that this power extends to replacing a sentence or order which for any reason appears to be invalid by another which the court has power to impose or make.

(2) Where a person is found guilty by a magistrates' court in a case in which he has pleaded not guilty or the court has proceeded in his absence under s.11(1) above, and it subsequently appears to the court that it would be in the interests of justice that the case should be heard again by different justices, the court may, subject to subs (4) below, so direct.

(3) Where a court gives a direction under subs (2) above–

(a) the finding of guilty and any sentence or other order imposed or made in consequence thereof shall be of no effect; and

(b) section 10(4) above shall apply as if the trial of the person in question had been adjourned.

(4) The powers conferred by subs (1) and (2) above shall be exercisable only within the period of 28 days beginning with the day on which the sentence or order was imposed or made or the person was found guilty, as the case may be, and only–

(a) by a court constituted in the same manner as the court by which the sentence or order was imposed or made or, as the case may be, by which the person in question was found guilty, or

(b) where that court comprised three or more justices of the peace, by a court which consists of or comprises a majority of those justices.

(5) Where a sentence or order is varied under subs (1) above, the sentence or other order, as so varied, shall take effect from the beginning of the day on which it was originally imposed or made, unless the court otherwise directs.

COMMENTARY

Whatever the powers of justices to re-open conviction at common law their only powers in this regard now are contained in this section the terms of which must be strictly complied with: *R v Maidstone Justices, ex p. Booth* (1980) 144 JP 354.

s.142(1): It is suggested that the power to vary sentence is not confined to reducing sentence but includes in a proper case the imposition of a more severe sentence or of an additional order ancillary to sentence: *cf R v Reilly* [1982] 3 WLR 149; *R v May* (1981) 3 Cr App R (S) 165. The power to vary sentence must be exercised in the presence of the offender, unless it is waived either expressly or impliedly, eg by absconding *R v May, supra.*

s.142(2): The powers under this subsection arise in two circumstances: a finding of guilt following a plea of not guilty or a finding of guilt in the absence of the accused (whether a plea of not guilty was entered at an earlier stage or not). It has no application to pleas of guilty, in particular *Written Pleas of Guilty* (Chapter 5, *ante*): see *R v Epping and Ongar JJ ex p. C Shippam* (1986) 150 JP 425; but see the comments in the introduction to this chapter and in Chapter 11, *post.*

The Home Office circular on the Act quotes 'examples of situations where the use of this power might be appropriate . . . where a conviction is announced prematurely, perhaps because a submission of no case to answer is misunderstood as constituting the whole defence case, or where a defendant is convicted in his absence but then arrives and presents new facts justifying a rehearing. The subsection does not apply where a defendant has pleaded guilty in person and seeks to change his plea after sentence.' HOC 230/1972.

A magistrate was wrong in refusing to direct a re-hearing under this subsection where the defendant was convicted in her absence after having arrived at court a half hour late: *R v Camberwell Magistrates' Court, ex p. Ibrahim* (1984) 148 JP 400.

Found guilty, not acquitted: *R v Gravesend Justices, ex p. Dexter* [1977] Crim LR 298.

The court may . . . so direct As to the composition of the court, see s.142(4).

s.142(3): Section 10(4) . . . shall apply thus the accused may be remanded in all cases and must be remanded where the offence is triable either way and the accused was first brought to court in custody or surrendered to custody or the accused had earlier been remanded.

s.142(4): Within the period of 28 days beginning ie at any time during the 28 days starting with and including the day of conviction or sentence: *cf Trow v Ind Coope* [1967] 2 All ER 900. The period cannot be extended by the clerk giving written notice of the court's intention to act under this section: *Bradburn v Richards* [1976] Crim LR 62.

A court constituted in the same manner, where the original court comprised three or more justices of the peace, the second court must consist of or comprise a majority of those justices: *Morris v Grant* [1983] RTR 433.

MENTAL HEALTH ACT 1983   8.35

Remand to Hospital for Report on Accused's Mental Condition

35. (1) Subject to the provisions of this section, the Crown Court or a magistrates' court may remand an accused person to a hospital specified by the court for a report on his mental condition.

(2) For the purposes of this section an accused person is–

(a) in relation to the Crown Court, any person who is awaiting trial before the court for an offence punishable with imprisonment or who has been arraigned before the court for such an offence and has not yet been sentenced or otherwise dealt with for the offence on which he has been arraigned;

(b) in relation to a magistrates' court, any person who has been convicted by the court of an offence punishable on summary conviction with imprisonment and any person charged with such an offence if the court is satisfied that he did the act or made the omission charged or he has consented to the exercise by the court of the powers conferred by this section.

(3) Subject to subs (4) below, the powers conferred by this section may be exercised if–

(a) the court is satisfied, on the written or oral evidence of a registered medical practitioner, that there is reason to suspect that the accused person is suffering from mental illness, psychopathic disorder, severe mental impairment or mental impairment; and

(b) the court is of the opinion that it would be impracticable for a report on his mental condition to be made if he were remanded on bail;

but those powers shall not be exercised by the Crown Court in respect of a person who has been convicted before the court if the sentence for the offence of which he has been convicted is fixed by law.

(4) The court shall not remand an accused person to a hospital under this section unless satisfied, on the written or oral evidence of the registered medical practitioner who would be responsible for making the report or of some other person representing the managers of the hospital, that arrangements have been made for his admission to that hospital and for his admission to it within the period of seven days beginning with the date of his remand; and if the court is so satisfied it may, pending his admission, give directions for his conveyance to and detention in a place of safety.

(5) Where a court has remanded an accused person under this section it may further remand him if it appears to the court, on the written or oral evidence of the registered medical practitioner responsible for making the report, that a further remand is necessary for completing the assessment of the accused person's mental condition.

(6) The power of further remanding an accused person under this section may be exercised by the court without his being brought before the court if he is represented by counsel or a solicitor and his counsel or solicitor is given an opportunity of being heard.

(7) An accused person shall not be remanded or further remanded under this section for more than 28 days at a time or for more than 12 weeks in all; and the court may at any time terminate the remand if it appears to the court that it is appropriate to do so.

(8) An accused person remanded to hospital under this section shall be entitled to obtain at his own expense an independent report on his mental condition from a registered medical practitioner chosen by him and to apply to the court on the basis of it for his remand to be terminated under subs (7) above.

(9) Where an accused person is remanded under this section–

(a) a constable or any other person directed to do so by the court shall convey the accused person to the hospital specified by the court within the period mentioned in subs (4) above; and

(b) the managers of the hospital shall admit him within that period and thereafter detain him in accordance with the provisions of this section.

(10) If an accused person absconds from a hospital to which he has been remanded under this section, or while being conveyed to or from that hospital, he may be arrested, be brought as soon as practicable before the court that remanded him; and the court may thereupon terminate the remand and deal with him in any way in which it could have dealt with him if he had not been remanded under this section.

COMMENTARY

s.35(2): An offence punishable . . . with imprisonment see s.55(2), Chapter 8c.

s.35(3): Evidence see s.54, Chapter 8c.

Psychopathic disorder/severe mental impairment/mental impairment defined in s.1 of the Act (s.145(1)); see Chapter 8c.

s.35(4): Hospital defined in s.145(1) of the Act; see Chapter 8c. For information about hospitals see s.39, Chapter 8c.

:vidence see s.54, Chapter 8c.

lace of safety, defined in s.55(1): see Chapter 8c.

.35(9): **Constable** ie a police officer of any rank.

`he manager defined in s.145(1): see Chapter 8c.

MAGISTRATES' COURT RULES 1981
(SI 1981 No 552, as amended by SI's 1982 No 245, 1983 No 523, 1984 No 1552, 1985 Nos 1695 and 1944, 1986 No 1332)

Remittals to another magistrates' court for sentence, etc.   **8.36**
   19. (1) Where a magistrates' court remits an offender to some other magistrates' court under s.39 of the Act of 1980 after convicting him of an offence, the clerk of the convicting court shall send to the clerk of the other court–
   (a) a copy signed by the clerk of the convicting court of the minute or memorandum of the conviction and remittal entered in the register;
   (b) a copy of any note of the evidence given at the trial of the offender, any written statement tendered in evidence and any deposition;
   (c) such documents and articles produced in evidence before the convicting court as have been retained by that court;
   (d) any report relating to the offender considered by the convicting court;
   (e) if the offender is remitted on bail, a copy of the record made by the convincing court in pursuance of s.5 of the Bail Act 1976 relating to such bail and also any recognizance entered into by any person as his surety;
   (f) if the convicting court makes an order under s.28 of the Theft Act 1968 (orders for restitution), a copy signed by the clerk of the convicting court of the minute or memorandum of the order entered in the register;
   (g) a copy of any legal aid order previously made in the same case;
   (h) a copy of any legal aid application; and
   (i) any statement of means already submitted.

   (2) Where a magistrates' court remits an offender to some other magistrates court as aforesaid and the other court remits him back to the convicting court under subs (5) of the said s.39, the clerk of the other court shall send to the clerk of the convicting court–
   (a) a copy signed by the clerk of the other court of the minute or memorandum of the remittal back entered in the register,
   (b) if the offender is remitted back on bail, a copy of the record made by the other court in pursuance of s.5 of the Bail Act 1976 relating to such bail and also any recognizance entered into by any person as his surety;
   (c) all documents and articles sent in pursuance of para (1).

   (3) In this rule 'the offender', 'the convicting court' and 'the other court' have the same meanings as in the said s.39.

Documents to be sent on remand for medical inquiry   **8.37**
   24. On exercising the powers conferred by s.30 of the Act of 1980 a court shall–
   (a) where the accused is remanded in custody, send to the institution or place to which he is committed;
   (b) where the accused is remanded on bail, send to the institution or place at which, or the person by whom, he is to be examined,
a statement of the reasons why the court is of opinion that an inquiry ought to be made into his physical or mental condition and of any information before the court about his physical or mental condition.

COMMENTARY
**** form of statement is recommended in HOC 113/73, and 1/75.

8.38   **Notification of conviction before expiration of period of deferment**
          27. Where under s.1 of the Powers of Criminal Courts Act 1973 a court ha
          deferred passing sentence on an offender and before the expiration of th
          period of deferment he is convicted of any offence by a magistrates' court, th
          clerk of the court shall, if the court which deferred passing sentence on th
          earlier occasion was another magistrates' court or the Crown Court, giv
          notice of the conviction to the clerk of that magistrates' court or the appro
          priate officer of the Crown Court, as the case may be.

CHAPTER 8a

Binding Over

This topic is dealt with in wider terms in Chapter 7, *Disorder and Other Interferences*

Binding Over

INTRODUCTION   8a.00

Since the earliest times it has been recognised that a magistrate has power to *bind over* persons appearing before him *to keep the peace and be of good behaviour*. This power is variously described as deriving from the common law or from his commission. In addition, there are a number of statutory powers to bind over. The oldest as well as the most widely used is contained in the Justices of the Peace Act 1361. Whether magistrates' powers may be traced to this Act or to any pre-existing law or to their commission, the statute of Edward III is, in the words of Avory J in *Lansbury v Riley* (1914) 77 JP 440, at p.442, 'not exhaustive of the jurisdiction of magistrates in such circumstances'. Often, the higher courts have 'avoided' concerning themselves with the exact source of the

power, or even whether it is civil or criminal in nature: see eg *Veater*
Glennon (1981) 72 Cr App R 331; though there is authority for saying tha
the proceedings are 'civil': see *R v Marlowe JJ ex p. O'Sullivan* (1984)
Cr App R (S) 297 (even if generally thought of as *quasi-criminal*); so tha
the civil standard of proof (ie a preponderance of probabilities – se
Chapter 6, *ante*) applies: *ibid*.

'A binding of a party is a precautionary measure to prevent a futur
crime, and is not by way of punishment for something past . . .', pe
Blackburn J in *Ex p. Davis* (1871) 35 JP 551. It is, as has frequently bee
said, an act of *preventive justice*: see the comments of Lord Goddard C.
in *Wilson v Skeock* (1949) 113 JP at p.295. Thus a person brought befor
the court 'charged' with conduct likely to cause a breach of the peace ma
not be fined: *Davies v Griffiths* (1937) 101 JP 247.

A person may be bound over, as appropriate, to keep the peace *or* to b
of good behaviour, or, more commonly, to keep the peace *and* to be o
good behaviour.

8a.01   SURETY OF THE PEACE

'Surety for the peace is the acknowledging of a recognizance (or bond) t
the King (taken by a competent judge of record) for the keeping of th
peace; and it is called surety, of the word *securitas*, because the party tha
was in fear, is thereby the more secure and safe': Dalton's *Country Justic*
at p.263, quoted by Lord Lane CJ in *Veater v Glennon* (1981) 72 Cr Ap
R 331.

It has been said that '. . . the surety of the peace shall not be granted
but where there is a fear of some present or future danger, and not merel
for a battery or trespass that is past or for any breach of the peace that i
past, for this surety of the peace is only for the security of such as are i
fear': Dalt. c.116. Thus, a threat alone is insufficient; the complainan
must actually be in fear of bodily injury: *R v Dunn* (1840) 4 JP 728; eve
though this is believed to be merely contingent, eg upon some act of th
complainant: *R v Mallinson* (1851) 15 JP 66. However, the court ma
bind over where there is evidence that an accused had behaved in such
way as to bring about a likelihood of a breach of the peace and provide
that the justices come to the conclusion that there is a danger of it
repetition: *Mercer v Cox* (1981) NLJ 2 April; but not where there is n
evidence at all before the Court to make it apprehensive of a breach of th
peace – even where the defendant is prepared to consent to the bind-over
R v Marylebone Stipendiary Magistrate, ex p. O'Kunnu (1987) *The Times*
4 November.

Surety to keep the peace may be required following the persisten
holding of meetings likely to provoke disorder: *Davies v Griffiths* (1937
101 JP 247, even where the speaker commits no breach of the peace nor
directly, incites his followers to do so, so long as disorder is the *natura*
consequence of the speaker's acts: *Wise v Dunning* (1902) 66 JP 212.

8a.02   SURETY FOR GOOD BEHAVIOUR

This is wider than surety of the peace and does not, eg require proof o
actual fear of bodily harm: *Lansbury v Riley* (1914) 77 JP 440; *R*
Sandbach Justices, ex p. Williams (1935) 99 JP 251 (apprehension only o

act contrary to law). It may be required for such acts as inciting persons not to pay their rent: *Dillon's Case* (1886) 31 SJ 136; eavesdropping *R v County of London Quarter Sessions, ex p. Metropolitan Police Commissioner* [1948] 1 KB 670, *R v Sheldon and Bromfield JJ* [1964] 2 All ER 131; in circumstances where there is apprehension that the defendant may do anything contrary to law: *R v Sandbach Justices, ex p. Williams* (1935) 99 JP 251 (persistently obstructing police); publishing a libel calculated to cause a breach of the peace: *Haylock v Sparke* (1853) 17 JP 262; 'kerb crawling' and soliciting women believing them to be prostitutes: *Hughes v Holley* (1987) 151 JP 233 (now also an offence: see ss.1 and 2 Sexual Offences Act 1985). But no one ought to be bound to be of good behaviour for any rash, quarrelsome or unmannerly words unless they either lead directly to a breach of the peace or to scandalise the government: *Hawkin's Pleas of the Crown.*

INSTITUTION OF PROCEEDINGS 8a.03

A police officer has, like any citizen, power at common law to arrest anyone committing a breach of the peace in his presence or anyone reasonably suspected of being about to commit or renew a breach of the peace in his presence. Anyone so arrested may be brought before a magistrate to be dealt with in accordance with the 1361 Act. But note that where proceedings are 'instituted by a police force', then the Crown Prosecutor is under a *duty* to take them over: s.3(2) Prosecution of Offences Act 1985, see Chapter 2.

The power of *a magistrates' court* (as opposed to the power of *a magistrate*) on the *complaint* of any person to adjudge any other person to enter into a recognizance with or without sureties to keep the peace or be of good behaviour *towards the complainant* must be exercised by order on complaint: s.115(1) MCA 1980. Although it is sometimes assumed that this statute *creates a power* to bind over it is suggested that it *is merely regulatory of the procedure to bind over under pre-existing powers*. In contrast, where a magistrate acts of his *own motion* as a measure of preventive justice there is *no need for either a complaint or a complainant* and the procedure is in the discretion of the magistrate, subject only to the rules of natural justice.

Under the procedure by way of complaint, a summons may issue under s.51 MCA 1980, and if the defendant fails to appear in answer to the summons a warrant may be issued under s.55. There is no statutory authority for the issue of a warrant at first instance, that is, without the prior issue of a summons, but it is generally considered that where a complainant satisfies a justice that he is in bodily fear, the authority given by the Commission of the Peace is sufficient to justify the issue of a warrant.

CONDUCT OF THE PROCEEDINGS 8a.04

It is important to distinguish between the court's power to act *on complaint* as governed by s.115 MCA 1980, and its power to act of its own motion under the 1361 Act. 'In the former case there must be proof, in the latter case there need not be proof of the matters complained of, but nevertheless the order cannot be made capriciously', *per* Edmund Davies LJ, in *R v Aubrey-Fletcher, ex p. Thompson* (1969) 53 Cr App R 380.

The procedure *on complaint* is laid down in ss.51–57 MCA 1980 and r.4 MC Rules 1981. At the hearing, the complainant may give evidence of *earlier conduct* of the defendant and of any *previous orders*: *R v Dunn* (1840) 4 JP 728.

8a.05   **TAKING THE RECOGNIZANCE**

The security offered by the process of binding-over consists in the *recognizance* or bond, entered into either by the principal or by his sureties or both, *per* Lord Lane CJ in *Veater v Glennon* (1981) 72 Cr App R 331. The recognizance *need not* be taken at the time but may be fixed by the court and taken later by another court or prescribed official: s.119 MCA 1980.

8a.05a   **REFUSAL TO BE BOUND OVER**

If anyone ordered by a magistrates' court under s.115 of the MCA 1980 to enter into such a recognizance fails to comply with the order the court may commit him to custody for up to six months or until he sooner complies with the order: s.115(3), *ibid*. The sanction in the case of a failure to enter into a recognizance under the 1361 Act is the same, namely imprisonment, *per* Lord Lane CJ in *Veater v Glennon, supra*. But whether the person concerned *is* prepared to enter into the recognizance and to be of good behaviour etc is the 'acid test' – and it is wrong for the court to decide not to impose an order binding over a defendant to keep the peace merely because he indicates *an intention* to continue with the acts complained of: *Lanham v Bernard; Lanham v Toye* (1986) *The Times*, 23 June.

Where a person is committed in default of finding sureties under any power the court may on fresh evidence vary or dispense with the requirement for sureties: s.118 MCA 1980.

Persons aged 17–20 cannot be committed to prison for refusing to be bound over but may be ordered to be detained under the provisions of s.9 CJA 1982: *Howley v Oxford* (1985) 81 Cr App R 246. (Refusal is a 'kindred offence' to contempt within the meaning of s.9). Those aged below 17 cannot be either imprisoned or detained on refusal to be bound over, so that the court is powerless in such a situation: *Veater v Glennon, supra*.

8a.06   **BINDING OVER WITHOUT COMPLAINT**

Magistrates have power under the 1361 Act to bind over any person appearing before them even though no formal complaint has been made against them: *Ex p. Davis* (1871) 35 JP 551; *R v Hughes* [1879] 4 QBD 614 at 625; *Wilson v Skeock* (1949) 113 JP 294. Thus, they may bind over *the complainant* for a summons to show cause why another should not be bound over: *R v Wilkins, ex p. John* (1907) 71 JP 327. Unlike a bind over on complaint under s.115 MCA 1980 this power may be exercised by a *single justice, per* Lord Lane CJ in *Veater v Glennon* (1981) 72 Cr App R 331.

It is elementary justice that particularly a mere witness should at any rate be told what is passing through the justices' minds and should have an opportunity of dealing with it, *per* Lord Parker CJ, in *Sheldon v Bromfield Justices* [1964] 2 All ER 131 at p.134; *R v Keighley Justices, ex p. Stoyles* [1976] Crim LR 573. The same principles apply *a fortiori* to a private prosecutor. When magistrates bound over both prosecutor and defendant after the latter had been convicted of an assault arising from a motoring incident *without giving either party prior opportunity to comment on this course of action*, the Divisional Court quashed by *certiorari* the order with regard to the prosecutor, Lord Widgery CJ, commenting that 'it is high time that this particular error (*ie* of failing to warn the applicant of what was in the court's mind) should be eradicated because it is the easiest thing in the world for justices contemplating binding over to say what they have in mind and to ask the intended recipient what he has to say': *R v Hendon Justices, ex p. Gorchein* (1974) 138 JP 139. In *R v Liverpool City JJ, ex p. Fraser and Fraser* (1986) *The Times*, 11 December, Watkins LJ put the position as follows: '. . . There is no such thing as natural justice unless parties are told why it is that they are being in a sense punished. One recognises, of course, that a binding over is not a punishment in the strict sense, but if for some reason or another there is a breach of the terms, then punishment can follow and sometimes quite serious punishment. . . So it is no small thing for someone to be bound over. It must always, in my judgment, be recognised by courts seeking to bind over a person before them, that there must be full explanation given to the party as to why that course is being taken and it must be plain to the justices that the parties fully understand why that course is being adopted'.

There are many instances where, although the offence is not adequately proved, the conduct of the accused has, in the opinion of the bench justified the use of preventive justice, *per* Lord Widgery CJ, in *R v Woking Justices, ex p. Gossage* [1973] 1 QB 448:

'. . . a very clear distinction is drawn between, on the one part, persons who come before the justices as witnesses, and on the other, persons who came before the justices as defendants. Not only do the witnesses come with no expected prospect of being subjected to any kind of penalty, but also witnesses as such, although they may speak in evidence, cannot represent themselves through counsel and cannot call evidence on their own behalf. By contrast, the defendant comes before the court knowing that allegations are to be made against him, knowing that he can be represented if appropriate, and knowing that he can call evidence if he wishes. It seems to me that a rule which requires a witness to be warned of the possibility of a binding-over should not necessarily apply to a defendant in that different position . . . That is not to say that it would not be wise, and indeed courteous in these cases for justices to give such a warning, there certainly would be absolutely no harm in a case like the present, if the justices, returning to court, had announced they were going to acquit, but had immediately said 'We are however contemplating a binding-over, what have you got to say?'

Justices should make a binding-over order against a prosecutor *only in an exceptional case* when facts have emerged on a plea of guilty: *R v Preston Crown Court, ex p. Pamplin* [1981] Crim LR 338. But the justices' powers to bind over do not arise only at the conclusion of the case. In *R v Aubrey-Fletcher, ex p. Thompson* (1969) 53 Cr App R 380, a defendant was charged with using insulting words at Speakers' Corner, Hyde Park. The case had to be adjourned part heard before conviction and the magistrate granted bail. Being persuaded that it would be an invalid condition of bail that the defendant should not take part in meetings at Speakers' Corner, he bound him over to keep the peace for three months in the sum of £500. Granting *certiorari* to quash this order, the Divisional Court clearly accepted that such an order could be made at that stage in the proceedings provided it had by then emerged that there was likely to be a breach of the peace in the future.

While consent does not by itself confer jurisdiction to bind over, where there is reasonable apprehension of a breach of the peace the effect of consent is to relieve the magistrates of the duty to give the person bound opportunity to show cause why this should not be done: *R v South West London Magistrates' Court ex p. Brown and Others* [1974] Crim LR 313.

8a.07   A NOTE ON DISORDER IN COURT

Prior to the Contempt of Court Act 1981 (see Chapter 7), the only order magistrates could make with respect to disorderly behaviour in court was a bind-over. This may still have a place where the 1981 Act is inappropriate or to prevent future misbehaviour. It was said in Hawk PC c.61, p.237 that surety for good behaviour could be required for *disrespectful or unmannerly expressions in the face of the court or words out of court disparaging the magistrate in his office, and of obstructing officers of the court in the execution of their duty.* Where the behaviour consists of defaming a particular justice he should not comprise the court which orders the bind-over: *R v Lee* (1701) 12 Mod 514. In the case of other behaviour *in court* there is no objection to a magistrate who has witnessed it ordering the bind-over: *R v Butt* (1957) 41 Cr App R 82, unless the behaviour is disputed, when it should be tried by a different bench.

The need for a warning does not apply where the magistrate binds over applicants seeking cross summonses who engage in *verbal argument in the face of the court* which there is fear will lead to a breach of the peace: *R v North London Metropolitan Magistrate, ex p. Haywood* [1973] 3 All ER 50.

See further under *Contempt of Court and Other Interferences*, Chapter 7.

8a.08   STATUTORY POWERS

A bind-over is not a sentence, but there are various provisions giving power to bind over *on conviction*, eg, s.38(3) CJA 1925 and s.12 PCCA 1973 (this last with consent only).

The parent or guardian of a juvenile found guilty of any offence may, with his consent, be ordered to enter into a recognizance to take proper care of him and exercise proper control over him under s.7(7) CYPA 1969. Such an order can be made in the adult court: s.7(8).

8a.09   TERMS OF THE BIND-OVER

A bind-over may be in respect of the world in general or with respect to a named individual or individuals (I *Hawkins Pleas of the Crown* 129). A 'particularized' bind-over was impliedly approved by the High Court in *Wilson v Skeock* (1949) 113 JP 294, where the order commanded that the peace be kept 'towards His Majesty and all his liege people and especially towards (the respondent).' It is not possible to insert other conditions into an order of bind-over: *R v Ayu* [1958] 1 WLR 1264; *Edward Lister v David Healey Morgan* [1978] Crim LR 292; *Goodlad v Chief Constable of South Yorkshire* [1979] Crim LR 51. Thus, it is not possible *under the 1361 Act or otherwise* to bind over a convicted offender to return to his country of origin: *R v Ayu, supra; R v East Grinstead Justices, ex p. Doeve* [1969] 1 QB 136; *R v Brixton Prison (Governor), ex p. Havlide (orse Gruschwitz)* [1969] 1 All ER 109.

'There does not seem to be any authority or case in which a limitation (*ie* of time) has not been inserted,' *per* Pickford J, in *R v Edgar* (1913) 77 JP 356, where the Court of Criminal Appeal inserted a limitation of five years in an order made by the recorder of London. Six or 12 months are the more usual periods for magistrates' orders in practice.

AMOUNT OF THE BIND-OVER   8a.10

Before imposing a bind-over of anything *other than a nominal sum* the court should make inquiry of the defendant's means: *R v Central Criminal Court, ex p. Boulding* (1984) 79 Cr App R 100. There is no rule that the amount of the recognizance shall be no greater than the maximum fine for the appropriate offence: *R v Sandbach Justices, ex p. Williams* (1935) 99 JP 251.

LEGAL AID   8a.11

Legal aid may be granted in proceedings under s.115 MCA 1980: ss.28(2) and 30(11) LAA 1974; and in forfeiture proceedings under s.120 MCA 1980: ss.28, 30(12) LAA 1974.

DISCHARGE

A surety to a bind-over may apply *by complaint* for his discharge on the ground that the principal has been or is about to be in breach of the order: s.116 MCA 1980.

FORFEITURE   8a.12

Conduct in breach of a bind-over may be punished by estreatment of recognizance: s.120 MCA 1980.

APPEAL   8a.12a

There is a specific right of appeal to the Crown Court against an order to enter into recognizances to keep the peace or be of good behaviour under the Magistrates' Courts (Appeals from Binding Over Orders) Act 1956. There is *no appeal* from an *estreatment* of recognizance: *R v Durham JJ, ex p. Laurent* (1945) 109 JP 21. There is seemingly no right of appeal against the bind-over of a parent etc under s.7(7) CYPA 1969.

Statutory Provisions

JUSTICES OF THE PEACE ACT 1361   8a.13

First, that in every county of England shall be assigned for the keeping of the peace, one lord, and with him three or four of the most worthy in the county, with some learned in the law, and they shall have power to restrain the offenders, rioters, and all other barators and to pursue, arrest, take, and chastise them according to their trespass or offence; and to cause them to be imprisoned and duly punished according to the law and customs of the

realm, and according to that which to them shall seem best to do by their discretions and good advisement . . . and to take and arrest all those that they may find by indictment, or by suspicion, and to put them in prison; and to take of all them that be [not] of good fame, where they shall be found, sufficient surety and mainprise of their good behaviour towards the King and his people, and the other duly to punish; to the intent that the people be not by such rioters or rebels troubled nor endamaged, nor the peace blemished, nor merchants nor others passing by the highways of the realm disturbed, nor [put in the peril which may happen] of such offenders.
[*as amended by Sch.3 CLA 1967*].

COMMENTARY

For procedure, enforcement and appeal *see* introduction. This Act does not create any offence, *per* Lord Goddard CJ in *R v County of London Quarter Sessions, ex p. Commissioner of Metropolitan Police* [1948] 1 All ER 72; *R v London Sessions Appeal Committee, ex p. Beaumont* [1951] 1 KB 557.

Rioters . . . barators, these words 'appear to me to mean people who create a disturbance or brawlers.' And, whether or not the word 'not' is properly inserted before the words 'of good fame', 'there is clear authority . . . that . . . justices can bind over, whether the person is or is not of good fame,' *per* Lord Goddard CJ in *R v County of London Quarter Sessions, ex p. Commissioner of Metropolitan Police, supra.*

[Not] of good fame, the negative is usually added to correct what some regard as a lacuna. For the opposite view *see* article at 145 JPN 500, and the previous note.

8a.14
MAGISTRATES' COURTS (APPEALS FROM BINDING-OVER ORDERS) ACT 1956

Right of appeal to the Crown Court
1. (1) Where, under the Justices of the Peace Act 1361, or otherwise, a person is ordered by a magistrates' court (as defined in the Magistrates' Court Act, 1980) to enter into a recognizance with or without sureties to keep the peace or to be of good behaviour, he may appeal to the Crown Court.

(2) In the case of an appeal under this section–
(a) the other party to the proceedings which were the occasion of the making of the order shall be the respondent to the appeal;
(b) in relation to an appellant in custody for failure to comply with the order, so much of s.37 of the Criminal Justice Act, 1948, as relates to the release of convicted persons from custody pending an appeal to the Crown Court shall, with the necessary adaptations, apply as if the appeal were an appeal against a conviction.

(3) Nothing in this section shall apply in relation to any order an appeal from which lies to the Crown Court apart from the provisions of this section.

(4) . . .
[*as amended by Sch.7 CJA 1967, Sch.9 Courts Act 1971, Sch.7 MCA 1980*].

COMMENTARY

For the procedure on appeal, see r.7 Crown Court Rules 1971. An appeal against a bind-over is by way of re-hearing at which fresh evidence may be called as to whether the bind-over is necessary to prevent a future breach of the peace: *Shaw v Hamilton* [1982] 2 All ER 718. For abandonment of appeal *see* s.109 MCA 1980.

s.1(2): The other party to the proceedings, the justices themselves should appear and resist an appeal if they know that there is no one else who can do so: *R v Kent Justices, ex p. Metropolitan Police Commissioner* (1936) 100 JP 17. Where justices bound over a prosecutor they were entitled to appear at the appeal in the role of *amicus curiae* and should in an appropriate case state the surrounding circumstances so far as they are not in dispute: *R v Preston Crown Court, ex p. Pamplin* [1981] Crim LR 338.

MAGISTRATES' COURT ACT 1980

Binding-over to keep the peace or be of good behaviour   8a.15
115. (1) The power of a magistrates' court on the complaint of any person
to adjudge any other person to enter into a recognizance, with or without
sureties, to keep the peace or to be of good behaviour towards the complainant
shall be exercised by order on complaint.

(2) Where a complaint is made under this section, the power of the court to
remand the defendant under subs (5) of s.55 above shall not be subject to the
restrictions imposed by subs (6) of that section.

(3) If any person ordered by a magistrates' court under subs (1) above to
enter into a recognizance, with or without sureties, to keep the peace or to be
of good behaviour fails to comply with the order, the court may commit him to
custody for a period not exceeding six months or until he sooner complies with
the order.

COMMENTARY

This provision would not appear to create a new power to bind-over, but merely to regulate
the procedure under which bind-overs are made on the application of the party as opposed
to bind-overs ordered on the court's initiative. See generally the introduction.
    Legal aid may be granted by magistrates in these proceedings: ss.28(2) and 30(11) LAA
1974.

Persons under 21, in *Howley v Oxford* (1985) 81 Cr App R 246 it was held that a refusal twice
repeated, to enter into a recognizance is an offence *kindred to contempt* within s.9(1)(c)
CJA 1982 so as to justify the fixing by the magistrates of a term of detention.

s.115(1): Magistrates' court defined in s.148(1) of the Act.

A recognizance, with or without sureties, instead of taking the recognizance at the time, the
court may fix the amount in which principal and sureties are to be bound and thereafter the
recognizances may be taken by another court or by prescribed officials: s.119 MCA 1980.
Where the offender is committed to custody in default of finding sureties, the court may
later reduce or dispense with the sureties on fresh evidence: s.118. For the forfeiture of the
recognizances see s.120.

Towards the complainant, this section appears to refer to a particularised bind-over and not
a general one.

By order on complaint, the procedure on complaint is set out in ss. 51-57 of the Act (not
reproduced herein) and in r.14 MCR 1981. Costs are accordingly available under s.64.

s.115(2), the effect of this is that the court may issue a warrant or remand the defendant
notwithstanding that he has given evidence in the proceedings. Such a remand does not
constitute bail in criminal proceedings and is not covered by the Bail Act 1976. The
defendant's own recognizance may be taken.

s.115(3): fails to comply *ie* with the order to enter into recognizances, not breach of the
recognizance. Breach of recognizances is dealt with under s.120 and not otherwise: *R v
Ossett Justices, ex p. Tebb* [1972] Crim LR 39.

Commit him to custody, this means commit *to prison* or, where any enactment authorises or
requires committal to some other place of detention instead of committal to prison, to that
other place: s.150(1) of the Act. Committals to prison must be by warrant: r.94 MC Rules
1981. The requirement as to sureties may be varied or dispensed with by virtue of s.118,
infra.

Discharge of recognizance to keep the peace or be of good behaviour on   8a.16
complaint of surety.
    116. (1) On complaint being made to a justice of the peace for any area to
which this section applies by a surety to a recognizance to keep the peace or to
be of good behaviour entered into before a magistrates' court that the person
bound by the recognizance as principal has been, or is about to be, guilty of
conduct constituting a breach of the conditions of the recognizance, the justice
may, if the complaint alleges that the principal is, or is believed to be, in that

area, or if the recognizance was entered into before a magistrates' court for that area, issue a warrant to arrest the principal and bring him before a magistrates' court for that area or a summons requiring the principal to appear before such a court; but the justice shall not issue a warrant unless the complaint is in writing and substantiated on oath.

(2) The magistrates' court before which the principal appears or is brought in pursuance of such a summons or warrant as aforesaid may, unless it adjudges the recognizance to be forfeited, order the recognizance to be discharged and order the principal to enter into a new recognizance, with or without sureties, to keep the peace or to be of good behaviour.

(3) The areas to which this section applies are any county, any London commission area and the City of London.

COMMENTARY
s.116(1): Complaint, the procedure on complaint is set out in ss.51–57 and r.14 MC Rules 1981.

s.116(2): Forfeited ie under s.120.

Discharged, the clerk must send a copy of the order to the clerk of the court which made the order: r.82 MC Rules 1981.

8a.17 **Varying or dispensing with requirement as to sureties**
118. (1) Subject to subs (2) below, where a magistrates' court has committed a person to custody in default of finding sureties, the court may, on application by or on behalf of the person committed, and after hearing fresh evidence, reduce the amount in which it is proposed that any surety should be bound or dispense with any of the sureties or otherwise deal with the case as it thinks just.

(2) Subsection (1) above does not apply in relation to a person granted bail in criminal proceedings.

COMMENTARY
For order see Form 117.

s.118(1): The court a court of the same petty sessions area, even though composed of a different justice or justices: s.148(2) of the Act.

On application by complaint: r.83 MC Rules 1981. For summons, *see* Form 117.

Fresh evidence a restrictive view of this term has been adopted in the civil law as meaning something which has occurred subsequent to the original hearing and which was unknown to the party at that time: *see* eg *Johnson v Johnson* (1900) 64 JP 72; *Weightman v Weightman* (1906) 70 JP 120; and *Cross v Cross* (1935) 95 JP 86. It is difficult to believe that the legislature would have used this technical term in a 1952 statute – re-enacted in 1980 – (changing it from the former 'new evidence') otherwise than deliberately.

s.118(2): Bail in criminal proceedings defined in s.150(1) as having the same meaning as in the Bail Act 1976.

8a.18 **Forfeiture of recognizance**
120. (1) Where a recognizance to keep the peace or to be of good behaviour has been entered into before a magistrates' court or any recognizance is conditioned for the appearance of a person before a magistrates' court or for his doing any other thing connected with a proceeding before a magistrates' court, and the recognizance appears to the court to be forfeited, the court may, subject to subs (2) below, declare the recognizance to be forfeited and adjudge the persons bound thereby, whether as principal or sureties, or any of them, to pay the sum in which they are respectively bound.

(2) Where a recognizance is conditioned to keep the peace or to be of good behaviour, the court shall not declare it forfeited except by order made on complaint.

(3) The court which declares the recognizance to be forfeited may, instead of adjudging any person to pay the whole sum in which he is bound, adjudge him to pay only part of the sum or remit the sum.

(4) Payment of any sum adjudged to be paid under this section, including any costs awarded against the defendant, may be enforced, and any such sum shall be applied, as if it were a fine and as if the adjudication were a summary conviction of an offence not punishable with imprisonment and so much of s.85(1) above as empowers a court to remit fines shall not apply to the sum but so much thereof as relates to remission after a term of imprisonment has been imposed shall so apply; but at any time before the issue of a warrant of commitment to enforce payment of the sum, or before the sale of goods under a warrant of distress to satisfy the sum, the court may remit the whole or any part of the sum either absolutely or on such conditions as the court thinks just.

(5) A recognizance such as is mentioned in this section shall not be enforced otherwise than in accordance with this section, and accordingly shall not be transmitted to the Crown Court nor shall its forfeiture be certified to that Court.

COMMENTARY

Declare the recognizance forfeited, there is no right of appeal to the Crown Court against an order to forfeit a recognizance: *R v Durham Justices, ex p. Laurent* (1945) 109 JP 21. But *certiorari* will lie where an error in law is disclosed in the affidavits: *R v Southampton Justices, ex p. Green* [1975] 3 WLR 277.

s.120(2): By order made on complaint, for order, see Form 133. The effect of these words is that to forfeit a recognizance to keep the peace or be of good behaviour a summons may be issued under s.51 of the Act and the hearing must follow the procedure laid down in ss.53–57 and r.14 MC Rules 1981. *Certiorari* will issue to quash an order of forfeiture made without complaint: *R v Ossett Justices, ex p. Tebb* [1972] Crim LR 39. Proceedings for a bind-over are *civil proceedings* and the civil standard of proof is appropriate: *R v Marlowe Justices, ex p. O'Sullivan* (1984) 5 Cr App R (S) 297.

The person summoned must be told precisely what it was he had been bound over to do: in what way it is alleged that he has failed to comply with his promise. Clear evidence must be given of the nature of the breach alleged. Most important, the defendant must be asked whether he desires to give evidence and explain his conduct, whether he has any witnesses to call; whether he has any explanation to make: *R v McGregor* (1945) 109 JP 136. The mere fact that a man the subject of a bind-over consents to a bind-over on a subsequent charge (which was not proceeded with) does not amount to an admission of a breach of the peace justifying forfeiture of the earlier recognizance: *Jackson v Lilley* (1982) 146 JP 132.

Legal aid may be granted in proceedings for failing to comply with a recognizance to keep the peace or be of good behaviour: ss.28 and 30(12) LLA 1974.

s.120(4): Costs, costs may, by virtue of subs (2) be awarded to the successful party under s.64 but costs may also be awarded out of central funds under the Prosecution of Offences Act 1985: see Chapter 9, *post.*

Enforced as if it were a fine, notice must be given to a defendant if he is absent or time to pay is allowed: r.46 MC Rules 1981. An order of discharge in bankruptcy does not release the debt on the recognizance: s.28(1)(c) Bankruptcy Act 1914.

Remit recognizances estreated by higher courts may not be remitted by magistrates except with the permission of that court: s.47(8) CJA 1967. Any order of remission must be entered in the register or separate record: r.65 MC Rules 1981.

MAGISTRATES' COURTS RULES 1981

(SI 1981 No 552, as amended by SI 1982 No 245, SI 1983 No 523, SI 1984 No 1552, SI 1985 Nos 1695 and 1944 and 1986 No 1332)

Recognizance to keep the peace etc, taken by one court and discharged by another   **8a.19**

82. Where a magistrates' court acting for any petty sessions area makes an order under s.116 of the Act of 1980 discharging a recognizance entered into before a magistrates' court acting for any other petty sessions area, the clerk of

the court that orders the recognizance to be discharged shall send a copy of the order of discharge to the clerk of the court acting for that other petty sessions area.

8a.20   **Application to vary order for sureties or dispense with them**
   83. Where a person has been committed to custody in default of finding sureties and the order to find sureties was made at the instance of another person, an application under s.118 of the Act of 1980 shall be made by complaint against that other person.

COMMENTARY
By complaint ie in accordance with ss.51–57 of the MCA 1980.

CHAPTER 8b

Fines, Compensation and Property Orders

Note that sentences of youth custody and detention centre orders are both replaced by 'a sentence of detention in a young offender institution', by means of a new s.1(3) CJA 1982, inserted by [s.121] CJA 1988, when in force: see Appendix III and the insertions under statutory provisions in Chapter 8d. For confiscation orders see [s.70–88] of the 1988 Act: Appendix III.

Fines, Compensation and Property Orders

8b.00   INTRODUCTION

The fine is far and away the most commonly used penalty in magistrates' courts, whilst compensation is now a sentence in its own right should the court see fit to use it: see s.35(1) PCCA 1973. The Judicial Studies Board has issued the following advice concerning the two measures and the correct approach to their use:

Compensation and Fines

1. A compensation order may be combined with any of the other penalties, and if combined with a fine takes priority.

2. Compensation can only be awarded when the amount or the facts upon which it is to be assessed are undisputed or properly proved by evidence.

3. Consider the defendant's ability to pay; instalments should permit payments to be completed in 12 months.

4. Beware excessive total where a number of offences are charged (especially applied to Road Traffic Cases).

5. Have regard to consequences of disqualification, if defendant's means will be affected.

6. Consider fixing review of payments.

7. Can a term in default be fixed? If so, should this be done?

The Structure of a Decision (1987).

All these matters are treated within the text at appropriate points.

8b.01   THE FINE

Magistrates cannot impose unlimited fines, a maximum is prescribed by law for every offence. For an indictable offence tried in a magistrates' court this is 'the prescribed sum' laid down in s.32 MCA 1980 (ie level 5), except in the case of certain *criminal damage* offences *triable only summarily* by virtue of s.22 for which the maximum fine is laid down in s.33 (ie 3 months or £1000).

The Standard Scale   8b.02

There is a standard scale of fines for summary offences as follows:

Level on the scale	Amount of fine
1	£50
2	£100
3	£400
4	£1,000
5	£2,000

.37(2) CJA 1982. References in any enactment to a fine *on the standard cale* are to be construed accordingly: s.37(3).

Juveniles   8b.03

There is an overriding maximum fine for *young persons* of £400: ss.24(3), 6(1) MCA 1980; and for children of £100: ss.24(4) and 36(2).

Means of the offender   8b.04

A magistrates' court is required in *fixing* the amount of a fine to take into onsideration the means of the offender so far as they appear or are known to the court: s.35 MCA 1980. Notwithstanding the requirement to have regard to means in *fixing the fine*, fines cannot be *increased* on ccount of the offender's means, *infra*. This is the position in the Crown Court where there is no equivalent of s.35. Contrary to the accepted wisdom, there is, on a plain reading of that provision, at least an arguable ase that fines can be increased for the wealthy in magistrates courts: see the argument advanced by JB Jenkins at (1987) 151 JPN 515.

The means of the offender must be investigated before the amount of he fine is fixed: *R v Rizvi* (1979) 1 Cr App R (S) 307: it is not enough imply to adjust the rate of payment. Although there is no clear pro-ouncement on this, the balance of judicial authority is probably best ummarized by Devlin (*Sentencing Offenders in Magistrates' Courts* at .69): 'Although the fine may be mitigated by the offender's lack of neans, it cannot be inflated by his wealth.' (And see also Thomas at 1967] Crim LR 523 and his commentary on the case of *R v Tester* [1969] Crim LR 274 at p.275 and the case of *R v Fairbairn* [1981] Crim LR 190). n considering the offender's means the court is not necessarily confined o his present capacity: *R v Lewis* [1965] Crim LR 121. But it is wrong to ake account of the means of the offender's wife: *R v Baxter* [1974] Crim LR 611 or family: *R v Charalambous* [1985] Crim LR 328. It is suggested owever that any income of a dependant may be relevant as offsetting the offender's liability to maintain that person.

Save in exceptional circumstances it is desirable that fines should be apable of being paid *within 12 months* or thereabout: *R v Hewitt* (1971) 5 Cr App R 433; *R v Knight* (1980) 2 Cr App R (S) 82; *R v Owen* [1984] Crim LR 436; *R v Nunn* (1984) 5 Cr App R (S) 203. This places a practical eiling upon the fine which may be imposed on many offenders. But there s no reason why a fine should not 'mop-up' the proceeds of profit made by ot complying with the law: see *R v Garner* (1985) 7 Cr App R (S) 285.

COMPENSATION   8b.05

Upon conviction of any offence a court may, *instead of or in addition to* dealing with the offender in any other way, make a compensation order equiring him to pay compensation for any personal injury, loss, or

damage resulting from that offence or any other offence taken int
consideration: s.35(1) PCCA 1973. Compensation may thus be impose
as an order ancillary to sentence or as a sentence in its own right. Wher
the court considers that it would be appropriate both to impose a fine an
make a compensation order but the offender has insufficient means to pa
both the court must give preference to compensation, though it ma
impose a fine as well: s.35(4A). *Note* also the strengthened compensatio
provisions in [ss.102–103] CJA 1988, when in force, which, *inter alia*, wi
require the court to give reasons where it does not make a compensatio
order in circumstances where it is empowered to do so: see Appendix II
and the insertions to ss. 35–38 PCCA 1973 at 8b.65.

A compensation order may be made on application or on the court'
own motion: *ibid*, s.35(1). It must be of such amount as the cou
considers appropriate having regard to any evidence and representation
made by the parties: s.35(1A). A plea of guilty to a charge which contain
some specific value does not fix the offender with acceptance of that valu
for the purposes of compensation: *R v Kneeshaw* (1974) 58 Cr App R 43ᶜ
'. . . it would be expecting too much of an accused man to have this issu
in mind at such an early stage of the trial and to hold it against him as if h
had relinquished any right to argue the extent (of the property stolen)
per Lord Widgery CJ, *ibid*.

In a magistrates' court the amount of a compensation order may no
exceed £2,000 in respect of any offence of which the court has convicted th
offender: s.40 MCA 1980. A compensation order may include any damag
accruing to the property while out of the owner's possession by whomsc
ever caused in the case of offences under the Theft Act 1968: s.35(2) bu
except in these cases a motor vehicle accident may not be the subject of
compensation order: s.35(3)). Loss suffered by dependants of the dead i
excluded: s.35(3). Where applicable, it is in order for the court to hav
regard to the figures published by the Criminal Injuries Compensatio
Board: *R v Broughton* (1986) 8 Cr App R (S) 379. Normally the amoun
should be payable within a year: see under *Means, infra*.

The machinery of the compensation order is intended for clear an
simple cases, *per* Lord Widgery CJ in *R v Kneeshaw* (1974) 58 Cr App I
439. It must be remembered that the civil rights of the victim remain. In
great majority of cases the appropriate court to deal with the extent of th
loss is in the appropriate civil proceedings, *per* Lord Widgery CJ in *R
Kneeshaw, supra*. And see *R v Daly* (1974) 138 JP 245; *R v Grundy* (1974
138 JP 242. Compensation for loss of a hired car was quashed in *R
Donovan* [1982] RTR 126 because the amount of damages in such a cas
is notoriously open to argument. It is inappropriate where goods ar
recovered undamaged: *R v Boardman* [1987] Crim LR 430.

It is *inappropriate* to make a *substantial compensation order* togethe
with a significant sentence of *immediate imprisonment* because if a man i
saddled with such an order which he will have to meet when he comes ou
of prison he will be tempted to return to crime to meet it. If there is reaso
to suppose, that he has *proceeds of his crime* (or presumably othe
capital), that is a different matter, *per* Dunn LJ, in *R v Morgan* (1982)
Cr App R (S) 358.

8b.06   Means of the offender

In determining whether to make a compensation order and the amount t
be paid thereunder the court must have regard to the offender's means s
far as they are known to the court: s.35(4) PCCA 1973.

As long as a man has his normal health and is capable of earning something it is perfectly proper to make an order against him even though he is temporarily unemployed, although the court may have to be restricted by reason of the probability that his earnings will be small, *per* Lord Widgery CJ in *R v Bradburn* (1973) 57 Cr App R 948. In saying this Lord Widgery was merely inviting courts to keep in mind all the common sense features, and rehabilitation is one of these. Section 35(4) does not assimilate the principles on which compensation is assessed to those used for the assessment of fines, but orders should not be counterproductive in the sense that they result in the accused committing further offences in order to pay: *R v Oddy* (1974) 138 JP 515; and see *R v Miller* (1979) 68 Cr App R 56 at 57. Subject to this rule, it is not improper to make a compensation order, even when a person has been sentenced to a substantial term of imprisonment: *R v Wylie* [1975] RTR 94. In *R v Dallas-Cope* (1975) 139 JPN 171, the Court of Appeal upheld a trial judge's decision to treat as the appellant's means *money which his father said he was prepared to pay*. Potential earning capacity may be considered: *R v Ford* [1976] Crim LR 14. The court must take a broad picture of the defendant's assets; it need not make a precise calculation: *R v Howell* (1978) 66 Cr App R 179. In *R v Workman* (1979) 1 Cr App R (S) 335, a Crown Court compensation order was upheld where the offender had bought a house with the proceeds of crime even though there was no evidence that she could pay within a reasonable time.

The 'twelve-month rule' applies to the payment of compensation orders as it does to fines: *R v Holden* [1985] Crim LR 397; *R v Hills* (1986) 8 Cr App R (S) 199; although it is not a 'hard and fast' rule: *R v Broughton* (1986) 8 Cr App R (S) 379. Longer periods have been ordered in special cases: see *R v Making* (1982) 4 Cr App R (S) 180 – 2 years; *R v Pellant* (1984) *The Times*, 16 March – 90 weeks.

Discharge   8b.07

The court may at any later time *discharge* a compensation order or *reduce the amount payable in the light of civil proceedings or any recovery of property*: s.37 PCCA 1973. The effect of the order on civil proceedings is described in s.38. *Note* the new ss.37 and 38 substituted by [s.103] CJA 1988, 8b.67 and 8b.68.

Collection and enforcement   8b.08

A compensation order is treated for purposes of collection and enforcement *as if adjudged to be paid on a conviction* by a magistrates' court: s.41 Sch.9 Administration of Justice Act 1970. But see s.36 of the 1973 Act under which compensation orders are suspended pending appeal and note the new s.36 substituted by [s.103] CJA 1988: see 8b.66. The effect of a compensation order on any subsequent award of damages is dealt with in s.38, 8b.68.

PARENT'S RESPONSIBILITY FOR A JUVENILE   8b.09

The *parent or guardian* of a juvenile *must* be ordered to pay any fine, compensation or costs ordered: s.55(1) CYPA 1933. This duty does not arise if the court is satisfied that,

(a) the parent or guardian cannot be found; or
(b) that in the circumstances of the case it would be unreasonable to do

so. The parent or guardian must first be given *an opportunity c being heard* unless, having been required to attend, he has failed t do so: s.55(3).

Note [s.125] CJA 1988 which extends s.55(1) to fines imposed fc *breach of supervision* and *breach of community service:* see 8b.37 an Appendix III.

8b.10   **RESTITUTION**

Magistrates have power under s.28 Theft Act 1968 to order the restitutio of

(a) stolen property (as widely defined in s.24 of the Act); or
(b) of goods directly or indirectly representing stolen goods; or
(c) of the offender's money taken from him on arrest representing th value of the goods; or may make any combination of those orders

When an order is made under (a) above, the court may also order th payment out of the offender's money of a sum not greater than th amount by which the offender sold the goods to a purchaser in good fait or raised money on them from a lender in good faith: s.28(3). This powe extends to offences taken into consideration: s.6(3), (4) CJA 1972. Bu see the commentary to s.28(4) at 8b.40 concerning the factual basis fo such an order.

Note that under s.28(7) Theft Act 1968, as added by [s.155] CJA 1988 when in force, restitution orders can be made against the Crown: se 8b.40.

8b.11   **DEPRIVATION OF PROPERTY ORDER**

A magistrates' court convicting anyone of *an offence punishable o indictment with not less than two year's imprisonment* may, in addition t any other sentence or order, make an order under s.43 PCCA 197 depriving the offender of his rights in any property which:

(a) was in his possession or under his control at the time of his appre hension; and
(b) which had been used for the purpose of committing or facilitatin the commission of any offence; or
(c) was intended by him for that purpose.

The taking of steps *after* an offence has been committed for the purpos of disposing of any property to which it relates or of avoiding appre hension or detection is to be regarded as facilitating the commission of th offence: s.42(2). Orders under s.43 have been upheld by the Court o Appeal when the use of the property was an integral part of the offence: *I v Lidster* [1976] RTR 240 (car necessary to transport goods away fror place of theft); but not when the offence was committed on the spur of th moment: *R v Miele* [1976] RTR 238. Like a compensation order, deprivation of property order should not be made if there are compli cating factors: *R v Troth* [1980] RTR 389 (partnership property). Th court should consider *the value of any property to be forfeited* so that together with any fine imposed, it does not represent an undue penalty or the accused; *R v Miele, supra.* The intention of s.43 is to provide ar *additional* penalty: *R v Kingston upon Hull Stipendiary Magistrate, ex p*

Hartung [1981] RTR 262 (order that proceeds of sale of van be applied to fine and compensation with balance to defendant quashed). It is not intended as a compensation provision: *R v Thibault* (1983) 147 JP 173. The power does not extend to real property: *R v Khan* [1982] 3 All ER 969. It refers to the *accoutrements* of crime, ie the tools, instruments, or other physical means used to commit the crime. It does not extend to property used by others: *R v Slater* (1986) 8 Cr App R (S) 217.

Not later than six months from the date of the order anyone may apply to a magistrates' court for an order under the Police (Property) Act 1897 if he can satisfy the court that he did not consent to the offender having possession of the property or did not know and had no reason to suspect that it was to be used for the prohibited purpose: s.43(4) PCCA 1973.

Note [s.68] CJA 1988 which, when in force, substitutes a new s.43(1) and (1A), and [s.105] which adds a new s.43A to the 1973 Act and under which the proceeds of forfeiture may be ordered to be paid to victims of 'personal injury, loss or damage' where the offender's means are inadequate for a compensation order: see 8b.69 and Appendix III.

RIGHT OF APPEAL 8b.12

There is a specific right of appeal to the Crown Court against the making of fines, compensation, restitution and deprivation orders: s.108 MCA 1980.

It would be 'exceedingly improper' to issue process to enforce a fine where notice of appeal has been lodged: *Kendall v Wilkinson* (1855) 19 JP 467. In the case of both compensation and, with certain exceptions, restitution orders enforcement is stayed automatically until the expiry of the normal time for appeal or the determination of any appeal entered: s.36(2) PCCA 1973 and s.6(5) CJA 1972, respectively.

PROPERTY IN POSSESSION OF POLICE 8b.13

When any property has come into the possession of police in connection with their investigation of a suspected offence or under certain statutes a magistrates' court may order its delivery to the apparent owner or, if he cannot be ascertained, make any other order with respect to the property as may seem meet: s.1 Police (Property) Act 1897. Justices are discouraged from using this procedure in cases which involve a *real issue of law* or *any real difficulty* in determining whether a *particular person was or was not the owner: Raymond Lyons and Co Ltd v Metropolitan Police Commissioner* (1975) 139 JP 213.

Except by way of *case stated*, there is no right of appeal against an order under this Act: *Stupple JW & FT v Royal Insurance Co Ltd* [1970] 1 All ER 390. Civil proceedings may however be instituted, but not later than six months after the order: s.1(2) Police (Property) Act 1897.

ARRESTED PERSONS' PROPERTY 8b.14

A magistrates' court has power under s.48 MCA 1980 to *direct the return* of property taken from an accused person on arrest without warrant or after the issue of process where this is consistent with the interests of justice and the safe custody of the accused.

TIME TO PAY 8b.15

A fine or other sum ordered by the court is payable *immediately*. However, the court may *allow time for payment* or order payment *by instalments* of any sum adjudged to be paid by conviction: s.75(1) MCA 1980. When payment by instalment is ordered enforcement proceedings may be brought if there is default in any one payment: s.75(3). Further time to pay may be allowed under s.75(2), and instalments may be varied under s.85A. In practice, applications under these provisions are *usually made to the justices' clerk* who may make similar orders under the Justices' Clerks Rules 1970 (SI No 231). When time is allowed for payment or payment is allowed in instalments the court may at the time *fix a day on which, if the court's order is not complied with, the defaulter must attend court for a means inquiry or hearing*: s.86.

8b.16   SEARCH

When a magistrates' court has adjudged a sum to be paid by a conviction, it may order that the offender be searched. Any money found on him may, unless the court otherwise directs, be applied towards payment: s.80 MCA 1980.

8b.17   TRANSFER OF FINE

When a person has been adjudged by a summary conviction to pay a sum and *it appears that he is resident in a different petty sessions area*, the court may make a transfer of fine order making payment enforceable in the other area: s.89 MCA 1980. The 'other court' may make a further transfer of fine order: s.89(3). A transfer of fine order may be made to and from courts in Scotland and Northern Ireland: ss.90, 91. In practice most transfer of fine orders are made by the justices' clerk under the Justices Clerks Rules 1970.

8b.18   MONEY PAYMENT SUPERVISION ORDER

A person adjudged to pay a sum by a summary conviction may be placed under the supervision of such person as the court may from time to time appoint: s.88(1) MCA 1980. Such an order may be made *on conviction* or *subsequently*. A defaulter *under 21* years of age may not be committed to detention unless first placed under such supervision except where the court is satisfied that it is *undesirable* or *impracticable*: s.88(4).

8b.19   ENFORCEMENT

There is a common system for the enforcement of *all sums adjudged to be paid by a conviction of a magistrates' court*, a term which includes, not only the fine, but also costs and compensation: s.150(3) MCA 1980 and for 'confiscation orders' see [s.74] CJA 1988, when in force: Appendix III. The following sanctions are available to secure payment:

Attendance at an attendance centre: see 8c.00
Detention in police cells etc: see the table at 8d.53 and 8d.73
Distraint of goods: see 8b.21
Imprisonment: see 8b.22
A garnishee order: see 8b.28
Attachment of earnings: see 8b.30

It may be doubted whether it is open to a justices' clerk to bring proceedings to wind up a limited company as a means of enforcing a fine:

cf *Re a Company* (1915) 1 Ch 520 but *note* the new s.87A MCA 1980 inserted by [s.61] CJA 1988, when in force, which will enable this: see 8b.90 and Appendix III.

In addition 'road traffic' fines due from 'foreign lorry drivers' may be enforced by the informal method of notifying the Department of Transport that fines are outstanding and requesting that Department to ask the defaulter's home state to issue an 'exclusion order' under bilateral European agreements: see HOC 1/1987, reproduced at 8b.34.

Note [s.64] CJA 1988, when in force, will enable the execution of warrants by 'civilian enforcement officers' and [s.66] which makes fines imposed by coroners enforceable as if imposed by magistrates: see Appendix III.

Notice of fine   8b.20

Neither a warrant of distress nor a warrant of commitment may be issued until a *notice of fine* has been served on the offender where:

(a) the court is enforcing a Crown Court or coroner's court order;
(b) time was allowed for payment or payment by instalment was ordered; or
(c) where the offender was absent when the sum was adjudged to be paid: r.46(1) MC Rules 1981.

Distraint of goods   8b.21

Where defaults is made the court may issue a distress warrant: s.76(1) Magistrates' Courts Act 1980. The issue of such a warrant may be *postponed until such time and on such conditions as the court thinks just*: s.78.

For the rules governing warrants of distress see r.54 MC Rules 1981. For defects in a warrant of distress and irregularity in execution see s.78 MCA 1980. A distress warrant may be executed anywhere in England and Wales: s.125. Justices may refuse to issue a warrant of distress where it is known that there are no goods: *R v German* (1892) 56 JP 258.

There is *no authority for the use of force* in entering under a distress warrant, but entry may be gained by an unsecured door or window: *Long v Clarke* (1894) 58 JP 150, or by opening an outer door in the usual manner: *Ryan v Shilock* (1851) 16 JP 213. A closed but unsecured window may not be opened: *Nash v Lucas* (1867) LR 2 QB 590, but a partly opened window may be further opened: *Crabtree v Robinson* (1885) 50 JP 70. Once inside, an internal door may be forced: *Browning v Dann* (1735) 95 ER 107 (all cases of *landlord's right of distress*).

It has been said *obiter* that in order to exercise their discretion whether to enforce payment by prison or distraint of goods justices *must inquire into the means of the defaulter*. For distress, however, they do not have to be satisfied that there is no doubt about the defaulter's ability to pay. If the evidence reveals that there is a *reasonable likelihood* that the defaulter has assets available to satisfy the sum he owes, justices should proceed by way of distress rather than by way of committing the defaulter to prison. It should be borne in mind that in the case of a defaulter already serving a prison sentence, a concurrent prison sentence is no penalty at all: *R v Birmingham Justices, ex p. Bennett* (1983) 147 JP 279.

Imprisonment   8b.22

Where default is made the court may issue a warrant committing the defaulter to prison: s.76(1) MCA 1980. A warrant may issue *either* where the return on a distress warrant has been insufficient *or* instead of a distress warrant: s.76(2). The period for which a person may be committed to prison may not exceed the period set out in Sch.4: s.76(2). Consecutive terms may be imposed by virtue of s.133, but see the commentary to s.76(3). The court may *not* impose imprisonment for *less than five days*: s.132; but committals following part payment are not subject to the rule: r.55(5) MC Rules 1981.

Where a court has power to issue a warrant of commitment it may, *if it thinks it expedient to do so*, fix a term of imprisonment or detention and postpone the issue of the warrant until such time and on such conditions as it thinks just: s.77(2) MCA 1980. Where the issue of a warrant of commitment is suspended, it may not be issued thereafter unless the defaulter has been given an opportunity to make further representations to the court: see the cases mentioned under *Means inquiry* at 8b.24 and *note* [s.60] CJA 1988, when in force, which extends ss.77 and 82 and, *inter alia*, introduces a statutory code of procedure: see 8b.79, 8b.83 and Appendix III.

See also *Notice of fine* at 8b.20.

8b.23 Restrictions on commencement

At the time of conviction a warrant of commitment may issue in respect of a defaulter *only*:

(a) in the case of an offence punishable with *imprisonment* if the defaulter appears to have *sufficient means to pay forthwith*:

(b) it appears that he is *unlikely to remain long enough* at a place of abode in the United Kingdom *to enable payment to be enforced* by other methods; or

(c) he is sentenced to or is *already serving a custodial sentence*: s.82(1) MCA 1980.

After conviction such a warrant may issue *only*:

(a) when the defaulter is *serving a custodial sentence*; or

(b) *after a means inquiry* (see 8b.24): s.82(3) MCA 1980.

8b.24 Means inquiry before commitment

After conviction a warrant of commitment may not be issued or a term of imprisonment fixed in default except at a hearing at which the defaulter is present unless,

(a) he is in breach of postponed terms; or

(b) he is serving a custodial sentence:

These exceptions do not mean that the defaulter is not entitled to a hearing, merely that he is not *entitled* to be present at such a hearing. The cases which follow establish that he is entitled to make *representations* before the issue of the warrant. Good practice demands an actual hearing wherever possible, but as a minimum, since the issue of a warrant of commitment is a judicial act, natural justice requires that notice be given to the defaulter of an intention to issue such a warrant: *Re Hamilton; Re Forrest* [1981] AC 1038; *sub nom Forrest v Brighton Justices; Hamilton v Marylebone Magistrates' Court* (1981) 145 JP 356. Although this decision dealt only with warrants issued in the circumstances of para (b) of s.82(5) it applies equally to warrants issued under para (a): *Re Wilson* [1985] 2

WLR 694. The principle applies where the court adjourns the hearing and in the interim there has been a new development such as fresh information on which he may wish to comment: *R v Steyning Magistrates' Court, ex p. Hunter* (1985) 150 JP 129.

Attendance of a defaulter at a means inquiry may be secured by the issue of a summons or warrant: s.83(1). Either before or at the inquiry the magistrates' court, a justice of the peace or the justices' clerk may order the defaulter to furnish to the court, within a specified period, such statement of his means as the court may require: s.84(1) Justices' Clerks Rules 1970 (SI No 231). Any written statement of wages by an employer is evidence in the inquiry: s.100 MCA 1980.

When a means inquiry is held the warrant may not issue except,

(a) in the case of an offence punishable with *imprisonment* the defaulter appears to have *sufficient means to pay forthwith*; or
(b) the court
   (i) is satisfied that the default is due to the offender's *wilful refusal or culpable neglect*; and
   (ii) has *considered or tried all other methods* of enforcing payment and they appear inappropriate or unsuccessful: ss.77(2), 82(2) MCA 1980. *Note* that both (i) and (ii) must be satisfied. Thus, eg even '*wilful refusal*' does not relieve the court from considering or trying '*all other methods R v Norwich Justices, ex p. Tigger (formerly Lilly)* (1987) *The Times*, 26 June.

Note the methods of enforcement are listed in [s.60(3)] CJA 1988, when in force, which adds a new subs (4A) to s.82 MCA 1980: see 8b.83 and Appendix III. *Note* also the statutory code to be introduced by the 1988 Act.

Part payment   8b.25

When a defaulter has been imprisoned for his default payment of the sum due will secure his release: s.79(1) MCA 1980. Part payment secures a proportionate reduction of the term calculated in accordance with s.79(2), (3).

Defaulter under 21 years   8b.26

In the case of a defaulter *under 21*, references to detention under s.9 CJA 1982 are to be substituted for references to prison: s.96A MCA 1980. Anyone committed to such detention is to be detained in a remand centre, detention centre, youth custody centre or certain other places as the Secretary of State may from time to time direct: s.12(1) CJA 1982. A defaulter may not be so detained unless the court is of the opinion that *no other method of dealing with him is appropriate*: s.1(5). The alternative of detention under s.9 may not be imposed or a warrant of distress issued in the case of a defaulter under 21 *unless he has been placed under supervision in respect of the sum or the court is satisfied that supervision is undesirable or impracticable*: s.88(4) MCA 1980. Where a supervision order is made the defaulter may not be committed to custody without taking all reasonable steps to obtain a report: s.88(6).

Scotland and Northern Ireland   8b.27

Warrants of commitment to prison for fine default etc issued in England and Wales may be executed in Scotland or Northern Ireland and *vice versa*: Criminal Law Act 1977, ss.37A and 37B CLA 1977, respectively.

8b.28   Garnishee order

Payment of a sum adjudged to be paid by a conviction or order of magistrates' court may be enforced by the High Court and county court as if the sum were due to the clerk of the magistrates' court in pursuance of a judgment or order of the High Court or county court: s.87(1) MCA 1980. This authority does not extend to the issue of a writ of *fieri facias* or other process against goods or by imprisonment or attachment of earnings because these proceedings are available in the magistrates' court. In other situations, the justices' clerk ranks and stands in the same position as a judgment creditor, *semble* see *Gooch v Ewing (Allied Irish Bank Ltd, Garnishee)* [1985] 3 All ER 654.

The clerk must first be authorised by the court to bring these proceedings after a means inquiry: s.87(3).

8b.29   Remission

A fine may be remitted *in whole or in part* at a means inquiry if the court thinks it just to do so having regard to any change in the offender's circumstances since the conviction: MCA s.85(1). 'Fine' is defined narrowly in this context: s.85(2). Crown Court fines and recognizances may not be remitted except with the *consent* of that court: s.32(4) PCCA 1973.

A new s.85 MCA 1980 is substituted by [s.60] CJA 1988, when in force: see 8b.87 and Appendix III.

8b.30   ATTACHMENT OF EARNINGS

The procedure for making and administering attachment of earnings orders in all types of courts and proceedings is contained in the Attachment of Earnings Act 1971. The Act is supplemented so far as magistrates' courts are concerned by the Magistrates' Courts (Attachment of Earnings) Rules 1971 (SI No 809). References are to the 1971 Act and Rules. Only the provisions relevant to the *criminal jurisdiction of magistrates* are reproduced herein.

Attachment of earnings is a procedure under which the court may order an employer to deduct money from the earnings of the debtor. Sums which can be recovered include:

— fines and other sums adjudged to be paid on conviction
— sums treated as so adjudged, a term which includes costs, compensation, and recognizances, and
— legal aid contribution orders: s.1.

An attachment of earnings order may be made:

— on the application of the debtor or, if there has been default creditor: s.3; or, it is suggested
— after a means inquiry: s.1.

In any proceedings where the court has power to make or vary an attachment of earnings order it can order the debtor or anyone appearing to be his employer to supply details of his earnings: s.14.

An attachment of earnings order may be made against the *employer* of an employed person only as defined in s.6(2). It cannot be used in respect of:

— the self employed; or
— servicemen's pay, seamen's wages and certain other sums excepted by s.24.

The fact that a person is employed by the Crown does not exclude him from the procedure: s.22. The court has power to determine under s.16 whether payments to the debtor constitute *earnings* as defined in s.24.

An attachment of earnings order must name the employer to whom it is directed, stipulate a *normal deduction rate* and a *protected earnings rate*, as well as the particulars specified in r.7. The detailed rules by which these deductions are made are set out in Sch.3 of the Act. The employer is allowed to deduct *50p a week* from an employee's earnings (not from the debt) for his pains: s.7(4).

An attachment of earnings order 'ceases to have effect' when a warrant of commitment is issued: s.8; and it 'lapses' if the debtor leaves his employer: s.9. The employer is required to notify the court when this happens: s.7(2). The debtor is required to notify the court when he is re-employed: s.15; and the court may then redirect the order to the new employer under r.12. This power may be exercised by the justices' clerk: r.22(2)(d). The court may discharge or vary an attachment of earnings order by order on complaint: ss.9 and 19(1).

Frequently, a debtor may be under more than one attachment of earnings order. All orders in respect of fines and other sums adjudged to be paid on conviction may be consolidated under s.17, when the procedure set out in rr.15 and 17 applies. Orders made to obtain maintenance payments cannot be consolidated.

THE JUSTICES' CLERK 8b.31

The enforcement of fines is the *responsibility of the clerk to the justices*, as follows:

— Fines imposed by his own magistrates and those of other magistrates' courts transferred to his court may by transfer of fine orders: ss.80, 90, 91 MCA 1980.
— Fines of the Crown Court, Court of Appeal and House of Lords: s.32 PCCA 1973.
— Coroners' fines: s.49 CJA 1967. (For the enforcement of a fine for contempt imposed by a coroner see *R v HM Coroner for the Eastern District of the Metropolitan County of West Yorkshire, ex p. Smith* (1985) 149 JP 97).

SERVICEMAN 8b.32

Advice on the collection of fines from servicemen is given in HOC 149/70. If a financial penalty has been awarded against any person under the Army Act 1955, the Air Force Act 1955 or the Naval Discipline 1957 on his being convicted of a qualifying offence or as the parent or guardian of a person so convicted and no term of imprisonment was imposed in default, the military authorities can make a financial penalty enforcement order which is enforceable in a magistrates' court as if it had been a fine: s.133A Army Act 1955 and r.47 Magistrates' Courts Rules 1981. This method is only available when the person concerned is neither subject to service law nor is among certain categories of civilian. In practice it is of use mainly with regard to discharged servicemen.

8b.33
BANKRUPTCY

A fine is a *debt of record* due to the Crown: *Re Pascoe, Trustee in Bankruptcy v The Lords Commissioners of HM Treasury* (1944) 108 JP 126. Under the terms of s.382 Insolvency Act 1986, a 'bankruptcy debt' (in relation to an individual) comprises, *inter alia*:

(a) any debt or liability to which he is subject at the commencement of the bankruptcy.
(b) any debt or liability to which he may become subject after the commencement of the bankruptcy (including after his discharge from bankruptcy) by reason of any obligation incurred before the commencement of the bankruptcy.

In both bankruptcies (individuals) and windings-up (companies) a fine does not rank as a preferential debt: Sch.6 Insolvency Act 1986. On a discharge from bankruptcy the individual bankrupt is not released from any liability in respect of 'a fine imposed for an offence': s.281(4) Insolvency Act 1986.

The omission from the list of remedies against the *person* of the debtor, therefore, probably implies that a criminal court is not, by reason of bankruptcy, deprived of its power to enforce fines, although the trustee in bankruptcy may have a claim on after acquired property. Thus, the fact that bankruptcy proceedings are in progress does not prevent the court conducting a means inquiry, although the making of a bankruptcy order may be evidence of lack of means which prevents enforcement of the fine: *R v Woking Justices, ex p. Johnstone* (1942) 106 JP 232. But it is not necessarily conclusive: *James v James* (1963) 127 JP 352 (a case of maintenance arrears). Where an alternative of imprisonment has been imposed in default of payment of a fine the fact of bankruptcy proceedings is no bar to the issue of the warrant of commitment.

It has been suggested that fines paid into court after a bankruptcy order has been made should be rendered to the trustee in bankruptcy, but it is suggested that the better view is that this duty is overridden by s.61 of the Justices of the Peace Act 1979.

The Crown is *not obliged* to prove a fine in bankruptcy and when it does not do so and an alternative of imprisonment is imposed in default *habeas corpus* will not issue to secure the release of the defaulter: *Re Savundra* (1973) 58 Cr App R 54. Fines imposed on a company have no priority in a winding up: *Food Controller v Cork* [1923] AC 647.

8b.34
FOREIGN LORRY DRIVERS

Road traffic fines due from 'foreign lorry drivers' may, in addition to any of the methods described *supra*, be enforced by the informal method of notifying the Department of Transport that fines are outstanding and requesting that Department to ask the defaulter's home state to issue an 'exclusion order' under bilateral European agreements in accordance with the terms of HOC 1/1987, as follows:

Foreign Lorry Drivers: Enforcement of Fines for Traffic Offences

1. I am directed by the Secretary of State to say that the Department of Transport has drawn attention to cases in which magistrates' courts, acting under s.82(1)(b) of the Magistrates' Courts Act 1980, have committed

foreign lorry drivers to prison for default in paying fines imposed for road traffic offences. Such action is a subject of concern to several European governments. The purpose of this letter is to supply details of another sanction which can be brought to bear against such defaulters and their employers. Magistrates' courts might care to consider it as an alternative to committal in appropriate cases although the decision on what action to take in a particular case is, of course, entirely within the courts' discretion.

2. The suggested alternative to committal can be applied by virtue of bilateral agreements on road transport to which the United Kingdom is a party. Agreements are in force between the United Kingdom and all European countries except Albania and the Soviet Union. The agreements have international treaty status and are enforceable in international law. They require hauliers, (defined as persons including legal persons, who carry goods for hire or reward in connection with a trade or business), to ensure that the vehicles they operate comply with all the road traffic laws and regulations of the host country. Each agreement provides that when a haulier from one contracting state has infringed the other's road traffic law and regulations the host country may request the competent authorities in the haulier's home state to issue an immediate exclusion order. Where such a request is received the competent authority is obliged to act on it and to report the action taken to the authority making the request.

3. The Department of Transport is the competent authority for administering the agreements in the United Kingdom. It suggests that magistrates' courts might consider action under the agreements to be fitting in cases where foreign lorry drivers are fined for *non imprisonable* traffic offences but are unable to pay the fines at once or to make satisfactory arrangements for them to be paid.

4. Where a court decides that such action would be fitting and allows time for payment it should warn the defendant of the possible consequences for him and for his employer should the fine not be paid. If a fine is not paid within the time allowed the court should send details of the case (personal particulars of the offender and of his employer, offence, amount of fine and the date by which payment was due) to:

Freight Policy and Road Haulage Division
Room S16/09 Department of Transport
2 Marsham Street, London SW1P 3EB

5. The Division will at once request the competent authority in the defaulter's home state to issue an exclusion order. The giving of notice by the court is, of course, in addition to any other steps it may take to enforce payment of the fine e.g. issuing a warrant of arrest for the defaulter to attend a means inquiry which could be executed if he returned to England or Wales.

6. Courts are requested to notify the Department of Transport once a fine is paid so that steps may immediately be taken to cancel an existing exclusion order. The Department will inform the relevant court when an exclusion order is removed.

7. It is intended to keep the arrangements under careful review in the light of experience. For that purpose the information supplied by magistrates' courts about fines paid will help in monitoring whether the issue of exclusion orders is effective in securing the payment of outstanding fines.

8b.35   ## ORDERS 'OTHER THAN FOR THE PAYMENT OF MONEY'

Where a magistrates' court has power to *require* or *prohibit* the doing of *'anything'*, and makes an order accordingly, the provisions for enforcement are contained in s.63 MCA 1980. In summary, the powers of the court on disobedience are:

    (a) £50 per day of default, or a sum not exceeding £2,000;
    (b) committal to custody until remedied, or for up to two months.

Under (a) the aggregate of the daily impositions may not exceed £1,000 (s.6(3)); whilst under (b) the committal, on whichever basis, may not exceed 2 months in all, 'for doing or abstaining from doing the same thing . . .' (*ibid*).

Statutory Provisions

POLICE (PROPERTY) ACT 1897

8b.36   **Power to make orders with respect to property in possession of Police**
    1. (1) Where any property has come into the possession of the police in connection with their investigation of a suspected offence or under s.66 of the Metropolitan Police Act 1839, s.48 of the Act of the session of the second and third years of Her present Majesty, chapter 94 (local), for regulating the police in the city of London, a court of summary jurisdiction may, on application, either by an officer of police or by a claimant of the property, make an order for the delivery of the property to the person appearing to the magistrate or court to be the owner thereof, if the owner cannot be ascertained, make such order with respect to the property as to the magistrate or court may seem meet.

    (2) An order under this section shall not affect the right of any person to take within six months from the date of the order legal proceedings against any person in possession of property delivered by virtue of the order for the recovery of the property, but on the expiration of those six months the right shall cease.

    (3) In any part of the metropolitan police district for which a police court is established under the Metropolitan Police Courts Acts 1839 and 1840, the powers of a court of summary jurisdiction under this section shall be exercised by a metropolitan police magistrate.
    [*As amended by Sch.3 Theft Act 1968, s.58 Criminal Justice Act 1972, s.192(3) Consumer Credit Act 1974 and SI 1983 No 1551*]

COMMENTARY

See generally *Property in Possession of the Police*, 8b.13. This Act is excluded in relation to things retained by the police under s.139(3), (4) Customs and Excise Management Act 1979.
    The Police (Disposal of Property) Regulations 1975 (SI No 1474) provide for the disposal of property which has come into possession of police under s.43 PCCA 1973 and for which no successful application has been made within six months of the making of the order, as well as of property in any other case in respect of which the owner has not been ascertained and no order of a competent court has been made.

Costs, where the proceedings are begun by way of complaint (see *On application* below) costs may be ordered against the unsuccessful party by virtue of s.64 MCA 1980. An order of costs is inappropriate where the police do not object to the making of an order sought by the claimant, *per* Sir Stanley Rees in *R v Uxbridge Justices, ex p. Commissioner of Police for the Metropolis* [1981] 3 All ER 129. Where the police *go beyond their usual role of merely* *assisting the justices and actively oppose the order* there is no reason why the justices should not in the exercise of their discretion order costs: *Mercer v Oldham* [1984] Crim LR 232.

S.1(1): Any property, in practice, a wide definition of this term has been adopted: see eg 123 JPN 640.

In connection with their investigation of a suspected offence, these words are wide enough to cover property seized on arrest or under a search warrant or in proceedings under s.3 CYPA 1969, where the offence condition is alleged.

A court of summary jurisdiction, not confined to the court by or before which an offender was convicted.

On application, these words do not preclude the initiation of proceedings by way of complaint or the issue of a summons thereon: *R v Uxbridge Justices, ex p. Commissioner of Police for the Metropolis* [1981] 3 All ER 129. The complaint procedure is simply a convenient and accepted manner of bringing a civil matter before magistrates for an order, *per* Sir George Baker P, *ibid.* The complaint procedure is *not only permissible but compulsory* in all cases except where no complainant can be traced, *per* Sir Stanley Rees, *ibid*, Lord Denning MR dissenting.

An officer of police, this is designed to protect the police from actions of trover such as *Winter v Bancks* (1901) 65 JP 468.

A claimant, presumably not an offender who has been deprived of the property by an order of a court under s.43 PCCA 1973, having regard to the terms of s.43(3), *ibid.*

An owner, to be given its popular meaning. It does not include jewellers to whom a diamond ring was handed for valuation by a youth who was never seen again: *Raymond Lyons and Co Ltd v Metropolitan Police Commissioner* [1975] QB 321. The magistrates are not bound by any determination of ownership made in excess or jurisdiction by the court of trial: *R v Chester Justices, ex p. Smith* (1978) 142 JP 282.

S.1(2), the effect of this subsection is 'to make it clear that, after the period of six months, the right to possession, even against the true owner, enures irrevocably for the benefit of the claimant. . . For six months the defendant has a title defeasible at the suit of the true owner', *per* Holroyd Pearce J in *Irving v National Provincial Bank Ltd* [1962] 2 QB 73.

CHILDREN AND YOUNG PERSONS ACT 1933

Power to order parent or guardian to pay fine etc.   **8b.37**

55. (1) Where–
(a) a child or young person is convicted or found guilty of any offence for the commission of which a fine or costs may be imposed or a compensation order may be under s.35 of the Powers of Criminal Courts Act 1973; and
(b) the court is of opinion that the case would best be met by the imposition of a fine or costs or the making of such an order, whether with or without any other punishment,

it shall be the duty of the court to order that the fine, compensation or costs awarded be paid by the parent or guardian of the child or young person instead of by the child or young person himself, unless the court is satisfied–
(i) that the parent or guardian cannot be found; or
(ii) that it would be unreasonable to make an order for payment, having regard to the circumstances of the case.

(2) An order under this section may be made against a parent or guardian who, having been required to attend, has failed to do so, but, save as aforesaid, no such order shall be made without giving the parent or guardian an opportunity of being heard.

(3) A parent or guardian may appeal to the Crown Court against an order under this section made by a magistrates' court.

(4) . . .
[*As substituted by s.26 CJA 1982*].

(1A) Where but for this subsection–
(a) a court would order a child or young person to pay a fine under section
15(2A) of the Children and Young Persons Act 1969 (failure to comply
with requirement included in supervision order); or
(b) a court would impose a fine on a young person under s.16(3) of the
Powers of Criminal Courts Act 1973 (breach of requirements of com-
munity service order),
it shall be the duty of the court to order that the fine be paid by the parent or
guardian of the child or young person instead of by the child or young person
himself, unless the court is satisfied–
(i) that the parent or guardian cannot be found; or
(ii) that it would be unreasonable to make an order for payment, having
regard to the circumstances of the case.
[subs (1A) will be added by [s.125] CJA 1988 from a date to be appointed].

COMMENTARY

The effects of this section are summarised under *Parent's Responsibility* at 8b.09. It is wrong to use information contained in a probation report to decide a parent's responsibility under this section: *Lenihan v West Yorkshire Metropolitan Police* (1981) 3 Cr App R (S) 42. However, it is submitted that it would be proper for the court, if alerted to a fact by a comment in the report, to verify it by inquiry of the parent or otherwise and act upon whatever is disclosed thereby.

Orders under this section are *enforceable* as if adjudged to be paid on a conviction by a magistrates' court by virtue of s.41 Administration of Justice Act 1970 and Sch.9, *ibid*.

s.55(1): Child, means a person *under the age of 14 years*: s.107(1) of the Act.

Young person, means a person who has *attained the age of 14 years and is under the age of 17 years*: s.107(1).

Fine, subject to a maximum of £400 in the case of *a young person*: ss.24(3), 36(1) MCA 1980, £100 in the case of a *child*: ss.24(4), 36(2).

Guardian, includes any person who in the opinion of the court having cognizance of any case in relation to a child or young person as in which the child or young person is concerned, has for the time being the charge of and control over the child or young person: s.107(1) of the Act. This term has no application to a local authority which has a child in its care or to anyone except *an individual human person*: *Leeds City Council v West Yorkshire Metropolitan Police* [1982] 1 All ER 274 in which it was said *obiter*:

'(1) a local authority which allows a child, accommodated and maintained in a community home which it manages, to visit a parent (or other person) on holiday or for a weekend does not, merely by giving the leave, transfer charge and control to the parent (or other person); (2) but a local authority may, without terminating its statutory care, arrange with a parent (or guardian or relative or friend) to transfer charge and control to that person, in which event that person, willingly, accepts the de facto guardianship of the child and so assumes (or, if a parent, reassumes) the role of a 'parent or guardian' within the meaning of s.55; (3) it is, as the Divisional Court recognized in the present case, a question of fact whether the arrangements made between the parties constitute such a transfer of control'.

Unreasonable, while the court will usually be concerned with the degree of control exercised by or the responsibility shown by the parent or guardian towards his child it would, *it is suggested*, be unreasonable to order a parent or guardian to pay a sum of money which was beyond his means: and cf s.35 MCA 1980, s.35(4) PCCA 1973, *post*.

s.55(2): Opportunity of being heard, presumably on the question of whether he should be ordered to pay.

ARMY ACT 1955

8b.38   **Financial penalty enforcement orders**
133A. (1) If–
(a) a financial penalty has been awarded against any person under this Act, and

(b) the penalty was–
   (i) a fine awarded in respect of a qualifying offence (or in respect of such an offence together with other offences) on the conviction of a qualifying offence either of that person or of the person as whose parent or guardian that person is to pay the penalty; or
   (ii) stoppages or a compensation order awarded in respect of a qualifying offence, (whether on the conviction of any person of the offence or on a request by any person for the offence to be taken into consideration) and
(c) no term of imprisonment was imposed in default of payment, and
(d) no appeal is outstanding and the time provided for the giving of notice of appeal against the award has expired, and
(e) the whole or any part of the penalty remains unpaid or unrecovered, and
(f) the person against whom the award was made is a person to whom this section applies,

the Defence Council or an officer authorised by them may make an order (in this section referred to as a 'financial penalty enforcement order') for the registration of the penalty by the relevant court.

(2) This section applies to a person who is, or would be but for s.131 above, neither subject to service law nor a civilian to whom Part III of this Act is applied by s.209 below, Part II of the Air Force Act 1955 is applied by s.209 of that Act or Parts I and II of the Naval Discipline Act 1957, are applied by s.118 of that Act.

(3) In this section, 'qualifying offence' means–
(a) an offence under s.36 above committed outside the United Kingdom and consisting of or including acts or omissions that would constitute a comparable foreign offence or a local road traffic offence;
(b) an offence under s.70 above;
(c) an offence under any provision of this Act other than s.70 above consisting or of including acts or omissions which would also constitute an offence under s.70 above;

and for the purposes of this definition–
'comparable foreign offence' means an offence under the civil law of any place outside the United Kingdom which is comparable to an offence under the law of England and Wales; and
'local road traffic offence' means an offence under the civil law of any place outside the United Kingdom relating to road traffic.

(4) A financial penalty enforcement order shall contain a certificate issued on behalf of the Defence Council or by an officer authorised by them and stating–
(a) that a financial penalty has been awarded against the person named in the order;
(b) that the conditions specified in para (b) to (f) of subs (1) above are satisfied;
(c) the nature and amount of the penalty;
(d) the date on which and the offence or offences in respect of which it was awarded;
(e) if it was awarded against the person named in the order as the parent or guardian of some other person, the fact that it was so awarded and the name of that other person;
(f) sufficient particulars of the case (including particulars of any offences taken into consideration at the trial);
(g) the date of any payment or recovery of a sum on account of the penalty;
(h) the sum outstanding; and
(j) the authority to whom and address to which any stoppages or compensation included in the penalty will fall, on recovery, to be remitted under subs (7) below.

(5) A document purporting to be a financial penalty enforcement order and to be signed on behalf of the Defence Council or by an officer authorised by them shall be deemed to be such an order unless the contrary is proved, and a certificate under subs (4) above shall be evidence of the matters stated.

(6) Subject to subs (7) below, upon registration of a financial penalty enforcement order–
(a) service enforcement procedures shall cease to be available for the recovery of the sum certified as outstanding, and
(b) the sum shall be treated for all purposes as if it had been a fine imposed upon a conviction by the relevant court.

(7) Stoppages or compensation recovered under this section shall be remitted to the authority at the address specified in the certificate under subs (4) above.

(8) Where it appears from a financial penalty enforcement order that the penalty was imposed in respect of more than one offence, it shall be deemed for the purposes of enforcement to be a single penalty only.

(9) Where–
(a) a financial penalty enforcement order has been made against any person, and
(b) he ceases to be a person to whom this section applies at a time when the whole or any part of the certified sum is still outstanding,
service enforcement procedures shall apply to the amount outstanding as if it were a sum payable by way of a fine imposed by a civil court.

(10) In this section–
'financial penalty' means–
(a) a fine, including a fine imposed by virtue of para 13 of Sch.5A below;
(b) stoppages;
(c) a compensation order imposed by virtue of para 11 or 13 or Sch.5A below; or
(d) a fine together with stoppages or a compensation order;
'the relevant court' means–
(a) the magistrates' court in England or Wales,
(b) (*Scotland*), or
(c) (*Northern Ireland*)
within whose jurisdiction the person against whom a financial penalty enforcement order is made appears to the Defence Council or an officer authorised by them to reside or to be likely to reside;
'service enforcement procedures' means any procedure available by virtue of any of the following enactments, namely–
(a) ss.144, 146 and 209(4) nad (4A) below and ss.144, 146 and 209(4) and (4A) of the Air Force Act 1955, and
(b) ss.128A and 128B of the Naval Discipline Act 1957; and
'stoppages' does not include sums awards by virtue of s.147 or 148 below.
[*As inserted by Sch.8 Armed Forces Act 1976 and amended by Sch.1 Armed Forces Act 1986*].

(11) Where a fine has been awarded together with stoppages or a compensation order, this section shall have effect in relation to the fine and to the stoppages or compensation order as if they were separate penalties.

COMMENTARY

Analagous provisions are contained in s.133A Air Force Act 1955 and s.128F Naval Discipline Act 1957. For the duties of the clerk of a magistrates' court receiving a financial penalty enforcement order see r.47 MC Rules 1981.

CRIMINAL JUSTICE ACT 1967

Fines imposed by coroners   8b.39
49. A fine imposed by a coroner after the commencement of the Act under
s.19 of the Coroners Act 1887, shall be treated for purposes of its collection,
enforcement and remission as having been imposed by the magistrates' court
for the area in which the coroner's court was held, and the coroner shall as soon
as practicable after imposing the fine give particulars of the fine to the clerk of
that court.
[*This section will be repealed when Sch.15 CJA 1988 comes into force*].

COMMENTARY
The magistrates' clerk must serve written notice on the person fined: r.46(1) MC Rules
1981.

Section 19 of the Coroners Act 1887, subsection (5) reads: 'Where a recognizance is forfeited
at an inquest before a coroner, the coroner shall proceed in like manner under this section as
if he had imposed a fine under this section upon the person forfeiting that recognizance, and
the provisions of this section shall apply accordingly.'

THEFT ACT 1968   8b.40

Order for restitution
28. (1) Where goods have been stolen and either a person is convicted of
any offence with reference to the theft (whether or not the stealing is the gist of
his offence) or a person is convicted of any other offence but such offence as
aforesaid is taken into consideration in determining his sentence, the court by
or before which the offender is convicted may on the conviction whether or not
the passing of sentence is in other respects deferred exercise any of the
following powers–
  (a) the court may order anyone having possession or control of the goods to
      restore them to any person entitled to recover them from him; or
  (b) on the application of a person entitled to recover from the person
      convicted any other goods directly or indirectly representing the first-
      mentioned goods (as being the proceeds of any disposal or realisation of
      the whole of part of them or of goods so representing them), the court
      may order those other goods to be delivered or transferred to the
      applicant; or
  (c) the court may order that a sum not exceeding the value of the first-
      mentioned goods shall be paid, out of any money of the person convic-
      ted which was taken out of his possession on his apprehension, to any
      person who, if those goods were in possession of the person convicted,
      would be entitled to recover them from him.

(2) Where under subs (1) above the court has power on a person's conviction to make an order against him both under para (b) and under para (c) with
reference to the stealing of the same goods, the court may make orders under
both paragraphs provided that the person in whose favour the orders are made
does not thereby recover more than the value of those goods.

(3) Where under subs (1) above the court on a person's conviction makes an
order under para (a) for the restoration of any goods, and it appears to the
court that the person convicted has sold the goods to a person acting in good
faith, or has borrowed money on the security of them from a person so acting,
the court may order that there shall be paid to the purchaser or lender, out of
any money of the person convicted which was taken out of his possession on his
apprehension, a sum not exceeding the amount paid for the purchase by the
purchaser or, as the case may be, the amount owed to the lender in respect of
the loan.

(4) The court shall not exercise the powers conferred by this section unless

in the opinion of the court the relevant facts sufficiently appear from evidence given at the trial or the available documents, together with admissions made by or on behalf of any person in connection with any proposed exercise of the powers; and for this purpose 'the available documents' means any written statements or admissions which were made for use, and would have been admissible, as evidence at the trial, the deposition taken at any committal proceedings and any written statements or admissions used as evidence in those proceedings.

(5) . . .

(6) References in this section to stealing are to be construed in accordance with s.24(1) and (4) of this Act.

(7) *An order may be made under this section in respect of money owed by the Crown.*
[*As amended by Sch.5 CJA 1972; Sch.12 CLA 1977. Subs (7) will be added by [s.155] CJA 1988 from a date to be appointed*].

COMMENTARY

For the extension of the powers conferred by this section to offences taken into consideration see ss.6(3) and (4) CJA 1972 *infra*.

With certain exceptions orders made under this section are suspended until the expiration of the appeal period or the determination of any appeal: see s.6(5) CJA 1972 *infra*. The police have no power to retain property seized from an accused person an anticipation of an order *Malone v Commissioner of Police of the Metropolis* (1978) 69 Cr App R 4.

s.28(1), when the whole of the goods the subject of the charge are recovered, it is an incorrect exercise of discretion to make the offender pay compensation in respect of other goods: *R v Parker* (1970) 134 JP 497.

Goods, defined in s.40 Theft Act 1968 as including (except in so far as the context otherwise requires) money and every other description of property except land and including things severed from land by stealing.

Stolen, see s.28(6), and note thereto.

On the conviction, this means immediately after the conviction: *R v Church* (1970) 54 Cr App R 35.

Whether or not . . . deferred, thus an order may be made under this section as an exception to the general rule in *R v Dwyer* (1975) 60 Cr App R 39, that on a deferment all aspects of sentencing must be deferred.

s.28(1), 'In other words, if the convicted man is found in possession of some specific goods, and goods includes money, there is power to order its restitution', *per* Lord Parker CJ in *R v Thebith* (1970) 54 Cr App R 35.

Order disobedience to the order is punishable under s.63 MCA 1980, see 8b.35 and 8b.76.

s.28(1)(b), this envisages a case where the original specific goods have been realised or exchanged or have been, as it were, converted into other specific goods, *per* Lord Parker CJ in *R v Thebith, supra.*

s.28(1)(c) the powers conferred by this paragraph are exercisable without application: s.6(2) CJA 1972.

Taken out of his possession on his apprehension, this phrase envisages a case where on apprehension the offender is found in possession of money which cannot be shown to be money representing the realisation of the goods that were stolen, *per* Lord Parker CJ in *R v Thebith, supra.* It includes money in a safe deposit, even though not opened between deposit and apprehension: *R v Ferguson* (1970) 134 JP 608.

s.28(3), the powers conferred by this subsection are exercisable without application: s.6(2) CJA 1972.

s.28(4), referring to the pre-existing powers in the Larceny Act 1916, Widgery J said, in *Stamp v United Dominions Trust* [1967] 1 QB 418.

'Justices should hesitate before exercising this jurisdiction if the value of the goods in question is substantial, or if the application for an order is likely to raise difficult questions of law. There are many cases . . . where the civil courts are really better equipped to try an issue of this kind, and I would deprecate any suggestions in the future that magistrates should be too anxious to exercise their discretion to deal with such issues.'

Lord Parker CJ went further in saying: 'It seems to me that whenever difficult questions of law affecting title are likely to arise, as, for instance – and this is only an illustration – by a reason of the Hire Purchase Act 1964, no criminal court, whether Assizes, quarter sessions or magistrates, should embark on the consideration of making a restitution order.'
Similarly, in *R v Ferguson, supra*, Salmon J said:

'It is only in the plainest cases, where there can be no doubt that the money belonged to the convicted man, that the court would be justified in exercising its discretion in making an order for restitution. To do so in any case of doubt might cause the gravest injustice to a third party because the third party to whom the money may belong has no *locus standi* to appear before a criminal court. Nor is there any appropriate machinery available in the criminal courts for deciding the issue of who is the true owner. Discovery is sometimes a very important part of the necessary machinery for resolving issues of that sort, and discovery for this purpose can be obtained only in the civil courts. The civil courts are the correct forum for deciding matters of this kind':

(Order should not have been made where defendant raised the issue that the money belonged not to him but to his mistress, and where there was no evidence by which the contrary could have been proved beyond all reasonable doubt); and see *R v Calcutt and Varty* (1985) 7 Cr App R (S) 385 (order under s.28 must have a 'factual basis').

At the trial, the trial concludes when sentence is passed: *R v Church, supra.*

s.26(6), these provisions read as follows:

'24(1) The provisions of this Act relating to goods which have been stolen shall apply whether the stealing occurred in England or Wales or elsewhere, and whether it occurred before or after the commencement of this Act, provided that the stealing (if not an offence under this Act) amounted to an offence where and at the time when the goods were stolen; and references to stolen goods shall be construed accordingly.' '24(4) For purposes of the provisions of this Act relating to goods which have been stolen (including subss. (1) to (3) above) goods obtained in England or Wales or elsewhere by blackmail or in the circumstances described in s.15(1) of this Act shall be regarded as stolen; and 'steal', 'theft' and 'thief' shall be construed accordingly.'

Section 15(1) of the Act refers to goods obtained by criminal deception.

Effect on civil proceedings and rights   **8b.41**
    31. (2) Notwithstanding any enactment to the contrary, when property has been stolen or obtained by fraud or other wrongful means, the title to that or any other property shall not be affected by reason only of the conviction of the offender.

ADMINISTRATION OF JUSTICE ACT 1970

SCHEDULE 9:   **8b.42**
Enforcement of orders for costs, compensation etc.

PART I: CASES WHERE PAYMENT ENFORCEABLE AS ON SUMMARY CONVICTION
Miscellaneous orders for costs, compensation, damages etc.
    9. Where a court makes an order by virtue of regulations made under s.19(5) Prosecution of Offences Act 1985 for the payment of costs by an offender.
  10. Where under s.35 of the Powers of Criminal Courts Act 1973 a court orders the payment of compensation.
  12. Where under s.35 of the Children & Young Persons Act 1933, a court orders any fine, compensation or costs, or any sum awarded by way of satisfaction or compensation to be paid by the parent or guardian of a child or young person.
  13–21 . . .

[As amended by s.8(4) Criminal Damage Act 1971, Schs.5, 6 CJA 1972, Sch.1 Costs in Criminal Cases Act 1973, Sch.5 PCCA 1973 and Schs.1 and 2 Prosecution of Offences Act 1985].

COMMENTARY

The above orders are treated for the purposes of collection and enforcement as if adjudged to be paid on a conviction by a magistrates' court being:
(a) when the order is made by a magistrates' court, that court and
(b) in any other case such magistrates' court as may be specified in the order: s.41(1) Administration of Justice Act 1970.

ATTACHMENT OF EARNINGS ACT 1971

8b.43   **Courts with power to attach earnings**
    1. (3) A magistrates' court may make an attachment of earnings order to secure–
    (a) . . .
    (b) the payment of any sum adjudged to be paid by a conviction or treated (by any enactment relating to the collection and enforcement of fines, costs, compensation or forfeited recognizances) as so adjudged to be paid; or
    (c) the payment of any sum required to be paid by a legal aid contribution order.

(4) The following provisions of this Act apply, except where otherwise stated, to attachment of earnings order made, or to be made, by any court.

(5) Any power conferred by this Act to make an attachment of earnings order includes a power to make such an order to secure the discharge of liabilities arising before the coming into force of this Act.

COMMENTARY

s.1(3), it is suggested that this provision is authority for a magistrates' court to make an attachment of earnings order of its own motion. For orders on application, see s.3, *infra*.

Sums adjudged to be paid by a conviction, defined in s.150(3) MCA 1980 as applied by s.25(6) of this Act as including a reference to any costs, damages or compensation adjudged to be paid by the conviction or order.

Treated . . . as so adjudged, see eg s.41(1) Administration of Justice Act 1970.

Legal aid contribution order, can no longer be made as such, see formerly, ss.7, 8(2) Legal Aid Act 1982; and s.25, *infra*.

8b.44   **Principal definitions**
    2. In this Act–
    (a), (b) . . .
    (c) 'judgment debt' means a sum payable under–
        (i) a judgment or order enforceable by a court in England and Wales (not being a magistrates' court);
        (ii) an order of a magistrates' court for the payment of money recoverable summarily as a civil debt; or
        (iii) an order of any court which is enforceable as if it were for the payment of money so recoverable,
    but does not include any sum payable under a maintenance order or an administration order;
    (d) 'the relevant adjudication', in relation to any payment secured or to be secured by an attachment of earnings order, means the conviction, judgment, order or other adjudication from which there arises the liability to make the payment; and

(e) 'the debtor', in relation to an attachment of earnings order, or to proceedings in which a court has power to make an attachment of earnings order, or to proceedings arising out of such an order, means the persons by whom payment is required by the relevant adjudication to be made.

COMMENTARY
Judgment debt, may be enforced by attachment in the county court, but not in the magistrates' court: s.1, *supra.*

Application for order and conditions of court's power to make it   8b.45
3. (1) The following persons may apply for an attachment of earnings order–
  (a) the person to whom payment under the relevant adjudication is required to be made (whether directly or through an officer of any court);
  (b), (c) . . .
  (d) in the following cases the debtor–
    (i) where the application is to a magistrates' court; or
    (ii) where the application is to the High Court or a county court for an order to secure maintenance payments.

(2) . . .

(3) For an attachment of earnings order to be made on the application of any person other than the debtor it must appear to the court that the debtor has failed to make one or more payments required by the relevant adjudication.

(4)–(7) . . .

COMMENTARY
Relevant adjudication, see s.2, *supra.*

Apply, application is by way of complaint: s.19. For the court having jurisdiction, see r.4, *infra.*

Effect and contents of order   8b.46
6. (1) An attachment of earnings order shall be an order directed to a person who appears to the court to have the debtor in his employment and shall operate as an instruction to that person–
  (a) to make periodical deductions from the debtor's earnings in accordance with Part I of Sch.3 to this Act; and
  (b) at such times as the order may require, or as the court may allow, to pay the amounts deducted to the collecting officer of the court, as specified in the order.

(2) For the purposes of this Act, the relationship of employer and employee shall be treated as subsisting between two persons if one of them, as a principal and not as a servant or agent, pays to the other any sums defined as earnings by s.24 of this Act.

(3) An attachment of earnings order shall contain prescribed particulars enabling the debtor to be identified by the employer.

(4) Except where it is made to secure maintenance payments, the order shall specify the whole amount payable under the relevant adjudication (or so much of that amount as remains unpaid), including any relevant costs.

(5) The order shall specify–
  (a) the normal deduction rate, that is to say, the rate (expressed as a sum of money per week, month or other period) at which the court thinks it reasonable for the debtor's earnings to be applied to meeting his liability under the relevant adjudications; and

(b) the protected earnings rate, that is to say the rate (so expressed) below which, having regard to the debtor's resources and needs, the court thinks it reasonable that the earnings actually paid to him should not be reduced.

(6) . . .

(7) For the purposes of an attachment of earnings order, the collecting officer of the court shall be (subject to later variation of the order under s.9 of this Act)–
(a) in the case of an order made by the High Court, either–
    (i) the proper officer of the High Court, or
    (ii) the appropriate officer of such county court as the order may specify;
(b) in the case of an order made by a county court, the appropriate officer of that court; and
(c) in the case of an order made by a magistrates' court, the clerk either of that court or of another magistrates' court specified in the order.

(8) In subs (7) above 'appropriate officer' means an officer designated by the Lord Chancellor.
[*As amended by s.19(5) Administration of Justice Act 1977*].

COMMENTARY

s.6(1): Employment, see the commentary to s.24, *infra.*

Collecting officer, see s.6(7).

s.6(4): Prescribed particulars, see r.7.

s.6(4): Relevant costs, see s.25(2).

s.6(5): Debtor's resources, itwsa held in a civil case that in fixing the *normal deduction rate* the court should not consider the potential earnings of the debtor in some other occupation than that in which it is sought to attach his earnings: *Pepper v Pepper* [1960] 1 All ER 529.

Debtor's needs, see s.25(3). It was said in a civil case that there is no principle which prevents a *protected earnings rate* being fixed *below* the rate prescribed by the Supplementary Benefits Commission, but that in most cases it would be unreasonable to do so: *Billington v Billington* [1974] 2 WLR 53.

8b.47   **Compliance with order by employer**
    7. (1) Where an attachment of earnings order has been made, the employer shall, if he has been served with the order, comply with it; but he shall be under no liability for non-compliance before seven days have elapsed since the service.

(2) Where a person is served with an attachment of earnings order directed to him and he has not the debtor in his employment, or the debtor subsequently ceases be in his employment, he shall (in either case), within ten days from the date of service, as the case may be, the cesser, give notice of that fact to the court.

(3) Part II of Sch.3 to this act shall have effect with respect to the priority to be accorded as between two or more attachment of earnings orders directed to a person in respect of the same debtor.

(4) On any occasion when the employer makes, in compliance with the order a deduction from the debtor's earnings–
(a) he shall be entitled to deduct, in addition, [50p], or such other sum as may be prescribed by order made by the Lord Chancellor, towards his clerical and administration costs; and
(b) he shall give to the debtor a statement in writing of the total amount of the deduction.

COMMENTARY

Employer, defined in s.25, *infra.*

Comply, failure to comply with an order is an offence under s.23(2)(a).

Give notice, failure to give notice is an offence under s.23(2)(b).

In his employment, see s.6(2).

s.7(4): Such other sums, SI 1980 No 558 substitutes 50p (for the original 5p).

Interrelation with alternative remedies open to creditor 8b.48

8. (4) An attachment or earnings order made to secure the payment of a judgment debt shall cease to have effect on the making of an order of commitment or the issue of a warrant of commitment for the enforcement of the debt.

(5) An attachment of earnings order made to secure any payment specified in s.1(3)(b) or (c) of this Act shall cease to have effect on the issue of a warrant committing the debtor to prison for default in making that payment.

COMMENTARY

When an order ceases to have effect, notice must be given to the employer: r.6(2).

Judgment debt, defined in s.2, *supra.*

Variation, lapse and discharge of orders 8b.49

9. (1) The court may make an order discharging or varying an attachment of earnings order.

(2) Where an order is varied, the employer shall, if he has been served with notice of the variation, comply with the order as varied; but he shall be under no liability for non-compliance before seven days have elapsed since the service.

(3) (*Rules*).

(4) Where an attachment of earnings order has been made and the person to whom it is directed ceases to have the debtor in his employment, the order shall lapse (except as respects deduction from earnings paid after the cesser and payment to the collecting officer of amounts deducted at any time) and be of no effect unless and until the court again directs it to a person (whether the same as before or another) who appears to the court to have the debtor in his employment.

(5) The lapse of an order under subs (4) above shall not prevent its being treated as remaining in force for other purposes.

COMMENTARY

The court, see s.25 *infra.*

Discharge or vary, by complaint: s.19(1). For temporary variations see r.14, *infra.*

Comply, failure to comply is an offence under s.23(2)(a).

In his employment, see s.6(2).

The court again directs it to a person, the employer is required to notify the court when the debtor leaves his employment: s.7(2), and there is a corresponding duty on the debtor, who is also required to notify when he becomes re-employed: s.15. The court may of its own volition redirect an order to a new employer: r.12; and this power may be exercised by the justices clerk: r.22(2)(d).

Termination of employer's liability to make deductions 8b.50

12. (1) Where an attachment of earnings order ceases to have effect under s.8 or s.11 of the Act, the proper officer of the prescribed court shall give notice of the cesser to the person to whom the order was directed.

(2) Where, in the case of an attachment of earnings order made otherwise than to secure maintenance payments, the whole amount payable under the

relevant adjudication has been paid, and also any relevant costs, the court shall give notice to the employer that no further compliance with the order is required.

(3) Where an attachment of earnings order–
(a) ceases to have effect under s.8 or s.11 of this Act; or
(b) is discharged under s.9
the person to whom the order has been directed shall be under no liability in consequence of his treating the order as still in force at any time before the expiration of seven days from the date on which the notice required by subs (1) above or, as the case may be, a copy of the discharging order is served on him.

COMMENTARY

The prescribed court, see r.6(3), *supra.*

Relevant costs, see s.25(2).

The court, see s.25, *infra.*

8b.51   **Application of sums received by collecting officer**
13. (1) Subject to subs (3) below, the collecting officer to whom a person makes payments in compliance with an attachment of earnings order shall, after deducting such court fees, if any, in respect of proceedings for or arising out of the order, as are deductible from those payments, deal with the sums paid in the same way as he would if they had been paid by the debtor to satisfy the relevant adjudications.

COMMENTARY

Collecting officer, see s.6(7), *supra.*

8b.52   **Power of court to obtain statements of earnings etc.**
14. (1) Where in any proceedings a court has power to make an attachment of earnings order, it may–
(a) order the debtor to give to the court, within a specified period, a statement signed by him of–
(i) the name and address of any person by whom earnings are paid to him;
(ii) specified particulars as to his earnings and anticipated earnings and as to his resources and needs; and
(iii) specified particulars for the purpose of enabling the debtor to be identified by any employer of his;
(b) order any person appearing to the court to have the debtor in his employment to give to the court, within a specified period, a statement signed by him or on his behalf of specified particulars of the debtor's earnings and anticipated earnings.

(2) Where an attachment of earnings order has been made, the court may at any time thereafter while the order is in force (a) make such an order as described in subs (1)(a) or (b) above; and (b) order the debtor to attend before it on a day and at a time specified in the order to give the information described in subs (1)(a) above.

(3) In the case of an application to a magistrates' court for an attachment of earnings order, or for the variation or discharge of such an order, the power to make an order under subs (1) or subs (2) above shall be exercisable also before the hearing of the application, by a single justice.

(4) *(Rules).*

(5) In any proceedings in which a court has power to make an attachment of earnings order, and in any proceedings for the making, variation or discharge of such an order, a document purporting to be a statement given to the court in compliance with an order under subs (1)(a) or (b) above, or with any such

requirement of a notice of application for an attachment of earnings order as is mentioned in subs (4) above, shall, in the absence of proof to the contrary, be deemed to be a statement so given and shall be evidence of the facts stated therein.

[*As amended by s.53(1) Administration of Justice Act 1982*].

COMMENTARY

Order, for service of the order, see r.20. Failure to comply is an offence: s.23(2)(c).

Earnings, defined in s.24, *infra*.

Debtor's needs, see s.25(3), *infra*.

In his employment, see s.6(2), *supra*.

Single justice, ie for the same petty sessions area as the court: s.25(1). For the justices' clerk's powers to make orders under s.14(1) and (2), see r.22(2)(a), *infra*.

Obligation of debtor and his employers to notify changes of employment and earnings   **8b.53**

15. While an attachment of earnings order is in force–

(a) the debtor shall from time to time notify the court in writing of every occasion on which he leaves any employment, or becomes employed or re-employed, not later (in each case) than seven days from the date on which he did so;

(b) the debtor shall, on any occasion when he becomes employed or re-employed, include in his notification under para (a) above particulars of his earnings and anticipated earnings from the relevant employment; and

(c) any person who becomes the debtor's employer and knows that the order is in force and by what court it was made shall, within seven days of his becoming the debtor's employer or of acquiring that knowledge (whichever is the later) notify that court in writing that he is the debtor's employer, and include in his notification a statement of the debtor's earnings and anticipated earnings.

COMMENTARY

The court, see s.25(1), *infra*.

Notify, failure to comply may be an offence under s.23(2)(d)–(f).

Earnings, defined in s.24, *infra*.

Power of court to determine whether particular payments are earnings   **8b.54**

16. (1) Where an attachment of earnings order is in force, the court shall, on the application of a person specified in subs (2) below, determine whether payments to the debtor of a particular class or description specified by the application are earnings for the purpose of the order; and the employer shall be entitled to give effect to any determination for the time being in force under this section.

(2) The persons referred to in subs (1) above are–

(a) the employer;

(b) the debtor;

(c) the person to whom payment under the relevant adjudication is required to be made (whether directly or through an officer of any court; and

(d) . . .

(3) Where an application under this section is made by the employer he shall not incur any liability for non-compliance with the order as respects any payments of the class or description specified by the application which are made by him to the debtor while the application, or any appeal in consequence thereof, is pending but this subsection shall not, unless the court otherwise

orders, apply as respects such payments if the employer subsequently withdraws the application or, as the case may be, abandons the appeal.

COMMENTARY

The court, see s.25(1), *infra.*

Application, by complaint: s.19(3). For the power to award costs see s.21.

Employer, see s.25(1), *infra.*

8b.55   **Consolidated attachment orders**

    17. (1) The powers of a county court under ss.1 and (3) of this Act shall include power to make an attachment of earnings order to secure the payment of any number of judgment debts; and the powers of a magistrates' court under those sections shall include power to make an attachment of earnings order to secure the discharge of any number of such liabilities as are specified in s.1(3).

    (2) An attachment of earnings order made by virtue of this section shall be known as a consolidated attachment order.

    (3) (*Rules*).

COMMENTARY

A magistrates' court may only consolidate orders for the payment of sums adjudged to be paid be a conviction and sums treated as so adjudged as well as legal aid contribution orders. Rule 15(1) excludes payments under a magistrates' courts maintenance order from consolidation procedure. For the jurisdiction and procedure concerning consolidated orders see rr.15, 17. For the transfer of fines for this purpose see r.16. Before the court consolidates two or more orders *of its own motion* written notice must first be given to the debtor: r.15(8), *infra.*

8b.56   **Procedure on application**

    19. (1) Subject to rules of court made by virtue of the following subsection, an application to a magistrates' court of an attachment of earnings order, or an order discharging or varying an attachment of earnings order, shall be made by complaint.

    (2) (*Rules*).

    (3) An application to a magistrates' court for a determintion under s.16 of this Act shall be made by complaint.

    (4) For the purposes of s.51 of the Magistrates' Courts Act 1980 (which provides for the issue of a summons directed to the person against whom an order may be made in pursuance of a complaint)–

    (a) the power to make an order in pursuance of a complaint by the debtor for an attachment of earnings order, or the discharge or variation of such an order, shall be deemed to be a power to make an order against the person to whom payment under the relevant adjudication is required to be made (whether directly or through an officer of any court); and

    (b) the power to make an attachment of earnings order, or an order discharging or varying an attachment of earnings order, in pursuance of a complaint by any other person (including a complaint in proceedings to which s.3(4)(b) of this Act applies) shall be deemed to be a power to make an order against the debtor.

    (5) A complaint for an attachment of earnings order may be heard notwithstanding that it was not made within the six months allowed by s.127(1) of the Magistrates' Courts Act 1980.

    [*As amended by Sch.7 Magistrates' Courts Act 1980*].

COMMENTARY

Rules of court, see r.14(1), *infra*, concerning temporary variations of protected earnings.

Complaint, see s.51 MCA 1980.

Costs on application under section 16 8b.57
21. (1) On making a determination under s.16 of the Act, a magistrates' court may in its discretion make such an order as it thinks just and reasonable for payment by any of the persons mentioned in subs (2) of that section of the whole or any part of the costs of the determination (but subject to s.18(2)(b) of this Act).

(2) Costs ordered to be paid under this section shall–
  (a) in the case of costs to be paid by the debtor to the person in whose favour the attachment of earnings order in question was made, be deemed–
    (i) if the attachment of earnings order was made to secure maintenance payments, to be a sum due under the related maintenance order, and
    (ii) otherwise, to be a sum due to the clerk of the court; and
  (b) in any other case, be enforceable as a civil debt.

COMMENTARY
s.18(2)(b), relates to payments under a maintenance order.

Enforceable as a civil debt, ie by order on complaint under s.96 MCA 1980.

Persons employed under the Crown 8b.58
22. (1) The fact that an attachment of earnings order is made at the suit of the Crown shall not prevent its operation at any time when the debtor is in the employment of the Crown.

(2) Where a debtor is in the employment of the Crown and an attachment of earnings order is made in respect of him, then for the purposes of this Act–
  (a) the chief officer for the time being of the department, office or other body in which the debtor is employed shall be treated as having the debtor in his employment (any transfer of sum from one department, office or body to another being treated as a change of employment); and
  (b) any earnings paid by the Crown or a Minister of the Crown or out of the public revenue of the United Kingdom, shall be treated as paid by the said chief officer.

(3) If any question arises, in proceedings for or arising out of an attachment of earnings order, as to what department, office or other body is concerned for the purposes of this section, or as to who for those purposes is the chief officer thereof, the question shall be referred to and determined by the Minister for the Civil Service; but that Minister shall not be under any obligation to consider a reference under this subsection unless it is made by the court.

(4) A document purporting to set out a determination of the said Minister under subs (3) above and to be signed by an official of the Management and Personnel Office, shall, in any such proceedings as are mentioned in that subsection, be admissible in evidence and be deemed to contain an accurate statement of such a determination unless the contrary is shown.

(5) This Act shall have effect notwithstanding any enactment passed before 29 May, 1970 and preventing or avoiding the attachment or diversion of sums due to a person in respect of service under the Crown, whether by way of remuneration, pension or otherwise.
[*As amended by the Transfer of Functions (Minister for the Civil Service and Treasury Order 1981*].

COMMENTARY
In the employment, s.6(2), *supra.*

Meanings of 'earnings' 8b.59
24. (1) For the purposes of this Act, but subject tothe following subsection, 'earnings' are any sums payable to a person–

(a) by way of wages or salary (including any fees, bonus, commission, overtime pay or other emoluments payable in addition to wages or salary or payable under a contract of service);

(b) by way of pension (including an annuity in respect of past services, whether or not rendered to the person paying the annuity, and including periodical payments by way of compensation for the loss, abolition or relinquishment, or diminution in the emoluments of any office or employment);

(c) by way of statutory sick pay.

(2) The following shall not be treated as earnings–

(a) sums payable by any public department of the Government of Northern Ireland or of a territory outside the United Kingdom;

(b) pay or allowances payable to the debtor as a member of Her Majesty's forces;

(c) pension, allowances, or benefit payable under any enactment relating to social security);

(d) pension or allowances payable in respect of disablement or disability;

(e) except in relation to a maintenance order wages payable to a person as a seaman, other than wages payable to him as a seaman of a fishing boat;

(f) guaranteed minimum pension within the meaning of the Social Security Pensions Act 1975.

(3) In subs (2)(e) above, expressions used in the Merchant Shipping Act 1894, have the same meanings as in that Act.

[*As amended by Sch.4 Social Security Pensions Act 1975, s.39(1) Merchant Shipping Act 1979, s.86 Social Security Act 1986*].

COMMENTARY

The fact that the parties regard themselves as not in the relationship of employer/employee is not conclusive: cf. *Maurice Graham v Brunswick* (1974) 16 KLR 158 and *Ferguson v John Dawson and Partners (Contractors) Ltd* [1976] 1 WLR 1213.

s.24(1): Pension, an ill-health pension calculated by reference to length of service was held not to be excluded by reason of s.24(2)(d) of the Act from the definition of a pension in s.24(1)(b): *Miles v Miles* [1979] 1 All ER 865.

s.24 2(e): A seaman, apparently includes crews of cross-channel ferries.

8b.60   **General interpretation**

25. (1) In this Act, except where the context otherwise requires–

'administration order' means an order made under, and so referred to in, Part VI of the County Courts Act 1984;

'the court', in relation to an attachment of earnings order, means the court which made the order, subject to rules of court as to the venue for, and the transfer of, proceedings in county courts and magistrates' courts;

'debtor' and 'relevant adjudications' have the meanings given by s.2 of this Act;

'the employer', in relation to an attachment of earnings order, means the person who is required by the order to make deductions from earnings paid by him to the debtor;

'judgment debt' has the meaning given by s.2 of this Act;

'legal aid contribution order' means an order under ss.7 or 8(2) of the Legal Aid Act 1982;

'maintenance order' has the meaning given by s.2 of this Act;

'maintenance payments' means payments required under a maintenance order;

'prescribed' means prescribed by rules of court; and

'rules of court', in relation to a magistrates' court, means rules under s.144 of the Magistrates' Courts Act 1980;

and, in relation to a magistrates' court, references to a single justice are to a justice of the peace acting for the same petty sessions area as the court.

(2) Any reference in this Act to sums payable under a judgment to order, or to the payment of such sums, includes a reference to costs and the payment of them; and the references in s.6(4) and 12(2) to relevant costs are to any costs of the proceedings in which the attachment of earnings order in question was made, being costs which the debtor is liable to pay.

(3) References in ss.6(5)(b) and 14(1)(a) of this Act to the debtor's needs include references to the needs of any person for whom he must, or reasonably may, provide.

(4) Earnings which, in pursuance of a scheme under the Dock Workers (Regulations of Employment) Act 1946, are paid to a debtor by a body responsible for the local administration of a scheme acting as agent for the debtor's employer or as delegate of the body responsible for the general administration of the scheme shall be treated for the purposes of this Act as paid to the debtor by the last-mentioned body acting as principal.

(5) Any power to make rules which is conferred by this Act is without prejudice to any other power to make rules of court.

(6) This Act, so far as it relates to magistrates' courts, and Part III of the Magistrates' Courts Act 1980 shall be construed as if this Act were contained in that Part.

(7) References in this Act to any enactment include references to that enactment as amended by or under any other enactment, including this Act.
[*As amended by Sch.4 Legal Aid Act 1974, Sch.7 MCA 1980, s.14 Legal Aid Act 1982, Sch.2 County Courts Act 1984*].

SCHEDULE 3   **8b.61**
Deductions by Employer under Attachment of Earnings Order

PART I: SCHEME OF DEDUCTIONS
Preliminary definitions
1. The following three paragraphs have effect for defining and explaining, for purposes of this schedule, expressions used therein.

2. 'Pay-day', in relation to earnings paid to a debtor, means an occasion on which they are paid.

3. Attachable earnings', in relation to a pay-day, are the earnings which remain payable to the debtor on that day after deduction by the employer of–
(a) income tax;
(b) primary Class I contributions under Part I of the Social Security Act 1975;
(c) amounts deductible under any enactment or in pursuance of a request in writing by the debtor, for the purposes of a superannuation scheme, namely any enactment, rules deed or other instrument providing for payment of annuities or lump sums–
   (i) to the persons with respect to whom the instrument has effect on their retirement at a specified age or on becoming incapacitated at some earlier age, or
   (ii) to the personal representatives or the widows, relatives or dependents of such persons on their death or otherwise,
whether with or without any further or other benefits.
4. (1) On any pay-day–
(a) 'the normal deduction' is arrived at by applying the normal deduction rate (as specified in the relevant attachment of earnings order) with respect to the relevant period; and
(b) 'the protected earnings' are arrived at by applying the protected earnings rate (as so specified) with respect to the relevant period.

(2) For the purposes of this paragraph the relevant period in relation to any pay-day is the period beginning–

    (a) if it is the first pay-day of the debtor's employment with the employer, with the first day of the employment; or

    (b) if on the last pay-day earnings were paid in respect of a period falling wholly or partly after that pay-day, with the first day after the end of that period; or

    (c) in any other case, with the first day after the last pay-day, and ending–

        (i) where earnings are paid in respect of a period falling wholly or partly after the pay-day, with the last day of that period; or

       (ii) in any other case, with the pay-day.

Employer's deduction (other cases)

6. (1) The following provision shall have effect in the case of an attachment of earnings order to which para 5 above does not apply.

(2) If on a pay-day the attachable earnings exceed the sum of–

    (a) the protected earnings; and

    (b) so much of any amount by which the attachable earnings on any previous pay-day fell short of the protected earnings as has not been made good by virtue of this subparagraph in another previous pay-day,

then, in so far as the excess allows, the employer shall deduct from the attachable earnings the amount specified in the following subparagraph.

(3) The said amount is the sum of–

    (a) the normal deduction; and

    (b) so much of the normal deduction on any previous pay-day as was not deducted on that day and has not been paid by virtue of this subparagraph on any other previous pay-day.

(4) No deduction shall be made on any pay-day when the attachable earnings are equal to, or less than, the protected earnings.

PART II: PRIORITY AS BETWEEN ORDERS

7. Where the employer is required to comply with two or more attachment of earnings orders in respect of the same debtor, all or none of which orders are made to secure either the payment of judgment debts or payments under an administration order, then on any pay-day the employer shall, for the purpose of complying with Part I of this schedule–

    (a) deal with orders according to the respective dates on which they were made, disregarding any later order until an earlier one has been dealt with;

    (b) deal with any later order as if the earnings to which it relates were the residue of the debtor's earnings after the making of any deduction to comply with any earlier order.

8. Where the employer is required to comply with two or more attachment of earnings orders, and one or more (but not all) of those orders are made to secure either the payment of judgment debts or payments under an administration order, then on any pay-day the employer shall, for the purpose of complying with Part I of this schedule–

    (a) deal first with any order which is not made to secure the payment of a judgment debt or payments under an administration order (complying with para 7 above if there are two or more such orders); and

    (b) deal thereafter with any order which is made to secure the payment of a judgment debt or payments under an administration order as if the earnings to which it relates were the residue of the debtor's earnings after the making of any deduction to comply with an order having priority by virtue of subpara (a) above; and

    (c) if there are two or more orders to which subpara (b) above applies, comply with para 7 above in respect of those orders.

[*As amended by Social Security (Consequential Provisions) Act 1975, Sch.5 Social Security Pensions Act 1975, s.54 Administration of Justice Act 1982, s.32(2) Wages Act 1986*].

CRIMINAL JUSTICE ACT 1972

Restitution orders   **8b.62**
6. (1) The following provisions of this section shall have effect with respect
to s.28 of the Theft Act 1968 (which enables orders for the restitution and
certain other orders to be made in relation to stolen property).

(2) The powers conferred by–
(a) subsection (1)(c) of the said s.28 (payment to owner of stolen goods out
of money taken from the offender on his apprehension); and
(b) subsection (3) of that section (payment to purchaser of, and lender on
the security of, stolen goods out of money so taken),
shall be exercisable without any application being made in that behalf or on the
application of any person appearing to the court to be interested in the
property concerned.

(3) The powers conferred by the said s.28 shall be exercisable not only
where a person is convicted of an offence with reference to the theft of the
goods in question but also where, on the conviction of a person of any other
offence, the court takes an offence with reference to the theft of those goods
into consideration in determining sentence.

(4) Where an order is made under the said s.28 against any person in respect
to an offence taken into consideration in determining his sentence–
(a) the order shall cease to have effect if he successfully appeals against his
conviction of the offence or, if more than one, all the offences, of which
he was convicted in the proceedings in which the order was made;
(b) he may appeal against the order as if it were part of the sentence
imposed in respect of the offence or, if more than one, any of the
offences, of which he was so convicted.

(5) Any order under the said s.28 made by a magistrates' court shall be
suspended–
(a) in any case until the expiration of the period for the time being prescribed by law for the giving of notice of appeal against a decision of a
magistrates' court;
(b) where notice of appeal is given within the period so described, until the
determination of the appeal;
but this subsection shall not apply where the order is made under s.28(1)(a) or
(b) and the court so directs, being of the opinion that the title to the goods to be
restored or, as the case may be, delivered or transferred under the order is not
in dispute.

POWERS OF CRIMINAL COURTS ACT 1973

Powers etc., of Crown Court in relation to fines and forfeited recognizances   **8b.63**
31. (1) Subject to the provisions of this section, if the Crown Court imposes
a fine on any person or forfeits his recognizance, the court may make an order–
(a) allowing time for the payment of the amount of the fine or the amount
due under the recognizance;
(b) directing payment of that amount by instalments of such amounts and
on such dates respectively as may be specified in the order;
(c) in the case of a recognizance, discharging the recognizance or reducing
the amount due thereunder.

(2) Subject to the provisions of this section, if the Crown Court imposes a
fine on any person or forfeits his recognizance, the court shall make an order
fixing a term of imprisonment or of detention under s.9 of the Criminal Justice

Act 1982 (detention of persons aged 17 to 20 for default) which he is to undergo if any sum which he is liable to pay is not duly paid or recovered.

(3) No person shall on the occasion when a fine is imposed on him or his recognizance is forfeited by the Crown Court be committed to prison or detained in pursuance of an order under subs (2) above unless—
   (a) in the case of an offence punishable with imprisonment, he appears to the court to have sufficient means to pay the sum forthwith;
   (b) it appears to the court that he is unlikely to remain long enough at a place of abode in the United Kingdom to enable payment of the sum to be enforced by other methods; or
   (c) on the occasion when the order is made the court sentences him to immediate imprisonment, custody for life, youth custody or detention in a detention centre for that or another offence, or sentences him as aforesaid for an offence in addition to forfeiting his recognizance, or he is already serving a sentence of custody for life or a term—
       (i) of imprisonment;
       (ii) of youth custody;
       (iii) of detention in a detention centre; or
       (iv) a detention under s.9 of the Criminal Justice Act 1982.

(3A) Subject to subs (3B) and (3C) below, the periods set out in the second column of the following Table shall be the maximum periods of imprisonment or detention under subs (2) above applicable respectively to the amounts set out opposite thereto.

Table

An amount not exceeding £50 .... 7 days
An amount exceeding £50 but not exceeding £100 .... 14 days
An amount exceeding £100 but not exceeding £400 .... 30 days
An amount exceeding £400 but not exceeding £1,000 .... 60 days
An amount exceeding £1,000 but not exceeding £2,000 .... 90 days
An amount exceeding £2,000 but not exceeding £5,000 .... 6 months
An amount exceeding £5,000 but not exceeding £10,000 .... 9 months
An amount exceeding £10,000 .... 12 months

(3B) Where the amount due at the time imprisonment or detention is imposed is so much of a fine or forfeited recognizance as remains due after part payment, then, subject to subs (3C) below, the maximum period applicable to the amount shall be the period applicable to the whole sum reduced by such number of days as bears to the total number of days therein the same proportion as the part paid bears to the total sum.

(3C) In calculating the reduction required under subs (3b) above any fraction of a day shall be left out of account and the maximum period shall not be reduced to less than five days.

(4) Where any person liable for the payment of a fine or a sum due under a recognizance to which this section applies is sentenced by the court to, or is serving or otherwise liable to serve, a term of imprisonment or youth custody or a term of detention under ss.4 or 9 of the Criminal Justice Act 1982, the court may order that any term of imprisonment or detention fixed under subs (2) above shall not begin to run until after the end of the first-mentioned term.

(5) The power conferred by this section to discharge a recognizance or reduce the amount due thereunder shall be in addition to the powers conferred by any other Act relating to the discharge, cancellation, mitigation or reduction of recognizances or sums forfeited thereunder.

(6) Subject to subs (7) below, the powers conferred by this section shall not be taken as restricted by any enactment about committal by a magistrates' court to the Crown Court which authorises the Crown Court to deal with an offender in any way in which the magistrates' court might have dealt with him.

(7) Any term fixed under subs (2) above as respects a fine imposed in pursuance of such an enactment, that is to say a fine which the magistrates' court could have imposed, shall not exceed the period applicable to that fine (if imposed by the magistrates' court) under s.149(1) of the Customs and Excise Management Act 1979.

(8) This section shall not apply to a fine imposed by the Crown Court on appeal against a decision of a magistrates' court, but subs (2) to (3C) above shall apply in relation to a fine imposed or recognizance forfeited by the criminal division of the Court of Appeal, or by the House of Lords on appeal from that division, as they apply in relation to a fine imposed or recognizance forfeited by the Crown Court, and the references to the Crown Court in subs (2) and (3) above shall be construed accordingly.

[*As amended by Customs and Excise Management Act 1979 Sch.4, CJA 1982 s.69, SI 1984 No 447*].

(3A) *Table*

An amount not exceeding £50	*5 days*
An amount exceeding £50 but not exceeding £100	*7 days*
An amount exceeding £100 but not exceeding £400	*14 days*
An amount exceeding £400 but not exceeding £1,000	*30 days*
An amount exceeding £1,000 but not exceeding £2,000	*45 days*
An amount exceeding £2,000 but not exceeding £5,000	*3 months*
An amount exceeding £5,000 but not exceeding £10,000	*6 months*
An amount exceeding £10,000 but not exceeding £20,000	*12 months*
An amount exceeding £20,000 but not exceeding £50,000	*18 months*
An amount exceeding £50,000 but not exceeding £100,000	*2 years*
An amount exceeding £100,000 but not exceeding £250,000	*3 years*
An amount exceeding £250,000 but not exceeding £1 million	*5 years*
An amount exceeding £1 million	*10 years*

[*The Table in subs (3A) will be substituted by [s.59] CJA 1988 from a date to be appointed*].

Enforcement, etc., of fines imposed and recognizances forfeited by Crown Court   **8b.64**

32. (1) Subject to the provisions of subs (4) below, a fine imposed or a recognizance forfeited by the Crown Court after 31 December 1967, shall be treated for the purposes of collection, enforcement and remission of the fine or other sum as having been imposed or forfeited–

    (a) by a magistrates' court specified in an order made by the Crown Court; or

    (b) if no such order is made, by the magistrates' court by which the offender was committed to the Crown Court to be tried or dealt with;

and in the case of a fine as having been so imposed on conviction by the magistrates' court in question.

(2) The term of imprisonment or detention under s.9 of the Criminal Justice Act 1982 specified in any warrant of committment issued by a magistrates' court on a default in the payment of a fine imposed, or sum due under a recognizance forfeited, by the Court as the term which the offender is liable to serve shall be the term fixed by the latter court under s.31(2) of this Act or, if that term has been reduced under s.79(2) of the Magistrates' Courts Act 1980 (part payment) or s.85(1) of that Act (remission) that term as so reduced, notwithstanding that that term exceeds the period applicable to the case under s.149(1) of the Customs and Excise Management Act 1979 (maximum periods of imprisonment in default of payment of fines, etc.).

(3) The preceding provisions of this section shall apply in relation to a fine imposed or recognizance forfeited by the criminal division of the Court of Appeal, or by the House of Lords on appeal from that division, as they apply in relation to a fine imposed or recognizance forfeited by the Crown Court, and

references in those provisions to the Crown Court shall be construed accordingly.

(4) A magistrates' court shall not under ss.85(1) or 120 of the Magistrates' Courts Act 1980, as applied by subs (1) above, remit the whole or any part of a fine imposed or a sum due under a recognizance forfeited by the Crown Court without the consent of that court, and s.85(1) shall have effect accordingly.

(5) A fine imposed or a recognizance forfeited by the criminal division of the Court of Appeal on appeal from the Crown Court or by the House of Lords on appeal from that division shall be treated for the purposes of collection, enforcement and remission of the fine or other sum as having been imposed or forfeited by the Crown Court.

(6) . . .

[*As amended by Sch.4 Customs and Excise Management Act 1979, Sch.7 MCA 1980, Schs.14, 16 CJA 1982*].

COMMENTARY

Despite the side note, these provisions apply equally to fines and recognizances imposed by the Criminal Division of the Court of Appeal and the House of Lords: s.32(5). Fines and recognizances may be transferred to Scotland notwithstanding that an alternative of imprisonment has been imposed by the higher court: s.33, *infra*.

s.32(1), written notice must be served by the clerk of the court; r.46(1) MC Rules 1981.

A fine, the wide definition of this term in s.150(1) MCA 1980 does not apply to this provision, wherein this term bears its narrow meaning.

Treated . . . as having been so imposed on conviction by the magistrates' court, the effect of these words, it is *suggested*, is to import all the enforcement powers that magistrates possess *vis-a-vis* their own fines. The Crown Court is required by s.31 of this Act to impose an alternative of imprisonment in default of payment of any fine or recognizance. Occasionally it fails to do so through an oversight. In such cases, it is *suggested*, magistrates may in exercise of their powers under s.76 MCA 1980 impose an alternative of imprisonment not exceeding the periods set out in Sch.4, *ibid*. It would appear that in all cases a means inquiry is necessary before the issue of a warrant of commitment in view of the fact that s.82(5) MCA 1980 speaks of '*the court*' fixing an alternative of imprisonment. Written notice must usually be served on the person fined: r.46(1) MC Rules 1981.

Collection, thus the justices' clerk has power to extend the time in which payment is to be made: Justices' Clerks Rules 1970 (SI No 231).

Enforcement, see the note 'Treated . . . as having been so imposed on conviction etc'.

Remission, this applies s.85 MCA 1980, subject to s.32(4).

8b.65   **Compensation orders against convicted persons**
35. (1) Subject to the provisions of this Part of this Act and to s.40 of the Magistrates' Courts Act 1980 (which imposes a monetary limit on the powers of a magistrates' court under this section), a court by or before which a person is convicted of an offence, instead of or in addition to dealing with him in any other way, may, on application or otherwise, make an order (in this Act referred to as 'a compensation order') requiring him to pay compensation for any personal injury, loss or damage resulting from that offence or any other offence which is taken into consideration by the court in determining sentence *or to make payments for funeral expenses or bereavement in respect of a death resulting from any such offence, other than a death due to an accident arising out of the presence of a motor vehicle on a road; and a court shall give reasons, on passing sentence, if it does not make such an order in a case where this section empowers it to do so.*

(1A) Compensation under subs (1) above shall be of such amount as the court considers appropriate, having regard to any evidence and to any representations that are made by or on behalf of the accused or the prosecutor.

(2) In the case of an offence under the Theft Act 1968, where the property

in question is recovered, any damage to the property occurring while it was out of the owner's possession shall be treated for the purposes of subs (1) above as having resulted from the offence, however and by whomsoever the damage was caused.

(3) No compensation order shall be made in respect of loss suffered by the dependants of a person in consequence of his death, and no such order shall be made in respect of injury, loss or damage due to an accident arising out of the presence of a motor vehicle on a road, except such damage as is treated by subs (2) above as resulting from an offence under the Theft Act 1968.

(4) In determining whether to make a compensation order against any person, and in determining the amount to be paid by any person under such an order, the court shall have regard to his means so far as they appear or are known to the court.

(4A) Where the court considers–
(a) that it would be appropriate both to impose a fine and to make a compensation order; but
(b) that the offender has insufficient means to pay both an appropriate fine and appropriate compensation,
the court shall give preference to compensation (though it may impose a fine as well).

[*As amended by s.60 CLA 1977, Sch.8 MCA 1980, s.67 CJA 1982. The words in italics in subs (1) will be added by [s.102] CJA 1988 from a date to be appointed*].

(3) A compensation order may only be made in respect of injury, loss or damage (other than loss suffered by a person's dependants in consequence of his death) which was due to an accident arising out of the presence of a motor vehicle on a road, if–
(a) it is in respect of damage which is treated by subsection (2) above as resulting from an offence under the Theft Act 1968; or
(b) it is in respect of injury, loss or damage as respects which–
    (i) the offender is uninsured in relation to the use of the vehicle; and
    (ii) compensation is not payable under any arrangements to which the Secretary of State is a party;
and, where a compensation order is made in respect of injury, loss or damage due to such an accident, the amount to be paid may include an amount representing the whole or part of any loss of or reduction in preferential rates of insurance attributable to the accident.

(3A) A vehicle the use of which is exempted from insurance by section 144 of the Road Traffic Act 1972 is not uninsured for the purposes of subsection (3) above.

(3B) A compensation order in respect of funeral expenses may be made for the benefit of anyone who incurred the expenses.

(3C) A compensation order in respect of bereavement may only be made for the benefit of a person for whose benefit a claim for damages for bereavement could be made under section 1A of the Fatal Accidents Act 1976.

(3D) The amount of compensation in respect of bereavement shall not exceed the amount for the time being specified in section 1A(3) of the Fatal Accidents Act 1976.

(4) In determining whether to make a compensation order against any person, and in determining the amount to be paid by any person under such an order, it shall be the duty of the court–
(a) to have regard to his means so far as they appear or are known to the court; and
(b) in a case where it is proposed to make against him both a compensation order and a confiscation order under Part VIII of the Criminal Justice Act

*1988, shall also have regard to its duty under section 65(7) of that Act
(duty where the court considers that the offenders means are insufficient
to satisfy both orders in full to order the payment out of sums recovered
under the confiscation order of sums due under the compensation order).*
*[Subsection (3)–(4) will be substituted by [Sch.14] CJA 1988 from a date to be
appointed].*

COMMENTARY

For the principles upon which compensation orders should be made to see 8b.05. For the
making of a compensation order against a juvenile see s.55 CYPA 1933.

An order of compensation made under this section continues in force even though the
offender be dealt with later under s.6 PCCA 1973 (breach of requirements of probation
order) in respect of the original offence: *R v Evans* (1961) 125 JP 134. The court expressed
the view that similar considerations would apply in the case of a probationer dealt with
under s.8 (subsequent offence). However, where a probationer subsequently receives a
substantial sentence of imprisonment it is contrary to justice that a compensation order
should remain hanging over his head if he has no means of paying it: *R v Wallis* [1979] Crim
LR 732.

For the effect of a compensation order on subsequent civil proceedings, see s.38, *infra*.

There is a maximum of £2000 on any compensation order made by a magistrates' court:
s.40 MCA 1980. Orders under this section may be enforced as sums adjudged to be paid on a
conviction by a magistrates' court: s.41(1) and Sch.9 Administration of Justice Act 1970; but
only after the period of suspension of this Act. For the priority of payment of compensation
orders see s.139 MCA 1980.

s.29 Ancient Monuments and Archaeological Areas Act 1979 provides that: 'Where the
owner or any other person is convicted of an offence involving damage to a monument
situated in England and Wales which was at the time of the offence under the guardianship
of the Secretary of State or any local authority by virtue of this Act, any compensation order
made under s.35 PCCA 1973 (compensation orders against convicted persons) in respect of
that damage shall be made in favour of the Secretary of State or (as the case may require) in
favour of the local authority in question.'

s.35(1): Instead of, this makes clear that compensation may be a sentence in its own right.

A person, an order against two persons involving joint and several liability is not inconsistent
with the Act, but, in view of the payment difficulties to which it could give rise, should be
made only with reserve and not if substantial justice can be achieved by orders made
severally: *R v Grundy; R v Moorhouse* [1974] 1 WLR 139. Where there are a number of
claimants for compensation and the offender has insufficient means to satisfy them all, as a
general rule the compensation should be apportioned *pro rata* but this principle may be
departed from where there are strong grounds, eg where it would lead to one or more small
claimants being compensated to a wholly inadequate degree. Similarly, all co-defendants
ought to be ordered to pay *pro rata* unless one of them is more responsible than the others or
where the ability to pay is markedly different: *R v Amey; R v Meah* (1983) 76 Cr App R 206.

Convicted, includes a conviction resulting in a probation order or order of absolute or
conditional discharge. Such orders are not excluded by the effects of s.13(1) of the Act,
because the making of a compensation order is a 'purpose of the proceedings in which the
order is made'.

Personal injury, compensation for distress and anxiety was upheld in *Bond v Chief Constable of Kent* [1983] 1 WLR 40 though left undecided whether it was personal injury or
damage.

Loss, the word 'loss' is to be given its *ordinary meaning* and includes any loss resulting from
the offence provided it is not too remote. It is wide enough to allow the award of interest, at
least where the amount involved is large, the time elapsed is long and the defendant's means
warrant the additional sum: *R v Schofield* (1978) 142 JP 426. Compensation should not be
asked for in respect of costs in related civil proceedings: *Hammerton Cars Ltd v Redbridge
LBC and Another* [1974] 2 All ER 216. In *R v Lester* (1976) 63 Cr App R 144, doubts were
expressed about the propriety of ordering compensation in respect of offences under the
Trade Descriptions Act 1968; but see *R v Thomson Holidays Ltd, infra*. Compensation is
inappropriate in a handling charge where there is no evidence that the goods have suffered
any damage or are of less value: *R v Sharkey* [1976] Crim LR 388 (car disassembled into
component parts). Seemingly this does not prevent an order for the cost of reassembly or an
order for loss where the parts cannot be reassembled. Loss is not limited to the personal
liability of a defendant in civil proceedings: *R v Chappell* (1985) 80 Cr App R 31 (under-

payment of tax). There is no loss where stolen goods are recovered undamaged: *R v Boardman* [1987] Crim LR 430.

Resulting from that offence, thus any order must be related to a *specific offence*, whether convicted or taken into consideration: *R v Oddy* [1974] 1 WLR 1212; *R v Inwood* (1974) 50 Cr App R 70; *R v Parker* (1982) 3 Cr App R (S) 279; *R v Making* [1982] Crim LR 613.

This term is to be given a wide meaning. In particular, Parliament did not intend to introduce into the criminal law the concepts of causation which apply to the assessment of civil damages: *R v Thomson Holidays Ltd* [1974] QB 592 (compensation for lost holiday). The court must ask itself whether loss or damage can fairly be said to have resulted to anyone from the offence for which the accused has been convicted or taken into consideration (*ibid*). Thus, a handler of stolen goods may be ordered to pay compensation to someone who purchased those goods from him innocently who has had to return them to the owner: *R v Howell* (1978) 66 Cr App R 179. Similarly, the court could make a compensation order in respect of sums frequently obtained over a number of weeks from the Department of Health and Social Security where the defendant was charged only with the first fraud: *Rowlston v Kenny* (1982) 4 Cr App R (S) 85. However, suffering if caused by taking a controlled drug does not result from the offence of its possession: *Berkeley v Orchard* [1975] Crim LR 225.

Any other offence which is taken into consideration, this is confined to offences taken into consideration under formalised practice and does not extend to other offences not the subject of sample charges: *Director of Public Prosecutions v Anderson* [1978] AC 964.

s.35(1A), '. . . what Parliament has done (in subs (1A)) . . . is slightly to reduce the obligation which was laid down by this Court in *Vivian's* case, in which it was said that it had to be proved that the compensation was due': *per* Kilner Brown J in *R v Swann and Webster* (1984) 6 Cr App R (S) 22 at p.25. S.35(1A) was introduced to reduce the obligations as to proof required by *R v Vivian* [1979] 1 WLR 291. However, the court has no jurisdiction to make a compensation order without receiving any evidence that a crime has been committed: *M (a Minor) v Oxford* [1981] RTR 246.

The new subsection seems to contemplate that the court can make assessments and approximations where the evidence is scanty or incomplete. It can then make an order which is 'appropriate'. Where there are plain issues as to liability, it is for the prosecution to place evidence before the court: *R v Horsham Justices, ex p. Richards* [1985] 1 WLR 986.

s.35(2), note that compensation for damage here is not subject to the exclusion concerning road accident damage contained in s.35(3). Since s.35(2) refers to damage to 'the property', damage to other property, eg other cars involved in an accident with a stolen car (where this falls within s.35(3)) may not be awarded: *Quigley v Stokes* [1977] 2 All ER 317.

s.35(3): Accident, where two young men were convicted of criminal damage following their having driven a stolen car into a wall it was held that there is no power to order compensation under this section because it was properly described as an 'accident' even though recklessness was proved: *M (a Minor) v Oxford* [1981] RTR 246.

S.35(4), see under *Compensation at 8b.05 and Means of the Offender* at 8b.06. Whilst there is no 'hard and fast rule' compensation should normally be payable (by instalments) within around one year': see *R v Hills* (1986) 8 Cr App R (S) 199 and *R v Broughton* [1987] Crim LR 140.

Appeals in the case of compensation orders   8b.66

36. (2) A compensation order made by a magistrates' court shall be suspended–
   (a) in any case until the expiration of the period for the time being described by law for the giving of notice of appeal against a decision of a magistrates' court;
   (b) where notice of appeal is given within the period so prescribed, until the determination of the appeal.

(3) Where a compensation order has been made against any person in respect of an offence taken into consideration in determining his sentence–
   (a) the order shall cease to have effect if he successfully appeals against his conviction of the offence or, if more than one, all the offences, of which he was convicted in the proceedings in which the order was made;
   (b) he may appeal against the order as if it were part of the sentence imposed in respect of the offence or, if more than one, any of the offences, of which he was so convicted.

Enforcement and appeals

36. *(1) A person in whose favour a compensation order is made shall not be entitled to receive the amount due to him until (disregarding any power of a court to grant leave to appeal out of time) there is no further possibility of an appeal on which the order could be varied or set aside.*

(2) Rules under s.144 of the Magistrates' Courts Act 1980 may make provision regarding the way in which the magistrates' court for the time being having functions (by virtue of s.41(1) of the Administration of Justice Act 1970) in relation to the enforcement of a compensation order is to deal with money paid in satisfaction of the order where the entitlement of the person in whose favour it was made is suspended.

(3) The Court of Appeal may by order annul or vary any compensation order made by the court of trial, although the conviction is not quashed; and the order, if annulled, shall not take effect and, if varied, shall take effect as varied.

(4) Where the House of Lords restores a conviction, it may make any compensation order which the court of trial could have made.

(5) Where a compensation order has been made against any person in respect of an offence taken into consideration in determining his sentence–
 (a) the order shall cease to have effect if he successfully appeals against his conviction of the offence or, if more than one, all the offences, of which he was convicted in the proceedings in which the order was made;
 (b) he may appeal against the order as if it were part of the sentence imposed in respect of the offence or, if more than one, any of the offences, of which he was so convicted.
[s.36 is substituted by [s.103] CJA 1988 from a date to be appointed].

COMMENTARY

s.36(2), it is suggested that this does not prevent a justices' clerk accepting payment of compensation within this period, but it should not be paid out to the person entitled until the period has expired or any appeal determined.

Made by a magistrates' court, a compensation order made on appeal from magistrates' shall be treated for the purposes of this Act as if it had been made by a magistrates' court: s.57(5).

Period for the time being prescribed, ie 21 days: r.7 Crown Court Rules 1971.

Determination of the appeal, there may, of course, be no determination of an appeal by way of case stated which is not proceeded with. In such a case it is *suggested* that enforcement may properly be commenced from the expiration of the period when the case should have been lodged in the Crown Office, provided that no application is being made for an extension of that time.

8b.67   **Review of compensation orders**

37. At any time before a compensation order has been complied with or fully complied with, the magistrates' court for the time being having functions in relation to the enforcement of the order (by virtue of s.41(1) of the Administration of Justice Act 1970), may, on the application of the person against whom it was made, discharge the order, or reduce the amount which remains to be paid, if it appears to the court–
 (a) that the injury, loss or damage in respect of which the order was made has been held in civil proceedings to be less than it was taken to be for the purposes of the order; or
 (b) in the case of an order in respect of the loss of any property, that the property has been recovered by the person in whose favour the order was made.

Review of compensation orders

37. *At any time before the person against whom a compensation order has been made has paid into court the whole of the compensation which the order requires him to pay, but at a time when (disregarding any power of a court to* *grant leave to appeal out of time) there is no further possibility of an appeal on which the order could be varied or set aside, the magistrates' court for the time being having functions in relation to the enforcement of the order may, on the application of the person against whom it was made, discharge the order, or reduce the amount which remains to be paid, if it appears to the court–*

 (a) *that the injury, loss or damage in respect of which the order was made has been held in civil proceedings to be less than it was taken to be for the purposes of the order; or*

 (b) *in the case of an order in respect of the loss of any property, that the property has been recovered by the person in whose favour the order was made; or*

 (c) *that the means of the person against whom the order was made are insufficient to satisfy in full both the order and a confiscation order under Part VI of the Criminal Justice Act 1988 made against him in the same proceedings; or*

 (d) *that the person against whom the order was made has suffered a substantial reduction in his means which was unexpected at the time when the compensation order was made, and that his means seem unlikely to increase for a considerable period;*

but where the order was made by the Crown Court, a magistrates' court shall not exercise any power conferred by this section in a case where it is satisfied as mentioned in paragraph (c) or (d) above unless it has first obtained the consent of the Crown Court.

[s.37 is substituted by [s.103] CJA 1988 from a date to be appointed].

COMMENTARY

There is power to grant legal aid in respect of proceedings under this section: s.28(4) LAA 1974.

Application, to be by way of complaint: r.104 MC Rules 1981. That incorporates the provisions ss.51–57 MCA 1980. The terms of the rule would appear to leave the justice no discretion but to issue a summons whenever a complaint is made.

The property has been recovered, the amount of the compensation order may seemingly be reduced for partial recovery.

Effect of compensation order on subsequent award of damages in civil proceedings   8b.68

38. (1) This section shall have effect where a compensation order has been made in favour of any person in respect of any injury. loss or damage and a claim by him in civil proceedings for damages in respect thereof subsequently falls to be determined.

(2) The damages in the civil proceedings shall be assessed without regard to the order; but where the whole or part of the amount awarded by the order has been paid; the damages awarded in the civil proceedings shall not exceed the amount (if any) by which, as so assessed, they exceed the amount paid under the order.

(3) Where the whole or part of the amount awarded by the order remains unpaid and the court awards damages in the civil proceedings, then, unless the person against whom the order was made has ceased to be liable to pay the amount unpaid (whether in consequence of an appeal, of his imprisonment for default or otherwise), the court shall direct that the judgment–

 (a) if it is for an amount not exceeding the amount unpaid under the order, shall not be enforced; or

 (b) if it is for an amount exceeding the amount unpaid under the order, shall not be enforced as to a corresponding amount;

without the leave of the court.

Effect of compensation order on subsequent award of damages in civil proceedings

38. *(1) This section shall have effect where a compensation order has been made in favour of any person in respect of any injury, loss or damage and a claim* *by him in civil proceedings for damages in respect of the injury, loss or damage subsequently falls to be determined.*

(2) The damages in the civil proceedings shall be assessed without regard to the order; but the plaintiff may only recover an amount equal to the aggregate of the following–
(a) any amount by which they exceed the compensation; and
(b) a sum equal to any portion of the compensation which he fails to recover,
and may not enforce the judgment, so far as it relates to a sum such as is mentioned in para (b) above, without the leave of the court.
[s.38 is substituted by [s.100] CJA 1988 from a date to be appointed].

8b.69   **Power to deprive offender of property used, or intended for use, for purposes of crime**
43. (1) Where a person is convicted of an offence punishable on indictment with imprisonment for a term of two years or more and the court by or before which he is convicted is satisfied that any property which was in his possession or under his control at the time of his apprehension–
(a) has been used for the purpose of committing, or facilitating the commission of, any offence; or
(b) was intended by him to be used for that purpose;
the court may make an order under this section in respect of that property.

(2) Facilitating the commission of an offence shall be taken for the purposes of this section and s.44 of this Act to include the taking of any steps after it has been committed for the purpose of disposing of any property to which it relates or of avoiding apprehension or detection, and references in this or that section to an offence punishable with imprisonment shall be construed without regard to any prohibition or restriction imposed by or under any enactment on the imprisonment of young offenders.

(3) An order under this section shall operate to deprive the offender of his rights, if any, in the property to which it relates, and the property shall (if not already in their possession) be taken into the possession of the police.

(4) The Police (Property) Act 1897, shall apply, with the following modifications, to property which is in the possession of the police by virtue of this section–
(a) no application shall be made under s.1(1) of that Act any claimant of the property after the expiration of six months from the date on which the order in respect of the property was made under this section; and
(b) no such application shall succeed unless the claimant satisfies the court either that he had not consented to the offender having possession of the property or that he did not know, and had no reason to suspect, that the property was likely to be used for the purpose mentioned in subs (1) above.

(5) *(Regulations).*

(1) Subject to the following provisions of this section, where a person is convicted of an offence and–
(a) the court by or before which he is convicted is satisfied that any property which has been lawfully seized from him or which was in his possession or under his control at the time when he was apprehended for the offence or when a summons in respect of it was issued–
(i) has been used for the purpose of committing, or facilitating the commission of, any offence; or
(ii) was intended by him to be used for that purpose; or
(b) the offence, or an offence which the court has taken into consideration in determining his sentence, consists of unlawful possession of property which–
(i) has been lawfully seized from him; or

(ii) was in his possession or under his control at the time when he was apprehended for the offence of which he has been convicted or when a summons in respect of that offence was issued,
the court may make an order under this section in respect of that property, and may do so whether or not it also deals with the offender in respect of the offence in any other way.

(1A) In considering whether to make such an order in respect of any property a court shall have regard–
(a) to the value of the property; and
(b) to the likely financial and other effects on the offender of the making of the order (taken together with any other order that the court contemplates making).
[subs (1) will be substituted and subs (1A) will be added by [s.68] CJA 1988 from a date to be appointed].

COMMENTARY

See under *Deprivation of Property* in the introduction. An order under this section cannot be combined with a conditional discharge: *R v Savage* (1983) 5 Cr App R (S) 216.

s.43(1): An offence punishable on indictment, even if tried summarily; and s.43(2). This provision is confined to property which has been '. . . used for the purpose of committing any offence *by him* (the accused)', which does not include property '. . . used for the purpose of committing any offence *by anyone*': see *R v Slater* (1986) 8 Cr App R (S) 217.

At the time of his apprehension, thus, if the property was seized before the defendant was arrested no order may be made under this section: *R v Hinde* (1977) 64 Cr App R 213; *R v McFarlane* (1982) 4 Cr App R (S) 264. Likewise, if the proceedings were begun by way of summons: *R v Bramble* (1984) 6 Cr App R (S) 81.

Facilitating the commission of any offence, see s.43(2). An order was quashed because a car used to transport a woman to a place where she was indecently assaulted was not used for the purpose of committing or facilitating the commission of an offence: *R v Lucas* [1976] RTR 235.

s.43(3), the property will, subject to s.43(4) be disposed of in accordance with s.140 MCA 1980. However, an order may not be made as a means of securing payment of a fine: *R v Kingston Upon Hull Stipendiary Magistrate, ex p. Hartnung* [1981] RTR 262.

s.43(4): the Police (Property) Act 1897, supra, the effect is to apply the s.1 procedure for application to a magistrates' court subject to the six months' limitation imposed by s.43(4)(a).

Application of proceeds of forfeited property

8b.69a

43A. (1) Where a court makes an order under section 43 above in a case where–
(a) the offender has been convicted of an offence which has resulted in a person suffering personal injury, loss or damage; or
(b) any such offence is taken into consideration by the court in determining sentence,
the court may also make an order that any proceeds which arise from the disposal of the property and which do not exceed a sum specified by the court shall be paid to that person.

(2) The court may only make an order under this section if it is satisfied that but for the inadequacy of the means of the offender it would have made a compensation order under which the offender would have been required to pay compensation of an amount not less than the specified amount.

(3) An order under this section has no effect–
(a) before the end of the period specified in section 43(4)(a) above; or
(b) if a successful application under section 1(1) of the Police (Property) Act 1897 has been made.
[s.43A will be added by [s.105] CJA 1988 from a date to be appointed].

CRIMINAL LAW ACT 1977

8b.70　　　**Execution in different part of United Kingdom of warrants for imprisonment for non-payment of fine**

38A. (1) Subject to subs (6) below, a person against whom an extract conviction is issued in Scotland for imprisonment in default of payment of a fine may be arrested–

(a) in England and Wales, by any constable acting within his police area;

(b) in Northern Ireland, by any member of the Royal Ulster Constabulary or the Royal Ulster Constabulary Reserve;

and subs (4) and (5) of s.159 of the Magistrates' Courts Act (Northern Ireland) 1964 (execution without possession of the warrant and execution on Sunday) shall apply to the execution in Northern Ireland of any such extract conviction as those subsections apply in relation to the execution of a warrant for arrest.

(2) Subject to subs (6) below, a person against whom there has been issued in England, Wales or Northern Ireland a warrant committing him to prison in default of payment of a sum adjudged to be paid by a conviction may be arrested in Scotland, by any constable appointed for a police area, in like manner as if the warrant were an extract conviction for imprisonment issued in Scotland in default of payment of a fine.

(3) A person arrested by virtue of subs (1) above under an extract conviction or by virtue of subs (2) above under a warrant of commitment may be detained under it in any prison in the part of the United Kingdom in which he was arrested; and while so detained he shall be treated for all purposes as if he were detained under a warrant of commitment or extract conviction issued that part of the United Kingdom.

(4) An extract conviction or a warrant of commitment may be executed by virtue of this section whether or not it has been endorsed under s.4 of the Summary Jurisdiction (Process) Act 1881 or under s.27 of the Petty Sessions (Ireland) Act 1851.

(5) In this section–

'fine' includes any sum treated by any enactment as a fine for the purposes of its enforcement and any sum to be found as caution;

'imprisonment' includes, in the case of a person who is under the age of 21 years, detention;

'part of the United Kingdom' means England and Wales, Scotland or Northern Ireland;

'prison' means–

(i) in the case of a person who is under the age of 21 years arrested in Scotland, a young offenders institution; and

(ii) in the case of a person under that age arrested in England and Wales, any place in which he could be detained under s.12(10) of the Criminal Justice Act 1982;

(iii) in the case of a person under that age arrested in Northern Ireland, a young offenders centre; and

'sum adjudged to be paid by a conviction' has the meaning given by s.150(3) of the Magistrates' Courts Act 1980 or, in Northern Ireland, s.169(2) of the Magistrates' Courts (Northern Ireland) Act 1964.

(6) This section shall not apply to the arrest of persons under the age of 17 years.

[*As inserted by s.51 Criminal Justice (Scotland) Act 1980, and as amended by Sch.14 CJA 1982*].

COMMENTARY

The effects of this section are described in HOC 58/1981.

s.38A(1): Extract conviction, this is the Scottish equivalent of a warrant of commitment.

Further provision for execution of warrants of commitment for non-payment 8b.71
of sum adjudged to be paid by conviction in England and Wales or Northern
Ireland
  38B. (1) Subject to subs (6) below, a person against whom there has been
issued in England and Wales a warrant committing him to prison in default of
payment of a sum adjudged to be paid by a conviction may be arrested in
Northern Ireland by any member of the Royal Ulster Constabulary Reserve in
like manner as if the warrant committing him to prison in default of payment of
a sum adjudged to be paid by a conviction in Northern Ireland and Article
158(4) and (5) of the Magistrates' Courts (Northern Ireland) Order 1981
(execution without possession of the warrant and execution on Sunday) shall
apply to the execution in Northern Ireland of any such warrant which has been
issued in England and Wales as they apply in relation to the execution of a
warrant for arrest.

  (2) Subject to subs (6) below, a person against whom there has been issued
in Northern Ireland a warrant committing him to prison in default of payment
of a sum adjudged to be paid by a conviction may be arrested in England and
Wales by any constable acting within his police area in like manner as the
warrant were a warrant committing him to prison in default of payment of a
sum adjudged to be paid by a conviction in England and Wales.

  (3) A person arrested by virtue of subss (1) or (2) above under a warrant of
commitment may be detained under it in any prison in the part of the United
Kingdom in which he was arrested; and while so detained he shall be treated
for all purposes as if he were detained under a warrant of commitment issued in
that part of the United Kingdom.

  (4) A warrant of commitment issued by a court in Northern Ireland may be
executed in England and Wales by virtue of this section whether or not it has
been endorsed under s.27 of the Petty Sessions (Ireland) Act 1851.

  (5) In this section–
'part of the United Kingdom' means England and Wales or Northern Ireland;
'prison' means–
  (a) in the case of a person who is under the age of 21 years arrested in
      England and Wales, any place in which he could be detained under
      s.12(1) of the Criminal Justice Act 1982; and
  (b) in the case of a person under that age arrested in Northern Ireland, a
      young offenders centre; and
'sum adjudged to be paid by a conviction' has the meaning given by s.150(3) of
the Magistrates' Courts Act 1980 or, in Northern Ireland, Art 2(5) of the
Magistrates' Courts (Northern Ireland) Order 1981.

  (6) This section shall not apply to the arrest of persons under the age of 17
years.
[*As inserted by s.52 CJA 1982*].

COMMENTARY
'Both subs (1) and (2) (like subs (1) and (2) of s.38A) are intended to meet the situation
where, after a court in one jurisdiction has issued a warrant committing a defaulter to
prison, it becomes known that he is living in the other. (Prior to the issue of a warrant a
transfer of fine order may be made under ss.90 and 91 of the Magistrates' Courts Act 1980.)':
HOC 13/1983.

MAGISTRATES' COURTS ACT 1980

Fixing amount of fine 8b.72
  35. In fixing the amount of a fine, a magistrates' court shall take into
consideration among other things the means of the person on whom the fine is
imposed so far as they appear or are known to the court.

COMMENTARY
See under *Means of the Offender* at 8b.04.

A **fine,** this includes any *pecuniary penalty* or *pecuniary forfeiture* or *pecuniary compensation* payable under a conviction: s.150(1) MCA 1980.

8b.73   Restriction on fines in respect of young persons
  36. (1) Where a person under 17 years of age is found guilty by a magistrates' court of an offence for which, apart from this section, the court would have power to impose a fine of an amount exceeding £400, the amount of any fine imposed by the court shall not exceed £400.

  (2) In relation to a person under the age of 14 subs (1) above shall have effect as if for the words £400, in both the places where they occur, there were substituted the words '£100'; but this subsection shall cease to have effect on the coming into force of s.4 of the Children and Young Persons Act 1969 (which prohibits criminal proceedings against children).
  [*As amended by SI 1984 No 447*].

COMMENTARY
A **fine,** the wide definition of this term in s.150(1) of the Act is inapplicable. It therefore bears its ordinary or narrow meaning.

8b.74   Restriction on amount payable under compensation order of magistrates' court
  40. (1) The compensation to be paid under a compensation order made by a magistrates' court in respect of any offence of which the court has convicted the offender shall not exceed £2,000; and the compensation or total compensation to be paid under a compensation order or compensation orders made by a magistrates' court in respect of any offence or offences taken into consideration in determining sentence shall not exceed the difference (if any) between the amount or total amount which under the preceding provisions of this subsection is the maximum for the offence or offences of which the offender has been convicted and the amount or total amounts (if any) which are in fact ordered to be paid in respect of that offence or those offences.

  (2) In subs (1) above 'compensation order' has the meaning assigned to it by s.35(1) of the Powers of Criminal Courts Act 1973.
  [*As amended by SI 1984 No 447*].

COMMENTARY
s.40(1): the second part of s.40(1) merely extends the existing rule that the maximum financial burden which can be imposed on a defendant when offences are taken into consideration cannot exceed the maximum permitted without such other offences, except that where there are two or more substantive offences the amount available for compensation is the aggregate of the amounts allowable for each offence. Thus, eg where there are two offences one of which involves damage of say, £100, the court may order a total of up to £3,900 compensation in respect of offences taken into consideration.

8b.75   Return of property taken from accused
  48. Where a summons or warrant has been issued requiring any person to appear or be brought before a magistrates' court to answer to an information, or where any person has been arrested without a warrant for an offence and property has been taken from him after the issue of the summons or warrant or, as the case may be, on or after his arrest without a warrant, the police shall report the taking of the property, with particulars of the property, to the magistrates' court which deals with the case; and, if the court, being of opinion that the whole or any part of the property can be returned to the accused consistently with the interests of justice and the safe custody of the accused, so directs, the property, or such part of it as the court directs, shall be returned to the accused or to such other person as he may require.

COMMENTARY

This section may be accused, eg when a person committed for trial needs access to his money to pay for his defence: *Cf R v D'Eyncourt* [1888] 21 QBD 109.

After the issue of the summons etc, not before: *Arnell v Harris* (1945) 109 JP 14.

Orders other than for payment of money 8b.76

63. (1) Where under any Act passed after 31 December 1879 a magistrates' court has power to require the doing of anything other than the payment of money, or to prohibit the doing of anything, any order of the court for the purpose of exercising that power may contain such provisions for the manner in which anything is to be done, for the time within which anything is to be done, or during which anything is not to be done, and generally for giving effect to the order, as the court thinks fit.

(2) The court may by order made on complaint suspend or rescind any such order as aforesaid.

(3) Where any person disobeys an order of a magistrates' court made under an Act passed after 31 December 1879 to do anything other than the payment of money or to abstain from doing anything the court may–
  (a) order him to pay a sum not exceeding £50 for every day during which he is in default or a sum not exceeding £2,000; or
  (b) commit him to custody until he has remedied his default or for a period not exceeding two months;
but a person who is ordered to pay a sum for every day during which he is in default or who is committed to custody until he has remedied his default shall not by virtue of this section be ordered to pay more than £1,000 or be committed for more than two months in all for doing or abstaining from doing the same thing contrary to the order (without prejudice to the operation of this section in relation to any subsequent default).

(4) Any sum ordered to be paid under subs (3) above shall for the purposes of this Act be treated as adjudged to be paid by a conviction of a magistrates' court.

(5) The preceding provisions of this section shall not apply to any order for the enforcement of which provision is made by any other enactment.
[*As amended by SI No 447*].

COMMENTARY

The power under this section may be exercised either of the court's own motion or by order on complaint: s.17(1) Contempt of Court Act 1981.

There is no power to make consecutive commitments to prison under this section: *Head v Head* [1982] 3 All ER 14.

Instead of being committed to a prison a person under 21 but not less than 17 may be detained under s.9 CJA 1982.

Power to dispense with immediate payment 8b.77

75. (1) A magistrates' court by whose conviction or order a sum is adjudged to be paid may, instead of requiring immediate payment, allow time for payment, or other payment by instalments.

(2) Were a magistrates' court has allowed time for payment, the court may, on application by or on behalf of the person liable to make the payment, allow further time to order payment by instalments.

(3) Where a court has ordered payment by instalments and default is made in the payment of any one instalment, proceedings may be taken as if the default has been made in the payment of all the instalments then unpaid.

COMMENTARY

For the '12 months rule' see under *Means of the Offender* at 8b.06.

s.75(1): the clerk must give notice to the offender unless the offender is present and the fine is ordered to be paid forthwith: r.46(1) MC Rules 1981. Payment is to the clerk unless the court directs otherwise: r.48.

A sum is adjudged to be paid (on conviction), defined in s.150(3) *infra*.

s.75(2): On application, unless the court requires the applicant to attend, the application may be in writing r.51 MC Rules 1981; and to any magistrates' court acting for the same petty sessions area: s.148(2) MCA 1980.

Allow further time or order payment by instalments, either order must be recorded in the court register or any separate record kept for the purpose: r.65 MC Rules 1981. The defaulter must be notified in writing r.46(1). The clerk to the justices may allow further time for payment of a sum enforceable by a magistrates' court: Justices' Clerks Rules 1970 (SI No 231).

8b.78   **Enforcement of sums adjudged to be paid**
        76. (1) Subject to the following provisions of this Part of this Act, and to s.132 below, where default is made in paying a sum adjudged to be paid by a conviction or order of a magistrates' court, the court may issue a warrant of distress for the purpose of levying the sum or issue a warrant committing the defaulter to prison.

        (2) A warrant of commitment may be issued as aforesaid either–
        (a) where it appears on the return to a warrant of distress that the money and goods of the defaulter are insufficient to satisfy the sum with the costs and charges of levying the sum; or
        (b) instead of a warrant of distress.

        (3) The period for which a person may be committed to prison under such a warrant as aforesaid shall not, subject to the provisions of any enactment passed after 31 December 1879, exceed the period applicable to the case under Sch.4 to this Act.
        [*As amended by Sch.16 CJA 1982*].

COMMENTARY

For *Defaulters under 21*, see under that title in the introduction.

s.76(1): Default in paying, a certificate signed by the clerk is admissible to prove non-payment: s.99 MCA 1980.

Sum adjudged to be paid by a conviction, defined in s.150(3), *infra*.

The court, not necessarily the justices, or even the court which imposed the fine, but any court acting for the same petty sessions area: s.148(2).

Warrant of distress, see under *Distraint of goods* at 8b.20.

Warrant committing the defaulter to prison, see under *Imprisonment* at 8b.21. The warrant may be executed anywhere in England and Wales s.125(2) MCA 1980; and remains in force until executed or withdrawn: s.125(1) MCA 1980. For the contents of the warrant see: rr.95, 96 and forms 51, 52 MC Rules 1981.
    When a warrant of commitment is issued or an alternative of imprisonment is fixed *on the occasion of conviction*, the reasons for the court's action must be recorded in the register or separate record: r.65. A warrant of commitment in default cannot be suspended under s.22 PCCA 1973: *R v Nixon* (1969) 54 Cr App R 179; but it can be postponed under s.77, *infra*.
    Imprisonment runs from the date the prisoner is received by the prison: *Henderson v Preston* (1888) 52 JP 820. Where a prison cannot be taken to prison the same day an *express order* should be inserted in the warrant that the sentence is to reckoned from the date on which it was passed: HOC 22 April 1889 (56 JPN 586). It is not an abuse of power for an officer to fail to execute a warrant of commitment until after the defaulter has been released from a period of remand: *R v Leeds Prison Governor, ex p. Huntley* (1972) 136 JP 551. Dealing with the arrest of an absconding debtor, Vaughan Williams LJ was of opinion that a warrant would authorise the officer to break the door and go in and arrest the debtor inside: *Re Von Weissenfeld, ex p. Hendry* (1892) 36 SJ 276.

s.76(3): terms may be consecutive up to a maximum of six months, or 12 months if two or more of the sentences are indictable: s.133. The period fixed by the court must not exceed the maximum for the aggregated sum found on the warrant. If separate periods for separate fines are fixed separate warrants must be issued: *R v Southampton Justices, ex p. Davies*

(1981) 145 JP 247; although doubted by the House of Lords in *Forrest v Brighton Justices, infra*, this decision was nevertheless followed in *R v Midhurst Justices, ex p. Seymour* (1983) 147 JP 266, wherein it was said that the proper course for justices is to look at the whole of the circumstances, including the offence and the amount sought to be enforced. If they are satisfied that justice can be done by a term not exceeding the statutory maximum, it would be appropriate for it to be done on a single warrant. If after full consideration it was felt that the aggregate of sentences imposed should be such that it would exceed the maximum, it was inevitable that separate warrants in respect of each committal would have to be issued.

Provided that sentences are imposed on different days, there is in theory no limit to the aggregate of the terms of imprisonment that may be imposed: *Forrest v Brighton Justices; Hamilton v Marylebone Magistrates Court* (1981) 145 JP 356. Thus, when a fine was imposed at the same time as a sentence of imprisonment and an alternative in default of payment fixed at a later hearing the total period of imprisonment was not limited in accordance with s.133(1): *R v Metropolitan Stipendiary Magistrates for South Westminster, ex p. Green* (1977) 141 JP 151.

Postponement of issue of warrant   **8b.79**

77. (1) Where a magistrates' court has power to issue a warrant of distress under this Part of this Act, it may, if it thinks it expedient to do so, postpone the issue of the warrant until such time and on such conditions, if any, as the court thinks just.

(2) Where a magistrates' court has power to issue a warrant of commitment under this Part of this Act, if it thinks it expedient to do so, fix a term of imprisonment or detention under s.9 of the Criminal Justice Act 1982 (detention of persons aged 17 to 20 for default) and postpone the issue of the warrant until such time and on such conditions, if any, as the court thinks just.

(3) A magistrates' court shall have power at any time to do either or both of the following–
(a) to direct that the issue of the warrant of commitment shall be postponed until a time different from that to which it was previously postponed;
(b) to vary any of the conditions on which its issue is postponed,
but only if it thinks it just to do so having regard to a change of circumstances since the relevant time.

(4) In this section 'the relevant time' means–
(a) where neither of the powers conferred by subs (3) above has been exercised previously, the date when the issue of the warrant was postponed under subs (2) above; and
(b) in any other case, the date of the exercise or latest exercise of either or both of the powers.

(5) Without prejudice to the generality of subs (3) above, if on an application by a person in respect of whom issue of a warrant has been postponed it appears to a justice of the peace acting for the petty sessions area in which the warrant has been or would have been issued that since the relevant time there has been a change of circumstances which would make it just for the court to exercise one or other or both of the powers conferred by that subsection, he shall refer the application to the court.

(6) Where such an application is referred to the court, it shall be the duty of the clerk of the court–
(a) to fix a time and place for the application to be heard; and
(b) to give the applicant notice of the time and place which he fixes.

(7) Where such a notice has been given but the applicant does not appear at the time and place specified in the notice, the court may proceed with the consideration of the application in his absence.

(8) If a warrant of commitment in respect of the sum adjudged to be paid has been issued before the hearing of the application, the court shall have power to order that the warrant shall cease to have effect and, if the applicant has been arrested in pursuance of it, to order that he shall be released, but it shall only

make an order under this subsection if it is satisfied that the change of circum-
stances on which the applicant relies was not put before the court when it was
determining whether to issue the warrant.'.
[*As amended by Sch.14 CJA 1982*].
[*subs (3)–(8) will be added by [s.60] CJA 1988 from a date to be appointed*].

COMMENTARY

s.77(1): Power . . . under this Part of this Act, see ss.76 and 82.

s.77(2): the power to review a postponed warrant of commitment may be exercised from
time to time as occasion demands by virtue of s.12(1) Interpretation Act 1978: *Wilson ι
Colchester Justices* [1985] AC 750.

8b.80 **Defect in distress warrant and irregularity in its execution**
78. (1) A warrant of distress issued for the purpose of levying a sum
adjudged to be paid by the conviction or order of a magistrates' court shall not,
if it states that the sum has been so adjudged to be paid, be held void by reason
of any defect in the warrant.

(2) A person acting under a warrant of distress shall not be deemed to be a
trespasser from the beginning by reason only of any irregularity in the execution of the warrant.

(3) Nothing in this section shall prejudice the claim of any person for special
damages in respect of any loss caused by a defect in the warrant or irregularity
in its execution.

(4) If any person removes any goods marked in accordance with the rules as
articles impounded in the execution of a warrant of distress, or defaces or
removes any such mark, he shall be liable on summary conviction to a fine not
exceeding level 1 on the standard scale.

(5) If any person charged with the execution of a warrant of distress wilfully
retains from the proceeds of a sale of the goods on which distress is levied, or
otherwise exacts, any greater costs and charges than those properly payable,
or makes any improper charge, he shall be liable on summary conviction to a
fine not exceeding level 1 on the standard scale.
[*As amended by s.46 CJA 1982*].

COMMENTARY

Warrants of distress may be issued under s.76, *supra.*

s.78(1): Any defect, presumably not to be taken literally: compare the cases on s.123.

s.78(2): Trespasser from the beginning, ie *ab initio*; but *cf. Chic Fashions (West Wales) Ltd ι
Jones* [1968] 2 QB 299.

s.78(4): Goods marked in accordance with the rules, ie in accordance with r.54(8) MC Rules
1981.

8b.81 **Release from custody and reduction of detention on payment**
79. (1) Where imprisonment or other detention has been imposed on any
person by the order of a magistrates' court in default of payment of any sum
adjudged to be paid by the conviction or order of a magistrates' court or for
want of sufficient distress to satisfy such a sum, then, on the payment of the
sum, together with the costs and charges, if any, of the commitment and
distress, the order shall cease to have effect; and if the person has been
committed to custody he shall be released unless he is in custody for some
other cause.

(2) Where, after a period of imprisonment or other detention has been
imposed on any person in default of payment of any sum adjudged to be paid
by the conviction or order of a magistrates' court or for want of sufficient
distress to satisfy such a sum, payment is made in accordance with the rules of
part of the sum, the period of detention shall be reduced by such number or

days as bears to the total number of days in that period less one day the same proportion as the amount so paid bears to so much of the said sum, and the costs and charges of any distress levied to satisfy that sum, as was due at the time the period of detention was imposed.

(3) In calculating the reduction required under subs (2) above any fraction of a day shall be left out of account.

COMMENTARY
s.79(1): Other detention, in the case of a defaulter aged 17–20 see s.96A, *infra.* For detention in police cells etc, see ss.134–136 MCA 1980 in Chapter 8d.

s.79(2) and (3), the calculation is as follows:

$$\frac{\text{Sum paid}}{\text{Sum adjudged to be paid}} \times \text{Days of imprisonment less 1}$$

From the product deduct (1) any fraction, (2) then take the remaining whole number from the total days' imprisonment. The answer is the period of imprisonment still to be served.

Note the difference between this calculation and that for reducing the maximum period of imprisonment set out in para 2, Sch.4, *infra.* When the period of imprisonment is reduced by part payment to *less than five days,* the offender may alternatively be detained in a place certified by the Secretary of State under s.134: r.55(5) MC Rules 1981.

Payment is made in accordance with the rules, for persons entitled to receive payment, see r.55.

Application of money found on defaulter to satisfy sum adjudged   8b.82
80. (1) Where a magistrates' court has adjudged a person to pay a sum by a conviction or has ordered the enforcement of a sum due from a person under an affiliation order an order enforceable as an affiliation order, the court may order him to be searched.

(2) Any money found on the arrest of a person adjudged to pay such a sum as aforesaid, or on a search as aforesaid, or on his being taken to a prison or other place of detention in default of payment of such a sum or for want of sufficient distress to satisfy such a sum, may, unless the court otherwise directs, be applied towards payment of the said sum; and the balance, if any, shall be returned to him.

(3) A magistrates' court shall not allow the application as aforesaid of any money found on a person if it is satisfied that the money does not belong to him or that the loss of the money would be more injurious to his family than would be his detention.

COMMENTARY
s.80(1): Adjudged . . . to pay a sum by conviction, defined in s.150(3).

s.80(2): Other place of detention, see note to s.79.

For want of sufficient distress, see s.76, *supra.*

Unless the court otherwise directs, must be endorsed on the warrant: r.64 MC Rules 1981.

Restriction on power to impose imprisonment for default   8b.83
82. (1) A magistrates' court shall not on the occasion of convicting an offender of an offence issue a warrant of commitment for a default in paying any sum adjudged to be paid by the conviction unless–
  (a) in the case of an offence punishable with imprisonment, he appears to the court to have sufficient means to pay the sum forthwith;
  (b) it appears to the court that he is unlikely to remain long enough at a place of abode in the United Kingdom to enable payment of the sum to be enforced by other methods; or
  (c) on the occasion of that conviction the court sentences him to immediate imprisonment, youth custody or detention in a detention centre for that

or another offence or he is already serving a sentence of custody for life, or a term of imprisonment, youth custody, detention under s.9 of the Criminal Justice Act 1982 or detention in a detention centre.

(2) A magistrates' court shall not in advance of the issue of a warrant of commitment fix a term of imprisonment which is to be served by an offender in the event of a default in paying a sum adjudged to be paid by a conviction, except where it has power to issue a warrant of commitment forthwith, but postpones issuing the warrant under s.77(2) above.

(3) Where on the occasion of the offender's conviction a magistrates' court does not issue a warrant of commitment for a default in paying any such sum as aforesaid or fix a term of imprisonment under the said. s.77(2) which is to be served by him in the event of any such default it shall not thereafter issue a warrant of commitment for any such default or for want of sufficient distress to satisfy such a sum unless–

(a) he is already serving a sentence of custody for life, a term of imprisonment, youth custody, detention under s.9 of the Criminal Justice Act 1982 or detention in a detention centre; or

(b) the court has since the conviction inquired into his means in his presence on at least one occasion.

(4) Where a magistrates' court is required by subs (3) above to inquire into a person's means, the court may not on the occasion of the inquiry or at any time thereafter issue a warrant of commitment for a default in paying any such sum unless–

(a) in the case of an offence punishable with imprisonment, the offender appears to the court to have sufficient means to pay the sum forthwith; or

(b) the court–

    (i) is satisfied that the default is due to the offender's wilful refusal or culpable neglect; and

    (ii) has considered or tried all other methods of enforcing payment of the sum and it appears to the court that they are inappropriate or unsuccessful.

(4A) The methods of enforcing payment mentioned in subs (4)(b)(ii) above are–

(a) a warrant of distress under s.76 above;

(b) an application to the High Court or county court for enforcement under s.87 below;

(c) an order under s.88 below;

(d) an attachment of earnings order; and

(e) if the offender is under the age of 21, an order under s.17 of the Criminal Justice Act 1982 (attendance centre orders).

(5) After the occasion of an offender's conviction by a magistrates' court, the court shall not, unless–

(a) the court has previously fixed a term of imprisonment under s.77(2) above which is to be served by the offender in the event of a default in paying a sum adjudged tobe paid by the conviction; or

(b) the offender is serving a sentence of custody for life, a term of imprisonment, youth custody, detention under s.9 of the Criminal Justice Act 1982 or detention in a detention centre,

issue a warrant of commitment for a default in paying the sum or fix such a term except at a hearing at which the offender is present.

(5A) A magistrates' court may not issue a warrant of commitment under subs (5) above at a hearing which the offender is not present unless the clerk of the court has served on the offender a notice in writing stating that the court intends to hold a hearing to consider whether to issue such a warrant and giving the reason why the court so intends.

(5B) Where after the occasion of an offender's conviction by a magistrates' court the court holds a hearing for the purpose of considering whether to issue a warrant of commitment for default in paying a sum adjudged to be paid by the conviction, it shall consider such information about the offender's means as is available to it unless it has previously–
(a) inquired into the offender's means; and
(b) postponed the issue of the warrant of commitment under s.77(2) above.

(5C) A notice under subs (5A) above–
(a) shall state the time and place appointed for the hearing; and
(b) shall inform the offender that, if he considers that there are grounds why the warrant should not be issued, he may make representations to the court in person or in writing,
but the court may exercise its powers in relation to the issue of a warrant whether or not he makes representations.

(5D) Except as mentioned in subs (5E) below, the time stated in a notice under subs (5A) above shall not be earlier than 21 days after the issue of the notice.

(5E) Where a magistrates' court exercises in relation to an offender the power conferred by s.77(2) above and at the same hearing issues a notice under subs (5A) above in relation to him, the time stated in the notice may be a time on any day following the end of the period for which the issue of the warrant of commitment has been postponed.

(5F) A notice under subs (5A) above to be served on any person shall be deemed to be served on that person if it is sent by registered post or the recorded delivery service addressed to him at his last known address, notwithstanding that the notice is returned as undelivered or is for any other reason not received by that person.

(6) Where a magistrates' court issues a warrant of commitment on the ground that one of the conditions mentions in subs (1) or (4) above is satisfied, it shall state that fact, specifying the ground, in the warrant.
[As amended by Sch.14 CJA 1982].
[Subs (4A) and (5A)–(5F) will be inserted by [s.60] CJA 1988 from a date to be appointed].

COMMENTARY

s.82(1), an alternative of imprisonment fixed *at the time of conviction* should be a true and not an illusory alternative in the sense that it should not be imposed on a defendant who cannot possibly pay: *R v Hall* [1968] Crim LR 688.

Sum adjudged to be paid by the conviction, defined in s.150(3) as including costs, damages or compensation adjudged to be paid by the conviction or order.

A warrant of commitment, ie under s.76, *supra*.

Offence punishable with imprisonment, to be construed *without* regard to any prohibition or restriction on imprisonment of young offenders: s.150(6).

Forthwith, it is *suggested* that the use of this term in this subsection indicates that Parliament intended exception (a) to apply not only to cases where the defendant has the money on him or in his possessions which are in police custody, but also where he can, by making a telephone call or the like, cause such a sum to be paid into court the same day.

United Kingdom, ie Great Britain and Northern Ireland. It does not include the Channel Islands and the Isle of Man: s.2(2) Royal & Parliamentary Titles Act 1927.

Immediate imprisonment, ie a sentence of imprisonment which is not suspended under s.22 PCCA 1973. For application to defaulters aged 17–20 see s.96A, *infra*.

s.82(3): the effect of s.82(2) is that a court may fix a postponed alternative of custody only where it has power to issue a warrant of commitment forthwith.

s.82(3): This includes a custodial sentence and a committal in default of payment of fine, but not periods on remand or on committal for trial.

Inquired into his means, by at least *two justices* in open court: s.121 MCA 1980. For process to compel appearance before such an inquiry see s.83. Particulars of the inquiry must be entered in the court register or separate record: r.65 MC Rules 1981.

s.82(4): All other methods, see introduction. *Note* that under s.82(4)(b) *both* limbs (i) and (ii) must be satisfied. Thus, eg even a 'wilful refusal' does not relieve the court from considering or trying 'all other methods': *R v Norwich Justices, ex p. Tigger (Lilly)* (1987) *The Times*, 26 June.

s.82(5): this does not relieve the court of the obligation of conducting a hearing, merely of the need for the accused to be present. The defaulter must be given opportunity either in person or through a representative or in writing to make representations to the court, particularly where it is proposed to lodge a warrant consecutively to another term: *Forrest v Brighton Justices* (1981) 145 JP 356 (a case under para (b) of the subsection). However, it applies equally to warrants issued under para (b): *Re Wilson* [1985] 2 WLR 694. Particulars of the hearing must be recorded in the register or record: r.65 MC Rules 1981. The principle applies where the court adjourns the hearing and in the interim there has been a new development such as fresh information on which he may wish to comment: *R v Steyning Magistrates Court, ex p. Hunter* (1985) 150 JP 129.

8b.84   **Process for securing attendance of offender for purposes of section 82**
     83. (1) A magistrates' court may, for the purpose of enabling inquiry to be made under s.82 above or for securing the attendance of an offender at a hearing required to be held by subs (5) of that section–
     (a) issue a summons requiring the offender to appear before the court at the time and place appointed in the summons; or
     (b) issue a warrant to arrest him and bring him before the court.

     (2) On the failure of the offender to appear before the court in answer to a summons under this section the court may issue a warrant to arrest him and bring him before the court.

     (3) A warrant issued under this section may be executed in like manner, and the like proceedings may be taken with a view to its execution, in any part of the United Kingdom, as if it had been issued under s.13 above.

     (4) Notwithstanding anything in s.125 below, a warrant under this section shall cease to have effect when the sum in respect of which the warrant is issued is paid to the police officer holding the warrant.

COMMENTARY
s.83(1): Issue a summons, for form and service of the summons see rr.98–100 MC Rules 1981.

Issue a warrant. For signature and contents of the warrant see rr.95, 96, 100 MC Rules 1981. The warrant may be backed for bail: s.117 MCA 1980. It is suggested that the general right to bail (s.4 Bail Act 1976) does not apply to the endorsement of a warrant. Vaughan Williams LJ in the case of *Re Von Weissenfeld, ex p. Hendry* (1892) 36 SJ 276 expressed the opinion that a warrant for the arrest of an absconding debtor was authority to break open doors in pursuit thereof. For the need for the officer to be in possession of the warrant see notes to s.125(3) MCA 1980.

United Kingdom, ie Great Britain and Northern Ireland: s.2(2) Royal and Parliamentary Titles Act 1927. Isle of Man and Channel Islands not included.

8b.85   **Power to require statement of means**
     84. (1) A magistrates' court may, either before or no inquiring into a person's means under s.82 above, and a justice of the peace acting for the same petty sessions area as that court may before any such inquiry, order him to furnish to the court within a period specified in the order such a statement of his means as the court may require.

     (2) A person who fails to comply with an order under subs (1) above shall be liable on summary conviction to a fine not exceeding £50.

     (3) If a person in furnishing any statement in pursuance of an order under subs (1) above makes a statement which he knows to be false in a material

particular or recklessly furnishes a statement which is false in a material particular, or knowingly fails to disclose any material fact, he shall be liable on summary conviction to imprisonment for a term not exceeding four months or a fine not exceeding £100 or both.

(4) Proceedings in respect of an offence under subs (3) above may, notwithstanding anything in s.127(1) below, be commenced at any time within two years from the date of the commission of the offence or within six months from its first discovery by the prosecutor, whichever period expires the earlier.

COMMENTARY
s.84(1): An order under s.84(1) may be made *before the means inquiry* by the clerk to the justices: Justices' Clerks Rules 1970 (SI No 231).

Power to remit fine
85. (1) Where a fine has been imposed on conviction of an offender by a magistrates' court, the court may, on inquiring into his means or at a hearing under s.82(5) above, remit the whole or any part of the fine if the court thinks it just to do so having regard to any change in his circumstances since the conviction, and where the court remits the whole or part of the fine after a term of imprisonment has been fixed, it shall also reduce the term by an amount which bears the same proportion to the whole term as the amount remitted bears to the whole fine or, as the case may be, shall remit the whole term.

In calculating the reduction in a term of imprisonment required by this subsection any fraction of a day shall be left out of account.

(2) Notwithstanding the definition of 'fine' in s.150(1) below, references in this section to a fine do not include any other sum adjudged to be paid on conviction, whether as a pecuniary penalty, forfeiture, compensation or otherwise.

8b.86

Power to remit fines
85. *(1) Where a fine has been imposed on conviction of an offender by a magistrates' court, the court may at any time remit the whole or any part of the fine, but only if it thinks it just to do so having regard to a change of circumstances which has occurred–*

(a) *where any court is considering whether to issue a warrant of commitment after the issue of such a warrant in respect of the fine has been postponed under subs (2) of s.74 above, since the relevant time as defined in subs (4) of that section; and*

(b) *in any other case, since the date of the conviction.*

(2) Where the court remits the whole or part of the fine after a term of imprisonment has been fixed, it shall also reduce the term by an amount which bears the same proportion to the whole term as the amount remitted bears to the whole or, as the case may be, shall remit the whole term.

(3) In calculating the reduction in a term of imprisonment required by subs (2) above any fraction of a day shall be left out of account.

(4) Notwithstanding the definition of 'fine' in s.150(1) below, references, in this section to a fine do not include any other sum adjudged to be paid on conviction, whether as a pecuniary penalty, forfeiture, compensation or otherwise.'.

[s.85 is substituted by [s.60] CJA 1988 from a date to be appointed].

COMMENTARY
Note that in order for the court to exercise its powers under s.85(1) there must have been *a change in the defendant's circumstances since the conviction.* Orders of remission must be recorded in the register or record: r.65. Although s.85(1) does not refer to a means inquiry at which the offender is present' the court must first 'inquire into his means'. Possibly this could be done in the defendant's absence, eg on the basis of a probation officer's report. s.85(1) does not apply to the remission of forfeited recognizances s.120(4) MCA 1980.

Fines imposed *by the Crown Court* may only be remitted *with the consent* of that court: s.32(4) PCCA 1973.

8b.87   **Variation of instalments of sum adjudged to be paid by conviction**
     85A. Where under s.75 above a magistrates' court orders that a sum adjudged to be paid by a conviction shall be paid by instalments, the court, on an application made by the person liable to pay that sum, shall have power to vary that order by varying the number of instalments payable, the amount of any instalment payable, and the date on which any instalment becomes payable.
     [*As inserted by s.51 CJA 1982*].

COMMENTARY
This power may be exercised by the justices' clerk: Justices' Clerks Rules 1970 (SI No 213). Any direction under this section must be entered in the register: r.65 MC Rules 1981.

8b.88   **Power of magistrates' court to fix day for appearance of offender at means inquiry etc.**
     86. (1) A magistrates' court which has exercised in relation to a sum adjudged to be paid by a conviction either of the powers conferred by s.75(1) above shall have power, either then or later, to fix a day on which, if the relevant condition is satisfied, the offender must appear in person before the court for either or both of the following purposes, namely–
     (a) to enable an inquiry into his means to be made under s.82 above;
     (b) to enable a hearing required by subs (5) of the said s.82 to be held.

     (1A) Where the power which the court has exercised is the power to allow time for payment of a sum ('the adjudged sum'), the relevant condition is satisfied if any part of that sum remains unpaid on the day fixed by the court.

     (1B) Where the power which the court has exercised is the power to order payment by instalments, the relevant condition is satisfied if an instalment which has fallen due remains unpaid on the day fixed by the court.
     (a) to enable an inquiry into his means to be made under s.82 above;
     (b) to enable a hearing required by subs (5) of the said s.82 to be held.

     (2) Except as provided in subs (3) below, the power to fix a day under this section shall be exercisable only in the presence of the offender.

     (3) Where a day has been fixed under this section, the court may fix a later day in substitution for the day previously fixed, and may do so–
     (a) when composed of a single justice; and
     (b) whether the offender is present or not.

     (4) Subject to subs (5) below, if on the day fixed under this section–
     (a) the relevant condition is satisfied; and
     (b) the offender fails to appear in person before the court,
the court may issue a warrant to arrest him and bring him before the court; and subs (3) and (4) of s.83 above shall apply in relation to a warrant issued under this section.

     (5) Where under subs (3) above a later day has in the absence of the offender been fixed in substitution for a day previously fixed under this section, the court shall not issue a warrant under this section unless it is proved to the satisfaction of the court, on oath or in such other manner as may be prescribed that notice in writing of the substituted day was served on the offender not less than what appears to the court to be a reasonable time before that day.
     [*As amended by s.51 CJA 1982*].

COMMENTARY
This section applies not only to fines, but to all other sums adjudged to be paid on conviction such as costs and compensation.

s.86(1): Sum adjudged to be paid by a conviction, defined in s.150(3).

s.86(2): Presence of the offender, not merely of his counsel or solicitor: s.12.2.

s.86(3): Service of the notice of the substituted day may be effected in any manner as service.

s.86(5): Notice may be served in any manner in which a summons may be served under r.52 MC Rules 1981.

Enforcement of payment of fines by High Court and county court 8b.89

87. (1) Subject to the provision of subs (2) below, payment of a sum adjudged to be paid by a conviction of a magistrates' court may be enforced by the High Court or county court (otherwise than by issue of a writ of fieri facias or other process against goods or by imprisonment or attachment of earnings) as if the sum were due to the clerk of the magistrates' court in pursuance of a judgment or order of the High Court or county court, as the case may be.

(2) Subsection (1) above shall not be construed as authorising the enforcement by a county court of payment of a fine exceeding the county court limit.

(2A) In subs (2) above 'the county court limit' means the amount which for the time being is the county court limit for the purposes of s.16 of the County Courts Act 1984 (money recoverable by statute).

(3) The clerk of the magistrates' court shall not take proceedings by virtue of subs (1) above to recover any sum adjudged to be paid by a conviction of the court from any person unless authorised to do so by the court after an enquiry under s.82 above into that person's means.

(4) Any expenses incurred by the clerk of the magistrates' court in recovering any such sum shall be treated for the purposes of Part VI of the Justices of the Peace Act 1979 as expenses of the magistrates' courts committee.

[*As amended by Sch.5 Supreme Court Act 1981, Sch.2 County Courts Act 1984*].

COMMENTARY

s.87(1): A sum adjudged to be paid by a conviction defined in s.150(3).

Authorised to do so, such an order shall be entered in the register or record: r.65 MC Rules 1981, see form 63.

s.87(5), presumably no means inquiry is necessary in the case of a corporation.

Fines imposed on companies 8b.90

87A. *(1) Where–*

(a) a magistrates' court has, or is treated by any enactment as having, adjudged a company by a conviction to pay a sum; and

(b) the court has issued a warrant of distress under s.76(1) above for above for the purpose of levying the sum; and

(c) it appears on the return to the warrant that the money and goods of the company are insufficient to satisfy the sum with the costs and charges of levying the same,

the clerk of the court may make an application in relation to the company under s.9 or 124 of the Insolvency Act 1986 (administration or winding up). (application for administration order).

(2) Any expenses incurred under subs (1) above by the clerk of a magistrates' court shall be treated for the purposes of Part VI of the Justices of the Peace Act 1979 as expenses of the magistrates' courts committee.'.

[*s.87A will be inserted by [s.61] CJA 1988 from a date to be appointed*].

Supervision pending payment 8b.90a

88. (1) Where any person is adjudged to pay a sum by a summary conviction and the convicting court does not commit him to prison forthwith in default of payment, the court may either on the occasion of the conviction or on a subsequent occasion, order him to be placed under the supervision of such person as the court may from time to time appoint.

(2) An order placing a person under supervision in respect of any sum shall remain in force so long as he remains liable to pay the sum or any part of it unless the order ceases to have effect or is discharged under subs (3) below.

(3) An order under this section shall cease to have effect on the making of a transfer of fine order under s.89 below with respect to the sum adjudged to be paid and may be discharged by the court that made it, without prejudice in either case to the making of the new order.

(4) Where a person under 21 years old has been adjudged to pay a sum by a summary conviction and the convicting court does not commit him to detention under s.9 of the Criminal Justice Act 1982 forwith in default of payment, the court shall not commit him to such detention in default of payment of the sum, or for want of sufficient distress to satisfy the sum, unless he has been placed under supervision in respect of the sum or the court is satisfied that it is undesirable or impracticable to place him under supervision.

(5) Where a court, being satisfied as aforesaid, commits a person under 21 years old to such detention without an order under this section having been made, the court shall state the grounds on which it is so satisfied in the warrant of commitment.

(6) Where an order placing a person under supervision with respect to a sum is in force, a magistrates' court shall not commit him to prison in default of payment of the sum, or for want of sufficient distress to satisfy the sum, unless the court has before committing him taken such steps as may be reasonably practicable to obtain from the person appointed for his supervision an oral or written report on the offender's conduct and means and has considered any report so obtained, in addition, in a case where an inquiry is required by s.82 above, to that inquiry.
[*As amended by Sch.14 CJA 1982*].

COMMENTARY

The Departmental Committee on the Probation Service pointed out (in paras 94 and 95 of their report) that a money payment supervision order was *designed to minimise committals to prison for default in paying fines*, and that it was *in no sense a substitute for a probation order*. They recommended that a probation officer should be used for money payment supervision *only* where the limited supervision he could exercise might avoid a default otherwise likely to occur; eg where the offender was too incompetent or feckless to put aside the necessary savings.

s.88(1): Adjudged to pay a sum by a summary conviction, defined in s.150(3).

Order, unless made in the offender's presence, notice of the order must be delivered or served by post: r.56(1) MC Rules 1981. It must be recorded in the register or record kept for the purpose of recording fine enforcement: r.65.

Such person as the court may from time to time appoint, first, therefore, the order must be to a named person; though this may, it is *suggested*, be by description, as for example, 'the senior probation officer . . . petty sessional division'. Secondly, the court is empowered from time to time to change the named person and this should, it is suggested, be effected by written order. The duties of the supervising officer are set out in r.56(2).
    A supervising officer has authority to receive part payment of the fine unless a warrant of distress or commitment has issued: r.55(1); but must hand the money over to the clerk of the court: r.55(4).

s.88(4): Under 21-years-old, for the determination of age see s.150(4).

s.88(6): Commit him to prison, that is the act of fixing the term of imprisonment, even where this is postponed on terms: *R v Clerkenwell Stipendiary Magistrate, ex p. Mays* (1975) 139 JP 151. For application to defaulters aged 17–20 see s.96A, *infra*.

8b.91   **Transfer of fine order**
        89. (1) Where a magistrates' court has, or is treated by any enactment as having, adjudged a person by a conviction to pay a sum and it appears to the court that the person is residing in any petty sessions area other than that for

which the court acted, the court may make a transfer of fine order, that is to say, an order making payment enforceable in the petty sessions area in which it appears to the court that he is residing, and that area shall be specified in the order.

(2) As from the date on which a transfer of fine order is made with respect to any sum, all functions under this Part of this Act relating to that sum which, if no such order had been made, would have been exercisable by the court which made the order, or the clerk of that court, shall be exercisable by a court acting for the petty sessions area specified in the order, or the clerk of that court, as the case may be, and not otherwise.

(3) Where it appears to a court by which functions in relation to any sum are for the time being exercisable by virtue of a transfer of fine order that the person liable to pay the sum is residing in a petty sessions area other than that for which the court is acting, the court may make a further transfer of fine order with respect to that sum.

(4) In this section and ss.90 and 91 below, references to this Part of this Act do not include references to s.81(1) above.

COMMENTARY

For the procedure for making a transfer of fine order see r.57. The defendant's presence or consent is not necessary. An order under s.89 puts an end to any money payment supervision order: s.88(3).

For transfers to and from Scotland see ss.90 and 91, *infra*, respectively, as well as s.33 PCCA 1973.

s.89(1): Treated by any enactment as having, see, eg s.41(1) Administration of Justice Act 1970.

Adjudged . . . by a conviction to pay a sum, this term is defined in s.150(3).

Residing. Corporations can have a residence: see *Halsbury's Laws*, 4th ed, vol 9, at p.731.

A transfer of fine order, the order must be entered in the register or record kept for the purpose of recording particulars of fine enforcement: r.65. For form of order, see form 59.

s.89(2): This Part of this Act, comprises ss.75–96 inclusive, except s.81(1): s.89(4).

Transfer of fines to Scotland or Northern Ireland   8b.92

90. (1) Where a magistrates' court has, or is treated by any enactment as having, adjudged a person by a conviction to pay a sum, and it appears to the court that he is residing–
  (a) within the jurisdiction of a court of summary jurisdiction in Scotland, or
  (b) in any petty sessions district in Northern Ireland,
the court may order that payment of the sum shall be enforceable by that court of summary jurisdiction or, as the case may be, in that petty sessions district.

(2) An order under this section shall specify the court of summary jurisdiction by which or petty sessions district in which payment of the sum in question is to be enforceable; and if–
  (a) the sum is more than £100 or is a fine originally imposed by the Crown Court or the sheriff court, and
  (b) payment is to be enforceable in Scotland,
the court to be so specified shall be the sheriff court.

(3) Where an order is made under this section with respect to any sum, any functions under this Part of this Act relating to that sum which, if no such order has been made, would have been exercisable by the court which made the order or by the clerk of that court shall cease to be so exercisable.

COMMENTARY

For the duties of the clerk, see r.57.

s.90(1): Adjudged . . . by a conviction to pay a sum, see s.150(3).

Treated by any enactment, see note to s.89.

s.90(3): This Part of this Act, does not include s.81(1): s.89(4).

8b.93   Transfer of fines from Scotland or Northern Ireland
91. (1) Where a transfer of fine order under s.403 of the Criminal Procedure (Scotland) Act 1975 or Art 95 of the Magistrates' Courts (Northern Ireland) Order 1981 provides that payment of a sum shall be enforceable in a specified petty sessions area in England and Wales, a magistrates' court acting for that area, and the clerk of that court, shall, subject to the provisions of this section, have all the like functions under this Part of this Act in respect of the sum (including power to make an order under s.89 or 90 above) as if the sum were a sum adjudged to be paid by a conviction of that court and as if any order made under the said Act of 1975 or, as the case may be, the said Order of 1981 in respect of the sum before the making of the transfer of fine order had been made by that court.

(2) For the purpose of determining the period of imprisonment which may be imposed under this Act in default of payment of a fine originally imposed by a court in Scotland, Sch.4 to this Act shall have effect as if for the Table set out in para 1 there were substituted the Table set out in s.407 of the Criminal Procedure (Scotland) Act 1975.

(3) Where a transfer of fine order under s.403 of the Criminal Procedure (Scotland) Act 1975 or Art 950 of the Magistrates' Courts (Northern Ireland) Order 1981 provides for the enforcement in a petty sessions area in England and Wales of a fine originally imposed by the Crown Court, a magistrates' court acting for that area shall have all the like functions under this Part of this Act, exercisable subject to the like restrictions, as if it were the magistrates' court by which payment of the fine fell to be enforced by virtue of s.32(1) of the Powers of Criminal Courts Act 1973, and as if any order made under the said Act of 1975 or, as the case may be, the said Order of 1981 in respect of the fine before the making of the transfer of fine order had been made by that court.
[*As amended by Sch.6 Magistrates' Courts (Northern Ireland) Order 1981*].

COMMENTARY
For the duties of the clerk see r.57(3)(4).

s.91(1): This Part of this Act, does not include s.81(1): s.89(4).

s.91(2): The table, this corresponds with the Table in Sch.4, *infra*.

8b.94   Application of Part III to persons aged 17 to 20
96A. This Part of this Act shall have effect in relation to a person aged 17 or over but less than 21 as if any reference to committing a person to prison, or fixing a term of imprisonment for a default, where a reference to committing the person to, or, as the case may be, to fixing a term of, detention under s.9 of the Criminal Justice Act 1982; and any reference to warrants of commitment, or to periods of imprisonment imposed for default, shall be construed accordingly.
[*As inserted by Sch.14 CJA 1982*].

COMMENTARY
This Part of this Act, ie ss.75–96.

8b.95   Statement of wages to be evidence
100. A statement in writing to the effect that wages of any amount have been paid to a person during any period, purporting to be signed by or on behalf of his employer, shall be evidence of the facts therein stated in any proceedings taken before a magistrates' court–
    (a) for enforcing payment by the person to whom the wages are stated to have been paid of a sum adjudged to be paid by a summary conviction on order; or

(b) on any application made by or against that person for the making of an order in any matter of bastardy or an order enforceable as an affiliation order, or for the variation, revocation, discharge or revivial of such an order.

COMMENTARY
Sum adjudged to be paid by a summary conviction, defined in s.150(3).

Disposal of non-pecuniary forfeitures   **8b.96**
140. Subject to any enactment relating to customs or excise, anything other than money forfeited on a conviction by a magistrates' court or the forfeiture of which may be enforced by a magistrates' court shall be sold or otherwise disposed of in such manner as the court may direct; and the proceeds shall be applied as if they were a fine imposed under the enactment on which the proceedings for the forfeiture are founded.

Interpretation of other terms   **8b.97**
150. (3) Any reference in this Act to a sum adjudged to be paid by a conviction or order of a magistrates' court shall be construed as including a reference to any costs, damages or compensation adjudged to be paid by the conviction or order of which the amount is ascertained by the conviction or order; but this subsection does not prejudice the definition of 'sum adjudged to be paid by a conviction' contained in subs (8) of s.81 above for the purposes of that section.

SCHEDULE 4   **8b.98**

MAXIMUM PERIODS OF IMPRISONMENT IN DEFAULT OF PAYMENT
1. Subject to the following provisions of this schedule, the periods set out in the second column of the following table shall be the maximum periods applicable respectively to the amounts set out opposite thereto, being amounts due at the time the imprisonment or detention is imposed.

TABLE
An amount not exceeding £50 .... 7 days
An amount exceeding £50 but not exceeding £100 .... 14 days
An amount exceeding £100 but not exceeding £400 .... 30 days
An amount exceeding £400 but not exceeding £1,000 .... 60 days
An amount exceeding £1,000 but not exceeding £2,000 .... 90 days
An amount exceeding £2,000 but not exceeding £5,000 .... 6 months
An amount exceeding £5,000 but not exceeding £10,000 .... 9 months
An amount exceeding £10,000 .... 12 months

2. (1) Where the amount due at the time imprisonment or detention is imposed is so much of a sum adjudged to be paid by a summary conviction as remainss due after payment, then, subject to sub-para (2) below, the maximum period applicable to the amount shall be the period applicable to the whole sum reduced by such number of days as bears to the total number of days therein the same proportion as the part bears to the whole sum.

(2) In calculating the reduction required under sub-para (1) above any fraction of a day shall be left out of account and the maximum period shall not be reduced to less than five days.

(3) The maximum period applicable to a sum of any amount enforceable as a civil debt shall be six weeks.
[*As amended by Sch.14 CJA 1982 and SI 1984 No 447*].

TABLE
An amount not exceeding £50 .... 5 days
An amount exceeding £50 but not exceeding £100 .... 7 days
An amount exceeding £100 but not exceeding £400 .... 14 days

An amount exceeding £400 but not exceeding £1,000 .... *30 days*
An amount exceeding £1,000 but not exceeding £2,000 .... *45 days*
An amount exceeding £2,000 but not exceeding £5,000 .... *3 months*
An amount exceeding £5,000 but not exceeding £10,000 .... *6 months*
An amount exceeding £10,000 .... *12 months*
[*The Table will be substituted by [s.59] CJA 1988 from a date to be appointed*].

COMMENTARY
For the calculation of the alternative see the commentary to s.79(2) (3) of the Act at 8b.81, *supra*.

CRIMINAL JUSTICE ACT 1982

8b.99   **Abolition of enhanced penalties on subsequent conviction of summary offences under Acts of Parliament**
35. (1) Subject to subs (3) below, this section applies where under an Act a person convicted of a summary offence–
(a) is liable to a fine or maximum fine of one amount in the case of a first conviction and of a different amount in the case of a second or subsequent conviction; or
(b) is liable to imprisonment for a longer term in the case of a second or subsequent conviction; or
(c) is liable to imprisonment in the case of a second or subsequent conviction.

(2) Where this section applies, a person guilty of such an offence shall be liable on summary conviction–
(a) to a fine or, as the case may be, a maximum fine of an amount not exceeding the greatest amount;
(b) to imprisonment for a term not exceeding the longest or only term,
to which he would have been liable before this section came into force if his conviction has satisfied the conditions required for the imposition of a fine or maximum fine of that amount or imprisonment for that term.

(3) This section does not apply to offences under–
(a) ss. 33 to 36 of the Sexual Offences Act 1956 (brothel-keeping and prostitution); or
(b) s.1(2) of the Street Offences Act 1959 (loitering and soliciting for the purpose of prostitution).

COMMENTARY
Fine, is defined in s.47(1), *infra*.

8b.100   **The standard scale of fines for summary offences**
37. (1) There shall be a standard scale of fines for summary offences, which shall be known as 'the standard scale'.

(2) The scale at the commencement of this section is shown below.

Level on the scale	Amount of fine
1	£50
2	£100
3	£400
4	£1,000
5	£2,000

(3) Where any enactment (whether contained in an Act passed before or after this Act) provides–
(a) that a person convicted of a summary offence shall be liable on convic-

tion to a fine or a maximum fine by reference to a specified level on the standard scale; or

(b) confers power by subordinate instrument to make a person liable on conviction of a summary offence (whether or not created by the instrument) to a fine or maximum fine by reference to a specified level on the standard scale,

it is to be construed as referring to the standard scale for which this section provides as that standard scale has effect from time to time by virtue of either of this section or of an order under s.143 of the Magistrates' Courts Act 1980.
[*As amended by SI 1984 No 447*].

COMMENTARY
Fine, defined in s.47(1), *infra*.

Conversion of references to amounts to references to levels on scale   8b.101
46. (1) Where–
(a) either–
  (i) a relevant enactment makes a person liable to a fine or maximum fine on conviction of a summary offence; or
  (ii) a relevant enactment confers power by subordinate instrument to make a person liable to a fine or maximum fine on conviction of a summary offence (whether or not created by the instrument); and
(b) the amount of the fine or maximum fine for the offence is, whether by virtue of this Part of this Act or not, an amount shown in the second column of the standard scale,

a reference to the level in the first column of the standard scale corresponding to that amount shall be substituted for the reference in the enactment to the amount of the fine or maximum fine.

(2) Where a relevant enactment confers a power such as is mentioned in subs (1)(a)(ii) above, the power shall be construed as a power to make a person liable to a fine or, as the case may be, a maximum fine not exceeding the amount corresponding to the level on the standard scale to which the enactment refers by virtue of subs (1) above or not exceeding a lesser amount.

(3) If an order under s.143 of the Magistrates' Courts Act 1980 alters the sums specified in s.37(2) above, the second reference to the standard scale in subs (1) above is to be construed as a reference to that scale as it has effect by virtue of the order.

(4) In this section 'relevant enactment' means–
(a) any enactment contained in an Act passed before this Act;
(b) any enactment contained in this Act;
(c) any enactment contained in an Act passed on the same day as this Act; and
(d) any enactment contained in an Act passed after this Act but in the same Session as this Act.

(5) This section shall not affect so much of any enactment as (in whatever words) makes a person liable on summary conviction to a maximum fine not exceeding a specified amount for each period of a specified length during which a continuing offence is continued.
[*As amended by s.15 Companies Consolidation (Consequential Provisions) Act 1985*].

COMMENTARY
Fine, defined in s.47(1), *infra*.

Provisions supplementary to sections 35 to 46   8b.102
47. (1) In ss.35 to 40 and 46 above 'fine' includes a pecuniary penalty but does not include a pecuniary forfeiture or pecuniary compensation.

(2) Nothing in any provision contained in ss.35 to 46 above shall affect the punishment for an offence committed before that provision comes into force.

8b.103 **Construction of references to 'statutory maximum'**
74. (1) In any enactment (whether contained in an Act passed before or after this Act) 'statutory maximum', in relation to a fine on summary conviction for an offence in England and Wales, means the prescribed sum within the meaning of s.32 of the Magistrates' Court Act 1980 (£1,000 or another sum fixed by order under s.143 of that Act to take account of changes in the value of money).

COMMENTARY
Another sum, now £2,000: SI 1984 No 447.

8b.104 **Construction of references to 'the standard scale'**
75. In any enactment (whether contained in an Act passed before or after this Act) 'the standard scale'–
    (a) in relation to England and Wales, has the meaning given by s.37 of this Act,

8b.105 # MAGISTRATES' COURTS (ATTACHMENT OF EARNINGS) RULES 1971
(SI 1971 No 809)

Interpretation
2. (1) Sections 2 and 25(1) of the Act shall apply to the interpretation of these rules as they apply to the interpretation of the Act.

(2) The Interpretation Act 1978, shall apply to the interpretation of these Rules as it applies to the interpretation of an Act of Parliament.

(3) Any reference in these rules to 'the Act' is a reference to the Attachment of Earnings Act 1971.

(4) Any reference in these rules to any enactment or rule is a reference to that enactment or rule as amended by any enactment or rule.

(5) Any reference in these rules to a form in the schedule to these rules shall include a reference to a form to the like effect with such variations as the circumstances may require.

(6) Any reference in these rules to an attachment of earnings order shall be construed subject to the provisions of r.23.

Service of orders and notices
6. (1) Where a magistrates' court makes an attachment of earnings order or an order varying or discharging such an order, the clerk of the court shall cause a copy of the order to be served on the employer and shall send a copy of the order to the debtor.

(2) Where an attachment of earnings order made by a magistrates' court ceases to have effect as provided in s.8 or s.11 of the act, notice of cessation shall be given to the employer.

(3) The notice required by the preceding paragraph shall be given by the clerk of the magistrates' court.
    (a) which made or confirmed the maintenance order (in a case to which s.11(1)(c) of the Act applies;
    (b) in which the maintenance order is registered under any enactment in a case in which s.11(1)(a), (b) or (d) of the Act applies;
    (c) which issued the warrant of commitment or exercised the power conferred by [s.77(2) of the Magistrates' Courts Act 1980] (in a case to which s.8 of the Act applies).

Particulars of debtor
7. The particulars of the debtor for the purpose of enabling him to be identified which, so far as they are known, are to be included in an attachment of earnings order under s.6(3) of the Act shall be–
(a) full names and addresses;
(b) place of work;
(c) nature of work and works number, if any.

(8)–(11) . . .

Variation of attachment of earnings order on change of employment
12. Where an attachment of earnings order has lapsed under s.9(4) of the Act on the debtor's ceasing to be in the employment of the person to whom the order was directed and it appears to a magistrates' court,[1] acting for the same petty sessions area as the court which made the order, that the debtor has subsequently entered the employment of a person (whether the same as before or another), the court may, of its own motion, vary the order by directing it to that person and may make any consequential amendment to the order made necessary by this variation.

Discharge of attachment of earnings order by court of its own motion
13. (1) Where it appears to a magistrate's court[2] acting for the same petty sessions area as the magistrates' court which made the attachment of earnings order that the debtor is not in the employment of the person to whom the order is directed and that the likelihood of the debtor's entering the employment of any person is not such as to justify preserving the order, the court may, of its own motion, discharge the order.

(2) . . .

Temporary variation of protected earnings rate
14. (1) A justice of the peace[3] acting for the same petty sessions area as the magistrates' court which made the attachment of earnings order may, on a written application made by the debtor on the ground of a material change in the debtor's resources and needs since the order was made or last varied, by order (hereinafter referred to as a temporary variation order) vary the attachment of earnings order for a period of not more than four weeks by an increase of the protected earnings rate.

(2) (*Form*).

(3) The clerk of the magistrates' court which made the attachment of earnings order shall cause a copy of any temporary variation order to be served on the employer and give him notice if the temporary variation order is discharged[4].

(4) Where an application for the variation or discharge of an attachment of earnings order is made to a magistrates' court and there is in existence of temporary variation order in respect of the attachment of earnings order, the court may, of its own motion, discharge the temporary variation order.

1. See r.22, *infra*.   2. As applied by r.23, *infra*.   3. Or a justices' clerk, see r.22.   4. As adapted by r.23(4).

Consolidated attachment orders   **8b.106**
15. (1) In this rule references to an attachment of earnings order are references to such an order made by a magistrates' court and do not include such an order made to secure payments under a magistrate' court maintenance order.

(2) Where a magistrates' court has power to make an attachment of earnings order in respect of a debtor who is already subject to such an order (whether or not it is itself a consolidated attachment order) made by any

magistrates' court, the court may, subject to the provisions of this rule, discharge the existing order and make a consolidated attachment order in respect of that debtor.

(4) Where two or more attachment of earnings orders (whether or not they are themselves consolidated attachment orders) made by magistrates' courts are in existence in respect of one debtor, a magistrates' court acting for the same petty sessions area as one of these courts may, subject to the provisions of this rule, discharge the existing orders and make a consolidated attachment order in respect of that debtor.

(5) A magistrates' court may exercise the powers conferred under paras (2) to (4) of this rule either of its own motion or on the application of the debtor.

(6) A debtor may apply to a magistrates' court for a consolidated attachment order–
   (i) in a case to which paras (2) or (3) of this rule applies, during the hearing of the proceedings for the enforcement of the fine or other liability;
   (ii) in a case to which para (4) of this rule applies, by complaint.

(7) Where an employer applies in writing to the clerk of a magistrates' court which has power to make a consolidated attachment order requesting the court to make such an order, the clerk shall bring the application before the court, and, if it appears to the court that the application is justified, the court shall proceed as if it had determined of its own motion to make such an order.

(8) Before a magistrates' court exercises of its own motion the powers conferred under para (4) of this rule, it shall cause written notice to be given to the debtor of his right to make representations to the court.

(9) Where a magistrates' court has power to make a consolidated attachment order under paras (3) or (4) of this rule and a relevant attachment of earnings order has been made by a magistrates' court acting for another petty sessions area, the first mentioned court shall cause notice to be given to the clerk of the second mentioned court and shall not discharge that attachment of earnings order unless the enforcement of the sum to which the order relates is transferred to the first mentioned court under [s.89 of the Magistrates Courts Act 1980 (transfer of fines), para 7 of Sch.3 to the Legal Aid Act 1974] (transfer of enforcement of legal aid contribution orders) or r.16 of these rules as the case may be.

(10) Where a magistrates' court makes a consolidated attachment order, it shall specify in the order such normal deduction rate as the court thinks reasonable and this rate may be less than the sum of the normal deduction rates specified in any attachment of earnings orders discharged by the court.

Transfer of fines etc. with view to making consolidated attachment order
   16. (1) Where a magistrates' court has made or has power to make an attachment of earnings order to secure–
   (a) the payment of any sum adjudged to be paid by a conviction or treated (by any enactment relating to the collection and enforcement of fines, costs, compensation or forfeited recognizances) as so adjudged to be paid, or
   (b) the payment of any sum required to be paid by a legal aid contribution order,
and a magistrates' court acting for some other petty sessions area has made an attachment of earnings order in respect of the debtor, then, if the debtor does not reside in either petty sessions area, the first mentioned court[1] may make an order making payment of that sum enforceable in the petty sessions area for which the second mentioned court acted.

(2) As from the date on which an order is made under para (1) of this rule with respect to any sum, all functions under any enactment relating to that sum

which, if no such order has been made, would have been exercisable by a court acting for the petty sessions area specified in the order, or the clerk of that court, as the case may be, and not otherwise.

(3) The making of an order under para (1) of this rule with respect to any sum shall not prejudice the power to make a subsequent order with respect to that sum under that paragraph or under [s.89 of the Magistrates Courts Act 1980 of para 7 of Sch.3 to the Legal Aid Act 1974].

Disposal of sums paid under consolidated attachment orders

17. (1) A clerk of magistrates' court receiving a payment under a consolidated attachment order shall, subject to para (2) below, apply the money in payment of the sums secured by the order, paying first any sum previously secured by an attachment of earnings order which was discharged in consequence of the making of the consolidated attachment order.

(2) Where two or more attachment of earnings orders were discharged in consequence of the making of the consolidated attachment order the sums due under the orders shall be paid in the chronological order of the orders.

Method of making payment under attachment of earnings order

8b.107

18. (1) A clerk of a magistrates' court to whom any payment under an attachment of earnings order is to be made shall notify the employer[1] of the hours during which, and the place at which, payments are, subject to the provisions of this rule, to be made and received.

1. As adapted by r.23(5).

(2) If an employer sends by post any payments under an attachment of earnings order to a clerk of a magistrates' court, he shall do so at his own risk and expense.

Service of orders and notices

20. Where under s.14 of the Act (which relates to statements of earnings, etc.) an order is directed to the debtor or to a person appearing to be an employer of the debtor or where under these rules a copy of an order is to be served or a notice is to be given to any person–
  (a) service may be effected on, or notice may be given to a person, other than a corporation, by delivering it to the person to whom it is directed or by sending it by post in a letter addressed to him at his last known or usual place of abode or, in the case of an employer or a person appearing to be an employer of the debtor, at his place of business;
  (b) service may be effected on, or notice given to, a corporation by delivering the document at, or sending it to–
    (i) such office or place as the corporation may, for the purpose of this rule have specified in writing to the court in relation to the debtor or to a class or description of person to which he belongs, or
    (ii) the registered office of the corporation if that office is in England and Wales or, if there is no registered office in England and Wales, any place therein where the corporation trades or conducts its business.

County court records

21. (1) Where a clerk of a magistrates' court causes a copy of an order or notice to be given to any person under r.6 of these rules, he shall cause a copy of the order or notice to be given also the the County Court Registrar for the district in which the debtor resides.

(2) Where the clerk of a magistrates' court which has made an attachment of earnings order is informed of a debtor's change of address, he shall notify the new address to the County Court Registrar for the district in which the debtor resided before the change of address.

Justices' clerks

22. (1) The things specified in para (2) of this rule, being things authorised to be done by, to or before a single justice of the peace for a petty sessions area, may be done by, to or before the justices' clerk for that area.

(2) The things referred to in para (1) above are–

(a) the power to make an order under s.14(1) or (2) of the Act (power of court to obtain statements of earnings etc.) before the hearing of an application to a magistrates' court for an attachment of earnings order, or for the variation or discharge of such an order.

(b) the determination that a complaint for the discharge or variation of an attachment of earnings order be dealt with by a magistrates' court acting for another petty sessions area in accordance with r.9 of these rules;

(c) the giving of directions under r.10 or r.11 of these rules;

(d) the discharge or variation by the court of its own motion of an attachment of earnings order in accordance with r.12 or r.13 of these rules;

(e) the temporary variation of an attachment of earnings order by an increase of the protected earnings rate in accordance with r.14 of these rules;

(f) the making of an order under r.16 of these rules (transfer of fines etc. with view to making consolidated attachment order).

Application of these Rules to attachment of earnings orders in respect of fines etc.

23. (1) In the application of these Rules to attachment of earnings orders to secure–

(a) the payment of any sum adjudged to be paid by a conviction or treated by any enactment relating to the collection and enforcement of fines, costs, compensation or forfeited recognizances as so adjudged to be paid, or

(b) the payment of any sum required to be paid by a legal aid contribution order,

the exceptions and modifications specified in the following provisions of this Rule shall apply.

(2) Rules 4, 5, 8, 9, 10, 11 and 19 shall not apply.

(3) An attachment of earnings order shall be in the form numbered 2 in the schedule to these Rules.

(4) Rule 14 (temporary variations of protected earnings rate) shall have effect as if in para (3) the words 'and the clerk shall also send a copy to the person entitled to receive payments under the related maintenance order whether directly or through an officer of any court' were omitted.

(5) Rule 18 (method of making payment under attachment of earnings order) shall have effect as if in para (1) the words 'and the person entitled to receive payments under the related maintenance order' and para (3) were omitted.

8b.108   # MAGISTRATES' COURTS RULES 1981

SI 1981 no 552, as amended by SIs 1982 No 245, 1983 No 523, 1984 No 1552, 1985 Nos 1695 and 1944 and 1986 No 1332)

Notice to defendant of fine or forfeited recognizances

46. (1) Where under s.3(1) of the Powers of Criminal Courts Act 1973, s.49 of the Criminal Justice Act 1967 and s.19(5) of the Coroners Act 1887 a magistrates' court is required to enforce payment of a fine imposed or recognizance forfeited by the Crown Court or by a coroner or where a magistrates' court allows time for payment of a sum adjudged to ber paid by a summary conviction, or directs that the sum be paid by instalments, or where the offender is absent when a sum is adjudged to be paid by a summary conviction, the clerk of the court shall serve on the offender notice in writing stating the amount on the sum and, if it is to be paid by instalments, the amount of the instalments, the date on which the sum, or each of the instalments, is to be paid and the places and times at which payment may be made; and a warrant of distress or commitment shall not be issued until the preceding provisions of this rule have been complied with.

(2) A notice under this rule shall be served by delivering it to the offender or by sending it to him by post in a letter addressed to him at his last known or usual place of abode.

COMMENTARY
Compliance with this rule is mandatory, even on an adjourned means inquiry where the defendant is present in court: *R v Farnham Justices, ex p. Hunt* (1976) 140 JPN 453.

Absent, a defendant who is legally represented is deemed not to be absent: s.122 MCA 1980.

Notice in writing, see forms 46 and 133.

Registration and notification of financial penalty enforcement order
47. (1) The clerk of a magistrates' court receiving a financial penalty enforcement order made by the Defence Council or an officer authorised by them shall cause the said order to be registered in his courts by means of a memorandum entered in the register kept pursuant to r.66 and signed by him and shall send notice in writing to the Defence Council or the authorised officer, as appropriate, stating that the order has been so registered.

(2) Where a financial penalty enforcement order has been registered in accordance with the provisions of para (1), the clerk shall forthwith serve on the person against whom the order was made a notice of registration in the prescribed form.

(3) A notice required by para (2) shall be served on the person by delivering it to him or by sending it by post addressed to him at the address shown on the financial penalty enforcement order.

(4) In this rule 'financial penalty enforcement order' means an order made under s.133A(1) of the Army Act 1955, s.133A(1) of the Air Force Act 1955 or s.128F(1) of the Naval Discipline Act 1957.

COMMENTARY
Only s.133A Army Act 1955 is printed in this work: see generally HOC 129/1977 and form 47.

To whom payments are to be made
48. (1) A person adjudged by the conviction or order of a magistrates' court to pay any sum shall, unless the court otherwise directs, pay that sum, or any instalment of that sum, to the clerk of the court.

(2) Where payment of any sum or instalment of any sum adjudged to be paid by the conviction or order, of a magistrates' court is made to any person other than the clerk of the court, that person, unless he is the person to whom the court has directed payment to be made or, in the case of a child, is the person with whom the child has his home, shall, as soon as may be, account for and, if the clerk so requires, pay over the sum or instalment to the clerk of the court.

(3) Where payment of any sum adjudged to be paid by the conviction or order of a magistrates' court, or any instalment of such a sum, is directed to be made to the clerk of some other magistrates' court the clerk of the court that adjudged the sum paid shall pay over any sums received by him on account of the said sum or instalment to the clerk of that other court.

Duty of clerk to give receipt
49. The clerk of a magistrates' court shall give or send a receipt to any person who makes a payment to him in pursuance of a conviction or order of a magistrates' court and who asks for a receipt.

Application for further time
51. An application under s.75(2) of the Act of 1980, s.22 of the Act of 1978, s.12B(5) of the Guardianship of Minors Act 1871 or s.6A(5) of the Affiliation Proceedings Act 1957 may, unless the court requires the applicant to attend, be made in writing.

Notice of date of hearing of means inquiry etc.
52. Where a magistrates' court, under subs (1) of s.86 of the Act of 1980 (power of magistrates' court to fix day for appearance of offender at means inquiry etc.), has fixed a day on which an offender must appear in person before the court and, under subs (3) of that section, fixes a later day in substitution for the day previously fixed, service of the notice of the substituted day may be effected in any manner in which service of a summons may be effected under r.99(1).

8b.109   **Execution of distress warrant**
54. (1) A warrant of distress issued for the purpose of levying a sum adjudged to be paid by a summary conviction or order–
  (a) shall name or otherwise describe the person against whom the distress is to be levied;
  (b) shall be directed to the constables of the police area in which the warrant is issued or to the authorised persons for the police area specified in the warrant, or to a person named in the warrant and shall, subject to, and in accordance with, the provisions of this rule, require them to levy the said sum by distress and sale of the goods belonging to the said person;
  (c) may where it is directed to the constables of a police area, instead of being executed by any of those persons be executed by any person under the direction of a constable.

(2) The warrant shall authorise the person charged with the execution of it to take any money as well as any goods of the person against whom the distress is levied; and any money so taken shall be treated as if it were the proceeds of the sale of goods taken under the warrant.

(3) The warrant shall require the person charged with the execution to pay the sum to be levied to the clerk of the court that issued the warrant.

(4) There shall not be taken under the warrant the wearing apparel or bedding of any person or his family or the tools and implements of his trade: so however that if the tools and implements of his trade exceed in value £150 it shall be lawful to take such of the tools and implements as will leave in that person's possession tools and implements of his trade to the value of £150.

(5) The distress levied under any such warrant aforesaid shall be sold within such period beginning not earlier than the sixth day after the making of the distress as may be specified in the warrant, or if no period is specified in the warrant, within a period beginning on the sixth day and ending on the 14th day after the making of the distress.
Provided that with the consent in writing of the person against whom the distress is levied the distress may be sold before the beginning of the said period.

(6) The said distress shall be sold by public auction or in such other manner as the person against whom the distress is levied may in writing allow.

(7) Notwithstanding anything in the preceding provisions of this rule, the said distress shall not be sold if the sum for which the warrant was issued and the charges of taking and keeping the distress have been paid.

(8) Subject to any direction to the contrary in the warrant, where the distress is levied on household goods, the goods shall not, without the consent in writing of the person against whom the distress is levied, be removed from the house until the day of sale; and so much of the goods shall be impounded as is in the opinion of the person executing the warrant sufficient to satisfy the distress, by affixing to the articles impounded a conspicuous mark.

(9) The constable or other person charged with the execution of any such warrant as aforesaid shall cause the distress to be sold, and may deduct out of the amount realised by the sale all costs and charges incurred in effecting the sale; and he shall return to the owner the balance, if any, after retaining the amount of the sum for which the warrant was issued and the proper costs and charges of the execution of the warrant.

(10) The constable or other person charged with the execution of any such warrant as aforesaid shall as soon as practicable send to the clerk of the court that issued it a written account of the costs and charges incurred in executing it; and the clerk shall allow the person against whom the distress was levied to inspect the account within one month after the levy of the distress at any reasonable time to be appointed by the court.

(11) If any person pays or tenders to the constable or other person charged with the execution of any such warrant as aforesaid the sum mentioned in the warrant, or produces a receipt for that sum give by the clerk of the court that issued the warrant, and also pays the amount of the costs and charges of the distress up to the time of the payment or tender or the production of the receipt the constable or other person as aforesaid shall not execute the warrant, or shall cease to execute it, as the case may be.

COMMENTARY

The landlord does not have a first claim on the proceeds of sale: *Potts v Hickman* (1940) 105 JP 26 (distress warrant for rates). Certain property of public utilities is exempted from distraint by various statutes, *viz* s.35(2) Water Act 1945; Sch.4 Gas Act 1972; s.25 Electric Lighting Act 1882; s.16 Electric Lighting Act 1909; s.57 and Sch.4 Electricity Act 1947.

Para (1): A warrant of distress, issued under s.76 MCA 1980, see form 48.

The authorised persons, this is a reference to the persons employed by a local authority in that area or by the chief officer of police or the police authority for that area who are authorised by the chief officer of police to execute warrants: r.2(4).

Para (4): Bedding, includes a bedstead: *Davis v Harris* (1900) 64 JP 136.

Implements of his trade, implements exceeding the prescribed value may not be taken if they are the only chattel on the premises: *Lovell v Ritchings*]1906] 1 KB 480 (a cab used by a cab driver). A typewriter used as a 'sample' is not so protected: *Addison v Shepherd* (1908) 72 JP 39.

A written account of the costs and charges, see form 50.

Payment after imprisonment imposed

55. (1) The persons authorised for the purposes of s.79(2) of the Act of 1980 to receive a part payment are–
  (a) unless there has been issued a warrant of distress or commitment, the clerk of the court enforcing payment of the sum, or any person appointed under s.88 of that Act to supervise the offender;
  (b) where the issue of a warrant of commitment has been suspended on conditions which provide for payment to be made to the clerk of some other magistrates' court, that clerk;
  (c) any constable holding a warrant of distress or commitment or, where the warrant is directed to some other person, that person;
  (d) the governor or keeper of the prison or place in which the defaulter is detained, or other person having lawful custody of the defaulter:
Provided that–
  (i) the said governor or keeper shall not be required to accept any sum

tendered in part payment lunder the said subs (2) except on a week-da
betwen 9 o'clock in the morning and 5 o'clock in the afternoon; and
(ii) no person shall be required to receive in part payment under the sai
subs (2) an amount which, or so much of an amount as, will not procur
a reduction of the period for which the defaulter is committed o
ordered to be detained.

(2) Where a person having custody of a defaulter receives payment of an
sum he shall note receipt of the sum on the warrant of commitment.

(3) Where the clerk of a court other than the court enforcing payment of th
sums receives payment or any sum he shall inform the clerk of the other court

(4) Where a person appointed under s.88 of the Act of 1980 to supervise a
offender receives payment of any sum, he shall send it forthwith to the clerk o
the court which appointed him.

(5) If the period of imprisonment imposed on any person in default o
payment of a sum adjudged to be paid by a conviction or order of a magistrate
court, or for want of sufficient distress to satisfy such a sum, is reduced throug
part payments to less than five days, he may be committed either to a prison o
to a place certified by the Secretary of State under s.134 of the Act of 1980, o
if he is already in prison, the Secretary of State may transfer him to a place s
certified.

8b.110   **Order for supervision**
56. (1) Unless an order under s.88(1) of the Act of 1980 is made in th
offender's presence, the clerk of the court making the order shall deliver to th
offender, or serve on him by post, notice in writing of the order.

(2) It shall be the duty of any person for the time being appointed under th
said section to advise and befriend the offender with a view to inducing him t
pay the sum adjudged to be paid and thereby avoid committal to custody an
to give any information required by a magistrates' court about the offender
conduct and means.

COMMENTARY
Para (1): An order under s.88(1), ie money payment supervision order.

Serve on him by post, for proof of service, see r.67.

Notice in writing, see form 62.

Transfer of fine order
57. (1) The clerk of a magistrates' court which has made a transfer of fin
order under s.89 or 90 or s.90 as applied by s.91 of the Act of 1980 shall send t
the clerk of the court having jurisdiction under the order a copy of the orde
with a statement of the offence and the steps, if any, taken to recover the su
adjudged to be paid, and with such further information as is available and is i
the opinion of the first-mentioned clerk likely to assist the last-mentione
court.

(2) Where a magistrates' court has made a transfer of fine order in respect c
a sum adjudged to be paid by a court in Scotland or in Northern Ireland th
clerk of the magistrates' court shall send a copy of the order to the clerk of th
Scottish court or to the clerk of the Northern Irish court, as the case may b

(3) Where the clerk of a magistrates' court receives a copy of a transfer c
fine order (whether made in England and Wales, or in Scotland or in Norther
Ireland) specifying that court as the court by which payment of the sum i
question is to be enforceable, he shall thereupon, if possible, deliver or send b
post to the offender notice in writing in the prescribed form.

(4) Where under a transfer of fine order a sum adjudged to be paid by
Scottish court or by a Northern Ireland court is enforceable by a magistrate
court–

(a) if the sum paid, the clerk of the magistrates' court shall send it to the clerk of the Scottish court or to the clerk of the Northern Irish court, as the case may be;

(b) if the sum is not paid, the clerk of the magistrates' court shall inform the clerk of the Scottish court or the clerk of the Northern Irish court, as the case may be, of the manner in which the adjudication has been satisfied or that the sum, or any balance thereof, appears to be irrecoverable.

COMMENTARY

The order, see forms 59 and 60.

Notice in . . . the prescribed form, see form 61.

Particulars of fine enforcement to be entered in register

65. (1) Where the court on the occasion of convicting an offender of an offence issues a warrant of commitment for a default in paying a sum adjudged to be paid by the conviction or having power to issue such a warrant, fixes a term of imprisonment under s.77(2) of the Act of 1980, the reasons for the court's action shall be entered in the register, or any separate record kept for the purpose of recording particulars of fine enforcement.

(2) There shall be entered in the register, or any such record, particulars of any–

(a) means inquiry under s.82 of the Act of 1980;

(b) hearing under subs (5) of the said s.82;

(c) allowance of further time for the payment of a sum adjudged to be paid by a conviction;

(d) direction that such a sum shall be paid by instalments including any direction varying the number of instalments payable, the amounts of any instalments payable and the date on which any instalment becomes payable;

(e) distress for the enforcement of such a sum;

(f) attachment of earnings order for the enforcement of such a sum;

(g) order under that Act placing a person under supervision pending payment of such a sum;

(h) order under s.85(1) of that Act remitting the whole or any part of a fine;

(i) order under s.120(4) of that Act remitting the whole or any part of any sum enforceable under that section (forfeiture of recognizance);

(j) authority granted under s.87(3) of that Act authorising the taking of proceedings in the High Court or county court for the recovery of any sum adjudged to be paid by a conviction;

(k) transfer of a fine order made by the court;

(l) order transferring a fine to the court;

(m) order under s.32(1) of the Powers of Criminal Courts Act 1973 specifying the court for the purpose of enforcing a fine imposed of a recognizance forfeited by the Crown Court; and

(n) any fine imposed or recognizance forfeited by a coroner which has to be treated as imposed or forfeited by the court.

Application for review of compensation order

104. (1) An application under s.37 of the Powers of Criminal Courts Act 1973 for the review of a compensation order shall be by complaint.

(2) The justice to whom the complaint is made shall issue a summons directed to the person for whose benefit the compensation order was made, requiring him to show cause why the order should not be amended or revoked.

CHAPTER 8c

Non-custodial Orders

ATTENDANCE CENTRE ORDERS 8c.00

Where a magistrates' court would in the case of someone *over 21*, have power to pass a sentence of *imprisonment* to commit him to prison for default, or to deal with him for 'breach of probation' it may make an attendance centre order in respect of a person under 21: s.17(1) CJA 1982. Such an order can only be made in respect of an offender if the court has been notified that an attendance centre (as defined in s.16(2)) is available for the reception of persons of his description: s.17(1). An order may *not* be made on anyone who has been previously sentenced to youth custody, detention in a detention centre or to certain other custodial sentences unless there are special circumstances which warrant the making of the order in his case: s.17(3). There is no bar on a second attendance centre order.

The number of *hours* must be specified in the order: s.17(1); and these must:

— Not be less than 12 in aggregate, expect where the offender is a child: s.17(4)

— Not exceed 12 in aggregate except where the court considers 12 hours inadequate, when they must

    (a) Not exceed 24 where the offender is under 17 years of age, or

    (b) Not exceed 36 hours where the offender is under 21 but not less than 17: s.17(5).

Where a previous attendance centre order is still in force, the number of fresh hours may be determined without reference to any hours still outstanding: s.17(6). The Home Office advises that:

'The aims of the order are to impose, in loss of leisure over a considerable period, a punishment that is generally understood by young people and to encourage them, in a disciplined environment, to make more constructive use of their leisure time. The sentence will not normally be suitable for those who have a long record of offences or who need removal from bad home surroundings, nor can it, of itself, meet a requirement for sustained supervision. It can, however, be ordered as an alternative to custody for an offence of some gravity.'

[*The Sentence of the Court*, para 8.2].

The attendance centre must be specified in the order: s.17(1); and must be reasonably accessible to the person concerned having regard to his age, the means of access available to him and any other circumstances: s.17(7). The time of first attendance must be specified in the order: s.17(9). Subsequent times are fixed by the officer in charge having regard to the offender's circumstances: s.17(10). A copy of the order must be delivered or sent by the clerk of the court to the officer in charge of the attendance centre with a copy to the offender: s.17(12).

8c.01 Discharge and variation

An attendance centre order may be discharged by the court on application by the *offender* or the *officer in charge*: s.18(1) CJA 1982. A magistrates' court acting for the petty sessions area in which the attendance centre is situated has jurisdiction, as well as the court which made the order (s.18(3)) except where the order was made by the Crown Court and a direction is included in the order reserving this power to that court: *ibid*, s.18(4). An attendance centre order may in like manner be varied as respects the time of first attendance or the centre specified: s.18(5),(6). Where either type of application is made the court may deal with it without summoning the offender: s.18(7). The order of discharge or variation must be delivered or served by the clerk of the court: s.18(8).

8c.02 Breach

Failure *without reasonable excuse* to attend an attendance centre or breach of the centre's rules, if proved to the satisfaction of a magistrates' court, may result in the court:

(a) revoking the order (if made by a magistrates' court) and dealing with the offender for the original offence in any manner in which he could have been dealt with for that offence by the court which made the order if the order had not been made; or

(b) committal in custody or on bail to the Crown Court (if the order was made by that court) to be dealt with, under s.19(5) CJA 1982: s.19(3).

A summons or warrant may be issued to secure the attendance of the offender: s.19(1). The magistrates' court in question is the one in the area of which the attendance centre is situated or the magistrates' court which made the order: s.19(2). There is an appeal to the Crown Court against sentence under (a) above: s.19(6).

Note

That there is no power to *penalize* the offender for the breach *and* to allow the attendance centre order to *continue*.

8c.03 PROBATION

As an *alternative to sentencing* an offender aged 17 or over a court can place him on probation, that is to say, direct that for a specified period of from *six months to three years* he shall be under the supervision of a probation officer and subject to the conditions of the order: s.2 PCCA 1973.

Various *requirements* (often referred to as 'conditions') may be added, notably:

— 'good conduct' requirements under s.2(3);
— 'presenting', 'participating' and 'refraining' requirements: s.4A;
— treatment for mental condition: s.3;
— day centre requirements: s.4B; and

— residence requirements: s.2(5) – see the commentary to subs (5) at 8c.56 and note the effect of [s.129] CJA 1988, when in force, in relation to conditions of bail for assessment in a bail or probation hostel.

Compensation and damages *must not form part of the order*: s.2(4)); although these may be ordered separately under s.35: see Chapter 8b.65.

'Good conduct' requirements

8c.04

The order may require the probationer to comply during *all or any part of the probation period* with *such requirements as the court*, having regard to the circumstances of the case, *considers necessary* for securing the offender's *good conduct* or for *preventing* a repetition by him of the same or of other *offences*: s.2(3) PCCA 1973.

A schedule to the prescribed form of probation order gives the following 'specimen requirements which are commonly inserted' in probation orders:

1. The accused shall be of good behaviour and lead an industrious life.
2. The accused shall inform the probation officer immediately of any change of address or employment.
3. The accused shall comply with the instructions of the probation officer as to reporting to the officer and as to receiving visits from the probation officer at home: see SI 1981 No 553.

There is no power to include a condition that the defendant leaves the country and does not return: *R v McCartan* [1958] 1 WLR 933 (an Irish youth). Although it was stated in that case that such an order could be made under the Justices of the Peace Act 1361, there is in fact *no such power*: *R v Ayu* [1958] 1 WLR 1264: see Chapter 8a.

In *Cullen v Rogers* [1982] 2 All ER 570 HL Lord Bridge, in his leading speech, stated that the power to impose requirements is subject to limitations *viz*: (1) since the making of a probation order is a course taken by the court to *avoid the passing of a sentence* a requirement must not introduce such a custodial or other element as will amount in substance to the imposition of a sentence; (2) since it is the court alone which can define the requirements of the order, any discretion conferred on the probation officer must itself be confined within well defined limits. Thus a court cannot under the guise of a requirement imposed pursuant to s.2(3) require a probationer to perform such unpaid work as would appropriately be the subject of a community service order; (3) no requirement to reside in any sort of institution can properly be imposed under s.2(3); (4) a requirement to attend for a given number of hours at an institutional establishment and here to comply with instructions of a wholly unspecified character given by the probation officer would go far beyond the range of proper requirements on the ground both that it would involve a substantial element of custodial punishment and that it would subject the probationer to the unfettered discretionary control of the probation officer.

These limitations must now be read in light of the new specific powers to impose certain carefully limited requirements under s.4A ('presenting', 'participating', and 'refraining' requirements) and under s.4B, (day training centre requirement) – but the basic principle expounded in *Cullen v Rogers* that probation requirements should not be used to construct penalties or sentences holds good.

8c.05 **'Presenting', 'Participating' and 'Refraining' requirements**

The power to add requirements in s.2(3) PCCA 1973 now includes power to impose requirements that the probationer:

(a) *presents* himself to a specified person or persons at a specified place or places;

(b) *participates*, or

(c) *refrains from participating* in specified activities: s.4A.

This power is subject to stringent statutory conditions, including the willingness of the defendant to comply and, in the case of a 'presenting' or 'participating' requirement, the consent of anyone else whose co-operation is involved: s.4A(3). A probation officer *must be consulted* about the offender's circumstances and the feasibility of securing compliance with the requirement and the court *must be satisfied*, having regard to his report, as to feasibility: s.4A(2).

'Participating' and *'refraining'* orders have effect on days specified in the probation order or, if the order so specifies, throughout the probation period: s.4A(1). *'Presenting'* and *'participating'* requirements operate to require the probationer in accordance with the probation officer's instructions to present himself at a place, or to participate in activities, for not more than 60 *days* and, while there or while participating, to comply with the instructions of those in charge: s.4A(4) and (6).

8c.06 **Treatment for mental condition**

The court may include a requirement that the offender submit during the whole or a specified part of the probation period to *treatment by or under the direction of a duly qualified medical practitioner* with a view to the improvement of his mental condition: s.3(1) PCCA 1973. The court must be satisfied:

(i) on the evidence of an approved medical practitioner that the offender's mental condition is such as requires and may be susceptible to treatment but is not such as to warrant his detention under a hospital order; and

(ii) that arrangements *have been made* for the treatment (including where appropriate reception): s.3(1).

The treatment must be:

(a) as a *resident patient* in a hospital other than a special hospital or a mental nursing home;

(b) as a *non-resident patient* at a specified institution or place; or

(c) by or under the direction of a duly qualified medical practitioner: s.3(2).

While the probationer is a *resident patient* supervision is only nominal: s.3(4). The medical practitioner may change the institution or place of treatment: s.3(5); subject to notifying the probation officer: s.3(6).

An offender's mental condition may be proved in accordance with s.54(2)(3) Mental Health Act 1983: s.3(7) PCCA 1973. A requirement to submit to mental treatment may be added to a probation order once made, but only within three months of the original order: Sch.1, para 3(2). A *reasonable refusal* to comply with a requirement to submit to treatment for a mental condition cannot constitute a breach of the order in the circumstance mentioned in s.6(7). The supervising officer is *under a duty* to apply for the variation or cancellation of the requirement on receipt of certain reports in writing from the medical practitioner: Sch.1, para 4.

Day centre
8c.07

The order may require the probationer during the probation period to attend at a specified day centre: s.4B(1) PCCA 1973. A day centre means premises at which *non-residential facilities* are provided for use in connection with the rehabilitation of offenders and which are *provided or approved by the probation committee*: s.4B(6). Before imposing such a requirement, a probation officer *must be consulted* and the court *must be satisfied* that (a) arrangements can be made for attendance; and (b) the person in charge consents: s.4B(2).

Such a requirement operates to require the probationer in accordance with instructions from the probation officer to attend on not more than *60 days* at the day centre and, while there, to comply with the instructions of the person in charge: s.4B(3). It also includes a duty to attend elsewhere for activities in accordance with the instructions of those in charge: s.4B(5). The probation officer's instructions must so far as practicable avoid interference with work and education: s.4B(4).

Social inquiry report
8c.08

Strictly speaking, there is no legal requirement for a social inquiry report before a probation order is made except to the extent that this is necessary in regard to 'presenting', 'participating' and 'refraining' requirements: s.4A(2) PCCA 1973; and day centre requirements: s.4B(2). However, the Home Secretary has reminded magistrates of the view expressed by the Departmental Committee on the Probation Service that a social inquiry report *should normally be obtained* before a probation order is made: HOC 28/1971. See also the comments on *R v Gillam* [1981] Crim LR 55 and the further cases quoted at 8c.24, the rationale of which would appear to apply equally to both probation reports and community service reports. In practice, a probation report is usually desirable whether written or verbal. Whilst the former kind will generally require an adjournment of up to four weeks, the latter can, in appropriate cases, occur on the day of the hearing – what is sometimes known as a 'stand alone' report.

Explanations and willingness to comply
8c.09

Before making a probation order the court must first explain *in ordinary language* the effect of the order and of any breach. An order may not be made unless the offender *expresses his willingness* to comply with its requirements: s.2(1) PCCA 1973.

The aims of probation
8c.10

The fundamental aim of probation is to uphold the law and protect society by the probation service working with the offender to improve his behaviour. The particular object of placing an offender on probation is to leave him at liberty in the community but subject to certain requirements regarding his way of life, with skilled help available to him from the probation service to cope with the problems and difficulties that may have led to his offending, and with an obligation to co-operate with his supervising probation officer as regards reporting, receiving visits and heeding the advice given to him. This response to offending, through the discipline of supervision by a probation officer, seeks to strengthen the offender's resources so that he becomes a more responsible person. . . .

Probation officers are required to supervise and to 'advise, assist and befriend' the offenders placed under their care by the courts, and this supervision of offenders is one of the principal activities of the probation service. The success of supervision turns on the ability of the individual probation officer first to gain the offender's confidence and then to work with him to overcome some of the problems which may have given rise to the offence. It is in this process that the reality and strength of the consent given in court is tested and the offender's practical capacity and willingness to change revealed. The probation officer's basic skills are those of a social worker who deals with offenders both individually and in groups, seeking to introduce them to a range of positive influences and experiences suited to their particular needs. The probation officer may provide these from within his own service or enlist the help of other agencies in the wider community. The probation officer also seeks sources of help for difficulties over money, accommodation or employment. The service seeks to involve numbers of individuals and agencies in a voluntary capacity both to demonstrate the concern of the wider community and to make a variety of talents and facilities available to offenders and their families.

[*The Sentence of the Court*, para 6.2, 3.]

8c.11 Combining probation with other orders

Since a probation order is made '*instead of sentence*' it cannot be combined with any other sentence or order in lieu of sentence *on the same offence: R v McClelland* [1951] 1 All ER 557 (wrong to combine fine and probation). Ancillary orders such as disqualification, endorsement (s.102 RTA 1972) and compensation (s.12(4) PCCA 1973) may however be made on the same offence as a probation order.

A probation order may not be made on one offence and a suspended sentence on another: s.22(3) PCCA 1973. In the ordinary way a probation order must operate forthwith. It is, therefore, wrong to make such an order at the same time as passing a sentence of detention centre training which will postpone the effective commencement of probation: *R v Evans* [1959] 1 WLR 26; or at the same time as a sentence of imprisonment: *R v Emmett* (1968) *The Times*, 21 December. Otherwise, there seems to be no reason why a probation order on one offence should not be combined with a different disposition on another offence, such as a fine: *R v Bainbridge* [1979] LS Gaz 28.

8c.12 Breach of probation

Breach of any of the requirements of a probation order renders the probationer liable:

(a) to a fine of up to £400;

(b) to an attendance centre order (if available); or

(c) unless the order was made by the Crown Court, to be dealt with in any manner in which the court could have dealt with him if it had just convicted him of the original offence: s.6(3) PCCA 1973.

In the first two cases the probation order continues unaffected; in the third it is replaced by the subsequent order. If the probation order was made by the Crown Court the magistrates' court may commit the offender to that court on bail or in custody to be dealt with: s.6(4) and (5). A summons or warrant may issue to compel the attendance of a probationer at court for the purpose of dealing with an alleged breach, provided the information is laid during the probation period: s.6(1). Breach proceedings must be distinguished from the powers of the court on the commission of an offence during the probation period.

For breach resulting from refusal to undergo treatment for a mental conditon, see s.6(7).

Commission of a further offence 8c.13
Since a probation order is an alternative to sentence *the commission of a further offence during the probationary period* followed by conviction therefor renders the offender liable to be dealt with as for the original offence, but in this case the court has no option of punishing the offender and allowing the probation order to continue: s.8 PCCA 1973. In the case of a probationer who commits further offences during the currency of a probation order made by the Crown Court magistrates' powers are confined to committing him to the Crown Court or taking no action. Where one magistrates' court sentences an offender who was placed on probation by another magistrates' court the consent of the latter or of the supervising court is necessary: s.8(9). This consent may be given by the justices' clerk: Justices' Clerks Rules 1970 (SI No 231).

Amendment 8c.14
A probation order may be amended in accordance with Sch.1 to PCCA 1973: s.5. Where the amendment is to substitute a different division the court is required to act upon the application of the probation officer: para 2(1) of Sch.1. No summons is necessary. A justices' clerk may amend a petty sessions area: JC Rules 1970. Other amendments, except where cancelling or reducing the period of any requirement or on the application of the probationer, must be by summons and with the consent of the probationer: para 5(1) and (2) of Sch.1. Any requirement of a probation order may be cancelled or inserted: Sch.1, para 3(1). The probation period may not be reduced: *ibid*, Sch.1, para 3(2). A requirement to submit to treatment for a mental condition may only be inserted within three months of the original order: Sch.1, para 3(2).

Discharge 8c.15
A probation order may be *discharged* on the application of the probation officer or probationer: Sch.1, para 1 PCCA 1973. No summons is necessary.

It is the 'supervising court' which has jurisdiction to amend a probation order: Sch.1, para 2. It is the supervising court which can discharge the order where it was made by the court by or before which the probationer was convicted (para 1(2), Sch.1) except when the order was made by the Crown Court and it includes a direction reserving that power to the Crown Court. Orders made by the Crown Court following a committal for sentence may also be discharged by the supervising court. In all other cases the power to discharge resides in the court which made the order: Sch.1, para 1(4).

Conversion to conditional discharge 8c.16
When a probation order ceases to be appropriate the unexpired portion may be converted to a conditional discharge on the application either of the probationer or the probation officer: s.11(1) PCCA 1973. The hearing may be conducted in the absence of the probationer if the probation officer produces a written statement to the effect that the probationer understands and consents to the proceedings: s.11(3). But application may not be made while an appeal against the making of the probation order is pending: s.11(1A).

8c.17   **Scotland**

For a Scottish order relating to a person residing in England see s.389 Criminal Procedure (Scotland) Act 1975; and for English orders relating to persons residing in Scotland: s.10 PCCA 1973.

8c.18   **ABSOLUTE AND CONDITIONAL DISCHARGE**

When *punishment is inexpedient* and *probation inappropriate* an offender may be discharged either *absolutely* or *conditionally*, under s.7 PCCA 1973. On conviction of a further offence, a conditional discharge – which may be for *up to three years*, but, unlike a probation order, has no minimum period – has the same consequences as a probation order: s.8.

8c.19   **EFFECTS OF PROBATION AND DISCHARGE**

Neither probation nor discharge, absolute or conditional, count as a conviction, except for the purposes of the proceedings in which the order was made and certain specifically exempt purposes: s.13 PCCA 1973. But this effect is removed if the offender is subsequently sentenced for the original offence.

8c.20   **APPEAL**

Notwithstanding that they do not rank as 'convictions' (8c.19), there is a right of appeal to the Crown Court against the making of probation orders and orders for conditional or absolute discharge: s.108(1)(1A) MCA 1980.

8c.21   **SUPERVISION ORDER**

A *juvenile* may not be made the subject of a probation order. If supervision is considered desirable he should be remitted to the juvenile court under s.7(8) CYPA 1969. Supervision orders may be made in both care and criminal proceedings. Often in practice, in relation to the latter, with conditions of 'Intermediate treatment' under s.12 CYPA 1969 as an 'alternative custody'. An order made in *criminal proceedings* may fall to be considered in the adult court if the supervised person has attained the age of 18 and either (1) there is an application for the terms of the order to be varied; or (2) the supervised person has failed to comply with certain requirements of the order: s.15. Proceedings of this nature in respect of 17-year-olds and younger are dealt with in the juvenile court. The supervised person may be brought before the court by summons or warrant under s.16(2), but his attendance is unnecessary in the cases listed in s.16(5).

A modified version of the restrictions in CYPA 1933 on the reporting of juvenile court proceedings is applied to the adult court in relation to proceedings resulting from supervision orders by virtue of s.10(1)(b) CYPA 1969. To be effective the restriction *must be announced* by the court in the course of the proceedings: s.10(2).

8c.22   **COMMUNITY SERVICE**

A magistrates' court convicting anyone aged *16 or over* of an offence punishable with imprisonment may, instead of dealing with him in any other way, make a community service order, that is an order that he should perform unpaid work under the direction of the 'relevant officer':

s.4(1) PCCA 1973. (Such orders in respect of persons below 17 can only be made in the juvenile court: see s.7(8) CYPA 1969).

Pre-condition to a community service order   8c.23
The power is subject to the following pre-requisites:
  (a) the offender's consent;
  (b) the court being satisfied, *after consideration of a report by a probation officer or by a social worker* of a local authority social services department and after hearing from them, if necessary, that the offender is a suitable person to perform work under such an order; and
  (c) (in the case of an offender aged 17 or over) the court being satisfied that provision can be made for the work in the area in which the offender resides: s.14(2), (2A), PCCA 1973 (below 17 the requirements are a set out in s.14(2A)(b)(i) and (ii)).

Before making a community service order the court must explain *in ordinary language* its purpose and effect, what is required of the offender, the consequences of breach and the possibility of review: s.14(5) PCCA 1973.

Social inquiry report   8c.24
The report the court is required to obtain must be about the offender and his circumstances: s.14(2) PCCA 1973. In practice it will usually be a full social inquiry report. When a court adjourns a case after conviction for the purpose of obtaining a report in order to ascertain the offender's suitability for community service and the report shows the offender to be suitable for such an order, the court ought to make it because otherwise a feeling of injustice will be aroused: *R v Gillam* [1981] Crim LR 55; *R v Millwood* [1982] Crim LR 832. *R v Rennes* (1985) 7 Cr App R (S) 343. (even where magistrates then commit to the Crown Court for sentence, when the latter court is equally bound). It is otherwise where the sentencer makes clear that he expects that a custodial sentence will be imposed and does 'not create in the mind of anyone present in court the expectation of a non-custodial sentence': *R v Horton and Alexander* (1985) 7 Cr App R (S) 299.

Length of a community service order   8c.25
The number of hours must be specified in a community service order and, in the case of an offender aged 17 or over, must be not less than 40 nor more than 240: s.14(1A)(a), (b)(ii) PCCA 1973. For offenders aged 16, the limits are 40 to 120 hours: s.14(1A)(a), (b)(i). There is no statutory or other equivalent between the length of a custodial sentence and the number of hours appropriate to a community service order. But it has been held that, generally speaking, it is wrong to order a small number of community service hours where the alternative would have been a sentence of imprisonment. A short period of community service would usually be reserved in cases where the court was not minded otherwise to impose a custodial sentence: *R v Lawrence* (1982) 4 Cr App R (S) 69.

Similarly it has been advised that:

'The social inquiry report will include mention of factors relating to the offender or his circumstances which will influence his ability to complete orders of a particular length within a 12 month period. Because of the differences between offenders, there is no clearly established tariff for length of orders. The Court of Appeal has given guidance by suggesting

190 hours for burglary meriting 9–12 months imprisonment. It is important for the court to consider whether the community service order is being made as an alternative to a custodial sentence. If it is not, then this fact should be recorded in the court register . . . The Lord Chief Justice has said that if the alternative would not have been a custodial sentence, the order should be for a small number of hours only . . . If an offender has spent time in custody on remand, and the court decides to make a community service order, the Court of Appeal has decided that, in recognition of the time in custody, it is reasonable for the length of the order to be reduced.'

[*The Sentence of the Court*, paras 7.10, 7.12].

When two or more community service orders are made at the same time the court may order that the hours shall be served *concurrently* or *additionally*, so a later order may be made consecutive to an earlier order: *R v Evans* (1977) 141 JP 441, provided that the total period does not exceed 240 hours. Whilst it is sometimes said that *consecutive* orders can give rise to administrative difficulties it is suggested that *R v Evans* implicitly recognises that a later court may 'top-up' to 240 hours (or 120 hours) where such a course *is* appropriate.

8c.26 The relevant officer

The community service order must specify the relevant officer, that is a probation officer or a person appointed by the probation committee: s.14(4) PCCA 1973.

8c.27 The work

The work under a community service order must be performed *within 12 months* of the making of the order: s.15(2) PCCA 1973. The offender must perform the work at such times as he may be instructed by the relevant officer: s.15(1). The instructions must, so far as practicable, avoid any conflict with the offender's religious beliefs and any interference with his normal working or school hours: s.15(3).

8c.28 Aims of community service

In practice, community service is often used as an 'alternative' to custody (see eg *R v Lawrence, supra, R v Stewart* [1987] 1 WLR 559 where it was *equated* with imprisonment), even though, legally speaking, it is available in respect of any offence *punishable with imprisonment*: s.14; whether such a sentence is in mind or not. Thus, it is *suggested*, as a matter of practice, a careful record should be made of the basis on which the order is made in a particular case, to be made available in any future 'breach' or 'revocation' proceedings in which the court has to deal with the offender for the original offence: see also *R v Howard and Wade et al, infra*.

The Home Office advises that:

A community service order represents a substantial deprivation of time: the minimum of 40 hours is 10% more than the maximum 36 hours of a senior attendance centre order; the maximum of 240 hours is six times that minimum. The order also involves reparation to the community and a demanding regular commitment. When Parliament accepted the proposal for the introduction of a community service order, it was seen as a penal sanction that made serious demands on the offender and could thus be regarded as a realistic alternative for a custodial sentence. Through subsequent custom and practice, the order has come to be regarded as a

sentence in its own right. Various judgements of the Court of Appeal have indicated that a community service order can properly be made – if the court is satisfied that the offender is suitable – even for quite serious offences for which the alternative sentence might be a substantial term of imprisonment.
[*The Sentence of the Court*, para 7.5].

Combining with orders 8c.29

Community service is a sentence and as such may not be combined with any other sentence or order in lieu of sentence on the same offence. Thus it cannot be combined *on the same offence* with a fine: *R v Carnwell* (1979) 68 Cr App R 58. It would not seemingly be wrong to make a community service order on one offence and a fine on another. However, it is bad sentencing practice to make a community service order on one offence and a suspended prison sentence on another: *R v Starie* (1979) 1 Cr App R (S) 239; *R v Ray* (1984) 6 Cr App R (S) 26; *a fortiori* on implementing a suspended sentence: *R v Seymour* [1983] Crim LR 410.

Breach of community service 8c.30

Breach *without reasonable excuse* of any requirement of a community service order may be dealt with by a magistrates' court:
  (a) imposing a fine of up to £400 (which does not prejudice the continuance of the order); or
      if the order was made by a magistrates' court, by
  (b) dealing with the offender in any way in which he could have been dealt with on conviction if the order had not been made; or
      if the order was made by the Crown Court, by
  (c) committing the offender to the Crown Court to be dealt with s.16 PCCA 1973.

Note
There is no power to 'commit for sentence' in respect of breach of an order made in a magistrates' court: *R v Worcester Crown Court and Birmingham Magistrates' Court, ex p. Lamb* (1985) 7 Cr App R (S) 44. '. . . When the magistrates imposed a community service order they must have considered the possibility of committing the defendant to the Crown Court for sentence and have rejected that as an alternative. A next step would have been to have decided what penalty they ought themselves to impose or, as an alternative, to impose a community service order. That is what they did. It seems to me to follow that upon breach of that community service order they were limited to those courses of action that they themselves had power to take immediately prior to the institution of the community service order.': per Stocker J.

A custodial sentence may be expected on breach of a community service order *where the making of the order had saved the offender from an immediate custodial sentence: R v Howard and Wade* [1977] Crim LR 683; when 'some credit' should be given for the fact that a substantial portion of the community service order has been completed: *R v Whittingham* (1986) 8 Cr App (S) 116 (one third of hours worked); and see the further cases quoted in the commentary to s.16(3) in Chapter 8d. However, a custodial sentence is usually *inappropriate* where an offender has completed a *substantial proportion* of the work required: *R v Paisley* (1979) 1 Cr App R (S) 196; *R v Baines* [1983] Crim LR 756.

Where *the breach* of community service *is not sufficiently grave* to warrant a prison sentence the court will rarely be justified in activating a suspended sentence: *R v McElhorne* [1983] Crim LR 487.

If the offender breaches the community service order by failing to attend for work and the proceedings are outside the twelve months period contemplated by s.15(2), then this is tantamount to an election by the community service organiser to treat the order as at an end – and once the court is seized of the matter any hours subsequently worked can only go to mitigation: *R v Tebbut* (1988) *The Times*, 22 February. Custody may thus be appropriate even where a substantial proportion of the hours have been worked, *semble:* (63 out of 100, with 27 completed voluntarily after proceedings were commenced). But contrast the views expressed in *R v Pailsey* and *R v Baines, supra* and see the criticism of *R v Tebbut* at 152 JPN 164. The rule will not in any event apply where the court extends the period of 12 months under s.17(1), *semble:* see 8c.33.

8c.31 Revocation consequent upon a custodial sentence

Where a person subject to a community service order receives a custodial sentence from a magistrates' court other than the court named in the order and it appears on the application of the offender or the relevant officer that it would be in the interests of justice to do so having regard to circumstances which have arisen since the order was made the court may:

    (a) (if the order was made by a magistrates' court) *revoke* it; or

    (b) (if the order was made by the Crown Court) commit the offender to that court: s.17(4A) PCCA 1973.

8c.32 Other revocations

On application by the *offender* or the *relevant officer* at any time while the order is in force, the magistrates' court specified in the order may, if it appears to be *in the interests of justice* to do so:

    (a) (if the order was made by a magistrates' court) revoke the order or revoke the order and deal with the offender in any manner in which he could have been dealt with by the court of conviction if the order had not been made; or

    (b) (if the order was made by the Crown Court) commit the offender to that court: s.17(2) PCCA 1973.

8c.33 Extension

The *offender* or the *relevant officer* may at any time while the order is in force apply for the 12-month period *to be extended* and the court may so order if this appears *in the interests of justice* having regard to circumstances which have *arisen since it was made*: s.17(1) PCCA 1973. When the rule in *R v Tebbut* (1988) *The Times*, 22 February will not apply, semble; at least until the new and extended period has expired.

8c.34 Petty sessions areas

The petty sessions area in which the offender resides or will reside must be specified in the order: s.14(4) PCCA 1973; and on his removal to another area may be amended in accordance with s.17(5), (5A).

8c.35 Scotland

A Scottish court may make a community service order in respect of an offender residing in England and Wales by virtue of s.6 Community Service by Offenders (Scotland) Act 1978 (not reproduced herein). Breach of such an order may be punished by a court in this country:

..16(3) PCCA 1973. A court in England or Wales may make a community
ervice order in respect of an offender residing in Scotland: ss.14, 17A.

Northern Ireland 8c.36

A Northern Ireland court may make a community service order in respect
of an offender residing in England or Wales: Treatment of Offenders
Northern Ireland) Order 1976, as amended by Sch.13 CJA 1982 (not
eproduced herein). A magistrates' court in England or Wales may make
a community service order in respect of an offender residing in Northern
reland: s.17B PCCA 1973.

MEDICAL TREATMENT 8c.37

The mental condition of a defendant may affect both the issue of his guilt
or innocence and the disposition of his case on conviction. Insanity under
he M'Naghten rules is *probably* a defence to all crimes; though for
obvious reasons it is in practice pleaded only in cases of homicide. A
pecial defence statutorily confined to murder is that of 'diminished
esponsibility', under s.2 Homicide Act 1957. Neither of these defences
as any significant part to play in summary jurisdiction and they are not
dealt with in this work.

Magistrates may be concerned with two categories of abnormal mental
ondition:

(1) mental disorder (of certain specified forms) of a nature and degree
which warrants detention in a hospital for medical treatment; and

(2) a mental condition such as requires and may be susceptible to
treatment, but which is not sufficient to warrant such detention.

In the second category of case, *however trivial the offence*, the magis-
rates may, if they make a probation order, include in it a requirement
hat the offender shall submit, for the probation period, or any lesser
eriod fixed by the court, to treatment, whether residential or otherwise,
y or under the direction of a doctor: s.3 PCCA 1973; see also Treatment
or Mental Condition at 8c.06.

Hospital and guardianship orders 8c.38

A hospital order is an order for the admission of an offender to a hospital:
.37(4) Mental Health Act 1983. A guardianship order is an order placing
an offender under the guardianship of a local social services authority or
of any other person: s.37(6). The effects of these orders are described at
.40.

A hospital order or a guardianship order may be made by a magistrates'
ourt where a person is convicted of an offence punishable on summary
onviction with *imprisonment* and where certain conditions are satisfied:
.37(1). The court must be satisfied on the evidence of two registered
nedical practitioners that the offender is suffering from mental illness,
sychopathic disorder, severe mental impairment or mental impairment
nd that *either*:

(a) the mental disorder is of a nature or degree which makes it appropriate for him to be detained in hospital for medical treatment and,
in the case of psychopathic disorder or mental impairment, that the
treatment is likely to alleviate or prevent a deterioration of his
condition; or

(b) in the case of an offender aged 16 or over, that the mental disorder
is of a nature or degree which warrants his reception into guardianship; *and*

(c) in *either case* the court must also be of the opinion that the mos
suitable method of disposing of the case is a hospital or guard
ianship order: s.37(2).

Where the accused is suffering from mental illness or severe menta
impairment and the court is satisfied that he did the act or made th
omission charged it may if it thinks fit make the order *without convictin
the accused*: s.27(3). In addition to the evidence required at (a) or (b
above the court must be satisfied on the evidence of the registere
medical practitioner who would be in charge of the treatment, or of som
other person representing the managers of the hospital, that arrange
ments have been made for *admission within 28 days:* s.37(4). For th
requirements concerning medical evidence see s.54.

Pending admission the court may give directions for the offender'
conveyance to and detention in a *place of safety*: s.37(4). Before making
guardianship order the court must be satisfied that the authority or othe
person is *willing to receive the offender into guardianship* s.57(6). Whe
making either type of order the court may not pass a sentence c
imprisonment or other detention, or impose a fine, or make a supervisio
order concerning a juvenile, or to bind over his parent or guardian
s.37(8). This does not rule out any other order which the court has powe
to make.

8c.39 Interim hospital order

Where a person is *convicted* by a magistrates' court of an offence punish
able on summary conviction with *imprisonment* it may make an interir
hospital order if satisfied on the evidence of *two* registered medic;
practitioners that

(a) he is suffering from mental illness, psychopathic disorder, sever
    mental impairment or mental impairment; *and*

(b) there is no reason to suppose that the mental disorder is such that 1
    may be appropriate for a hospital order to be made: s.38(1) Ment;
    Health Act 1983.

An interim hospital order is an order authorizing admission to
specified hospital and detention there in accordance with s.38(1). For th
requirements concerning medical evidence see s.38(3) and (4), and s.5∠
A *further* interim order may be made without the offender being brougr
before the court if he is represented by counsel or solicitor who is given a
opportunity of being heard: s.38(2). An interim hospital order remains i
force for such period as the court specifies *not exceeding 12 week*;
s.38(5).It may be *renewed* for further periods of not more than *28 days at
time* if it appears on the evidence of the responsible medical officer tha
continuation is warranted: *ibid*. An interim hospital order may not cont
nue in force *for more than six months in all* and the court must terminate
on making a hospital order or deciding to deal with the offender in som
other way: s.38(5). Absconding is dealt with in s.38(7).

8c.40 Information about hospitals

On request from the Regional Health Authority, the court may obtai
information about hospitals which could receive persons under a hospit;
order or an interim hospital order: s.39 Mental Health Act 1983.

8c.41 Committal to Crown Court for a restriction order

Where the conditions for the making of a hospital order are satisfied but
appears having regard to the nature of the offence, the antecedents of th

offender and the risk of his committing further offences if set at large that a restriction order should accompany the hospital order a magistrates' court may, instead of making a hospital order, commit the offender in custody to the Crown Court to be dealt with: s.43(1) Mental Health Act 1983. The powers of the Crown Court are set out in s.43(2).

Magistrates may at the same time commit the offender for sentence under s.38 MCA 1980, where they are of the opinion that greater punishment should be inflicted on the offender unless a hospital order is made: s.43(4). Instead of committing the offender in custody he may be committed to a specified hospital if the court is satisfied on medical evidence that arrangements have been made for his reception: s.44.

Appeal 8c.42

Where the hospital order or a guardianship order is made *without convicting the accused* he has a right of appeal against the order under s.45 Mental Health Act 1983. In other cases there is a right of appeal under s.108 MCA 1980: see Appeal at 8c.46.

DEPORTATION 8c.43

A person aged *17 or over* who is not a British citizen is liable to deportation if he is cᴖnvicted of an offence which is punishable by *imprisonment* and a competent court *recommends deportation*: s.3(6) Immigration Act 1971. Such a person may be recommended for deportation by any court having power to sentence him for the offence unless the court commits him to be sentenced or further dealt with by another court: s.6(1). There are exceptions for certain existing residents: s.7; and for seamen, aircrew and other special cases: s.8. When any question arises whether or not a person is a British citizen or is entitled to any exemption *it lies with the person asserting it to prove that he is*: s.3(8). A court may not recommend deportation unless the offender has been given *not less than seven days written notice* of the legal provisions and the hearing may be adjourned for this purpose: s.6(2).

The following guidelines were laid down by Lawton LJ, in *R v Nazari* [1980] 1 WLR 1366:

'First the court must consider, as was said by Sachs LJ in *R v Caird* (1970) 54 Cr App R 499, whether the accused's continued presence in the United Kingdom is to its detriment. This country has no use for criminals of other nationalities, particularly if they have committed serious crimes or have long criminal records. That is self-evident. The more serious the crime and the longer the record the more obvious it is that there should be an order recommending deportation. On the other hand, a minor offence would not merit an order recommending deportation. In the Greater London area, for example, shoplifting is an offence which is frequently committed by visitors to this country. Normally an arrest for shoplifting followed by conviction, even if there were more than one offence being dealt with, would not merit a recommendation for deportation. But a series of shoplifting offences on different occasions may justify a recommendation for deportation. Even a first offence of shoplifting might merit a recommendation if the offender were a member of a gang carrying out a planned raid on a department store. Second, the courts are not concerned with the political systems which operate in other countries. They may be harsh; they may be soft; they may be oppressive; they may be the quintessence of democracy. The court has no knowledge of these matters over and above that which is common knowledge, and that may be wrong. In our judgment it would be undesirable for this court or any other court to express views about regimes which exist outside the United Kingdom of Great Britain and Northern Ireland. It is for the Home Secretary to decide in each case whether an offender's return to his country of origin would have consequences which would make his compulsory return unduly harsh. The Home Secretary has opportunities of informing himself about what is happening in other countries which the courts do not have.

The sentencer may consider the consequences of deportation on the offender: *R v Thoseby and Krawczyk* (1979) 1 Cr App R (S) 280 (defendants had married residents of UK). However, fears of the treatment the offender will receive if deported are matters for the Secretary of State and not the court: *R v Caird* (1970) 54 Cr App R 499; *R v Antypas* (1972) 57 Cr App R 207; *R v Sabharwal* [1973] Crim LR 132; *R v Nazari, supra.* It was not the intention of the (pre-existing legislation) that a recommendation for deportation should be part of the punishment for the offence in the sense that the court should give a reduced sentence when a recommendation was made. Courts should sentence the prisoner to the penalty he deserves and then deal with the recommendation quite separately: *R v Edgehill* [1963] 1 All ER 181.

There is no power to make a recommendation when the executive act cannot follow thereupon. Thus a recommendation may not be made where a deportation order is still in force: *R v Kelly* [1966] 1 WLR 1556.

A recommendation may be made in respect of a national of an EEC member state. However the Secretary of State's powers are limited by the EEC restrictions upon interference with the free movement of workers in accordance with art 48 of the Treaty of Rome. By virtue of art 3(2) of Directive 62/221 previous criminal convictions do not by themselves justify a recommendation although they may be evidence that the continued presence of the accused represents a present threat to public policy: *R v Boucherel [1978] 2 WLR 251 (European Ct); and see R v Secretary of State for the Home Department, ex p. Santillo* [1981] 2 All ER 897. It is inappropriate to make a recommendation for deportation on a national of a member state of the EEC solely for failure to obtain a special residence permit: *R v Pieck* [1981] 3 All ER 46 (European Ct).

8c.44   The attitude of the Secretary of State

The Secretary of State has made the following statement of principle:

STATEMENT OF IMMIGRATION RULES

FOR CONTROL

AFTER ENTRY

Laid before Parliament under s.3(2) of the Act.

Consideration of the merits

48. In considering whether deportation is the right course on the merits, the public interest will be balanced against any compassionate circumstance of the case. While each case will be considered in the light of the particular circumstances, the aim is an exercise of the power of deportation that is consistent and fair as between one person and another, although one case will rarely be identical with another in all material respects.

49. Most of the cases in which deportation may be the appropriate course fall into two main categories. There are, first, those cases which come to notice following a conviction for a criminal offence and in which it is fitting that, because of his conduct, a person should no longer be allowed to remain here, in defiance of the immigration control.

Deportation following a conviction

50. In considering whether to give effect to a recommendation for deportation made by a court on conviction the Secretary of State will take into account every relevant factor, including–

age
length of residence in the United Kingdom
personal history, including character, conduct and employment record
domestic circumstances
the nature of the offence of which the person was convicted
previous criminal record
compassionate circumstances
any representations received on the person's behalf.
In certain circumstances, particularly in the case of young or first offenders, supervised departure, with a prohibition on re-entry, may be arranged as an alternative to the deportation recommended by the court provided that the person is willing to leave the country.

51. Where the court has not recommended deportation there may nevertheless be grounds, in the light of all the relevant information and subject to the right of appeal, for curtailment of stay or a refusal to extend stay followed, after departure, by a prohibition on re-entry.

'While any recommendation of a court will of course be most carefully considered in relation to the circumstances of the case, he would not normally think it right to deport an offender sentenced to borstal training or to be sent to a detention centre; it would, in his view, be inappropriate to require an offender to serve either of these sentences, which could be designed to fit him for future life in this country, and then to deport him at the end of it.': HOC 215/1972.

Detention pending deportation   8c.45

When a recommendation for deportation is in force in respect of anyone not detained pursuant to a sentence or released on bail and the court *fails to direct otherwise* he must be detained pending the making of the order unless the Secretary of State directs his release: Sch.3 para 1 Immigration Act 1971. The court may direct the release of a person recommended for deportation but only on prescribed conditions: Sch.3, para 4.

Appeal   8c.46

A recommendation for deportation is *treated as a sentence* for the purpose of appeal: s.6(5)(a) Immigration Act 1971; and an appeal against a recommendation lies therefore to the Crown Court under s.108 MCA 1980. No deportation order may be made until the expiration of the 21 day period for appeal, or pending the determination of the appeal: s.6(6) Immigration Act 1971.

A person ordered to be deported following a recommendation has a right of appeal under s.17 (not included herein) to the appellate authorities set up under the Immigration Appeals Act 1969 on the ground only that he ought to be removed to a country or territory other than that specified in the removal directions.

Statutory Provisions

CHILDREN AND YOUNG PERSONS ACT 1969

8c.47   **Variation and discharge of supervision orders**
15. (1), (2), (2A) (*Concern the juvenile court*).

(3) If while a supervision order is in force in respect of a supervised person who has attained the age of 18 it appears to a magistrates' court other than a juvenile court, on the application of the supervisor or the supervised person, that it is appropriate to make an order under this subsection, the court may make an order discharging the supervision order or varying it by–

(a) inserting in it a provision specifying the duration of the order or altering or cancelling such a provision already included in it; or

(b) substituting for the provisions of the order by which the supervisor is designated or by virtue of which he is selected such other provisions in that behalf as could have been included in the order if the court had then had power to make it and were exercising the power; or

(c) substituting for the name of an area included in the order in pursuance of s.18(2)(a) of this Act the name of any other area of a local authority or petty sessions area, as the case may be, in which it appears to the court that the supervised person resides or will reside; or

(d) cancelling any provision included in the order by virtue of s.18(2)(b) of this Act or inserting in it any provision prescribed for the purposes of that paragraph; or

(e) cancelling any requirement included in pursuance of s.12(1) or (2) of this Act.

(4) If while a supervision order is in force in respect of a supervised person who has attained the age of eighteen it is proved to the satisfaction of a magistrates' court other than a juvenile court, on the application of the supevisor, that the supervised person has failed to comply with any requirement included in the supervision order in pursuance of s.12 or s.18(2)(b) of this Act, the court may–

(a) whether or not it also makes an order under subs (3) of this section, order him to pay a fine of an amount not exceeding £100 or, subject to subs (1) of the following section, make an attendance centre order in respect of him;

(b) if it also discharges the supervision order, make an order imposing on him any punishment which it could have imposed on him if it had then had power to try him for the offence in consequence of which the supervision order was made and had convicted him in the exercise of that power;

and in a case where the offence in question is of a kind which the court has no power to try without appropriate consents, the punishment imposed by virtue of para (b) of this subsection shall not exceed that which any court having power to try such an offence could have imposed in respect of it and shall not in any event exceed imprisonment for a term of six months and a fine of £2,000.

(5) (*Concerns the juvenile court*).

(6) The preceding provisions of this section shall have effect subject to the provisions of the following section.
[*As amended by ss.37, 58(5) CLA 1977 and SI 1984 No 19*].

15. (3)(e) *cancelling any requirement included in pursuance of section 12, 12A, 12B or 12C of this Act.*

(4) *If while a supervision order made under section 7(7) of this Act or made by a court on discharging a care order made under that section is in force in*

respect of a person who has attained the age of 18 it is proved to the satisfaction of a magistrates' court (not being a juvenile court), on the application of the supervisor, that the supervised person has failed to comply with any requirement included in the supervision order in pursuance of section 12, 12A, 12B, 12C or 18(2)(b) of this Act, the court–

    (a) whether or not it also makes an order under subsection (3) of this section, order him to pay a fine of an amount not exceeding £100 or, subject to section 16A(1) of this Act, may make an attendance centre order in respect of him;

    (b) if it also discharges the supervision order, may make an order imposing on him any punishment other than a sentence of detention in a young offender institution which it could have imposed on him if it had then had power to try him for the offence in consequence of which the supervision order was made and had convicted him, in the exercise of that power;

and in a case where the offence in question is of a kind which the court has no power to try without appropriate consents–

    (i) the punishment imposed by virtue of paragraph (b) of this subsection shall not exceed that which any court having power to try such an offence could have imposed in respect of it; and

    (ii) if the punishment imposed is a fine, it shall not in any event exceed £2,000.

(4A) If while a supervision order is in force in respect of a person it is proved to the court under subsection (2A) or (4) above that the supervised person has failed to comply with any requirement included in the supervision order in pursuance of section 2A(3)(a) of this Act directing the supervised person to participate in specified activities, the court may, if it also discharges the supervision order, make an order imposing on him any sentence which it could have imposed on him if it had then had power to try him for the offence in consequence of which the supervision order was made and had convicted him, or found him guilty, in the exercise of that power.

(4B) In a case where the offence in question is of a kind which the court has no power to try or has no power to try without appropriate consents, the sentence imposed shall not exceed that which any court having power to try such an offence could have imposed in respect of it and shall not in any event exceed a custodial sentence for a term of six months and a fine–

    (a) if the offender has not attained the age of 18, of £400; and

    (b) if he has attained that age, of £2,000.

(4C) A court may not make an order by virtue of subsection (4A) of this section unless the court which made the supervision order made a statement under section 12D(1) of this Act.

(4D) For the purposes of subsection (4C) above a certificate under section 12D of this Act shall be evidence of the making of the statement to which it relates.

[s.15 (3)(e) and (4) are to be substituted and subs (4A)–(4D) are to be added by Sch.10 Part III] CJA 1988 from a date to be appointed.]

COMMENTARY

Proceedings under this section in the adult court are governed by the restrictions on reporting applicable to juvenile courts: s.49 CYPA 1933 as applied by s.10 CYPA 1969 and this fact must be announced in the course of the proceedings: s.10(2). For the right to appeal against an order under this section see s.16(8), *infra*.

s.15(3): Supervision order, has the meaning assigned to it by s.11 of the Act: s.70(1), *ibid*. Supervision orders to which this subsection apply will have been made by the juvenile court under s.7(7) of the Act.

Attained the age of 18, for the determination of age, see s.99 CYPA 1933. Variations under the age of 18 are made in the juvenile court under: s.15(1), even though the supervised person is no longer a juvenile.

A magistrates' court, as to which court see s.16(11), *infra*.

The **application of . . . a supervised person,** or his parent or guardian: s.70(2).

s.15(3)(b): Such other provisions, see ss.12 and 18 of the Act.

Make an attendance centre order, under s.17 CJA 1982, see: also s.16(10), *infra.*

8c.48   **Provisions supplementary to s.15**

16. (1) Where the supervisor makes an application or reference under the preceding section to a court he may bring the supervised person before the court and subject to subs (5) of this section a court shall not make an order under that section unless the supervised person is present before the court.

(2) Without prejudice to any power to issue a summons or warrant apart from this subsection, a justice may issue a summons or warrant for the purpose of securing the attendance of a supervised person before the court to which any application or reference in respect of him is made under the preceding section; but subss (3) and (4) of s.55 of the Magistrates' Courts Act, 1980 (which among other things restrict the circumstances in which a warrant may be issued) shall apply with the necessary modifications to a warrant under this subsection as they apply to a warrant under that section and as if in sub (3) after the word 'summons' there were inserted the words 'cannot be served or'.

(3) Where the supervised person is arrested in pursuance of a warrant issued by virtue of the preceding subsection and cannot be brought immediately before the court referred to in that subsection, the person in whose custody he is–
   (a) may make arrangements for his detention in a place of safety for a period of not more than 72 hours from the time of the arrest (and it shall be lawful for him to be detained in pursuance of the arrangements); and
   (b) shall within that period, unless within it the relevant infant is brought before the court aforesaid, bring him before a justice;
and the justice shall either direct that he be released forthwith or–
   (i) if he has not attained the age of 18, make an interim order in respect of him;
   (ii) if he has attained that age, remand him.

(4) (*Concerns the juvenile court*).

(5) A court may make an order under the preceding section in the absence of the supervised person if the effect of the order is confined to one or more of the following, that is to say–
   (a) discharging the supervision order;
   (b) cancelling a provision included in the supervision order in pursuance of s.12 or s.18(2)(b) of this Act;
   (c) reducing the duration of the supervision order or any provision included in it in pursuance of the said s.12;
   (d) altering in the supervision order the name of any area;
   (e) changing the supervisor.

(6) (*Concerns the juvenile court*).

(7) Where the supervised person has attained the age of 14, then except with his consent a court shall not make an order under the preceding section containing provisions which insert in the supervision order a requirement authorised by s. 12(4) of this Act or which alter such a requirement already included in the supervision order otherwise than by removing it or reducing its duration.

(8) The supervised person may appeal to the Crown Court against–
   (a) any order made under the preceding section, except an order made or which could have been made in the absence of the supervised person and an order containing only provisions to which he consented in pursuance of the preceding subsection;
   (b) the dismissal of an application under that section to discharge a supervision order.

(9) Where an application under the preceding section for the discharge of a

supervision order is dismissed, no further application for its discharge shall be made under that section by any person during the period of three months beginning with the date of the dismissal except with the consent of a court having jurisdiction to entertain such an application.

(10) In para (b) of subs (2A) and para (a) of subs (4) of the preceding section 'attendance centre order' means such an order to attend an attendance centre as is mentioned in subs (1) of s.17 of the Criminal Justice Act 1982; and the provisions of that section shall accordingly apply for the purpose of each of those paragraphs as if for the words from 'has power' to 'probation order' in subs (1) there were substituted the words 'considers it appropriate to make an attendance centre order in respect of any person in pursuance of s.15(2A) or (4) of the Children and Young Persons Act 1969, and for references to an offender there were substituted references to the supervised person and as if subs (13) were omitted.

(11) In this and the preceding section references to a juvenile court or any other magistrates' court, in relation to a supervision order, are references to such a court acting for the petty sessions area for the time being named in the order in pursuance of s.18(2) of this Act; and if while an application to a juvenile court in pursuance of the preceding section is pending the supervised person to whom it related attains the age of 17 or 18, the court shall deal with the application as if he had not attained the age in question.
[*as amended by Sch.9 Courts Act 1971, Sch.12 CLA 1977, Sch.7 MCA 1980, Sch.14 CJA 1982.*]

16. (5) (b) *cancelling a provision included in the supervision order in pursuance of section 12, 12A, 12B or 12C or section 18(2)(b) of this Act;*
    (c) *reducing the duration of the supervision order or any provision included in it in pursuance of the said section 12, 12A, 12B or 12C;*
[*S.16(5)(b) and (c) are to be amended by [Sch.10, Part II] CJA 1988 from a date to be appointed.*]

Application of sections 17 to 19 of Criminal Justice Act 1982
16A. *(1) The provisions of section 17 of the Criminal Justice Act 1982 (attendance centre orders) shall apply for the purposes of section 15(2A)(b) and (4A) of this Act but as if—*
   (a) in subsection (1), for the words from 'has power' to 'probation order' there were substituted the words 'considers it appropriate to make an attendance centre order in respect of any person in pursuance of section 15(2A) or (4) of the Children and Young Persons Act 1969';
   (b) for references to an offender there were substituted references to a supervised person; and
   (c) subsection (13) were omitted.

(2) Sections 18 and 19 of the Criminal Justice Act 1982 (discharge and variation of attendance centre order and breach of attendance centre orders or attendance centre rules) shall also apply for the purposes of each of those pararaphs but as if—
   (a) for the references to an offender there were substituted references to the person in respect of whom the attendance centre order has been made; and
   (b) there were omitted—
      (i) from subsections (3) and (5) of section 19, the words ', for the offence in respect of which the order was made,' and 'for that offence'; and
      (ii) from subsection (6), the words 'for an offence'.
[*Section 16A is to be added by Sch.10, Part IV] CJA 1988 from a date to be appointed.*]

COMMENTARY
Proceedings under this section in the adult court are governed by the restrictions on reporting applicable to juvenile courts: s.40 MCA 1933, as applied by s.10 CYPA 1969. This fact must be announced in the course of proceedings: s.10(2).

s.16(3): Place of safety This means a community home provided by a local authority or a controlled community home, any police station or any hospital, surgery or any other suitable place, the occupier of which is willing temporarily to receive a child or young person: s.107(1) CYPA 1933.

Remand him, ie under s.128 MCA 1980.

Is present Appearance by counsel or solicitor under s.122 MCA 1980 is not enough.

Requirements authorised by s.12(4), this relates to medical treatment.

Order which could have been made in absence, see s.16(5).

8c.49 **Supplementary provisions relating to supervision orders**
   18. (3) A court which makes a supervision order or an order varying or discharging a supervision order shall forthwith send a copy of its order–
   (a) to the supervised person and, if the supervised person is a child, to his parent or guardian; and
   (b) to the supervisor and any person who has ceased to be the supervisor by virtue of the order; and
   (c) to any local authority who is not entitled by virtue of the preceding paragraph to such a copy and whose area is named in the supervision order in pursuance of the preceding subsection or has ceased to be so named by virtue of the court's order; and
   (d) where the supervised person is required by the order, or was required by the supervision order before it was varied or discharged, to reside with an individual or to undergo treatment by or under the direction of an individual or at any place, to the individual or the person in charge of that place; and
   (e) where a petty sessions area named in the order or discharged order in pursuance of subs (2) of this section is not that for which the court acts, to the clerk to the justices for the petty sessions area so named;
   and, in a case falling within para (e) of this subsection, shall also send to the clerk to the justices in question such documents and information relating to the case as the court considers likely to be of assistance to them.

IMMIGRATION ACT 1971

8c.50 **General provisions for regulation and control**
   3. (6) Without prejudice to the operation of subs (5) above, a person who is not a British citizen shall also be liable to deportation from the United Kingdom if, after he has attained the age of 17, he is convicted of an offence for which he is punishable with imprisonment and on his conviction is recommended for deportation by a court empowered by this Act to do so.

   (7) (*Power to make orders in Council*).

   (8) When any question arises under this Act whether or not a person is a British citizen, or is entitled to any exemption under this Act, it shall lie on the person asserting it to prove that he is.
   [*as amended by s.39(3), Sch.4 British Nationality Act 1981*].

COMMENTARY

s.3(6): Liable to deportation, by order of the Secretary of State under s.5.

Attained the age of 17, ie on the relevant anniversary of his birth: s.9 Family Law Reform Act 1969; and see s.6(3)(a), *infra*.

Convicted, a conviction followed by an order of probation, absolute or conditional discharge is a conviction for the purposes of deportation recommendations notwithstanding s.13 PCCA 1973: *R v Akan* [1973] 1 QB 491; and see s.6(3), *infra*.

An offence for which he is punishable by imprisonment, to be determined without regard to restrictions on the imprisonment of young offenders or of persons not previously sentenced to imprisonment: s.6(3)(b). An offence triable either way punishable by imprisonment only on conviction on indictment eg 'fraudulent use' of a vehicle excise licence contrary to s.26 Vehicles (Excise) Act 1971, would not appear to fall within the terms of the statute if tried summarily. An offender dealt with otherwise than by imprisonment in respect of an offence punishable by imprisonment would however be liable to be recommended for deportation. Although the occasions must be rare when it would be right for justices not to make a recommendation in the case of an offender convicted of an offence under s.24 of the Act (remaining in the United Kingdom without leave), justices have a complete discretion in the matter: *Khan v Shea* (1968) *The Times*, 1 November.

Recommended for deportation ie under s.6(1), *infra*.

Recommendations by court for deportation   **8c.51**
   6. (1) Where under s.3(6) above a person convicted of an offence is liable to deportation on the recommendation of a court, he may be recommended for deportation by any court having power to sentence him for the offence unless the court commits him to be sentenced or further dealt with for that offence by another court:
(Proviso applies to Scotland).

   (2) A court shall not recommend a person for deportation unless he has been given not less than seven days notice in writing stating that a person is not liable to deportation if he is a British citizen, describing the persons who are partial and stating (so far as material) the effect of s.3(8) above and s.7 below; but the powers of adjournment conferred by s.10(3) of the Magistrates' Courts Act 1980, s.179 or 380 of the Criminal Procedure (Scotland) Act 1975 or any corresponding enactment for the time being in force in Northern Ireland shall include power to adjourn, after convicting an offender, for the purpose of enabling a notice to be given to him under this subsection or, if a notice was given to him less than seven days previously, for the purpose of enabling the necessary seven days to elapse.

   (3) For purposes of s.3(6) above–
   (a) a person shall be deemed to have attained the age of 17 at the time of his conviction if, on consideration of any available evidence, he appears to have done so to the court making or considering a recommendation for deportation; and
   (b) the question whether an offence is one for which a person is punishable with imprisonment shall be determined without regard to any enactment restricting the imprisonment of young offenders or persons who have not previously been sentenced to imprisonment,
and for purposes of deportation a person who on being charged with an offence is found to have committed it shall, notwithstanding any enactment to the contrary and notwithstanding that the court does not proceed to conviction, be regarded as a person convicted of the offence, and references to conviction shall be construed accordingly.

   (4) . . .

   (5) Where a court recommends or purports to recommend a person for deportation, the validity of the recommendation shall not be called in question except on an appeal against the recommendation or against the conviction on which it is made; but the recommendation shall be treated as a sentence for the purpose of any enactment providing an appeal against sentence.

   (6) A deportation order shall not be made on the recommendation of a court so long as an appeal or further appeal is pending against the recommendation or against the conviction on which it was made; and for this purpose an appeal or further appeal shall be treated as pending (where one is competent but has not been brought) until the expiration of the time for bringing that appeal or, in Scotland, until the expiration of 28 days from the date of the recommendation.

   (7) *(Applies to Scotland)*.
[*as amended by Sch.5, CJA 1972, Sch.9 Criminal Procedure (Scotland) Act 1975, Sch.7 MCA 1980, Sch.4 British Nationality Act 1981, Sch.16 CJA 1982.*]

COMMENTARY

s.6(1): For the principles upon which the court should exercise its discretion see the introduction. It is advisable in general that legal aid should be granted when a recommendation is being considered: *R v Edgehill* [1963] 1 All ER 181. Normally, if a court is minded to make a recommendation it would be desirable for his advocate to be given the opportunity of making any submissions he may wish in that respect, *per* Megaw LJ in *R v Antypas* (1972) 57 Cr App R 207; but this is not a rule of law: *R v Newham Justices, ex p. Akhtar* (1982) 25 June, unreported.

A suggested certificate of recommendation is attached to HOC 215/1972. Once a recommendation has been made the provisions of Sch.3 apply with respect to detention or control.

Commits him to be sentenced or further dealt with, thus where magistrates commit an offender to the Crown Court they may *not* at the same time make a recommendation for deportation.

s.6(2): Notice:

'12. The service of a notice will, as at present, be the duty of the police, and the Secretary of State has suggested to chief officers of police the use of the form of notice which is enclosed with this circular. He has suggested, further, that where a person is charged with an offence of illegal entry under s.24(1)(a) of the Act, or of overstaying or breach of conditions under s.24(1)(b) or where, in a particular case, they consider it desirable to do so, the police should normally serve the notice forthwith, as a matter of course; but that, in all other cases, where notice has not been served on a person who appears to the police to be liable for deportation, and who is charged with an offence punishable with imprisonment, they should be prepared to provide the court with whatever information they have about his liability, and should seek the court's direction on whether the notice should be served. The direction will be sought at the end of the accused person's first court appearance on the charge, ie when he is convicted or, as the case may be, when he is remanded or committed for sentence or trial.

'13. Where a notice has been served on a person, the prosecution will so inform the court when giving, after conviction, particulars of the character and antecedents of the offender. The court will also be given any information that the prosecution may have bearing on the offender's liability to deportation.

'14. It is also desirable that the governor of a prison or remand centre should be informed whenever a person in his custody has been, or is about to be, served with a notice under s.6(2) of the Act. Accordingly, it is requested that, when proceedings are adjourned to enable a notice to be given to the prisoner or to enable the necessary seven days after the service of a notice to elapse, the purpose of the adjournment should be indicated on the warrant of commitment on remand.'

HOC 215/1972 (which also contains a recommended form of notice). Acknowledgement of the notice should be attached to the papers sent to the appeal court: *R v Edgehill, supra.*

s.6(4): Any rule of practice, see *R v Assa Singh* [1965] 1 All ER 938.

8c.52 **Exemption from deportation for certain existing residents**

7. (1) Notwithstanding anything in s.3(5) or (6) above but subject to the provisions of this section, a Commonwealth citizen or citizen of the Republic of Ireland who was such a citizen at the coming into force of this Act and as then ordinarily resident in the United Kingdom–

    (a), (b) . . .; and

    (c) shall not on conviction of an offence be recommended for deportation under s.3(6) if at the time of the conviction he had for the last five years been ordinarily resident in the United Kingdom and Islands.

(2) A person who has at any time become ordinarily resident in the United Kingdom or in any of the Islands shall not be treated for the purposes of this section as having ceased to be so by reason only of his having remained there in breach of the immigration laws.

(3) The 'last five years' beore the material time under subs (1)(b) or (c) above is to be taken as a period amounting in total to five years exclusive of any time during which the person claiming exemption under this section was undergoing imprisonment or detention by virtue of a sentence passed for an offence on a conviction in the United Kingdom and Islands, and the period for which he was imprisoned or detained by virtue of the sentence amounted to six months or more.

(4) For purposes of subs (3) above–

(a) 'sentence' includes any order made on conviction of an offence; and

(b) two or more sentences for consecutive (partly consecutive) terms shall be treated as a single sentence; and

(c) a person shall be deemed to be detained by virtue of a sentence–

   (i) at any time when he is liable to imprisonment or detention by virtue of the sentence, but is unlawfully at large; and

   (ii) (unless the sentence is passed after the material time) during any period of custody by which under any relevant enactment the term to be served under the sentence is reduced.

In para (c)(ii) above 'relevant enactment' means s.67 of the Criminal Justice Act 1967 (or, before that section operated, s.17(2) of the Criminal Justice Administration Act 1962) and any similar enactment which is for the time being or has (before or after the passing of this Act) been in force in any part of the United Kingdom and Islands.

(5) Nothing in this section shall be taken to exclude the operation of s.3(8) above in relation to an exemption under this section.

COMMENTARY

s.7(1)(c): Islands, defined in s.33, *infra.*

Ordinarily resident, *illegal residence* cannot amount to *ordinary residence: R v Bangoo* [1976] Crim LR 746.

Exceptions for seamen, aircrews and other special cases   **8c.53**

   8. (2) (*Rule making power*).

(3) The provisions of this Act relating to those who are not British citizens shall not apply to any person so long as he is a member of a mission (within the meaning of the Diplomatic Privileges Act 1964), a person who is a member of the family and forms part of the household of such a member, or a person otherwise entitled to the like immunity from jurisdiction as is conferred by that Act on a diplomatic agent.

(4) . . .

(5) Where a person having a limited leave to enter or remain in the United Kingdom becomes entitled to an exemption under this section, that leave shall continue to apply after he ceases to be entitled to the exemption, unless it has by then expired; and a person is not to be regarded for purposes of this Act as having been settled in the United Kingdom at any time when he was entitled under the former immigration laws to any exemption corresponding to any of those afforded by subs (3) or (4)(b) or (c) above or by any order under subs (2) above.

(5A) (*Rules*).

(6) In this section 'the home forces' means any of Her Majesty's forces other than a Commonwealth force or a force raised under the law of any associated state; 'Commonwealth force' means a force of any country to which provisions of the Visiting Forces Act 1952, apply without an Order in Council under s.1 of the Act; and 'visiting force' means a body, contingent or detachment for the time being present in the United Kingdom on the invitation of Her Majesty's Government in the United Kingdom.

[*as amended by s.39(4), Sch.4 British Nationality Act 1981*].

COMMENTARY

s.8(3): Consular officers, etc., are exempted by the Immigration (Exemption from Control) Order 1972 (SI No 1613).

Interpretation   **8c.54**

   33. (1) For purposes of this Act, except in so far as the context otherwise requires–

'aircraft' includes hovercraft, 'airport' includes hoverport and 'port' includes airport;

'captain' means master (of a ship) or commander (of an aircraft);

'certificate of patriality' means such a certificate as is referred to in s.3(9) above;

'crew', in relation to a ship or aircraft, means all persons actually employed in the working or service of the ship or aircraft, including the captain, and 'member of the crew' shall be construed accordingly;

'entrant' means a person entering or seeking to enter the United Kingdom, and 'illegal entrant' means a person unlawfully entering or seeking to enter in breach of a deportation order or of the immigration laws, and includes also a person who has so entered;

'entry clearance' means a visa, entry certificate or other document which, in accordance with the immigration rules, is to be taken as evidence of a person's eligibilty, though not a British citizen, for entry into the United Kingdom (but does not include a work permit);

'immigration laws' means this Act and any law for purposes similar to this Act which is for the time being or has (before or after the passing of this Act) been in force in any part of the United Kingdom and Islands;

'immigration rules' means the rules for the time being laid down as mentioned in s.3(2) above;

'the Islands' means the Channel Islands and the Isle of Man, and 'the United Kingdom and Islands' means the United Kingdom and the Islands taken together;

'legally adopted' means adopted in pursuance of an order made by any court in the United Kingdom and Islands or by an adoption specified as an overseas adoption by order of the Secretary of State under s.4 of the Adoption Act 1958;

'limited leave' and 'indefinite leave' mean respectively leave under this Act to enter to remain in the United Kingdom which is, and one which is not, limited as to duration;

'settled' shall be construed in accordance with subs (2A) below;

'ship' includes every description of vessel used in navigation;

'United Kingdom passport' means a current passport issued by the Government of the United Kingdom, or by the Lieutenant Governor of any of the Islands or by the Government of any territory which is for the time being a dependent territory within the meaning of the British Nationality Act 1981;

'work permit' means a permit indicating in accordance with the immigration rules, that a person named in it is eligible, though not a British citizen, for entry into the United Kingdom for the purpose of taking employment.

(2) It is hereby declared that, except as otherwise provided in this Act, a person is not to be treated for the purposes of any provision of this Act as ordinarily resident in the United or in any of the Islands at a time when he is there in breach of the immigration laws.

(2A) Subject to s.8(5) above, references to a person being settled in the United Kingdom are references to his being ordinarily resident there without being subject under the immigration laws to any restriction on the period for which he may remain.

(3), (4) . . .

(5) This Act shall not be taken to supersede or impair any power exercisable by Her Majesty in relation to aliens by virtue of Her prerogative.
[*as amended by Sch.4 British Nationality Act 1981*]

COMMENTARY

Settled, by virtue of s.33(2) an illegal entrant is not settled in this country: *Azam v Secretary of State* [1974] AC 18.

SCHEDULE 3   8c.55

1. . . .

DETENTION OR CONTROL PENDING DEPORTATION
2. (1) Where a recommendation for deportation made by a court is in force
in respect of any person, and that person is neither detained in pursuance of
the sentence or order of any court nor for the time being released on bail by any
court having power so to release him, he shall, unless the court by which the
recommendation is made otherwise directs or a direction is given under
sub-para (1A) below, be detained pending the making of a deportation order
in pursuance of the recommendation, unless the Secretary of State directs him
to be released pending further consideration of his case.

(2)–(4) . . .

3. . . .

POWERS OF COURTS PENDING DEPORTATION
4. Where the release of a person recommended for deportation is directed
by a court, he shall be subject to such restrictions as to residence and as to
reporting to the police as the court may direct.

5. (1) On an application made–
(a) by or on behalf of a person recommended for deportation whose release
    was so directed; or
(b) by a constable; or
(c) by an immigration officer,
the appropriate court shall have the powers specified in sub-para (2) below.

(2) The powers mentioned in sub-para (1) above are–
(a) if the person to whom the application relates is not subject to any such
    restrictions imposed by a court as are mentioned in para 4 above, to
    order that he shall be subject to any such restrictions as the court may
    direct; and
(b) if he is subject to such restrictions imposed by a court by virtue of that
    paragraph or this paragraph–
    (i) to direct that any of them shall be varied or shall cease to have
        effect; or
    (ii) to give further directions as to his residence and reporting.

6. (1) In this Schedule 'the appropriate court' means, except in a case to
which sub-para (2) below applies, the court which directed release.

(2) This sub-paragraph applies where the court which directed release was–
(a) the Crown Court;
(b) the Court of Appeal;
(c) the High Court of Justiciary;
(d) the Crown Court in Northern Ireland; or
(e) the Court of Appeal in Northern Ireland.

(3) Where the Crown Court or the Crown Court in Northern Ireland
directed release, the appropriate court is–
(a) the court that directed release; or
(b) a magistrates' court acting for the commission area or county court
    division where the person to whom the application relates resides.

(4), (5) . . .

7. (1) A constable or immigration officer may arrest without warrant any
person who is subject to restrictions imposed by a court under this Schedule
and who at the time of the arrest is in the relevant part of the United Kingdom–
(a) if he has reasonable grounds to suspect that that person is contravening
    or has contravened any of those restrictions; or

(b) if he has reasonable grounds for believing that that person is likely to contravene any of them.

(2) In sub-para (1) above 'the relevant part of the United Kingdom' means–

(a) England and Wales, in a case where a court with jurisdiction in England or Wales imposed the restrictions;

(b) Scotland, in the case where a court with jurisdiction in Scotland imposed them; and

(c) Northern Ireland, in a case where a court in Northern Ireland imposed them.

8. (1) A person arrested in England or Wales or Northern Ireland in pursuance of para 7 above shall be brought as soon as practicable and in any event within 24 hours after his arrest before a justice of the peace for the petty sessions area or district in which he was arrested.

(2) In reckoning for the purposes of this paragraph any period of 24 hours, no account shall be taken of Christmas Day, Good Friday or any Sunday.

9. (*Scotland*).

10. Any justice of the peace or court before whom a person is brought by virtue of paras 8 or 9 above–

(a) if of the opinion that that person is contravening, has contravened or is likely to contravene any restriction imposed on him by a court under this Schedule, may direct–

  (i) that he be detained; or

  (ii) that he be released subject to such restrictions as to his residence and reporting to the police as the court may direct; and

(b) if not of that opinion, shall release him without altering the restrictions as to his residence and his reporting to the police.

[*as amended by Sch.10 CJA 1982*].

COMMENTARY

Para 2, the exclusion in para 2(1) of Sch.3 from the need to detain persons 'released on bail by any court' does not apply to bail on an irrelevant charge: *R v Secretary of State for the Home Office, ex p. Giambe* (1981) 3 Cr App R (S) 260. It is nowhere stated where persons shall be detained in pursuance of para 2, or who shall convey them there. The para has effect without any order or warrant of the court.

Para 4, the power to direct release is not a power to grant bail. Thus, the court cannot demand the defendant's recognizances, take a surety or impose conditions other than those allowed in para 4.

POWERS OF CRIMINAL COURTS ACT 1973

8c.56   **Probation**

2. (1) Where a court by or before which a person of or over 17 years of age is convicted of an offence (not being an offence the sentence for which is fixed by law) is of opinion that having regard to the circumstances, including the nature of the offence and the character of the offender, it is expedient to do so, the court may, instead of sentencing him, make a probation order, that is to say, an order requiring him to be under the supervision of a probation officer for a period to be specified in the order of not less than six months nor more than three years.

For the purposes of this subsection the age of a person shall be deemed to be that which it appears to the court to be after considering any available evidence.

(2) A probation order shall name the petty sessions area in which the offender resides or will reside; and the offender shall (subject to the provisions of Sch.1 to this Act relating to probationers who change their residence) be required to be under the supervision of a probation officer appointed for or assigned to that area.

In this Act 'supervising court' means, in relation to a probation order, a magistrates' court acting for the petty sessions area for the time being named in the order.

(3) Subject to the provisions of subs (4) below and subs 3, 4A and 4B of this Act a probation order may in addition require the offender to comply during the whole or any part of the probation period with such requirements as the court, having regard to the circumstances of the case, considers necessary for securing the good conduct of the offender or for preventing a repetition by him of the same offence or the commission of other offences.

(4) Without prejudice to the power of the court under s.35 of this Act to make a compensation order, the payment of sums by way of damages for injury or compensation for loss shall not be included among the requirements of a probation order.

(5) Without prejudice to the generality of subs (3) above, a probation order may include requirements relating to the residence of the offender, but–
(a) before making an order containing any such requirements, the court shall consider the home surroundings of the offender; and
(b) where the order requires the offender to reside in an approved probation hostel or any other institution, the period for which he is so required to reside shall be specified in the order.

(6) Before making a probation order, the court shall explain to the offender in ordinary language the effect of the order (including any additional requirements proposed to be inserted therein and that if he fails with it or commits another offence he will be liable to be sentenced for the original offence; and the court shall not make the order unless he expressed his willingness to comply with its requirements.

(7) The court by which a probation order is made shall forthwith give copies of the order to a probation officer assigned to the court, and he shall give a copy to the offender, to the probation officer responsible for the supervision of the offender and to the person in charge of any institution in which the probationer is required by the order to reside; and the court shall, except where it is itself the supervising court, send to the clerk to the justices for the petty sessions area named in the order a copy of the order, together with such documents and information relating to the case as it considers likely to be of assistance to the supervising court.
[*as amended by s.57, Schs.12, 13 CLA 1977, Probation Orders (Variation of Statutory Limits) Order 1978 (SI No 474) Schs.11, 16 (JA 1982)*].

COMMENTARY
For the use of probation see the introduction.

s.2(1): Convicted, for effects of a probation order on the conviction see s.3.

Instead of sentencing him, these words do not take away the court's powers to order the offender to pay *costs* or *compensation*: s.12(4).

Probation order, see form 64.

A probation officer, selected in accordance with Sch.3, Part I, para 9, his duties are set out in para 8, *ibid*.

A period, the period may not be reduced by amendment or extended more than three years from the original date, but the order may be discharged altogether (Sch.1 to the Act, *infra*) or its unexpired portion converted to a conditional discharge under s.11, *infra*. The minimum period, now six months, was reduced from one year by the Probation Orders (Variation of Statutory Limits) Order 1978 (SI No 474) HOC 67/1978 refers.

s.2(3): Such requirements as the court . . . considers necessary, see under *Good Conduct Requirements* at 8c.04.

s.2.(5): Approved probation hostel, the Home Office advise:
Approved probation hostels (run by the probation service or by voluntary organisations

and approved by the Secretary of State) provide a stable and supportive environment in which groups of between 15 and 25 offenders may learn how to get on with their contemporaries and other people, including those in authority, and may be helped to develop regular work habits and to achieve satisfaction in work and at leisure. The emphasis is upon helping the resident through group and individual contact both inside and outside the hostel to move towards a more adequate way of life and away from a pattern of offending. Probationers in hostels are expected to go to daily employment (or to full-time education or training) outside the hostel. They contribute from their earnings towards their board and lodging and are helped to take responsibility for their own affairs.

A number of hostels however provide for more inadequate offenders who are unlikely to be able to obtain and keep ordinary employment in the community. Residents in these hostels initially receive full-time training on the premises aimed at the acquisition of basic work habits, but commonly go to outside employment during the later stages of their stay.

Residence in a probation hostel is likely to be of benefit to offenders who are socially or emotionally immature or who, by reason of their background, are likely to be socially isolated and to lack family or community support. It is expected that offenders will have had a number of previous convictions and may also have had experience of custodial treatment. However, residents are not in legal custody, and hostels are unlikely to be suitable for the more serious offenders or those who require special care by reason of a high degree of personal disturbance or addiction to drugs or alcohol.

(*The Sentence of the Court*).

Note that [s.129] CJA 1988, when in force, amends s.3 and Sch.1 Bail Act 1976 so as to empower courts to require a defendant who as a condition of bail is required to reside in a bail or probation hostel to enable a report to be made on his suitability, to receive a disposal which would involve a condition of hostel residence to comply with the rules of the hostel; see s.3[6ZA] Bail Act 1976 at 3.48.

s.2.(6): Willingness to comply, this is *not exactly the same as the offender's consent*. Note also that the court should explain, not only the normal conditions of a probation order, but also any special requirements imposed in the particular case. There is no 'consent' where the offender is not given a free choice: *R v Marquis* [1974] 2 All ER 1216, where the offender was (wrongly) given the impression that the only alternative was a custodial one; but consent is not vitiated by a reference to the possibility of imprisonment where this is a 'realistic alternative': *R v Barnett* (1986) 8 Cr App R (S) 200, distinguishing *R v Marquis, supra*.

s.2(7): this subsection does not apply to orders made in respect of offenders who reside or will reside in Scotland, as to which see s.10(7), *infra*. The normal rule that orders made on appeal are made by the court from which the appeal is brought does not apply to s.2(7): s.12(2), *infra*.

8c.57   **Probation orders requiring treatment for mental condition**

    3.   (1) Where the court is satisfied, on the evidence of a duly qualified medical practitioner approved for the purpose of s.12 of the Mental Health Act 1983, that the mental condition of an offender is such as requires and may be susceptible to treatment but is not such as to warrant his detention in pursuance of a hospital order under Part III of that Act, the court may, if it makes a probation order, include in it a requirement that the offender shall submit, during the whole of the probation period or during such part of that period as may be specified in the order, to treatment by or under the direction of a duly qualified medical practitioner with a view to the improvement of the offender's mental condition.

    (2) The treatment required by any such order shall be such one of the following kinds of treatment as may be specified in the order, that is to say–
    (a) treatment as a resident patient in a hospital within the meaning of the Mental Health Act 1983, or mental nursing home within the meaning of the Nursing Homes Act 1975, not being a special hospital within the meaning of the National Health Service Act 1977;
    (b) treatment as a non-resident patient at such institution or place as may be specified in the order; or
    (c) treatment by or under the direction of such duly qualified medical practitioner as may be specified in the order;
but the nature of the treatment shall not be specified in the order except as mentioned in paras (a), (b) or (c) above.

(3) A court shall not by virtue of this section include in a probation order a requirement that an offender shall submit to treatment for his mental condition unless it is satisfied that arrangements have been made for the treatment intended to be specified in the order (including arrangements for the reception of the offender where he is to be required to submit to treatment as a resident patient).

(4) While the probationer is under treatment as a resident patient in pursuance of a requirement of the probation order, the probation officer responsible for his supervision shall carry out the supervision to such extent only as may be necessary for the purpose of the discharge or amendment of the order.

(5) Where the medical practitioner by whom or under whose direction a probationer is being treated for his mental condition in pursuance of a probation order is of opinion that part of the treatment can be better or more conveniently given in or at an institution or place not specified in the order, being an institution or place in or at which the treatment of the probationer will be given by or under the direction of a duly qualified medical practitioner, he may, with the consent of the probationer, make arrangements for him to be treated accordingly; and the arrangements may provide for the probationer to receive part of his treatment as a resident patient in an institution or place notwithstanding that the institution or place is not one which could have been specified for that purpose in the probation order.

(6) Where any such arrangements as are mentioned in subs (5) above are made for the treatment of a probationer–
- (a) the medical practitioner by whom the arrangements are made shall give notice in writing to the probation officer responsible for the supervision of the probationer, specifying the institution or place in or at which the treatment is to be carried out; and
- (b) the treatment provided for by the arrangements shall be deemed to be treatment to which he is required to submit in pursuance of the probation order.

(7) Subsections (2) and (3) of s.54 of the Mental Health Act 1983, shall have effect with respect to proof for the purposes of subs (1) above of an offender's mental condition as they have effect with respect to proof of an offender's mental condition for the purposes of s.37(2)(a) of that Act.

(8) The provisions of this section shall apply in relation to a probation order made or amended by virtue of s.10 of this Act only so far as indicated in subs (3) of that section, and except as provided by this section or s.10 a court shall not include in a probation order a requirement that the probationer shall submit to treatment for his mental condition.
[*as amended by Sch.4 Mental Health Act 1983*].

COMMENTARY

For the effects of this section see *Treatment for Mental Condition* at 8c.06.

s.3(1): A duly qualified medical practitioner, see s.55 Medical Act 1983.

s.3(5), it is not necessary to amend the order. Notice must however be given under s.3(6).

Requirements in probation orders 8c.58

4A. (1) Without prejudice to the generality of s.2(3) above, the power conferred by that subsection includes power, subject to the provisions of this section, to require the probationer–
- (a) to present himself to a person or persons specified in the order at a place or places so specified;
- (b) to participate or refrain from participating in activities specified in the order–
  - (i) on a day or days so specified; or
  - (ii) during the probation period or such portion of it as may be so specified.

(2) A court shall not include in a probation order a requirement such as is mentioned in subs (1) above unless it has first consulted a probation officer as to–

    (a) the offender's circumstances; and

    (b) the feasibility of securing compliance with the requirements, and is satisfied, having regard to the probation officer's report, that it is feasible to secure compliance with them.

(3) A court shall not include a requirement such as is mentioned in subs (1)(a) above or a requirement to participate in activities if it would involve the co-operation of a person other than the probationer and the probation officer responsible for his supervision, unless that other person consents to its inclusion.

(4) A requirement such as is mentioned in subs(1)(a) above shall operate to require the probationer–

    (a) in accordance with instructions given by the probation officer responsible for his supervision, to present himself at a place for not more than 60 days; and

    (b) while there, to comply with instructions given by, or under the authority of, the person in charge of the place.

(5) A place specified in the order shall have been approved by the probation committee for the area in which the premises are situated as providing facilities suitable for persons subject to probation orders.

(6) A requirement to participate in activities shall operate to require the probationer–

    (a) in accordance with instructions given by the probation officer responsible for his supervision, to participate in the activities for not more than 60 days; and

    (b) while participating, to comply with instructions given by, or under the authority of, the person in charge of the activities.

(7) Instructions given by a probation officer under subs (4) or (6) above shall, as far as practicable, be such as to avoid any interference with the times, if any, at which the probationer normally works or attends a school or other educational establishment.

[*as inserted by Sch.11 CJA 1982*].

COMMENTARY

See under '*Presenting*', '*Participating*' and '*Refraining*' *Requirements* at 8c.03.

s.4A(1), all three types of requirement authorised by this subsection may be included in the same probation order. These requirements must however be carefully formulated and may not exceed the clear words of the statute.

s.4A(2) Consulted a probation officer, presumably concerning the requirement. Normally the 'consultation' will take the form of a social inquiry report, but a written report is not essential, for example where the offender and the offender's present circumstances are already sufficiently known to the probation officer.

The feasibility of compliance, note that the court's conclusion must 'have regard' to the probation officer's report. This does not mean that the probation officer has a veto, but the circumstances in which a court could be satisfied as to the feasibility of compliance in face of clear advice from a probation officer that compliance would not be feasible must be rare.

s.4A(3): Consents, there is no prescribed procedure for obtaining or proving a third person's consent, but the court will clearly be satisfied if the probation officer reports that he has explained what is contemplated to the person concerned and that the latter has given his consent. The court would also accept such a statement from an advocate, where he speaks of his own knowledge.

s.4A(4): 60 days, it is *suggested* that the effect of this subsection is that directions may be given by the probation officer in respect of not more than 60 days. It is not seemingly intended that the court should stipulate a period. The probation officer is under no obligation to use all the days.

s.4A(6), see note to s.4A(4). In this case the overall length of time must be specified by the court: see s.4A(1).

Probation orders requiring attendance at day centre   **8c.59**

4B. (1) Without prejudice to the generality of ss.2(3) and 4A above, the power conferred by s.2(3) above includes power, subject to the provisions of this section, to require the probationer during the probation period to attend at a day centre specified in the order.

(2) A court shall not include such a requirement in a probation order unless–
(a) it has consulted a probation officer; and
(b) it is satisfied–
  (i) that arrangements can be made for the probationer's attendance at a centre; and
  (ii) that the person in charge of the centre consents to the inclusion of the requirements.

(3) A requirement under subs (1) above shall operate to require the probationer–
(a) in accordance with instructions given by the probation officer responsible for his supervision, to attend on not more than 60 days at the centre specified in the order; and
(b) while attending there to comply with instructions given by, or under the authority of, the person in charge of the centre.

(4) Instructions given by a probation officer under subs(3) above shall, so far as is practicable, be such as to avoid any interference with the times, if any, at which the probationer normally works or attends a school or other educational establishment.

(5) References in this section to attendance at a day centre include references to attendance elsewhere than at the centre for the purpose of participating in activities in accordance with instructions given by, or under the authority of, the person in charge of the centre.

(6) In this section 'day centre' means premises at which non-residential facilities are provided for use in connection with the rehabilitation of offenders and which–
(a) are provided by a probation committee; or
(b) have been approved by the probation committee for the area in which the premises are situated as providing facilities suitable for persons subject to probation orders.
[*as amended by Sch.11 CJA 1982*].

COMMENTARY
See under *Day Centre* at 8c.07.

s.4B(2): Consulted a probation officer, see the note to s.4A, *supra*.

Consents, see the note to s.4A(3), *supra*.

s.4B(3): 60 days, see the note to s.4A(4), *supra*.

Discharge and amendment of probation orders   **8c.60**

5. (1) The provisions of Sch.1 to this Act shall have effect in relation to the discharge and amendment of probation orders.

(2) Where, under the following provisions of this Part of this Act, a probationer is sentenced for the offence for which he was placed on probation, the probation order shall cease to have effect.

COMMENTARY
The making of a deportation order does not discharge a probation order *R v Bissett* [1973] Crim LR 132.

s.5(2): **Sentenced,** a further probation order is not a sentence: s.2(1), *supra.*

Cease to have effect, but not any order for costs or compensation: *R v Evans* [1961] 2 WLR 213.

8c.61   **Breach of requirement of probation order**
          6. (1) If at any time during the probation period it appears on information to a justice of the peace on whom jurisdiction is conferred by subs (2) below that the probationer has failed to comply with any of the requirements of the order, the justice may issue a summons requiring the probationer to appear at the place and time specified therein, or may, if the information is in writing and on oath, issue a warrant for his arrest.

          (2) The following justices shall have jurisdiction for the purposes of subs (1) above, that is to say–
          (a) if the probation order was made by a magistrates' court any justice acting for the petty sessions area for which that court or the supervising court acts;
          (b) in any other case, any justice acting for the petty sessions area for which the supervising court acts;
and any summons or warrant issued under this section shall direct the probationer to appear or be brought before a magistrates' court acting for the petty sessions area for which the justice issuing the summons or warrants acts.

          (3) If it is proved to the satisfaction of the magistrates' court before which a probationer appears or is brought under this section that the probationer has failed to comply with any of the requirements of the probation order, then, subject to the following provisions of this subsection, that court may deal with him in respect of the failure in any one of the following ways, that is to say:
          (a) it may impose on him a fine not exceeding £400;
          (b) [subject to subs (10) below, it may make a community service order in respect of him;]
          (c) in a case to which s.17 of the Criminal Justice Act 1982 applies, it may make an order under that section requiring him to attend at an attendance centre; or
          (d) where the probation order was made by a magistrates' court, it may deal with him for the offence in respect of which the probation order was made, in any manner in which it could deal with him if it had just convicted him of that offence.

          (4) Where the probation order was made by the Crown Court and a magistrates' court has power to deal with the probationer under subs (3)(a), (b) or (c) above in respect of a failure to comply with any of the requirements of the order, the magistrates' court may instead commit him to custody or release him on bail until he can be brought or appear before the Crown Court.

          (5) A magistrates' court which deals with a probationer's case under subs (4) above shall send to the Crown Court a certificate signed by a justice of the peace, certifying that the probationer has failed to comply with such of the requirements of the probation order as may be specified in the certificate, together with such other particulars of the case as may be desirable; and a certificate purporting to be so signed shall be admissible as evidence of the failure before the Crown Court.

          (6) Where by virtue of subs (4) above the probationer is brought or appears before the Crown Court, and it is proved to the satisfaction of the court that he has failed to comply with any of the requirements of the probation order, the court may deal with him in respect of the failure in any one of the following ways, that is to say:
          (a) it may impose on him a fine not exceeding £400;
          (b) [subject to subs (10) below, it may make a community service order in respect of him;] or

(c) it may deal with him for the offence in respect of which the probation order was made in any manner in which it could deal with him if he had just been convicted before the Crown Court of that offence.

(7) A probationer who is required by the probation order to submit to treatment for his mental condition shall not be treated for the purposes of this section as having failed to comply with that requirement on the ground only that he has refused to undergo any surgical, electrical or other treatment if, in the opinion of the court, his refusal was reasonable having regard to all the circumstances; and without prejudice to the provisions of s.8 of this Act, a probationer who is convicted of an offence committed during the probation period shall not on that account be liable to be dealt with under this section in respect of a failure to comply with any requirement of the probation order.

(8) Any exercise by a court of its powers under subs (3)(a), (b) or (c) or (6)(a) or (b) above shall be without prejudice to the continuance of the probation order.

(9) A fine imposed under subs (3)(a) above in respect of a failure to comply with the requirements of a probation order shall be deemed for the purposes of any enactment to be a sum adjudged to be paid by a conviction.

(10) Section 14(2) of this Act and, so far as applicable, the other provisions of this Act relating to community service orders shall have effect in relation to a community service order under this section as they have effect in relation to a community service order in respect of an offender, but as if the power conferred by ss.16 and 17 of this Act to deal with the offender for the offence in respect of which the community service order was made were a power to deal with the probationer for the failure to comply with the requirements of the probation order in respect of which the community service order was made. [*as amended by Sch.14 CJA 1982, SI 1984 No 19*].

COMMENTARY

Legal aid may be granted in proceedings under this section: ss.28, 30(12). For *Costs* see Chapter 9.

Where a magistrates' court deals with a person under this section in respect of an order made by another court, the clerk must notify the other court: r.28(2) MC Rules 1981.

s.6(1): Any time during the probation period, thus, an information laid after the probation period is *out of time.*

Issue a summons, for the contents and service of the summons see rr.98, 99 MC Rules 1981 and form 71. S.4 Summary Jurisdiction (Process) Act 1881 applies to this section as it applies to process issued under s.53 PCCA 1973.

Issue a warrant, for the contents of the warrant, see rr.95, 96 MC Rules 1981 and form 72. The warrant may be endorsed for bail: s.118 MCA 1980.

The supervising court, defined in s.2(2), *supra.* Whenever a probationer is dealt with under this section by a magistrates' court other than the court which made the order, the clerk of that court shall notify the original court: r.28(2) MC Rules 1981.

s.6(3): Proved to the satisfaction of the court, the Court of Criminal Appeal has laid down the following procedure:

'Where a prisoner is brought before a court for breach of a probation order (the breach alleged) should be put to him . . . in the clearest possible terms and he should be asked to say whether he admits it or not. The terms in which the matter should be put to him are: first, to say where he was convicted and what happened to him, then to tell him how the breach is alleged to have taken place, and, if it be by a further conviction, then to tell him the time of the conviction and the adjudication of the court. He should next be asked to say whether he admits those acts. If that is done, there is no further difficulty. If that is not done, then, of course, it being a trial, albeit without a jury, the prisoner will have to be asked whether he desires to give evidence or call witnesses, and the court will have to pronounce on whether they find the breach of the order has been proved. But it is desirable that the proceedings should begin by the matter being put clearly to the prisoner and for him to be asked whether he admits the allegation with regard to it'.

per Byrne J in *R v Devine* [1956] 1 All ER 548n, *R v Long* [1960] 1 All ER 452, *R v Chapman and Pidgley* [1960] 1 QB 681, *R v Holmes* [1965] 1 WLR 1512 and *R v Bruce* [1967] Crim LR 356. For the court's powers under s.6(3) when dealing with an adult offender convicted when under 17 of an offence which, if he had been an adult, could not have been tried summarily, see s.9, *infra*.

s.6(3)(b): Has not yet been brought into force.

s.6(3)(d): This includes power to make a further probation order, the original order becoming ineffective by virtue of s.5(2), *supra: R v Havant Justices, ex p. Jacobs* [1957] 1 WLR 365. But, if a man who has broken the terms of a probation order is again put on probation without proper reflection: 'it greatly weakens the force of probation orders, it brings the machinery of the probation service into contempt and public harm would result therefrom': *R v Thompson* [1969] 1 All ER 60. In the event of the offender being sentenced in respect of the original offence any order for compensation made at the same time will continue in force: *R v Evans* [1961] 2 WLR 213.

The defendant has a right to appeal to the Crown Court against sentence: s.108 MCA 1980.

s.4(4) Legal aid may be granted by magistrates in respect of the proceedings in the Crown Court: ss.28 and 30(12) LAA 1974.

Commit him to custody General right to bail applies s.4(3) and Sch.1 Bail Act 1976.

For the place to which defendants under 21 years of age should be committed see s.27 CJA 1948. Committals to prison must be by warrant: r.94 MC Rules 1981. For the contents of the warrant see rr.95, 96.

The Crown Court, the location of the Crown Court is specified in the Directions of the Lord Chief Justice, paras 5–9: see Chapter 4.

s.6(5): A certificate, see form 74.

Admissible as evidence, but *not conclusive* evidence: *R v Devine* [1956] 1 All ER 548, *R v Chapman and Pidgley* [1960] 1 QB 68, *R v Tucker* [1967] Crim LR 473.

s.6.(7): A probationer who is convicted of an offence for the method of dealing with such offenders, see s.8, *infra*.

8c.62   **Absolute and conditional discharge**

   7. (1) Where a court by or before which a person is convicted of an offence (not being an offence the sentence for which is fixed by law) is of opinion, having regard to the circumstances including the nature of the offence and the character of the offender, that it is inexpedient to inflict punishment and that a probation order is not appropriate, the court may make an order discharging him absolutely, or, if the court thinks fit, discharging him subject to the condition that he commits no offence during such period, not exceeding three years from the date of the order, as may be specified therein.

   (2) An order discharging a person subject to such a condition is in this Act referred to as 'an order for conditional discharge', and the period specified in any such order (subject to s.8(1) of this Act) as 'the period of conditional discharge'.

   (3) Before making an order for conditional discharge the court shall explain to the offender in ordinary language that if he commits another offence during the period of conditional discharge he will be liable to be sentenced for the original offence.

   (4) Where, under the following provisions of this Part of this Act, a person conditionally discharged under this section is sentenced for the offence in respect of which the order for conditional discharge was made, that order shall cease to have effect.

   (5) . . .
   [*as amended by s.57(2) CLA 1977*].

COMMENTARY

An order under this section may be combined with a disqualification for holding or obtaining a driving licence: s.102 RTA 1972. Costs and compensation may also be ordered: s.12(4), *infra*.

On making an order of conditional discharge the court may allow persons who consent to do so to give security for the good behaviour of the offender: s.12(1), *infra*. No other conditions may be imposed by virtue of this section. An order for conditional discharge cannot be made except in the *presence* of the defendant in view of the terms of s.7(3). An order for conditional discharge is not a 'sentence' from which appeal may be made to the Crown Court: s.108 MCA 1980, although the conviction itself may be challenged where the plea was one of not guilty: s.108(1).

s.7(1): Convicted, to be construed in the case of a child or young person as including a reference to a person *found guilty* of an offence: s.59(1) CYPA 1933. For the effects of an order under s.7 on conviction, see s.13, *infra*.

Inexpedient to inflict punishment, thus, by analogy with a probation order, an order for conditional discharge may not be accompanied by a fine except in respect of a separate offence. An order under this section cannot be coupled with an order of deprivation of property: *R v Hunt* [1978] Crim LR 697; *R v Savage* (1983) 5 Cr App R (S) 216.

s.7(3): the requirement for the court to give the explanation is merely a statement of good practice and in *R v Wehner* (1977) 141 JP 24 an order was upheld where the task of explanation had been delegated to counsel.

Liable to be sentenced for the original offence, for the power to deal with an offender who has committed a further offence during the period of conditional discharge, see s.8.

Commission of further offences by probationer or person conditionally discharged   8c.63

8. (1) If it appears to the Crown Court, where that court has jurisdiction in accordance with subs (2) below, or to a justice of the peace having jurisdiction in accordance with that subsection, that a person in whose case a probation order or an order for conditional discharge has been made has been convicted by a court in any part of Great Britain of an offence committed during the relevant period, and has been dealt with in respect of that offence, that court or justice may, subject to subs (3) below, issue a summons requiring that person to appear at the place and time specified therein or a warrant for his arrest.

In this section 'the relevant period' means, in relation to a probation order, the probation period, and in relation to an order for conditional discharge, the period of conditional discharge.

(2) Jurisdiction for the purposes of sub (1) above may be exercised–
(a) if the probation order or order for conditional discharge was made by the Crown Court, by that court;
(b) if the order was made by a magistrates' court, by a justice acting for the petty sessions area for which that court acts;
(c) in the case of a probation order, by whatever court it was made, by a justice acting for the petty sessions area for which the supervising court acts.

(3) A justice of the peace shall not issue a summons under this section except on information and shall not issue a warrant under this section except on information in writing and on oath.

(4) Subject to subs (5) below, a summons or warrant issued under this section shall direct the person to whom it relates to appear or to be brought before the court by which the probation order or the order for conditional discharge was made.

(5) In the case of a probation order made by a magistrates' court, a summons or warrant issued by a justice acting for the petty sessions area for which the supervising court acts may specify the supervising court instead of the court which made the order.

(6) If a person in whose case a probation order or an order for conditional discharge has been made by the Crown Court is convicted by a magistrates' court of an offence committed during the relevant period, the magistrates' court may commit him to custody or release him on bail until he can be brought or appear before the Crown Court; and if it does so the magistrates' court shall

send to the Crown Court a copy of the minute or memorandum of th
conviction entered in the register, signed by the clerk of the court by whom the
register is kept.

(7) Where it is proved to the satisfaction of the court by which a probation
order or an order for conditional discharge is made, or the satisfaction of that
court or the supervising court in the case of a probation order made by a
magistrates' court, that the person in whose case the order was made has been
convicted of an offence committed during the relevant period, the court may
deal with him, for the offence for which the order was made, in any manner in
which it could deal with him if he had just been convicted by or before that
court of that offence.

(8) If a person in whose case a probation order or an order for conditional
discharge has been made by a magistrates' court is convicted before the Crown
Court of an offence committed during the relevant period, or is dealt with by
the Crown Court for any such offence in respect of which he was committed for
sentence to the Crown Court, the Crown Court may deal with him, for the
offence for which the order was made, in any manner in which the magistrates
court could deal with him if it had just convicted him of that offence.

(9) If a person in whose case a probation order or an order for conditional
discharge has been made by a magistrates' court is convicted by another
magistrates' court of any offence committed during the relevant period, that
court may, with the consent of the court which made the order or, in the case of
a probation order, with the consent of that court or of the supervising court
deal with him, for the offence for which the order was made, in any manner in
which the court could deal with him if it had just convicted him of that offence

COMMENTARY

Although the commission of a further offence is, technically, a breach of a requirement of
probation order, it may not be so dealt with under s.6, but under s.8: s.6(7), *supra*.
  'When an accused commits an offence while on probation it is usually desirable that
  court should consider whether he is to be dealt with for the original offence, for if he is
  not, two consequences ensue. First, the original offence cannot thereafter be treated as
  conviction. Second, the probation officer's responsibilities under the probation order
  continue, even though the accused may have been sent to prison for the offence in respec
  of which he is before the court, unless and until the probation order is discharged.' *R*
  Calvert [1963] 1 WLR 151.

Legal aid may be granted in these proceedings: ss.28 and 30(12) LAA 1974. For *Costs* se
Chapter 9.

s.8(1): Great Britain, ie England, Scotland and Wales: Union with Scotland Act 1706; s.
Wales and Berwick Act 1745.

Has been dealt with, not *'sentenced'*. Therefore if an offender is placed on probation o
discharged absolutely or conditionally in respect of the second offence he may still be deal
with under this section. The terms of s.13(1), *infra*, exempt 'any subsequent proceeding
which may be taken against the offender under the preceding provisions of this Act': and *R*
Wilcox (1964) 21 November, unreported.

Issue a summons warrant, see the notes to s.6, *supra*, and forms 78, 79.

s.8(2): Petty sessions area, see the note to s.6, *supra*.

s.8(3): On information, see form 77. Unlike proceedings under s.6, *supra*, this may be laid
after the relevant period has expired.

s.8(6): Commit him to custody, general right to bail (s.4 Bail Act 1976) does not apply. For
the place to which defendants *under 21 years* should be committed see s.27 CJA 1948
Committals to custody must be by warrant: r.94 MC Rules 1981. For the contents of th
warrant see rr.95, 96, and form 82.

Release him on bail See the note to s.6, *supra*.

The Crown Court, for the location of the Crown Court see paras 5–9 of the directions of th
Lord Chief Justice reproduced in Chapter 4.
  When committing under s.8(6) there is power to commit for sentence also in respect o

certain other offences at the same time under s.56 CJA 1967.

Legal aid may be granted in respect of the proceedings in the Crown Court: ss.28 and 30(12) LAA 1974.

s.8(7): Proved to the satisfaction of the court, see the Commentary on s.6.

The supervising court, defined in s.2(2). If that court deals with the probationer under this section, it must notify the court which made the order: r.28(2) MC Rules 1981.

Convicted a conviction resulting in an order of conditional discharge does not count as a conviction for the purposes of this section because of the first words of s.13(3), *post: R v Wilcox* (1965) 25 January (unreported). The same applies to an order of absolute discharge and a probation order.

An offence committed during the relevant period, even though the conviction may be outside that period: *R v Lee* [1976] Crim LR 521.

Any manner in which the court could deal with him, the court should first make proper inquiry of the facts of the earlier offence: *R v Laval* [1977] Crim LR 527. By analogy with s.6, *supra,* this includes the power to make a further probation order, as a result of which the original order becomes ineffective: *R v Havant Justices, ex p. Jacobs* [1957] 1 WLR 365. But such an order should not be made lightly: *R v Thompson* [1969] 1 All ER 60. Where an offender is put on probation on two separate occasions, a sentence for the original offence not being imposed at the second occasion, the offender falls to be dealt with under this section for both if he should later commit a third offence: *R v Keeley* [1960] 1 WLR 749; (the second probation order being 'ineffective' only in so far as supervision is concerned in respect of orders which are concurrent).

'The sentence (upon commission of a further offence) should in general be made consecutive and should be more than a nominal one': *R v Stuart* (1965) 129 JP197; and see also *R v Fry* [1955] 1 WLR 28. The sentence does not affect any order for compensation made on the original occasion: *R v Evans* [1961] 2 WLR 213 (although this was a case under s.6, *supra,* the court expressed the view that it seemed immaterial in this respect whether the offender was dealt with under s.6 or s.8). For the court's powers when dealing with an adult convicted when under 17 of an offence which, if he had been an adult, could not have been dealt with summarily, see s.9, *infra.*

The defendant has a right to appeal to the Crown Court against sentence when dealt with by magistrates for the original offence: s.108 MCA 1980.

s.8(9): The consent of the court, the justices' clerk may give consent when the order was made after the offender attained 17: Justices' Clerks Rules 1970 (SI No 231).

Any manner in which the court could deal with him, see note to s.8(7).

Breach of conditional discharge by young offenders   8c.64

9. (1) Where an order for conditional discharge has been made by a magistrates' court in the case of an offender under 17 years of age in respect of an offence triable only on indictment in the case of an adult any powers exercisable by that or any other court in respect of the offender after he has attained the age of 17 years under subss (7), (8) or (9) of s.8 of this Act shall be those which should be exercisable if that offence were an offence triable either way and had been tried summarily.

For the purposes of this section the age of an offender at a particular time shall be deemed to be or to have been that which appears to the court after considering any available evidence or to or to have been his age at that time. [*as amended by Sch.12 CLA 1977*].

COMMENTARY

The effect of this section is that when a juvenile offender is given a conditional discharge for an offence triable, in the case of an adult, on indictment only, and later commits a further offence as an adult, the court will have the same powers as in the case of an offender convicted summarily of an indictable offence, namely imprisonment for a term not exceeding six months or a fine not exceeding £2,000, or both, or any alternative to those sentences.

An offence triable either way, defined in Sch.1 Interpretation Act 1978.

Probation orders relating to persons residing in Scotland   8c.65

10. (1) Where the court by which a probation order is made under s.2 of this Act is satisfied that the offender resides or will reside in Scotland, subs (2) of that section shall not apply to the order, but the order shall specify as the appropriate court for the purposes of this section a court of summary jurisdiction (which, in the case of an offender convicted on indictment, shall be the sheriff court) having jurisdiction in the place in Scotland in which the offender resides or will reside.

(2) Where a probation order has been made under s.2 of this Act and the supervising court is satisfied that the probationer proposes to reside or is residing in Scotland, the power of that court to amend the order under Sch.1 to this Act shall include power to amend it by substituting for the provisions required by s.2(2) of this Act the provisions required by subs (1) above; and the court may so amend the order without summoning the probationer and without his consent.

(3) A probationer order made or amended by virtue of this section may include a requirement that the probationer shall submit to treatment for his mental condition, and–
  (a) subsections (1), (3) and (7) of s.3 of this Act and ss.184(2) or 385(2) of the Criminal Procedure (Scotland) Act 1975 (which makes equivalent provision to that made by s.3(2) of this Act) shall apply to the making of an order which includes any such requirement by virtue of this subsection as they apply to the making of an order which includes any such requirement by virtue of s.3 of this Act and ss.184 or 385 of that Act respectively; and
  (b) subsections (4) to (6) of ss.184 or 385 of that Act (functions of supervising officer and medical practitioner where such a requirement has been imposed) shall apply in relation to a probationer who is undergoing treatment in Scotland in pursuance of a requirement imposed by virtue of this subsection as they apply in relation to a probationer undergoing such treatment in pursuance of a requirement imposed by virtue of ss.184 or 385 of that Act.

(4) Sections 5(1) and 6(1) and (2) of this Act shall not apply to any order made or amended by virtue of this section; but the provisions of the Criminal Procedure (Scotland) Act 1975 except ss.186(2)(b), 187, 387(2)(b) and 388 (sentencing the probationer for the offence for which the order was made), shall apply to the order as if it were a probation order made under ss.183 or 384 of that Act and as if the court specified in the order as the appropriate court had been named as such under subs (2) of that section.

(5) If in the case of a probation order made or amended by virtue of this section the appropriate court (as defined by the Criminal Justice (Scotland) Act 1975) is satisfied that the probationer has failed to comply with any requirement of the probation order, the court may, instead of dealing with him in any manner authorised by that Act, commit him to custody or release him on bail until he can be brought or appear before the court in England and Wales by which the probation order was made, and, if it so commits him or releases him on bail,–
  (a) the court shall send to the court in England and Wales a certificate certifying that the probationer has failed to comply with such of the requirements of the probation order as may be specified in the certificate; together with such other particulars of the case as may be desirable;
  (b) that court shall have the same powers as if the probationer had been brought or appeared before it in pursuance of a warrant or summons issued under s.6(1) of this Act;
and a certificate purporting to be signed by the clerk of the appropriate court shall be admissible as evidence of the failure before the court which made the probation order.

(6) In relation to a probation order made or amended by virtue of this section, the appropriate court (as defined by the Criminal Justice (Scotland) Act 1975) shall have jurisdiction for the purposes of s.8(1) of this Act.

(7) The court by which a probation order is made or amended by virtue of this section shall send three copies of the order as made or amended to the clerk of the court specified in the order as the appropriate court, together with such documents and information relating to the case as it considers likely to be of assistance to that court; and s.2(7) of this Act, or para 6 of Sch.1 to this Act, as the case may be, shall not apply to any such order.

(8) Where a probation order which is amended by virtue of subs (2) above is an order to which the provisions of this Act apply by virtue of ss.188 or 389 of the Criminal Procedure (Scotland) Act 1975 (probation orders under that Act relating to persons residing in England and Wales) then, notwithstanding anything in that section or this section, the order shall, as from the date of the amendment, have effect in all respects as if it were an order made under ss.183 or 384 of that Act in the case of a person residing in Scotland, and as if the court specified as the appropriate court in the order as so amended had been named as such under subs (2) of that section.
[*as amended by Sch.9 Criminal Procedure (Scotland) Act 1975*].

COMMENTARY
The appropriate court, defined in s.462(1) Criminal Procedure (Scotland) Act 1975.

s.10(5), see notes to s.8, *supra.*

For *Costs,* see Chapter 9.

Substitution of conditional discharge for probation

8c.66

11. (1) Where on an application made by the probationer or the probation officer it appears to the court having power to discharge a probation order that the order is no longer appropriate in the case of a probationer, the court may make, in substitution for the probation order, an order discharging him in respect of the original offence, subject to the condition that he commits no offence between the making of the order under this section and the expiration of the probation period.

(1A) No application may be made under subs (1) above while an appeal against the probation order is pending.

(2) A person in respect of whom an order is made under this section shall so long as the condition mentioned in subs (1) above continues in force be treated in all respects and in particular for the purposes of s.8 of this Act as if the original order made in his case had been an order for conditional discharge made by the court which made the original order and as if the period of conditional discharge were the same as the probation period.

(3) Where an application under this section is made by the probation officer, it may be heard in the absence of the probationer if the officer produces to the court a statement by him that he understands the effect of an order under this section and consents to the application being made.

(4) On the making of an order under this section the appropriate officer of the court shall forthwith give copies of the order to the probation officer, who shall give a copy to the person in respect of whom the order is made and to the person in charge of any institution in which that person was required by the probation order to reside.
[*as amended by s.66 CJA 1982*].

COMMENTARY
When a magistrates' court makes an order under this section the clerk must notify the court which made the original order: r.28(1) MC Rules 1981.

s.11(1) The application must be by complaint: r.103. For the order, see form 69.

The court having power to discharge, ie the supervising court except where the convicting court was the Crown Court which included in the order a direction to the contrary: Sch.1.

8c.67   **Supplementary provision as to probation and discharge**
12. (1) Any court may, on making a probation order or an order for conditional discharge under this Part of this Act, if it thinks it expedient for the purpose of the reformation of the offender, allow any person who consents to do so to give security for the good behaviour of the offender.

(2) For the purposes of this Act, except s.2(7) and para 1 of Sch.1, where a probation order or an order for conditional discharge has been made on appeal, the order shall be deemed to have been made by the court from which the appeal was brought.

(3) . . .

(4) Nothing in ss.2 or 7 of this Act shall be construed as taking away any power of the court, on making a probation order in respect of an offender or discharging an offender absolutely or conditionally, to order him to pay costs or compensation.

COMMENTARY

Security for . . . good behaviour, a provision in addition to the court's common law powers.

8c.68   **Effects of probation and discharge**
13. (1) Subject to subs (2) below and to s.50(1A) of the Criminal Appeal Act 1968 and s.108(1A) of the Magistrates' Courts Act 1980, a conviction of an offence for which an order is made under the Part of this Act placing the offender on probation or discharging him absolutely or conditionally shall be deemed not to be a conviction for any purpose other than the purposes of the proceedings in which the order is made and of any subsequent proceedings which may be taken against the offender under the preceding provisions of this Act and for the purposes of s.1(2)(bb) of the Children and Young Persons Act 1969.

(2) Where the offender was of or over 17 years of age at the time of his conviction of the offence in question and is subsequently sentenced under this Part of this Act for that offence, subs (1) above shall cease to apply to the conviction.

(3) Without prejudice to the preceding provisions of this section, the conviction of an offender who is placed on probation or discharged absolutely or conditionally under this Part of this Act shall in any event be disregarded for the purpose of any enactment or instrument which imposes any disqualification or disability upon convicted persons, or authorises or requires the imposition of any such disqualification or disability.

(4) The proceding provisions of this section shall not effect–
(a) any right of any offender placed on probation or discharged absolutely or conditionally under this Part of this Act to rely on his conviction, in bar of any subsequent proceedings for the same offence;
(b) the restoration of any property in consequence of the conviction of any such offender; or
(c) the operation, in relation to any such offender, of any enactment or instrument in force at the commencement of this Act which is expressed to extend to persons dealt with under s.1(1) of the Probation of Offenders Act 1907, as well as to convicted persons.

(5) In this section 'enactment' includes an enactment contained in a local Act and 'instrument' means an instrument having effect by virtue of an Act. [*as amended by Sch.14 CJA 1982, Sch.3 Health and Social Services and Social Security Adjudications Act 1983*].

COMMENTARY

'The section absolves the offender from legal consequences which otherwise would flow from the conviction': Morrison and Hughes on *The Criminal Justice Act 1948*, cited with approval in *R v Harris* [1950] 2 All ER 816. An applicant for a firearms certificate may thus ruthfully deny a conviction for which he was given a conditional discharge: *R v Kitt* [1977] Crim LR 220; and see *R v Maizone* [1974] Crim LR 112.

This section is excluded by s.1(4) Rehabilitation of Offenders Act 1974 so as to permit offenders whose convictions are spent to rely upon the additional protection of that Act; also s.11(5) Civil Evidence Act 1968, so as to allow a conviction which would otherwise be caught by it to be admissible to prove in civil proceedings the commission of the offence. The other effects of this section are not excluded.

For the purpsoe of proving 'known character' under s.15 Prevention of Crimes Act 1871, a certificate of conviction which resulted in an order of conditional discharge is not admissible by virtue of this section, but it would not be objectionable if a witness gave evidence to the following effect: 'I was present at the court on the day named when the accused was there. *I heard him confess* to a charge of having been found in possession of certain implements of housebreaking and he was discharged subject to the condition that he commit no further offence during the period of 12 months thereafter': *R v Harris, supra*.

s.13(1): Notwithstanding this subsection, convictions resulting in a probation order or order of absolute or conditional discharge must be taken into account in determining liability to punishment or disqualification under the Road Traffic Acts: s.102 RTA 1972.

This section does not prevent an appeal against the making of an order for conditional discharge or a probation order: s.108(1A) MCA 1980.

Because of the effects it is 'undesirable and, indeed, wrong, to take breaches of probation or of conditional discharge into consideraiton. They should be separately dealt with and separate sentences passed so that the original offences may rank as convictions': *R v Webb* [1953] 2 QB 390.

The preceding provisions of this Act Notably s.8, *supra*, which deals with the commission of a further offence during the probation period.

s.13(2): 17 years of age For the determination of age see s.150(4) MCA 1980.

The time of his conviction, ie when his plea of guilty is accepted or when the charge is found proved: *R v Sheridan* [1937] 1 KB 223. The reasoning in *R v Sheridan* was disapproved of by the House of Lords in *S (an Infant) v Manchester City Recorder* (1970) 134 JP 3. This does not affect the fact that the term 'conviction' in s.13(1) is used in what Lord Upjohn described as *its secondary sense*, ie the time at which a plea of guilty is made or when the case is proved.

s.13(3): Notwithstanding this subsection, disqualification and endorsement under the Road Traffic Act may be ordered at the same time as a probation order or order of absolute or conditional discharge: s.102(1) RTA 1972. A recommendation for deportation by a court is not a disqualification or disability within the meaning of this subsection: *R v Akan* [1972] 3 All ER 285. The provision does not prevent a disciplinary tribunal from looking at the facts which led to the conviction: *R v Statutory Committee of Pharmaceutical Society of Great Britain, ex p. Pharmaceutical Society of Great Britain* [1981] 2 All ER 805.

Community service orders in respect of convicted persons   8c.69

14. (1) Where a person of or over 16 years of age is convicted of an offence punishable with imprisonment, the court by or before which he is convicted may, instead of dealing with him in any other way (but subject to subs (2) below) make an order (in this Act referred to as 'a community service order') requiring him to perform unpaid work in accordance with the subsequent provisions of this Act.

The reference in this subsection to an offence punishable with imprisonment shall be construed without regard to any prohibition or restriction imposed or under any enactment on the imprisonment of young offenders.

(1A) The number of hours which a person may be required to work under a community service shall be specified in the order and shall be in the aggregate–
(a) not less than 40; and
(b) not more–
(i) in the case of an offender aged sixteen, than 120; and
(ii) in other cases, than 240.

(2) A court shall not make a community service order in respect of any offender unless the offender consents and after considering a report by a probation officer or by a social worker of a local authority social services department about the offender and his circumstances and, if the court thinks it

necessary, hearing a probation officer or a social worker of a local authority social services department, the court is satisfied that the offender is a suitable person to perform work under such an order.

(2A) Subject to ss.17A or 17B below,–

(a) a court shall not make a community service order in respect of an offender who is of or over seventeen years of age unless the court is satisfied that provision for him to perform work under such an order can be made under the arrangements for persons to perform work under such orders which exist in the petty sessions area in which he resides or will reside: and

(b) a court shall not make a community service order in respect of an offender who is under seventeen years of age unless–

(i) it has been notified by the Secretary of State that arrangements exist for persons of the offender's age who reside in the petty sessions area in which the offender resides or will reside to perform work under such orders; and

(ii) it is satisfied that provision can be made under the arrangements for him to do so.

(3) Where a court makes community service orders in respect of two or more offences of which the offender has been convicted by or before the court, the court may direct that the hours of work specified in any of those orders shall be concurrent with or additional to those specified in any other of those orders, but so that the total number of hours which are not concurrent shall not exceed the maximum specified in para (b)(i) or (ii) of subs (1A) above.

(4) A community service order shall specify the petty sessions area in which the offender resides or will reside; and the functions conferred by the subsequent provisions of this Act on the relevant officer shall be discharged by a probation officer (whether under this subsection or by virtue of s.17(5) of this Act), or by a person appointed for the purposes of those provisions by the probation and aftercare committee for that area.

(5) Before making a community service order the court shall explain to the offender in ordinary language–

(a) the purpose and effect of the order (and in particular the requirements of the order as specified in s.15 of this Act);

(b) the consequences which may follow under s.16 if he fails to comply with any of those requirements; and

(c) that the court has under s.17 the power to review the order on the application either of the offender or of a probation officer.

(6) The court by which a community service order is made shall forthwith give copies of the order to a probation officer assigned to the court and he shall give a copy to the offender and to the relevant officer; and the court shall, except where it is itself a magistrates' court acting for the petty sessions area specified in the order, send a copy to the clerk to the justices for the petty sessions area specified in the order a copy of the order, together with such documents and information relating to the case as it considers likely to be of assistance to the court acting for that area in exercising its functions in relation to the order.

(7) . . .

(8) Nothing in subs (1) above shall be construed as preventing a court which makes a community service order in respect of any offence from making an order for costs against, or imposing any disqualification on, the offender or from making in respect of the offence an order under ss.35, 39, 43 or 44 of this Act, or under s.28 of the Theft Act 1968.

[*as amended by Schs.11, 16 CJA 1982*].

COMMENTARY

For the use of community service see the introduction. Community service orders may be amended or revoked in accordance with s.17, *infra*. Breach is punishable under s.16.

Scotland and Northern Ireland: for the adaptation of this section to an offender residing in Scotland or Northern Ireland, see ss.17A, 17B, respectively.

s.14(1): 16 years of age, for the determination of age see s.150(4) MCA 1980.

A community service order, see form 92.

In the aggregate, this apparently refers to the possibility of consecutive orders. There is no objection in principle to one order being made consecutive to another made on an earlier occasion: *R v Evans* (1977) 141 JP 441.

s.14(2): report, see *R v Gillam* and further cases quoted in *Social Inquiry Report* at 8c.08.

s.14(3): Where a court makes, this appears to be confined to orders made on the same occasion. But there is no objection to a later order being made consecutive to an earlier order: *R v Evans, supra,* so, however, that the total period does not exceed 240 hours.

s.14(6): this subsection is *directory* only: a community service order properly made and explained to the defendant comes into force at the time it is spoken in court: *Walsh v Barlow* [1985] 1 WLR 90.

s.14(8): the sections quoted refer to orders of compensation, restitution, criminal bankruptcy and deprivation of property.

Obligations of persons subject to community service order   **8c.70**
    15. (1) An offender in respect of whom a community service order is in force shall–
    (a) report to the relevant officer and subsequently from time to time notify him of any change of address; and
    (b) perform for the number of hours specified in the order such work at such times as he may be instructed by the relevant officer.

    (2) Subject to s.17(1) of this Act, the work required to be performed under a community service order shall be performed during the period of 12 months beginning with the date of the order but, unless revoked, the order shall remain in force until the offender has worked under it for the number of hours specified in it.

    (3) The instructions given by the relevant officer under this section shall, so far as practicable, be such as to avoid any conflict with the offender's religious beliefs and any interference with the times, if any, at which he normally works or attends a school or other educational establishment.
[*as amended by Sch.12 CLA 1977*].

COMMENTARY
For breach of the requirements of a community service order, see s.16, *infra*.

s.15(1): The relevant officer, see s.14(4), *supra*.

s.15(2): Remains in force, by virtue of s.15(2) an order remains in force *until the hours are worked*.

Breach of requirements of community service order   **8c.71**
    16. (1) If at any time while a community service order is in force in respect of an offender it appears on information to a justice of the peace acting for the petty sessions area for the time being specified in the order that the offender has failed to comply with any of the requirements of s.15 of this Act (including any failure satisfactorily to perform the work which he has been instructed to do), the justice may issue a summons requiring the offender to appear at the place and time specified therein, or may, if the information is in writing and on oath, issue a warrant for his arrest.

    (2) Any summons or warrant issued under this section shall direct the offender to appear or be brought before a magistrates' court acting for the petty sessions area for the time being specified in the community service order.

    (3) If it is proved to the satisfaction of the magistrates' court before which an offender appears or is brought under this section that he has failed without reasonable excuse to comply with any of the requirements of s.15 the court

may, without prejudice to the continuance of the order, impose on him a fine not exceeding £400 or may–

(a) if the community service order was made by a magistrates' court, revoke the order and deal with the offender, for the offence in respect of which the order was made, in any manner in which he could have been dealt with for that offence by the court which made the order if the order had not been made;

(b) if the order was made by the Crown Court, commit him to custody or release him on bail until he can be brought or appear before the Crown Court.

(4) A magistrates' court which deals with an offender's case under subs (3)(b) above shall send to the Crown Court a certificate signed by a justice of the peace certifying that the offender has failed to comply with the requirements of s.15 in the respect specified in the certificate, together with such other particulars of the case as may be desirable; and a certificate purporting to be so signed shall be admissible as evidence of the failure before the Crown Court.

(5) . . .

(6) A person sentenced under subs (3)(a) above for an offence may appeal to the Crown Court against the sentence.

(7) . . .

(8) A fine imposed under this section shall be deemed for the purposes of any enactment to be a sum adjudged to be paid by a conviction.
[*as amended by SI 1984 No 19*].

COMMENTARY

Legal aid may be granted, ss.28 and 30(12) LAA 1974.

For *Costs*, see Chapter 9.

s.16(1): At any time while a community service order is in force, see the note to s.15(2), *supra*; and see the comments concerning *R v Tebbit* (1988) *The Times*, 22 February and the position where the offender completes the hours voluntarily after the 12 months has expired, see further 8c.30.

Issue a summons, for the content and service see rr.98, 99, MCA 1980. Process may be served in Scotland in accordance with s.4 Summary Jurisdiction (Process) Act 1881: s.53 PCCA 1973.

Issue a warrant, for contents see rr.95, 96 MC Rules 1981. The warrant may be backed for bail: s.118, MCA 1980. The warrant is a warrant 'in connexion with an offence' within the meaning of s.125(4) MCA 1980, and can be executed by a police officer, although not in his possession: *Jones v Kelsey* (1987) 151 JPN 175.

s.16(3): for the purposes of this Act a community service order made on appeal from a magistrates' court shall be treated as if made by a magistrates' court: s.57(5) of the Act.

Proved to the satisfaction of the court, formal proof of breach is required, so that, once the prosecution have closed their case, they may not, save for purely technical matters, be allowed to re-open it: *R v Gainsborough Justices, ex p. Green* (1983) 147 JP 434. *Cf.* the note to s.6(3), *supra*. Note that s.15 contains a multiplicity of requirements, viz (a) to report to the relevant officer; (b) subsequently from time to time to notify him of any change of address; (c) to perform for the number of hours specified in the order such work at such times as he may be instructed; and (d) to perform the work during the period of twelve months beginning with the date of the order. The first three requirements arise under subs (1), the fourth under subs (2).

s.16(3)(a): the terms of this subsection appear to preclude a further community service order. Otherwise the powers of the court are limited to those available to the original court at the time the order was made.

Where the community service order was made as an 'alternative to custody', of which the offender was aware, a custodial sentence can be expected on breach: *R v Howard and Wade* [1977] Crim LR 683; when 'some credit' should be given for the fact that a significant portion of the order has completed: *R v Wittingham* (1986) 8 Cr App R (S) 116 (one third of hours worked).

However, a custodial sentence may be inappropriate where a *substantial* proportion has been completed: *R v Paisley* (1979) 1 Cr App (S) 196; *R v Baines* [1983] Crim LR 487; *R v Anderson* (1982) 4 Cr App R (S) 252 (126 hours worked out of 180); *R v Cook* (1985) 7 Cr App R (S) 249 (61 out of 80 – 'a question of fact in every case' – 3 months sentence made to run concurrently). It is an error to assume that credit has been given because a sentence of imprisonment has been suspended. The correct approach is to fix the correct term, then to go on to consider suspension: *R v Williams* (1986) 8 Cr App R (S) 257 (80 per cent completed – sentence reduced from 12 months suspended to 3 months suspended). But even a suspended sentence will be inappropriate where this would subject the offender to risks long after the offence: *R v Robinson* (1986) 8 Cr App R (S) 327.

In the event of the offender being sentenced in respect of the original offence any compensation order made at the same time will continue in force: *cf R v Evans* [1961] 1 All ER 313. There is a right of appeal to the Crown Court against a sentence under s.16(3)(a): s.16(6); but there is *no power to commit for sentence* in respect of breach of an order made by a magistrates' court: see *R v Worcester Crown Court and Birmingham Magistrates' Court ex p. Lamb* (1985) 7 Cr App R (S) 44; *R v Daniels* (1986) 8 Cr App R (S) 257.

If the offender breaches the community service order by failing to attend for work and the proceedings are outside the 12 month period contemplated by s.15(2) then this is tantamount to an election by the community service organiser to treat the order as at an end – and once the court is seized of the matter any hours subsequently worked can only go to mitigation: *R v Tebbit* (1988) *The Times*, 22 February.

Commit him to custody, the general right to bail applies: s.4(4) Bail Act 1976 and bail may only be withheld in the circumstances mentioned in Sch.1, *ibid*. For the place to which defendants *under 21 years* of age should be committed see s.27 CJA 1948. Committals to prison must be by warrant: r.94 MC Rules 1981. For contents, see form 95.

Release him on bail, if the defendant is released on bail the clerk must notify the governor of the appropriate prison, etc: r.87 MC Rules 1981. Forfeiture of recognizances is a matter for the Crown Court.

s.16(4): A certificate, see form 93. May be signed by the justices' clerk: Justices' Clerks' Rules 1970 (SI No 231).

Amendment and revocation of community service orders, and substitution of other sentences

8c.72

17. (1) Where a community service order is in force in respect of any offender and, on the application of the offender or the relevant officer, it appears to a magistrates' court acting for the petty sessions area for the time being specified in the order that it would be in the interests of justice to do so having regard to circumstances which have arisen since the order was made, the court may extend, in relation to the order, the period of 12 months specified in s.15(2) of this Act.

(2) Where such an order is in force and on any such application it appears to a magistrates' court acting for the petty sessions area so specified that, having regard to such circumstances, it would be in the interests of justice that the order should be revoked or that the offender should be dealt with in some other manner for the offence in respect of which the order was made, the court may–
    (a) if the order was made by a magistrates' court, revoke the order or revoke it and deal with the offender for that offence in any manner in which he could have been dealt with for that offence by the court which made the order if the order had not been made;
    (b) if the order was made by the Crown Court, commit him to custody or release him on bail until he can be brought or appear before the Crown Court;
and where the court deals with his case under para (b) above it shall send to the Crown Court such particulars of the case as may be desirable.

(3) Where an offender in respect of whom such an order is in force–
    (a) is convicted of an offence before the Crown Court; or
    (b) is committed by a magistrates' court to the Crown Court for sentence and is brought or appears before the Crown Court; or
    (c) by virtue of subs (2)(b) above, is brought or appears before the Crown Court,

and it appears to the Crown Court to be in the interests of justice to do so, having regard to circumstances which have arisen since the order was made, the Crown Court may revoke the order or revoke the order and deal with the offender, for the offence in respect of which the order was made, in any manner in which he could have been dealt with for that offence by the court which made the order if the order had not been made.

(4) A person sentenced under subs (2)(a) above for any offence may appeal to the Crown Court against the sentence.

(4A) Where–
(a) an offender in respect of whom a community service order is in force is convicted of an offence before a magistrates' court other than a magistrates' court acting for the petty sessions area for the time being specified in the order; and
(b) it appears to the court, on the application of the offender or the relevant officer, that it would be in the interests of justice to do so having regard to circumstances which have arisen since the order was made,
the court may–
 (i) if the order was made by a magistrates' court, revoke it; and
 (ii) if the order was made by the Crown Court, commit him in custody or release him on bail until he can be brought or appear before the Crown Court;
and where the court deals with his case under sub-para (ii) above, it shall send to the Crown Court such particulars of the case as may be desirable.

(4B) Where by virtue of subs (4A)(c)(ii) above the offender is brought or appears before the Crown Court and it appears to the Crown Court to be in the interests of justice to do so, having regard to circumstances which have arisen since the order was made, the Crown Court may revoke the order.

(5) If–
(a) a magistrates' court acting for the petty sessions area for the time being specified in a community service order is satisfied that the offender proposes to change, or has changed, his residence from that petty sessions area to another petty sessions area; and
(b) the conditions specified in subs (5A) below are satisfied,
the court may, and on the application of the relevant officer shall, amend the order by substituting the other petty sessions area for the area specified in the order.

(5A) The conditions referred to in subs (5) above are–
(a) if the offender is of or over 17 years of age, that it appears to the court that provision can be made for him to perform work under the community service order under the arrangements which exist for persons who reside in the other petty sessions area to perform work under such orders; and
(b) if the offender is under 17 years of age–
 (i) that the court has been notified by the Secretary of State that arrangement exist for persons of his age who reside in the other petty sessions area to perform work under such orders; and
 (ii) it appears to the court that provision can be made under the arrangements for him to do so.

(6) Where a community service order is amended by a court under subs (5) above the court shall send to the clerk to the justices for the new area specified in the order a copy of the order, together with such documents and information relating to the case as it considers likely to be of assistance to a court acting for that area in exercising its functions in relation to the order.

(7) Where a magistrates' court proposes to exercise its powers under subs (1) or (2) above otherwise than on the application of the offender it shall summon him to appear before the court and, if he does not appear in answer to the summons, may issue a warrant for his arrest.

[*as amended by Sch.12 CLA 1977, Sch.12 CJA 1982*].

COMMENTARY

Legal aid may be granted ss.28, 30(12) Legal Aid Act 1974. For *Costs*, see Chapter 9.

Note that the exercise of the court's powers under s.17(1) or (2) is dependent on circumstances having arisen *'since the order was made'*. For the purposes of this Act, a community service order made on appeal from magistrates shall be treated as if made by a magistrates' court: s.57(5) PCCA 1973.

s.17(1): In force, see s.15(2).

On the application of . . . the relevant officer, a summons must issue under s.17(7). The issue of a warrant, however, is *continent on non-appearance* in answer to a summons. 'Relevant officer' is defined in s.14(4), *supra. Note* that the court has *no power* to act on its own motion.

Circumstances which have arisen, these can include in a proper case breach of the requirements of the order: *R v Goscombe* (1981) 3 Cr App R (S) 61, CA, but, if so, the matter should be put on a proper evidentiary basis: *R v Jackson* [1984] Crim LR 573 CA.

Extend . . . the period of 12 months, when the rule in *R v Tebbit* (1988) *The Times,* 22 February, noted in relation to s.16(1) *supra,* will not apply, *semble.*

s.17(2): In force, see s.15(2).

Any such application, ie an application by the offender or the relevant officer: *R v Grays Justices ex p. Aldwinkle* (1984) *The Times,* 1 December.

s.17(2)(a): Deal with the offender . . . in any manner in which he could have been dealt with, see the note to s.16(3)(a), *supra* s.17(4) gives a right of appeal to the Crown Court against sentence.

Commit him to custody or release him on bail, general right to bail s.4 Bail Act 1976 does not seemingly apply. Otherwise, see the notes to s.16, *supra.*

s.17(3): Convicted, does not include probation orders and orders of absolute and conditional discharge: s.13.

s.17(4A): note that the conviction need not be in respect of a subsequent offence, but the *interests of justice test* relates to circumstances which have arisen since the order was made. These circumstances may relate to the offence but need not.

s.17(7): process may be served in Scotland: s.4 Summary Jurisdiction (Process) Act 1881: s.53 of the Act.

Making and amendment of community service orders relating to persons residing in Scotland   8c.73

17A. (1) Where a court considering the making of a community service order is satisfied that the offender resides, or will be residing when the order comes into force, in Scotland, s.14 above shall have effect as if the following subsection were substituted for subs (2A)–

'(2A) A court shall not make a community service order in respect of any offender unless–
(a) the court has been notified by the Secretary of State that arrangements exist for persons who reside in the locality in Scotland in which the offender resides, or will be residing when the order comes into force, to perform work under community service orders made under s.1 of the Community Service by Offenders (Scotland) Act 1978; and
(b) it appears to the court that provision can be made for him to perform work under those arrangements.'

(2) Where a community service order has been made and–
(a) a magistrates' court acting for a petty sessions area for the time being specified in it is satisfied that the offender proposes to reside or is residing in Scotland;
(b) that court has been notified by the Secretary of State that arrangements exist for persons who reside in the locality in Scotland in which the offender proposes to reside or is residing to perform work under community service orders made under s.1 of the Community Service by Offenders (Scotland) Act 1978;

(c) it appears to that court that provision can be made for him to perform work under the community service order under those arrangements,

it may amend the order by specifying that the unpaid work required to be performed by the order be so performed.

(3) A community service order made or amended in accordance with this section shall–

(a) specify the locality in Scotland in which the offender resides or will be residing when the order or the amendment comes into force; and

(b) require the regional or islands council in whose area the locality specified under para (a) above is situated to appoint or assign an officer who will discharge in respect of the order the functions in respect of community service orders conferred on the local authority officer by the Community Service by Offenders (Scotland) Act 1978.

[*as inserted by Sch.13 CJA 1982*].

8c.74 **Making and amendment of community service orders relating to persons residing in Northern Ireland**

17B. (1) Where a court considering the making of a community service order is satisfied that the offender resides or will be residing when the order comes into force, in Northern Ireland, it shall not make the order unless it is also satisfied that he is of or over 17 years of age.

(2) Where the court is satisfied that he is of or over that age, s.14 above shall have effect as if the following subsection were substituted for subs (2A)–

'(2A) A court shall not make a community service order in respect of any offender unless it appears to the court that provision can be made by the Probation Board for Northern Ireland (in this section referred to as 'the Probation Board') for him to perform work under the order.'

(3) Where a community service order has been made–

(a) a magistrates' court acting for a petty sessions area for the time being specified in it is satisfied that the offender has attained the age of 17 years and proposes to reside or is residing in Northern Ireland;

(b) it appears to that court that provision can be made by the Probation Board for him to perform work under the order,

it may amend the order by specifying that the unpaid work required to be performed by the order be so performed.

(4) A community service order made or amended in accordance with this section shall–

(a) specify the petty sessions district in Northern Ireland in which the offender resides or will be residing when the order or the amendment comes into force; and

(b) require the Probation Board to select an officer who will discharge in respect of the order the functions in respect of community service orders conferred on the relevant officer by the Treatment of Offenders (Northern Ireland) Order 1976.

[*as inserted by Sch.13 CJA 1982*].

8c.75 **Community service orders relating to persons residing in Scotland or Northern Ireland – general**

17C. (1) Where a community service order is made or amended in the circumstances specified in ss.17A or 17B of this Act, the court which makes or amends the order shall send three copies of it as made or amended to the home court, together with such documents and information relating to the case as it considers likely to be of assistance to that court.

(2) In this section–

'home court' means–

(a) if the offender resides in Scotland, or will be residing in Scotland at the

relevant time, the sheriff court having jurisdiction in the locality in which he resides or proposes to reside; and
(b) if he resides in Northern Ireland,or will be residing in Northern Ireland at the relevant time, the court of summary jurisdiction acting for the petty sessions district in which he resides or proposes to reside; and
'the relevant time' means the time when the order or the amendment to it comes into force.

(3) A community service order made or amended in the circumstances specified in ss.17A or 17B of this Act shall be treated, subjct to the following provisions of this section, as if it were a community service order made in the part of the United Kingdom in which the offender resides, or will be residing at the relevant time; and the legislation relating to community service orders which has effect in that part of the United Kingdom shall apply accordingly.

(4) Before making or amending a community service order in those circumstances the court shall explain to the offender in ordinary language–
(a) the requirements of the legislation relating to community service orders which has effect in the part of the United Kingdom in which he resides or will be residing at the relevant time;
(b) the powers of the home court under that legislation, as modified by this section; and
(c) its own powers under this section,
and an explanation given in accordance with this section shall be sufficient without the addition of an explanation under s.14(5) above.

(5) The home court may exercise in relation to the community service order any power which it could exercise in relation to a community service order made by a court in the part of the United Kingdom in which the home court exercises jurisdiction, by virtue of the legislation relating to such orders which has effect in the part of the United Kingdom in which it has jurisdiction except–
(a) a power to vary the order by substituting for the number of hours' work specified in it any greater number than the court which made the order could have specified;
(b) a power to revoke the order; and
(c) a power to revoke the order and deal with the offender for the offence in respect of which it was made in any manner in which he could have been dealt with for that offence by the court which made the order if the order had not been made.

(6) If at any time while legislating relating to community service orders which has effect in one part of the United Kingdom applies by virtue of subs (3) above to a community service order made in another part–
(a) it appears to the home court–
(i) if that court is in Scotland, on evidence on oath from the local authority officer under the Community Service by Offenders (Scotland) Act 1978; and
(ii) if it is in Northern Ireland, upon a complaint being made to a justice of the peace acting for the petty sessions district for the time being specified in the order, that the offender has failed to comply with any of the requirements of the legislation applicable to the order; or
(b) it appears to the home court on the application of the offender or–
(i) if that court is in Scotland, of the local authority officer; and
(ii) if it is in Northern Ireland, of the relevant officer, as defined in the Treatment of Offenders (Northern Ireland) Order 1976, that it would be in the interests of justice to exercise a power mentioned in subs (5)(b) or (c) above,
the home court may require the offender to appear before the court by which the order was made.

(7) Where an offender is required by virtue of subs (6) above to appear before the court which made a community service order, that court–

(a) may issue a warrant for his arrest; and

(b) may exercise any power which it would exercise in respect of the community service order if the offender resides in the part of the United Kingdom where the court has jurisdiction,

and any enactment relating to the excise of such powers shall have effect accordingly.

[*as inserted by Sch.3 CJA 1982*].

SCHEDULE 1

8c.76   **Discharge and Amendment of Probation Orders**

DISCHARGE

1. (1) A probation order may be discharged, in accordance with the following provisions of this paragraph, on an application made by the probation officer or by the probationer.

(1A) No application may be made under sub-para (1) above while an appeal against the probation order is pending.

(2) Where the probation order made by the court by or before which the probationer was convicted, or on appeal or by the Crown Court, where a magistrates' court has committed an offender to it for sentence, or by a magistrates' court to which the offender has been remitted for sentence under s.39 of the Magistrates' Courts Act 1980, the power to discharge the order shall, subject to sub-para (3) below, be exercised by the supervising court.

(3) Where the court before which the probationer was convicted or the court from which the appeal is brought is the Crown Court or where the Crown Court made the order following the offender's committal to it for sentence by a magistrates' court and there is included in the order a direction that the power be reserved to that court, the power to discharge the order shall be exercised by the Crown Court.

(4) In any other case the power to discharge the order shall be exercised by the court by which the order was made.

AMENDMENT

2. (1) Subject to sub-para (2) below, if the supervising court is satisfied that a probationer proposes to change, or has changed his residence from the petty sessions area named in the probation order to another petty sessions area, the court may, and on the application of the probation order officer shall, by order amend the probation order by substituting for the petty sessions area named in the order the petty sessions area where the probationer proposes to reside or is residing.

(1A) No order may be made under sub-para (1) above while an appeal against the probation order is pending.

(2) If the probation order contains requirements which, in the opinion of the court, cannot be complied with unless the probationer continues to reside in the area named in the order, the court shall not amend the order under this paragraph unless, in accordance with the following provisions of this schedule, it cancels those requirements or substitutes for those requirements other requirements which can be complied with if the probationer ceases to reside in that area.

(3) Where a probation order is amended under this paragraph, the old supervising court shall send to the clerk to the justices for the new area named in the order a copy of the order, together with such documents and information relating to the case as it considers likely to be of assistance to the new supervising court.

3. (1) Without prejudice to the provisions of para 2 above, but subject to sub-para (2) below, the supervising court may, on an application made by the probation officer or by the probationer, by order amend a probation order by cancelling any of the requirements of the order or by inserting in the order (either in addition to or in substitution for any such requirement) any require-ment which the court could include under ss.2, 3, 4A or 4B of this Act if it were then making the order.

(1A) No application may be made under sub-para (1) above while an appeal against the probation order is pending.

(2) The power of the supervising court under this paragraph to amend a probation order shall be subject to the following restrictions–
    (a) the court shall not amend a probation order by reducing the probation period, or by extending that period beyond the end of three years from the date of the original order;
    (b) (*Repealed*).
    (c) the court shall not amend a probation order by inserting therein a requirement that the probationer shall submit to treatment for his mental condition unless the amending order is made within three months after the date of the original order.

4. Subject to para 4A below, where the medical practitioner by whom or under whose direction a probationer is being treated for his mental condition in pursuance of any requirement of the probation order is of opinion–
    (a) that the treatment of the probationer should be continued beyond the period specified in that behalf in the order, or
    (b) that the probationer needs different treatment, being treatment of a kind to which he could be required to submit in pursuance of a probation order, or
    (c) that the probationer is not susceptible to treatment, or
    (d) that the probationer does not require further treatment,
or where the practitioner is for any reason unwilling to continue to treat or direct the treatment of the probationer, he shall make a report in writing to that effect to the probation officer and the probation officer shall apply to the supervising court for the variation or cancellation of the requirement.

(4A) No application may be made under para 4 above while an appeal against the probation order is pending.

GENERAL
5. (1) Subject to sub-para (2) below, where the supervising court proposes to amend a probation order under this schedule, otherwise than on the application of the probationer, it shall summon him to appear before the court; and the court shall not amend a probation order unless the probationer expresses his willingness to comply with the requirements of the order as amended.

(2) This paragraph shall not apply to an order cancelling a requirement of the probation order or reducing the period of any requirement, or substituting a new petty sessions area for the area named in the probation order.

6. (1) On the making of an order discharging or amending a probation order, the clerk to the court shall forthwith–
    (a) if the order discharges the probation order or amends it otherwise than by substituting a new petty sessions area for the area named in the probation order, give copies of the discharging or amending order to the probation officer;
    (b) if the order amends the probation order in the manner excepted by head (a) above, send copies of the amending order to the clerk to the justices for the new petty sessions area;
and in the case falling within head (b) above the clerk to the justices for the new petty sessions area shall give copies of the amending order to the probation officer.

(2) A probation officer to whom in accordance with sub-para (1) abov
copies of an order are given shall give a copy to the probationer and to th
person in charge of any institution in which the probationer is or was require
by the order to reside.

7. (*Repealed*).
[*as amended by Schs.12, 13, CLA 1977, s.66, Schs.11, 16 CJA 1982*].

COMMENTARY

Para 1, no procedure is prescribed for discharge, in particular it is *not stated to be o
complaint.* Copies of the order must be given to the probation officer and by him to th
former probationer: paras 6(1) and (2). The normal rule that orders made on appeal ar
deemed to be made by the court appealed against does not apply to this paragraph: s.12(2
supra.

Para 2(1) see r.39 Probation Rules 1984, *infra.* The justices' clerk may amend a probatio
order by substituting a different petty sessions area under para 2(1): Jutsices' Clerks Rule
1970 (SI No 231).

Para 3, certain applications by the probation officer must be by way of summons: para 5
There would, however, seem to be no power to issue a warrant on non-appearance.

Para 5, failure to secure an expression of 'willingness to comply' renders the variation voic
R v Emmett (1968) *The Times*, 21 December.

SCHEDULE 3

8c.77   Part I

PROBATION OFFICERS

8. (1) It shall be the duty of probation officers to supervise the probationer
and other persons placed under their supervision and to advise, assist an
befriend them, to inquire, in accordance with any directions of the court, int
the circumstances or home surroundings of any person with a view to assistin
the court in determining the most suitable method of dealing with his case, t
advise, assist and befriend, in such cases and in such manner as may b
prescribed, persons who have been released from custody and to perform suc
other duties as may be prescribed or may be imposed by any enactment o
instrument.

(2) In sub-para (1) above 'enactment' includes an enactment contained in
local Act and 'instrument' means an instrument having effect by virtue of a
Act.

9. The probation officer who is to be responsible for the supervision of an
probation shall be selected under arrangements made by the probation an
after-care committee for the probation and after-care area which includes th
petty sessions area for the time being named in the order from among th
probation officers appointed for or assigned to that petty sessions area; and,
the probation officer so selected dies or is unable for any reason to carry out h
duties, another probation officer shall be selected in like manner from amon;
the probation officers appointed for or assigned to that petty sessions area.
[*as amended by Sch.12 CLA 1977*].

CRIMINAL PROCEDURE (SCOTLAND) ACT 1975

8c.78   **Probation orders relating to persons residing in England**

289. (1) Where the court by which a probation order is made under s.384 o
this Act is satisfied that the offender has attained the age of 17 years and reside
or will reside in England, subs (2) of the said section shall not apply to th
order, but the order shall contain a requirement that he be under the supervi
sion of a probation officer appointed for or assigned to the petty sessions are
in which the offender resides or will reside; and that area shall be named in th
order.

(2) Where a probation order has been made under s.384 of this Act and the court in Scotland by which the order was made or the appropriate court is satisfied that the probationer has attained the age of 17 years and proposes to reside or is residing in England, the power of that court to amend the order under Sch.5 to this Act shall include power to insert the provisions required by subs (1) of this section; and the court may so amend the order without summoning the probationer and without his consent.

(3) A probation order made or amended by virtue of this section may, notwithstanding s.385(8) of this Act, include a requirement that the probationer shall submit to treatment for his mental condition, and–
  (a) subsections (1), (3) and (7) of the said s.385 and s.3(2) of the Powers of Criminal Courts Act 1973 (all of which regulate the making of probation orders which include any such requirement) shall apply to the making of an order which includes any such requirement by virtue of this subsection as they apply to the making of an order which includes any such requirement by virtue of s.385 of this Act and s.3 of the said Act of 1973 respectively; and
  (b) subsections (4) to (6) of s.3 of the said Act of 1973 (functions of supervising officer and medical practitioner where such a requirement has been imposed) shall apply in relation to a probationer who is undergoing treatment in England in pursuance of a requirement imposed by virtue of this subsection as they apply in relation to a probationer undergoing such treatment in pursuance of a requirement imposed by virtue of that section.

(4) Sections 386(1) and 387(1) of this Act shall not apply to any order made or amended under this section; but subject as hereinafter provided the provisions of the Powers of Criminal Courts Act 1973 (ecept s.8 of that Act) shall apply to the order as if it were a probation order made under s.2 of that Act:
  Provided that s.6(2)(a), (3)(d) and (6) of that Act shall not apply to any such order and s.6(4) and (5) of that Act shall have effect respectively in relation to any such order as if for the first reference in s.6(4) to the Crown Court there were substituted a reference to a court in Scotland and as if for the second such reference therein and for both such references in s.6(5) there were substituted references to the court in Scotland by which the probation order was made or amended under this section.

(5) If it appears on information to a justice acting for the petty sessions area for which the supervising court within the meaning of the Powers of Criminal Court Act 1973 acts that a person in whose case a probation order has been made or amended under this section has been convicted by a court in any part of Great Britain of an offence committed during the period specified in the order, he may issue a summons requiring that person to appear, at the place and time specified therein, before the court in Scotland by which the probation order was made or, if the information is in writing and on oath, may issue a warrant for his arrest, directing that person to be brought before the last-mentioned court.

(6) If a warrant for the arrest of a probationer issued under s.388 of this Act by a court is executed in England, and the probationer cannot forthwith be brought before that court, the warrant shall have effect as if it directed him to be brought before a magistrates' court for the place where he is arrested; and the magistrates' court shall commit him to custody or release him on bail (with or without sureties) until he can be brought or appear before the court in Scotland.

(7) The court by which a probation order is made or amended in accordance with the provisions of this section shall send three copies of the order to the clerk to the justices for the petty sessions area named therein, together with such documents and information relating to the case as it considers likely to be of assistance to the court acting for that petty sessions area.

(8) Where a probation order which is amended under subs (2) of this section is an order to which the provisions of this Act apply by virtue of s.10 of the Powers of Criminal Courts Act 1973 (which relates to probation orders under that Act relating to persons residing in Scotland) then notwithstanding anything in that section or this section, the order shall, as from the date of the amendment, have effect in all respects as if it were an order made under s.2 of that Act in the case of a person residing in England.

COMMENTARY

s.289(1): Petty sessions area, this has the same meaning as in s.390(8) CYPA 1969.

s.289(6): Warrant issued under s.388, ie in respect of the commission of a further offence by a probationer.

CRIMINAL JUSTICE ACT 1982

8c.79   **Provision, regulation and management of attendance centres**
     16. (1) The Secretary of State may continue to provide attendance centres.

(2) In this Act 'attendance centre' means a place at which offenders under 21 years of age may be required to attend and be given under supervision appropriate occupation or instruction, in pursuance of orders made–
   (a) by the Crown Court or magistrates' courts under s.17 below;
   (b) by juvenile courts or other magistrates' courts under ss.15(2A) or (4) of the Children and Young Persons Act 1969 (attendance centre orders made on breach of requirements in supervision orders); or
   (c) by magistrates' courts under s.6(3)(c) of the Powers of Criminal Courts Act 1973 (attendance centre orders made on breach of requirements in probation orders).

8c.80   **Attendance centre orders**
     17. (1) Subject to ss. (3) and (4) below, where a court–
   (a) would have power, but for s.1 above, to pass a sentence of imprisonment on a person who is under 21 years of age or to commit such a person to prison in default of payment of any sum of money or for failing to do or abstain from doing anything required to be done or left undone; or
   (b) has power to deal with any such person under s.6 of the Powers of Criminal Courts Act 1973 for failure to comply with any of the requirements of a probation order,
the court may, if it has been notified by the Secretary of State that an attendance centre is available for the reception of persons of his description, order him to attend at such a centre, to be specified in the order, for such number of hours as may be so specified.

(2) An order under this section is referred to in this Act as an 'attendance centre order'.

(3) No attendance centre order shall be made in the case of an offender who has been previously sentenced–
   (a) to imprisonment;
   (b) to detention under s.53 of the Children and Young Persons Act 1933;
   (c) to Borstal training;
   (d) to youth custody or custody for life under this Act; or
   (e) to detention in a detention centre,
unless it appears to the court that there are special circumstances (whether relating to the offence or to the offender) which warrant the making of such an order in his case.

(4) The aggregate number of hours for which an attendance centre order may require an offender to attend at an attendance centre shall not be less than 12 except where he is under 14 years of age and the court is of opinion that 12 hours would be excessive, having regard to his age or any other circumstances.

(5) The aggregate number of hours shall not exceed 12 except where the court is of opinion, having regard to all the circumstances, that 12 hours would be inadequate, and in that case shall not exceed 24 where the offender is under 17 years of age, or 36 hours where the offender is under 21 but not less than 17 years of age.

(6) A court may make an attendance centre order in respect of an offender before a previous attendance centre order made in respect of him has ceased to have effect, and may determine the number of hours to be specified in the order without regard–
(a) to the number specified in the previous order; or
(b) to the fact that that order is still in effect.

(7) An attendance centre order shall not be made unless the court is satisfied that the attendance centre to be specified in it is reasonably accessible to the person concerned, having regard to his age, the means of access available to him and any other circumstances.

(8) The times at which an offender is required to attend at an attendance centre shall be such as to avoid interference, so far as practicable, with his school hours or working hours.

(9) The first such time shall be a time at which the centre is available for the attendance of the offender in accordance with the notification of the Secretary of State and shall be specified in the order.

(10) The subsequent times shall be fixed by the officer in charge of the centre, having regard to the offender's circumstances.

(11) An offender shall not be required under this section to attend at an attendance centre on more than one occasion on any day, or for more than three hours on any occasion.

(12) Where a court makes an attendance centre order, the clerk of the court shall deliver or send a copy of the order to the officer in charge of the attendance centre specified in it, and shall also deliver a copy to the officer or send a copy by registered post or the recorded delivery service addressed to the offender's last or usual place of abode.

(13) Where an offender has been ordered to attend at an attendance centre in default of the payment of any sum of money–
(a) on payment of the whole sum to any person authorised to receive it, the attendance centre order shall cease to have effect;
(b) on payment of a part of the sum to any such person, the total number of hours for which the offender is required to attend at the centre shall be reduced proportionately, that is to say by such number of complete hours as bears to the total number the proportion most nearly approximating to, without exceeding the proportion which the part bears to the said sum.

COMMENTARY

For the effects of this section see *Attendance Centre Orders* at 8c.00.

s.17(1): Attendance centre, defined in s.16(2), *supra.*

21 years of age, for the determination of age, see s.1(6), *supra.*

Notified by the Secretary of State, up to date lists are issued to courts on a regular basis.

s.17(3): Sentenced to imprisonment, including a suspended and partly suspended sentence.

s.17(7): Reasonably accessible, the Home Office consider 10 miles or a journey of 45 minutes to be the most that a boy could reasonably be expected to travel (15 miles or 90 minutes in the case of a 14 year old). HOC 136/1977.

Discharge and variation of attendance centre orders   **8c.81**
18. (1) An attendance centre order may be discharged on an application made by the offender or the officer in charge of the relevant attendance centre.

(2) An application under subs (1) above shall be made to one of the courts specified in subs (3) below or to the Crown Court under subs (4) below, and the discharge of such an order shall be by order of the court.

(3) Subject to subs (4) below, the power to discharge an attendance centre order shall be exercised–
(a) by a magistrates' court acting for the petty sessions area in which the relevant attendance centre is situated; or
(b) by the court which made the order.

(4) Where the court which made the order is the Crown Court and there is included in the order a direction that the power to discharge the order is reserved to that court, the power shall be exercised by that court.

(5) An attendance centre order may, on the application of the offender or of the officer in charge of the relevant attendance centre, be varied by a magistrates' court acting for the petty sessions area in which the relevant attendance centre is situated; and an attendance centre order made by a magistrates' court may also be varied, on such an application, by that court.

(6) The power to vary an attendance centre order is a power by order–
(a) to vary the day or hour specified in the order for the offender's first attendance at the relevant attendance centre; or
(b) if the court is satisfied that the offender proposes to change or has changed his residence, to substitute for the relevant attendance centre an attendance centre which the court is satisfied is reasonably accessible to the offender, having regard to his age, the means of access available to him and any other circumstances.

(7) Where an application is made under this section by the officer in charge of an attendance centre, the court may deal with it without summoning the offender.

(8) It shall be the duty of the clerk to a court which makes an order under this section–
(a) to deliver a copy to the offender or send a copy by registered post or the recorded delivery addressed to the offender's last or usual place of abode; and
(b) to deliver or send a copy–
  (i) if the order is made by virtue of subss (1) or (6)(a) above, to the officer in charge of the relevant attendance centre; and
  (ii) if it is made by virtue of subs (6)(b) above, to the officer in charge of the attendance centre which the order was varied will require the offender to attend.

(9) In this section 'the relevant centre', in relation to an attendance centre order, means the attendance centre specified in the order or sustituted for the attendance center so specified by an order may by virtue of subs (6)(b) above.

8c.82   **Breaches of attendance centre orders or attendance centre rules**
    19. (1) Where an attendance centre order has been made and it appears on information to a justice acting for a relevant petty sessions area that the offender–
(a) has failed to attend in accordance with the order; or
(b) while attending has committed a breach of rules made under s.16(3) above which cannot be adequately dealt with under those rules,
the justice may issue a summons requiring the offender to appear at the place and time specified in the summons before a magistrates' court acting for the area or, if the information is in writing and on oath, may issue a warrant for the offender's arrest requiring him to be brought before such a court.

(2) For the purposes of this section a petty sessions area is a relevant petty sessions area in relation to an attendance centre order–

(a) if the attendance center which the offender is required to attend by an order made by virtue of s.17(1) or 18(6)(b) above is situated in it; or

(b) if the order was made by a magistrates' court acting for it.

(3) If it is proved to the satisfaction of the magistrates' court before which an offender appears or is brought under this section that he has failed without reasonable excuse to attend as mentioned in para (a) of subs (1) above or has committed such a breach of rules as is mentioned in para (b) of that subsection, that court–

(a) if the attendance centre order was made by a magistrates' court, may revoke it and deal with him, for the offence in respect of which the order was made, in any manner in which he could have been dealt with for that offence by the court which made the order if the order had not been made;

(b) if the order was made by the Crown Court, may commit him in custody or release him on bail until he can be brought or appear before the Crown Court.

(4) A magistrates' court which deals with an offender's case under subs (3)(b) above shall send to the Crown Court a certificate signed by a justice of the peace giving particulars of the offender's failure to attend or, as the case may be, the breach of the rules which he has committed, together with such other particulars of the case as may be desirable; and a certificate purporting to be so signed shall be admissible as evidence of the failure or the breach before the Crown Court.

(5) Where by virtue of subs (3)(b) above the offender is brought or appears before the Crown Court and it is proved to the satisfaction of the court that he has failed to attend as mentioned in para (a) of subs (1) above or has committed such a breach of rules as is mentioned in para (b) of tha subsection, that court may revoke the attendance centre order and deal with him, for the offence in respect of which the order was made, in any manner in which it could have dealt with him for that offence if it had not made the order.

(6) A person sentenced under subs (3)(a) above for an offence may appeal to the Crown Court against the sentence.

MENTAL HEALTH ACT 1983

Application of Act: 'mental disorder' 8c.83
1. (1) The provisions of this Act shall have effect with respect to the reception, care and treatment of mentally disordered patients, the management of their property and other related matters.

(2) In this Act – 'mental disorder' means mental illness, arrested or incomplete development of mind, psychopathic disorder and any other disorder or disability of mind and 'mentally disordered' shall be construed accordingly; 'severe mental impairment' means a state of arrested or incomplete development of mind which includes severe impairment of intelligence and social functioning and is associated with abnormally aggressive or seriously irresponsible conduct on the part of the person concerned and 'severely mentally impaired' shall be construed accordingly; 'mental impairment' means a state of arrested or incomplete development of mind (not amounting to severe mental impairment) which includes significant impairment of intelligence and social functioning and is associated with abnormally aggressive or seriously irresponsible conduct on the part of the person concerned and 'mentally impaired' shall be construed accordingly; 'psychopathic disorder' means a persistent disorder or disability of mind (whether or not including significant impairment of intelligence) which results in abnormally aggressive or seriously irresponsible conduct on the part of the person concerned; and other expressions shall have the meanings assigned to them in s.145 below.

(3) Nothing in subs (2) above shall be construed as implying that a person may be dealt with under this Act as suffering from mental disorder, or from any form of mental disorder described in this section, by reason only of promiscuity or other immoral conduct, sexual deviancy or dependence on alcohol or drugs.

COMMENTARY

Mental illness, is not further defined.

8c.84   **Power of courts to order hospital admission or guardianship**

37. (1) Where a person is convicted before the Crown Court of an offence punishable with imprisonment other than an offence the sentence for which is fixed by law, or is convicted by a magistrates' court of an offence punishable on summary conviction with imprisonment, and the conditions mentioned in subs (2) below are satisfied, the court may by order authorise his admission to and detention in such hospital as may be specified in the order or, as the case may be, place him under the guardianship of a local social services authority or of such other person approved by a local social services authority as may be so specified.

(2) The conditions referred to in subs (1) above are that–

(a) the court is satisfied, on the written or oral evidence of two registered medical practitioners, that the offender is suffering from mental illness, psychopathic disorder, severe impairment or mental impairment and that either–

   (i) the mental disorder from which the offender is suffering is of a nature or degree which makes it appropriate for him to be detained in a hospital for medical treatment and, in the case of a psychopathic disorder or mental impairment, that such treatment is likely to alleviate or prevent a deterioration of his condition; or

   (ii) in the case of an offender who has attained the age of 16 years, the mental disorder is of a nature or degree which warrants his reception into guardianship under this Act; and

(b) the court is of the opinion, having regard to all the circumstances including the nature of the offence and the character and antecedents of the offender, and to the other available methods dealing with him, that the most suitable method of disposing of the case is by means of an order under this section.

(3) Where a person is charged before a magistrates' court with any act or omission as an offence and the court would have power, on convicting him of that offence, to make an order under subs (1) above in his case as being a person suffering from mental illness or severe mental impairment, then, if the court is satisfied that the accused did the act or made the omission charged, the court may, if it thinks fit, make such an order without convicting him.

(4) An order for the admission of an offender to a hospital (in this Act referred to as 'a hospital order') shall not be made under this section unless the court is satisfied on the written or oral evidence of the registered medical practitioner who would be in charge of his treatment or some other person representing the managers of the hospital that arrangements have been made for his admission to that hospital in the event of such an order being made by the court, and for his admission to it within the period of 28 days beginning with the date of the making of such an order; and the court may, pending his admission within that period, give such directions as it thinks fit for his conveyance to and detention in a place of safety.

(5) If within the said period of 28 days it appears to the Secretary of State that by reason of an emergency or other special circumstances it is not practicable for the patient to be received into the hospital specified in the order, he may give directions for the admission of the patient to such other

hospital as appears to be appropriate instead of the hospital so specified; and where such directions are given–
  (a) the Secretary of State shall cause the person having the custody of the patient to be informed, and
  (b) the hospital order shall have effect as if the hospital specified in the directions were substituted for the hospital specified in the order.

(6) An order placing an offender under the guardianship of a local social services authority or of any other person (in this Act referred to as 'a guardianship order') shall not be made under this section unless the court is satisfied that that authority or person is willing to receive the offender into guardianship.

(7) A hospital order or guardianship order shall specify the form or forms of mental disorder referred to in subs (2)(a) above from which, upon the evidence taken into account under that subsection, the offender is found by the court to be suffering; and no such order shall be made unless the offender is described by each of the practitioners whose evidence is taken into account under that subsection as suffering from the same one of those forms of mental disorder, whether or not he is also described by either of them as suffering from another of them.

(8) Where an order is made under this section, the court shall not pass sentence of imprisonment or impose a fine or make a probation order in respect of the offence or make any such order as is mentioned in paras (b) or (c) of s.7(7) of the Children and Young Persons Act 1969 in respect of the offender, but may make any other order which the court has power to make apart from this section; and for the purposes of this subsection 'sentence of imprisonment' includes any sentence or order for detention.

COMMENTARY

This section allows the court to make a hospital order or a guardianship order on anyone convicted of an offence punishable with imprisonment. Alternatively, a magistrates' court may make either order without proceeding to conviction if satisfied under s.37(3) that the accused is suffering from mental illness or severe mental impairment and that he did the act or made the omission charged.

For the effects of a hospital order and a guardianship order, see s.40, *infra*.

Legal aid should be offered when magistrates are considering making a hospital order: *R v King's Lynn Justices, ex p. Fysh* [1964] Crim LR 143.

The disorder need not be the cause of the offence in question: *R v Hatt* [1962] Crim LR 647.

For the information to be sent to the hospital (or the local authority in the case of a guardianship order) see r.31(1)(2) MC Rules 1981. The adult court may not make an order under this section in respect of a juvenile but should remit him to a juvenile court: s.7(8) CYPA 1969.

For directions which should be added to orders under this section, see s.40, *infra*, and notes.

s.37(1): Offence punishable on summary conviction with imprisonment, to be construed without regard to any prohibition or restriction relating to the imprisonment of young offenders: s.55(2).

Hospital defined in s.145, *infra*. For information about hospitals, see s.39, *infra*.

Local social services authority, defined in s.145(1).

s.37(2): Written or oral evidence, see s.54, *infra*. *Note* s.37 (7), also.

Justices act *outside their jurisdiction* if they make a hospital order without disclosing to an unrepresented defendant the substance of the reports or fail to inform him of his rights of cross-examination: *R v King's Lynn Justices, ex p. Fysh* [1964] Crim LR 143. There is power to order costs from central funds in respect of the doctor's reports: s.19 POA 1985 and r.25 Costs in Criminal Cases (General Regulations 1986 (SI No 1335) (oral reports) and s.32(2) CJA 1967 (written reports).

Psychopathic disorder/severe mental impairment/mental impairment, defined in s.1(2), *supra*; and see note s.1(3), also.

s.37(3) This provision allows a magistrates' court to make a hospital order without embarking on a trial and without (in the case of an offence triable either way) the defendant's consent to summary trial: *R v Lincolnshire (Kesteven) Justices, ex p. O'Connor* [1983] 1 All ER 901. Lord Lane CJ stressed that the circumstances in which such a course would be appropriate will be rare and will usually require the assent of the defendant's legal representative. The power also applies where the defendant has elected to be tried by a judge and jury: *R v Ramsgate Justices, ex p. Kazmarek* (1985) 149 JP 16, in which Mann J reserved the question of whether the power is available in respect of an offence triable only on indictment.

s.37(4): Written or oral evidence, see s.54, *infra.*

Managers, defined in s.145(1), *infra.*

s.37(8): Order . . . mentioned in paras (b) or (c) or s.7(7), ie a supervision order or an order that a parent or guardian be bound over to keep proper control.

8c.85   **Interim hospital orders**

38. (1) Where a person is convicted before the Crown Court of an offence punishable with imprisonment (other than an offence the sentence of which is fixed by law) or is convicted by a magistrates' court of an offence punishable on summary conviction with imprisonment and the court before or by which he is convicted is satisfied, on the written or oral evidence of two registered medical practitioners—

   (a) that the offender is suffering from mental illness, psychopathic disorder, severe mental impairment or mental impairment; and

   (b) that there is reason to suppose that the mental disorder from which the offender is suffering is such that it may be appropriate for a hospital order to be made in his case,

the court may, before making a hospital order or dealing with him in some other way, make an order (in this Act referred to as 'an interim hospital order') authorising his admission to such hospital as may be specified in the order and his detention there in accordance with this section.

   (2) In the case of an offender who is subject to an interim hospital order the court may make a hospital order without his being brought before the court if he is represented by counsel or a solicitor and his counsel or solicitor is given an opportunity of being heard.

   (3) At least one of the registered medical practitioners whose evidence is taken into account under subs (1) above shall be employed at the hospital which is to be specified in the order.

   (4) An interim hospital order shall not be made for the admission of an offender to a hospital unless the court is satisfied, on the written or oral evidence of the registered medical practitioner who would be in charge of his treatment or of some other person representing the managers of the hospital that arrangements have been made for his admission to that hospital and for his admission to it within the period of 28 days beginning with the date of the order; and if the court is so satisfied the court may, pending his admission, give directions for his conveyance to and detention in a place of safety.

   (5) An interim hospital order—

   (a) shall be in force for such period, not exceeding 12 weeks, as the court may specify when making the order; but

   (b) may be renewed for further periods of not more than 28 days at a time if it appears to the court, on the written or oral evidence of the responsible medical officer, that the continuation of the order is warranted;

but no such order shall continue in force for more than six months in all and the court shall terminate the order if it makes a hospital order in respect of the offender or decides after considering the written or oral evidence of the responsible medical officer to deal with the offender in some other way.

   (6) The power of renewing an interim hospital order may be exercised

without the offender being brought before the court if he is represented by counsel or a solicitor and his counsel or solicitor is given an opportunity of being heard.

(7) If an offender absconds from a hospital in which he is detained in pursuance of an interim hospital order, or while being conveyed to or from such a hospital, he may be arrested without warrant by a constable and shall, after being arrested, be brought as soon as practicable before the court that made the order; and the court may thereupon terminate the order and deal with him in any way in which it could have dealt with him if no such order had been made.

COMMENTARY

s.38(1): An offence punishable . . . with imprisonment, see the note to s.37.

Written or oral evidence, see s.54, *infra*; and see s.38(3).

Psychopathic disorder/severe mental impairment/mental impairment, defined in s.1(1), *supra*; and note s.1(3).

Hospital, defined in s.145(1), *infra*.

s.38(2): A hospital order, defined in s.37(4), s.145(1).

s.38(4): Written or oral evidence, see s.54, *infra*.

Information as to hospitals   8c.86
39. (1) Where a court is minded to make a hospital order or interim hospital order in respect of any person it may request–
    (a) the Regional Health Authority for the region in which that person resides or last resided; or
    (b) any other Regional Health Authority that appears to the court to be appropriate,
to furnish the court with such information as that Authority has or can reasonably obtain with respect to the hospital or hospitals (if any) in its region or elsewhere at which arrangements could be made for the admission of that person in pursuance of the order, and that Authority shall comply with any such request.

(2) In its application to Wales subs (1) above shall have effect as if for any reference to any such Authority as is mentioned in paras (a) or (b) of that subsection there were substituted a reference to the Secretary of State, and as if for the words 'in its region or elsewhere' there were substituted the words 'in Wales'.

COMMENTARY

The clerk of the court should contact the Regional Medical Officer for the Regional Health Authority covering the area from which the offender seems to come: HOC 69/1983.

s.39(1): Hospital order/interim hospital order, defined in s.37, *supra*: s.145(1).

Effect of hospital orders, guardianship orders and interim hospital orders   8c.87
40. (1) A hospital order shall be sufficient authority–
    (a) for a constable, an approved social worker or any other person directed to do so by the court to convey the patient to the hospital specified in the order within a period of 28 days; and
    (b) for the managers of the hospital to admit him at any time within that period and thereafter detain him in accordance with the provisions of this Act.

(2) A guardianship order shall confer on the authority or person named in the order as guardian the same powers as a guardianship application made and accepted under Part II of this Act.

(3) Where an interim hospital order is made in respect of an offender–

(a) a constable or any other person directed to do so by the court shall convey the offender to the hospital specified in the order within the period mentioned in s.38(4) above; and

(b) the managers of the hospital shall admit him within that period and thereafter detain him in accordance with the provisions of s.38 above.

(4) A patient who is admitted to a hospital in pursuance of a hospital order, or placed under guardianship by a guardianship order, shall, subject to the provisions of this subsection, be treated for the purposes of the provisions of this Act mentioned in Part I of Sch.1 to this Act as if he had been so admitted or placed on the date of the order in pursuance of an application for admission for treatment or a guardianship application, as the case may be, duly made under Part II of this Act, but subject to any modifications of those provisions specified in that Part of that Schedule.

(5) Where a patient is admitted to a hospital in pursuance of a hospital order, or placed under guardianship by a guardianship order, any previous application, hospital order or guardianship order by virtue of which he was liable to be detained in a hospital or subject to guardianship shall cease to have effect; but if the first-mentioned order, or the conviction on which it was made, is quashed on appeal, this subsection shall not apply and s.22 above shall have effect as if during any period for which the patient was liable to be detained or subject to guardianship under the order, he had been detained in custody as mentioned in that section.

COMMENTARY

After consultation with the Home Office, the Department of Health and Social Security and the Lord Chancellor's Department, the Lord Chief Justice directed that an additional direction be given by the court under this section addressed to the governor of the prison which is to hold the person pending admission to hospital, which reads as follows:

'but if at any time it appears to the person in whose custody the defendant is detained in a place of safety that the defendant might not be admitted to hospital in pursuance of this order within 28 days of this date, that person shall within 21 days of this date (or at once if it becomes apparent only after 21 days that the defendant might not be admitted to hospital) report the circumstances to the Chief Clerk of the Court and unless otherwise directed by the Chief Clerk shall bring the defendant before the Court forthwith so as to enable it within 28 days of this date to make such order as may be necessary.'

The Home Office have advised that:

'Magistrates' courts have re-sentencing powers, analogous to those of the Crown Court under [s.142 of the Magistrates' Courts Act 1980.] The Secretary of State has no authority to interpret the law, but he takes the view that this provision can properly be applied in these circumstances. It is open to magistrates' courts to make a request in similar terms by means of an addendum to [Form 35 of the Magistrates' Courts (Forms) Rules 1981]. Prison authorities have been asked to inform the clerk to the justices of the impending possible frustration of a hospital order, but the suggested addendum for Form 35 would be a useful additional safeguard': HOC 66/1980.

s.40(1): A constable, ie a police officer of any rank.

Approved social worker, defined in s.145(1), *infra.*

8c.88   **Powers of magistrates' courts to commit for restriction order**

43. (1) If in the case of a person of or over the age of 14 years who is convicted by a magistrates' court of an offence punishable on summary conviction with imprisonment–

(a) the conditions which under s.37(1) above are required to be satisfied for the making of a hospital order are satisfied in respect of the offender but

(b) it appears to the court, having regard to the manner of the offence, the antecedents of the offender and the risk of his committing further offences if set at large, that if a hospital order is made a restriction order should also be made,

the court may, instead of making a hospital order or dealing with him in any other manner, commit him in custody to the Crown Court to be dealt with in respect of the offence.

(2) Where an offender is committed to the Crown Court under this section, the Crown Court shall inquire into the circumstances of the case and may–

    (a) if that court would have power so to do under the foregoing provisions of this Part of this Act upon the conviction of the offender before that court of such an offence as is described in s.37(1) above, make a hospital order in his case, with or without a restriction order;

    (b) if the court does not make such an order, deal with the offender in any other manner in which the magistrates' court might have dealt with him.

(3) The Crown Court shall have the same power to make orders under ss.35, 36 and 38 above in the case of a person committed to the court under this section as the Crown Court has under those sections in the case of an accused person within the meaning of ss.35, 36 above or of a person convicted before that court as mentioned in s.38 above.

(4) The power of a magistrates' court under s.38 of the Magistrates' Courts Act 1980 (which enables such a court to commit an offender to the Crown Court where the court is of the opinion that greater punishment should be inflicted for the offence than the court has power to inflict) shall also be exercisable by a magistrates' court where it is of the opinion that greater punishment should be inflicted as aforesaid on the offender unless a hospital order is made in his case with a restriction order.

(5) The power of the Crown Court to make a hospital order, with or without a restriction order, in the case of a person convicted before that court of an offence may, in the same circumstances and subject to the same conditions, be exercised by such a court in the case of a person committed to the court under s.5 of the Vagrancy Act 1824 (which provides for the committal to the Crown Court of persons who are incorrigible rogues within the meaning of that section.)

COMMENTARY

The magistrates have power to grant legal aid in respect of the proceedings in the Crown Court: s.28(7) CAA 1974. As to the desirability of legal aid, see the note to s.60, *supra*. For the documents to be sent to the Crown Court, see r.18 MC Rules 1981.

A restriction order was upheld against a subnormal psychopath with a persistent history of absconding in *R v Toland* [1974] Crim LR 196.

s.43(1): An offence punishable on summary conviction with imprisonment, to be construed without regard to any prohibition or restriction relating to the imprisonment of young offenders: s.55(2).

Commit him to custody, alternatively, if satisfied that arrangements have been made for his admission, the court may direct that the offender be admitted to hospital and give instructions for his production at the Crown Court: s.44, *infra*.

Committal to hospital under section 43   8c.89

44. (1) Where an offender is committed under s.43(1) above and the magistrates' court by which he is committed is satisfied on written and oral evidence that arrangements have been made for the admission of the offender to a hospital in the event of an order being made under this section, the court may, instead of committing him in custody, by order direct him to be admitted to that hospital, specifying it, and to be detained there until the case is disposed of by the Crown Court, and may give such directions as it thinks fit for his production from the hospital to attend the Crown Court by which his case is to be dealt with.

(2) The evidence required by subs (1) above shall be given by the registered medical practitioner who would be in charge of the offender's treatment or by some other person representing the managers of the hospital in question.

(3) The power to give directions under s.37(4) above, s.37(5) above and s.40(1) above shall apply in relation to an order under this section as they apply in relation to a hospital order, but as if references to the period of 28 days mentioned in s.40(1) above were omitted; and subject as aforesaid an order under this section shall, until the offender's case is disposed of by the Crown Court, have the same effect as a hospital order together with a restriction order, made without limitation of time.

COMMENTARY
s.44(2): Evidence, see s.54, *infra.*

8c.90   **Appeals from magistrates' courts**
   45. (1) Where on the trial of an information charging a person with an offence a magistrates' court makes a hospital order or guardianship order in respect of him without convicting him, he shall have the same right of appeal against the order as if it had been made on his conviction; and on any such appeal the Crown Court shall have the same powers as if the appeal had been against both conviction and sentence.

(2) An appeal by a child or young person with respect to whom any such order has been made, whether the appeal is against the order or against the finding upon which the order was made, may be brought by him or by his parent or guardian on his behalf.

COMMENTARY
Where there is a conviction, appeal is under s.108 MCA 1980.

8c.91   **Further provisions as to persons remanded by magistrates' courts**
   52. (1) This section has effect where a transfer direction has been given in respect of any such person as is described in para (b) of s.48(2) above; and that person is in this section referred to as 'the accused'.

(2) Subject to subs (5) below, the transfer direction shall cease to have effect on the expiration of the period of remand unless the accused is committed in custody to the Crown Court for trial or to be otherwise dealt with.

(3) Subject to subs (4) below, the power of further remanding the accused under s.128 of the Magistrates' Courts Act 1980 may be exercised by the court without his being brought before the court; and if the court futher remands the accused in custody (whether or not he is brought before the court) the period of remand shall, for the purposes of this section, be deemed not to have expired.

(4) The court shall not under subs (3) above further remand the accused in his absence unless he has appeared before the court within the previous six months.

(5) If the magistrates' court is satisfied, on the written or oral evidence of the responsible medical officer–
   (a) that the accused no longer requires treatment in hospital for mental disorder; or
   (b) that no effective treatment for his disorder can be given in the hospital to which he has been removed,
the court may direct that the transfer direction shall cease to have effect notwithstanding that the period of remand has not expired or that the accused is committed to the Crown Court as mentioned in subs (2) above.

(6) If the accused is committed to the Crown Court as mentioned in subs (2) above and the transfer direction has not ceased to have effect under subs (5) above, s.51 above shall apply as if the transfer direction given in his case were a direction given in respect of a person falling within that section.

(7) The magistrates' court may, in the absence of the accused, inquire as examining justices into an offence alleged to have been committed by him and commit him for trial in accordance with s.6 of the Magistrates' Courts Act 1980 if–

    (a) the court is satisfied, on the written or oral evidence of the responsible medical officer, that the accused is unfit to take part in the proceedings; and

    (b) where the court proceeds under subs (1) of that section, the accused is represented by counsel or a solicitor.

COMMENTARY

.52(1): A transfer direction, ie a direction by the Secretary of State under s.48 removing a prisoner to a hospital.

ara (b) of s.48(2), this deals with persons remanded in custody by magistrates.

.52(4): Written or oral evidence, see s.54, *infra.*

Requirements as to medical evidence 8c.92

54. (1) The registered medical practitioner whose evidence is taken into account under s.35(3)(a) above and at least one of the registered medical practitioners whose evidence is taken into account under ss.36(1), 37(2)(a), 38(1) and 51(6)(a) above and whose reports are taken into account under ss.47(1) and 48(1) above shall be a practitioner approved for the purposes of s.12 above by the Secretary of State as having special experience in the diagnosis or treatment of mental disorder.

(2) For the purposes of any provision of this Part of this Act under which a court may act on the written evidence of–

    (a) a registered medical practitioner or a registered medical practitioner of any description; or

    (b) a person representing the managers of a hospital,

a report in writing purporting to be signed by a registered medical practitioner or a registered medical practitioner of such a description or by a person representing the managers of a hospital may, subject to the provisions of this section, be received in evidence without proof of the signature of the practitioner or that person and without proof that he has the requisite qualifications or authority or is of the requisite description; but the court may require the signatory of any such report to be called to give oral evidence.

(3) Where, in pursuance of a direction of the court, any such report is tendered in evidence otherwise than by or on behalf of the person who is the subject of the report, then–

    (a) if that person is represented by counsel or a solicitor; a copy of the report shall be given to his counsel or solicitor;

    (b) if that person is not so represented, the substance of the report shall be disclosed to him or, where he is a child or young person, to his parent or guardian if present in court; and

    (c) except where the report relates only to arrangements for his admission to a hospital, that person may require the signatory of the report to be called to give oral evidence, and evidence to rebut the evidence contained in the report may be called by or on behalf of that person.

COMMENTARY

ustices act *outside their jurisdiction* if they make a hospital order without disclosing to an unrepresented defendant the substance of the reports or fail to inform him of his rights of cross-examination: *R v King's Lynn Justices, ex p. Fysh* [1964] Crim LR 143.

Interpretation of Part III 8c.93

55. (1) In this Part of this Act–

'child' and 'young person' have the same meaning as in the Children and Young Persons Act 1933;

'civil prisoner' has the meaning given to it by s.48(2)(c) above;
'guardian', in relation to a child or young person, has the same meaning as in
the Children and Young Persons Act 1933;
'place of safety', in relation to a person who is not a child or a young person,
means any police station, prison or remand centre, or any hospital the managers of which are willing temporarily to receive him, and in relation to a child
or young person has the same meaning as in the Children and Young Persons
Act 1933;
'responsible medical officer', in relation to a person liable to be detained in a
hospital within the meaning of Part II of this Act, means the registered medical
practitioner in charge of the treatment of the patient.

(2) Any reference to this Part of this Act to an offence punishable on
summary conviction with imprisonment shall be construed without regard to
any prohibition or restriction imposed by or under any enactment relating to
the imprisonment of young offenders.

(3) Where a patient who is liable to be detained in a hospital in pursuance of
an order or direction under this Part of this Act is treated by virtue of any
provision of this Part of this Act as if he had been admitted to the hospital in
pursuance of a subsequent order or direction under this Part of this Act or a
subsequent application for admission for treatment under Part II of this Act,
he shall be treated as if the subsequent order, direction or application had
described him as suffering from the form or forms of mental disorder specified
in the earlier order or direction or, where he is treated as if he had been so
admitted by virtue of a direction under s.42(1) above, such form of mental
disorder as may be specified in the direction under that section.

(4) Any reference to a hospital order, a guardianship order or a restriction
order in s.40(2), (4) or (5), s.41(3) to (5), or s.42 above or s.69(1) below shall
be construed as including a reference to any order or direction under this Part
of this Act having the same effect as the first-mentioned order; and the
exceptions and modifications set out in Sch.1 to this Act in respect of the
provisions of this Act described in that Schedule accordingly include those
which are consequential on the provisions of this subsection.

(5) Section 34(2) above shall apply for the purpose of this Part of this Act as
it applies for the purposes of Part II of this Act.

(6) References in this Part of this Act to persons serving a sentence of
imprisonment shall be construed in accordance with s.47(5) above.

(7) Section 99 of the Children and Young Persons Act 1933 (which relates
to the presumption and determination of age) shall apply for the purposes of
this Part of this Act as it applies for the purposes of that Act.

8c.94   **Interpretation**
              145. (1) In this Act, unless the context otherwise requires–
'absent without leave' has the meaning given to it by s.18 above and related
expressions shall be construed accordingly;
'application for admission for assessment' has the meaning given in s.2 above;
'application for admission for treatment' has the meaning given in s.3 above;
'approved social worker' means an officer of a local social services authority
appointed to act as an approved social worker for the purposes of this Act;
'hospital' means–
  (a) any health service hospital within the meaning of the National Health
      Service Act 1977; and
  (b) any accommodation provided by a local authority and used as a hospital
      by or on behalf of the Secretary of State under that Act;
and 'hospital within the meaning of Part II of this Act' has the meaning given in
s.34 above;
'interim hospital order' has the meaning given in s.38 above;

'local social services authority' means a council which is a local authority for the purpose of the Local Authority Social Services Act 1970;
'the managers' means–
  (a) in relation to a hospital vested in the Secretary of State for the purposes of his functions under the National Health Service Act 1977, and in relation to any accommodation provided by a local authority and used as a hospital by or on behalf of the Secretary of State under that Act, the District Health Authority or special health authority responsible for the administration of the hospital;
  (b) in relation to a special hospital, the Secretary of State;
  (c) in relation to a mental nursing home registered in pursuance of the Nursing Homes Act 1975, the person or persons registered in respect of the home;
and in this definition 'hospital' means a hospital within the meaning of Part II of this Act;
'medical treatment' includes nursing, and also includes care, habilitation and rehabilitation under medical supervision;
'mental disorder', 'severe mental impairment', 'mental impairment' and 'psychopathic disorder' have the meanings given in s.1 above;
'mental nursing home' has the same meaning as in the Nursing Homes Act 1975;
'nearest relative', in relation to a patient, has the meaning given in Part II of this Act;
'patient' (except in Part VII of this Act) means a person suffering or appearing to be suffering from mental disorder;
'restriction direction' has the meaning given to it by s.49 above;
'restriction order' has the meaning given to it by s.41 above;
'special hospital' has the same meaning as in the National Health Service Act 1977;
'standard scale' has the meaning given in s.75 of the Criminal Justice Act 1982;
'transfer direction' has the meaning given to it by s.47 above.

(2) 'Statutory maximum' has the meaning given in s.74 of the Criminal Justice Act 1982 and for the purpose of s.128(4)(a) above–
  (a) subs (1) of s.74 shall have effect as if after the words 'England and Wales' there were inserted the words 'or Northern Ireland'; and
  (b) s.32 of the Magistrates' Courts Act 1980 shall extend to Northern Ireland.

(3) In relation to a person who is liable to be detained or subject to guardianship by virtue of an order or direction under Part III of this Act (other than under ss.35, 36 or 38), any reference in this Act to any enactment contained in Part II of this Act or in ss.66 or 67 above shall be construed as a reference to that enactment as it applies to that person by virtue of Part III of this Act.

MAGISTRATES' COURTS RULES 1981
(SI 1981 No 552 as amended by SI's 1982 No 245, 1983 No 523, 1984 No 1552, 1985 Nos 1695 and 1944 and 1986 No 1332)

Committal to Crown Court for order restricting discharge, etc.　　　**8c.95**
  18. Where a magistrates' court commits an offender to the Crown Court either–
  (a) under s.43(1) of the Mental Health Act 1983 with a view to the making of a hospital order with an order restricting his discharge; or
  (b) under s.38 of the Act of 1980, as modified by subs (4) of the said s.67, with a view to the passing of a more severe sentence than the magistrates' court has power to inflict if such an order is not made
the clerk of the court shall send to the appropriate officer of the Crown Court–
  (i) the copies, documents and articles specified in r.17;

(ii) any written evidence about the offender given by a medical practitioner under s.37(2)(a) of the Mental Health Act 1983 or a copy of a note of any oral evidence so given;

(iii) the name and address of the hospital the managers of which have agreed to admit the offender if a hospital order is made; and

(iv) if the offender has been admitted to a hospital under s.68 of that Act, the name and address of that hospital.

8c.96   **Notification of discharge, etc., of probation order or order for conditional discharge**

28. (1) Where a magistrates' court discharges a probation order or makes an order under s.11 of the Powers of Criminal Courts Act 1973 substituting an order for conditional discharge for a probation order and, in either case, the probation order was not made by that court, the clerk of the court shall–

(a) if the probation order was made by another magistrates' court, notify the clerk of that court; or

(b) if the probation order was made by the Crown Court, notify the appropriate officer of the Crown Court.

(2) Where a magistrates' court deals with a person under ss.6 or 8 of the said Act of 1973 in relation to a probation order or order for conditional discharge which was not made by that court the clerk of the court shall give notice of the result of the proceedings to the clerk of the court by which the order was made.

(3) The clerk of a magistrates' court receiving a notice under this rule shall note the decision of the other court in the register against the entry in respect of the original order.

8c.97   **Documents to be sent under Mental Health Act 1983**

31. (1) The court by which a hospital order is made under s.37 of the Mental Health Act 1983 shall send to the hospital named in the order such information in the possession of the court as it considers likely to be of assistance in dealing with the patient to whom the order relates, and in particular such information about the mental condition, character and antecedents of the patient and the nature of the offence.

(2) The court by which a guardianship order is made under the said s.60 shall send to the local health authority named therein as guardian or, as the case may be, the local health authority for the area in which the person so named resides, such information in the possession of the court as it considers likely to be of assistance in dealing with the patient to whom the order relates and in particular such information about the mental condition, character and antecedents of the patient and the nature of the offence.

(3) The court by which an offender is ordered to be admitted to hospital under s.43 of the said Act of 1983 shall send to the hospital such information in the possession of the court as it considers likely to assist in the treatment of the offender until his case is dealt with by the Crown Court.

8c.98   **Application for substitution of conditional discharge for probation**

103. An application to a magistrates' court under s.11 of the Powers of Criminal Courts Act 1973 for the substitution of an order of conditional discharge for a probation order shall be by complaint.

8c.99   **Cessation of transfer direction**

110. Where a magistrates' court directs, under s.52(5) of the Mental Health Act 1983, that a transfer direction given by the Secretary of State under s.48 of that Act in respect of a person remanded in custody by a magistrates' court shall cease to have effect, the clerk of the court shall give notice in writing of the court's direction to the managers of the hospital specified in the Secretary of State's direction and, where the period of remand has not expired or the person has been committed to the Crown Court for trial or to be otherwise dealt with, to the governor of the prison to which persons of the sex of that person are committed by the court if remanded in custody or committed in custody for trial.

PROBATION RULES 1984
(SI 1984 No 647)

Reports   8c.100
38. (1) A probation officer shall make a report concerning the progress of any person under his supervision to the supervising court or to the court which made the order placing the person under his supervision not being the supervising court, if so requested by either court.

(2) A probation officer shall make a report to the supervising court or to a justice acting for the petty sessions area for which the supervising court acts when it appears to him that a person under his supervision has failed to comply with the requirements of a probationer or a supervision order, or that a person in respect of whom a community service order is in force has failed to comply with the requirements of s.15 of the Powers of Criminal Courts Act 1973.

Applications to court   8c.101
39. (1) If a probation officer becomes aware that a person under his supervision proposes to change or has changed his residence from the petty sessions area named in the order placing him under his supervision to another petty sessions area, he shall apply, in the case of a probationer to the supervising court to amend the order in accordance with para 2(1) of Sch.1 to the Powers of Criminal Courts Act 1973, and in the case of a person placed under his supervision by a supervision order to a juvenile court to amend the order in pursuance of s.15 of the Children and Young Persons Act 1969 unless–
  (a) the probation officer has reason to believe that the person under supervision is unlikely to reside there for a reasonable time; or
  (b) the probation officer has ascertained from, in the case of a probationer, the supervising court, or, in the case of a person placed under his supervision by a supervision order, a juvenile court acting for the petty sessions area named in the order, that that court and the court having jurisdiction in the petty sessions area where the person under supervision proposes to reside or is residing are satisfied that, having regard to the special circumstances of the case, it is desirable that the person should remain under his supervision.

(2) If a probation officer becomes aware that a person in respect of whom a community service order is in force in relation to which that officer is responsible for discharging the functions of the relevant officer proposes to change or has changed his residence from the petty sessions area specified in the community service order to another petty sessions area in England and Wales or to Scotland or to Northern Ireland, he shall apply to a magistrates' court acting for the petty sessions area for the time being specified in the community service order to amend the order in pursuance of s.17(5) or 17A(3) or 17B(3) of the Powers of Criminal Courts Act 1973.

(3) Where it appears to a probation officer that an application can properly be made for the discharge or amendment (otherwise than as provided by the foregoing paragraphs of this Rule) of a probation or supervision order relating to a person under his supervision or of a community service order in relation to which he is responsible for discharging the functions of the relevant officer, the probation officer shall make such application unless the person under supervision, or in respect of whom the community service order is in force as the case may be, or any other person makes the application.

CHAPTER 8d

Custodial Sentences

Custodial Sentences

INTRODUCTION   8d.00

Sentencing is not – and cannot be – an exact *science*. It has often been described as more akin to an *art*, though it would be misleading, from this, to suppose that it can be an intuitive process. The requirement for magistrates to give statutory reasons in specified cases – together with the trend towards 'structured decision making' and the preference of many courts for sentencing in *days* rather than *months* – has done much to change the way in which custodial decisions are reached. Many factors may affect a particular decision, ranging from the general principals of sentencing, eg deterrence, retribution, *infra*, through legal rulings and 'guideline judgments' concerning particular kinds of offences, to the availability of and/or confidence, or otherwise, in what have become known as *'alternatives to custody'* (see Chapter 8c), and even to local attitudes and practices in so far as these are consistent with more general considerations. Always, in conjunction with the wider principles, the *individual merits* must receive proper attention, and increasingly offence 'labels' are tending to become less significant than they once were, in favour of the particular circumstances of offences: see eg *R v Bradbourn* (1985) 7 Cr App R (S) 180 (a 'young offender' case). It is important to emphasise that custodial sentencing is not just a matter of deciding *whether such a sentence should be imposed*, but for *how long*, and that each of these questions demands equal attention. Deprivation of individual liberty is a drastic step, and whilst some offences will themselves dictate that there is no other appropriate course, describing the decision making process as *an art* may sometimes have served to mask a degree of imprecision.

It is *suggested* that a sound knowledge of custodial sentencing is as relevant to the '*Mode of Trial*' decision (see 4.02), as it is to the process of sentencing itself. It is unusual for magistrates' aggregate powers not to enable a total of 12 months imprisonment for an adult, or 12 months youth custody for a young offender (ie because, in practice, with cases of this level of seriousness, there are likely to be at least two offences charged; and two 'either way' offences enable 12 months in aggregate: see s.133 MCA 1980 – although there are some exceptions where a single offence may only attract, eg 3 months, cf Social Security 'fraud' provisions). From some of the cases noted under the titles *Custodial offences for particular offences*, 8d.34 and *Restrictions on custodial sentences for young offenders*, 8.17 it can be seen that some offences which may have attracted sentences of longer than six or 12 months custody some years ago, might now fall within – or sufficiently close to – magistrates' maximum sentencing powers for them to assume jurisdiction at the 'mode of trial' stage. These changes are a relevant consideration in relation to that decision, and within the matters set out s.19(3) MCA 1980: see 4.46.

The classic purposes of sentencing are usually stated as *retribution, deterrence, prevention* and *rehabilitation*. But, commenting on the second of these, *The Sentence of the Court* (4th ed, at paras 3.5, 3.6) states:

'The incapacitation effect of custody of course operates whatever the deterrent effect – the offender is taken away from society. But it is modest. A Home Office study has estimated that if all sentences of imprisonment were reduced by 6 months . . . the annual increase in convictions would be only 1.6 per cent. These findings omit offences which are not "cleared up", and should therefore be viewed with caution. They do, however, suggest that no realistic increase in prison terms would make a substantial impact on crime rates simply by virtue of locking up the particular offenders caught, convicted and sentenced . . . It is, of course, very difficult in conducting studies of this kind to adjust for all the potentially relevant variables, and it would be wrong to conclude from these results that sentences are never an effective deterrent in individual cases or that deterrence is not relevant to sentencing – still less that the general deterrent effect on the population of the existing structure of penalties is non-existent. What they might be taken to suggest is rather that a sentence should not normally be justified on merely deterrent or therapeutic grounds – either that the offender will be "cured" or that others need to be discouraged from similar crimes. It may be that properly reflecting the relative gravity of the offence, and fairness between different offenders, are more important aims in the individual case.'

The Judicial Studies Board has advised magistrates as follows:

'The Object of the Sentence
Consider the need to
— Punish the offender
— Deter the offender
— Deter others
— Rehabilitate the offender
— Compensate the victim
— Protect the public
— Reflect public concern
and decide on the relative importance of these considerations in each case.'
[*The Structure of a Decision* (1986)]

and has put forward the following guidelines for custodial sentences:

'Custodial Sentences
1. If considering custody for a person under 21 consult the Clerk as to statutory requirements and statement of reasons.
2. If considering custody:
   (a) must the defendant be given a chance to be represented?
   (b) impose custody only if necessary – would CSO be equally appropriate?
   (c) give reasons for imprisonment if not previously imposed
   (d) impose the shortest appropriate term
   (e) can the sentence be suspended wholly or in part? (only applies to offenders of 21 and over)
   (f) if more than one offence, should sentences run concurrently or consecutively? (should be concurrent unless good reasons for making consecutive eg offences of different types or offences on bail)
   (g) is it appropriate to give a discount for guilty plea?'

[*The Structure of a Decision* (1986)]

All these matters are dealt with in the text at appropriate points, with the exception of that mentioned in 'g'. It is a well established principle in the Crown Court that a discount should be awarded for a guilty plea and it is clear from the advice that this is intended to apply in the magistrates' court also. There is no 'set discount', but the reports of appeal cases disclose regular discounts of up to one third of the sentence which would otherwise have been imposed: and see under *The plea*, 8d.27.

In *R v Sargeant* (1974) 60 Cr App R 74 Lawton LJ said, at p. 77, that the classic principles of sentencing are summed up in four words, *retribution, deterrence, prevention* and *rehabilitation*:

'I will start with retribution. The Old Testament concept of an eye for an eye and a tooth for a tooth no longer plays any part in our criminal law. There is, however, another aspect of retribution which is frequently overlooked; it is that society, through the courts, must show its abhorrence of particular types of crime, and the only way in which the courts can show this is by the sentences they pass. The courts do not have to reflect public opinion. On the other hand courts must not disregard it. Perhaps the main duty of the court is to lead public opinion. Anyone who surveys the criminal scene at the present time must be alive to the appalling problem of violence. Society, we are satisfied, expects the courts to deal with violence. The weapons which the courts have at their disposal for doing so are few. We are satisfied that in most cases fines are not sufficient punishment for senseless violence . . .

I turn now to the element of deterrence . . . There are two aspects of deterrence: deterrence of the offender and deterrence of likely offenders. Experience has shown over the years that deterrence of the offender is not a very useful approach, because those who have their wits about them usually find the closing of prison gates an experience which they do not want again. If they learn that lesson, there is unlikely to be a high degree of recidivism anyway. So far as deterrence of others is concerned, it is the experience of the courts that deterrent sentences are of little value in respect of offences which are committed on the spur of the moment, either in hot blood or in drink or both. Deterrent sentences may very well be of considerable value where crime is premeditated. Burglars, robbers and users of firearms and weapons may very well be put off by deterrent sentences . . .

We come now to the element of prevention. Unfortunately it is one of the facts of life that there are some offenders for whom neither deterrence nor rehabilitation works. They will go on committing as long as they are able to do so. In those cases the only protection which the public has is that such persons should be locked up for a long period . . .

Finally, there is the principle of rehabilitation. Some 20 to 25 years ago there was a view abroad, held by many people in executive authority, that short sentences were of little value, because there was not enough time to give in prison the benefit of training. That view is no longer held as firmly as it was.'

IMPRISONMENT

8d.01   For adults (ie those aged 21 and over) only

A sentence of imprisonment, *which includes a suspended sentence and a partly suspended sentence*, may not be passed on a person under 21, nor may such a person be committed to prison for any reason: s.1(1) CJA 1982. But this does not prevent the committal to prison of a person under 21 who is *remanded* in custody or *committed* to custody *for trial or sentence* s.1(2)).

8d.02   Maximum and minimum sentences

The *maximum* term of imprisonment which may be imposed by a magistrates' court is usually set out in the statute creating the offence. However, a magistrates' court does not have power to impose imprisonment for more than six months in respect of any one offence: s.31 MCA 1980. Section 34 makes it clear that the court is not bound to impose the maximum sentence. A magistrates' court may not impose imprisonment for *less than five days*: s.132.

But see *Concurrent and Consecutive Sentences*, 8d.03.

8d.03   Concurrent and consecutive sentences

Sentences of imprisonment and youth custody may be ordered to take effect *concurrently* or, subject to limits, *consecutively*: s.133 MCA 1980. The effects are:

(i)   sentences of imprisonment and youth custody, including suspended sentences and partly suspended sentences, imprisonment or detention in default of payment of a fine, may be consecutive to others imposed at the same time or earlier:

(ii) where two or more consecutive periods are imposed by the same magistrates' court they may not in total exceed *six months*, or *12 months* if two or more of the sentences are for offences *triable either way* (except offences tried summarily under s.22(2), ie criminal damage of a value below £400).

(iii) these limitations (of six or 12 months) do not apply when the sentence is consecutive to an earlier sentence (including a suspended sentence from an earlier occasion now being activated).

The High Court has given guidance *as to the form in which consecutive sentences should be pronounced*:

Attention has been drawn to a difficulty which sometimes arises when a sentence is expressed to begin 'at the expiration of the term of imprisonment you are now serving', or words to the same effect. If, as sometimes happens, the prisoner is already subject to two or more consecutive terms of imprisonment the effect of such a formula is that the new sentence will begin at the expiration of the term that he is *then* serving which may be the first of two conseutive terms. This will often not be the intention of the court giving the new sentence. It is suggested that the simplest course would be to use some such formula as '*consecutive to the total period of imprisonment to which you are already subject.*' The only exception to the use of such a formula would be if the intention was that the new sentence should be concurrent with one of the previous sentences:

Practice Note [1959] 2 All ER 144.

As to the need to indicate clearly *the total effective period* of detention, the Court of Criminal Appeal has issued the following guidance in relation to trials on indictment:

The attention of this court has been drawn to the fact that in many cases when a prisoner has been sentenced on more than one count only one sentence, say three years' imprisonment, is recorded on the indictment without indicating whether it is 'concurrent on each count' or otherwise. No doubt this is because the court in question has been concentrating on the total period of imprisonment appropriate and has omitted specifically to say that it is intended to be concurrent on each count. While in the absence of any reference to a sentence being consecutive it is no doubt intended to be concurrent, we think that this should, to avoid confusion, be expressly stated in the presence of the prisoner and entered on the indictment. Clerks of the peace and clerks of assize should, therefore, in such a case consult the court before the prisoner leaves the dock and ask the court to state expressly that the sentence is concurrent on all counts, or as the case may be, and then make the appropriate entry on the indictment:

Practice Direction [1962] 1 All ER 417; and see *Re Hastings* [1958] 1 WLR 372.

In the ordinary way consecutive sentences should not be passed for what is in effect one act and one offence: *R v Cowburn* [1959] Crim LR 590; *R v Hussain* [1962] Crim LR 712. Thus, if two charges 'arise out of precisely the same facts and involve, so to speak, the same criminality on the part of the (defendant)' there is no possible reason for passing consecutive sentences: *R v Torr* [1966] 1 WLR 52 (obtaining goods by false pretences and obtaining credit by false pretences in respect of the same transaction). On the other hand, consecutive sentences may properly be passed for the theft of a car and the subsequent obtaining of money by deception through its sale: *R v Bishoppe* [1973] Crim LR 583; and for burglary and going equipped therefor: *R v Ferris* [1973] Crim LR 642. If an assault on a police officer is part and parcel of a substantive offence (in that case robbery) and is to be treated as an aggravation of it this can be reflected in the sentence for the original offence and the sentence for the assault may be ordered concurrently. On the other hand when the offender assaults the police in an effort to escape, the sentence for the substantive offence can be fixed independently of that for the assault and the sentence for the assault can be dealt with by a separate and consecutive sentence: *R v Kastercum* (1972) 56 Cr App R 298; *R v Hill* (1983) *The Times*, 30 June. Similarly, consecutive sentences may be justified where the offender (i) takes a vehicle without consent and (ii) drives it while disqualified and whilst unfit: *R v Dillon* (1985) 149 JP 182.

A multiplicity of short consecutive sentences should not be passed in respect of a number of similar offences forming a series of transactions. It is the overall picture that matters and the court should decide what the overall sentence should be: *R v Brown* (1970) 50 Cr App R 176; *R v Simpson* [1969] Crim LR 383.

It is wrong to impose a sentence of imprisonment consecutive to one of detention in a detention centre (which, it seems, would be possible in magistrates' courts where detention is already being served). The correct course is to order the imprisonment to commence forthwith: *R v Raisis* [1969] 1 WLR 1805. Likewise, it was wrong to make one sentence *partly* consecutive to another: *R v Gregory and Mills* (1969) 133 JP 337.

Restrictions on first prison sentence   8d.04

A sentence of imprisonment may not be passed on a person on whom such a sentence has not previously been passed by any court in the United Kingdom unless the court is of the opinion that no other method of dealing with him is appropriate: s.20(1) PCCA 1973.

8d.05   Social inquiry reports, legal representation and legal aid

For the purposes of s.20(1) PCCA 1973, the court must obtain and
consider information about the offender's circumstances and must take
into account any information before the court which is relevant to his
character and his *physical and mental condition*: s.20(1). Where a sentence of imprisonment is passed in such a case, the court *must state the
reason for its opinion* that no other method is appropriate *and the reason
must be specified in the warrant and the register*: s.20(2).

The court must obtain a social inquiry report unless of the opinion that
this is *unnecessary*: s.20A(1), (2). The report must be from a probation
officer: s.20A(7). If the court does not obtain a social inquiry report it
must state in open court the reason for its opinion why it was unnecessary:
s.20A(3). The reason must be specified in the warrant and entered in the
register: s.20A(4). Failure to obtain a social inquiry report does not
invalidate sentence, but the appeal court must obtain one unless this is
considered unnecessary: s.20A(5).

The court may not pass a sentence of imprisonment, *including a
suspended sentence and a partly suspended sentence* on an *unrepresented*
offender unless, having been informed of his right to apply for legal aid
and having had the opportunity to do so, he refused or failed to apply or
was refused legal aid on grounds of means: s.21.

8d.06   The need for shorter sentences

In recent years, realisation of the limited rehabilitative effects of
imprisonment and the pressure on prison accommodation have led the
judges to examine more carefully the types of offender who should
receive a custodial sentence and the length of such sentences. In *R v Bibi*
(1980) 71 Cr App R 363 Lord Lane CJ said,

> Many offenders can be dealt with equally justly and effectively by a sentence of six or nine
> months' imprisonment as by one of 18 months or three years. We have in mind not only
> the obvious case of the first offender for whom any prison sentences, however short,
> might be an adequate punishment and deterrent, but other types of case as well. The less
> serious types of factory or shopbreaking; the minor cases of sexual indecency; the more
> petty frauds where small amounts of money are involved; the fringe participant in more
> serious crime; all these are examples of cases where the shorter sentence would be
> appropriate. There are, on the other hand, some offences for which, generally speaking,
> only the medium or longer sentences will be appropriate. For example, most robberies;
> most offences involving serious violence; use of a weapon to wound; burglary of private
> dwelling-houses; planned crime for wholesale profit; active large scale trafficking in
> dangerous drugs. These are only examples. It would be impossible to set out a catalogue
> of those offences which do and those which do not merit more severe treatment. So much
> will, obviously, depend upon the circumstances of each individual offender and each
> individual offence. What the court can and should do is to ask itself whether there is any
> compelling reason why a shorter sentence should not be passed. We are not aiming at
> uniformity of sentence; that would be impossible. We are aiming at uniformity of
> approach. (18 months upheld for burglary of a department store).

In *R v Upton* (1980) 71 Cr App R 102, Lord Lane CJ said:

> . . . the time has come to appreciate that non-violent petty offenders should not be
> allowed to take up what has become valuable space in prison. If there really is no
> alternative, as we believe to be the case here, to an immediate prison sentence, then it
> should be as short as possible. Sentencing judges should appreciate that overcrowding in
> many of the penal establishments in this country is such that a prison sentence, however
> short, is a very unpleasant experience indeed for the inmates. (Six months' imprisonment
> too long for small theft by deputy manager of supermarket).

8d.07   Suspended Sentences

When passing a prison sentence a magistrates' court may order that its
operation shall be suspended for a period of *one to two years*: s.22 PCCA

1973; but *only* where a sentence of imprisonment would have been appropriate in the absence of this power: s.22(2); and see *R v Jeffrey* (1985) 7 Cr App R (S) 11.

A court passing a suspended sentence for one offence may not make a probation order in respect of another: s.22(3).

When a court passes a suspended sentence its *first duty* is to consider *what would be the appropriate immediate custodial sentence,* to pass that, and *then to go on* to consider whether there are grounds for suspending it. What the court must not do is pass a longer custodial sentence than it would otherwise do, simply because it is suspended: *R v Mah Wing* (1983) 5 Cr App R (S) 347. It has been held in relation to a trial on indictment that a *fine may be imposed in addition* to a suspended sentence *on the same offence*: *R v Leigh* (1970) 54 Cr App R 169; *R v Ffoulkes* [1976] Crim LR 458. The same principle must apply in the magistrates' court, *semble*.

There is nothing wrong in principle in passing a forthwith sentence of imprisonment on an offender already subject to a suspended sentence, even when he is not in breach of the latter: *R v Gibbons* [1969] Crim LR 210; *R v Sorrell* (1971) 55 Cr App R 573. It has been said that the former rule that it was wrong to pass two prison sentences, one suspended and the other forthwith must be regarded as superseded by the thinking in the Criminal Law Act 1977 which allows for partly suspended sentences: *R v Ipswich Crown Court, ex p. Williamson* (1982) 4 Cr App R (S) 348. But this decision, which seems to involve tortuous logic, must be doubted after the case of *R v Crawley* [1985] Crim LR 58 which decided that it is *not correct* to pass an immediate sentence of imprisonment on one offence and extend the operational period of a suspended sentence on another.

Breach of a suspended sentence 8d.08

If within the operational period of a suspended sentence the offender commits in Great Britain an offence punishable with imprisonment, the suspended sentence must be ordered to take effect unaltered, either consecutively to or concurrently with any other sentence, *unless* the court is of opinion that this would be *unjust* in view of all the circumstances, including the facts of the subsequent offence, when it may mitigate the sentence or make no order: s.23 PCCA 1973.

The *comparative triviality* of an offence committed during the operational period of a suspended sentence may be a good ground for declining to put a suspended sentence into operation, particularly when the later offence is *in a different category* to the first offence: *R v Moylan* [1970] 1 QB 143. But the *mere fact* that it is of a different character to the original offence is no ground for refraining from bringing the suspended sentence into operation: *R v Saunders* (1970) 54 Cr App R 247; and see *R v Williams* [1969] Crim LR 669; *R v Griffiths* (1969) 133 JP 507; *R v Stevens* (1970) 55 Cr App R 154; *R v Peck* [1970] Crim LR 172; *R v Cobbold* [1971] Crim LR 436; *R v Barton* [1974] Crim LR 555; *R v Craine* (1981) 3 Cr App R (S) 198.

It is not a pre-condition to the *activation* of a suspended sentence that a custodial sentence should be passed for the later offence: *R v Cobbold* [1971] Crim LR 436; *R v Isaacs* [1980] Crim LR 666 (fine for subsequent offence); compare *R v McElhorne* (1983) 5 Cr App R (S) 53; *R v Seymour* [1983] Crim LR 410 (community service orders): *R v Stewart* (1984) 6 Cr App R (S) 166; and *R v Jagodzinski* (1986) 8 Cr App R (S) 150. It seems from these last two cases that where a person commits a further offence during the operational period of a suspended sentence which does not itself warrant a sentence of imprisonment, then this will be *strong evidence* that it may be unjust to activate the suspended sentence. When the suspended sentence was passed by the *Crown Court*, a magistrates' court dealing with the offender may commit him to the Crown Court or take no action except to notify that court: s.24. There is power in s.25 for the Crown Court or a magistrates' court to compel the appearance of an offender who falls to be dealt with.

8d.09 *Concurrent* and *consecutive* suspended sentences

Supended sentences, like other prison sentences may be ordered to be either *concurrent* or *consecutive*: s.133 MCA 1980. It is imperative when passing two or more suspended sentences to indicate, eg for the purposes of s.57(2) PCCA 1973, whether *as between themselves* they are to be served *consecutively* or *concurrently*: *R v Wilkinson* [1970] 1 QB 123. But it is against the spirit and intention of the Act to impose a suspended sentence, whether consecutive to or concurrent with a prison sentence then being served: *R v Sapiano* (1968) 32 Cr App R 674; *R v Morris* [1970] Crim LR 172. Similarly, when passing a suspended sentence (as opposed to ordering that it shall be put into effect) it is wrong to order that it shall take effect consecutively to any other suspended sentence already imposed: *R v Blakeway* [1969] 2 All ER 1133; *R v Towner* [1970] Crim LR 358. As to ordering that suspended sentences *take effect* consecutively see s.23(2), *infra* and the commentary thereto.

8d.10 Suspended sentence supervision order

Although a magistrates' court *cannot* make a suspended sentence supervision order, it does have certain functions with respect thereto. When a suspended sentence of imprisonment is passed for a term *in excess of six months on a single offence*, the Crown Court may at the same time make a suspended sentence supervision order in accordance with s.26 PCCA 1973. Such an order may stipulate a period of supervision not longer than the operational period of the suspended sentence during which the offender will be under the supervision of a probation officer. The suspended sentence supervision order must specify the petty sessions area in which the offender resides. A copy of the order together with relevant documents and information must be sent to the clerk of the magistrates' court: s.26(4), (5). The magistrates' court may, *and on the application of the supervising officer, must* amend the order when the offender moves to another area: s.26(6), (7). The order *may* be discharged by the magistrates' court unless the Crown Court included in the order *a direction to the contrary*: s.27(9). Failure without reasonable cause to comply with any requirement of a suspended sentence supervision order may be punished by a fine of up to £400: s.27(3).

Note: a suspended sentence supervision order is *not* a type of suspended sentence, but an order ancillary to a suspended sentence.

8d.11 Partly suspended sentence

When passing a sentence of imprisonment on an offender who has attained the *age of 21* for a term of *not less than three months and not more than two years* a court may order that, after he has served part of his sentence in prison, the *remainder* of it should be held *in suspense*: s.47(1) CLA 1977. The part to be served must be *not less than 28 days* and the part held in suspense *not less than one quarter* of the whole term: s.47(2). A partly suspended sentence may not be passed unless a wholly suspended sentence would be inappropriate: s.47(1A).

Partly suspended sentences are subject to the restrictions on passing any prison sentence, and to the requirement concerning legal representation: s.47(1B). Where a court passes a partly suspended sentence it may not make a probation order in respect of any other offence: Sch.9, para 1. Imposing a partly suspended sentence on a person already subject to an effective sentence rarely serves any purpose and should be discouraged: *R v Young* [1985] Crim LR 526. It is *undesirable* to sentence an offender to a substantive term of imprisonment and a partly suspended sentence at the same time: *R v McCarthy* (1982) 4 Cr App R (S) 364.

The following guidelines were laid down by Lord Lane CJ in *R v Clarke* [1983] 3 All ER 232:

> Before imposing a partly suspended sentence the court should ask itself the following question: First of all, is this a case where a custodial sentence is really necessary? If it is not it should pass a non-custodial sentence. But if it is necessary then the court should ask itself secondly this: can we make a community service order as an equivalent to imprisonment, or can we suspend the whole sentence? That problem requires very careful consideration. It is easy to slip into a partly suspended sentence because the court does not have the courage of its own convictions. That temptation must be resisted. If it is possible to make a community service order or to suspend the whole of the sentence, then of course, that should be done. If not, then the third point arises: what is the shortest sentence the court can properly impose? In many cases, of which an obvious example is the case of the first offender for whom a short term of imprisonment is a sufficient shock, without any suspension, that would be enough. Sometimes 14 or 28 days may suffice, which is shorter than the shortest term which is at present available under s.47.
>
> In that case that should be the order of the court, without any partial suspension at all. The imposition of a very short term will also make possible the ordering of a fine or a compensation order in addition, when such a course is appropriate. If imprisonment is necessary, and if a very short sentence is not enough, and if it is not appropriate to suspend the sentence altogether, then partial suspension should be considered. Great care must be taken to ensure that the power is not used in a way which may serve to increase the length of sentence. It is not possible satisfactorily to forecast the precise way in which the provisions of s.47 might be used. In general the type of case that we have in mind is where the gravity of the offence is such that at least three months' imprisonment is merited, but when there are mitigating circumstances which point towards a measure of leniency not sufficient to warrant total suspension. Examples are always dangerous, but we venture very tentatively to suggest a few: first of all, some serious 'one off' acts of violence which are usually met with the immediate terms of imprisonment: some cases of burglary which at present warrant 18 months' or two years' imprisonment, where the offender is suitably qualified in terms of his record: some cases of fraud on public departments or some credit card frauds, where a short immediate sentence would be insufficient; some cases of handling involving medium-range sums of money; some thefts involving breach of trust; some cases of stealing from employers. All these are examples of cases where it may be possible to suspend part of the sentence without harm to the public and with benefit to the prisoner.
>
> We would like to echo the words of the Advisory Council on the Penal System in para 282 of their report on the review of maximum penalties: 'We view the partially suspended sentence as a legitimate means of exploiting one of the few reliable pieces of criminological knowledge – that many offenders sent to prison for the first time do not subsequently re-offend. We see it not as a means of administering a 'short, sharp shock', nor as a substitute for a wholly suspended sentence, but as espcially applicable to serious first offenders or first-time prisoners who are bound to have to serve some time in prison, but who may well be effectively deterred by eventually serving only a small part or even the minimum sentence appropriate to the offence. This, in our view, must be its principal role. We would like to add another type of offender: prisoners whose last term of imprisonment was some considerable time ago. We think that the power can be used on occasions where something more than a short sentence of immediate imprisonment is required to mark public disapproval and as a deterrent to others, but where the circumstances of the particular offender are such that some short term of immediate imprison-

ment, coupled with the threat involved in the suspension of the remainder, is enough to punish him for what he has done and to deter him in the future.

8d.12   Breach of partly suspended sentence

If at any time after the making of the order an offender is convicted of an offence punishable with imprisonment committed *during the whole period of the original sentence* a competent court may restore the part of the sentence held in suspense and order him to serve it: s.47(3) CLA 1977. The 'whole period' of a sentence is defined in s.47(6); and the 'competent court' in Sch.9, para 2. If the court is of the opinion that in view of all the circumstances, including the facts of the subsequent offence it would be *unjust* fully to restore the part of the sentence held in suspense it must either restore the lesser part or declare, with reasons given, its decision to make no order: s.47(4). The court restoring part of a partly suspended sentence may direct that it take effect immediately or consecutively to another sentence: s.47(5). NB that once an order has been made restoring part of a sentence no further such order may be made: s.47(4A).

8d.13   Restrictions on first prison sentence

Note The *Restrictions* set out at 8d.17 apply equally to *suspended* and *partly suspended sentences*; and see *Social inquiry reports, legal representation and legal aid*, 8d.20.

8d.14   YOUNG OFFENDERS (AGES 17 TO 20, INCLUSIVE)

The only custodial sentences for young offenders are *detention centre orders* and *youth custody sentences*. Broadly speaking, detention centre orders are for short sentences and youth custody for long. While training is part of the regime of both types of sentence it is clear from HOC 42/1983 that training is not intended to be the purpose for which young offenders should receive these sentences. It would be wrong in principle therefore for a court to decide that a youth custody or a detention centre regime was the more suitable for the offender and then to fix a length of sentence which would allow that. Instead, the court should first determine the length of sentence in accordance with the same principles as a sentence of imprisonment and the institution in which the young offender should serve a sentence of that length will then fall to be determined according to law, ie on whether it is up to 4 months (detention centre), or more than 4 months (youth custody). But *note* the effects of the CJA 1988 when in force: 8d.15, 8d.16.

Since a partially suspended sentence is not available for a young offender the proper approach where such a sentence would have been passed in the case of an adult is to pass an immediate sentence of the sort of length that would have been the un-suspended portion of a partially suspended sentence: *R v Dobbs and Hitchings* (1983) 5 Cr App R (S) 378; *R v Trew* [1985] Crim LR 168.

8d.15   Youth custody

A sentence of *youth custody* may be passed on an offender *under 21* years of age but *not less than 15* years convicted of an offence which is punishable with imprisonment in the case of a person aged 21 or over where the court considers a sentence of *more than four months* (or sentences of more than 4 months in aggregate) to be appropriate: s.6(1) CJA 1982.

The court must be of the opinion, for *reasons which must be stated in open court*, that the only appropriate method of dealing with the offender is to pass a custodial sentence: s.6(1). In addition, the *Restrictions on Custodial Sentences for Young Offenders*, 8d.17, must be satisfied.

The usual term of youth custody is a term exceeding four months: s.7(5). By s.7(6) the term in certain limited circumstances may be for less than this period but not less than 21 days as follows:

(i) a sentence of four months or less would be appropriate, but a detention centre order is precluded because of the offender's physical or mental condition or because he is serving or has served a sentence of youth custody for certain other sentences: s.6(2); or

(ii) the offender is *female* and has attained the age of 17: s.6(4).

The maximum term of youth custody may not exceed the maximum period of imprisonment which may be imposed in the case of someone over 21: s.7(1) CJA 1982. Magistrates' courts are limited to a maximum of six months' youth custody for any one offence: s.31 MCA 1980. If a longer sentence is called for they may in certain circumstances commit the offender to the Crown Court for sentence in accordance with s.38 (*Committal for Sentence*, Chapter 8e).

The court has the same power to pass consecutive sentences of youth custody as if they were sentences of imprisonment: s.7(2) CJA 1982; see *Concurrent and consecutive sentences*, 8d.03. A sentence of imprisonment on someone over 21 may be made consecutive to a sentence of youth custody *already being served*: s.7(3). The place in which a youth custody sentence is to be served is determined in accordance with s.12 of the 1982 Act. This gives effect to the Secretary of State's undertaking that anyone receiving a term of between four and 18 months youth custody will be guaranteed a place in a youth custody centre. Others may have to serve their sentence in a remand centre or prison. There is *no power to suspend* a sentence of youth custody, but the issue of a warrant of commitment on a fine etc default may be postponed on terms: see 8b.19.

Note that youth custody and detention centre are both replaced by detention in a young offender institution' under the CJA 1988 when in force: see 8d.74 *et seq* and Appendix III.

Detention centre   8d.16

A *detention centre order* may be made on a *male* offender aged *14 to 20 years* convicted of an offence punishable in the case of a person of 21 years with imprisonment: s.4(1) CJA 1982. The court must consider that a custodial sentence of no more than four months is the only appropriate method of dealing with him: s.4(1). The *Restrictions on Custodial Sentences for Young Offenders* must first be satisfied: 8d.17.

There is no requirement for the offender to receive a medical examination before a detention centre order is made, but an order may not be made where detention would be unsuitable because of the offender's mental or physical condition: s.4(5)(a) CJA 1982. Advice and arrangements concerning securing a medical report from a 'police surgeon' on the day of conviction are contained in HOC 122/1983.

A detention centre order may not be made if the offender is serving or has ever served a sentence of youth custody or certain other offences: s.4(5)(b). This latter prohibition may be overridden where there are special circumstances, whether relating to the offence or to the offender, which warrant the making of a detention centre order in his case: s.4(6).

There is no prohibition on the making of a second or subsequent detention centre order.

The *minimum* period is 21 days: s.4(3). The *maximum* term is four months: s.4(1); so long as this does not exceed the maximum term of imprisonment had the offender been 21: s.4(2).

Consecutive detention centre orders are allowed by s.5(1); so long as they do not exceed in *aggregate* a period of four months: s.5(2). Any excess is automatically remitted if the offender is younger than 15: s.5(3). In the case of an offender aged 15 or older, a sentence of excess length is deemed to be one of youth custody: s.5(4).

There is *no power* to suspend a detention centre order, although the issue of a warrant of commitment to detention in default of payment etc may be postponed on terms: see Chapter 9. A magistrates' court *may not* in a person's absence make a detention centre order: s.11(3) MCA 1980.

Administratively, detention centres are divided into *senior detention centres* (for offenders aged 17–20) and *junior detention centres* (for offenders aged 14–16). There are *no detention centres for females*. The detention centres available to each court are listed in HOC 18/1985 (amendments to which are notified to courts on a regular basis) – see HOC 6/1986 (for senior centres) and HOC 82/1986 (for junior centres)), which also requests courts, *after* making a detention centre order, to ascertain whether a place is available and suggests the procedure to be followed if it is not. The detention centre regime is described in GOC 9/1985.

Note that youth custody and detention centre are both replaced by 'detention in a young offender institution' under the CJA 1988 when in force: see 8d.74 *et seq* and Appendix III.

8d.17 **Restrictions on custodial sentences for young offenders**

Since 1982, no-one below the age of 21 can be sentenced to imprisonment and there are severe restrictions concerning the circumstances in which sentences of *youth custody* or *detention centre orders* can be used. It should be noted that these restrictions will be further enhanced by [s.121] CJA 1988: see Appendix III and the insertions to s.1(4) CJA 1982 at 8d.74. Although the Court of Appeal was at first slow to respond to the provisions of s.1(4) CJA 1982, *infra*, there are now quite literally hundreds of appeal rulings in which the criteria set out in that sub-section have been examined and elaborated upon. It is also impossible for either magistrates or practitioners to comprehend the true extent or import of the young offender restrictions without a good knowledge of the availability of local 'community alternatives', as they are usually styled. Given the shifts in sentencing patterns which have taken place in relation to juvenile offenders since 1982 (in broad figures the substitution of 'alternatives' for around fifty per cent of custodial dispositions) it seems safe to assume that the young offender age group, ie 17 to 20 inclusive, is likely to be the next group to feel the full effect of the restrictions. The provisions are summarised below, followed by a selection of the more significant appeal cases.

No court may pass a youth custody sentence or make a detention centre order unless it is of the opinion that *no other method* of dealing with the offender *is appropriate* because:

    (a) it appears to the court that he is *unable or unwilling* to respond to non-custodial sentences; or

(b) because a custodial sentence is necessary for the *protection of the public*; or

(c) because the offence was *so serious* that a non-custodial sentence cannot be justified: s.1(4) CJA 1982. The court must then go on to state the reason why a particular head applies and to record this in the register and the warrant, *infra*.

The court must first obtain a social inquiry report: s.2(2) CJA 1982, save where in the circumstances of the case, it is of opinion that this is *unnecessary*: s.2(3). The report can be either from a probation officer or a social worker of a local authority social services department: s.2(1). The court must also obtain and consider information about the circumstances and take into account any information before the court relevant to the offender's character and his physical and mental condition: s.2(1). Legal representation/legal aid must also be offered: see next section.

The reason why no other method is appropriate must be stated in open court: s.2(4), and recorded in the warrant of commitment and the court register: s.2(7). The reasons must explain why exceptions apply, not merely which one(s). Sentencers must have regard to the criteria in s.1(4), whether or not they are brought to their attention: *R v Bradbourn* (1985) 7 Cr App R (S) 180; *R v Passmore* (1985) 7 Cr App R (S) 377 (a 'drastic step' to take away a young man's liberty for the first time).

The position can thus be seen as a series of hurdles, all of which must be surmounted before a custodial sentence can be used, viz:
— a social enquiry report, unless 'unnecessary'
— the offer of legal representation/legal aid
— the decision that no other method is appropriate
— a statutory 'ground' for this, ie
  '*unable or unwilling*'; or
  '*protection of the public*'; or
  '*so serious*'
— a reason for the 'ground'; and then
— a correct announcement and record of the reason.

Note also the effect on the 'hurdles' of the CJA 1988, when in force.

The vast majority of the appeal cases deal with the '*so serious*' exception, although there is some judicial guidance on the application of the two remaining heads.

Whilst every case must turn on its facts, some indication of the trend since 1983 (when the provisions first came into force) can be seen from the following outline summaries of the main points from the more significant appeal decisions.

[*The next paragraph is 8d.20*]

Social inquiry reports, legal representation and legal aid 8d.20

A youth custody sentence may not be passed or a detention centre order made unless a social inquiry report has been obtained or dispensed with: s.2(2) CJA 1982, and unless, in the case of an unrepresented defendant unless he has knowingly refused or failed to apply for legal aid or has had an application for legal aid refused on the ground of means: s.3 CJA 1982.

Cases on s.1(4) CJA 1982

Burglary and theft 8d.21

A single domestic burglary involving the taking of a video recorder was not 'so serious', and a community service order would have been appropriate, despite a recommendation against this in the social inquiry report:

R v Bates (1985) 7 Cr App R (S) 105; similarly a domestic burglary (bathroom suite) and a school burglary (equipment valued at £508) were not 'so serious', and a community service order would have been appropriate: *R v Grimes* (1986) 7 Cr App R (S) 137. Neither did the 'protection' criteria apply and such offences were '. . . not offences at the upper end of the scale of criminality': per Russell J, *ibid*; and see *R v Moffett* (1984) 6 Cr App R (S) 90 (probation). In *R v Seymour* [1983] Crim L R 635, a community service order was substituted for an eighteen months sentence of youth custody on a burglar with a 'bad record' of offending where he was 'beginning to realise' where his offending would lead to. But contrast *R v Pilford* (1985) 7 Cr App R (S) 23 (16 year old who was part of a gang which was engaged in several burglaries of dwellings and with 6 previous convictions 'richly deserved' 12 months' youth custody).

In the somewhat individual circumstances of *R v Hart and Hart* (1984) 5 Cr App R (S) 385, 12 months' youth custody was appropriate for two brothers who had committed relatively minor burglaries, but who were mentally subnormal and 'in need of training in a contained environment', and because they were 'a problem to the community'. Section 1(4) was not expressly mentioned, and it is *suggested* that no guidance of any general import emerges from this anomalous case.

In *R v Bradbourn* (1985) 7 Cr App R (S) 180, a shop assistant slipped £2 from the till into her handbag. A conditional discharge was substituted for the original sentence of 3 months youth custody after one month had been served. Holding that the offence was not 'so serious', Lawton LJ commented that further guidelines to explain the criteria were unnecessary and would only lead to greater difficulties – '. . . courts can recognise an elephant when they see one, but may not find it necessary to define it'. But Lawton LJ did add that the phrase 'so serious' etc: '. . . comes to this: the kind of offence which when committed by a young person would make right-thinking members of the public, knowing all the facts, feel that justice had not been done by the passing of any sentence other than a custodial one'.

Offence 'labels' are not important, rather it is the circumstances of the particular offence, *ibid*. Even some robberies might not be 'so serious': *ibid*.

A 'gross breach of trust' and 'cunning' will, however, attract custody: *R v Dunning* [1984] Crim LR 635 (18 month's youth custody for receptionist who altered cheques amounting to £66,650 to pay them into her own account).

One of the few appeal cases to mention the 'unable or unwilling' criterion is *R v Munday* (1985) 7 Cr App R (S) 216, where the offender, aged 17, pleaded guilty to six offences of theft of ladies clothing of a total value of £168, committed during a single afternoon. After first rejecting the 'protection' and 'so serious' criteria, the Court of Appeal went on to state that a recent previous conviction for a single offence of theft was '. . . too slender a basis for saying that he was unable or unwilling to respond to non-custodial penalties': per Lord Lane CJ. Fines were substituted, the appellant having served 2 months of a 6 months' sentence of youth custody.

8d.22   Robbery and violence

In *R v Willis* (1984) 6 Cr App R (S) 68, 12 months' youth custody was upheld for robbery with an imitation firearm under the 'so serious' criteria, although the 'protection' criteria was said not to be met; similarly in *R v Bright* (1984), unreported, where 6 months youth custody was upheld when imposed for threatening a cashier by pretending to have a gun. Some robberies may not be 'so serious': *obiter* in *R v Bradbourn, supra*; but *note*, however that more serious forms of robbery – particularly where violence has been used – have consistently attracted *long* sentences in the Crown Court.

A group attack on a stranger causing actual bodily harm was 'so serious' as to merit 3 months detention centre – despite a recommendation for community service – in *R v Jeoffroy* (1985) 7 Cr App R (S) 135; and see *R v Dobbs and Hitchings* (1983) 5 Cr App R (S) 378 (9 months youth custody where three youths attacked a man out walking his dog causing grievous bodily harm); '. . . Young men who behaved in such a way should lose their liberty straight away . . . society must mark its disapproval of young bullies who beat up inoffensive citizens': per Lord Lane CJ, *ibid*; see also *R v English* (1985) 7 Cr App R (S) 65 (attack with jack handle – racial overtones); *R v Senior* [1984] Crim L R 439 (2 months for unprovoked attack *by* girl of 17).

Apparently serious offences have, however, sometimes resulted in rulings that non-custodial dispositions *are* appropriate: see, eg *R v McDermot* (1984) 6 Cr App R (S) 377 (12 months' youth custody for 'revenge attack' on proprietor of fish-bar with piece of wood causing wounding to scalp 'not wrong in principle', but Court of Appeal varied sentence to a community service order – a 'classical example where community service should have been considered . . . Taking into account all the circumstances, including . . . that the appellant was serving an apprenticeship': per Otton J); and see *R v West* (1983) 5 Cr App R (S) 206 and *R v Shenton* (1982) 4 Cr App R (S) 294 (community service where 'isolated offences); and *R v Gittings* [1985] Crim L R 246 ('glassing' under provocation – but 12 months youth custody correct on breach of original community service order).

As with adult offenders (see 8d.42), 'glassing' is 'so serious' and normally attracts custody: *R v Power* (1983) *The Times*, 25 May; *R v Allen* (1983) unreported, 14 October (6 months). But see *R v Gittings, supra*. Similarly, 'mugging' attracts custody even though actual injury may be slight: *R v Fleming and Dodge* (1984) 6 Cr App R (S) 222 (juveniles); and a *substantial* period of custody where there are aggravating features: *R v Spencer* (1985) 7 Cr App R (S) 1 (£3 taken from man walking his dog, man assaulted – 3 years); *R v O'Brien* (1984) 6 Cr App R (S) 274 (two separate 'street robberies' and assaults on 90 and 83 year old women, taking £790 and £1 – 5 years).

There is need for custodial sentences to deter those who use violence at or near football grounds: see *R v Wood* (1984) 6 Cr App R (S) 2 – an extended extract from which is reproduced under *Sentencing for Particular Offences* 8d.34.

Criminal damage and arson   8d.23

In *R v Travis and Others* (1985) 7 Cr App R (S) 149 three months detention centre orders were the correct sentence for 'tyre-slashing' by a group who damaged the tyres of 18 cars causing £1,000 worth of damage, irrespective of the effect on the offenders' (aged 15 to 17) education (as to which see also *R v Innes and Hopkins, infra*; but contrast the view taken in relation to an apprenticeship in *R v McDermot, supra*).

A number of appeal rulings established that whether 'arson' is 'so serious' depends not on the 'label', but on the particular circumstances.

In *R v Dewberry and Stone* (1985) 7 Cr App R (S) 202, a youth custody sentence of 12 months was replaced by a community service order in respect of a 17 year old who set fire to a parka against a temporary classroom, thereby doing £200 worth of damage. But, in respect of a juvenile who had additionally committed a separate offence which resulted in damage valued at £67,000 to another classroom, his offences were 'so serious'. In his case, 12 months' youth custody was substituted for 18 months' detention under s.53 CYPA 1933 (the 6 months' difference not justifying the use of s.53); see also *R v Swallow* (1985) 7 Cr App R (S) 22 (£66,000 damage to cafe – 12 months); *R v Innes and Hopkins* (1985) 7 Cr App R (S) 52 (£90,000 damage to school – 12 months – wrong to treat offenders differently because they were 'educated and had a promising future'). But *note* that it is the *intention* which is decisive, not the amount or value of the damage, since the result may be 'unfortunate': see *R v Swallow, supra*.

8d.24   Other offences

In *R v Emery* [1985] RTR 415, taking a motor vehicle without consent and reckless driving were held not to be 'so serious', despite evading the police during the events in question (community service substituted after 46 days of a 6 months' sentence had been served). But compare *R v Warrior* [1984] Crim LR 188 (9 months for driving whilst disqualified – but *note* that no reference was made to s.1(4) CJA 1982).

Where unlawful sexual intercourse occurred following drink, pornographic films and sexual activity, sentences of 9 months youth custody were upheld: *R v Forrest and Gray* [1984] Crim LR 764 (the offences were 'serious enough themselves').

In *R v Hooper* [1984] Crim LR 637 (permitting premises to be used for smoking cannabis), 3 months was 'absolutely right' – but a probation order was made because the appellant had found a job whilst on bail.

8d.25   Supervision on release

Anyone *under 22* years of age released from youth custody or detention centre otherwise than on licence will be under the supervision of a probation officer or social worker for various periods of time between three to 12 months: s.15 CJA 1982.

Failure without reasonable excuse to comply with requirements laid down by the Secretary of State is a summary offence punishable by a fine of £400 (level 3) or an appropriate custodial sentence not exceeding 30 days: s.15(11). The appropriate custodial sentence is stipulated in s.15(12) and the 21-day minimum period is waived for his offence: s.7(7). If breach proceedings result in a custodial sentence, such a sentence entails no extra supervision: s.15(13).

FACTORS AFFECTING SENTENCE

8d.26   Previous convictions

So far as a prison sentence is concerned previous convictions are *relevant to the likelihood* of redemption and the effectiveness of training, but where the object of a sentence is punitive or deterrent 'a man must not be sentenced on his record, he must be sentenced on the facts which have come out in evidence, or, alternatively, have been put before the court after a plea of guilty': *R v Griffiths*, 29 November 1966 (unreported). And see *R v Queen* (1981) 3 Cr App R (S) 245. In other words, 'a man has to be sentenced for the offences which he has committed': *R v Disbrey* [1967] Crim LR 431

Dealing with a man who, the court said, it was manifest had been sentenced on his record, Lawton LJ said in the case of *R v Lister*, 5 October 1972 (unreported): 'That is not a correct way of sentencing and the court wishes to emphasise that the proper way of sentencing is to look first at the offence itself and the circumstances in which it was committed, then to assess the proper sentence for the offence on the basis that there are no mitigating circumstances; and finally to look to see what the mitigating circumstances are, if any, to reduce the assessed sentence to give effect to the mitigating circumstances; see also *R v Webster* (1985) 7 Cr App R (S) 359.

The view that an offender should be sentenced for the *offence* and not on the basis of his *previous record* – which has gained increasing acceptance and support in recent years – is, however, difficult to reconcile with one significant provision affecting magistrates' courts, ie s.38 MCA 1980 under which liability to committal to the Crown Court for sentence depends exclusively on the *character* and *antecedents* of the offender, and not on the gravity of the offence, which can only be considered at the 'mode of trial' stage: see 4.02. *Character* and *antecedents* are wider than *previous convictions*, see *Previous convictions and antecedents* at 8.07, but it would be to ignore day to day reality to say that *previous convictions* are not the single biggest factor in committals by magistrates to the Crown Court for sentence. But if their relevance and effect is to reduce the scope for mitigation, then common practice is wrong apparently and s.38 is itself anomalous, *semble*.

The plea   8d.27

A principle grounded more in practical and economic factors than any sound tenets of justice is that whereby a person who pleads guilty is entitled to a 'discount' on account of that plea. The position concerning discounts is clearly set out in several appeal rulings on sentences imposed in the Crown Court. Insofar as magistrates are concerned there can be no difference in principle and, indeed, Skinner J, in an address to the Summer Conference of the Magistrates' Association in 1985 urged magistrates' courts to follow the Crown Court approach (although a working party of that Assocaition has suggested, more recently, that whilst the principle may be appropriate in the Crown Court – as in the magistrates' court in so far as custodial sentences are concerned – it may not be appropriate in relation to the generally smaller fines imposed in summary proceedings). The guidelines indicated by Skinner J are as follows:

1. A plea of guilty can be a potent mitigating factor and should normally result in a reduction in sentence in all cases except standard motoring offences such as exceeding the speed limit or using a motor vehicle without third party insurance. An early admission of guilt enhances the mitigating power of the plea.

2. The justification for such a discount is two-fold:
   (i) An admission can, and usually will, result in a substantial saving of court and police time.
   (ii) A recognition of guilt by an offender is an essential first step on the road to reformation.

3. The amount of reduction will vary greatly from case to case. When the evidence against an offender largely comes from his confession, it should be substantial. One example is the man charged with indecent

assault on a child as to which the child is the only witness. If by confessing at an early stage, he provides corroboration of the child and by pleading guilty he saves the child from giving evidence, a substantial discount should be, and should be said to be, given. Another, the dishonest clerk or servant (eg a club steward) who avoids the necessity of a lengthy examination of his employer's books and papers by admitting the nature and extent of his defalcations should similarly be given substantial credit for his (albiet belated) frankness. In such cases, a reduction of a six month's sentence to one of four months could be justified or of a fine from £200 to £150. On the other hand, where an offender has been caught red-handed and has no realistic alternative to pleading guilty, the allowance will be very much smaller, even minimal. The thief caught in the driving seat trying to start someone else's car or the burglar arrested inside the burgled premises are examples.

4. While the fact that a discount has been given should always be stated, the amount of the reduction should never be specified. Where, however, the offender's frankness results in a non-custodial sentence, or the suspension of what would otherwise have been an immediate custodial sentence, this can and should be made clear: 'Had it not been for your pleas of guilty and frankness with the police, you would have gone to prison today. As it is, however, we find it possible to suspend . . ./ make a community service order . . .', is a formula which can be used.

5. It is clear that a plea of guilty (especially when accompanied by other mitigating factors, eg good character) may enable a non-custodial sentence to be passed instead of one of immediate custody. In that case, the mitigating force of the plea will usually have been exhausted before the non-custodial options fall to be considered; but the principle also operates in cases where even without the plea, the sentence would have been non-custodial. The example of a fine has already been given: it should be reduced to allow for the plea. The number of hours work to be performed under a community service order should be scaled down in an appropriate case. Such a discount would not be appropriate in the case of a probation order: generally speaking the length of the order should be geared to the needs of the offender and the needs of the community to have some control over him. Any discount can be given if it becomes necessary to sentence him for the original offences on a breach of the order (a probation order not being, technically, 'a sentence').

[*The Magistrate*, vol. 41 no. 10, October 1985].

In *R v Harper* [1967] 3 All ER 619, reducing a sentence of imprisonment, Lord Parker CJ said: 'It is quite improper to use language which may convey that an accused is being sentenced because he has pleaded not guilty or because he has run his defence in a particular way. It is, however, proper to give an accused a lesser sentence if he has shown genuine remorse, amongst other things, by pleading guilty'; see also *R v Behman* (1967) 117 NLJ 834. However, 'it is undoubtedly right that a confession of guilt [in the context a plea changed from not guilty to guilty] should tell in favour of an accused person, for that is clearly in the public interest', *per* Edmund Davies LJ in *R v de Han* [1967] 3 All ER 618 sentence varied from four-and-a-half to three years when there was a change of plea after four prosecution witnesses had given evidence). The reduction cannot be expressed in percentage terms because of the individual nature of sentencing: *R v Williams* [1983] Crim LR 693. The principle applies to youth custody sentences also: *R v Stewart* [1983] Crim LR 830. For more recent re-iteration of the principle, see, eg *R v Pilford*

(1985) 7 Cr App R (S) 23; *R v Reynolds* (1985) 7 Cr App R (S) 23; and *R v Storey* (1986) 8 Cr App R (S) 301, where it was stated that '. . . the pressure on the Crown Courts resulting from the increasing number of criminal offences is such that great importance attaches to a substantial proportion of guilty defendants acknowledging their guilt': per Nolan J.

There are conflicting decisions whether it is proper to suspend a sentence of imprisonment on an offender who pleaded guilty, while not suspending it on a co-defendant who pleaded not guilty: *R v Hollymen* (1979) 1 Cr App R (S) 289 and *R v Tonks* (1979) 1 Cr App R (S) 293.

As to 'remorse', see eg *R v Alcock* [1967] Crim LR 66; or the lack of it: *R v O'Leary* [1965] Crim LR 56 – long held to be relevant to sentence. Failure to name an accomplice may be material to sentence if it is in defiance of the law, but not through fear: *R v Hogwood* [1969] Crim LR 209.

Conduct of the defence 8d.28

It is well established that the fact that the defence consists of an attack on the integrity of a police officer or the character of the prosecution witnesses should not be taken into account when passing sentence: *R v Harper* [1967] 3 All ER 619; *R v Scott* [1983] Crim LR 568; and see *R v Evans* (1986) 8 Cr App R (S) 197 (allegation that drugs 'planted' by police). Nor should sentence be increased because of the offenders 'attitude to society': *ibid.*

Similarly, it is *wrong to increase* the sentence simply because the court believes the defendant to have committed perjury during his trial: *R v Quinn* (1932) 23 Cr App R 196; *R v Dunbar* (1966) 51 Cr App R 57.

Prevalence of the offence 8d.29

The prevalence of a particular type of offence in a locality may be a ground for increasing the sentence: *R v Green* (1912) 76 JP 351; *R v Withers* (1935) 25 Cr App R 53. But for a single court deliberately to adopt a change of policy (eg by determining to sentence first offenders to imprisonment for driving under the influence of alcohol) in matters which affect every part of the country alike is improper: *R v Lavin* (1967) 51 Cr App R 378.

Wealth 8d.30

It is wrong to impose a prison sentence simply because the offender is too rich to be hurt by a fine: *R v Hanbury* (1979) 1 Cr App R (S) 243; or because he is too poor to pay an adequate fine: *R v Reeves* (1972) 56 Cr App R 366; *R v McGowan* [1975] Crim LR 113. The case of *R v Gormley* [1973] Crim LR 644 suggests that this course is not wrong where imprisonment is being imposed for another offence. For an argument that – contrary to popular conceptions – there *is* power in magistrates, as opposed to the Crown Court, to increase fines for wealthy offenders see the article by J B Jenkins at 151 JPN 515.

Different standards of immigrants 8d.31

Once in this country, this country's laws must apply. While a first transgression may be treated sympathetically, thereafter the defendant would be expected to conform strictly with English standards: *R v Derriviere* (1969) 53 Cr App R 637. The same standards of conduct are expected of people of all colours: *R v Mack* [1974] Crim LR 557.

8d.32 **'Curative' element**

In relation to offences of dishonesty, sentences of imprisonment – except when there is an element of protection of the public involved – are normally intended to be the corrct sentence for the particular crime and not to include a curative element. This has nothing to do with special cases such as possessing drugs or cases where the protection of the public is involved: *R v Ford* [1969] 1 WLR 1703 (sentence of imprisonment on chronic alcoholic wrongly invoked to allow for treatment). But when there is a background of alcoholism the court must determine what are the limits of a proper sentence in respect of the offence charged. Within those limits it may be proper to *increase sentence* in order to enable a cure to be undertaken while the accused is in prison, *per* Lord Widgery CJ, in *R v Moylan* [1970] 1 QB 143.

It is not the function of the courts to use their sentencing powers to dispose of those who are socially inconvenient: *R v Clarke* (1975) 61 Cr App R 320.

8d.33 **'Political' offences**

Strongly held *opinions* and *high motives* do not justify deliberate disobedience of the law: *R v Gruffydd and Others* (1972) 56 Cr App R 585 (a Welsh language/road signs case; *R v Francis* (1985) 7 Cr App R (S) 222 (vicar's wife who cut fence at Greenham Common). But the fact that the accused may be a danger to society by reason of his political views is not a reason for increasing sentence: *R v King and Simpkins* (1973) 57 Cr App R 696.

Young men in universities or in any walk of life have no licence to assault policemen and deliberate use of violence, when in support of political issues, should, save for wholly exceptional mitigation, result in immediate custodial sentences: *R v Coleman* [1975] Crim LR 349. In *R v Stock* [1984] Crim LR 64 the appropriate sentence for the deliberate burglary and ransacking of a university office by animal rights campaigners was 28 days suspended for two years.

8d.34 **SENTENCING FOR PARTICULAR OFFENCES**

From time to time, the Court of Appeal (and occasionally the High Court) has offered guidance on how the courts should approach sentencing in particular classes of offence; although it has equally emphasised that it is the individual circumstances of particular offences, and not their 'labels which are of greater importance. The following is a selection from the cases. Where both older and more recent cases are quoted, the latter may indicate a trend towards a less punitive approach, sometimes bringing cases within the sentencing powers of magistrates, particularly where magistrates possess powers of up to 12 months custody in aggregate: see s.133 MCA 1980, and the comments in the *Introduction*, 8d.00. Court of Appeal decisions specifically relating to 'Young Offenders' (17 to 20 inclusive, in the present context) are dealt with separately: 8d.14.

8d.35 **(a)** *Dishonesty* **or** *'abuse'* **by those in a position of trust**

The 'guideline judgment' is *R v Barrick* (1985) 7 Cr App R (S) 142, where it was stated *inter alia* that, in general, a term of imprisonment is inevitable, save in very exceptional circumstances, or where the amount of money obtained was small. The following were stated to be relevant considerations:

In determining what the proper level of sentence should be: (i) the quality and degree of trust reposed in the offender including his rank; (ii) the period over which the fraud or the thefts have been perpetrated; (iii) the use to which the money or property dishonestly taken was put; (iv) the effect upon the victim; (v) the impact of the offences on the public and public confidence; (vi) the effect on fellow-employees or partners; (vii) the effect on the offender himself; (viii) his own history; (ix) those matters of mitigation special to himself such as illness; being placed under great strain by excessive responsibility or the like; where, as sometimes happens, there has been a long delay, say over two years, between his being confronted with his dishonesty by his professional body or the police and the start of his trial; finally, any help given by him to the police. The amount stolen is not necessarily a conducive yardstick to the appropriate sentence: thefts by postmen errode confidence in the public service and cause at least disappointment and sometimes distress or worse to those directly affected: see *R v Rendall* (1973) 57 Cr App R 714; *R v Temple* (1986) 8 Cr App R (S) 305 (theft of £3,000 of cheques and forgery by sorter – 30 months imprisonment upheld); but cf *R v Poulter* (1985) 7 Cr App R (S) 260 (12 months sufficient for postman who also opened letters containing small sums to total value of £100).

A suspended sentence is generally inappropriate: *R v Howard* (1979) 1 Cr App R (S) 364 (postman), save where the sums involved are small: *R v Bowler* (1972) 57 Cr App R 275 (bus conductor). In *R v Orsler* (1981) 3 Cr App R (S) 204, a sentence of 12 months imprisonment was upheld on a postman for stealing postal packets involving small sums of money; and see *R v Brinkley* (1986) 8 Cr App R (S) 105 (foreman – £6,000 – 12 months); *R v Chatfield* (1985) 7 Cr App R (S) 262 (honorary secretary of community centre stole £350 from funds over two and a half years – 4 months immediate imprisonment upheld); *R v Colley* (1985) 7 Cr App R (S) 264 (accounts clerk – £1,000 – immediate 6 months); *R v Bagnall* (1985) 7 Cr App R (S) 40 (shop assistant – £1,700 over several months – 2 months immediate imprisonment appropriate); *R v Mason* (1986) 8 Cr App R (S) 226 (employee – £10,000 – 12 months, including one third discount for guilty plea); *R v Berry* (1986) 8 Cr App R (S) 303 (57 year old secretary of weekly savings club – £3,000 plus – 12 months with 6 suspended). But contrast *R v Hills* (1986) 8 Cr App R (S) 199 where a book-keeper who obtained £6,000 by a 'sophisticated deception' over a period was given 100 hours community service and ordered to pay £5,000 compensation. Reducing the compensation to £1,400 on appeal, Michael Davies J described the appellant as 'fortunate' to have received the community service order and not imprisonment.

For analogous 'abuses' of trust, see eg *R v Rhodes* (1985) 7 Cr App R (S) 341: indecent assault by 47 year old choirmaster on choirboy merited 12 months immediate custody; and *R v Gavin* (1986) 8 Cr App R (S) 211: indecency with 'cubs' and friend's children – 12 months; and cf the cases of 'family' indecency noted at the end of the section on *Unlawful sexual intercourse*, 8d.47.

Thefts involving danger to the public   8d.36

Although the value of the goods stolen may be small, the offence may be serious: *R v Holmes* [1966] Crim LR 457 (larceny of battery from railway warning device); *R v Yardley* [1968] Crim LR 48 (railway signal wire). The court will 'uphold any substantial sentences that are given for these offences connected with telephone kiosks. It is something which 'must be stamped out, and deterrent sentences given': *R v French* 31 January 1966 (unreported).

8d.37 Social security frauds

This type of offence is prevalent and deterrent sentences have become essential: *R v Williams* [1970] Crim LR 357. Where the public is swindled out of a large sum of money by a large and sustained deceit an immediate custodial sentence is inevitable: *R v Grafton* (1979) 1 Cr App R (S) 305 (pretending to be unemployed when in work, the defendant fraudulently obtained £3,000 over two years). But the sentence may be short: *R v McDonald* (1981) 144 JPN 337.

A lowering of the general level of sentences is discernable in recent years: cf. eg *R v Mitchell* (1985) 7 Cr App R (S) 368 (£5,000 benefit over 2 years attracted 9 months imprisonment for a man already on probation for, *inter alia*, deception); *R v Burns* (1983) 5 Cr App R (S) 370 ('usually' 6 months is appropriate); see also *R v Balfour-Acheampong* (1986) 8 Cr App R (S) 313 (six months where in part-time work); *R v Ford* (1986) 8 Cr App R (S) 1 (12 months imprisonment in respect of £7,265 supplementary benefit obtained over a substantial period. But the situation may be different where there is not merely 'non-disclosure', but a '. . . calculated and clever series of frauds', as where the names of several deceased persons were used to obtain benefit: *R v Adams* (1985) 7 Cr App R (S) 411 (two years youth custody); see also *R v Stafford* (1985) 7 Cr App R (S) 62 (15 months correct for man registered as unemployed, but also receiving substantial sums from the DHSS for taking in lodgers in a house he owned in London). Further guidance was offered by Lord Lane CJ in *R v Stewart (Livingstone)* (1987) *The Times*, 27 March (in which it was stated, *inter alia*, that the aim was to achieve parity with the proper sentences for other types of fraud, as exemplified, eg by *R v Barrick, supra*) it was stated that the court should consider the following matters:

(i) the plea;

(ii) the amount involved and length of time over which the defalcations are persisted in;

(ii) the circumstances in which the offence began (there is a plain difference between a claim false from the beginning and one which becomes false due to a change of situation);

(iv) the use to which the money is put (was it spent on necessities or unnecessary luxuries?);

(v) previous character;

(vi) matters special to the offender, such as illness, disability, family difficulties, etc;

(vii) any voluntary repayment of the amounts overpaid.

Additionally, prosecuting counsel could assist the court by indicating what steps, if any, the Department proposed to take to recover their loss from the offender. He could also seek to help the court on whether a compensation order could be made and, if so, in what amount. 'Merely as suggestions', it was also stated that, in approaching sentencing, the court should consider the following questions:

(i) is a custodial sentence really necessary? This was more likely to be the case with respect to charges heard in the Crown Court;

(ii) if a custodial sentence is necessary, can the court make a community service order as an equivalent to imprisonment, or can it suspend the whole sentence? A suspended sentence or (especially

a community service order may be an ideal form of punishment in many of these cases;
(iii) where immediate imprisonment is necessary, what is the shortest sentence which the court can impose? A short term of up to nine or 12 months will usually be sufficient in a contested case where the overpayment is less than, say, £10,000. A partly suspended sentence may well be appropriate where a short immediate sentence is insufficient.

Burglary of inhabited dwellings   8d.38
This offence is treated as a serious crime particularly if accompanied by vandalism. However, a less stringent attitude has been taken of late where the defendant is young or has no previous convictions. Thus in *R v Plant* (1982) 146 JPN 207 six months imprisonment was held to be adequate for a man with no previous convictions convicted of a single burglary of a dwelling house.
In *R v Seymour* (1983) 5 Cr App R (S) 85 it was said that:

Where one has an offence of burglary committed by a young man of 18 years who has already had so substantial a past record of burglary offences, the court naturally thinks long and hard before taking the view that a sentence other than a custodial sentence, so as to remove the convicted burglar from circulation for a time for the protection of the public, should be imposed. A sentence other than a custodial one is perhaps justified, however, particularly in the case of a young offender, if there is any indication that he is beginning to realise the extent of his past criminality and the situation to which offences of a similar nature will take him if they are persisted in. The Powers of Criminal Courts Act 1937* also requires the court to consider, when deciding whether or not to imprison a young man of this age, whether any other alternative sentence might be appropriate, and only pass a sentence of imprisonment if the court is forced to the conclusion that none other would be appropriate. (*Since replaced by the enhanced provisions of s.1(4) CJA 1982. Persons under 21 may not be sentenced to imprisonment: s.1(1), but only to youth custody or detention, *post*).

'Going equipped' (for theft, etc)   8d.39
This offence is a very important piece of protective justice and will lose its value and effect unless it is clearly recognised that it attracts a significant sentence which will deter others: *R v Person* [1969] Crim LR 553.

Violence   8d.40
Generally speaking deterrent sentences are called for. Whilst much will also depend on the severity of the attack (ie whether assault *simpliciter*, actual bodily harm, grievous bodily harm) the following decisions deal with some of the more common forms of violent attack:

(i) On licensees: 8d.41
R v Thompson [1974] Crim LR 720 (glasses and fittings smashed in public house; a glass thrown at landlord's face); *R v Williams* (1980) 2 Cr App R (S) 150 (four months for kicking and punching which knocked out a tooth).

(ii) 'Glassing':   8d.42
Offences involving the use of glass, even if used impetuously and without any real premeditation are serious and almost invariably result in immediate imprisonment: *R v Fleet* (1985) 7 Cr App R (S) 245 ('malicious wounding' – three years reduced to two); and see *R v McLoughlin* (1985) 7 Cr App R (S) 67 (2 years where glass was 'unbroken' and charge under s.20 OAPA 1861) but compare *R v Gittings* [1985] Crim LR 246 noted in relation to young offenders at 8d.22.

8d.43 *(iii) On 'late night' bus etc crews:*
Bus conductors (and bus drivers also) in charge of buses in the very early hours of the morning are vulnerable to attacks by young men. It is clearly the duty of the courts to extend to such conductors and drivers such protection as they can. One measure of protection which they can and should extend is to impress upon defendants in cases such as this that the penalty for using violence of any kind towards such persons will be met by immediate prison sentences: *R v Tremlett* (1983) 5 Cr App R (S) 199 (six months imprisonment upheld for assault with a pool cue).

Note Criminal damage to late night trains has also attracted custody: see *R v Hough* (1986) 8 Cr App R (S) 359.

8d.44 *(iv) At football matches:*
. . . the time has come for the courts to impose sentences which may deter those who are minded to use violence at or near football grounds. Unless there are expectional mitigating circumstances – and it is not easy to see what they could be – youths between the ages of 17 and 21 who are convicted of any offence involving violence towards police officers or others trying to maintain order or to spectators who are not themselves involved in the violence should receive a custodial sentence. In most cases a short detention centre order should be adequate; but if any weapon has been used or a disabling injury was caused or there is evidence that the convicted youth is addicted to the use of violence, a youth custody order would be appropriate. If the injury should be such as to amount to grievous bodily harm, as is likely to arise from stabbing, a longish sentence may be necessary.
per Lawton LJ in *R v Wood* (1984) 6 Cr App R (S) 3, at p.5.
It has been said that unlawful violence on the field of play must be discouraged as much as violence on the terraces: *R v Johnson* (1986) 8 Cr App R (S) 343 (6 months immediate custody for police officer who bit off part of an opponent's ear during a rugby union match).

8d.45 *(v) Assaults on police:*
A sentence of imprisonment for an attack deliberately made on a police officer inflicting upon him harm, no matter how slight, is never wrong in principle: *R v McKenlay* (1979) 1 Cr App R (S) 161 (sentence of six months suspended on a picketing journalist who punched and butted an officer). An immediate sentence is usually appropriate: *R v Bird* (1979) 1 Cr App R (S) 348 (six months upheld for actual bodily harm at incident outside a dance hall). It is inappropriate to suspend a prison sentence when there is deliberate violence, even in the course of evading arrest: *R v Bell* [1973] Crim LR 318 (knee in the groin). In *R v Aguilar* (1985) 7 Cr App R (S) 178 for driving a car at a police officer and 'zig-zagging' with him on the bonnet, 6 months imprisonment, with half suspended, was held to be the appropriate sentence. The mitigation was the defendant's 'excellent record' and the fact that he 'repented immediately'.

8d.46 *(vi) Weapons:*
Carrying a knife is a serious matter, and if it is used severe punishment must be imposed: *R v Nuttall* [1968] Crim LR 282. Violence involving the use of weapons such as bottles in public or semi-public places will inevitably be visited with condign punishment: *R v Lachtay* [1983] Crim LR 766 (six months upheld for hitting victim on head at dance with bottle); see also *R v English* (1985) 7 Cr App R (S) 65 (5 months youth custody on 20 year old for attack on restaurant proprietor with jack handle causing bruising to arm and small puncture wound). Kicking has often been equated in severity with 'weapons': cf eg *R v Jeoffroy* (1985) 7 Cr App R (S) 135 (3 month detention centre orders for unprovoked attack on

couple by gang outside dance hall); and see *'Glassing'* at 8d.42, *supra*. It has been held that custody was appropriate for *possession* of an offensive weapon by a man with a record of violence (11 previous convictions for actual bodily harm, threatening behaviour and possession), who 'could not call on his record in mitigation': see *R v Webster* (1985) 7 Cr App R (S) 359 (12 months immediate imprisonment upheld for 'simple possession' of 'Stanley knife').

Note Even *where no weapon is used* custody may be appropriate for an isolated instance of serious violence: see eg *R v Roberts* (1986), unreported (single punch fracturing jaw in two places); *R v Johnson* (1986) 8 Cr App R (S) 343 (biting off part of ear).

Unlawful sexual intercourse

8d.47

A sentence of a punitive nature is *inappropriate* when there is a virtuous friendship which ends in unlawful sexual intercourse between young people, but a man who abuses a position of trust for sexual gratification ought to receive something near the maximum sentence of two years. In between there are various degrees of guilt. Thus, a casual pick-up by a youth of a girl at a dance is dealt with by a fine. A man in his twenties or older can expect a much stiffer fine, and if the girl is under 15, he can expect to go to prison for a short term. A young man who deliberately sets out to seduce a girl under 16 can expect to go to detention, the older man to prison: *R v Taylor* (1977) 64 Cr App R 183; and see *R v O'Grady* (1978) 66 Cr App R 279 (young man of good character had sex with 'passionate' 14-year-old once. Given absolute discharge after he had spent Christmas in detention).

Substantial sentences have been given where family relationships have been abused, ranging from 15 months for an isolated offence by a 30 year old man with his wife's step-sister aged 14: *R v Dewar* (1986) 8 Cr App R (S) 311; to six years for sustained indecent conduct by a 51 year old man culminating in intercourse with a 13 year old step-daughter (indictable only): *R v Luff* (1986) 8 Cr App R (S) 318. Cf also indecent assaults by man aged 58 on step-daughter aged 12 and wife's grand-daughter aged 7 which attracted nine months in *R v Smith (Frederick William)* (1986) 8 Cr App R (S) 325; and see *R v Vinson* (1981) 3 Cr App R (S) 315.

Drugs

8d.48

The 'guideline' judgment is to be found in *R v Aramah* (1983) 76 Cr App R 190 from which the following are merely extracts:

Possession of heroin, morphine etc: (Simple possession). It is at this level that the circumstances of the individual offender become of much greater importance. Indeed the possible variety of considerations is so wide, including often those of a medical nature, that we feel it impossible to lay down any practical guidelines. On the other hand the maximum penalty for simple possession of class 'A' drugs is seven years' imprisonment and/or a fine, and there will be very many cases where deprivation of liberty is both proper and expedient.

CLASS 'B' DRUGS, PARTICULARLY CANNABIS: We select this from amongst the class 'B' drugs as being the drug most likely to be exercising the minds of the courts. Importation of cannabis: Importation of very small amounts for personal use can be dealt with as if it were simple possession, with which we will deal later.

After dealing with the prison sentences appropriate to a number of sellers to importation and wholesale supply. His Lordship said: 'Supplying a number of small sellers – wholesaling if you like – comes at the top of the bracket. At the lower end will be the retailer of a small amount to a consumer. Where there is no commercial motive (for example, where cannabis is supplied at a party), the offence may well be serious enough to justify a short custodial sentence. Possession of cannabis: When only small amounts are involved being for personal use, the offence can often be met by a fine. If the history shows, however, a persisting flouting of law, imprisonment may become necessary.'

It is not appropriate as a general rule to impose a sentence of imprisonment where the offence is possession of cannabis in very small quantities for personal consumption. The proper penalty in the ordinary course is a financial one. If however there was a continuous and persistent defiance of the law there might come a time where there would be no alternative to a custodial sentence: *R v Robinson-Coupar and Baxendale* [1982] Crim LR 536.

8d.49 Obscene publications

In the judgment of this court, the only way of stamping out this filthy trade is by imposing sentences of imprisonment on first offenders and all connected with the commercial exploitation of pornography: otherwise frontmen will be put up and the real villains will hide behind them. It follows, in our judgement, that the salesmen, projectionists, owners and suppliers behind the owners should on conviction lose their liberty. For first offenders sentences need only be comparatively short, but persistent offenders should get the full rigour of the law. In addition courts should take the profit out of this illegal filthy trade by imposing very substantial fines. Before leaving this matter we wish to make one or two further observations. We wish to make it clear that the guidelines we have indicated apply to those who commercially exploit pornography. We do not suggest that sentences of imprisonment would be appropriate for a newsagent who is carrying on a legitimate trade in selling newspapers and magazines and who has the odd pornographic magazines in his possession, probably because he has been careless in not looking to see what he is selling. If he is discovered to have the odd pornographic magazine in the midst of the articles of trade which he is properly and lawfully selling, he can be discouraged, and usually should be, by a substantial fine from repeating his carelessness. Nor do we suggest that a young man who comes into possession of a pornographic video tape and who takes it along to his rugby or cricket club to amuse his friends by showing it should be sentenced to imprisonment. On conviction he too can be dealt with by the imposition of a fine. The matter might be very different if owners or managers of clubs were to make a weekly practice of showing 'blue' films to attract custom. Like the pornographers of Soho they would be engaging in the commercial exploitation of pornography.

per Lawton J in *R v Holloway* (1982) 4 Cr App R (S) 128 (six months upheld on a man convicted of six offences of having obscene books and videos for sale). In *R v Cowan* [1982] Crim LR 766, three months was considered appropriate for an owner of a sex shop with no similar previous convictions. In *R v Calleja* (1985) 7 Cr App R (S) 13, 12 months immediate custody was upheld (together with a fine of £5,000 'to deprive . . . of at least part of the proceeds') in respect of managing a cinema showing obscene films (second conviction).

8d.50 Drink driving

There is no principle that a custodial sentence should not be imposed on a first conviction for driving with excess alcohol in the body, but the circumstances of these offences vary infinitely. The surrounding circumstances must also be looked at: *R v Nokes* [1978] RTR 101 (183 mg alcohol/100 ml blood: six months' imprisonment upheld when defendant drove erratically at high speed in built-up area. No previous convictions for drink). Circumstances which may indicate a custodial sentence (particularly when they occur together) are: high blood/alcohol reading: *R v Tupa* [1974] RTR 153 (289 mg/100 ml) dangerous driving: *R v Jenkins* [1978] RTR 104; *R v Pashley* [1974] RTR 149; and repeated offending: *R v Sylvester* (1979) 1 Cr App R (S) 250; *R v Peverill* 4 December 1975, unreported. Without such aggravating features a custodial sentence is inappropriate: *R v Thomas* [1973] RTR 325.

Reckless driving

8d.51

A short forthwith prison sentence is right in principle for deliberately ramming a car from behind in the fast lane of a motorway: *R v Till* (1982) 4 Cr App R (S) 158 (but three months too long for a man of good character): and see *R v O'Sullivan, R v Burtoft* [1983] Crim LR 827. In *R v Carrier* (1985) 7 Cr App R (S) 57, 12 months imprisonment was held to be the appropriate sentence where the driver of a car 'persistently overtook' two motorcyclists and then slowed down, until a collision occurred and a motorcyclist and his passenger were injured; and see *R v O'Sullivan, supra* (police chase – two months imprisonment upheld); *R v Bilton* (1985) 7 Cr App R (S) 103, (16 months for overturning car after consuming 14 pints of beer – passenger paralysed from the waist down). An anomalous distinction is drawn between such cases and 'causing death by reckless driving', which attracts higher penalties, generally for purely fortuitous reasons. The maximum penalty for careless driving may be justified where the charge is reduced from one of reckless driving: cf *R v Stevens* (1985) 7 Cr App R (S) 346.

Harrassment of tenants

8d.52

The use of threats and force to get tenants out is one of the worst forms of this offence. In such cases loss of liberty is the appropriate penalty: *R v Brennan* (1979) 1 Cr App R (S) 103 (sentence reduced to three months when the two appellants and another went to the house with an alsatian dog and ordered the tenants out).

Note The fact that the Lord Chief Justice or the higher courts have indicated that a particular offence should be visited by a particular sentence in no way fetters the discretion of magistrates: *R v Acting Deputy Chairman, South East London Quarter Sessions, ex p. Abraham* [1970] Crim LR 116 (sentence quashed where deputy chairman expressed himself as if so bound). In *R v De Havilland* (1983) 5 Cr App R (S) 109, Dunn LJ said that the sentencer retains his discretion within the guidelines laid down by the Court of Appeal or even to depart from them if the particular circumstances of the case justify it.

DETENTION FOR SHORTER PERIODS

8d.53

A magistrates' court has various powers to detain for short periods under three separate provisions of MCA 1980, as follows:

	Detention in police cells s.134	Detention in court or police station s.135	Committal to custody overnight s.136
Available in lieu of sentence of imprisonment and youth custody . . .	Yes	Yes	No
Available for non-payment of a fine . . .	Yes (2)	Yes (2)	Yes (1)
Place of detention . . .	Certified police cells, bridewell or similar place	Precincts of the courthouse or any police station	In a police station
Maximum period of detention . . .	Four days	Until 8 pm or such earlier time as is necessary to give offender reasonable opportunity of returning to his abode the same day	Until 8 pm if arrested between midnight and 8 am. Otherwise until 8 am next morning

(1) For persons aged 21 and over only
(2) For persons aged 17 and over

Note that s.134 will cease to have effect when [s.48] CJA 1988 comes into force (see Appendix III) and that s.136 will be amended by [s.64]: see 8d.73.

8d.54 Juveniles

Magistrates sitting in the adult court may not pass any custodial sentence, in respect of a juvenile. Instead, they should remit the offender to the juvenile court to be dealt with: s.7(8) CYPA 1969 which confines the adult court's powers to fines, absolute or conditional discharges and parental bind-overs: see Chapter 8b.

8d.55 CHARGE AND CONTROL ORDERS

Where a person, the subject of a care order made in criminal proceedings or in care proceedings based on the offence condition, is convicted of an offence punishable with imprisonment the court may make an order restricting the classes of person who may have charge and control of the offender for a period not exceeding six months: s.20A(1) CYPA 1969. This is achieved by adding to the care order a condition that the power of the local authority to allow a parent, guardian, relative or friend to have charge or control

(a) shall not be exercisable; or
(b) shall not be exercisable except to allow charge and control to a specified parent, guardian, relative or friend.

Where such a direction has been given and the defendant commits another such offence the court may replace the condition with another: s.20A(2).

These powers may not be exercised unless the court is of opinion that it is appropriate to do so because of the seriousness of the offence *and* that no other method of dealing with the person is appropriate. To determine this the court must obtain and consider information about the circumstances: s.20A(3). Nor may these powers be exercised with respect to an unrepresented defendant unless he has knowingly failed or refused to apply for legal aid or has been refused legal aid on grounds of means: s.20A(4), (8). The order must be explained to the defendant before it is made: s.20A(5).

The subject of the order, his parent or guardian and the local authority may apply to the juvenile court for its revocation: s.20A(6). The local authority may appeal to the Crown Court against the making of the order: s.20A(7). The subject of the order may appeal under s.108 MCA 1980.

Statutory Provisions

CHILDREN AND YOUNG PERSONS ACT 1969

Power of court to add condition as to charge and control of offender in care   **8d.56**

20A. (1) Where a person to whom a care order relates which was made–

(a) by virtue of subs (3) of s.1 of this Act in a case where the court which made the order was of the opinion that the condition mentioned in subs (2)(f) of that section was satisfied; or

(b) by virtue of s.7(7) of this Act, is convicted or found guilty of an offence punishable with imprisonment in the case of a person over 21

the court which convicted or finds him guilty of that offence may add to the care order a condition under this section that the power conferred by s.21(2) of the Child Care Act 1980 (power of local authority to allow a parent, guardian, relative or friend charge and control) shall for such period not exceeding six months as the court may specify in the condition–

(c) not be exercisable; or

(d) not be exercisable to allow the person to whom the order relates to be under the charge and control of a specified parent, guardian, relative or friend.

(2) Where–

(a) the power conferred by subs (1) above has been exercised; and

(b) before the period specified in the condition has expired the person to whom the care order relates is convicted or found guilty of another offence punishable with imprisonment in the case of a person over 21

the court may replace the condition with another condition under his section.

(3) A court shall not exercise the powers conferred by this section unless the court is of opinion that it is appropriate to exercise those powers because of the seriousness of the offence and that no other method of dealing with the person to whom the care order relates is appropriate; and for the purpose of determining whether any other method of dealing with him is appropriate the court shall obtain and consider information about the circumstances.

(4) A court shall not exercise the said powers in respect of a person who is not legally represented in that court unless either–

(a) he applied for legal aid and the application was refused on the ground that it did not appear his means were such that he required assistance; or

(b) having been informed of his right to apply for legal aid and had the opportunity to do so, he refused or failed to apply.

(5) Before adding a condition under this section to a care order a court shall explain to the person to whom the care order relates the purpose and effect of the condition.

(6) At any time when a care order includes a condition under this section–

(a) the person to whom the order relates;
(b) his parent or guardian, acting on his behalf; or
(c) the local authority in whose care he is, may apply to a juvenile court for the revocation or variation of the condition.

(7) The local authority may appeal to the Crown Court against the imposition of a condition under this section by a magistrates' court or against the terms of such a condition.

(8) For the purposes of this section a person is to be treated as legally represented in court if, but only if, he has the assistance of counsel or a solicitor to represent him in the proceedings in that court at some time after he is convicted or found guilty and before any power conferred by this section is exercised, and in this section 'legal aid' means legal aid for the purposes of proceedings in that court, whether the whole proceedings or the proceedings on or in relation to the exercise of the power; but in the case of a person committed to the Crown Court for sentence or trial, it is immaterial whether he applied for legal aid in the Crown Court to, or was informed of his right to apply by, that court or the court which committed him.
[*as inserted by s.22 CJA 1982*].

or
  (c) *by virtue of section 15(1) of this Act in a case where-*
      (i)   *the supervision order for which the care order was substituted was made under section 7(7) of this Act; and*
      (ii) *the offence in respect of which the supervision order was made was punishable with imprisonment in the case of a person over 21,.*
[*subs(1)(c) will be amended by [Sch.14] CJA 1988 from a date to be appointed*].

COMMENTARY

The effect of this section is described under *Charge and Control Orders* 8d.55.

s.20A(1): Care order, defined in s.70(1) as 'an order committing (a person) to the care of a local authority'.

s.20A(3): this relates to care orders made in care proceedings based on the offence condition (s.1(2)(f)).

Section 7(7): this relates to care orders made in criminal proceedings.

Section 21(2) of the Child Care Act 1980 reads:
'Without prejudice to the generality of subs (1) above, but subject to s.20A of the Children and Young Persons Act 1969 (power of court to add condition as to charge and control), a local authority may allow a child in their care, either for a fixed period or until the local authority otherwise determine, to be under the charge and control of a parent, guardian, relative or friend.

Subs (1) of s.21 reads:
A local authority shall discharge their duty to provide accommodation and maintenance for a child in their care in such one of the following ways as they think fit, namely,
  (a) by boarding him out on such terms as to payment by the authority and otherwise as the authority may, subject to the provisions of this Act and regulations thereunder, determine; or
  (b) by maintaining him in a community home or in any such home as is referred to in s.80 of this Act; or
  (c) by maintaining him in a voluntary home (other than a community home) the managers of which are willing to receive him;
or by making such other arrangements as seem appropriate to the local authority and shall secure, subject to s.18 of this Act, that any accommodation which they provide is, so far as practicable, near the child's home.

Charge and control, DHSS circular LAC (83) 6 dated 5 April 1983 comments:
'Local authorities may make any arrangements for the juvenile's accommodation during the currency of the order except placements with parents, guardians, relatives or friends not specified in the order, and this will include boarding out or placement outside the community home system. The currency of an order does not prohibit home leave, provided that responsibility for the juvenile's charge and control is not transferred, and

local authorities may make reasonable provision for home visits, though in doing so they are asked not to be insensitive to the wishes of the courts.'

s.21A(3): The seriousness of the offence, thus it could not be appropriate to make an order under this section in respect of a relatively trivial offence.

No other method . . . appropriate, this seems to indicate that an order under this section is a sentence in its own right and cannot, for example, be combined with an attendance centre order on the same offence. It is suggested that it does not rule out the making of orders for costs, compensation and other ancillary matters.

s.21A(7): the offender himself may appeal to the Crown Court under s.108 MCA 1980.

POWERS OF CRIMINAL COURTS ACT 1973

Restriction on imposing sentences of imprisonment on persons who have not previously served prison sentences   8d.57

20. (1) No court shall pass a sentence of imprisonment on a person of or over 21 years of age on whom such a sentence has not previously been passed by a court in any part of the United Kingdom unless the court is of opinion that no other method of dealing with him is appropriate; and for the purpose of determining whether any other method of dealing with any such person is appropriate the court shall obtain and consider information about the circumstances, and shall take into account any information before the court which is relevant to his character and his physical and mental condition.

(2) Where a magistrates' court passes a sentence of imprisonment on any such person as is mentioned in subs (1) above, the court shall state the reason for its opinion that no other method of dealing with him is appropriate, and cause that reason to be specified in the warrant of commitment and to be entered in the register.

(3) For the purposes of this section–
(a) a previous sentence of imprisonment which has been suspended and which has not taken effect under s.23 of this Act or under s.19 of the Treatment of Offenders Act (Northern Ireland) 1968 shall be disregarded; and
(b) 'sentence of imprisonment' does not include a committal or attachment for contempt of court.

(4) . . .

(5) For the purposes of this section the age of a person shall be deemed to be that which it appears to the court to be after considering any available evidence.
[*as amended by Sch.14 CJA 1982*].

COMMENTARY

s.20(1): A sentence of imprisonment, does not include a committal in default of payment of any sum of money, or for want of sufficient distress to satisfy any sum of money, or for failure to do or abstain from doing anything required to be done or left undone: s.57(1) PCCA 1973; and note s.20(3).

21 years of age, see s.20(5).

United Kingdom, ie Great Britain and Northern Ireland: Royal and Parliamentary Titles Act 1927.

No other method of dealing with him is appropriate, the obligation is merely a duty to *think twice* before passing a prison sentence: *Vassall v Harris* [1964] Crim LR 322; *Morris v The Crown Office* [1970] 1 All ER 1079.

Shall obtain and consider information, it is suggested that this provision goes primarily to the matters which the prosecutor normally lays before the court on a plea of guilty: see Chapter 8. But see also s.20A *infra*, which requires a social inquiry report to be obtained for the purpose of determining whether there is any appropriate method of dealing with an offender other than imprisonment, unless this is 'unnecessary'.

s.20(2): the provisions of s.20(2) are *not mandatory but directory only*: cf *Morris v The Crown Office* [1970] 1 All ER 1079. Failure to state reasons would not be sufficient grounds for quashing the sentence: *R v Jackson (alias Rintoul)* (1966) 130 JP 284; *R v Chesterfield Justices, ex p. Hewitt* [1973] Crim LR 181.

The register, means the register of proceedings before a magistrates' court required by rules made under s.15 Justices of the Peace Act 1979 to be kept by the clerk of the court: s.57(1) PCCA 1973.

8d.58   **Social inquiry report for purposes of s.20**
    20A. (1) Subject to subs (2) below, the court shall in every case obtain a social inquiry report for the purpose of determining under s.20(1) above whether there is any appropaite method of dealing with an offender other than imprisonment.

    (2) Subs (1) above does not apply if, in the circumstances of the case, the court is of the opinion that it is unnecessary to obtain a social inquiry report.

    (3) Where a magistrates' court passes a sentence of imprisonment on a person of or over 21 years of age on whom such a sentence has not previously been passed by a court in any part of the United Kingdom without obtaining a social inquiry report, it shall state in open court the reason for its opinion that it was unnecessary to obtain such a report.

    (4) A magistrates' court shall cause a reason stated under subs (3) above to be specified in the warrant of commitment and to be entered in the register.

    (5) No sentence shall be invalidated by the failure of a court to comply with subs (1) above, but any other court on appeal from that court shall obtain a social inquiry report if none was obtained by the court below, unless it is of the opinion that in the circumstances of the case it is unnecessary to do so.

    (6) In determining whether it should deal with the appellant otherwise than by passing a sentence of imprisonment on him the court hearing the appeal shall consider any social inquiry report obtained by it or by the court below.

    (7) In this section 'social inquiry report' means a report about a person and his circumstances made by a probation officer.
    [*as inserted by s.62 CJA 1982*].

COMMENTARY
s.20A(1): Social inquiry report, defined in s.20A(7).

s.20A(2): Unnecessary, compare the comment to s.2(3) CJA 1982, *infra*.

8d.59   **Restriction on imposing sentence of imprisonment, [Borstal training] or detention on persons not legally represented**
    21. (1) A magistrates' court on summary conviction or the Crown Court on committal for sentence or on conviction on indictment shall not pass a sentence of imprisonment, on a person who is not legally represented in that court and has not been previously sentenced to that punishment by a court in any part of the United Kingdom, unless either–
        (a) he applied for legal aid and the application was refused on the ground that it did not appear his means were such that he required assistance; or
        (b) having been informed of his right to apply for legal aid and had the opportunity to do so, he refused or failed to apply.

    (2) For the purposes of his section a person is to be treated as legally represented in court if, but only if, he has the assistance of counsel or a solicitor to represent him in the proceedings in that court at some time after he is found guilty and before he is sentenced, and in subs (1)(a) and (b) above 'legal aid' means legal aid for the purposes of proceedings in that court, whether the whole proceedings or the proceedings on or in relation to sentence; but in the case of a person committed to the Crown Court for sentence or trial, it is

immaterial whether he applied for legal aid in the Crown Court to, or was informed of his right to apply by, that court or the court which committed him.

(3) For the purposes of this section–

(a) a previous sentence of imprisonment which has been suspended and which has not taken effect under s.23 of this Act or under s.19 of the Treatment of Offenders Act (Northern Ireland) 1968 shall be disregarded;

(b) 'sentence of imprisonment' does not include a committal or attachment for contempt of court.

as amended by Sch.16 CJA 1982].

COMMENTARY

Corresponding provisions for offenders *under 21* are contained in s.3 CJA 1982, *infra.* Failure to comply with the terms of this section renders a sentence invalid: *R v Birmingham Justices, ex p. Wyatt* (1975) 140 JP 46.

s.21(1): Pass a sentence of imprisonment, includes a *suspended sentence*; and see s.21(3)(a).

Not legally represented, representation after conviction and before sentence is sufficient: s.21(2); legal aid must be offered: see s.21(1).

United Kingdom, ie Great Britain and Northern Ireland: Royal and Parliamentary Titles Act 1927.

s.21(2), in view of the terms of s.21(2), the magistrates' court should inform the Crown Court whether the accused had the opportunity to apply at the magistrates' court for legal aid in the Crown Court proceedings and what the outcome was: HOC 237/1972.

Suspended sentences of imprisonment   **8d.60**

22. (1) Subject to subs (2) below, a court which passes a sentence of imprisonment for a term of not more than two years for an offence may order that the sentence shall not take effect unless, during a period specified in the order, being not less than one year or more than two years from the date of the order, the offender commits in Great Britain another offence punishable with imprisonment and thereafter a court having power to do so orders under s.23 of this Act that the original sentence shall take effect; and in this part of this Act 'operational period', in relation to a suspended sentence, means the period so specified.

(2) A court shall not deal with an offender by means of a suspended sentence unless the case appears to the court to be one in which a sentence of imprisonment would have been appropriate in the absence of any power to suspend such a sentence by an order under subs (1) above.

(3) A court which passes a suspended sentence on any person for an offence shall not make a probation order in his case in respect of another offence of which he is convicted by or before the court or for which he is dealt with by the court.

(4) On passing a suspended sentence the court shall explain to the offender in ordinary language his liability under s.23 of this Act if during the operational period he commits an offence punishable with imprisonment.

(5) Where a court has passed a suspended sentence on any person, and that person is subsequently sentenced to borstal training, he shall cease to be liable to be dealt with in respect of the suspended sentence unless the subsequent sentence or any conviction or finding on which it was passed is quashed on appeal.

(6) Subject to any provision to the contrary contained in the Criminal Justice Act 1967, this Act or any enactment passed or instrument made under enactment after 31 December 1967–

(a) a suspended sentence which has not taken effect under s.23 of this Act shall be treated as a sentence of imprisonment for the purposes of all enactments and instruments made under enactments except any enactment or instrument which provides for disqualification for or loss of office, or forfeiture of pensions, of persons sentenced to imprisonment; and

(b) where a suspended sentence has taken effect under that section, the offender shall be treated for the purposes of the enactments and instruments excepted by para (a) above as having been convicted on the ordinary date on which the period allowed for making an appeal against an order under that section expires or, if such an appeal is made, the date on which it is finally disposed of or abandoned or fails for non-prosecution.

COMMENTARY

See generally *Suspended Sentences*, 8d.07.

s.22(1): A sentence of imprisonment, defined in s.57(1) PCCA 1973: see the note to s.20, *supra*. It does *not include* a committal to prison for non-payment of a fine: *R v Nixon* [1976] Crim LR 117; nor the imprisonment of an incorrigible rogue: *R v Graves* [1976] Crim LR 697.

Great Britain, ie England, Scotland and Wales: Union with Scotland Act 1706; as Wales and Berwick Act 1746. Excluding the Channel Islands and the Isle of Man.

Offence punishable with imprisonment, see the note to s.23, *post.*

This Part of this Act, ie ss.1–46 inclusive.

s.22(2): gives effect to the decision in *R v O'Keefe* [1969] 2 QB 20 in which it was said that before deciding to impose a suspended sentence *all other possibilities must first be rejected. Only when the court has decided it is a case for imprisonment can it go on to the final question: is immediate imprisonment required or can it be suspended?*

s.22(4): for a model form of explanation see *R v Crosby and Hayes* (1975) 60 Cr App R 235.

8d.61   **Power of court on conviction of further offence to deal with suspended sentence**
    23. (1) Where an offender is convicted of an offence punishable with imprisonment committed during the operational period of a suspended sentence and either he is so convicted by or before a court having power under s.24 of this Act to deal with him in respect of the suspended sentence or he subsequently appears or is brought before such a court, then, unless the sentence has already taken effect, the court shall consider his case and deal with him by one of the following methods–

(a) the court may order that the suspended sentence shall take effect with the original term unaltered;

(b) it may order that the sentence shall take effect with the substitution of a lesser term for the original term;

(c) it may by order vary the original order under s.22(1) of this Act by substituting for the period specified therein a period expiring not later than two years from the date of the variation; or

(d) it may make no order with respect to the suspended sentence;

and a court shall make an order under para (a) of this subsection unless the court is of opinion that it would be unjust to do so in view of all the circumstances, including the facts of the subsequent offence, and where it is of that opinion the court shall state its reasons.

(2) Where a court orders that a suspended sentence shall take effect, with or without any variation of the original term, the court may order that that sentence shall take effect immediately or that the term thereof shall commence on the expiration of another term of imprisonment passed on the offender by that or another court.

(3)–(5) (*Repealed*). (6) . . .

(7) Where a court deal with an offender under this section in respect of a suspended sentence the appropriate officer of the court shall notify the

appropriate officer of the court which passed the sentence of the method adopted.

(8) Where on consideration of the case of an offender a court makes no order with respect to a suspended sentence, the appropriate officer of the court shall record that fact.

(9) For the purposes of any enactment conferring rights of appeal in criminal cases any order made by a court with respect to a suspended sentence shall be treated as a sentence passed on the offender by that court for the offence for which the suspended sentence was passed.
[*as amended by s.13, Sch.16 CJA 1982*].

COMMENTARY

Legal aid may be granted in these proceedings: ss.28(2), 30(12) LAA 1974. For *Costs* see Chapter 9.

s.23(1): Convicted, it was formerly held that a suspended sentence cannot be brought into operation as as result of a conviction during the period of suspension which resulted in a probation order or an order of absolute or conditional discharge, having regard to the fact that this is deemed not to be a 'conviction' by s.13(1) PCCA 1973. To the extent that a probation order may be made by justices where a previous suspended sentence has been made by the Crown Court, this holds good as does the statement that it ought to be a rule of practice for magistrates' courts that whenever they are minded to make an order which will not enable a suspended sentence (passed by a higher court) to be brought into operation, namely absolute or conditional discharge or probation, their proper course is to refrain from making one or other of those orders and to commit under s.56 of the 1967 Act so that the court that imposed the sentence can deal with the whole matter together: *R v Tarry* [1970] 2 QB 561. *R v Salmon* (1973) 57 Cr App R 953. The rule in *Tarry* was applied in *R v Stewart* (1984) 6 Cr App R 166. (Where it was held to be wrong to make a community service order upon conviction of an offender who was thereby in breach of a suspended sentence passed by the Crown Court). Yet, more recently, where this *has* occurred, it has been held wrong for the Crown Court to then activate the suspended sentence – at least where the new offence is '. . . not of any great importance': see *R v Cresswell* (1986) 8 Cr App R (S) 29.

But where the probation order is made by the same court which deals with the suspended sentence in the same proceedings, the position is otherwise: *R v Barnes* (1986) 8 Cr App R (S) 88, where Lord Lane CJ explained that: '. . . However there was a difference between the circumstances in *Tarry* and those of the present case: in *Tarry*, the probation order had been made in the magistrates' court, and the suspended sentence was activated by assizes. In the present case, the suspended sentence was dealt with by the court which made the probation order, and in the same proceedings. Section 13(1) provided that a conviction followed by a probation order was deemed not to be a conviction "for any purpose other than the purposes of the proceedings in which the order is made . . ." In the present case, the probation order was made in the same proceedings as the order dealing with the suspended sentence, and accordingly was within the exception in section 13(1). The probation order was therefore a "conviction" entitling the court to use its powers in relation to the suspended sentence under section 23(1). Although the order extending the operational period of the suspended sentence was therefore technically lawful, it was an undesirable order to make in the circumstances, as it would result in a suspended sentence and a probation order running at the same time.'

Save only when it is *unjust* to do so, a suspended sentence must be put into effect on conviction of an imprisonable offence, whether a sentence of imprisonment is imposed therefor or not: *R v Cobbold* [1971] Crim LR 436 (fine for subsequent offence); *R v Isaacs* [1980] Crim LR 666. But see now *R v McElhorne* (1983) 5 Cr App R (S) 53; *R v Seymour* [1983] Crim LR 410; *R v Jagodzinski* (1986) 8 Cr App R (S) 150. It seems from these later cases that where a person commits a further offence during the operational period of a suspended sentence which does not itself warrant a sentence of imprisonment, then this will be '*strong evidence*' that it may be *unjust* to activate the suspended sentence.

The operational period, defined in s.22(1), *supra*.

A suspended sentence, means a sentence to which s.22(1) applies: s.57(1).

Offence punishable with imprisonment, to be construed without regard to any prohibition or restriction on the imprisonment of offenders: s.57(4).

An offence triable either way which carries imprisonment in the Crown Court but not in the magistrates' court, such as an offence under s.14(1)(b) Trqde Description Act 1968 or s.26 Vehicles (Excise) Act 1971, is only an offence punishable by imprisonment when the offender is convicted in the Crown Court: *R v Melbourne* [1980] Crim LR 510. For the offence of failing to provide a laboratory specimen see *R v Hugsons* [1977] Crim LR 684. A certificate purporting to be signed by or on behalf of the Lord Advocate that an offence is punishable in Scotland with imprisonment or is so punishable on indictment for a specified term is evidence of the matter so specified: s.52.

Brought before such a court, ie under s.25, *infra*.

Unless the sentence has already taken effect, the extension of the operational period under s.23(1)(c) in respect of one offence committed in breach of a suspended sentence does not constitute a taking effect of that sentence for the purpose of a quite different offence in breach: *R v McDonald* (1971) 55 Cr App R 575.

The court shall consider his case
'Whilst, of course, it is never part of the function of a court which may have to consider activating a suspended sentence in any way to review its propriety, nonetheless, there are cases where justice cannot be done without fitting into the pattern of events leading to the further conviction the facts which led to the suspended sentence. To that extent, therefore, it may then be necessary on the second occasion for the court to inform itself of the circumstances in which the suspended sentence was passed in order that such proper assessment may be made of the overall position so as to determine the sentence to be passed and make plain the grounds on which it is acting.'
per Sachs LJ in *R v Munday* (1971) 56 Cr App R 220 (revised judgment); and see *R v Metcalfe* [1971] Crim LR 112.

Deal with him, whenever a person is dealt with under s.23(1) otherwise than by method (a) the court's reason must be entered in the register. When the sentence was passed by another court, the clerk of that court must be notified: r.29(1) MC Rules 1981. See generally the note *Dealt With* to s.25, *infra*.

Order that the suspended sentence shall take effect, see forms 89, 90. *Note* that the court is not 'imposing imprisonment'. It follows that the power to impose consecutive sentences under s.133 MCA 1980 does not apply – but see s.23(2), *infra*. If the offender is subject to a suspended sentence supervision order the clerk must notify the court which made the order: r.30(1) MC Rules 1981. A court which activates a suspended sentence may not make an order under s.47 CLA 1977 suspending that sentence in part: *R v Senior* (1984) 6 Cr App R (S) 15.

A lesser term, but not less than five days: s.132 MCA 1980. If the offender is subject to a suspended sentence supervision order the clerk must notify the court which made the order: r.30(1) When two or more suspended sentences passed on the same occasion were ordered by the earlier court to be served consecutively, they are, by the operation of s.57(2) PCCA 1973, to be treated as a single term, eg for the purposes of a reduction of length of sentence when a later court comes to put them into effect: *R v Gall* (1970) 54 Cr App R 292. Periods spent in custody prior to the passing of the suspended sentence do not justify a later court from putting into effect a lesser term: *R v Deering* [1976] Crim LR 638. The fact that the subsequent offence was committed near the end of the operational period of the suspended sentence may be a reason for reducing the length of the activated sentence *R v Beacock* (1979) 1 Cr App R (S) 198. Although not unlawful it is wrong in principle to pass an immediate sentence of imprisonment on the later offences and extend the operational period of a suspended sentence: *R v Treays* [1981] Crim LR 511.

Vary the original order, see form 91. It is *not good practice* when passing a forthwith sentence of imprisonment to vary the operational period of an earlier suspended sentence: *R v Goodlad* (1973) 137 JP 704; following *R v Sapiano* (1968) 52 Cr App R 674.

Make no order, for the effect of such a course see the note *Dealt With* to s.25, *infra*. When an offender in breach of suspended sentences is made the subject of a community service order on the occasion of the later offence, the court deciding under s.23(1)(d) to make no order regarding the breach of the suspended sentences, a later court may not purport to reconsider and activate the suspended sentences when dealing with the offence for which the community service order was imposed: *R v Peterborough Justices, ex p. Casey* (1979) 1 Cr App R (S) 268; *R v Folan* [1980] 1 All ER 217.

The facts of the subsequent offence, see under *Breach of suspended sentence*, 8d.08.

s.23(2): the sentence for the original offence may thus be consecutive to any passed by the court, whether on the same occasion or previously or passed by any other court. The proper course is to sentence the offender for the second offence first and then to order that the suspended sentence take effect either concurrently or consecutively: *R v Ithell* [1969] 1

WLR 272. 'It (is) wrong in principle when an order bringing into force a suspended sentence (is) made for that sentence to be made concurrent unless there (are) some very special circumstances', *per* Lord Parker CJ in *R v Brown* [1969] Crim LR 20; *R v Smith* (1977) 64 Cr App R 217. It is *suggested* that this power cannot extend to two or more suspended sentences passed on the same occasion and expressed by the earlier court to be concurrent. The maximum periods of imprisonment referred to in s.133 MCA 1980 do not apply to an order under s.23(2).

When an offender subject to a suspended sentence is convicted of a number of offences, *some committed before* and *some after* the date of the suspended sentence, the suspended sentence can be put into effect consecutively to the sentences for all the other offences: *R v Drablow* [1969] Crim LR 501.

To avoid confusion, the *Practice Direction* [1962] 1 All ER 417 (noted under s.133 MCA 1980, *infra*) should be followed: *R v Corry* [1973] Crim LR 381. There is *no power* to antedate the commencement of a suspended sentence when ordering it to be put into effect: *R v Bell* [1969] Crim LR 670. When consecutive sentences are imposed the sentencer's duty is to make sure that the *totality* is not excessive, which he may do either by reducing the period of the instant or the suspended sentence: *R v Bocskei* (1970) 54 Cr App R 519.

s.23(7): For a recommended form of notice see Annex A to HOC 209/1967.

The appropriate officer of the court, means in relation to a magistrates' court the clerk of the court: s.57(1) PCCA 1973.

s.23(9): creates a right of appeal against orders made under s.23.

Court by which suspended sentence may be dealt with 8d.62

24. (1) An offender may be dealt with in respect of a suspended sentence by the Crown Court or, where the sentence was passed by a magistrates' court, by any magistrates' court before which he appears or is brought.

(2) Where an offender is convicted by a magistrates' court of an offence punishable with imprisonment and the court is satisfied that the offence was commited during the operational period of a suspended sentence passed by the Crown Court–

    (a) the court may, if it thinks fit, commit him in custody or on bail to the Crown Court; and

    (b) if it does not, shall give written notice of conviction to the appropriate officer of the Crown Court.

(3) For the purposes of this section and of s.25 of this Act a suspended sentence passed on an offender on appeal shall be treated as having been passed by the court by which he was originally sentenced.

COMMENTARY

s.24(1): When the sentence was passed by a magistrates' court, as to suspended sentences passed on appeal see s.24(3).

Is brought, ie under s.25, *infra*.

s.24(2): The operational period, defined in s.22(1), *supra*.

Commit, there is power to grant legal aid in respect of the proceedings in the Crown Court: ss.28(7), 30(12) LAA 1974. When committing to the Crown Court under s.24(2), the court may also commit the offender to be dealt with in respect of (a) if the offence concerned was an offence triable either way any other offence whatsoever, and (b) if the offence concerned was a summary offence (i) any offence punishable with imprisonment (ii) any disqualifiable offence and (iii) any breach of a suspended sentence imposed by magistrates: s.56(1) CJA 1967.

For the power to impose interim disqualification of road traffic offenders, see s.103 RTA 1972.

For the location of the Crown Court see the Directions of the Lord Chief Justice, paras 5–9, reproduced at 4.02.

In custody or on bail, see the notes to s.38 MCA 1980, *infra*.

Procedure where court convicting of further offence does not deal with 8d.63 suspended sentence

25. (1) If it appears to the Crown Court, where that court has jurisdiction in accordance with subs (2) below, or to a justice of the peace having jurisdiction in accordance with that subsection, that an offender has been convicted in Great Britain of an offence punishable with imprisonment committed during the operational period of a suspended sentence, that court or justice may, subject to the following provisions of this section, issue a summons requiring the offender to appear at the place and time specified therein, or a warrant for his arrest.

(2) Jurisdiction for the purposes of subs (1) above may be exercised–
(a) if the suspended sentence was passed by the Crown Court, by that court;
(b) if it was pased by a magistrates' court, by a justice acting for the area for which that court acted.

(3) Where an offender is convicted by a court in Scotland of an offence punishable with imprisonment and the court is informed that the offence was committed during the operational period of a suspended sentence passed in England or Wales, the court shall give written notice of the conviction to the appropriate officer of the court by which the suspended sentence was passed.

(4) Unless he is acting in consequence of a notice under subs (3) above, a justice of the peace shall not issue a summons under this section except on information and shall not issue a warrant under this section except on information in writing and on oath.

(5) A summons or warrant issued under this section shall direct the offender to appear or to be brought before the court by which the suspended sentence was passed.

COMMENTARY

s.25(1): for the location of the court to which the offender should be summoned or brought see s.25(5), and paras 5–9 of the directions given by the Lord Chief Justice, reproduced in Chapter 4.

Great Britain, see note to s.22, *supra.*

An offence punishable with imprisonment, see note to s.22, *supra.*

The operational period, defined in s.22(1), *supra.*

Dealt with, under s.23(1), *supra.* If an offender has been convicted of an imprisonable offence during the operational period of a suspended sentence and the convicting court decides to make no order under s.23(1), the effect of these words is to prevent any other court having concurrent jurisdiction from issuing process. It does not, it is suggested, prevent the suspended sentence being brought into force later if the offender should commit any further offence during the operational period.

A summons/warrant, see Chapter 2.

s.25(3): The court by which the suspended sentence was passed, as to suspended sentences made on appeal, see s.24(3), *supra.*

The appropriate officer of the court, see note to s.23, *supra.*

s.25(4): On information, see form 84. G S Wilkinson in an article at 132 JPN 529 suggested that the period of limitation prescribed by s.127(1) MCA 1980 does not apply to an information laid under this section.

8d.64 **Suspended sentence supervision orders**
26. (1) Where a court passes on an offender a suspended sentence for a term of more than six months for a single offence, the court may make a suspended sentence supervision order (in this Act referred to as 'a supervising order') placing the offender under the supervision of a supervising officer for a period specified in the order, being a period not exceeding the operational period of the suspended sentence.

(2) (*Order making power*).

(3) A supervision order shall specify the petty sessions area in which the offender resides or will reside; and the supervising officer shall be a probation

officer appointed for or assigned to the area for the time being specified in the order (whether under this subsection or by virtue of subs (6) below).

(4) An offender in respect of whom a supervision order is in force shall keep in touch with the supervising officer in accordance with such instructions as he may from time to time be given by that officer and shall notify him of any change of address.

(5) The court by which a supervision order is made shall forthwith give copies of the order to a probation officer assigned to the court, and he shall give a copy to the offender and the supervising officer; and the court shall, except where it is itself a magistrates' court acting for the petty sessions area specified in the order, send to the clerk to the justices for the petty sessions area specified in the order a copy of the order, together with such documents and information relating to the case as it considers likely to be of assistance to a court acting for that area in exercising its functions in relation to the order.

(6) If a magistrates' court acting for the petty sessions area for the time being specified in a supervision order is satisfied that the offender proposes to change, or has changed, his residence from that petty sessions area to another petty sessions area, the court may, and on the application of the supervising officer shall, amend the order by substituting the other petty sesions area for the area specifed in the order.

(7) Where a supervision order is amended by a court under subs (6) above the court shall send to the clerk to the justices for the new area specified in the order a copy of the order, together with such documents and information relating to the case as it considers likely to be of assistance to a court acting for that area in exercising its functions in relation to the order.

(8) A supervision order shall cease to have effect if before the end of the period specified in it–
   (a) a court orders under s.23 of this Act that a suspended sentence passed in the proceedings in which the order was made shall have effect; or
   (b) the order is discharged or replaced under the subsequent provisions of this section.

(9) A supervision order may be discharged, on the application of the supervising officer or the offender–
   (a) if it was made by the Crown Court and includes a direction reserving the power of discharging it to that court, by the Crown Court;
   (b) in any other case by a magistrates' court acting for the petty sessions area for the time being specified in the order.

(10) Where under s.23 of this Act a court deals with an offender in respect of a suspended sentence by varying the operational period of the sentence or by making no order with respect to the sentence, the court may make a supervision order in respect of the offender–
   (a) in place of any such order made when the suspended sentence was passed; or
   (b) if the court which passed the sentence could have made such an order but did not do so; or
   (c) if that court could not then have made such an order but would have had power to do so if subs (1) above had then had effect as it has effect at the time when the offender is dealt with under s.23.

(11) On making a supervision order the court shall in ordinary language explain its effect to the offender.

COMMENTARY

Since a magistrates' court cannot impose a single sentence longer than six months (s.31 MCA 1980) it cannot make a suspended sentence supervision order. The functions of magistrates with regard to such orders are confined to discharge, variation and breach proceedings.

s.26(1): A suspended sentence, means a sentence to which an order under s.22(1) applies: s.57(1) PCCA 1973.

s.26(4): a summons or warrant may issue for breach of requirement and a fine may be imposed under s.27, *infra*.

s.26(9): the clerk of the discharging court must notify the court which made the original order: r.30(2) MC Rules 1981.

8d.65 **Breach of requirement of suspended sentence supervision order**
    27. (1) If at any time while a supervision order is in force in respect of an offender it appears on information to a justice of the peace acting for the petty sessions area for the time being specified in the order that the offender had failed to comply with any of the requirements of s.26(4) of this Act, the justice may issue a summons requiring the offender to appear at the place and time specified therein, or may, if the information is in writing and on oath, issue a warrant for his arrest.

    (2) Any summons or warrant issued under this section shall direct the offender to appear or be brought before a magistrates' court acting for the petty sessions area for the time being specified in the supervision order.

    (3) If it is proved to the satisfaction of the court before which an offender appears or is brought under this section that he has failed without reasonable cause to comply with any of the requirements of s.26(4) the court may, without prejudice to the continuance of the order, impose on him a fine not exceeding £400.

    (4) A fine imposed under this section shall be deemed for the purposes of any enactment to be a sum adjudged to be paid by a conviction.
    [*as amended by Sch.14 CJA 1982*].

COMMENTARY

Process under this section may be served or executed in Scotland under s.4 Summary Jurisdiction (Process) Act 1881: s.53 PCCA 1973.

s.27(1): At any time while a supervision order is in force, thus no action may be taken for breach of requirements after the expiry of the supervision order. Supervision order is defined in s.26(1), *supra*.

Summons/warrant, see Chapter 2.

s.27(3): legal aid may be granted in these proceedings: ss.28(2), 30(12) LAA 1974. For *Costs* see Chapter 9.

A fine, the clerk of the 'fining court' must notify the court which made the original order: r.30(3) MC Rules 1981.

CRIMINAL LAW ACT 1977

8d.66 **Prison sentence partly served and partly suspended**
    47. (1) Subject to subs (1A) below, where a court passes on an adult a sentence of imprisonment for a term of not less than three months and not more than two years, it may order that, after he has served part of the sentence in prison, the remainder of it shall be held in suspense.

    (1A) A court shall not make an order under this section unless the case appears to the court to be one in which an order under s.22 of the Powers of Criminal Courts Act 1973 (sentences wholly suspended) would be inappropriate.

    (1B) Subs (1A) above is without prejudice to s.20 of the Powers of Criminal Courts Act 1973 (restriction on imposing sentences of imprisonment on persons who have not previously served prison sentences).

    (2) The part of the sentence to be served in prison shall be not less than twenty eight days and the part to be held in suspense shall be not less than

one-quarter of the whole term, and the offender shall not be required to serve the latter part unless it is restored under subs (3) below; and this shall be explained to him by the court, using ordinary language and stating the substantial effect of that subsection.

(3) If at any time after the making of the order he is convicted of an offence punishable with imprisonment and committed during the whole period of the original sentence, then (subject to subs (4) and (4A) below) a court which is competent under this subsection may restore the part of the sentence held in suspense and order him to serve it.

(4) If a court considering the offender's case with a view to exercising the powers of subs (3) above, is of opinion that (in view of all the circumstances, including the facts of the subsequent offence) it would be unjust fully to restore the part of the sentence held in suspense, it shall either restore a lesser part or declare, with reasons given, its decision to make no order under the subsection.

(4A) If an order restoring part of a sentence has been made under subs (3) above, no order restoring any further part of it may be made.

(5) Where a court exercises those powers, it may direct that the restored part of the original sentence is to take effect as a term to be served either immediately or on the expiration of another term of imprisonment passed on the offender by that or another court.

(6) 'Adult' in this section means a person who has attained the age of 21; and 'the whole period' of a sentence is the time which the offender would have had to serve in prison if the sentence had been passed without an order under subs (1) above and he had no remission under s.25(1) of the Prison Act 1952 (industry and good conduct in prison).

(7) Schedule 9 to this Act has effect with respect to procedural, sentencing and miscellaneous matters ancillary to those dealt with above in this section, including in particular the courts which are competent under subs (3) above.

(8) This section and para 1 to 6 of Sch.9 to this Act and the Powers of Criminal Courts Act 1973 shall be construed and have effect as if this section and those paragraphs of the Schedule were contained in that Act.

(9)–(11) (*Orders*).
[*as amended by s.30 CJA 1982*].

COMMENTARY

See *Partly suspended sentences*, 8d.11.

s.47(1): A sentence of imprisonment, by virtue of PCCA 1973, as applied by s.47(8), this term does *not include* a committal in default of payment of any sum of money or for want of sufficient distress to satisfy any sum of money, or for failure to do, or abstain from doing, anything required to be done or left undone.
For consecutive terms, see Sch.9, para 3A, *infra*.

s.47(2): there is no rule of law requiring that if part of a sentence is to be suspended it is to be the greater part: *R v Lunn* (1982) 4 Cr App R (S) 343.

s.47(4): Make no order, the *reason* for the court's decision must be entered in the register: r.29 (1A) MC Rules 1981.

s.47(6): Attained the age, a person attains a given age at the commencement of the relevant anniversary of the date of his birth: s.9 Family Law Reform Act 1969.

The whole period, includes the time before the offender was released from prison, even though he had absconded: *R v Taylor* [1984] Crim LR 693.

SCHEDULE 9

8d.67   **Matters ancillary to Section 47**
PROBATION ORDERS

1. Where a court makes an order under s.47(1) above with respect to a sentence of imprisonment, it shall not make a probation order in the offender's case in respect of another offence of which he is convicted by or before that court, or for which he is dealt with by that court.

COURTS COMPETENT TO RESTORE SENTENCE HELD IN SUSPENSE

2. (1) In relation to a sentence of imprisonment part of which is held in suspense, the courts competent under s.47(3) above are–

(a) the Crown Court; and

(b) where the sentence was passed by a magistrates' court, any magistrates' court before which the offender appears or is brought.

(2) Where an offender is convicted by a magistrates' court of an offence punishable with imprisonment and the court is satisfied that the offence was committed during the whole period of a sentence passed by the Crown Court with an order under s.47(1) above–

(a) it may, if it thinks fit, commit him to custody or on bail to the Crown Court; and

(b) if it does not, it shall give written notice of the conviction to the appropriate officer of that court.

(3) For the purposes of this and the next following paragraph, a sentence of imprisonment passed on an offender with an order under s.47(1) above shall be treated as having been passed (with such an order) by the court which originally sentenced him.

RECALL OF OFFENDER ON RE-CONVICTION

3. (1) If it appears to the Crown Court, where that court has jurisdiction in accordance with subpara (2) below, or to a justice of the peace having jurisdiction in accordance with that sub-paragraph that an offender has been convicted in Great Britain of an offence punishable with imprisonment committed during the whole period of a sentence passed with an order under s.47(1) above and that he has not been dealt with in respect of the part of the sentence held in suspense, that court or justice may, subject to the following provisions of this paragraph, issue a summons requiring the offender to appear at the place and time specified therein, or a warrant for his arrest.

(2) Jurisdiction for the purposes of sub-para (1) above may be exercised–

(a) if the sentence was passed by the Crown Court, by that court;

(b) if it was passed by a magistrates' court, by a justice acting for the area for which that court acted,

(3) Where an offender is convicted by a court in Scotland of an offence punishable with imprisonment and the court is informed that the offence was committed during the whole period of a sentence passed in England and Wales with an order under s.47(1) above, the court shall give written notice of the conviction to the appropriate officer of the court by which the original sentence was passed.

(4) Unless he is acting in consequence of a notice under sub-para (3) above, a justice of the peace shall not issue a summons under this paragraph except on information and shall not issue a warrant under this paragraph except on information in writing and on oath.

(5) A summons or warrant issued under this paragraph shall direct the offender to appear or to be brought before the court by which the original sentence of imprisonment was passed.

CONSECUTIVE SENTENCES OF IMPRISONMENT

3A. (1) This paragraph applies where–

(a) an offender is serving consecutive sentences of imprisonment; and
(b) at least one of the sentences was passed with an order under s.47(1) of this Act.

(2) Where this paragraph applies the offender shall, so far as the consecutive sentences are concerned, be treated for the purposes–
(a) of computing the date when he should be released from prison; and
(b) of calculating the term of imprisonment liable to be restored under s.47(3) of this Act,
as if he had been sentenced to a single term of imprisonment with an order under s.47(1) of this Act of which the part which he is immediately required to serve in prison were the aggregate–
(i) of the part which he is required to serve in prison of any consecutive sentence passed with an order under s.47(1) of this Act; and
(ii) of the whole term of any other consecutive sentence
and of which the part which is held in suspense were the aggregate of all parts of the sentences which were ordered to be held in suspense under that section.

(3) Section 47(6) of this Act shall have effect, in relation to any consecutive sentence passed with an order under s.47(2) of this Act, as if for the words following the word 'prison' there were substituted the following words 'if–
(a) none of the sentences to which he is subject had been passed with an order under subs (1) above; and
(b) he had not had, in respect of any sentence passed with such an order, any remission under s.25(1) of the Prison Act 1952 (industry and good conduct in prison)'.

(4) In this paragraph 'a consecutive sentence' means a sentence which is one of two or more sentences of imprisonment the terms of which have been ordered to run consecutively.

MISCELLANEOUS (PROCEDURAL)
4. Where the offender is before the Crown Court with a view to the exercise by that court of its powers under s.47(3) above, any question whether and, if so, when he has been convicted of an offence shall be determined by the court and not by the verdict of a jury.

5. Where the offender has been before a court with a view to its exercising those powers, the appropriate officer shall–
(a) if the court decided not to exercise the powers, record that fact; and
(b) whether or not it exercised them, notify the appropriate officer of the court which passed the original sentence as to the manner in which the offender was dealt with.

6. For the purposes of any enactment conferring rights of appeal in criminal cases, the restoration by a court under s.47(3) above of a part of a sentence held in suspense shall be treated as a sentence passed on the offender by that court for the original offence, that is to say the offence for which the original sentence was passed with an order under s.47(1) above.

MISCELLANEOUS (CONSEQUENTIAL)
7. Subject to s.60(1C) of the Criminal Justice Act 1967 (release on licence) where a sentence of imprisonment is passed with an order under s.47(1) above, it is still to be regarded for all purposes as a sentence of imprisonment for the term stated by the court, notwithstanding that part of it is held in suspense by virtue of the order; and, for the avoidance of doubt, a sentence of which part is held in suspense by virtue of such an order is not to be regarded as falling within the expression 'suspended sentence' for the purposes of any legislation, instrument or document.

8. Where an offender is sentenced to imprisonment with an order under s.47 above and, having served part of the sentence in prison, is discharged under s.25(1) of the Prison Act 1952 (remission for industry and good

conduct), the remainder of the sentence being held in suspense, the sentence is not to be regarded as expiring under that section.

9–11 . . .
[*as amended by Sch.14 CJA 1982*].

MAGISTRATES' COURTS ACT 1980

8d.68 **General limit on power of magistrates' court to impose imprisonment**
    31. (1) Without prejudice to s.133 below, a magistrates' court shall not have power to impose imprisonment or youth custody for more than six months in respect of any one offence.

(2) Unless expressly excluded, subs (1) above shall apply even if the offence in question is one for which a person would otherwise be liable on summary conviction to imprisonment or youth custody for more than six months.

(3) Any power of a magistrates' court to impose a term of imprisonment for non-payment of a fine, or for want of sufficient distress to satisfy a fine, shall not be limited by virtue of subs (1) above.

(4) In subs (3) above 'fine' includes a pecuniary penalty but does not include a pecuniary forfeiture for pecuniary compensation.
[*as amended by Sch.14 CJA 1982*].

COMMENTARY
s.31(1): this does not affect the power in s.133 MCA 1980 to pass consecutive sentences in excess of six months in aggregate.

Impose imprisonment, means pass a sentence of imprisonment or fix a term of imprisonment for failure to pay any sum of money, or for want of sufficient distress to satisfy any sum of money, or for failure to do or abstain from doing anything required to be done or left undone: s.150(1).

s.31(3): Fine, see s.31 (4).

8d.69 **Minimum term**
    132. A magistrates' court shall not impose imprisonment for less than five days.

COMMENTARY
Impose imprisonment: see note to s.31, *supra*. Committals in default following part payment of a fine are not subject to this restriction: r.55(5) MC Rules 1981. Nor are orders of detention under s.134, 135, 136 MCA 1980.

8d.70 **Consecutive terms of imprisonment**
    133. (1) A magistrates' court imposing imprisonment or youth custody on any person may order that the term of imprisonment or youth custody shall commence on the expiration of any other term of imprisonment or youth custody imposed by that or any other court; but where a magistrates' court imposes two or more terms of imprisonment or youth custody to run consecutively the aggregate of such terms shall not, subject to the provisions of this section, exceed six months.

(2) If two or more of the terms imposed by the court are imposed in respect of an offence triable either way which was tried summarily otherwise than in pursuance of s.22(2) above, the aggregate of the terms so imposed and any other terms imposed by the court may exceed six months but shall not, subject to the following provisions of this section, exceed 12 months.

(2A) *In relation to the imposition of terms of detention in a young offender institution subsection (2) above shall have effect as if the reference to an offence triable either way were a reference to such an offence or an offence triable only on indictment.*

(3) The limitations imposed by the preceding subsections shall not operate to reduce the aggregate of the terms that the court may impose in respect of any offences below the term which the court has power to impose in respect of any one of those offences.

(4) Where a person has been sentenced by a magistrates' court to imprisonment and a fine for the same offence a period of imprisonment imposed for non-payment of the fine, or for want of sufficient distress to satisfy the fine, shall not be subject to the limitations imposed by the preceding subsections.

(5) For the purposes of this section a term of imprisonment shall be deemed to be imposed in respect of an offence if it is imposed as a sentence or in default of payment of a sum adjudged to be paid by the conviction or for want of sufficient distress to satisfy such a sum.
[as amended by Sch.14 CJA 1982. Subs (2A) will be added by [Sch.13, para 56] CJA 1988 from a date to be appointed].

COMMENTARY

For the use of *concurrent and consecutive sentences* see 8.03.

s.133(1): this subsection limits only the total imprisonment etc imposed on the same occasion: *Forrest v Brighton Justices* [1981] 2 All ER 711 (alternatives of imprisonment in default of payment of fine).

Imposing imprisonment, see the note to s.31, *supra* and *R v Metropolitan Stipendiary Magistrate for South Westminster, ex p. Green* [1977] 1 All ER 353.

s.133(2): An offence triable either way, see note to s.38, *supra.*

In pursuance of s.22(2), this refers to certain offences of criminal damage.

Detention in police cells, etc   **8d.71**
   134. (1) A magistrates' court having power to impose imprisonment on any person may instead of doing so order him to be detained for any period not exceeding four days in a place certified by the Secretary of State to be suitable for the purpose.

(2) The Secretary of State may certify under this section any police cells, bridewell or similar place provided by him and on the application of any other police authority, any such place provided by that authority.

(3) A woman or girl shall not be detained in any such place except under the supervision of women.
   Section 6(b) of the Interpretation Act 1978 (feminine includes masculine) does not apply for the purposes of this subsection.

(4) (*Regulations*).

(5), (6) . . .

(7) Subsection (2) above shall, in its application to the City of London, have effect as if for the references therein to the police authority there were substituted references to the Commissioner of Police for the City of London.

(8) This section shall have effect in relation to a person aged 17 or over but less than 21 as if references in it to imprisonment were references to youth custody.
[as amended by Sch.14 CJA 1982. Note that s.134 will 'cease to have effect' when [Sch.15] CJA 1988 comes into force: see Appendix III].

COMMENTARY

s.134(1): Power to impose imprisonment, see note to s.31, *supra.*

   Imprisonment here includes youth custody: s.134(8).

Detained . . .in a place certified, an order under this section is not a sentence of imprisonment and may not be suspended under s.22 PCCA 1973. Committal must be by warrant: r.94 MC Rules 1981; see form 57. The order of detention should be so described in the register: HOC 35/52/C.

The making of such an order does not deprive the court of its powers to order costs or compensation: s.150(7) MCA 1980.

s.134(2): Police authority, defined in s.62 and Sch.8 Police Act 1964; and see s.134(7).

8d.72 **Detention of offender for one day in court-house or police station**

135. (1) A magistrates' court that has power to commit to prison a person convicted of an offence, or would have that power but for ss.82 or 88 above, may order him to be detained within the precincts of the court-house or at any police station until such hour, not later than 8 o'clock in the evening of the day on which the order is made, as the court may direct, and, if it does so, shall not, where it has power to commit him to prison, exercise that power.

(2) A court shall not make such an order under this section as will deprive the offender of a reasonable opportunity of returning to his abode on the day of the order.

(3) This section shall have effect in relation to a person aged 17 or over but less than 21 as if references in it to prison were references to detention under s.9 of the Criminal Justice Act 1982 (detention of persons aged 17 to 20 for default).

[as amended by Sch.14 CJA 1982].

COMMENTARY

s.135(1): Power to commit to prison, eg by way of sentence of imprisonment or in default of payment of fines or under s.75(3) or 84 MCA 1980. This term includes detention under s.9 CJA (detention of persons aged 17–20 for default) but not, seemingly, as a sentence for persons of that age.

Or would have that power but for, thus, an order under this section is not subject to the restrictions on imposing alternatives to a fine on conviction, the need to hold a means inquiry, or the need to receive a report from a fines supervision officer.

Order him to be detained, no warrant is necessary. The order of detention should be so described in the register. HOC 35/53C. The making of such an order does not deprive the court of the power to order payment of costs or compensation: s.150(7) of the Act.

8d.73 **Committal to custody overnight at police station for non-payment of sum adjudged by conviction**

136. (1) A magistrates' court that has power to commit to prison a person in default of payment of a sum adjudged to be paid by a summary conviction, or would have that power but for ss.82 or 88 above, may issue a warrant for his detention in a police station, and, if it does so, shall not, where it has power to commit him to prison, exercise that power.

(2) A warrant under this section, unless the sum adjudged to be paid by the conviction is sooner paid–
    (a) shall authorise any police constable to arrest the defaulter and take him to a police station, and
    (b) shall require the officer in charge of the station to detain him there until 8 o'clock in the morning of the day following that on which he is arrested, or, if he is arrested between midnight and 8 o'clock in the morning, until 8 o'clock in the morning of the day on which he is arrested.

(4) The Secretary of State may make regulations for the inspection of places certified by him under this section, for the treatment of persons detained in them and generally for the purpose of carrying this section into effect.

(5) Any expenses incurred in the maintenance of persons detained under this section shall be defrayed out of moneys provided by Parliament.

(6) ...

(7) Subsection (2) above shall, in its application to the City of London, have effect as if for the references therein to the police authority there were sustituted references to the Commissioner of Police for the City of London.
Note
Subs (2)(a) shall be amended to read as follows by [s.64(2)] CJA 1988 from a date to be appointed:
   (a) shall authorise any police constable or any person who–
      (a) is employed by an authority of a prescribed class;
      (b) is authorised in the prescribed manner to execute such warrants; and
      (c) is acting within the area for which the authority that employs him performs its functions.

COMMENTARY

The power under this section may be used for enforcing payment of fines, compensation and costs, but not as an alternative to a sentence of imprisonment.

s.136(1): Power to commit to prison, this *excludes offenders under 21:* s.1(1) CJA 1982.

Or would have that power but for, see note to s.135, *supra.*

Issue a warrant, see form 58.

CRIMINAL JUSTICE ACT 1982

General restriction on custodial sentences   **8d.74**
   1. (1) Subject to subs (2) below, no court shall pass a sentence of imprisonment on a person under 21 years of age or commit such a person to prison for any reason.

   (2) Nothing in subs (1) above shall prevent the committal to prison of a person under 21 years of age who is remanded in custody or committed in custody for trial or sentence.

   (3) No court shall pass a sentence of Borstal training.

   (3A) Subject to section 53 of the Children and Young Persons Act 1933 (Punishment of certain grave crimes), the only custodial orders that a court may make where a person under 21 years of age is convicted or found guilty of an offence are–
   (a) a sentence of detention in a young offender institution under section 1A below; and
   (b) a sentence of custody for life under section 8 below.

   (4) Where a person under 21 years of age is convicted or found guilty of an offence, the court may not–
   (a) make a detention centre order in respect of him under s.4 below;
   (b) pass a youth custody sentence on him under s.6 below; or
   (c) pass a sentence of custody for life on him under s.8(2) below,
unless it is of the opinion that no other method of dealing with him is appropriate because it appears to the court that he is unable or unwilling to respond to non-custodial penalties or because a custodial sentence is necessary for the protection of the public or because the offence was so serious that a non-custodial sentence cannot be justified.

   (4) A court may not–
   (a) pass a sentence of detention in a young offender institution; or
   (b) pass a sentence of custody for life under section 8(2) below,
unless it is satisfied–
      (i) that the circumstances, including the nature and the gravity of the offence, are such that if the offender were aged 21 or over the court would pass a sentence of imprisonment; and
      (ii) that he qualifies for a custodial sentence.

   (4A) An offender qualifies for a custodial sentence if–

(a) *he has a history of failure to respond to non-custodial penalities and is unable or unwilling to respond to them; or*

(b) *only a custodial sentence would be adequate to protect the public from serious harm from him; or*

(c) *the offence of which he has been convicted or found guilty was so serious that a non-custodial sentence for it cannot be justified.*

(5) No court shall commit a person under 21 years of age to be detained under s.9 below unless it is of the opinion that no other method of dealing with him is appropriate.

(6) For the purpose of any provision of this Act which requires the determination of the age of a person by the court or the Secretary of State his age shall be deemed to be that which it appears to the court or the Secretary of State (as the case may be) to be after considering any available evidence.

[*subs (3A) and (4A) will be added by [s.121] CJA 1988 from a date to be appointed and subs (4) will be substituted from that date.*]

8d.74a   **Detention in a young offender institution**

1A. (1) Subject to section 8 below and to section 53 of the Children and Young Persons Act 1933, where–

(a) *a male offender under 21 but not less than 14 years of age or a female offender under 21 but not less than 15 years of age is convicted of an offence which is punishable with imprisonment in the case of a person aged 21 or over; and*

(b) *the court is satisfied of the matters referred to in section 1(4) above, the sentence that the court is to pass is a sentence of detention in a young offender institution.*

(2) Subject to section 1B(1) and (2) below, the maximum term of detention in a young offender institution that a court may impose for an offence is the same as the maximum term of imprisonment that it may impose for that offence.

(3) Subject to subsection (4) below and section 1B(3) below, a court shall not pass a sentence for an offender's detention in a young offender institution for less than 21 days.

(4) A court may pass a sentence of detention in a young offender institution for less than 21 days for an offence under section 15(11) below.

(5) Subject to section 1B(4) below, where–

(a) *an offender is convicted of more than one offence for which he is liable to a sentence of detention in a young offender institution; or*

(b) *an offender who is serving a sentence of detention in a young offender institution is convicted of one or more further offences for which he is liable to such a sentence,*

the court shall have the same power to pass consective sentences of detention in a young offender institution as if they were sentences of imprisonment.

(6) Where an offender who–

(a) *is serving a sentence of detention in a young offender institution; and*

(b) *is aged over 21 years,*

is convicted of one or more further offences for which he is liable to imprisonment, the court shall have the power to pass one or more sentences of imprisonment to run consecutively upon the sentence of detention in a young offender institution.

[*s.1A will be added by [s.121] CJA 1988 from a date to be appointed. See also the transitional provisions in [Sch.8, Pt. II] CJA 1988*].

8d.74b   **Special provision for offenders under 17**

1B. (1) In the case of a male offender under 15 the maximum term of detention in a young offender institution that a court may impose is whichever is the lesser of–

(a) the maximum term of imprisonment the court may impose for the offence; and

(b) 4 months.

(2) In the case of an offender aged 15 or 16 the maximum term of detention in a young offender institution that a court may impose is whichever is the lesser of–

(a) the maximum term of imprisonment the court may impose for the offence; and

(b) 12 months.

(3) Where an offender is a female under 17 a court shall not pass a sentence for her detention in a young offender institution whose effect would be that she would be sentenced to a total term of four months or less.

(4) A court shall not pass a sentence of detention in a young offender institution on an offender whose effect would be that the offender would be sentenced to a total term which exceeds–

(a) if the offender is male and under 15, 4 months; and

(b) if the offender is aged 15 or 16, 12 months.

(5) Where the total term of detention in a young offender institution to which an offender is sentenced exceeds–

(a) in the case of a male offender under 15, 4 months; and

(b) in the case of an offender aged 15 or 16, 12 months,

so much of the term as exceeds 4 or 12 months, as the case may be, shall be treated as remitted.

(6) In this section 'total term' means–

(a) in the case of an offender sentenced (whether or not on the same occasion) to two or more terms of detention in a young offender institution which are consecutive or wholly or partly concurrent, the aggregate of those terms;

(b) in the case of any other offender, the term of the sentence of detention in a young offender institution in question.

[s.1B will be inserted by [s.121] CJA 1988 from a date to be appointed].

COMMENTARY

For the effects of s.1 see under *Restrictions on custodial sentences for young offenders* **8d.17**.

s.1(4): For the purpose of this subsection the court must obtain and consider certain information (s.2(1), *infra*) *and, unless it is unnecessary,* obtain a social inquiry report (s.2(2), (3)).

Before making a detention centre order or passing a youth custody sentence, the court must consider that a custodial sentence is the only appropriate method of dealing with the offender: ss.1(4), 4(1), 6(1), *infra*. The test involves two further hurdles. ie first, one of the exceptions set out in s.1(4) must apply, ie '*inability or unwillingness*' to respond to non-custodial measures, '*protection of the public*', or that the offence was '*so serious*' that a non-custodial sentence cannot be justified; second the court must 'state in open court' its reason for such a conclusion: see s.2(4), *infra*. Sentencers must have regard to the criteria in s.1(4), whether or not they are brought to their attention: *R v Bradbourn* (1985) 7 Cr App R (S) 180; *R v Passmore* (1985) 7 Cr App R (S) 377 (a 'drastic step' to take away a young man's liberty for the first time); and see generally the cases on s.1(4), *Restrictions on custodial sentences for young offenders*, 8d.17.

s.1(5) for the purpose of this subsection, the court must obtain and consider certain information: s.2(1), *infra*.

Social inquiry reports etc   8d.75

2. (1) For the purpose of determining whether there is any appropriate method of dealing with a person under 21 years of age other than a method whose use in the case of such a person is restricted by s.1(4) or (5) above the court shall obtain and consider information about the circumstances and shall take into account any information before the court which is relevant to his character and his physical and mental condition.

(2) Subject to subs (3) below, the court shall in every case obtain a social inquiry report for the purpose of determining whether there is any appropriate method of dealing with a person other than a method whose use is restricted by s.1(4) above.

(3) Subsection (2) above does not apply if, in the circumstances of the case, the court is of the opinion that it is unnecessary to obtain a social inquiry report.

(4) Where a magistrates' court deals with a person under 21 years of age by a method whose use in the case of such a person is restricted by section 1(4) above, it shall state in open court that no other method of dealing with him is appropriate because it appears to the court that he is unable or unwilling to respond to non-custodial penalties or because a custodial sentence is necessary for the protection of the public or because the offence was so serious that a non-custodial sentence cannot be justified.

(4) Where–
(a) the Crown Court passes a sentence of detention in a young offender institution or a sentence of custody for life under section 8(2) below, or
(b) a magistrates' court passes a sentence of detention in a young offender institution,
it shall be its duty–
(i) to state in open court that it is satisfied that he qualifies for a custodial sentence under one or more of the paragraphs of section 1(4A) above, the paragraph or paragraphs in question and why it is so satisfied; and
(ii) to explain to the offender in open court and in ordinary language why it is passing a custodial sentence on him.

(5) Where a magistrates' court deals with a person under 21 years of age by a method whose use in the case of such a person is restricted by s.1(5) above, it shall state in open court the reason for its opinion that no other method of dealing with him is appropriate.

(6) Where a magistrates' court deals with a person under 21 years of age by a method whose use in the case of such a person is restricted by s.1(4) above without obtaining a social inquiry report, it shall state in open court the reason for its opinion that it was unnecessary to obtain such a report.

(7) A magistrates' court shall cause a reason stated under subs (4), (5) or (6) above to be specified in the warrant of commitment and to be entered in the register.

(8) No sentence or order shall be invalidated by the failure of a court to comply with subs (2) above, but any other court on appeal from that court shall obtain a social inquiry report if none was obtained by the court below, unless it is of the opinion that in the circumstances of the case it is unnecessary to do so.

(9) In determining whether it should deal with the appellant by a method different from that by which the court below dealt with him the court hearing the appeal shall consider any social inquiry report obtained by it or by the court below.

(10) In this section 'social inquiry report' means a report about a person and his circumstances made by a probation officer or by a social worker of a local authority social services department.
[*subs (4) will be substituted by [s.121] CJA 1988 from a date to be appointed*].

COMMENTARY

s.2(1): it would seem that this merely re-enacts the practice at common law concerning the usual matters presented to the court by the prosecution and the defence.

s.2(2): Social inquiry report, defined in s.2(1) in terms which are *not confined to a written report*. However, unless the defendant and his circumstances are already well known to the reporting officer, the calling for a 'stand-down' report should be approached with caution.

s.2(3): Unnecessary, not merely inconvenient. Where a defendant in the course of a long trial put his character in issue and the judge went into his background, a report was held to be unnecessary: *R v Peter* [1975] Crim LR 593. A judge failed to comply with this section where no report was available due, in part, to industrial action and in part to local practice and where there was no suggestion that the report was unnecessry: *R v Massheder* [1984] Crim LR 185.

s.2(4): this appears to require the court to stipulate, not only which of the s.1(4) criteria it relies on, but the reason why it does so: see s.2(7).

s.2(5): see also s.2(7).

s.2(6): see also s.2(7).

s.2(10): see the note '*Social inquiry report*', *supra*.

Restrictions on imposing custodial sentences on persons under 21 not legally represented   8d.76

   3. (1) A magistrates' court on summary conviction or the Crown Court on committal for sentence or on conviction on indictment shall not–
(a) make a detention centre order under s.4 below;
(b) pass a youth custody sentence under s.6 below;
(c) pass a sentence of custody for life under s.8(2) below; or
(d) make an order for detention under s.53(2) of the Children and Young Persons Act 1933,
in respect of or on a person who is not legally represented in that court, unless either–
  (i) he applied for legal aid and the application was refused on the ground that it did not appear his means were such that he required assistance; or
 (ii) having been informed of his right to apply for legal aid and had the opportunity to do so, he refused or failed to apply.

   (2) For the purposes of this section a person is to be treated as legally represented in a court if, but only if, he has the assistance of counsel or a solicitor to represent him in the proceedings in that court at some time after he is found guilty and before he is sentenced, and in subs (1)(i) and (ii) above 'legal aid' means legal aid for the purposes of proceedings in that court, whether the whole proceedings or the proceedings on or in relation to sentence; but in the case of a person committed to the Crown Court for sentence or trial, it is immaterial whether he applied for legal aid in the Crown Court to, or was informed of his right to apply by, that court or the court which committed him.

COMMENTARY
Compare the notes to s.21 PCCA 1973, *supra*.

Orders for detention of male offenders aged 14 to 20   8d.77
   4. (1) Where–
(a) a male offender under 21 but not less than 14 years of age is convicted of an offence which is punishable with imprisonment in the case of a person aged 21 or over; and
(b) the court considers–
  (i) that the only appropriate method of dealing with him is to pass a custodial sentence on him; but
 (ii) that the term of such a sentence should be no more than four months,
the order that the court is to make, subject to the provisions of this section and to s.5(2) below, is an order for his detention in a detention centre for such period, not exceeding four months, as it considers appropriate.

   (2) If the maximum term of imprisonment that a court could impose for an offence is less than four months, the maximum term of detention it may specify for that offence in a detention centre order is the same as the maximum term of imprisonment.

(3) Subject to subs (4) below, no order may be made under this section for the detention of an offender in a detention centre for less than 21 days.

(4) A court may order the detention of an offender in a detention centre for less than 21 days for an offence under s.15(11) below.

(5) Subject to subs (6) below, a court shall not make an order under this section for the detention of an offender in a detention centre–
    (a) if it considers that his detention in such a centre would be unsuitable because of his mental or physical condition; or
    (b) if he is serving or has ever served a sentence–
        (i) of imprisonment;
        (ii) of detention under s.53 of the Children and Young Persons Act 1933 (detention on conviction of certain grave crimes);
        (iii) of Borstal training;
        (iv) of youth custody under s.6 below; or
        (v) of custody for life under s.8 below.

(6) A court may make an order under this section for the detention in a detention centre of an offender who has served a sentence of a description specified in subs 5(b) above if it appears to the court that there are special circumstances (whether relating to the offence or to the offender) which warrant the making of such an order in his case.

(7) An order under this section is referred to in this Act as a 'detention centre order'.

COMMENTARY

The effects of this section are summarised in *Detention Centres*, 8d.16. For the limitations on passing a detention centre see ss.1(4), 2(1)–(4), (6), (7). For restrictions on sentencing an *unrepresented defendant* see s.3.

For the determination of age see s.1(1), *supra*.

s.4(1): Four months, ie calendar months: Sch.1 Interpretation Act 1978.

s.4(5): where a detention center order is precluded by this subsection, a youth custody sentence may be passed for less than the usual period of youth custody: ss.6(2) and 7(6).

Note the effects of the CJA 1988, when in force, see the amendments to s.1 CJA 1982, *supra* and Appendix III. A detention centre order as such becomes redundant in favour of the 'generic' sentence of detention in a *young offender institution*.

8d.78   **Consecutive terms and aggregate periods of detention**
    5. (1) Subject to the provisions of this section, any court which makes a detention centre order may direct that the term of detention under the order shall commence on the expiration of a term of detention under another detention centre order.

(2) No court shall–
    (a) make a detention centre order in respect of an offender who is subject to another such order; or
    (b) give a direction under subs (1) above,
if the effect would be that the offender would be ordered to be detained in a detention centre for more than four months at a time.

(3) If a court makes such an order or gives such a direction in respect of an offender aged less than 15 years, so much of the aggregate of all the terms of detention in a detention centre to which he is subject as exceeds four months shall be treated as remitted.

(4) If a court makes such an order or gives such a direction in respect of an offender aged 15 years or over, he shall be treated for all purposes as if he had been sentenced to a term of youth custody equal to the aggregate of all the terms of detention in a detention centre to which he is subject.

(5) Where–

(a) an offender not less than 15 years of age is serving a term of detention in a detention centre; and

(b) on his conviction of an offence the court by which he is convicted considers that the only appropriate method of dealing with him is to pass a custodial sentence on him; and

(c) the length of sentence which the court considers appropriate is such that the period for which he would be ordered to be detained by virtue of the sentence, together with the period for which any detention centre order to which he is subject directed that he should be detained, would exceed four months,

the sentence that the court is to pass is a youth custody sentence for the term which it considers appropriate.

(6) Where a court passes a youth custody sentence on an offender under subs (5) above, it shall direct that any detention centre order to which he is subject at the time of conviction for which the youth custody sentence is imposed shall be treated for all purposes as if it had been a sentence of youth custody.

(7) Where a detention centre order is treated as a sentence of youth custody by virtue of this section, the portion of the term of detention imposed by the order which the offender has already served shall be deemed to have been a portion of a term of youth custody.

COMMENTARY

The effect of this section is to permit consecutive detention centre orders to be made subject to an *overriding aggregate of four months*. Excess terms are *automatically converted* to youth custody if the offender is 15 or older (s.5(4)); the excess is remitted if he is under that age (s.5(3)).

Youth custody: offenders aged 15 to 20   **8d.79**
    6. (1) Subject to s.8 below and to s.53 of the Children and Young Persons Act 1933, where–

(a) a person under 21 but not less than 15 years of age is convicted of an offence which is punishable with imprisonment in the case of a person aged 21 or over; and

(b) the court considers for reasons which shall be stated in open court that the only appropriate method of dealing with the offender is to pass a custodial sentence; and

(c) either–

    (i) the court considers that it would be appropriate to sentence the offender to a term of more than four months, or where the offender has been convicted of more than one offence, to terms of more than four months in the aggregate; or

    (ii) the case falls within subss (2) or (4) below, the sentence that the court is to pass is a sentence of youth custody.

(2) A case falls within this subsection where the offender is male and the court determines–

(a) that a sentence of four months or less would be appropriate; but

(b) that a detention centre order is precluded by s.4(5) above.

(3) If a court passes a sentence of youth custody on an offender because it considers that his detention in a detention centre would be unsuitable because of his mental condition, it shall certify in the warrant of commitment that it passed the sentence of youth custody for that reason.

(4) A case falls within this subsection if the offender is female and has attained the age of 17 years.

(5) A sentence under this section is referred to in this Act as a 'youth custody sentence'.

COMMENTARY

For the effects of this section see under *Youth custody*, 8d.15. For the determination of age, see s.1(6), *supra*. For the place of detention, see s.12, *infra*. *Note* the effects of the CJA 1988, when in force, see the amendments to s.1 CJA 1982, *supra* and Appendix III to this work. Youth custody, as such becomes redundant in favour of the 'generic' sentence of *detention in a young offender institution*.

s.6.(1): Reasons, see s.1(4), *supra*.

s.6.(2): if the offender is sentenced to youth custody because a detention centre order would be unsuitable by reason of his mental condition, the place of detention is to be determined in accordance with s.12(3), *supra*.

8d.80
Youth custody: length of term

7. (1) Subject to subs (8) below, the maximum term of youth custody that a court may impose for an offence is the same as the maximum term of imprisonment that it may impose for that offence.

(2) Subject to subs (8) below, where–
(a) an offender is convicted of more than one offence for which he is liable to a sentence of youth custody; or
(b) an offender who is serving a youth custody sentence is convicted of one or more further offences for which he is liable to such a sentence,
the court shall have the same power to pass consecutive youth custody sentences as if they were sentences of imprisonment.

(3) Where an offender who–
(a) is serving a youth custody sentence; and
(b) is aged over 21 years,
is convicted of one or more further offences for which he is liable to imprisonment, the court shall have the power to pass one or more sentences of imprisonment to run consecutively upon the youth custody sentence.

(4) Subject to subs (6) and (7) below, a court shall not pass a youth custody sentence on an offender whose effect would be that he would be sentenced to a total term which is less than the usual term of youth custody.

(5) The usual term of youth custody is a term exceeding four months.

(6) If a case falls within s.6(2) or (4) above, the term of youth custody in which the offender is sentenced may be less than the usual term but not less than 21 days.

(7) A court may pass a sentence of youth custody for less than 21 days for an offence under s.15(11) below.

(8) (*Juvenile court*).

(9) In subs (4) above 'total term' means–
(a) in the case of an offender sentenced to two or more terms of youth custody which are consecutive or wholly or partly concurrent, the aggregate of those terms;
(b) in the case of any other offender, the term of the youth custody sentence in question.

COMMENTARY

For the determination of age, see s.1(6), *supra*.

s.7(2):The same power, ie consecutive terms may be passed up to six months in aggregate or twelve months if two or more of the offences are triable either way: s.133 MCA 1980, *supra*.

s.7(4): Total term, s.9(9).

The usual term of youth custody, see s.7(5).

8d.81
Detention of persons aged 17 to 20 for default or contempt

9. (1) In any case where, but for s.1(1) above, a court would have power–

(a) to commit a person under 21 but not less than 17 years of age to prison for default in payment of a fine or any other sum of money; or
(b) to make an order fixing a term of imprisonment in the event of such a default by such a person; or
(c) to commit such a person to prison for contempt of court or any kindred offence,

the court shall have power, subject to s.1(5) above, to commit him to be detained under this section or, as the case may be, to make an order fixing a term of detention under this section in the event of default, for a term not exceeding the term of imprisonment.

COMMENTARY

For the determination of age, see s.1(6), *supra*.

9(1), *Note* that the making of an order under s.9 is subject to s.1(5), *supra* (no other method appropriate). That in turn attracts ss.2(1), (5) and (7).

Contempt of court, see under s.12 Contempt of Court Act 1981 or under s.97(4) MCA 1980.

Kindred offence, this clearly applies to offences under s.63(3) (disobedience of an order of the court); and to a refusal to be bound over: *Howley v Oxford* (1985) 81 Cr App R 246.

Detained under this section, see s.12(1), *infra*.

Accommodation of young offenders and defaulters etc   8d.82

12. (1) Subject to subs (11) below, a male offender sentenced to youth custody shall be detained in a youth custody centre–
(a) if the terms of his youth custody sentence is more than four but not more than 18 months; and
(b) if the term is not treated by virtue of s.67 of the Criminal Justice Act 1967 as reduced to less than 21 days.
unless the Secretary of State gives a direction for his detention in a prison under subs (4) below.

(2) (*Juveniles*).

(3) Subject to subs (11) below, an offender who has been sentenced to youth custody because the court considered that his detention in a detention centre would be unsuitable because of his mental condition is to be detained in a youth custody centre or in a remand centre as the Secretary of State may from time to time direct unless–
(a) the term of his youth custody sentence is treated by virtue of s.67 of the Criminal Justice Act 1967 as reduced to less than 21 days; or
(b) he has been sentenced under s.15(11) below to youth custody for less than 21 days; or
(c) the Secretary of State gives a direction for his detention in a prison under subs (4) below.

(4) The Secretary of State may from time to time direct that–
(a) an offender who falls to be detained in a youth custody centre by virtue of subs (1) above; or
(b) an offender who falls to be detained in a youth custody centre or a remand centre by virtue of subs (2) or (3) above,
is instead to be detained for any temporary purpose in a prison.

(5) Any offender sentenced to youth custody, other than an offender who falls to be detained in a youth custody centre by virtue of subs (1) above or an offender who falls to be detained in a youth custody centre or a remand centre by virtue of subs (2) or (3) above, is to be detained–
(a) in a youth custody centre;
(b) in a remand centre; or
(c) in a prison,
as the Secretary of State may from time to time direct.

(6), (7) . . .

(8) Where a detention centre order has been made in respect of an offender aged 15 years or over, the Secretary of State may from time to time direct that he shall be detained for any temporary purpose in a youth custody centre of a prison instead of a detention centre.

(9) Where in the case of an offender aged 15 years or over–
(a) either–
    (i) a detention centre order has been made; and
    (ii) the term for which he is ordered to be detained is treated by virtue of s. 67 of the Criminal Justice Act 1967 as reduced to less than 2 days; or
(b) he is ordered under s.15(11) below to be detained in a detention centre for less than 21 days,
the Secretary of State may from time to time direct that he is to be detained (otherwise than for a temporary purpose) in a remand centre, a youth custody centre or (where the offender is aged 17 or over) a prison instead of a detention centre.

(10) A person in respect of whom an order has been made under s.9 above is to be detained–
(a) in a remand centre;
(b) in a detention centre;
(c) in a youth custody centre; or
(d) in any place in which a person aged 21 years or over could be imprisoned or detained for default in payment of a fine or any other sum of money
as the Secretary of State may from time to time direct.

(11) This section is without prejudice–
(a) to s.22(2)(b) of the Prison Act 1952 (removal to hospital etc); and
(b) to s.43(3) of that Act (detention in remand centre for a temporary purpose or for the purpose of providing maintenance and domestic services).

8d.83   **Release of young offenders**
15. (1) Subject to subs (1) below, if subs (2), (3) or (4) below applies to a person under 22 years of age who is released from a term of detention under a detention centre order of a term of youth custody, he shall be under the supervision of a probation officer or a social worker of a local authority social services department.

(2) This subsection applies to a person who was neither granted remission nor released on licence.

(3) This subsection applies to a person who was granted remission.

(4) This subsection applies to a person–
(a) who was under 21 years of age when sentence was passed on him; and
(b) who is released on licence; and
(c) whose licence expires less than 12 months after his release.

(5) The supervision period ends on the offender's 22nd birthday if it has not ended before.

(6) Subject to subs (5) above, where subs (2) above applies, the supervision period begins on the offender's release and ends three months from his release.

(7) Subject to subs (5) above and to subs (9) below, where subs (3) above applies, the supervision period begins on the offender's release and ends–
(a) three months from his release; or
(b) on the date on which his sentence would have expired if he had not been granted remission,
whichever is the later.

(8) Subject to subs (5) above and to subs (9) below, where subs (4) above applies, the supervision period begins when the offender's licence expires and ends on the date on which he would have been released if he had never been granted remission or released on licence.

(9) If the date mentioned in subs (7(b) or (8) above is more than 12 months from the date of the offender's release, the supervision period ends 12 months from the date of his release.

(10) While a person is under supervision by virtue of this section, he shall comply with such requirements, if any, as may for the time being be specified in a notice from the Secretary of State.

(11) A person who without reasonable excuse fails to comply with a requirement imposed under subs (1) above shall be guilty of an offence and liable on summary conviction–
(a) to a fine not exceeding £200; or
(b) to an appropriate custodial sentence for a period not exceeding 30 days *but not liable to be dealt with in any other way.*

(12) In subsection (11) above 'appropriate custodial sentence' means–
(a) a sentence of imprisonment, if the offender has attained the age of 21 years when he is sentenced; and
(b) a detention centre order or a youth custody sentence, if he has not then attained that age.

(13) A person released from a custodial sentence passed under subs (11) above shall not be liable to a period of supervision in consequence of his conviction under that subsection, but his conviction shall not prejudice any liability to supervision to which he was previously subject, and that liability shall accordingly continue until the end of the supervision period.

(14) In this section–
'licence' means a licence under s.60 of the Criminal Justice Act 1967; and
'remission' means remission under rules made by virtue of s.47 of the Prison Act 1952.
[*the words in italics in subs (11) will be added by Sch.14 CJA 1988 when in force*].

COMMENTARY
For the determination of age, see s.1(6).

.15(11): **An appropriate custodial sentence,** see s.15(12).

MAGISTRATES' COURTS RULES 1981
(SI 1981 No 552, as amended by SI 1982 No 245, 1983 No 253, 1984 No 1552, 1985 Nos 1695 and 1944 and 1986 No 1332)

Entries in register in respect of suspended sentence   **8d.84**
29. (1) Where under s.23 of the Powers of Criminal Courts Act 1973 a magistrates' court deals with a person in respect of a suspended sentence otherwise than by making an order under subs (1)(a) of that section, the court shall cause to be entered in the register its reasons for its opinion that it would be unjust to make such an order.

(1A) Where a magistrates' court, in dealing with a person under s.47(3) to (5) of the Criminal Law Act 1977 in respect of a partly suspended sentence, decides under subs (4) to make no order under subs (3), the court shall cause to be entered in the register its reasons for its decision.

(2) Where an offender is dealt with under the said s.23 or the said s.47(3) to (5) in respect of a suspended or partly suspended sentence passed by a magistrates' court, the clerk of the court shall note this in the register against the original entry in respect of the suspended or partly suspended sentence, or

where the suspended or partly suspended sentence was not passed by tha court, shall notify the clerk of the court by which it was passed who shall note in the register against the original entry in respect of the suspended or partl suspended sentence.

(3) In this Rule 'partly suspended sentence' means a sentence of which pal has been ordered under s.47(1) of the Criminal Law Act 1977 to be held i suspense.

8d.85 **Suspended sentence supervision orders**
30. (1) Where a magistrates' court makes an order under s.23(1)(a) or (b of the Powers of Criminal Courts Act 1973 in respect of a person who is subjec to a suspended sentence supervision order, the clerk of the court shall note th in the register against the original entry in respect of the suspended sentenc supervision order, or where that order was not made by that court, shall–
   (a) if the order was made by another magistrates' court, notify the clerk c that court who shall note the court register accordingly; or
   (b) if the order was made by the Crown Court, notify the appropriate office of the Crown Court.

(2) Where a magistrates' court discharges a suspended sentence supervisio order under s.26(9) of the said Act of 1973, the clerk of the court shall note i the register against the original entry in respect of that order, or where tha order was not made by that court, shall–
   (a) if the order was made by another magistrates' court, notify the clerk c that court who shall note the court register accordingly; or
   (b) if the order was made by the Crown Court, notify the appropriate office of the Crown Court.

(3) Where a magistrates' court fines a person under s.27 of the said Act c 1973 for breach of the requirements of a suspended sentence supervision orde which was not made by that court, the clerk of the court shall–
   (a) if the order was made by another magistrates' court, notify the clerk c that court; or
   (b) if the order was made by the Crown Court, notify the appropriate office of the Crown Court.

8d.86 **Committal to custody to be by warrant**
94. (1) A justice of the peace shall not commit any person to a prisor detention centre, remand centre or place certified under s.134 of the Act c 1980 or to the custody of a constable under s.128(7) of the Act except by warrant of commitment.

8d.87 **Warrant of commitment**
97. (1) A warrant of commitment issued by a justice of the peace–
   (a) shall name or otherwise describe the person committed;
   (b) shall contain a statement of the offence with which the perso committed is charged, or of which he has been convicted, or of any othe ground on which he is committed;
   (c) shall be directed to a person named in the warrant or to the constables c the police area in which the warrant is issued or to the authorise persons for the police area specified in the warrant and to the governc or keeper of the prison or place of detention specified in the warran and shall require–
      (i) the named person or the constables or authorised persons to arre the person committed, if he is at large, and convey him to tha prison or place and deliver him with the warrant to the governor c keeper;
      (ii) the governor or keeper to keep in custody the person committe until that person be delivered in due course of law, or until th

happening of an event specified in the warrant, or for the period specified in the warrant, as the case may be.

(2) A warrant of commitment may be executed by conveying the person committed to any prison or place of detention in which he may lawfully be detained and delivering him there together with the warrant; and so long as any person is detained in any such prison or place other than that specified in the warrant, the warrant shall have effect as if that other prison or place were the prison or place specified in it.

(3) Notwithstanding the preceding provisions of this rule, a warrant of commitment issued in pursuance of a valid conviction, or of a valid order requiring the person committed to do or abstain from doing anything, shall not, if alleges that the person committed has been convicted, or order to do or abstain from doing that thing, be held void by reason of any defect in the warrant.

(4) The governor or keeper of the prison or place of detention at which any person is delivered in pursuance of a warrant of commitment shall give to the constable or other person making the delivery a receipt for that person.

(5) Notwithstanding the preceding provisions of this rule, a warrant of a justice of the peace to commit to custody any person who to the justice's knowledge is already detained in a prison or other place of detention shall be delivered to the governor or keeper of the prison or place of detention in which that person is detained.

COMMENTARY

Para (1): A statement of the offence, as to what constitutes a sufficient statement of offence, see r.100.

Para (3): Any defect, it is 'good sense and good law' to lodge a *fresh warrant* after the defendant has been committed to correct a defect or informality: *Ex p. Cross* (1857) 21 JP 407; *Ex p. Smith* (1858) 27 LJMC 196. 'When magistrates commit . . . on several charges, the committals are several and distinct and, if one is bad, the others are not necessarily invalidated', *per* Lord Hewart, CJ in *R v Phillips, R v Quayle* (1938) 102 JP 467.

Para (5): the provisions of this paragraph are administrative in content and do not prevent a warrant being executed later which was not lodged with a prison while the subject was there on remand: *R v Leeds Prison Governor, ex p. Huntley* [1927] 1 WLR 1016.

CHAPTER 8e

Committal for Sentence

Committal for Sentence

8e.00   **INTRODUCTION**

A magistrates' court has power to commit a convicted offender to the Crown Court for sentence:

(i) in the case of most offences triable either way, where it is of opinion that greater punishment should be inflicted than it has power to inflict – ie 'committal for sentence', or 'greater punishment' under s.38 MCA 1980; and

(ii) in the case of a wide range of offences, when the offender is at the same time being committed to the Crown Court for sentence – ie 'committal to be dealt with' under s.56 CJA 1967.

Both varieties of committal are discussed, *infra*, but *note* that the provisions creating some summary offences allow for committal for sentence – so that, legally speaking, it is possible, in the extreme, to have a committal for sentence in respect of such a summary offence with the either way offence being committed to the Crown Court to be dealt with. This, of course, is the very reverse of the normal run of cases, where a summary offence becomes 'attached' to either way offences which are committed for sentence. A summary of the provisions is set out below.

The offender must be committed to the most convenient location of the Crown Court: see the *Directions of the Lord Chief Justice*, para 8, reproduced in Chapter 4.

Note also the effects of [s.40 CJA] 1988, when in force, which will enable the committal to the Crown Court of summary matters 'to be dealt with' following committal for trial of an either way offence; and s.41 of the 1988 Act which will amend s.56 CJA 1967: see 8e.05 and Appendix III.

COMMITTAL FOR GREATER PUNISHMENT 8e.01

If upon summary conviction of anyone not less than 17 years old of an offence triable either way other than one excluded by the s.33 MCA 1980 (offences of criminal damage of a value below £400 [£2,000 – CJA 1988, when in force]) a magistrates' court is of opinion that the *character* and *antecedents* of the offender are such that greater punishment should be inflicted than is within the court's powers, it may commit him in custody or on bail to the Crown Court for sentence: s.38. The power to commit for sentence rests entirely upon the character and antecedents of the offender and not the gravity of the offence. Grave offences, the High Court has said repeatedly, should not be tried summarily: see *Mode of Trial* at Chapter 4.

Lord Parker CJ expressed the view that magistrates, when committing for sentence, should *state in open court any local reasons*, such as that the crime had become particularly prevalent in the area, which had led them to take this course, and these should be sent by the clerk with the committal papers to the Crown Court (see *The Magistrate* Vol XXV at p.163). The communication of other reasons was impliedly approved in *R v Leith* (1983) 1 March, 147 JPN 193. The Home Secretary recommends that courts should, as normal practice, consider a social inquiry report before committing an offender to the Crown Court for sentence: HOC 28/1971.

There is no power to commit a corporation to the Crown Court for sentence: s.3 MCA 1980.

On committal, the Crown Court may deal with the offender in any manner in which it could have dealt with him if he had just been convicted of the offence on indictment: s.42(1) PCCA 1973.

COMMITTAL TO BE DEALT WITH 8e.02

A magistrates' court which commits an offender to the Crown Court 'to be sentenced or otherwise dealt with' may at the same time commit him to that court to be dealt with as follows:
(a) If the 'relevant offence' (ie the offence in respect of which the offender is already to be committed for sentence) is *an offence triable either way*:

In respect of any offence – see s.56(1)(a).
(b) If the 'relevant offence is a *summary offence*:

In respect of – an offence triable either way; or
– an offence punishable with imprisonment; or
– a disqualifiable road traffic offence; or
– any suspended sentence in respect of which the committing court has power to deal with the offender (ie under s.24 PCCA 1973): see s.56(1)(b).

Under (b), the Crown Court may then deal with the offender in respect of the other offences in any way in which he could have been dealt with in the magistrates' court for those additional offences: s.56(5); see *R v Cattell* (1986) 8 Cr App R (S) 269; and *cf* the ruling in *Arthur v Stringer* (1986) *The Times*, 11 October in relation to *Appeals to the Crown Court*, Chapter 11. The Crown Court could not eg wait for the offender to reach a greater age in order to pass a more severe sentence.

For the enactments to which s.56(1)(b) applies, see s.56(2).

8e.03   # OTHER OFFENCES

When an offender is committed for sentence under these or any other provisions, other related offences which cannot be so committed should be dealt with by the magistrates or by adjournment until the decision of the Crown Court is known.

8e.04   # ANCILLARY ORDERS

There is a discretionary power to order the *interim disqualification* of a road traffic offender upon committal to the Crown Court for sentence: s.103 RTA 1972. Any other powers which the magistrates might otherwise have exercised must on a committal for sentence or a committal to be dealt with be left to the Crown Court: s.56(5) CJA 1967.

Statutory Provisions

8e.05   # CRIMINAL JUSTICE ACT 1967

Committal for sentence for offences tried summarily

56. (1) Where a magistrates' court ('the committing court') commits a person in custody or on bail to the Crown Court under any enactment to which this section applies to be sentenced or otherwise dealt with in respect of an offence ('the relevant office'), the committing court–

(a) if the relevant offence is an offence triable either way, may also commit him, in custody or on bail as the case may require, to the Crown Court to be dealt with in respect of any other offence whatsoever in respect of which the committing court has power to deal with him (being an offence of which he has been convicted by that or any other court); or

(b) if the relevant offence is a summary offence, may commit him, as aforesaid, to the Crown Court to be dealt with in respect of–

  (i) any other offence of which the committing court has convicted him, being either an offence punishable with imprisonment or an offence in respect of which the committing court has a power or duty to order him to be disqualified under s.93 of the Road Traffic Act 1972 or s.19 of the Transport Act 1981 (disqualification for certain motoring offences); or

  (ii) any suspended sentence in respect of which the committing court has under s.24(1) of the Powers of Criminal Courts Act 1973 power to deal with him.

(2) The enactments to which this section applies are the Vagrancy Act 1824 (incorrigible rogues), ss.37 and 38 of the Magistrates' Courts Act 1980 (committal for sentence), s.62(6) of this Act and s.8(6) (probationer convicted of subsequent offence) and s.24(2) (committal to be dealt with in respect of a suspended sentence) of the Powers of Criminal Courts Act 1973.

(3) . . . (4) (*Repealed*).

(5) Where under subs (1) of this section a magistrates' court commits a person to be dealt with by the Crown Court in respect of an offence, the latter court may after inquiring into the circumstances of the case deal with him in any way in which the magistrates' court might have dealt with him, and without prejudice to the foregoing provision, where under that subsection or any enactment to which this section applies a magistrates' court so commits a person, any duty or power which, apart from this subsection, would fall to be discharged or exercised by the magistrates' court shall not be discharged or exercised by that court but shall instead be discharged or may instead be exercised by the Crown Court.

(6) Any duty imposed or power conferred by virtue of the last foregoing subsection on the Crown Court, in a case where an offender has been committed to the court under s.37 of the Magistrates' Courts Act 1980, shall be discharged or may be exercised by the court notwithstanding that it sentences him to borstal training and in that or any other case shall be discharged or may be exercised notwithstanding anything in any other enactment and, in particular, in ss.93 and 101 of the Road Traffic Act 1972 or s.19 of the Transport Act 1981.

(7)–(12) (*Repealed*).

(13) In this section–
'disqualified' means disqualified for holding or obtaining a licence under Part II of the Road Traffic Act 1972 or s.19 of the Transport Act 1981.
[*As amended by Sch.1 Vehicles and Driving Licences Act 1969, Schs.8 and 11 Courts Act 1971, Schs.7 and 9 RTA 1972, Sch.5 PCCA 1973, s.46 CLA 1977, Sch.7 MCA 1980, Sch.9 Transport Act 1981*].

56. (1) . . . (a) *if the relevant offence is an indictable offence, may also commit him in custody or on bail as the case may require, to the Crown Court to be dealt with in respect of any other offence whatsoever in respect of which the committing court has power to deal with him (being an offence of which he has been convicted by that or any other court); or* . . .

(2) *The enactments to which this section applies are the Vagrancy Act 1824 (incorrigible rogues), ss.37 and 38 of the Magistrates' Courts Act 1980 (committal for sentence), s.62(6) of this Act, s.8(6) of the Powers of Criminal Courts Act 1973 (probationer convicted of subsequent offence) and s.24(2) of that Act and para 2(2)(a) of Schedule 9 to the Criminal Law Act 1977 (committal to be dealt with in respect of a wholly or partly suspended sentence).*
[*Subsections (1)(a) and (2) will be amended by s.41 CJA 1988 from a date to be appointed*].

COMMENTARY

s.56(1): any enactment to which this section applies, s.56 applies only where the defendant has been committed for sentence or to be dealt with under one of the enactments mentioned in s.56(2) and not to a committal for trial: *R v Thorne* [1969] Crim LR 188.

An offence triable either way/a summary offence, defined in Sch.1 Interpretation Act 1978.

Commit him in custody or on bail, see notes to s.38 MCA 1980, *infra*, and Form 96. For the location of the Crown Court to which the offender should be committed see paras 3–9 of the directions of the Lord Chief Justice reproduced at Chapter 4. For the document to be sent to the higher court see r.17 MC Rules 1981.

To be dealt with, on a committal under this section the Crown Court is restricted to the powers which the magistrates could have exercised: *R v Ward* (1969) 53 Cr App R 23; *R v Cattell* (1986) 8 Cr App R (S) 269; and *cf.* the analogous rule in relation to *Appeals to the Crown Court*, Chapter 11; as to which see *Arthur v Stringer* (1986) *The Times* 11 October whilst the Crown Court may increase sentence on an appeal, it cannot impose a sentence which would only have been available to the magistrates had the offender already attained a greater age than his age at the time of conviction.

An offence punishable with imprisonment, to be construed in relation to any offender without regard to any prohibition or restriction imposed by or under any enactment on the imprisonment of offenders of his age: s.104(4) of the Act.

s.56(2): Section 62(6) of this Act, deals with prisoners on licence: 'If a person subject to a licence under ss.60 or 61 of this Act is convicted by a magistrates' court of an offence punishable on indictment with imprisonment, the court may commit him in custody or on bail to the Crown Court for sentence in accordance with s.42 PCCA 1973. (*power of the Crown Court to sentence persons convicted by magistrates' courts of indictable offences*)'.

s.8(6): it is *suggested* that the words in brackets following this reference do not limit its scope and that it applies to persons committed to the Crown Court following commission of an offence during the operational period of an order of conditional discharge as well as a probation order.

s.56(5), thus the magistrates may not, for example, commit to the Crown Court for sentence while at the same time making a restitution order: *R v Blackpool Justices, ex p. Charlson and Gregory* [1972] 1 WLR 1456. Magistrates must be *scrupulously careful* to leave all questions of sentence to the Crown Court: *R v Brogan* [1975] 1 WLR 393. But the magistrates have power to make an interim order of disqualification and endorsement – see s.103 RTA 1972.

8e.06   Power of Crown Court on committal for sentence
42. (1) Where an offender is committed by a magistrates' court for sentence under s.38 of the Magistrates' Courts Act 1980, or s.62 of the Criminal Justice Act 1967, the Crown Court shall inquire into the circumstances of the case and shall have power to deal with the offender in any manner in which it could deal with him if he had just been convicted of the offence on indictment before the court.

(2) . . .
[*As amended by Sch.7 MCA 1980, Sch.14 CJA 1982*].

COMMENTARY
The Crown Court may issue a warrant for the arrest of a person bailed who fails to appear: s.13(3) Courts Act 1971.

8e.07   Evidence with respect of offences punishable in Scotland
52. For the purposes of this Act a certificate purporting to be signed by or on behalf of the Lord Advocate that an offence is punishable in Scotland with imprisonment or is punishable in Scotland on indictment with imprisonment for a term specified in the certificate shall be evidence of the matter so certified.

8e.08   MAGISTRATES' COURTS ACT 1980

Committal for sentence on summary trial of offence triable either way
38. Where on the summary trial of an offence triable either way (not being an offence as regards which this section is excluded by s.33 above), a person who is not less than 17 years old is convicted of the offence, then, if on obtaining information about his character and antecedents the court is of opinion that they are such that greater punishment should be inflicted for the offence than the court has power to inflict, the court may, in accordance with s.56 of the Criminal Justice Act 1967, commit him in custody or on bail to the Crown Court for sentence in accordance with the provisions of s.42 of the Powers of Criminal Courts Act 1973.

8e.09   COMMENTARY
Where justices purport to commit for sentence in a case where they have no such power the proceedings are a nullity: *R v South Greenhoe JJ, ex p. Director of Public Prosecutions* [1950] 2 KB 558; *R v Jones (Gwyn)* [1969] 2 QB 33.

An order may be made under this section in addition to a committal to the Crown Court with a view to a restriction order s.37 Mental Health Act 1983.

When magistrates commit an offender to the Crown Court under this section, they may also commit him in respect of any other offence whatsoever: s.56(1) CJA 1967.

When committing under this power the magistrates relinquish all other powers and duties with respect to the offender to the Crown Court s.56(5) CJA 1967, *infra*. But they do have power to order *interim disqualification* under s.103 RTA 1972.

Appeal, a committal under this section is not an 'order made on conviction' and there is, therefore, no right to appeal against such a committal: *R v London Sessions Appeal Committee, ex p. Rogers* [1951] 2 KB 74; the remedy of a man wrongly committed is by way of prerogative order: *R v Warren* [1954] 1 WLR 531; *R v Jones (Gwyn), supra*. But there is a right of appeal against conviction on a plea of not guilty and if dealt with before the normal time for appeal has expired the Crown Court should, before passing sentence, ascertain whether the defendant intends to appeal against conviction: *R v Faithful* [1950] 2 All ER 1251. A plea of guilty which is not unambiguous may be changed even after a committal for sentence, but the proper court to order this at that late stage is the Crown Court and not the magistrates' court: *R v Mutford and Lothingland Justices, ex p. Harber* [1971] 2 QB 291; *R v Inner London Crown Court, ex p. Sloper* (1979) 69 Cr App R 1.

Legal aid The magistrates have power to grant legal aid in respect of the proceedings in the Crown Court: s.28(7) LAA 1974.
'If a lower court has it in mind, having regard to the gravity of the offence charged or the number of offences which are charged or for other reasons, that a heavy sentence is called for, it is most desirable that the accused should be offered legal aid . . . and we take the view that, in the circumstances already indicated, the court should take it on itself to offer legal aid to the accused so that, albeit there may be guilty pleas before the court, any matters which even remotely tell in favour of the accused may be properly advanced through a skilled advocate to the court and so may be properly brought adequately to their attention and then considered by them',
per Edmund Davies LJ in *R v Serghiou* [1966] 3 All ER 637; and see *R v Green* [1968] 2 All ER 77, at p 80.

The justices' duty It is the duty of justices to make proper inquiry of the facts before agreeing to summary trial, particularly in the case of assaults: *R v Hartlepool Justices, ex p. King* [1973] Crim LR 637 (*certiorari* issued to quash a committal for sentence when the justices regretted their decision for summary trial after hearing the facts of the case). However, in *R v Lymm JJ, ex p. Brown* [1973] 1 WLR 1039 it was held that failure to make inquiry about the sufficiency of punishment did not inhibit the power to commit for sentence where the court later learnt that the offender was a police officer. When, following a plea of guilty, the magistrates learned that the circumstances of the offence were graver than they had believed (head injuries) and that the accused had failed to show remorse, these factors did not justify a committal for sentence because they did not relate to the character and antecedents of the offender: *R v Warrington Justices, ex p. Mooney* (1980) 2 Cr App R (S) 40. There must be some change of circumstances from the situation as it was known to the magistrates when they decided to try the case summarily: *R v Derby Magistrates, ex p. McCarthy* (1980) 2 Cr App R (S) 140; *R v Derby and South Derbyshire Magistrates, ex p. McCarthy and McGovern* (1981) 145 JPN 735. Information about the defendant's character and antecedents which come to the court's attention when making the mode of trial decision cannot be a basis for committing him to the Crown Court for sentence: *R v Guildhall Justices, ex p. Cooper* (1983) 147 JP 466.

An offence triable either way, defined in Sch.1 Interpretation Act 1978 as meaning an offence which, if committed by an adult, is triable either on indictment or summarily.   **8e.10**

Excluded by s.33, this relates to certain offences of criminal damage tried summarily.

A person, the powers under this section do not apply to a corporation: para 5 of Sch.3 MCA 1980.

Not less than 17 years old, for the determination of age, see s.150(4) MCA 1980.

Character and antecedents, '"character" . . . relates to something more than the fact that a person has been previously convicted, and the word "antecedents" is as wide as can be conceived', *per* Lord Goddard CJ in *R v Vallett* [1951] 1 All ER 231 (a 'shameless thief' who asked for 96 other offences to be taken into consideration). Thus, an offender who asked for 19 other offences to be taken into consideration involving a systematic fraud of £5,000 could be committed under this section: *R v Harlow Justices, ex p. Galway* [1975] Crim LR 288. Equally, a defendant with no previous convictions not asking for offences to be taken into consideration may be committed under this section in respect of a series of thefts over a long period: *R v King's Lynn Justices, ex p. Carter* [1969] 1 QB 488. That decision is not a charter for magistrates to deal with cases summarily rather than commit them for trial: *per* Lord Parker CJ in *R v Tower Bridge Magistrate, ex p. Osman* [1971] 1 WLR 1109: see also under The Justices' Duty above.

Greater punishment, a suspended sentence coupled with a supervision order (which can only be for a period in excess of six months) is greater punishment than a forthwith sentence for a lesser period: *R v Rugby Justices, ex p. Prince* [1974] 2 All ER 116.

In accordance with s.56 of the Criminal Justice Act 1967, for the documents to be sent to the Crown Court, see r.17(1) MC Rules 1981.

On bail, 'in the opinion of this court the cases must be rare when justices can properly commit (under this section) on bail because the whole purpose of the committal is to have the man sent to prison for a longer period than the justices can send him to prison', *per* Lord Parker CJ in *R v Coe* [1969] 1 All ER 65. The general right to bail does not apply: s.4(2) Bail Act 1976.
The High Court has power to admit to bail where it is offered on unacceptable terms: s.22 CJA 1967. The Crown Court has similar powers under s.13(4) Courts Act 1971. If the

defendant is committed on bail, the governor of the appropriate prison, etc., must be notified: r.17(3). Forfeiture of recognizances is a matter for the Crown Court.

In custody, the general right to bail does not apply: s.4(2) Bail Act 1976. Committals must be by warrant: r.94. For the form of warrant, see Form 39. For the place of commitment of persons *under 21 years* see s.27 CJA 1948.

To the Crown Court, for the location of the Crown Court to which the offender should be committed see paras 5–9 of the directions of the Lord Chief Justice reproduced at Chapter 4.

8e.11   MAGISTRATES' COURTS RULES 1981

(SI 1981 No 552, as amended by SI 1982 No 245, SI 1983 No 523, SI 1984 No 1552, SI 1985 Nos 1695 and 1944, and SI 1986 No 1332.)

Committals for sentence, etc.

17. (1) Where a magistrates' court commits an offender to the Crown Court under the Vagrancy Act 1824, ss.37 or 38 of the Act of 1980, ss.56(1) or 61(6) of the Criminal Justice Act 1967, s.24(2)(a) of the Powers of Criminal Courts Act 1973 or s.6 of the Bail Act 1976 after convicting him of an offence, the clerk of the magistrates' court shall send to the appropriate officer of the Crown Court–

(a) a copy signed by the clerk of the magistrates' court of the minute or memorandum of the conviction entered in the register;

(b) a copy of any note of the evidence given at the trial of the offender, any written statement tendered in evidence and any deposition;

(c) such documents and articles produced in evidence before the court as have been retained by the court;

(d) any report relating to the offender considered by the court;

(e) if the offender is committed on bail, a copy of the record made in pursuance of s.5 of the said Act of 1976 relating to such bail and also any recognizance entered into by any person as his surety;

(f) if the court imposes under s.56(8) of the Criminal Justice Act 1967 an interim disqualification for holding or obtaining a licence under Part III of the Road Traffic Act 1972, a statement of the date of birth and sex of the offender;

(g) if the court makes an order under s.28 of the Theft Act 1968 (orders for restitution), a copy signed by the clerk of the convicting court of the minute or memorandum of the order entered in the register;

(h) a copy of any contribution order previously made in the case under s.7 of the Legal Aid Act 1982.

(2) Where a magistrates' court commits an offender to the Crown Court under the Vagrancy Act 1824, ss.8(6) or 24(2) of the Powers of Criminal Courts Act 1973, ss.37 or 38 of the Act of 1980 or ss.56(1) or 62(6) of the Criminal Justice Act 1967 and the magistrates' court on that occasion imposes, under s.56(8) of the Criminal Justice Act 1967, an interim disqualification for holding or obtaining a licence under Part III of the Road Traffic Act 1972, the clerk of the magistrates' court shall give notice of the interim disqualification to the appropriate officer of the Crown Court.

(3) Where a magistrates' court commits a person on bail to the Crown Court under any of the enactments mentioned in para (2) or under s.6(4) of the Powers of Criminal Courts Act 1973 or under s.6 of the Bail Act 1976 the clerk of the magistrates' court shall give notice thereof in writing to the governor of the prison to which persons of the sex of the person committed are committed by that court if committed in custody for trial and also, if the person committed is under the age of 21, to the governor of the remand centre to which he would have been committed if the court had refused him bail.

COMMENTARY

The Home Office also request justices' clerks to notify the liaison probation officer at the Crown Court of the particulars contained in HOC No 28/71, para 36.

Any note of the evidence, 'in the case of committal for sentence or borstal training it is really essential that all the information that was before the committing justices should be before the Crown Court, and accordingly, any notes of evidence taken by the clerk and any documents put in at the hearing should be sent, as no doubt they generally are. Our opinion on this matter was, we think, made clear in the case of *R v Dorset Quarter Sessions, ex p. O'Brien': Practice Note* [1956] 1 All ER 448.

CHAPTER 9

Costs and Witnesses' Allowances

Note Comparable provision concerning costs orders is made in relation to the Crown Court and the higher courts by the 1985 Act. Except where of direct relevance to summary proceedings, those provisions have been excluded from the text of the Act and the 1986 regulations, and from further treatment in this work.

Costs and Witnesses' Allowances

INTRODUCTION   9.00

The law of costs in criminal cases is now contained in Part II, Prosecution of Offences Act 1985 ('POA 1985') and the Costs in Criminal Cases (General) Regulations 1986 (SI 1986 No 1335) ('1986 Regulations'). There is one important interconnecting provision contained in s.32(2) CJA 1967 concerning *written* medical reports, but this apart, the POA 1985 and the 1986 Regulations represent the full code although this code does not deal with *Quantum* beyond setting basic statutory criteria for the various types of orders for costs and – in certain instances – providing a mechanism for the *'Determination'* of costs: see under those headings, 9.07.

The 1985 Act abolished the Costs in Criminal Cases Act 1973, but cases decided under the old law will still hold good where apposite, and in so far as the new provisions allow for this. Thus, eg, it is wrong for costs to be used as disguised penalty: *R v Highgate Justices, ex p. Petrou* [1954] 1 All ER 406; *R v Whalley* (1972) 56 Cr App R 304; costs should not be out of proportion to the subject matter or to any financial penalty: *ibid*; unless there is some especial reason for a high award *Hoad v Kenny* (1986) 21 April (unreported, but discussed at 150 JPN 580); and costs ordered to be paid by a defendant should normally be payable within about a year: see *R v Nottingham Justices, ex p. Fohmann* (1987) 151 JP 49.

The question of 'punitive' costs *supra* must be distinguished from the separate new concept of *'Costs Thrown Away'* (see under 9.05) whereby courts can control 'improper acts and omissions' by either party during the proceedings.

The statutory provisions govern the *general costs* incurred by a party – ie legal expenses, travelling costs, etc; *witnesses' expenses* and *allowances*; and the special position of *medical, professional* and other *expert witnesses* and *interpeters*. All these matters, to which detailed legal rules apply, are discussed under appropriate headings, *post*.

The relationship between costs and witnesses' allowances would appear to be as follows. Whilst an award of costs to a party may well include the amount of any loss or expenses incurred by his witnesses where this has been born by him, specific provisions allow for the reimbursement of defence witnesses direct from central funds by the justices' clerk. The intention seems to be that, in the normal course, such witnesses will be paid out of central funds so that witnesses' expenses etc being paid for and claimed by the defendant ought to be a rarity. However, a successful *private prosecutor* – who cannot have his witnesses paid for out of central funds – may wish to make a claim against the defendant whereas a Crown Prosecutor might claim that an order should be made against the defendant in order to recover monies disbursed by him to prosecution witnesses pursuant to the Crown Prosecution Service (Witnesses' Allowances) Regulations 1986 (SI 1986 No 405, as amended by SI 1986 No 842) and Costs Orders made thereunder.

COSTS FROM CENTRAL FUNDS AND COSTS   9.01
'INTER PARTES'

Sections 16–19 POA 1985 set out the circumstances in which costs may be awarded from central funds:

— *in favour of a defendant* (s.16);

— *in favour of a prosecutor* (other than a public authority such as the Crown Prosecution Service, which can no longer receive a central funds order in its favour) (s.17);

— *against the accused* (s.18); and

— '*in other circumstances*' (s.19 and the 1986 Regulations).

Section 19 gives the Lord Chancellor wide powers to make regulations specifying 'other circumstances' in which costs may be awarded. That power has been exercised via Part II of the 1986 Regulations to enable orders for '*Costs Thrown Away*' 9.05, where '. . . one party to criminal proceedings has incurred costs as a result of an unnecessary or improper act or omission by, or on behalf of, another party to the proceedings'. The relevant provisions here are s.19(1) POA 1985 and r.3, which are outlined under the heading mentioned.

Costs Thrown Away apart, awards between the parties themselves can now only be made against the defendant and in accordance with s.18 POA 1985, under which a convicted person may be ordered to pay all or part of the costs of the prosecutor. *There is no longer any power to award costs against a prosecutor* (other than costs thrown away, *post*). The remedy for a person who is acquitted, or who has the proceedings against him abandoned in any way, is to obtain an order for the payment of his costs from central funds in accordance with s.16 POA 1985 – which extends to the payment of costs from central funds in both *indictable* and *summary* cases.

As to *Quantum* – the amount of any costs – the provisions contain basic criteria for the various types of awards of costs and these are set out under 9.08: see, eg s.16(6) which, in relation to a 'defendant's costs order', provides that the order shall be for the payment from central funds '. . . of such amount as the court considers reasonably sufficient to compensate him for any expenses properly incurred by him in the proceedings'. But the provisions do not go any further than this in relation to the precise amount to be ordered, which in certain cases *must* be fixed by the court, but in others *may* be left for *Determination* by the clerk to the justices, see 9.10.

9.02   **'DEFENDANT'S COSTS ORDER'**

As indicated, 'unnecessary acts and omissions' apart, there is no power to order a prosecutor – public or private – to pay the defendant's costs. But under s.16 POA 1985, the court may make what is defined as 'a defendant's costs order', ie an order for the payment of the defendant's costs *from central funds* in any case – *summary* or *indictable*, where:

— (a) an information is not proceeded with;

— (b) examining justices determine not to commit for trial; or

— (c) the court dismisses the information: s.16(1)(a), (b).

Situation (a) would include proceedings which are out of time because the information was laid outside the six months limit for summary offences contained in s.127 MCA 1980: see *Patel v Blakey* (1987) *The Times*, 26 February (because s.127 goes to the 'consequences' of the information, not its validity); or withdrawn; or 'discontinued' under s.23 POA 1985 and the Magistrates' Courts Discontinuance of Proceedings Rules 1986 (SI 1986 No 367): as to which see *Discontinuance* at 2.03, *ante*. Where a case *is* 'discontinued', the defendant has a right to apply for the proceedings to be 'continued', but it is considered that it is not necessary –

ind probably quite inappropriate – for him to do this simply in order to be ible to apply for costs. This last application, it is suggested, can be made iy a straightforward notice or letter to the clerk to the justices, who may n turn refer it to the court on an *ex parte* basis. It may be otherwise where he clerk has some specific reason to suppose that the prosecutor might vish to put forward reasons why central funds costs should be disallowed, ir reduced in accordance with s.16(6). It is suggested that the prosecutor hould be notified by the clerk of the date and time when a defendant's :osts application in respect of a discontinued matter is to be placed before he court so that he may make representations should he wish to do so. There seems to be no reason why applications should not be dealt with *in vriting* and without attendance in appropriate cases.

The court may order all or part of the costs. It may reduce the amount if the 'defendant's costs order' where it is of opinion that '. . . there are :ircumstances which make it inappropriate that the person in whose avour the order is made should recover the full amount . . .' s.16(6).)therwise the order must be for the payment of such amount as the court ionsiders to be '. . . reasonably sufficient to compensate (the defendant) or any expenses properly incurred by him in the proceedings'. Any :xpenses covered by legal aid must be disregarded (but not, eg personal ravelling or other out of pocket expenses): s.16(8). The defendant will be iound by the prevailing rates and scales of witnesses' allowances, even vhere disbursed by him personally, *semble*: cf reg 16(1). Generally, it ieems that the spirit of *Practice Note (Justices: Defendant's Costs)* [1982] 3 All ER 1152 issued by Lord Lane CJ and concerning the analogous irovisions of the Costs in Criminal Cases Act 1973 still applies. The *Practice Note* states that a successful defendant should normally get his :osts *unless there is a positive reason for the court to order otherwise*; and iets out three specific instances:

— (1) where the defendant's own conduct has brought suspicion on himself and has misled the prosecution into thinking that the case against him is stronger than it is;
— (2) where there is ample evidence to support a conviction, but the defendant is acquitted on a technicality which has no merit; and
— (3) where the defendant is acquitted on one charge but convicted of another. In this last case the court should make whatever order seems just, having regard to the relative importance of the two or more charges and the conduct of the parties generally.

As to *Quantum*, see 9.07. It should be noted, however, that in relation o (a) the situation where a case is 'not proceeded with' (only) – ie ..16(1)(a) – the overall measure of a 'defendant's costs order' is not the isual expenses 'incurred in the proceedings' (see s.16(6)), but those incurred 'in or about the defence': s.16(10). On one view, this latter neasure is wider in scope, possibly eg, including loss of earnings, profits, :xpenses incurred in interviewing witnesses, establishing the defence etc, vhereas the former would not. But on another view, the difference in vording is simply to accommodate the fact that proceedings in the full ense will not have occurred, so that no change in substance concerning :he measure of costs is intended. The true position is yet to be resolved by iuthority.

Subject to the exceptions which follow, whenever an order for the iayment of the defendant's costs from central funds is made, the amount if the order *may* be fixed by the court *by agreement* with the defendant: iee s.16(9)(a), or be left to be 'determined' by the justices' clerk or his appointee in his role as taxing officer, or 'determining authority': see s.16(9)(b), and r.5. But the court *must* fix the amount at the time of the order whenever it makes a reduction under s.16(6): s.16(7) (as it *must* also do when ordering *Prosecution costs against the defendant* (at 9.04 see s.18(3); and *'Costs Thrown Away'* (at 9.05) s.19 and r.3, *post*).

PROSECUTION COSTS

9.03 **(i) Prosecution Costs from Central Funds**

As already indicated a public authority prosecutor cannot recover cost from central funds: s.17(2). 'Public authority' is defined in s.17(6) a meaning:

(a) a police force (as defined in s.3 POA 1985);

(b) the Crown Prosecution Service or any other government department;

(c) a local authority or other authority or body constituted for pur poses of–

　(i) the public service or of local government; or

　(ii) carrying on under national ownership any industry or under taking or part of an industry or undertaking; or

(d) any other authority or body whose members are appointed by Her Majesty or by any Minister of the Crown or government depart ment or whose revenues consist wholly or mainly of money pro vided by Parliament.

Section 17(6)(c)(iii) refers to 'nationalised industries' or undertakings the present ones (subject to any further privatisation) being as follows:

British Railways Board
British Shipbuilders
British Steel Corporation
British Waterways Board
Central Electricity Generating Board
Civil Aviation Authority
Electricity Council
National Bus Company
National Coal Board
Oil and Pipelines Agency
Post Office
Scottish Transport Group
South of Scotland Electricity Board
North of Scotland Hydro-Electric Board
United Kingdom Atomic Energy Authority

But in the case of private prosecutions involving an *indictable* offence, the court can reimburse the prosecutor and any witnesses attending on his behalf from central funds irrespective of whether the accused is ordered to pay any costs: see s.17(1) and r.16(1). It should be stressed that costs cannot be awarded out of central funds, even to a private prosecutor, in respect of summary offences. Presumably, the principle that a private prosecutor should get his costs paid from central funds unless he has misconducted himself (eg acted spitefully or brought the proceedings unreasonably) applies as it did to the Costs in Criminal Cases Act 1973: c the *Practice Note* [1982] 3 All ER 1152.

The amount which the court should order to be paid is such as it considers *reasonably sufficient to compensate the prosecutor for any expenses properly incurred by him in the proceedings*: s.17(1). Where the

ourt considers it appropriate, it may specify the amount of costs but only
f the prosecutor agrees to that amount: s.17(4)(a). If the prosecutor does
ot agree to the amount, or the court does not consider it appropriate to
pecify the amount, then the costs are left for the justices' clerk to
letermine in his role as determining officer: s.17(4)(b) and r.5. In assess-
ng the amount, the court is bound by regulations as to the amount of
vitnesses expenses which may be ordered, see r.16(1) and the rates and
cales of allowances, as contained in the Lord Chancellor's Department
Circular, JC(86)(7).

If the court is of the opinion that circumstances make it inappropriate
or the private prosecutor to recover the full amount of his costs (eg a
onviction in some cases but not in others) the court must assess what
mount in its opinion would be just and reasonable. It must then specify
he amount and cannot leave this to be determined by the justices' clerk.
Where a case has been instituted by a private prosecutor and has then
een taken over by the Crown Prosecutor, the private prosecutor may
ecover from central funds the costs incurred up until the time that the
ase was taken over, but no expenses incurred after that date.

ii) Prosecution costs against the defendant   9.04

The costs thrown away provisions of s.19 POA 1985 and r.3 of the 1986
Regulations apart, the only species of '*inter partes*' costs now remaining is
he order for the accused to pay costs to the prosecutor. This power exists
vhere any person is convicted of an offence and is governed by s.18 of the
Act. The court may make such order for costs as it considers 'just and
easonable', but the amount *must* be specified by the court: see s.18(3) –
nd thus cannot be left for 'determination' by the justices' clerk.

The court has a discretion how much to order and is not bound by
egulations in determining the amount. The court must have regard to the
neans of the accused and, it has been suggested, any order as to costs
hould be in such amount that the offender can pay within a reasonable
ime, namely about a year: see *R v Nottingham Justices, ex p. Fohmann*
1987) 151 JP 49. See also the general principles concerning 'punitive
osts' and 'proportionality' at 9.00.

There are the following restrictions:
— where under the conviction the court orders payment of any sum as a
   fine, penalty, forfeiture or compensation not exceeding £5, then *no
   costs may be ordered unless* in the particular circumstances the court
   considers it right to do so: s.18(4); and
— with a juvenile, the amount of any costs may not exceed the amount of
   any fine imposed on him: s.18(5), but it is arguable that this ought not
   to affect the situation where a parent or guardian is ordered to pay the
   costs pursuant to s.55 CYPA 1933.

The award of costs *against a defendant* and *in favour of the prosecution*
s extended in its application by r.14. The full list of circumstances in
vhich costs may be so ordered by magistrates is as follows:
   (a) Where the accused is *convicted* of any offence by magistrates:
       s.18(1)(a);
   (b) Where an offender is *dealt with* under ss.6, 8 or 10 Powers of
       Criminal Courts Act 1973 (probation orders, conditional dis-
       charges): r.14(3)(a);
   (c) In proceedings under s.16 or s.17 of the 1973 Act (community
       service orders): r.14(3)(b);

(d) Where an offender is dealt with under s.23(1) or s.27 of the 197
Act or under s.47 Criminal Law Act 1977 (suspended and par
tially suspended sentences): r.14(3)(c),

Note Dealing with an offender for breach of an attendance centre
order under s.19(3)(a) CJA 1982 is not covered; *contrast* the position
in relation to the Crown Court when dealing with an offender under
s.19(5) *ibid*: see r.14(3)(d).

9.05   **'COSTS THROWN AWAY'**

Section 19(1) Prosecution Offences Act 1985 enables the Lord Chan
cellor to make regulations providing for awards of costs between
parties in respect of *costs thrown away*, a power which has been exer
cised via r.3 of the 1986 Regulations. A court may order costs to b
paid by either party at *any time during criminal proceedings* where it i
satisfied that one party has incurred costs as a result of an *unnecessar*
or improper act or omission by, or on behalf of, the other party to th
proceedings: r.3(1). The court must give both parties the opportunit
to make representations: r.3(1); and must take into account any othe
order as to costs (including any legal aid order) made in respect of th
proceedings: r.3(2). The court *must specify* the amount of costs: r.3(3)
and at the conclusion of the case it must take into account any earlie
orders for costs before it makes its final order: r.3(4).

The use of such costs orders is a means of control in the hands of th
court with which, eg to curb unwarranted delay and other abuses a
against the other party, but one which needs to be exercised wit
discretion. The situation should be distinguished from the general rul
against the use of costs in disguise for a penalty and the authoritie
thereon, noted at 9.00 – though the principle that courts should no
seek to use cost powers in disguise for the ultimate penalty woul
appear to hold good, even in relation to r.3.

With a juvenile, the general rule is that costs cannot exceed th
amount of any fine imposed: see r.3(5) – but this only applies *pos*
conviction, whereas r.3 applies *at any time during the proceedings*
Ironically, perhaps, the provision whereby a parent may be ordered t
pay a fine or costs operates only on a 'finding of guilt': see s.55 CYP
1933.

9.06   **COSTS IN 'OTHER CIRCUMSTANCES'**

Section 19 POA 1985 gives wide powers to the Lord Chancellor t
make regulations concerning '*Costs Thrown Away*', 9.05, the paymen
of *Witnesses' Allowances*, 9.12, and to extend the operation of an
aspect of ss.16 to 21 of the Act to 'any category of proceedings i
which an offender is before a magistrates' court . . .' and with appro
priate modifications. This last power has been used to extend the *Pros*
ecution costs against the defendant provisions of s.18, 9.04, to variou
'breach' occasions – to wit of conditional discharge, probation order
community service and suspended sentence: see r.14(3), and the ful
list at 9.25. The use of the power to make regulations in relation to th
two other matters mentioned is incorporated into the text under thos
headings.

QUANTUM – INCLUDING CLAIMS AND 'DETERMINATION'

9.07

An outline of each type of costs order is given under appropriate headings, *supra*. For ease of reference, this section assembles those provisions relevant to *quantum* and adds information concerning the 'determination' provisions.

The basic criteria

9.08

The statutory provisions can be separated into two kinds: firstly, those governing the position where *the court* itself exercises its *own powers* to fix the amount of the relevant costs order, whether this be for payment from central funds or '*inter partes*'; secondly, the regulations under which *the justices' clerk* 'determines' the actual amount of costs to be paid from central funds in those situations where the court makes an order for costs but leaves the amount to be settled out of court. The subject matter overlaps – ie the court or the justices' clerk may be faced with fixing the amount – in relation to (1) defendant's costs orders; and (2) private prosecution costs, in either case from central funds. Whilst there is some difference in wording as between the respective provisions under which the court and the clerk are empowered to act, it is considered that no difference in principle was intended as between the two methods. It may be that the court in acting at the time of the order – and by agreement of the party entitled – is apt to perform a less sophisticated assessment, albeit that there is no reason why it should not call on the justices' clerk to advise in the light of his knowledge of taxation.

Each of the provisions creating a power to award costs lays down what can be described as a 'basic measure' for costs, whilst the regulations concerning determination provide a further general yardstick for the justices' clerk in those cases where the amount of costs falls to be determined by him. Beyond this – and in contrast to the rates and scales for *Witnesses' Allowances*, 9.12, – the statutory provisions do not seek to prescribe further, leaving the precise amount to be awarded in the discretion of the court or the clerk.

The various 'basic measures' are as follows:

(1) *Defendant's Costs Order* (see, generally 9.02) under s.16 – which is **9.08a** *always* for payment from central funds:
The amount may be fixed by *the court* with the agreement of the defendant in accordance with s.16(9)(a) or may be left for determination by the clerk under s.16(9)(b).

The 'basic measure' is '. . . such amount as is *reasonably sufficient* to compensate the defendant *for any expenses properly incurred by him in carrying on the proceedings*': see s.16(6). This is subject to any deduction under s.16(7) (when the court itself *must* fix the amount of the award of costs and cannot leave this for determination by the clerk); and subject to any deduction in respect of costs covered by legal aid: s.16(8).

When this type of costs order is made in circumstances where '. . . the information is not proceeded with as envisaged by s.16(1)(a)' – the words '. . . *in or about the defence*' must be substituted for the words '*in carrying on the proceedings*': s.16(10); for two possible interpretations of the distinction, see under '*Defendant's Costs Order*', at 9.02.

Where the amount of costs is left for determination by the justices' clerk, r.7(2) provides that he '. . . shall allow such costs . . . as (he) considers *reasonably sufficient* to compensate the applicant *for any expenses properly incurred in the proceedings'* for work done and disbursements made. He must also take account of those matters set out under '*Determination*' at 9.10. There must be allowed '. . . *a reasonable amount* in respect of all costs *reasonably incurred* . . . *in the proceedings*', with any doubts being resolved *against* the applicant: r.7(3).

It is considered that r.7 is not intended to override the 'basic measure' contained in s.16(6), *supra*, but to be applied subject to it – ie s.16(6) sets the basis for the award, r.7 lays down how the clerk should assess whether amounts actually incurred were properly incurred. Generally, any distinction would seem to be illusory in any event. But this is otherwise and a potential conflict appears to arise where the award relates to s.16(1)(a), ie where 'the information is not proceeded with'. Here the special 'basic measure' introduced by s.16(10) – the costs incurred '. . . in or about the defence' – is at variance with r.7(1), which refers to expenses incurred 'in the proceedings'. The conflict does not appear to have been foreseen by the legislature, but can be avoided by treating the two provisions in the way suggested – ie by assuming that r.7(1) is intended to be read subject to s.16(6), as amended by s.16(10). The alternative of treating r.7(1) as replacing s.16(a) leads, in the particular circumstances of s.16(1)(a) and s.16(10), to the anomalous result that determinations by the clerk would be on a basis which has been expressly rejected via s.16(10) in the case of the court.

Where the amount is fixed by the court, there is no reason why it should not seek advice from the justices' clerk – as determining officer – even though the fixing of the amount by the court by agreement appears to be intended as a less sophisticated exercise than determination.

Note In all cases, account *may* be taken of any order for *costs thrown away* made during the proceedings in accordance with r.3: r.3(4), and see (3) at 9.08c.

9.08b (2) *Prosecution Costs* (see generally 9.03):

(i) *From central funds*, under s.17(1) in respect of successful *private prosecutions* only of *indictable offences only*. The amount may be fixed by the court: s.17(4)(a) or left for determination by the clerk under s.17(4)(b). Under s.17, the 'basic measure' is '. . . such amount as the court considers *reasonably sufficient* to compensate the prosecutor for any expenses properly incurred by him *in the proceedings*'. This is subject to any reduction under s.17(3) (when the court itself *must* fix the amount of costs and cannot leave this for determination by the justices' clerk). If the case is taken over by the Crown Prosecutor, the private prosecutor cannot recover for expenses incurred thereafter: s.17(5).

Here, the phrase '. . . in the proceedings' would, eg exclude the costs of investigaiton, interviewing of witnesses and other similar pre-court preparations. But no difficulties of the kind adverted to at (1), *supra*, arise where the amount of costs is left for determination by the justices' clerk as envisaged by s.17(4)(b) in accordance with r.7, since that regulation uses the words 'in the proceedings' also. This aspect apart, the remarks in relation to the determining officer's function are as for (1), *supra* – in particular the suggestion that the court may seek advice from the justices' clerk in his capacity as determining officer when fixing the amount of costs itself.

(ii) *Against the defendant* under s.18, when the award *must* be made by the court itself and is *inter partes*., The only measure is '. . . such order as to costs to be paid by the accused to the prosecutor as it considers *just and reasonable*': s.18(1). This is subject to the limitations set out in s.18 (4) and (5), ie the prohibition on costs where other financial orders do not exceed £5: see s.18(4); and the prohibition on costs exceeding the amount of any fine in the case of a juvenile: see s.18(5).

Note In all cases under both (2)(i) and (ii), *supra*, account *may* be taken of an order in respect of *costs thrown away* made during the proceedings under r.3: r.3(4) and see (3), *post*.

(3) *'Costs Thrown Away'* (see generally at 9.05) under s.19 and r.3.   **9.08c**

The amount *must* be fixed by the court and costs are payable *'inter partes'*. The amount is fixed in accordance with r.3(1) as follows: '. . . . where the court is satisfied that costs have been incurred in respect of the proceedings by one of the parties as a result of an unnecessary or improper act or omission by, or on behalf of, another party to the proceedings, the court may, after hearing the parties, order that all or part of the costs so incurred by that party shall be paid to him by the other party'.

The amount should thus correspond to the costs incurred by 'the other party', a term which could, *semble*, include a co-accused. The order is subject to any other order as to costs (including legal aid) which has been made in respect of the proceedings, which must be taken into account by the court: r.3(2); and the costs thrown away *may* be taken into account when making any other order as to costs in the proceedings: r.3(4).

Whilst r.3 represents a means of control in the hands of the court, it is considered that the general rule against the use of costs in a punitive fashion – mentioned at the beginning of the Introduction, 9.00 – still applies to this kind of order. The only proper use of orders for costs thrown away is in accordance with the terms of r.3(1), to compensate another party for the amount of costs incurred *as a result of the act or omission of another party*.

Orders for costs thrown away against *convicted* juveniles are restricted to the amount of any fine imposed on the juvenile: r.3(5).

Claiming costs   9.09

Once the order has been obtained – and assuming that the situation is not one of those, *ante*, where the court has fixed the order at the time of making the order for costs – the onus is on the claimant (in practical terms his solicitor) to submit his claim to the 'appropriate authority' – ie in relation to magistrates' courts, the justices' clerk: r.5(2)(d) – for determination of the amount. Generally, the claim cannot be entertained '. . . unless submitted within three months' of the date of the order: r.6(1); although this limit can be extended 'for good reason' by the clerk: r.12(1). Where there is no good reason, an extension is still possible in 'exceptional circumstances': see r.12(2).

The claim – which should be in such form and manner as the clerk may direct (see r.6(2)) – must summarise the items of work done by a solicitor and state the date on which done, the time taken and the sums claimed, and the circumstances and amounts of any disbursements, including counsel's fees: r.6(3). Any 'special circumstances' should be specified: r.6(4). Receipts or any other documents in support must accompany the claim: r.6(2). The clerk may require the applicant to supply further particulars, information and documents: r.6(5).

9.10 **'Determination'**

'Determination' is the description given to the taxing of an award of costs by the justices' clerk or his appointee in those circumstances where the amount of the award of costs has not been fixed by the court at the time when the order for costs was made. It thus applies only to the central funds costs situations envisaged by s.16(9)(b) POA 1985 (defendants' costs) and s.17(4)(b) (private prosecution costs). It does not apply to situations where the court *must* fix the amount of the costs order, ie where it wishes to reduce costs under s.16(6) or s.17(3), or when it makes an order against the accused under s.18, for *costs thrown away* under s.19 and r.3. The officer making the determination must consider the applicant's claim and any other accompanying information and allow such costs as he considers '*reasonably sufficient* to compensate the applicant for any expenses properly incurred by him in the proceedings' in respect of work reasonably done and for disbursements reasonably incurred. The officer must take into account all the relevant circumstances of the case including the nature, importance, complexity or difficulty of the work and the time involved: r.7(2). It should be noted that 'disbursements' do not include payments out of central funds under Part V of the 1986 Regulations to witnesses, interpreters, medical practitioners etc – although it would seem that, eg a defendant who paid his own witnesses' expenses from his own pocket in ignorance of the central fund provisions should be entitled to recover – within the allowance limits – such amounts by way of 'disbursements'. This approach may not apply in relation to character witnesses, cf r.15.

When determining costs for the purposes of r.7 '. . . there shall be allowed a reasonable amount in respect of all costs reasonably incurred and any doubts which the appropriate authority may have as to whether the costs were reasonably incurred or were reasonable in amount shall be resolved against the applicant'. Justices' clerks have been issued with *Costs from Central Funds – Notes for the Guidance of Justices' Clerks* (generally known as Taxing Officers' Notes for Guidance 'TONG'), which give detailed advice on common taxing occurrences: Lord Chancellor's Department: Costs from Central Funds (83)1.

The following is one of the few reported cases concerning the taxation of costs in criminal cases (based on the old costs provisions), and is reproduced by kind permission of the *Law Society's Gazette*:

'In case No 830316 the taxing master on appeal dealt with a case in which the defendant, who was not in receipt of legal aid, had been acquitted of charges of theft and awarded his costs out of central funds. The taxing master's decision discusses the principles which apply in central funds taxation where the defendant is not in receipt of legal aid. It will be noted that the principles were applied to the work done in both the magistrates' court and the Crown Court.

Reasons for Decision

1. The defendant, a man of good character and a headmaster of a school, was committed for trial on 3 February 1983 and was on 14 March 1983, after a trial lasting five days acquitted of charges of theft. It was a heavy shoplifting case which had serious personal and professional implications. There were difficulties over the police evidence and the owners of the shop were subject to judicial criticism. He was awarded his costs out of central funds in the Crown Court and in the court below. The bulk

of the preparatory work was done by a senior solicitor and a claim was made for the cost of his time at a rate of £33 an hour with an uplift for care and conduct of 50%. Some of the Crown Court work was done by an articled clerk and the cost of her time was claimed at £17 an hour with a similar uplift. Time spent in travelling and waiting by the senior solicitor was claimed at £22 an hour and by the articled clerk at £10 an hour, in each case with an uplift of 50%. Both the senior solicitor and the articled clerk attended the Crown Court trial and the attendance was claimed on an hourly basis at the rates I have mentioned plus the same uplift. Letters were claimed at a unit charge of £3 each.

2. The taxing officer allowed all the work claimed but not at the rates asked for. For the work done in the magistrates' court he allowed a rate of £30 for the senior solicitor for preparatory work and court attendance and £20 for travelling and waiting. Those rates were allowed as charging rates, that is, nothing was added for care and conduct. For the work done in the Crown Court the taxing officer allowed a rate of £33 for the senior solicitor for preparatory work with travelling and waiting time at £22 an hour. His attendance at court was allowed at £30 an hour. The time spent by the articled clerk in preparation was allowed at £17 an hour with travelling and waiting time at £10 an hour. Her attendance at court was allowed at £15 an hour. The letters throughout were allowed at £2 each.

3. The taxing officer chose these rates and declined to allow anything for care and conduct for these reasons:
'I feel that although being costs out of central funds I am not bound by the Legal Aid in Criminal Proceedings (Costs) Regulations 1982, I must keep within the spirit of them and not stray too far away from the standard rates fixed by them . . . it follows from this approach that I have disallowed all care and conduct claimed'.

4. The taxing officer was correct in saying that the 1982 regulations do not apply to taxation of costs out of central funds. He was wrong in principle to fix his rates by references to those prescribed by these regulations. They are wholly irrelevant. The taxation should have proceeded on the ordinary common fund basis and the well known principles and authorities relevant thereto. The Costs in Criminal Cases Act 1973 provides in s.3(2)(*a*) that the costs payable shall be such sums as may be reasonably sufficient to compensate the defendant for the expenses properly incurred by him in carrying on the proceedings. The test of reasonableness has accordingly to be applied from that viewpoint and in accordance with the principles laid down in *Francis v Francis and Dickerson* [1956] 3 All ER 836. The taxing officer having decided what level of fee-earner was proper to the case should have assessed the time spent on preparation and allowed it at an expense rate appropriate to such a fee-earner at the time the work was done. He should then have assessed the relevant factors set out in para 8 of TONG and allowed a proper sum for care and conduct. The method is wholly different from the procedure prescribed by the scheme of the 1982 regulations. While, of course, consistency of assessment between various methods of taxation is desirable, it remains the duty of the taxing officer to follow the principles proper to the basis of taxation with which he is concerned and he must not seek to change these principles because the result might lead to a lack of consistency.

5. On that basis I have concluded that the work of preparation is to be allowed at a rate of £30 an hour for the work done by the senior solicitor and £15 an hour for the work done by the articled clerk. Travelling time is

to be allowed at two-thirds of those rates. Letters are to be allowed at £3 each as claimed. The appropriate allowance for care and conduct is, having regard to all the relevant circumstances, 50%. The allowances to be made are to be recalculated on these bases and the extra sum thrown up paid to the defendant plus VAT.

6. Attendance at court both in the Crown Court and below was claimed at an hourly rate plus care and conduct. In the light of what is said in para 97 of TONG and in *R v Wilkinson* [1980] 1 WLR 396 that claim was wrong in principle and the appellant so conceded before me. What is to be allowed is a proper daily allowance having regard to the time spent in relation to the normal court day. I had in mind certain allowances which seemed to me proper and I indicated to the appellant that the result would probably entitle him to a further small sum, but having looked again at the times involved and what was allowed, bearing in mind that the taxing officer's allowances were made on an hourly basis, I have concluded that the difference is too small to warrant my interference and accordingly I allow nothing further for any of these items.

Once *quantum* has been ascertained, the officer must notify the applicant of the costs payable and authorise payment accordingly: r.8(1). Unlike the position in relation to other determinations, eg in relation to Crown Court awards of costs, there is no provision for 'redetermination' (see r.9), neither is there any special channel of appeal against decisions by the clerk – although, on general principle, *judicial review* would appear to be available where, eg the determining officer has considered irrelevant matters or failed to consider relevant ones.

9.11 Enforcement

Orders for costs are enforceable in accordance with the provisions of s.41 Administration of Justice Act 1970, and Sch.9 to that Act, which treats the various types of order as either 'enforceable as on summary conviction', or 'enforceable as a civil debt'. Schedule 9 is set out in full in the section *Statutory Provisions* at 9.22.

9.12 WITNESSES' ALLOWANCES – INCLUDING MEDICAL REPORTS

Apart from the allowable rates and scales of payments, the law applicable to witnesses' allowances is contained in Part V of the 1986 Regulations. The 'rates and scales' of payment are fixed separately by the Lord Chancellor with the consent of the Treasury under powers given by r.17.

Many of the regulations provide for an allowance to be paid provided that it does not exceed the appropriate rate or scale as set by the Lord Chancellor, referred to in the regulations as the 'relevant amount'. The current rates and scales contained in the *Guide to Allowances under Part V of the Costs in Criminal Cases (General) Regulations 1986*, Appendix One thereto, as amended, are reproduced at the end of the section on *Statutory Provisions* at 9.40.

As a rule, a witness, interpreter or doctor should be granted expenses properly incurred to the extent allowed under the regulations unless the court directs otherwise: r.16(1). With the exception of a written medical report, allowances are paid on a *temporal* basis: see r.16(2), (3).

It should be noted that it no longer matters whether a case is indictable or summary; but that witnesses *called by the prosecution* – as opposed to the defence – cannot have expenses paid out of central funds *on the authorisation of the court* unless the prosecutor is a 'private prosecutor', ie, one in whose favour the court can order costs out of central funds under s.17 POA 1985. Since most prosecutions will be by public bodies, few prosecution witnesses will be paid by the court. So far as witnesses called by the Crown Prosecution Service are concerned, the Crown Prosecution Service (Witnesses' Allowances) Regulations 1986 (SI 1986 No 405, as amended by SI 1986 No 842) (not reproduced herein) make provision for the payment of witnesses from central funds by the service.

The following are not treated as witnesses for the purposes of payment under Part V of the 1986 Regulations:
  (a) someone who is only a *character witness*. However, he can qualify as a witness if the court *certifies* that the interests of justice required his attendance;
  (b) members of *police* forces attending court *in that capacity*;
  (c) full-time *prison officers* attending *in that capacity*;
  (d) *prisoners* on the occasions on which they are conveyed to court in custody; r.15.

But where a witness *is* treated as within that definition for the purpose of the regulations, it does not matter whether the witness was in fact called to give evidence provided he was *a person properly attending* to give evidence: *ibid*.

Those eligible for payment can be divided into the following *categories*, which are *not necessarily mutually exclusive*:
  (i) witnesses
  (ii) professional witnesses (not all 'professions' being included, 9.14 *post*)
  (iii) expert witnesses
  (iv) doctors
  (v) prosecutors and defendants
  (vi) interpreters; and
  (vii) others
The allowances of each of these are considered below.

Witnesses – in general 9.13

Witnesses can claim for the following:
  (a) A loss allowance (not available to professional or expert witnesses) not exceeding the relevant amount in respect of expenditure incurred as a result of attending court apart from the cost of travel, lodging and subsistence which is dealt with separately: r.18(1)(a)(i).
  (b) A loss allowance (not available to professional or expert witnesses) *not exceeding the relevant amount* in respect of (a) loss of earnings and (b) loss of benefit under the legislation on National Insurance: r.18(1)(a)(ii).
  (c) A subsistence allowance (not available to professional or expert witnesses) *not exceeding the relevant amount*: r.18(1)(b).
  (d) *Travelling expenses*. In effect, the witness can choose whether he wishes to use his own private vehicle or to go by public transport. If he adopts the former course he may be allowed an appropriate private vehicle allowance not exceeding the relevant amount. If he chooses the latter, he will be allowed the fare actually paid subject to two exceptions. First, if he travels by rail, only the *second class* fare will be allowed *unless the court otherwise directs*. Secondly, if he goes by air, he will only be allowed his fare if (a) there was no

reasonable alternative mode of travel and the class of fare was reasonable in all the circumstances or (b) travel by air was more economical because of its consequent effect in reducing the allowances otherwise payable due to the time saved by this method of transport. If the air fare is not allowed there may be allowed such amount as the court considers reasonable.

A witness will only be allowed the fare actually paid for a hired vehicle (together with any reasonable gratuity paid) in cases of urgency or where public transport is not reasonably available. If either of those criteria are not satisfied he can only be allowed the fare for travel by public transport (ie not the mileage allowance which he could have claimed in respect of his own vehicle).

The court has a discretion to allow reasonable additional amounts where, in the opinion of the court, a witness is suffering from a serious illness or where heavy exhibits have to be taken to court.

9.14 Professional witnesses

Professional witnesses are defined as witnesses *practising* as members of *certain professions only* and attending to give *professional evidence* as to matters of *fact*. The professions concerned are the legal and medical professions, dentists, veterinary surgeons and accountants: r.15.

Such witnesses are eligible for the following allowances:
(a) A professional witness allowance not exceeding the relevant amount: r.19.
(b) A night allowance not exceeding the relevant amount if the witness is necessarily absent from home overnight: r.21.

9.15 Expert Witnesses

(a) The court may make an allowance for attending to give expert evidence and for work in connection with its preparation of such an amount as it considers reasonable having regard to the nature and difficulty of the case and the work necessarily involved: r.20(1).
(b) The night allowance that applies to *professional witnesses, supra* also applies to expert witnesses.

9.16 Medical Practitioners

(a) The expert witnesses' allowance for attendance and preparation, *supra*, applies to doctors giving *oral* reports for the purpose of s.30 MCA 1980: r.20(2).
(b) If a doctor in fact receives an expert witnesses attendance and preparation allowance, he also qualifies for a night allowance not exceeding the relevant amount if he is necessarily absent from his home overnight: r.21(2).
(c) A travelling allowance not exceeding the relevant amount may be allowed to a doctor making an oral report: r.24(7).
(d) *Allowances for written reports* in accordance with r.25. Note that such allowances cannot be claimed by prison doctors: r.25(3). An allowance not exceeding the relevant amount may be paid for a written report made in response to a *request by a court* under s.32(2) Criminal Justice Act 1967. It is suggested that this includes the practical situation where a solicitor arranges a written report following a request to him by the court to do this. Section 32(2), when read in conjunction with s.32(3) covers, in effect, reports for all purposes involving a medical element. A doctor who makes

such a written report may be allowed a travelling allowance not exceeding the relevant amount: r.25(2).

Prosecutors and defendants 9.17

A person in whose favour an order under s.16 or s.17 the 1985 Act is *in fact made*, may be allowed the same subsistence and travelling allowances that would have been available to him if he had attended as an ordinary witness: r.23.

Interpreters 9.18

The provisions apply only to interpreters who are required due to the defendant's 'lack of English': see r.16(1)(b).

(a) The expert witnesses' attendance and preparation allowance applies, *mutatis mutandis* to an interpreter – in effect the 'interpreter's fee', which is to be a sum determined by the court: r.20(2)(a).

(b) An interpreter who *in fact receives* the above allowance may be allowed the professional or expert witnesses' night allowance if he is necessarily absent from his home overnight: r.21(2).

(c) An interpreter may be allowed a travelling allowance not exceeding the relevant amount: r.24(7).

Others 9.19

Anyone, (apart from a police officer or a full-time prison officer attending in such capacities or a prisoner who is conveyed to court in custody), who in the opinion of the court, necessarily attends for the purposes of the proceedings otherwise than to give evidence, may be allowed the same loss and subsistence allowances as an ordinary witness. However, he may not claim other allowances, eg for travelling: r.18(2),(3).

Statutory Provisions

CRIMINAL JUSTICE ACT 1967

Amendments of Costs in Criminal Cases Act 1952 9.20

32. (2) Section 33 of the Courts-Martial (Appeals) Act 1968 to apply in relation to a registered medical practitioner making a written report to a Court in pursuance of a request to which this subsection applies.

(3) The last foregoing subsection applies to a request to a registered medical practitioner to make a written or oral report on the medical condition of an offender or defendant, being a request made by a court–

(a) for the purpose of determining whether or not to make an order under s.3 of the Powers of Criminal Courts Act 1973 (probation orders requiring treatment for mental condition) of s.60 of the Mental Health Act 1959 (hospital orders and guardianship orders) or otherwise for the purpose of determining the most suitable method of dealing with an offender; or

(b) in exercise of the powers conferred by s.30 of the Magistrates' Courts Act 1980 (remand of a defendant for medical examination and requirement of such an examination on committing a defendant for trial on bail).

[*as amended by Sch.11 Courts Act 1971, Schs.1 and 2 Costs in Criminal Cases Act 1973, Sch.5 Powers of Criminal Courts Act 1973, Sch.7 MCA 1980 and Sch.1 Prosecution of Offences Act 1985*].

COMMENTARY

The Costs in Criminal Cases Act 1973 has been repealed and replaced by Part II Prosecution of Offences Act 1985: see s.19(3), *post*. As to written medical reports, see also r.25 Costs in Criminal Cases (General) Regulations 1986, *post*.

s.32(3(a): s.60 Mental Health Act 1959: see now s.37 of the Mental Health Act 1983, Chapter 8, *ante*.

ADMINISTRATION OF JUSTICE ACT 1970

9.21   **Recovery of costs and compensation awarded by magistrates, Crown Court, etc**
41. (1) In the cases specified in Part I of Schedule 9 to this Act (being cases where, in criminal proceedings, a court makes an order against the accused for the payment of costs, compensation, etc) any sum required to be paid by such an order as is there mentioned shall be treated, for the purposes of collection and enforcement, as if it had been adjudged to be paid on a conviction by a magistrates' court, being–
   (a) where the order is made by a magistrates' court, that court; and
   (b) in any other case, such magistrates' court as may be specified in the order.

(2) In the cases specified in Part II of the said Schedule (being cases where a court make an order against the prosecutor in criminal proceedings, and certain cases where an order for costs arises out of an appeal to the Crown Court in proceedings which are not criminal) any sum required to be paid by such an order as is there mentioned shall be enforceable as if the order were for the payment of money recoverable summarily as a civil debt.

(3) Without prejudice to the foregoing subsections, but subject to subsection (4) below, in the cases specified in Schedule 9 to this Act any sum required to be paid by such an order as is there mentioned shall be enforceable by the High Court or a county court (otherwise than by issue of a writ of *feri facias* or other process against goods or by imprisonment or attachment of earnings) as if the sum were due in pursuance of a judgment or order of the High Court or county court, as the case may be.

(4) Subsection (3) above shall not authorise the enforcement by a county court of payment of any sum exceeding the county court limit on the amount of any penalty recoverable by statute in a county court.

(4A) In subsection (4) above 'the county court limit' means the amount which for the time being is the county court limit for the purposes of section 16 of the County Courts Act 1984.

(5) References in subsections (1) and (2) above to orders mentioned in Schedule 9 to this Act include references to orders made before the day appointed under section 54 of this Act for the coming into force of this section, except an order in the case of which the person entitled to payment has before that day begun proceedings for its enforcement; and in relation to such a case the enactments in force immediately before that day with reference to the enforcement of such an order shall continue to apply notwithstanding any repeal effected by this Act, without prejudice however to section 13(6) of this Act.

For the purpose of the operation of subsection (1) above with respect to an order made (otherwise than by a magistrates' court) before the day so appointed, the order shall be deemed to specify the magistrates' court for the petty sessions area in which the person subject to the order for the time being resides.

(8) In any of the cases specified in Part I of Schedule 9 to this Act, a court (other than a magistrates' court) which makes such an order as is there mentioned may, if it thinks that the period for which the person subject to the order is liable apart from this subsection (c) to be committed to prison for

default under the order is insufficient, specify a longer period for that purpose, but not exceeding twelve months; and then, in the case of default–
    (a) the specified period shall be sustituted as the maximum for which the person may be imprisoned under section 76 of the Magistrates' Courts Act 1980 (distress or committal); and
    (b) paragraph 2 of Schedule 4 to that Act shall apply, with the necessary modifications, for the reduction of the specified period where, at the time of the person's imprisonment, he has made part payment under the order.

(9) Where a magistrates' court has power to commit a person to prison for default in paying a sum due under an order enforceable as mentioned in this section, the court shall not exercise the power unless it is satisfied that all other methods of enforcing payment have been tried or considered and either have proved unsuccessful or are likely to do so.
[as amended by Sch.13 Criminal Law Act 1977, Sch.7 MCA 1980, and Sch.2 County Courts Act 1984].

(8) Subject to subsection (8A) below, where in the case specified in paragraph 10 of Schedule 9 to this Act the Crown Court thinks that the period for which the person subject to the order is liable apart from this subsection to be committed to prison for default under the order is insufficient, it may specify a longer period for that purpose; and then, in the case of default–
    (a) the specified period shall be substituted as the maximum for which the person may be imprisoned under section 76 of the Magistrates' Courts Act 1980; and
    (b) paragraph 2 of Schedule 4 to that Act shall apply, with any necessary modifications, for the reduction of the specified period where, at the time of the person's imprisonment, he has made part payment under the order.

(8A) The Crown Court may not specify under subsection (8) above a period of imprisonment longer than that which it could order a person to undergo on imposing on him a fine equal in amount to the sum required to be paid by the order.
[as amended by [s.104] CJA 1988 from a date to be appointed].

COMMENTARY

s.41(2): 'recoverable . . . as civil debt' note that s.12 Administration of Justice Act 1970 contains restrictions on committal for default; also that pursuant to ss.1 and 2 Attachment of Earnings Act 1971, county courts but not magistrates' courts may make attachment of earnings orders in respect of costs under s.41(2).

SCHEDULE 9   **9.22**

ENFORCEMENT OF ORDERS FOR COSTS, COMPENSATION, ETC

PART I

CASES WHERE PAYMENT ENFORCEABLE AS ON SUMMARY CONVICTION

Costs awarded by magistrates
    1. Where a magistrates' court, on the summary trial of an information, makes an order as to costs to be paid by the accused to the prosecutor.

    1A. Where a magistrates' court makes an order as to costs to be paid by the accused in exercise of any power in that behalf conferred by regulations made under section 19(1) of the Prosecution of Offences Act 1985.

    2. Where an appellant to the Crown Court against conviction or sentence by a magistrates' court abandons his appeal and the magistrates' court orders him to pay costs to the other party to the appeal.

Costs awarded by the Crown Court
    3. Where a person appeals to the Crown Court against conviction or sen-

tence by a magistrates' court and the Crown Court make an order as to costs to be paid by him.

4. Where a person is prosecuted or tried on indictment before the Crown Court and is convicted, and the court makes an order as to costs to be paid by him.

4A. Where the Crown Court makes an order as to costs to be paid by the accused in exercise of any power in that behalf conferred by regulations made under section 19(1) of the Prosecution of Offences Act 1985.

Costs awarded by Court of Appeal (Criminal Division) or House of Lords
6. Where the criminal division of the Court of Appeal makes an order as to costs to be paid by–
    (a) an appellant;
    (b) an applicant for leave to appeal to that court; or
    (c) in the case of an application for leave to appeal to the House of Lords, an applicant who was the appellant before the criminal division.

Miscellaneous orders for costs, compensation, damages, etc
9. Where a court makes an order by virtue of regulations made under section 19(5) of the Prosecution of Offences Act 1985 for the payment of costs by an offender.

10. Where under s.35 of the Powers of Criminal Courts Act 1973 a court orders the payment of compensation.

12. Where under section 55 of the Children and Young Persons Act 1933 a court orders any fine, damages, compensation or costs, or any sum awarded by way of satisfaction or compensation to be paid by the parent or guardian of a child or young person.

PART II
CASES WHERE COSTS ENFORCEABLE SUMMARILY AS CIVIL DEBT

Costs awarded by magistrates
13. Where a magistrates' court makes an order as to costs to be paid by the prosecutor in exercise of any power in that behalf conferred by regulations made under section 19(1) of the Prosecution of Offences Act 1985.

14. Where an appellant to the Crown Court from a magistrates' court (otherwise than against conviction or sentence) abandons his appeal and the magistrates' court orders him to pay costs to the other party to the appeal.

15. *Repealed.*

Costs awarded by the Crown Court
16. Any order for the payment of costs made by the Crown Court, other than an order falling within Part I above, or an order for costs to be paid out of money provided by Parliament.

Costs awarded by Court of Appeal (Criminal Division)
16A. Where the criminal division of the Court of Appeal makes an order as to costs to be paid by the respondent or, in the case of an application for leave to appeal to the House of Lords, an applicant who was the respondent before the criminal division, and does so in exercise of any powers in that behalf conferred by regulations made under section 19(1) of the Prosecution of Offences Act 1985.
[*as amended by the Courts Act 1971, the CJA 1972, the Costs in Criminal Cases Act 1973, Sch.13 CLA 1977, and Schs.1 and 2 Prosecution of Offences Act 1985*].

PROSECUTION OF OFFENCES ACT 1985

Defence costs 9.23

16. (1) Where–

(a) an information laid before a justice of the peace for any area, charging any person with an offence, is not proceeded with;

(b) a magistrates' court inquiring into an indictable offence as examining justices determines not to commit the accused for trial;

(c) a magistrates' court dealing summarily with an offence dismisses the information;

that court or, in a case falling within paragraph (a) above, a magistrates' court for that area, may make an order in favour of the accused for a payment to be made out of central funds in respect of his costs (a 'defendant's costs order').

(2) (Crown Court).

(3) (Crown Court – Costs on appeal).

(4) (Court of Appeal).

(5) (Higher courts).

(6) A defendant's costs order shall, subject to the following provisions of this section, be for the payment out of central funds, to the person in whose favour the order is made, of such amount as the court considers reasonably sufficient to compensate him for any expenses properly incurred by him in the proceedings.

(7) Where a court makes a defendant's costs order but is of the opinion that there are circumstances which make it inappropriate that the person in whose favour the order is made should recover the full amount mentioned in subsection (6) above, the court shall–

(a) assess what amount would, in its opinion, be just and reasonable; and

(b) specify that amount in the order.

(8) Where a defendant's costs order is made in favour of a legally assisted person, any expenses incurred on his behalf pursuant to the legal aid order in question shall be disregarded in determining (for the purposes of this section) the amount of the expenses incurred by him in the proceedings.

(9) Subject to subsection (7) above, the amount to be paid out of central funds in pursuance of a defendant's costs order shall–

(a) be specified in the order, in any case where the court considers it appropriate for the amount to be so specified and the person in whose favour the order is made agrees the amount; and

(b) in any other case, be determined in accordance with regulations made by the Lord Chancellor for the purposes of this section.

(10) Subsection (6) falls above shall have effect, in relation to any case falling within subsection (1)(a) or (2)(a) above, as if for the words 'in the proceedings' there were substituted the words 'in or about the defence'.

(11) Where a person ordered to be retried is acquitted at his retrial, the costs which may be ordered to be paid out of central funds under this section shall include–

(a) any costs which, at the original trial, could have been ordered to be so paid under this section if he had been acquitted; and

(b) if no order was made under this section in respect of his expenses on appeal, any sums for the payment of which such an order could have been made.

COMMENTARY

s.16(1)(a) 'not proceeded with': note that in relation to this subsection *only*, the measure of a 'defendant's costs order' in the expenses incurred 'in or about the defence', and not the more usual expenses incurred 'in the proceedings' see s.16(6), (10), and the comments in the

Introduction, at 9.00. Section 16(1)(a) applies to the situation where an information is 'out of time' because it is laid outside the six months time limit for summary offences contained in s.127 MCA 1980: see *Patel v Blakey* (1987) *The Times*, 26 February; and to withdrawals and 'discontinued' proceedings: see *Defendant's Costs Order*, 9.02.

s.16(6): see commentary to s.16(1). '. . . compensate him', etc. Other things being equal, a solicitor who defends himself is entitled to all of his costs, including those incurred in the course of conducting his own case: *R v Stafford, Stone and Eccleshall Justices, ex p. Robinson* (1987) *The Times*, 6 November. 'It was right to say that solicitors' expenses properly could be held to include their own fees such as they would otherwise be earning on behalf of the firm': per Simon Brown J, *ibid*. See also *R v Stockport Magistrates' Court, ex p. Cooper* (1984) 148 JP 261 and *London Scottish Benefit Society v Chorley* (1884) 13 QBD 872 (a civil case).

The Court of Appeal – relying on 16(4) – ordered costs to be paid to a third party, the appellants' mother, where she had put up the money for his appeal and he was bankrupt and would therefore forfeit any costs received: *R v Jain* (1987) *The Times*, 10 December. Section 16(1) and r.4 are in sufficiently similar terms to allow magistrates' to make a 'third party defendants' costs order' in appropriate circumstances, *semble*.

s.16(9)(a): for the amount of the award, see under *Quantum, etc* in the *Introduction* at 9.00.

s.16(9)(b): 'determined in accordance with regulations': see r.7 in Part III, Prosecution of Offences Regulations 1986 SI 1986 No 1335, *post* and for the amount of the award, see *Quantum – Including Claims and 'Determination'* at 9.07. The 'determining authority' is the justices' clerk, see r.5(2)(d); or his appointee: r.5(3).

s.16(10): see the commentary to s.16(1), *supra*.

9.24   **Prosecution costs**
          17. (1) Subject to subsection (2) below, the court may–
          (a) in any proceedings in respect of an indictable offence; and
          (b) (Higher courts).
order the payment out of central funds of such amount as the court considers reasonably sufficient to compensate the prosecutor for any expenses properly incurred by him in the proceedings.

(2) No order under this section may be made in favour of–
(a) a public authority; or
(b) a person acting–
      (i) on behalf of a public authority; or
      (ii) in his capacity as an official appointed by such an authority.

(3) Where a court makes an order under this section but is of the opinion that there are circumstances which make it inappropriate that the prosecution should recover the full amount mentioned in subsection (1) above, the court shall–
(a) assess what amount would, in its opinion, be just and reasonable; and
(b) specify that amount in the order.

(4) Subject to subsection (3) above, the amount to be paid out of central funds in pursuance of an order under this section shall–
(a) be specified in the order, in any case where the court considers it appropriate for the amount to be so specified and the prosecutor agrees the amount; and
(b) in any other case, be determined in accordance with regulations made by the Lord Chancellor for the purposes of this section.

(5) Where the conduct of proceedings to which subsection (1) above applies is taken over by the Crown Prosecution Service, that subsection shall have effect as if it referred to the prosecutor who had the conduct of the proceedings before the intervention of the Service and to expenses incurred by him up to the time of intervention.

(6) In this section 'public authority' means–
(a) a police force within the meaning of section 3 of this Act;
(b) the Crown Prosecution Service or any other government department;

(c) a local authority or other authority or body constituted for purposes of–
   (i) the public service or of local government; or
   (ii) carrying on under national ownership any industry or undertaking or part of an industry or undertaking; or
(d) any other authority or body whose members are appointed by Her Majesty or by any Minister of the Crown or government department or whose revenues consist wholly or mainly of money provided by Parliament.

COMMENTARY

s.17(1): 'To compensate the prosecutor for any expenses properly incurred by him in the proceedings': note that the Crown Prosecutor will pay his own witnesses and that the amount which he may recover in this regard is thus limited to the accounts laid down pursuant to the Crown Prosecution Service (Witnesses' Allowances) Regulations 1986 SI 1986 No 405, as amended by SI 1986 No 842.

s.17(2): public authority': as defined in s.17(6), *post*. For a list of 'nationalised industries and undertakings', see 9.03.

s.17(4)(a): For the amount of the award, see under *Quantum, etc* in the *Introduction*, 9.00.

s.17(4)(b): 'determined in accordance with regulations': see r.7 Prosecution of Offences Regulations 1986 SI 1986 No 1335, *post*, and for the amount of the award, see *Quantum – Including Claims and 'Determination'*, 9.07: The 'determining authority' is the justices clerk: r.5(2)(d); or his appointee: r.5(3).

s.17(5): note the position where the Crown Prosecutor takes over proceedings from a private prosecutor. The latter may not claim for any expenses (eg 'a watching brief') incurred *after* the takeover.

s.17(6)(c)(ii): for a list of 'nationalised industries and undertakings', see 9.03.

Award of costs against accused   **9.25**
   18. (1) Where–
   (a) any person is convicted of an offence before a magistrates' court;
   (b) (Crown Court)
the court may make such order as to the costs to be paid by the accused to the prosecutor as it considers just and reasonable.

   (2) (Court of Appeal)

   (3) The amount to be paid by the accused in pursuance of an order under this section shall be specified in the order.

   (4) Where any person is convicted of an offence before a magistrates' court and–
   (a) under the conviction the court orders payment of any sum as a fine, penalty, forfeiture or compensation; and
   (b) the sum so ordered to be paid does not exceed £5;
the court shall not order the accused to pay any costs under this section unless in the particular circumstances of the case it considers it right to do so.

   (5) Where any person under the age of seventeen is convicted of an offence before a magistrates' court, the amount of any costs ordered to be paid by the accused under this section shall not exceed the amount of any fine imposed on him.

   (6) (Costs).

COMMENTARY

Note The circumstances in which s.18 applies are extended by r.14, *post*, to a number of 'breach' situations. The full list of circumstances in which costs may be so ordered by magistrates is as follows:

(a) Where the accused is *convicted* of any offence by magistrates: s.18(1)(a);
(b) Where an offender is *dealt with* under ss.6, 8 or 10 Powers of Criminal Courts Act 1973 (probation orders conditional discharges): r.14(3)(a);

(c) In proceedings under s.16 or s.17 of the 1973 Act (community service orders): r.14(3)(b);
(d) Where an offender is dealt with under s.23(1) or s.27 of the 1973 Act or under s.47 Criminal Law Act 1977 (suspended and partially suspended sentences): r.14(3)(c).

s.18(3): note that the amount *must* be fixed by the court.

9.26   **Provision for orders as to costs in other circumstances**
     19. (1) The Lord Chancellor may by regulations make provision empowering magistrates' courts, the Crown Court and the Court of Appeal, in any case where the court is satisfied that one party to criminal proceedings has incurred costs as a result of an unnecessary or improper act or omission by, or on behalf of, another party to the proceedings, to make an order as to the payment of those costs.

(2) Regulations made under subsection (1) above may, in particular–
(a) allow the makings such an order at any time during the proceedings;
(b) make provision as to the account to be taken, in making such an order, of any other order as to costs (including any legal aid order) which has been made in respect of the proceedings;
(c) make provision as to the account to be taken of any such order in the making of any other order as to costs in respect of the proceedings; and
(d) contain provisions similar to those in section 18(4) and (5) of this Act.

(3) The Lord Chancellor may by regulations make provision for the payment out of central funds, in such circumstances and in relation to such criminal proceedings as may be specified, of such sums as appear to the court to be reasonably necessary–
(a) to compensate any witness in the proceedings, *and for any other person who in the opinion of the court necessarily attends for the purpose of the proceedings otherwise than to give evidence,* for the expense, trouble or loss of time properly incurred in or incidental to his attendance;
(b) to cover the proper expenses of an interpreter who is required because of the accused's lack of English;
(c) to compensate a duly qualified medical practitioner who–
  (i) makes a report otherwise than in writing for the purpose of section 30 of the Magistrates' Courts Act 1980 (remand for medical examination); or
  (ii) makes a written report to a court in pursuance of a request to which section 32(2) of the Criminal Justice Act 1967 (report by medical practitioner on medical condition of offender) applies;
for the expenses properly incurred in or incidental to his reporting to the court.
(3A) In subsection (3)(a) above 'attendance' means attendance at the court or elsewhere.

(4) *Court of Appeal.*

(5) The Lord Chancellor may by regulations provide that any provision made by or under this Part which would not otherwise apply in relation to any category of proceedings in which an offender is before a magistrates' court or the Crown Court shall apply in relation to proceedings of that category, subject to any specified modifications.
[*the words in italics in subs (3)(a) and subs (3A) will be inserted by [s.158] CJA 1988, when in force*].

COMMENTARY
s.19(1): '. . . by regulation'; ie currently the Costs in Criminal Cases Regulations 1986, SI 1986 No 1335, reproduced *post.* In relation to s.19 (1), *Costs Thrown Away,* see r.3, and 9.05.

s.19(2): the regulations do all of those things referred to in s.19(2)(a) to (d), so that it is important to work directly from these regulations, which are reproduced *post.*

s.19(3): the comments at s.19(2) *supra* are equally applicable in relation to subs (3). The present rates and scales of witnesses' allowances are contained in Appendix One and Two to the Guide to Allowances reproduced at the end of this chapter.

s.19(3)(c)(i): medical 'report otherwise than in writing': see r.16(1)(c). Reports *in writing* may be paid for out of central funds in accordance with s.32(2)CJA 1967, *supra* and r.25.

s.19(5): 'any category of proceedings': see r.14 which extends the operation of s.18 (prosecution costs against a defendant) to those 'breach' situations contained in the list reproduced in the commentary to that section.

Interpretation etc
9.27
21. (1) In this Part–
'defendant's costs order' has the meaning given in section 16 of this Act;
'legal aid order' means an order under any provision of section 28 of the Legal Aid Act 1974 and includes, in relation to proceedings in a Divisional Court of the Queen's Bench Division, any certificate or other instrument under which legal aid is given;
'legally assisted person' means a person to whom aid is ordered to be given by a legal aid order;
'proceedings' includes–
  (a) proceedings in any court below; and
  (b) in relation to the determination of an appeal by any court, any application made to that court for leave to bring the appeal; and
'witness' means any person properly attending to give evidence, whether or not he gives evidence or is called at the instance of one of the parties or of the court, but does not include a person attending as a witness to character only unless the court has certified that the interests of justice required his attendance.

COSTS IN CRIMINAL CASES (GENERAL) REGULATIONS 1986
9.28
(SI No 1335)

1. (2), (3) (Appeal to the Court of Appeal).

(4) For the purposes of sections 16 and 17 of this Act, the costs of any party to proceedings shall be taken to include the expense of compensating any witness for the expenses, trouble or loss of time properly incurred in or incidental to his attendance.

(5) Where, in any proceedings in a criminal cause or matter or in either of the cases mentioned in subsection (6) below, an interpreter is required because of the accused's lack of English, the expenses properly incurred on his employment shall not be treated as costs of any party to the proceedings.

(6) The cases are–
(a) where an information charging the accused with an offence is laid before a justice of the peace for any area but not proceeded with and the expenses are incurred on the employment of the interpreter for the proceedings on the information; and
(b) where the accused is committed for trial but not tried and the expenses are incurred on the employment of the interpreter for the proceedings in the Crown Court.

COMMENTARY
s.21(1): 'witness' note that the definition does not include a *character witness* unless *the court has certified that the interests of justice require his attendance.*

s.21(5): 'interpreter'; '. . . expenses properly incurred' in the situations described in s.21(5) and (6), the expenses of interpreters are thus to be paid for *out of central funds*, and at their actual rate and are not to be treated as the costs of either party.

COSTS UNNECESSARILY OR IMPROPERLY INCURRED

9.29   **Unnecessary or improper acts and omissions**
3. (1) Subject to the provisions of this regulation, where at any time during criminal proceedings–
(a) a magistrates' court,
(b) (Crown Court)
(c) (Court of Appeal)
is satisfied that costs have been incurred in respect of the proceedings by one of the parties as a result of an unnecessary or improper act or omission by, or on behalf of, another party to the proceedings, the court may, after hearing the parties, order that all or part of the costs so incurred by that party shall be paid to him by the other party.

(2) Before making an order under paragraph (1), the court shall take into account any other order as to costs (including any legal aid order) which has been made in respect of the proceedings.

(3) An order made under paragraph (1) shall specify the amount of costs to be paid in pursuance of the order.

(4) Where an order under paragraph (1) has been made, the court may take that order into account when making any other order as to costs in respect of the proceedings.

(5) No order under paragraph (1) shall be made by a magistrates' court which requires a person under the age of seventeen who has been convicted of an offence to pay an amount by way of costs which exceeds the amount of any fine imposed on him.

COMMENTARY
R.3(4): note that the court *may* take account of an order under r.3(1) when making '. . . any other order as to costs', ie under s.16 (defendant's costs order), s.17 (private prosecution costs), or s.18 (costs against a defendant).

PART III

COSTS OUT OF CENTRAL FUNDS

9.30   **Application and definitions**
4. This Part of these Regulations applies to costs payable out of central funds in pursuance of an order made under or by virtue of Part II of the Act and in this Part of these Regulations–
'applicant' means the person in whose favour a costs order has been made;
'appropriate authority' has the meaning assigned to it by regulation 5;
'costs order' means an order made under or by virtue of Part II of the Act for the payment of costs out of central funds;
'disbursements' do not include any payment made out of central funds to a witness, interpreter or medical practitioner in accordance with Part V of these Regulations'
'presiding judge' means the judge who presided at the hearing in respect of which the costs are payable; and
'taxing master' means a taxing master of the Supreme Court.

The appropriate authority
5. (1) Costs shall be determined by the appropriate authority in accordance with these Regulations.

(2) Subject to paragraph (3), the appropriate authority shall be–
(a) (Court of Appeal)
(b) (Divisional Court)
(c) (Crown Court)
(d) the justices' clerk in the case of proceedings in a magistrates' court.

(3) The appropriate authority may appoint or authorise the appointment of determining officers to act on its behalf under these Regulations in accordance with directions given by it or on its behalf.

Claims for costs

6. (1) Subject to regulation 12, no claim for costs shall be entertained unless it is submitted within three months of the date on which the costs order was made.

(2) Subject to paragraph (3), a claim for costs shall be submitted to the appropriate authority in such form and manner as it may direct and shall be accompanied by any receipts or other documents in support of any disbursements claimed.

(3) A claim shall–
(a) summarise the items of work done by a solicitor;
(b) state, where appropriate, the dates on which items of work were done, the time taken and the sums claimed, and
(c) specify any disbursements claimed, including counsel's fees, the circumstances in which they were incurred and the amounts claimed in respect of them.

(4) Where there are any special circumstances which should be drawn to the attention of the appropriate authority, the applicant shall specify them.

(5) The applicant shall supply such further particulars, information and documents as the appropriate authority may require.

COMMENTARY

R.6(1): '. . . within 3 months' ie subject to any extension by the justices' clerk pursuant to the power conferred by r.12, *post.*

Determination of costs

7. (1) The appropriate authority shall consider the claim, any further particulars, information or documents submitted by the applicant under regulation 6 and shall allow such costs in respect of–
(a) such work as appears to it to have been actually and reasonably done; and
(b) such disbursements as appear to it to have been actually and reasonably incurred,
as it considers reasonably sufficient to compensate the applicant for any expenses properly incurred by him in the proceedings.

(2) In determining costs under paragraph (1) the appropriate authority shall take into account all the relevant circumstances of the case including the nature, importance, complexity or difficulty of the work and the time involved.

(3) When determining costs for the purpose of this regulation, there shall be allowed a reasonable amount in respect of all costs reasonably incurred and any doubts which the appropriate authority may have as to whether the costs were reasonably incurred or were reasonable in amount shall be resolved against the applicant.

Payment of costs

8. (1) Having determined the costs payable to an applicant in accordance with these Regulations, the appropriate authority shall notify the applicant of the costs payable and authorise payment accordingly.

(2) (Redetermination – not applicable to magistrates' courts).

9. (Redetermination – not applicable to magistrates' courts).

10. (Appeals to a taxing master – not applicable to magistrates' courts).

11. (Further appeals to the High Court – not applicable to magistrates' courts).

Time Limits
12. (1) Subject to paragraph (2), the time limit within which there must be made or instituted–
(a) a claim for costs by the applicant under regulation 6 . . .;
(b) (taxing matters)
(c) (Appeals to the High Court)
may, for good reason, be extended by the appropriate authority . . . may, in exceptional circumstances, extend the time limit.

13. (House of Lords).

PART IV

MISCELLANEOUS APPLICATIONS OF THE ACT

9.31   **Application of sections 16, 17 and 18 of the Act**
14. (1), (2) (Crown Court)
(3) Section 18 of the Act shall apply to proceedings in a magistrates' court or Crown Court–
(a) for dealing with an offender under section 6, 8 or 10 of the Powers of Criminal Courts Act 1973 (probation orders and orders for conditional discharge);
(b) under section 16 or 17 of the Powers of Criminal Courts Act (1973 (community service orders);
(c) under section 23(1) or 27 of the Powers of Criminal Courts Act 1973 or section 47 of the Criminal Law Act 1977 for dealing with an offender in respect of a suspended or partially suspended sentence or for breach of a suspended sentence supervision order; or
(d) under section 19(5) of the Criminal Justice Act 1982 for dealing with an offender in respect of a breach of an attendance centre order,
as if the offender had been tried in those proceedings for the offence for which the order was made or the sentence passed.

(4) Section 16 of the Act shall apply to proceedings in a magistrates' court or the Crown Court in which it is alleged that an offender required to enter into a recognisance to keep the peace or be of good behaviour has failed to comply with a condition of that recognisance, as if that failure were an indictable offence.

PART V

ALLOWANCES TO WITNESSES

9.32   **Definitions**
15. In this Part of these Regulations–
'expenses' include compensation to a witness for his trouble or loss of time and out of pocket expenses;
'proceedings in a criminal cause or matter' includes any case in which–
(a) an information charging the accused with an offence is laid before a justice of the peace for any area but not proceeded with; or
(b) the accused is committed for trial but not tried;
'professional witness' means a witness practising as a member of the legal or medical profession or as a dentist, veterinary surgeon or accountant who attends to give professional evidence as to matters of fact;
'private prosecutor' means any person in whose favour an order for the payment of costs out of central funds could be made under section 17 of the Act;
'the relevant amount' has the meaning assigned to it by regulation 17;

'witness' means any person properly attending to give evidence, whether or not he gives evidence or is called at the instance of one of the parties or of the court, but does not include–
  (a) a person attending as a witness to character only unless the court has certified that the interests of justice required his attendance;
  (b) a member of a police force attending court in his capacity as such;
  (c) a full-time officer of an institution to which the Prison Act 1952(a) applies attending court in his capacity as such; or
  (d) a prisoner in respect of any occasion on which he is conveyed to court in custody.

General
16.(1) Where, in any proceedings in a criminal cause or matter in a magistrates' court, the Crown Court, a Divisional Court of the Queen's Bench Division, the Court of Appeal or the House of Lords–
  (a) a witness attends at the instance of the accused, a private prosecutor or the court; or
  (b) an interpreter is required because of the accused's lack of English; or
  (c) a medical practitioner makes a report otherwise than in writing,
the expenses properly incurred by that witness, interpreter or medical practitioner shall be allowed out of central funds in accordance with this Part of these Regulations, unless the court directs that the expenses are not to be allowed out of central funds.

(2) Subject to paragraph (3), any entitlement to an allowance under this Part of these Regulations shall be the same whether the witness, interpreter or medical practitioner attends on the same day in one case or more than one case.

(3) Paragraph (2) shall not apply to allowances under regulation 25.

COMMENTARY
R.16(3): 'regulation 25': ie written medical reports pursuant to s.32(2) CJA 1967.

Determination of rates or scales of allowances payable out of central funds
17. The Lord Chancellor shall, with the consent of the Treasury, determine the rates or scales of allowances payable out of central funds to witnesses, interpreters or medical practitioners and a reference in this Part of these Regulations to an allowance not exceeding the relevant amount means an amount calculated in accordance with the rates or scales so determined.

COMMENTARY
R.17: 'rates or scales of allowance': the current rates and scales are contained in Appendix One and Appendix Two to the *Guide to Allowances*, reproduced at the end of this Chapter.

Witnesses other than professional or expert witnesses
18. (1) A witness (other than a witness to whom regulation 19 or 20 applies) may be allowed–
  (a) a loss allowance not exceeding the relevant amount in respect of
    (i) any expenditure incurred (other than on travelling, lodging or subsistence) to which the witness would not otherwise be subject; or
    (ii) any loss of earnings or of benefit under the enactments relating to National Insurance; and
  (b) a subsistence allowance not exceeding the relevant amount.

COMMENTARY
R.18: 'relevant amount': see r.17 *supra* and the commentary thereto.

(2) Any other person who in the opinion of the court necessarily attends for the purpose of any proceedings otherwise than to give evidence may be

allowed the same allowances under paragraph (1) as if he attended as a witness other than a professional or expert witness.

(3) Paragraph (2) shall not apply to–
(a) a member of a police force attending court in his capacity as such;
(b) a full-time officer of an institution to which the Prison Act 1952 applies attending court in his capacity as such, or
(c) a prisoner in respect of any occasion on which he is conveyed to court in custody.

Professional witnesses
19. A professional witness may be allowed a professional witness allowance not exceeding the relevant amount.

COMMENTARY
R.19: 'relevant amount': see r.17 *supra*, and the commentary thereto.

9.33   **Expert witnesses etc**
20. (1) The court may make an allowance in respect of an expert witness for attending to give expert evidence and for work in connection with its preparation of such an amount as it may consider reasonable having regard to the nature and difficulty of the case and the work necessarily involved.

(2) Paragraph (1) shall apply, with the necessary modifications, to–
(a) an interpreter, or
(b) a medical practitioner who makes a report otherwise than in writing for the purpose of section 30 of the Magistrates' Courts Act 1980(a)
as it applies to an expert witness.

Night allowances
21. (1) A professional or expert witness who is necessarily absent from his place of residence overnight may be allowed a night allowance not exceeding the relevant amount.

(2) An interpreter or medical practitioner who receives an allowance under regulation 20 may be allowed the same night allowance as if he attended as a professional or expert witness.

COMMENTARY
R.21: 'relevant amount': see r.17 *supra*, and the commentary thereto.

Seamen
22. (1) A seaman who is detained on shore as a witness may be allowed–
(a) an allowance not exceeding the relevant amount in respect of any loss of earnings, unless for special reasons the court allows a greater sum; and
(b) an allowance not exceeding the sum actually and reasonably incurred for his maintenance, for the time during which he is necessarily detained on shore.

(2) No allowance shall be paid under regulation 18 to a seaman who is paid an allowance under paragraph (1).

COMMENTARY
R.22: 'relevant amount': see r.17 *supra*, and the commentary thereto.

Prosecutors and defendants
23. A person in whose favour an order is made under section 16, 17 or 19(4) of the Act may be allowed the same subsistence allowance and travelling expenses as if he attended as a witness other than a professional or expert witness.

Travelling expenses

24. (1) Subject to paragraphs (2) and (3), a witness who travels to or from court by public transport (including by air) may be allowed the fare actually paid.

(2) Unless the court otherwise directs, only the second class fare shall be allowed under paragraph (1) for travel by railway.

(3) A witness who travels to or from court by air may be allowed the fare actually paid only if–
- (a) there was no reasonable alternative to travel by air and the class of fare paid was reasonable in all the circumstances; or
- (b) travel by air was more economical in the circumstances taking into account any savings of time resulting from the adoption of such mode of travel and its consequent effect in reducing the amount of allowances payable under the other provisions of this Part of these Regulations,

and, where the air fare is not allowed, there may be allowed such amount as the court considers reasonable.

(4) A witness who travels too or from court by hired vehicle may be allowed–
- (a) the fare actually paid and any reasonable gratuity so paid in a case of urgency or where public transport is not reasonably available; or
- (b) in any other case, the amount of fare for travel by public transport.

(5) A witness who travels to or from court by private vehicle may be allowed an appropriate private vehicle allowance not exceeding the relevant amount.

(6) Where–
- (a) a witness is in the opinion of the court suffering from a serious illness; or
- (b) heavy exhibits have to be taken to court,

the court may allow reasonable additional sums in excess of those allowed under paragraphs (1) to (5).

(7) An interpreter or a medical practitioner who incurs travelling expenses in providing the court with a report otherwise than in writing may be allowed a travelling allowance not exceeding the relevant amount.

COMMENTARY
R.24 (7): 'relevant amount': see r.17 *supra*, and the commentary thereto.

Written medical reports

25. (1) A medical practitioner who makes a written report to a court in pursuance of a request to which section 32(2) of the Criminal Justice Act 1967 applies may be allowed a medical report allowance not exceeding the relevant amount.

(2) A medical practitioner who makes a report to which paragraph (1) applies and incurs travelling expenses in connection with the preparation of that report may be allowed a travelling allowance not exceeding the relevant amount.

(3) Nothing in this regulation shall apply to a report by the medical officer of an institution to which the Prison Act 1952 applies.

COMMENTARY
R.25 (1), (2): 'relevant amount': see. r.17, *supra* and the commentary thereto. Section 32(2) CJA 1967 (written reports) is reproduced at the beginning to this section at 9.20. Reports 'otherwise than in writing' are governed by s.19(3)(c)(i), r.20(2)(b).

PART VI

RECOVERY OF SUMS PAID OUT OF THE
LEGAL AID FUNDS OR CENTRAL FUNDS

Directions by the Lord Chancellor
26. (1) The Lord Chancellor shall recover in accordance with direction
given by him any sums paid out of the legal aid fund or central funds where a
costs order has been made against a party to proceedings in favour of–
  (a) a legally assisted person, or
  (b) a person in whose favour an order for the payment of costs out of central
      funds has been made.

(2) Directions given by the Lord Chancellor under this regulation may be
given generally or in respect of a particular case and may require the payment
of sums due under a costs order and stipulate the mode of payment and the
person to whom payment is to be made.

Recovery of sums due under a costs order
27. Where the person required to make a payment in respect of sums due
under a costs order fails to do so, the payment may be recovered summarily by
the Lord Chancellor as a sum adjudged to be paid as a civil debt by order of a
magistrates' court.

9.34   **GUIDE TO ALLOWANCES UNDER PART V, COSTS IN
CRIMINAL CASES (GENERAL) REGULATIONS 1986**

This *Guide* to the rates and scales of allowance was originally issued by the
Lord Chancellor's Department in November 1986 – Appendix One and
Appendix Two are published as amended, and as at the dates given in brackets
against any particular amount.

PART I – GENERAL

1.1 Introduction. These notes provide guidance for court staff who have to
calculate the amounts of allowances payable under Part V of the Costs in
Criminal Cases (General) Regulations 1986; they should not be taken as a
definitive statement of the law. The notes supplement the information given
from time to time in LCD Circulars issued under the Costs in Criminal Cases
(General) Regulations 1986.

1.2 The Regulations. The Costs in Criminal Cases (General) Regulations
1986 are made under s.19 and 20 of the Prosecution of Offences Act 1985.
They follow, in the main, the Costs in Criminal Cases (Allowances) Regulations 1977; the primary difference is that unless a case is privately prosecuted,
the expenses of prosecution witnesses must *not* be paid from central funds. The
rates or scales applied by the Regulations are determined administratively by
the Lord Chancellor with the concurrence of the Treasury under r.17.

1.3 The rates and scales of allowances effective from time to time are notified
to courts by the Lord Chancellor's Department. The rates in force at the time
of publication are contained in Appendix One to these notes. These should be
updated as new rates are published.

1.4 The Regulations apply to both summary and indicatable cases but they do
not apply to payments made under a legal aid order. Witnesses' expenses may
not be paid under a legal aid order where payment can be made under another
enactment eg out of central funds (see s.37(3) Legal Aid Act 1974).

1.5 The Regulations provide at (r.16(1)) that the expenses properly incurred by a witness or interpreter called on behalf of a defendant, a private prosecutor or the court or a medical practitioner (who makes a report otherwise than in writing to which s.34(5) of the Mental Health (Amendment) Act 1982, or s.30 of the Magistrates' Courts Act 1980, or s.32(2) of the Criminal Justice Act 1967 applies) shall be allowed out of central funds *unless the court directs that the expenses are not to be allowed out of central funds*. Therefore there is no requirement for the court to make an order for the payment of those expenses. In general, an allowance should be the same if the witness, interpreter or medical practitioner attends on the same day in one case or more than one case (see rr.16(2) and 16(3)).

1.6 Court staff should note the definitions in r.15 of terms used through Part V of the Regulations.

PART II – ALLOWANCES

1. REGULATION 18 – WITNESSES OTHER THAN PROFESSIONAL OR EXPERT WITNESSES

18(1) – ORDINARY WITNESSES

9.35

2.1 An ordinary witness is a person required to attend court to give evidence as a witness to events or circumstances which are relevant to a particular case. It is important to note that this may include a person who could on another occasion be called to give evidence as a professional or expert witness eg a doctor who has witnessed a robbery and is called as a witness to the event and not in a professional capacity. In such circumstances only the allowances for an ordinary witness may be paid.

2.2 Financial Loss Allowance. A financial loss allowance is payable to an ordinary witness to compensate for any expenditure (other than travelling, lodging or subsistence) to which the witness would not otherwise have been subject, or for any loss of earnings or benefit under the enactments relating to National Insurance. In the case of an employed person it should normally be possible to determine the appropriate payment without requiring written verification of the loss of earnings from the employer. In some circumstances however the court may wish to call for written evidence particularly in the case of a witness who is not an employee (eg a self-employed person), but it may not be possible in all such cases to require proof of an actual financial loss. It can be assumed, for example, that a tradesperson's absence from a shop or place of business will ordinarily entail a loss of income. Witnesses employed on shift work may face particular difficulties in returning to work. A witness may be unable to work an early morning shift because of the time he is required to attend court and may also be unable to return to a shift later in the day because of uncertainty about the time of release from court. An attendance at court may result in a double absence from employment. Courts should be prepared to exercise discretion in such cases. Overall, whilst it is important to ensure that no more than the loss actually incurred is reimbursed, the amount allowed should be fixed having regard to the individual circumstances of the witness.

2.3 There is a maximum amount, depending on the period of absence, fixed by the Regulations. As a result, it is recognised that the financial loss allowance may not fully reimburse all witnesses for their loss of earnings. Its purpose is to provide compensation and to relieve hardship as a result of discharging a public duty in attending court to give evidence. Courts may wish to note that any allowance paid does not count as earned income and is not subject therefore to income tax.

2.4 The financial loss allowance is not payable in cases of hypothetical loss. For example, a person in the process of seeking employment may not claim for a loss of earnings which might have occurred had the witness been free to seek employment rather than having to attend court. However, discretion should be exercised in the case of a witness who is not in regular employment but turns up and is taken on each day if some evidence is produced that work was available.

2.5 The financial loss allowance also covers financial losses other than earnings. For example, a loss allowance may be paid to someone who has had to employ a babysitter to cover absences from home. Similarly the costs of cancelling a driving test may be reimbursed where a witness was obliged to attend court on the same day as the test since it was an expense incurred as a result of giving evidence. A financial loss may also result from the cancellation of a holiday. Evidence of the financial loss or additional expenditure should normally be produced.

2.6 Subsistence Allowance. A daily subsistence allowance (based on the length of absence from home to work) is payable to an ordinary witness whilst travelling to and from court and attending court. The allowance compensates for money spent on meals and/or refreshments whilst attending court and is subject to a maximum limit. Payment of the allowance recognises that witnesses attending court may be unable to take advantage of normal arrangements. The allowance is not separately payable to a professional or expert witness, since it forms part of the allowances payable under rr.19 and 20 respectively.

2.7 Where an ordinary witness has to spend a night away from home an overnight subsistence allowance is payable, but day subsistence cannot be claimed in addition to an overnight allowance covering the same period. The overnight subsistence allowance covers a period of absence of up to 24 hours including compensation for money spent on meals/refreshment taken during that period and is subject to a maximum limit. Where the absence exceeds 24 hours, the appropriate day subsistence or a further overnight allowance whichever is appropriate, is payable in addition.

18(2) & (3) – OTHER PERSONS ATTENDING COURT

2.8 Persons attending otherwise than to give evidence. Any person who in the opinion of the court necessarily attends on behalf of a defendant or a private prosecutor for the purposes of the case otherwise than to give evidence may be allowed the same travelling and subsistence allowances as if he attends to give evidence other than professional or expert evidence (ie an ordinary witness allowance). Examples are a parent of a minor witness, a person accompanying a disabled witness, or someone who has charge of bulky, expensive or dangerous exhibits.

2.9 Character Witnesses. A character witness is only entitled to receive payment from central funds where the court certifies that the interests of justice required his attendance.

2.10 Persons Not Entitled to Allowances. No payments in respect of loss of earnings, travelling or subsistence can be made to:
- (a) a prosecution witness, except where the case is conducted by a private prosecutor;
- (b) a member of a police force attending court in his capacity as such;
- (c) a whole time officer of an institution to which the Prison Act 1952 applies, attending court in his capacity as such; or
- (d) a prisoner in respect of any occasion on which he is conveyed to court in custody.

REGULATION 19 – PROFESSIONAL WITNESSES

9.36

3.1 A professional witness is defined by r.15 as a person practising as a member of the legal or medical profession, or as a dentist, a veterinary surgeon, or as an accountant, who attends to give professional evidence. The allowance is not payable to a member of a profession who attends as an ordinary witness (see para 2.1). Salaried hospital, medical or dental staff of the National Health Service who attend to give professional evidence should be treated as professional witnesses since such attendance is outside the scope of the hospital and specialist services. An accountant should be a member of one of the following bodies: the Institute of Chartered Accounts for England and Wales, the Institute of Chartered Accountants for Scotland, the Chartered Institute of Public Finance and Accountancy, the Institute of Cost and Management Accountants or the Association of Certified Accountants. A pharmacist is not considered to be a professional witness despite the need to keep a pharmacy open during his period of absence.

3.2 Professional Witness Allowance. The level of allowance is dependent on two factors:

   (i) the length of time the witness is absent from a place of residence or practice; and

  (ii) whether or not the witness employs a professional person to take care of the practice during the absence.

3.3 Two scales of allowances are provided. The first sets the maximum amount which may be paid to compensate a professional witness who attends on any day to give evidence (in one or more cases) for an absence from a profesional practice or residence. The maximum amount payable is dependent on the period of the absence.

3.4 The second scale, which is an alternative, applies only where the witness necessarily incurs expense in the provision of a professional person to take care of a practice during the period of absence. The maximum amount payable again depends on the period of absence of the witness from the practice, but where it is not possible or practicable to employ a locum for only half a day, full reimbursement of the costs of employing the locum should be made, subject to the overriding maximum amount per day.

3.5 Since it is not uncommon for a locum to cover only part of the work of a practice (for example, a doctor may be absent for four hours but employ a locum only to cover a two-hour surgery and may re-arrange home visits to a time when they can be undertaken personally), discretion exists as to which allowance may be paid even when a locum is engaged. But a *professional witness cannot receive both allowances.* The allowance must be either an amount to compensate for the absence, or the cost of employing a locum, depending on the circumstances. Where a claim is made for the cost of engaging a locum, the witness should provide proof of the expense. [Note: see para 5.1 for overnight allowances].

REGULATION 20 – EXPERT WITNESSES AND INTERPRETERS ETC

9.37

20(i) – EXPERT WITNESSES

4.1 An expert witness is a person of any calling, profession or trade who gives evidence because of his expertise. In most cases one would expect that the witness has been called by the defence or a private prosecutor specifically to give an independent and expert view on some technical matter in the case. It is not, however, always easy to distinguish an expert witness from a professional witness. The 'Oxford Companion to Law' describes expert evidence as 'evidence given to a court by a person skilled and experienced in some professional or technical sphere of the conclusions he has reached on the basis of his knowledge, from facts reported to him or discovered by him by tests, measurements or similar means'. Courts might find the following example to be of some assistance. A consultant doctor giving factual evidence of a defendant's medical condition, perhaps in mitigation, is a professional witness. A consultant doctor giving an *opinion* based on the factual evidence of a defendant's medical condition as to the probable effect on the defendant's actions or state of mind should be regarded as an expert witness. Armed Forces and prison medical officers, meteorologists and other specialists called to give evidence in a professional capacity who are salaried employees of a government department do not incur a loss or expense and should not be paid a professional or expert witness allowance. Court staff should note that no payment from central funds should be made to an expert witness called by a prosecutor, other than by a private prosecutor.

4.2 Expert Witness Allowance. An expert witness may be allowed a fee for attending to give expert evidence and for work in connection with its preparation. It is normal practice to pay an attendance fee which is inclusive of preparation work, but exceptionally a 'qualifying fee' may be paid in addition. A qualifying fee provides payment where extensive time is spent researching relevant material and preparing to give evidence.

4.3 Where the expert witness has prepared a written report for which a separate fee may be payable regard should be had to this in determining the payment for attending to give evidence. Likewise, where the expert is a pathologist, regard should be had to any fee paid for conducting a post mortem examination.

4.4 No rates or scales of allowance for expert witnesses are set under the Regulations; the amount to be paid is a matter for discretion. In determining the payment to be made, regard should be had to the nature and difficulty of the case, the work necessarily involved, and such factors as whether there is a reasonable choice of experts available and whether considerable travelling is involved.

4.5 As there are no prescribed scales of allowance for expert witnesses, guidance is given in Appendix Two to assist officers determining the fees payable by providing a point of reference on *quantum* for use when exercising discretion in determining claims. Guidance on points of principle is already available in the Taxing Officers' Notes for Guidance (paras 128–134), the Notes for Guidance of Justices Clerks (paras 52–53) and published decisions of the Taxing Masters. The figures shown in Appendix Two are based upon allowances made in the Spring of 1986. It is intended that the information will be reviewed annually.

9.38   **20(2) – INTERPRETERS & MEDICAL PRACTITIONERS WHO MAKE REPORTS OTHER THAN IN WRITING**

4.6 The amounts allowed to interpreters (including sign language interpreters) for the accused are at the discretion of the court. This is to allow courts to pay the going rates for interpreters and thus ensure a regular and sufficient supply of people qualified in the necessary languages. The discretion recognises that the availability and expense of obtaining an interpreter in one place will not be the same as in another place. The only exception to the court's discretion is in respect of fees for Welsh language interpreters in Courts in Wales. For these there is a prescribed allowance determined by the Lord Chancellor. To assist courts guidance is given in Appendix Two by providing a point of reference for use when exercising discretion in determining claims.

4.7 Similarly, in the unusual circumstances where a medical practitioner makes a report other than in writing for the purpose of s.30 of the Magistrates' Courts Act 1980, the amounts payable are at the discretion of the court. However, courts should use the professional witness allowance determined by the Lord Chancellor as a point of reference when assessing the amount to be paid.

4.8 Court staff should note that where a witness for a defendant or a private prosecutor requires an interpreter, payment of the interpreter's fees (which are at the discretion of the court) can be made under r.16(1), if the court considers it to be an expense properly incurred by that witness.

REGULATION 21 – NIGHT ALLOWANCES

5.1 21(1) – Expert and Professional Witness Overnight Allowance. A professional or expert witness is not entitled to a financial loss allowance nor day subsistence since the allowances paid to them under either r.19 or 20 cover these. An expert or professional witness may, however, be eligible for an overnight allowance less the daily subsistence allowance. The maximum amount is prescribed in Appendix One.

5.2 Interpreters' and Medical Practitioners' Overnight Allowance. Regulation 21(2) provides that an interpreter or medical practitioner who receives an allowance under r.20 may be allowed the *same* night allowance as if he attended as a professional witness.

REGULATION 22 – SEAMEN WITNESSES

6.1 22(1)(a) – Loss of Wages Allowance. This allowance compensates a seaman, who is prevented from joining a ship because he is detained on shore to give evidence, for loss of wages. There is a maximum daily rate which may be paid for the time during which he is, and is likely to be, detained on shore and therefore unable to join his ship or an alternative ship. There is, however, discretion to exceed the maximum daily allowance for special reasons. The circumstances in which special reasons may arise are not well documented, but it does appear that these may cover, for example, the need to pay off and re-hire a crew where the witness is a self-employed single vessel owner who undertakes intermittent contracts. However, special reasons do not include the simple fact that a seaman may earn more than the maximum daily rate; the provision is not intended to place a seaman in a better position than an ordinary witness who may not be able to recover full loss of earnings because of the maximum limit.

6.2 22(1)(b) – Maintenance Allowance. In addition to loss of wages, a seaman missing his ship may also claim an allowance not exceeding the sum actually and reasonably incurred for his maintenance on shore. There is no limitation on the amount of this allowance, but courts should have regard to the normal cost of such maintenance and should not exceed the sum actually incurred. The daily subsistence and financial loss allowances payable to an ordinary witness cannot be paid to a seaman, who receives a loss of wages or maintenance allowance but reasonable travelling expenses may be allowed (see para 8.1).

6.3 Seaman Recalled from Ship. The position of a seaman called to give evidence when actually aboard a ship is unclear. It is suggested that such a witness should be treated as an ordinary witness – to whom financial loss allowance, subsistence and reasonable travelling costs may be allowed – unless as a result of being called to give evidence the witness is unable to rejoin his ship. In the latter case it may be appropriate to class the witness as a seaman detained on shore.

9.38a

REGULATION 23 – PROSECUTORS AND DEFENDANTS

7.1 Allowances to Prosecutors and Defendants. Any private prosecutor or defendant whose costs are ordered by a court to be paid out of central funds, may be allowed the same *travelling and subsistence* allowances as if he attended to give evidence other than professional or expert evidence (ie an ordinary witness subsistence allowance, plus travelling expenses). Loss of earnings cannot be recovered out of central funds as they are not 'expenses properly incurred by him in the proceedings'.

REGULATION 24 – TRAVELLING EXPENSES

8.1 Travelling Allowances. Travelling allowances are payable in addition to other allowances to any witness (including a professional or expert witness) and to any other person who receives an allowance under r.18(2) who incurs expenditure travelling to and from court.

8.2 24(1) and (2) – Public Transport. Where a witness travels to or from court by public transport (including by air but excluding taxis or other hired vehicles), travelling expenses may be allowed to reimburse the fare actually paid, but only a second class fare for rail travel is to be allowed unless the court otherwise directs.

8.3 24(3) – Travel by Air. The cost of travel by air may be allowed *only if* the court is of the opinion that:
> '(a) there was no reasonable alternative to travel by air and the class of fare paid was reasonable in all the circumstances; or
> (b) travel by air was more economical in the circumstances taking into account any savings of time resulting from the adoption of such mode of transport and its consequent effect in reducing the amount of allowances payable under these Regulations'.

The above considerations apply to travel on internal or international flights. Where it is considered that air travel was not reasonable, then the appropriate rate for travel by another means of public transport should be paid together with the appropriate subsistence allowance for the time the journey would have taken.

8.4 However, witnesses are expected to take advantage, where possible, of cheap fares. The system of international air fares is complex and it is difficult to lay down any hard and fast rules. Broadly speaking, however, the position is that the more money expended on an air ticket the greater the flexibility purchased in terms of late booking facilities, flight availability and the sum that is refundable in the event of short notice cancellation. The court should therefore allow what is reasonable in all the circumstances bearing in mind that the most economical fare might not always be appropriate; a last minute cancellation of a trial might mean the loss of the full amount of the cheapest fare, but only a percentage of an ordinary or standard fare. Moreover a witness notified at short notice of the date an attendance is required may be unable to take advantage of cheap tickets.

8.5 24(4) – Hired Vehicles. In a case of urgency, or where no alternative means of transport is reasonably available, a witness may travel to or from court by a hired vehicle or taxi and the actual cost of the hire or the fare, and any reasonable gratuity, may be allowed. Where, however, the witness chooses without good reason to travel by hired vehicle only the amount of the fare for travel by the appropriate public service may be reimbursed.

8.6 24(5) – Private Motor Vehicles. A witness may choose to travel to court using a private motor vehicle. Where a private motor vehicle is used the expense incurred may be reimbursed by payment of a mileage rate. There are two categories of mileage rate – public transport rate and standard rate.

8.7 The standard rate of mileage may *only* be paid where the use of a private motor vehicle was necessary (for example, because no public transport was available), or where a considerable saving of time is made (for example, where the witness would have been required to stay overnight, or leave and return at unreasonable hours, if public transport was used), or the use of a private motor vehicle was otherwise reasonable (for example, in the case of elderly or disabled witnesses, or witnesses carrying exhibits).

8.8 In all other cases, public transport rates apply. The public transport rate is a rate per mile calculated to be equivalent to the average cost of public transport. Thus, where the court at which a witness is required to attend is reasonably accessible by public transport, though the witness may choose to use a private motor vehicle, reimbursement is limited to the public transport cost.

8.9 Separate scales of standard rates and public transport rates are provided for motor cars and motor-cycles. For motor cars there is only one standard rate and one public transport rate regardless of engine capacity. For motor-cycles a scale of rates is provided depending on engine capacity.

8.10 **Passenger Supplement.** A passenger supplement per mile may be paid where the witness carries passengers to whom a travelling allowance would otherwise be payable. The supplement may be paid in addition to both public transport rates and standard rates.

8.11 **Car parking fees.** Car parking fees actually and reasonably incurred may be paid, but *only* where the use of a private motor vehicle was necessary or otherwise reasonable, ie where standard rate of mileage has been allowed.

8.12 **24(6) – Special Circumstances.** There are two exceptions to the general rules governing payment of travelling expenses. Where, in the opinion of the court, a person is suffering from a serious illness, or where *heavy* exhibits have to be carried to court, an amount in excess of the normal allowances may be paid.

8.13 **24(7) – Interpreters etc.** Travelling allowances are also payable to any interpeter or medical practitioner who provides a report *otherwise than in writing* for the purposes of s.30 of the Magistrates' Courts Act 1980 who incurs expenditure in travelling to or from court or in making the report.

REGULATION 25 – WRITTEN MEDICAL REPORTS   9.39

9.1 **25(1) – Allowances for Written Reports by Medical Practitioners.**   A registered medical practitioner who is requested by a court to make a written medical report in pursuance of a request to which s.32(2) of the Criminal Justice Act 1967 applies in connection with:
  (a) s.3 of the Powers of Criminal Courts Act 1973 (probation orders requiring treatment for mental condition),
  (b) s.37 of the Mental Health Act 1983 (hospital orders and guardianship orders); or
  (c) s.12(4) of the Children and Young Persons Act 1969 (supervision orders requiring treatment for mental condition).
may be paid an allowance not exceeding the maximum amount. A higher maximum is set for consultants. A separate allowance is set for reports to determine fitness for a detention centre.

9.2 The fees provide generally for up to two hours' work, including any travelling time. In difficult cases where more than two hours' work has necessarily been undertaken, higher fees (but not exceeding the daily maximum) may be paid on a pro rata basis at the discretion of the appropriate officer of the court, but the appropriate officer should be satisfied that payment of a higher fee is justified. In exceptional cases, a senior medical officer in a DHSS regional office may be consulted for advice.

9.3 25(2) – Travelling Expenses. Where a medical practitioner incurs travelling expenses in preparing a report, he may receive travelling expenses. A mileage rate is fixed where a private motor car is used.

9.4 By virtue of r.25(3), a medical officer of an institution covered by the Prison Act 1952 may not claim any of the allowances under r.25.

APPENDIX ONE

9.40   **CURRENT ALLOWANCES**

[Published as amended and as at the date given in brackets against any particular amount. The figures should be amended from time to time as new rates are published]

REGULATION 18: ORDINARY WITNESS AND OTHER PERSONS FINANCIAL LOSS

Period of absence		Maximum amount	New Rates	
	5.10.87			
Not exceeding 4 hours	(LCD JC(87)4)	£13.75		
Exceeding 4 hours	ditto	£27.50		

REGULATION 18: ORDINARY WITNESS AND

OTHER PERSONS SUBSISTENCE ALLOWANCE

		Maximum amount		
	16.11.87			
Not exceeding 5 hours	(see LCD JC(87)5)	£1.50		
Exceeding 5 hours but not exceeding 10 hours	ditto	£2.85		
Over 10 hours	ditto	£6.25		
Overnight (Inner London, within a five-mile radius of Charing Cross)	ditto	£55.75		
Overnight (elsewhere)	ditto	£47.10		

REGULATION 19: PROFESSIONAL WITNESS ALLOWANCES

(a) <u>Professional witness allowance where locum fees are</u>
<u>not claimed</u>

Period of absence		Maximum amount	New Rates
Not exceeding 2 hours	11.8.86	£33.70	
Exceeding 2 hours but not exceeding 4 hours	ditto	£49.20	
Exceeding 4 hours but not exceeding 6 hours	ditto	£73.90	
Exceeding 6 hours	ditto	£98.40	

(b) Professional witness allowance where locum fees
are claimed

Not exceeding 4 hours	11.8.86	£49.20	
Exceeding 4 hours	ditto	£98.40	

REGULATION 20: EXPERT WITNESS AND
INTERPRETERS ETC. ALLOWANCE

Discretionary (see Appendix Two and
paragraphs 4.1. to 4.7)

REGULATION 21: EXPERT AND PROFESSIONAL WITNESS
AND INTERPRETERS ETC. OVERNIGHT ALLOWANCE

		Maximum amount	
Inner London, within a five-mile radius of Charing Cross	16.11.87 (LCD JC(87)5)	£49.50	
Elsewhere	ditto	£40.95	

REGULATION 22: SEAMAN WITNESS ALLOWANCES

		Maximum amount	
Loss allowance	5.10.87 (LCD JC(87)4)	£27.50	
Maintenance allowance		At the discretion of the court, but not exceeding the sum actually and reasonably incurred.	

REGULATION 24: TRAVELLING ALLOWANCES

(a) Public transport rate

	Maximum amount	Rate per mile	New Rates	
Motor-cycles – engine capacity not exceeding 150cc	1.7.87 (LCD JC(87)3)	11p		
Motor-cycles – engine capacity exceeding 150cc but not exceeding 250cc	ditto	15.3		
Motor-cycles – engine capacity exceeding 250cc	ditto	15.6		
Motor cars	ditto	15.6		

(b) Standard rate

(i) For all motor-cycles where the engine capacity does not exceed 250cc the appropriate public transport rates apply. For all motor-cycles with an engine capacity exceeding 250cc, in circumstances where the use of such a motor-cycle results in a substantial saving of time or is otherwise reasonable	8.87 (LCD JC(87)3)	21.3p		
(b) For all motor cars in circumstances where the use of a car results in a substantial saving of time or is otherwise reasonable	ditto	34.4p		
(c) Passenger supplement for passengers carried and to whom an allowance would otherwise have been payable:				
The first passenger	ditto	2p		
Each additional passenger	ditto	1p		
(d) Parking fees actually and reasonably incurred in cases where the use of a motor car results in substantial saving of time or is otherwise reasonable may be reimbursed				

REGULATION 25: WRITTEN MEDICAL REPORTS

	Maximum amount	New Rates
(a) Report in pursuance of a request to which section 32(2) of the Criminal Justice Act 1967 applies	11.8.86	
Consultant	£33.70	
Other registered medical practitioner	£24.60	

Daily maximum

(b) *Higher fees* (where more than 2 hours work necessary undertaken)	
Consultant	£134.80
Other registered medical practitioner	£98.40
(c) **Examination and report to determine fitness for detention centre training**	
All registered medical practitioners	£16.60

REGULATION 25(2): MILEAGE ALLOWANCE

		Rate per mile
Preparing report under regulation 25(1)	1.7.87 (LCD JC(87)3)	34.4p

APPENDIX TWO

GUIDANCE FOR TAXING/DETERMINING OFFICERS WHEN ASSESSING EXPERT

WITNESS AND OTHER ALLOWANCES

1. As there are no prescribed scales for the allowance for the remuneration of expert witnesses and certain other persons such as interpreters, the attached guidance is issued to assist taxing/determining officers by providing a point of reference on *quantum* for use when exercising their discretion in determining such claims.

2. The figures shown are based upon allowances made in the Spring of 1986 throughout England and Wales. It is intended that the information will be revised annually.

3. The rate bands shown cover a wide field of skill and, in some cases, a number of different kinds of skills. The bands show the fees which were allowed in the majority of cases. A few exceptional cases were, however, paid for at figures outside the band shown.

4. In exercising their discretion, taxing/determining officers are to bear in mind that each case must be considered individually. They are to take into account all the relevant circumstances surrounding the claim including such things as the work done, the status or experience of the person doing the work, and the availability of such persons in the area of the country concerned.

5. In cases of difficulty, taxing/determining officers should seek advice from the Circuit Taxing Co-ordinator, or his assistant, through their Chief Clerk.

		Allowance	New Rates
A. Expert Witnesses			
1. **Consultant medical practitioner, psychiatrist, pathologist**	1.4.86		
Preparation (Examination and report)	ditto	£31-£42 per hour	
Attendance at Court (Full day)	ditto	£158-210	
2. **Handwriting, Fire expert (assessor), Explosives**			
Preparation	ditto	£26-£37 per hour	
Attendance at Court (Full day)	ditto	£131-£184	
3. **Forensic scientist, surveyor, accountant, engineer, medical practitioner, architect**			
Preparation	ditto	£21-£42 per hour	
Attendance at Court (Full day)	ditto	£105-£210	
4. **Fingerprint**			
Preparation	ditto	£16-£26 per hour	
Attendance at Court (Full day)	ditto	£79-£131	
B. Others			
5. **Interpreter**	ditto	£8.50-£16 per hour (with a minimum of 3 hours for those employed regularly in this capacity)	

[Note: Fees in respect of Welsh language interpreters in courts in Wales are provided for in the Welsh Courts Act 1942, as amended by the Administration of Justice Act 1977].

PART III – FURTHER GUIDANCE

Note: The notes are issued by the Lord Chancellor's Department. In cases of difficulty, courts are invited to contact Circuit Taxing Co-ordinators, or their assistants, for further guidance. Comments and enquiries in relation to the notes should be addressed to: Legal Services Division, Lord Chancellor's Department, Neville House, Page Street, London SW1P 4LS.

CHAPTER 10

Legal Aid

Legal Aid

10.00

INTRODUCTION

So far as criminal proceedings are concerned, a person *unable to afford* (see *Means test* at 10.18) to instruct a solicitor privately may be assisted in the following ways:

    by legal *representation and advice* under a legal aid order;

    by legal *advice and assistance* under the 'green form' scheme; and

    by legal *representation* on the part of a solicitor acting under the 'green form' scheme and authorised by the court

Legal aid in civil proceedings and proceedings in the High Court arising rom criminal proceedings such as appeal by way of case stated and application for judicial review is outside the scope of this work. **Referen-es are to sections of the Legal Aid Act 1974 and to the Legal Aid in Criminal Proceedings (General) Regulations 1968 (SI No 1231), unless otherwise stated. No account has been taken of the forthcoming Legal Aid Act 1988.**

LEGAL AID ORDERS 10.01

The proceedings in which a legal aid order may be made in criminal and related matters are set out in s.28.

Not all proceedings which are criminal in nature are covered, although t does extend to some quasi-criminal proceedings, eg failure to comply with a bind-over to keep the peace or be of good behaviour, as well as to some purely civil matters, notably care proceedings in the juvenile court. It is therefore important in any case of doubt to check that the proceedings for which legal aid is sought fall within the ambit of s.28. Magistrates can grant legal aid not only for proceedings before their own courts, but also for certain proceedings in the Crown Court, including trial on indictment, appeals and committals for sentence.

APPLICATIONS FOR LEGAL AID 10.02

The power to determine an application for legal aid for proceedings in a magistrates court may be exercised by

  (i) the court: s.28.
  (ii) the justices' clerk: r.1(4).

Application to the court may be made orally: r.1(2) in which case it *may* be referred to the justices' clerk: r.1(5). Where the application is made to the *court*, or referred to the *court*, *infra*, justices should not proceed to try the defendant on a not guilty plea if they have heard of previous convictions, or, *semble*, other information about his past which could prejudice a fair hearing: *R v Blyth Valley Juvenile Court ex p. S* (1987) 151 JPN 382.

Application to the clerk must be in prescribed form: r.1(1). The justices' clerk may either:

  (i) make the order:
  (ii) refer the application to the court or to a justice of the peace; or
  (iii) where review by the legal aid committee is available, refuse to make the order: r.1(6). The term *justices' clerk* includes a person duly authorised to act on his behalf: 4.31(1).

Corresponding arrangements for legal aid for proceedings in the *Crown Court* are set out in r.2 except that, because of the absence of review by the legal aid committee, (see *Review* at 10.11), the clerk may not refuse such an application.

A parent or guardian may apply on behalf of a juvenile: s.40(2).

There is power in the court to make a legal aid order *without application*: r.5. This is useful, eg in the case of the mentally ill. A statement of means (*infra*) is however still necessary under s.29(4), except where the applicant appears to be *incapable* of furnishing one by reason of his physical or mental condition.

Obligatory grant 10.03

Subject to means (see *Means test,* at 10.18), a legal aid order *must* be made:

  (i) when an applicant is committed for trial on a charge of *murder*;

(ii) before conviction upon a *remand or committal in custody* if he ha
      already been remanded in custody unrepresented; and
(iii) before a remand or *committal in custody for inquiries befor
      sentence*: s.29(1).

Murder apart, there is no charge on which legal aid *must* be granted

In the case referred to in (ii) above, legal aid may be confined to th
purposes of the bail proceedings: s.29(1A). In such a case the order ma
not include the services of counsel: s.30(2).

10.04   The interests of justice – the 'Widgery criteria'
Subject to means (see *Means test* at 10.18) a legal aid order *may* be made i
it appears *desirable in the interests of justice*: s.29(1)(1A)(2).

The Departmental Committee on Legal Aid in Criminal Proceeding
(the Widgery Committee) stated that in their view the following factor;
indicate that legal aid is desirable in the interest of justice:

(a) the charge is *a grave one* in the sense that the accused is in *rea*
    jeopardy of losing his *liberty* or *livelihood* or suffering *seriou*
    damage to his reputation;
(b) the charge raises *a substantial question of law*:
(c) the accused is *unable to follow the proceedings* and state his owr
    case because of his inadequate knowledge of English, menta*
    illness or other mental or physical disability;
(d) the nature of the defence involves the *tracing and interviewing o*
    witnesses or *expert cross-examination* of a witness for the pros
    ecution; and
(e) legal representation is desirable *in the interest of someone othe*
    than the accused as, eg in the case of sexual offences against youn*
    children when it is undesirable that the accused should cross
    examine the witness in person.

10.05   *Persons committed for trial or sentence*
The Committee recommended that the general practice should be t
grant legal aid to persons committed for trial or sentence who are finan-
cially eligible, and that while the courts should retain discretion to refuse
legal aid on grounds other than means this should be exercised only ir
rare cases. They considered that the existing practice of assigning counse
only to unrepresented persons is unsatisfactory and that it is advisable
that full legal aid should be provided in such cases. The Committee
further recommended that the grant of legal aid in such cases should be
considered by the justices at the time of committal.

10.06   *Committal proceedings*
The Committee recommended that (a) the application for legal aic
should be considered before the plea is taken and before any election fo*
summary trial or trial on indictment is made; (b) subject to the test of
means, legal aid should normally be granted for the preliminary hearing
in the case of offences triable only on indictment and (c) where an offence
can be tried either summarily or on indictment, the same criteria should
be applied as for a summary trial.

10.07   *Juvenile courts*
The Committee took the view that the grant of legal aid in juvenile courts
should be governed by the same general principles as in adult courts.

Appeals to the Crown Court   **10.08**
The Committee concluded that the only criteria, other than means, which
it is practicable to apply are those suggested for the grant of legal aid in
magistrates' courts.

Trials on indictment   **10.09**
The Committee also recommended that where a person who is charged
with an offence triable only on indictment does not apply for legal aid
before his appearance in court and is unrepresented, the examining
justices should inquire on his first appearance whether he has been
informed of the facilities for legal aid and whether he wishes to apply for
it. On committing a person for trial or sentence the court should likewise
inquire whether he wishes to apply for legal aid in the court of trial. In any
other cases which appear to fulfil the criteria for the grant of legal aid, the
court should satisfy itself that a failure to apply for legal aid is not the
consequence of ignorance of the facilities available.

Case law on grant   **10.10**
In addition, the High Court have stated that legal aid should be offered
where:
   (a) the magistrates are considering making a recommendation for
       deportation: *R v Edgehill* [1963] 1 All ER 181;
   (b) where the defendant is resident abroad with no experience of
       English courts; *R v Phillips* [1965] Crim LR 109;
   (c) a hospital order is being considered: *R v King's Lynn Justices ex p.*
       Fysh [1964] Crim LR 143;
   (d) on committal for sentence: *R v Serghiou* [1966] 3 All ER 637.
    In *R v Briggs Justices, ex p. Lynch* (1984) 148 JP 214 it was held that,
since a serving soldier convicted of an offence of indecent exposure is
likely to find himself discharged from the service, he should be granted
legal aid. Decisions on the grant of legal aid should be taken on the basis
of *an adequate knowledge of the facts* and the arrangements must be such
that the courts are properly acquainted with the precise nature of the
charges and the grounds of the application, if necessary by calling upon
the prosecution for information: *R v Highgate Justices, ex p. Lewis* (1978)
142 JP 78. The High Court will not interfere to upset the exercise by
magistrates of their discretion: *R v Macclesfield Justices, ex p. Green-
halgh* (1980) 144 JP 142; *R v Cambridge Crown Court, ex p. Hagi* (1980)
144 JP 145.

Review   **10.11**
An applicant *refused* legal aid on the *interests of justice* test for proceedings in a magistrates' court *in respect of an indictable offence* may apply
for *review* to the appropriate criminal legal aid committee. Such application must be made not later than *21 days* before the date fixed for the trial
or the inquiry, where such a date had been fixed when the application was
made: r.6E(2). This time limit may be waived or altered by the committee
for good reason: r.6F(3). The justices' clerk and the applicant must
supply whatever further particulars the committee requires r.6G. The
date of the accused's first appearance in court can never be the date fixed
for trial etc: *R v Bury Justices, ex p. N (A Minor)* [1986] 3 WLR 965; so
that only a court itself can fix the trial or inquiry date, *semble* – and there
must therefore always be a right to apply for review where legal aid is
refused before this has happened.

10.12   What legal aid consists of

Once a legal aid order is made, the court must assign any solicitor selected by the assisted person who is willing to act, except that a single solicitor or counsel may be assigned to two or more persons whose cases are heard together, unless the *interests of justice require separate representation*: rr.8, 14.

Legal aid consists of legal representation including advice on the preparation of the case. It also gives 'authority' (ie discretion to the solicitor) to give advice on whether there appear to be reasonable grounds of appeal, as well as assistance in the preparation of a notice of appeal or in making application for a case to be stated, if given or made within the ordinary time: s.30(1), (5). Legal aid before *magistrates* is normally confined to the services of a solicitor, but where in any indictable offence there are circumstances which make the case *unusually grave or difficult* the court may order representation by solicitor and counsel if this appears desirable: s.30(2). Not more than one counsel may be assigned in magistrates' courts. Legal aid for proceedings in the *Crown Court* is limited to one counsel, but two may be ordered by a magistrates' court on a charge of murder: r.13 (the Crown Court has power to order two counsel in other cases). The selection of counsel is a matter for the solicitor: r.9. A refusal to allow counsel may result in a reference to the criminal legal aid committee (*infra*). Legal aid may be confined to the services of a solicitor (without counsel) in proceedings in the Crown Court at which solicitors have a right to audience: s.30(3).

10.13   'Through' orders

Examining justices may make a legal aid order covering the committal proceedings and the proceedings in the Crown Court: s.2 LAA 1982.

10.14   Amendment and revocation

A legal aid order may be *amended* by the court substituting a different solicitor or counsel, either on the application of the assisted person or otherwise: s.31(1). An order may be *revoked* on the application of the legally assisted person or if the solicitor or counsel withdraws and the court thinks it undesirable by reason of the assisted person's conduct to substitute another: s.31(2). A contribution order may be made in respect of an amended or revoked order: s.31(3). A refusal to amend or revoke a legal aid order may result in a reference to the legal aid committee (*infra*).

10.15   Reference to the Criminal Legal Aid Committee

Certain applications by a legally assisted person or his solicitor, if not granted by the clerk, may have to be referred to the criminal legal aid committee. They are applications for:
— representation by counsel under s.30(2), and
— amendment or revocation of a legal aid order under s.31: r.14A.

Reference of a refused application must be made to the court instead of the committee where:
— an application has already been refused by the committee;
— the application was made less than 14 days before the date fixed for the trial in the magistrates' court or for the committal proceedings where that date had been fixed at the time of the application; or
— in the case of proceedings in the Crown Court, the application was made more than 14 days after the committal for trial or sentence or the date of giving notice of appeal: r.14A(3).

Back-dating

10.16

Under present case law, no payment may be made under a legal aid order for work undertaken by a solicitor before the solicitor was assigned: *R v Rogers* [1979] 1 All ER 693 (Master Matthews); confirmed in *R v Gibson* [1983] 1 All ER 1038, CA (which distinguished the power of the Crown Court to back-date a legal aid order); and *Welch v Redbridge Justices* (1984) 148 JP 474 (in which the court left open the question of whether a clerk or a justice granting legal aid can give the order the earlier date on which the application was made). But see now s.30(9A) LAA 1974, as inserted by s.46 Administration of Justice Act 1985, which enables regulations to be made under which the Lord Chancellor may prescribe circumstances in which legal aid may be 'deemed to include representation or advice . . . previously provided by counsel or a solicitor not then assigned . . .'.

Statement of means

10.17

Before making a legal aid order the court *must* require the applicant to furnish a statement of means in prescribed form unless it appears that he is by reason of his physical or mental condition incapable of doing so: s.29(4). Where the applicant is *under 16* the court has a *discretion* to call for a statement of means from him or any *'appropriate contributor'* or from both, or may waive the requirement altogether: s.29(5). An appropriate contributor is defined in s.40 as meaning his father, any person who has been adjudged to be his putative father and (whether or not he is legitimate) his mother. Where an applicant *fails* to furnish a statement of means he may be treated as if his disposable income and disposable capital exceeded the prescribed limits and as if the amount of the contribution were such as the court might determine: s.7(5) LAA 1982.

The court or the proper officer of the court *may demand evidence* of any information given in a statement of means and if it is not provided the legally assisted person's disposable income may be treated as exceeding the statutory limits and the contribution may be such as the court or the proper officer may determine: r.4A. A legal aid application form should be seen by the trial court *only after conviction* and only for the purpose of dealing with a legal aid application: *R v Winter* [1980] Crim LR 659. The form ought not to be used for the purpose of cross-examining the applicant as to his credit: *R v Stubbs* [1981] 1 All ER 424. Where a witness is properly cross-examined on his application form – eg in a prosecution arising from a statement therein – he is entitled to be given the normal warning against self-incrimination: *ibid*. It was also suggested *obiter* that applications for criminal legal aid may be *privileged*: *ibid*.

Means test

10.18

A legal aid order may not be made unless it appears that the applicant's disposable income and disposable capital are such that he requires assistance in meeting the costs which he may incur for that purpose: s.29(2). Disposable income and disposable capital are concepts defined in r.31(1). The financial limits are now contained in the Legal Aid in Criminal Proceedings (General) (Amendment) Regulations 1987 (SI No 422).

Contribution orders

10.19

Where a court makes an order giving legal aid to a person whose disposable income or disposable capital exceeds prescribed limits it *must* make a legal aid *contribution order*: s.7(1). The amount is determined by rr.18–20 and the second Schedule in the case of a legally assisted person who has not attained the age of 16 the court may, instead of or in addition to making a legal aid contribution order against him, make such an order against any appropriate contributor: s.7(3). The contribution is payable in one sum or by instalments: s.7(2).

Payments out of *disposable income* are payable by instalments within a period not exceeding the contribution period: r.22(1); which is six months: r.31. Any contributions payable out of *disposable capital* must be paid immediately if the sum is readily available or, if it is not, at such time as the court or its proper officer considers reasonable: r.22(2). Where a sum is required to be paid on the making of the legal aid contribution order the court may direct that the legal aid order *shall not take effect* until it is paid: s.9(2) LAA 1982.

In a letter to courts from the Lord Chancellor's Department dated 19 March 1987 (LCD (87)1), court staff were issued with instructions for the calculation of legal aid contributions and these were amended by a later circular issued on 14 March 1988 (LCD JC (88)1) so as to read as follows:

10.20 Instructions to court staff for calculation of legal aid contribution (LCD JC (88)1)

Part One

1. *INCOME*

   Enter here the total average weekly net income of the applicant, including that of his spouse (where appropriate). Do *not* include any income which is to be disregarded under paragraph 3 of Schedule 2, Part II. (eg attendance allowance, mobility allowance, housing benefit and constant attendance allowance paid as an increase to a disablement pension)

   Total net income   £.............. (A)

2. *ALLOWANCES FROM INCOME*

   Enter here the total amount of allowances against income under the following headings:–

   (1) *Maintenance of dependants*

   (a)   Spouse living with the applicant
         (including common law marriage) ....
                                    £30.95 per week   £.............. (1)

   (b) Dependant children living with applicant:–

18 and over	£32.55	£.............. (2)
16 and 17	£24.25	£.............. (3)
11 to 15	£20.15	£.............. (4)
under 11	£13.45	£.............. (5)

   (c) Any other dependants for whom the
        applicant must provide
                                                     £.............. (6)

   (d) Total dependant's allowances   £..............(B)

   (2) *Housing expenses*

   Enter the total amount spent on rent, mortgage repayments, rates, or lodging. Allow only half the cost of lodging charges if the cost of meals is included. Deduct any amount met by housing benefit or received by any rate rebate.   £..............(C)

(3) *Travelling expenses*
Enter the total amount spent on travelling to and
from the place of employment £.............. (D)

(4) *Any other expenses for which allowance should
be made* £.............. (E)
Total Allowances from Income
(B + C + D + E) £.............. (F)

. CAPITAL
Enter here the total capital of the applicant, including that of his
spouse (where appropriate). Do *not* include those capital resources to
be disregarded under paras 2 and 3 of Sch.2, Part III. (ie death grant,
maternity grant, value of main residence, furniture, personal clothing
and tools of trade).
Total Capital £.............. (G)

'art Two
. *CALCULATION OF CONTRIBUTION FROM INCOME*
The total disposable income is (A) – (F) = £.............. (H)
(a) If (H) is less than £50, the contribution is NIL.
(b) If (H) is £50 or more, weekly contribution is as
shown in the table below.
Total weekly contribution £.............. (J)
(c) If the defendant received green form advice and
was liable to pay a contribution the sum due
should be deducted from the first instalment(s)
of contribution.

. *CALCULATION OF CONTRIBUTION FROM CAPITAL*
(1) If (G) is £3,000 or less, the contribution is NIL.
(2) If (G) exceeds £3,000, the contribution is the full
amount of the excess.
(3) If the applicant is in receipt of income support,
supplementary benefit or family credit, the contribution is NIL

*WEEKLY INSTALMENT OF CONTRIBUTION OUT OF
DISPOSABLE INCOME*

NORMAL WEEKLY DISPOSABLE INCOME			WEEKLY CONTRIBUTION
Exceeding £50 but not exceeding	£56		£1
£56		£60	£2
£60		£64	£3
£64		£68	£4
£68		£72	£5
£72		£76	£6
£76		£80	£7
£80		£84	£8
£84		£88	£9
£88		£92	£10
£92		£96	£11
£96		£100	£12
£100		£104	£13
£104		£108	£14
£108		£112	£15

The weekly instalment of contribution shall be increased by £1 for each £4 or part of £4 by which average weekly disposable income exceeds £112. [NB the above rates are adjusted at intervals to remain in line with inflation, so that it is important to know what the current amounts are.]

10.21 Over-payment

Where the contribution made under a legal aid contribution order exceeds the cost of legal aid, the difference must be repaid: s.7(6) LAA 1982 and r.26A.

10.22 Variation and revocation of contribution orders

A contribution order may be *varied* in light of further information about the assisted person's disposable income or disposable capital, or of any change in them: s.8(1) LAA 1982. Similarly, where no contribution order was made at first one may be made later if it subsequently appears that his means warrant it: s.8(2). A contribution order may be *revoked* where it subsequently appears that it should not have been made: s.8(3). The court which may exercise these powers is specified in s.8(4). At the conclusion of the proceedings the court may remit outstanding sums and in the event of acquittal order repayment: s.8(5).

10.23 Failure to pay a contribution order

A notice may be served on anyone who *fails* to pay a contribution order and the court may *revoke* the legal aid order *where it appears just to do so*. Before revoking the order the court must be satisfied of the matters set out in s.9(3) LAA 1982, ie that the applicant was and is able to pay, but has failed or refused to do so. A legal aid contribution order payable under the former scheme is enforceable as if it were a sum ordered to be paid by the order of the collecting court: s.35(1), Sch.3. The 'collecting court' is defined in s.32(5).

10.24 ADVICE AND ASSISTANCE – THE 'GREEN FORM' SCHEME

A solicitor may give advice and assistance to a client who fulfils prescribed means qualifications. This scheme, which is known by the name of the green form used for ascertaining means, is provided for in ss.1, 2 and 2A.

It is for the solicitor to determine (by use of the Law Society's green form) whether the party to the proceedings falls within the financial limit meriting assistance as set out in s.1. He is then entitled to give assistance up to the financial limit set in s.3. Before exceeding this limit he must first obtain approval of the area committee of the Law Society. Advice and assistance may not be given under this section to a child, that is anyone under the upper limit of compulsory school age, unless authorised by the general committee: r.8(1) of the Legal Advice and Assistance (No 2) Regulations 1980.

10.25 ASSISTANCE BY WAY OF REPRESENTATION

Advice and assistance under the 'green form' scheme does not extend to legal representation *unless given in compliance with a request made to the solicitor by the court* at a time when the solicitor is present within the precincts of the court: r.19. Legal Advice and Assistance Regulation (No 2) 1980.

Statutory Provisions

LEGAL AID ACT 1974

Persons eligible for advice and assistance 10.26

1. (1) Advice and assistance to which this section applies shall, subject to and in accordance with the provisions of this Part of this Act, be available in England and Wales for any person if–

(a) his disposable income does not exceed £118 a week, or

(b) he is (directly or indirectly) in receipt of supplementary benefit under the Supplementary Benefits Act 1976 or of income support or family credit

and (in either case) his disposable income does not exceed £825.

(2) and (3) *(Regulations)*

[*Sch.7 Supplementary Benefits Act 1976, Sch.1 LAA 1979, s.45 Administration of Justice Act 1985, s.86 Social Security Act 1986 and numerous SI's*].

COMMENTARY

Disposable income/capital defined in s.11 of the Act (not reproduced herein).

Any person Corporate and unincorporated bodies are excluded by s.25.

Scope and general conditions of advice and assistance 10.27

2. (1) Subject to subs (2) and s.2A below and to any prescribed exceptions or conditions, s.1 above applies to any oral or written advice given by a solicitor, or, if and so far as may be necessary, by counsel–

(a) on the application of English law to any particular circumstances which have arisen in relation to the person seeking advice, and

(b) as to any steps which that person might appropriately take (whether by way of settling any claim, bringing or defending any proceedings, making an agreement, will or other instrument or transaction, obtaining further legal or other advice or assistance, or otherwise) having regard to the application of English law to those circumstances,

and applies to any assistance given by a solicitor, or, if and so far as may be necessary, by counsel to any person in taking any such steps as are mentioned in para (b) above, whether the assistance is given by taking any such steps on his behalf or by assisting him in taking them on his own behalf.

(2) Notwithstanding anything in subs (1) above, s.1 above does not apply to any advice or assistance given to a person in connection with any proceedings before a court or tribunal–

(a) . . .

(b) in the case of criminal proceedings, or any proceedings mentioned in subs (3), (6), or (6A) of s.28 below, at a time when a legal aid order made in respect of him for the purposes of those proceedings is in force.

(3), (4) *(Repealed)*

(5) Except as previously provided by this Part of this Act or by regulations made under it–

(a) the fact that the services of counsel or a solicitor are given by way of advice or assistance shall not affect the relationship between or the rights of counsel, solicitor and client or any privilege arising out of such relationships, and

(b) the rights conferred by this Part of this Act on a person receiving advice or assistance shall not affect the rights or liabilities of other parties to any proceedings or the principles on which the discretion of any court or tribunal is normally exercised.

(6) In this section 'legal aid certificate' means a certificate required, in accordance with regulations made under s.20 below, to be obtained as a condition of entitlement to legal aid, 'legal aid order' means an order made under s.28 below.
[*as amended by s.1(1) Sch.1 LAA 1979*].

COMMENTARY

See under *Advice and Assistance – The 'Green Form' scheme* at 10.24.

s.2(1) Advice under this subsection can with the approval of the court be extended to legal representation in accordance with the Legal Advice and Assistance (No 2) Regulations 1980; *see* under s.2A, *infra*. Where this is done payment for the advice and assistance is made as part of the costs of legal aid and any sum paid by the client is credited towards any legal aid contribution order: s.12 LAA 1982.

10.28 **Representation in proceedings**
2A. (1) In this Part of this Act 'assistance by way of representation' means any assistance given to a person by taking on his behalf any step in the institution or conduct of any proceedings before a court or tribunal, or of any proceedings in connection with a statutory inquiry, whether by representing him in those proceedings or by otherwise taking any step on his behalf (as distinct from assisting him in taking such a step on his own behalf).

(2) Without prejudice to s.2(2) above and subject to any prescribed exceptions, s.1 above does not apply to any assistance by way of representation unless it is approved by an appropriate authority in accordance with regulations made for the purposes of this section; and regulation so made may make different provisions for different cases or classes of cases.

(3), (4) (*Regulations*)

(5) Where a person receives any assistance by way of representation in any civil proceedings before a court or any proceedings before a tribunal, then, except in so far as regulations otherwise provide, his liability by virtue of an order for costs made against him with respect to the proceedings shall not exceed the amount (if any) which is a reasonable one for him to pay having regard to all the circumstances, including the means of all the parties and their conduct in connection with the dispute, and regulations shall make provision as to the court, tribunal or person by whom that amount is to be determined and the extent to which any determination of that amount is to be final.

(6) For the purposes of any inquiry under subs (5) above as to the means of a person against whom an order for costs has been made, his dwelling house and household furniture and the tools and implements of his trade shall be left out of account except in such cases and to such extent as may be prescribed, and except as so prescribed they shall, in all parts of the United Kingdom, be protected from seizure in execution to enforce the order.

(7) . . .
[*as inserted by s.1 Legal Aid Act 1979*].

COMMENTARY

s.1(2A)(2): The appropriate authority, defined in r.16 Legal Advice and Assistance Regulations (No 2) 1980. This is normally the general committee; however, r.19 states that:

'The approval of a general committee shall not be required for assistance by way of representation given by a solicitor to any party to proceedings (whether criminal or civil) before a magistrates' court or to proceedings (whether criminal or civil) before a magistrates' court or to proceedings before a county court, provided that the cost of such assistance does not exceed the limit imposed by virtue of s.3(2) of the Act, where the assistance is given in compliance with a request which is made to the solicitor by the court or given in accordance with a proposal which is made by the solicitor and approved by the court and which in either case–

(a) is so made or approved at a time (whether at or after the beginning of the proceedings) when the solicitor is present within the precincts of the court, but

(b) is not made or approved at any such time as is mentioned in s.2(2)(a) or (b) of the Act'.

Regulation 27 and Sch.6 (costs) would not seem to apply to criminal proceedings.

Power to order legal aid to be given 10.29

28. (1) The following provisions of this section have effect with respect to the giving of legal aid in connection with criminal proceedings and the proceedings mentioned in subss (3), (6) and (6A) below, but any power conferred by those provisions to give such aid shall be exercisable only in the circumstances mentioned in sub (1) of s.19 below and subject to the provisions of subss (1A) to (4) of that section.

(2) Where a person is charged with an offence before a magistrates' court or appears or is brought before a magistrates' court to be dealt with, the court may order that he shall be given legal aid for the purpose of the proceedings before the court and any juvenile court to which the case is remitted in pursuance of s.56(1) of the Children and Young Persons Act 1933 or, in the circumstances mentioned in para (c) of s.29(1) below, for the purpose of so much of those proceedings as related to the grant of bail.

(3) *(Juvenile Court)*

(4) Where a person makes an application to a magistrates' court under s.37 of the Powers of Criminal Courts Act 1973 (review of compensation orders), the court may order that he shall be given legal aid for the purpose of the proceedings before the court.

(5) Where a person convicted or sentenced by a magistrates' court desires to appeal to the Crown Court, either of those courts may order that he shall be given legal aid for the purpose of the appeal, and, where any such person gives notice of appeal, either of those courts may order that the other party to the appeal shall be given legal aid for the purpose of resisting the appeal.

(6) Where a person desires to appeal to the Crown Court in pursuance of ss.2(12), 3(8), 21(4) or 31(6) of the Children and Young Persons Act of 1969 or under s.21A of the Child Care Act 1980, the Crown Court or the court from whose decision the appeal lies may order that he be given legal aid for the purposes of the appeal.

(6A) *(Juvenile Court)*.

(7) Where a person is committed to or appears before the Crown Court for trial or sentence, or appears or is brought before the Crown Court to be dealt with, the court which commits him or the Crown Court may order that he shall be given legal aid for the purpose of the trial or other proceedings before the Crown Court.

(7A) Where a notice of transfer is given under s.4 of the Criminal Justice Act 1987, the magistrates' court in whose jurisdiction the offence was charged or the Crown Court may order that the person charged shall be given legal aid for the purpose of the trial.

(8)–(11) . . .

(11A) In any case where a person is liable to be committed or fined–
(a) by a magistrates' court under s.12 of the Contempt of Court Act 1981;
(b) by a county court under s.30, 127 or 157 of the County Courts Act 1959; or
(c) by any superior court for contempt in the face of that or any order court or tribunal,
the court may order that he shall be given legal aid for the purposes of the proceedings.

(12) In the following provisions of this Part of this Act 'legal aid order' means an order made under any provision of this section and 'legally assisted person' means a person to whom legal aid is ordered to be given by such an order.

[*as amended by s.65 Children Act 1975, s.11 Bail Act 1976, s.25 (2) CJA 1982, Sch.2 CJA 1987*].

COMMENTARY

s.28(2): charged with an offence see the extended definition of this term in s.30(10), (11), *infra*. Legal aid ordered under this subsection includes proceedings on an application for bail to the Crown Court following a full argument certificate: s.30(1A). Counsel are not included for this purpose, except where they were allowed in the magistrates' court: s.30(1B).

To be dealt with defined in s.30(12), *infra*.

The proceedings before the court Examining justices can make a 'through' order which covers both the committal proceedings and the proceedings in the Crown Court: s.2 LAA 1982. This term includes by virtue of s.2(1) European Communities Act 1972, proceedings before the European Court upon a reference by a magistrates' court to that court: *R v Marlborough Street Stipendiary Magistrate, ex p. Bouchereau* (1977) 142 JP 27.

s.28(5), the wide terminology of this subsection ('desires to appeal') suggests that legal aid may be granted before notice of appeal has been served. It could thus cover an application for leave to appeal out of time. Legal aid may only be granted on appeals to the Crown Court under this Part of the Act. Appeals by way of case stated are dealt with under Part 1 (civil legal aid), even where they arise from criminal proceedings.

A person convicted this includes a juvenile found guilty: s.59 CYPA 1933.

Sentenced defined in s.30(12), *infra*.

Appeal for the documents to be transmitted to the Crown Court see r.17, *infra*. Any notes of evidence taken must be supplied to the defence: r.16.

The other party to the appeal presumably this would extend to the original prosecutor in third party proceedings: *R v Recorder of Derby, ex p. Spalton* (1944) 108 JP 193; *R v Epsom Justices, ex p. Dawnier Motors Ltd* (1961) 125 JP 40.

s.28(7): Committed . . . for trial defined in Sch.1 Interpretation Act 1978 as meaning, committed in custody or on bail by a magistrates' court pursuant to s.6 MCA 1980, or by any judge, or other authority having power to do so with a view to trial before a judge and jury. For the documents to be transmitted to the Crown Court see r.17 General Regulation, *infra*.

Committed . . . for . . . sentence defined in s.40(1), *infra*. For the documents to be transmitted to the Crown Court see r.17, *infra*.

s.28(11A), prospectively added by s.13 Contempt of Court Act 1981 from a day to be appointed.

10.30   **Circumstances in which legal aid may be ordered to be given**
        29. (1) Subject to the following provisions of this section, the power to make a legal aid order shall be exercisable by a court having the power under s.28 above where it appears to the court desirable to do so in the interests of justice, and a court having that power shall make such an order–
        (a) where a person is committed for trial on a charge of murder; or
        (b) . . .
            or
        (c) where a person charged with an offence before a magistrates' court is brought before the court in pursuance of a remand in custody on an occasion when he may be again remanded or committed in custody and is not (but wishes to be) legally represented before the court, not having been legally represented before the court when he was so remanded; or
        (d) where a person who is to be sentenced or dealt with for an offence before a magistrates' court or the Crown Court is to be kept in custody to enable inquiries or a report to be made to assist the court in sentencing or dealing with him for the offence;
        (e) where a child is brought before a juvenile court under s.21A of the Child Care Act 1980 and is not (but wishes to be) legally represented before that court.

(1A) Nothing in subs (1) above shall require a magistrates' court, in the circumstances mentioned in para (c) of that subsection, to order that the person charged before it be given legal aid for the purposes of the proceedings before that court and any juvenile court (as distinct from legal aid for the purpose of so much of those proceedings as relates to the grant of bail) or, in those circumstances, to make a legal aid order after the conviction of that person.

(2) A court shall not make a legal aid order for the giving of aid to any person for any purpose unless it appears to the court that his disposable income and disposable capital are such that he requires assistance in meeting the costs which he may incur for that purpose.

(3) (*Repealed*)

(4) Without prejudice to subs (2) above, before a court makes a legal aid order for the giving of aid to any person, the court shall require him to furnish a written statement of his means in a prescribed form unless it appears to the court that he is by reason of his physical or mental condition incapable of doing so.

(5) Subsections (3) and (4) above shall have effect in their application to a person who has not attained the age of 16, as if the words 'he', 'him' and 'his' referred to that person and a person who is an appropriate contributor in relation to him or such of them as the court selects, and as if in subs (4) for the words 'shall' there were substituted the word 'any' and the words from 'unless' onwards were omitted; and the court may require that a statement furnished by an appropriate contributor in pursuance of subs (4) shall specify both his means and those of the person who has not attained the age of 16.

(5A) Paragraphs (c) and (d) of subs (1) above shall have effect in their application to a person who has not attained the age of 18 as if the references to a remand in custody and to being remanded, committed or kept in custody included references to being committed under s.23 of the Children and Young Persons Act 1969 to the care of a local authority or to a remand centre.

(6) Where a doubt arises whether a legal aid order should be made for the giving of aid to any person, the doubt shall be resolved in that person's favour. [*as amended by s.1 Bail Act 1976, Sch.12 Criminal Law Act 1977, s.25(2) CJA 1982, s.14(4) LAA 1982*].

COMMENTARY

s.29(1): A legal aid order defined in s.28(12), *supra*.

The interests of justice see under this heading in the introduction.

Committed for trial see note to s.28, *supra*.

s.29(2): Any indictable offence it was formerly held that this includes an offence which can be tried either summarily or on indictment: *R v Guildhall Justices, ex p. Marshall* (1976) 140 JP 274. The present definition of 'indictable offence' in Sch.1 Interpretation Act 1978 confirms this decision.

s.29(4): A written statement of his means the penalty for false statements is in s.90 CJA 1967, as applied by s.42(3) of this Act.
  In the case of persons under 16 see s.7(4) LAA 1982.
  For the treatment of persons who fail to furnish a statement of means, see s.7(5) LAA 1982.

Attained the age of 16 for juveniles who subsequently attain this age see s.40(3) LAA 1982, *infra*.

Appropriate contributor defined in s.40(1), *infra*.

Scope of legal aid and supplementary provisions as to legal aid order   10.31
  30. (1) For the purposes of this Part of this Act legal aid, in relation to any proceedings to which a person is party, shall be taken, subject to the following

provisions of this section, as consisting of representation by a solicitor and counsel assigned by the court, including advice on the preparation of that person's case for those proceedings.

(1A) Legal aid which may be ordered to be given to any person for the purpose of any proceedings by a legal aid order under s.28(2) above, whether or not in the circumstances mentioned in s.29(1)(c) above, shall include, in the event–

(a) of his being remanded in custody in those proceedings; and
(b) of the court issuing a certificate under s.5(6A) of the Bail Act 1976 (refusal of fully argued bail application),

legal aid for the purpose of proceedings in connection with an application for bail to the Crown Court.

(1B) Notwithstanding anything in subs (1) above, legal aid in connection with an application for bail to the Crown Court shall not include representation by counsel except in a case where by virtue of subs (2)(a) below legal aid ordered to be given for the purposes of the proceedings before the magistrates' court included representation by counsel.

(2) Notwithstanding anything in subs (1) above, legal aid ordered to be given for the purposes of any proceedings before a magistrates' court shall not include representation by counsel except–

(a) in the case of any indictable offence, where the court is of the opinion that, because of circumstances which make the case unusually grave or difficult, representation by both solicitor and counsel would be desirable; and
(b) . . .

and legal aid ordered to be given for the purpose of so much of any proceedings before a magistrates' court as relates to the grant of bail shall not include representation by counsel.

(3) Where the Crown Court makes a legal aid order under s.28(5), (6) or (7) above, the court may, in cases of urgency where it appears to the court that there is no time to instruct a solicitor, order that the legal aid to be given shall consist of representation by counsel only, and where a magistrates' court or the Crown Court makes a legal aid order under any of those subsections for the purpose of proceedings in the Crown Court, being proceedings at which solicitors have a right of audience, the court may order that the legal aid to be given shall consist of representation by a solicitor only.

(4) . . .

(4A) Where a court makes a legal aid order under s.28(11A) above, the court may order that the legal aid to be given shall consist of representation by counsel only or, in any court where solicitors have a right of audience, by a solicitor only; and the court may assign for the purpose any counsel or solicitor who is within the precincts of the court at the time when the order is made.

(5) A legal aid order under s.28(2) or (3) above for the purposes of proceedings before a magistrates' court shall be authority for the solicitor assigned by the court to give advice on the question whether there appear to be reasonable grounds of appeal from any determination in those proceedings and assistance by him in the giving of a notice of appeal or making of an application for a case to be stated, being a notice given or application made within the ordinary time for doing so.

(6) Where legal aid is ordered to be given to any person for the purpose of an appeal to the Crown Court by a legal aid order under s.28(5) or (6) above and the Crown Court–

(a) in the case of an order under s.28(5), confirms or varies his conviction or sentence, or
(b) in the case of an order under s.28(6), dismisses the appeal or otherwise alters the order to which the appeal relates,

the legal aid order shall be authority for counsel or the solicitor assigned to him to give advice on the question whether there appear to be reasonable grounds of appeal from the decision of the Crown Court and, if such grounds appear to exist, assistance in the making of an application for a case to be stated.

(7) Legal aid which may be ordered to be given to any person for the purpose of any proceedings by a legal aid order under s.28(7) above shall, in the event of his being convicted or sentenced in those proceedings, include advice on the question whether there appear to be reasonable grounds of appeal and–

(a) if such grounds appear to exist, assistance in the preparation of an application for leave to appeal or in the giving of a notice of appeal;

(b) while the question is being considered, assistance in the making of a provisional application or the giving of a provisional notice.

(7A) Where a certificate that a case is fit for appeal has been issued under the Criminal Appeal Act 1968 or under s.81(1B) of the Supreme Court Act 1981, legal aid which may be ordered to be given by a legal aid order under s.28(7) above shall include legal aid for the purposes of an application for the grant of bail by the Crown Court.

(8) Legal aid which may be ordered to be given to any person for the purpose of any appeal by a legal aid order under s.28(8) or (9) above may, without prejudice to subs (1) above, consist in the first instance of advice, by counsel or a solicitor assigned by the court, on the question whether appear to be reasonable grounds of appeal and assistance by that solicitor in the preparation of an application for leave to appeal or in the giving of a notice of appeal.

(9), (9A) . . .

(10) The reference in s.28(2) above to a person charged with an offence before a magistrates' court includes a reference to a person summoned or arrested for an offence and under a duty to appear or a liability to be brought before a magistrates' court in respect of that offence; and the power to make a legal aid order under that subsection shall, in the case of a person arrested for an offence who has not appeared or been brought before a magistrates' court, be exercisable by the magistrates' court to which an application for legal aid is made in pursuance of regulations under this part of the Act.

(11) Any reference in s.28(2) above to a person charged with an offence includes a reference to a person against whom proceedings are instituted under s.115 of the Magistrates' Court Act, 1980 (binding over), in respect of an actual or apprehended breach of the peace or other misbehaviour, and any such reference to a person brought before a magistrates' court to be dealt with includes a reference to a person brought before a metropolitan stipendiary magistrate to be dealt with under s.9 of the Extradition Act 1970, or s.7 of the Fugitive Offenders Act 1967 (hearing of extradition and similar proceedings).

(12) In ss.28 and 29 above–
'dealt with' means dealt with under ss.6, 8, 16, 17(1) or (2), 23 or 27 of the Powers of Criminal Courts Act 1973 or s.47(3) of the Criminal Law Act 1977, or dealt with for a failure to comply with a condition of a recognizance to keep the peace or be of good behaviour.

'Sentence' includes an order of a court in respect of which an appeal lies (with or without leave) to another court, and 'sentenced' shall be construed accordingly.

[*as amended by s.1 Bail Act 1976, Sch.1 Administration Act 1977, Schs 1, 7 MCA 1980, ss.29, 60 CJA 1982, s.4 LAA 1982, s.46 Administration of Justice Act 1985*].

COMMENTARY

s.30(1): Solicitor and counsel assigned by the court see s.28, *infra*. the court must assign any solicitor willing to act who is selected by the assisted person: r.8 General Regulations 1968;

except that the court may assign a single counsel or solicitor to two or more persons whose cases are heard together *unless the interests of justice require separate representations*: *ibid*, r.14; and except a solicitor or barrister excluded by a complaints tribunal: see s.47 Solicitors Act 1974, as amended by s.44 Administration of Justice Act 1985 (solicitors) and s.42, *ibid* (barristers). As to the selection of counsel, see rr.9 and 10 General Regulations 1968.

Not more than one counsel may be assigned in magistrates' courts: r.13; and only in the circumstances stipulated in s.30(2), *infra*. Two counsel may be assigned for proceedings in the Crown Court, but where the legal aid order is made by the magistrates' court, only on a charge of murder: r.13.

s.30(2): except in a murder case, before justices can exercise their discretion affirmatively to order representation by counsel under s.30(2)(a) the applicant has to show both that the case is of unusual gravity or difficulty and that that circumstance leads to the conclusion that such representation is desirable in the particular proceedings under consideration – whether for summary trial before the justices or for committal proceedings. Where there is no conceivable reason for opposing a s.6(2) committal, no matter how grave or difficult the case might be, it is difficult to see how there can be any conceivable reason for assigning counsel at that stage. Certainly, the mere multiplicity of simple, straightforward charges cannot make it desirable for counsel to be instructed. However, the facts in relation to a single charge may be so complex that it is desirable that counsel should at least advise whether there are good grounds for opposing a committal under s.6(2): *R v Guildford Justices, ex p. Scott* [1975] Crim LR 286. In the case of committal proceedings for alleged murder it should be recognised as a rule of practice that legal aid should include representation by counsel: *R v Derby Justices, ex p. Kooner* [1970] 3 WLR 598.

An application under this subsection may be referred to the appropriate criminal legal aid committee: r.14A(2).

Indictable offence, defined in Sch.1 Interpretation Act 1978 as meaning an offence which, if committed by an adult, is triable on indictment, whether it is exclusively so triable or triable either way.

s.30(3): Proceedings at which solicitors have a right of audience, the *Practice Direction* [1972] 1 All ER 708 states that:

1. A solicitor may appear in, conduct, defend and address the court in (*a*) criminal proceedings in the Crown Court on appeal from a magistrates' court or on committal of a person for sentence or to be dealt with, if he, or any partner of his, or any solicitor in his employment or by whom he is employed, appeared on behalf of the defendant in the magistrates' court; (*b*) civil proceedings in the Crown Court on appeal from a magistrates' court if he, or any partner of his, or any solicitor in his employment or by whom he is employed, appeared in the proceedings in the magistrates court.

2. The rights of audience conferred by this direction are in addition to and not in derogation from the rights of audience conferred by the *Practice Direction* dated 7 December 1971 (which concerned sittings of the Crown Court at Caernarvon, Barnstaple, Bodmin, Doncaster and (in certain respects) Lincoln).

s.30(4A): prospectively added by s.13 Contempt of Court Act 1981 from a day to be appointed.

s.30(5): The ordinary time, ie 21 days after the day on which the decision was given: r.7 Crown Court Rules 1971 (appeal to the Crown Court) s.111 MCA 1980 (appeal by way of case stated).

s.30(11): alleged breaches of bind-over are dealt with under ss.28(2) and 30(12) of this Act.

s.30(12): Dealt with, These provisions of PCCA 1973 refer to breach of probation (s.6) commission of further offence when on probation or conditional discharge (s.8), breach of community service order (s.16) and certain amendments thereto (s.17(1) and (2)), dealing with suspended sentences (s.23) and suspended sentence supervision orders (s.27), S.47(3) CLA 1977 deals with partly suspended sentences.

10.32   **Amendment and revocation of legal aid order**
         31. (1) A court having power to make a legal aid order may on the application of the legally assisted person or otherwise amend any such order by substituting for any legal representative or representatives previously assigned to him any legal representative or representatives whom the court could have assigned to him if it had been making the legal order.

         (2) A court having power to make a legal aid order may revoke any such order–

(a) on the application of the legally assisted person; or

(b) if the only legal representative or all the legal representatives for the time being assigned to him withdraw from the case and it appears to the court that, because of his conduct, it is not desirable to amend the order under subs (1) above.

(3) The amendment or revocation of a legal aid order under this section shall not affect the right of any legal representative previously assigned to the legally assisted person to remuneration for work done before the date of the amendment or revocation, as the case may be.

[*as amended by Sch. LAA 1982*].

COMMENTARY

Subsections (1) and (2) of this section are two quite different methods of dealing with a legal aid order: the first one is simply of substitution, the second of revocation, *per* Slynn J in *R v Swindon Justices, ex p. Preece* (1977) 141 JPN 529. A copy of the amending or revoking order must be sent or delivered to the solicitor and the legally aided person must be notified: r.6 General Regulations, *infra*. An application under this subsection may be referred to the appropriate criminal legal aid committee: r.14A(2).

s.3(1): Court having power to make a legal aid order, see s.28(2)–(11), *supra*.

Legal aid order/legally assisted person, defined in s.28(12), *supra*.

s.31(2): before the court can exercise its powers under this subsection either an application must be received from the legally aided person for revocation or alternatively the legal representative(s) must withdraw *and* it must appear to the court because of the conduct of the legally assisted person that it is not desirable to amend the order under subs (1): *R v Swindon Justices, ex p. Preece, supra*.

Power to order payment of contributions   10.33

32. (1)–(4) (*Repealed*)

(5) In this Part of the Act 'collecting court' in relation to a legal aid contribution order, means a magistrates' court specified in that order; and the court so specified shall be–

(a) in a case where the court making the order is itself a magistrates' court, that court;

(b) in a case where the order is made on an appeal from a magistrates' court, or in respect of a person who was committed (whether for trial or otherwise by a magistrates' court) to the Crown Court, the court from which the appeal is brought or, as the case may be, which committed him; and

(c) in any other case, a magistrates court nominated by the court making the order.

[*as amended by Sch.12 CLA 1977, Sch. LAA 1982*].

Enforcement of legal aid contribution orders   10.34

35. (1) Subject to subs (4) below, any sum required to be paid by a legal aid contribution order shall be recoverable as if it had been adjudged to be paid by an order of the collecting court, subject to and in accordance with the provisions of Sch.3 to this Act.

(2) Without prejudice to subs (1) above, but subject to the following subsections, payment of any sum required to be paid by a legal aid contribution order shall be enforceable by the High Court or a county court (otherwise than by issue of a write of *fieri facias* or other process against goods or by imprisonment of attachment of earnings) as if the sum were due to the clerk of the collecting court in pursuance of a judgment or order of the High Court or county court, as the case may be.

(3) Subsection (2) above shall not authorise the enforcement by a County Court of payment of any sum exceeding the amount which for the time being is the County Court limit for the purposes of s.16 of the County Courts Act 1984.

(4) Where a legal aid contribution order has been made in respect of a member of Her Majesty's armed forces and the Secretary of State notifies the collecting court that any sum payable under the order will be recovered by deductions from the person's pay, the collecting court shall not enforce payment of any sum unless and until the Secretary of State subsequently notifies it that the person is no longer a member of those forces and that that sum has not been fully recovered.

(5) The clerk of the collecting court shall not take proceedings by virtue of subs (2) above to recover any sum required to be paid by a legal aid contribution order unless authorised to do so.

(6) Any expenses incurred by the clerk of the magistrates' court in recovering any sum so required to be paid shall be treated for the purposes of Part VI of the Justices of the Peace Act 1979, as expenses of the magistrates' court committee.

(7) Any sum paid by way of contribution towards costs to a clerk of the magistrates' court shall be paid by him to the Lord Chancellor and subs (4) of s.61 of the Justices of the Peace Act 1979 (regulations as to accounts of justices' clerks) shall apply in relation to sums payable to the Lord Chancellor under this subsection as it applies in relation to sums payable to the Secretary of State under that section.

(8) . . .

[*as amended by Sch.2 Justices of the Peace Act 1979, SI 1980 No 705*].

COMMENTARY

s.35(1): A legal aid contribution order ie an order under ss.7 or 8(2) LAA 1982.

Recoverable as if it has been adjudged to be paid by an order ie in accordance with s.76 MCA 1980.

The collecting court defined in s.32(5), *supra*.

s.35(2): A writ of *fieri facias* **etc.** These remedies are excluded because corresponding remedies are available under Sch.3.

s.35(7) see Justices' Clerks (Accounts) Regulations 1973 (not reproduced herein).

10.35　　**Recovery of costs and refund of contributions**
　　　　36. (1) Where a legally assisted person is given legal aid for the purposes of any proceedings, any sums due under an order for costs made in his favour with respect of those proceedings shall be paid–
　　　　(a) in the case of proceedings in a magistrates' court, to the Lord Chancellor
　　　　(b) in the case of proceedings not falling within para (a) above, to the Secretary of State.

(2) If the total contribution made by or in respect of a legally assisted person in respect of any costs is more than the difference between the costs incurred on his behalf and the sums due in respect of costs under any such order as is mentioned in subs (1) above, the excess shall be repaid–
　　　　(a) where the contribution was made by one person only, to him; and
　　　　(b) where the contribution was made by two or more persons, to them in proportion to the amounts contributed by them.

[*as amended by SI 1980 No 705*].

COMMENTARY

The whole section has been prospectively repealed by s.14(4) LAA 1982 from a date to be appointed.

10.36　　**Solicitors and counsel**
　　　　38. (1) Any practising barrister or solicitor may be assigned to act for a legally assisted person unless he is for the time being excluded by virtue of subs

(2) below as being unfit so to act by reason of his conduct when acting for legally assisted persons or his professional conduct generally.

(2) *(Rules)*

(3) . . .

(4) *(Rules)*

(5), (6) . . .

COMMENTARY

Excluded ie by a complaints tribunal set up under the Legal Aid in Criminal Proceedings (Complaints Tribunal) Rules 1968: r.7 General Regulations, *infra*. See also s.47 Solicitors Act 1974, as amended by s.44 Administration of Justice Act 1985 (solicitors); and *ibid*, s.42 (barristers).

Interpretation of Part II   **10.37**
    40. In this Part of this Act, except so far as the context otherwise requires–
'appropriate contributor', in relation to a person who has not attained the age of 16, means his father, any person who has been adjudged to be his putative father, and (whether or not he is legitimate) his mother;
'committed for sentence' means committed under the Vagrancy Act, 1824, ss.37 or 38 of the Magistrates' Court Act, 1980, s.67 of the Mental Health Act, 1959, s.62(6) of the Criminal Justice Act 1967 or ss.6, 8, 16, 17(2)(b) or 24 of the Powers of Criminal Courts Act 1973;
'legal aid contribution order' means an order under ss.7 or 8(2) of the Legal Aid Act 1982;
'legal aid fund' means the legal aid fund established under Part 1 of this Act;
'prescribed' means prescribed by regulations made under this Part of this Act.

(2) Any power to make an application in pursuance of this Part of this Act which is exercisable by a person who has not attained the age of 17 shall also be exercisable by his parent or guardian apart from this subsection; and in this subsection 'guardian' has the same meaning as in s.70(2) of the Children and Young Persons Act 1969.

(3) A person who attains the age of 16 after a legal aid order is made in respect of him or, in a case where such an order is made in pursuance of an application, after the application is made, shall be treated for the purposes of this Part of this Act, in relation to the order, as not having attained that age.

(4) . . .
[*as amended by Sch.7 MCA 1980, s.14 Legal Aid Act 1982*].

COMMENTARY

s.40(2): Guardian, section 70(2) of the 1969 Act provides that this term 'includes any person who was a guardian of the child or young in question at the time when any supervision order, care order or warrant to which the application relates was orginally made.'

Attained the age of 17, for the ascertainment of age s.150(3) MCA 1980.

SCHEDULE 3

Enforcement of legal aid contribution orders   **10.38**

General provisions as to enforcement
    1. In this schedule 'collecting court' and 'legal aid contribution order' have the same meanings as in Part II of this Act.
    2. The collecting court may, in relation to a legal aid contribution order, exercise the power of s.75 of the Magistrates' Courts Act 1980, (power to dispense with immediate payment); and for the purposes of that section any provision made by the court which made the order as to time for payment, or payment by instalments, shall be treated as made by the collecting court.

3. Sections 93 (complaint for arrears), 94 (effect of committal on arrears) and 95 (power to remit arrears) of the Magistrates' Court Act 1980, shall apply as if a legal aid contribution order were enforceable as an affiliation order.

4. Any costs awarded, under s.64 of the Magistrates' Court Act 1980, on the hearing of a complaint for the enforcement of a legal aid contribution order shall be enforceable as a sum required to be paid by that order.

5. Sections 17 and 18 of the Maintenance Orders Act 1958, (not more than one committal for same arrears, and power to review committals), shall apply as if a legal aid contribution order were a maintenance order.

6. Section 80 of the Magistrates' Court Act 1980, (application of money found on defaulter to satisfy sum adjudged) shall apply as if a legal aid contribution order were enforceable as an affiliation order.

Transfer of enforcement proceedings to different court
7. (1) Where it appears to the collecting court that a person subject to a legal aid contribution order is residing in a petty sessions area other than that for which the court acts, the court may make a transfer order under this paragraph, that is to say an order making payment under the legal aid contribution order enforceable in that other petty sessions area (which area shall be specified in the transfer order).

(2) As from the date of a transfer order under this paragraph the court which made the order shall cease to be the collecting court for the purposes of the legal aid contribution order and of s.35 above and this schedule and be replaced as such by a magistrates' court acting for the petty sessions area specified in the transfer order.
[*as amended by Sch.7 MCA 1980, s.14 LAA 1982*].

LEGAL AID ACT 1982

10.39 **Advice and representation by duty solicitors**
1. (1) A scheme under s.15 of the Legal Aid Act 1974 (in this Act referred to as 'the principal Act') may provide–
  (a) for the making, by committees set up under the scheme, of arrangements whereby advice and representation to which this section applies is provided by solicitors in attendance at magistrates' courts; and
  (aa) for the making, by such committees, of arrangements whereby advice and assistance under s.1 of the principal Act is provided for persons–
     (i) such as are mentioned in s.29 of the Police and Criminal Evidence Act 1984; or
     (ii) arrested and held in custody who–
        (i) exercise the right to consult a solicitor conferred on them by s.58(1) of that Act, or
        (ii) are permitted to consult a representative of a solicitor, and
  (b) for the remuneration out of the legal aid fund or by the Lord Chancellor of solicitors providing advice and representation or advice and assistance under the arrangements.

(1A) A scheme under s.15 of the principal Act which relates to advice and representation at magistrates' courts may provide that arrangements made under it may be so framed as to preclude solicitors from providing such advice and representation if they do not also provide advice and assistance in pursuance of arrangements made by virtue of a scheme under that section which relates to the provision of advice and assistance for persons such as are mentioned s.29 of the Police and Criminal Evidence Act 1984 and for persons arrested and held in custody.

(2) This section applies to such advice and representation in connection with criminal proceedings before magistrates' courts as may be specified by the

scheme, being advice and representation for persons, or any class of persons, in respect of whom no legal aid order is for the time being in force in relation to the proceedings in question and to whom advice and assistance in respect of those proceedings is not being given under s.1 of the principal Act.

(3), (4)

(5) A magistrates' court shall comply with such directions given to it by the Lord Chancellor as he thinks requisite for securing that effect is given at that court to any arrangements made under subs (1) above for the provision of advice and representation at the court.

(6) . . .

(7) Sections 2(5), 15(1), 20(1) and (2)(a), (c) and (d), 22 and 23 of the principal Act (ancillary provisions relation to advice and assistance under s.1 of that Act) shall apply also in relation to advice and representation provided pursuant to this section.
[as amended by s.59 PACE Act 1984].

Legal aid for committal proceedings and trials   **10.40**
   2. (1) A magistrates' court inquiring into an offence as examining justices may make a legal aid order under s.28(2) of the principal Act which applies, or amend an order already made by the court under that provision so that it applies, both to the proceedings before the court and, in the event of the defendant being committed for trial, to his trial before the Crown Court.

(2) Legal aid ordered to be given to a person by virtue of this section shall, in the event of his being convicted by the Crown Court, include such advice and assistance as is mentioned in s.30(7) of the principal Act.

COMMENTARY
s.2(1) this is a discretionary power. The court can still limit the legal aid order to the committal proceedings only, if that seems desirable.

Examining justices thus, in the case of an offence triable either way a 'through' legal aid order cannot be made *until the mode of trial decision has been taken.*

Legal aid contribution orders   **10.41**
   7. (1) Where a court makes a legal aid order giving legal aid to a person whose disposable income or disposable capital exceeds the limits prescribed in relation to such income and capital respectively the court shall, subject to the provisions of this section, make an order ('a legal aid contribution order') requiring him to make a payment (in this Act referred to as 'a contribution') in respect of the costs of the legal aid.

(2) The contribution which a legal aid contribution order requires a person to make shall be of such amount as is applicable in his case in accordance with regulations made for the purposes of this section; and any such contribution shall be paid in one sum or by instalments as may be prescribed.

(3) In a case where the legally assisted person has not attained the age of sixteen, the court may, instead of or in addition to making a legal aid contribution order against him, make such an order against any person who is an appropriate contributor in relation to him and whose disposable income or disposable capital exceeds the limits referred to in subs (1) above.

(4) Where a court makes a legal aid order for the giving of legal aid to a person who has attained the age of sixteen and does so without first requiring him to furnish a statement of his means under s.29(4) of the principal Act because it appears to the court that he is by reason of his physical or mental condition incapable of doing so–
   (a) no legal aid contribution order need be made at the time when the legal aid order is made; but

(b) if it subsequently appears to the court having power to make a legal aid contribution order under s.8(2) below that he has become capable of furnishing such a statement, that court may require him to do so.

(5) Where a person fails to furnish a statement which he is required to furnish under subs (4) above or under s.29(5) of the principal Act (statements by appropriate contributors) he shall be treated, for the purposes of any legal aid contribution order made in connection with the legal aid order in relation to which the requirement was imposed, as if his disposable income and disposable capital exceeded the limits referred to in subs (1) above and as if the amount of the contribution applicable in his case were such as the court may determine.

(6) Subject to s.13(5) below, where the costs of the legal aid in respect of which a legal aid contribution was made are less than the contribution made under the order, the difference between the contribution and those costs shall be repaid–
(a) where the contribution was made by one person only, to him; and
(b) where the contribution was made by two or more persons, to them in proportion to the amounts contributed by them.

(7), (8) (*Regulations*).

COMMENTARY

The amount of a legal aid contribution order must be determined in accordance with rr.18–20 General Regulations 1968; and the second Schedule.

s.7(3): Appropriate contributor the definition in s.40(1) LAA is applied by s.16(4) of this Act.

10.42   **Variation and revocation of legal aid contribution orders**
8. (1) A legal aid contribution order made against a person in connection with a legal aid order may be varied–
(a) in the light of any further information as to his disposable income or disposable capital at the time when the legal aid contribution order was made; or
(b) in the light of any change in his disposable income or disposable capital at any time within such period beginning with the date of the legal aid order as may be prescribed for the purposes of this section ('the pre-scribed period').

(2) Where no legal aid contribution order has been made against a person in connection with a legal aid order at the time when that order was made–
(a) because his disposable income or disposable capital did not exceed (or was then believed not to exceed) the limits referred to in subs (1) of s.7 above; or
(b) because of subs (4)(a) of that section,
a legal aid contribution order may be made against that person at any subsequent time if it appears that his disposable income or disposable capital at any time within the prescribed period exceeds or exceeded the limits referred to in subs (1) of that section.

(3) Where a legal aid contribution order has been made against a person and it subsequently appears that his disposable income or disposable capital at the time when the order was made was such that no legal aid contribution order should have been made in his case, the order shall be revoked; but if the order is revoked subs (2) above shall apply as if the order has never been made.

(4) The powers conferred by the foregoing provisions of this section shall be exercisable by the court that made the legal aid order in question except that–
(a) where the relevant proceedings are being heard or have been concluded in a different court, those powers shall, subject to para (b) below, be exercisable by that court; and

(b) where any sum in respect of a contribution under a legal aid contribution order falls due at a time after the conclusion of the relevant proceedings, the power conferred by subs (1) above to vary the order so far as relates to any sum falling due as aforesaid shall be exercisable by the collecting court.

(5) At the conclusion of the relevant proceedings the court in which those proceedings are concluded may, if it thinks fit–

(a) remit any sum due under a legal aid contribution order from a legally assisted person which falls to be paid after the conclusion of those proceedings or, if that person has been acquitted, remit or order the repayment of any sum due from or paid by him under such an order;

(b) remit or order the repayment of any sum due from or paid by an appropriate contributor under such an order:

and where a legally assisted person successfully appeals against his conviction the court which allows his appeal may remit or order the repayment of any sum due from or paid by him or an appropriate contributor under such an order.

(6) Where the legal aid order in connection with which a legal aid contribution order was made is revoked, the foregoing provision of this section shall have effect as if the relevant proceedings had then been concluded.

(7) Where a legal aid contribution order is revoked, or is varied to an amount less than what has already been paid, any sum paid or, as the case may be, overpaid under the order shall be repaid.

(8) For the purposes of this section the relevant proceedings, in relation to a legal aid contribution order, are the proceedings for the purposes of which legal aid was ordered to be given by the legal aid order in connection with which the legal aid contribution order was made except that where those proceedings are proceedings before a magistrates' court which result–

(a) in the legally assisted person being committed to the Crown Court for trial or sentence; or

(b) in his case being remitted to a juvenile court in pursuance of s.56(1) of the Children and Young Persons Act 1933 or s.2(1) of the Children and Young Persons Act 1969

the relevant proceedings include the proceedings before the Crown Court or that juvenile court.

Enforcement of legal aid contribution orders 10.43

9. (1) Any sum due under a legal aid contribution order shall not be recoverable, and payment of any such sum shall not be enforced, under s.35 of the principal Act until–

(a) the conclusion of the relevant proceedings; or

(b) if earlier, the revocation of the legal aid order in connection with which the legal aid contribution order was made.

(2) Where a sum in respect of a contribution under a legal aid contribution order made in connection with a legal aid order is required to be paid on the making of the legal aid contribution order, the court may direct that the legal aid order shall not take effect until that sum is paid.

(3) Where a sum in respect of a contribution under a legal aid contribution order made in connection with a legal aid order is required to be paid by the legally assisted person at any subsequent time before the conclusion of the relevant proceedings and is not paid at that time, the court in which those proceedings are being heard may revoke the legal aid order but shall not do so unless satisfied, after affording the legally assisted person an opportunity of making representations in such manner as may be prescribed–

(a) that he was at the time able to pay the sum in question; and

(b) that he is able to pay the whole or part of it but has failed or refused to do so.

(4) The revocation of a legal aid order under subs (3) above shall not affec: the right of any legal representative previously assigned to the legally assistec person to remuneration for work done before the date of the revocation.

(5) The collecting court may defer recovering any sum due under a legal aic contribution order if an appeal is pending in respect of the relevant proceed ings or if the legally assisted person has been ordered to be retried.

(6) In this section 'the relevant proceedings' has the same meaning as in s.ξ above.

10.44

LEGAL AID IN CRIMINAL PROCEEDINGS (GENERAL) REGULATIONS 1968
SI No 1231
(as amended by SI 1970, No 1980, SI 1976 No 790, SI 1980 Nos 661, 705, 1651, SI 1983 No 1863, SI 1984 No 1716, SI 1985 No 1632, SI 1986 No 274).

Many of the terms used in these regulations are defined in r.31 *infra*. Note tha: the term 'the proper officer of the court' usually includes both the justices clerk and anyone authorised by him to act on his behalf. By contrast, in r.? (proceedings in the Crown Court) the justices' clerk is defined in such a way a: to exclude the power of that officer to delegate his function.

NOTE: These and the succeeding regulations made under former legislation are kept in effect by s.42(2) LAA 1974. References have been altered so as tc refer to that Act.

10.45

Proceedings in a magistrates' court
1. (1) An application for a legal aid order in respect of proceedings in ε magistrates' court under s.73(2) or (3A) of the Act (magistrates' court pro ceedings) may be made to the justices' clerk–
   (a) If the application is made by a parent or guardian on behalf of a persor who has not attained the age of 17 years, in Form 1 in the Schedule o: these regulations.
   (b) if the application is made by any other person, in Form 1 in the Schedulε to these Regulations.

(2) An application for a legal aid order may be made orally to the court.

(3) A legal aid order shall not be made until the court, a justice of the peacε or the justices' clerk has considered the statement of means of the applican: except where the applicant is not required under s.29(4) and (5) of the 197↔ Act to furnish a statement of means.

(4) Subject to the provisions of this regulation, the powers of the court t∈ determine an application for a legal aid order may be exercised by the justices clerk or a justice of the peace to whom the clerk has referred the application

(5) Where an application for a legal aid order is made orally to the court, th∈ court may refer it to the justices' clerk for determination.

(6) The justices' clerk considering an application for a legal aid order.
   (a) shall make an order or refer the application to the court or a justice o: the peace; or
   (b) may, where review under regulation 6H would be available, refuse tc make an order.

(7), (8)

(9) In this regulation the expression 'justice of the peace' means a justice o: the peace who is entitled to sit as a member of the magistrates' court and 'lega aid order' means a legal aid order within the meaning of para (1) of thi: regulation.

COMMENTARY

r.1(6)(b): Review, there is a right to apply for review where the application is refused on the *interests of justice* ground and it was made 'not later than 21 days before' the date *fixed for trial* or *committal proceedings*: see rr.6C(1)(a), 6D and 6E(2) *post*, and *R v Bury Justices, ex p. N (A Minor)* [1986] 3 WLR 965.

Proceedings in the Crown Court   **10.46**
2. (1) An application for a legal aid order under s.73(3), (3B) or (4) of the Act (proceedings in the Crown Court) may be made–
 (a) (i) to the appropriate officer of the Crown Court, or
   (ii) in the case of an appeal to the Crown Court, to the justices' clerk;
 (b) (i) if the application is made by a parent or guardian on behalf of a person who has not attained the age of 17 years, in Form 2 in the Schedule to these Regulations.
   (ii) if the application is made by any other person, in Form 2 in the Schedule to these Regulations.

(2) An application for a legal aid order may be made orally to the Crown Court, or to the magistrates' court at the conclusion of the proceedings in that court.

(3) . . .

(4) A legal aid order shall not be made until the court, a judge of the court, the proper officer of the court or, where the application is made to the magistrates' court or justices' clerk, a justice of the peace has considered the statement of means of the applicant except where the applicant is not required under s.29(4) and (5) of the 1974 Act to furnish a statement of means.

(5) Subject to the provisions of this regulation, the powers of the court to determine an application for a legal aid order may be exercised by a judge of the court, the proper officer of the court, or, where the application is made to the magistrates' court or justices' clerk, a justice of the peace.

(6) Where an application for a legal aid order is made orally to the court, the court may refer it to the proper officer of the court for determination.

(7) The proper officer of the court considering an application for a legal aid order shall–
 (a) make an order; or
 (b) *(repealed)*
 (c) except where the proper officer of the court is a justices' clerk, refer the application to a judge of the court, if he is, to the magistrates' court or a justice of the peace.

(8), (9) *(repealed)*

(10) In this regulation the expression 'magistrates' court' means the court which committed or convicted the applicant, 'justice of the peace' means a justice of the peace who is entitled to sit as a member of the magistrates' court, 'justices clerk' means the clerk to the magistrates' court, and 'legal aid order' means a legal aid order within the meaning of para (1) or (3) of this regulation, as the case may be.

Statement of means   **10.47**
4. (1) A statement of means submitted by an applicant or an appropriate contributor shall be in Form 5 in the Schedule to these regulations.

(2) *(repealed)*

(3) If an applicant who has attained the age of 16 years does not furnish a statement of means at the time that he makes an application for legal aid, he shall be required to do so by a proper officer of the court to whom or to whose court he is making the application, unless he has already submitted such a

statement in pursuance of a previous application in respect of the same case where no legal aid order has previously been made and revoked.

(4) If a statement of means of an applicant who has not attained the age of 16 years or an appropriate contributor is not furnished at the time that the applicant makes an application for legal aid, either or both may be required to furnish one by the proper officer of the court to whom or to whose court the application is made unless the person who has not furnished a statement at that time has already submitted a statement in pursuance of a previous application in respect of the same case where no legal aid order has previously been made or revoked.

10.48 **Provision of information**
4A. (1) The court or the proper officer of the court may require the applicant, the legally assisted person or the appropriate contributor to provide evidence of any information given in a statement of means or of any change in his financial circumstances at any time after the submission of a statement of means and such additional information as the court or the proper officer of the court may require.

(2) Where the applicant, the legally assisted person or the appropriate contributor fails to provide evidence or information required under para (1), he may be treated as though his disposable income and disposable capital exceeded the limits prescribed in reg 19(3) and as if the contribution payable by him were such amount as the court or the proper officer of the court may determine or redetermine.

10.49 **General powers to make legal aid order**
5. Subject to the provisions of reg 4 of these Regulations, nothing in reg 1, 2, 3 or 25D of these Regulations shall affect the power of a court or a judge of the court or the Registrar (subject to the provisions of s.75 of the Act) to make a legal aid order, whether an application has been made for legal aid or not, or the right of an applicant whose application has been refused or whose legal aid order has been revoked under s.9(3) of the 1982 Act to apply to the court at the trial or other proceedings.

10.50 **Legal aid order**
6. A legal aid order shall be in Form 6A or 6B in the Schedule and a copy of it shall, subject to reg 6H(3) and 22(3), be sent to:
  (a) the legally assisted person or, where the application was made by his parent or guardian, the parent or guardian;
  (b) the solicitor assigned or counsel (where counsel only is assigned): and
  (c) where the legal aid order is made by a criminal legal aid committee, to the proper officer of the court to which the application for legal aid was made.

10.51 **Amendment of legal aid orders**
6A. (1) An order amending a legal aid order shall be in Form 7 in the Schedule and a copy of it shall be sent to–
  (a) the legally assisted person or, where the application was made by his parent or guardian, the parent or guardian;
  (b) the solicitor assigned by the legal aid order or to counsel (where counsel only is assigned) and to any solicitor and counsel assigned by the amended legal aid order; and
  (c) where the legal aid order is amended by the criminal legal aid committee, to the proper officer of the court to which the application for amendment was made.

(2) Where a new solicitor or counsel only is assigned by an order amending a legal aid order–

(a) counsel originally assigned shall send all papers and other things in his possession relating to the proceedings to the solicitor who instructed him or to counsel newly assigned (where counsel only was assigned); and

(b) the solicitor originally assigned shall send all papers and other things in his possession relating to the proceedings to the solicitor newly assigned or to counsel (where counsel only is assigned by the amended legal aid order).

Revocation of legal aid orders   **10.52**
6B. (1) An order revoking a legal aid order shall be in Form 8 in the Schedule and a copy of it shall be sent to–

(a) the legally assisted person or, where the application was made by his parent or guardian, the parent or guardian;

(b) the solicitor assigned or to counsel (where counsel only is assigned), and

(c) where the legal aid order is revoked by the criminal legal aid committee, to the proper officer of the court to which the application for revocation or amendment was made.

(2) Where a legal aid order is revoked–

(a) the counsel assigned shall send all the papers and other things in his possession relating to the proceedings to the solicitor assigned or (where no solicitor was assigned) to the legally assisted person; and

(b) the solicitor assigned shall send all papers and other things in his possession relating to the proceedings to the legally assisted person.

Notification of refusal of legal aid   **10.53**
6C. (1) Where an application for a legal aid order is refused the proper officer of the court shall notify the applicant or, where the application was made by his parent or guardian, the parent or guardian, stating that the application has been refused on one or both of the following grounds, that–

(a) it does not appear to the court or the proper officer of the court desirable to make an order in the interests of justice; or

(b) it does not appear to the court or the proper officer of the court that the applicant's disposable income and disposable capital are such that he requires assistance in meeting the costs he may incur,

and shall inform him of the provision, if any, of these regulations which relate to the circumstances in which he may apply to a criminal legal aid committee for the decision to be reviewed.

(2) Notification of refusal, and determination of contribution under reg 6D, shall be in Form 14A in the Schedule.

(3) A copy of Form 14A and, where an application for review under reg 6E may be made, of Form 1 shall be sent to the applicant or, where the application was made by his parent or guardian, the parent or guardian and to his solicitor, if any.

Determination of contribution where legal aid is refused   **10.54**
6D. Where a magistrates' court, justice of the peace or a justices' clerk has refused to make a legal aid order on the grounds specified in reg 6C(1)(a) above, there shall nevertheless be determined, where an application for a review under reg 6E may be made, and in accordance with reg 18, 19 and 22, the applicant's disposable income, disposable capital and the amount of any contribution that would have been payable and the manner in which it would be so payable by the applicant or an appropriate contributor had a legal aid order been made.

Application for review   **10.55**
6E. (1) Where an application for a legal aid order has been refused after being considered for the first time by a magistrates' court, justice of the peace

or a justices' clerk, the applicant may, subject to para (2), apply for review to the appropriate criminal legal aid committee.

(2) An application for review shall only lie to a criminal legal aid committee where–
(a) the applicant is charged with an indictable offence or an offence triable either way, and
(b) the application for a legal aid order has been refused on the grounds specified in reg 6C(1)(a); and
(c) the application for a legal aid order was made no later than 21 days before the date fixed for the trial of an information or the inquiry into an offence as examining justices, where such a date had been fixed at the time that the application was made.

COMMENTARY

r. 6E(2)(c): Date fixed for . . . trial, etc, this can never be the date of the accused's *first appearance* before the court; only a *court* can fix the trial etc date, *semble: R v Bury Justices, ex p. N (A Minor)* [1986] 3 WLR 965. Thus where legal aid is refused before *first appearance*, there is always a right to apply for review.

10.56   **Procedure for application for review**
6F. (1) An application for review shall be made by giving notice in Form 14B in the Schedule to the appropriate criminal legal aid committee within 14 days of the date of notification of refusal to make a legal aid order.

(2) The applicant or, where the application was made by his parent or guardian, the parent or guardian shall also send to the appropriate criminal legal aid committee the following documents–
(a) a copy of the application for legal aid; and
(b) a copy of Form 14A (notification of refusal and determination of contribution).

(3) The time limit within which the application for review must be made may, for good reason, be waived or altered by the criminal legal aid committee.

10.57   **Provision of information**
6G. The justices' clerk and the applicant or, where the application was made by his parent or guardian, the parent or guardian shall supply such further particulars, information and documents as the criminal legal aid committee may require.

10.58   **Determination of review**
6H. (1) The criminal legal aid committee shall, on a review, reconsider the application for legal aid and
(a) refuse the application; or
(b) make a legal aid order

(2) Where the criminal legal aid committee makes a legal aid order, it shall make a legal aid contribution order in accordance with any determination made under reg 6D.

(3) Where the magistrates' court, justice of the peace or justices' clerk has made a determination under reg 6D that any legal aid order granted be withheld until a contribution from disposable capital is paid, the criminal legal aid committee shall send the legal aid order to the appropriate justices' clerk.

(4) The criminal legal aid committee shall give notice of its decision and the reason for it to–
(a) the applicant or, where the application was made by his parents or guardian, to the parent or guardian;
(b) his solicitor, if any, and
(c) the justices' clerk of the magistrates' court to which the application for legal aid was made.

Exclusion of solicitors and counsel   **10.59**
7. (1) The proper officer of each court shall keep a list of solicitors and
counsel, notified to him by the Lord Chancellor, who are for the time being
excluded from acting for legally assisted persons under s.82 of the Act.

(2) Any reference in these Regulations to solicitors or counsel shall not
apply to solicitors or counsel so excluded.

Assignment of solicitor   **10.60**
8. Subject to the provisions of reg 11 and 14 of these Regulations, any
person in respect of whom a legal aid order is made, entitling him to the
services of a solicitor, may select any solicitor who is willing to act and such
solicitor shall be assigned to him.

Selection of counsel   **10.61**
9. Where a legal aid order is made in respect of the services of solicitor and
counsel, the solicitor may instruct any counsel who is willing to act:
Provided that in the case of proceedings in the Court of Appeal or House of
Lords, counsel may be assigned by the court or person making or amending the
legal aid order.

Assignment of counsel only   **10.62**
10. (1) Where a legal aid order in respect of proceedings in the Crown
Court is made or amended so as to provide for representation by counsel only,
counsel shall be assigned by the court or person making or amending the legal
aid order.

(2) Where a legal aid order in respect of proceedings in the Court of Appeal
is made or amended so as to provide for representation by counsel only,
counsel shall be assigned by the court, a judge of the court or the Registrar.

Assignment of two counsel   **10.63**
13. (1) Except as provided by para (2) of this regulation, a legal aid order
shall not provide for the services of more than one counsel.

(2) In trials in the Crown Court or appeals to the House of Lords or the
Court of Appeal, an order may provide for the services of two counsel–
(a) on a charge of murder; or
(b) where it appears to the court or person making the legal aid order that
    the case is one of exceptional difficulty, gravity or complexity and that
    the interests of justice require that the legally assisted person shall have
    the services of two counsel,
but an order made by a magistrates court (or amended by such a court under
para (3) of this regulation) may not provide for the services of more than one
counsel except on a charge of murder.

(3) Where, in such a case as is specified in para (2) of this regulation, a legal
aid order provides for the services of one counsel, it may be amended to
provide for the services of two counsel.

Assignment of one solicitor or counsel to more than one legally   **10.64**
assisted person
14. A solicitor may be assigned to two or more legally assisted persons
whose cases are heard together, unless the interests of justice require that such
persons be separately represented.

COMMENTARY
This provision *overrides* the right of the legally assisted person (r.8) to choose his solicitor: *R
v Solihull Justices, ex p. Johnson* (1976) 140 JPN 189, in which Lane LJ added that it is for
the *appointed* and not the *disappointed* solicitor to point out any conflict of interest. Where
the applicant's wishes are overridden by this regulation he must be assigned a solicitor

chosen by another defendant: *Baker v West Sussex Justices* (1984) 148 JP 129. This regulation does *not* override the solicitor's right to select counsel in the Crown Court: *R v O'Brien and Oliffe* (1985) 149 JP 289.

10.65 **Application in respect of legal representation**
14A. (1) An application by a legally assisted person or his solicitor for–
(a) representation by counsel in accordance with s.30(2) of the 1974 Act; or
(b) the amendment or revocation of a legal aid order under s.31 of the 1974 Act,
shall be made to the proper officer of the court.

(2) The proper officer of the court considering an application under para (1) shall–
(a) grant it; or
(b) where para (3) applies, refer it to the appropriate criminal legal aid committee; or
(c) refer it to the court.

(3) Any application under para (1) which is not granted shall be referred to a criminal legal aid committee unless–
(a) an application under the same sub-paragraph of para (1) has previously been refused by a criminal legal aid committee in the same proceedings; or
(b) the application was made–
(i) in the case of proceedings in the Crown Court, more than 14 days after the committal for trial or sentence or the date of giving of notice of appeal; or
(ii) in the case of proceedings in the magistrates' court, less than 14 days before the date fixed for trial of an information or the inquiry into an offence as examining justices, where such a date had been fixed at the time the application was made; or
(c) the application is an application in respect of proceedings in the Court of Appeal or in the House of Lords.

10.66 **Reference to criminal legal aid committee**
14B. (1) The proper officer of the court, in referring an application to a criminal legal aid committee, shall send to the secretary the following documents–
(a) a copy of the legal aid order;
(b) any papers presented to the proper officer of the court by the legally assisted person or his solicitor in support of the application; and
(c) any other relevant documents or information.

(2) The proper officer of the court and the legally assisted person or his solicitor shall supply such further particulars, information and documents as the criminal legal aid committee may require.

10.67 **Reference to criminal legal aid committee**
14C. (1) The criminal legal aid committee shall consider any application referred to it under reg 14A and any further particulars, information or documents submitted to it under reg 14B and any other relevant information and shall grant or refuse the application and, where necessary, amend or revoke the legal aid order accordingly.

(2) The criminal legal aid committee shall notify the proper officer of the court and the legally assisted person and his solicitor of its decision.

10.68 **Power of criminal legal aid committee to authorise expenditure**
14D. (1) Where it appears to a legally assisted person's solicitor necessary for the proper conduct of proceedings in a magistrates' court or in the Crown Court to incur costs by taking any of the following steps–

(a) obtaining a report or opinion of one or more experts or tendering expert evidence;

(b) employing a person to provide a report or opinion (otherwise than as an expert);

(c) bespeaking transcripts of shorthand notes or tape recordings of any proceedings, including police questioning of suspects; or

(d) performing an act which is either unusual in its nature or involves unusually large expenditure,

he may apply to the appropriate criminal legal aid committee for authority to do so.

(2) If a criminal legal aid committee authorises the taking of any step specified in para (1), it shall also authorise the maximum fee payable for any such report, opinion, expert evidence, transcript or act.

Restriction on payment   10.69

14E. Where a legal aid order has been made, the legally assisted person's solicitor or counsel shall not receive or be a party to any payment for work done in connection with the proceedings in respect of which the legal aid order was made except such payments as are made–

(a) out of the legal aid fund by the Lord Chancellor in accordance with s.37 of the 1974 Act; or

(b) in respect of any expenses or fees incurred in

(i) preparing, obtaining or considering any report, opinion or further evidence, whether provided by an expert witness or otherwise; or

(ii) bespeaking a transcript of shorthand notes or tape recordings of any proceedings, including police questioning of suspects:

provided that the assisted person's solicitor or counsel (where counsel only is assigned) has previously made an application under reg 14D for authority to incur such expenses or fees which has been refused by the criminal legal aid committee.

Powers exercisable by secretaries   10.70

14F. (1) Where a criminal legal aid committee is required or entitled to perform any function under these regulations, that function, may, subject to para (2), be performed on behalf of the committee by the secretary.

(2) Paragraph (1) shall not empower a secretary to–

(a) refuse an application to the committee under reg 14A; or

(b) refuse an application for review under reg 6(H)(1).

15. . . .

Notes of evidence and depositions   10.71

16. Where a legal aid order is made in respect of an appeal to the Crown Court, the justices' clerk shall supply, on the application of the solicitor assigned to the appellant or respondent on whose application such an order was made, copies of any notes of evidence or depositions taken in the proceedings in the magistrates' court.

Transfer of documents   10.72

17. Where a person is committed by a lower court to a higher court or appeals or applies for leave to appeal from a lower court to a higher court, the proper officer of the lower court shall send to the proper officer of the higher court the following documents (if any):–

(a) a copy of any legal aid order previously made in the same case;

(b) a copy of any contribution order previously made;

(c) a copy of any legal aid application which has been refused;

(d) any statement of means already submitted.

10.73   **Determination of contributions**
     18. (1) The court or the proper officer of the court shall, in making a legal aid order or where reg 25 applies, determine the amount of any contribution payable in respect of the costs of the legal aid by the applicant, the legally assisted person or the appropriate contributor in accordance with reg 19.

     (2) Where the applicant or the legally assisted person has paid or is liable to pay a contribution under s.4(2) of the 1974 Act in respect of legal advice and assistance in the same proceedings, any contribution he is liable to make, or an appropriate contributor is liable to make on his behalf, under s.7(1) of the 1982 Act shall be reduced by the total amount of any contribution already paid or liable to be paid under s.4(2) of the 1974 Act.

10.74

     19. (1) The court or the proper officer of the court shall consider the statement of means of the applicants, the legally assisted person or the appropriate contributor, and any other relevant information, and, subject to para (2), determine his disposable income and disposable capital in accordance with the Second Schedule.

     (2) The court or the proper officer of the court shall not determine–
     (a) disposable income and disposable capital where the applicant, the legally assisted person or the appropriate contributor is in receipt of supplementary benefit; or
     (b) disposable income where the applicant, the legally assisted person or the appropriate contributor is in receipt of family income supplement; unless he is required to make a re-determination under reg 25A below.

     (3) The applicant, the legally assisted person or the appropriate contributor shall make a contribution–
     (a) if his disposable income exceeds the average weekly sum of £48, of such an amount as shall be determined by the proper officer in accordance with the Third Schedule; and
     (b) if his disposable capital exceeds £3,000, of such an amount as is equal to the excess.

10.75   **Legal aid contribution orders**
     20. (1) The court or the proper officer of the court shall make a legal aid contribution order in respect of any contribution determined under reg 18 above.

     (2) A legal aid contribution order shall be in Form 9 in the Schedule and a copy shall be sent to the person ordered to make the contribution, to the legally assisted person's solicitor and to the collecting court.

     21. . . .

10.76   **Payment of contributions**
     22. (1) Any contribution payable out of disposable income shall be payable by weekly instalments (or, at the discretion of the court or the proper officer of the court, by two-weekly or monthly instalments) within the period not exceeding the contribution period, with the first such instalment falling due 7 days from the making of the legal aid order or of the legal aid contribution order, whichever is the later.

     (2) Any contribution payable out of disposable capital shall be paid immediately if the sum is readily available or, if it is not, at such time as the court or the proper officer of the court considers to be reasonable in all the circumstances.

     (3) Where a contribution out of disposable capital is payable immediately, the court or the proper officer of the court may withhold the legal aid order until such payment is made.

(4) Where a legal aid order is withheld under para (3), the court or the proper officer of the court shall give notice of this fact in Form 10 in the Schedule to–

(a) the assisted person or, where the application was made by his parent or guardian, the parent or guardian; and

(b) the solicitor assigned or counsel (where counsel only is assigned).

Payment of contributions 10.77

23. (1) Except where para (2) applies, contributions shall be payable to the proper officer of the collecting court.

(2) Where the legal aid order is withheld until a contribution out of disposable capital is made, such payment shall be made to the proper officer of the court making the legal aid order, unless that court otherwise directs.

Change in financial circumstances 10.78

24. The legally assisted person or the appropriate contributor shall inform the court or the proper officer of the court of any change in his financial circumstances which has occurred since the submission of his statement of means which he has reason to believe–

(a) might make him liable to pay contribution in respect of the costs of the legal aid, where such a contribution is not already payable; or

(b) might affect the terms of any legal aid contribution order made in connection with a legal aid order.

Determination where no contribution previously payable 10.79

25. The court or the proper officer of the court shall determine the amount of any contribution payable in respect of the costs of the legal aid by a legally assisted person or an appropriate contributor who is not already liable to make such a contribution where–

(a) further information has become available as to the amount of disposable income and disposable capital available at the time when the legal aid order was made; or

(b) the circumstances upon which the disposable income or disposable capital were determined at the time the legal aid order was made have altered within the contribution period:

and it appears likely that, were such determination to be made, the legally assisted person or the appropriate contributor would be liable to make a contribution in respect of the costs of the legal aid.

Redetermination of contribution 10.80

25A. The court or the proper officer of the court shall redetermine the amount of any contribution payable by a legally assisted person or an appropriate contributor under a legal aid order where–

(a) further information has become available as to the amounts of disposable income and disposable capital available at the time when the legal aid contribution order was made; or

(b) the circumstances upon which the disposable income or disposable capital were determined at the time when the legal aid contribution order was made have altered within the contribution period so that–

(i) his disposable income may have increased by an amount greater than £400 or decreased by an amount greater than £200; or

(ii) his disposable capital may have increased by an amount greater than £200;

unless it appears to be unlikely that any significant change in the liability to make a contribution would result from such a redetermination, and shall vary or revoke the legal aid contribution order accordingly.

Note at the time of going to press the Lord Chancellor had laid amending regulations before Parliament. These will add a subpara (c) to reg 25A which will require the redetermination of a contribution order where the legally assisted person or appropriate contributor has ceased to receive supplementary benefit, income support or family credit.

10.81 **Effect of error or mistake**
25B. Where it appears to the court or the proper officer of the court that there has been some error or mistake in the determination of the legally assisted person's or the appropriate contributor's disposable income, disposable capital or contribution and that it would be just and equitable to correct the error or mistake, the court or the proper officer of the court may vary or revoke the legal aid contribution order accordingly.

10.82 **Variation and revocation of legal aid contribution orders**
25C. (1) Where the legal aid contribution order is revoked or varied to an amount less than that already paid the court or the proper officer of the court shall order the repayment of any sum paid or overpaid as the case may be.

(2) Where–
(a) the legal aid contribution order is varied to an amount greater than that previously payable; or
(b) a legal aid contribution order is made after a determination under reg 25,
and any payment is to be made out of disposable income, the court or the proper officer of the court may, for the purposes of such payment, extend the period provided in reg 22 within which such payment must be made.

(3) An order varying or revoking a legal aid contribution order shall be in Form 11 in the Schedule and a copy of it shall be sent to the person ordered to make the contribution, to the legally assisted person's solicitor and to the proper officer of the collecting court.

10.83 **Refusal to pay contributions**
25D. (1) When any sums due under a legal aid contribution order before the conclusion of the proceedings have not been paid by the legally assisted person, the court or the proper officer of the court may–
(a) serve notice on the legally assisted person requiring him to comply with the legal aid contribution order and pay any sums due under it within 7 days of receiving such notice; and
(b) if he does not do so, serve notice on him inviting him to make representations giving reasons for not complying with the legal aid contribution order.

(2) A notice under para (1)(a) shall be in Form 12 and a notice under para (1)(b) in Form 13 in the Schedule and copies shall be sent to the legally assisted person and to his solicitor or counsel (where counsel only is assigned).

(3) The court shall consider any representations made under para 1(b) above and, if satisfied that it would be just so to do, may revoke the legal aid order in accordance with s.9(3) of the 1982 Act.

10.83a **Termination of contribution period**
(1) Where the contribution period has not ended and–
(a) the court remits any sum due under a legal aid contribution order which falls to be paid after the conclusion of the relevant proceedings;
(b) the legally assisted person is sentenced to an immediate term of imprisonment or a sentence of youth custody or detention in a detention centre; or
(c) the legally assisted person or an appropriate contributor begins to receive supplementary benefit, income support or family credit (in this regulation referred to as 'income-related benefits'),
the contribution period shall be deemed to have ended on the date of that remission or sentence or on the date receipt of income-related benefits commenced.

(2) The court making any such remission or passing any such sentence shall inform the collecting court that the contribution period is to be deemed to have ended on the date of that remission or sentence.

(3) Without prejudice to regulation 24, the legally assisted person or appropriate contributor shall inform the collecting court of the date on which receipt of income-related benefits commenced.

Repayment of contributions 10.84
26A. The collecting court or the proper officer of the collecting court, on receiving notification of the amount of the costs of the legal aid determined by the appropriate authority under the 1982 Regulations, shall, in accordance with s.7(6) of the 1982 Act, repay to the legally assisted person or the appropriate contributor, as the case may be, the amount, if any, by which any contribution paid exceeds those costs.

Recovery of costs 10.85
27. Where a court makes an order that the costs of a legally aided person shall be paid by any other person, the proper officer of that court shall notify the authority from whose funds the costs of legal aid are to be paid or, in the case of an order made by a magistrates' court, the Law Society, of the order and of the name and address of the person by whom the costs are to be paid.

Enforcement of orders for payment of costs 10.86
28. Where a person ordered to pay the costs of a legally aided person does not pay them in accordance with s.79(1) of the Act, they may be recovered summarily by the aforesaid authority referred to in reg 27 of these Regulations or the Law Society, as the case may be, as a sum adjudged to be paid as a civil debt by order of a magistrates' court.

Notification of fund into which costs are to be paid 10.87
29. Where any court makes such an order as is referred to in reg 27 of these Regulations, the court shall cause the person against whom the order is made to be informed of the fund into which the payment must be made in accordance with s.79(1) of the Act.

Legal aid records 10.88
30. (1) The proper officer of each court shall keep a record, in the manner and form directed from time to time by the Lord Chancellor of all cases in which an application for legal aid was made to the court or a legal aid order was made under reg 5 of these Regulations, by the court without application; and shall send to the Lord Chancellor such information from such record as the Lord Chancellor shall from time to time direct.

Interpretation 10.89
31. (1) In these Regulations, unless the context otherwise requires–
'the Act' means the Criminal Justice Act 1967;
'the 1974 Act' means the Legal Aid Act 1974;
'the 1982 Act' means the Legal Aid Act 1982;
'applicant' means, in relation to an application for legal aid made on behalf of a person who has not attained the age of 17 years by his parent or guardian, that person and in the case of any other application for legal aid the person making the application;
'appropriate authority' means an officer or body authorised to determine costs under the 1982 Regulations;
'appropriate contributor' has the meaning assigned to it by s.84(1) of the Act;
'appropriate criminal legal aid committee' means the criminal legal aid committee in whose area is situated the court to which an application for or concerning a legal aid order has been made;

'collecting court' has the meaning assigned to it by s.32(5) of the 1974 Act;
'contribution' means a payment in respect of the costs of the legal aid;
'contribution period' means the period of 6 months commencing with the date of the making of the legal aid order;
'Court of Appeal' means the criminal division of the Court of Appeal;
'criminal legal aid committee' means a criminal legal aid committee appointed by the Council of the Law Society under the provisions of a scheme made under s.15 of the 1974 Act;
'disposable capital' means capital calculated in accordance with the Second Schedule which is available for the making of a contribution;
'disposable income' means income calculated in accordance with the Second Schedule which is available for the making of a contribution;
'family income supplement' means any supplement under the Family Income Supplements Act 1970;
'guardian' has the same meaning as in s.87 of the Child Care Act 1980;
'judge of the court' means–
  (i) in the case of the Court of Appeal, a Lord Justice of Appeal or a judge of the Queen's Bench Division of the High Court;
  (ii) in the case of the Crown Court, a judge of the High Court, a circuit judge, a recorder or an assistant recorder;
'justices clerk' includes a person duly authorised by the justices' clerk to act on the justices' clerk's behalf to the extent that he is so authorised;
'legal aid contribution order' means an order made under s.7(1) of the 1982 Act;
'legal aid fund' has the meaning assigned to it by s.84 of the Act;
'legal aid order' means an order made under s.73 of the Act and includes an order made solely for the purpose described in s.74(8) of the Act;
'legally assisted person' has the meaning assigned to it by s.73(9) of the Act;
'person concerned' means the person whose disposable income and disposable capital are to be determined or the person whose resources are to be treated as the resources of any other person under these Regulations;
'proper officer' means the Clerk of the Parliaments, the Registrar of Criminal Appeals, the appropriate officer of the Crown Court or the justices' clerk (as the case may be);
'Registrar' means the Registrar of Criminal Appeals;
'the 1982 Regulations' means the Legal Aid in Criminal Proceedings (Costs) Regulations 1982;
'secretary' means the secretary of the appropriate criminal legal aid committee and includes any person duly authorised to act on the secretary's behalf to the extent that he is so authorised;
'statement of means' means a statement of means submitted in accordance with reg 4 of these Regulations;
'supplementary benefit' means supplementary benefit under the Supplementary Benefits Act 1976.

(1A) An applicant who attains the age of 16 years after the date on which the application is made shall be treated for the purposes of these Regulations as not having attained that age.

(2) The Interpretation Act 1978 shall apply to the interpretation of these Regulations as it applies to the interpretation of an Act of Parliament.

(3) Any reference in these Regulations to an enactment is a reference thereto as amended.

10.90   **Determination in private and in absence of legally assisted person**
  32. Where it is provided by these regulations that any matter may be determined otherwise than by a court, it may be determined in private and in the absence of the applicant or legally assisted person or appropriate contributor.

SECOND SCHEDULE

Part 1: General 10.91

1. (1) In computing the disposable income and disposable capital of the person concerned the resources of any spouse of his shall be treated as his resources unless–

(a) the person concerned and the spouse are living separate and apart; or

(b) the spouse has a contrary interest in the proceedings in respect of which an application for legal aid has been made; or

(c) in all the circumstances of the case it would be inequitable to do so.

(2) If the spouse fails to provide information as to his resources at the request of the proper officer, the proper officer may make an estimate, on the basis of any information then available, of the likely resources of the spouse.

2. If it appears to the proper officer that the person concerned has with intent to reduce the amount of his disposable income or disposable capital–

(a) directly or indirectly deprived himself of any resources; or

(b) converted any part of his resources into resources which under these regulations are to be wholly or partly disregarded, or in respect of which nothing is to be included in determining the resources of that person;

the resources of which he has so deprived himself or which he has so converted shall be treated as part of his resources or as not so converted as the case may be.

Part II: Disposable Income 10.92

1. (1) The income of the person concerned shall be that which he received during the contribution period.

(2) The income received during the contribution period may be estimated on the basis of the income received by the person concerned during the three months prior to the commencement of the contribution period.

2. (1) Income from any trade, business or gainful occupation other than employment at a wage or salary shall be the profit therefrom which accrues during the contribution period.

(2) The income received during the contribution period may be estimated on the basis of the profits made in the last accounting period for which accounts have been made up.

3. In computing disposable income there shall be disregarded–

(a) attendance allowance paid under the Social Security Acts 1975–1980;

(b) mobility allowance paid under the Social Security Acts 1975–1980;

(c) any rebate or allowance paid under Part II of the Social Security and Housing Benefits Act 1982 and any rebate; and

(d) constant attendance allowance paid as an increase to a disablement pension under s.61 of the Social Security Act 1975.

4. In computing disposable income there shall be deducted–

(a) the total amount of any tax payable on that income;

(b) the total amount of any contribution payable under the Social Security Acts 1975–1980;

(c) reasonable expenses of travelling to and from the place of employment;

(d) the amount of any contribution paid, whether under a legal obligation or not, to an occupational pension scheme within the meaning of the Social Security Pension Act 1975; and

(e) reasonable expenses in respect of the making of reasonable provision for the care of any dependant child living with the person concerned because of that person's absence from home by reason of employment.

5. In computing disposable income there shall be a deduction in respect of the main or only dwelling in the case of a householder of the amount of the net rent payable, or such part thereof as is reasonable in the circumstances.

(2) In this rule 'rent' means–

(a) the annual rent payable; and

(b) a sum in respect of yearly outgoings borne by the householder including in particular, rates, a reasonable allowance towards any necessary expenditure on repairs and insurance and any annual instalment (whether of interest or of capital) payable in respect of a mortgage debt or heritable security charged on the house in which the householder resides or has an interest therein.

(3) Where any amount of the rent or rates is met by a rebate or allowance under Part II of the Social Security and Housing Benefits Act 1982, or by any rate rebate, the amount so met shall be deducted from the rent to be considered under para (1) of this rule.

6. If the person concerned is not a householder, there shall be a deduction in respect of the costs of his living accommodation of such an amount as is reasonable in the circumstances.

7. (1) In computing disposable income, there shall be a deduction in respect of the maintenance of the spouse of the person concerned, if the spouses are living together, in respect of the maintenance of any dependant child and in respect of the maintenance of any dependant relative of the person concerned being (in either of such cases) a member of his household at the following rates–

(a) in the case of a spouse at the rate equivalent to 25 per cent above the amount specified for the time being in col (3) of para 6 of Part IV of Sch.4 to the Social Security Act 1975 (increase for adult dependant of Category A retirement pension); and

(b) in the case of a dependant child or a dependant relative, at the rate equivalent to 25 per cent above the amount specified for the time being in para 3 of Sch.1 to the Supplementary Benefit (Requirements) Regulations 1980 appropriate to the age of the child or relative;

provided that the proper officer may reduce such rate by taking into account the income and other resources of the dependant child or other dependant to such extent as appears to the officer to be just and equitable.

(2) In ascertaining whether a child is a dependant child and whether a person is a dependant relative regard shall be had to their income and other resources.

8. If a person concerned is making and, throughout such period as the proper officer may consider adequate, has regularly made bona fide payments for the maintenance of a spouse who is living apart, of a former spouse, of a child or of a relative who is not (in any such cases) a member of the household of the person concerned there shall be a deduction at the rate of such payments or at such rate, not exceeding the rate of such payments, as in all the circumstances is reasonable.

9. In computing disposable income, there shall be a deduction in respect of any sum or sums payable by the person concerned under an order made by or arising from any conviction before the High Court, county court, Crown Court or a magistrates' court in proceedings otherwise that those in respect of which the legal aid order was granted.

10. Where the person must or may reasonably provide for any other matter the proper officer may make an allowance of such amount he considers to be reasonable in the circumstances of the case.

11. In computing the income from any source there shall be disregarded such amount, if any, as the proper officer considers to be reasonable having regard to the nature of the income or to any other circumstances of the case.

10.93   **Part III: Disposable Capital**

1. (1) In computing the capital of the person concerned there shall be included the amount or value of every resource of a capital nature belonging to him on the date of the assessment.

(2) So far as any such resource does not consist of money, the amount or value thereof shall be taken to be the amount which that resource would realise if sold in the open market, or if there is only a restricted market for the resource, the amount which it would realise in that market, after deduction of any expenses incurred in the sale, or if such amount cannot be ascertained, an amount which appears to the proper officer to be reasonable.

2. In computing such capital there shall be disregarded–
(a) a death grant payable to a person under s.32 of the Social Security Act 1975;
(b) any maternity grant payable under s.21 of the Social Security Act 1975;
(c) any savings of mobility allowance paid under the Social Security Act 1975 which the person concerned intended to use in connection with mobility; and
(d) for a period not exceeding 12 months from the date of receipt, any arrears of–
   (i) attendance or mobility allowance under the Social Security Act 1975; and
   (ii) supplementary benefit.

3. Save where it is reasonable in the circumstances, nothing shall be included in the amount of capital of the person concerned in respect of the value of the assets of any business owned in whole or party by him.

4. Save in exceptional circumstances, nothing shall be included in the amount of capital of the person in respect of–
(a) the household furniture and effects of the main or only residence occupied by him;
(b) articles of personal clothing; and
(c) the personal tools and equipment of his trade.

5. In computing the amount of capital of the person concerned, the value of any interest in the main or only residence in which he resides shall be wholly disregarded.

6. In computing such capital there shall be disregarded such an amount of capital, if any, as the proper officer considers to be reasonable having regard to the nature of the capital or to any other circumstances of the case.

THIRD SCHEDULE

Contributions from disposable income   **10.94**
The weekly instalment payable by the applicant or the appropriate contributor under s.7(1) of the 1982 Act, where his disposable income falls within a range specified in the first column of the following table, is the amount specified in relation to that range in the second column.

Average Disposable Income			Weekly Contribution	**10.95**
Exceeding £50 but not exceeding	£56		£1	
£56	£60		£2	
£60	£64		£3	
£64	£68		£4	
£68	£72		£5	
£72	£76		£6	
£76	£80		£7	
£80	£84		£8	
£84	£88		£9	
£88	£92		£10	
£92	£96		£11	
£96	£100		£12	
£100	£104		£13	
£104	£108		£14	
£108	£112		£15	

The weekly instalment shall be increased by £1 for each £4 or part of £4 by which disposable income exceeds £112.

CHAPTER 11

Appeals

Appeals

11.00
INTRODUCTION

There are three principal avenues via which decisions of magistrates may be questioned: appeal to the Crown Court, appeal to the High Court by way of *case stated* and applications to the High Court for *judicial review*. Occasionally, the High Court has also been prepared to grant a *declaration* concerning some aspect of the law affecting criminal procedure, although it cannot, as yet, be said that any well established rules exist concerning the existence of this particular 'remedy' in relation to criminal proceedings.

11.01
APPEAL TO THE CROWN COURT

A person *convicted* by a magistrates' court may appeal to the Crown Court, if he *pleaded guilty, against sentence*, and if he pleaded *not guilty, against conviction and sentence* s.108 MCA 1980, 'Sentence' is defined in s.108(3) as including, with certain exceptions, any order made on conviction. Other orders of magistrates may be the subject of separate rights of appeal: see, for example, the Magistrates' Courts (Appeal from Binding Over Orders) Act 1956. Appeal is made by giving *written notice* to the magistrates' clerk and to the prosecutor not later than *21 days* after the day on which the decision appealed against was given r.7(3) Crown Court Rules 1982. Where the hearing was adjourned after conviction *time runs from the date of sentence*; but this period may be extended by the Crown Court: r.7(5).

Justices have a right to appear at the appeal and support their decision without rendering themselves liable to costs: *R v Kent Justices, ex p. Commissioner of Metropolitan Police* (1936) 100 JP 17; *R v Goodall and Others, Sussex Justices* (1874) 38 JP 616.

Appeal is by way of rehearing. The powers of the Crown Court are set out in s.48 Supreme Court Act 1981. While the Crown Court may *increase* sentence, it may not exceed the magistrates' maximum powers. Neither may it adjourn until the appellant is aged 21 so as to avoid the statutory restriction (s.1(1) CJA 1982) on imposing imprisonment, including a suspended sentence, on persons who were below that age at the time when they appeared before the magistrates: *Arthur v Stringer* (1986) *The Times*, 11 October. Section 48 gives the Crown Court power to 'confirm, reverse or vary' the *whole* of the decision of the magistrates' court on the occasion that sentence was imposed; whether the defendant chooses to appeal against the whole or only part of the decision: *Dutta v Westcott* (1986) 8 Cr App R (S) 191 (attempt to appeal only the traffic offence for which disqualified so as to take advantage of penalty points system). *Note* the effect of [s.148] CJA 1988 which, when in force, amends s.48(2) Supreme Court Act 1981 so that the Crown Court will be able to alter any part of the decision of the justices including 'a determination not to impose a separate penalty': see 11.20 and Appendix III.

Decisions are *enforced* by the magistrates' courts, except in so far as they are dealt with by process already issued: s.110 MCA 1980.

An appeal to the Crown Court may be abandoned by notice in writing to the clerk and prosecutor not later than the third day before the day fixed for hearing: r.11 Crown Court Rules 1982; and failing this the Crown Court may itself grant *leave* to abandon: *ibid*. If there is no abandonment and the appellant fails to appear, the Crown Court may proceed to hear the appeal in his absence, even increasing the sentence if appropriate: see *R v Guildford Crown Court, ex p. Brewer* (1987) *The Times*, 26 October. For the effect of abandonment see s.109 MCA 1980.

There is no corresponding right of appeal to the Crown Court on the part of the prosecutor. However, such an appeal may, rarely, be conferred by statute as eg by s.283(4) Customs and Excise Act 1952, and s.78 Animal Health Act 1981.

The death of the informant does not abate the appeal: *R v Truelove* (1880) 44 JP 346.

It was held in *Hawkins v Bepey and Others* [1980] 1 WLR 419, that the death of the police officer who had preferred the information did not cause the appeal to lapse when the officer was acting on behalf of the chief constable whose order he had to obey.

APPEAL BY WAY OF CASE STATED   11.02

Any party or any person *aggrieved* by the conviction, order, determination or other proceeding of a magistrates' court may question any proceeding before a magistrates' court on the ground that it is *wrong in law* or is in *excess of jurisdiction* by applying to the justices to state a case for the opinion of the High Court: s.111 MCA 1980, but not where the issue is essentially one of fact: see *James v Chief Constable of Kent* (1986) *The Times*, 7 June. The justices may refuse to state a case where they consider the application *frivolous*: s.111(5). If they agree to state a case, they may require the appellant to enter into recognisances conditioned for the prosecution of his appeal: s.114; but justices must have regard to the applicant's means in fixing the amount of this recognisance, and in deciding whether to fix any recognisance at all; *R v Newcastle upon Tyne Justices ex p. Skinner* (1986) 150 JPN 783. There is no statutory procedure for abandonment analogous to that in s.109, nor have magistrates power to order costs against an appellant who fails to prosecute his appeal. They may however forfeit his recognisance under s.120.

When there is a *denial of natural justice* the correct remedy is *not* case stated, but judicial review: *R v Wandsworth Justices, ex p. Read* [1942] 1 KB 281; and see *R v Dorking Justices, ex p. Harrington* [1983] 3 WLR 370. Magistrates have no power to state a case on an interlocutory matter. The following advice concerning the relationship and interaction of the two remedies was given by May LJ in *Streames v Copping* (1985) 148 JP 305 at 310:

'Where either party contends that justices have no jurisdiction to hear and determine an information or complaint, and the justices uphold that contention, then the remedy available to the party aggrieved is to ask for leave to apply for judicial review seeking a finding from the Divisional Court that the justices were wrong to decline jurisdiction and an order for mandamus directing them to hear the information or complaint. Where, upon such a contention, justices decide that they do have jurisdiction to hear and dispose of the matter, they should not accede to an application there and then by the party against whom they have decided to adjourn any further hearing and state a case on the jurisdiction point. They should in general proceed to hear and determine the matter before them on whatever evidence is adduced and then, if either party is dissatisfied, he can apply to the justices to state a case under s.111(1). The party against whom the justices decided that they did have jurisdiction at the outset of course always has the concurrent right to apply to the Divisional Court for leave to seek judicial review in the nature of prohibition. In some cases, if the party aggrieved did take that course, it might be desirable for the justices to adjourn their further hearing of the substantive matter until after the determination of the judicial review proceedings; in most cases, however, nothing will be lost if the justices do complete their hearing. It may be that on the facts they will decide the substantive issue in favour of the party contending that they had had no jurisdiction. If they do not, then all the issues can be determined by the Divisional Court on a case stated, at a substantial saving of time and money. Apart from questions of jurisdiction, where justices are asked to, and do rule on a point of law in the course of a hearing before them – for instance, on a question of the admission of evidence, or the construction of a statute or document – they should not at that stage, with nothing more, accede to an application by the party against whom they have ruled for an adjournment and for them to state what I can describe as an 'interlocutory' case. If they purport to do so, then for the reasons I have given I do not think that this court has jurisdiction to hear it. The justices, having made their ruling, should complete the hearing and determination of the matter before them, and then state a case thereafter if they are asked to do so. In a very special instance, if the party aggrieved sought and obtained leave to apply for prohibition, then the justices might be wise to adjourn the matter pending the hearing of the application for judicial review, but they should not state a case under s.111(1) until after their final determination of the information or complaint before them.'

See also Lord Reid in *Atkinson v US Government* [1969] 3 All ER 1317 at 1324; and *Piggott v Simms* [1972] Crim LR 595; *Davies v May* (1937) 101 JP 250.

A *sentence* outside the normal limits of discretion may be an error of law which can be challenged by way of case stated: *Universal Salvage Ltd and Robinson v Boothby* (1984) 148 JP 347 (maximum penalty imposed despite a finding that the defendant believed on reasonable grounds he was acting lawfully); applying *R v St Alban's Crown Court, ex p. Cinnamond* (1981) 145 JP 277; and see *R v Tottenham Justices, ex p. Joshi* (1982) 4 Cr App R (S) 19. However, since there is a statutory framework for appeals from the sentence of a magistrates' court in the course of which the Crown Court has full power to review sentence *certiorari* may be refused except where that procedure does not exist or has been exhausted: *R v Battle Magistrates' Court, ex p. Shepherd and Another* (1983) 5 Cr App R (S) 124.

An application to state a case must be made within 21 days after the day on which the decision of the magistrates' court was given: s.111(2) MCA 1980. It must be *in writing* signed by or on behalf of the applicant and it must *identify the question or questions of law or jurisdiction on which the opinion of the High Court is sought:* r.77(1) MC Rules 1981. Thereafter the drawing up of the case proceeds by strictly regulated time limits contained in rr.77, 79 MC Rules 1981. Once received by the appellant the case must be lodged with the Crown Office within 10 days and within four days of lodging notice of entry a copy of the case must be served on the respondent: RSC Order 56, r.6. A single Judge has jurisdiction to extend the time for lodging a case: *Devlin v F* [1982] 2 All ER 450. Application is by originating motion RSC Order 56, r.8. The appeal is heard by a Divisional Court of the Queen's Bench Division: r.5. It has power to send the case back for amendment: s.10 Summary Jurisdiction Act 1857. The magistrates have *no right to be heard* at the appeal: *Smith v Smith* (1886) 50 JP 260.

Once a defendant has applied for a case to be stated *he forfeits his right to appeal to the Crown Court,* s.111(4) MCA 1980.

The appellant is not to be deprived of his right to appeal merely by reason of the prosecutor's death: *Garnsworthy v Pyne* (1870) 35 JP 21. A case was struck out where the respondent had died before argument: *Finchley UDC v Blyton* (1913) 77 JPN 556 (but without reference to *Garnsworthy v Pyne, supra*). In *Hodgson v Lakeman* (1943) 107 JP 27, the Divisional Court held that they had jurisdiction to allow the appellant's executors to proceed with his appeal after his death. But there must be some legal interest, such as a pecuniary penalty, to justify the action of the executor and a sentence of imprisonment is not enough: *R v Rowe* [1955] 1 QB 573.

The powers of the High Court in respect of a case stated are set out in s.6 Summary Jurisdiction Act 1857, which provides *inter alia* that the magistrates shall not be liable to costs (but see the note to that section). The order is enforceable as if it were a decision of the magistrates' court: s.112 MCA 1980.

JUDICIAL REVIEW   11.03

The High Court also exercises a controlling jurisdiction over the actions of magistrates by way of the prerogative orders of *mandamus, prohibition* and *certiorari* (formerly prerogative writs of the same names: s.11 Administration of Justice (Miscellaneous Provisions) Act 1933. A prerogative order is obtained by way of an *application for judicial review* under RSC Order 53. The leave of the court must first be obtained under r.3. Application must be made promptly and *normally within three months* from the date when grounds for the application first arose: r.4. Application is by originating motion to a Divisional Court of the Queen's Bench Division: r.5.

When the facts are complicated it is far more convenient if appeal is by way of case stated, rather than judicial review: *R v Felixstowe Justices, ex p. Baldwin* (1980) 22 October, unreported. All the prerogative orders are discretionary remedies, so that even if all else 'succeeds', the remedy may yet be denied by the High Court: see eg *R v Lewes Magistrates' Court, ex p. Oldfield* (1987) *The Times,* 6 May, where a prosecutor was refused judicial review although it was held that the justices had erred in dismissing 42 summonses – due to the overall delay in getting matters before the High Court. It has been said that 'judicial review is concerned, not with the decision, but with the decision making process': per Lord Brightman in *Chief Constable of North Wales v Evans* [1982] 1 WLR 1155.

Mandamus   11.04

The order of *mandamus* is appropriate when the High Court is asked to

compel an inferior tribunal such as a magistrates' court to perform its
duty, eg where it has wrongly declined jurisdiction. *Mandamus* will not be
granted in committal proceedings to review the decisions of the magistrate (in this case allowing a particular line of cross examination) until the
proceedings have run their course: *R v Wells Street Stipendiary Magistrate, ex p. Seillon* [1978] 3 All ER 257.

11.05   *Prohibition*

Prohibition may be used to *restrain* magistrates from exceeding their
jurisdiction so long as the matter is still capable of being corrected and has
not been finally determined: *R v North, ex p. Oakey* (1927) 43 TLR 60.
Prohibition has been granted to prevent oppressive and unfair prosecutions: *R v Cwmbran Justices, ex p. Pope* (1979) 143 JP 638. But the
High Court will be slow to exercise this jurisdiction where the allegation is
of oppressive and vexatious process, if only because the justices themselves have ample power to stop the proceedings: *R v Bury Justices, ex p.
Anderton* (1987) *The Times*, 4 April.

11.06   *Certiorari*

An order of *certiorari* issues to *remove* to the High Court any decision or
action of justices for review where there can be demonstrated an *excess of
jurisdiction, an error of law* or *a denial of natural justice: R v West Sussex
Quarter Sessions, ex p. Albert and Maud Johnson Trust Ltd* (1973) 137 JP
784. Instead of quashing a conviction upon which an unlawful sentence
was imposed the High Court may amend the conviction by substituting
any sentence which the magistrates' courts had power to impose: s.16
Administration of Justice Act 1960; *R v Birmingham Justices, ex p. Wyatt*
[1975] 3 All ER 897.

   Certiorari will not be granted if an objection was not taken before the
court below, unless the party was unaware of the absence of jurisdiction:
R v Inner London Quarter Sessions, ex p. D'Souza (1969) 54 Cr App R
193. Thus *certiorari* will not issue where a defendant, knowing that a
justice was interested in the proceedings failed to take objection before
the magistrates' court: *R v Byles ex p. Hollidge* (1912) 77 JP 40. But
certiorari has been issued where no point was taken but the applicant
later discovered that evidence was wholly unreliable: *R v Kingston upon
Thames Justices ex p. Khana* (1985) *The Times*, 21 November (faulty
calibration of intoximeter); and see *R v Knightsbridge Crown Court, ex p.
Goonatilleke* [1986] 1 QB 1 (police officer dismissed for 'disgraceful
conduct' and who had later committed offences of dishonety said in
evidence that he had no particular reason for leaving the police); and see
R v Liverpool Crown Court ex p. Roberts [1986] Crim LR 622 (failure by
prosecution to declare 'previous inconsistent statement').

   Certiorari will not issue as a matter of course where there is a more
convenient statutory remedy: *R v Brighton Justices, ex p. Robinson*
[1973] 1 WLR 69. (cases heard without defendant's knowledge may be
reopened under s.14(1) MCA 1980). In *R v Wells St Justices, ex p. Collett*
[1981] RTR 272 *certiorari* was refused where the accused had not availed
herself of the remedy in s.142 MCA 1980, (power to rectify mistakes).

   A mistakenly announced 'conviction' by justices following a submission of no case to answer does not make them *functi officio* and
certiorari is therefore unnecessary: *R v Midhurst Justices, ex p. Thompson
and Another* (1974) 138 JP 359. *Certiorari* was issued to quash a conviction where there was no fault on the part of the magistrates, merely the

prosecutor, on the basis that this had caused a clear denial of natural justice: *R v Leyland Justices, ex p. Hawthorn* (1979) 68 Cr App R 269.

Certiorari will *not* issue where a conflict of evidence has to be resolved: *R v Abingdon (County) Magistrates' Court, ex p. Leonard Arthur Clifford* [1978] Crim LR 165.

The High Court will not interfere by way of *certiorari* while proceedings before a magistrate are in progress and not yet finally determined, whether those proceedings are committal proceedings: (*R v Carden* (1879) QBD 1; *R v Highbury Corner Magistrates' Court, ex p. Boyce* (1984) 148 JP 420) or summary trial (*R v Rochford Justices, ex p. Buck* (1979) 68 Cr App R 114). *Certiorari* may be used to correct a breach of the rules of natural justice even when this constitutes a refusal to grant an adjournment: *R v Thames Magistrates' Court, ex p. Polemis* [1974] 1 WLR 1371. *Certiorari* as a remedy for excessively long adjournments cannot be ruled out: see *R v Ali* (1987) *The Times*, 6 July.

However, unless the proceedings are a *nullity*, the High Court will not interfere by way of judicial review to upset an acquittal: *R v Dorking Justices, ex p. Harrington* [1983] 3 WLR 370; and see *R v Cardiff Magistrates' Court ex p. Cardiff City Council* (1987) *The Times*, 24 February where *certiorari* was granted to quash an acquittal on the basis of nullity where the justices had failed to put the defendant to his election under the mode of trial provisions of ss.18 to 23 MCA 1980. Where proceedings are *not a* nullity, the appropriate remedy is an appeal *by way of case stated, semble.*

The justices may make and file an affidavit setting forth the grounds of the decision and any material facts: s.2 Review of Justices' Decisions Act 1872, but if they appear by counsel they may be liable in costs. In a circular letter dated 17 June 1981 the Lord Chancellor's Secretary of Commissions reminded justices' clerks that it is generally unnecessary and even undesirable for the justices to be represented, but that if the Divisional Court indicates that they should be, the Treasury Solicitor will normally make the necessary arrangements. When justices have appeared at the suggestion of the court and costs have been awarded against them or their clerk the Lord Chancellor has power at his discretion to defray such costs out of moneys provided by Parliament. (s.54(2) Justices of the Peace Act 1979).

DECLARATION 11.07

Where eg proceedings are conducted under the *Written Plea* procedure provided for by s.12 MCA 1980 (see Chapter 5), the rectification powers under s.142 MCA 1980 are not available. The accused is not 'found guilty' as required by s.142(2), and the power to re-open a case to rectify mistakes does not apply where proceedings are a complete nullity (see, generally, Chapter 8). In arriving at these conclusions, the Divisional Court in *R v Epping and Ongar Justices, ex p. C. Shippam Ltd* (1986) 150 JP 425, went on to consider what remedy might exist. Woolf LJ quoted with approval the following words of Connor LJ in *R v Seisdon Justices, ex p. Derek Dougan* [1983] 1 All ER 6, where a failure to notify a defendant of an adjourned hearing date following which magistrates had proceeded in the defendant's absence – but where the case was outside the 28 day limit provided for in s.142 – had resulted in a *declaration* of nullity being granted:

'. . . Because of the failure to comply with the provisions of the 1980 Act and Rules . . . the purported trial was a nullity and the justices were entitled to do what they proposed to do, namely to make provision to hear the case again. That being the position, the proper remedy in this court (is) to grant a declaration, rather than to quash the conviction because there was no conviction to quash . . . the proceedings . . . were a nullity and the justices were free to restore the case for hearing according to law'.

In *ex p. Shippam, supra*, Woolf LJ said '. . . It seems that those words would equally apply here. Having regard to the fact that that court granted a declaration that the conviction was a nullity, it appears to me that the appropriate remedy here is to grant the application; not to make the order for *certiorari* but to grant a declaration . . . It should not, however, be thought, by reason of the fact that I consider the appropriate remedy to be a declaration, to be indicating that the result would be any different if in fact the court was to grant an order of *certiorari*'. By this, Woolf LJ was indicating that the magistrates were free to deal with the matter afresh on the basis of the original information, *semble*.

Thus, whilst the full scope of the *declaration* in relation to criminal proceedings remains uncertain, the existence of the remedy cannot be discounted in relation to nullity. But if by nullity is meant that proceedings are *void* as opposed to *voidable*, it is an open question whether magistrates cannot simply proceed to treat them as such under their inherent discretion. The passage quoted from *ex p. Dougan supra*, suggests that this course is permissible, though it must be recognised that a *declaration* guarantees the position. In contrast, *certiorari* was granted in respect of an acquittal held to be a nullity (failure to observe the 'mode of trial' provisions) in *R v Cardiff Magistrates' Court, ex p. Cardiff City Council* (1987) *The Times*, 24 February.

A declaration was granted, in a different context, in *R v Felixstowe Justices, ex p. Leigh* (1987) 151 JP 65 (see *The rule against anonymity*, Chapter 1), to declare unlawful the withholding of justices' identities to *bona fide* inquirers.

11.08   **BAIL ON APPEAL**

After an appellant has given notice of appeal to the Crown Court *or* has applied to a magistrates' court to state a case, the magistrates may release him on bail: s.113 MCA 1980. Magistrates have no power to grant bail pending the hearing of an application for a prerogative order: *Blythe v Lancaster Appeal Committee* [1944] 1 All ER 587. The *general right to bail* does not apply to bail pending appeal: see s.4 Bail Act 1976; Chapter 3.

The High Court has power to admit to bail anyone refused bail by magistrates or offered it on unacceptable terms: s.22 CJA 1967; also anyone convicted and sentenced by a magistrates' court who has applied for an order of *certiorari* or who has applied for leave to make such application: s.37 CJA 1948. The Crown Court may grant bail to anyone who has appealed to it: s.81 Supreme Court Act 1981.

SUMMARY JURISDICTION ACT 1857

11.09   **Superior Court to determine the questions on the case**
        6. The Court to which a case is transmitted under the Magistrates' Courts Act 1980, shall hear and determine the question or questions of law arising thereon, and shall thereupon reverse, affirm, or amend the determination in respect of which the case has been stated, or remit the matter to the justice or justices, with the opinion of the Court thereon, or may make such other order in relation to the matter, and may make such orders as to costs, as to the Court may seem fit; and except as provided by the Administration of Justice Act 1960, all such orders shall be final and conclusive on all parties. Provided always, that no justice or justices of the peace, who shall state and deliver a case in pursuance of the Magistrates' Courts Act 1980, shall be liable to any

costs in respect or by reason of such appeal against his or their determination. [*As amended by s.131 MCA 1952, s.19(1) Administration of Justice Act 1960, Sch.7 MCA 1980*].

COMMENTARY

See generally under *Appeal by way of Case Stated* at 11.02. The authority and jurisdiction vested in a superior court by this section may be exercised by a judge in chambers s.8 of the Act. *Certiorari* is not necessary for a case to be stated: *ibid*, s.10.

For the court's power to award costs see Chapter 9, *Costs*.

Appeal from the decision of the High Court lies, with leave, to the House of Lords, where a point of law of *general public importance* is involved: s.1 Administration of Justice Act 1960.

Shall hear and determine, the High Court have power, on application, to send a case back to the justices to repair an omission: *Yorkshire Tyre and Axle Co v Rotherham Board of Health* (1858) 22 JP 625; *Christie v St Luke's Chelsea* (1858) 22 JP 496; *Townsend v Read* (1861) 25 JP 455; *Spicer v Warbey* (1953) 117 JP 92.

Remit the matter to the magistrates, who can be *compelled* to act thereupon by *mandamus; R v Corser* (1892) 8 TLR 563. Where the remission contains a suggestion that the case shall be heard by a fresh bench, the new bench need not begin the hearing *de novo* but may start at the moment when evidence is first called, omitting the preliminaries regarding choice of venue and the taking of the plea: *R v Bradfield and Sonning Justices, ex p. Jones* [1976] RTR 144.

There is *no power* in the High Court to order a retrial, although they may order that a hearing shall be resumed if, eg the magistrates wrongfully failed to hear the defence: *Rigby v Woodward* (1957) 121 JP 129; *Maydew v Flint* (1985) 80 Cr App R 49.

In the Irish case *R v Waterford Justices* (1900) 2 Ir R 307 it was held that when a case is remitted to justices with a direction to convict on the basis that they came to a wrong conclusion from the facts, there remains a right to appeal to quarter sessions against the findings of facts.

Make such other order, when substituting a conviction for an acquittal this provision was held to be wide enough to allow the making of an order of absolute discharge: *Coote v Winfield* [1980] RTR 42.

Costs, but see *Edge v Edwards* (1932) 96 JPN 350 (Costs awarded when the justices failed to amend the case by removing admittedly erroneous matters). Although not stated, this decision presumably rested on the fact that the justices had not 'stated and delivered a case in pursuance of' the Act.

Amendment of case   **11.10**
7. The court for the opinion of which a case is stated shall have power, if they think fit, to cause the case to be sent back for amendment and thereupon the same shall be amended accordingly, and judgment delivered after it shall have been amended.

REVIEW OF JUSTICES' DECISIONS ACT 1872

Affidavit of ground of justices' decision
2. Whenever the decision of any justice or justices is called in question in any Superior Court of Common Law by a rule to show cause or other process issued upon an ex parte application, it shall be lawful for any such justice to make and file in such court an affidavit setting forth the grounds of the decision so brought under review, and any facts which he may consider to have a material bearing upon the question at issue, without being required to pay any fee in respect of filing such affidavit and such affidavit may be forwarded by post to one of the Masters of the Court for the purpose of being so filed.

[*As amended by s.52 Statute Law Revision (No 2) Act 1893, Sch.11 Finance Act 1949*].

COMMENTARY

A dissenting justice has no right to file an affidavit: *R v Waddingham etc, Gloucestershire Justices and Tustin* (1896) 60 JPN 372.

11.11   **Consideration of affidavit**
              3. Whenever any such affidavit has been filed as aforesaid, the Court shall,
              before making the rule absolute against the justice or justices, or otherwise
              determining the matter so as to overrule or set aside the acts or decisions of the
              justice or justices to which the application relates, take into consideration the
              matter set forth in such affidavit, notwithstanding that no counsel appear on
              behalf of the said justices.

MAGISTRATES' COURTS ACT 1980

11.12   **Right of appeal to the Crown Court**
              108. (1) A person convicted by a magistrates' court may appeal to the
              Crown Court–
                  (a) if he pleaded guilty, against his sentence;
                  (b) if he did not, against the conviction or sentence.

(1A) Section 13 of the Powers of Criminal Courts Act 1973 (under which a
conviction of an offence for which a probation order or an order for conditional or absolute discharge is made is deemed not to be a conviction except for
certain purposes) shall not prevent an appeal under this section, whether
against conviction or otherwise.

(2) A person sentenced by a magistrates' court for an offence in respect of
which a probation order or an order for conditional discharge has been
previously made may appeal to the Crown Court against the sentence.

(3) In this section 'sentence' includes any order made on conviction by a
magistrates' court, not being–
    (a) *(Repealed)*
    (b) an order for the payment of costs;
    (c) an order under s.2 of the Protection of Animals Act 1911 (which enables
        a court to order the destruction of an animal); or
    (d) an order made in pursuance of any enactment under which the court has
        no discretion as to the making of the order or its terms.
[*As amended by s.66, Sch.1 CJA 1982*].

COMMENTARY

See generally under *Appeal to the Crown Court* at 11.01. The right of appeal to the Crown
Court is of statutory origin: *R v Warwickshire Justices* (1856) 20 JP 693. Save where given by
statute, the Crown Court has no jurisdiction to hear an appeal, *per* Lord Widgery CJ in *R v
Crown Court at Lewes, ex p. Rogers* [1974] 1 WLR 196. The rights given by this Act are not
in derogation of any other statutory right of appeal: *Harris v Cooke* (1918) 83 JP 72;
Mittelmann v Dennman (1920) 84 JP 30; *Cockhill v Davies* (1943) 107 JP 130; but see
s.111(4), *infra*.
    Magistrates have power to grant legal aid in an appeal to the Crown Court both to the
defendant and to 'the other party', s.28(5) Legal Aid Act.

s.108(1): Pleaded guilty, *Ambiguous plea:* The Crown Court may determine whether a
defendant's plea was correctly recorded by the magistrates: *R v Durham Quarter Sessions,
ex p. Virgo* [1952] 2 QB 1 and may then remit the case to the magistrates for rehearing as a
plea of not guilty. The terms of the order of remission are immaterial: *R v Tottenham
Justices, ex p. Rubens* [1970] 1 WLR 800. The same principles apply to appeals against
conviction following committals for sentence: *R v Fareham Justices, ex p. Long* [1976] Crim
LR 269.
    When, on appeal against sentence, a defendant wishes to change his plea to one of not
guilty, asserting that the previous guilty plea was equivocal, the Crown Court should first be
satisfied that there was credible *prima facie* evidence that the original plea was one of 'guilty,
but . . .'. If there was no such evidence that was the end of the matter and the court could
proceed to deal with the appeal against sentence. There might, however, be rare cases when
prima facie evidence of equivocality was produced. If the Crown Court then remitted the
matter to the justices with a view to a retrial, the justices, having before them their own
opinion of what happened, would be likely to say that there was no equivocality and decline
to act. Thus an unseemly conflict would arise between the two courts. It was essential that in
such cases the Crown Court should seek help from the justices by way of affidavits from the

justices' clerk or the chairman of the bench or both as to what occurred in the magistrates' court. Only when it had considered such evidence, should the Crown Court come to a conclusion as to the equivocality of the plea. It should not remit before such evidence had been considered. Cases in which it would be proper to remit were likely to be out of the ordinary; and it might well be that in most cases the proper forum for determining the question of equivocality was the Divisional Court rather than the Crown Court, *per* Lord Lane, CJ in *R v Rochdale Justices, ex p. Allwork* (1982) 146 JP 33; and see *R v Plymouth Justices, ex p. Whitton* (1980) 71 Cr App R 322. But when the ground of appeal is the ambiguity of the plea the Crown Court exceed their jurisdiction by remitting a case to magistrates with a direction that a plea of not guilty should be entered if they fail to make any inquiry to ascertain whether anything took place before the magistrates' court which would cast doubt on the plea of guilty. The inquiry in each case is was to what took place before the magistrates' court to see whether the court acted properly in accepting an apparent plea of guilty as an equivocal plea and where no such inquiry is held the magistrates act properly in refusing to accept the remission: *R v Marylebone Justices, ex p. Westminster City Council* (1971) 135 JP 239; and see *R v Coventry Crown Court, ex p. Manson* (1978) 67 Cr App R 356.

Plea under duress, when the accused is making a plea of guilty under pressure and threats he does not make a free plea and the trial starts without there being a proper plea at all: *R v Inns* (1975) 60 Cr App R 231 (pressure from the judge).

Sentence, does not include a committal in default of payment of any sum of money, or for want of sufficient distress to satisfy any sum of money, or for failure to do or abstain from doing anything required to be done or left undone: s.150(1). It includes a recommendation for deportation: s.66(5)(a) Immigration Act 1971; and see subs (3) of this section. The mere fact that the sentence is invalid does not deprive the Crown Court of the power to hear an appeal: *R v Birmingham Justices, ex p. Wyatt* [1975] 3 All ER 897.

Conviction, includes a finding of guilt in respect of a juvenile, s.59 CYPA 1933.

s.108(3): Order made on conviction, this means an order made as a consequence of conviction and not simply at the time of conviction: *R v London Sessions Appeal Committee, ex p. Beaumont* [1951] 1 KB 557; *R v Harmann* [1959] 2 All ER 738. Thus, it excludes a binding over to be of good behaviour, even though made at the time of conviction: *R v London Sessions, supra*; although appeal against such an order is now provided for separately by the Magistrates' Courts (Appeal From Binding Over Orders) Act 1956.

A committal for sentence under s.38 of this Act is not an order made on conviction: *R v London Sessions, ex p. Rogers* [1951] 2 KB 74. There is a right of appeal under this section from a discretionary order of disqualification for holding or obtaining a driving licence: *R v Surrey Quarter Sessions, ex p. Commissioner of Police of the Metropolis* (1962) 126 JP 269. s.94(1) RTA 1972 give a separate right of appeal against 'mandatory' orders of disqualification.

A direction under s.40(3) Education Act 1944, that a child should be brought before a juvenile court in respect of his failure to attend school regularly is not, *it is suggested*, an order made on conviction.

The payment of costs, the prosecutor has a right of appeal when costs ordered against him in committal proceedings exceed £25: Sch.2 POA 1985. This applies only to a discharge, not to a case when the prosecution is not proceeded with: *R v Crown Court at Lewes, ex p. Rogers* [1974] 1 WLR 196.

Abandonment of appeal   **11.13**

109. (1) Where notice to abandon an appeal has been duly given by the appellant–

  (a) the court against whose decision the appeal was brought may issue process for enforcing that decision, subject to anything already suffered or done under it by the appellant; and

  (b) the said court may, on the application of the other party to the appeal, order the appellant to pay to that party such costs as appear to the court to be just and reasonable in respect of expenses properly incurred by that party in connection with the appeal before notice of the abandonment was given to that party.

(2) In this section 'appeal' means an appeal from a magistrates' court to the Crown Court, and the reference to a notice to abandon an appeal is a reference to a notice shown to the satisfaction of the magistrates' court to have been in accordance with Crown Court rules.

COMMENTARY

Unless an abandonment of appeal is a nullity by virtue of mistake or fraudulent inducement, the Crown Court cannot entertain appeal once it has been validly abandoned: *R v Essex Quarter Sessions, ex p. Larkin* [1962] 1 QB 712.

s.109(1): Notice to abandon, under r.11 Crown Court Rules 1982, *infra*. And see subs (2) of this section.

Costs, costs on appeal are enforceable by whatever magistrates' court is specified in the order as sums adjudged to be paid on a conviction of that court: s.41 and Sch.9 Administration of Justice Act 1970.

See also the Commentary to r.11 Crown Court Rules 1982, *post*.

11.14   **Enforcement of decision of the Crown Court**
110. After the determination by the Crown Court of an appeal from a magistrates' court the decision appealed against as confirmed or varied by the Crown Court, or any decision of the Crown Court substituted for the decision appealed against, may, without prejudice to the powers of the Crown Court to enforce the decision, be enforced–
(a) by the issue by the court by which the decision appealed against was given of any process that it could have issued if it had decided the case as the Crown Court decided it;
(b) so far as the nature of any process already issued to enforce the decision appealed against permits, by that process;
and the decision of the Crown Court shall have effect as if it had been made by the magistrates' court against whose decision the appeal is brought.

COMMENTARY

Any process, such enforcement action to be commenced *within six months* of the completion of taxation: *McVittie v Rennison* (1941) 104 JP 455. When a defendant has been released on bail after notice of appeal, the warrant is exhausted and the sentence, if confirmed on appeal, requires a fresh warrant: *R v Pentonville Prison Governor* (1902) 67 JP 206; *Demer v Cook* (1903) 88 LT 629.

11.15   **Statement of case by magistrates' court**
111. (1) Any person who was a party to any proceeding before a magistrates' court or is aggrieved by the conviction, order, determination or other proceeding of the court may question the proceeding on the ground that it is wrong in law or is in excess of jurisdiction by applying to the justices composing the court to state a case for the opinion of the High Court on the question of law or jurisdiction involved; but a person shall not make an application under this section in respect of a decision against which he has a right of appeal to the High Court or which by virtue of any enactment passed after 31 December, 1879 is final.

(2) An application under subs (1) above shall be made within 21 days after the day on which the decision of the magistrates' court is given.

(3) For the purpose of subs (2) above, the day on which the decision of the magistrates' court is given shall, where the court has adjourned the trial of an information after conviction, be the day on which the court sentences or otherwise deals with the offender.

(4) On the making of an application under this section in respect of a decision any right of the applicant to appeal against the decision to the Crown Court shall cease.

(5) If the justices are of opinion that an application under this section is frivolous, they may refuse to state a case, and, if the applicant so requires, shall give him a certificate stating that the application has been refused; but the justices shall not refuse to state a case if the application is made by or under the direction of the Attorney General.

(6) Where justices refuse to state a case, the High Court may, on the

application of the person who applied for the case to be stated, make an order of *mandamus* requiring the justices to state a case.

COMMENTARY 11.16

See generally under *Appeal by way of Case Stated*, 11.02. 'The stating of the case, like any other form of appeal, is a matter arising entirely from statute', *per* Lord Goddard CJ, in *Card v Salmon* [1953] 1 All ER 324.

A legal aid order for proceedings before magistrates is authority for the solicitor to give assistance in the making of an application for a case to be stated within the ordinary time for doing so: s.30(5) Legal Aid Act 1974. Legal aid for the conduct of the proceedings themselves is available under the civil scheme contained in Part I of the Act.

s.111(1): Proceeding, this word is to be construed as meaning where it first appears 'or proceedings – something to which there are parties' and in the second and third places as 'adjudication or decision': *Atkinson v United States Government* [1969] 3 All ER 1317 at 1324 HL, *per* Lord Reid.

A magistrates' court, this means any justice or justices of the peace acting under any enactment or by virtue of his or their commission or under the common law: s.148 MCA 1980. The consolidating Act of 1952 did not change the previously established rule in *Card v Salmon* [1953] 1 QB 392 that examining magistrates have no power to state a case: *Atkinson v United States Government* [1969] 3 All ER 1317 (an extradition case); followed in *Dewing v Cummins* [1971] RTR 295.

Person . . . aggrieved, not necessarily a party, but 'person whose legal rights are directly affected by the decision', *per* Bruce J, in *Drapers' Co v Hadder* (1892) 57 JP 200. Thus a person adversely affected by an order of restitution of stolen property may be a person aggrieved: *Moss v Hancock* (1899) 63 JP 517. Although the prosecutor is *not* a person aggrieved, he is a *party to the proceedings: R v Newport (Salop) Justices, ex p. Wright* (1929) 93 JP 179. An informant under s.3 Obscene Publications Act 1959, is not a *person aggrieved* though he is a *party to the proceedings: Burke v Cooper* [1962] 1 WLR 700.

'Where the prosecution ask for a case against a defendant who has taken advantage of [third party proceedings], it is essential that the prosecution should join the third party as a party to the case if the result of the case may be a remission to the justices for re-hearing or with a direction to convict, because otherwise the defendant will lose his right to proceed against the third party at the rehearing', *per* Lord Goddard CJ, in *Elkington v Kesley* [1948] 2 KB 256 (a case turning upon what is now s.8 Food Act 1984).

For a discussion of the term 'person aggrieved' in the context of a civil appeal see *R v London Sessions Appeal Committee, ex p. Westminster City Council* [1951] 2 KB 508 and *R v Dorset Quarter Sessions Appeal Committee, ex p. Weymouth Corporation* [1960] 2 QB 230.

Wrong in law, it is a question of law when justices fail to draw the only conclusion which could be drawn from the facts by reasonable persons honestly applying their minds to the question; where, in other words, the decision is *perverse: Bracegirdle v Oxley* [1947] KB 349. A point of law constituting a valid defence to a criminal charge may be entertained providing it depends on the facts stated in the case: *Knight v Halliwell* (1874) 38 JP 470; which no evidence could alter: *Kates v Jeffrey* (1914) 78 JP 310; but not otherwise: *Mottram v Eastern Counties Rail Co* (1859) 24 JP 40. Despite *dicta* to the contrary in *Ross v Moss* [1965] 2 QB 396, it was held in *Whitehead v Haines* [1965] 1 QB 200, that it would not be right for the Divisional Court to decline to entertain and determine a point of law open on the facts found in the case to an appellant convicted on a criminal charge which, if sound, might afford him a defence, merely because that legal objection to the charge had first been appreciated after his conviction. But case stated may not be used where the issue is essentially one of *fact: James v Chief Constable of Kent* (1986), *The Times*, 7 June, where Woolf LJ felt it necessary to '. . . emphasise that justices must exercise care and discretion in reaching a decision whether to state a case'.

Excess of jurisdiction, a refusal of jurisdiction should be challenged by way of case stated: *R v Wisbech Justices* (1890) 54 JP 743; *R v Clerkenwell Metropolitan Stipendiary Magistrates ex p. DPP* [1984] QB 821.

Applying to the justices composing the court, the application must be in writing and signed and must be sent to the magistrates' clerk: r.76 MC Rules 1981. Even under the former law the names of the justices need not be stated and error in naming them is not fatal provided the application is clearly made: *R v Oxford (Bullingdon) Justices, ex p. Bird* [1948] 1 KB 100.

State a case, the procedure for stating the case is laid down in rr.76–80 MC Rules 1981. The contents of the case are prescribed by r.81. There is no reason why half a dozen different cases heard by the same magistrate on the same day against different people should not be included in one case stated, assuming always, of course, that they raise precisely the same point: *Director of Public Prosecutions v Lamb* (1941) 105 JP 251.

It is not for the inferior court to direct what shall be done upon hearing of the case: *R v Headington Union* (1883) 47 JPN 756. The High Court will not offer a decision on a *hypothetical question* at the request of the parties which is 'essentially in the nature of an *obiter dictum* and would not be binding upon any other court': *Tindall v Wright* (1922) 86 JP 108. Nor will a special case be entered by the Crown Office where it is stated in alternative form: *Sheffield Waterworks Co v Sheffield Union* (1887) 31 SJ 271.

s.111(2): Within 21 days after, that is, not counting the day of decision but including the 21st day: *Goldsmiths' Co v West Metropolitan Rail Co* (1904) 68 JP 41; *Stewart v Chapman* (1951) 115 JP 473, Sunday must be counted even though it is the last of the days: *Peacock v R* (1858) 22 JP 403; *Ex p. Simpkin* (1859) 24 JP 262; *Wynne v Ronaldson* (1865) 29 JP 566. The High Court has no power to extend the period: *Michael v Gowland* (1977) 141 JP 343. Nor, it is suggested, have the magistrates any discretion to state a case where *application* is made outside this period. As to the need for the question(s) of law or jurisdiction to be identified within the 21 days see the notes to r.76 MC Rules 1981, *infra*.

s.111(4): this provision is not avoided by simultaneously asking for a case to be stated and appealing to the Crown Court: *R v Winchester Crown Court, ex p. Lewington* [1982] 1 All ER 1277. However, an appeal by case stated does not bar an appeal to the Crown Court against sentence: *ibid*; and *Sivalingham v DPP* [1975] CLY 2037.

s.111(5): Frivolous, justices cannot refuse to state a case on an arguable point of law: *R v Petersfield Justices, ex p. Levy* [1981] RTR 204. A magistrate may decline to state a case where he has followed a decision binding upon him on the same point from which there is no right of appeal: *R v Shiel* (1900) 19 Cox 507; 82 LT 587; but this does not apply where the authority followed was not the final court of appeal: *R v Watson, ex p. Bretherton* (1944) 109 JP 38. For an example of a frivolous point see *R v Newport (Salop) Justices, ex p. Wright* (1929) 93 JP 179; and compare the meaning of this term in the Court of Appeal in *R v Taylor* [1979] Crim LR 649 (Not confined to *foolish* or *silly* but extends to a point of law which cannot possibly succeed on argument). If the justices refuse improperly to state a case they may be ordered to do so by *mandamus*.

11.17 **Effect of decision by High Court on case stated by magistrates' court**
112. Any conviction, order, determination or other proceeding of a magistrates' court varied by the High Court on an appeal by case stated, and any judgment or order of the High Court on such an appeal, may be enforced as if it were a decision of the magistrates' court from which the appeal was brought.

11.18 **Bail on appeal or case stated**
113. (1) Where a person has given notice of appeal to the Crown Court against the decision of a magistrates' court or has applied to a magistrates' court to state a case for the opinion of the High Court, then, if he is in custody, the magistrates' court may grant him bail.

(2) If a person is granted bail under subs (1) above, the time and place at which he is to appear (except in the event of the determination in respect of which the case is stated being reversed by the High Court) shall be–
    (a) if he has given notice of appeal, the Crown Court at the time appointed for the hearing of the appeal;
    (b) if he has applied for the statement of a case, the magistrates' court at such time within 10 days after the judgment of the High Court has been given as may be specified by the magistrates' court;
and any recognizance that may be taken from him or from any surety for him shall be conditioned accordingly.

(3) Subsection (1) above shall not apply where the accused has been committed to the Crown Court for sentence under s.37 or 38 above.

(4) Section 37(6) of the Criminal Justice Act 1948 (which relates to the currency of a sentence while a person is released on bail by the High Court) shall apply to a person released on bail by a magistrates' court under this section pending the hearing of a case stated as it applies to a person released on bail by the High Court under s.22 of the Criminal Justice Act 1967.

COMMENTARY

See generally *Bail Pending Appeal*, 11.08.

s.113(1): Notice of appeal, that is, under r.7 Crown Court Rules 1982, *infra*.

Applied . . . to state a case, that is, under s.111, *supra*.

May grant him bail, although it is not obligatory, the Home Office recommend that a defendant refused bail should be informed of his right to apply to a High Court Judge: HOC 88/49.

s.113(2): Within 10 days after, that is, excluding the day of judgment but including the 10th day.

s.113(4): the effect of this is to exclude time spent on bail from any sentence of imprisonment. As to the effect of bail on appeal to the Crown Court see *R v Pentonville Prison Governor* (1903) 67 JP 206.

Recognizances and fees on case stated   11.19

114. Justices to whom application has been made to state a case for the opinion of the High Court on any proceeding of a magistrtes' court shall not be required to state the case until the applicant has entered into a recognizance, with or without sureties, before the magistrates' court, conditioned to prosecute the appeal without delay and to submit to the judgment of the High Court and pay such costs as that Court may award; and (except in any criminal matter the clerk of a magistrates' court shall not be required to deliver the case to the applicant until the applicant has paid him the fees payable for the case and for the recognizances.

COMMENTARY

Shall not be required, thus magistrates may state a case before or even without a recognizance.

Recognizance, see form 118. The recognizance will be in time if entered into before the case is stated and delivered: *Stanhope v Thorsbey* (1866) 30 JP 342; but not later. *Walker v Delacombe* (1894) 58 JP 88. When a recognizance was entered into with a surety and the appellant went bankrupt and his surety died, the magistrate could not insist on a further recognizance: *R v Kettle, ex p. Ellis* (1905) 69 JP 55. Justices must have regard to the applicant's means in fixing the amount of a recognizance, or in deciding whether to require a recognizance at all: *R v Newcastle upon Tyne Justices, ex p. Skinner* (1986) 150 JPN 783.
   In the case of a corporation, a director or other agent may be appointed by the board of directors under s.74(2) Law of Property Act 1925, to enter into the recognizance: *Southern Counties Deposit Bank Ltd. v Boaler* (1895) 59 JP 536.
   Failure to prosecute the appeal without delay renders the recognizance liable to forfeiture in accordance with s.120 MCA 1980. An order of forfeiture of such a recognizance may *seemingly* be made without complaint.

The fees, no fees are chargeable in any criminal matter. Sch.6, Part II, para 2 of the 1981 Act. That provision applies to fees on a case stated in a criminal matter: *R v Preston Justices, ex p. Pamplin* [1981] Crim LR 338.

SUPREME COURT ACT 1981

Appeals to the Crown Court   11.20

48. (1) The Crown Court may, in the course of hearing any appeal, correct any error or mistake in the order or judgment incorporating the decision which is the subject of the appeal.

(2) On the termination of the hearing of an appeal the Crown Court–
(a) may confirm, reverse or vary the decision appealed against; or
(b) may remit the matter with its opinion thereon to the authority whose decision is appealed against; or
(c) may make such other order in the matter as the court thinks just, and by such order exercise any power which the said authority might have exercised.

(3) Subsection (2) has effect subject to any enactment relating to any such appeal which expressly limits or restricts the powers of the court on the appeal.

(4) If the appeal is against a conviction or a sentence, the preceding provisions of this section shall be construed as including power to award any punishment, whether more or less severe than that awarded by the magistrates' court whose decision is appealed against, if that is a punishment which that magistrates' court might have awarded.

(5) This section applies whether or not the appeal is against the whole of the decision.

(6) In this section 'sentence' includes any order made by a court when dealing with an offender, including–
  (a) a hospital order under Part III of the Mental Health Act 1983 with or without a restriction order and an interim hospital order under that Act; and
  (b) a recommendation for deportation made when dealing with an offender.

(7) The fact that an appeal is pending against an interim hospital order under the said Act of 1983 shall not affect the power of the magistrates' court that made it to renew or terminate the order to deal with the appellant on its termination; and where the Crown Court quashes such an order but does not pass any sentence or make any other order in its place the Court may direct the appellant to be kept in custody or released on bail pending his being dealt with by that magistrates' court.

(8) Where the Crown Court makes an interim hospital order by virtue of subs (8)–
  (a) the power of renewing or terminating the order and of dealing with the appellant on its termination shall be exercisable by the magistrates' court whose decision is appealed against and not by the Crown Court; and
  (b) that magistrates' court shall be treated for the purposes of s.38(7) of the said Act of 1983 (absconding offenders) as the court that made the order.
[*As amended by Sch.3 Mental Health (Amendment) Act 1982, Sch.4 Mental Health Act 1983*].

48. (2) *On the termination of the hearing of an appeal the Crown Court–*
  (a) *may confirm, reverse or vary any part of the decision appealed against, including a determination not to impose a separate penalty in respect of an offence: or*
[*Subsection 48(2)(a) will be amended by s.148 CJA 1988 from a date to be appointed.*]

COMMENTARY

See generally under *Appeal to the Crown Court*, 11.01.
  For the court's power to award costs see *Costs*, Chapter 9.
  An appeal to quarter sessions was always treated as a rehearing, although there was no statutory authority for this, but in an appeal against sentence it is usual to hear only the matters affecting sentence: *Paprika Ltd v Board of Trade* (1944) 108 JP 104. And see *Rugmann v Drover* [1951] 1 KB 380; *Sirros v Moore* [1975] QB 118.

s.48(2): Confirm, reverse or vary etc see *Arthur v Stringer* (1986) *The Times*, 11 October; and *Dutta v Westcott* (1986) 8 Cr App R (S) 191, noted in *Appeal to the Crown Court*, 11.01.

With opinion, the fact that this phraseology is used by the superior court does not make its decision any less binding on the magistrates: *R v Tottenham Justices, ex p. Rubens* [1971] 1 All ER 879.

Make such other order . . . as the court thinks just, compare the similar wording of an appeal provision in a civil matter in *Fulham Metropolitan Borough Council v Santilli* (1933) 97 JP 174.

The Crown Court has no power on appeal to commit an offender to themselves for sentence under s.38 MCA 1980: *R v Bullock* [1963] 3 All ER 506; nor any power to amend after conviction an information which is bad on its face: *Meek v Powell* (1952) 116 JP 116; *Garfield v Maddocks* (1973) 137 JP 461 (explaining *Wright v Nicholson* (1970) 134 JP 85 as being *per incuriam* on this point); or which charges the wrong offence.

Exercise any power, the substitution of a suspended sentence for a forthwith sentence of imprisonment has the effect of a new order under para (c), which runs from the date of the Crown Court order: *R v Burn* [1976] Crim LR 754.

Subs (4): thus, if the defendant was not legally represented or otherwise within the terms of s.21 PCCA 1973 when he appeared before the magistrates' court the Crown Court may not on appeal pass a first sentence of imprisonment: *R v Birmingham Justices, ex p. Wyatt* [1975] 3 All ER 897; neither may the Crown Court adjourn until the appellant is 21 years of age so as to avoid the restriction on imposing imprisonment on persons below that age (s.1(1) CJA 1982) as it applied in the magistrates' court: *Arthur v Stringer* (1986) *The Times*, 11 October.

MAGISTRATES' COURTS RULES 1981
(As amended by SI 1981 No 552, SI 1982 No 245, SI 1983 No 523, SI 1984 No 1552, SI 1985 Nos 1695 and 1944, and SI 1986 No 1332.)

Form of conviction or order   **11.21**
16. (1) A form of summary conviction or order made on complaint shall be drawn up if required for an appeal or other legal purpose, and if drawn up shall be in such one of the prescribed forms as is appropriate to the case.

(2) Where the conviction is of an offence that could not have been tried summarily without the consent of the accused, the conviction shall contain a statement that the accused consented to the summary trial.

COMMENTARY
Note also the effect of r.100, which applies to convictions: *Cole v Wolkind* [1981] Crim LR 252.

'The courts have always been more particular about the necessity for accuracy and more rigid in their decisions with regard to convictions than they have been with regard to processes of the court . . . which are designed to bring persons before the court', *per* Humphrey J, in *Atterton v Browne* (1945) 109 JP 25. But the record is never conclusive in matters of a criminal nature, *per* Lord Denning MR in *Sirros v Moore* [1975] QB 118. The decision should set out with sufficient particularity the nature of the offence. It is not sufficient merely to recite the wording of the statute: the conviction must include sufficient details to identify the ingredients necessary to constitute the offence: *Newman v Lord Hardwicke* (1838) 8 Ad & El 124; *Charter v Greame* (1849) 13 JP 232; *R v Mackenzie* (1892) 56 JP 712; *Smith v Moody* (1903) 67 JP 69. The conviction should also (i) show the jurisdiction: *R v Fuller* (1845) 9 JP 140; (ii) state the venue: *R v Casterton (Inhabitants)* (1844) 6 QB 507; and (iii) state the costs ordered: *R v Hampshire Justices* (1862) 32 LJMC 46; 7 LT 391. It is not necessary to recite the date of laying of the informations: *Wray v Toke* (1848) 12 JP 804.

A number of defendants may be included in the same conviction so long as the separate penalties are stated clearly: *R v Cridland* (1857) 21 JP 404; but it is not enough to recite 'Messrs Harrison and Company'; *R v Harrison & Co.* (1800) 8 Term Rep. 508. A conviction may be drawn up in correct form even after one has been delivered to the defendant so long as the earlier conviction has not been quashed for informality: *R v Allen* (1812) 15 East 333; *Charter v Greame* (1849) 13 JP 232.

Para (1): Other legal purpose, a defendant has a right to a copy of his conviction: *R v Midlam* (1765) 3 Burr 1720.

Documents to be sent to Crown Court   **11.22**
74. (1) A clerk of a magistrates' court shall as soon as practicable send to the appropriate officer of the Crown Court any notice of appeal to the Crown Court given to the clerk of the court.

(2) The clerk of a magistrates' court shall send to the appropriate officer of the Crown Court, with the notice of appeal, a statement of the decision from which the appeal is brought and of the last known or usual place of abode of the parties to the appeal.

(3) Where any person, having given notice of appeal to the Crown Court, has been granted bail for the purposes of the appeal the clerk of the court from whose decision the appeal is brought shall before the day fixed for the hearing of the appeal send to the appropriate officer of the Crown Court–

(a) in the case of bail in criminal proceedings, a copy of the record made in pursuance of s.5 of the Bail Act 1976 relating to such bail;

(b) in the case of bail otherwise than in criminal proceedings, the recognizance entered into by the appellant relating to such bail.

(4) Where, in any such case as is referred to in para 3(b), the recognizance in question has been entered into otherwise than before the magistrates' court from whose decision the appeal is brought, or the clerk of that court, the person who took the recognizance shall send it forthwith to that clerk.

(5) Where a notice of appeal is given in respect of a hospital order or guardianship order made under s.60 of the Mental Health Act 1959, the clerk of the magistrates' court from which the appeal is brought shall send with the notice to the appropriate officer of the Crown Court any written evidence considered by the court under subs (1)(a) of the said s.60.

(6) Where a notice of appeal is given in respect of an appeal against conviction by a magistrates' court the clerk of the court shall send with the notice to the appropriate officer of the Crown Court any admission of facts made for the purposes of the summary trial under s.10 of the Criminal Justice Act 1967.

COMMENTARY

'We hope . . . that clerks to justices will send their notes to the clerk of the peace when there is an appeal, so that he can show them to the chairman or recorder if he requires them before the hearing . . . and also will give them to the court during the hearing if it becomes necessary or desirable for the court to see what happened below': *Practice Note* [1956] 1 All ER 448. The purpose of this is to help decide applications for legal aid and estimate the length of the case. It is undesirable when trying an appeal for the court to have before it any notes of the hearing in the magistrates' court unless this is necessary to see what a witness had said or what had transpired in the court below: *ibid.*

See also generally: Notes of Evidence, Chapter 1.

Notice of appeal, ie under r.7 Crown Court Rules 1982. So long as the document is a notice of appeal' there is seemingly a duty on the clerk to transmit it to the Crown Court even if he believes it to be invalid, eg because it is out of time.

Statement of the decision see r.16 as to the form of conviction or order.

11.23 Abandonment of appeal

75. Where notice to abandon an appeal has been given by the appellant, any recognizance conditioned for the appearance of the appellant at the hearing of the appeal shall have effect as if conditioned for the appearance of the appellant before the court from whose decision the appeal was brought at a time and place to be notified to the appellant by the clerk of that court.

COMMENTARY

Notice to abandon. ie, under r.11 Crown Court Rules 1982. *Note* that a failure to give notice of abandonment means that the Crown Court may proceed to hear and determine an appeal in the appellant's absence, including increasing sentence: *R v Guildford Crown Court, ex p. Brewer* (1987) *The Times,* 26 October.

11.24 Application to state case

76. (1) An application under s.111(1) of the Act of 1980 shall be made in writing and signed by or on behalf of the applicant and shall identify the question or questions of law or jurisdiction on which the opinion of the High Court is sought.

(2) Where one of the questions on which the opinion of the High Court is sought is whether there was evidence on which the magistrates' court could

come to its decision, the particular finding of fact made by the magistrates' court which it is claimed cannot be supported by the evidence before the magistrates' court shall be specified in such application.

(3) Any such application shall be sent to the clerk of the magistrates' court whose decision is questioned.

COMMENTARY

Para (1): Identify the question, despite a line of cases which suggests that the appeal may not proceed unless the question or questions of law or jurisdiction have been identified within the period laid down by the Act (*Shippington v Gouvenot-Gardinér* (1977) 15 February; *Taylor v Phillips* (1977) 141 JPN 711; *R v Flint Justices, ex p. Baker* (1980) 144 JPN 303; *Bristol & West Building Society and Brian Simmons v Hickmott* (1981) 144 JP 443) the better view would seem to be that this rule is *directory* rather than *mandatory* (*R v Bromley Magistrates' Court, ex p. Waitrose Ltd* [1980] 3 All ER 464; *Robinson v Whittle* [1980] 1 WLR 1476) in the sense that there must be a 'substantial compliance' with the rule: *R v Croydon Justices, ex p. Lefore Holdings Ltd* [1980] 1 WLR 1465 (In that case the clerk must have realised that there could not have been any other question because that was the only question at the hearing). Each case has to be looked at on its merits but the object of the rule was the speeding up of justice, not to curtail the opportunities for doing justice, *per* Lawton LJ, *ibid.*

Consideration of draft case   **11.25**

77. (1) Within 21 days after receipt of an application made in accordance with r.76, the clerk of the magistrates' court whose decision is questioned, shall, unless the justices refuse to state a case under s.111(5) of the Act of 1980, send a draft case in which are stated the matters required under r.81 to the applicant or his solicitor and shall send a copy thereof to the respondent or his solicitor.

(2) Within 21 days after receipt of the draft case under para (1), each party may make representations thereon. Any such representations shall be in writing and signed by or on behalf of the party making them and shall be sent to the clerk.

(3) Where the justices refuse to state a case under s.111(5) of the Act and they are required by the High Court by order of *mandamus* under s.111(6) to do so, this rule shall apply as if in paragraph (1)–
(a) for the words 'receipt of an application made in accordance with r.76' there were substituted the words 'the date on which an order of *mandamus* under s.116(6) of the Act of 1980 is made'; and
(b) the words 'unless the justices refuse to state a case under s.111(5) of the Act of 1980' were omitted.

COMMENTARY

Although these rules are *directory* rather than *mandatory* the High Court will refuse to hear a case when the party seeking to have the case heard has himself been the author of the delay: *Parsons v FW Woolworth & Co Ltd* [1980] 1 WLR 1472.

Para (1): Within 21 days after, that is, not counting the day of the decision but including the 21st day: *Goldsmith's Co v West Metropolitan Railway* (1904) 68 JP 41; *Stewart v Chapman* (1951) 115 JP 473; Sunday must be counted even though it is the last day: *Peacock v R* (1858) 22 JP 403; *Ex p. Simpkin* (1859) 24 JP 262; *Wynne v Ronaldson* (1865) 29 JP 566.

The clerk of the magistrates' court, that is, the justices' clerk. 'The intention is that as a general rule, but not invariably, the justices' clerk should prepare the first draft of the case, unless the justices wish to do so themselves. The Lord Chief Justice has expressed the view that this will usually be the most expeditious way of proceeding'. HOC 55/1975.

Send, see r.80.

Preparation and submission of final case   **11.26**

79. (1) If the clerk of a magistrates' court is unable to send to the applicant a draft case under para (1) of r.77 within the time required by that paragraph, he shall do so as soon as practicable thereafter and the provisions of that rule shall apply accordingly; but in that event the clerk shall attach to the draft case, and to the final case when it is sent to the applicant or his solicitor under r.78(3), a statement of the delay and the reasons therefor.

(2) If the clerk of a magistrates' court receives an application in writing from or on behalf of the applicant or the respondent for an extension of the time within which representations on the draft case may be made under para (2) of r.77, together with reasons in writing therefor, he may by notice in writing send to the applicant or respondent as the case may be to extend the time and the provisions of that paragraph and of r.78 shall apply accordingly; but in that event the clerk shall attach to the final case, when it is sent to the applicant or his solicitor under r.78(3), a statement of the delay and the reasons therefor.

11.27   **Service of documents**
80. Any document required by r.76 to 79 to be sent to any person shall either be delivered to him or be sent by post in a registered letter or by recorded delivery service and, if sent by post to an applicant or respondent, shall be addressed to him at his last known or usual place of abode.

11.28   **Content of case**
81. (1) A case stated by the magistrates' court shall state the facts found by the court and the question or questions of law or jurisdiction on which the opinion of the High Court is sought.

(2) Where one of the questions on which the opinion of the High Court is sought is whether there was evidence on which the magistrates' court could come to its decision, the particular finding of fact which it is claimed cannot be supported by the evidence before the magistrates' court shall be specified in the case.

(3) Unless one of the questions on which the opinion of the High Court is sought is whether there was evidence on which the magistrates' court could come to its decision, the case shall not contain a statement of evidence.

COMMENTARY

The form of a case stated (Form 155) is prescribed in The Magistrates' Courts (Forms) Rules 1981 (SI 1981, No 553, as amended). It should be strictly followed.

'It is necessary to draw attention to [r.81 MC Rules 1981], the terms of which are frequently disregarded. Every magistrates' case should contain a full statement of the facts proved or admitted, and should not contain any statement of the evidence unless it is to be contended that there was no evidence to support a particular finding of fact. The case should follow [Form 155 of the Schedule to the Magistrates' Courts (Forms) Rules 1981] as closely as possible; and see *Laird (Inspector of Factories) v Simms (Gomersal) Ltd* (1988) *The Times*, 7 March.'

[Practice Note (1972) 136 JP 39]
Contents
If a respondent thinks that certain facts found by the justices – and not merely evidence which was submitted to them – have been omitted from the case, he can apply to the High Court for a reassessment of the case on stating in an affidavit the findings of fact which, in his opinion, have been omitted: *per* Lord Goddard CJ in *Spicer v Warbey* (1953) 117 JP 92; and see s.7 Summary Jurisdiction Act 1857. According to Woolf LJ in *James v Chief Constable of Kent* (1986) *The Times*, 7 June, in stating a case, it is important '. . . to recreate the impression given before the justices'.

State the facts found, this is inappropriate where the appeal is founded on a submission of no case to answer, as to which see the unreported case of *Smith and Smith v Luck* (1976) 140 JPN 384.

CROWN COURT RULES 1982
(As amended by SI 1982 No 1109)

Application of Part II **11.29**
6. (1) Subject to the following provisions of this Rule, this Part of these Rules shall apply to every appeal which by or under any enactment lies to the Crown Court from any court, tribunal or person.

(2) Without prejudice to r.7(5), this Part of these Rules shall have effect subject to the provisions of the enactments specified in Part I of Sch.3 (being enactments which make special procedural provisions in respect of certain appeals) and those enactments shall have effect subject to the amendments set out in Part II of that Schedule (being amendments reproducing amendments made by r.6(2) of, and Part II of Sch.1 to, the Crown Court Rules 1971).

Notice of appeal **11.30**
7. (1) An appeal shall be commenced by the appellant's giving notice of appeal in accordance with the following provisions of this rule.

(2) The notice required by the preceding paragraph shall be in writing and shall be given–
  (a) in a case where the appeal is against a decision of a magistrates' court, to the clerk of the magistrates' court;
  (b) in the case of an appeal under s.81B of the Licensing Act 1964 against a decision of licensing justices, to the clerk of the justices;
  (c) in any other case, to the appropriate officer of the Crown Court; and
  (d) in any case, to any other party to the appeal.

(3) Notice of appeal shall be given not later than 21 days after the day on which the decision appealed against is given and, for this purpose, where the court has adjourned the trial of an information after conviction, that day shall be the day on which the court sentences or otherwise deals with the offender.
  Provided that, where a court exercises its power to defer sentence under s.1(1) of the Powers of Criminal Courts Act 1973, that day shall, for the purposes of an appeal against conviction, be the day on which the court exercises that power.

(4) A notice of appeal shall state–
  (a) in the case of an appeal arising out of a conviction by a magistrates' court, whether the appeal is against conviction or sentence or both; and
  (b) in the case of an appeal under an enactment listed in Part III of Sch.3, the grounds of appeal.

(5) The time for giving notice of appeal (whether prescribed under para (3), or under an enactment listed in Part I of Sch.3) may be extended, either before or after it expires, by the Crown Court, on an application made in accordance with para (6).

(6) An application for an extension of time shall be made in writing, specifying the grounds of the application and sent to the appropriate officer of the Crown Court.

(7) Where the Crown Court extends the time for giving notice of appeal, the appropriate officer of the Crown Court shall give notice of the extension to–
  (a) the appellant;
  (b) in the case of an appeal from a decision of a magistrates' court, to the clerk of that court;
  (c) in the case of an appeal under s.81B of the Licensing Act 1964 from a decision of licensing justices, to the clerk to the justices,
and the appellant shall give notice of the extension to any other party to the appeal.

COMMENTARY

For the documents to be sent to the Crown Court see r.74 MC Rules, *supra*.

It would be 'exceedingly improper' for a justice to issue process to enforce a sentence after notification of appeal: *Kendal v Wilkinson* (1855) 19 JP 467.

Notice of appeal, it was held in relation to the previous legislation that the superior court is exclusive judge of the sufficiency of the description of the notice and that, therefore, *certiorari* will not lie: *R v Durham Justices* (1981) 55 JPN 277.

Any other party, service on his solicitor is insufficient if he is no longer instructed: *R v Oxfordshire Justices* (1893) 57 JP 712. In third party proceedings it is necessary that substantive notice of appeal be given to the original prosecutor as well as to the third party: *R v The Recorder of Derby, ex p. Spalton* (1944) 108 JP 193; and this applies even where the third party procedure goes only to penalty: *R v Epsom Justices, ex p. Dawnier Motors Ltd.* [1961] 1 QB 201; see also the notes to s.111 MCA 1980, *supra*.

Para (5) For the exercise of the higher court's discretion: see *R v Middlesex Quarter Sessions Chairman, ex p. M* [1967] Crim LR 474.

11.31   **Entry of appeal and notice of hearing**
            8. On receiving notice of appeal, the appropriate officer of the Crown Court shall enter the appeal and give notice of the time and place of the hearing to–
            (a) the appellant;
            (b) any other party to the appeal;
            (c) in the case of an appeal from a decision of the magistrates' court, to the clerk of that court;
            (d) in the case of an appeal under s.81B of the Licensing Act 1964 from a decision of the licensing justices, to the clerk to the justices.

11.32   **Abandonment of appeal**
            11. (1) Without prejudice to the power of the Crown Court to give leave for an appeal to be abandoned, an appellant may abandon an appeal by giving notice in writing, in accordance with the following provisions of this Rule, not later than the third day before the day fixed for hearing the appeal.

            (2) The notice required by the preceding paragraph shall be given–
            (a) in a case where the appeal is against a decision of a magistrates' court, to the clerk of the magistrates' court;
            (b) in the case of an appeal under s.21 of the Licensing Act 1964, or in the case of an appeal under s.81B of that Act against a decision of licensing justices, to the clerk to the licensing justices;
            (c) in any other case, to the appropriate officer of the Crown Court; and
            (d) in any case, to any other party to the appeal;
            and, in the case of an appeal mentioned in sub-para (a) or (b), the appellant shall send a copy of the notice to the appropriate officer of the Crown Court.

            (3) For the purposes of determining whether notice of abandonment was given in time there shall be disregarded any Saturday, Sunday and any day which is specified to be a bank holiday in England and Wales under s.1(1) of the Banking and Financial Dealings Act 1971.

COMMENTARY

The only *right* that an appellant has to abandon an appeal is the right which he exercises by giving notice in writing not later than the third day before the hearing. Any other application may or may not be granted in the court's *discretion*. It will only be in the most exceptional circumstances that the judge would be entitled to decline to give leave to abandon where the application is made before the hearing begins. Once the hearing has started it will only be in exceptional circumstances that leave will be granted: *R v Manchester Crown Court, ex p. Welby and Smith* (1981) 3 Cr App R (S) 194. But if there is no abandonment and the appellant fails to appear, the Crown Court may proceed to hear the appeal in his absence, even increasing sentence if appropriate: *R v Guildford Crown Court, ex p. Brewer*, (1987) *The Times*, 26 October.

Any other party see the note to r.7, *supra*.

CHAPTER 12

Warrants under the Police and Criminal Evidence Act 1984 and Criminal Justice Act 1987 – including an outline of investigative powers

Warrants under the PACE Act 1984 and CJA 1987

INTRODUCTION   **12.00**

The *investigation* of crime by the police and the *arrest* of suspects is governed by the Police and Criminal Evidence Act 1984 and the *Codes of*

Practice made by the Home Secretary under s.66 of the Act, see Appendix I. Once a suspect has been arrested, the *Police Detention* provisions contained in ss.34 to 52 PACE Act 1984 come into play and these are discussed under that title in Chapter 3, *Detention, Remands, Custody and Bail*, where they logically precede such later considerations. Also, quite apart from those provisions relating specifically to the issue of warrants, *infra*, the Act and codes have potential relevance for all criminal trials, since a breach by the police may affect the question of whether a court is prepared to receive evidence. As to the considerations affecting the exclusion of otherwise admissible evidence – principally under ss.76 and 78 PACE Act 1984 – see Chapter 6, *Evidential Matters*. References in Part 1 of this chapter are to the PACE Act 1984, unless otherwise stated.

Under the Criminal Justice Act 1987, the Director of Serious Fraud is given, at his own discretion, a dual role as *investigator* and *prosecutor* in cases of 'complex or serious fraud' (not further defined). Those provisions of the 1987 Act relating to the Director's discretion to require the *Transfer to the Crown Court*, without the need for committal proceedings etc, of cases for trial are dealt with under that title in Chapter 4, *Mode of Trial, Committal for Trial and Transfer to the Crown Court*. As with the PACE Act 1984, justices are given powers under the CJA 1987 to grant warrants on application. Under the 1987 Act, however, the provisions are limited to 'documents', as widely defined in s.12(18), and application for a warrant can only be made where the Director has the conduct of the proceedings. The procedures under both Acts involve compliance with strict criteria, as set out in the text, *infra*. References in Part 2 are to the 1987 Act which, at the time of going to press, is only partially in force, ie in so far as concerns this work as follows: s.1 (appointment of Director): see Criminal Justice Act 1987 (Commencement No 1) Order 1987 (SI No 1061), s.2 (Director's investigative powers), s.3 (disclosure of information, and certain other minor and consequential amendments: Criminal Justice Act 1987 (Commencement No 2) Order 1988 (SI No 397).

PART 1: PACE ACT 1984

12.01   Codes of Practice

The Secretary of State has made four Codes of Practice in accordance with ss.66, 67. The Code of Practice for *Detention, Treatment and Questioning* by Police (Code 'C') is mentioned at 3.00, in relation to *Police Detention* and *Justices' Warrants of Further Detention*. The remaining codes deal with the following matters:

The Exercise by Police Officers of Statutory Powers of *Stop and Search* (Code 'A').

The *Searching of Premises* by Police Officers and the Seizure of Property Found by Police Officers on Persons or Premises (Code 'B').

The *Identification of Persons by Police* (Code 'D').

All four Codes are printed in Appendix I. They flesh out the Act and consist of a text and *Notes for Guidance*. The latter do not form part of the Code but are guidance to police officers and others about its application and interpretation. Failure on the part of a police officer to comply with any provision of a Code cannot of itself render him liable to any criminal or civil proceedings: s.67(10), but it can render him liable to disciplinary proceedings: s.67(8). Protection against double jeopardy is given by s.104.

The provisions of a Code are *admissible in civil and criminal proceedings* and any provision of the Code may be taken into account if it appears to be relevant to any questions arising in the proceedings: s.67(11); eg whether evidence was improperly obtained and should be excluded under s.76 (confessions) or s.78 ('unfair' evidence).

Serious arrestable offences

12.02

Many of the more important police powers are only exercisable in relation to a serious arrestable offence. Thus, the powers to issue a *search warrant* under s.8, to detain for longer than 24 hours without charge, to *delay access to a solicitor* or *notification of arrest*, and to conduct a *road check* are all referable to the concept of the *'serious arrestable offence'*.

A serious arrestable offence is defined in s.116 as follows:
  (i) the following offences are always serious: treason, murder, manslaughter, rape, kidnapping; incest with a girl under 13, buggery with a boy under 16 or without consent, indecent assault constituting an act of gross indecency: (Sch.5, Pt I); and causing explosions likely to endanger life, unlawful sexual intercourse with a girl under 13, possessing firearms with intent to injure, using them to resist arrest or carrying them with criminal intent, causing death by reckless driving, hostage taking and hijacking (Sch.5, Pt II).
  (ii) *any other arrestable offence is serious only* if its commission has led or is likely to lead to:
  (a) *serious harm* to the security of the state or to public order;
  (b) *serious interference* with the administration of justice or with the investigation of an offence;
  (c) the *death* of any person;
  (d) *serious injury* to any person;
  (e) *substantial financial gain* to any person; or
  (f) *serious financial loss* to any person.
Loss is serious if, having regard to all the circumstances, it is serious for the person who suffers it. Injury includes any disease and any impairment of a person's physical or mental condition.

An *arrestable* offence is defined in s.24 as an offence:
  (i) for which the *sentence is fixed by law*;
  (ii) for which a person of 21 years of age or over (not previously convicted) may be sentenced to *imprisonment for a term of 5 years*; or
  (iii) certain offences listed in s.24(2) including conspiracy and attempting to commit these offences and inciting, aiding, abetting, counselling or procuring their commission.

Safeguards concerning warrants of search and entry

12.03

All warrants to enter and search premises, whether under PACE Act 1984 or any other provision, must comply with s.15. In particular, a constable applying for a warrant must–
  state the ground on which he makes the application and the enactment under which the warrant would issue;
  specify the premises; and
  identify as far as is practicable, the articles or persons to be sought.
The application *must* be *ex parte* and supported by *an information in writing*. The constable must answer *on oath* any questions that the justice or judge asks him. The warrant may authorise an entry on *one occasion only*.

If an application is refused it may not be renewed unless supported by additional grounds. Code 'B', para 2.8, Appendix I, *post*.

Entry and search under any search warrant must be *within one month* from the date of issue: s.16(3). The manner of execution of all search warrants is governed by s.16. Reasonable force may be used if necessary: s.117.

Two copies must be made of a warrant: s.15(7), and the constable must supply to the occupier or, if he is not present, the person in charge a copy of the warrant or, if no one is in charge, leave a copy in a prominent position in the premises: s.16(5), (6), (7). The warrant must be endorsed with a statement as to whether the articles or persons sought were found and whether any articles were seized other than articles which were sought: s.16(9). After execution or expiry of the time authorised for execution the warrant must be returned to the justices' clerk or the appropriate officer of the court: s.16(10); who must retain it for 12 months: s.16(11); and allow the occupier of the premises to inspect it on request: s.16(12).

See, generally, Code 'B', Appendix I, *post*.

12.04 Warrants to search for evidence

A justice of the peace *may* issue a warrant authorising a constable to enter and search premises if he is satisfied that there are *reasonable grounds for believing* that a serious arrestable offence has been committed and that there is material on the premises which is likely to be of *substantial value* to the investigation of the offence and is *likely to be relevant* evidence: s.8. In addition, the justice must have *reasonable grounds for believing* that any of the conditions in s.8(3) is satisfied, namely that:

(a) it is not practicable to communicate with any person entitled to grant entry to the premises;

(b) it is practicable to communicate with such a person but it is not practicable to communicate with any person entitled to grant access to the evidence;

(c) entry to the premises will not be granted unless a warrant is produced; or

(d) the purpose of a search may be frustrated or seriously prejudiced unless a constable can secure immediate entry to the premises.

12.05 Specially protected material

Neither a warrant under s.8 nor a warrant under any pre-existing power may be granted in respect of items subject to *legal privilege, excluded material* and *special procedure material*: s.9(2). However a constable may obtain access to excluded material or special procedure material by making an application to a circuit judge for a production order and/or a search warrant in accordance with s.9, Sch.1 (not reproduced herein).

Items subject to legal privilege are defined in s.10 in conventional terms.

Excluded material is, in summary, any personal records, human tissue, human fluids and journalistic material held in confidence. Personal records are defined in s.12 and journalistic material in s.14: s.11.

'Special procedure material' means, in summary:

(a) journalistic material other than excluded material; and

(b) material acquired or created in the course of a trade, profession or other occupation or for the purpose of any office, held in confidence or subject to a restriction on disclosure or an obligation of secrecy: s.14.

Entry and search without warrant 12.06

A constable may enter and search any premises (as defined in s.23) without a warrant for the purposes of:
- (a) executing a warrant of arrest and commitment;
- (b) arresting a person for an arrestable offence;
- (c) recapturing a person unlawfully at large;
- (d) saving life or limb or preventing serious damage to property; and
- (e) arresting a person for certain offences, notably offences under the Public Order Act 1986, ss.1 to 5 (offensive conduct including riot, violent disorder, affray, fear or provocation of violence or harassment, alarm or distress) and offences under ss.6–8 of the Criminal Law Act 1977 (offences relating to entering or remaining on property): s.17(1).

The power is only exercisable if the constable has reasonable grounds for believing that the person whom he is seeking is on the premises and, in the case of offences under the Act of 1977, by a uniformed officer: s.17(2), (3). The power to search is confined to the extent that is reasonably required for the purpose: s.17(4).

At common law a constable may enter premises to deal with or prevent a breach of the peace and this power is expressly preserved by s.17(6).

A constable may also enter and search any premises occupied or controlled by a person who is under arrest for an arrestable offence if he has reasonable grounds for suspecting that there is on the premises evidence other than items subject to legal privilege relating to the offence or some other offence connected with or similar to that offence: s.18(1). This power may only be exercised on the *written authority* of a police officer of the rank of inspector or above: s.18(4). No authority is needed for entry and search *before* the arrested person is taken to the police station if his presence elsewhere is necessary for the effective investigation of the offence: s.18(5).

See, generally, Code 'B', Appendix I, *post*.

Search of premises with consent 12.07

This is expressly provided for and governed by Code 'B', para 4, Appendix I, *post*.

Seizure of property 12.08

A constable enjoys the following powers under PACE Act 1984; namely to *seize and retain* anything:
- (i) any article which he discovers in the course of a search under s.1 and which he has reasonable grounds for suspecting to be a stolen or prohibited article: s.1(6).
- (ii) for which a search has been authorised by a justices' warrant under s.8: s.8(2).
- (iii) for which he may under s.18 search for after entering premises following an arrest: s.18(2).
- (iv) he finds in the exercise of the power in s.32 to search an arrested person whom he believes may present a danger to himself or others: s.32(8).
- (v) *other than an item subject to legal privilege* which he finds in the course of searching an arrested person for anything which he might use for escape or which might be evidence: s.32(9).

(vi) for which a search has been authorised by a circuit judge: Sch.1, para 13.

In addition, a constable lawfully on any premises may seize anything which is on the premises if he has reasonable grounds for believing that:

(i) it has been obtained in consequence of the commission of an offence; and

(ii) it is necessary to seize it in order to prevent it being *concealed, lost, damaged, altered or destroyed*;

or

(i) it is evidence in relation to the offence; and

(ii) it is necessary to seize it to prevent it being *concealed, lost, altered or destroyed*: s.19(1), (3).

Any power to seize conferred on a constable who has entered premises includes a power to require a print-out of computerized information: s.20.

The Act also regulates the use of all powers to seize property. Thus, items which a constable has reasonable grounds for believing to be subject to legal privilege may not be seized under any enactment: s.19(6). Information about and access to seized property must be provided on request to the occupier of premises or the custodian or controller of the property: s.21. Anything seized or taken away by a constable may be retained so long as is necessary in all the circumstances: s.22(1); but under s.22(4), property is exempted from retention if a photograph or copy would be sufficient. The remaining rules governing retention are contained in s.22(2).

See, generally, Code 'B', para 6, Appendix I, *post*.

12.09 Stop and search

If a constable in uniform has reasonable grounds for suspecting that he will find stolen or prohibited articles he may *search any person or vehicle* for them and may *detain any person or vehicle* for that purpose: s.1(2), (3). A prohibited article is defined in s.1(7), (8), (9) as an offensive weapon and articles used or intended for theft and certain similar crimes. As to what constitutes reasonable grounds for suspicion: see Code 'A', Annex B, Appendix I, *post*.

The power may be exercised in any place to which the public or any section of the public have access or in any other place to which people have ready access but which is not a dwelling: s.1(1). Restrictions are imposed on the exercise of the power in gardens, yards and other land associated with dwellings: s.1(4), (5). *Note* that s.1 of the 1984 Act will be extended to searches for articles with blades or sharp points by [ss.132 and 133] CJA 1988 when in force.

12.10 Regulation of powers

The constable must take reasonable steps before beginning a search under this or similar provisions to bring to the attention of the appropriate person:

– his identity

– the object of the search

– the grounds for making it; and

– unless it is impracticable, the entitlement to a copy of the record: s.2(2)–(4).

The appropriate person is the person searched or, in the case of a vehicle, the person in charge: s.2(5). A person may not be required under this or similar powers to remove any of his clothing in public other than an outer coat, jacket or gloves: s.2(9).

After searching an unattended vehicle the constable must leave a notice in or on the vehicle: s.2(6). A written record must be kept of any search and must be made on the spot or as soon as practicable thereafter: s.3(1), (2). The searched person or owner of the vehicle is entitled to a copy of the record on demand within 12 months of the search: s.3(8), (9).

Road checks   12.11

A uniformed constable has power under s.159 RTA 1972, to stop a person driving a motor vehicle, or a cyclist. The exercise in a locality of this power in such a way as to stop during a period all vehicles or vehicles selected by any criterion is described as a road check: s.4(2) PACE Act 1984.

A road check may only be authorised in writing by a police officer of the rank of superintendent or above, but an officer below the rank of superintendent may authorise a road check if it appears to him that it is required as a matter of urgency: s.4(3), (5). He must as soon as is practicable inform an officer of the rank of superintendent or above who may authorise the road check to continue: s.4(6), (7), (8).

A road check may only be authorised for the purpose of ascertaining whether a vehicle is carrying a person:

(a) who has committed an offence other than a road traffic offence or a vehicle excise offence;

(b) who is a witness to such an offence;

(c) who intends to commit such an offence; or

(d) who is unlawfully at large: s.4(1), (3).

The superintendent must have reasonable grounds for believing that the offence is a serious arrestable offence and that the person in question is or is about to be in the locality: s.4(4). The authority may not last for more than 7 days at a time: s.4(11).

Reasonable force may be used if necessary in the exercise of the power: s.117.

Arrest without warrant   12.12

The powers of summary arrest, ie arrest without warrant, depend on whether the offence concerned is an *arrestable offence* and whether *the person arresting is a constable or not*.

Anyone may arrest without warrant a person *in the act* of committing an arrestable offence or anyone whom he has reasonable grounds for suspecting to be committing such an offence: s.24(4). Where an arrestable offence *has been committed* anyone may arrest without warrant anyone guilty of the offence or anyone whom he has reasonable grounds for suspecting to be guilty of the offence: s.24(5).

Where a constable has reasonable grounds for suspecting that an arrestable offence has been committed he may arrest without warrant anyone whom he has *reasonable grounds for suspecting* to be guilty of the offence: s.24(6). A constable may arrest without warrant anyone who is about to commit an arrestable offence or whom he has *reasonable grounds to suspect* to be about to commit such an offence: s.24(7).

Where a constable has reasonable grounds for believing that an offence which is *not* an arrestable offence has been committed or attempted he may arrest anyone whom he has reasonable grounds to suspect of *having committed or attempted to commit the offence or of being in the course of doing so* if it appears to him that service of a summons is impracticable or inappropriate because any of the general arrest conditions is satisfied: s.25(1), (2). The general arrest conditions are contained in s.25(3). They concern doubts about the identity or address of the arrested person, the prevention of certain offences and the protection of the young and vulnerable.

Reasonable force may be used if necessary by a constable in exercise of a power of arrest conferred on him as such by s.117.

Certain statutory powers of arrest without warrant are saved by Sch.2: s.26(2). In addition, there are the following powers of arrest without warrant:

(i) at common law for breach of the peace:

'. . . every citizen in whose presence a breach of the peace is being, or reasonably appears about to be, committed has the right to take reasonable steps to make the person who is breaking or threatening to break the peace refrain from doing so; and those reasonable steps in appropriate cases will include detaining him against his will. At common law this is not only the right of every citizen, it is also his duty, although, except in the case of a citizen who is a constable, it is a duty of imperfect obligation;'

per Lord Diplock in *Albert v Lavin* [1981] 3 All ER 878 at 880.

(ii) under various statutes, eg Sexual Offences Act 1956, s.41, Customs and Excise Management Act 1979, s.138(1).

Note

For *Procedure on Arrest*, including the power to search an arrested person, see under that title at Chapter 3, *Detention, Remands, Custody and Bail.*

PART 2: CJA 1987

12.13 JUSTICES' WARRANTS TO SEARCH FOR DOCUMENTS UNDER THE ACT

A note on the Serious Fraud Office

Section 1 CJA 1987 creates a 'Serious Fraud Office' and makes provision for the appointment of a 'Director of Serious Fraud' who will discharge his function under the superintendence of the Attorney-General. The Director has wide power to *investigate* any suspected offence involving 'complex or serious fraud' (not further defined), should he see fit in conjunction with the police or any other person. The Director may also *institute* and *conduct* any related criminal proceedings, including taking over proceedings already in existence at any stage. The role is thus a hybrid of investigator and prosecutor (*cf.* the Crown Prosecutor, Chapter 2). Section 1(15) invokes Sch.1 to the Act (not reproduced herein) which, *inter alia*, regulates the Serious Fraud Office, requires the Director to report annually to Parliament, and sets out the procedures as between the new office and the existing agencies.

The Director's investigative powers under s.1 are supplemented by a number of specific powers and entitlements under s.2. Thus, eg he may require a person whose affairs are under investigation, or any other person whom he believes to have information relevant to an investigation under s.1, by notice in writing, to attend before him and to answer questions or otherwise furnish information relevant to the investigation. Similarly, he may require the production of documents, take copies and require an explanation of them. Contained in s.3 are detailed provisions concerning disclosure of information by and to public bodies and officers, eg the Commissioners of Inland Revenue.

Applications for warrants 12.14

By s.2(4), a justice of the peace is empowered in response to information on oath from a member of the Serious Fraud Office to issue a warrant for a constable – generally accompanied by a member of the Office – to enter premises, by force if necessary, and to search for and to seize documents. The warrant will then authorise the constable to take possession of '. . . any documents appearing to be documents of the description specified in the information or to take . . . any steps which may appear necessary for preserving them and preventing interference with them': see s.2(5). The circumstances in which a justice may issue a warrant are set out in s.2(4). The justice must be:

'. . . satisfied, in relation to any documents, that there are reasonable grounds for believing–
(a) that–
  (i) a person has failed to comply with an obligation under s.2 to produce them;
  (ii) it is not practicable to serve a notice . . . in relation to them; or
  (iii) the service of such a notice in relation to them might seriously prejudice the investigation; and
(b) that they are on premises specified in the information'.

The term 'documents' is defined so as to include information recorded in any form for the purposes of the issue of a warrant, search and seizure: see s.2(18).

Protection for those under investigation or otherwise 12.15
assisting the Director

A general summary offence, punishable by imprisonment of up to six months and/or a fine of up to £2,000 (level 5), of failing without reasonable excuse to comply with a requirement imposed under s.2 is created by s.2(13).

In so far as evidence *against* a person is concerned, the use to which a statement made by a person in response to a requirement under s.2 may be put is circumscribed by s.2(8) of the Act. The statement may only be used against him on a prosecution for offences created by s.2(14) of the Act of making false or misleading statements, knowingly or recklessly. Such offences are triable either way and punishable on indictment with two years' imprisonment or a fine, or summarily up to the usual maximum six months' imprisonment and/or a fine of £2,000. Further offences of 'falsification', 'concealment' and 'destruction' of relevant documents – where the person knows that an investigation by the police or by the Serious Fraud Office into serious or complex fraud '. . . is being *or is likely* to be carried out' are created by s.2(16), in this instance triable either way, but subject to a higher maximum punishment of seven years' imprisonment on indictment. By way of an exception to the offence, the subsection casts the burden on the accused to prove that he had no intention of concealing the facts disclosed by the documents from the investigators.

No one can be required to disclose any information, or to produce any document which he would be entitled to refuse to disclose or produce on grounds of legal professional privilege 'in proceedings in the High Court', with the exception that a lawyer may be required to furnish the name of his client: s.2(9). Bankers' confidence is nominally respected by s.2(10), which exempts documents in respect of which a 'duty of confidence' is owed unless either the 'customer' consents to disclosure or production or the Director has authorised the making of the requirement. The intention seems to be that this authority will be made in person by the Director, although there is a saving where this is impracticable, when a member of the Serious Fraud Office 'designated by him' may make the authorisation. This contrasts with the general functions of the Director which, under s.1 and s.2, can be discharged by members of his Office, or in some cases, other delegates.

12.16   POLICE AND CRIMINAL EVIDENCE ACT 1984

Power of constable to stop and search persons, vehicles etc
1. (1) A constable may exercise any power conferred by this section–
  (a) in any place to which at the time when he proposes to exercise the power the public or any section of the public has access, on payment or otherwise, as of right or by virtue of express or implied permission; or
  (b) in any other place to which people have ready access at the time when he proposes to exercise the power but which is not a dwelling.

(2) Subject to subs (3) to (5) below, a constable–
  (a) may search–
    (i) any person or vehicle;
    (ii) anything which is in or on a vehicle,
      for stolen or prohibited articles; and
  (b) may detain a person or vehicle for the purpose of such a search.

(3) This section does not give a constable power to search a person or vehicle or anything in or on a vehicle unless he has reasonable grounds for suspecting that he will find stolen or prohibited articles.

(4) If a person is in a garden or yard occupied with and used for the purposes of a dwelling or on other land so occupied and used, a constable may not search him in the exercise of the power conferred by this section unless the constable has reasonable grounds for believing–
  (a) that he does not reside in the dwelling: and
  (b) that he is not in the place in question with the express or implied permission of a person who resides in the dwelling.

(5) if a vehicle is in a garden or yard occupied with and used for the purposes of a dwelling or on other land so occupied and used, a constable may not search the vehicle or anything in or on it in the exercise of the power conferred by this section unless he has reasonable grounds for believing–
  (a) that the person in charge of the vehicle does not reside in the dwelling; and
  (b) that the vehicle is not in the place in question with the express or implied permission of a person who resides in the dwelling.

(6) If in the course of such a search a constable discovers an article which he has reasonable grounds for suspecting to be a stolen or prohibited article, he may seize it.

(7) An article is prohibited for the purposes of this Part of this Act if it is–
  (a) an offensive weapon; or
  (b) an article–

  (i) made or adapted for use in the course of or in connection with an offence to which this sub-paragraph applies; or

  (ii) intended by the person having it with him for such use by him or by some other person.

(8) The offences to which subs (7)(b)(i) above applies are–

(a) burglary;

(b) theft;

(c) offences under s.12 of the Theft Act 1968 (taking motor vehicle or other conveyance without authority); and

(d) offences under s.15 of that Act (obtaining property by deception).

(9) In this Part of this Act 'offensive weapon' means any article–

(a) made or adapted for use for causing injury to persons; or

(b) intended by the person having it with him for such use by him or some other person.

1.(2) Subject to subsections (3) to (5) below, a constable–

(a) may search–

  (i) any person or vehicle;

  (ii) anything which is in or on a vehicle, for stolen or prohibited articles or an article to which subsection (8A) below applies; and

(b) may detain a person or vehicle for the purpose of such a search.

(3) This section does not give a constable power to search a person or vehicle or anything in or on a vehicle unless he has reasonable grounds for suspecting that he will find stolen or prohibited articles or any article to which subsection (8A) below applies.

(6) If in the course of such a search a constable discovers an article which he has reasonable grounds for suspecting to be a stolen or prohibited article or an article to which subsection (8A) below applies he may seize it.

(8A) This subsection applies to any article in relation to which a person has committed, or is committing or is going to commit an offence under s.128 of the Criminal Justice Act 1988.

[Subsections 1(2)(a), (3) and (6) are to be amended and subs (8A) added by s.129 CJA 1988 from a date to be appointed].

COMMENTARY

See generally the Code 'A', Appendix I.

Constable, includes a police officer of any rank. He need not be in uniform.

Prohibited weapon, see s.1(7).

Offensive weapon, see s.1(9).

Offence, see s.1(8).

Vehicle, extends to vessels, aircraft and hovercraft: s.2(10), *post.*

s.(3): Reasonable grounds for suspecting, see Annex B, Code of Practice: Appendix 1).

Search a person, as to the removal of clothing, see s.2(9)(a), *post.*

Provisions relating to search under s.1 and other powers   **12.17**

2. (1) A constable who detains a person or vehicle in the exercise–

(a) of the power conferred by s.1 above; or

(b) of any other power–

  (i) to search a person without first arresting him; or

  (ii) to search a vehicle without making an arrest,

need not conduct a search if it appears to him subsequently–

  (i) that no search is required; or

  (ii) that a search is impracticable.

  (2) If a constable contemplates a search, other than a search of an unattended vehicle, in the exercise–

   (a) of the power conferred by s.1 above; or

   (b) of any other power, except the power conferred by s.6 below and the power conferred by s.27(2) of the Aviation Security Act 1982–

      (i) to search a person without first arresting him; or

      (ii) to search a vehicle without making an arrest,

it shall be his duty, subject to subs (4) below, to take reasonable steps before he commences the search to bring to the attention of the appropriate person–

      (i) if the constable is not in uniform, documentary evidence that he is a constable; and

      (ii) whether he is in uniform or not, the matters specified in subs (3) below;

and the constable shall not commence the search until he has performed that duty.

   (3) The matters referred to in subs (2)(ii) above are–

   (a) the constable's name and the name of the police station to which he is attached;

   (b) the object of the proposed search;

   (c) the constable's grounds for proposing to make it; and

   (d) the effect of s.3(7) or (8) below, as may be appropriate.

   (4) A constable need not bring the effect of s.3(7) or (8) below to the attention of the appropriate person if it appears to the constable that it will not be practicable to make the record in s.3(1) below.

   (5) In this section 'the appropriate person' means–

   (a) if the constable proposes to search a person, that person; and

   (b) if he proposes to search a vehicle, or anything in or on a vehicle, the person in charge of the vehicle.

   (6) On completing a search of an unattended vehicle or anything in or on such a vehicle in the exercise of any such power as is mentioned in subs (2) above a constable shall leave a notice–

   (a) stating that he has searched it;

   (b) giving the name of the police station to which he is attached;

   (c) stating that an application for compensation for any damage caused by the search may be made to that police station; and

   (d) stating the effect of s.3(8) below.

   (7) The constable shall leave the notice inside the vehicle unless it is not reasonably practicable to do so without damaging the vehicle.

   (8) The time for which a person or vehicle may be detained for the purposes of such a search is such time as is reasonably required to permit a search to be carried out either at the place where the person or vehicle was first detained or nearby.

   (9) Neither the power conferred by s.1 above nor any other power to detain and search a person without first arresting him or to detain and search a vehicle without making an arrest is to be construed–

   (a) as authorising a constable to require a person to remove any of his clothing in public other than an outer coat, jacket or gloves; or

   (b) as authorising a constable not in uniform to stop a vehicle.

   (10) This section and s.1 above apply to vessels, aircraft and hovercraft as they apply to vehicles.

COMMENTARY

Constable, includes a police officer of any rank.

Appropriate person, see s.2(5).

Vehicle, see s.2(10).

Vessel, see s.118, *post.*

Duty to make records concerning searches **12.18**

3. (1) Where a constable has carried out a search in the exercise of any such power as is mentioned in s.2(1) above, other than a search–
(a) under s.6 below; or
(b) under s.27(2) of the Aviation Security Act 1982.
he shall make a record of it in writing unless it is not practicable to do so.

(2) If–
(a) a constable is required by subs (1) above to make a record of a search; but
(b) it is not practicable to make the record on the spot,
he shall make it as soon as practicable after the completion of the search.

(3) The record of a search of a person shall include a note of his name, if the constable knows it, but a constable may not detain a person to find out his name.

(4) If a constable does not know the name of a person whom he has searched, the record of the search shall include a note otherwise describing that person.

(5) The record of a search of a vehicle shall include a note describing the vehicle.

(6) The record of a search of a person or a vehicle–
(a) shall state–
    (i) the object of the search;
    (ii) the grounds for making it;
    (iii) the date and time when it was made;
    (iv) the place where it was made;
    (v) whether anything, and if so what, was found;
    (vi) whether any, and if so what, injury to a person or damage to property appears to the constable to have resulted from the search; and
(b) shall identify the constable making it.

(7) If a constable who conducted a search of a person made a record of it, the person who was searched shall be entitled to a copy of the record if he asks for one before the end of the period specified in subs (9) below.

(8) If–
(a) the owner of a vehicle which has been searched or the person who was in charge of the vehicle at the time when it was searched asks for a copy of the record of the search before the end of the period specified in subs (9) below; and
(b) the constable who conducted the search made a record of it,
the person who made the request shall be entitled to a copy.

(9) The period mentioned in subs (7) and (8) above is the period of 12 months beginning with the date on which the search was made.

(10) The requirements imposed by this section with regard to records of searches of vehicles shall apply also to records of searches of vessels, aircraft and hovercraft.

COMMENTARY
Vessel, see s.118, *post.*

Road checks **12.19**

4. (1) This section shall have effect in relation to the conduct of road checks by police officers for the purpose of ascertaining whether a vehicle is carrying–
(a) a person who has committed an offence other than a road traffic offence or a vehicles excise offence;
(b) a person who is a witness to such an offence;

(c) a person intending to commit such an offence; or

(d) a person who is unlawfully at large.

(2) For the purposes of this section a road check consists of the exercise in a locality of the power conferred by s.159 of the Road Traffic Act 1972 in such a way as to stop during the period for which its exercise in that way in that locality continues all vehicles or vehicles selected by any criterion.

(3) Subject to subs (5) below, there may only be such a road check if a police officer of the rank of superintendent or above authorises it in writing.

(4) An officer may only authorise a road check under subs (3) above–

(a) for the purpose specified in subs (1)(a) above, if he has reasonable grounds–

  (i) for believing that the offence is a serious arrestable offence; and

  (ii) for suspecting that the person is, or is about to be, in the locality in which vehicles would be stopped if the road check were authorised;

(b) for the purpose specified in subs (1)(b) above, if he has reasonable grounds for believing that the offence is a serious arrestable offence;

(c) for the purpose specified in subs (1)(c) above, if he has reasonable grounds–

  (i) for believing that the offence would be a serious arrestable offence; and

  (ii) for suspecting that the person is, or is about to be, in the locality in which vehicles would be stopped if the road check were authorised;

(d) for the purpose specified in subs (1)(d) above, if he has reasonable grounds for suspecting that the person is, or is about to be, in that locality.

(5) An officer below the rank of superintendent may authorise such a road check if it appears to him that it is required as a matter of urgency for one of the purposes specified in subs (1) above.

(6) If an authorisation is given under subs (5) above, it shall be the duty of the officer who gives it–

(a) to make a written record of the time at which he gives it; and

(b) to cause an officer of the rank of superintendent or above to be informed that it has been given.

(7) The duties imposed by subs (6) above shall be performed as soon as it is practicable to do so.

(8) An officer to whom a report is made under subs (6) above may, in writing, authorise the road check to continue.

(9) If such an officer considers that the road check should not continue, he shall record in writing–

(a) the fact that it took place; and

(b) the purpose for which it took place.

(10) An officer giving an authorisation under this section shall specify the locality in which vehicles are to be stopped.

(11) An officer giving an authorisation under this section, other than an authorisation under subs (5) above–

(a) shall specify a period, not exceeding seven days, during which the road check may continue; and

(b) may direct that the road check–

  (i) shall be continuous; or

  (ii) shall be conducted at specified times,

  during that period.

(12) If it appears to an officer of the rank of superintendent or above that a road check ought to continue beyond the period for which it has been authorised he may, from time to time, in writing specify a further period, not exceeding seven days, during which it may continue.

(13) Every written authorisation shall specify–
(a) the name of the officer giving it;
(b) the purpose of the road check; and
(c) the locality in which vehicles are to be stopped.

(14) The duties to specify the purposes of a road check imposed by subs (9) and (13) above includes duties to specify any relevant serious arrestable offence.

(15) Where a vehicle is stopped in a road check, the person in charge of the vehicle at the time when it is stopped shall be entitled to obtain a written statement of the purpose of the road check if he applies for such a statement not later than the end of the period of twelve months from the day on which the vehicle was stopped.

(16) Nothing in this section affects the exercise by police officers of any power to stop vehicles for purposes other than those specified in subs (1) above.

COMMENTARY
See generally the Code 'A', Appendix I.

Road checks, see s.4(2).

s.1(4): Reasonable grounds . . . for suspecting, see Code 'A', Annex B, Appendix I

Serious arrestable offence, defined in s.116, *post.*

Statutory undertakers etc   12.20
6. (1) A constable employed by statutory undertakers may stop, detain and search any vehicle before it leaves a goods area included in the premises of the statutory undertakers.

(2) In this section 'goods area' means any area used wholly or mainly for the storage or handling of goods.

(3) For the purposes of s.6 of the Public Stores Act 1875, any person appointed under the Special Constables Act 1923 to be a special constable within any premises which are in the possession or under the control of British Nuclear Fuels Limited shall be deemed by a constable deputed by a public department and any goods and chattels belonging to or in the possession of British Nuclear Fuels Limited shall be deemed to be Her Majesty's Stores.

(4) (*Northern Ireland*).

COMMENTARY
Statutory undertaking, defined in s.7(3), *post.*

Goods area, see s.6(2).

Premises, see s.23, *post.*

Part I – supplementary   12.21
7. (3) In this Part of this Act 'statutory undertakers' means persons authorised by any enactment to carry on any railway, light railway, road transport, water transport, canal, inland navigation, dock or harbour undertaking.

Power of justice of the peace to authorise entry and search of premises   12.22
8. (1) If on an application made by a constable a justice of the peace is satisfied that there are reasonable grounds for believing–
(a) that a serious offence has been committed; and
(b) that there is material on premises specified in the application which is likely to be of substantial value (whether by itself or together with other material) to the investigation of the offence; and

(c) that the material is likely to be relevant evidence; and
(d) that it does not consist of or include items subject to legal privilege, excluded material or special procedure material; and
(e) that any of the conditions specified in subs (3) below applies,

he may issue a warrant authorising a constable to enter and search the premises.

(2) A constable may seize and retain anything for which a search has been authorised under subs (1) above.

(3) The conditions mentioned in subs (1)(e) above are–
(a) that it is not practicable to communicate with any person entitled to grant entry to the premises;
(b) that it is practicable to communicate with a person entitled to grant entry to the premises but it is not practicable to communicate with any person entitled to grant access to the evidence;
(c) that entry to the premises will not be granted unless a warrant is produced;
(d) that the purpose of a search may be frustrated or seriously prejudiced unless a constable arriving at the premises can secure immediate entry to them.

(4) In this Act 'relevant evidence', in relation to an offence, means anything that would be admissible in evidence at a trial for the offence.

(5) The power to issue a warrant conferred by this section is in addition to any such power otherwise conferred.

COMMENTARY

The issue of a search warrant under this section is governed by the safeguards in s.15 *post*. For execution, see s.16. A warrant issued under this section includes power to require a print-out of computerised information: see s.20, *post*.

Constable, includes a police officer of any rank.

Serious arrestable offence, defined in s.116.

Premises, defined in s.23: s.118(1).

Relevant evidence, defined in s.8 (4).

Items subject to legal privilege, defined in s.10: s.118(1).

Excluded material, defined in s.11.'

Special procedure material, defined in s.14.

Premises, partially defined in s.23: s.118(1).

12.23 **Special provisions as to access**
9. (1) A constable may obtain access to excluded material or special procedure material for the purposes of a criminal investigation by making an application under Schedule 1 below and in accordance with that Schedule.

(2) Any Act (including a local Act) passed before this Act under which a search of premises for the purposes of a criminal investigation could be authorised by the issue of a warrant to a constable shall cease to have effect so far as it relates to the authorisation of searches–
(a) for items subject to legal privilege; or
(b) for excluded material; or
(c) for special procedure material consisting of documents or records other than documents.

COMMENTARY

Access, the provisions are for the protection of the person against whom the order is sought, not for the protection of the suspect: *R v Manchester Crown Court, ex p. Taylor* (1988) *The Times*, 17 February.

Constable, includes a police officer of any rank.

Excluded material, defined in s.11, *post.*

Special procedure material, defined in s.14.

Schedule 1, not reproduced herein.

Meaning of 'items subject to legal privilege' 12.24
10. (1) Subject to subs (2) below, in this Act 'items subject to legal privilege' means–
  (a) communications between a professional legal adviser and his client or any person representing his client made in connection with the giving of legal advice to the client;
  (b) communications between a professional legal adviser and his client or any person representing his client or between such an adviser or his client or any such representative and any other person made in connection with or in contemplation of legal proceedings and for the purposes of such proceedings; and
  (c) items enclosed with or referred to in such communications and made–
    (i) in connection with the giving of legal advice; or
    (ii) in connection with or in contemplation of legal proceedings and for the purposes of such proceedings,
when they are in the possession of a person who is entitled to possession of them.

(2) Items held with the intention of furthering a criminal purpose are not items subject to legal privilege.

Meaning of 'excluded material' 12.25
11. (1) Subject to the following provisions of this section, in this Act 'excluded material' means–
  (a) personal records which a person has acquired or created in the course of any trade, business, profession or other occupation or for the purposes of any paid or unpaid office and which he holds in confidence;
  (b) human tissue or tissue fluid which has been taken for the purposes of diagnosis or medical treatment and which a person holds in confidence;
  (c) journalistic material which a person holds in confidence and which consists–
    (i) of documents; or
    (ii) of records other than documents.

(2) A person holds material other than journalistic material in confidence for the purposes of this section if he holds it subject–
  (a) to an express or implied undertaking to hold it in confidence; or
  (b) to a restriction on disclosure or an obligation of secrecy contained in any enactment, including an enactment contained in an Act passed after this Act.

(3) A person holds journalistic material in confidence for the purposes of this section if–
  (a) he holds it subject to such an undertaking, restriction or obligation; and
  (b) it has been continuously held (by one or more persons) subject to such an undertaking, restriction or obligation since it was first acquired or created for the purposes of journalism.

COMMENTARY
Personal records, defined in s.12, *post.*

Holds in confidence, defined in s.11(2).

Journalistic material, defined in s.13.

Documents, defined in s.118(1).

12.26   Meaning of 'personal records'
12. In this Part of this Act 'personal records' means documentary and other records concerning an individual (whether living or dead) who can be identified from them and relating–
  (a) to his physical or mental health;
  (b) to spiritual counselling or assistance given or to be given to him; or
  (c) to counselling or assistance given or to be given to him, for the purposes of his personal welfare, by any voluntary organisation or by any individual who–
      (i) by reason of his office or occupation has responsibilities for his personal welfare; or
      (ii) by reason of an order of a court has responsibilities for his supervision.

12.27   Meaning of 'journalistic material'
13. (1) Subject to subs (2) below, in this Act 'journalistic material' means material acquired or created for the purposes of journalism.

(2) Material is only journalistic material for the purposes of this Act if it is in the possession of a person who acquired or created it for the purposes of journalism.

(3) A person who receives material from someone who intends that the recipient shall use it for the purposes of journalism is to be taken to have acquired it for those purposes.

12.28   Meaning of 'special procedure material'
14. (1) In this Act 'special procedure material' means–
  (a) material to which subs (2) below applies; and
  (b) journalistic material, other than excluded material.

(2) Subject to the following provisions of this section, this subsection applies to material, other than items subject to legal privilege and excluded material, in the possession of a person who–
  (a) acquired or created it in the course of any trade, business, profession or other occupation or for the purpose of any paid or unpaid office; and
  (b) holds it subject–
      (i) to an express or implied undertaking to hold it in confidence; or
      (ii) to a restriction or obligation such as is mentioned in s.11(2)(b) above.

(3) Where material is acquired–
  (a) by an employee from his employer and in the course of his employment; or
  (b) by a company from an associated company,
it is only special procedure material if it was special procedure material immediately before the acquisition.

(4) Where material is created by an employee in the course of his employment, it is only special procedure material, if it would have been special procedure material had his employer created it.

(5) Where material is created by a company on behalf of an associated company, it is only special procedure material if it would have been special procedure material had the associated company created it.

(6) A company is to be treated as another's associated company for the purposes of this section if it would be so treated under s.302 of the Income and Corporation Taxes Act 1970.

COMMENTARY
Journalistic material, defined in s.13, *ante.*
Items subject to legal privilege, defined in s.10: s.118(1).

Excluded material, defined in s.11.

Associated company, see s.14(6).

Search warrants – safeguards   **12.29**
   15. (1) This section and s.16 below have effect in relation to the issue to constables under any enactment, including an enactment contained in an Act passed after this Act, of warrants to enter and search premises; and an entry on or search of premises under a warrant is unlawful unless it complies with this section and s.16 below.

   (2) Where a constable applies for any such warrant, it shall be his duty–
   (a) to state–
      (i) the ground on which he makes the application; and
      (ii) the enactment under which the warrant would be issued;
   (b) to specify the premises which it is desired to enter and search; and
   (c) to identify, so far as is practicable, the articles or persons to be sought.

   (3) An application for such a warrant shall be made *ex parte* and supported by an information in writing.

   (4) The constable shall answer on oath any question that the justice of the peace or judge hearing the application asks him.

   (5) A warrant shall authorise an entry on one occasion only.

   (6) A warant–
   (a) shall specify–
      (i) the name of the person who applies for it;
      (ii) the date on which it is issued;
      (iii) the enactment under which it is issued; and
      (iv) the premises to be searched; and
   (b) shall identify, so far as is practicable, the article or persons to be sought.

   (7) Two copies shall be made of a warrant.

   (8) The copies shall be clearly certified as copies.

COMMENTARY
Premises, partially defined in s.23, *post*: s.118(1).

s.15(4): see Code 'B', para 2.6, Appendix I which elaborates on these requirements.

Execution of warrants   **12.30**
   16. (1) A warrant to enter and search premises may be executed by any constable.

   (2) Such a warrant may authorise persons to accompany any constable who is executing it.

   (3) Entry and search under a warrant must be within one month from the date of its issue.

   (4) Entry and search under a warrant must be at a reasonable hour unless it appears to the constable executing it that the purpose of a search may be frustrated on an entry at a reasonable hour.

   (5) Where the occupier of premises which are to be entered and searched is present at the time when a constable seeks to execute a warrant to enter and search them, the constable–
   (a) shall identify himself to the occupier and, if not in uniform, shall produce to him documentary evidence that he is a constable;
   (b) shall produce the warrant to him; and
   (c) shall supply him with a copy of it.

   (6) Where–

(a) the occupier of such premises is not present at the time when a constable seeks to execute such a warrant; but

(b) some other person who appears to the constable to be in charge of the premises is present,

subs (5) above shall have effect as if any reference to the occupier were a reference to that other person.

(7) If there is no person present who appears to the constable to be in charge of the premises, he shall leave a copy of the warrant in a prominent place on the premises.

(8) A search under a warrant may only be a search to the extent required for the purpose for which the warrant was issued.

(9) A constable executing a warrant shall make an endorsement on it stating–

(a) whether the articles or persons sought were found; and

(b) whether any articles were seized, other than articles which were sought.

(10) A warrant which–

(a) has been executed; or

(b) has not been executed within the time authorised for its execution, shall be returned–

(i) if it was issued by a justice of the peace, to the clerk to the justices for the petty sessions area for which he acts; and

(ii) if it was issued by a judge, to the appropriate officer of the court from which he issued it.

(11) A warrant which is returned under subs (10) above shall be retained for 12 months from its return–

(a) by the clerk to the justices, if it was returned under para (i) of that subsection; and

(b) by the appropriate officer, if it was returned under para (ii).

(12) If during the period for which a warrant is to be retained the occupier of the premises to which it relates asks to inspect it, he shall be allowed to do so.

COMMENTARY

Constable, includes a police officer of any rank.

Month, ie a calendar month: Sch.1 Interpretation Act 1978.

Premises, partially defined in s.23: s.118(1).

Endorsement, Attaching a separate document to the warrant is not endorsement: *R v Metropolitan Police Commissioner, ex p. Melia* [1957] 1 WLR 1065.

s.16(4), see Code 'B', para 5(a), Appendix I, *post.*

s.16(5), shall identify himself, etc. But not where there are reasonable grounds for believing that this would frustrate the object of the search, or endanger the constable or others: *R v Longman* (1988) *The Times,* 8 March.

12.31   **Entry for purpose of arrest etc**

17. (1) Subject to the following provisions of this section, and without prejudice to any other enactment, a constable may enter and search any premises for the purpose–

(a) of executing

(i) a warrant of arrest issued in connection with or arising out of criminal proceedings; or

(ii) a warrant of commitment issued under s.76 of the Magistrates' Courts Act 1980;

(b) of arresting a person for an arrestable offence;

(c) of arresting a person for an offence under–

  (i) section 1 (prohibition of uniforms in connection with political objects) of the Public Order Act 1936;
  (ii) any enactment contained in ss.6 to 8 or 10 of the Criminal Law Act 1977 (offences relating to entering and remaining on property);
  (iii) section 4 of the Public Order Act 1986 (fear of provocation of violence);
(d) of recapturing a person who is unlawfully at large and whom he is pursuing; or
(e) of saving life or limb or preventing serious damage to property.

(2) Except for the purpose specified in para (e) of subs (1) above, the powers of entry and search conferred by this section–
(a) are only exercisable if the constable has reasonable grounds for believing that the person whom he is seeking is on the premises; and
(b) are limited, in relation to premises consisting of two or more separate dwellings, to powers to enter and search–
  (i) any parts of the premises which the occupiers of any dwelling comprised in the premises use in common with the occupiers of any other such dwelling; and
  (ii) any such dwelling in which the constable has reasonable grounds for believing that the person whom he is seeking may be.

(3) The powers of entry and search conferred by this section are only exercisable for the purposes specified in subs (1)(c)(ii) above by a constable in uniform.

(4) The power of search conferred by this section is only a power to search to the extent that is reasonably required for the purpose for which the power of entry is exercised.

(5) Subject to subs (6) below, all the rules of common law under which a constable has power to enter premises without a warrant are hereby abolished.

(6) Nothing in subs (5) above affects any power of entry to deal with or prevent a breach of the peace.
[*As amended by Sch.3 Public Order Act 1986*].

COMMENTARY
Reasonable force may be used, if necessary, in the exercise of the power under this section: s.117, *post*. 'Force' in this context means the application of energy to an obstacle: *Swales v Cox* [1981] 1 All ER 115.

Constable, includes a police officer of any rank.

Premises, partially defined in s.23: s.118(1).

Arrestable offence, defined in s.24: s.118(1). For an example of entry based on reasonable grounds for suspecting the commission of such an offence see *Kynaston v DPP* (1987) *The Times*, 4 November.

Breach of the peace, see under *Arrest without Warrant*, 12.12.

Entry and search after arrest   **12.32**
18. (1) Subject to the following provisions of this section, a constable may enter and search any premises occupied or controlled by a person who is under arrest for an arrestable offence, if he has reasonable grounds for suspecting that there is on the premises evidence, other than items subject to legal privilege, that relates–
(a) to that offence; or
(b) to some other arrestable offence which is connected with or similar to that offence.

(2) A constable may seize and retain anything for which he may search under subs(1) above.

(3) The power to search conferred by subs (1) above is only a power to

search to the extent that is reasonably required for the purpose of discovering such evidence.

(4) Subject to subs (5) below, the powers conferred by this section may not be exercised unless an officer of the rank of inspector or above has authorised them in writing.

(5) A constable may conduct a search under subs (1) above–
(a) before taking the person to a police station; and
(b) without obtaining an authorisation under subs (4) above,
if the presence of that person at a place other than a police station is necessary for the effective investigation of the offence.

(6) If a constable conducts a search by virtue of subs (5) above, he shall inform an officer of the rank of inspector or above that he has made the search as soon as practicable after he has made it.

(7) An officer who–
(a) authorises a search; or
(b) is informed of a search under subs (6) above,
shall make a record in writing–
 (i) of the grounds for the search; and
(ii) of the nature of the evidence that was sought.

(8) If the person who was in occupation or control of the premises at the time of the search is in police detention at the time the record is to be made, the officer shall make the record as part of his custody record.

COMMENTARY

The power to search under s.18 includes power to require a print-out of computerised information: see s.20, *post*.

Constable, includes a police officer of any rank.

Premises, partially defined in s.23: s.118(1).

Arrestable offence, defined in s.24: s.118(1).

Items subject to legal privilege, defined in s.10; s.118(1).

12.33   **General power of seizure etc**
19. (1) The powers conferred by subs (2), (3) and (4) below are exercisable by a constable who is lawfully on any premises.

(2) The constable may seize anything which is on the premises if he has reasonable grounds for believing–
(a) that it has been obtained in consequence of the commission of an offence; and
(b) that it is necessary to seize it in order to prevent it being concealed, lost, damaged, altered or destroyed.

(3) The constable may seize anything which is on the premises if he has reasonable grounds for believing–
(a) that it is evidence in relation to an offence which he is investigating or any other offence; and
(b) that it is necessary to seize it in order to prevent the evidence being concealed, lost, altered or destroyed.

(4) The constable may require any information which is contained in a computer and is accessible from the premises to be produced in a form in which it can be taken away and in which it is visible and legible if he has reasonable grounds for believing–
(a) that–
 (i) it is evidence in relation to an offence which he is investigating or any other offence; or
(ii) it has been obtained in consequence of the commission of an offence; and

(b) that it is necessary to do so in order to prevent it being concealed, lost, tampered with or destroyed.

(5) The powers conferred by this section are in addition to any power otherwise conferred.

(6) No power of seizure conferred on a constable under any enactment (including an enactment contained in an Act passed after this Act) is to be taken to authorise the seizure of an item which the constable execising the power has reasonable grounds for believing to be subject to legal privilege.

COMMENTARY
Premises, partially defined in s.23, *post*: s.118(1).

Item . . . subject to legal privilege, defined in s.10, *ante*: s.118(1).

Extension of powers of seizure to computerised information 12.34
20. (1) Every power of seizure which is conferred by an enactment to which this section applies on a constable who has entered premises in the exercise of a power conferred by an enactment shall be construed as including a power to require any information contained in a computer and accessible from the premises to be produced in a form in which it can be taken away and in which it is visible and legible.

(2) This section applies–
(a) to any enactment contained in an Act passed before this Act;
(b) to s.8 and 18 above;
(c) to para 14 of Sch.1 to this Act; and
(d) to any enactment contained in an Act passed after this Act.

COMMENTARY
Premises, partially defined in s.23, *post:* s.118(1).

Access and copying 12.35
21. (1) A constable who seizes anything in the exercise of a power conferred by any enactment, including an enactment contained in an Act passed after this Act, shall, if so requested by a person showing himself–
(a) to be the occupier of premises on which it was seized; or
(b) to have had custody or control of it immediately before the seizure,
provide that person with a record of what he seized.

(2) The officer shall provide the record within a reasonable time from the making of the request for it.

(3) Subject to subs (8) below, if a request for permission to be granted access to anything which–
(a) has been seized by a constable; and
(b) is retained by the police for the purpose of investigating an offence,
is made to the officer in charge of the investigation by a person who had custody or control of the thing immediately before it was so seized or by someone acting on behalf of such a person, the officer shall allow the person who made the request access to it under the supervision of a constable.

(4) Subject to subs (8) below, if a request for a photograph or copy of any such thing is made to the officer in charge of the investigation by a person who had custody or control of the thing immediately before it was so seized, or by someone acting on behalf of such a person, the officer shall–
(a) allow the person who made the request access to it under the supervision of a constable for the purpose of photographing or copying it; or
(b) photograph or copy it, or cause it to be photographed or copied.

(5) A constable may also photograph or copy, and have photographed or copied, anything which he has power to seize, without a request being made under subs (4) above.

(6) Where anything is photographed or copied under subs (4)(b) above, the photograph or copy shall be supplied to the person who made the request.

(7) The photograph or copy shall be so supplied within a reasonable time from the making of the request.

(8) There is no duty under this section to grant access to, or to supply a photograph or copy of, anything if the officer in charge of the investigation for the purposes of which it was seized has reasonable grounds for believing that to do so would prejudice–
(a) that investigation;
(b) the investigation of an offence other than the offence for the purposes of investigating for which the thing was seized; or
(c) any criminal proceedings which may be brought as a result of–
    (i) the investigation of which he is in charge; or
    (ii) any such investigation as is mentioned in para (b) above.

COMMENTARY
Premises, partially defined in s.23 *post*: s.118(1).

12.36   **Retention**
    22. (1) Subject to subs (4) below, anything which has been seized by a constable or taken away by a constable following a requirement made by virtue of ss.19 or 20 above may be retained so long as is necessary in all the circumstances.

(2) Without prejudice to the generality of subs (1) above–
(a) anything seized for the purposes of a criminal investigation may be retained, except as provided by subs (4) below–
    (i) for use as evidence at a trial for an offence; or
    (ii) for forensic examination or for investigation in connection with an offence; and
(b) anything may be retained in order to establish its lawful owner, where there are reasonable grounds for believing that it has been obtained in consequence of the commission of an offence.

(3) Nothing seized on the ground that it may be used–
(a) to cause physical injury to any person;
(b) to damage property;
(c) to interfere with evidence; or
(d) to assist in escape from police detention or lawful custody,
may be retained when the person from whom it was seized is no longer in police detention or the custody of a court or is in the custody of a court but has been released on bail.

(4) Nothing may be retained for either of the purposes mentioned in subs (2)(a) above if a photograph or copy would be sufficient for that purpose.

(5) Nothing in this section affects any power of a court to make an order under s.1 of the Police (Property) Act 1897.

12.37   **Meaning of 'premises' etc**
    23. In this Act–
'premises' includes any place and, in particular, includes–
(a) any vehicle, vessel, aircraft or hovercraft;
(b) any offshore installation; and
(c) any tent or movable structure; and
'offshore installation' has the meaning given to it by s.1 of the Mineral Workings (Offshore Installations) Act 1971.

12.38   **Arrest without warrant for arrestable offences**
    24. (1) The powers of summary arrest conferred by the following subsections shall apply–

(a) to offences for which the sentence is fixed by law;
(b) to offences for which a person of 21 years of age or over (not previously convicted) may be sentenced to imprisonment for a term of five years (or might be so sentenced but for the restrictions imposed by s.33 of the Magistrates' Courts Act 1980); and
(c) to the offences to which subs (2) below applies,
and in this Act 'arrestable offences' means any such offence.

(2) The offences to which this subsection applies are–
(a) offences for which a person may be arrested under the customs and excise Acts, as defined in s.1(1) of the Customs and Excise Management Act 1979;
(b) offence under the Official Secrets Act 1911 and 1920 that are not arrestable offences by virtue of the term of imprisonment for which a person may be sentenced in respect of them;
(c) offences under s.22 (causing prostitution of women) or 23 (procuration of a girl under 21) of the Sexual Offences Act 1956;
(d) offences under s.12(1) (taking motor vehicle or other conveyance without authority etc) or 25(1) (going equipped for stealing, etc) of the Theft Act 1968; and
(e) offences under s.1 of the Public Bodies Corrupt Practices Act 1889 (corruption in office) or s.1 of the Prevention of Corruption Act 1906 (corrupt transactions with agents).

(3) Without prejudice to s.2 of the Criminal Attempts Act 1981, the powers of summary arrest conferred by the following subsections shall also apply to the offences of–
(a) conspiring to commit any of the offences mentioned in subs (2) above;
(b) attempting to commit any such offence;
(c) inciting, aiding, abetting, counselling or procuring the commission of any such offence;
and such offences are also arrestable offences for the purposes of this Act.

(4) Any person may arrest without a warrant–
(a) anyone who is in the act of committing an arrestable offence;
(b) anyone whom he has reasonable grounds for suspecting to be committing such an offence.

(5) Where an arrestable offence has been committed, any person may arrest without a warrant–
(a) anyone who is guilty of the offence;
(b) anyone whom he has reasonable grounds for suspecting to be guilty of it.

(6) Where a constable has reasonable grounds for suspecting that an arrestable offence has been committed, he may arrest without a warrant anyone whom he has reasonable grounds for suspecting to be guilty of the offence.

(7) A constable may arrest without a warrant–
(a) anyone who is about to commit an arrestable offence;
(b) anyone whom he has reasonable grounds for suspecting to be about to commit an arrestable offence.

[*As amended by Sch.6 Sexual Offences Act 1985. Subs (2)(e) will be repealed by [Sch.15] CJA 1988 when in force*].

COMMENTARY

For the power of a constable to enter and search premises for the purpose of arresting a person for an arrestable offence, see s.17, *ante*.

s.24(6): it was held under the pre-existing law that it is not necessary that the constable who first suspects an arrestable offence and seeks to arrest should be the one who effects entry: *R v Francis* [1972] Crim LR 549.

Arrestable offence, see s.24(1), (3).

12.39 **General arrest conditions**

25. (1) Where a constable has reasonable grounds for suspecting that any offence which is not an arrestable offence has been committed or attempted, or is being committed or attempted, he may arrest the relevant person if it appears to him that service of a summons is impracticable or inappropriate because any of the general arrest conditions is satisfied.

(2) In this section 'the relevant person' means any person whom the constable has reasonable grounds to suspect of having committed or having attempted to commit the offence or of being in the course of committing or attempting to commit it.

(3) The general arrest conditions are–

(a) that the name of the relevant person is unknown to, and cannot be readily ascertained by, the constable;

(b) that the constable has reasonable grounds for doubting whether a name furnished by the relevant person as his name is his real name;

(c) that–

    (i) the relevant person has failed to furnish a satisfactory address for service; or

    (ii) the constable has reasonable grounds for doubting whether an address furnished by the relevant person is a satisfactory address for service;

(d) that the constable has reasonable grounds for believing that arrest is necessary to prevent the relevant person–

    (i) causing physical injury to himself or any other person;

    (ii) suffering physical injury;

    (iii) causing loss or damage to property;

    (iv) committing an offence against public decency; or

    (v) causing an unlawful obstruction of the highway;

(e) that the constable has reasonable grounds for believing that arrest is necessary to protect a child or other vulnerable person from the relevant person.

(4) For the purposes of subs (3) above an address is a satisfactory address for service if it appears to the constable–

(a) that the relevant person will be at it for a sufficiently long period for it to be possible to serve him with a summons; or

(b) that some other person specified by the relevant person will accept service of a summons for the relevant person at it.

(5) Nothing in subs (3)(d) above authorises the arrest of a person under subpara (iv) of that paragraph except where members of the public going about their normal business cannot reasonably be expected to avoid the person to be arrested.

(6) This section shall not prejudice any power of arrest conferred apart from this section.

COMMENTARY

Arrestable offence, defined in s.24, *ante*: s.118(1).

The relevant person, defined in s.25(2).

The general arrest conditions, see s.25(3).

A satisfactory address, see s.25(4).

Note

For provisions from s.27 onwards, including definitions (s.118); 'serious arrestable offences' (s.116); and Codes of Practice (s.66), Chapter 3, *Detention, Remands, Custody and Bail*; and for the Codes themselves, see Appendix I.

CRIMINAL JUSTICE ACT 1987

Serious Fraud Office **12.40**
   1. (1) A Serious Fraud Office shall be constituted for England and Wales and Northern Ireland.

(2) The Attorney General shall appoint a person to be the Director of the Serious Fraud Office (referred to in this Part of this Act as 'the Director'), and he shall discharge his functions under the superintendence of the Attorney General.

(3) The Director may investigate any suspected offence which appears to him on reasonable grounds to involve serious or complex fraud.

(4) The Director may, if he thinks fit, conduct any such investigation in conjunction either with the police or with any other person who is, in the opinion of the Director, a proper person to be concerned in it.

(5) The Director may–
   (a) institute and have the conduct of any criminal proceedings which appear to him to relate to such fraud; and
   (b) take over the conduct of any such proceedings at any stage.

(6) The Director shall discharge such other functions in relation to fraud as may from time to time be assigned to him by the Attorney General.

(7) The Director may designate for the purposes of subs (5) above any member of the Serious Fraud Office who is–
   (a) a barrister in England and Wales or Northern Ireland;
   (b) a solicitor of the Supreme Court; or
   (c) a solicitor of the Supreme Court of Judicature of Northern Ireland.

(8) Any member so designated shall, without prejudice to any functions which may have been assigned to him in his capacity as a member of that Office, have all the powers of the Director as to the institution and conduct of proceedings but shall exercise those powers under the direction of the Director.

(9) Any member so designated who is a barrister in England and Wales or a solicitor of the Supreme Court shall have, in any court, the rights of audience enjoyed by solicitors holding practising certificates and shall have such additional rights of audience in the Crown Court in England and Wales as may be given by virtue of subs (11) below.

(10)–(14) Crown Court; Northern Ireland.

(15) Schedule 1 to this Act shall have effect.

(16) For the purposes of this section (including that Schedule) references to the conduct of any proceedings include references to the proceedings being discontinued and to the taking of any steps (including the bringing of appeals and making of representations in respect of applications for bail) which may be taken in relation to them.

(17) (Northern Ireland).

COMMENTARY
.1.(3): Serious or complex fraud, not further defined.

.1(16): Discontinued, compare the power of Crown Prosecutors in relation to criminal proceedings generally under s.23 POA 1985, but under s.1(16) of the 1987 Act discontinuance is not limited to any particular stage of the proceedings, *semble.*

Director's investigative powers **12.41**
   2. (1) The powers of the Director under this section shall be exercisable, but only for the purposes of an investigation under s.1 above, in any case in

which it appears to him that there is good reason to do so for the purpose of investigating the affairs, or any aspect of the affairs, of any person.

(2) The Director may by notice in writing require the person whose affairs are to be investigated ('the person under investigation') or any other person whom he has reason to believe has relevant information to attend before the Director at a specified time and place and answer questions or otherwise furnish information with respect to any matter relevant to the investigation.

(3) The Director may by notice in writing require the person under investigation or any other person to produce at a specified time and place any specified documents which appear to the Director to relate to any matter relevant to the investigation or any documents of a specified class which appear to him so to relate; and–
  (a) if any such documents are produced, the Director may–
      (i) take copies or extracts from them;
      (ii) require the person producing them to provide an explanation of any of them;
  (b) if any such documents are not produced, the Director may require the person who was required to produce them to state, to the best of his knowledge and belief, where they are.

(4) Where, on information on oath laid by a member of the Serious Fraud Office, a justice of the peace is satisfied, in relation to any documents, that there are reasonable grounds for believing–
  (a) that–
      (i) a person has failed to comply with an obligation under this section to produce them;
      (ii) it is not practicable to serve a notice under subs (3) above in relation to them; or
      (iii) the service of such a notice in relation to them might seriously prejudice the investigation; and
  (b) that they are on premises specified in the information,
he may issue such a warrant as is mentioned in subs (5) below.

(5) The warrant referred to above is a warrant authorising any constable–
  (a) to enter (using such force as is reasonably necessary for the purpose) and search the premises, and
  (b) to take possession of any documents appearing to be documents of the description specified in the information or to take in relation to any documents so appearing any other steps which may appear to be necessary for preserving them and preventing interference with them.

(6) (Execution of warrants).

(7) (Definitions relating to s.2(6)).

(8) A statement by a person in response to a requirement imposed by virtue of this section may only be used in evidence against him–
  (a) on a prosecution for an offence under subs (14) below; or
  (b) on a prosecution for some other offence where in giving evidence he makes a statement inconsistent with it.

(9) A person shall not under this section be required to disclose any information or produce any document which he would be entitled to refuse to disclose or produce on grounds of legal professional privilege in proceedings in the High Court, except that a lawyer may be required to furnish the name and address of his client.

(10) A person shall not under this section be required to disclose information or produce a document in respect of which he owes an obligation of confidence by virtue of carrying on any banking business unless–

(a) the person to whom the obligation of confidence is owed consents to the disclosure or production; or

(b) the Director has authorised the making of the requirement or, if it is impracticable for him to act personally, a member of the Serious Fraud Office designated by him for the purposes of this subsection has done so.

(11) Without prejudice to the power of the Director to assign functions to members of the Serious Fraud Office, the Director may authorise any competent investigator (other than a constable) who is not a member of that Office to exercise on his behalf all or any of the powers conferred by this section, but no such authority shall be granted except for the purpose of investigating the affairs, or any aspect of the affairs, of a person specified in the authority.

(12) No person shall be bound to comply with any requirement imposed by a person exercising powers by virtue of any authority granted under subs (11) above unless he has, if required to do so, produced evidence of his authority.

(13) to (17) Offences.

(18) In this section, 'documents' includes information recorded in any form and, in relation to information recorded otherwise than in legible form, references to its production include references to producing a copy of the information in legible form.

(19) (Scotland).

COMMENTARY

s.2(4): Information on oath . . . by a member of the Serious Fraud Office, note s.2(11) which allows the Director to assign functions outside of members of his own office and to authorise outsiders to 'exercise . . . all or any of the powers conferred by this section'.

Failed to comply with an obligation, ie the power to issue warrants under the head created by s.2(4)(a)(i) operates by reference to obligations imposed in response to a legitimate request by a member of the Serious Fraud Office under s.2(2)(3), and in relation to an investigation under s.1: see s.2(1). A justice being asked for a warrant should be provided with an account of these prior steps and stages if he is to have any power to issue the warrant.

Disclosure of information   12.42

3. (2) Where the Serious Fraud Office has the conduct of any prosecution of an offence which does not relate to inland revenue, the court may not prevent the prosecution from relying on any evidence under s.78 of the Police and Criminal Evidence Act 1984 (discretion to exclude unfair evidence) by reason only of the fact that the information concerned was disclosed by the Commissioners of Inland Revenue or an officer of those Commissioners for the purposes of any prosecution of an offence relating to inland revenue.

(3)–(5) Not reproduced.

COMMENTARY

Section 78 PCEA 1984, ie the discretion to exclude 'unfair evidence'; see *Evidential Matters*, Chapter 6. This does not mean that such evidence cannot be excluded under s.78, but it cannot be excluded 'by reason only' of the matters set out in s.3(2) of the 1987 Act.

Note
Sections 4 and 5, and relevant parts of Sch.1, which deal with *Transfer to the Crown Court* and the *Procedure for Transfer*, respectively, are reproduced in Chapter 4, and see under those titles in the introduction to that chapter, generally.

Appendix I

Codes of Practice under the PACE ACT 1984

A1.00   Codes of practice issued by the Home Secretary under s.66 PACE Act 1984. The four *separate* codes relate to the following:

A1.01   **A**   The exercise by police officers of statutory powers of *stop and search*;

A1.02   **B**   The *searching of premises* by police officers and the *seizure of property* found by police officers on persons or premises;

A1.03   **C**   The *detention, treatment and questioning* of persons by police officers;

A1.04   **D**   The *identification* of persons by police officers.

Note   The codes supercede former provision, including the Judges' Rules. They reflect the views of the Royal Commission on Criminal Procedure, which reported in 1981 and the philosophy of the PACE Act 1984, in providing for clear and workable guidelines for the police, balanced by strengthened safeguards for the public.

Under s.67 of the Act, police officers are liable to disciplinary proceedings for failure to comply with any provision of the codes, although such a failure '. . . shall not of itself render him liable to criminal or civil proceedings': s.67(8), (9) and (10). But under s.67(11):

'In all criminal and civil proceedings any such code shall be admissible in evidence; and if any provision of such a code appears to the court or tribunal conducting the proceedings to be relevant to any question arising in the proceedings it shall be taken into account in determining that question.' 'Relevant questions' would include, eg whether to exclude a confession, or to exclude evidence as unfair under ss.76 and 78 PACE Act 1984, respectively: see, generally, Chapter 6, *Evidential Matters*.

Appendix I also includes, at A1.05 the *Draft Code* on *'Tape Recording'* issued under s.60(1)(a) PACE Act 1984 together with a note on *R v Rampling* (1987) *The Times*, 29 August.

A CODE OF PRACTICE FOR THE EXERCISE BY POLICE OFFICERS OF STATUTORY POWERS OF STOP AND SEARCH

A1.01

1. General

1.1 This code of practice must be readily available at all police stations for consultation by police officers, detained persons and members of the public.

1.2 The notes for guidance included are not provisions of this code, but are guidance to police officers and others about its application and interpretation. Provisions in the annexes to the code are provisions of this code.

1.3 This code governs the exercise by police officers of statutory powers to search a person without first arresting him or to search a vehicle without making an arrest. The main stop and search powers in existence at the time when this code was prepared are set out in Annex A, but that list should not be regarded as definitive.

1.4 This code does *not* apply to the following powers of stop and search:
  (i) Aviation Security Act 1982, s.27(2);
  (ii) Police and Criminal Evidence Act 1984, s.6(1) (which relates specifically to powers of constables employed by statutory undertakers on the premises of the statutory undertakers).

1.5 The exercise of the powers to which this code applies requires reasonable grounds for suspicion that articles of a particular kind are being carried. Annex B provides guidance about this.

1.6 Nothing in this code affects the ability of an officer to speak to or question a person in the course of his duties without detaining him or exercising any element of compulsion.

Note for Guidance
1A It is important to ensure that powers of stop and search are used responsibly and sparingly and only where reasonable grounds for suspicion genuinely exist. Over use of the powers is as likely to be harmful to police effort in the long term as misuse; both can lead to mistrust of the police among sections of the community. It is also particularly important to ensure that any person searched is treated courteously and considerately if police action is not to be resented.

2. Action before a search is carried out

2.1 Where an officer has the reasonable grounds for suspicion necessary to exercise a power of stop and search he may detain the person concerned for the purposes of and with a view to searching him. There is no power to stop or detain a person against his will in order to find grounds for a search.

2.2 Before carrying out a search the officer may question the person about his behaviour or his presence in circumstances which gave rise to the suspicion, since he may have a satisfactory explanation which will make a search unnecessary. If, as a result of any questioning preparatory to a search, or other circumstances which come to the attention of the officer, there cease to be reasonable grounds for suspecting that an article is being carried of a kind for which there is a power of stop and search, no search may take place.

2.3 The reasonable grounds for suspicion which are necessary for the exercise of the initial power to detain may be confirmed or eliminated as a result of the questioning of a person detained for the purposes of a search (or such questioning may reveal reasonable grounds to suspect the possession of a different kind of unlawful article from that originally suspected); but the reasonable grounds for suspicion without which any search or detention for the purposes of a search is unlawful cannot be retrospectively provided by such questioning during his detention or by his refusal to answer any question put to him.

2.4 Before any search of a detained person or attended vehicle takes place the officer must give the person to be searched or in charge of the vehicle the following information:
  (i) his name and the name of the police station to which he is attached;
  (ii) the object of the search; and
  (iii) his grounds for undertaking it.

2.5 If the officer is not in uniform he must show his warrant card.

2.6 Unless it appears to the officer that it will not be practicable to make a record of the search, he must also inform the person to be searched (or the owner or person in charge of a vehicle that is to be searched, as the case may be) that he is entitled to a copy of the record of the search if he asks for it within a year. If the person wishes to have a copy and is not given one on the spot, he should be advised to which police station he should apply.

2.7 If the person to be searched, or in charge of a vehicle to be searched, does not understand what is being said, the officer must take reasonable steps to bring the information in paragraphs 2.4 to 2.6 to his attention. If the person has someone with him then the officer must take reasonable steps to bring the information in paragraphs 2.4 to 2.6 to his attention. If the person has someone with him then the officer must establish whether that person can interpret.

Note for Guidance
2A In some circumstances preparatory questioning may be unnecessary, but in general a brief conversation or exchange will be desirable as a means of avoiding unsuccessful searches. Where a person is lawfully detained for the purpose of a search, but no search in the event takes place, the detention will not thereby have been rendered unlawful.

3. Conduct of the search

3.1 Every reasonable effort must be made to reduce to the minimum the embarrassment that a person being searched may experience.

3.2 Although force may only be used as a last resort, reasonable force may be used if necessary to conduct a search or to detain a person or vehicle for the purposes of a search. A compulsory search may be made only if it has been established that the person is unwilling to co-operate (eg by opening a bag).

3.3 The length of time for which a person or vehicle may be detained will depend on the circumstances, but must in all circumstances be reasonable and not extend beyond the time taken for the search. The thoroughness and extent of a search must depend on what is suspected of being carried, and by whom. If the suspicion relates to a particular article, for example an offensive weapon, which is seen to be slipped into a person's pocket then, in the absence of other grounds for suspicion or an opportunity for the article to be moved elsewhere, the search must be confined to that pocket. In the case of a small article which can readily be concealed, such as a drug, and which might be concealed anywhere on the person, a more extensive search may be necessary. [See *Note 3B*].

3.4 The search must be conducted at the place where the person or vehicle was first detained or nearby.

3.5 Searches in public must be restricted to superficial examination of outer clothing. There is no power to require a person to remove any clothing in public other than an outer coat, jacket or gloves. Where on reasonable grounds it is considered necessary to conduct a more thorough search (eg by requiring someone to take off a T-shirt or headgear), this should be done out of public view (eg in a police van or a nearby police station if there is one). Any search involving the removal of more than an outer coat, jacket, gloves, headgear or footwear may only be made by an officer of the same sex as the person searched and may not be made in the presence of anyone of the opposite sex. [See *Note 3A*].

Notes for Guidance
3A A search in the street itself should be regarded as being in public for the purposes of paragraph 3.5 above, even though it may be empty at the time a search begins. Although there is no power to require a person to do so, there is nothing to prevent an officer from asking a person voluntarily to remove more than an outer coat, jacket or gloves in public.
3B As a search of a person in public should be a superficial examination of outer clothing, such searches should normally be capable of completion within one minute or so.

4. Action after a search is carried out

(a) General

4.1 An officer who has carried out a search must make a written record. In some cases this may not be possible such as in situations involving public disorder occurring in seaside areas during Bank Holiday weekends or the search of football supporters entering or leaving a ground. [See *Note 4A*].

4.2 The record must be completed as soon as practicable – on the spot unless circumstances (eg other immediate duties or very inclement weather) make this impracticable.

4.3 The record must be made on the form provided for this purpose (the national search record).

4.4 In order to complete the search record the officer should normally seek the name, address, and date of birth of the person searched, but under the search procedures there is no obligation on a person to provide these details and no power to detain him if he is unwilling to do so.

4.5 The following information can always, and must, be included in the record of a search even if the person does not wish to identify himself or give his date of birth:
    (i) the name of the person searched, or (if he withholds it) a description of him;
    (ii) where the person searched is white, Afro-Caribbean or Asian, a note to that effect;
    (iii) when a vehicle is searched, a description of it;
    (iv) the object of the search;
    (v) the grounds for making it;
    (vi) the date and time it was made;
    (vii) the place where it was made;
    (viii) its result;
    (ix) a note of any injury or damage to property resulting from it;
    (x) the identity of the officer making it. [See *Note 4B*].

4.6 A record is required for each person and each vehicle searched. If, for example, a person is in a vehicle and both are searched, two records must be completed.

4.7 The record of the grounds for making a search must, briefly but informatively, explain the reason for suspecting the person concerned, whether by reference to his behaviour or other circumstances.

(b) Unattended vehicles

4.8 After searching an unattended vehicle, or anything in or on it, an office must leave a notice in it (or on it, if things in or on it have been searched without opening it) recording the fact that it has been searched.

4.9 The notice should include the name of the police station to which the officer concerned is attached and state where a copy of the record of the search may be obtained and where any application for compensation should be directed.

4.10 The vehicle must if practicable be left secure.

Notes for Guidance

4A Nothing in this code affects the routine searching of persons entering sports grounds or other premises with their consent, or as a condition of entry.

4B Where a search is conducted by more than one officer the identity of all officers engaged in the search must be recorded on the search record.

Annex A

Summary of main stop and search powers [1.3]

POWER	OBJECT OF SEARCH	EXTENT OF SEARCH	WHERE EXERCISABLE
Unlawful articles general			
1 Public Stores Act 1875, s.6	HM Stores stolen or unlawfully obtained	Persons, vehicles and vessels	Anywhere where the constabulary powers are exercisable*
2 Firearms Act 1968, s.47	Firearms	Persons and vehicles	A public place**
3 Misuse of Drugs Act 1971, s.23	Controlled drugs	Persons and vehicles	Anywhere
4 Customs and Excise Management Act 1979, s.163	Goods: (a) on which duty has not been paid; (b) being unlawfully removed, imported or exported; (c) otherwise liable to forfeiture to HM Customs and Excise	Vehicles and vessels only	Anywhere*
Customs and Excise Management Act 1979, s.164****	Goods: (a) on which duty has not been paid; (b) the importation or exportation of which is restricted or prohibited by law	Persons only	At entry to or departure from UK; on board or at landing from ships or aircraft; in dock areas or Customs and Excise airports; at entry to, departure from or within approved wharves, transit sheds or free zones; or when travelling to or from any place beyond the N. Ireland boundary.
5 Aviation Security Act 1982, s.27(1)	Stolen or unlawfully obtained goods	Airport employees and vehicles carrying airport employees or aircraft or any vehicle in a cargo area whether or not carrying an employee	Any designated airport
6 Police and Criminal Evidence Act 1984, s.1	Stolen goods; articles for use in certain Theft Act offences; offensive weapons	Persons and vehicles	Where there is public access***

Police and Criminal Evidence Act 1984, s.6(3) (by a constable of the United Kingdom Atomic Energy Authority Constabulary in respect of property owned or controlled by British Nuclear Fuels plc)	HM Stores (in the form of goods and chattels belonging to British Nuclear Fuels plc)	Persons, vehicles and vessels	Anywhere where the constabulary powers are exercisable*
7 Sporting Events (Control of Alcohol etc.) Act 1985, s.7	Intoxicating liquor	Persons, coaches and trains	Designated sports grounds or coaches and trains travelling to or from a designated sporting event
Evidence of game and wildlife offences			
8 Poaching Prevention Act 1862, s.2	Game or poaching equipment	Persons and vehicles	A public place
9 Deer Acts 1963, s.5 and 1980, s.4	Evidence of offences under the Act	Persons and vehicles	Anywhere except dwellings
10 Conservation of Seals Act 1970, s.4	Seals or hunting equipment	Vehicles only	Anywhere
11 Badgers Act 1973, s.10	Evidence of offences under the Act	Persons and vehicles	Anywhere
12 Wildlife and Countryside Act 1981, s.19	Evidence of wildlife offences	Persons and vehicles	Anywhere except dwellings
Other			
13 Prevention of Terrorism (Temporary Provisions) Act 1984, Schedule 3	Evidence of offences under the Act	Persons and vehicles	Anywhere

* Including, in the case of a vessel, territorial waters.
** Anywhere in the case of reasonable suspicion of offences of carrying firearms with criminal intent or trespassing with firearms.
*** Any place where the public is at the time entitled to go or places other than dwellings where people have ready access at the time (unless land attached to a dwelling where the person or vehicle is permitted to be).
**** Police may only search under the directions of an officer of Customs and Excise.

Reasonable grounds for suspicion [1.5]

1. Reasonable suspicion does not require *certainty* that an unlawful article is being carried; nor does the officer concerned have to be satisfied of this beyond reasonable doubt. Reasonable suspicion, in contrast to *mere* suspicion must be founded on fact. There must be some concrete basis for the officer's suspicion, related to the individual person concerned, which can be considered and evaluated by an objective third person. Mere suspicion, in contrast, is a hunch or instinct which cannot be explained or justified to an objective observer. An officer who has such a hunch or instinct may well be justified in continuing to keep the person under observation or speak to him, but additional grounds which bring up mere suspicion to the level of reasonable suspicion are needed before he may exercise the powers dealt with in this code.

2. Reasonable suspicion may arise from the nature of the property observed or being carried or suspected of being carried coupled with other factors including the time, the place or the suspicious behaviour of the person concerned or those with him. The decision to search must be based on all the facts which, to a careful officer, bear on the likelihood that an article of a certain kind will be found, and not only on what can be seen at the time. So an officer with prior knowledge of the behaviour of someone he sees in a certain situation, or acting on information received (such as a description of a suspected offender) may have reasonable grounds for searching him although another officer would not.

3. Reasonable suspicion cannot be supported on the basis simply of a higher than average chance that the person has committed or is committing an offence, for example because he belongs to a group within which offenders of a certain kind are relatively common, or because of a combination of factors such as these. For example, a person's colour of itself can never be a reasonable ground for suspicion. The mere fact alone that a person is carrying a particular kind of property or is dressed in a certain way or has a certain hairstyle is likewise not of itself sufficient. Nor is the fact that a person is known to have a previous conviction for unlawful possession of an article.

4. The degree or level of suspicion required to establish the reasonable grounds justifying the exercise of powers of stop and search is no less than the degree or level of suspicion required to effect an arrest without warrant for any of the suspected offences to which these powers relate. The powers of stop and search provide an opportunity to establish the commission or otherwise of certain kinds of offences without arrest and may therefore render arrest unnecessary.

5. Paragraph 4 above is subject to the principle that where a police officer has reasonable grounds to suspect that a person is in *innocent* possession of a stolen or prohibited article, the power of stop and search exists notwithstanding that there would be no power of arrest. However every effort should be made to secure the voluntary production of the article before the power is resorted to.

A1.02 **B** CODE OF PRACTICE FOR THE SEARCHING OF PREMISES BY POLICE OFFICERS AND THE SEIZURE OF PROPERTY FOUND BY POLICE OFFICERS ON PERSONS OR PREMISES

6. Seizure and retention of property
    (a) Seizure   6.1
    (b) Retention   6.6
    (c) Rights of owners etc.   6.8
7. Action to be taken after searches   7.1
8. Search registers   8.1

1. General

1.1 This code of practice must be readily available at all police stations for consultation by police officers, detained persons and members of the public.

1.2 The notes for guidance included are not provisions of this code, but are guidance to police officers and others about its application and interpretation.

1.3 This code applies to the following searches of premises:
    (a) searches of premises undertaken for the purposes of an investigation into an alleged offence, with the occupier's consent, other than routine scenes of crime searches and searches following the activation of burglar or fire alarms or bomb threat calls;
    (b) searches of premises under the powers conferred by sections 17, 18 and 32 of the Police and Criminal Evidence Act 1984;
    (c) searches of premises undertaken in pursuance of a search warrant issued in accordance with section 15 of, or Schedule 1 to, that Act.
'Premises' is a wide term which may include vessels and, in certain circumstances, vehicles.

2. Search warrants and production orders

(a) Action to be taken before an application is made
2.1 Where information is received which appears to justify an application, the officer concerned must take reasonable steps to check that the information is accurate, recent and has not been provided maliciously or irresponsibly. An application may not be made on the basis of information from an anonymous source where corroboration has not been sought.

2.2 The officer shall ascertain as specifically as is possible in the circumstances the nature of the articles concerned and their location.

2.3 The officer shall also make enquiries to establish what, if anything, is known about the likely occupier of the premises and the nature of the premises themselves; and whether they have been previously searched and if so how recently; and to obtain any other information relevant to the application.

2.4 No application for a search warrant may be made without the authority of an officer of at least the rank of inspector (or, in a case of urgency where no officer of this rank is readily available, the senior officer on duty). No application for a production order or warrant under Schedule 1 to the Police and Criminal Evidence Act 1984 may be made without the authority of an officer of at least the rank of superintendent.

2.5 Except in a case of urgency, if there is reason to believe that a search might have an adverse effect on relations between the police and the community then the local police community liaison officer shall be consulted before it takes place.

(b) Making an application
2.6 An application for a search warrant must be supported by an information in writing, stating:
    (i) the enactment under which the application is made;
    (ii) as specifically as is reasonably practicable the premises to be searched and the object of the search; and
    (iii) the grounds on which the application is made (including, where the purpose of the proposed search is to find evidence of an alleged offence, an indication of how the evidence relates to the investigation).

2.7 An application for a search warrant under paragraph 12(a) of Schedule 1 to the Police and Criminal Evidence Act 1984 shall also, where appropriate, indicate why it is believed that service of notice of an application for a production order may seriously prejudice the investigation.

2.8 If an application is refused, no further application may be made for a warrant to search those premises unless supported by additional grounds.

Note for Guidance
2A The identity of an informant need not be disclosed when making an application, but the

officer concerned should be prepared to deal with any questions the magistrate or judge may have about the accuracy of previous information provided by that source or other related matters.

3. Entry without warrant

(a) Making an arrest etc.
3.1 The conditions under which an officer may enter and search premises without warrant are as set out in section 17 of the Police and Criminal Evidence Act 1984.

(b) Search after arrest of premises in which arrest takes place
3.2 The powers of an officer to search premises in which he has arrested a person are as set out in section 32 of the Police and Criminal Evidence Act 1984.

(c) Search after arrest of premises of arrested person
3.3 The powers of an officer to search premises occupied or controlled by a person who has been arrested for an arrestable offence are as set out in section 18 of the Police and Criminal Evidence Act 1984. The record of the search required by section 18(7) of the Act shall be made in the custody record, where this is one.

4. Search with consent

4.1 Subject to paragraph 4.3 below, if it is proposed to search premises with the consent of a person entitled to grant entry to the premises the consent must be given in writing. [See *Note 4B*].

4.2 Before seeking consent the officer in charge of the search shall state the purpose of the proposed search and inform the person concerned that he is not obliged to consent and that anything seized may be produced in evidence. If at the time the person is not suspected of an offence, the officer shall tell him so when stating the purpose of the search.

4.3 It is unnecessary to seek consent under paragraphs 4.1 and 4.2 above where in the circumstances this would cause disproportionate inconvenience to the person concerned. [See *Note 4C*].

Notes for Guidance
4A In the case of a lodging house or similar accommodation a search should not be made on the basis solely of the landlord's consent unless the tenant is unavailable and the matter is urgent.
4B Where it is intended to search premises under authority of a warrant or a power of entry and search without warrant, and co-operation of the occupier of the premises is obtained in accordance with paragraph 5.4 below, there is no additional requirement to obtain written consent as at paragraph 4.1 above.
4C Paragraph 4.3 is intended in particular to apply, for example, to circumstances where police have arrested someone in the night after a pursuit and it is necessary to make a brief check of gardens along the route of the pursuit to see whether stolen or incriminating articles have been discarded.

5. Searching of premises: general considerations

(a) Time of searches
5.1 Searches made under warrant must be made within one month from the date of issue of the warrant.

5.2 Searches must be made at a reasonable hour unless this might frustrate the purpose of the search. [See *Note 5A*]

5.3 A warrant authorises an entry on one occasion only.

(b) Entry other than with consent
5.4 The officer in charge shall first attempt to communicate with the occupier or any other person entitled to grant access to the premises by explaining the authority under which he seeks entry to the premises and ask the occupier to allow him to do so, unless:
    (i) the premises to be searched are known to be unoccupied;
    (ii) the occupier and any other person entitled to grant access are known to be absent; or
    (iii) there are reasonable grounds for believing that to alert the occupier or any other person entitled to grant access by attempting to communicate with him would frustrate the object of the seach or endanger the officers concerned or other persons.

5.5 Where the premises are occupied the officer shall identify himself and, if not in uniform, show his warrant card; and state the purpose of the search and the grounds for undertaking it, before a search begins.

5.6 Reasonable force may be used if necessary to enter premises if the officer in charge is satisfied that the premises are those specified in any warrant or other written authority and where:

   (i) the occupier or any other person entitled to grant access has refused a request to allow entry to his premises;

   (ii) it is impossible to communicate with the occupier or any other person entitled to grant access; or

   (iii) any of the provisions of sub-paragraphs 5.4(i) to (iii) apply.

5.7 Where the search is to be made under warrant the occupier shall, if present, be given a copy of it. If he is not present the copy shall be left in a prominent place on the premises. The warrant itself shall be endorsed to show that this has been done.

(c) Conduct of searches

5.8 Premises may be searched only to the extent necessary to achieve the object of the search, having regard to the size and nature of whatever is sought. A search under warrant may not continue under the authority of that warrant once all the things specified in it have been found, or the officer in charge of the search is satisfied that they are not on the premises.

5.9 Searches must be conducted with due consideration for the property and privacy of the occupier of the premises searched, and with no more disturbance than necessary. Reasonable force may be used only where this is necessary because the co-operation of the occupier cannot be obtained or is insufficient for the purpose.

5.10 If the occupier wishes to ask a friend, neighbour or other person to witness the search then he must be allowed to do so, unless the officer in charge has reasonable grounds for believing that this would seriously hinder the investigation. A search need not be delayed for this purpose unreasonably.

(d) Leaving premises

5.11 If premises have been entered by force the officer in charge shall, before leaving them, satisfy himself that they are secure either by arranging for the occupier or his agent to be present or by any other appropriate means.

(e) Search under Schedule 1 to the Police and Criminal Evidence Act 1984

5.12 An officer of the rank of inspector or above shall take charge of and be present at any search under a warrant issued under this Schedule. He is responsible for ensuring that the search is conducted with discretion and in such a manner as to cause the least possible disruption to any business or other activities carried on in the premises.

5.13 After satisfying himself that material may not be taken from the premises without his knowledge, the officer in charge of the search shall ask for the documents or other records concerned to be produced. He may also, if he considers it to be necessary, ask to see the index to files held on the premises, if there is one; and the officers conducting the search may inspect any files which, according to the index, appear to contain any of the material sought. A more extensive search of the premises may be made only if the person responsible for them refuses to produce the material sought, or to allow access to the index; if it appears that the index is inaccurate or incomplete; or if for any other reason the officer in charge has reasonable grounds for believing that such a search is necessary in order to find the material sought. [See *Note 5B*]

Notes for Guidance

5A In determining at what time to make a search, the officer in charge should have regard, among other considerations, to the times of day at which the occupier of the premises is likely to be present, and should not search at a time when he, or any other person on the premises, is likely to be asleep unless not doing so is likely to frustrate the purpose of the search.

5B In asking for documents to be produced in accordance with paragraph 5.13 above, officers should direct the request to a person in authority and with responsibility for the documents.

5C If the wrong premises are searched by mistake, everything possible should be done at the earliest opportunity to allay any sense of grievance. In appropriate cases assistance should be given to obtain compensation.

6. Seizure and retention of property

(a) Seizure

6.1 Subject to paragraph 6.2 below, an officer who is searching any premises under any statutory power or with the consent of the occupier may seize:

   (a) anything covered by a warrant; and

(b) anything which he has reasonable grounds for believing is evidence of an offence or has been obtained in consequence of the commission of an offence.

Items under (b) may only be seized where this is necessary to prevent their concealment, alteration, loss, damage or destruction.

6.2 No item may be seized which is subject to legal privilege (as defined in section 10 of the Police and Criminal Evidence Act 1984).

6.3 An officer who decides that it is not appropriate to seize property because of an explanation given by the person holding it, but who has reasonable grounds for believing that it has been obtained in consequence of the commission of an offence by some person, shall inform the holder of his suspicions and shall explain that, if he disposes of the property, he may be liable to civil or criminal proceedings.

6.4 An officer may photograph or copy, or have photographed or copied, any document or other article which he has power to seize in accordance with paragraph 6.1 above.

6.5 Where an officer considers that a computer may contain information that could be used in evidence, he may require the information to be produced in a form that can be taken away and in which it is visible and legible.

(b) Retention
6.6 Subject to paragraph 6.7 below anything which has been seized in accordance with the above provisions may be retained only for as long as is necessary in the circumstances. It may be retained, among other purposes:
　　(i) for use as evidence at a trial for an offence;
　　(ii) for forensic examination or for other investigation in connection with an offence; or
　　(iii) where there are reasonable grounds for believing that it has been stolen or obtained by the commission of an offence, in order to establish its lawful owner.

6.7 Property shall not be retained in accordance with sub-paragraphs 6.6(i) and (ii) (ie for use as evidence or for the purposes of investigation) if a photograph or copy would suffice for those purposes.

(c) Rights of owners etc.
6.8 If property is retained the person who had custody or control of it immediately prior to its seizure must on request, be provided with a list or description of the property within a reasonable time.

6.9 He or his representative must be allowed supervised access to the property to examine it or have it photographed or copied, or must be provided with a photograph or copy, in either case within a reasonable time of any request and at his own expense, unless the officer in charge of an investigation has reasonable grounds for believing that this would prejudice the investigation of an offence or any criminal proceedings. In this case a record of the grounds must be made.

Note for Guidance
6A　Any person claiming property seized by the police may apply to a magistrates' court under the Police (Property) Act 1897 for its possession, and should, where appropriate, be advised of this procedure.

7. Action to be taken after searches

7.1 Where premises have been searched in circumstances to which this code applies, other than in the circumstances covered by paragraph 4.3 above, the officer in charge of the search shall, on arrival at a police station, make or have made a record of the search. The record shall include:
　　(i) the address of the premises searched;
　　(ii) the date, time and duration of the search;
　　(iii) the authority under which the search was made. Where the search was made in the exercise of a statutory power to search premises without warrant, the record shall include the power under which the search was made; and where the search was made under warrant, or with written consent, a copy of the warrant or consent shall be appended to the record or kept in a place identified in the record;
　　(iv) the names of the officers who conducted the search;
　　(v) the names of any persons on the premises if they are known;
　　(vi) either a list of any articles seized or a note of where such a list is kept and, if not covered by a warrant, the reason for their seizure;
　　(vii) whether force was used and, if so, the reason why it was used;
　　(viii) details of any damage caused during the search, and the circumstances in which it was caused.

7.2 Where premises have been searched under warrant, the warrant shall be endorsed to show:

- (i) whether any articles specified in the warrant were found;
- (ii) whether any other articles were seized;
- (iii) the date and time at which it was executed;
- (iv) the names of the officers who executed it; and
- (v) whether a copy was handed to the occupier or left on the premises and if so where on them.

7.3 Any warrant which has been executed or which has not been executed within one month of its issue shall be returned, if it was issued by a justice of the peace, to the clerk to the justices for the petty sessions area concerned or, if issued by a judge, to the appropriate officer of the court from which he issued it.

8. Search registers

8.1 A search register shall be maintained at each sub-divisional police station. All records which are required to be made by this code shall be made, copied or referred to in the register.

C CODE OF PRACTICE FOR THE DETENTION, TREATMENT AND QUESTIONING OF PERSONS BY POLICE OFFICERS

A1.03

1. General

1.1 All persons in custody must be dealt with expeditiously, and released as soon as the need for detention has ceased to apply.

1.2 This code of practice must be readily available at all police stations for consultation by police officers, detained persons and members of the public

1.3 The notes for guidance included are not provisions of this code, but are guidance to police officers and others about its application and interpretation. Provisions in the annexes to this code are provisions of this code.

1.4 If an officer has any suspicion, or is told in good faith, that a person of any age may be mentally ill or mentally handicapped, or mentally incapable of understanding the significance of questions put to him or his replies, then that person shall be treated as a mentally ill or mentally handicapped person for the purposes of this code.

1.5 If anyone appears to be under the age of 17 then he shall be treated as a juvenile for the purposes of this code in the absence of clear evidence to show that he is older.

1.6 If a person appears to be blind or seriously visually handicapped, deaf, unable to read or unable to communicate orally with the officer dealing with him at the time, he should be treated as such for the purposes of this code in the absence of clear evidence to the contrary.

1.7 In this code 'the appropriate adult' means:
  (a) in the case of a juvenile:
      (i) his parent or guardian (or, if he is in care, the care authority or organisation);
      (ii) a social worker; or
      (iii) failing either of the above, another responsible adult who is not a police officer or employed by the police.
  (b) in the case of a person who is mentally ill or mentally handicapped:
      (i) a relative, guardian or other person responsible for his care or custody;
      (ii) someone who has experience of dealing with mentally ill or mentally handicapped persons but is not a police officer or employed by the police; or
      (iii) failing either of the above, some other responsible adult who is not a police officer or employed by the police.
[See *Note 1C*]

1.8 Whenever this code requires a person to be given certain information he does not have to be given it if he is incapable at the time of understanding what is said to him or is violent or likely to become violent or is in urgent need of medical attention, but he must be given it as soon as practicable.

1.9 Any reference to a custody officer in this code includes an officer who is performing the functions of a custody officer.

1.10 In its application to persons who are in custody at police stations, this code applies whether or not they have been arrested for an offence, except section 16 which applies solely to persons in police detention.

Notes for Guidance
1A Although certain sections of this code (eg section 9 – Treatment of detained persons) apply specifically to persons in custody at police stations, those there voluntarily to assist with an investigation should be treated with no less consideration (eg offered refreshments at appropriate times) and enjoy an absolute right to obtain legal advice or communicate with anyone outside the police station.
1B This code does not affect the principle that all citizens have a duty to help police officers to prevent crime and discover offenders. This is a civic rather than a legal duty; but when a police officer is trying to discover whether, or by whom, an offence has been committed, he is entitled to question any person from whom he thinks useful information can be obtained, subject to the restrictions imposed by this code. A person's declaration that he is unwilling to reply does not alter this entitlement.
1C In the case of persons who are mentally ill or mentally handicapped, it may in certain circumstances be more satisfactory for all concerned if the appropriate adult is someone who has experience or training in their care rather than a relative lacking such qualifications. But if the person himself prefers a relative to a better qualified stranger his wishes should if practicable be respected.

2. Custody records

2.1 A separate custody record must be opened as soon as practicable for each person who is brought to a police station under arrest or is arrested at the police station having attended there voluntarily. All information which has to be recorded under this code must be recorded as soon as practicable, in the custody record unless otherwise specified.

2.2 In the case of any action requiring the authority of an officer of a specified rank, his name and rank must be noted in the custody record.

2.3 The custody officer is responsible for the accuracy and completeness of the custody record and for ensuring that the record or a copy of the record accompanies a detained person if he is transferred to another police station. The record shall show the time of and reason for transfer and the time a person is released from detention.

2.4 When a person leaves police detention he or his legal representative shall be supplied on request with a copy of the custody record as soon as practicable. This entitlement lasts for twelve months after his release. [See *Note 2A*]

2.5 All entries in custody and written interview records must be timed and signed by the maker.

2.6 Any refusal by a person to sign either a custody or an interview record when asked to do so in accordance with the provisions of this code must itself be recorded.

Note for Guidance
2A The person who has been detained, the appropriate adult, or legal representative who gives reasonable notice of a request to inspect the original custody record after the person has left police detention, should be allowed to do so.

3. Initial action

(a) Detained persons: normal procedure
3.1 When a person is brought to a police station under arrest or is arrested at the police station having attended there voluntarily, the custody officer must inform him of the following rights and of the fact that they need not be exercised immediately:
    (i) the right to have someone informed of his arrest in accordance with section 5 below;
    (ii) the right to consult a solicitor in accordance with section 6 below; and
    (iii) the right to consult this and the other codes of practice.
[See *Note 3D*]

3.2 The custody officer must also give the person a written notice setting out the above three rights, the right to a copy of the custody record in accordance with paragraph 2.4 above and the caution in the terms prescribed in section 10 below. The custody officer shall ask the person to sign the custody record to acknowledge receipt of this notice. [See *Note 3E*]

3.3 If the custody officer authorises a person's detention he must inform him of the grounds as soon as practicable and in any case before that person is then questioned about any offence.

3.4 The person shall be asked to sign on the custody record to signify whether or not he wants legal advice at this point.

(b) Detained persons: special groups
3.5 If the person does not understand English or appears to be deaf and the custody officer cannot communicate with him then the custody officer must as soon as practicable call an interpreter, and ask him to provide the information required above.

3.6 If the person is a juvenile, is mentally handicapped or is suffering from mental illness then the custody officer must as soon as practicable inform the appropriate adult of the grounds for his detention and his whereabouts, and ask the adult to come to the police station to see the person. If the appropriate adult is already at the police station when information is given to the person as required in paragraphs 3.1 to 3.3 above then the information must be given to the detained person in his presence. If the appropriate adult is not at the police station when the information is given then the information must be given to the detained person again in the presence of the appropriate adult once that person arrives.

3.7 If the person is blind or seriously visually handicapped or is unable to read, the custody officer should ensure that his solicitor, relative, the appropriate adult or some other person likely to take an interest in him is available to help in checking any documentation. Where this code requires written consent or signification, then the person who is assisting may be asked to sign instead if the detained person so wishes. [See *Note 3F*]

3.8 In the case of a juvenile who is known to be subject to a supervision order, reasonable steps must also be taken to notify the person supervising him.

(c) Persons attending a police station voluntarily
3.9 Any person attending a police station voluntarily for the purpose of assisting with an investigation may leave at will unless placed under arrest. If it is decided that he would not be allowed to do so then he must be informed at once that he is under arrest and brought before the custody officer. If he is not placed under arrest but is cautioned in accordance with section 10 below, the officer who gives the caution must at the same time inform him that he is not under arrest, that he is not obliged to remain at the police station but that if he remains at the police station he may obtain legal advice if he wishes. [See *Note 3G*]

(d) Documentation
3.10 The grounds for a person's detention shall be recorded, in his presence if practicable.

3.11 Action taken under paragraphs 3.5 to 3.8 shall be recorded.

Notes for Guidance
3A If the juvenile is in the care of a local authority or voluntary organisation but is living with his parents or other adults responsible for his welfare then, although there is no legal obligation on the police to inform them, they as well as the authority or organisation should

normally be contacted unless suspected of involvement in the offence concerned. *Even if a juvenile in care is not living with his parents, consideration should be given to informing them as well.*

3B Section 7 of this code contains special additional provisions for Commonwealth citizens and foreign nationals.

3C Most local authority Social Services Departments can supply a list of interpreters who have the necessary skills and experience to interpret for the deaf at police interviews.

3D The right to consult the codes of practice under paragraph 3.1 above does not entitle the person concerned to delay unreasonably, necessary investigative or administrative action while he does so.

3E When the custody officer gives the person a copy of the notice referred to in paragraph 3.2, he should also give him a copy of a notice explaining the arrangements for obtaining legal advice.

3F Blind or seriously visually handicapped persons may be unwilling to sign police documents. The alternative of their representative signing on their behalf seeks to protect the interests of both police and suspects.

3G If a person who is attending a police station voluntarily (in accordance with paragraph 3.9) asks about his entitlement to legal advice, he should be given a copy of a notice explaining the arrangements for obtaining legal advice.

4. Detained persons' property

(a) Action

4.1 The custody officer is responsible for:
 (a) ascertaining:
   (i) what property a detained person has with him when he comes to the police station (whether on arrest, re-detention on answering to bail, commitment to prison custody on the order or sentence of a court, on lodgement at the police station with a view to his production in court from such custody, or on arrival at a police station on transfer from detention at another station or from hospital);
   (ii) what property he might have acquired for an unlawful or harmful purpose while in custody.
 (b) the safekeeping of any property which is taken from him and which remains at the police station.

To these ends the custody officer may search him or authorise his being searched to the extent that he considers necessary (provided that a search of intimate parts of the body or involving the removal of more than outer clothing may only be made in accordance with Annex A to this code). A search may only be carried out by an officer of the same sex as the person searched. [See *Note 4A*]

4.2 A detained person may retain clothing and personal effects at his own risk unless the custody officer considers that he may use them to cause harm to himself or others, interfere with evidence, damage property or effect an escape or they are needed as evidence. In this event the custody officer can withhold such articles as he considers necessary. If he does so he must tell the person why.

4.3 Personal effects are those items which a person may lawfully need to use or refer to while in detention but do not include cash and other items of value.

(b) Documentation

4.4 The custody officer is responsible for recording all property brought to the police station that a detained person had with him, or had taken from him on arrest. The detained person shall be allowed to check and sign the record of property as correct.

4.5 If a detained person is not allowed to keep any article of clothing or personal effects the reason must be recorded.

Notes for Guidance

4A Paragraph 4.1 is not to be taken as requiring each detained person to be searched. Where for example a person is to be detained for only a short period and is not to be placed in a cell, the custody officer may at his discretion decide not to search the person. In such a case the custody record will be endorsed 'not searched', paragraph 4.4. will not apply, and the person will be invited to sign the entry. Where the person detained refuses to sign, the custody officer will be obliged to ascertain what property he has on him in accordance with paragraph 4.1.

4B Paragraph 4.4 does not require the custody officer to record on the custody record, property in the possession of the person on arrest, if by virtue of its nature, quantity or size, it is not practicable to remove it to the police station.

4C Paragraph 4.1 above is not to be taken as requiring that items of clothing worn by the person be recorded unless withheld by the custody officer in accordance with paragraph 4.2.

5. Right not to be held incommunicado

(a) Action

5.1 Any person to whom paragraphs 2.1 and 3.9 apply may on request have one person known to him or who is likely to take an interest in his welfare informed at public expense as soon as practicable of his whereabouts. If the person cannot be contacted the person who has made the request may choose up to two alternatives. If they too cannot be contacted the custody officer has discretion to allow further attempts until the information has been conveyed. [See *Notes 5C and 5D*]

5.2 The exercise of the above right in respect of each of the persons nominated may be delayed only in accordance with Annex B to this code.

5.3 The above right may be exercised on each occasion that a person is taken to another police station.

5.4 The person may receive visits at the custody officer's discretion. [See *Note 5B*].

5.5 Where an enquiry as to the whereabouts of the person is made by a friend, relative or person with an interest in his welfare, this information shall be given, if he agrees and if Annex B does not apply. [See *Note 5D*]

5.6 The person shall be supplied on request with writing materials. Any letter or other message shall be sent as soon as practicable unless Annex B applies.

5.7 He may also speak on the telephone for a reasonable time to one person unless Annex B applies. [See *Note 5E*]

5.8 Before any letter or message is sent, or telephone call made, the person shall be informed that what he says in any letter, call or message (other than in the case of a communication to a solicitor) may be read or listened to as appropriate and may be given in evidence. A telephone call may be terminated if it is being abused. The costs can be at public expense at the discretion of the custody officer.

(b) Documentation

5.9 A record must be kept of:
  (a) any request made under this section and the action taken on it;
  (b) any letters or messages sent, calls made or visits received; and
  (c) any refusal on the part of a person to have information about himself or his whereabouts given to an outside enquirer.

Notes for Guidance

5A An interpreter may make a telephone call or write a letter on a person's behalf.

5B In the exercise of his discretion the custody officer should allow visits where possible in the light of the availability of sufficient manpower to supervise a visit and any possible hindrance to the investigation.

5C If the person does not know of anyone to contact for advice or support or cannot contact a friend or relative, the custody officer should bear in mind any local voluntary bodies or other organisations who might be able to offer help in such cases. But if it is specifically legal advice that is wanted, then paragraph 6.1 below will apply.

5D In some circumstances it may not be appropriate to use the telephone to disclose information under paragraphs 5.1 and 5.5 above.

5E The telephone call at paragraph 5.7 is in addition to any communication under paragraphs 5.1 and 6.1.

6. Right to legal advice

(a) Action

6.1 Subject to paragraph 6.2, any person may at any time consult and communicate privately, whether in person, in writing or on the telephone with a solicitor. [See *Note 6B*]

6.2 The exercise of the above right may be delayed only in accordance with Annex B to this code.

6.3 A person who asks for legal advice may not be interviewed or continue to be interviewed until he has received it unless:
  (a) Annex B applies; or
  (b) an officer of the rank of superintendent or above has reasonable grounds for believing that:
    (i) delay will involve an immediate risk of harm to persons or serious loss of, or damage to, property; or
    (ii) where a solicitor, including a duty solicitor, has been contacted and has agreed

to attend, awaiting his arrival would cause unreasonable delay to the processes of investigation; or

(c) the solicitor nominated by the person, or selected by him from a list:
    (i) cannot be contacted;
    (ii) has previously indicated that he does not wish to be contacted; or
    (iii) having been contacted, has declined to attend;
       and the person has been advised of the Duty Solicitor Scheme (where one is in operation) but has declined to ask for the duty solicitor, or the duty solicitor is unavailable; or

(d) the person has given his agreement in writing or on tape that the interview may be started at once.
    [See *Notes 6A and 6B*]

6.4 Where sub-paragraph 6.3(b)(i) applies, once sufficient information to avert the risk has been obtained, questioning must cease until the person has received legal advice or sub-paragraphs 6.3(a), (b)(ii), (c) or (d) apply.

6.5 Where a person has been permitted to consult a solicitor and the solicitor is available at the time the interview begins or is in progress, he must be allowed to have his solicitor present while he is interviewed.

6.6 The solicitor may only be required to leave the interview if his conduct is such that the investigating officer is unable properly to put questions to the suspect. [See *Note 6D*]

6.7 If the investigating officer considers that a solicitor is acting in such a way, he will stop the interview and consult an officer not below the rank of superintendent, if one is readily available, and otherwise an officer not below the rank of inspector who is not connected with the investigation. After speaking to the solicitor, the officer who has been consulted will decide whether or not the interview should continue in the presence of that solicitor. If he decides that it should not, the suspect will be given the opportunity to consult another solicitor before the interview continues and that solicitor will be given an opportunity to be present at the interview.

6.8 The removal of a solicitor from an interview is a serious step and if it occurs, the officer of superintendent rank or above who took the decision will consider whether the incident should be reported to The Law Society. If the decision to remove the solicitor has been taken by an officer below the rank of superintendent, the facts must be reported to an officer of superintendent rank or above who will similarly consider whether a report to The Law Society would be appropriate.

6.9 In this code 'solicitor' means a solicitor qualified to practise in accordance with the Solicitors Act 1974. If a solicitor wishes to send a clerk or legal executive to provide advice on his behalf, then the clerk or legal executive shall be admitted to the police station for this purpose unless an officer of the rank of inspector or above considers that such a visit will hinder the investigation of crime and directs otherwise. Once admitted to the police station, the provisions of paragraphs 6.3 to 6.7 apply.

6.10 If the inspector refuses access to a clerk or legal executive or a decision is taken that such a person should not be permitted to remain at an interview, he must forthwith notify a solicitor on whose behalf the clerk or legal executive was to have acted or was acting, and give him an opportunity of making alternative arrangements.

(b) Documentation
6.11 Any request for legal advice and the action taken on it shall be recorded.

6.12 If a person has asked for legal advice and an interview is commenced in the absence of a solicitor or his representative (or the solicitor or his representative has been required to leave an interview) a record shall be made in the interview record.

Notes for Guidance
6A In considering whether sub-paragraphs 6.3(b)(i) and (ii) apply, the officer should where practicable ask the solicitor for an estimate of the time that he is likely to take in coming to the station, and relate this information to the time for which detention is permitted, the time of day (ie whether the period of rest required by paragraph 12.2 is imminent) and the requirements of other investigations in progress. If it appears that it will be necessary to begin an interview before the solicitor's arrival he should be given an indication of how long police would be able to wait before sub-paragraphs 6.3(b)(i) and (ii) apply so that he has an opportunity to make arrangements for legal advice to be provided by someone else.
6B A person who asks for legal advice should be given an opportunity to consult a specific solicitor (for example, his own solicitor or one known to him) or the duty solicitor where a Duty Solicitor Scheme is in operation. If advice is not available by these means, or he does not

wish to consult the duty solicitor, the person should be given an opportunity to choose a solicitor from a list of those willing to provide legal advice. If this solicitor is unavailable, he may choose up to two alternatives. If these attempts to secure legal advice are unsuccessful, the custody officer has discretion to allow further attempts until a solicitor has been contacted who agrees to provide legal advice.

6C   Procedures undertaken under section 8 of the Road Traffic Act 1972 do not constitute interviewing for the purposes of this code.

6D   In considering whether paragraph 6.6 applies, a solicitor is not guilty of misconduct if he seeks to challenge an improper question to his client or the manner in which it is put or he wishes to give his client further legal advice, and should not be required to leave an interview unless his interference with its conduct clearly goes beyond this.

6E   In a case where an officer takes the decision to exclude a solicitor, he must be in a position to satisfy the court that the decision was properly made. In order to do this he may need to witness what is happening himself.

7.   Citizens of independent Commonwealth countries or foreign nationals

(a)   Action

7.1   A citizen of an independent Commonwealth country or a national of a foreign country (including the Republic of Ireland) may communicate at any time with his High Commission, Embassy or Consulate.

7.2   If a citizen of an independent Commonwealth country has been detained for more than 24 hours he must be asked if he wishes the police to inform his High Commission of his whereabouts and the grounds for his detention. If so, the custody officer is responsible for ensuring that the High Commission is informed by telephone.

7.3   If a national of a foreign country with which a consular convention is in force is detained, the appropriate Consulate shall be informed as soon as practicable, subject to paragraph 7.6 below.

7.4   Any other foreign national who is detained must be informed as soon as practicable of his right to communicate with his consul if he so wishes. He must also be informed that the police will notify his consul of his arrest if he wishes.

7.5   Consular officers may visit one of their nationals who is in police detention to talk to him and, if required, to arrange for legal advice. Such visits shall take place out of the hearing of a police officer.

7.6   Notwithstanding the provisions of consular conventions, where the person is a political refugee (whether for reasons of race, nationality, political opinion or religion) or is seeking political asylum, a consular officer shall not be informed of the arrest of one of his nationals or given access to or information about him except at the person's express request.

(b)   Documentation

7.7   A record shall be made when a person is informed of his rights under this section and of any communications with a High Commission, Embassy or Consulate.

Notes for Guidance

7A   The exercise of the rights in this section may not be interfered with even though Annex B applies.

7B   A list of countries with which a consular convention is in force is set out in the Home Office Consolidated Circular to the Police on Crime and Kindred Matters.

8.   Conditions of detention

(a)   Action

8.1   So far as is practicable, not more than one person shall be detained in each cell.

8.2   Cells in use must be adequately heated, cleaned and ventilated. They must be adequately lit, subject to such dimming as is compatible with safety and security to allow persons detained overnight to sleep. No additional restraints should be used within a locked cell unless absolutely necessary, and then only approved handcuffs.

8.3   Blankets, mattresses, pillows and other bedding supplied should be of a reasonable standard and in a clean and sanitary condition. [See *Note 8B*]

8.4   Access to toilet and washing facilities must be provided.

8.5   If it is necessary to remove a person's clothes for the purposes of investigation, for hygiene or health reasons or for cleaning, replacement clothing of a reasonable standard of comfort and cleanliness shall be provided. A person may not be interviewed unless adequate clothing has been offered to him.

8.6 At least two light meals and one main meal shall be offered in any period of 24 hours. Whenever necessary, advice shall be sought from the police surgeon on medical or dietary matters. As far as practicable, meals provided shall offer a varied diet and meet any special dietary needs or religious beliefs that the person may have; he may also have meals supplied by his family or friends at his or their own expense. [See *Note 8B*]

8.7 Brief outdoor exercise shall be offered daily if practicable.

8.8 A juvenile shall not be placed in a police cell unless no other secure accommodation is available and the custody officer considers that it is not practicable to supervise him if he is not placed in a cell. He may not be placed in a cell with a detained adult.

8.9 Reasonable force may be used if necessary for the following purposes:
  (i) to secure compliance with reasonable instructions, including instructions given in pursuance of the provisions of a code of practice; or
  (ii) to prevent escape, injury, damage to property or the destruction of evidence.

8.10 Persons detained should be visited every hour, and those who are drunk, every half hour. [See *Note 8A*]

(b) Documentation
8.11 A record must be kept of replacement clothing and meals offered.

8.12 If a juvenile is placed in a cell, the reason must be recorded.

Notes for Guidance
8A Whenever possible juveniles and other persons at risk should be visited more regularly.
8B The provisions in paragraphs 8.3 and 8.6 respectively regarding bedding and a varied diet are of particular importance in the case of a person detained under the Prevention of Terrorism (Temporary Provisions) Act 1984. This is because such a person may well remain in police custody for some time.

9. Treatment of detained persons

(a) General
9.1 If a complaint is made by or on behalf of a detained person about his treatment since his arrest, or it comes to the notice of any officer that he may have been treated improperly, a report must be made as soon as practicable to an officer of the rank of inspector or above who is not connected with the investigation. If the matter concerns a possible assault or the possibility of the unnecessary or unreasonable use of force then the police surgeon must also be called as soon as practicable.

(b) Medical treatment
9.2 The custody officer must immediately call the police surgeon (or, in urgent cases, send the person to hospital or call the nearest available medical practitioner) if a person brought to a police station or already detained there:
  (a) appears to be suffering from physical or mental illness; or
  (b) is injured; or
  (c) does not show signs of sensibility and awareness or fails to respond normally to questions or conversation (other than through drunkenness alone); or
  (d) otherwise appears to need medical attention.
This applies even if the person makes no request for medical attention and whether or not he has recently had medical treatment elsewhere (unless brought to the police station direct from hospital). [See *Note 9A*]

9.3 If it appears to the custody officer, or he is told, that a person brought to the police station under arrest may be suffering from an infectious disease of any significance he must take steps to isolate the person and his property until he has obtained medical directions as to where the person should be taken, whether fumigation should take place and what precautions should be taken by officers who have been or will be in contact with him.

9.4 If a detained person requests a medical examination the police surgeon must be called as soon as practicable. He may in addition be examined by a medical practitioner of his own choice at his own expense.

9.5 If a person is required to take or apply any medication in compliance with medical directions, the custody officer is responsible for its safe keeping and for ensuring that he is given the opportunity to take or apply it at the appropriate times. No police officer may administer controlled drugs subject to the Misuse of Drugs Act 1971 for this purpose. A person may administer such drugs to himself only under the personal supervision of the police surgeon.

9.6 If a detained person has in his possession or claims to need medication relating to a heart condition, diabetes, epilepsy or a condition of comparable potential seriousness then, even though paragraph 9.2 may not apply, the advice of the police surgeon must be obtained.

(c) Documentation
9.7 A record must be made of any arrangements made for an examination by a police surgeon under paragraph 9.1 above and of any complaint reported under that paragraph together with any relevant remarks by the custody officer.

9.8 A record must be kept of any request for a medical examination under paragraph 9.4, of the arrangements for any examination made, and of any medical directions to the police.

9.9 Subject to the requirements of section 4 above the custody record shall include not only a record of all medication that a detained person has in his possession on arrival at the police station but also a note of any such medication he claims he needs but does not have with him.

Notes for Guidance
9A The need to call a police surgeon need not apply to minor ailments.
9B It is important to remember that a person who appears to be drunk or behaving abnormally may be suffering from illness or the effect of drugs or may have sustained injury (particularly head injury) which is not apparent, and that someone needing or addicted to certain drugs may experience harmful effects within a short time of being deprived of their supply. Police should therefore always call the police surgeon when in any doubt, and act with all due speed.
9C If a medical practitioner does not record his clinical findings in the custody record, the record must show where they are recorded.
9D All officers dealing with detained persons are of course under a duty to observe not only the above provisions but also those set out in the Police Discipline Code.

10. Cautions

(a) When a caution must be given
10.1 A person whom there are grounds to suspect of an offence must be cautioned before any questions about it (or further questions if it is his answers to previous questions that provide grounds for suspicion) are put to him for the purpose of obtaining evidence which may be given to a court in a prosecution. He therefore need not be cautioned if questions are put for other purposes, for example, to establish his identity, his ownership of, or responsibility for, any vehicle or the need to search him in the exercise of powers of stop and search.

10.2 When a person who is not under arrest is initially cautioned before or during an interview at a police station or other premises he must at the same time be told that he is not under arrest, is not obliged to remain with the officer but that if he does, may obtain legal advice if he wishes.

10.3 A person must be cautioned upon arrest for an offence unless:
  (a) it is impracticable to do so by reason of his condition or behaviour at the time; or
  (b) he has already been cautioned immediately prior to arrest in accordance with paragraph 10.1 above.

(b) Action: general
10.4 The caution shall be in the following terms:
  'You do not have to say anything unless you wish to do so, but what you say may be given in evidence.'
Minor deviations do not constitute a breach of this requirement provided that the sense of the caution is preserved. [See *Notes 10C and 10D*]

10.5 When there is a break in questioning under caution the interviewing officer must ensure that the person being questioned is aware that he remains under caution. If there is any doubt the caution should be given again in full when the interview resumes. [See *Note 10A*]

(c) Documentation
10.6 A record shall be made when a caution is given under this section, either in the officer's pocket book or in the interview record as appropriate.

Notes for Guidance
10A In considering whether or not to caution again after a break, the officer should bear in mind that he may have to satisfy a court that the person understood that he was still under caution when the interview resumed.

10B It is not necessary to give or repeat a caution when informing a person who is not under arrest that he may be prosecuted for an offence.

10C If it appears that a person does not understand what the caution means, the officer who has given it should go on to explain it in his own words.

10D In case anyone who is given a caution is unclear about its significance, the officer concerned should explain that the caution is given in pursuance of the general principle of English law that a person need not answer any questions or provide any information which might tend to incriminate him, and that no adverse inferences from this silence may be drawn at any trial that takes place. The person should not, however, be left with a false impression that non co-operation will have no effect on his immediate treatment as, for example, his refusal to provide his name and address when charged with an offence may render him liable to detention.

11. Interviews: general

(a) Action

11.1 No police officer may try to obtain answers to questions or to elicit a statement by the use of oppression, or shall indicate, except in answer to a direct question, what action will be taken on the part of the police if the person being interviewed answers questions, makes a statement or refuses to do either. If the person asks the officer directly what action will be taken in the event of his answering questions, making a statement or refusing to do either, then the officer may inform the person what action the police propose to take in that event provided that that action is itself proper and warranted.

11.2 As soon as a police officer who is making enquiries of any person about an offence believes that a prosecution should be brought against him and that there is sufficient evidence for it to succeed, he shall without delay cease to question him.

(b) Interview records

11.3 (a) An accurate record must be made of each interview with a person suspected of an offence, whether or not the interview takes place at a police station.

(b) if the interview takes place in the police station or other premises:
    (i) the record must state the place of the interview, the time it begins and ends, the time the record is made (if different), any breaks in the interview and the names of all those present; and must be made on the forms provided for this purpose or in the officer's pocket book or in accordance with the code of practice for the tape recording of police interviews with suspects;
    (ii) the record must be made during the course of the interview, unless in the investigating officer's view this would not be practicable or would interfere with the conduct of the interview, and must constitute either a verbatim record of what has been said or, failing this, an account of the interview which adequately and accurately summarises it.

11.4 If an interview record is not made during the course of the interview it must be made as soon as practicable after its completion.

11.5 Written interview records must be timed and signed by the maker.

11.6 If an interview record is not completed in the course of the interview the reason must be recorded in the officer's pocket book.

11.7 Any refusal by a person to sign an interview record when asked to do so in accordance with the provisions of this code must itself be recorded.

12. Interviews in police stations

(a) Action

12.1 If a police officer wishes to interview, or conduct enquiries which require the presence of, a detained person the custody officer is responsible for deciding whether to deliver him into his custody.

12.2 In any period of 24 hours a detained person must be allowed a continuous period of at least 8 hours for rest, free from questioning, travel or any interruption arising out of the investigation concerned. This period should normally be at night. The period of rest may not be interrupted or delayed unless there are reasonable grounds for believing that it would:
    (i) involve a risk of harm to persons or serious loss of, or damage to, property;
    (ii) delay unnecessarily the person's release from custody; or
    (iii) otherwise prejudice the outcome of the investigation.

If a person is arrested at a police station after going there voluntarily, the period of 24 hours runs from the time of arrival at the police station and not the time of his arrest.

12.3 A detained person may not be supplied with intoxicating liquor except on medical directions. No person who is unfit through drink or drugs to the extent that he is unable to appreciate the significance of questions put to him and his answers may be questioned about an alleged offence in that condition except in accordance with Annex C. [See *Note 12C*]

12.4 As far as practicable interviews shall take place in interview rooms which must be adequately heated, lit and ventilated.

12.5 Persons being questioned or making statements shall not be required to stand.

12.6 Before the commencement of an interview each interviewing officer shall identify himself and any other officers present by name and rank to the person being interviewed.

12.7 Breaks from interviewing shall be made at recognised meal times. Short breaks for refreshment shall also be provided at intervals of approximately two hours, subject to the interviewing officer's discretion to delay a break if there are reasonable grounds for believing that it would:
  (i) involve a risk of harm to persons or serious loss of, or damage to property;
  (ii) delay unnecessarily the person's release from custody; or
  (iii) otherwise prejudice the outcome of the investigation.

12.8 If in the course of the interview a complaint is made by the person being questioned or on his behalf, concerning the provisions of this code then the interviewing officer shall:
  (i) record it in the interview record; and
  (ii) inform the custody officer, who is then responsible for dealing with it in accordance with section 9 of this code.

(b) Documentation
12.9 A record must be made of the times at which a detained person is not in the custody of the custody officer, and why; and of the reason for any refusal to deliver him out of that custody.

12.10 A record must be made of any intoxicating liquor supplied to a detained person, in accordance with paragraph 12.3 above.

12.11 Any decision to delay a break in an interview must be recorded, with grounds, in the interview record.

12.12 Where the person interviewed is in the police station at the time that a written record of the interview is made, he shall be given the opportunity to read it and to sign it as correct or to indicate the respects in which he considers it inaccurate, but no person shall be kept in custody for this sole purpose. If the interview is tape recorded the arrangements set out in the relevant code of practice apply. [See *Note 12B*]

12.13 All written statements made at police stations under caution shall be written on the forms provided for the purpose.

12.14 All written statements made under caution shall be taken in accordance with Annex D to this code.

12.15 Where the appropriate adult or another third party is present at an interview and is still in the police station at the time that a written record of the interview is made, he shall be asked to read it (or any written statement taken down by a police officer) and sign it as correct or to indicate the respects in which he considers it inaccurate. If the person refuses to read or sign the record as accurate or to indicate the respects in which he considers it inaccurate, the senior officer present shall record on the record itself, in the presence of the person concerned, what has happened. If the interview is tape recorded the arrangements set out in the relevant code of practice apply.

Notes for Guidance
12A The purpose of any interview is to obtain from the person concerned his explanation of the facts, and not necessarily to obtain an admission.
12B If the interview has been contemporaneously recorded and the record signed by the person interviewed in accordance with paragraph 12.12 above, or has been tape recorded, it is normally unnecessary to ask for a written statement. Statements under caution should normally be taken in these circumstances only at the person's express wish. An officer may, however, ask him whether or not he wants to make such a statement.
12C The police surgeon can give advice about whether or not a person is fit to be interviewed in accordance with paragraph 12.3 above.

13. Persons at risk: juveniles, and those who are mentally ill or mentally handicapped

13.1 A juvenile or a person who is mentally ill or mentally handicapped, whether suspected or not, must not be interviewed or asked to provide or sign a written statement in the absence of the appropriate adult unless Annex C applies. If he is cautioned in accordance with section 10 above in the absence of the appropriate adult, the caution must be repeated in the adult's presence (unless the interview has by then already finished).

13.2 If, having been informed of the right to legal advice under paragraph 3.6 above, the appropriate adult considers that legal advice should be taken, then the provisions of section 5 of this code apply:

13.3 Juveniles may only be interviewed at their places of education in exceptional circumstances and then only where the principal or his nominee agrees and is present.

Notes for Guidance

13A Where the parents or guardians of a person at risk are themselves suspected of involvement in the offence concerned, or are the victims of it, it may be desirable for the appropriate adult to be some other person.

13B It is important to bear in mind that, although juveniles or persons who are mentally ill or mentally handicapped are often capable of providing reliable evidence, they may, without knowing or wishing to do so, be particularly prone in certain circumstances to provide information which is unreliable, misleading or self-incriminating. Special care should therefore always be exercised in questioning such a person, and the appropriate adult involved, if there is any doubt about a person's age, mental state or capacity. Because of the risk of unreliable evidence it is also important to obtain corroboration of any facts admitted whenever possible.

13C The appropriate adult should be informed that he is not expected to act simply as an observer. The purposes of his presence are, first, to advise the person being questioned and to observe whether or not the interview is being conducted properly and fairly; and, secondly, to facilitate communication with the person being interviewed.

13D A juvenile should not be arrested at his place of education unless this is unavoidable. In this case the principal or his nominee must be informed.

14. Interpreters

(a) Foreign languages

14.1 Unless Annex C applies, a person must not be interviewed in the absence of a person capable of acting as interpreter if:
(a) he has difficulty in understanding English;
(b) the interviewing officer cannot himself speak the person's own language; and
(c) the person wishes an interpreter to be present.

14.2 The interviewing officer shall ensure that the interpreter makes a note of the interview at the time in the language of the person being interviewed for use in the event of his being called to give evidence, and certifies its accuracy. The person shall be given an opportunity to read it or have it read to him and sign it as correct or to indicate the respects in which he considers it inaccurate. If the interview is tape recorded the arrangements set out in the relevant code of practice apply.

14.3 In the case of a person making a statement in a language other than English:
(a) the interpreter shall take down the statement in the language in which it is made;
(b) the person making the statement shall be invited to sign it; and
(c) an official English translation shall be made in due course.

(b) The deaf

14.4 If a person is deaf or there is doubt about his hearing ability, he must not be interviewed in the absence of an interpreter unless he agrees in writing to be interviewed without one or Annex C applies. (Information on obtaining the services of a suitably qualified interpreter for the deaf is given in *Note for Guidance 3C*.)

14.5 The interviewing officer shall ensure that the interpreter makes a note of the interview at the time for use in the event of his being called to give evidence and certifies its accuracy. The person shall be given an opportunity to read it and sign it as correct or to indicate the respects in which he considers it inaccurate.

(c) Additional rules for detained persons

14.6 All reasonable attempts should be made to make clear to the detained person that interpreters will be provided at public expense.

14.7 Where paragraph 6.1 applies and the person concerned cannot communicate with the solicitor, whether because of language or hearing difficulties, an interpreter must be called. The interpreter may not be a police officer when interpretation is needed for the purposes of obtaining legal advice. In all other cases a police officer may only interpret if he first obtains the detained person's (or the appropriate adult's) agreement in writing or if the interview is tape recorded in accordance with the relevant code of practice.

14.8 When a person who has difficulty in understanding English is charged with an offence and the custody officer cannot himself speak the person's language, arrangements must also be made for an interpreter to explain as soon as practicable the offence concerned and any other information given by the custody officer.

(d) Documentation
14.9 Action taken to call an interpreter under this section and any agreement to be interviewed in the absence of an interpreter must be recorded.

Note for Guidance
14A If the interpreter is needed as a prosecution witness at the person's trial, a second interpreter must act as the court interpreter.

15. Questioning: special restrictions

15.1 If a person has been arrested by one police force on behalf of another and the lawful period of detention in respect of that offence has not yet commenced in accordance with section 41 of the Police and Criminal Evidence Act 1984 no questions may be put to him about the offence while he is in transit between the forces except in order to clarify any voluntary statement made by him.

15.2 If a person is in police detention at a hospital he may not be questioned without the agreement of a responsible doctor. [See *Note 15A*]

Note for Guidance
15A If questioning takes place at a hospital under paragraph 15.2 (or on the way to or from a hospital) the period concerned counts towards the total period of detention permitted.

16. Reviews and extensions of detention

(a) Action
16.1 The review officer is responsible under section 40 of the Police and Criminal Evidence Act 1984 for determining whether or not a person's detention continues to be necessary. In reaching a decision he shall provide an opportunity to the detained person himself to make representations (unless he is unfit to do so because of his condition or behaviour) and to his solicitor or the appropriate adult if available at the time. Other persons having an interest in the person's welfare may make representations at the review officer's discretion.

16.2 The same persons may make representations to the officer determining whether further detention should be authorised under section 42 of the Act.

(b) Documentation
16.3 The grounds for and extent of any delay in conducting a review shall be recorded.

16.4 Any written representations shall be retained.

16.5 A record shall be made as soon as practicable of the outcome of each review and application for a warrant of further detention or its extension.

Notes for Guidance
16A An application for a warrant of further detention or its extension should be made between 10am and 9pm, and if possible during normal court hours. It will not be practicable to arrange for a court to sit specially outside the hours of 10am to 9pm. If it appears possible that a special sitting may be needed (either at a weekend, Bank/Public Holiday or on a weekday outside normal court hours but between 10am and 9pm) then the clerk to the justices should be given notice and informed of this possibility, while the court is sitting if possible.
16B If in the circumstances the only practicable way of conducting a review is over the telephone then this is permissible, provided that the requirements of section 40 of the Police and Criminal Evidence Act 1984 are observed.

17. Charging of detained persons

(a) Action
17.1 When an officer considers that there is sufficient evidence to prosecute a detained person he should without delay bring him before the custody officer who shall then be

responsible for considering whether or not he should be charged. Any resulting action should be taken in the presence of the appropriate adult if the person is a juvenile or mentally ill or mentally handicapped.

17.2 When a detained person is charged with or informed that he may be prosecuted for an offence he shall be cautioned in the terms of paragraph 10.4 above.

17.3 At the time a person is charged he shall be given a written notice showing particulars of the offence with which he is charged and including the name of the officer in the case, his police station and the reference number for the case. So far as possible the particulars of the charge shall be stated in simple terms, but they shall also show the precise offence in law with which he is charged. The notice shall begin with the following words:

'You are charged with the offence(s) shown below. You do not have to say anything unless you wish to do so, but what you say may be given in evidence.'

If the person is a juvenile or is mentally ill or mentally handicapped the notice shall be given to the appropriate adult.

17.4 If at any time after a person has been charged with or informed he may be prosecuted for an offence a police officer wishes to bring to the notice of that person any written statement made by another person or the content of an interview with another person, he shall hand to that person a true copy of any such written statement or bring to his attention the content of the interview record, but shall say or do nothing to invite any reply or comment save to caution him in the terms of paragraph 10.4 above. If the person cannot read then the officer may read it to him. If the person is a juvenile or mentally ill or mentally handicapped the copy shall also be given to, or the interview record brought to the attention of, the appropriate adult.

17.5 Questions relating to an offence may not be put to a person after he has been charged with that offence, or informed that he may be prosecuted for it, unless they are necessary for the purpose of preventing or minimising harm or loss to some other person or to the public or for clearing up an ambiguity in a previous answer or statement, or where it is in the interests of justice that the person should have put to him and have an opportunity to comment on information concerning the offence which has come to light since he was charged or informed that he might be prosecuted. Before any such questions are put he shall be cautioned in the terms of paragraph 10.4 above.

17.6 Where a juvenile is charged with an offence and the custody officer authorises his continuing detention he must try to make arrangements for the juvenile to be taken into the care of a local authority to be detained pending appearance in court unless he certifies that it is impracticable to do so in accordance with section 38(6) of the Police and Criminal Evidence Act 1984. [See *Note 17A*]

(b) Documentation

17.7 A record shall be made of anything a detained person says when charged.

17.8 Any questions put after charge and answers given relating to the offence shall be contemporaneously recorded in full on the forms provided and the record signed by that person or, if he refuses, by the interviewing officer and any third parties present. If the questions are tape recorded the arrangements set out in the relevant code of practice apply.

17.9 If it is not practicable to make arrangements for the transfer of a juvenile into local authority care in accordance with paragraph 17.6 above the custody officer must record the reasons and make out a certificate to be produced before the court together with the juvenile.

Note for Guidance

17A Neither a juvenile's unruliness nor the nature of the offence with which he is charged provides grounds for the custody officer to retain him in police custody rather than seek to arrange for his transfer to the care of the local authority.

Annex A

Intimate and strip searches [4.1]

(a) Action

1. Body orifices may be searched only if an officer of the rank of superintendent or above has reasonable grounds for believing:

    (a) that an article which could cause physical injury to a detained person or others at the police station has been concealed; or

    (b) that the person has concealed a Class A drug which he intended to supply to another or to export; and

    (c) that in either case an intimate search is the only practicable means of removing it.

The reasons why an intimate search is considered necessary shall be explained to the person before the search takes place.

2. An intimate search may only be carried out by a registered medical practitioner, State Registered Nurse, or State Enrolled Nurse, unless an officer of at least the rank of superintendent considers that this is not practicable and the search is to take place under sub-paragraph 1(a) above.

3. An intimate search under sub-paragraph 1(a) above may take place only at a hospital, surgery, other medical premises or police station. A search under sub-paragraph 1(b) may take place only at a hospital, surgery or other medical premises.

4. An intimate search at a police station of a juvenile or a mentally ill or mentally handicapped person may take place only in the presence of the appropriate adult of the same sex. In the case of a juvenile, the search may take place in the absence of the appropriate adult only if the juvenile signifies in the presence of the appropriate adult that he prefers the search to be done in his absence and the appropriate adult agrees.

5. A strip search (that is a search involving the removal of more than outer clothing) may take place only if the custody officer considers it to be necessary to remove an article which the detained person would not be allowed to keep.

6. Where an intimate search under sub-paragraph 1(a) above or a strip search is carried out by a police officer, the officer must be of the same sex as the person searched. No person of the opposite sex who is not a medical practitioner or nurse shall be present, nor shall anyone whose presence is unnecessary.

(b) Documentation
7. In the case of an intimate search the custody officer shall as soon as practicable record which parts of the person's body were searched, who carried out the search, who was present, the reasons for the search and its result.

8. In the case of a strip search he shall record the reasons for the search and its result.

9. If an intimate search is carried out by a police officer, the reason why it is impracticable for a suitably qualified person to conduct it must be recorded.

Annex B
Delay in notifying arrest or allowing access to legal advice

(A) Persons detained under the Police and Criminal Evidence Act 1984

(a) Action
1. The rights set out in sections 5 or 6 of the code (or both) may be delayed if the person is in police detention in connection with a serious arrestable offence, has not yet been charged with an offence and an officer of the rank of superintendent or above has reasonable grounds for believing that the exercise of each right:
  (i) will lead to interference with or harm to evidence connected with a serious arrest-able offence or interference with or physical harm to other persons;
  (ii) will lead to the alerting of other persons suspected of having committed such an offence but not yet arrested for it; or
  (iii) will hinder the recovery of property obtained in consequence of the commission of such an offence.
[See *Note B3*]

2. Access to a solicitor may not be delayed on the grounds that he might advise the person not to answer any questions or that the solicitor was initially asked to attend the police station by someone else, provided that the person himself then wishes to see the solicitor.

3. These rights may be delayed only for as long as is necessary and, subject to paragraph 6 below, in no case beyond 36 hours after the relevant time as defined in section 41 of the Police and Criminal Evidence Act 1984. If the above grounds cease to apply within this time, the person must as soon as practicable be asked if he wishes to exercise either right and action must be taken in accordance with the the relevant section of the code.

4. A detained person must be permitted to consult a solicitor for a reasonable time before any court hearing.

(b) Documentation
5. The grounds for action under this Annex shall be recorded and the person informed of them as soon as practicable.

(B) Persons detained under the Prevention of Terrorism (Temporary Provisions) Act 1984

(a) Action

6. The rights set out in sections 5 or 6 of this code (or both) may be delayed if paragraph 1 above applies or if an officer of the rank of superintendent or above has reasonable grounds for believing that the exercise of either right:

    (a) will lead to interference with the gathering of information about the commission, preparation or instigation of acts of terrorism; or

    (b) by alerting any person, will make it more difficult to prevent an act of terrorism or to secure the apprehension, prosecution or conviction of any person in connection with the commission, preparation or instigation of an act of terrorism.

7. These rights may be delayed only for as long as is necessary and in no case beyond 48 hours from the time of arrest. If the above grounds cease to apply within this time, the person must as soon as practicable be asked if he wishes to exercise either right and action must be taken in accordance with the relevant section of this code.

(b) Documentation

8. Paragraph 5 above applies.

9. Any reply given by a person under paragraph 7 above must be recorded and the person asked to endorse the record in relation to whether he wishes to receive legal advice at this point.

Notes for Guidance

B1 Even if Annex B applies in the case of a juvenile, or a person who is mentally ill or mentally handicapped, action to inform the appropriate adult must nevertheless be taken in accordance with paragraph 3.6 of the code.

B2 In the case of Commonwealth citizens and foreign nationals, see Note 7A.

B3 Police detention is defined in section 118(2) of the Police and Criminal Evidence Act 1984.

Annex C
Urgent interviews

1. If, and only if, an officer of the rank of superintendent or above considers that delay will involve an immediate risk of harm to persons or serious loss of or serious damage to property:

    (a) a person heavily under the influence of drink or drugs may be interviewed in that state; or

    (b) an arrested juvenile or a person who is mentally ill or mentally handicapped may be interviewed in the absence of the appropriate adult; or

    (c) a person who has difficulty in understanding English or who has a hearing disability may be interviewed in the absence of an interpreter.

2. Questioning in these circumstances may not continue once sufficient information to avert the immediate risk has been obtained.

3. A record shall be made of the grounds for any decision to interview a person under paragraph 1 above.

Note for Guidance

C1 The special groups referred to in Annex C are all particularly vulnerable. The provisions of the Annex, which override safeguards designed to protect them and to minimise the risk of interviews producing unreliable evidence, should be applied only in exceptional cases of need.

Annex D
Written statements under caution [12.14]

(a) Written by a person under caution

1. A person shall always be invited to write down himself what he wants to say.

2. Where the person wishes to write it himself, he shall be asked to write out and sign before writing what he wants to say, the following:

    'I make this statement of my own free will. I understand that I need not say anything unless I wish to do so and that what I say may be given in evidence.'

3. Any person writing his own statement shall be allowed to do so without any prompting except that a police officer may indicate to him which matters are material or question any ambiguity in the statement.

(b) Written by a police officer

4. If a person says that he would like someone to write it for him, a police officer shall write the statement, but, before starting, he must ask him to sign, or make his mark, to the following:

'I, ..., wish to make a statement, I want someone to write down what I say. I understand that I need not say anything unless I wish to do so and that what I say may be given in evidence.'

5. Where a police officer writes the statement, he must take down the exact words spoken by the person making it and he must not edit or paraphrase it. Any questions that are necessary (eg to make it more intelligible) and the answers given must be recorded contemporaneously on the statement form.

6. When the writing of a statement by a police officer is finished the person making it shall be asked to read it and to make any corrections, alterations or additions he wishes. When he has finished reading it he shall be asked to write and sign or make his mark on the following certificate at the end of the statement:

'I have read the above statement, and I have been able to correct, alter or add anything I wish. This statement is true. I have made it of my own free will.'

7. If the person making the statement cannot read, or refuses to read it, or to write the above mentioned certificate at the end of it or to sign it, the senior police officer present shall read it over to him and ask him whether he would like to correct, alter or add anything and to put his signature or make his mark at the end. The police officer shall then certify on the statement itself what has occurred.

Annex D
Summary of provisions relating to mentally ill and mentally handicapped persons

1. If an officer has any suspicion or is told in good faith that a person of any age, whether or not in custody, may be mentally ill or mentally handicapped, or cannot understand the significance of questions put to him or his replies, then he shall be treated as a mentally ill or mentally handicapped person. [1.4]

2. In the case of a person who is mentally ill or mentally handicapped, 'the appropriate adult' means:
   (a) a relative, guardian or some other person responsible for his care or custody;
   (b) someone who has experience of dealing with mentally ill or mentally handicapped persons but is not a police officer or employed by the police; or
   (c) failing either of the above, some other responsible adult who is not a police officer or employed by the police.
   [1.7(b)]

3. If the custody officer authorises the detention of a person who is mentally handicapped or is suffering from mental illness he must as soon as practicable inform the appropriate adult of the grounds for the person's detention and his whereabouts, and ask the adult to come to the police station to see the person. If the appropriate adult is already at the police station when information is given as required in paragraphs 3.1 to 3.3 the information must be given to the detained person in his presence. If the appropriate adult is not at the police station when the information is given then the information must be given to the detained person again in the presence of the appropriate adult once that person arrives. [3.6]

4. If a person brought to a police station appears to be suffering from mental illness, or is incoherent other than through drunkenness alone, or if a detained person subsequently appears to be mentally ill, the custody officer must immediately call the police surgeon or, in urgent cases, send the person to hospital or call the nearest available medical practitioner. [9.2]

5. A mentally ill or mentally handicapped person must not be interviewed or asked to provide or sign a written statement in the absence of the appropriate adult unless an officer of the rank of superintendent or above considers that delay will involve an immediate risk of harm to persons or serious loss of or serious damage to property. Questioning in these circumstances may not continue in the absence of the appropriate adult once sufficient information to avert the risk has been obtained. A record shall be made of the grounds for any decision to begin an interview in these circumstances. [13.1 and Annex C]

6. If the appropriate adult, having been informed of the right to legal advice, considers that legal advice should be taken, the provisions of section 6 of the code apply as if the mentally ill or mentally handicapped person had requested access to legal advice. [13.2]

7. If the detention of a mentally ill or mentally handicapped person is reviewed by a review officer or a superintendent, the appropriate adult must, if available at the time, be given an opportunity to make representations to the officer about the need for continuing detention. [16.1 to 16.2]

8. If the custody officer charges a mentally ill or mentally handicapped person with an offence or takes such other action as is appropriate when there is sufficient evidence for a prosecution this must be done in the presence of the appropriate adult. The written notice embodying any charge must be given to the appropriate adult. [17.1 to 17.3]

9. An intimate search of a mentally ill or mentally handicapped person may take place only in the presence of the appropriate adult of the same sex. [Annex A, paragraph 4]

Notes for Guidance
E1 It is important to bear in mind that although persons who are mentally ill or mentally handicapped are often capable of providing reliable evidence, they may, without knowing or wishing to do so, be particularly prone in certain circumstances to provide information which is unreliable, misleading or self-incriminating. Special care should therefore always be exercised in questioning such a person, and the appropriate adult involved, if there is any doubt about a person's mental state or capacity. Because of the risk of unreliable evidence, it is important to obtain corroboration of any facts admitted whenever possible. [Note 13B]
E2 Because of the risks referred to in Note E1, which the presence of the appropriate adult is intended to minimise, officers of superintendent rank or above should exercise their discretion to authorise the commencement of an interview in the adult's absence only in exceptional cases, where it is necessary to avert an immediate risk of serious harm. [Annex C, sub-paragraph 1(b) and Note C1]
E3 The appropriate adult should be informed that he is not expected to act simply as an observer. The purposes of his presence are, first, to advise the person being interviewed and to observe whether or not the interview is being conducted properly and fairly; and, secondly, to facilitate communication with the person being interviewed. [Note 13C]
E4 In the case of persons who are mentally ill or mentally handicapped, it may in certain circumstances be more satisfactory for all concerned if the appropriate adult is someone who has experience or training in their care rather than a relative lacking such qualifications. But if the person himself prefers a relative to a better qualified stranger his wishes should if practicable be respected. [Note 1C]

D CODE OF PRACTICE FOR THE IDENTIFICATION OF PERSONS BY POLICE OFFICERS   A1.04

1. General

1.1 This code of practice must be readily available at all police stations for consultation by police officers, detained persons and members of the public.

1.2 The notes for guidance included are not provisions of this code, but are guidance to police officers and others about its application and interpretation. Provisions in the annexes to the code are provisions of this code.

1.3 If an officer has any suspicion, or is told in good faith, that a person of any age may be mentally ill or mentally handicapped, or mentally incapable of understanding the significance of questions put to him or his replies, then that person shall be treated as a mentally ill or mentally handicapped person for the purposes of this code.

1.4 If anyone appears to be under the age of 17 then he shall be treated as a juvenile for the purposes of this code in the absence of clear evidence to show that he is older.

1.5 In this code 'the appropriate adult' means:
    (a) in the case of a juvenile:
        (i) his parent or guardian (or, if he is in care, the care authority or organisation);
       (ii) a social worker; or
      (iii) failing either of the above, another responsible adult who is not a police officer or employed by the police.
    (b) in the case of a person who is mentally ill or mentally handicapped:
        (i) a relative, guardian or some other person responsible for his care or custody;
       (ii) someone who has experience of dealing with mentally ill or mentally handicapped persons but is not a police officer or employed by the police; or
      (iii) failing either of the above, some other responsible adult who is not a police officer or employed by the police.

1.6 Any reference to a custody officer in this code includes an officer who is performing the functions of a custody officer. Any reference to a solicitor in this code includes a clerk or legal executive except in Annex C, paragraph 7.

1.7 Where a record is made under this code of any action requiring the authority of an officer of specified rank, his name and rank must be included in the record.

1.8 All records must be timed and signed by the maker.

1.9 In the case of a detained person records are to be made in his custody record unless otherwise specified.

1.10 In the case of any procedure requiring a suspect's consent, the consent of a person who is mentally ill or mentally handicapped is only valid if given in the presence of the appropriate adult; and in the case of a juvenile the consent of his parent or guardian is required as well as his own (unless he is under 14, in which case the consent of his parent or guardian is sufficient in its own right). [See *Note 1A*]

1.11 In the case of any procedure requiring information to be given to a suspect, it must be given in the presence of the appropriate adult if the suspect is mentally ill, mentally handicapped or a juvenile. If the suspect is deaf or there is doubt about his hearing ability or ability to understand English, and the officer cannot himself speak the person's language, the information must be given through an interpreter.

1.12 Any procedure involving the participation of a person (whether as a suspect or witness) who is mentally ill, mentally handicapped or a juvenile must take place in the presence of the appropriate adult; but the adult must not be allowed to prompt any identification of a suspect by a witness.

1.13 Nothing in this code affects any procedure under:
   (i) sections 5 to 12 of the Road Traffic Act 1972, as amended;
  (ii) paragraph 18 of Schedule 2 to the Immigration Act 1971; or
 (iii) paragraph 5 of Schedule 3 to the Prevention of Terrorism (Temporary Provisions) Act 1984.

1.14 In this code references to photographs include optical disc computer printouts.

Note for Guidance
1A For the purposes of paragraph 1.10 above consent may be given, in the case of a juvenile in the care of a local authority or voluntary organisation, by that authority or organisation.

2. Identification by witnesses
(a) Suspect at the police station: the decision as to the method of identification
2.1 In a case which involves disputed identification evidence a parade must be held if the suspect asks for one and it is practicable to hold one. A parade may also be held if the officer in charge of the investigation considers that it would be useful.

2.2 Arrangements for the parade and its conduct shall be the responsibility of an officer in uniform not below the rank of inspector who is not involved with the investigation ('the identification officer'). No officer involved with the investigation of the case against the suspect may take any part in the arrangements for, or the conduct of, the parade.

2.3 A parade need not be held if the identification officer considers that, whether by reason of the unusual appearance of the suspect or for some other reason, it would not be practicable to assemble sufficient people who resembled him to make a parade fair.

2.4 If a suspect refuses or, having agreed, fails to attend an identification parade or the holding of a parade is impracticable, arrangements must if practicable be made to allow the witness an opportunity of seeing him in a group of people. Such a group identification may also be arranged if the officer in charge of the investigation considers, whether because of fear on the part of the witness or for some other reason, that it is, in the circumstances, more satisfactory than a parade.

2.5 If neither a parade nor a group identification procedure is arranged, the suspect may be confronted by the witness. Such a confrontation does not require the suspect's consent, but may not take place unless neither a parade nor a group identification is practicable, whether because the suspect has withheld his consent to them or his co-operation, or for some other reason.

2.6 A witness must not be shown photographs or photofit, identikit or similar pictures for identification purposes if there is a suspect already available to be asked to stand on a parade or participate in a group identification.

(b) Notice to suspect
2.7 Before (a) a parade takes place or (b) a group identification is arranged, the identification officer shall explain to the suspect:
    (i) the purpose of the parade or group identification;
   (ii) the procedures for holding it (including his right to have a solicitor or friend present);
  (iii) where appropriate the special arrangements for juveniles;
  (iv) where appropriate the special arrangements for mentally ill and mentally handicapped persons;
   (v) the fact that he does not have to take part in either procedure and, if it is proposed to hold a group identification, his entitlement to a parade if this can practicably be arranged; and
  (vi) the fact that, if he does not consent to take part in a parade or other group identification, he may be confronted by a witness and his refusal may be given in evidence in any subsequent trial, where a witness might be given an opportunity of identifying him in court.

2.8 This information must also be contained in a written notice which must be handed to the suspect. The identification officer shall give the suspect a reasonable opportunity to read the notice, after which he shall be asked to sign a second copy of the notice to indicate whether or not he is willing to attend the parade or participate in the group identification. The signed copy shall be retained by the identification officer.

(c) Conduct of a parade or other group identification
2.9 Any parade or other group identification must be carried out in accordance with Annex A.

(d) Confrontation by a witness
2.10 Any confrontation must be carried out in accordance with Annex B.

(e) Street identification
2.11 A police officer may take a witness to a particular neighbourhood or place to observe the persons there to see whether he can identify the person whom he said he saw on the relevant occasion. Care should be taken however not to direct the witness's attention to any individual. Where the suspect is at a police station, the provisions of paragraphs 2.1 to 2.10 must apply.

(f) Showing of photographs etc.
2.12 If photographs or photofit, identikit or similar pictures are shown to a witness for identification purposes this must be done in accordance with Annex C.

(g) Documentation
2.13 The identification officer will make a record of the parade or group identification on the forms provided.

2.14 If the identification officer considers that it is not practicable to hold a parade he shall tell the suspect why and record the reason.

2.15 A record shall be made of a person's refusal to take part in a parade or other group identification.

3. Identification by fingerprints
(a) Action
3.1 A person's fingerprints may be taken only with his consent or if paragraph 3.2 applies. If he is at a police station consent must be in writing. In either case the person must be informed of the reason before they are taken and that they will be destroyed if paragraph 3.4 applies. He must be told that he may witness their destruction if he asks to do so within one month of being cleared or informed that he will not be prosecuted.

3.2 Powers to take fingerprints without consent from any person over the age of ten years are provided by section 61 of the Police and Criminal Evidence Act 1984. Reasonable force may be used if necessary.

3.3 Section 27 of the Police and Criminal Evidence Act 1984 describes the circumstances in which a constable may require a person convicted of a recordable offence to attend at a police station in order that his fingerprints may be taken. [See *Note 3A*]

3.4 The fingerprints of a person and all copies of them taken in that case must be destroyed if:
    (a) he is prosecuted for the offence concerned and cleared; or
    (b) he is not prosecuted (unless he admits the offence and is cautioned for it).
An opportunity of witnessing the destruction must be given to him if he wishes and if, in accordance with paragraph 3.1, he applies within one month of being cleared or informed that he will not be prosecuted.

3.5 References to fingerprints include palm prints.

(b) Documentation
3.6 A record must be made as soon as possible of the reason for taking a person's fingerprints without consent and of their destruction. If force is used a record shall be made of the circumstances and those present.

Note for Guidance
3A References to recordable offences in this code relate to those offences for which convictions are recorded in national police records. (See section 27(4) of the Police and Criminal Evidence Act 1984.)

4. Identification by photographs
(a) Action
4.1 The photograph of a person who has been arrested may be taken at a police station only with his written consent or if paragraph 4.2 applies. In either case he must be informed of the reason for taking it and that the photograph will be destroyed if paragraph 4.4 applies. He must be told that he may witness the destruction of the photograph if he asks to do so within one month of being cleared or informed that he will not be prosecuted.

4.2 The photograph of a person who has been arrested may be taken without consent if:
    (i) he is arrested at the same time as other persons, or at a time when it is likely that other persons will be arrested, and a photograph is necessary to establish who was arrested, at what time and at what place;

(ii) he has been charged with or reported for a recordable offence and has not yet been released or brought before a court [See *Note 3A*]; or

(iii) he is convicted of such an offence and his photograph is not already on record as a result of (i) or (ii). There is no power of arrest to take a photograph in pursuance of this provision which applies only where the person is in custody as a result of the exercise of another power (eg arrest for fingerprinting under section 27 of the Police and Criminal Evidence Act 1984).

4.3 Force may not be used to take a photograph.

4.4 Where a person's photograph has been taken in accordance with this section, the photograph, negatives and all copies taken in that particular case must be destroyed if:
(a) he is prosecuted for the offence and cleared; or
(b) he is not prosecuted (unless he admits the offence and is cautioned for it).
An opportunity of witnessing the destruction must be given to him if he so requests provided, in accordance with paragraph 4.1, he applies within one month of being cleared or informed that he will not be prosecuted.

(b) Documentation
4.5 A record must be made as soon as possible of the reason for taking a person's photograph under this section without consent and of the destruction of any photographs.

5. Identification by body samples, swabs and impressions

(a) Action
5.1 Dental impressions and intimate samples may be taken from a person in police detention only:
(i) with his written consent;
(ii) if an officer of the rank of superintendent or above considers that the offence concerned is a serious arrestable offence; and
(iii) there are reasonable grounds for suspecting that such an impression, sample or swab will tend to confirm or disprove the suspect's involvement in it.
Before the impression, sample or swab is taken, the person must be informed of the grounds on which the required authority has been given, including the nature of the suspected offence.

5.2 Before a person is asked to provide an intimate sample or swab he must be warned that a refusal may be treated, in any proceedings against him, as corroborating relevant prosecution evidence. [See *Note 5A*]

5.3 Except for samples of urine or saliva, the above samples and swabs may be taken only by a registered medical or dental practitioner as appropriate.

5.4 A non-intimate sample, as defined in paragraph 5.11 or a body impression other than fingerprints, may be taken from a detained suspect only with his written consent or if paragraph 5.5 below applies. Even if he consents, an officer of the rank of inspector or above must have reasonable grounds for believing that such a sample or impression will tend to confirm or disprove the suspect's involvement in a particular offence.

5.5 A non-intimate sample or a body impression may be taken without consent if the offence in connection with which the suspect is detained is a serious arrestable offence and an officer of the rank of superintendent or above has reasonable grounds for believing that the sample or impression will tend to confirm or disprove his involvement in it.

5.6 The suspect must be informed, before the sample or impression is taken, of the grounds on which the relevant authority has been given, including the nature of the suspected offence, and that the sample or impression will be destroyed if paragraph 5.8 applies.

5.7 Where paragraph 5.5 applies, reasonable force may be used if necessary to take non-intimate samples and body impressions.

5.8 Where a sample or impression has been taken in accordance with this section, it and all copies of it taken in that particular case must be destroyed:
(a) if he is prosecuted for the offence concerned and cleared; or
(b) if he is not prosecuted (unless he admits the offence and is cautioned for it).

(b) Documentation
5.9 A record must be made as soon as practicable of the reason for taking a sample or impression and of its destruction. If force is used a record shall be made of the circumstances and those present. Consent to the taking of a sample or impression must be recorded in writing.

5.10 A record must be made of the giving of a warning required by paragraph 5.2 above.

(c) General
5.11 The following terms are defined in section 65 of the Police and Criminal Evidence Act 1984 as follows:
  (a) 'intimate sample' means a sample of blood, semen or any other tissue fluid, urine, saliva or pubic hair, or a swab taken from a person's body orifice;
  (b) 'non-intimate sample' means:
    (i) a sample of hair other than pubic hair;
    (ii) a sample taken from a nail or from under a nail;
    (iii) a swab taken from any part of a person's body other than a body orifice;
    (iv) a footprint or a similar impression of any part of a person's body other than a part of his hand.

5.12 Where clothing needs to be removed in circumstances likely to cause embarrassment to the person, no person of the opposite sex, who is not a medical practitioner or nurse, shall be present, nor shall anyone whose presence is unnecessary.

Note for Guidance
5A In warning a person who refuses to provide an intimate sample or swab in accordance with paragraph 5.2, the following form of words may be helpful:
  'You do not have to [provide this sample] [allow this swab to be taken], but I must warn you that if you do not do so, a court may treat such a refusal as supporting any relevant evidence against you'.

Annex A
Identification parades and group identifications [2.9]
(a) General
1. A suspect must be given a reasonable opportunity to have a solicitor or friend present, and the identification officer shall ask him to indicate on a second copy of the notice to suspect whether or not he so wishes.

2. A parade may take place either in a normal room or in one equipped with a screen permitting witnesses to see members of the parade without being seen. The procedures for the composition and conduct of the parade are the same in both cases, subject to paragraph 7 below (except that a parade involving a screen may take place only when the suspect's solicitor, friend or appropriate adult is present or the parade is recorded on video).

(b) Parades involving prison inmates
3. If an inmate is required for identification, and there are no security problems about his leaving the establishment, he may be asked to participate in a parade. (Group identification, however, may not be arranged other than in the establishment or inside a police station.)

4. A parade may be held in a Prison Department establishment, but shall be conducted as far as practicable under normal parade rules. Members of the public shall make up the parade unless there are serious security or control objections to their admission to the establishment. In such cases, or if a group identification is arranged within the establishment, other inmates may participate.

(c) Conduct of a parade
5. Immediately before the parade, the identification officer must remind the suspect of the procedures governing its conduct and caution him in the terms of paragraph 10.4 of the code of practice for the detention, treatment and questioning of persons by police officers.

6. All unauthorised persons must be strictly excluded from the place where the parade is held.

7. Once the parade has been formed, everything afterwards in respect of it shall take place in the presence and hearing of the suspect and of any interpreter, solicitor, friend or appropriate adult who is present (unless the parade involves a screen, in which case everything said to or by any witness at the place where the parade is held must be said in the hearing and presence of the suspect's solicitor, friend or appropriate adult or be recorded on video).

8. The parade shall consist of at least eight persons (in addition to the suspect) who so far as possible resemble the suspect in age, height, general appearance and position in life. One suspect only shall be included in a parade unless there are two suspects of roughly similar appearance in which case they may be paraded together with at least twelve other persons. In no circumstances shall more than two suspects be included in one parade and where there are separate parades they shall be made up of different persons.

9. Where all members of a similar group are possible suspects, separate parades shall be held for each member of the group unless there are two suspects of similar appearance when they may appear on the same parade with at least twelve other members of the group who are not suspects. Where police officers in uniform form an identification parade, any numerals or other identifying badge shall be concealed.

10. When the suspect is brought to the place where the parade is to be held, he shall be asked by the identification officer whether he has any objection to the arrangements for the parade or to any of the other participants in it. The suspect may obtain advice from his solicitor or friend, if present, before the parade proceeds. Where practicable, steps shall be taken to remove the grounds for objection. Where it is not practicable to do so, the officer shall explain to the suspect why his objections cannot be met.

11. The suspect may select his own position in the line. Where there is more than one witness, the identification officer must tell the suspect, after each witness has left the room, that he can if he wishes change position in the line. Each position in the line must be clearly numbered, whether by means of a numeral laid on the floor in front of each parade member or by other means.

12. The identification officer is responsible for ensuring that, before they attend the parade, witnesses are not able to:
  (i) communicate with each other about the case or overhear a witness who has already seen the parade;
  (ii) see any member of the parade;
  (iii) on that occasion see or be reminded of any photograph or description of the suspect or be given any other indication of his identity; or
  (iv) see the suspect either before (or after) the parade.

13. The officer conducting a witness to a parade must not discuss with him the composition of the parade, and in particular he must not disclose whether a previous witness has made any identification.

14. Witnesses shall be brought in one at a time. Immediately before the witness inspects the parade, the identification officer shall tell him that the person he saw may or may not be on the parade and if he cannot make a positive identification he should say so. The officer shall then ask him to walk along the parade at least twice, taking as much care and time as he wishes. When he has done so the officer shall ask him whether the person he saw in person on an earlier relevant occasion is on the parade.

15. The witness should make an identification by indicating the number of the person concerned.

16. If the witness makes an identification after the parade has ended the suspect and, if present, his solicitor, interpreter, or friend shall be informed. Where this occurs, considera-tion should be given to allowing the witness a second opportunity to identify the suspect.

17. If a witness wishes to hear any parade member speak, adopt any specified posture or see him move, the identification officer shall first ask whether he can identify any persons on the parade on the basis of appearance only. When the request is to hear members of the parade speak, the witness shall be reminded that the participants in the parade have been chosen on the basis of physical appearance only. Members of the parade may then be asked to comply with the witness's request to hear them speak, to see them move or to adopt any specified posture.

18. When the last witness has left, the suspect shall be asked by the identification officer whether he wishes to make any comments on the conduct of the parade.

(d) Conduct of a group identification
19. The arrangements for a group identification are the sole responsibility of the identifica-tion officer and must as far as practicable satisfy the requirements of *(c)* above.

(e) Documentation
20. If a parade is held without a solicitor or a friend of the suspect being present, a colour photograph of the parade shall be taken unless any of the parade members objects. A copy of the photograph shall be supplied on request to the suspect or his solicitor within a reasonable time.

21. Where a photograph is taken in accordance with paragraph 20, at the conclusion of the proceedings the negative will be destroyed.

22. If the identification officer asks any person to leave a parade because he is interfering with its conduct the circumstances shall be recorded.

23. A record must be made of all those present at a parade or group identification whose names are known to the police.

24. If prison inmates make up a parade the circumstances must be recorded.

25. A record of the conduct of any parade or group identification must be made on the forms provided.

Annex B
Confrontation by a witness [2.5 and 2.10]

1. The identification officer is responsible for the conduct of any confrontation of a suspect by a witness.

2. The suspect shall be confronted independently by each witness, who shall be asked 'Is this the person?'. Confrontation must take place in the presence of the suspect's solicitor, interpreter or friend, where he has one, unless this would cause unreasonable delay.

3. Confrontation may take place either in a normal room or one equipped with a screen permitting a witness to see the suspect without being seen. In both cases the procedures are the same except that a room equipped with a screen may be used only when the suspect's solicitor, friend or appropriate adult is present or the confrontation is recorded on video.

Annex C
Showing of photographs [2.12]

(a) Action
1. An officer of the rank of sergeant or above shall be responsible for supervising and directing the showing of photographs. The actual showing may be done by a constable.

2. Only one witness shall be shown photographs at any one time. He shall be given as much privacy as practicable and shall not be allowed to communicate with or overhear any other witness in the case.

3. The witness shall be shown not less than twelve photographs at a time. These photographs shall either be in an album or loose photographs mounted in a frame and shall, as far as possible, all be of a similar type. If the photographs include that of a person suspected by the police of the offence concerned, the other photographs shall resemble the suspect as closely as possible.

4. When the witness is shown the photographs, he shall be told that the photograph of the person he saw may or may not be amongst them. He shall not be prompted or guided in any way but shall be left to make any selection without help.

5. If a witness makes a positive identification from photographs, then, unless the person identified is otherwise eliminated from enquiries, other witnesses shall not be shown photographs. But both they and the witness who has made the identification shall be asked to attend an identification parade or group identification if practicable unless there is no dispute about the identification of the suspect.

6. Where the use of a photofit, identikit or similar picture has led to there being a suspect available who can be asked to appear on a parade, or participate in a group identification the picture shall not be shown to other potential witnesses.

7. Where a witness attending an identification parade has previously been shown photographs or photofit, identikit or similar pictures then the suspect and his solicitor must be informed of this fact before any committal proceedings or summary trial.

8. Any photographs used shall be retained for production in court if necessary, whether or not an identification is made.

(b) Documentation
9. Whether or not an identification is made, a record shall be kept of the showing of photographs and of any comment made by the witness.

A1.05   **TAPE RECORDING**

Draft code of practice issued under section 60(1)(a) of the Police and Criminal Evidence Act 1984

Foreword

This booklet contains a code of practice in respect of the tape-recording by the police of their interviews at police stations with suspected persons. It is issued in pursuance of the duty placed upon the Home Secretary by Section 60(1)(a) of the Police and Criminal Evidence Act.

The code's provisions must be followed in all areas where interviews with suspects are required to be recorded by virtue of the provisions of an order made under Section 60(1)(b) of the 1984 Act.

1. General

1.1 This code of practice must be readily available for consultation by police officers, detained persons and members of the public at all police stations to which an order made under Section 60(1)(b) of the Police and Criminal Evidence Act, 1984, applies.

1.2 The notes for guidance included are not provisions of this code. They form guidance to police officers and others about its application and interpretation.

1.3 Nothing in this code shall be taken as detracting in any way from the requirements of the Code of Practice for the Detention, Treatment and Questioning of Persons by Police Officers (Code C). [See *Note 1A*]

Note for Guidance
1A The Code of Practice for the Detention, Treatment and Questioning of Persons by Police Officers is contained in the booklet 'Police and Criminal Evidence Act, 1984 (s.66): Codes of Practice' published by Her Majesty's Stationery Office, 1985.

2. Recording and the sealing of master tapes

2.1 Tape recording of interviews shall be carried out openly to instil confidence in its reliability as an impartial and accurate record of the interview. [See *Note 2A*]

2.2 The master tape will be sealed before it leaves the presence of the suspect. A second tape will be used as a working copy. The master tape is either one of the two tapes used in a twin deck machine, or the only tape used in a single deck machine. The working copy is either the second tape used in a twin deck machine, or a copy of the master tape made by a single deck machine. [See *Notes 2B and 2C*]

Notes for Guidance
2A Police officers will wish to arrange that, as far as possible, tape recording arrangements are unobtrusive. It must be clear to the suspect, however, that there is no opportunity to interfere with the tape recording equipment or the tapes.
2B The purpose of sealing the master tape before it leaves the presence of the suspect is to establish his confidence that the integrity of the tape is preserved. Where a single deck machine is used the working copy of the master tape must be made in the presence of the suspect and without the master tape having left his sight. The working copy shall be used for making further copies where the need arises. The recorder will normally be capable of recording voices and a time coding or other security device.
2C Throughout this code any reference to 'tapes' shall be construed as 'tape', as appropriate, where a single deck machine is used.

3. Interviews to be tape recorded

3.1 Tape recording shall be used at police stations for any interview:
   (a) with persons who have been cautioned in respect of indictable offences or offences triable either way. [See *Notes 3A and 3B*];
   (b) which takes place as a result of a police officer exceptionally putting further questions to a suspect about an offence described in sub-paragraph (a) above after he has been charged with, or informed he may be prosecuted for, that offence. [See *Note 3C*];
   (c) which takes place in which a police officer wishes to bring to the notice of a person, after he has been charged with, or informed he may be prosecuted for, an offence described in sub-paragraph (a) above, any written statement made by another person, or the content of an interview with another person. [See *Note 3D*]

3.2 The custody officer may authorise the interviewing officer not to tape record the interview:
   (a) where it is not reasonably practicable to do so because of failure of the equipment or the non-availability of a suitable interview room or recorder and the authorising officer considers on reasonable grounds that the interview should not be delayed until the failure has been rectified or a suitable room or recorder becomes available. [See *Note 3E*]
   (b) where it is clear from the outset that no prosecution will ensue.
In all cases the custody officer shall make a note of the reasons for not tape recording in specific terms. [See *Note 3F*]

3.3 In circumstances where an interview takes place with a person voluntarily attending the police station and the police officer has grounds to believe that person has become a suspect (ie the point at which he should be cautioned in accordance with paragraph 10.1 of Code C) the continuation of the interview shall be tape recorded, unless the custody officer gives authority in accordance with the provisions of paragraph 3.2 above for the continuation of the interview not to be recorded.

3.4 The whole of each interview shall be tape recorded, including the taking and reading back of statements.

Notes for Guidance
3A Nothing in this code is intended to preclude tape recording at police discretion of interviews at police stations with persons cautioned in respect of offences not covered by paragraph 3.1, or responses made by interviewees after they have been charged with, or informed they may be prosecuted for, an offence, provided that this code is complied with.
3B Attention is drawn to the restrictions in paragraph 12.3 of Code C on the questioning of persons unfit through drink or drugs to the extent that they are unable to appreciate the significance of questions put to them or of their answers.
3C Circumstances in which a suspect may be questioned about an offence after being charged with it are set out in paragraph 17.5 of Code C.
3D Circumstances in which a person's attention may be drawn after charge to a statement made by another person are set out in paragraph 17.4 of Code C. One method of bringing the content of an interview with another person to the notice of a suspect may be to play him a tape recording of that interview.
3E Where practicable, priority should be given to tape recording interviews with persons who are suspected of more serious offences.
3F A decision not to tape record an interview for any reason may be the subject of comment in court. The authorising officer should therefore be prepared to justify his decision in each case.

4. The interview

4.1 When the suspect is brought into the interview room the police officer shall without delay, but in the sight of the suspect, load the tape recorder with previously unused tapes and set it to record. The tapes must be unwrapped or otherwise opened in the presence of the suspect. [See *Notes 4A and 4B*]

4.2 The police officer shall then tell the suspect formally about the tape recording. He shall say:
(a) that the interview is being tape recorded;
(b) his name and rank, and the name and rank of any other police officer present;
(c) the name of the suspect and any other party present (eg a solicitor);
(d) the date, time of commencement and place of the interview;
(e) that the suspect will be given a notice about what will happen to the tapes.
[See *Note 4C*]

4.3 The police officer shall then caution the suspect in the following terms:
'You do not have to say anything unless you wish to do so, but what you say may be given in evidence'.

4.4 If the suspect is deaf or there is doubt about his hearing ability, the police officer shall take a contemporaneous note of the interview in accordance with the requirements of Code C, as well as tape record it in accordance with the provisions of this code. [See *Note 4D and 4E*]

4.5 If the suspect raises objections to the interview being tape recorded either at the outset, or during the interview, or during a break in the interview, the police officer shall explain the fact that the interview is being tape recorded and that the provisions of this code require that the suspect's objections should be recorded on tape. When any objections have been recorded on tape or the suspect has refused to have his objections recorded, the police officer may turn off the recorder. In this eventuality he shall say that he is turning off the recorder and give his reasons for doing so and then turn it off. The police officer may then make a contemporaneous written record of the interview in accordance with section 11 of Code C. If, however, the police officer reasonably considers that he may proceed to put the questions to the suspect with the tape recorder still on, he may do so. [See *Note 4D*]

4.6 If in the course of an interview a complaint is made by the person being questioned, or on his behalf, concerning the provisions of this code or of Code C, then the officer shall act in accordance with paragraph 12.8 of Code C. [See *Notes 4E and 4F*]

4.7 If the suspect indicates that he wishes to tell the police officer about matters not directly connected with the offence of which he is suspected and that he is unwilling for these matters to be recorded on tape, he shall be given the opportunity to tell the police officer about these matters after the conclusion of the formal interview.

4.8 When the recorder indicates that the tapes have only a short time left to run, the police officer shall tell the suspect that the tapes are coming to an end and round off that part of the interview. If the police officer wishes to continue the interview but does not already have a second set of tapes, he shall obtain a set. The suspect shall not be left unattended in the interview room. The police officer will remove the tapes from the tape recorder and insert the new tapes which shall be unwrapped or otherwise opened in the suspect's presence. The tape recorder shall then be set to record on the new tapes. Care must be taken, particularly when a number of sets of tapes have been used, to ensure that there is no confusion between the tapes. This may be done by marking the tapes with an identification number immediately they are removed from the tape recorder.

4.9 When a break is to be taken during the course of an interview and the interview room is to be vacated by the suspect, the fact that a break is to be taken, the reason for it and the time shall be recorded on tape. The tapes shall then be removed from the tape recorder and the procedures for the conclusion of an interview set out in paragraph 4.14 below followed.

4.10 When a break is to be a short one and both the suspect and a police officer are to remain in the interview room the fact that a break is to be taken, the reasons for it and the time shall be recorded on tape. The tape recorder shall be turned off; there is, however, no need to remove the tapes and when the interview is recommenced the tape recording shall be continued on the same tapes. The time at which the interview recommences shall be recorded on tape.

4.11 When there is a break in questioning under caution the interviewing officer must ensure that the person being questioned is aware that he remains under caution. If there is any doubt the caution must be given again in full when the interview resumes. [See *Notes 4G and 4H*]

4.12 If there is a failure of equipment which can be rectified quickly, for example by inserting new tapes, the appropriate procedures set out in paragraph 4.7 shall be followed, and when the recording is resumed the officer shall explain what has happened and record the time the interview recommences. If, however, it will not be possible to continue recording on that particular tape recorder and no replacement recorder or recorder in another interview room is readily available, the interview may continue unrecorded. In such circumstances the procedures in paragraph 3.2 above for seeking the authority of the custody officer will be followed.

4.13 Where tapes are removed from the recorder in the course of an interview, they shall be retained and the procedures set out in paragraph 4.15 below followed.

4.14 At the conclusion of the interview, the suspect shall be offered the opportunity to clarify anything he has said and to add anything he may wish.

4.15 At the conclusion of the interview, including the taking and reading back of any written statement, the time shall be recorded and the tape recorder switched off. The master tape shall be sealed with an exhibit label and treated as an exhibit in accordance with the force standing orders. The police officer shall sign the label and ask the suspect and any third party present to sign it also. If the suspect refuses to sign the label, an officer of at least the rank of inspector (or in his absence the officer in charge of the police station) who is independent of the investigation shall be called into the interview room and asked to sign it.

4.16 The suspect shall be handed a notice which explains the use which will be made of the tape recording and the arrangements for access to it.

Notes for Guidance

4A   The police officer should attempt to estimate the likely length of the interview and ensure that the appropriate number of unused tapes and labels with which to seal the master copies are available in the interview room.

4B   As the tape recording may be used for evidential purposes and as transcriptions will not necessarily be made, the police officer may wish to take notes during the interview as an aide memoire.

4C   It will be helpful for the purpose of voice identification if the officer asks the suspect and any other persons present to identify themselves.

4D   This provision is intended to give the deaf equivalent rights of first hand access to the full interview record as other suspects.

4E   The provisions of paragraphs 14.1, 14.4 and 14.7 of Code C on interpreters for the deaf or the interviews with suspects who have difficulty in understanding English continue to apply. In a tape recorded interview there is no requirement on the interviewing officer to ensure that the interpreter makes a separate note of interview as prescribed in paragraph 14.2 of Code C. But it is advisable to suggest to the interpreter that he does so, in case he is required to give evidence in court.

4F The officer should bear in mind that a decision to continue recording against the wishes of the suspect may be the subject of comment in court.

4G Wherever possible the tape recorder should be left to run until the custody officer has entered the interview room and spoken to the person being interviewed. Continuation or termination of the interview should be at the direction of the interviewing officer, pending action by an inspector under paragraph 9.1 of Code C.

4H Where the complaint is about a matter not connected with this code of practice or Code C, the decision to continue with the interview is at the discretion of the interviewing officer. Where the interviewing officer decides to continue with the interview, the person being interviewed shall be told that the complaint will be brought to the attention of the custody officer at the conclusion of the interview. When the interview is concluded, the interviewing officer must, as soon as practicable, inform the custody officer of the existence and nature of the complaint made.

4J In considering whether to caution again after a break, the officer should bear in mind that he may have to satisfy a court that the person understood that he was still under caution when the interview resumed.

4K The officer should bear in mind that it may be necessary to show to the court that nothing occurred during a break in an interview or between interviews which influenced the suspect's recorded evidence. The officer should consider, therefore, after a break in an interview or at the beginning of a subsequent interview summarising on tape the reason for the break and confirming this with the suspect.

4L If one of the tapes breaks during the interview two copies of the other (unbroken) tape shall be made in the presence of the suspect and then one of them sealed, together with the broken tape, and used as the master tape.

5. After the interview

5.1 The police officer shall make a note in his notebook of the fact that the interview has taken place and has been recorded, its time, duration and date, and the identification number of the master tape.

5.2 Where no proceedings follow in respect of the person whose interview was recorded, the tapes must nevertheless be kept securely in accordance with paragraph 6.1 and guidance note 6A.

5.3 Where such proceedings do follow, the officer shall prepare a statement and summary. The statement shall set out the fact that the interview has taken place and has been recorded, its time, duration and date, and the identification number of the master tape. The summary shall either be incorporated into the police officer's statement or produced as a separate document exhibited to the statement. [See *Note 5A and 5B*]

5.4 Where the police officer's evidence of the interview is accepted by the defence, the evidence shall refer to the fact that the interview was tape recorded and shall be presented to the court in the form of the summary. Where the police officer's evidence of the interview is not accepted by the defence, the police officer shall refer to the fact that the interview was tape recorded and shall produce the master tape as an exhibit. The officer shall inform the court of any transcription which has been made. [See *Note 5C*].

Notes for Guidance

5A Prior to preparing the summary, the officer may refresh his memory of the interview by listening to the working copy of the tape. The purpose of using the tape will be to act as a check on the accuracy of the summary, which may be written either in the third person or may quote verbatim questions and answers from the interview. The summary shall not, however, comprise a transcript of the whole or substantial parts of the interview unless it is so short that a summary would serve little purpose.

5B Where the interview can satisfactorily be summarised briefly, it will generally be appropriate to incorporate the summary into the police officer's witness statement. Where, however, the summary is necessarily lengthy it will often be more helpful to the orderly presentation of the evidence for the summary to be prepared as a separate document. In any cases of doubt whether the interview has produced evidence that is relevant, the Crown Prosecutor shall be consulted. Where a decision is made to transcribe the tape, a summary will not be necessary.

5C The summary shall be prepared on the basis that it shall be used first to enable the prosecutor to make informed decisions about the case on the basis of what was said at the interview; secondly, to enable the prosecutor to comply with the rules of advanced disclosure and committal proceedings; and thirdly, where the summary is accepted by the defence, to be used for the conduct of the case by the prosecution, the defence, and the court. The summary shall, therefore, comprise a balance account of the interview, including points in mitigation and/or defence made by the suspect. Where an admission is made the question as well as the answer containing the admission shall be recorded verbatim in the summary. Where there is prejudicial or inadmissible material in the interview the officer shall, by means of a covering report, bring such matters to the attention of the prosecutor.

5D Production of the tape as an exhibit will have the effect in court proceedings of producing the content of the whole interview.

6. Tape security

Each police station at which interviews with suspects are recorded shall make arrangements for master tapes to be kept securely and their movements accounted for on the same basis as other material which may be used for evidential purposes, in accordance with force standing orders.

6.2 A police officer has no authority to break the seal on a master tape. If it is necessary to gain access to the master tape, the police officer shall arrange for its seal to be broken in the presence of a representative of the Crown Prosecution Service. The defendant or his legal adviser shall be informed and given an opportunity to be present. If the defendant or his legal representative is present he shall be invited to reseal and sign the master tape. If he refuses or is not present this shall be done by the representative of the CPS. [See *Notes 6A and 6B*]

6.3 Where no criminal proceedings result it is the responsibility of the chief officer of police, in agreement with the Chief Crown Prosecutor, to establish arrangements for the breaking of the seal on the master tape, where this becomes necessary.

Notes for Guidance
6A This section is concerned with the security of the master tape which will have been sealed with an exhibit label at the conclusion of the interview. Care should, however, be taken of working copies of tapes, since their loss or destruction may lead unnecessarily to the need to have access to master tapes.
6B If the tape has been delivered to the crown court for their keeping after committal for trial the Crown Prosecutor will apply to the Chief Clerk of the Crown Court Centre for the release of tape for unsealing by the Crown Prosecutor.
6C 'Crown Prosecutor' in this part of the code shall be taken to mean any other body or person with a statutory responsibility for prosecution for whom the police conduct any tape recorded interviews.

Appendix II

Code for Crown Prosecutors

Introduction

1. This Code is issued pursuant to s.10 of the Prosecution of Offences Act 1985, and as provided for in s.10(3) of the Act will be included in the Director's annual report to the Attorney-General. In accordance with s.9 of the Act, the report will be laid before Parliament and published. The Code, therefore, is a public declaration of the principles upon which the Crown Prosecution Service will exercise its functions. Its purpose is to promote efficient and consistent decision-making so as to develop and thereafter maintain public confidence in the Service's performance of its duties. Amendments to the Code may be made from time to time.

2. The principles endorsed by the Attorney-General's criteria for prosecution, which have hitherto guided all who prosecute on behalf of the public, have been drawn upon to indicate the basis upon which decisions are to be made. Having regard, however, to the specific statutory duties with which the Service is charged, it is right that the Code should be, and be seen to be, an independent body of guidance designed for and aimed directly at those who prosecute in its name.

3. Crown Prosecutors at every level in the Service will have great scope for the exercise of discretion at various stages of the prosecution process and in respect of many different functions. The responsible use of that discretion, based on clear principles, can better serve both justice, the interests of the public and the interests of the offender, than the rigid application of the letter of the law. The misuse of discretionary powers, on the other hand, can have severe consequences not only for those suspected of crime, but also for the public at large and the reputation of justice and the Service itself.

The evidential sufficiency criteria

4. When considering the institution or continuation of criminal proceedings the first question to be determined is the sufficiency of the evidence. A prosecution should not be started or continued unless the Crown Prosecutor is satisfied that there is admissible, substantial and reliable evidence that a criminal offence known to the law has been committed by an identifiable person. The Crown Prosecution Service does not support the proposition that a bare *prima facie* case is enough, but rather will apply the test of whether there is a realistic prospect of a conviction. When reaching this decision the Crown Prosecutor as a first step will wish to satisfy himself that there is no realistic expectation of an ordered acquittal or a successful submission in the magistrates' court of no case to answer. He should also have regard to any lines of defence which are plainly open to, or have been indicated by, the accused and any other factors which in his view would affect the likelihood or otherwise of a conviction.

5. The Crown Prosecutor in evaluating the evidence should have regard to the following matters:

    (i) In respect of any evidence, having regard to the requirements of the Police and Criminal Evidence Act 1984 and Codes of Practice, are there grounds for believing that breaches of the requirements may lead to the exclusion of the evidence under Pt VIII of the Act? The Act and its Codes of Practice contain provisions for the detention, treatment and questioning of persons by the police which are designed to ensure the proper treatment of people in police custody and the reliability of evidence derived from confessions or other statements made to the police. Crown Prosecutors will wish to satisfy themselves that confession evidence has been properly obtained and is not exposed to the suggestion of oppressive behaviour. In considering other evidence, Crown Posecutors will need to consider whether it has been obtained improperly and, if it may have been, whether a court might feel it right to exclude it on the grounds that its admission would have an adverse effect on the fairness of the proceedings. The possibility that certain evidence might be excluded should be taken into account when the suffiency of evidence to justify the proceedings is initially reviewed, and, if it is crucial to the case, may substantially affect the decision whether or not to proceed.

  (ii) If the case depends in part on admissions by the accused, are there any grounds for believing that they are of doubtful reliability having regard to the age, intelligence and apparent understanding of the accused?

 (iii) Does it appear that a witness is exaggerating, or that his memory is faulty, or that he is either hostile or friendly to the accused, or may be otherwise unreliable?

 (iv) Has a witness a motive for telling less than the whole truth?

  (v) Are there matters which might properly be put to a witness by the defence to attack his credibility?

 (vi) What sort of impression is the witness likely to make? How is he likely to stand up to cross-examination? Does he suffer from any physical or mental disability which is likely to affect his credibility?

 (vii) If there is conflict between eye-witnesses, does it go beyond what one would expect and hence materially weaken the case?

(viii) If there is a lack of conflict between eye witnesses, is there anything which causes suspicion that a false story may have been concocted?

 (ix) Are all the necessary witnesses available and competent to give evidence, including any who may be abroad?

  (x) Where child witnesses are involved, are they likely to be able to give sworn evidence?

 (xi) If identity is likely to be an issue, how cogent and reliable is the evidence of those who purport to identify the accused?

 (xii) Are the facts of the case such that the public would consider it oppressive to proceed against the accused?

(xiii) Where two or more defendants are charged together, is there a realistic prospect of the proceedings being severed? If so, is the case sufficiently proved against each defendant should separate trials be ordered?

6. This list is not of course exhaustive, and the factors to be considered will depend on the circumstances of each individual case, but it is introduced to indicate that, particularly in borderline cases, the Crown Prosecutor must be prepared to look beneath the surface of the statements. He must also draw, so far as is possible, on his own experience of how evidence of the type under consideration is likely to 'stand-up' in court before reaching a conclusion as to the likelihood of a conviction.

The Public Interest Criteria

7. Having satisfied himself that the evidence itself can justify proceedings, the Crown Prosecutor must then consider whether the public interest requires a prosecution. The Crown Prosecution Service will be guided by the view expressed in a House of Commons debate by Lord Shawcross when he was Attorney-General, and subsequently endorsed by his successors:

'It has never been the rule in this country – I hope it never will be – that suspected criminal offences must automatically be the subject of prosecution. Indeed the very first regulations under which the Director of Public Prosecutions worked provided that he should . . . prosecute "wherever it appears that the offence or the circumstances of its commission is or are of such a character that a prosecution in respect thereof is required in the public interest". That is still the dominant consideration.' (HC Deb, Vol 483, col 681, 29 January 1951.)

He continued by saying that regard must be had to 'the effect which the prosecution, successful or unsuccessful as the case may be, would have upon public morale and order, and with any other considerations affecting public policy'.

8. The factors which can properly lead to a decision not to prosecute will vary from case to case, but broadly speaking, the graver the offence, the less likelihood there will be that the public interest will allow of a disposal less than prosecution, for example, a caution. Where, however, an offence is not so serious as plainly to require prosecution, the Crown Prosecutor should always apply his mind to the public interest and should strive to ensure

that the spirit of the Home Office Cautioning Guide-lines is observed. If the case falls within any of the following categories this will be an indication that proceedings may not be required, subject of course to the particular circumstances of the case.

(i) Likely Penalty

When the circumstances of an offence are not particularly serious, and a court would be likely to impose a purely nominal penalty, Crown Prosecutors should carefully consider whether the public interest would be better served by a prosecution or some other form of disposal such as, where appropriate, a caution. This applies particularly where the offence is triable on indictment when Crown Prosecutors should also weigh the likely penalty with the likely length and cost of the proceedings.

(ii) Staleness

Regard must be had not only to the date when the last known offence was committed, but also the length of time which is likely to elapse before the matter can be brought to trial. The Crown Prosecutor should be slow to prosecute if the last offence was committed three or more years before the probable date of trial, unless, despite its staleness, an immediate custodial sentence of some length is likely to be imposed. Less regard will be paid to staleness, however, if it has been contributed to by the accused himself, the complexity of the case has necessitated lengthy police investigation or the particular characteristics of the offence have themselves contributed to the delay in its coming to light. Generally, the graver the allegation the less significance will be attached to the element of staleness.

(iii) Youth

The stigma of a conviction can cause irreparable harm to the future prospects of a young adult, and careful consideration should be given to the possibility of dealing with him or her by means of caution.

(iv) Old age and infirmity

(a) The older or more infirm the offender, the more reluctant the Crown Prosecutor should be to prosecute unless there is a real possibility of repetition or the offence is of such gravity that it is impossible to overlook. In general, proceedings should not be instituted where a court is likely to pay such regard to the age or infirmity of the offender as to induce it to impose only a nominal penalty, although there may be exceptional circumstances, such as where the accused still holds a position of some importance, when proceedings are required in the public interest regardless of what penalty may be imposed.

(b) It will also be necessary to consider whether the accused is likely to be fit enough to stand his trial. The Crown Prosecutor should have regard to any medical reports which have been made available by the defence solicitor and may arrange through him for an independent medical examination where this is necessary.

(v) Mental illness or stress

(a) Whenever the Crown Prosecutor is provided with a medical report to the effect that an accused or a person under investigation is suffering from some form of mental illness or psychiatric illness and that the strain of criminal proceedings may lead to a considerable worsening of his condition, such a report should receive anxious consideration. This is a difficult field because in some instances the accused may have become mentally disturbed or depressed by the mere fact that his misconduct has been discovered and the Crown Prosecutor may be dubious about a prognosis that criminal proceedings will adversely affect his condition to a significant extent. Where, however, the Crown Prosecutor is satisfied that the probable effect upon the defendant's mental health outweighs the interests of justice in that particular case, he should not hesitate to discontinue proceedings. An independent medical examination may be sought, but should generally be reserved for cases of such gravity as plainly to require prosecution but for clear evidence that such a course would be likely to result in a permanent worsening of the accused's condition.

(b) The Crown Prosecutor should not pay as much regard to evidence of mental instability not coupled with a prognosis as to the adverse effect of proceedings, as such instability may increase the likelihood that the offence will be repeated. The accused's mental state will, of course, be relevant in considering any issue of *mens rea* or fitness to plead.

(vi) Sexual offences

(a) Whenever two or more persons have participated in the offence in circumstances rendering both or all liable to prosecution the Crown Prosecutor should take into account each person's age, the relative ages of the participants and whether or not there was any element of seduction or corruption when deciding whether, and if so in respect of whom, proceedings should be instituted.

(b) Sexual assaults upon children should always be regarded seriously, as should offences against adults, such as rape, which amount to gross personal violation. In such cases, where the Crown Prosecutor is satisfied as to the sufficiency of the evidence there will seldom be any doubt that prosecution will be in the public interest.

(vii) Complainant's attitude
In some cases it will be appropriate for the Crown Prosecutor to have regard to the attitude of a complainant who notified the police but later expresses a wish that no action be taken. It may be that in such circumstances proceedings need not be pursued unless either there is suspicion that the change of heart was actuated by fear or the offence was of some gravity.

(viii) Peripheral defendants
Where an allegation involves several accused, as a general rule the Crown Prosecutor should have regard to the need to ensure that proceedings are continued only against those whose involvement goes to the heart of the issue to be placed before the court. The inclusion of defendants on the fringe of the action and whose guilt in comparison with the principal offenders is minimal can lead to additional delay and cost, as well as unnecessarily clouding the essential features of the case.

9. Finally, if, having weighed such of the above factors as may appertain to the case, the Crown Prosecutor is still in doubt as to whether proceedings are called for, he will throw into the scales the attitude of the local community and any information about the prevalance of the particular offence in the area or nationally. Should doubt still remain, the scales will normally be tipped in favour of prosecution as if the balance is so even, it could properly be said that the final arbiter must be the court.

Discontinuance

10. The use by the Crown Prosecutor of his power to terminate proceedings whether by using the procedure under s.23 of the Prosecution of Offences Act 1985 or the continuing power to withdraw or offer no evidence, is in many ways the most visible demonstration of the Service's fundamental commitment towards ensuring that only fit and proper cases are taken to trial. Unless, of course, advice has been given at a preliminary stage, the police decision to institute proceedings should never be met with passive acquiescence but must always be the subject of review. Furthermore the discretion to discontinue is a continuing one, and even when proceedings are under way Crown Prosecutors should continue to exercise their reviewing function. There may be occasions when time and other practical constraints limit the depth of the initial review of the case. It is important that cases should be kept under continuous review, not least because the emergence of new evidence or information may sometimes cast doubt on the propriety of the initial decision to proceed. Crown Prosecutors must be resolute when made aware of evidence or information of this nature and should not hesitate to bring proceedings to an end in appropriate cases. Public confidence in the Service can only be maintained if there is no doubting its commitment to taking effective action at whatever stage whenever it is right to do so. Prosecutions instituted in circumstances apparently falling outside the spirit of the Home Office Cautioning Guide-lines should be queried with the police and may be discontinued where the Crown Prosecutor is satisfied that proceedings would not be in the public interest. It will be the normal practice to consult the police whenever it is proposed to discontinue proceedings instituted by them. The level of consultation will depend on the particular circumstances of the case or the accused, but the final decision will rest with the Crown Prosecutor.

11. The broad heading of discontinuance also includes the question of the acceptance of pleas. To a large extent this area is bound up with charging practice – the selection of charges will sometimes affect the scope of the discretion to accept pleas, but equally there will always be occasions calling for the judicious exercise of that discretion. This could include, for example, the situation where charges are preferred in the alternative or where the defendant is prepared to admit part only of the ingredients of a particular offence itself amounting to another offence; burglary reducing to theft by virtue of a denial of the element of trespass is a common example. The over-riding consideration will be to ensure that the court is never left in the position of being unable to pass a proper sentence consistent with the gravity of the defendant's actions; having accepted a plea, the Crown Prosecutor must not then open the case on the basis that what the defendant actually did was something more serious than appears in the charge. Administrative convenience in the form of a rapid guilty plea should not take precedence over the interests of justice, but where the court is able to deal adequately with an offender on the basis of a plea which represents a criminal involvement not inconsistent with the alleged facts, the resource advantages both to the Service and the courts generally will be an important consideration.

Charging Practice

12. It is axiomatic that there must be available admissible evidence which supports all the ingredients of the offence or offences charged. The Service will exercise its discretion on the choice of charge on the basis of the following principles:

    (i) Every effort should be made to keep the number of charges as low as possible. A multiplicity of charges imposes an unnecessary burden on the administration of the courts as well as upon the prosecution, and often tends to obscure the essential features of the case. Where the evidence discloses a large number of offences of a similar nature, the use of specimen charges should always be considered. Where numerous different types of offence are disclosed, the ability to present the case in a clear, simple manner should remain a key objective.

   (ii) Multiplicity of charging should never be used in order to obtain leverage for the offering of a plea of guilty.

  (iii) The charges laid should adequately reflect the gravity of the defendant's conduct and will normally be the most serious revealed by the evidence. Provided, however, that the offence charged is not inappropriate to the nature of the facts alleged and the court's sentencing powers are adequate, the Crown Prosecutor should take into account matters such as speed of trial, mode of trial and sufficiency of proof which may properly lead to a decision not to prefer or continue with the gravest possible charge. The Crown Prosecutor should also take into account probable lines of defence when exercising his discretion.

Mode of trial

13. Where an offence is triable either on indictment or summarily, the magistrates' court must consider which mode of trial appears more suitable, having regard to the matters mentioned in s.19(3) of the Magistrates' Courts Act 1980 and any representations made by the prosecutor or accused. The aim of the Crown Prosecutor when making representations as to venue should be to assist the Court in the exercise of its judicial discretion and in making such representations he should focus on those matters to which the court is obliged to have regard, namely:

    (i) The nature of the case.

   (ii) Whether the circumstances make the offence one of serious character.

  (iii) Whether the magistrates' powers of punishment would be adequate; this must not, of course, extend to any expression of view by the Crown Prosecutor as to the nature or range within which the punishment should fall.

  (iv) Any other circumstances which appear to make the offence more suitable for trial in one way than another.

While the attraction of an expeditious disposal should never be the sole reason for a request for summary trial, the Crown Prosecutor is entitled to have regard to the delay in the adminstration of justice likely to be occasioned by proceeding on indictment, together with the additional cost and possible adverse effect upon witnesses.

14. Where the case involves co-accused additional considerations may apply. As a general principle it will be in the interests of justice for all co-accused to be tried at the same Court. Accordingly, if the court decides that one accused should be tried on indictment, the Crown Prosecutor should generally urge that mode of trial for his co-accused. Summary trial in these circumstances is only likely to be requested by the Crown Prosecutor rarely and will generally arise where the role of one defendant in the offence or offences is out of all proportion to that of his co-accused and where his absence seems unlikely to have any adverse effect on their trial or sentence.

Juveniles

15. It is a long standing statutory requirement that the courts shall have regard to the welfare of the juvenile appearing before them, in criminal as in civil proceedings. It is accordingly necesary that in deciding whether or not the public interest requires a prosecution the welfare of the juvenile should be fully considered.

16. There may be positive advantages for the individual and for society, in using prosecution as a last resort and in general there is in the case of juvenile offenders a much stronger presumption in favour of methods of disposal which fall short of prosecution unless the seriousness of the offence or other exceptional circumstances dictate otherwise. The objective should be to divert juveniles from court wherever possible. Prosecution should always be regarded as a severe step.

17. The Home Office has issued guidelines to the police on cautioning juvenile offenders and on related decision making. Where the police are unable to make an immediate decision

to caution, the guide-lines suggest that there may be advantages in their seeking the advice and views of other interested agencies, such as the Social Services Department, the Probation Service and the Education Welfare Service, on whether to caution or institute proceedings. Where the Crown Prosecutor decides that the public interest does not require the institution or continuation of proceedings against a juvenile and it appears that there has been no prior consultation, the Crown Prosecutor should consider whether to ask the police to bring the circumstances of the individual's involvement to the attention of the appropriate agency. Crown Prosecutors should be aware of the general arrangements and procedures for inter-agency consultation in their areas and are encouraged to contribute their experience to the development and improvement of such arrangements. Crown Prosecutors must satisfy themselves that the spirit of the Cautioning Guide-lines has been applied before continuing a prosecution instituted by the police against a juvenile. The Crown Prosecutor should, taking account of the views of all the agencies concerned of which he is aware and having regard to the Cautioning Guide-lines, refer back to the police any case where he considers that a lesser disposal, eg a caution, would be an adequate response and, in the final analysis, will not hesitate to exercise his power to discontinue proceedings where he is satisfied that a prosecution is not required in the public interest. When considering whether or not to continue proceedings, the Crown Prosecutor should have regard to the circumstances of any previous cautions the juvenile may have been given by the police. Where these are such as to indicate that a less formal disposal in respect of the present offence would prove inadequate, a prosecution will be appropriate.

18. It will never be right to prosecute a juvenile solely to secure access to the welfare powers of the court. Where the Crown Prosecutor thinks that there may be grounds for care proceedings and that this might better serve the public interest and welfare of the individual he should invite the police to put this possibility to the local social services authority.

Mode and venue of trial considerations affecting juveniles

19. (i) Juveniles charged alone: Where the juvenile has attained the age of 14 and is charged with certain grave offences (as defined by s.53(2) of the Children and Young Persons Act 1933) other than homicide, it is the court's duty, having heard representations, to consider whether it ought to be possible to sentence the juvenile up to the maximum adult sentence (s.24(1)(a) of the Magistrates' Courts Act 1980). Accordingly, the Crown Prosecutor should put the relevant facts dispassionately before the court and generally assist as required by the court.

(ii) Juveniles charged with adults: A charge against a juvenile may be heard in an adult magistrates' court if an adult is charged at the same time where either is charged with aiding, abetting, etc the other's offence, or where the juvenile is charged with an offence arising out of circumstances which are the same as, or connected with, those giving rise to an offence with which the adult is charged at the same time. There is also a discretion to commit for trial where the juvenile is charged with an indictable offence jointly with an adult and the court considers it necessary in the interests of justice to commit them both for trial. In making representations as to venue in these circumstances, the prime task of the Crown Prosecutor will be to assist the court in its judicial considerations. In reaching his decision as to the mode of trial to be requested, the Crown Prosecutor will wish to take several factors into account. These will include, for example, the respective ages of the adult and the juvenile, the seriousness of the offence, the likely plea, whether there are existing charges against the juvenile before the juvenile court and the need to deal with the juvenile as expeditiously as possible consistent with the interests of justice.

Appendix III

Criminal Justice Bill/Act 1988

Reproduced below are those sections of the Criminal Justice Bill/Act 1988 which are relevant to the work of magistrates' courts. The text has been taken from the Bill as amended by Standing Committee H and printed on 29 March 1988. The section numbers have been printed in square brackets to indicate that the number may be changed between this print of the Bill and the Act receiving Royal Assent.

The following provisions of the Act will come into force on the day it receives the Royal Assent: ss.65, 66, 101(1) so far as it relates to the substitution of two new offences for s.26 Drug Trafficking Offences Act 1986, 127, 130 so far as it relates to the Local Government Finance Act 1982, 134, 135, 158, 159, 160, 161, 162(1) part, 163–165. The following provisions will come into force two months after the date of Royal Assent: ss.43–47, 57, 63, 67, 132, 133, 150, 152, 153, 162 (1) part and (2) part. The rest of the Act will come into force on a day or days to be appointed.

PART I

[1.]–[21.] *Extradition*
[NB Certain of the *Extradition* provisions apply to magistrates' courts, justices and stipendiary magistrates – but the view is taken that these are beyond the scope of a general work on criminal procedure and *Extradition* has not previously been dealt with in this work.]

PART II

DOCUMENTARY EVIDENCE IN CRIMINAL PROCEEDINGS

First-hand hearsay
[22.] (1) Subject–
(a) to subsection (4) below;
(b) to paragraph 1A of Schedule 2 to the Criminal Appeal 1968 (evidence given orally at original trial to be given orally at retrial); and
(c) to section 69 of the Police and Criminal Evidence Act 1984 (evidence from computer records),
a statement made by a person in a document shall be admissible in criminal proceedings as evidence of any fact of which direct oral evidence by him would be admissible if–
  (i) the requirements of one of the paragraphs of subsection (2) below are satisfied;
  (ii) the requirements of subsection (3) below are satisfied.

(2) The requirements mentioned in subseciton (1)(i) above are–
(a) that the person who made the statement is dead or by reason of his bodily or mental condition unfit to attend as a witness;
(b) that–
  (i) the person who made the statement is outside the United Kingdom; and
  (ii) it is not reasonably practicable to secure his attendance;

(c) that the person who made the statement cannot reasonably be expected (having regard to the time which has elapsed since he made the statement and to all the circumstances) to have any recollection of the matters dealt with in the statement; or

(d) that, all reasonable steps have been taken to find the person who made the statement, but that he cannot be found.

(3) The requirements mentioned in subsection (1)(ii) above are–

(a) that the statement was made to a police officer or some other person charged with the duty of investigating offences or charging offenders; and

(b) that the person who made it does not give oral evidence through fear or because he is kept out of the way.

(4) Subsection (1) above does not render admissible a confession made by an accused person that would not be admissible under section 76 of the Police and Criminal Evidence Act 1984.

Business etc. documents
[23.] (1) Subject–
(a) to subsections (3) and (4) below;
(b) to paragraph 1A of Schedule 2 to the Criminal Appeal Act 1968; and
(c) to section 69 of the Police and Criminal Evidence Act 1984,
a statement in a document shall be admissible in criminal proceedings as evidence of any fact of which direct oral evidence would be admissible, if the following conditions are satisfied–

(i) the document was created or received by a person in the course of a trade, business, profession or other occupation, or as the holder of a paid or unpaid office; and

(ii) the information contained in the document as supplied by a person (whether or not the maker of the statement) who had, or may reasonably be supposed to have had, personal knowledge of the matters dealt with.

(2) Subsection (1) above applies whether the information contained in the document was supplied directly or indirectly but, if it was supplied indirectly, only if each person through whom it was supplied received it–

(a) in the course of a trade, business, profession or other occupation; or

(b) as the holder of a paid or unpaid office.

(3) Subsection (1) above does not render admissible a confession made by an accused person that would not be admissible under section 76 of the Police and Criminal Evidence Act 1984.

(4) A statement prepared otherwise than under section 28, 29 or 30 below for the purposes–
(a) of pending or contemplated criminal proceedings; or
(b) of a criminal investigation,
shall not be admissible by virtue of subsection (1) above unless–

(i) the requirements of one of the paragraphs of subsection (2) of section 22 above are satisfied; or

(ii) the requirements of subsection (3) of that section are satisfied.

Principles to be followed by court
[24.] (1) If, having regard to all the circumstances–
(a) the Crown Court–
(i) on a trial on indictment;
(ii) on an appeal from a magistrates' court; or
(iii) on the hearing of an application under section 6 of the Criminal Justice Act 1987 (applications for dismissal of charges of fraud transferred from magistrates' courts to Crown Court); or
(b) the criminal division of the Court of Appeal; or
(c) a magistrates' court on a trial of an information,
is of the opinion that in the interests of justice a statement which is admissible by

virtue of section 22 or 23 above nevertheless ought not to be admitted, it may direct that the statement shall not be admitted.

(2) Without prejudice to the generality of subsection (1) above, it shall be the duty of the court to have regard–
  (a) to the nature and source of the document containing the statement and to whether or not, having regard to its nature and source and to any other circumstances that appear to the court to be relevant, it is likely that the document is authentic;
  (b) to the extent to which the statement appears to supply evidence which would otherwise not be readily available;
  (c) to the relevance of the evidence that it appears to supply to any issue which is likely to have to be determined in the proceedings; and
  (d) to any risk, having regard in particular to whether it is likely to be possible to controvert the statement if the person making it does not attend to give oral evidence in the proceedings, that its admission or exclusion will result in unfairness to the accused or, if there is more than one, to any of them.

Statements in documents that appear to have been prepared for purposes of criminal proceedings or investigations
[25.] Where a statement which is admissible in criminal proceedings by virtue of section 22 or 23 above appears to the court to have been prepared, otherwise than under section 28, 29 or 30 below, for the purposes–
  (a) of pending or contemplated criminal proceedings; or
  (b) of a criminal investigation,
the statement shall not be given in evidence in any criminal proceedings without the leave of the court, and the court shall not give leave unless it is of the opinion that the statement ought to be admitted in the interests of justice; and in considering whether its admission would be in the interests of justice, it shall be the duty of the court to have regard–

  (i) to the contents of the statement;
  (ii) to any risk, having regard in particular to whether it is likely to be possible to controvert the statement if the person making it does not attend to give oral evidence in the proceedings, that its admission or exclusion will result in unfairness to the accused or, if there is more than one, to any of them; and

Proof of statements contained in documents
[26.] Where a statement contained in a document is admissible as evidence in criminal proceedings, it may be proved–
  (a) by the production of that document; or
  (b) (whether or not that document is still in existence) by the production of a copy of that document, or of the material part of it,
authenticated in such manner as the court may approve; and it is immaterial for the purposes of this subsection how many removes there are between a copy and the original.

Documentary evidence– supplementary
[27.] (1) Nothing in this Part of this Act shall prejudice–
  (a) the admissibility of a statement not made by a person while giving oral evidence in court which is admissible otherwise than by virtue of this Part of this Act; or
  (b) any power of a court to exclude at its discretion a statement admissible by virtue of this Part of this Act.

(2) Schedule 2 to this Act shall have effect for the purpose of supplementing this Part of this Act.

PART III

OTHER PROVISIONS ABOUT EVIDENCE IN CRIMINAL PROCEEDINGS

Issue of letters of request
[**28.**] (1) Where on an application made in accordance with the following provisions of this section it appears to a justice of the peace or judge that criminal proceedings–
(a) have been instituted; or
(b) are likely to be instituted if evidence is obtained for the purpose,
he may order that a letter of request shall be issued to a court or tribunal or appropriate authority specified in the order and exercising jurisdiction in a place outside the United Kingdom, requesting it to assist in obtaining for the purposes of the proceedings evidence specified in the letter.

(2) In subsection (1) above 'appropriate authority' means any central authority designated by a state to receive requests for asistance in legal matters.

(3) An application for an order under this section may be made by a prosecuting authority.

(4) If proceedings have already been instituted, a person charged with an offence in the proceedings may make such an application.

(5) Without prejudice to the generality of any enactment conferring power to make them–
(a) Crown Court Rules;
(b) Criminal Appeal Rules; and
(c) rules under section 144 of the Magistrates' Courts Act 1980,
may make such provision as appears to the authority making any of them to be necessary or expedient for the purposes of this section and in particular for the appointment of a person before whom evidence may be taken in pursuance of a letter of request.

(6) In exercising the discretion conferred by section 24 above in relation to a statement contained in evidence taken in pursuance of a letter of request, the court shall have regard–
(a) to whether it was possible to challenge the statement by questioning the person who made it; and
(b) to whether the local law allowed the parties to the criminal proceedings to be legally represented when the evidence was being taken.

Expert reports
[**29.**] (1) An expert report shall be admissible as evidence in criminal proceedings, whether or not the person making it attends to give oral evidence in those proceedings.

(2) If it is proposed that the person making the report shall not give oral evidence, the report shall only be admissible with the leave of the court.

(3) For the purpose of determining whether to give leave the court shall have regard–
(a) to the contents of the report;
(b) to the reasons why it is proposed that the person making the report shall not give oral evidence;
(c) to any risk, having regard in particular to whether it is likely to be possible to controvert statements in the report if the person making it does not attend to give oral evidence in the proceedings, that its admission or exclusion will result in unfairness to the accused or, if there is more than one, to any of them; and
(d) to any other circumstances that appear to the court to be relevant.

(4) An expert report, when admitted, shall be evidence of any fact or opinion of which the person making it could have given oral evidence.

(5) In this section 'expert report' means a written report by a person dealing wholly or mainly with matters on which he is (or would if living be) qualified to give expert evidence.

[**30.**] *Form of evidence and glossaries (for juries).*

[**31.**] *Evidence through closed circuit television links (for trials on indictment and appeals).*

Evidence of persons under 14 in committal proceedings
[**32.**] The following section shall be substituted for section 103 of the Magistrates' Courts Act 1980–

'Evidence of persons under 14 in committal proceedings for assault, sexual offences etc.
103. (1) In any proceedings before a magistrates' court inquiring into an offence to which this section applies as examining justices–
(a) a child shall not be called as a witness for the prosecution; but
(b) any statement made by or taken from a child shall be admissible in evidence of any matter of which his oral testimony would be admissible,
except in a case where the application of this subsection is excluded under subsection (3) below.

(2) This section applies–
(a) to an offence which involves an assault, or injury or a threat of injury to, a person;
(b) to an offence under section 1 of the Children and Young Persons Act 1933 (cruelty to persons under 16);
(c) to an offence under the Sexual Offences Act 1956, the Indecency with Children Act 1960, the Sexual Offences Act 1967, section 54 of the Criminal Law Act 1977 or the Protection of Children Act 1978; and
(d) to an offence which consists of attempting or conspiring to commit, or of aiding, abetting, counselling, procuring or inciting the commission of, an offence falling within paragraph (a), (b) or (c) above.

(3) The application of subsection (1) above is excluded–
(a) where at or before the time when the statement is tendered in evidence the defence objects to its admission; or
(b) where the prosecution requires the attendance of the child for the purpose of establishing the identity of any person; or
(c) where the court is satisfied that it has not been possible to obtain from the child a statement that may be given in evidence under this section; or
(d) where the inquiry into the offence takes place after the court has discontinued to try it summarily and the child has given evidence in the summary trial.

(4) Section 28 above shall not apply to any statement admitted in pursuance of subsection (1) above.

(5) In this section 'child' means a person under the age of 14.'.

Abolition of requirement of corroboration for unsworn evidence of children
[**33.**] (1) The proviso to subsection (1) of section 38 of the Children and Young Persons Act 1933 (under which, where the unsworn evidence of a child of tender years admitted by virtue of that section is given on behalf of the prosecution, the accused is not liable to be convicted unless that evidence is corroborated by some other material evidence in support thereof implicating him) shall cease to have effect.

(2) Any requirement whereby at a trial on indictment it is obligatory for the court to give the jury a warning about convicting the accused on the uncorroborated evidence of a child is abrogated in relation to cases where such a

warning is required by reason only that the evidence is the evidence of a child.

(3) Unsworn evidence admitted by virtue of section 38 of the Children and Young Persons Act 1933 may corroborate evidence (sworn or unsworn) given by any other person.

PART IV

[33.]–[34.] *Reference of sentencing questions to Court of Appeal.*

PART V

JURISDICTION, IMPRISONMENT, FINES, ETC.

Jurisdiction

Certain either way offences relating to motor vehicles to be summary offences
   [36.] (1) In section 12 of the Theft Act 1968 (taking motor vehicle or other conveyance without authority etc.)–
   (a) in subsection (2), for the words 'on conviction on indictment be liable to imprisonment for a term not exceeding three years.' there shall be substituted the words 'be liable on summary conviction to a fine not exceeding level 5 on the standard scale, to imprisonment for a term not exceeding six months, or to both.'; and
   (b) at the end of subsection (4) there shall be added the words 'and if he is found guilty of it, he shall be liable as he would have been liable under subsection (2) above on summary conviction.'.

(2) In Schedule 4 to the Road Traffic Act 1972 (prosecution and punishment of offences) as it applies in England and Wales, the following shall be substituted for columns 3 and 4 of the entry relating to offences under section 99(b) (driving while disqualified)–
'Summarily   6 months or level 5 on the standard scale or both.'.

Criminal damage etc. as summary offences
   [37.] (1) In subsection (1) of section 22 of the Magistrates' Courts Act 1980 (under which, where an offence of or related to criminal damage is charged and it appears to a magistrates' court clear that the value involved does not exceed the relevant sum, the court is required to proceed as if the offence charged were triable only summarily) in the second paragraph (which states the relevant sum) for '£400' there shall be substituted '£2,000'.

(2) Subsection (1) above does not apply to an offence charged in respect of an act done before this section comes into force.

(3) The following subsection shall be inserted after subsection (10) of that section–
'(11) Where–
   (a) the accused is charged on the same occasion with two or more scheduled offences and it appears to the court that they constitute or form part of a series of two or more offences of the same or a similar character; or
   (b) the offence charged consists in incitement to commit two or more scheduled offences,
this section shall have effect as if any reference in it to the value involved were a reference to the aggregate of the values involved.'.

(4) Subsection (3) above does not apply where any of the offences are charged in respect of acts done before this section comes into force.

Common assault and battery to be summary offences
   [38.] Common assault and battery shall be summary offences and a person guilty of either of them shall be liable to a fine not exceeding level 5 on the standard scale, to imprisonment for a term not exceeding six months, or to both.

Power to join in indictment count for common assault etc.

[39.] (1) A court charging a person with a summary offence to which this section applies may be included in an indictment if the charge–

(a) is founded on the same facts or evidence as a count charging an indictable offence; or

(b) is part of a series of offences of the same or similar character as an indictable offence which is also charged,

but only if (in either case) the facts or evidence relating to the offence were disclosed in an examination or deposition taken before a justice in the presence of the person charged.

(2) Where a count charging an offence to which this section applies is included in an indictment, the offence shall be tried in the same manner as if it were an indictable offence; but the Crown Court may only deal with the offender in respect of it in a manner in which a magistrates' court could have dealt with him.

(3) The offences to which this section applies are–

(a) common assault;

(b) an offence under section 12(1) of the Theft Act 1968 (taking motor vehicle or other conveyance without authority etc.);

(c) an offence under section 99(b) of the Road Traffic Act 1972 (driving a motor vehicle while disqualified);

(d) an offence mentioned in the first column of Schedule 2 to the Magistrates' Courts Act 1980 (criminal damage etc.) which would otherwise be triable only summarily by virtue of section 22(2) of that Act; and

(e) any summary offence specified under subsection (4) below.

(4) The Secretary of State may by order made by statutory instrument specify for the purposes of this section any summary offence which is punishable with imprisonment or involves obligatory or discretionary disqualification from driving.

(5) A statutory instrument containing an order under this section shall be subject to annulment in pursuance of a resolution of either House of Parliament.

Power of Crown Court to deal with summary offence where person committed for either way offence

[40.] (1) Where a magistrates' court commits a person to the Crown Court for trial on indictment for an offence triable either way or a number of such offences, it may also commit him for trial for any summary offence with which he is charged and which–

(a) is punishable with imprisonment or involves obligatory or discretionary disqualification from driving; and

(b) arises out of circumstances which appear to the court to be the same as or connected with those giving rise to the offence, or one of the offences, triable either way.

whether or not evidence relating to that summary offence appears on the depositions or written statements in the case; and the trial of the information charging the summary offence shall then be treated as if the magistrates' court had adjourned it under section 10 of the Magistrates' Courts Act 1980 and had not fixed the time and place for its resumption.

(2) Where a magistrates' court commits a person to the Crown Court for trial on indictment for a number of offences triable either way and exercises the power conferred by subsection (1) above in respect of a summary offence, the magistrates' court shall give the Crown Court and the person who is committed for trial a notice stating which of the offences triable either way appears to the court to arise out of circumstances which are the same as or connected with those giving rise to the summary offence.

(3) A magistrates' court's decision to exercise the power conferred by subsection (1) above shall not be subject to appeal or liable to be questioned in any court.

(4) The committal of a person under this section in respect of an offence to which section 39 above applies shall not preclude the exercise in relation to the offence of the power conferred by that section; but where he is tried on indictment for such an offence, the functions of the Crown Court under this section in relation to the offence shall cease.

(5) If he is convicted on the indictment, the Crown Court shall consider whether the conditions specified in subsection (1) above were satisfied.

(6) If it considers that they were satisfied, it shall state to him the substance of the summary offence and ask him whether he pleads guilty or not guilty.

(7) If he pleads guilty, the Crown Court shall convict him, but may deal with him in respect of that offence only in a manner in which a magistrates' court could have dealt with him.

(8) If he does not plead guilty, the powers of the Crown Court shall cease in respect of the offence.

(9) The Crown Court shall inform the clerk of the magistrates' court of the outcome of any proceedings under this section.

(10) Where the Court of Appeal allows an appeal against conviction of an offence triable either way which arose out of circumstances which were the same as or connected with those giving rise to a summary offence of which the appellant was convicted under this section–
  (a) it shall set aside his conviction of the summary offence and give the clerk of the magistrates' court notice that it has done so; and
  (b) it may direct that no further proceedings in relation to the offence are to be undertaken;
and the proceedings before the Crown Court in relation to the offence shall thereafter be disregarded for all purposes.

(11) A notice under subsection (10) above shall include particulars of any direction given under paragraph (b) of that subsection in relation to the offence.

(12) The references to the clerk of the magistrates' court in this section are to be construed in accordance with section 141 of the Magistrates' Courts Act 1980.

Amendments relating to committal for sentence
[41.] (1) Section 56 of the Criminal Justice Act 1967 shall be amended as follows.

(2) In subsection (1), for the words 'offence triable either way' there shall be substituted the words 'indictable offence'.

(3) In subsection (2), for the words from 'and sections 8(6)' to the end there shall be substituted the words ', section 8(6) of the Powers of Criminal Courts Act 1973 (probationer convicted of subsequent offence) and section 24(2) of that Act and paragraph 2(2)(a) of Schedule 9 to the Criminal Law Act 1977 (committal to be dealt with in respect of a wholly or partly suspended sentence)'.

[42.] *Power of Court of Appeal to order retrial.*

[43.] *Firearms offences* – see the Table of Commonplace Offences, Chapter 13.

[44.] *Increase in Maximum term of imprisonment for cruelty to children and young persons.*

Maximum term of imprisonment on summary conviction under Prevention of Crime Act 1953 and maximum fine under Restriction of Offensive Weapons Act 1959
[45.] (1) In section 1(1)(a) of the Prevention of Crime Act 1953 'six months' shall be substituted for 'three months'.

(2) The maximum fine that may be imposed for an offence under section 1 o'
the Restriction of Offensive Weapons Act 1959 shall be a fine not exceeding leve'
5 on the standard scale.

(3) This section shall not have effect in relation to anything done before i'
comes into force.

Corruption
[46.] (1) The following paragraph shall be substituted for paragraph (a) o'
section 2 of the Public Bodies Corrupt Practices Act 1889 (penalty for corruptio»
in office)–
'(a) be liable–
>   (i) on summary conviction, to imprisonment for a term not exceeding (
>   months or to a fine not exceeding the statutory maximum, or to both
>   and
>   (ii) on conviction on indictment, to imprisonment for a term not exceed
>   ing 7 years or to a fine, or to both; and'.

(2) In subsection (1) of section 1 of the Prevention of Corruption Act 190(
(punishment of corrupt transactions with agents) for the words from 'shall b(
liable' to the end of the subsection there shall be substituted the words 'shall b(
liable–
(a) on summary conviction, to imprisonment for a term not exceeding (
     months or to a fine not exceeding the statutory maximum, or to both; anc
(b) on conviction on indictment, to imprisonment for a term not exceeding '
     years or to a fine, or to both.'.

(3) Nothing in this section shall affect the punishment for an offence com'
mitted before this section comes into force.

Increase in penalty for insider dealing
[47.] (1) In section 8(1)(a) of the Company Securities (Insider Dealing) Ac'
1985 (under which the maximum term of imprisonment for insider dealin¡
offences is 2 years) for '2' there shall be substituted '7'.

(2) Nothing in subsection (1) above shall affect the punishment for an offenc(
committed before this section comes into force.

Repeal of s.134 of Magistrates' Courts Act 1980
[48.] Section 134 of the Magistrates' Courts Act 1980 (under which a magis
trates' court having power to impose imprisonment on any person may instead o'
doing so order him to be detained for any period not exceeding 4 days in a plac(
certified by the Secretary of State to be suitable for the purpose) shall cease t(
have effect.

[49.] *Suspended and partly suspended sentences on certain civilians in courts*
martial and Standing Civilian Courts.
This provision gives power to the Secretary of State, *inter alia*, to mak(
regulations under which 'courts' (not further defined) may deal with suc»
sentences.

Maximum fines under subordinate legislation

Statutory maximum as penalty on summary conviction for offences triable eithe
way under subordinate legislation
[50.] (1) For an offence triable either way under a subordinate instrumen»
made before the commencement of this section, the maximum fine which may b(
imposed on summary conviction shall by virtue of this subsection be the statutor)
maximum unless the offence is one for which by virtue of the instrument a large'
maximum fine may be imposed on summary conviction.

(2) Where apart from this section the maximum fine would be one amount i»

the case of a first conviction and a different amount in the case of a second or subsequent conviction, subsection (1) above shall apply irrespective of whether the conviction is a first, second or subsequent one.

(3) Subsection (1) above shall not affect so much of any instrument as (in whatever words) makes a person liable on summary conviction to a fine not exceeding a specified amount for each period of a specified length during which a continuing offence is continued after conviction or the occurrence of any other specified event.

(4) Where there is under any enactment (however framed or worded) contained in an Act passed before the commencement of this section a power by subordinate instrument to impose penal provisions, being a power which allows the creation of offences triable either way, the maximum fine which may in the exercise of that power be authorised on summary conviction in respect of an offence triable either way shall by virtue of this subsection be the statutory maximum unless some larger maximum fine can be authorised on summary conviction of such an offence by virtue of an enactment contained in an Act passed before the commencement of this section.

(5) Where there is under any enactment (however framed or worded) contained in an Act passed before the commencement of this section a power by subordinate instrument to create offences triable either way, the maximum fine for an offence triable either way so created may be expressed as a fine not exceeding the statutory maximum.

(6) Subsection (5) above has effect in relation to exercises of powers before as well as after the commencement of this section.

(7) Nothing in this section shall affect the punishment for an offence committed before the commencement of this section.

(8) In this Part of this Act 'fine' includes a pecuniary penalty but does not include a pecuniary forfeiture or pecuniary compensation.

Penalties on conviction for summary offences under subordinate legislation – conversion of references to amounts to references to levels on scale
[51.] (1) Where under a relevant subordinate instrument the maximum fine on conviction of a summary offence specified in the instrument is an amount shown in the second column of the standard scale, the reference in the instrument to the amount of the maximum fine shall be construed as a reference to the level in the first column of the standard scale corresponding to that amount.

(2) In subsection (1) above 'relevant subordinate instrument' means any instrument made by virtue of an enactment or instrument after 30 April 1984 and before the commencement of this section.

(3) Subsection (1) above shall not affect so much of any instrument as (in whatever words) makes a person liable on summary conviction to a fine not exceeding a specified amount for each period of a specified length during which a continuing offence is continued after conviction or the occurrence of any other specified event.

(4) Where there is–
(a) under any enactment (however framed or worded) contained in an Act passed before the commencement of this section;
(b) under any instrument (however framed or worded) made by virtue of such an enactment,
a power to provide by subordinate instrument that a person, as regards any summary offence (whether or not created by the instrument) shall be liable on conviction to a fine, a person may be so made liable to a fine not exceeding a specified level on the standard scale.

(5) Subsection (4) above has effect in relation to exercises of powers before as well as after the commencement of this section.

Powers to specify maximum fines for summary offences under subordinate instruments – conversion of references to amounts to references to levels on scale – England and Wales

[52.] (1) Where an instrument which was made under an enactment on or after 11 April 1983 but before this section came into force confers on any authority other than a harbour authority a power by subordinate instrument to make a person liable to a fine on conviction of a summary offence of an amount shown in the second column of the standard scale, as that scale had effect when the instrument was made, a reference to the level in the first column of the standard scale which then corresponded to that amount shall be substituted for the reference in the instrument conferring the power to the amount of the fine.

(2) If an order under section 143 of the Magistrates' Courts Act 1980 alters the sums specified in section 37(2) of the Criminal Justice Act 1982, the second reference to the standard scale in subsection (1) above is to be construed as a reference to that scale as it has effect by virtue of the order.

(3) This section shall not affect so much of any instrument as (in whatever words) makes a person liable on summary conviction to a maximum fine not exceeding a specified amount for each period of a specified length during which a continuing offence is continued.

Fines under secondary subordinate instruments – England and Wales

[54.] (1) This section applies to any instrument (however framed or worded) which–
  (a) was made before 11 April 1983 (the date of the commencement of sections 35 to 50 of the Criminal Justice Act 1982); and
  (b) confers on any authority other than a harbour authority a power by subordinate instrument to make a person, as regards any summary offence (whether or not created by the latter instrument), liable on conviction to a maximum fine of a specified amount not exceeding £1,000,
but does not affect so much of any such instrument as (in whatever words) confers a power by subordinate instrument to make a person liable on conviction to a fine for each period of a specified length during which a continuing offence is continued.

(2) The maximum fine to which a subordinate instrument made by virtue of an instrument to which this section applies may provide that a person shall be liable on conviction of a summary offence is–
  (a) if the specified amount is less than £25, level 1 on the standard scale;
  (b) if it is £25 or more but less than £50, level 2;
  (c) if it is £50 or more but less than £200, level 3;
  (d) if it is £200 or more but less than £400, level 4; and
  (e) if it is £400 or more, level 5.

(3) Subject to subsection (5) below, where an instrument to which this section applies confers a power by subordinate instrument to make a person, as regards a summary offence, liable on conviction to a fine in respect of a specified quantity or a specified number of things, that fine shall be treated for the purposes of this section as being the maximum fine to which a person may be made liable by virtue of the instrument.

(4) Where an instrument to which this section applies confers a power to provide for different maximum fines in relation to different circumstances or persons of different descriptions, the amounts specified as those maximum fines are to be treated separately for the purposes of this section.

(5) Where an instrument to which this section applies confers a power by subordinate instrument to make a person, as regards a summary offence, liable on conviction to a fine in respect of a specified quantity or a specified number of things but also confers a power by subordinate instrument to make a person, as regards such an offence, liable on conviction to an alternative fine, this section shall have effect in relation–

(a) to the alternative fine; and
(b) to any amount that the instrument specifies as the maximum fine for which a subordinate instrument made in the exercise of the power conferred by it may provide,

as well as in relation to the fine mentioned in subsection (3) above.

(6) Section 36 of the Criminal Justice Act 1982 (abolition of enhanced penalties under subordinate instruments) shall have effect as if the references in it to an Act included references to an instrument and the reference in subsection (2) to the coming into force of the section were a reference, in relation to an instrument conferring a power such as is mentioned in subsection (1), to the coming into force of this section.

[55.] *Scotland.*

[56.] *Powers of harbour authorities to provide for maximum fines up to level 4 on standard scale.*

[57.] *Byelaws relating to the burning of crop residues* (Stubble burning etc.).

[58.] *Power to alter exceptionally high maximum fines.*

Default in payment of fines etc.

Increased periods of imprisonment for default
[59.] (1) In the Tables in section 31(3A) of the Powers of Criminal Courts Act 1973 and paragraph 1 of Schedule 4 to the Magistrates' Courts Act 1980, for the entries relating to amounts not exceeding £10,000 there shall be substituted–
'An amount not exceeding £50 .... 5 days
An amount exceeding £50 but not exceeding £100 .... 7 days
An amount exceeding £100 but not exceeding £400 .... 14 days
An amount exceeding £400 but not exceeding £1,000 .... 30 days
An amount exceeding £1,000 but not exceeding £2,000 .... 45 days
An amount exceeding £2,000 but not exceeding £5,000 .... 3 months
An amount exceeding £5,000 but not exceeding £10,000 .... 6 months'.

(2) In the Table in section 31(3A) of the Powers of Criminal Courts Act 1973, for the entry relating to an amount exceeding £10,000 there shall be substituted–
'An amount exceeding £10,000 but not exceeding £20,000 .... 12 months
An amount exceeding £20,000 but not exceeding £50,000 .... 18 months
An amount exceeding £50,000 but not exceeding £100,000 .... 2 years
An amount exceeding £100,000 but not exceeding £250,000 .... 3 years
An amount exceeding £250,000 but not exceeding £1 million .... 5 years
An amount exceeding £1 million .... 10 years'.

Default – procedure
[60.] (1) The Magistrates' Courts Act 1980 shall be amended as follows.

(2) The following subsections shall be added after section 77(2)–

'(3) A magistrates' court shall have power at any time to do either or both of the following–
(a) to direct that the issue of the warrant of commitment shall be postponed until a time different from that to which it was previously postponed;
(b) to vary any of the conditions on which its issue is postponed,
but only if it thinks it just to do so having regard to a change of circumstances since the relevant time.

(4) In this section 'the relevant time' means–
(a) where neither of the powers conferred by subsection (3) above has been exercised previously, the date when the issue of the warrant was postponed under subsection (2) above; and

(b) in any other case, the date of the exercise or latest exercise of either or both of the powers.

(5) Without prejudice to the generality of subsection (3) above, if on an application by a person in respect of whom issue of a warrant has been postponed it appears to a justice of the peace acting for the petty sessions area in which the warrant has been or would have been issued that since the relevant time there has been a change of circumstances which would make it just for the court to exercise one or other or both of the powers conferred by that subsection, he shall refer the application to the court.

(6) Where such an application is referred to the court, it shall be the duty of the clerk of the court–
(a) to fix a time and place for the application to be heard; and
(b) to give the applicant notice of the time and place which he fixes.

(7) Where such a notice has been given but the applicant does not appear at the time and place specified in the notice, the court may proceed with the consideration of the application in his absence.

(8) If a warrant of commitment in respect of the sum adjudged to be paid has been issued before the hearing of the application, the court shall have power to order that the warrant shall cease to have effect and, if the applicant has been arrested in pursuance of it, to order that he shall be released, but it shall only make an order under this subsection if it is satisfied that the change of circumstances on which the applicant relies was not put before the court when it was determining whether to issue the warrant.'.

(3) The following subsection shall be inserted after subsection (4) of section 82 (restriction on power to impose imprisonment for default)–

'(4A) The methods of enforcing payment mentioned in subsection (4)(b)(ii) above are–
(a) a warrant of distress under section 76 above;
(b) an application to the High Court or county court for enforcement under section 87 below;
(c) an order under section 88 below;
(d) an attachment of earnings order; and
(e) if the offender is under the age of 21, an order under section 17 of the Criminal Justice Act 1982 (attendance centre orders).'

(4) The following subsections shall be inserted after subsection (5) of that section–

'(5A) A magistrates' court may not issue a warrant of commitment under subsection (5) above at a hearing at which the offender is not present unless the clerk of the court has first served on the offender a notice in writing stating that the court intends to hold a hearing to consider whether to issue such a warrant and giving the reason why the court so intends.

(5B) Where after the occasion of an offender's conviction by a magistrates' court the court holds a hearing for the purpose of considering whether to issue a warrant of commitment for default in paying a sum adjudged to be paid by the conviction, it shall consider such information about the offender's means as is available to it unless it has previously–
(a) inquired into the offender's means; and
(b) postponed the issue of the warrant of commitment under section 77(2) above.

(5C) A notice under subsection (5A) above–
(a) shall state the time and place appointed for the hearing; and
(b) shall inform the offender that, if he considers that there are grounds why the warrant should not be issued, he may make representations to the court in person or in writing, but the court may exercise its powers in

relation to the issue of a warrant whether or not he makes representations.

(5D) Except as mentioned in subsection (5E) below, the time stated in a notice under subsection (5A) above shall not be earlier than 21 days after the issue of the notice.

(5E) Where a magistrates' court exercises in relation to an offender the power conferred by section 77(2) above and at the same hearing issues a notice under subsection (5A) above in relation to him, the time stated in the notice may be a time on any day following the end of the period for which the issue of the warrant of commitment has been postponed.

(5F) A notice under subsection (5A) above to be served on any person shall be deemed to be served on that person if it is sent by registered post or the recorded delivery service addressed to him at his last known address, notwithstanding that the notice is returned as undelivered or is for any other reason not received by that person'.

(5) The following section shall be substituted for section 85–

'Power to remit fine
85. (1) Where a fine has been imposed on conviction of an offender by a magistrates' court, the court may at any time remit the whole or any part of the fine, but only if it thinks it just to do so having regard to a change of circumstances which has occurred–
  (a) where the court is considering whether to issue a warrant of commitment after the issue of such a warrant in respect of the fine has been postponed under subsection (2) of section 74 above, since the relevant time as defined in subsection (4) of that section; and
  (b) in any other case, since the date of the conviction.

(2) Where the court remits the whole or part of the fine after a term of imprisonment has been fixed, it shall also reduce the term by an amount which bears the same proportion to the whole term as the amount remitted bears to the whole or, as the case may be, shall remit the whole term.

(3) In calculating the reduction in a term of imprisonment required by subsection (2) above any fraction of a day shall be left out of account.

(4) Notwithstanding the definition of 'fine' in section 150(1) below, references in this section to a fine do not include any other sum adjudged to be paid on conviction, whether as a pecuniary penalty, forfeiture, compensation or otherwise.'.

(6) In section 121(2) (magistrates' court to consist of at least 2 justices when holding an inquiry into the means of an offender for the purposes of section 82) after the word 'above' there shall be inserted the words 'or determine under that section at a hearing at which the offender is not present whether to issue a warrant of commitment'.

Fines on companies

[**61.**] (1) The following section shall be inserted after section 87 of the Magistrates' Courts Act 1980–

'Fines imposed on companies
87A. (1) Where–
  (a) a magistrates' court has, or is treated by any enactment as having, adjudged a company by a conviction to pay a sum; and
  (b) the court has issued a warrant of distress under section 76(1) above for the purpose of levying the sum; and
  (c) it appears on the return to the warrant that the money and goods of the company are insufficient to satisfy the sum with the costs and charges of levying the same,

the clerk of the court may make an application in relation to the company under section 9 or 124 of the Insolvency Act 1986 (administration or winding up). (application for administration order).

(2) Any expenses incurred under subsection (1) above by the clerk of a magistrates' court shall be treated for the purposes of Part VI of the Justices of the Peace Act 1979 as expenses of the magistrates' courts committee.'.

(3) The words 'or by the clerk of a magistrates' court in the exercise of the power conferred by section 87A of the Magistrates' Courts Act 1980 (enforcement of fines imposed on companies)' shall be inserted–
  (a) before the words 'or by all' in section 9(1) of the Insolvency Act 1986;
  (b) after the word 'contributories' in section 124(1) of that Act.

[62.] *Fixed penalty notices.*

[63.] *Increase of maximum fine under s.32 Game Act 1831.*

Powers of civilian fine enforcement officers
  [64.] (1) The following paragraph shall be inserted after the first paragraph of subsection (2) of section 125 (warrants) of the Magistrates' Courts Act 1980–
    'A warrant of arrest, warrant of commitment or warrant of distress which is issued by a justice of the peace for the enforcement of a fine may also be executed by a person who–
    (a) is employed by an authority of a prescribed class;
    (b) is authorised in the prescribed manner to execute such warrants; and
    (c) is acting within the area for which the authority that employs him performs its functions.'.

(2) In section 136(2)(a) of that Act (by virtue of which a warrant for the detention of a fine defaulter overnight in a police station may be executed by any police constable) after the word 'constable' there shall be inserted the words 'or any person who–
    (a) is employed by an authority of a prescribed class;
    (b) is authorised in the prescribed manner to execute such warrants; and
    (c) is acting within the area for which the authority that employs him performs its functions.'

[65.] *Fisheries offences on River Tweed.*

Fines imposed and recognizances forfeited by coroners
  [66.] (1) A fine imposed by a coroner, including a fine so imposed before this section comes into force, shall be treated for the purpose of its collection, enforcement and remission as having been imposed by the magistrates' court for the area in which the coroner's court was held, and the coroner shall as soon as practicable after imposing the fine give particulars of the fine to the clerk of that court.

(2) A coroner shall proceed in the like manner under subsection (1) above in relation to a recognizance forfeited at an inquest held before him, including a recognizance so forfeited before this section comes into force, as if he had imposed a fine upon the person forfeiting that recognizance, and subsection (1) above shall apply accordingly.

[67.] *Causing death by reckless driving – increased minimum disqualification period.*

Forfeiture

Forfeiture – general
  [68.] The following subsections shall be substituted for section 43(1) of the Powers of Criminal Courts Act 1973–

'(1) Subject to the following provisions of this section, where a person is convicted of an offence and–
(a) the court by or before which he is convicted is satisfied that any property which has been lawfully seized from him or which was in his possession or under his control at the time when he was apprehended for the offence or when a summons in respect of it was issued–
   (i) has been used for the purpose of committing, or facilitating the commission of, any offence; or
   (ii) was intended by him to be used for that purpose; or
(b) the offence, or an offence which the court has taken into consideration in determining his sentence, consists of unlawful possession of property which–
   (i) has been lawfully seized from him; or
   (ii) was in his possession or under his control at the time when he was apprehended for the offence of which he has been convicted or when a summons in respect of that offence was issued,
the court may make an order under this section in respect of that property, and may do so whether or not it also deals with the offender in respect of the offence in any other way.

(1A) In considering whether to make such an order in respect of any property a court shall have regard–
(a) to the value of the property; and
(b) to the likely financial and other effects on the offender of the making of the order (taken together with any other order that the court contemplates making).'

Forfeiture for drug offences

[69.] In section 27(1) of the Misuse of Drugs Act 1971 (forfeiture on conviction of an offence under that Act) after the words 'under this Act' there shall be inserted the words 'or a drug trafficking offence, as defined in section 38(1) of the Drug Trafficking Offences Act 1986'.

PART VI

CONFISCATION OF THE PROCEEDS OF AN OFFENCE

Confiscation orders

[70.] (1) The Crown Court and a magistrates' court shall each have power, in addition to dealing with an offender in any other way, to make an order under this section requiring him to pay such sum as the court thinks fit.

(2) The Crown Court may make such an order against an offender where–
(a) he is found guilty of any offence to which this Part of this Act applies; and
(b) it is satisfied–
   (i) that he has benefited from that offence or from that offence taken together with some other offence of which he is convicted in the same proceedings, or which the court takes into consideration in determining his sentence, and which is not a drug trafficking offence; and
   (ii) that his benfit is at least the minimum amount.

(3) A magistrates' court may make such an order against an offender where–
(a) he is convicted of an offence listed in Schedule 4 to this Act; and
(b) it is satisfied–
   (i) that he has benefited from that offence or from that offence taken together with some other offence listed in that Schedule of which he is convicted in the same proceedings, or which the court takes into consideration in determining his sentence; and
   (ii) that his benefit is at least the minimum amount.

(4) For the purposes of this Part of this Act a person benefits from an offence if he obtains property as a result of or in connection with its commission and his benefit is the value of the property so obtained.

(5) Where a person derives a pecuniary advantage as a result of or in connection with the commission of an offence, he is to be treated for the purposes of this Part of this Act as if he had obtained as a result of or in connection with the commission of the offence a sum of money equal to the value of the pecuniary advantage.

(6) The sum which an order made by a court under this section requires an offender to pay must be at least the minimum amount, but must not exceed–
(a) the benefit in respect of which it is made; or
(b) the amount appearing to the court to be the amount that might be realised at the time the order is made,
whichever is the less.

(7) For the purposes of this Part of this Act the minimum amount is £10,000 or such other amount as the Secretary of State may specify by order made by statutory instrument.

(8) A statutory instrument containing an order made by the Secretary of State under this section shall be subject to annulment in pursuance of a resolution of either House of Parliament.

(9) In this Part of this Act–
(a) an order made by a court under this section is referred to as a 'confiscation order';
(b) 'drug trafficking offence' has the same meaning as in the Drug Trafficking Offences Act 1986;
(c) references to an offence to which this Part of this Act applies are references to any offence which–
    (i) is listed in Schedule 4 to this Act; or
    (ii) if not so listed, is an indictable offence, other than a drug trafficking offence; and
(d) a person against whom proceedings have been instituted for an offence to which this Part of this Act applies is referred to (whether or not he has been convicted) as 'the defendant'.

Making of confiscation orders
[71.] (1) A court shall not make a confiscation order unless the prosecutor has given written notice to the court to the effect that it appears to him that, were the court to consider that it ought to make such an order, it would be able to make an order requiring the offender to pay at least the minimum amount.

(2) If the prosecutor gives the court such a notice, the court shall determine whether it ought to make a confiscation order.

(3) When considering whether to make a confiscation order the court may take into account any information that has been placed before it showing that a victim of an offence to which the proceedings relate has instituted, or intends to institute, civil proceedings against the defendant in respect of loss, injury or damage sustained in connection with the offence.

(4) If the court determines that it ought to make such an order, the court shall, before sentencing or otherwise dealing with the offender in respect of the offence or, as the case may be, any of the offences concerned, determine the amount to be recovered in his case by virtue of this section and make a confiscation order for that amount specifying the offence or offences.

(5) Where a court makes a confiscation order against a defendant in any proceedings, it shall be its duty, in respect of any offence of which he is convicted in those proceedings, to take account of the order before–
(a) imposing any fine on him; or
(b) making any order involving any payment by him, other than an order under section 35 of the Powers of Criminal Courts Act 1973 (compensation orders); or
(c) making any order under–

(i) section 27 of the Misuse of Drugs Act 1971 (forfeiture orders); or

(ii) section 43 of the Powers of Criminal Courts Act 1973 (deprivation orders),

but subject to that shall leave the order out of account in determining the appropriate sentence or other manner of dealing with him.

(6) No enactment restricting the power of a court dealing with an offender in a particular way from dealing with him also in any other way shall by reason only of the making of a confiscation order restrict the court from dealing with an offender in any way it considers appropriate in respect of an offence to which this Part of this Act applies.

(7) Where–

(a) a court makes both a confiscation order and an order for the payment of compensation under section 35 of the Powers of Criminal Courts Act 1973 against the same person in the same proceedings; and

(b) it appears to the court that he will not have sufficient means to satisfy both the orders in full,

it shall direct that so much of the compensation as will not in its opinion be recoverable because of the insufficiency of his means shall be paid out of any sums recovered under the confiscation order.

Statements, etc. relevant to making confiscation orders

72. (1) Where–

(a) a defendant has been convicted of an offence to which this Part of this Act applies and the prosecutor tenders to the court a statement as to any matters relevant–

(i) to determining whether the defendant has benefited from the offence or from any other offence to which this Part of this Act applies of which he is convicted in the same proceedings or which is taken into consideration in determining his sentence; or

(ii) to an assessment of the value of the defendant's benefit from the offence or any other offence to which this Part of this Act applies of which he is so convicted or which is so taken into consideration; and

(b) the defendant accepts to any extent any allegation in the statement;

the court may, for the purposes of so determining or making such an assessment, treat his acceptance as conclusive of the matters to which it relates.

(2) Where–

(a) a statement is tendered under subsection (1)(a) above, and

(b) the court is satisfied that a copy of that statement has been served on the defendant,

the court may require the defendant to indicate to what extent he accepts each allegation in the statement and, so far as he does not accept any such allegation, to indicate any matters he proposes to rely on.

(3) If the defendant fails in any respect to comply with a requirement under subsection (2) above, he may be treated for the purposes of this section as accepting every allegation in the statement apart from–

(a) any allegation in respect of which he has complied with the requirement; and

(b) any allegation that he has benefited from an offence or that any property was obtained by him as a result of or in connection with the commission of an offence.

(4) Where–

(a) there is tendered to the court by the defendant a statement as to any matters relevant to determining the amount that might be realised at the time the confiscation order is made; and

(b) the prosecutor accepts to any extent any allegation in the statement;

the court may, for the purposes of that determination, treat the acceptance by the prosecutor as conclusive of the matters to which it relates.

(5) An allegation may be accepted or a matter indicated for the purposes of this section either–
(a) orally before the court; or
(b) in writing in accordance with rules of court.

(6) If the court is satisfied as to any matter relevant for determining the amount that might be realised at the time the confiscation order is made (whether by an acceptance under this section or otherwise), the court may issue a certificate giving the court's opinion as to the matters concerned and shall do so if satisfied that the amount that might be realised at the time the confiscation order is made is less than the amount the court assesses to be the value of the defendant's benefit from the offence or, if more than one, all the offences in respect of which the order may be made.

Definition of principal terms used

[**73.**] (1) In this Part of this Act, 'realisable property' means, subject to subsection (2) below–
(a) any property held by the defendant; and
(b) any property held by a person to whom the defendant has directly or indirectly made a gift caught by this Part of this Act.

(2) Property is not realisable property if–
(a) an order under section 43 of the Powers of Criminal Courts Act 1973 (deprivation orders);
(b) an order under section 27 of the Misuse of Drugs Act 1971 (forfeiture orders); or
(c) an order under section 223 or 436 of the Criminal Procedure (Scotland) Act 1975 (forfeiture of property),
is in force in respect of the property.

(3) For the purposes of this Part of this Act the amount that might be realised at the time a confiscation order is made is–
(a) the total of the values at that time of all the realisable property held by the defendant, less
(b) where there are obligations having priority at that time, the total amounts payable in pursuance of such obligations,
together with the total of the values at that time of all gifts caught by this Part of this Act.

(4) Subject to the following provisions of this section, for the purposes of this Part of this Act the value of property (other than cash) in relation to any person holding the property–
(a) where any other person holds an interest in the property, is–
(i) the market value of the first-mentioned person's beneficial interest in the property, less
(ii) the amount required to discharge any incumbrance (other than a charging order) on that interest; and
(b) in any other case, is its market value.

(5) References in this Part of this Act to the value at any time (referred to in subsection (6) below as 'the material time') of any property obtained by a person as a result of or in connection with the commission of an offence are references to–
(a) the value of the property to him when he obtained it adjusted to take account of subsequent changes in the value of money; or
(b) where subsection (6) below applies, the value there mentioned,
whichever is the greater.

(6) If at the material time he holds–
(a) the property which he obtained (not being cash); or
(b) property which, in whole or in part, directly or indirectly represents in his hands the property which he obtained,
the value referred to in subsection (5)(b) above is the value to him at the material time of the property mentioned in paragraph (a) above or, as the case may be, of

the property mentioned in paragraph (b) above, so far as it so represents the property which he obtained, but disregarding any charging order.

(7) Subject to subsection (12) below, references in this Part of this Act to the value at any time (referred to in subsection (8) below as 'the material time') of a gift caught by this Part of this Act are references to–
   (a) the value of the gift to the receipient when he received it adjusted to take account of subsequent changes in the value of money; or
   (b) where subsection (8) below applies, the value there mentioned,
whichever is the greater.

(8) Subect to subsection (12) below, if at the material time he holds–
   (a) the property which he received (not being cash); or
   (b) property which, in whole or in part, directly or indirectly represents in his hands the property which he received;
the value referred to in subsection (7) above is the value to him at the material time of the property mentioned in paragraph (a) above or, as the case may be, of the property mentioned in paragraph (b) above so far as it so represents the property which he received, but disregarding any charging order.

(9) For the purposes of subsection (3) above, an obligation has priority at any time if it is an obligation of the defendant to–
   (a) pay an amount due in respect of a fine, or other order of a court, imposed or made on conviction of an offence, where the fine was imposed or order made before the confiscation order; or
   (b) pay any sum which would be included among the preferential debts (within the meaning given by section 386 of the Insolvency Act 1986) in the defendant's bankruptcy commencing on the date of the confiscation order or winding up under an order of the court made on that date.

(10) A gift (including a gift made before the commencement of this Part of this Act) is caught by this Part of this Act if–
   (a) it was made by the defendant at any time after the commission of the offence or, if more than one, the earliest of the offences to which the proceedings for the time being relate; and
   (b) the court considers it appropriate in all the circumstances to take the gift into account.

(11) The reference in subsection (10) above to an offence to which the proceedings for the time being relate includes, where the proceedings have resulted in the conviction of the defendant, a reference to any offence which the court takes into consideration when determining his sentence.

(12) For the purpsoes of this Part of this Act–
   (a) the circumstances in which the defendant is to be treated as making a gift include those where he transfers property to another person directly or indirectly for a consideration the value of which is significantly less than the value of the consideration provided by the defendant; and
   (b) in those circumstances, the preceding provisions of this section shall apply as if the defendant had made a gift of such share in the property as bears to the whole property the same proportion as the difference between the values referred to in paragraph (a) above bears to the value of the consideration provided by the defendant.

Enforcement, etc. of confiscation orders

Application of procedure for enforcing fines
[74.] (1) Where the Crown Court orders the defendant to pay an amount under this Part of this Act, sections 31(1) to (3C) and 32(1) and (2) of the Powers of Criminal Courts Act 1973 (powers of Crown Court in relation to fines and enforcement of Crown Court fines) shall have effect as if that amount were a fine imposed on him by the Crown Court.

(2) Where a magistrates' court orders the defendant to pay an amount under this Part of this Act, that amount shall be treated as a fine for the purposes of section 31(3) of the Magistrates' Courts Act 1980 (general limit on the power of a magistrates' court to impose imprisonment not to apply in the case of imprisonment in default).

(3) Where–
(a) a warrant of commitment is issued for a default in payment of an amount ordered to be paid under this Part of this Act in respect of an offence; and
(b) at the time the warrant is issued, the defendant is liable to serve a term of custody in respect of the offence;
the term of imprisonment or of detention under section 9 of the Criminal Justice Act 1982 (detention of persons aged 17 to 20 for default) to be served in default of payment of the amount shall not begin to run until after the term mentioned in paragraph (b) above.

(4) The reference in subsection (3) above to the term of custody which the defendant is liable to serve in respect of the offence is a reference to the term of imprisonment, youth custody or detention under section 4 or 9 of the Criminal Justice Act 1982 which he is liable to serve in respect of the offence; and for the purposes of this subsection–
(a) consecutive terms and terms which are wholly or partly concurrent shall be treated as a single term; and
(b) there shall be disregarded–
    (i) any sentence suspended under section 22(1) of the Powers of Criminal Courts Act 1973 which has not taken effect at the time the warrant is issued;
   (ii) in the case of a sentence of imprisonment passed with an order under section 47(1) of the Criminal Law Act 1977, any part of the sentence which the defendant has not at that time been required to serve in prison; and
  (iii) any term of imprisonment or detention fixed under section 31(2) of the Powers of Criminal Courts Act 1973 for which a warrant of commitment has not been issued at that time.

(5) In the application of Part III of the Magistrates' Courts Act 1980 to amounts payable under confiscation orders–
(a) such an amount is not a sum adjudged to be paid by a conviction for the purposes of section 81 (enforcement of fines imposed on young offenders) or a fine for the purposes of section 85 (remission of fines); and
(b) in section 87 (enforcement by High Court or county court), subsection (3) shall be omitted.

(6) This section applies in relation to confiscation orders made by the criminal division of the Court of Appeal, or by the House of Lords on appeal from that division, as it applies in relation to confiscation orders made by the Crown Court, and the reference in subsection (1) above to the Crown Court shall be construed accordingly.

[75.]–[96.] *Miscellaneous provisions relating to charging orders and restraint orders – including in relation to 'confiscation orders'.*

Miscellaneous and supplemental

Authorisation of delay in notifying arrest etc.
[97.] (1) The Police and Criminal Evidence Act 1984 shall be amended as follows.

(2) In section 56(5A) (which authorises delay in notifying arrest for a drug trafficking offence)–
(a) after the word 'offence', in the second place where it occurs, there shall be inserted the words 'or an offence to which Part VI of the Criminal Justice

Act 1988 applies (offences in respect of which confiscation orders under that Part may be made)'; and
(b) the following paragraphs shall be substituted for paragraphs (a) and (b)–
'(a) where the offence is a drug trafficking offence, that the detained person has benefited from drug trafficking and that the recovery of the value of that person's proceeds of drug trafficking will be hindered by telling the named person of the arrest; and
(b) where the offence is one to which Part VI of the Criminal Justice Act 1988 applies, that the detained person has benefited from the offence and that the recovery of the value of the property obtained by that person from or in connection with the offence or of the pecuniary advantage derived by him from or in connection with it will be hindered by telling the named person of the arrest.'

(3) In section 58(8A) (which authorises delay in access to legal advice on arrest for a drug trafficking offence)–
(a) after the word 'offence', in the second place where it occurs, there shall be inserted the words 'or an offence to which Part VI of the Criminal Justice Act 1988 applies'; and
(b) the following paragraphs shall be substituted for paragraphs (a) and (b)–
'(a) where the offence is a drug trafficking offence, that the detained person has benefited from drug trafficking and that the recovery of the value of that person's proceeds of drug trafficking will be hindered by the exercise of the right conferred by subsection (1) above; and
(b) where the offence is one to which Part VI of the Criminal Justice Act 1988 applies, that the detained person has benefited from the offence and that the recovery of the value of the property obtained by that person from or in connection with the offence or of the pecuniary advantage derived by him from or in connection with it will be hinderd by the exercise of the right conferred by subsection (1) above.'

(4) Without prejudice to section 20(2) of the Interpretation Act 1978, the Police and Criminal Evidence Act 1984 (Application to Customs and Excise) Order 1985 shall apply to sections 56 and 58 of the Police and Criminal Evidence Act 1984 as those sections have effect by virtue of this section.

[98.] *Power to inspect Land Register etc.*

[99.] *Abolition of power to make criminal bankruptcy order.*

[100.] *Part VI – Interpretation.*

[101.] *Amendments of Drug Trafficking Offences Act 1986 and Criminal Justice (Scotland) Act 1987.*

PART VII

COMPENSATION BY COURT AND CRIMINAL INJURIES COMPENSATION BOARD

Powers of court

Compensation orders
[102.] (1) At the end of subsection (1) of section 35 of the Powers of Criminal Courts Act 1973 there shall be added the words 'or to make payments for funeral expenses or bereavement in respect of a death resulting from any such offence, other than a death due to an accident arising out of the presence of a motor vehicle on a road; and a court shall give reasons, on passing sentence, if it does not make such an order in a case where this section empowers it to do so'.

(2) The following subsections shall be substituted for subsection (3) of that section–

'(3) A compensation order may only be made in respect of injury, loss or damage (other than loss suffered by a person's dependants in consequence of his death) which was due to an accident arising out of the presence of a motor vehicle on a road, if–

    (a) it is in respect of damage which is treated by subsection (2) above as resulting from an offence under the Theft Act 1968; or

    (b) it is in respect of injury, loss or damage as respects which–

        (i) the offender is uninsured in relation to the use of the vehicle; and

        (ii) compensation is not payable under any arrangements to which the Secretary of State is a party;

and, where a compensation order is made in respect of injury, loss or damage due to such an accident, the amount to be paid may include an amount representing the whole or part of any loss of or reduction in preferential rates of insurance attributable to the accident.

(3A) A vehicle the use of which is exempted from insurance by section 144 of the Road Traffic Act 1972 is not uninsured for the purposes of subsection (3) above.

(3B) A compensation order in respect of funeral expenses may be made for the benefit of anyone who incurred the expenses.

(3C) A compensation order in respect of bereavement may only be made for the benefit of a person for whose benefit a claim for damages for bereavement could be made under section 1A of the Fatal Accidents Act 1976.

(3D) The amount of compensation in respect of bereavement shall not exceed the amount for the time being specified in section 1A(3) of the Fatal Accidents Act 1976.'.

Enforcement of compensation orders
[103.] The following sections shall be substituted for sections 36 to 38 of the Powers of Criminal Courts Act 1973–

'Enforcement and appeals

36. (1) A person in whose favour a compensation order is made shall not be entitled to receive the amount due to him until (disregarding any power of a court to grant leave to appeal out of time) there is no further possibility of an appeal on which the order could be varied or set aside.

(2) Rules under section 144 of the Magistrates' Courts Act 1980 may make provision regarding the way in which the magistrates' court for the time being having functions (by virtue of section 41(1) of the Administration of Justice Act 1970) in relation to the enforcement of a compensation order is to deal with money paid in satisfaction of the order where the entitlement of the person in whose favour it was made is suspended.

(3) The Court of Appeal may by order annul or vary any compensation order made by the court of trial, although the conviction is not quashed; and the order, if annulled, shall not take effect and, if varied, shall take effect as varied.

(4) Where the House of Lords restores a conviction, it may make any compensation order which the court of trial could have made.

(5) Where a compensation order has been made against any person in respect of an offence taken into consideration in determining his sentence–

    (a) the order shall cease to have effect if he successfully appeals against his conviction of the offence or, if more than one, all the offences, of which he was convicted in the proceedings in which the order was made;

    (b) he may appeal against the order as if it were part of the sentence imposed in respect of the offence or, if more than one, any of the offences, of which he was so convicted.

Review of compensation orders
37. At any time before the person against whom a compensation order has

been made has paid into court the whole of the compensation which the order requires him to pay, but at a time when (disregarding any power of a court to grant leave to appeal out of time) there is no further possibility of an appeal on which the order could be varied or set aside, the magistrates' court for the time being having functions in relation to the enforcement of the order may, on the application of the person against whom it was made, discharge the order, or reduce the amount which remains to be paid, if it appears to the court–

(a) that the injury, loss or damage in respect of which the order was made has been held in civil proceedings to be less than it was taken to be for the purposes of the order; or

(b) in the case of an order in respect of the loss of any property, that the property has been recovered by the person in whose favour the order was made; or

(c) that the means of the person against whom the order was made are insufficient to satisfy in full both the order and a confiscation order under Part VI of the Criminal Justice Act 1988 made against him in the same proceedings; or

(d) that the person against whom the order was made has suffered a substantial reduction in his means which was unexpected at the time when the compensation order was made, and that his means seem unlikely to increase for a considerable period;

but where the order was made by the Crown Court, a magistrates' court shall not exercise any power conferred by this section in a case where it is satisfied as mentioned in paragraph (c) or (d) above unless it has first obtained the consent of the Crown Court.

Effect of compensation order on subsequent award of damages in civil proceedings

38. (1) This section shall have effect where a compensation order has been made in favour of any person in respect of any injury, loss or damage and a claim by him in civil proceedings for damages in respect of the injury, loss or damage subsequently falls to be determined.

(2) The damages in the civil proceedings shall be assessed without regard to the order; but the plaintiff may only recover an amount equal to the aggregate of the following–

(a) any amount by which they exceed the compensation; and

(b) a sum equal to any portion of the compensation which he fails to recover, and may not enforce the judgment, so far as it relates to a sum such as is mentioned in paragraph (b) above, without the leave of the court.'

[**104.**] *Discretion of Crown Court to specify extended period of imprisonment in default of compensation.*

Compensation for victim out of forfeited property

Power to make order applying proceeds of sale of property forfeited by offender for benefit of victim

[**105.**] (1) The following section shall be inserted after section 43 of the Powers of Criminal Courts Act 1973–

'Application of proceeds of forfeited property

43A. (1) Where a court makes an order under section 43 above in a case where–

(a) the offender has been convicted of an offence which has resulted in a person suffering personal injury, loss or damage; or

(b) any such offence is taken into consideration by the court in determining sentence,

the court may also make an order that any proceeds which arise from the disposal of the property and which do not exceed a sum specified by the court shall be paid to that person.

[106.]–[115.] *Criminal Injuries Compensation Scheme.*

[116.]–[120.] *Amendments of law relating to juries.*

PART IX

YOUNG OFFENDERS

Custodial sentences for young offenders
[121.] (1) Part I of the Criminal Justice Act 1982 shall be amended as mentioned in subsections (2) to (5) below.

(2) The following subsection shall be inserted after subsection (3) of section 1—

'(3A) Subject to section 53 of the Children and Young Persons Act 1933 (punishment of certain grave crimes), the only custodial orders that a court may make where a person under 21 years of age is convicted or found guilty of an offence are–
(a) a sentence of detention in a young offender institution under section 1A below; and
(b) a sentence of custody for life under section 8 below.'.

(3) The following subsections shall be substituted for subsection (4) of that section–
'(4) A court may not–
(a) pass a sentence of detention in a young offender institution; or
(b) pass a sentence of custody for life under section 8(2) below, unless it is satisfied–
(i) that the circumstances, including the nature and the gravity of the offence, are such that if the offender were aged 21 or over the court would pass a sentence of imprisonment; and
(i) that he qualifies for a custodial sentence.

(4A) An offender qualifies for a custodial sentence if–
(a) he has a history of failure to respond to non-custodial penalties and is unable or unwilling to respond to them; or
(b) only a custodial sentence would be adequate to protect the public from serious harm from him; or
(c) the offence of which he has been convicted or found guilty was so serious that a non-custodial sentence for it cannot be justified.'.

(4) The following sections shall be inserted after section 1–
'Detention in a young offender institution
1A. (1) Subject to section 8 below and to section 53 of the Children and Young Persons Act 1933, where–
(a) a male offender under 21 but not less than 14 years of age or a female offender under 21 but not less than 15 years of age is convicted of an offence which is punishable with imprisonment in the case of a person aged 21 or over; and
(b) the court is satisfied of the matters referred to in section 1(4) above,
the sentence that the court is to pass is a sentence of detention in a young offender institution.

(2) Subject to section 1B(1) and (2) below, the maximum term of detention in a young offender institution that a court may impose for an offence is the same as the maximum term of imprisonment that it may impose for that offence.

(3) Subject to subsection (4) below and section 1B(3) below, a court shall not pass a sentence for an offender's detention in a young offender institution for less than 21 days.

(4) A court may pass a sentence of detention in a young offender institution for less than 21 days for an offence under section 15(11) below.

(5) Subject to section 1B(4) below, where–

(a) an offender is convicted of more than one offence for which he is liable to a sentence of detention in a young offender institution; or

(b) an offender who is serving a sentence of detention in a young offender institution is convicted of one or more further offences for which he is liable to such a sentence,

the court shall have the same power to pass consecutive sentences of detention in a young offender institution as if they were sentences of imprisonment.

(6) Where an offender who–

(a) is serving a sentence of detention in a young offender institution; and

(b) is aged over 21 years,

is convicted of one or more further offences for which he is liable to imprisonment, the court shall have the power to pass one or more sentences of imprisonment to run consecutively upon the sentence of detention in a young offender institution.

Special provision for offenders under 17

1B. (1) In the case of a male offender under 15 the maximum term of detention in a young offender institution that a court may impose is whichever is the lesser of–

(a) the maximum term of imprisonment the court may impose for the offence; and

(b) 4 months.

(2C) In the case of an offender aged 15 or 16 the maximum term of detention in a young offender institution that a court may impose is whichever is the lesser of–

(a) the maximum term of imprisonment the court may impose for the offence; and

(b) 12 months.

(3) Where an offender is a female under 17 a court shall not pass a sentence for her detention in a young offender institution whose effect would be that she would be sentenced to a total term of four months or less.

(4) A court shall not pass a sentence of detention in a young offender institution on an offender whose effect would be that the offender would be sentenced to a total term which exceeds–

(a) if the offender is male and under 15, 4 months; and

(b) if the offender is aged 15 or 16, 12 months.

(5) Where the total term of detention in a young offender institution to which an offender is sentenced exceeds–

(a) in the case of a male offender under 15, 4 months; and

(b) in the case of an offender aged 15 or 16, 12 months,

so much of the term as exceeds 4 or 12 months, as the case may be, shall be treated as remitted.

(6) In this section 'total term' means–

(a) in the case of an offender sentenced (whether or not on the same occasion) to two or more terms of detention in a young offender institution which are consecutive or wholly or partly concurrent, the aggregate of those terms;

(b) in the case of any other offender, the term of the sentence of detention in a young offender institution in question.

Accommodation of offenders sentenced to detention in a young offender institution

1C. (1) Subject to section 22(2)(b) of the Prison Act 1952 (removal to hospital etc.), an offender sentenced to detention in a young offender institution shall be detained in such an institution unless a direction under this section is in force in relation to him.

(2) The Secretary of State may from time to time direct that an offender sentenced to detention in a young offender institution shall be detained in a prison or remand centre instead of a young offender institution, but if he is under 17 at the time of the direction, only for a temporary purpose.'

(5) The following subsection shall be substituted for section 2(4)–

'(4) Where–

(a) the Crown Court passes a sentence of detention in a young offender institution or a sentence of custody for life under section 8(2) below, or

(b) a magistrates' court passes a sentence of detention in a young offender institution,

it shall be its duty–

    (i) to state in open court that it is satisfied that he qualifies for a custodial sentence under one or more of the paragraphs of section 1(4A) above, the paragraph or paragraphs in question and why it is so satisfied; and

    (ii) to explain to the offender in open court and in ordinary language why it is passing a custodial sentence on him.'.

(6) The amendments and transitional provisions in Schedule 8 to this Act shall have effect.

[122.] *Detention of young offenders in Scotland.*

Abolition of power of court to commit juvenile to remand centre instead of local authority care.

[123.] Section 22(5) of the Children and Young Persons Act 1969 shall cease to have effect.

Amendment of section 53(2) of Children and Young Persons Act 1933

[124.] The following words shall be substituted for the words in section 53(2) of the Children and Young Persons Act 1933 (punishment of certain grave offences) from the beginning of the subsection to 'law'–

'(2) Where–

(a) a young person is convicted on indictment of any offence punishable in the case of an adult with imprisonment for fourteen years or more, not being an offence the sentence for which is fixed by law; or

(b) a child is convicted of manslaughter,'

Payment of fine by parent or guardian

[125.] The following subsection shall be inserted after subsection (1) of section 55 of the Children and Young Persons Act 1933 (power to order parent or guardian to pay fine etc.)–

'(1A) Where but for this subsection–

(a) a court would order a child or young person to pay a fine under section 15(2A) of the Children and Young Persons Act 1969 (failure to comply with requirement included in supervision order); or

(b) a court would impose a fine on a young person under section 16(3) of the Powers of Criminal Courts Act 1973 (breach of requirements of community service order),

it shall be the duty of the court to order that the fine be paid by the parent or guardian of the child or young person instead of by the child or young person himself, unless the court is satisfied–

    (i) that the parent or guardian cannot be found; or

    (ii) that it would be unreasonable to make an order for payment, having regard to the circumstances of the case.'.

[126.] *Supervision.*

[127.] *Signature of orders.*

[128.] *Computation of sentence.*

Part X

Probation and the Probation Service, etc.

Bail: hostel conditions
[129.] (1) In section 3 of the Bail Act 1976 (grant of bail) the following subsection shall be inserted after subsection (6)–

'(6ZA) Where he is required under subsection (6) above to reside in a bail hostel or probation hostel, he may also be required to comply with the rules of the hostel.'.

(2) In paragraph 8 of Schedule 1 to that Act (restrictions on bail conditions) at the end of sub-paragraph (1) there shall be added the words 'or, where the condition is that the defendant reside in a bail hostel or probation hostel, that it is necessary to impose it to assess his suitability for being dealt with for the offence in a way which would involve a period of residence in a probation hostel.'.

[130.] *Administration of the probation service.*

Part XI

Miscellaneous

[131.] *Compensation for miscarriages of justice.*

Articles with blades or points and offensive weapons

Offence of having article with blade or point in public place
[132.] (1) Subject to subsection (4) below, any person who has an article to which this section applies with him in a public place shall be guilty of an offence.

(2) Subect to subsection (3) below, this section applies to any article which has a blade or is sharply pointed except a folding pocketknife.

(3) This section applies to a folding pocketknife if the cutting edge of its blade exceeds 3 inches.

(4) It shall be a defence for a person charged with an offence under this section to prove that he had good reason or lawful authority for having the article with him in a public place and, without prejudice to the generality of this subsection, to prove that he had it with him in that place–
(a) for use at work;
(b) for religious reasons; or
(c) as part of any national costume.

(5) A person guilty of an offence under subsection (1) above shall be liable on summary conviction to a fine not exceeding level 3 on the standard scale.

(6) In this section 'public place' includes any place to which at the material time the public have or are permitted access, whether on payment or otherwise.

(7) This section shall not have effect in relation to anything done before it comes into force.

Extension of constable's power to stop and search
[133.] (1) In section 1 of the Police and Criminal Evidence Act 1984 (powers of constable to stop and search)–
(a) the words 'or any article to which subsection (8A) below applies' shall be inserted–
    (i) in subsection (2)(a), after the word 'articles'; and
    (ii) at the end of subsection (3);
(b) in subsection (6), after the word 'article', in the second place where it occurs, there shall be inserted the words 'or an article to which subsection (8A) below applies'; and

(c) the following subsection shall be inserted after subsection (8)–
    '(8A) This subsection applies to any article in relation to which a person has committed, or is committing or is going to commit an offence under section 132 of the Criminal Justice Act 1988.'

(2) In section 5(2)(a)(ii) of that Act (annual reports to contain total numbers of searches for offensive weapons) after the word 'weapons' there shall be inserted the words 'or articles to which section 1(8A) above applies'.

Offensive weapons
[134.] (1) Any person who manufactures, sells or hires or offers for sale or hire, exposes or has in his possession for the purpose of sale or hire, or lends or gives to any other person, a weapon to which this section applies shall be guilty of an offence and liable on summary conviction to imprisonment for a term not exceeding six months or to a fine not exceeding level 5 on the standard scale or both.

(2) The Secretary of State may by order made by statutory instrument direct that this section shall apply to any description of weapon specified in the order except–
(a) any weapon subject to the Firearms Act 1968; and
(b) crossbows.

(3) A statutory instrument containing an order under this section shall not be made unless a draft of the instrument has been laid before Parliament and has been approved by a resolution of each House of Parliament.

(4) The importation of a weapon to which this section applies is hereby prohibited.

(5) It shall be a defence for any weapon charged in respect of any conduct of his relating to a weapon to which this section applies–
(a) with an offence under subsection (1) above; or
(b) with an offence under section 50(2) or (3) of the Customs and Excise Management Act 1979 (improper importation),
to prove that his conduct was only for the purposes of functions carried out on behalf of the Crown or of a visiting force.

(6) In this section–
the reference to the Crown includes the Crown in right of Her Majesty's Government in Northern Ireland; and
'visiting force' means any body, contingent or detachment of the forces of a country–
(a) mentioned in subsection (1)(a) of section 1 of the Visiting Forces Act 1952; or
(b) designated for the purposes of any provision of that Act by Order in Council under subsection (2) of that section,
which is present in the United Kingdom (including United Kingdom territorial waters) or in any place to which subsection (7) below applies on the invitation of Her Majesty's Government in the United Kingdom.

(7) This subsection applies to any place on, under or above an installation in a designated area within the meaning of section 1(7) of the Continental Shelf Act 1964 or any waters within 500 metres of such an installation.

(8) This section shall not have effect in relation to anything done before it comes into force.

(9) In the application of this section to Northern Ireland the reference in subsection (2) above to the Firearms Act 1968 shall be construed as a reference to the Firearms (Northern Ireland) Order 1981.

Power of justice of the peace to authorise entry, and search of premises for offensive weapons
[135.] (1) If on an application made by a constable a justice of the peace (including, in Scotland, the sheriff) is satisfied that there are reasonable grounds for believing–

   (a) that there are on premises specified in the application–
       (i) knives such as are mentioned in section 1(1) of the Restriction of Offensive Weapons Act 1959; or
      (ii) weapons to which section 134 above applies; and
   (b) that an offence under section 1 of the Restriction of Offensive Weapons Act 1959 or section 134 above has been or is being committed in relation to them; and
   (c) that any of the conditions specified in subsection (3) below applies,
he may issue a warrant authorising a constable to enter and search the premises.

(2) A constable may seize and retain anything for which a search has been authorised under subsection (1) above.

(3) The condition mentioned in subsection (1)(b) above are–
   (a) that it is not practicable to communicate with any person entitled to grant entry to the premises;
   (b) that it is practicable to communicate with a person entitled to grant entry to the premises but it is not practicable to communicate with any person entitled to grant access to the knives or weapons to which the application relates;
   (c) that entry to the premises will not be granted unless a warrant is produced;
   (d) that the purpose of a search may be frustrated or seriously prejudiced unless a constable arriving at the premises can secure immediate entry to them.

(4) Subsection (1)(a)(i) shall be omitted in the application of this section to Northern Ireland.

[136.] *Assistance to Isle of Man and Channel Islands.*

Transferred charges
[137.] (1) The Criminal Justice Act 1987 shall be amended as follows.

(2) In Section 4(1) (under which, on a notice of transfer in a fraud case, the functions of a magistrates' court, subject to certain exceptions, cease in relation to the case) after '5(3)' there shall be inserted, '(7A)'.

(3) In section 5(6) and (7) (effect of notice of transfer on requirement to appear before examining justices) for the words 'examining justices' there shall be substituted the words 'a magistrates' court'.

(4) The following subsection shall be inserted after section 5(7)–
   '(7A) If the notice states that the requirement is to continue, when the person charged appears before the magistrates' court, the court shall have–
   (a) the powers and duty conferred on a magistrates' court by subsection (3) above, but subject as there provided; and
   (b) power to enlarge, in the surety's absence, a recognizance conditioned in accordance with section 128(4)(a) of the Magistrates' Courts Act 1980 so that the surety is bound to secure that the person charged appears also before the Crown Court.'.

[138.] *Power to petition for winding-up etc on information obtained by Director of Serious Fraud Office.*

[139.] *Evidence before courts-martial etc.*

Amendments of Police and Criminal Evidence Act 1984

Searches of detained persons
[140.] In section 54 of the Police and Criminal Evidence Act 1984 (searches of detained persons)–
   (a) the following paragraph shall be substituted for subsection (1)(b)–

'(b) arrested at the station or detained there under section 47(5) above.';
and

(b) the following subsections shall be inserted after subsection (6)–

'(6A) A person who is in custody at a police station or is in police detention
otherwise than at a police station may at any time be searched in ordered to
ascertain whether he has with him anything which he could use for any of the
purposes specified in subsection (4)(a) above.

(6B) Subject to subsection (6C) below, a constable may seize and retain, or
cause to be seized and retained, anything found on such a search.

(6C) A constable may only seize clothes and personal effects in the circumstances specified in subsection (4) above.'.

Computer data about fingerprints

[**141.**] (1) The following subsection shall be substituted for subsection (5) of
section 64 of the Police and Criminal Evidence Act 1984 (destruction of
fingerprints etc.)–

'(5) If fingerprints are destroyed–
(a) any copies of the fingerprints shall also be destroyed; and
(b) any chief officer of police controlling access to computer data relating to
    the fingerprints shall make access to the data impossible, as soon as it is
    practicable to do so.'.

(2) The following subsections shall be inserted after subsection (6) of that
section–

'(6A) If–
(a) subsection (5)(b) above falls to be complied with; and
(b) the person to whose fingerprints the data relate asks for a certificate that
    it has been complied with,
such a certificate shall be issued to him by the responsible chief officer of police
or a person authorised by him or on his behalf for the purposes of this section.

(6B) In this section–
'chief officer of police' means the chief officer of police for an area mentioned
in Schedule 8 to the Police Act 1964; and
'the responsible chief officer of police' means the chief officer of police in
whose area the computer data were put on to the computer.'.

Provisions relating to Customs and Excise

Bail for persons in customs detention

[**142.**] At the end of section 114(2)(b) of the Police and Criminal Evidence Act
1984 there shall be added the words 'and
(c) that in relation to customs detention (as defined in any order made under
    this subsection) the Bail Act 1976 shall have effect as if references in it to a
    constable were references to an officer of Customs and Excise of such grade
    as may be specified in the order.'.

Customs and Excise power of arrest

[**143.**] (1) If–
(a) a person–
    (i) has been released on bail in criminal proceedings for an offence falling
        within subsection (4) below; and
    (ii) is under a duty to surrender into customs detention; and
(b) an officer of Customs and Excise has reasonable grounds for believing that
    that person is not likely to surrender to custody,
he may be arrested without warrant by an officer of Customs and Excise.

(2) A person arrested in pursuance of subsection (1) above shall be brought as
soon as practicable and in any event within 24 hours after his arrest before a
justice of the peace for the petty sessions area in which he was arrested.

(3) In reckoning for the purposes of subsection (2) above any period of 24 hours, no account shall be taken of Christmas Day, Good Friday or any Sunday.

(4) The offences that fall within this subsection are–
(a) an offence against section 5(2) of the Misuse of Drugs Act 1971 (possession of controlled drugs); and
(b) a drug trafficking offence.

(5) In this section and section 144 below 'drug trafficking offence' means a drug trafficking offence as defined by section 38(1) of the Drug Trafficking Offences Act 1986 other than an offence under section 24 of that Act (assisting another to retain the benefit of drug trafficking).

Remands of suspected drug offenders to customs detention
[**144.**] (1) Subject–
(a) to subsection (2) below; and
(b) to section 4 of the Bail Act 1976,
where–
> (i) a person is brought before a magistrates' court on a charge of an offence against section 5(2) of the Misuse of Drugs Act 1971 or a drug trafficking offence; and
> (ii) the court has power to remand him,

it shall have power, if it considers it appropriate to do so, to remand him to customs detention, that is to say, commit him to the custody of a customs officer for a period not exceeding 192 hours.

(2) This section does not apply where a charge is brought against a person under the age of 17.

(3) In the application of this section to Northern Ireland, for the words from the beginning of subsection (1) above to '1976' there shall be substituted the words 'Subject to subsection (2) below,'.

(4) The definition of 'drug trafficking offence' in section 38(1) of the Drug Trafficking Offences Act 1986 shall extend to Northern Ireland for the purposes of this section but shall have effect in relation to Northern Ireland as if–
(a) the reference in paragraph (e) to section 1 of the Criminal Law Act 1977 were a reference to Article 9 of the Criminal Attempts and Conspiracy (Northern Ireland) Order 1983; and
(b) the reference in paragraph (f) to section 1 of the Criminal Attempts Act 1981 were a reference to Article 3 of that Order.

Bail and custody

Court to give reasons for granting bail to a person accused of serious offence
[**145.**] The following paragraph shall be inserted after paragraph 9 (decisions as to grant or refusal of bail) of Part I of Schedule 1 to the Bail Act 1976–
'9A (1) If–
(a) the defendant is charged with an offence to which this paragraph applies; and
(b) representations are made as to any of the matters mentioned in paragraph 2 of this Part of this Schedule; and
(c) the court decides to grant him bail,
the court shall state the reasons for its decision and shall cause those reasons to be included in the record of the proceedings.

(2) The offences to which this paragraph applies are–
(a) murder;
(b) manslaughter;
(c) rape;
(d) attempted murder; and
(e) attempted rape.'.

Decisions where bail refused on previous hearing
[**146.**] The following new Part shall be inserted after Part II of Schedule 1 to the
Bail Act 1976–

'PART IIA

DECISIONS WHERE BAIL REFUSED ON PREVIOUS HEARING

If the court decides not to grant the defendant bail, it is the court's duty to
consider, at each subsequent hearing while the defendant is a person to whom
section 4 above applies and remains in custody, whether he ought to be granted
bail, but the court need not hear arguments as to fact or law which it has heard
previously.'

Remands in custody for more than eight days
[**147.**] (1) The following section shall be inserted after section 128 of the
Magistrates' Courts Act 1980–

'Remands in custody for more than eight days
    128A (1) The Secretary of State may by order made by statutory instrument
provide that this section shall have effect–
        (a) in an area specified in the order; or
        (b) in proceedings of a description so specified,
in relation to any accused person ('the accused') who has attained the age of 17.

(2) A magistrates' court may remand the accused in custody for a period
exceeding 8 clear days if–
        (a) it has previously remanded him in custody for the same offence; and
        (b) he is before the court,
but only if, after affording the parties an opportunity to make representations,
it has set a date on which it expects that it will be possible for the next stage in
the proceedings, other than a hearing relating to a further remand in custody or
on bail, to take place, and only–
        (i) for a period ending not later than that date; or
        (ii) for a period of 28 clear days,
whichever is the less.

(3) Nothing in this section affects the right of the accused to apply for bail
during the period of the remand.

(4) A statutory instrument containing an order under this section shall not
be made unless a draft of the instrument has been laid before Parliament and
been approved by a resolution of each House.'.

(2) After paragraph 9A of Schedule 1 to the Bail Act 1976 there shall be
inserted–

'Cases under section 128A of Magistrates' Courts Act 1980

9B Where the court is considering exercising the power conferred by section
128A of the Magistrates' Courts Act 1980 (power to remand in custody for
more than 8 clear days), it shall have regard to the total length of time which the
accused would spend in custody if it were to exercise the power.'.

[**148.**]–[**149.**] *Appeals.*

Reports of criminal proceedings

Anonymity in rape etc. cases
[**150.**] (1) The Sexual Offences (Amendment) Act 1976 shall be amended as
follows.

(2) The following subsections shall be substituted for subsection (1) of section
4 (anonymity of complainants in rape etc. cases)–

'(1) Except as authorised by a direction given in pursuance of this section–
(a) after an allegation that a woman has been the victim of a rape offence has been made by the woman or by any other person neither the woman's name nor her address nor a still or moving picture of her shall during her lifetime–
    (i) be published in England and Wales in a written publication available to the public; or
    (ii) be broadcast or included in a cable programme in England and Wales,
if that is likely to lead members of the public to identify her as an alleged victim of such an offence; and
(b) after a person is accused of a rape offence no matter likely to lead members of the public to identify a woman as the complainant in relation to that accusation shall during her lifetime–
    (i) be published in England and Wales in a written publication available to the public; or
    (ii) be broadcast or included in a cable programme in England and Wales;
but nothing in this subsection prohibits the publication or broadcasting or inclusion in a cable programme of matter consisting only of a report of criminal proceeedings other than proceedings at, or intended to lead to, or on an appeal arising out of, a trial at which the accused is charged with the offence.

(1A) In subsection (1) above 'picture' includes a likeness however produced.'.

(3) The following subsections shall be inserted after subsection (5) of that section–

'(5A) Where a person is charged with an offence under subsection (5) of this section in respect of the publication or broadcast of any matter or the inclusion of any matter in a cable programme, it shall be a defence, subject to subsection (5B) below, to prove that the publication, broadcast or cable programme in which the matter appeared was one in respect of which the woman had given written consent to the appearance of matter of that description.

(5B) Written consent is not a defence if it is proved that any person interfered unreasonably with the woman's peace or comfort with intent to obtain the consent.'.

(4) In subsection (3) of that section–
(a) the words 'before the Crown Court at which a person is charged with a rape offence' and 'relating to the complainant' shall cease to have effect; and
(b) for the words 'an acquittal of a defendant at' there shall be substituted the words 'the outcome of'.

(5) Section 6 (anonymity of defendants in rape etc. cases) shall cease to have effect.

(6) In section 7(2), in the definition of a 'rape offence', for the words 'and incitement to rape' there shall be substituted the words, 'incitement to rape, conspiracy to rape and burglary with intent to rape'.

[151.] *Judicial review of Contempt Act orders relating to trial on indictment.*

Possession of indecent photograph of child

Summary offence of possession of indecent photograph of a child
[152.] (1) It is an offence for a person to have any indecent photograph of a child in his possession.

(2) Where a person is charged with an offence under subsection (1) above, it shall be a defence for him to prove–
(a) that he had a legitimate reason for having the photograph in his possession; or

(b) that he had not himself seen the photograph and did not know, nor had any cause to suspect, it to be indecent; or

(c) that the photograph was sent to him without any prior request made by him or on his behalf and that he did not keep it for an unreasonable time.

(3) A person shall be liable on summary conviction of an offence under this section to a fine not exceeding level 5 on the standard scale.

(4) Sections 1(3), 2(3), 3 and 7 of the Protection of Children Act 1978 shall have effect as if any reference in them to that Act included a reference to this section.

(5) Possession before this section comes into force is not an offence.

[153.] *Scotland.*

[154.] *Enforcement of Video Recordings Act 1984.*

Restitution orders

Application of restitution orders to the Crown
[155.] The following subsection shall be added at the end of section 28 of the Theft Act 1968–

'(7) An order may be made under this section in respect of money owed by the Crown.'.

[156.] *Alteration of names of petty sessions areas.*

[157.] *Officers of inner London magistrates' courts.*

[158.] *Costs and expenses of prosecution witnesses and other persons.*

[159.] *Acquisition of easements etc under Prison Act 1952.*

[160.]–[162.] *General and Supplementary.*

Commencement
[163.] Subject to the following provisions of this section, this Act shall come into force on such day as the Secretary of State may by order made by statutory instrument appoint and different days may be appointed in pursuance of this subsection for different provisions or different purposes of the same provision.

(2) An order under this section may make such transitional provision as appears to the Secretary of State to be necessary or expedient in connection with any provision thereby brought into force other than a provision contained in sections 106 to 115 above or in Schedule 6 or 7 to this Act.

(3) The Secretary of State may by regulations made by statutory instrument make such provision as he considers necessary or expedient in preparation for or in connection with the coming into force of any provision contained in those sections or Schedules.

(4) A statutory instrument containing any such regulations shall be subject to annulment in pursuance of a resolution of either House of Parliament.

(5) The following provisions shall come into force on the day this Act is passed–
section 65;
section 66;
section 101(1), so far as it relates to the substitution of two new sections for section 26 of the Drug Trafficking Offences Act 1986;
section 127;
section 130, so far as it relates to the Local Government Finance Act 1982;
section 134;
section 135;

section 158;
section 159;
section 160;
section 161;
subsection (1) of section 162, so far as relating to the following–
the extension of references in the Children and Young Persons Act 1933 to the offences mentioned in Schedule 1 to that Act so as to include offences under Part I of the Child Abduction Act 1984;
the Visiting Forces Act 1952;
section 29 of the Children and Young Persons Act 1969;
section 6(1) of the Juries Act 1974;
the Child Care Act 1980;
sections 37 and 133 of the Magistrates' Courts Act 1980;
the Police and Criminal Evidence Act 1984;
the Prosecution of Offences Act 1985; subsection (2) of that section, so far as relating to the following–
section 49 of the Criminal Justice Act 1967;
section 29 of the Children and Young Persons Act 1969;
this section;
sections 164 and 165.

(6) The following provisions–
section 43;
section 44;
section 45;
section 46;
section 47;
section 57;
section 63;
section 67;
section 132;
section 133;
section 150;
sections 152 and 153;
subsection (1) of section 162, so far as relating to the Sexual Offences (Amendment) Act 1976, the Protection of Children Act 1978 and the Magistrates' Court Act 1980;
subsection (2) of that section, so far as relating to the following–
the Prevention of Corruption Act 1916;
section 28(3) of the Criminal Justice Act 1972;
the Sexual Offences (Amendment) Act 1976;
the Protection of Children Act 1978;
the Cable and Broadcasting Act 1984;
section 24(2)(e) of the Police and Criminal Evidence Act 1984,
shall come into force at the end of the period of two months beginning with the day this Act is passed.

[164.] *Extent.*

[165.] *Citation.*

SCHEDULES

[1.] *Extradition and fugitive offenders.*

[SCHEDULE 2]

DOCUMENTARY EVIDENCE – SUPPLEMENTARY

1. Where a statement is admitted as evidence in criminal proceedings by virtue of Part II of this Act–

(a) any evidence which, if the person making the statement had been called as a witness, would have been admissible as relevant to his credibility as a witness shall be admissible for that purpose in those proceedings;

(b) evidence may, with the leave of the court, be given of any matter which, if that person had been called as a witness, could have been put to him in cross-examination as relevant to his credibility as a witness but of which evidence could not have been adduced by the cross-examining party; and

(c) evidence tending to prove that that person, whether before or after making the statement, made (whether orally or not) some other statement which is inconsistent with it shall be admissible for the purpose of showing that he has contradicted himself.

2. A statement which is given in evidence by virtue of Part II of this Act shall not be capable of corroborating evidence given by the person making it.

3. In estimating the weight, if any, to be attached to such a statement regard shall be had to all the circumstances from which any inference can reasonably be drawn as to its accuracy or otherwise.

(4) Without prejudice to the generality of any enactment conferring power to make them–

(a) Crown Court Rules;

(b) Criminal Appeal Rules; and

(c) rules under section 144 of the Magistrates' Courts Act 1980,

may make such provision as appears to the authority making any of them to be necessary or expedient for the purposes of Part II of this Act.

5. Expressions used in Part II of this Act and in Part I of the Civil Evidence Act 1968 are to be construed in Part II of this Act in accordance with section 10 of that Act.

6. In Part II of this Act 'confession' has the meaning assigned to it by section 82 of the Police and Criminal Evidence Act 1984.

[3.] *Reference of sentencing questions to Court of Appeal.*

[SCHEDULE 4]

CONFISCATION ORDERS

PART I

OFFENCES IN RESPECT OF WHICH MAGISTRATES' COURTS MAY MAKE CONFISCATION ORDERS

Enactment	Description of offence
LOCAL GOVERNMENT (MISCELLANEOUS PROVISIONS) ACT 1982 (c. 30.)	
Schedule 3–	Offences relating to sex establishments.
VIDEO RECORDINGS ACT 1984 (c. 39.)	
Section 9	Supplying video recording of unclassified work.
Section 10	Possession of video recording of unclassified work for the purposes of supply.
CINEMAS ACT 1985 (c. 13.)	
Section 10(1)(a)	Use of unlicensed premises for exhibition which requires a licence.

Part II

Orders Varying List of Offences

1. The Secretary of State may by order made by statutory instrument amend Part I of this Schedule by removing any offence from or adding any offence to the offences listed in it.

2. A statutory instrument containing an order under paragraph 1 above shall be subject to annulment in pursuance of a resolution of either House of Parliament.

[5.] *Drug trafficking.*

[6.] *Criminal Injuries Compensation Board.*

[7.] *Compensation.*

[SCHEDULE 8]

Custodial Sentences for Young Offenders

Part I

Amendments

General

1. Subject to paragraphs 2 and 3 below, in any enactment–
(a) for a reference to a detention centre or to a youth custody centre or to both there shall be substituted a reference to a young offender institution; and
(b) for a reference (however expressed) to a detention centre order or to a sentence of youth custody or to both there shall be sustituted a reference to a sentence of detention in a young offender institution.

2. Nothing in paragraph 1(a) above applies–
(a) to section 71AA of the Army Act 1955 or the Air Force Act 1955;
(b) to paragraph 10 of Schedule 5A to either of those Acts; or
(c) to section 43AA of the Naval Discipline Act 1957 or paragraph 10 of Schedule 4A to that Act.

3. Nothing in paragraph 1(b) above applies–
(a) to section 21 of the Firearms Act 1968;
(b) to Schedule 1 to the Juries Act 1974;
(c) to section 5 of the Rehabilitation of Offenders Act 1974; or
(d) to section 17(3) of the Criminal Justice Act 1982.

4.–17. *Not reproduced here.*

[9.] *Scotland.*

[10.] *Supervision.*

[11.] *Probation service.*

[12.] *Assessors of compensation for miscarriages of justice.*

[13.] *Courts-martial.*

[14.] *Amendments.*

[15.] *Repeals.*

INDEX

(References are to paragraphs)